5/15 #3

D1538300

Mobil 1998
TRAVEL GUIDE®

Northwest
and Great Plains

**IDAHO • IOWA • MINNESOTA • MONTANA
NEBRASKA • NORTH DAKOTA • OREGON
SOUTH DAKOTA • WASHINGTON • WYOMING**

ALBERTA • BRITISH COLUMBIA • MANITOBA

Fodor's Travel Publications, Inc.

Guide Staff

General Manager: Diane E. Connolly
Editorial/Inspection Coordinators: Sara D. Hauber, Doug Weinstein
Inspection Assistant: Brenda Piszczek
Editorial Assistants: Korrie Klier, Julie Raio, Kathleen Rose, Kristin Schiller,
 Elizabeth Schwar
Creative Director: Fabrizio La Rocca
Cover Design: John Olenyik
Cover Photograph: ©Greg Vaughn

Acknowledgments

We gratefully acknowledge the help of our more than 100 field representatives for their efficient and perceptive inspection of every lodging and dining establishment listed; the establishments' proprietors for their coorperation in showing their facilities and providing information about them; the many users of previous editions of the *Mobil Travel Guide* who have taken the time to share their experiences; and for their time and information, the thousands of chambers of commerce, convention and visitors bureaus, city, state, and provincial tourism offices, and government agencies who assisted in our research.

Mobil

and Pegasus, the flying Red Horse, are trademarks of Mobil Oil Corporation. All rights reserved. Reproduction by any means including but not limited to photography, electrostatic copying devices, or electronic data processing is prohibited. Use of the information contained herein for solicitation of advertising or listing in any other publication is expressly prohibited without written permission from Mobil Corporation. Violations of reserved rights are subject to prosecution.

Copyright

Copyright © 1960, 1961, 1962, 1963, 1964, 1965, 1966, 1967, 1968, 1969, 1970, 1971, 1972, 1973, 1974, 1975, 1976, 1977, 1978, 1979, 1980, 1981, 1982, 1983, 1984, 1985, 1986, 1987, 1988, 1989, 1990, 1991, 1992, 1993, 1994, 1995, 1996, 1997, 1998 by Mobil Corporation.

All rights reserved, including the right of reproduction in whole or in part in any form.

Published in 1998 by Fodor's Travel Publications, Inc.
201 E. 50th St.
New York, NY 10022

Northwest and Great Plains
ISBN 0-679-03503-6
ISSN 0076-9819

Printed in the United States of America
10 9 8 7 6 5 4 3 2 1

Contents

Northwest and Great Plains

Maps

Larger, more detailed maps are available at many Mobil service stations

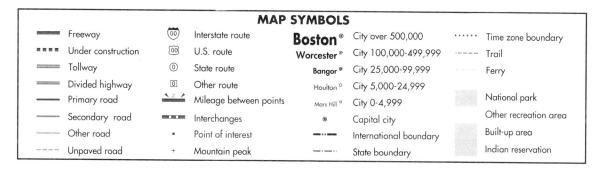

MAP SYMBOLS

Freeway	Interstate route	**Boston** ® City over 500,000
Under construction	U.S. route	**Worcester** ® City 100,000-499,999
Tollway	State route	**Bangor** ® City 25,000-99,999
Divided highway	Other route	Houlton ○ City 5,000-24,999
Primary road	Mileage between points	Mars Hill ○ City 0-4,999
Secondary road	Interchanges	⊛ Capital city
Other road	Point of interest	International boundary
Unpaved road	Mountain peak	State boundary

Time zone boundary
Trail
Ferry
National park
Other recreation area
Built-up area
Indian reservation

PACIFIC OCEAN

CANADA

BRITISH COLUMBIA

ALBERTA SASKATCHEWAN MAN

Vancouver Kamloops Calgary Saskatoon

Victoria Bellingham Lethbridge Medicine Hat Regina

Seattle WASHINGTON Spokane Great Falls NORTH DAKOTA Minot

Tacoma Olympia Yakima Lewiston Missoula MONTANA Bismarck

Portland Salem Butte Billings SOUTH DAKOTA Pierre

Eugene OREGON Boise IDAHO Idaho Falls Rapid City

Medford Twin Falls Pocatello WYOMING Casper NEBRASKA

Eureka Redding Logan Ogden Laramie Cheyenne

Chico Reno Salt Lake City Provo

San Francisco Oakland Sacramento Stockton NEVADA UTAH Denver COLORADO KANSAS

San Jose Carson City Grand Junction

Salinas Fresno Colorado Springs Pueblo

CALIFORNIA Las Vegas St. George Santa Fe

San Luis Obispo Bakersfield Flagstaff Albuquerque Amarillo Lawton

Santa Barbara ARIZONA NEW MEXICO Clovis Lubbock Wichita Falls

Los Angeles San Bernardino Riverside Indio Phoenix Roswell

Long Beach Tucson Alamogordo Abilene

San Diego El Centro Yuma Las Cruces TEXAS

Tijuana BAJA CALIFORNIA El Paso Odessa San Angelo

SONORA Juárez San Antonio

Nuevo Casas Grandes CHIHUAHUA Chihuahua Del Rio Piedras Negras

MEXICO COAHUILA Nuevo Laredo Laredo

Monclova McAllen

DURANGO Gomez Palacio Monterrey NUEVO LEON

Saltillo

SINALOA Durango ZACATECAS TAMAULIPAS

Mazatlán Ciudad Victo

HAWAII

Wailua Honolulu Hilo

PACIFIC OCEAN

0 100 Miles
0 200 Kilometers

© 1998 GeoSystems Global Corp.

ALASKA YUKON

Nome Fairbanks Dawson Whitehorse

Anchorage Valdez B.C.

Juneau

Kodiak

ALEUTIAN ISLANDS

PACIFIC OCEAN

R.U.S. U.S. CAN. U.S.

BERING SEA

0 250 500 Miles
0 250 500 750 Kilometers

© 1998 GeoSystems Global Corp.

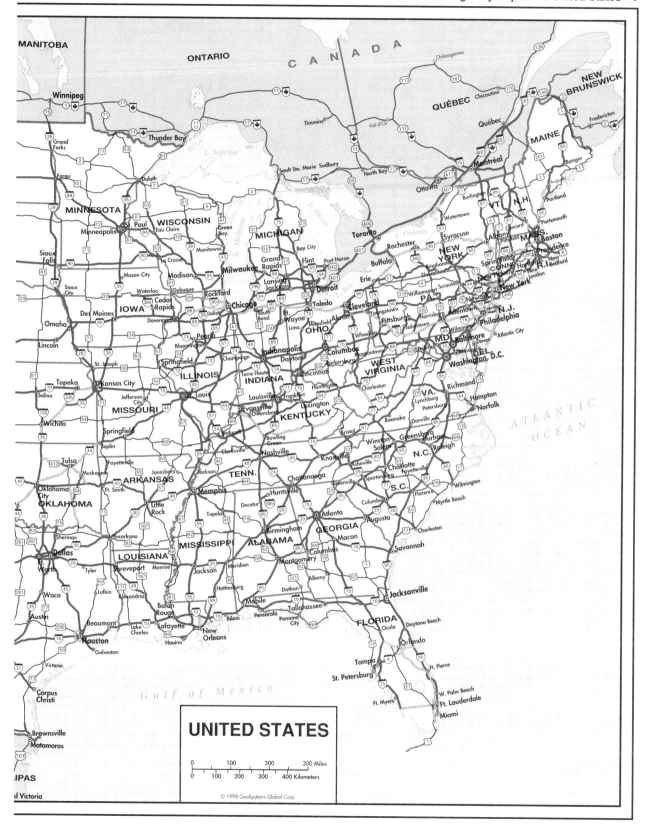

UNITED STATES

0   100   200   300 Miles
0   100   200   300   400 Kilometers

© 1998 GeoSystems Global Corp.

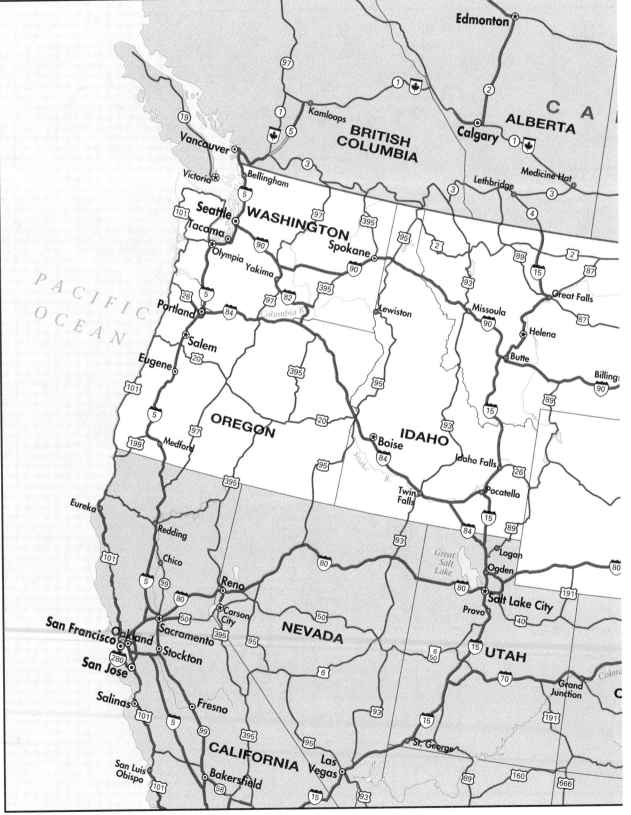

NORTHWEST & GREAT PLAINS

0   100   200 Miles

0   100   200   300 Kilometers

© 1998 GeoSystems Global Corp.

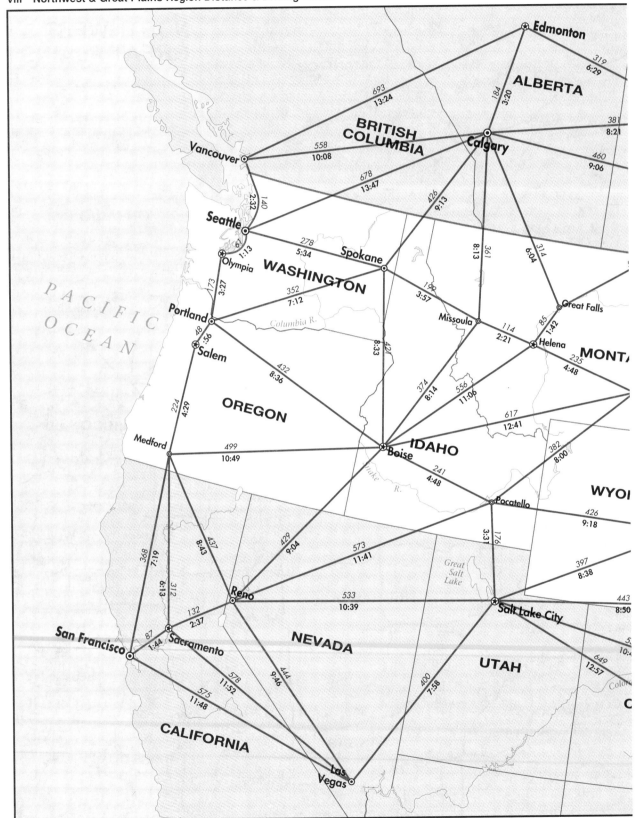

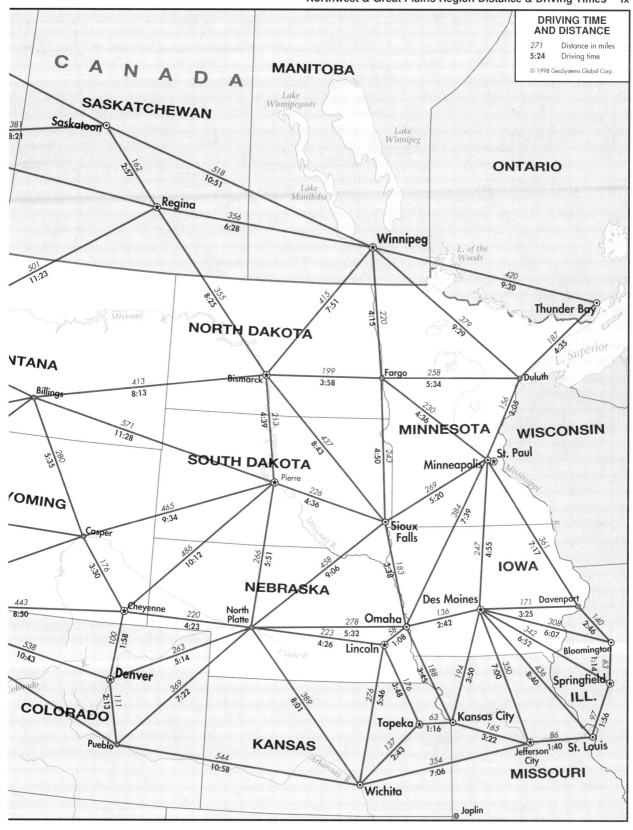

DRIVING TIME AND DISTANCE
271 Distance in miles
5:24 Driving time
© 1998 GeoSystems Global Corp.

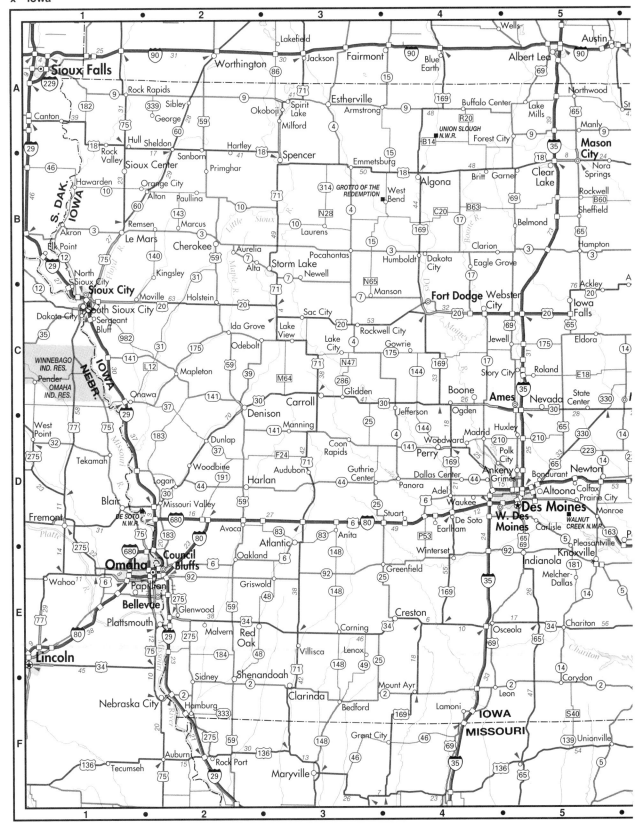

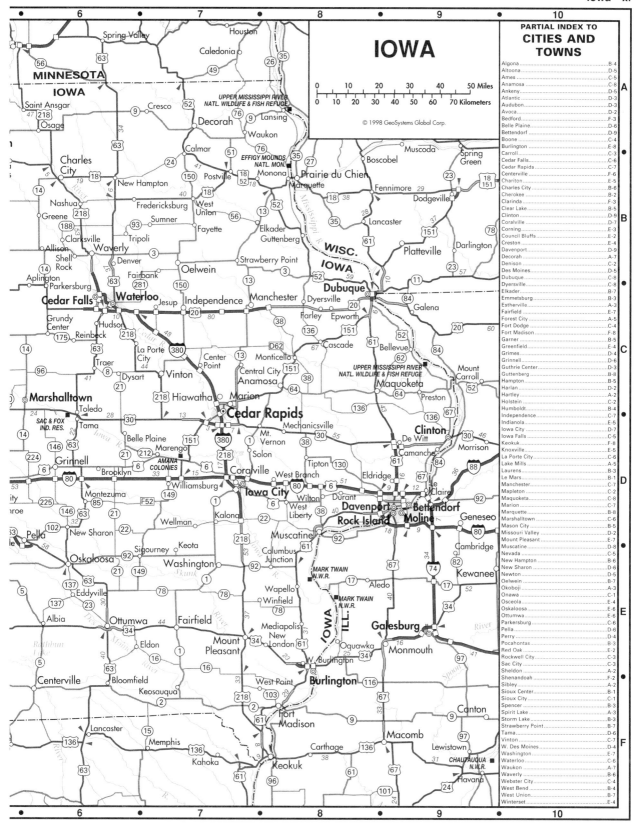

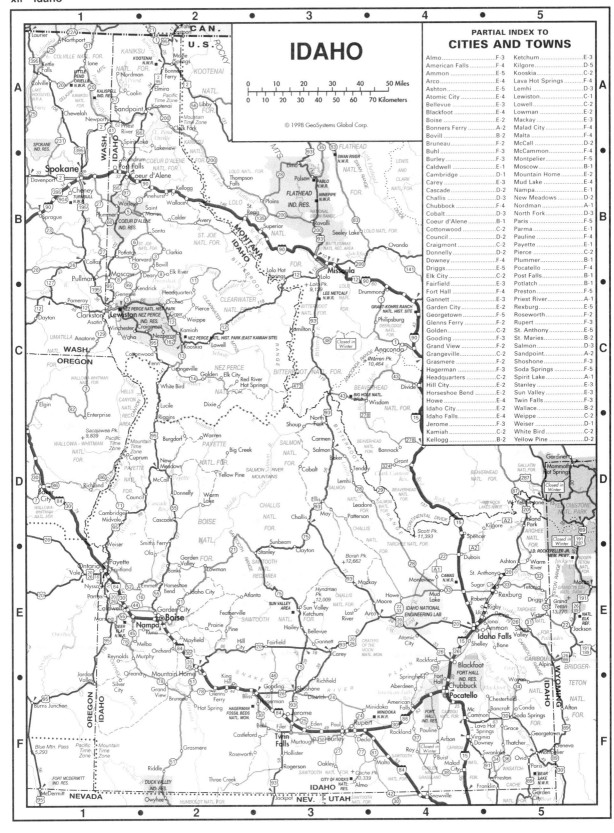

IDAHO

© 1998 GeoSystems Global Corp.

MINNEAPOLIS/
ST. PAUL

© 1998 GeoSystems Global Corp.

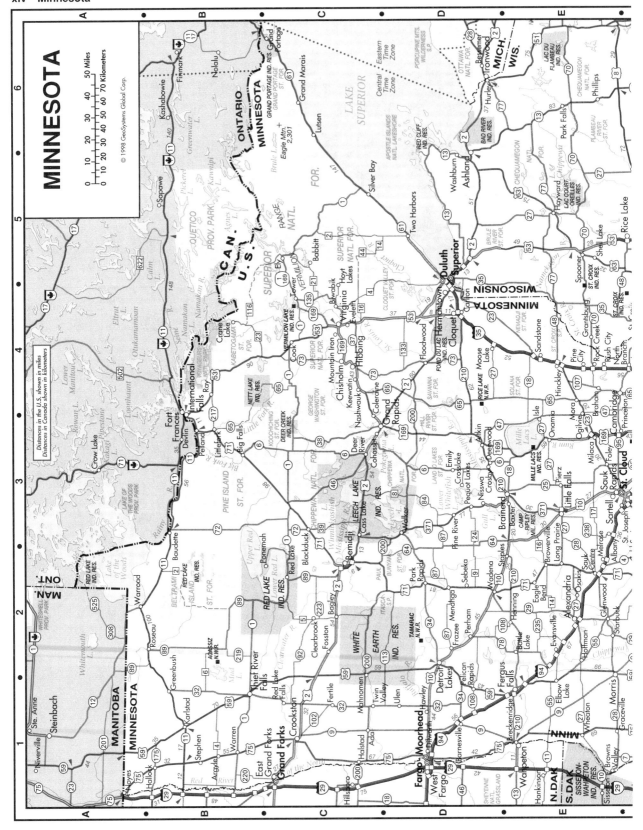

MINNESOTA

© 1998 GeoSystems Global Corp.

0 10 20 30 40 50 60 70 Kilometers
0   10   20   30   40   50 Miles

Distances in the U.S. shown in miles
Distances in Canada shown in kilometers

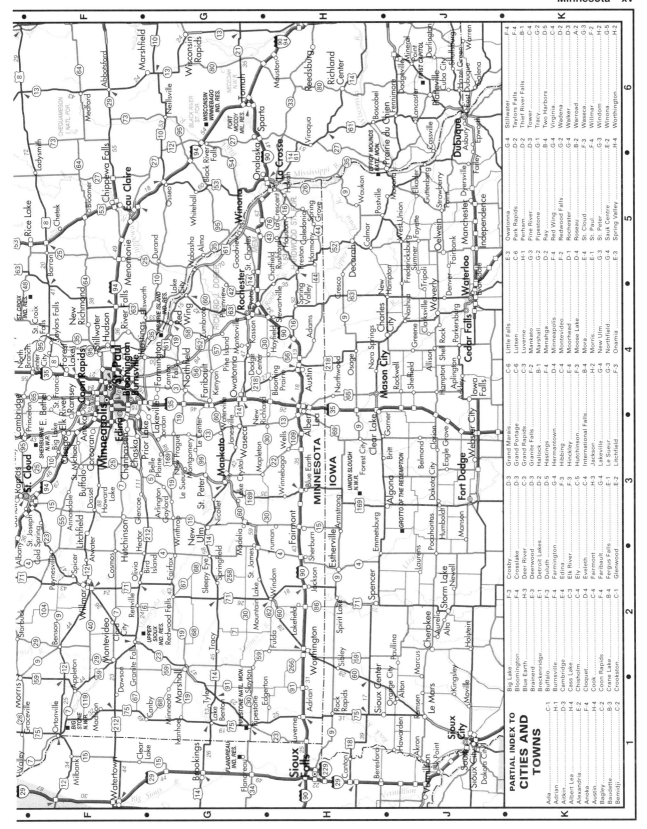

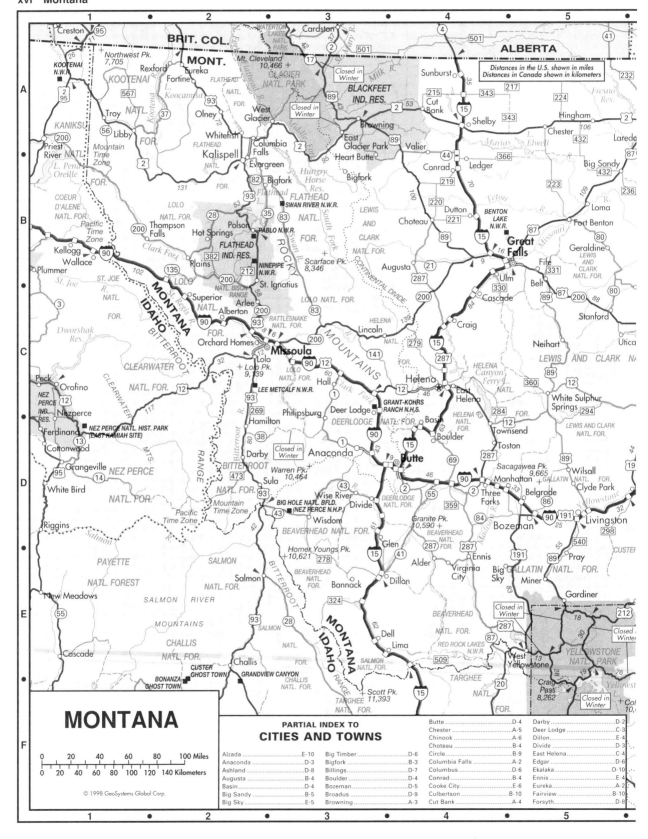

MONTANA

0 20 40 60 80 100 Miles
0 20 40 60 80 100 120 140 Kilometers

© 1998 GeoSystems Global Corp.

PARTIAL INDEX TO
CITIES AND TOWNS

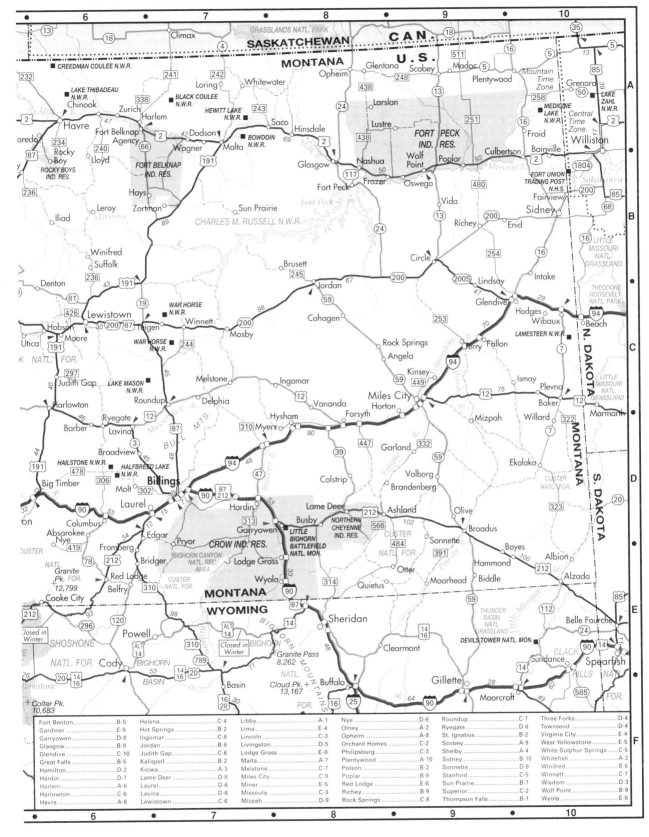

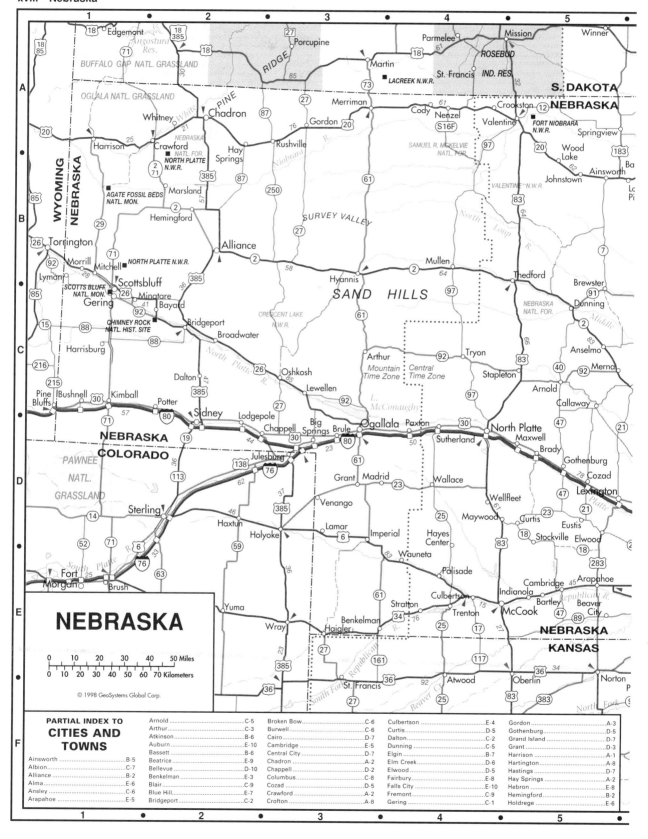

NEBRASKA

0 10 20 30 40 50 Miles

0 10 20 30 40 50 60 70 Kilometers

© 1998 GeoSystems Global Corp.

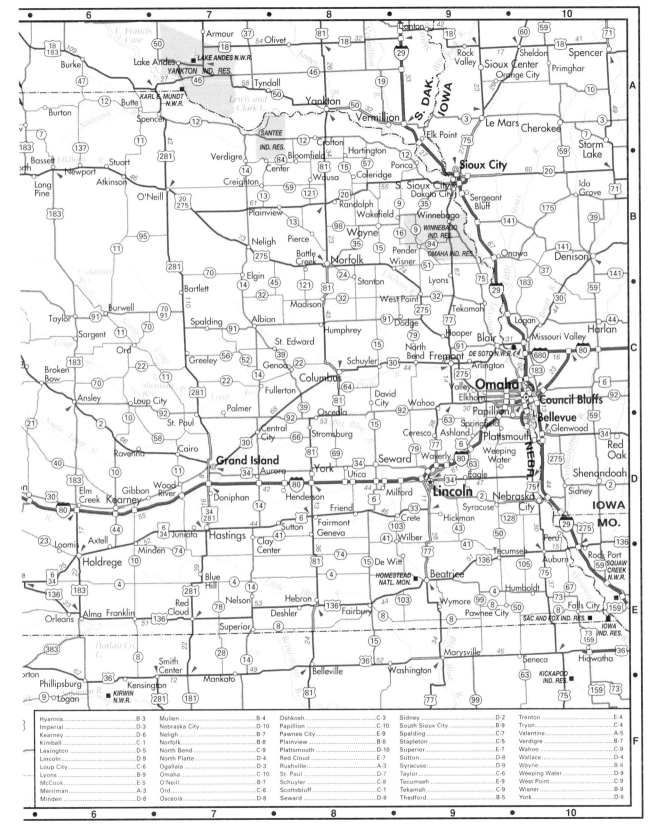

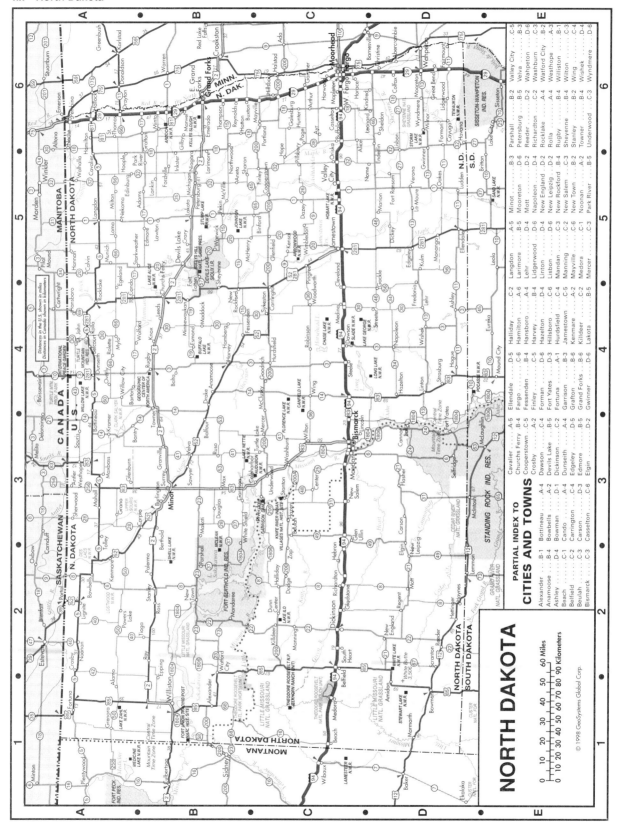

NORTH DAKOTA

PARTIAL INDEX TO CITIES AND TOWNS

Alexander	A-4
Anamoose	B-4
Ashley	D-4
Beach	C-1
Belfield	C-2
Beulah	B-3
Bismarck	C-3
Bottineau	A-4
Bowbells	A-2
Bowman	D-1
Cando	A-4
Carrington	C-4
Carson	D-3
Casselton	C-3
Cavalier	A-5
Churchs Ferry	B-4
Cooperstown	C-5
Crosby	A-2
Dawson	C-4
Devils Lake	B-5
Dickinson	D-2
Dunseith	A-4
Edgeley	D-5
Edmore	B-5
Elgin	D-2
Ellendale	A-5
Fargo	B-4
Fessenden	C-5
Finley	C-5
Forman	D-5
Fort Yates	D-3
Fortuna	A-1
Garrison	A-4
Grafton	A-5
Grand Forks	B-5
Gwinner	D-2
Halliday	D-5
Hamilton	C-6
Hansboro	B-4
Harvey	C-5
Hazelton	D-4
Hillsboro	B-5
Hurdsfield	C-6
Jamestown	B-3
Kenmare	C-5
Killdeer	C-2
Lakota	D-6
Langdon	C-2
Larimore	A-6
Lehr	B-4
Lidgerwood	D-6
Linton	D-4
Lisbon	D-2
Mandan	C-6
Manning	D-2
Mayville	C-5
Medora	C-2
Mercer	C-3
Minot	A-5
Mooreton	B-5
Mott	D-2
Napoleon	D-4
New England	A-4
New Leipzig	D-2
New Rockford	B-3
New Salem	C-6
New Town	B-2
Noonan	A-2
Park River	B-5
Parshall	B-3
Petersburg	D-6
Reeder	D-2
Richardton	D-4
Rocklake	A-4
Rolla	B-4
Rugby	B-4
Sheyenne	C-3
Stanley	C-4
Towner	B-4
Underwood	C-3
Valley City	C-5
Velva	B-5
Wahpeton	D-2
Watford City	B-2
Westhope	A-4
Williston	C-3
Wing	B-4
Wishek	D-4
Wyndmere	D-6

© 1998 GeoSystems Global Corp.

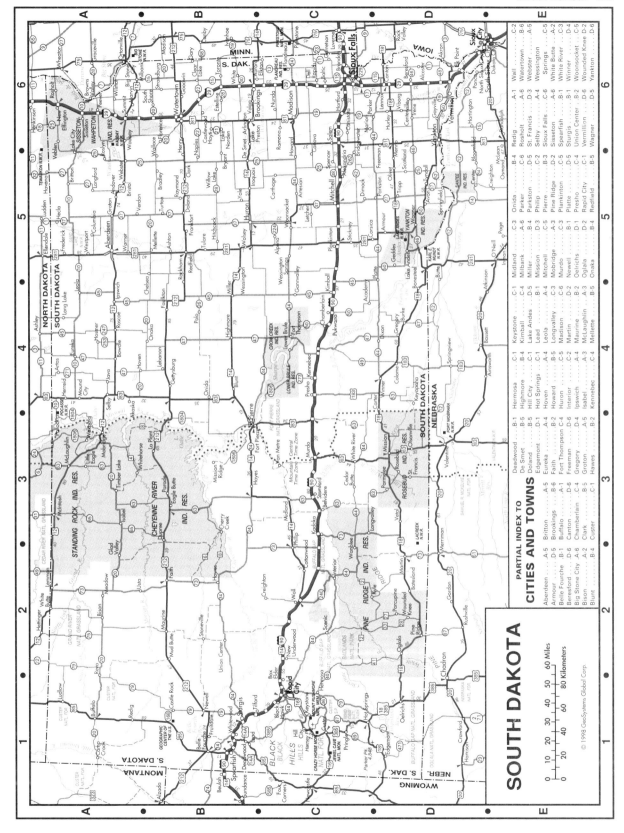

SOUTH DAKOTA

PARTIAL INDEX TO

CITIES AND TOWNS

Aberdeen	A-5	Britton	A-5	Midland	C-1
Armour	D-5	Brookings	B-6	Milbank	C-4
Belle Fourche	B-1	Buffalo	A-1	Miller	D-5
Beresford	D-6	Canton	C-4	Mission	B-1
Big Stone City	A-6	Chamberlain	C-4	Mitchell	A-4
Bison	A-2	Clark	B-5	Mobridge	C-3
Blunt	B-4	Custer	C-1	Murdo	A-3
				Madison	C-6
Deadwood	B-1	Hermosa	B-1	Martin	D-2
De Smet	B-5	Highmore	B-4	Maurine	A-4
Doland	C-1	Hill City	B-5	McLaughlin	A-3
Edgemont	D-1	Hot Springs	D-1	Mellette	B-5
Eureka	A-4	Hoven	A-4		
Faith	B-2	Howard	A-5	Newell	B-1
Fort Thompson	C-4	Huron	C-5	Oelrichs	D-1
Freeman	D-6	Interior	C-2	Oglala	A-3
Gregory	D-4	Ipswich	A-4	Onaka	B-4
Groton	B-5	Isabel	A-3	Onida	C-3
Hawes	C-1	Kennebec	B-2	Parker	A-6
Keystone	C-1			Parkston	D-5
Kimball	B-4			Philip	D-3
Lake Andes	C-1			Pierre	C-5
Lead	A-4			Pine Ridge	A-6
Leola	A-4			Plankinton	C-3
Longvalley	C-3			Platte	B-1
Madison	A-5			Presho	D-5
				Rapid City	C-4
				Redfield	B-4
Redig	B-4	Wall	A-1
Rosholt	C-6	Watertown	A-6
St. Francis	D-5	Webster	A-5
Selby	C-2	Wessington	A-4
Sioux Falls	C-6	Springs	C-5
Sisseton	A-2	White Butte	A-6
Spearfish	B-1	White River	C-3
Sturgis	D-5	Winner	D-4
		Woonsocket	C-5
		Wounded Knee	D-6
Union Center	B-2	Yankton	D-6
Vermillion	D-6	
Wagner	B-5	

© 1998 GeoSystems Global Corp.

Scale: 0 10 20 30 40 50 60 Miles
0 20 40 60 80 Kilometers

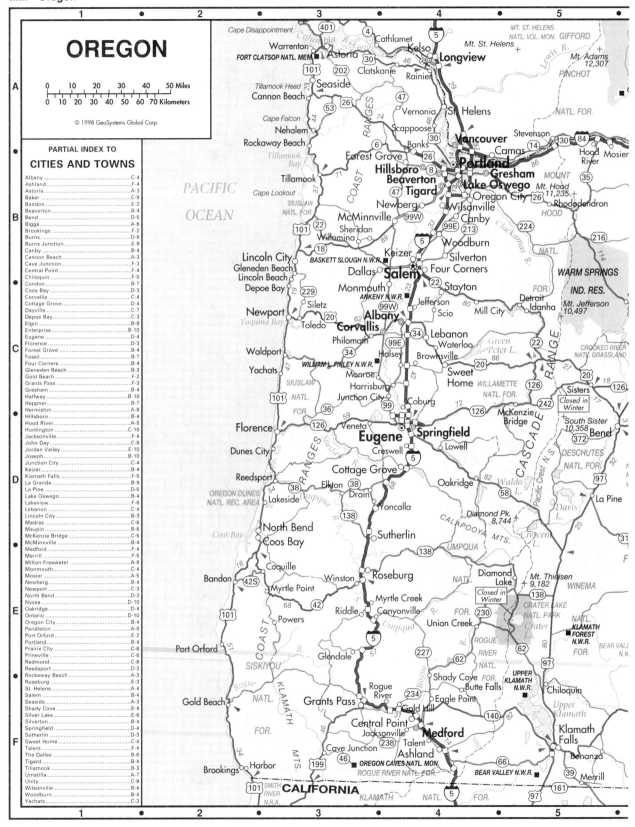

OREGON

0   10   20   30   40   50 Miles

0 10 20 30 40 50 60 70 Kilometers

© 1998 GeoSystems Global Corp.

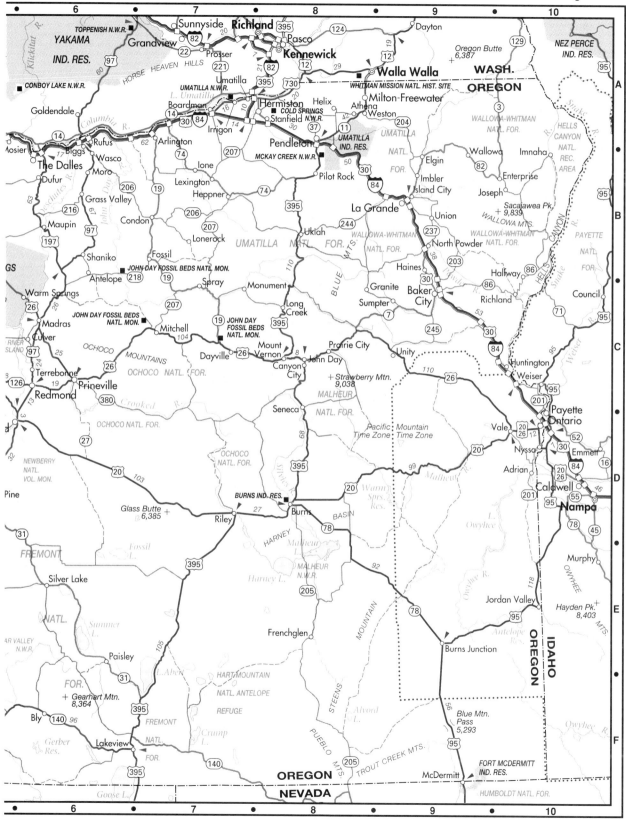

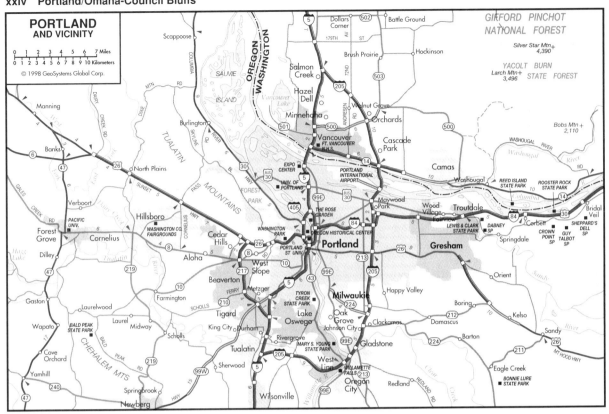

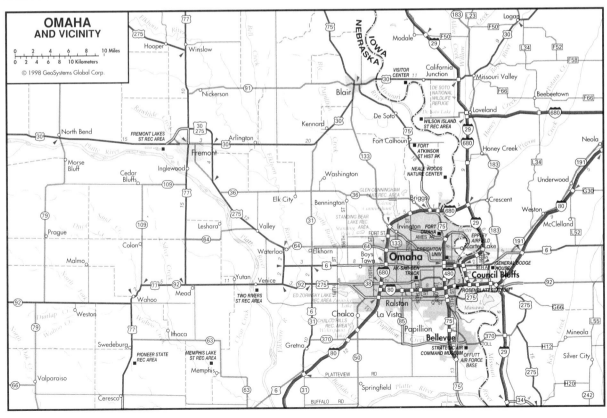

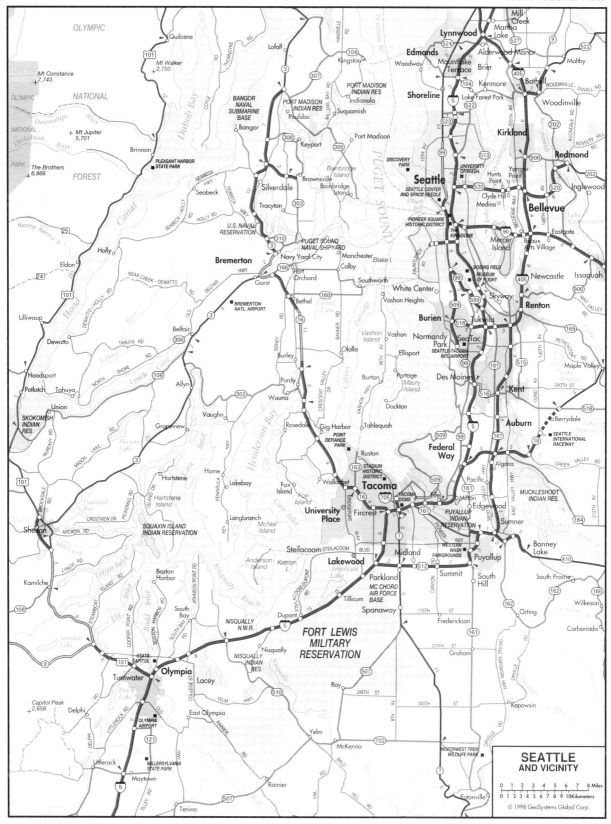

SEATTLE
AND VICINITY

0 1 2 3 4 5 6 7 8 Miles
0 1 2 3 4 5 6 7 8 9 10 Kilometers

© 1998 GeoSystems Global Corp.

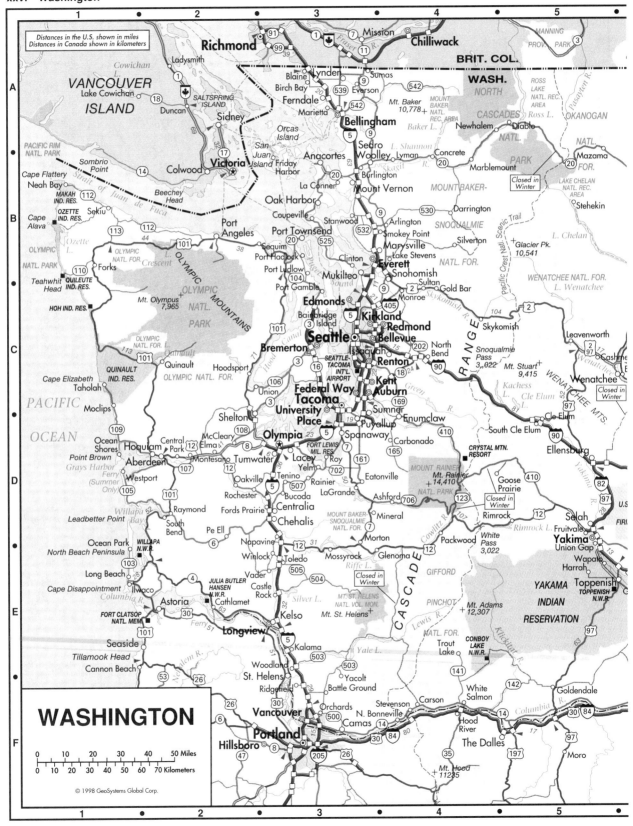

WASHINGTON

© 1998 GeoSystems Global Corp.

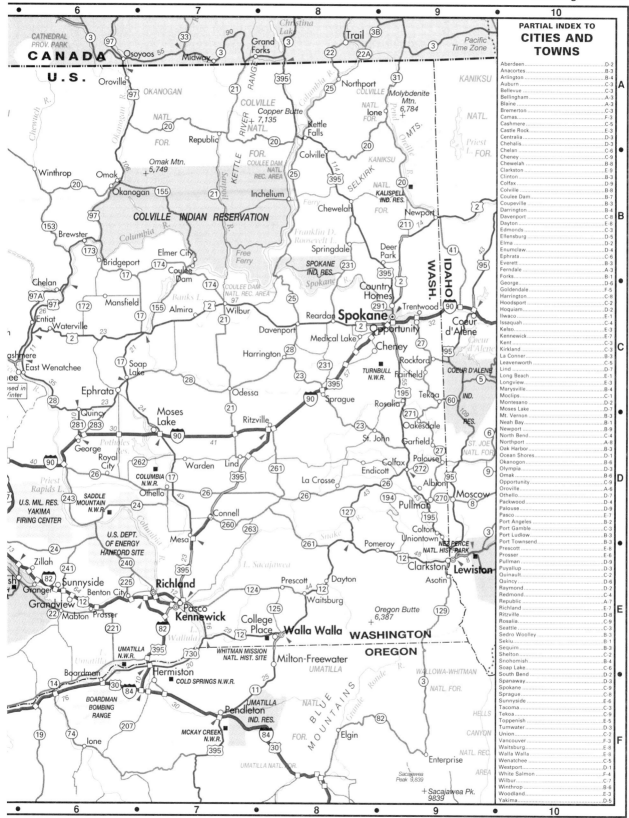

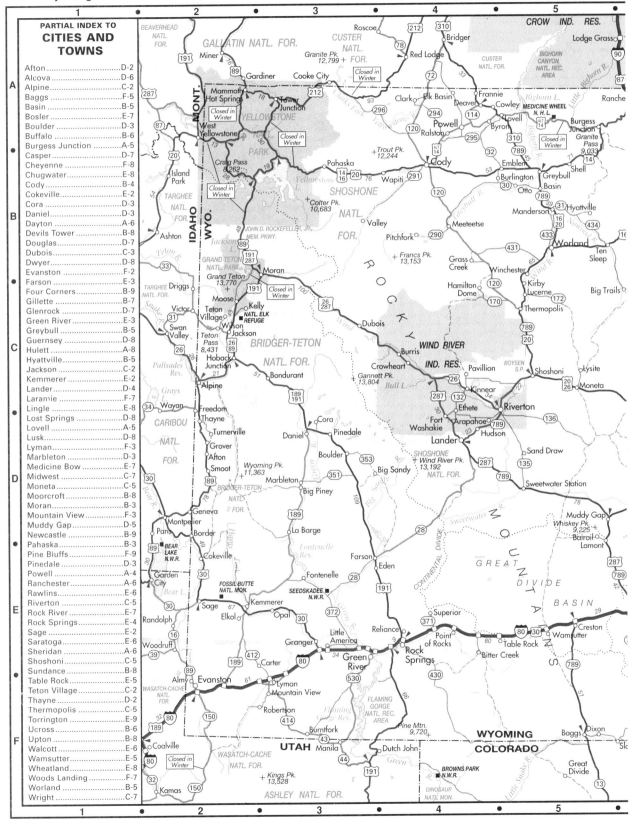

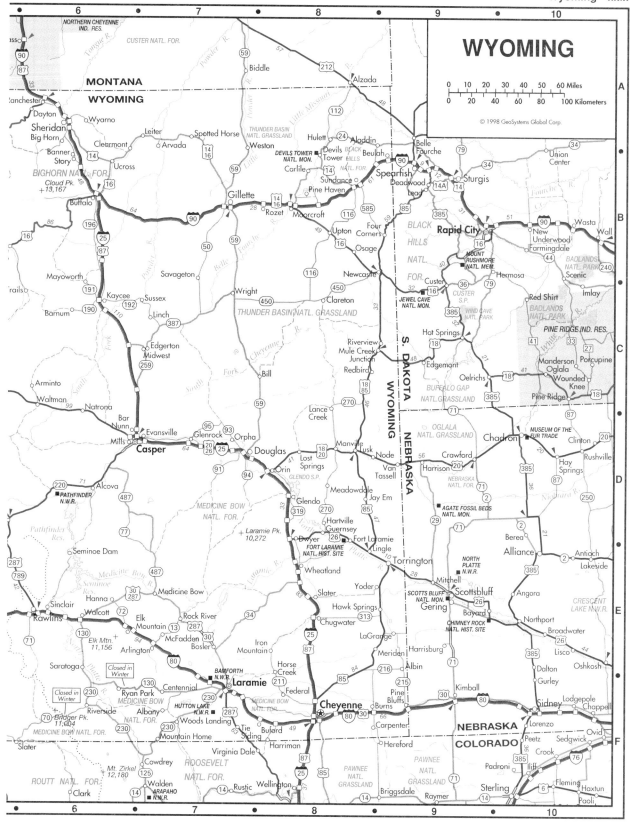

WYOMING

0 10 20 30 40 50 60 Miles
0   20   40   60   80 100 Kilometers

© 1998 GeoSystems Global Corp.

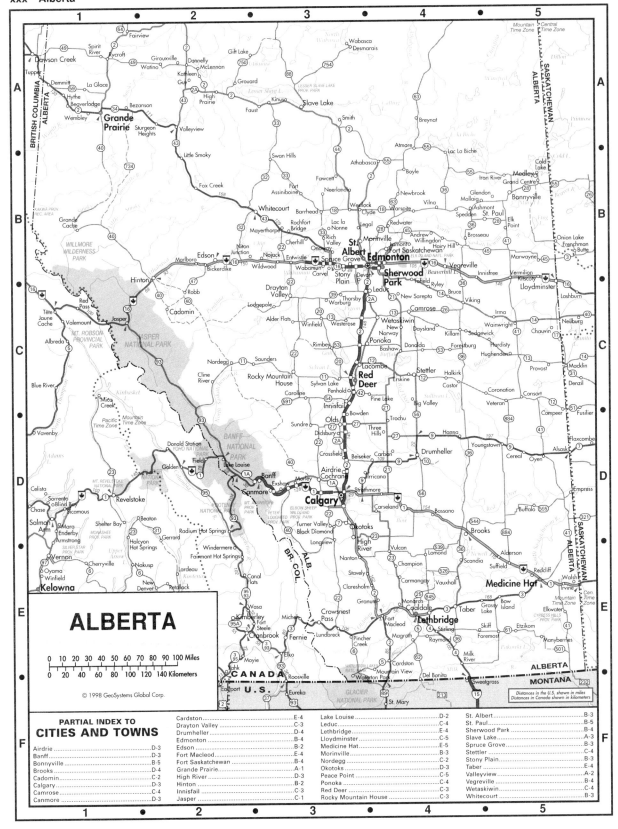

ALBERTA

0 10 20 30 40 50 60 70 80 90 100 Miles
0   20   40   60   80   100   120   140 Kilometers

© 1998 GeoSystems Global Corp.

Distances in the U.S. shown in miles
Distances in Canada shown in kilometers

PARTIAL INDEX TO
CITIES AND TOWNS

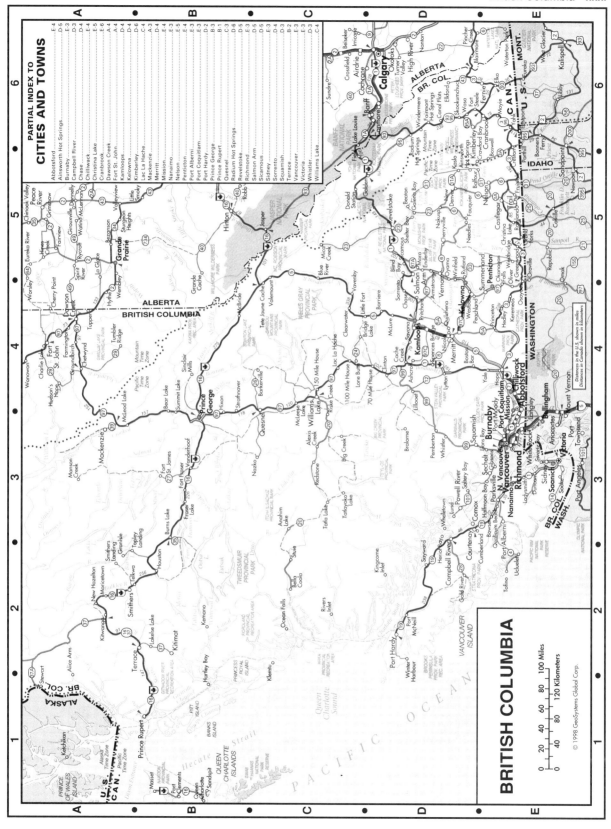

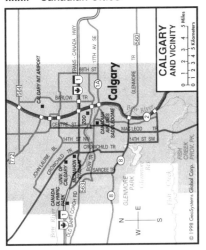

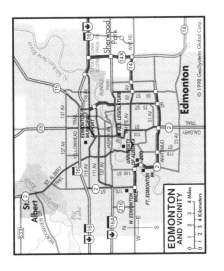

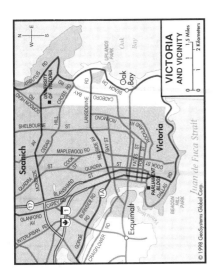

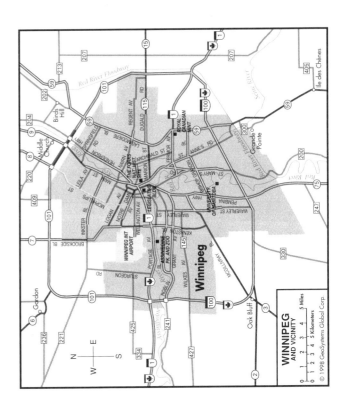

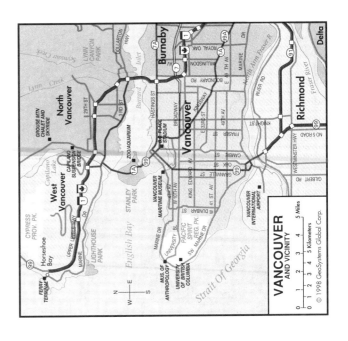

Before a long trip,
it's always smart to stop at Mobil.

On its ten-year, billion-mile mission, the International Space Station won't make pit stops, and its air system can't ever break down. So the grease for its fans and motors isn't a detail. It had to pass nearly as many tests as astronauts do, and in the end a Mobil synthetic won the job. What excites us is that we didn't create this grease for outer space. You can buy the same stuff (Mobilith SHC® 220) for your bicycle, bus or paper mill. Which, to us, shows the value of how we do research, trying to make things better than necessary. Nobody asked us to develop synthetic lubes, but we pursued it because that's how real innovation works. You aim to exceed present-day expectations so that when the future arrives, you're already there. To learn more, visit www.mobil.com.

© 1997 Mobil Corporation

Mobil The energy
to make a difference

when racing began, our decals were a lot easier to read.

...ank Duryea's race car streamed across the finish line at a breathtaking ...bil helped get it there. Of course, Mobil Motor Oil has protected some- ...sophisticated engines since then. In fact, Mobil 1 is the official oil of Team ...ccessful team in Indy history. So whether you work in racing or race to ...K-MOBIL and find out more about any of our advanced oils. After all, ...really only one place to promote our name. Under the hood.

A Word to Our Readers

hether you're going on an extended family vacation, a weekend getaway, or a business trip, you need good, solid information on where to stay and eat and what to see and do. It would be nice if you could take a corps of well-seasoned travelers with you to suggest lodgings and activities, or ask a local restaurant critic for advice on dining spots, but since these options are rarely practical, the *Mobil Travel Guide* is the next best thing. It puts a huge database of information at your disposal and provides the value judgments and advice you need to use that information to its fullest.

Published by Fodor's Travel Publications, Inc., in collaboration with Mobil Corporation, the sponsor since 1958, these books contain the most comprehensive, up-to-date information possible on each region. In fact, listings are revised and ratings reviewed annually, based on inspection reports from our field representatives, evaluation by senior staff, and comments from more than 100,000 readers. These incredible data are then used to develop the *Mobil Travel Guide*'s impartial quality ratings, indicated by stars, which Americans have trusted for decades.

Space limitations make it impossible for us to include every fine hotel and restaurant, so we have picked a representative group, all above-average for their type. There's no charge to any establishment for inclusion, and only places that meet our standards are chosen. Because travelers' needs differ, we make every effort to select a variety of establishments and provide the information to decide what's right for you. If you're looking for a lodging at a certain price or location, or even one that offers 24-hour room service, you'll find the answers you need at your fingertips. Take a minute to read the next section, How to Use This Book; it'll make finding the information you want a breeze.

Also look at Making the Most of Your Trip, the section that follows. It's full of tips from savvy travelers that can help you save money, stay safe, and get around more easily—the keys to making any trip a success.

Of course, the passage of time means that some establishments will close, change hands, remodel, improve, or go downhill. Though every effort has been made to ensure the accuracy of all information when it was printed, change is inevitable. Always call and confirm that a place is open and that it has the features you want. Whatever your experiences at any of the establishments we list—and we hope they're terrific—or if you have general comments about our guide, we'd love to hear from you. Use the convenient postage-paid card near the end of this book, or drop us a line at the *Mobil Travel Guide,* Fodor's Travel Publications, Inc., 4709 W. Golf Road, Suite 803, Skokie, IL 60076.

So pack this book in your suitcase or toss it next to you on the front seat. If it gets dog-eared, so much the better. We here at the *Mobil Travel Guide* wish you a safe and successful trip.

Bon voyage and happy driving,

THE EDITORS

Welcome

For 40 years, the *Mobil Travel Guide* has provided travelers in North America with reliable advice on finding good value, quality service, and the attractions that give a destination its special character. During this time, our teams of culinary and hospitality experts have worked hard to develop objective and exacting standards. In so doing, they seek to fully meet the desires and expectations of a broad range of customers.

At Mobil, we demonstrate the energy to make a difference through a commitment to excellence that allows us to bring the best service and products to the people we serve. We believe that the ability to respond to and anticipate customers' needs is what distinguishes good companies from truly great ones.

It is our hope, whether your travels are for business or leisure, over a long distance or a short one, that this book will be your companion, dependably guiding you to quality and value in lodging and dining.

Finally, I ask that you help us improve the guides. Please take the time to fill out the customer feedback form at the back of this book or contact us on the Internet at www.mobil.com/travel.

Lucio A. Noto
Chairman and
Chief Executive Officer
Mobil Corporation

How to Use This Book

The *Mobil Travel Guide* is easy to use. Each state chapter begins with a general introduction that both provides a general geographical and historical orientation to the state and covers basic statewide tourist information, from state recreation areas to seat-belt laws. The balance of each chapter is devoted to the travel destinations within the state—cities and towns, state and national parks, and tourist regions—which, like the states themselves, are arranged alphabetically.

What follows is an explanation of the wealth of information you'll find within those travel destinations—information on the area, on things to see and do there, and on where to stay and eat.

Maps and Map Coordinates

The first thing you'll notice is that next to each destination is a set of map coordinates. These refer to the appropriate state map in the front of this book. In addition, there are maps of selected larger cities in the front section as well as maps of key neighborhoods within the sections on the cities themselves.

Destination Information

Because many travel destinations are so close to other cities and towns where visitors might find additional attractions, accommodations, and restaurants, cross-references to those places are included whenever possible. Also listed are addresses and phone numbers for travel-information resources—usually the local chamber of commerce or office of tourism—as well as pertinent vital statistics and a brief introduction to the area.

What to See and Do

More than 11,000 museums, art galleries, amusement parks, universities, historic sites and houses, plantations, churches, state parks, ski areas, and other attractions are described in the *Mobil Travel Guide.* A white star on a black background ★ signals that the attraction is one of the best in the state. Since municipal parks, public tennis courts, swimming pools, and small educational institutions are common to most towns, they are generally excluded.

Following the attraction's description are the months and days it's open, address/location and phone number, and admission costs (see the inside front cover for an explanation of the cost symbols). Note that directions are given from the center of the town under which the attraction is listed, which may not necessarily be the town in which the attraction is located. Zip codes are listed only if they differ from those given for the town.

Events

Events—categorized as annual, seasonal, or special—are highlighted. An annual event is one that's held every year for a period of usually no longer than a week to 10 days; festivals and fairs are typical entries. A seasonal event is one that may or may not be annual and that is held for a number of weeks or months in the year, such as horse racing, summer theater, concert or opera festivals, and professional sports. Special event listings occur infrequently and mark a certain date or event, such as a centennial or other commemorative celebration.

Major Cities

Additional information on airports and transportation, suburbs, and neighborhoods, including a list of restaurants by neighborhood, may be included for large cities.

Lodging and Restaurant Listings

ORGANIZATION

For both lodgings and restaurants, when a property is in a town that does not have its own heading, the listing appears under the town nearest its location with the address and town in parentheses immediately after the establishment name. In large cities, lodgings located within 5 miles of major, commercial airports are listed under a separate "Airport" heading, following the city listings.

LODGING CLASSIFICATIONS

Each property is classified by type according to the characteristics below. Because the following features and services are found at most motels, lodges, motor hotels, and hotels, they are not shown in those listings:

- Year-round operation with a single rate structure unless otherwise quoted
- European plan (meals not included in room rate)
- Bathroom with tub and/or shower in each room
- Air-conditioned/heated, often with individual room control
- Cots
- Daily maid service
- Phones in rooms
- Elevators

Motels and Lodges. Accommodations are in low-rise structures with rooms easily accessible to parking (usually free). Properties have outdoor room entry and small, functional lobbies. Service is often limited, and dining may not be offered in lower-rated motels and lodges. Shops and businesses are found only in higher-rated properties, as are bellhops, room service, and restaurants serving three meals daily.

Lodges differ from motels primarily in their emphasis on outdoor recreational activities and in location. They are often found in resort and rural areas rather than in major cities or along highways.

Motor Hotels. Offering the convenience of motels along with many of the features of hotels, motor hotels range from low-rise structures offering limited services to multistory buildings with a wide range of services and facilities. Multiple building entrances, elevators, inside hallways, and parking areas (generally free) near access doors are some of the features of a motor hotel. Lobbies offer sitting areas and 24-hour desk and switchboard services. Often bellhop and valet services as well as restaurants serving three meals a day are found. Expanded recreational facilities and more than one restaurant are available in higher-rated properties.

The distinction between motor hotels and hotels in metropolitan areas is minor.

Hotels. To be categorized as a hotel, an establishment must have most of the following facilities and services: multiple floors, a restaurant and/or coffee shop, elevators, room service, bellhops, a spacious lobby, and recreational facilities. In addition, the following features and services not shown in listings are also found:

- Valet service (one-day laundry/cleaning service)
- Room service during hours restaurant is open
- Bellhops
- Some oversize beds

Resorts. These specialize in stays of three days or more and usually offer American Plan and/or housekeeping accommodations. Their emphasis is on recreational facilities, and a social director is often available. Food services are of primary importance, and guests must be able to eat three meals a day on the premises, either in restaurants or by having access to an on-site grocery store and preparing their own meals.

Inns. Frequently thought of as a small hotel, an inn is a place of homelike comfort and warm hospitality. It is often a structure of historic significance, with an equally interesting setting. Meals are a special occasion, and refreshments are frequently served in late afternoon. Rooms are usually individually decorated, often with antiques or furnishings representative of the locale. Phones, bathrooms, and TVs may not be available in every room.

Guest Ranches. Like resorts, guest ranches specialize in stays of three days or more. Guest ranches also offer meal plans and extensive outdoor activities. Horseback riding is usually a feature; there are stables and trails on the ranch property, and trail rides and daily instruction are part of the program. Many guest ranches are working ranches, ranging from casual to rustic, and guests are encouraged to participate in ranch life. Eating is often family-style and may also include cookouts. Western saddles are assumed; phone ahead to inquire about English saddle availability.

Cottage Colonies. These are housekeeping cottages and cabins that are usually found in recreational areas. Any dining or recreational facilities are noted in our listing.

DINING CLASSIFICATIONS

Restaurants. Most dining establishments fall into this category. All have a full kitchen and offer table service and a complete menu. Parking on or near the premises, in a lot or garage, is assumed. When a property offers valet or other special parking features, or when only street parking is available, it is noted in the listing.

Unrated Dining Spots. These places, listed after Restaurants in many cities, are chosen for their unique atmosphere, specialized menu, or local flavor. They include delis, ice-cream parlors, cafeterias, tearooms, and pizzerias. Because they may not have a full kitchen or table service, they are not given a *Mobil Travel Guide* rating. Often they offer extraordinary value and quick service.

QUALITY RATINGS

The *Mobil Travel Guide* has been rating lodgings and restaurants on a national basis since the first edition was published in 1958. For years the guide was the only source of such ratings, and it remains among the few guidebooks to rate restaurants across the country.

All listed establishments were inspected by experienced field representatives or evaluated by a senior staff member. Ratings are based upon their detailed inspection reports of the individual properties, on written evaluations of staff members who stay and dine anonymously, and on an extensive review of comments from our readers.

You'll find a key to the rating categories, ★ through ★★★★★, on the inside front cover. All establishments in the book are recommended. Even a ★ place is above average, usually providing a basic, informal experience. Rating categories reflect both the features the property offers and its quality in relation to similar establishments.

For example, lodging ratings take into account the number and quality of facilities and services, the luxury of appointments, and the attitude and professionalism of staff and management. A ★ establishment provides a comfortable night's lodging. A ★★ property offers more than a facility that rates one star, and the decor is well planned and integrated. Establishments that rate ★★★ are professionally managed and staffed and often beautifully appointed; the lodging experience is truly excellent and the range of facilities is extensive. Properties that have been given ★★★★ not only offer many services but also have their own style and personality; they are luxurious, creatively decorated, and superbly maintained. The ★★★★★ properties are among the best in the United States, superb in every respect and entirely memorable, year in and year out.

Restaurant evaluations reflect the quality of the food and the ingredients, preparation, and presentation as well as service levels and the property's decor and ambience. A restaurant that has fairly simple goals for menu and decor but that achieves those goals superbly might receive the same number of stars as a restaurant with somewhat loftier ambitions but whose execution falls somewhat short of the mark. In general, ★ indicates a restaurant that's a good choice in its area, usually fairly simple and perhaps catering to a clientele of locals and families; ★★ denotes restaurants that are more highly recommended in their area; ★★★ restaurants are of national caliber, with professional and attentive service and a skilled chef in the kitchen; ★★★★ reflects superb dining choices, where remarkable food is served in equally remarkable surroundings; and ★★★★★ represents that rarefied group of the best restaurants in the country, where in addition to near perfection in every detail, there's that special something extra that makes for an unforgettable dining experience. A list of the four-star and five-star establishments in this region is located just before the state listings.

Each rating is reviewed annually and each establishment must work to maintain its rating (or improve it). Every effort is made to assure that ratings are fair and accurate; the designated ratings are published purely as an aid to travelers.

In general, properties that are very new or have recently undergone major management changes are considered difficult to assess fairly and are often listed without ratings.

Good Value Check Mark. In all locales, you'll find a wide range of lodging and dining establishments with a ✔ in front of a star rating. This indicates an unusually good value at economical prices as follows:

In Major Cities and Resort Areas

Lodging: average $105–$125 per night for singles; average $115–$140 per night for doubles

Restaurants: average $25 for a complete lunch; average $40 for a complete dinner, exclusive of beverages and gratuities

Local Area Listings

Lodging: average $50–$60 per night for singles; average $60–$75 per night for doubles

Restaurants: average $12 for a complete lunch; average $20 for a complete dinner, exclusive of beverages and gratuities

LODGINGS

Each listing gives the name, address, directions (when there is no street address), neighborhood and/or directions from downtown (in major cities), phone number (local and 800), fax number, number and type of rooms available, room rates, and seasons open (if not year-round). Also included are details on recreational and dining facilities on property or nearby, the presence of a luxury level, and credit-card information. A key to the symbols at the end of each listing is on the inside front cover. (Note that Mobil Corporation credit cards cannot be used for payment of meals and room charges.)

All prices quoted in the *Mobil Travel Guide* publications are expected to be in effect at the time of publication and during the entire year; however, prices cannot be guaranteed. In some localities there may be short-term price variations because of special events or holidays. Whenever possible, these price changes are noted. Certain resorts have complicated rate structures that vary with the time of year; always confirm listed rates when you make your plans.

RESTAURANTS

Listings give the name, address, directions (when there is no street address), neighborhood and/or directions from downtown (in major cities), phone number, hours and days of operation (if not open daily year-round), reservation policy, cuisine (if other than American), price range for each meal served, children's meals (if offered), specialties, and credit card information. Additionally, special features such as chef ownership, ambience, and entertainment are noted. By carefully reading the detailed restaurant information and comparing prices, you can easily determine whether the restaurant is formal and elegant or informal and comfortable for families.

TERMS AND ABBREVIATIONS IN LISTINGS

The following terms and abbreviations are used consistently throughout the listings:

A la carte entrees With a price, refers to the cost of entrees/main dishes only that are not accompanied by side dishes.

AP American plan (lodging plus all meals).

Bar Liquor, wine, and beer are served in a bar or cocktail lounge and usually with meals unless otherwise indicated (e.g., "wine, beer").

Business center The property has a designated area accessible to all guests with business services.

Business servs avail The property can perform/arrange at least two of the following services for a guest: audiovisual equipment rental, binding, computer rental, faxing, messenger services, modem availability, notary service, obtaining office supplies, photocopying, shipping, and typing.

Cable Standard cable service; "premium" indicates that HBO, Disney, Showtime, or similar services are available.

Ck-in, ck-out Check-in time, check-out time.

Coin lndry Self-service laundry.

Complete meal Soup and/or salad, entree, and dessert, plus nonalcoholic beverage.

Continental bkfst Usually coffee and a roll or doughnut.

Cr cds: A, American Express; C, Carte Blanche; D, Diners Club; DS, Discover; ER, enRoute; JCB, Japanese Credit Bureau; MC, MasterCard; V, Visa.

D Followed by a price, indicates room rate for a "double"—two people in one room in one or two beds (the charge may be higher for two double beds).

Downhill/x-country ski Downhill and/or cross-country skiing within 20 miles of property.

Each addl Extra charge for each additional person beyond the stated number of persons at a reduced price.

Early-bird dinner A meal served at specified hours, typically around 4:30–6:30 pm.

Exc Except.

Exercise equipt Two or more pieces of exercise equipment on the premises.

Exercise rm Both exercise equipment and room, with an instructor on the premises.

Fax Facsimile machines available to all guests.

Golf privileges Privileges at a course within 10 miles

Hols Holidays

In-rm modem link Every guest room has a connection for a modem that's separate from the phone line.

Kit. or kits. A kitchen or kitchenette that contains stove or microwave, sink, and refrigerator and that is either part of the room or a separate room. If the kitchen is not fully equipped, the listing will indicate "no equipt" or "some equipt".

Luxury level A special section of a hotel, covering at least an entire floor, that offers increased luxury accommodations. Management must provide no less than three of these four services: separate check-in and check-out, concierge, private lounge, and private elevator service (key access). Complimentary breakfast and snacks are commonly offered.

MAP Modified American plan (lodging plus two meals).

Movies Prerecorded videos are available for rental.

No cr cds accepted No credit cards are accepted.

No elvtr In hotels with more than two stories, it's assumed there are elevators; only their absence is noted.

No phones Phones, too, are assumed; only their absence is noted.

Parking There is a parking lot on the premises.

Private club A cocktail lounge or bar available to members and their guests. In motels and hotels where these clubs exist, registered guests can usually use the club as guests of the management; the same is frequently true of restaurants.

Prix fixe A full meal for a stated price; usually one price is quoted.

Res Reservations.

S Followed by a price, indicates room rate for a "single," i.e., one person.

Semi-a la carte Meals include vegetable, salad, soup, appetizer, or other accompaniments to the main dish.

Serv bar A service bar, where drinks are prepared for dining patrons only.

Serv charge Service charge is the amount added to the restaurant check in lieu of a tip.

Table d'hôte A full meal for a stated price, dependent upon entree selection; no a la carte options are available.

Tennis privileges Privileges at tennis courts within 5 miles.

TV Indicates color television; B/W indicates black-and-white television.

Under certain age free Children under that age are not charged for if staying in room with a parent.

Valet parking An attendant is available to park and retrieve a car.

VCR VCRs in all guest rooms.

VCR avail VCRs are available for hookup in guest rooms.

Special Information for Travelers with Disabilities

The *Mobil Travel Guide* symbol [D] shown in accommodation and restaurant listings indicates establishments that are at least partially accessible to people with mobility problems.

The *Mobil Travel Guide* criteria for accessibility are unique to our publication. Please do not confuse them with the universal symbol for wheelchair accessibility. When the [D] symbol appears following a listing, the establishment is equipped with facilities to accommodate people using wheelchairs or crutches or otherwise needing easy access to doorways and rest rooms. Travelers with severe mobility problems or with hearing or visual impairments may or may not find facilities they need. Always phone ahead to make sure that an establishment can meet your needs.

All lodgings bearing our [D] symbol have the following facilities:

- ISA-designated parking near access ramps
- Level or ramped entryways to building
- Swinging building entryway doors minimum 3'0"
- Public rest rooms on main level with space to operate a wheelchair; handrails at commode areas
- Elevators equipped with grab bars and lowered control buttons
- Restaurants with accessible doorways; rest rooms with space to operate wheelchair; handrails at commode areas

- Minimum 3'0" width entryway to guest rooms
- Low-pile carpet in rooms
- Telephone at bedside and in bathroom
- Bed placed at wheelchair height
- Minimum 3'0" width doorway to bathroom
- Bath with open sink—no cabinet; room to operate wheelchair
- Handrails at commode areas; tub handrails
- Wheelchair accessible peephole in room entry door
- Wheelchair accessible closet rods and shelves

All restaurants bearing our D symbol offer the following facilities:

- ISA-designated parking beside access ramps
- Level or ramped front entryways to building
- Tables to accommodate wheelchairs
- Main-floor rest rooms; minimum 3'0" width entryway
- Rest rooms with space to operate wheelchair; handrails at commode areas

In general, the newest properties are apt to impose the fewest barriers.

To get the kind of service you need and have a right to expect, do not hesitate when making a reservation to question the management in detail about the availability of accessible rooms, parking, entrances, restaurants, lounges, or any other facilities that are important to you, and confirm what is meant by "accessible." Some guests with mobility impairments report that lodging establishments' housekeeping and maintenance departments are most helpful in describing barriers. Also inquire about any special equipment, transportation, or services you may need.

Making the Most of Your Trip

A few diehard souls might fondly remember the trip where the car broke down and they were stranded for a week, or the vacation that cost twice what it was supposed to. For most travelers, though, the best trips are those that are safe, smooth, and within their budget. To help you make your trip the best it can be, we've assembled a few tips and resources.

Saving Money

ON LODGING

After you've seen the published rates, it's time to look for discounts. Many hotels and motels offer them—for senior citizens, business travelers, families, you name it. It never hurts to ask—politely, that is. Sometimes, especially in late afternoon, desk clerks are instructed to fill beds, and you might be offered a lower rate, or a nicer room, to entice you to stay. Look for bargains on stays over multiple nights, in the off-season, and on weekdays or weekends (depending on location). Many hotels in major metropolitan areas, for example, have special weekend package plans, which offer considerable savings on rooms and may include breakfast, cocktails, and meal discounts. Prices change frequently throughout the year, so phone ahead.

Another way to save money is to choose accommodations that give you more than just a standard room. Rooms with kitchen facilities enable you to cook some meals for yourself, reducing restaurant costs. A suite might save money for two couples traveling together. Even hotel luxury levels can provide good value, as many include breakfast or cocktails in the price of the room.

State and city sales taxes as well as special room taxes can increase your room rates as much as 25% per day. We are unable to bring this specific information into the listings, but we strongly urge that you ask about these taxes when placing reservations in order to understand the total price to you.

Watch out for telephone-usage charges that hotels frequently impose on long-distance calls, credit-card calls, and other phone calls—even those that go unanswered. Before phoning from your room, read the information given to you at check-in, and then be sure to read your bill carefully before checking out. You won't be expected to pay for charges that weren't spelled out. (On the other hand, it's not unusual for a hotel to bill you for your calls after you return home.) Consider using public telephones in hotel lobbies; the savings may outweigh the inconvenience.

ON DINING

There are several ways to get a less-expensive meal at a more-expensive restaurant. Early-bird dinners are popular in many parts of the country and offer considerable savings. If you're interested in sampling a ★★★★ or ★★★★★ establishment, consider going at lunchtime. While the prices then are probably relatively high, they may be half of those at dinner and come with the same ambience, service, and cuisine.

PARK PASSES

While many national parks, monuments, seashores, historic sites, and recreation areas may be used free of charge, others charge an entrance fee (ranging from $1 to $5 per person to $5 to $15 per carload) and/or a "use fee" for special services and facilities. If you plan to make several visits to federal recreation areas, consider one of the following National Park Service money-saving programs:

Park Pass. This is an annual entrance permit to a specific unit in the National Park Service system that normally charges an entrance fee. The pass admits the permit holder and any accompanying passengers in a private noncommercial vehicle or, in the case of walk-in facilities, the holder's spouse, children, and parents. It is valid for entrance fees only. A Park Pass may be purchased in person or by mail from the National Park Service unit at which the pass will be honored. The cost is $15 to $20, depending upon the area.

Golden Eagle Passport. This pass, available to people who are between 17 and 61, entitles the purchaser and accompanying passengers in a private noncommercial vehicle to enter any outdoor NPS unit that charges an entrance fee and admits the purchaser and family to most walk-in fee-charging areas. Like the Park Pass, it is good for one year and does not cover use fees. It may be purchased from the National Park Service, Office of Public Inquiries, Room 1013, US Department of the Interior, 18th and C Sts NW, Washington, DC 20240, phone 202/208–4747; at any of the 10 regional offices throughout the country; and at any NPS area that charges a fee. The cost is $50.

Golden Age Passport. Available to citizens and permanent residents of the United States 62 years or older, this is a lifetime entrance permit to fee-charging recreation areas. The fee exemption extends to those accompanying the permit holder in a private noncommercial vehicle or, in the case of walk-in facilities, to the holder's spouse and children. The passport also entitles the holder to a 50% discount on use fees charged in park areas but not to fees charged by concessionaires. Golden Age Passports must be obtained in person. The applicant must show proof of age, i.e., a driver's license, birth certificate, or signed affidavit attesting to age (Medicare cards are not acceptable proof). Passports are available at most park service units where they're used, at National Park Service headquarters (see above), at park system regional offices, at National Forest Supervisors' offices, and at most Ranger Station offices. The cost is $10.

Golden Access Passport. Issued to citizens and permanent residents of the United States who are physically disabled or visually impaired, this passport is a free lifetime entrance permit to fee-charging recreation areas. The fee exemption extends to those accompanying the permit holder in a private noncommercial vehicle or, in the case of walk-in facilities, to the holder's spouse and children. The passport also entitles the holder to a 50% discount on use fees charged in park areas but not to fees charged by concessionaires. Golden Access Passports must be obtained in person. Proof of eligibility to receive federal benefits is required (under programs such as Disability Retirement, Compensation for Military Service-Connected Disability, Coal Mine Safety and Health Act, etc.), or an affidavit must be signed attesting to eligibility. These passports are available at the same outlets as Golden Age Passports.

FOR SENIOR CITIZENS

Look for the senior-citizen discount symbol in the lodging and restaurant listings. Always call ahead to confirm that the discount is being offered, and be sure to carry proof of age. At places not listed in the book, it never hurts to ask if a senior-citizen discount is offered. Two organizations provide additional information for mature travelers: the American Association of Retired Persons (AARP), 601 E St NW, Washington, DC 20049, phone 202/434–2277, and the National Council of Senior Citizens, 8403 Cosville, Ste 1200, Silver Springs, MD 20910, phone 301/528-8800.

Tipping

Tipping is an expression of appreciation for good service, and often service workers rely on tips as a significant part of their income. However, you never need to tip if service is poor.

IN HOTELS

Doormen in major city hotels are usually given $1 for getting you a cab. Bellhops expect $1 per bag, usually $2 if you have only one bag. Concierges are tipped according to the service they perform. It's not mandatory to tip when you've asked for suggestions on sightseeing or restaurants or help in making reservations for dining. However, when a concierge books you a table at a restaurant known to be difficult to get into, a gratuity of $5 is appropriate. For obtaining theater or sporting event tickets, $5–$10 is expected. Maids, often overlooked by guests, may be tipped $1–$2 per day of stay.

AT RESTAURANTS

Coffee shop and counter service wait staff are usually given 8%–10% of the bill. In full-service restaurants, tip 15% of the bill, before sales tax. In fine restaurants, where the staff is large and shares the gratuity, 18%–20% for the waiter is appropriate. In most cases, tip the maitre d' only if service has been extraordinary and only on the way out; $20 is the minimum in upscale properties in major metropolitan areas. If there is a wine steward, tip him or her at least $5 a bottle, more if the wine was decanted or if the bottle was very expensive. If your busboy has been unusually attentive, $2 pressed into his hand on departure is a nice gesture. An increasing number of restaurants automatically add a service charge to the bill in lieu of a gratuity. Before tipping, carefully review your check.

AT AIRPORTS

Curbside luggage handlers expect $1 per bag. Car-rental shuttle drivers who help with your luggage appreciate a $1 or $2 tip.

Staying Safe

The best way to deal with emergencies is to be prepared enough to avoid them. However, unforeseen situations do happen, and you can prepare for them.

IN YOUR CAR

Before your trip, make sure your car has been serviced and is in good working order. Change the oil, check the battery and belts, and make sure tires are inflated properly (this can also improve gas mileage). Other inspections recommended by the car's manufacturer should be made, too.

Next, be sure you have the tools and equipment to deal with a routine breakdown: jack, spare tire, lug wrench, repair kit, emergency tools, jumper cables, spare fan belt, auto fuses, flares and/or reflectors, flashlights, first-aid kit, and, in winter, a windshield scraper and shovel.

Bring all appropriate and up-to-date documentation—licenses, registration, and insurance cards—and know what's covered by your insurance. Also bring an extra set of keys, just in case.

En route, always buckle up!

If your car does break down, get out of traffic as soon as possible—pull well off the road. Raise the hood and turn on your emergency flashers or tie a white cloth to the roadside door handle or antenna. Stay near your car. Use flares or reflectors to keep your car from being hit.

IN YOUR LODGING

Chances are slim that you will encounter a hotel or motel fire. The ▨ in a listing indicates that there were smoke detectors and/or sprinkler systems in the rooms we inspected. Once you've checked in, make sure that any smoke detector in your room is working properly. Ascertain the locations of fire extinguishers and at least two fire exits. Never use an elevator in a fire.

For personal security, use the peephole in your room's door.

PROTECTING AGAINST THEFT

To guard against theft wherever you go, don't bring any more of value than you need. If you do bring valuables, leave them at your hotel rather than in your car, and if you have something very expensive, lock it in a safe. Many hotels have one in each room; others will store your valuables in the hotel's safe. And of course, don't carry more money than you need; use traveler's checks and credit cards, or visit cash machines.

For Travelers with Disabilities

A number of publications can provide assistance. Fodor's *Great American Vacations for Travelers with Disabilities* ($19.50) covers 38 top U.S. travel destinations, including parks, cities, and popular tourist regions. It's available from bookstores or by calling 800/533–6478. The most complete listing of published material for travelers with disabilities is available from *The Disability Bookshop*, Twin Peaks Press, Box 129, Vancouver, WA 98666, phone 360/694–2462. A comprehensive guidebook to the national parks is *Easy Access to National Parks: The Sierra Club Guide for People with Disabilities* ($16), distributed by Random House.

The Reference Section of the National Library Service for the Blind and Physically Handicapped (Library of Congress, Washington, DC 20542, phone 202/707–9275 or 202/707–5100) provides information and resources for persons with mobility problems and hearing and vision impairments, as well as information about the NLS talking-book program (or visit your local library).

Traveling to Canada

Citizens of the United States do not need visas to enter Canada, but proof of citizenship—passport, birth certificate, or voter registration card—is required. A driver's license is not acceptable. Naturalized citizens will need their naturalization certificates or their U.S. passport to reenter the United States. Children under 18 who are traveling on their own should carry a letter from a parent or guardian giving them permission to travel in Canada.

Travelers entering Canada in automobiles licensed in the United States may tour the provinces for up to three months without fee. Drivers are advised to carry their motor vehicle registration card and, if the car is not registered in the driver's name, a letter from the registered owner authorizing use of the vehicle. If the car is rented, carry a copy of the rental contract stipulating use in Canada. For your protection, ask your car insurer for a Canadian Non-resident Interprovince Motor Vehicle Liability Insurance Card. This card ensures that your insurance company will meet minimum insurance requirements in Canada.

The use of seat belts by drivers and passengers is compulsory in all provinces. A permit is required for the use of citizens' band radios. Rabies vaccination certificates are required for dogs or cats.

No handguns may be brought into Canada. If you plan to hunt, sporting rifles and shotguns plus 200 rounds of ammunition per person will be admitted duty-free. Hunting and fishing licenses must be obtained from the appropriate province. Each province has its own regulations concerning the transportation of firearms.

The Canadian dollar's rate of exchange with the U.S. dollar varies; contact your local bank for the latest figures. Since customs regulations can change, it's recommended that you contact the Canadian consulate or embassy in your area. Offices are located in Atlanta, Boston, Buffalo, Chicago, Dallas, Detroit, Los Angeles, Minneapolis, New York City, Seattle, and Washington, DC. For the most current and detailed listing of regulations and sources, ask for the annually revised brochure "Canada: Travel Information," which is available upon request.

Important Toll-Free Numbers
and On-Line Information

HOTELS AND MOTELS

Adam's Mark 800/444–2326
Web www.adamsmark.com
Best Western ....800/528–1234, TDD 800/528–2222
Web www.bestwestern.com
Budgetel Inns 800/428–3438
Web www.budgetel.com
Budget Host 800/283–4678
Clarion 800/252–7466
Web www.clarioninn.com
Comfort 800/228–5150
Web www.comfortinn.com
Courtyard by Marriott 800/321–2211
Web www.courtyard.com
Days Inn 800/325–2525
Web www.travelweb.com/daysinn.html
Doubletree 800/528–0444
Web www.doubletreehotels.com
Drury Inns 800/325–8300
Web www.drury-inn.com
Econo Lodge 800/446–6900
Web www.hotelchoice.com
Embassy Suites 800/362–2779
Web www.embassy-suites.com
Exel Inns of America 800/356–8013
Fairfield Inn by Marriott 800/228–2800
Web www.marriott.com
Fairmont Hotels 800/527–4727
Forte 800/225–5843
Four Seasons 800/332–3442
Web www.fourseasons.com
Friendship Inns 800/453–4511
Web www.hotelchoice.com
Hampton Inn 800/426–7866
Web www.hampton-inn.com
Hilton ....800/445–8667, TDD 800/368–1133
Web www.hilton.com
Holiday Inn ....800/465–4329, TDD 800/238–5544
Web www.holiday-inn.com
Howard Johnson ....800/654–4656, TDD 800/654–8442
Web www.hojo.com
Hyatt & Resorts 800/233–1234
Web www.hyatt.com
Inns of America 800/826–0778
Inter-Continental 800/327–0200
Web www.interconti.com
La Quinta ....800/531–5900, TDD 800/426–3101
Web www.laquinta.com
Loews 800/235-6397
Web www.loewshotels.com
Marriott 800/228–9290
Web www.marriott.com
Master Hosts Inns 800/251–1962

Meridien 800/225–5843
Motel 6 .... 800/466–8356
Nikko International 800/645–5687
Web www.hotelnikko.com
Omni 800/843–6664
Web www.omnirosen.com
Park Inn 800/437–7275
Web www.p-inns.com/parkinn.html
Quality Inn 800/228–5151
Web www.qualityinn.com
Radisson 800/333–3333
Web www.radisson.com
Ramada ....800/228–2828, TDD 800/228–3232
Web www.ramada.com/ramada.html
Red Carpet/Scottish Inns 800/251–1962
Red Lion 800/547–8010
Web www.travelweb.com/travelweb/rl/common/redlion.html
Red Roof Inn 800/843–7663
Web www.redroof.com
Renaissance 800/468–3571
Web www.niagara.com/nf.renaissance
Residence Inn by Marriott 800/331–3131
Web www.marriott.com
Ritz-Carlton 800/241–3333
Web www.ritzcarlton.com
Rodeway 800/228–2000
Web www.rodeway.com
Sheraton 800/325–3535
Web www.sheraton.com
Shilo Inn 800/222–2244
Signature Inns 800/822–5252
Web www.signature-inns.com
Sleep Inn 800/221–2222
Web www.sleepinn.com
Super 8 .... 800/848–8888
Web www.super8motels.com/super8.html
Susse Chalet 800/258–1980
Web www.sussechalet.com
Travelodge/Viscount 800/255–3050
Web www.travelodge.com
Vagabond 800/522–1555
Westin Hotels & Resorts 800/937-8461
Web www.westin.com
Wyndham Hotels & Resorts 800/822–4200
Web www.travelweb.com

AIRLINES

Air Canada 800/776–3000
Web www.aircanada.ca
Alaska 800/426–0333
Web www.alaska-air.com/home.html
Aloha 800/367–5250
American 800/433–7300
Web www.americanair.com/aahome/aahome.html

America West...800/235–9292
Web www.americawest.com
British Airways 800/247–9297
Web www.british-airways.com
Canadian 800/426–7000
Web www.cdair.ca
Continental 800/525–0280
Web www.flycontinental.com
Delta 800/221–1212
Web www.delta-air.com
Hawaiian 800/367–5320
IslandAir 800/323–3345
Mesa..800/637–2247
Northwest 800/225–2525
Web www.nwa.com
SkyWest...800/453–9417
Southwest 800/435–9792
Web www.iflyswa.com
TWA 800/221–2000
Web www.twa.com
United 800/241–6522
Web www.ual.com
USAir..800/428–4322
Web www.usair.com

TRAINS

Amtrak 800/872–7245
Web www.amtrak.com

BUSES

Greyhound...800/231–2222
Web www.greyhound.com

CAR RENTALS

Advantage..800/777–5500
Alamo 800/327–9633
Web www.goalamo.com
Allstate 800/634–6186
Avis...800/331–1212
Web www.avis.com
Budget..800/527–0700
Web www.budgetrentacar.com
Dollar 800/800–4000
Web www.dollarcar.com
Enterprise 800/325–8007
Web www.pickenterprise.com
Hertz 800/654–3131
Web www.hertz.com
National 800/328–4567
Web www.nationalcar.com
Payless...800/237–2804
Rent-A-Wreck 800/535–1391
Web www.rent-a-wreck.com
Sears 800/527–0770
Thrifty 800/367–2277
Web www.thrifty.com
Ugly Duckling 800/843–3825
U-Save 800/272–8728
Value..800/327–2501
Web www.go-value.com

Four-Star and Five-Star Establishments

in the Northwest and Great Plains

IDAHO

★★★★ Lodging
Coeur d'Alene Resort on the Lake, *Coeur d'Alene*

MINNESOTA

★★★★ Lodging
The Saint Paul, *St Paul*

MONTANA

★★★★ Lodging
Flathead Lake Lodge, *Bigfork*

OREGON

★★★★ Lodgings
5th Avenue Suites, *Portland*
Salishan, *Lincoln City*
Tu Tu'Tun Lodge, *Gold Beach*
Vintage Plaza, *Portland*

★★★★ Restaurants
The Dining Room at Salishan (Salishan), *Lincoln City*

Genoa, *Portland*
Meadows (Sunriver Resort), *Bend*

WASHINGTON

★★★★★ Lodging
Four Seasons Olympic Hotel, *Seattle*

★★★★ Lodgings
Alexis Hotel, *Seattle*
Bellevue Club, *Bellevue*
Domaine Madeleine, *Port Angeles*
Hotel Vintage Park, *Seattle*
Inn at the Market, *Seattle*
Salish Lodge and Spa, *North Bend*
Sorrento, *Seattle*
Sun Mountain Lodge, *Winthrop*
Woodmark Hotel on Lake Washington, *Bellevue*

★★★★ Restaurants
Fullers (Sheraton), *Seattle*
Rover's, *Seattle*
Saleh al Lago, *Seattle*
Shoalwater, *Long Beach*

WYOMING

★★★★ Lodgings
Jenny Lake Lodge, *Grand Teton National Park*
Lost Creek Ranch, *Grand Teton National Park*
Rusty Parrot, *Jackson*

★★★★ Restaurant
Alpenhof, *Jackson*

WESTERN CANADA

★★★★ Lodgings
The Aerie, *Victoria*
Four Seasons, *Vancouver*
Hotel Macdonald, *Edmonton*
Pan Pacific Vancouver, *Vancouver*
Sooke Harbour House, *Victoria*
Sutton Place, *Vancouver*
The Westin Bayshore Hotel, *Vancouver*

★★★★ Restaurant
Sooke Harbour House, *Victoria*

Idaho

Population: 1,006,749
Land area: 82,413 square miles
Elevation: 710-12,662 feet
Highest point: Borah Peak (Custer County)
Entered Union: July 3, 1890 (43rd state)
Capital: Boise
Motto: It is forever
Nickname: The Gem State
State flower: Syringa
State bird: Mountain bluebird
State tree: White pine
State fair: Eastern, Early September, 1998, in Blackfoot; Western, Mid-August, 1998, in Boise.
Time zone: Mountain and Pacific
Web: www.visitid.org

When Idaho Territory was created (it included much of Montana and Wyoming as well as the present state), President Abraham Lincoln had difficulty finding a governor who was willing to come to this wild and rugged land. Some appointees, including Gilman Marston and Alexander H. Conner, never appeared.

They had good reason to be timorous—the area was formidable and still is. For there is not just one Idaho—there are at least a half dozen: a land of virgin rain forests (more than one-third of the state is wooded); a high desert covering an area bigger than Rhode Island and Delaware combined; gently sloping farmland, where soft Pacific winds carry the pungency of growing alfalfa; an alpine region of icy, isolated peaks and densely forested valleys hiding more lakes and streams than have been named, counted or even discovered; an atomic energy testing station as modern as tomorrow, only a few miles from the Craters of the Moon, where lava once poured forth and congealed in fantastic formations; and the roadless, nearly uninhabited, 2.3-million-acre Frank Church-River of No Return Wilderness, where grizzly bear, moose and bighorn sheep still run wild.

Stretching southward from Canada for nearly 500 miles, varying dramatically in terrain, altitude and climate, Idaho has the deepest canyon in North America (Hells Canyon, 7,913 feet), the largest stand of white pine in the world (in Idaho Panhandle National Forests), the finest big-game area in the country (Chamberlain Basin and Selway), the largest wilderness area in the United States (the Frank Church-River of No Return Wilderness) and the largest contiguous irrigated area in the US (created by American Falls and several lesser dams). Idaho's largest county, named after the state itself, would hold the entire state of Massachusetts; its second-largest county, Owyhee, would hold New Jersey.

In addition to superlative scenery, fishing and hunting, the visitor will find such diversions as buried bandit treasure, lost gold mines, hair-raising boat trips down the turbulent Salmon River (the "River of No Return") and ghost mining towns. For those who prefer something less strenuous, Sun Valley and Coeur d'Alene have luxurious accommodations.

Millions of years ago herds of mammoth and mastodon, camels and a species of enormous musk ox, roamed the Idaho area. When Lewis and Clark entered the region in 1805, they found fur-bearing animals in such great numbers that they got in each other's way. The promise of riches in furs brought trappers, who fought the animals, the Native Americans, the country and each other with equal gusto. They were aided and abetted by the great fur companies, including the legendary Hudson's Bay Company. The first gold strike in the Clearwater country in 1860, followed by rich strikes in the Salmon River and Florence areas, the Boise Basin and Coeur d'Alene (still an important mining area in the state), brought hordes of miners who were perfectly willing to continue the no-holds-barred way of life initiated by fur trappers. Soon afterward the shots of warring sheepmen and cattlemen mingled with those of miners.

Mining, once Idaho's most productive and most colorful industry, has yielded its economic reign, but the state still produces large amounts of silver, zinc, pumice, antimony and lead. It holds great reserves (268,000 acres) of phosphate rock in the US. Copper, thorium, limestone, asbestos, graphite, talc, tungsten, cobalt, nickel, cinnabar, bentonite and a wealth of other important minerals are found here. Gems, some of the finest quality, include agate, jasper, garnets, opals, onyx, sapphires and rubies.

Today, Idaho's single largest industry is farming. On more than 3.5 million irrigated acres, the state produces an abundance of potatoes, beets, hay, vegetables, fruit and livestock. The upper reaches of the Snake River Valley, once a wasteland of sagebrush and greasewood, are now among the West's most fertile farmlands. Manufacturing and processing of farm products, timber and minerals is an important part of the state's economic base. Tourism is also important to the economy.

When to Go/Climate

Summer and fall are usually pleasant times to visit Idaho, although it can snow at almost any time of year here. The state's varied topography makes for a wide range of weather conditions. Winter temperatures are cold but not so cold as to make outdoor acitivities uncomfortable.

CALENDAR HIGHLIGHTS

FEBRUARY

Pacific Northwest Sled Dog Championship Races (Priest Lake Area). At Priest Lake Airport. Approximately 100 teams from the US and Canada compete in various races from 1/2-mile to 35 miles. Phone Chamber of Commerce, 208/443-3191.

Lionel Hampton/Chevron Jazz Festival (Moscow). University of Idaho. Four-day festival hosted by Lionel Hampton featuring all-star headliners and student performers. Phone 208/885-6765.

APRIL

Cowboy Poet Festival (St Anthony). Entertainment, clogging demonstrations. Phone South Fremont Chamber of Commerce, 208/624-3494.

JUNE

Western Days (Twin Falls). Three-day event featuring shoot-out, barbecue contests, dances, parade. Phone 800/255-8946.

National Oldtime Fiddlers' Contest (Weiser). High School gym. One of the oldest such contests in the country, attracting some of the nation's finest fiddlers. Also parade, barbecue, arts and crafts. Phone 800/437-1280.

Boise River Festival (Boise). Night-time parade, contests, entertainment, fireworks. Phone 208/338-8887.

JULY

smART Festival (St Maries). St Maries City Park. Paintings and crafts by local and regional artists featured in juried art show. Food; entertainment; swimming. Phone 208/245-3417.

Snake River Stampede (Nampa). Among nation's top professional rodeos. All seats reserved. Phone 208/466-8497.

AUGUST

Shoshone-Bannock Indian Festival (Blackfoot). Ft Hall Indian Reservation. Tribes from many western states and Canada gather for this festival. Dancing, parades, rodeo, Native American queen contest, buffalo feast and other events. Phone 208/785-2080.

Western Idaho Fair (Boise). Largest fair in state. Four entertainment stages, grandstand for nationally known musicians. Livestock, rodeo, agricultural pavilion, antique tractors, indoor and outdoor commercial exhibits, midway rides. Phone 208/376-3247.

SEPTEMBER

Eastern Idaho State Fair (Blackfoot). 70-acre fairground. Livestock, machinery exhibits, 4-, 6-, and 8-horse hitch competition, racing (parimutuel betting), rodeo, tractor pull, demolition derby, parade, nightly outdoor musical shows. Phone 208/785-2480.

AVERAGE HIGH/LOW TEMPERATURES (°F)

BOISE

Jan 36/22	May 71/44	Sept 77/48
Feb 44/28	June 81/52	Oct 65/39
Mar 53/32	July 90/58	Nov 49/31
Apr 61/37	Aug 88/57	Dec 38/23

POCATELLO

Jan 32/14	May 68/40	Sept 75/43
Feb 38/20	June 78/47	Oct 63/34
Mar 47/26	July 88/53	Nov 45/26
Apr 58/32	Aug 86/51	Dec 34/16

Parks and Recreation Finder

Directions to and information about the parks and recreation areas below are given under their respective town/city sections. Please refer to those sections for details.

Key to abbreviations: I.P. = Interstate Park; N.B.C. = National Battlefield & Cemetery; N.B.P. = National Battlefield Park; N.F. = National Forest; N.G. = National Grassland; N.H. = National Historical Park; N.H.S. = National Historic Site; N.M. = National Monument; N.Mem. = National Memorial; N.M.P. = National Military Park; N.P. = National Park; N.Pres. = National Preserve; N.R. = National Recreational Area; N.R.R. = National Recreational River; N.Res. = National Reserve; N.S. = National Seashore; N.S.R. = National Scenic River; N.S.T. = National Scenic Trail; N.V.M. = National Volcanic Monument; S.B. = State Beach; S.C.P. = State Conservation Park; S.G. = State Garden; S.H.A. = State Historic Area; S.H.P. = State Historic Park; S.N.A. = State Natural Area; S.P. = State Park; S.R. = State Reserve; S.R.A. = State Recreation Area; S.Res.P. = State Resort Park; S.R.P. = State Rustic Park.

NATIONAL PARK AND RECREATION AREAS

Place Name	Listed Under
Boise N.F.	BOISE
Caribou N.F.	MONTPELIER, POCATELLO
Challis N.F.	CHALLIS
City of Rocks N.Res.	BURLEY
Clearwater N.F.	LEWISTON
Craters of the Moon N.M.	same
Idaho Panhandle N.F.	COEUR D'ALENE, PRIEST LAKE AREA, ST MARIES
Nez Perce N.F.	GRANGEVILLE
Nez Perce N.H.	LEWISTON
Payette N.F.	McCALL
Salmon N.F.	SALMON
Sawtooth N.F.	BELLEVUE, BURLEY, STANLEY
Targhee N.F.	ASHTON

STATE RECREATION AREAS

Place Name	Listed Under
Bear Lake S.P.	MONTPELIER
Bruneau Dunes S.P.	MOUNTAIN HOME
Eagle Island S.P.	BOISE
Farragut S.P.	COEUR D'ALENE
Harriman S.P.	ASHTON
Hells Gate S.P.	LEWISTON
Henry's Lake S.P.	ASHTON
Heyburn S.P.	ST MARIES
Lucky Peak S.P.	BOISE
Massacre Rocks S.P.	AMERICAN FALLS
Old Mission S.P.	KELLOGG
Ponderosa S.P.	McCALL
Priest Lake S.P. (Dickensheet, Indian Creek, and Lionhead units)	PRIEST LAKE AREA
Round Lake S.P.	SANDPOINT

Water-related activities, hiking, riding, various other sports, picnicking, visitor centers and camping are available in most of these areas. Camping: $14/site/night with all hookups; $10/site/night with water; $7/site/night for primitive site. Extra vehicle $5/night. 15-day maximum stay at most parks. Reservations available only at Bear Lake, Farragut, Hells Gate, Ponderosa and Priest Lake parks ($6 fee). Motorized vehicle entrance fee (included in camping fee), $2/day or $30 annual pass; no entrance fee for persons walking, riding a bicyle or horseback riding. All camping parks in the Idaho system feature at least one site designed for use by the disabled. Most visitor centers and restrooms also accommodate the disabled. For further information contact the Idaho Dept of Parks & Recreation, PO Box 83720, Boise 83720-0065; 208/334-4199 or 800/VISIT-ID.

SKI AREAS

Place Name	Listed Under
Bogus Basin Ski Resort	BOISE
Brundage Mt Ski Area	McCALL

Grand Targhee Ski and Summer Resort	DRIGGS
Lookout Pass Ski Area	WALLACE
Pebble Creek Ski Area	POCATELLO
Pomerelle Ski Area	BURLEY
Schweitzer Mountain Resort	SANDPOINT
Silver Mountain Ski Area	KELLOGG
Snowhaven Ski Area	GRANGEVILLE
Soldier Mt Ski Area	MOUNTAIN HOME
Sun Valley Resort	SUN VALLEY AREA

FISHING & HUNTING

Nowhere in Idaho is the outdoor enthusiast more than an hour drive from a clear-water fly-fishing stream. From 2,000 lakes, 90 reservoirs and 16,000 miles of rivers and streams, anglers take several million fish each year. Kokanee, trout (steelhead, rainbow, Kamloops, cutthroat, brown, brook, Dolly Varden and Mackinaw), bass, perch, channel catfish and sunfish are the most common varieties, with trout the most widespread and certainly among the scrappiest. Big game includes white-tailed and mule deer, elk, antelope, bighorn sheep, mountain goat and black bear. There are 12 kinds of upland game birds; ducks, Canada geese and doves in season.

Nonresident fishing license: season $51.50; 1-day $7.50; each addl day $3/day; 3-day salmon/steelhead $31.50. Nonresident hunting license: game $101.50; turkey tag $36.50; deer tag $226.50; elk tag $326.50; other tag fees required for some game. There are nonresident quotas for deer and elk; apply mid-Dec. State permit validation is required for hunting waterfowl and some upland bird species, $6.50; archery and muzzleloader permits, $9. Prices may vary; for full information contact the Idaho Dept of Fish and Game, 600 S Walnut St, Box 25, Boise 83707; 208/334-3700 or 800/635-7820.

RIVER EXPEDITIONS

See Grangeville, Lewiston, Pocatello, Salmon, Stanley, Sun Valley Area and Weiser. For further information contact Idaho Outfitters and Guides Assn, PO Box 95, Boise 83701; 800/71-IDAHO.

Driving Information

Safety belts are mandatory for all persons in front seat of vehicle. Children under 4 years must be in an approved safety seat anywhere in vehicle. For further information phone 208/334-8100.

INTERSTATE HIGHWAY SYSTEM

The following alphabetical listing of Idaho towns in *Mobil Travel Guide* shows that these cities are within 10 miles of the indicated Interstate highways. A highway map, however, should be checked for the nearest exit.

Highway Number	Cities/Towns within 10 miles
Interstate 15	Blackfoot, Idaho Falls, Lava Hot Springs, Pocatello.
Interstate 84	Boise, Burley, Caldwell, Jerome, Mountain Home, Nampa, Twin Falls.
Interstate 86	American Falls, Pocatello.
Interstate 90	Coeur d'Alene, Kellogg, Wallace.

Additional Visitor Information

Idaho Division of Tourism Development, PO Box 83720, 700 W State St, Boise 83720-0093, publishes a number of attractive and helpful pamphlets, among them an Idaho Travel Guide. Phone 208/334-2470 or 800/71-IDAHO.

Visitor centers in Idaho are located in or near the Oregon/Idaho, Washington/Idaho and Utah/Idaho borders, as well as throughout the state. Visitors who stop by will find information and brochures helpful in planning stops at points of interest.

American Falls (F-4)

(For accommodations see Pocatello)

Pop 3,757 **Elev** 4,404 ft **Area code** 208 **Zip** 83211
Information Chamber of Commerce, 239 Idaho St, PO Box 207; 208/226-7214.

After a party of American Fur Company trappers was caught in the current of the Snake River and swept over the falls here, the fur company gave its name to both the community and the falls. American Falls boasts an important hydroelectric plant and is the capital of a vast dry-farming wheat belt; agricultural reclamation projects stretch westward for 170 miles.

What to See and Do

American Falls Dam. Impounds 25-mi-long lake; Willow Bay Recreation Area has swimming (beaches); fishing; boating (ramp; fee); picnicking; camping (hookups; fee). I-86 exit 40, follow signs on ID 39 Bypass. Phone 208/226-7214.

Indian Springs. Hot mineralized springs, pools and baths; camping. (May-Labor Day, daily) 4 mi S on ID 37. Phone 208/226-2174. ¢¢

Massacre Rocks State Park. 995 acres. Along the Old Oregon Trail, emigrants carved their names on Register Rock. Nearby, at Massacre Rocks, is the spot where a wagon train was ambushed in 1862. River, juniper-sagebrush area; extensive bird life. Waterskiing; fishing; boating (ramps). Hiking, bird-watching, picnicking. 52 tent & trailer sites (dump station). Interpretive programs; information center. Standard fees. (Daily) 12 mi SW on I-86 at exit 28. Phone 208/548-2672. ¢

Trenner Memorial Park. Honors engineer who played key role in development of area; miniature power station, fountain, lava terrace. Near Idaho Power Co plant, SW of dam. **Free.**

Annual Event

Portneuf Muzzleloader Blackpowder Rendezvous. Massacre Rocks State Park. 1st wkend June.

Arco (E-4)

Settled 1879 **Pop** 1,016 **Elev** 5,318 ft **Area code** 208 **Zip** 83213

Arco, seat of Butte County, was the first town to be lighted by power derived from atomic energy. Wildcat Peak casts its shadow on this pleasant little community located in a bend of the Big Lost River. Visitors pause here while exploring the Craters of the Moon National Monument (see), 20 miles southwest.

What to See and Do

Craters of the Moon National Monument. (see). 20 mi SW on US 20/26/93.

Experimental Breeder Reactor Number 1 (EBR-1). The first nuclear reactor developed to generate electricity (Dec 20, 1951). Visitor center exhibits include the original reactor and three other nuclear reactors, equipment and control rm as well as displays on the production of electricity. Self-guided or 1-hr tours (Memorial Day wkend-Labor Day, daily; rest of yr, by appt). 18 mi SE via US 20/26. Contact INEL Tours, PO Box 1625, Idaho Falls 83415-3695; 208/526-0050. **Free.**

Ashton (E-5)

(For accommodations see Driggs, Rexburg, St Anthony)

Pop 1,114 **Elev** 5,260 ft **Area code** 208 **Zip** 83420
Information Chamber of Commerce, City Hall, 64 N 10th St, PO Box 689; 208/652-3987.

Ashton's economy is centered on the flow of products from the rich agricultural area that extends to Blackfoot. Equally important to the town, which has a view of the Twin Teton Peaks in Wyoming, is the influx of vacationers bound for the Targhee National Forest, Warm River recreation areas and the Bear Gulch winter sports area. A Ranger District office of the forest is located here.

What to See and Do

Harriman State Park. Located in the heart of a 16,000-acre wildlife refuge; home of the rare trumpeter swan. Nature is the main attraction here with Golden and Silver lakes, wildflowers, lodgepole pines and thriving wildlife. The world-famous fly-fishing stream, Henry's Fork of the Snake River, winds through the park. Historic Railroad Ranch. Hiking, horseback riding; cross-country skiing. (Daily) Standard fees. 19 mi N on US 20/191, S of Island Park. Phone 208/558-7368. Per vehicle ¢

Henry's Lake State Park. This 586-acre park offers waterskiing; boating (ramp). Hiking; picnicking; 50 campsites (26 with hookups, 24 without hookups); dump station). (Mid-May-Oct, daily) Standard fees. 37 mi N on US 20, then 1 mi W; N of Island Park, on the S shore of famous fishing area, Henry's Lake. Phone 208/558-7368 or 208/558-7532 (summer). Per vehicle ¢

⭐ **Targhee National Forest.** Approx 1.8 million acres include two wilderness areas: Jedediah Smith (W slope of the Tetons, adj Grand Teton National Park) and Winegar Hole (grizzly bear habitat, bordering Yellowstone National Park); no motorized vehicles allowed in wilderness areas. Fishing (including trout fishing on Henry's Fork of the Snake River and Henry's Lake Reservoir), big game hunting, camping (fee), picnicking, winter sports; Grand Targhee Resort (see DRIGGS) ski area. Float trips on the Snake River; boating, sailing, waterskiing and canoeing on the Palisades Reservoir; outfitters and guides for the Jedediah Smith Wilderness. N on US 20/191. For further information contact the Supervisor, 420 N Bridge St, PO Box 208, St Anthony 83445; 208/624-3151. In the forest are

Big Springs. Source of North Fork of Snake River which gushes from subterranean cavern at constant 52°F; it quickly becomes 150 ft wide. Schools of salmon and rainbow trout can be seen from the bridge. The stream was designated the first National Recreation Water Trail. Moose, deer, sandhill cranes, trumpeter swans and bald eagles can be seen along the banks. 33 mi N on US 20/191 to Mack's Inn, then 5 mi E on paved road.

Upper Mesa Falls. North Fork of Snake River takes a 114-ft plunge here; scenic overlook. 18 mi NE on ID 47 on forest service land.

Lower Mesa Falls. North Fork drops another 65 ft here; scenic overlook; camping. 14 mi NE on ID 47.

Bellevue (E-3)

(For accommodations see Sun Valley Area; also see Shoshone)

Pop 1,275 **Elev** 5,190 ft **Area code** 208 **Zip** 83313

What to See and Do

Sawtooth National Forest. Elevations from 6,000-12,100 ft. Swimming, water sports; fishing; boating. Nature trails. Downhill and cross-country skiing, snowmobiling. Picnicking; saddle and pack trips; hunting. Camping.

Fee at certain designated campgrounds. N & W. Contact Forest Supervisor, 2647 Kimberly Rd E, Twin Falls 83301-7976; 208/737-3200. **Free.**

Blackfoot (E-4)

(For accommodations see Idaho Falls, Pocatello)

Founded 1878 **Pop** 9,646 **Elev** 4,504 ft **Area code** 208 **Zip** 83221
Information Chamber of Commerce, Riverside Plaza, #1, PO Box 801; 208/785-0510.

Blackfoot's economy has been stimulated by the establishment of an atomic reactor center, about 45 miles west (see ARCO), and deep-well drilling techniques that have increased agricultural productivity. The town, once called Grove City, was established in anticipation of the Utah Northern Railroad's arrival on Christmas Day. Its present name is linked to a legend about Native Americans who crossed a fire-blackened range. To the south is the 528,000-acre Fort Hall Indian Reservation. Excellent Shoshone and Bannock handicraft work is available at local stores and at the tribal office in Fort Hall agency on US 91.

What to See and Do

Bingham County Historical Museum. Restored 1905 homestead containing gun collection, Native American artifacts, early 20th-century furnishings and kitchen utensils. (Mar-Nov, Wed-Fri; closed hols) 190 N Shilling Ave. Phone 208/785-8065. **Donation.**

Parks. Airport, Rodeo grounds, racetrack; picnicking, playground, golf. **Jensen Grove,** Parkway Dr, ½ mi N via I-15 exit 93. Boating, waterskiing, paddleboat rentals, varied water activities. Airport Rd, on Snake River.

Annual Events

Blackfoot Pride Days. Mid-Late June.

Shoshone-Bannock Indian Festival. Ft Hall Indian Reservation, S on I-15, Simplot Rd exit 80, then 2 mi W. Tribes from many western states and Canada gather for this festival. Dancing, parades, rodeo, Native American queen contest, buffalo feast and other events. Phone 208/785-2080. Early Aug.

Eastern Idaho State Fair. 70-acre fairground, N of town. Livestock, machinery exhibits, 4-, 6- and 8-horse hitch competition, racing (parimutuel betting), rodeo, tractor pull, demolition derby, parade, nightly outdoor musical shows. Phone 208/785-2480. 8 days beginning Sat before Labor Day.

Boise (E-2)

(See also Nampa)

Settled 1862 **Pop** 125,738 **Elev** 2,726 ft **Area code** 208 **E-mail** admin@boisecvb.org **Web** www.boise.org
Information Convention and Visitors Bureau, 168 N 9th St, Suite 200, PO Box 2106, 83701; 208/344-7777 or 800/635-5240.

Capital and largest city in Idaho, Boise (BOY-zee) is also the business, financial, professional and transportation center of the state. It is home to Boise State University (1932) and the National Interagency Fire Center, the nation's logistical support center for wildland fire suppression. Early French trappers labeled this still tree-rich area as *les bois* (the woods). Established during gold rush days, Boise was overshadowed by nearby Idaho City until designated the territorial capital in 1864. Abundant hydroelectric power stimulated manufacturing, with electronics, steel fabrication and mobile homes the leading industries. Several major companies have their headquarters here. Lumber, fruit, sugar beets and livestock are other mainstays of the economy; the state's main dairy region lies to the west of

Boise. Natural hot water from the underground springs (with temperatures up to 170°F) heats some of the homes in the eastern portion of the city. A Ranger District office and the headquarters of the Boise National Forestare located here.

Extending alongside the Boise River is the Greenbelt, a trail used for hiking, skating, biking and walking. When complete, the 22-mile trail will connect Eagle Island State Park on the west side of the city with Lucky Peak State Park on the east side of the city.

What to See and Do

Basque Museum and Cultural Center (1864). The only museum in North America dedicated solely to Basque heritage; historical displays, paintings by Basque artists, changing exhibits, restored boarding house used by Basque immigrants in 1900s. (Tues-Sat, limited hrs, phone ahead; closed major hols) 607 Grove St. Phone 208/343-2671. ¢

Bogus Basin Ski Resort. 6 double chairlifts, high-speed quad, paddle tow; patrol, school, rentals; 2 lodges, restaurants, bar; day care. Longest run 1.5 mi; vertical drop 1,800 ft. Night skiing. (Dec-mid-Apr, daily) Cross-country trails. 16 mi N on Bogus Basin Rd. Phone 208/342-2100 (snow conditions) or 800/367-4397 (exc ID). ¢¢¢¢

Boise National Forest. This 2,646,341-acre forest includes the headwaters of the Boise and Payette rivers, 2 scenic byways, abandoned mines and ghost towns and access to the Sawtooth Wilderness and the Frank Church-River of No Return Wilderness. Trout fishing, hunting; swimming; rafting. Skiing; snowmobiling. Mountain biking; motorized trail biking; hiking. Picnicking. Camping. 18 mi SE on ID 21. For further information contact the Supervisor, 1750 Front St, 83702; 208/364-4100.

Discovery Center of Idaho. Hands-on exhibits explore various principles of science; large bubblemaker, catenary arch, magnetic sand. (Daily exc Mon; closed hols) 131 Myrtle St. Phone 208/343-9895. ¢¢

Eagle Island State Park. This 546-acre park was once a prison farm. Situated between the north and south channels of the Boise River, the park has cottonwoods, willows and a variety of native flowers, as well as an abundance of wildlife including the great blue heron, eagle, hawk, beaver, muskrat, fox and weasel. Facilities include 15-acre man-made lake (no fishing), swimming beach, water slide (fee); picnicking, concession. No pets. No glass beverage bottles. (Memorial Day-Labor Day, daily) 8 mi W via ID 20/26 to Linder Rd. Phone 208/939-0696. ¢

Idaho Botanical Gardens. Eleven themed and display gardens including meditation, cactus, rose, water and butterfly/hummingbird gardens; 3/4-mi nature trail, plaza. (Mid-Apr-mid-Oct, daily) 2355 N Penitentiary Rd. Phone 208/343-8649. ¢¢

🎫 **Julia Davis Park.** Rose garden, tennis courts, picnicking, (shelters), playground. Boat rentals, bandshell. Between Capitol Blvd & Broadway on the Boise River. Phone 208/384-4240. On grounds are

Zoo Boise. Home to 285 animals; large birds of prey area; otter exhibit; primates; variety of cats; petting zoo. Education center; gift shop. (Daily; closed Jan 1, Thanksgiving, Dec 25) 355 N Julia Davis Dr. Phone 208/384-4260. ¢¢

Idaho State Historical Museum. History of Idaho and Pacific Northwest. 10 historical interiors; Native American exhibits; fur trade, mining, ranching, forestry displays. (Daily) 610 N Julia Davis Dr. Phone 208/334-2120. **Donation.**

Boise Art Museum. Northwest, Asian and American art featured in changing and permanent exhibits. (Daily exc Mon; closed hols) 670 S Julia Davis Dr. Phone 208/345-8330. ¢¢

Boise Tour Train. Narrated, 1-hr tour of the city and historical areas aboard motorized 1890s-style tour train. Departure point in Julia Davis Park. (Memorial Day-Labor Day, daily; early May-Memorial Day & after Labor Day-Oct, wkends) Phone 208/342-4796. ¢¢¢

Lucky Peak State Park. A 237-acre park comprised of 3 units: Spring Shores Marina (boating, day use), Sandy Point (swimming beach below dam) and Discovery unit (picnicking, 3 group shelters, river). Standard fees. 10 mi SE on ID 21. Phone 208/344-0240. Per vehicle ¢

M-K Nature Center. River observatory allows visitors to view activities of fish life; aquatic and riparian ecology displays; also visitor center with hands-on computerized exhibits; nature trails. (Daily) 600 S Walnut St. Phone 208/334-2225. Grounds **Free.** Visitor center ¢¢

Old Idaho Penitentiary (1870). Self-guided tour through the cells, compounds and other areas of the prison. Guided tours by appt (Memorial Day-Labor Day). Displays about famous inmates, lawmen and penal methods. Slide show on history. (Daily; closed state hols) Under 13 only with adult. 2¹/₂ mi E via Warm Springs Ave (ID 21) to 2445 Old Penitentiary Rd. Phone 208/368-6080. ¢¢

St Michael's Episcopal Cathedral (1900). Tiffany window in south transept is fine example of this type of stained glass. (Mon-Fri, call for schedule) 518 N 8th St. Phone 208/342-5601.

State Capitol (1905-1922). Neo-classical design, faced with Boise sandstone; mounted statue of George Washington in lobby on second floor. Murals on fourth floor symbolically tell state's past, present and future. Changing exhibits. Self-guided tours (daily exc Sun). Guided tours (Mon-Fri, by appt). 8th & Jefferson Sts. Phone 208/334-2470. **Free.**

Table Rock. Provides panoramic view of entire valley, 1,100 ft below. Road may be closed in winter. 4 mi E at end of Shaw Mt Rd.

World Center for Birds of Prey. Originally created to prevent the extinction of the peregrine falcon; scope has been expanded to include national and international conservation of birds of prey and their environments. Visitors can see the breeding chamber of California condors and other raptors at the interpretive center; gift shop. (Daily exc Mon; closed Jan 1, Thanksiving, Dec 25) 5666 W Flying Hawk Lane, I-84, exit 50 to S Cole Rd, then 6 mi S. Phone 208/362-TOUR. ¢¢

Annual Events

Boise River Festival. Night-time parade, contests, entertainment, fireworks. Phone 208/338-8887. Last full wkend June.

Western Idaho Fair. Phone 208/376-3247. Mid-Aug.

Seasonal Events

Thoroughbred racing. Les Bois Park. 5610 Glenwood Rd. Wed & Sat evenings; matinees Sun. Simulcast racing yr-round (daily). Phone 208/376-RACE (7223). May-mid-Aug.

Idaho Shakespeare Festival. Amphitheater. Repertory theater. Phone 208/336-9221. June-Sept.

Motels

★ ★ **BEST REST.** *8002 Overland Rd (83709), near Air Terminal Airport.* 208/322-4404; FAX 208/322-7487; res: 800/733-1418. 86 rms, 2 story. June-mid-Sept: S $50; D $56; under 18 free; ski plans; lower rates rest of yr. Crib free. Pet accepted. TV; cable (premium), VCR (movies). Pool; whirlpool. Restaurant adj open 24 hrs. Ck-out 11 am. Business servs avail. Sundries. Gift shop. Barber, beauty shop. Cr cds: A, C, D, DS, MC, V.

D ⟋ 🏊 ⊠ 🐾 SC

✔★ ★ **BEST WESTERN AIRPORT.** *2660 Airport Way (83705), near Air Terminal Airport.* 208/384-5000; FAX 208/384-5566. 50 rms, 2 story. S $53; D $59; each addl $4; under 19 free. Crib free. TV; cable (premium). Pool. Complimentary continental bkfst. Restaurant opp open 24 hrs. Ck-out 1 pm. In-rm modem link. Coin lndry. Free airport, RR station, bus depot transportation. Some refrigerators. Cr cds: A, C, D, DS, MC, V.

D 🏊 ✕ ⊠ 🐾 SC

★ ★ **BEST WESTERN SAFARI.** *1070 Grove St (83702).* 208/344-6556; FAX 208/344-7240. 104 rms, 3 story. May-mid-Sept: S $49-$63; D $55-$65; each addl $5; suites $73-$125; under 18 free; higher rates special events; lower rates rest of yr. Crib free. TV; cable (premium). Heated pool; whirlpool, sauna. Complimentary continental bkfst. Complimentary coffee in rms. Restaurant nearby. Ck-out 1 pm. Meeting rms. Business servs avail. Free airport, RR station, bus depot transportation. Downhill/x-country ski 16 mi. Refrigerators. Cr cds: A, C, D, DS, MC, V.

★ ★ **BEST WESTERN VISTA.** *2645 Airport Way (83705), near Air Terminal Airport.* 208/336-8100; FAX 208/342-3060. 87 rms, 2 story. S $65; D $71; each addl $4; under 19 free; higher rates River Festival. Crib free. TV; cable (premium). Indoor pool; whirlpool. Complimentary continental bkfst. Restaurant nearby. Ck-out 1 pm. Meeting rms. Business servs avail. In-rm modem link. Free airport, RR station, bus depot transportation. Exercise equipt; weight machine, stair machine, sauna. Cr cds: A, C, D, DS, MC, V.

D ⚊ ✈ ✕ ⋈ 🔥 SC

★ ★ **BOISE RIVER INN.** *1140 Colorado Ave (83706).* 208/344-9988; FAX 208/336-9471. 88 kit. suites, 2 story. S, D $53-$58; each addl $5; wkly rates. Crib free. TV. Heated pool. Complimentary continental bkfst. Restaurant nearby. Ck-out noon. Coin lndry. Balconies. Picnic tables, grills. On river. Cr cds: A, D, DS, MC, V.

⚊ ⋈ 🔥 SC

✔ ★ **COMFORT INN.** *2526 Airport Way (83705), near Air Terminal Airport.* 208/336-0077; FAX 208/342-6592. 60 rms, 2 story. Apr-Oct: S $46-$50; D $50-$58; each addl $6; suites $60-$75; under 18 free; lower rates rest of yr. Crib $2. TV; cable (premium), VCR avail. Indoor pool; whirlpool. Complimentary continental bkfst. Restaurant adj open 24 hrs. Ck-out 11:30 am. Free airport, RR station, bus depot transportation. Downhill ski 20 mi. Refrigerator in suites. Cr cds: A, C, D, DS, ER, JCB, MC, V.

D ⚊ ✈ ⋈ 🔥 SC

✔ ★ **ECONO LODGE.** *2155 N Garden (83706).* 208/344-4030; FAX 208/342-1635. 52 rms, 3 story. S $38; D $45; each addl $6; under 18 free. Crib free. TV; cable (premium), VCR avail. Complimentary continental bkfst. Restaurant nearby. Ck-out 11:30 am. Cr cds: A, C, D, DS, JCB, MC, V.

D ✕ 🔥 SC

★ ★ **HOLIDAY INN.** *3300 Vista Ave (83705), near Air Terminal Airport.* 208/344-8365; FAX 208/343-9635. 265 rms, 2 story. S, D $75-$105; each addl $5; under 18 free; wknd rates. Crib free. Pet accepted. TV; cable (premium), VCR avail. 2 pools, 1 indoor. Restaurant 6 am-11 pm. Rm serv. Bar 11-1 am. Ck-out noon. Coin lndry. Valet serv. Meeting rms. Business servs avail. Bellhops. Sundries. Free airport transportation. Downhill ski 20 mi. Exercise equipt; bicycles, stair machine. Cr cds: A, C, D, DS, JCB, MC, V.

D ✔ ⚊ ✈ ⋈ 🔥 SC

★ ★ **INN AMERICA.** *2275 Airport Way (83705), I-84, exit 53, near Air Terminal Airport.* 208/389-9800; FAX 208/338-1308; res: 800/469-4667. 73 rms, 3 story. S $37.95-$41.95; D $43.95-$49.95; each addl $4; under 18 free; higher rates: Boise River Fest, NCAA events. Crib free. TV; cable (premium), VCR avail. Heated pool. Restaurant nearby. Ck-out 1 pm. Coin lndry. Business servs avail. In-rm modem link. Valet serv. Sundries. Free airport transportation. Downhill/x-country ski 20 mi. Cr cds: A, C, D, DS, MC, V.

D ⚊ ⚊ ✈ ⋈ 🔥 SC

★ **QUALITY INN AIRPORT SUITES.** *2717 Vista Ave (83705), near Air Terminal Airport.* 208/343-7505; FAX 208/342-4319. 79 suites, 2 story, 50 kit. units. May-Oct: suites, kit. units $57-$64; under 18 free; wkly rates; lower rates rest of yr. Crib $2. Pet accepted, some restrictions; $10. TV; cable (premium), VCR avail. Pool. Complimentary continental bkfst. Restaurant nearby. Ck-out noon. Coin lndry. Free airport transportation. Refrigerators. Cr cds: A, C, D, DS, ER, JCB, MC, V.

⚊ ⚊ ✈ ⋈ 🔥 SC

★ ★ **RESIDENCE INN BY MARRIOTT.** *1401 Lusk Ave (83707), Yale at Capitol Blvd.* 208/344-1200; FAX 208/384-5354. 104 rms, 2 story. S $120; D $120-$150; family rates. Crib free. Pet accepted, some restrictions; $10/day. TV; cable (premium), VCR avail. Pool; whirlpool. Restaurant nearby. Ck-out noon. Coin lndry. Meeting rms. Business servs avail. Free airport, RR station, bus depot transportation. Downhill/x-country ski 20 mi. Lawn games. Refrigerators. Private patios, balconies. Picnic tables, grills. Cr cds: A, D, DS, MC, V.

⚊ ⚊ ⚊ ⋈ 🔥 SC

★ **RESTON.** *1025 S Capitol Blvd (83706), opp Boise State Univ.* 208/344-7971; FAX 208/345-6846. 126 rms, 2 story. S $69; D $77; each addl $5; suites $85-$160; under 18 free. Crib free. Pet accepted; $50. TV; cable (premium), VCR avail (movies). Heated pool; whirlpool, sauna, poolside serv. Complimentary continental bkfst. Bar 5 pm-2 am; entertainment Fri, Sat. Ck-out noon. Meeting rms. Business servs avail. Free airport transportation. Downhill ski 20 mi. Health club privileges. Cr cds: A, C, D, DS, MC, V.

D ✔ ⚊ ⚊ ⋈ 🔥 SC

★ ★ **RODEWAY INN.** *1115 N Curtis Rd (83706).* 208/376-2700; FAX 208/377-0324. 98 rms, 2 story. S $65-$75; D $75-$85; each addl $10; suites $75-$140; under 18 free. Crib free. TV; cable (premium). Indoor/outdoor pool; whirlpool, sauna. Complimentary full bkfst. Restaurant 6:30 am-10 pm. Rm serv. Bar; entertainment. Ck-out noon. Meeting rms. Business servs avail. In-rm modem link. Bellhops. Valet serv. Free airport, RR station, bus depot transportation. Putting green. Private patios, balconies. Cr cds: A, C, D, DS, JCB, MC, V.

D ⚊ ⋈ 🔥 SC

★ ★ **SHILO INN AIRPORT.** *4111 Broadway (83705), near Air Terminal Airport.* 208/343-7662; FAX 208/344-0318. 126 rms, 4 story, 88 suites. S, D $70-$75; each addl $10; suites $75-$85; under 13 free; higher rates NCAA events. Pet accepted; $7. TV; cable (premium), VCR avail (movies). Pool; whirlpool. Complimentary continental bkfst. Restaurant adj open 24 hrs. Ck-out noon. Coin lndry. Meeting rms. Business servs avail. Valet serv. Free airport, RR station, bus depot transportation. Exercise equipt; weight machine, bicycles, sauna. Bathrm phones; some refrigerators, wet bars. Cr cds: A, C, D, DS, ER, JCB, MC, V.

D ✔ ⚊ ✈ ✕ ⋈ 🔥 SC

★ ★ **SHILO INN RIVERSIDE.** *3031 Main St (83702).* 208/344-3521; FAX 208/384-1217. 112 rms, 3 story. S, D $55-$79; each addl $10; under 12 free. Crib free. Pet accepted; $7. TV; cable (premium), VCR (movies). Indoor pool; whirlpool. Complimentary continental bkfst. Restaurant nearby. Ck-out noon. Coin lndry. Meeting rms. Business servs avail. Valet serv. Free airport, RR station, bus depot transportation. Downhill/x-country ski 15 mi. Exercise equipt; weights, bicycles, sauna, steam rm. Refrigerators. Private patios, balconies (many overlook river). Cr cds: A, C, D, DS, ER, JCB, MC, V.

✔ ⚊ ✔ ⚊ ✕ 🔥 SC

★ **SLEEP INN.** *2799 Airport Way (83705), near Air Terminal Airport.* 208/336-7377; FAX 208/336-2035; res: 800/321-4661. 69 rms, shower only, 2 story. S $53; D $57; each addl $4; under 19 free; higher rates Boise River Festival. Crib free. TV; cable (premium), VCR (movies). Complimentary continental bkfst. Restaurant nearby. Ck-out 1 pm. Business servs avail. Free airport, bus depot transportation. Some refrigerators. Cr cds: A, C, D, DS, JCB, MC, V.

D ✕ ⋈ 🔥 SC

✔ ★ **SUPER 8 LODGE-BOISE AIRPORT.** *2773 Elder St (83705), near Air Terminal Airport.* 208/344-8871; FAX 208/344-8871, ext. 444. 110 rms, 3 story. S $45.88; D $49.88-$58.88; each addl $2. Crib free. Pet accepted, some restrictions; $20. TV; cable (premium), VCR avail. Heated pool. Restaurant opp 6 am-10 pm. Ck-out 11 am. Business servs avail. Cr cds: A, C, D, DS, MC, V.

D ✔ ⚊ ⋈ 🔥 SC

✔ ★ **TRAVELODGE-BOISE CENTER.** *1314 Grove St (83702).* 208/342-9351; FAX 208/336-5828. 50 rms, 40 with shower only, 2 story. May-mid-Sept: S $39; D $44-$52; each addl $5; under 18 free; lower rates rest of yr. Crib free. TV; cable (premium). Pool. Complimentary coffee in rms. Restaurant nearby. Ck-out noon. Cr cds: A, C, D, DS, ER, JCB, MC, V.

⚊ ⋈ 🔥 SC

★ ★ **UNIVERSITY INN.** *2360 University Dr (83706), adj to Boise State Univ.* 208/345-7170; FAX 208/345-5118; res: 800/345-7170. 80 rms, 2 story. S $46.50-$65.50; D $55.50-$65; each addl $7; suites $65-$71; under 18 free. TV; cable (premium). Heated pool; whirlpool, poolside serv. Restaurant 6 am-9 pm; Sun 7 am-3 pm. Rm serv. Bar. Ck-out noon. Business servs avail. Valet serv. Free airport transportation. Downhill ski 20 mi. Cr cds: A, C, D, DS, MC, V.

⬛ ⬛ ⬛ ⬛ SC

Motor Hotels

★ ★ ★ **BOISE PARK SUITE HOTEL.** *424 E Park Center Blvd (83706).* 208/342-1044; FAX 208/342-2763; res: 800/342-1044. 238 kit. units, 3 story. S, D $120; wkend, wkly rates; higher rates Boise River Festival. Crib free. TV; cable (premium). Pool; whirlpool. Complimentary continental bkfst. Complimentary coffee in rms. Restaurant nearby. Bar 5-10 pm. Ck-out noon. Coin lndry. Meeting rms. Business center. In-rm modem link. Valet serv. Free airport, RR station, bus depot transportation. Exercise equipt; weights, bicycles. Minibars. Cr cds: A, D, DS, MC, V.

⬛ ⬛ ⬛ ⬛ ⬛ SC ⬛

★ ★ ★ **DOUBLETREE.** *1800 Fairview Ave (83702).* 208/344-7691; FAX 208/336-3652. 182 rms, 3-7 story. S $88-$108; D $103-$123; each addl $15; suites $195; under 18 free; wkend rates. Crib free. TV; cable. Heated pool. Restaurant 6 am-11 pm. Rm serv. Bar 3 pm-2 am. Ck-out noon. Meeting rms. Business servs avail. Bellhops. Valet serv. Free airport, RR station, bus depot transportation. Downhill ski 16 mi. Exercise equipt; weights, stair machine. Balconies. Cr cds: A, C, D, DS, ER, JCB, MC, V.

⬛ ⬛ ⬛ ⬛ ⬛

★ ★ ★ **DOUBLETREE-RIVERSIDE.** *2900 Chinden Blvd (83714).* 208/343-1871; FAX 208/344-1079. 304 rms, 2 story. S $104-$114; D $119-$129; each addl $15; suites $165-$395; under 18 free. Crib $10. Pet accepted, some restrictions. TV; cable. Heated pool; wading pool, whirlpool, poolside serv. Restaurant 6 am-11 pm. Rm serv. Bar. Ck-out noon. Convention facilities. Business servs avail. In-rm modem link. Bellhops. Valet serv. Sundries. Free airport, RR station, bus depot transportation. Downhill ski 16 mi. Exercise equipt; weight machine, bicycles. Some bathrm phones, refrigerators. Private patios, balconies. Beautifully landscaped grounds; on Boise River. Cr cds: A, C, D, DS, ER, JCB, MC, V.

⬛ ⬛ ⬛ ⬛ ⬛ ⬛ ⬛

★ ★ ★ **OWYHEE PLAZA HOTEL.** *1109 Main St (83702).* 208/343-4611; FAX 208/336-3860; res: 800/233-4611 (exc ID), 800/821-7500 (ID). 100 rms, 3 story. S $65-$107; D $75-$117; each addl $10; suites $200-$375; under 18 free. Crib free. Pet accepted. TV; cable (premium). VCR avail. Heated pool; poolside serv. Restaurants 6 am-10 pm. Rm serv. Bars; entertainment. Ck-out noon. Meeting rms. Business servs avail. In-rm modem link. Bellhops. Valet serv. Sundries. Beauty shop. Free airport transportation. Downhill/x-country ski 20 mi. Balconies. Built 1910. Cr cds: A, MC, V.

⬛ ⬛ ⬛ ⬛ ⬛ SC

Hotels

★ ★ **DOUBLETREE AND PARK CENTER.** *475 W Park Center Blvd (83706).* 208/345-2002; FAX 208/345-8354. 158 rms, 6 story. S $95-$110; D $105-$120; each addl $10; suites $165; under 12 free; wkend rates. Crib free. TV; cable (premium), VCR avail. Heated pool. Complimentary continental bkfst. Bar. Ck-out 1 pm. Meeting rm. Business servs avail. Free airport, RR station, bus depot transportation. Downhill/x-country ski 20 mi. Exercise equipt; weights, bicycles. Refrigerator in suites. Opp river. Cr cds: A, C, D, DS, ER, JCB, MC, V.

⬛ ⬛ ⬛ ⬛ ⬛ ⬛ SC

★ ★ **PLAZA SUITE.** *409 S Cole Rd (83709).* 208/375-7666; res: 800/376-3608. 39 suites, 4 story. Suites $70-$180; each addl $7.50; under 2 free. Crib free. TV; cable (premium), VCR avail. Indoor pool. Coffee in

rms. Ck-out 1 pm. Meeting rms. Business servs avail. In-rm modem link. Free airport transportation. Downhill ski 20 mi. Cr cds: A, C, D, DS, MC, V.

⬛ ⬛ ⬛ ⬛ ⬛ SC

★ ★ **STATEHOUSE INN.** *981 Grove St (83702).* 208/342-4622; FAX 208/344-5751; res: 800/243-4622. 88 rms, 6 story. S $75-$85; D $80-$100; each addl $10; suites $175; under 18 free. Crib free. TV; cable (premium), VCR. Complimentary full bkfst. Restaurant 6 am-10 pm. Bar 3 pm-midnight. Ck-out 1 pm. Meeting rms. Business servs avail. Free garage parking. Free airport, RR station, bus depot transportation. Exercise equipt; weights, bicycles, whirlpool, sauna. Some refrigerators, minibars. Cr cds: A, C, D, DS, MC, V.

⬛ ⬛ ⬛ ⬛ ⬛ SC

Inn

★ ★ **IDAHO HERITAGE INN.** *109 W Idaho St (83702).* 208/342-8066; FAX 208/343-2325. 6 rms, 2 with shower only, 3 story. S, D $65-$95; each addl $10. TV in some rms. Complimentary coffee in rms. Complimentary full bkfst; afternoon refreshments. Restaurant nearby. Ck-out 11 am, ck-in 3 pm. Luggage handling. Downhill/x-country ski 20 mi. Picnic tables. Built 1904; many antiques. Former home of Senator Frank Church. Cr cds: A, DS, MC, V.

⬛ ⬛ ⬛ ⬛

Restaurants

★ ★ **MILFORD'S FISH HOUSE.** *405 S 8th St #100.* 208/342-8382. Hrs: 5-10 pm. Closed major hols. Res accepted. Bar. Complete meals: dinner $12.95-$32.95. Specializes in fresh Northwest seafood. Outdoor dining. Former railroad freight warehouse. Cr cds: A, MC, V.

★ **OÑATI.** *(3544 Chinden Blvd, Garden City) 2 mi NW on Chinden Blvd.* 208/343-6464. Hrs: 11:30 am-2 pm, 5:30-10 pm; Sat from 5:30 pm. Closed Sun; Jan 1, July 4, Dec 24. Res accepted. Basque menu. Bar. Complete meals: lunch $4.25-$7.95, dinner $9.95-$16. Specializes in lamb shank, baked lamb, seafood. Basque-style dancing. Basque artwork on display. Cr cds: A, DS, MC, V.

⬛

★ **PEG-LEG ANNIE'S.** *3019 N Cole Rd (83711).* 208/375-3050. Hrs: 11:30 am-10 pm; Fri, Sat to 11 pm. Closed Sun; major hols. Res accepted. Bar to 1 am. Semi-a la carte: lunch $5-$8.50, dinner $7.95-$10. Child's meals. Specializes in baby back pork ribs, prime rib, chicken. Outdoor dining. Memorabilia from 1930s & 1940s; photos, musical instruments. Cr cds: A, C, DS, MC, V.

⬛

✓★ **RICK'S CAFE AMERICAIN AT THE FLICKS.** *646 Fulton St, in theater complex.* 208/342-4288. Hrs: 4:30-9:30 pm; Sat, Sun from noon. Res accepted. Wine, beer. Semi-a la carte: lunch, dinner $5-$15. Specializes in pasta, vegetarian lasagne. Outdoor dining. Designed after Humphrey Bogart's famous cafe in Casablanca; movie memorabilia, directors chairs, hologram image. Totally nonsmoking. Cr cds: A, C, D, DS, MC, V.

Bonners Ferry (A-2)

(See also Sandpoint)

Settled 1864 **Pop** 2,193 **Elev** 1,777 ft **Area code** 208 **Zip** 83805
Information Visitors Center, PO Box X; 208/267-5922.

E.L. Bonner offered ferry service from this point on the Kootenai River, near the northern tip of the state, and gave this community its name. Today Bonners Ferry services the agricultural and lumbering districts of Boundary County, of which it is the county seat. From here the broad, flat and fertile

Kootenai Valley stretches north to British Columbia. This is a scenic area featuring many lakes and streams; fishing, hunting and hiking are popular pastimes. A Ranger District office of the Idaho Panhandle National Forest-Kaniksu (see PRIEST LAKE AREA) is located here.

What to See and Do

Kootenai National Wildlife Refuge. This 2,774-acre refuge was created as a resting area for waterfowl during migration. Its wide variety of habitat supports many species of birds and mammals, including bald eagles. Auto tour (4½ mi). Hunting, fishing. 5 mi W on Riverside Rd. For further information contact Refuge Mgr, HCR 60, Box 283; 208/267-3888. **Free.**

Moyie Falls. Park and look down into 400-ft canyon at spectacular series of plunges. Greater flow during the spring runoff. 9 mi E on US 2, then N at Moyie Springs on small road; watch for sign for overlook just E of first bridge over Moyie River.

Annual Event

Kootenai River Days. 3 wks June.

Motels

★ ★ ★ **BEST WESTERN KOOTENAI RIVER INN & CASINO.** Kootenai River Plaza. 208/267-8511. 47 rms, 2 story. May-Sept: S $76.50; D $84.50-$90.50; each addl $6; suites from $250; under 13 free; lower rates rest of yr. Crib $6. TV; cable. Indoor pool; whirlpool, poolside serv. Restaurant 6 am-9 pm. Rm serv. Bar. Ck-out noon. Meeting rms. Exercise equipt; bicycles, rowing machine, sauna. Bathrm phone in suites. Private patios, balconies. Cr cds: A, C, D, DS, MC, V.

[D] [⚡] [≋] [✕] [↖] [⚞] [SC]

★ **KOOTENAI VALLEY.** Rte 4, Box 4740, S on US 95. 208/267-7567. 22 rms, 3 kit. units. June-Sept: S $55; D $65-$125; each addl $5; kit. units $75-$90; wkly rates; higher rates special events; lower rates rest of yr. Crib free. TV; cable (premium). Playground. Restaurant adj 4:30 am-8 pm. Ck-out 11 am. Business servs avail. Picnic tables. Cr cds: MC, V.

[D] [↖] [⚞] [SC]

✔★ **SUNSET.** (2705 Hwy 3E (Canyon St), Creston BC CAN V0B 1G0) 33 mi N via US 2/95 to ID 1, then 7 mi N. 250/428-2229; FAX 250/428-2251; res: 800/663-7082. 24 rms, 2 story, 7 kit. units. June-mid-Sept: S $45; D $50-$54; each addl $4; kit. units $5 addl; lower rates rest of yr. Crib $4. Pet accepted. TV; cable (premium), VCR avail (free movies). Heated pool. Complimentary coffee in rms. Ck-out 11 am. Business servs avail. In-rm modem link. Refrigerators. Cr cds: A, C, D, DS, ER, MC, V.

[D] [⚡] [≋] [↖] [⚞]

★ **TOWN & COUNTRY.** Rte 4, Box 4664, US 95. 208/267-7915. 11 rms, 5 kits. Mar-Oct: S $47; D, kit. units $49-$59; each addl $5; lower rates rest of yr. TV; cable. Complimentary coffee. Restaurant nearby. Ck-out 11 am. Cr cds: A, D, DS, MC, V.

[↖] [⚞]

Restaurant

✔★ **PANHANDLE.** 7168 Main St. 208/267-2623. Hrs: 6 am-8 pm; Sat, Sun from 7 am. Closed some major hols. Semi-a la carte: bkfst $2-$6.95, lunch $4-$9, dinner $6-$12. Specializes in chicken-fried steak, fish & chips, homemade soups. Salad bar. Cr cds: DS, MC, V.

Buhl (F-3)

(For accommodations see Twin Falls)

Pop 3,516 **Elev** 3,793 ft **Area code** 208 **Zip** 83316
Information Chamber of Commerce, 716 US 30 E; 208/543-2185.

Named for Frank Buhl, an early empire builder, this community processes the outpouring of farm goods produced in the farmlands of "Magic Valley." A Ranger District office of Nevada's Humboldt National Forest is located here.

What to See and Do

Balanced Rock. This 40-ft rock tower, resembling the mushroom cloud of an atomic bomb, rests on 18-by-36-inch base; picnic area nearby. 12 mi SW on local roads.

Annual Events

Sagebrush Days. Rodeo, sidewalk sales, Rodeo Queen contest, fireworks, parade. Wk of July 4.

Twin Falls County Fair and Rodeo. 6 mi E in Filer. Carnival, 4-H exhibits, flower, art and antique shows; RCA rodeo. 4 days beginning Wed after Labor Day.

Burley (F-3)

(See also Twin Falls)

Pop 8,702 **Elev** 4,165 ft **Area code** 208 **Zip** 83318 **E-mail** mcidcham@cyberhighway.net **Web** www.cyberhighway.net/~mcidcham/
Information Mini-Cassia Chamber of Commerce, 324 Scott Ave, Rupert, 83350; 208/678-7230 or 800/333-3408.

Created by a 210,000-acre irrigation project that turned a near-desert area into a thriving agricultural center ideal for alfalfa, grain, sugar beet and potatoes. Burley is a center for potato processing and has one of the largest sugar beet processing plants in the world. A Ranger District office of the Sawtooth National Forest is located here.

What to See and Do

Boating. 30 mi of the Snake River, with constant water levels, provide great boating opportunities throughout the summer.

Cassia County Historical Museum. Railroad cars; pioneer cabins; wagon collection, other pioneer relics. (Apr-mid-Nov, Tues-Sat; closed July 4) E Main & Hiland Ave. Phone 208/678-7172. **Donation.**

City of Rocks National Reserve. A pioneer stopping place, this 25-sq-mi area of granite spires and sculptured rock formations resembles a city carved from stone; granite walls are inscribed with messages and names of westward-bound settlers, and remnants of the California Trail are still visible. Well-known for technical rock climbing. Hiking. Picnicking. Primitive camping. 22 mi S on ID 27 to Oakley, then 16 mi S and follow signs; or 32 mi S on ID 77 to Almo, then 2 mi W and follow signs. Phone 208/824-5519.

Sawtooth National Forest. Fishing, camping, hiking, horseback riding, snowmobiling, cross-country and downhill skiing, scenic views. Includes Howell Canyon, Lake Cleveland and four other glacial lakes. Fee for certain designated campgrounds. 9 mi E on US 30 to Declo, then 15 mi S on ID 77; other areas E & W. For further information contact the Supervisor, 2647 Kimberly Rd E, Twin Falls 83301-7976; 208/737-3200. In forest is

Pomerelle Ski Area. Double, triple chairlifts, rope tow; patrol, school, rentals; cafeteria. Longest run 2.2 mi; vertical drop 1,000 ft. (Mid-Nov-Mar, daily; Apr, wkends) Night skiing (Jan-mid-Mar, Tues-Sat). 25 mi SE on ID 77, off I-84 exit 216. Phone 208/638-5599 (office) or 208/638-5555 (recorded snow report). ¢¢¢¢¢

Annual Events

Idaho Powerboat Regatta. Burley Marina. Boat racers from throughout the western US compete in this American Power Boat Association's national championship series event. Last wkend June.

Cassia County Fair & Rodeo. County Fairgrounds, E end of E 10th & E 12th Sts. Racing, parimutuel betting. 3rd wk Aug.

Motor Hotel

★ ★ **BEST WESTERN BURLEY INN.** *800 N Overland Ave, I-84 exit 208.* 208/678-3501; FAX 208/678-9532. 126 rms, 2 story. S $58-$68; D $64-$74; each addl $6; suites $88; under 18 free. Crib free. Pet accepted. TV; cable (premium). Heated pool. Playground. Restaurant 6-1:30 am. Rm serv. Bar 4 pm-1 am. Ck-out noon. Coin lndry. Meeting rms. Business servs avail. Lawn games. Trailer facilities. Cr cds: A, C, D, DS, ER, MC, V.

Caldwell (E-1)

(See also Boise, Nampa)

Founded 1883 **Pop** 18,400 **Elev** 2,369 ft **Area code** 208 **Zip** 83605
Information Chamber of Commerce, 300 Frontage Rd, PO Box 819, 83606; 208/459-7493.

Caldwell, seat of Canyon County, is situated in the triangle formed by the confluence of the Snake and Boise rivers. Founded by the Idaho and Oregon Land Improvement Company, the town was named for the company's president, C.A. Caldwell. Livestock, diversified agriculture and vegetable-processing plants are mainstays of the economy.

What to See and Do

Albertson College of Idaho (1891). (800 students) Oldest 4-yr college in state. Private liberal arts college. Evans Mineral Collection, the Orma J. Smith Natural Science Museum and a planetarium are in Boone Science Hall; Blatchley Hall houses the Rosenthal Gallery of Art (Sept-May, inquire for hrs). On Cleveland Blvd at 20th St. Phone 208/459-5500.

Ste Chapelle Winery & Vineyards. Vineyards spread over slopes of the beautiful Snake River Valley. Reception area; tasting room; 24-ft cathedral windows offer spectacular view of valley and distant Owyhee Mts. Half-hr tours. (Daily) 12 mi S via ID 55. Phone 208/459-7222. **Free.**

Succor Creek Canyon. Two-mile stretch of spectacular canyon scenery and interesting earth formations. An abundance of prehistoric fossils has been found here. 33 mi W on ID 19, just across Oregon line.

Warhawk Air Museum. Displays World War II aviation artifacts. (Daily; call for schedule) 4917 Aviation Way, Caldwell Industrial Airport. Phone 208/454-2854. ¢

Annual Events

Little Britches Rodeo. 2nd wk July.

Canyon County Fair. Late July.

Night Rodeo. 2nd or 3rd wk Aug.

Motels

★ ★ **COMFORT INN.** *901 Specht Ave.* 208/454-2222; FAX 208/454-9334. 65 rms, 3 story. Mid-May-mid-Sept: S $58-$79; D, kit. units $68-$89; each addl $8; suites $89-$130; under 18 free; lower rates rest of yr. Crib free. Pet accepted. TV; cable. Indoor pool; whirlpool. Complimentary continental bkfst. Restaurant adj open 24 hrs. Ck-out 1 pm. Coin lndry. Meeting rms. Sundries. Gift shop. Exercise equipt; weight machine, bicycles, sauna. Health club privileges. Some refrigerators, minibars. Picnic tables, grills. Cr cds: A, C, D, DS, ER, JCB, MC, V.

✔ ★ **SUNDOWNER.** *1002 Arthur St.* 208/459-1585; FAX 208/454-9487. 67 rms, 2 story. S $40; D $42; each addl $2. Crib free. TV. Pool. Complimentary continental bkfst. Restaurant nearby. Some refrigerators. Cr cds: A, C, D, DS, MC, V.

Challis (D-3)

Founded 1876 **Pop** 1,073 **Elev** 5,288 ft **Area code** 208 **Zip** 83226

Cloud-capped mountains, rocky gorges and the Salmon River make this village one of the most picturesque in the Salmon River "Grand Canyon" area. This is the seat of Custer County and the headquarters for Challis National Forest. Two Ranger District offices of the forest are also located here.

What to See and Do

Challis National Forest. More than 2½ million acres of forest land surrounds Challis on all sides, crossed by US 93 & ID 75. Hot springs, ghost towns, nature viewing via trails; portion of the Frank Church-River of No Return Wilderness, camping, picnicking, hunting and trout fishing. Guides, outfitters avail in Challis and vicinity. Idaho's highest point is here—Mt Borah (12,665 ft). For further information contact the Recreation Staff Officer, Forest Supervisor Bldg, HC 63, Box 1671; 208/879-2285. Flowing through the forest is the

Middle Fork of the Salmon Wild and Scenic River. One of the premier whitewater rafting rivers in the US. Permits are required to float this river (apply Oct-Jan, permits issued June-Sept by lottery; fee). For permit information contact Middle Fork Ranger, PO Box 750; 208/879-5204.

Grand Canyon in miniature. Walls cut 2,000 ft down on either side. Best seen at dusk. 10-13 mi S & SE on US 93.

Motels

★ **NORTHGATE INN.** *HC 63, Box 1665, ¼ mi N on US 93.* 208/879-2490. 56 rms, 3 story. S $34; D $37-$40; each addl $4; under 12 free. Crib free. TV; cable. Complimentary continental bkfst. Ck-out 11 am. Meeting rm. Cr cds: A, D, DS, MC, V.

✔ ★ **VILLAGE INN.** *Box 6, 6 blks NW on US 93.* 208/879-2239. 54 rms, 6 kits. S $30-$42; D $42-$52; each addl $2; kit. units $2 addl; under 3 free. Pet accepted. TV; cable (premium). Restaurant 6 am-10 pm. Ck-out 11 am. Meeting rm. Downhill ski 7 mi; x-country ski 10 mi. Some refrigerators. Cr cds: A, C, D, DS, MC, V.

Coeur d'Alene (B-1)

(See also Kellogg; also see Spokane, WA)

Settled 1878 **Pop** 24,563 **Elev** 2,152 ft **Area code** 208 **Zip** 83814
Information Coeur d'Alene Area Chamber of Commerce, PO Box 850, 83816; 208/664-3194.

Nestled amid lakes and rivers, Coeur d'Alene (cor-da-LANE) is a tourist and lumbering community, but particularly a gateway to a lush vacation area in the Idaho Panhandle. Irrigation has opened vast sections of nearby countryside for agricultural development; grass seed production is of major importance. This is the headquarters for the three Idaho Panhandle National Forests, and there are three Ranger District offices here.

What to See and Do

Coeur d'Alene Greyhound Park. Parimutuel betting; clubhouse, restaurant, concessions. (Evenings exc Mon; matinees Sat & Sun) 11 mi W via I-90, at Idaho/Washington state line. Phone 208/773-0545. ¢

Farragut State Park. 4,000 acres on S end of Lake Pend Oreille; some open landscape, heavy woods. Swimming, bathhouse; fishing; boating (ramps). Hiking and bicycle route; cross-country skiing, sledding and snowshoeing in winter. Model airplane field. Picnicking. Tent & trailer sites (hookups Apr-mid-Oct, dump station; res recommended). Campfire programs; interpretive displays and talks; information center. (Daily) Standard fees. 20 mi N on US 95, then 4 mi E on ID 54, in Athol. Phone 208/683-2425. Per vehicle ¢

Idaho Panhandle National Forests—Coeur d'Alene. Camping (fee), cabins, picnicking, boating, fishing, hiking, cross-country skiing, snowmobiling trails. Visitors are welcome at the Coeur d'Alene Tree Nursery, 1 mi NW on Ramsey Rd. N on US 95 & E on I-90. Contact the Forest Supervisor, 1201 Ironwood Dr; 208/765-7223.

Other national forests that lie in the Panhandle are Kaniksu (see PRIEST LAKE AREA) and St Joe (see ST MARIES).

Lake Coeur d'Alene. Partially adj to the Idaho Panhandle National Forest. This lake, 26 mi long with a 109-mi shoreline, is considered one of the loveliest in the country. Popular for boating, fishing, swimming. Municipal beach, picnic grounds at point where lake and town meet. At S end of lake is

St Joe River. One of the rivers that feed Lake Coeur d'Alene. Trout and lovely scenery abound. Stretch between Lake Chatcolet and Round Lake is said to be the world's highest navigable river.

Lake Coeur d'Alene Cruises, Inc. Makes 6-hr trip up Lake Coeur d'Alene into the St Joe River (mid-June-early Sept, Wed & Sun; mid-May-Oct, Sun only). Also 90-min lake cruises (mid-May-mid-Oct, daily). Dinner cruises (June-mid-Sept, Mon). Sun brunch cruises (mid-June-Sept). City dock, E of City Park. Phone 208/765-4000. ¢¢¢¢-¢¢¢¢¢

Museum of North Idaho. Exhibits feature steamboating, timber industry and Native American history. Also, a big game trophy collection. (Apr-Oct, Tues-Sat) 115 NW Blvd, adj to City Park, near waterfront. Phone 208/664-3448. ¢ Admission includes

Ft Sherman Museum. North Idaho College campus. Housed in old powder house of Ft Coeur d'Alene (ca 1880). Exhibits include log cabin once used by US Forest Service firefighters. Logging, mining and pioneer implements are among featured exhibits. (May-Sept, Tues-Sat) Phone 208/664-3448.

◪ **Scenic drives.** Some of the most spectacular drives are S on US 97, along E shore of Lake Coeur d'Alene; E on US 10, through Fourth of July Canyon; and N, along US 95. In any direction from city.

Silverwood Theme Park. Turn-of-the-century park and village with Victorian buildings including restaurants, saloon, general store, theater featuring old newsreels and classic movies, aircraft museum, air shows and entertainment; adj amusement park with rides and attractions. (Memorial Day wkend-Labor Day, daily) 15 mi N on I-95, in Athol. Phone 208/683-3400. ¢¢¢¢

Annual Events

Art on the Green. 1st wkend Aug.

Northern Idaho Fair. Late Aug.

Motels

★ ★ **COEUR D'ALENE INN.** *414 W Appleway, at jct US 95 & I-90. 208/765-3200; FAX 208/664-1962; res: 800/251-7829.* 122 rms, 2 story. S $105-$115; D $115-$130; each addl $10; under 19 free. Crib free. TV; cable (premium). Heated pool. Restaurant 6 am-1 pm. Rm serv. Bar; entertainment. Ck-out noon. Meeting rms. Business center. In-rm modem link. Sundries. Airport, RR station, bus depot transportation. Cr cds: A, C, D, DS, JCB, MC, V.

🄳 ⊠ 🏌 🖂 🐾 🚶

★ ★ **COMFORT INN.** *280 W Appleway. 208/765-5500; FAX 208/664-0433.* 51 rms, 2 story, 7 suites, 21 kit. units. May-Oct: S $94; D $104-$115; each addl $10; suites $174-$205; kit. units $104-$115; under 19 free; higher rates special events; lower rates rest of yr. Crib free. Pet accepted. TV; cable (premium), VCR avail. Pool; wading pool, whirlpool, sauna. Playground. Complimentary continental bkfst. Restaurant adj open 24 hrs. Ck-out noon. Coin lndry. Meeting rm. Valet serv. Gift shop. Lawn games. Refrigerator, minibar in suites. Picnic tables. Cr cds: A, C, D, DS, ER, JCB, MC, V.

🄳 🐾 ⊠ 🖂 🐾 SC

★ ★ **DAYS INN.** *2200 Northwest Blvd. 208/667-8668; FAX 208/765-0933.* 61 rms, 2 story. June-Aug: S $75; D $80; each addl $5; under 13 free; lower rates rest of yr. Crib free. Pet accepted. TV; VCR avail. Complimentary continental bkfst. Ck-out noon. Meeting rms. Valet serv. Sundries. Exercise equipt; bicycles, stair machine, whirlpool, sauna. Cr cds: A, C, D, DS, JCB, MC, V.

🄳 🐾 🏌 🖂 🐾 SC

★ **FLAMINGO.** *718 Sherman Ave. 208/664-2159; res: 800/955-2159.* 14 rms, 3 kits, 6 bungalows. May-Sept: S, D $65.50-$85.50; each addl $5; 2-bedrm suites $90-$105; kit. units $5-$7 addl; 2-4-bedrm bungalows $110-$150; wkly rates winter only; lower rates rest of yr. Crib $1. TV; cable (premium), VCR avail. Pool. Coffee avail. Restaurant nearby. Ck-out 11 am. Airport transportation. Some refrigerators. Cr cds: A, C, D, DS, MC, V.

⊠ 🖂 🔥

✔★ **MOTEL 6.** *416 Appleway. 208/664-6600; FAX 208/667-9446.* 109 rms, 2 story. S $37.99; D $43.99; each addl $3; under 18 free. Crib free. TV; cable (premium). Pool. Restaurant adj 6 am-10 pm. Ck-out noon. Cr cds: A, C, D, DS, MC, V.

🄳 ⊠ 🖂 🔥

★ ★ **RIVERBEND INN.** *(W 4105 Riverbend Ave, Post Falls 83854) 10 mi W via I-90 exit 2 to Riverbend Ave. 208/773-3583; FAX 208/773-1306; res: 800/243-7666.* 71 rms, 2 story. S $63; D $75; each addl $5; under 12 free; package plans. Crib free. TV; cable (premium). Heated pool; whirlpool. Complimentary continental bkfst. Ck-out noon. Coin lndry. Valet serv. Cr cds: A, C, D, DS, MC, V.

🄳 ⊠ 🖂 🐾 SC

★ ★ **SHILO INN.** *702 W Apple Way. 208/664-2300; FAX 208/667-2863.* 139 rms, 4 story. May-Oct: S, D $99-$165; each addl $12; kit. units $115-$125; under 13 free; wkly rates; ski, golf plans; lower rates rest of yr. Crib free. TV; cable (premium), VCR avail. Indoor pool; whirlpool. Complimentary continental bkfst. Restaurant adj 6 am-11 pm. Ck-out noon. Coin lndry. Meeting rms. Business servs avail. Valet serv. Airport, bus depot transportation. Exercise equipt; weight machine, bicycles, sauna. Bathrm phones, wet bars. Cr cds: A, C, D, DS, ER, JCB, MC, V.

🄳 ⊠ 🏌 🖂 🐾 SC

★ ★ **SUNTREE INN.** *(W 3705 5th Ave, Post Falls 83854) 10 mi W via I-90 exit 2, then E on 5th Ave. 208/773-4541; FAX 208/773-0235; res: 800/888-6630.* 100 rms, 2-4 story. June-Sept: S $59.90; D $64.90;

each addl $5; under 15 free; package plans; lower rates rest of yr. Crib $5. Pet accepted, some restrictions; $35. TV; cable (premium), VCR avail. Indoor pool; whirlpool. Complimentary continental bkfst. Restaurant opp open 24 hrs. Ck-out 1 pm. Game rm. Cr cds: A, D, DS, MC, V.

⬡ ⬡ ⬡ ⬡ SC

★ **SUPER 8.** *505 W Appleway.* *208/765-8880.* 95 units, 3 story. June-Sept: S $62.88; D $73.88-$76.88; each addl $5; suites $75.88-$85.88; under 12 free; wkly rates winter; lower rates rest of yr. Crib free. TV; cable (premium), VCR avail. Complimentary coffee. Ck-out 11 am. Cr cds: A, C, D, DS, MC, V.

⬡ ⬡ SC

Motor Hotel

★ ★ **BEST WESTERN TEMPLIN'S.** *(414 E 1st Ave, Post Falls 83854)* W via I-90, exit 5. *208/773-1611; FAX 208/773-4192.* 167 rms, 2-3 story. May-mid-Sept: S $93-$112; D $100-$121; each addl $7; suites $125-$350; under 12 free; lower rates rest of yr. Crib $7. Pet accepted, some restrictions. TV; cable (premium). Indoor pool; whirlpool. Restaurant 6 am-10 pm. Rm serv. Bar 10-1 am; entertainment. Ck-out noon. Meeting rms. Business servs avail. In-rm modem link. RR station, bus depot transportation. Tennis. Exercise equipt; weights, bicycles, sauna. Lawn games. Some refrigerators; bathrm phone in suites. Private patios, balconies. Picnic tables. On river; marina, guest docking, boat rentals. Cr cds: A, C, D, DS, ER, JCB, MC, V.

⬡ ⬡ ⬡ ⬡ ⬡ ⬡ ⬡ ⬡ SC

Inn

★ ★ **BLACKWELL HOUSE.** *820 Sherman Ave.* *208/664-0656.* 8 rms, 2 share bath, 3 A/C, 5 air-cooled, 3 story, 3 suites. No elvtr. No rm phones. MAP: S $70-$104; D $75-$125; each addl $10; suites $75-$125; wkly rates. Children over 12 yrs only. TV in lobby; cable. Complimentary full bkfst; afternoon refreshments. Complimentary coffee in rms. Restaurant opp 6 am-11 pm. Ck-out noon, ck-in 2 pm. Luggage handling. Some street parking. Restored, late-Victorian house (1904); music rm, sitting rm, antiques. Gazebo. Cr cds: A, DS, MC, V.

⬡ ⬡

Resort

★ ★ ★ **COEUR D'ALENE RESORT ON THE LAKE.** *115 S 2nd St.* *208/765-4000; FAX 208/667-2707; res: 800/688-5253.* E-mail dburnett@cdaresort.com; web www.cdaresort.com. With its 6½ acres of private beachfront park and floating boardwalk abutting a marina, this is a favorite getaway for Pacific Northwesterners. The pricier tower rooms offer more space than the smaller standard accommodations. 338 rms, 18 story. Mid-June-Sept: S, D $150-$350; each addl $10; suites $350-$2,750; under 18 free; lower rates rest of yr. Crib free. TV; cable (premium), VCR avail (movies). 2 heated pools, 1 indoor; wading pool, whirlpool, poolside serv, lifeguard. Playground adj. Supervised child's activities (Apr-Oct). Restaurants 6-2 am (also see BEVERLY'S). Rm serv. Bars; entertainment. Ck-out noon, ck-in after 3 pm. Convention facilities. Business center. Valet serv. Shopping arcade. Airport, bus depot transportation. Tennis. 18-hole golf. Marina. Boat rentals. Tour boats. Seaplane rides. X-country ski on site. Bowling. Exercise rm; instructor, weight machines, bicycles, sauna, steam rm. Massage. Refrigerators. Balconies. Atrium areas. Cr cds: A, C, D, DS, MC, V.

⬡ ⬡ ⬡ ⬡ ⬡ ⬡ ⬡ ⬡ ⬡ ⬡

Restaurants

✓★ ★ **3RD STREET CANTINA.** *201 N 3rd St.* *208/664-0581.* Hrs: 11 am-9 pm; Fri, Sat to 10:30 pm. Closed Thanksgiving, Dec 25. Mexican menu. Bar to 10 pm. Semi-a la carte: lunch, dinner $4.25-$11.95. Child's

meals. Specializes in fajitas, carnitas. Tropical, Mexican decor; authentic Mexican artwork. Cr cds: A, C, D, DS, MC, V.

D

★ ★ ★ **BEVERLY'S.** *(See Coeur d'Alene Resort on the Lake)* *208/765-4000.* Hrs: 11 am-10 pm. Res accepted. Northwestern cuisine. Bar. Wine cellar. Complete meals: lunch $6.50-$15.95, dinner $15.95-$35.95. Child's meals. Specialties: broiled salmon with shiitake mushrooms, smoke-roasted sturgeon, tenderloin of beef. Display kitchen. Panoramic view of lake. Cr cds: A, C, D, DS, JCB, MC, V.

D

✓★ **IRON HORSE.** *407 Sherman Ave.* *208/667-7314.* Hrs: 7 am-10 pm; Sat from 8 am; Sun 9 am-9 pm. Closed Jan 1, Dec 25. Bar 11-2 am. Semi-a la carte: bkfst $2.95-$6.95, lunch $3.50-$6.50, dinner $4.95-$15.95. Child's meals. Specializes in prime rib, seafood. Outdoor dining. RR train decor. Cr cds: MC, V.

SC

★ ★ **JIMMY D'S.** *320 Sherman Ave.* *208/664-9774.* Hrs: 9 am-11 pm; Sun brunch to 2 pm. Closed Jan 1, Thanksgiving, Dec 25. Bar. Semi-a la carte: bkfst, lunch $3-$7, dinner $8-$17. Sun brunch $4-$7. Specialties: fresh seafood fettucine, pasta. Outdoor dining. Sidewalk cafe atmosphere. Cr cds: A, DS, MC, V.

D

Craters of the Moon National Monument (E-3)

(18 mi SW of Arco on US 20/26/93)

So named because it resembles the surface of the moon as seen through a telescope, this 83-square-mile monument has spectacular lava flows, cinder cones and other volcanic creations. Geologists believe a weak spot in the earth's crust permitted outbursts of lava at least 8 times during the last 15,000 years. These eruptions produced the lava flows, the 25 cinder cones, spatter cones, lava tubes, natural bridges and tree molds within the monument. Geological and historical exhibits are on display at the visitor center (daily; closed winter hols). Autos may follow the 7-mile loop drive; closed by snow in winter. Interpretive programs of nature walks, campfire talks (mid-June-Labor Day). Campground (no hookups) near entrance (mid-May-Oct; fee). Golden Eagle, Golden Age, Golden Access passports accepted (see MAKING THE MOST OF YOUR TRIP). For further information contact PO Box 29, Arco 83213; 208/527-3257. Per vehicle ¢¢

Driggs (E-5)

(See also Ashton, Rexburg, St Anthony)

Pop 846 **Elev** 6,116 ft **Area code** 208 **Zip** 83422

A Ranger District office of the Targhee National Forest (see ASHTON) is located here.

What to See and Do

Grand Targhee Ski and Summer Resort. 3 chairlifts, surface lift; patrol, school, rentals; 3 lodges, 3 restaurants, cafeteria, bar; nursery; hot tubs, heated outdoor pool. Longest run 2.7 mi; vertical drop 2,200 ft. (Mid-Nov-late Apr, daily) Second mountain for powder skiing only. Cross-country trails; snowboard half-pipe. Summer activities include fishing, rafting, horseback riding, biking, hiking, golf, tennis, music festivals (July-Aug); chairlift rides (June-Aug, daily). Half-day rates. 12 mi E on county road, in Alta, WY. Phone 307/353-2300 or 800/TARGHEE. ¢¢¢¢

Motels

✔★ **BEST WESTERN TETON WEST.** *476 N Main St. 208/354-2363; FAX 208/354-2962.* 42 rms, 2 story, 2 kits. S $50; D $60-$63; each addl $4; kit. units $100; under 12 free; ski plans. Crib $4. Pet accepted; $25 deposit. TV; cable (premium). Indoor pool; whirlpool. Complimentary continental bkfst. Restaurant nearby. Ck-out noon. Meeting rm. Downhill ski 10 mi; x-country ski 5 mi. Cr cds: A, C, D, DS, MC, V.

★ **INTERMOUNTAIN LODGE.** *34 Ski Hill Rd. 208/354-8153.* 14 kit. units, showers only. No A/C. Mid-June-mid-Sept, mid-Nov-mid-Apr: kit. units $59; each addl $5; family rates; lower rates rest of yr. Crib avail. TV; VCR avail. Complimentary coffee in lobby. Ck-out 11 am. Coin lndry. Downhill/x-country ski 10 mi. Whirlpool. Picnic tables. Totally nonsmoking. Cr cds: A, DS, MC, V.

★ ★ **SUPER 8 TETON WEST.** *133 N ID 33. 208/354-8888.* 22 rms, 2 story. Mid-June-mid-Sept: S, D $75; under 12 free; higher rates wk of Dec 25; lower rates rest of yr. Crib $4. TV; cable (premium). Whirlpool. Complimentary continental bkfst. Ck-out noon. Coin lndry. Downhill/x-country ski 13 mi. Refrigerators, microwaves. Cr cds: A, D, DS, MC, V.

★ **TETON MOUNTAIN VIEW LODGE.** *(510 Egbert Ave, Tetonia 83452)* 7 mi N. *208/456-2741; res: 800/625-2232; FAX 208/456-2232.* E-mail tmvl@axxess.net. 24 rms, 10 with shower only, 2 story. July-Sept: S $79.95; D $89.95; each addl $5; suite $109.95; under 16 free; wkly rates; lower rates rest of yr. Crib free. Pet accepted, some restrictions. TV; cable. Complimentary coffee in lobby. Restaurant nearby. Ck-out noon. Whirlpool. Cr cds: DS, MC, V.

Resort

★ ★ ★ **GRAND TARGHEE.** *(Box SKI, Alta WY 83422)* 12 mi E on Ski-Hill Rd *(lodge is accessible only from ID). 307/353-2300; FAX 307/353-8148; res: 800/827-4433.* 96 rms, 1-4 story, 32 kit. units. Late Nov-late Apr: S, D $59-$152; kit. units $143-$362; under 14 free; ski plans; lower rates June-Oct. Closed rest of yr. Crib free. TV, VCR avail (movies). Heated pool; whirlpools. Supervised child's activities, ages 6-12. Complimentary coffee in rms. Dining rms 7:30 am-9 pm. Box lunches. Picnics. Bar 11:30 am-10 pm; entertainment. Ck-out 11 am, ck-in 4 pm. Grocery. Coin lndry. Package store (winter only). Meeting rms. Business servs avail. Concierge. Gift shops. Airport transportation. Tennis. Downhill/x-country ski on site (rentals). Dog sled rides (winter). Horse stables. Hiking. Rec rm. Game rm. Child day care (2 months-5 yr). Exercise equipt; weight machine, treadmill, sauna. Massage. Balconies. Picnic tables. In Targhee National Forest, adj to Grand Teton National Park. Cr cds: A, DS, MC, V.

Guest Ranch

★ ★ ★ **TETON RIDGE RANCH.** *(200 Valley View Rd, Tetonia 83452)* N on ID 33, then 1.7 mi E on unnumbered road toward Leigh Creeks, then turn at first left going N to Dry Ridge, follow signs to ranch. *208/456-2650; FAX 208/456-2218.* 6 units. July-Aug, AP: S $350; D $475; each addl $100; lower rates rest of yr. Closed Nov-mid-Dec, Apr-May. Children over 12 yrs only. Pet accepted, some restrictions. TV in public rms; cable (premium). Setups. Ck-out, ck-in noon. Grocery. Guest lndry. Package store 9 mi. Meeting rms. Airport transportation. Downhill ski 20 mi; x-country ski on site. Sleighing. Horse stables. Hiking. Mountain bikes (rentals). Rec rm. Fishing/hunting guides, clean & store. Balconies. Secluded mountain valley ranch situated on west side of Grand Tetons. No cr cds accepted.

Fort Hall

(see Blackfoot)

Grangeville (C-2)

Founded 1876 **Pop** 3,226 **Elev** 3,390 ft **Area code** 208 **Zip** 83530
Information Chamber of Commerce, US 95 & Pine St, PO Box 212; 208/983-0460.

Grangeville is a light industry and agricultural community. It was a focal point in the Nez Perce Indian War and a gold rush town in the 1890s when rich ore was found in the Florence Basin and the Elk City areas. The seat of Idaho County, it is also the gateway to several wilderness areas. The headquarters and two Ranger District offices of the Nez Perce National Forest are located here.

What to See and Do

Hells Canyon National Recreation Area. Created by the Snake River, at the Idaho/Oregon border, Hells Canyon is the deepest gorge in North America—1¹/₂ mi from He Devil Mt (elevation 9,393 ft) to the Snake River at Granite Creek (elevation 1,408 ft). Overlooks at Heavens Gate, west of Riggins, and in Oregon (see JOSEPH, OR). The recreation area includes parts of the Nez Perce and Payette National Forest in Idaho and the Wallowa-Whitman National Forest in Oregon. Activities include float trips, jet boat tours, auto tours, backpacking and horseback riding; boat trips into canyon from Lewiston, Grangeville and Riggins, also via Pittsburg Landing or the Hells Canyon Dam (see WEISER). Developed campgrounds in Oregon and Idaho; much of the area is undeveloped, some is designated wilderness. Be sure to inquire about road conditions before planning a trip; some roads are rough and open for a limited season. Access approx 16 mi S on US 95 to White Bird, then W on County 493 to Pittsburg Landing; access also from Riggins, from US 95 take Rd 241 (Race Creek) N of Riggins; paved access via ID 71 from Cambridge (see WEISER). For further information contact Hells Canyon National Recreation Area, 88401 Hwy 82, Enterprise, OR 97828, phone 541/426-4978; or 2535 Riverside Dr, Box 699, Clarkston, WA 99403, phone 509/758-0616. For river information and float reservations, phone 509/758-1957.

✪ **Nez Perce National Forest.** More than 2.2 million acres with excellent fishing, camping, cabins (fee at some campgrounds), picnicking, cross-country skiing and snowmobiling. The Salmon (the River of No Return) Selway, South Fork Clearwater and Snake rivers, all classified as wild and scenic, flow through or are adjacent to the forest. S on US 95. Pack and float trips are avail; contact the Idaho Outfitters and Guides Assn, PO Box 95, Boise 83701; 208/342-1438. High elevations are open only in summer and fall; low elevations are open Mar-Nov. For further information contact Office of Information, Rte 2, Box 475; 208/983-1950.

Skiing. Snowhaven. T-bar, rope tow; patrol, school, rentals; cafeteria. Vertical drop 400 ft. (Dec-early Mar, Fri-Sun) Night skiing; half-day rates. 7 mi SE via Fish Creek Rd. Phone 208/983-2299. ¢¢-¢¢¢

White Bird Hill. Site of the famous Whitebird Battle of the Nez Perce Indian Wars. View of Camas Prairie, canyons, mountains and Seven Devils Peaks. Self-guided tour brochures avail from Chamber of Commerce. 5 mi S on US 95.

Annual Events

Border Days. Three-day rodeo & parades, dances. Art-in-the-park; food. Phone 208/983-0460. July 4 wkend.

Oktubberfest. Three-day event features tub races on Main St, arts & crafts, street dance, entertainment. Last wkend Sept.

Idaho City (E-2)

(For accommodations see Boise)

Settled 1862 **Pop** 322 **Elev** 3,906 ft **Area code** 208 **Zip** 83631
Information Chamber of Commerce, PO Box 70; 208/392-4148.

Flecks of gold persist in the gravel beneath most of Idaho City, and the community is steeped in gold rush lore. From the 18-square-mile Boise Basin, said to have produced more gold than all of Alaska, Idaho City's fame once spread far and wide. Idaho City also is home to the state's first Pioneer Lodge (established 1864) and the birthplace of the Grand Lodge of Idaho (established 1867).

What to See and Do

Boise Basin Museum (1867). Restored building houses artifacts of gold rush era. Walking tours of Idaho City avail (fee). (Memorial Day-Labor Day, daily; May & Sept, wkends only; rest of yr, by appt) Montgomery & Wall Sts. Phone 208/392-4550. ¢

Boise National Forest. Surrounding area. Fishing, hunting, swimming, camping, skiing and snowmobiling. A Ranger District office of the forest is located here. Contact the Supervisor, 1750 Front St, Boise 83702.

Boot Hill. Restored 40-acre cemetery, last resting place of many gunfight victims.

Gold Hill. Rich Boise Basin placer ground. 1 mi N on Main St.

Idaho Falls (E-4)

(See also Blackfoot, Pocatello, Rexburg)

Pop 43,929 **Elev** 4,710 ft **Area code** 208
Information Chamber of Commerce, 505 Lindsay Blvd, PO Box 50498, 83405; 208/523-1010 or 800/634-3246.

An industrial, transportation and trading center in the upper Snake River Valley, Idaho Falls is a center of potato production and headquarters for the Idaho Operations Office of the Department of Energy. The Idaho National Engineering Laboratory is located on the Lost River Plains, 30 miles west on US 20. Potato processing is important; stockyards here are the state's largest; and one of the nation's leading safety research centers for nuclear reactors is located here. A Ranger District office of Targhee National Forest (see ASHTON) is also in Idaho Falls.

What to See and Do

Bonneville Museum. Displays of early county, state and city history; natural history; Native American artifacts; early settler and mountain-man relics; replica of early (ca 1890) Idaho Falls (Eagle Rock); 30-min video on county history and other subjects of local interest. Art exhibits featuring works of area artists; special and traveling exhibits. (Mon-Fri; also Sat afternoons; closed Jan 1, Thanksgiving, Dec 25) 200 N Eastern Ave. Phone 208/522-1400. ¢

Heise Hot Springs. Mineral water pool, freshwater pools; water slide; golf; camping; fishing. (Mid-May-Sept) Fee for activities. 23 mi E on US 26, in Ririe. Phone 208/538-7312.

Idaho Falls. Falls run for 1,500 ft along Snake River. Picnic tables nearby.

Tautphaus Park. Zoo (fee); amusement rides (Memorial Day wkend-Labor Day wkend; fee); picnic and barbecue areas; lighted tennis courts and softball diamonds; horseshoe pits; ice-skating, hockey (seasonal). Park (daily; closed Jan 1, Thanksgiving, Dec 25). Rollandet Ave or South Blvd. **Free.**

The Lavas. Lava-created caves, fissures and rock flows, fringed by dwarf trees. Native American relics are also plentiful. 10 mi S via US 91 to Shelley, then 4 mi W on local road.

Annual Event

War Bonnet Roundup. Sandy Downs Park Rodeo Grounds. Rodeo. 4 nights early Aug.

Motels

★ ★ **AMERITEL INN.** *645 Lindsay Blvd (83402). 208/523-1400; res: 800/600-6001; FAX 208/523-0004.* Web www.ameritelinns.com. 126 rms, 4 story, 43 suites. June-Sept: S, D $99.75; each addl $8; suites $119-$229; under 12 free; lower rates rest of yr. Crib free. TV; cable (premium). Complimentary continental bkfst. Complimentary coffee in rms. Restaurant nearby. Ck-out noon. Meeting rms. Business servs avail. In-rm modem link. Bellhops. Sundries. Free airport transportation. Exercise equipt; weights, rowers. Indoor pool; whirlpool. Bathrm phones; some microwaves. Cr cds: A, D, DS, MC, V.

D ≈ 犬 ⇥ 🐾 SC

★ ★ **BEST WESTERN COTTONTREE INN.** *900 Lindsay Blvd (83402), near Fanning Field Airport. 208/523-6000; FAX 208/523-0000.* 94 rms, 3 story, 9 suites, 6 kit. units. S, D $65-$75; each addl $5; suites $90-$110; kit. units $90-$110; under 18 free. Crib $8. TV; cable (premium). Indoor pool; whirlpool. Complimentary continental bkfst. Restaurant nearby. Ck-out noon. Coin lndry. Meeting rms. Business servs avail. Valet serv. Free airport transportation. Exercise equipt; weight machine, bicycles. Microwaves avail. Near river. Cr cds: A, C, D, DS, MC, V.

D ≈ 犬 ✕ ⇥ 🐾 SC

★ ★ **COMFORT INN.** *195 S Colorado (83402), I-15, exit 118, near Fanning Field Airport. 208/528-2804.* 56 rms, 2 story, 14 suites. June-Sept: S $56; D $61; each addl $7; suites $65-$120; under 12 free; lower rates rest of yr. Crib free. Pet accepted, some restrictions. TV; cable. Indoor pool; whirlpool. Complimentary continental bkfst. Restaurant nearby. Ck-out 11 am. Refrigerators. Cr cds: A, D, DS, MC, V.

D 🐾 ≈ ⇥ 🐾 SC

★ ★ **HAMPTON INN.** *2500 Channing Way (83404). 208/529-9800; FAX 208/529-9455.* 63 rms, 3 story, 7 suites. Late May-Aug: S $59; D $64; suites $74-$99; under 18 free; lower rates rest of yr. Crib free. TV; cable (premium). Complimentary continental bkfst. Restaurant nearby. Ck-out noon. Meeting rm. Business servs avail. Bellhops. Exercise equipt; weight machine, bicycle. Indoor pool; whirlpool. Refrigerator, microwave in suites. Cr cds: A, C, D, DS, MC, V.

D ≈ 犬 ⇥ 🐾 SC

Motor Hotel

★ ★ ★ **SHILO INN.** *780 Lindsay Blvd (83402). 208/523-0088; FAX 208/522-7420.* 161 suites, 4 story. S, D $89-$120; each addl $12; under 12 free. Crib free. Pet accepted, some restrictions; $7. TV; cable (premium). Indoor pool; whirlpool. Complimentary full bkfst. Coffee in rms. Restaurant 6 am-10 pm. Rm serv. Bar 11-1 am. Ck-out noon. Coin lndry. Meeting rms. Business servs avail. Bellhops. Valet serv. Sundries. Free airport transportation. Exercise equipt; weight machine, bicycles, sauna. Bathrm phones; refrigerators, microwaves. Balconies. On river. Cr cds: A, C, D, DS, ER, MC, V.

D 🐾 ≈ 犬 ⇥ 🐾 SC

Restaurant

★ **JAKERS.** *851 Lindsay Blvd. 208/524-5240.* Hrs: 11:30 am-2 pm, 5-10 pm; Fri, Sat to 10:30 pm; Sun 4-9 pm. Closed Jan 1, Thanksgiving, Dec 25. Res accepted. Bar 11:30 am-midnight. Semi-a la carte: lunch $2.25-$7.95, dinner $8.95-$22.95. Child's meals. Specialties:

pan-fried shrimp, prime rib, steaks & ribs. Contemporary rustic decor. Cr cds: A, DS, MC, V.

Jerome (F-3)

(See also Shoshone, Twin Falls)

Pop 6,529 **Elev** 3,781 ft **Area code** 208 **Zip** 83338
Information Chamber of Commerce, 101 W Main St, Suite 6; 208/324-2711.

What to See and Do

Jerome County Historical Museum. Located in historic Pioneer Hall building. Changing displays. Guided tours. (May-Sept, daily exc Sun; rest of yr, Tues-Sat) 220 N Lincoln. Phone 208/324-5641. **Free.**

Malad Gorge State Park. More than 650 acres with the 2½-mi-long, 250-ft-deep Malad Gorge. Footbridge spans waterfall at Devil's Washbowl. Interpretive trails, picnicking. (Schedule varies, phone ahead) 26 mi W on I-84 to Tuttle exit 147. Phone 208/837-4505.

Annual Events

Horse Racing. Jerome County Fairgrounds. Parimutuel racing. Phone 208/324-7209. 2 wkends mid-June.

Jerome County Fair. Concert, rodeo, carnival, parade. Phone 208/324-7209. First wk Aug.

Seasonal Event

Chariot Races. Jerome County Fairgrounds. Phone 208/324-7209. Wkends, Dec-Feb.

Motels

★ ★ **BEST WESTERN SAWTOOTH INN & SUITES.** *3057 S Lincoln. 208/324-9200; FAX 208/324-9292.* 57 rms, 2 story. June-Sept: S $59; D $69; each addl $5; suites $69-$79; under 18 free; higher rates: Jerome County Fair, 1st wk July; lower rates rest of yr. Crib free. Pet accepted, some restrictions. TV; cable (premium). Complimentary continental bkfst. Restaurant nearby. Ck-out noon. Meeting rms. Business servs avail. Bellhops. Coin lndry. Exercise equipt; treadmill, stair machine. Indoor pool; whirlpool. Some refrigerators, microwaves. Cr cds: A, C, D, DS, JCB, MC, V.

★ ★ **SLEEP INN.** *1200 Centennial Spur. 208/324-6400.* 73 rms, 3 story. May-Sept: S $45-$55; D $49-$59; each addl $5; under 19 free; lower rates rest of yr. Crib free. TV; cable (premium), VCR (movies). Restaurant adj open 24 hrs. Ck-out noon. Meeting rm. Business servs avail. In-rm modem link. Sundries. Coin lndry. Whirlpool. Cr cds: A, C, D, DS, JCB, MC, V.

Kellogg (B-2)

(See also Coeur d'Alene, Wallace)

Pop 2,591 **Elev** 2,308 ft **Area code** 208 **Zip** 83837 **E-mail** kellogg@nidlink.com **Web** www.nidlink.com/~kellogg
Information Greater Kellogg Area Chamber of Commerce, 608 Bunker Ave; 208/784-0821.

In this rich mining region are the country's largest silver and lead mines. One of the state's most violent miners' strikes took place here in 1899. Today, the former mining town is being transformed into a ski resort.

What to See and Do

Old Mission State Park (1850). A 100-acre park. Tours of the Coeur d'Alene Mission of the Sacred Heart, a restored Native American mission; oldest existing building in state. Picnicking; information center; interpretive programs; history trail. Standard fees. (Daily) 10 mi W off I-90 exit 39, in Cataldo. Phone 208/682-3814.

Silver Mountain Ski Area. Double, quad, 3 triple chairlifts, surface lift; patrol, school, rentals; lodges, restaurants, cafeteria, bar, nursery. 50 trails, longest run 2.5 mi; vertical drop 2,200 ft. (Mid-Nov-Apr, daily) Summer activities include amphitheater performances; hiking, mountain biking; 3-mi gondola rides. ½ mi SW, off I-90 exit 49. Phone 208/783-1111. ¢¢¢¢

Sunshine Mine Disaster Memorial. Double life-size statue constructed of steel is memorial to all miners; created by Kenn Lonn, a native of Kellogg. The helmet's light burns perpetually and the miner holds a typical jack-leg drill. 3 mi E on I-90, exit 54, Big Creek.

Motel

★ **SILVERHORN.** *699 W Cameron. 208/783-1151; FAX 208/784-5081; res: 800/437-6437.* 40 rms. S $52; D $56-$61; each addl $4; under 12 free. Crib $3. Pet accepted. TV; cable. Restaurant 5 am-11 pm. Rm serv. Ck-out noon. Business servs avail. Valet serv. Free lndry facilities. Gift shop. Downhill/x-country ski 3 mi. Whirlpool. Cr cds: A, C, D, DS, MC, V.

Ketchum
(see Sun Valley Area)

Lava Hot Springs (F-4)

(For accommodations see Pocatello)

Pop 420 **Elev** 5,060 ft **Area code** 208 **Zip** 83246

Hot water pouring out of the mountains and bubbling up in springs, believed to be the most highly mineralized water in the world, makes Lava Hot Springs a busy year-round resort. Fishing, hunting, swimming, camping and golf are available in the surrounding area.

What to See and Do

Lava Hot Springs. Outdoor mineral pools, fed by 30 different springs, range from 104°-112°F. Olympic-size swimming pool with diving tower (Memorial Day-Labor Day). (Daily; closed Thanksgiving, Dec 25) ½ mi E on US 30N. Phone 208/776-5221. ¢¢

South Bannock County Historical Center. Museum artifacts, photographs, transcripts and memorabilia trace history of town from the era of Native American and fur trappers to its development as a resort area. Slide show and guided walking tour (by appt). (Daily) 110 Main St. Phone 208/776-5254. **Donation.**

Lewiston (C-1)

(See also Moscow; also see Clarkston, WA)

Founded 1861 **Pop** 28,082 **Elev** 739 ft **Area code** 208 **Zip** 83501 **E-mail** lewcoc@valley-internet.net

Information Chamber of Commerce, 2207 E Main St; 208/743-3531 or 800/473-3543.

The Clearwater River, starting in the Bitterroot Mts and plunging through the vast Clearwater National Forest, joins the Snake River at Lewiston. The two rivers and the mountains that surround the town give it one of the most picturesque settings in the state. A thriving tourist trade supplements Lewiston's grain, lumber and livestock industries.

What to See and Do

⊠ **Auto tours.** The Lewis & Clark Hwy (US 12) parallels the famous Lewis & Clark Trail east to Montana. Interpretive signs along the way explain the human and natural history of the canyon. A Forest Service Information Station is at Lolo Pass on the Idaho/Montana border. The Chamber of Commerce has maps for other tours.

Castle Museum. Three-story, handmade cement block house built in 1906 and patterned after Scottish castle; embossed metal ceilings, antiques. (Apr-Oct, daily; rest of yr, by appt) 23 mi N on ID 3 in Juliaetta; 1 blk off main hwy. Phone 208/276-3081. **Donation.**

Clearwater National Forest. About 1,850,000 acres with trout fishing, hunting. Skiing, snowmobiling trails. Camping (fee for some developed campsites), cabins, picnicking. Pack trips. Higher elevations accessible July-Sept; lower elevations accessible Mar-Oct or Nov. Lolo Pass Visitor Center and Lochsa Historical Ranger Station on US 12 (mid-May-mid-Sept; daily). US 12 in Orofino. For further information contact the Supervisor, 12730 US Hwy 12, Orofino 83544; 208/476-4541.

Hells Canyon Excursions. Jet boat trips and fishing charters into Hells Canyon National Recreation Area (see GRANGEVILLE). For information contact the Chamber of Commerce.

Hells Gate State Park. 960 acres on Snake River, 40 mi N of Hells Canyon National Recreation Area (see GRANGEVILLE). Swimming, fishing, boating (marina, concession, ramp). Hiking and paved bicycle trails; horseback riding area. Picnicking, playground. Tent & trailer campsites (hookups, dump station; 15-day max). Information center, interpretive programs, exhibits; excursion boats. Park (Mar-Nov). Standard fees. 4 mi S on Snake River Ave. Phone 208/799-5015.

Luna House Museum. On site of first hotel in town (1861). Exhibits on Nez Perce and pioneers; displays on town and county history. (Tues-Sat; closed hols) 3rd & C Sts. Phone 208/743-2535. **Free.**

Nez Perce National Historical Park. The park is composed of 38 separate sites scattered throughout Washington, Oregon, Montana and Idaho. All of the sites relate to the culture and history of the Nez Perce; some relate to the westward expansion of the nation into homelands. Headquarters, 11 mi E on US 95 in Spalding, has visitor center and museum (daily; closed Jan 1, Thanksgiving, Dec 25). Phone 208/843-2261. **Free.**

Annual Events

Lewiston Round Up. Lewiston Round Up grounds, 7000 Tammany Creek Rd. Wkend after Labor Day.

Nez Perce County Fair. 4 days late Sept.

Motels

★ ★ **HOWARD JOHNSON.** *1716 Main St.* 208/743-9526; FAX 208/746-6212; res: 800/634-7669. 66 rms, 1-2 story, 4 kit. units. S $56.50-

$61.50; D $60.50-$65.50; each addl $5; under 12 free. Pet accepted. TV; cable. Complimentary continental bkfst. Heated pool. Ck-out noon. Free lndry facilities. Airport, bus depot transportation. Refrigerators. Cr cds: A, C, D, DS, ER, MC, V.

🐾 ≈ 🛏 🐾 SC

★ ★ **RIVERVIEW.** *1325 Main St.* 208/746-3311; FAX 208/746-7955; res: 800/806-7666. 75 rms, 4 story. S $35.50; D $47.50-$51.50; each addl $6; under 12 free. Crib $5. Pet accepted. TV; cable (premium). Heated pool. Complimentary continental breakfast. Coffee in rms. Restaurant nearby. Ck-out noon. Meeting rm. Cr cds: A, D, DS, MC, V.

🐾 ≈ 🛏 🐾 SC

★ ★ **SACAJAWEA SELECT INN.** *1824 Main St, near Nez Perce County Regional Airport.* 208/746-1393; FAX 208/743-3620; res: 800/333-1393. 90 rms, 2 story. S $42-$45; D $49-$52; each addl $2; suites $65. Crib $3. Pet accepted, some restrictions; $2/day. TV; cable. Heated pool; whirlpool. Restaurant 6 am-10 pm. Bar 11-1 am; closed Sun. Ck-out noon. Coin lndry. Meeting rms. Valet serv. Airport transportation. Exercise equipt; bicycles, stair machine. Refrigerators. Cr cds: A, D, DS, MC, V.

D 🐾 ≈ 🏃 ✈ 🛏 🔥

✔★ **SUPER 8.** *3120 North-South Hwy (US 12).* 208/743-8808. 62 rms, 2 story. Apr-Sept: S $38.88; D $47.88-$51.88; each addl $4; under 12 free; higher rates special events; lower rates rest of yr. Crib free. TV; cable, in-rm movies. Complimentary coffee. Ck-out 11 am. Refrigerator in suites. On river. Cr cds: A, C, D, DS, ER, JCB, MC, V.

D 🐾 🛏 🔥 SC

Motor Hotel

★ ★ ★ **GRAND PLAZA HOTEL.** *621 21st St, near Nez Perce County Regional Airport.* 208/799-1000; FAX 208/799-1000, ext. 131. 136 rms, 4 story. S $75-$95; D $80-$100; each addl $10; suites $99-$400; under 18 free; wkly rates; ski, golf plans. Crib free. TV; cable. 2 pools, 1 indoor; whirlpool, poolside serv. Restaurant 6 am-10 pm. Rm serv. Bar 3 pm-1:30 am. Ck-out noon. Coin lndry. Meeting rms. Bellhops. Valet serv. Concierge. Sundries. Free airport, RR station, bus depot transportation. Exercise rm; instructor, weights, bicycles. Some bathrm phones. Cr cds: A, C, D, DS, ER, MC, V.

D ≈ 🏃 🏃 ✈ 🛏 🐾 SC

Restaurants

✔★ **COUNTRY COOKERY.** *1516 Main St.* 208/743-4552. Hrs: 6 am-9 pm. Semi-a la carte: bkfst $2.25-$6.95, lunch $3-$7, dinner $5-$15. Child's meals. Specializes in barbecued beef. Country decor. Player piano (1917). Cr cds: MC, V.

D SC

★ ★ **JONATHAN'S.** *301 D Street.* 208/746-3438. Hrs: 11 am-10 pm; Fri-Sun from 4 pm. Closed Sun; Dec 25. Continental menu. Bar to 2 am. Semi-a la carte: lunch $3.95-$9.95, dinner $5.95-$29.95. Specializes in Northwestern seafood dishes, char-broiled steak. Cr cds: A, DS, MC, V.

D

McCall (D-2)

Pop 2,005 **Elev** 5,030 ft **Area code** 208 **Zip** 83638 **E-mail** mccallcc@cyberhighway.net **Web** www.mccall.net/chamber

Information Chamber of Commerce, PO Box D; 208/634-7631.

At the southern tip of Payette Lake, McCall is a resort center for one of the state's chief recreational areas. Fishing, swimming, boating and waterskiing are available on Payette Lake. McCall is also the headquarters for

Payette National Forest, and three Ranger District offices of the forest are located here.

What to See and Do

Brundage Mt Ski Area. Triple, 2 double chairlifts, Pomalift, rope tow; patrol, school, rentals; bar, cafeteria; nursery. (Mid-Nov-mid-Apr, daily) 8 mi NW via ID 55, unnumbered road. Phone 208/634-4151 or 208/634-5650 (snow conditions). ¢¢¢¢

Cascade Dam Reservoir. Fishing, boating. 25 mi S on ID 55, in Cascade.

Pack trips into Idaho primitive areas. Check with Chamber of Commerce for list of outfitters.

Payette National Forest. More than 2.3 million acres surrounded by the Snake and Salmon rivers, the River of No Return Wilderness, Hells Canyon National Recreation Area and the Boise National Forest. Trout and salmon fishing in 300 lakes and 3,000 mi of streams; 2,100 mi of hiking trails; hunting, camping and picnic areas; boating, winter sports. For further information contact the Supervisor, PO Box 1026; 208/634-0700.

Ponderosa State Park. Approx 1,280 acres. Large stand of ponderosa pines. Swimming, waterskiing; fishing; boating (ramps). Hiking; cross-country skiing. Picnicking. Camping (exc winter; res accepted Memorial Day-Labor Day); tent & trailer sites (hookups; 15-day max; dump station). Park (daily). 2 mi NE, on Payette Lake. Standard fees. Contact Park Manager, PO Box A; 208/634-2164.

River rafting. Salmon River Outfitters. Offers 5- and 6-day guided raft trips along the Salmon River. For information and reservations, contact PO Box 307, Columbia, CA 95310; 209/795-4041. ¢¢¢¢

Annual Events

Winter Carnival. Parades, fireworks; ice sculptures, snowmobile and ski races, snowman-building contest, carriage & sleigh rides, ball. 10 days early Feb.

Music Festival. Fiddle music; Western, swing, Irish, folk, blues and jazz; square dancing. 3rd wkend July.

Motels

★★ **BEST WESTERN.** 415 3rd St. 208/634-6300; FAX 208/634-2967; res: 800/528-1234. 77 rms, 2 story. Mid-June-mid-Sept: S $70-$120; D $75-$125; under 18 free; higher rates Winter Carnival; lower rates rest of yr. Crib $3. Pet accepted, some restrictions. TV; cable (premium), VCR avail. Indoor pool; whirlpool. Complimentary coffee in lobby. Ck-out 11 am. Coin lndry. Meeting rms. Business servs avail. In-rm modem link. Downhill ski 10 mi. Exercise equipt; weight machine, bicycles. Refrigerators. Cr cds: A, C, D, DS, ER, JCB, MC, V.

D ⊁ ≈ ⛌ ⊠ ⋒ SC

✔★ **WOODSMAN.** Box 884, 1/2 mi S on ID 55. 208/634-7671. 63 rms, 1-2 story. No A/C. S $32-$55; D $55; family, wkly rates. TV, some B/W; cable. Restaurant 7 am-10 pm. Ck-out 11 am. Airport, bus depot transportation. Downhill ski 10 mi; x-country ski on site. Cr cds: A, DS, MC, V.

⊁ ⊠ ⋒

Lodge

★★★ **SHORE.** PO Box 1006, 501 W Lake St. 208/634-2244; FAX 208/634-7504; res: 800/657-6464. 116 rms, 2-3 story. No A/C. June-Labor Day: S, D $79-$139; each addl $10; suites $139-$175; under 12 free; ski plans; lower rates rest of yr. Crib free. TV; cable. Heated pool; whirlpool. Dining rm 7 am-10 pm. Rm serv. Bar 11-2 am. Ck-out 11 am. Meeting rms. Free airport, bus depot transportation. Tennis. Downhill ski 9 mi; x-country ski 4 mi. Exercise equipt; weight machine, bicycle, sauna. Some refrigerators. Some balconies. On Payette Lake; private beach, swimming. Cr cds: A, DS, MC, V.

⊁ ▸ ⋇ ≈ ⛌ ⊠ ⋒ SC

Inn

★★ **HOTEL McCALL.** 1101 N 3rd St, on ID 55. 208/634-8105. 22 rms, 6 share bath, 3 story. S, D $57-$120; each addl $15; under 3 free; ski plan. TV; cable (premium), VCR avail. Complimentary bkfst. Restaurant nearby. Ck-out 11 am, ck-in 2 pm. Downhill ski 10 mi; x-country ski 4 mi. Garden patio, sun deck. Overlooks Payette Lake. Totally nonsmoking. Cr cds: A, MC, V.

D ▸ ⊠ ⋒

Restaurant

★★ **THE MILL.** 1/2 mi S on ID 55. 208/634-7683. Hrs: 6-10 pm. Closed Thanksgiving, Dec 25. Bar. Semi-a la carte: dinner $7.95-$29.95. Child's meals. Specializes in steak, prime rib, seafood. Entertainment wkends. Photo collection of history of the Northwest. Family-owned. Cr cds: A, C, D, DS, MC, V.

Montpelier (F-5)

Founded 1864 **Pop** 2,656 **Elev** 5,964 ft **Area code** 208 **Zip** 83254

Information Bear Lake Convention & Visitors Bureau, PO Box 26, Fish Haven 83287; 208/945-2333 or 800/448-2327.

Located in the highlands of Bear Lake Valley, Montpelier is surrounded by lakes, rivers, creeks and grazing ranges. The average yearly temperature is 46°F. First called Clover Creek, then Belmont, it was finally designated by the Mormon leader Brigham Young as Montpelier, after the capital of Vermont. There are Mormon tabernacles throughout this area. Phosphate is mined extensively nearby. A Ranger District office of the Caribou National Forest is located here.

What to See and Do

Bear Lake. Covering 71,000 acres, this 20-mi-long, 200-ft-deep body of water lies across the Idaho/Utah border. Fishing for Mackinaw, cutthroat, whitefish and the rare Bonneville cisco. 20 mi S on US 89. On N shore is

Bear Lake State Park. Provides swimming beach, waterskiing, fishing, boating (ramp), picnicking. Park (mid-May-mid-Sept). Camping on E shore (dump station, hookups). Standard fees. Phone 208/945-2790.

Bloomington Lake. Spring-fed lake of unknown depth. Camping, fishing. 12 mi S on US 89, then W on local road, W of Bloomington.

Caribou National Forest. Camping (fee at certain designated campsites), hunting, fishing, picnicking, winter sports. W, N & S of US 89; N & S of US 30. For further information contact Ranger District, 431 Clay St; 208/847-0375. Within the forest is

Minnetonka Cave. Cave is 1/2 mi long and has 9 rms; 40°F. Guided tours (mid-June-Labor Day, daily). 10 mi W of St Charles off US 89. Phone 208/847-0375. ¢¢

Annual Events

Oregon Trail Rendezvous Pageant. Fri closest to July 24.

Bear Lake County Fair and Rodeo. 3rd wkend Aug.

Motel

★ **BEST WESTERN CREST.** 243 N 4th St. 208/847-1782; FAX 208/847-3519. 65 rms, 2 story. May-Oct: S $53; D $58-$63; each addl $6; suites $80; under 12 free; lower rates rest of yr. Crib $6. Pet accepted, some restrictions. TV; cable (premium), VCR avail (movies). Restaurant opp 6 am-10 pm. Ck-out 11 am. Meeting rm. Business servs avail. In-rm modem link. Exercise equipt; stair machine, weights. Whirlpool. Some refrigerators. Cr cds: A, C, D, DS, JCB, MC, V.

D ✆ 🏋 🛏 🐾 SC

Moscow (B-1)

Pop 18,519 **Elev** 2,583 ft **Area code** 208 **Zip** 83843
Information Chamber of Commerce, PO Box 8936; 208/882-1800.

Moscow is the seat of Latah County in the heart of the Palouse Hills country and beautiful Paradise Valley. A monument at 810 B St marks the site of old Ft Russell, where settlers sought refuge from Chief Joseph and the Nez Perce in 1877.

What to See and Do

Appaloosa Museum & Heritage Center. Exhibit of paintings and artifacts relating to the appaloosa horse; early cowboy equipment; saddle collection; Nez Perce clothing, tools. (June-Aug, daily exc Sun; rest of yr, Mon-Fri; closed most hols) Also houses national headquarters of the Appaloosa Horse Club, Inc. Moscow-Pullman Hwy. Phone 208/882-5578. **Free.**

Latah County Historical Society. Period furnishings, exhibits and artifacts depicting local history. Local history and genealogy library. Museum (Tues-Sat, limited hrs; closed major hols); library, 327 E 2nd St (Tues-Fri). McConnell Mansion (1886), 110 S Adams St. Phone 208/882-1004. **Donation.**

University of Idaho (1889). (11,000 students) Graduate and undergraduate programs. On campus is a major collection of big game specimens from the estate of well-known hunter Jack O'Connor; art gallery and performing arts center; mining, forestry and wildlife exhibits in the mining and forestry buildings; 18,000-seat, covered Kibbie-ASUI Activities Center with award-winning barrel-arch dome. Tours (daily). W off US 95. Phone 208/885-6424.

Annual Events

Lionel Hampton/Chevron Jazz Festival. University of Idaho. Four-day festival hosted by Lionel Hampton featuring all-star headliners and student performers. Phone 208/885-6765. Late Feb.

Rendezvous in the Park. In East City Park. Arts & crafts festival, juried art shows, silent movies, concerts under the stars. Phone 208/882-1178. 2nd & 3rd wkends July.

Latah County Fair. Fairgrounds, E of town. Phone 208/883-0694. 2nd wk Sept, after Labor Day.

Seasonal Event

Idaho Repertory Theater. E.W. Hartung Theater, University of Idaho. Shakespeare, musicals, dramas, comedies. Phone 208/885-7212 or 800/345-7402. July-early Aug.

Motels

★ ★ **BEST WESTERN-UNIVERSITY INN.** 1516 Pullman Rd. 208/882-0550; FAX 208/883-3050. 173 units, 2 story. S $63-$79; D $70-$86; each addl $7; suites $150-$350; under 18 free. TV; cable (premium). Pet accepted. Indoor pool; wading pool, whirlpool, sauna. Restaurant open 24 hrs. Rm serv. 2 bars 11-2 am; entertainment. Ck-out noon. Meeting rms. Business servs avail. Valet serv. Airport, bus depot transportation. Some refrigerators. Cr cds: A, C, D, DS, MC, V.

D ✆ 🏊 🎿 🛏 🐾 SC

✔ ★ **HILLCREST.** 706 N Main St. 208/882-7579; FAX 208/882-0310; res: 800/368-6564. 35 rms. S $28-$42; D $32-$52; family, wkly rates; higher rates: special events, university football games. TV; cable.

Restaurant nearby. Ck-out 11 am. Business servs avail. Some refrigerators. Cr cds: A, MC, V.

🛏 🐾 SC

★ ★ **MARK IV MOTOR INN.** 414 N Main St. 208/882-7557; FAX 208/883-0684. 86 units, 2 story. S $41-$51; D $44.50-$61; each addl $5; suites $50-$87; under 11 free; higher rates special events. TV; cable. Indoor pool; whirlpool. Restaurant 6 am-10 pm. Rm serv. Bar 3:30 pm-midnight. Ck-out noon. Meeting rm. Business servs avail. Free airport, bus depot transportation. Cr cds: A, C, D, DS, MC, V.

D 🏊 🛏 🐾 SC

★ **SUPER 8.** 175 Peterson Dr. 208/883-1503; FAX 208/883-4769. 60 rms, 3 story. No elvtr. S $36.88; D $44.88-$68.88; each addl $3; under 12 free; higher rates special events. Crib free. TV; cable. Ck-out 11 am. Meeting rms. Cr cds: A, C, D, DS, MC, V.

D 🛏 🐾 SC

Mountain Home (E-2)

(See also Boise)

Pop 7,913 **Elev** 3,143 ft **Area code** 208 **Zip** 83647
Information Desert Mountain Visitor Center, 2900 American Legion Blvd, PO Box 3; 208/587-4464.

A transportation center in the Boise-Owyhee Valley of southwest Idaho, Mountain Home affords a fine starting point for side trips. Within a few hours' drive are forested ranges of the Boise National Forest, sand dunes, ghost towns, reservoirs and canyons; a Ranger District office of the forest (see BOISE) is located here.

What to See and Do

Bruneau Canyon. A 61-mi gorge, 2,000 ft deep, but narrow enough in places to toss a rock across. **Bruneau Dunes State Park** (4,800 acres) has small lakes, sand dunes and the highest single structured dune in North America (470 ft). Fishing for bass and bluegill, boating (ramps; no motors); nature trails; picnicking. Tent & trailer sites (15-day max; hookups, dump station). Information center, interpretive programs (by appt). Standard hrs, fees. 20 mi S on ID 51 to Bruneau, then SE on local road, near Bruneau. Phone 208/366-7919.

Elmore County Historical Foundation Museum. Contains historical information about Mountain Home and Elmore County. (Mar-Dec, Fri & Sat afternoons) 180 S 3rd St E. Phone City Hall, 208/587-2104. ¢

Fishing, swimming, boating. Strike Reservoir, 23 mi S on ID 51; or Anderson Ranch Reservoir, 22 mi NE on ID 20.

Soldier Mt Ski Area. 2 double chairlifts, rope tow; patrol, school, rentals; snowmaking; cafeteria, concession. Longest run 2 mi; vertical drop 1,400 ft. Half-day rates. (Mid-Nov-Apr, Thurs-Sun & hols; Christmas & Easter wks, daily) NE on US 20 to Fairfield, then 10 mi N on Soldier Creek Rd. Phone 208/764-2300. ¢¢¢¢

Motels

★ ★ **BEST WESTERN-FOOTHILLS MOTOR INN.** 1080 US 20, I-84 exit 95. 208/587-8477; FAX 208/587-5774. 76 rms, 2 story. S $56-$62; D $65-$72; each addl $5; suites $130; under 12 free. Crib $5. TV; cable (premium). Pool; whirlpool, sauna. Complimentary continental bkfst. Complimentary coffee in rms. Ck-out 11 am. Business servs avail. Cr cds: A, C, D, DS, ER, JCB, MC, V.

D 🏊 🛏 🐾 SC

✔ ★ **HILANDER MOTEL & STEAK HOUSE.** 615 S 3rd St W. 208/587-3311. 34 rms, 2 story, 4 kits. S $35; D $39; each addl $4; kit. units

$42-$59. Crib $4. TV; cable. Restaurant 4-11 pm. Rm serv. Bar to 1 am. Ck-out 11 am. Refrigerators avail. Cr cds: A, C, D, DS, MC, V.

★ **SLEEP INN.** *1180 US 20. 208/587-9743; FAX 208/587-7382.* 60 rms, shower only, 2 story. May-Sept: S $55; D $60; each addl $5; family, wkly rates; ski plan; lower rates rest of yr. Crib $5. TV; cable (premium), VCR. Pool privileges. Complimentary continental bkfst. Restaurant adj open 24 hrs. Ck-out noon. Meeting rm. Business servs avail. In-rm modem link. Refrigerators. Cr cds: A, C, D, DS, ER, JCB, MC, V.

Nampa (E-1)

(See also Boise)

Founded 1885 **Pop** 28,365 **Elev** 2,490 ft **Area code** 208
Information Chamber of Commerce, 1305 3rd St S, PO Box A, 83653; 208/466-4641.

Nampa, the largest city in Canyon County, is located in the heart of the agriculturally rich Treasure Valley of southwestern Idaho.

What to See and Do

Canyon County Historical Society Museum. Historical artifacts and memorabilia inside a 1903 train depot once used as offices of the Union Pacific Railroad. (Tues-Sat, limited hrs) 1200 Front St. Phone 208/467-7611. **Donation.**

Deer Flat National Wildlife Refuge. Thousands of migratory waterfowl pause at this 10,500-acre refuge while on their journey (Oct-Dec). Wildlife observation. Fishing, hunting in season. Visitor center (Mon-Fri; closed hols). 5 mi SW off I-84. Phone 208/467-9278. **Free.** Within the refuge is

Lake Lowell. Approx 8,800 acres. Picnicking, waterskiing, boating, sailing (mid-Apr-Sept, daily).

Lakeview Park. A 90-acre park with gardens, sports facilities, tennis, archery range, picnic areas. Pool (June-Labor Day; fee). Antique fire engine, locomotive, steam roller, jet fighter plane on display. Amphitheater. Park (daily). Garrity Blvd & 16th Ave N. Phone 208/465-2215. **Free.**

Annual Event

Snake River Stampede. Among nation's top professional rodeos. All seats reserved. For tickets contact PO Box 231, 83653; 208/466-8497. Tues-Sat, 3rd wk July.

Motels

(Rates may be higher Snake River Stampede)

✔★ **DESERT INN.** *115 9th Ave S (83651). 208/467-1161; FAX 208/467-5268.* 40 rms, 2 story. S $39-$42; D $44-$52; each addl $5; under 12 free. TV. Pool. Complimentary continental bkfst. Restaurant adj 6 am-10 pm. Ck-out 11 am. Valet serv. Cr cds: A, C, D, DS, MC, V.

★ **SHILO INN.** *617 Nampa Blvd (83687). 208/466-8993; FAX 208/465-3239.* 61 rms, 3 story. No elvtr. S, D $53-$75; each addl $8; under 13 free. Crib free. Pet accepted. TV; cable. Heated pool; whirlpool, sauna, steam rm. Complimentary continental bkfst. Ck-out noon. Coin lndry. Valet serv. Free airport transportation. Cr cds: A, C, D, DS, ER, JCB, MC, V.

★★ **SHILO INN.** *1401 Shilo Dr (83687). 208/465-3250; FAX 208/465-5929.* 83 suites, 4 story, 8 kits. S, D $59-$73; each addl $10; kit. suites $85; under 13 free. Crib free. Pet accepted. TV; cable. Indoor pool; whirlpool. Complimentary coffee in lobby. Restaurant adj 6 am-10 pm. Rm serv. Ck-out noon. Coin lndry. Meeting rms. Sundries. Free airport, RR station, bus depot transportation. Exercise equipt; weight machine, bicycles, sauna. Bathrm phones, refrigerators; many wet bars. Cr cds: A, C, D, DS, ER, JCB, MC, V.

Pocatello (F-4)

(See also Blackfoot, Idaho Falls)

Founded 1882 **Pop** 46,080 **Elev** 4,464 ft **Area code** 208
Information Greater Pocatello Chamber of Commerce, 343 W Center St, PO Box 626, 83204; 208/233-1525.

At the heart of the intermontane transportation system is Pocatello. Once the site of a reservation, the city was named for the Native American leader who granted the railroad rights of way and building privileges. A Ranger District office and the headquarters of the Caribou National Forest are located here.

What to See and Do

Caribou National Forest. Scenic drives, pack trips, camping (fee in some designated developed campgrounds), picnic grounds, hunting, fishing, downhill and cross-country skiing, snowmobiling. S, W & E of city. For further information contact the Forest Supervisor, 250 S 4th Ave, Suite 187, 83201; 208/236-7500. In forest is

Pebble Creek Ski Area. Triple, 2 double chairlifts; beginner-to-expert trails; patrol, school, rentals; restaurant, bar; day care. Longest run 1½ mi; vertical drop 2,000 ft. Night skiing. Half-day rates. (2nd wk Dec-early Apr; daily exc Mon) 10 mi SE on I-15 to Inkom, then 5 mi E on Green Canyon Rd. Phone 208/775-4452. ¢¢¢¢

Idaho State University (1901). (11,155 students) Undergraduate and graduate programs. Art gallery in Fine Arts Bldg has changing exhibits (academic yr, daily; summer by appt, phone 208/236-3532); art gallery in Student Union Bldg (daily); both galleries free. On campus is 12,000-seat Holt Arena, indoor football stadium and sports arena. Tours. 741 S 7th Ave. For information, schedules phone 208/236-3620. Also here is

Idaho Museum of Natural History. Exhibits on Idaho fossils, especially large mammals of the Ice Age; Native American basketry & beadwork; "Discovery Room" for educational activities; pre-arranged tours; museum shop. (Mon-Fri; closed hols) Phone 208/236-3168 or 208/236-2262. **Free.**

Rocky Mountain River Tours. 6-day wilderness rafting tours; equipment provided. Middlefork Salmon River Canyon. For schedule, fee and other information, phone 208/345-2400.

Ross Park. Zoo; swimming pool (June-Aug), water slide; playground; picnic area with shelter; band shell. Park (daily). Fee for some activities. S 2nd Ave. Phone 208/234-6232. On upper level are

Old Ft Hall Replica. Reproduction of 1834 Hudson's Bay Trading Post; period displays. (June-mid-Sept, daily; Apr-May, Tues-Sat) ¢

Bannock County Historical Museum. Relics of the early days of Pocatello and Bannock County; Bannock and Shoshone display. (Memorial Day-Labor Day, daily; rest of yr, Tues-Sat, limited hrs; closed hols, also mid-Dec-mid-Jan) Phone 208/233-0434. ¢

Standrod House. Restored Victorian mansion lavishly decorated with woodwork and marble; furnished with antiques. (Tues-Fri) 648 N Garfield Ave. Phone 208/233-4198. ¢

Annual Events

Shoshone-Bannock Indian Festival. Begins 2nd Wed Aug.

Bannock County Fair and Rodeo. North: Bannock County Fairgrounds. South: Downey Fairgrounds. Carnival, rodeo, exhibits, food booths, livestock and horse shows. Mid-Aug.

Seasonal Event

Summer Band Concert Series. Guy Gates Memorial Band Shell, in lower level of Ross Park. Sun, July-Aug.

Motels

★ ★ **AMERITEL INN.** *1440 N Bench Rd (83201), I-15 exit 71.* 208/234-7500; FAX 208/234-0000; res: 800/600-6001. Web www.ameritel inns.com. 148 rms, 3 story, 14 kit. units. June-Aug: S, D $79; each addl $8; suites, kit. units $109-$189; under 13 free; lower rates rest of yr. Crib free. TV; cable (premium). Indoor pool; whirlpool. Complimentary continental bkfst. Restaurant nearby. Ck-out noon. Coin lndry. Meeting rms. In-rm modem link. Valet serv. Free airport transportation. Exercise equipt; weight machine, bicycle. Some refrigerators; microwaves avail. Cr cds: A, D, DS, MC, V.

D ⛫ ✕ ⊠ 🏋 SC

✔★ ★ **COMFORT INN.** *1333 Bench Rd (83201).* 208/237-8155. 52 rms, 2 story, 14 suites. June-Sept: S $59; D $69; suites $74; under 18 free; lower rates rest of yr. Crib free. Pet accepted. TV; cable (premium). Indoor pool; whirlpool. Complimentary continental bkfst. Restaurant nearby. Ck-out 11 am. Microwaves avail. Cr cds: A, C, D, DS, ER, MC, V.

D ✔ ⛫ ⊠ 🏋

★ ★ **HOLIDAY INN.** *1399 Bench Rd (83201).* 208/237-1400; FAX 208/238-0225. 202 rms, 2 story. S, D $69; each addl $6; suites $139; under 18 free; wkly, wkend, hol rates. Crib free. Pet accepted, some restrictions; $25 deposit. TV; cable (premium), VCR avail. Complimentary continental bkfst. Complimentary coffee in rms. Restaurant 6 am-2 pm, 5-10 pm. Rm serv 6 am-10 pm. Bar 5 pm-1 am. Ck-out noon. Meeting rms. Business servs avail. Bellhops. Sundries. Coin lndry. Free airport transportation. Indoor putting green. Exercise equipt; bicycle, stair machine, sauna. Indoor pool; whirlpool. Game rm. Cr cds: A, C, D, DS, JCB, MC, V.

✔ ⛫ ✕ ⊠ 🏋 SC

★ **SUPER 8.** *1330 Bench Rd (83201).* 208/234-0888; FAX 208/232-0347. 80 rms, 3 story, 8 suites. S $42.88; D $46.88-$50.88; each addl $4; suites $64.88; under 12 free. Crib free. Pet accepted, some restrictions; $2. TV; cable. Complimentary continental bkfst. Ck-out 11 am. Microwaves avail. Cr cds: A, C, D, DS, MC, V.

D ✔ ⊠ 🏋 SC

Motor Hotels

★ ★ ★ **BEST WESTERN COTTONTREE INN.** *1415 Bench Rd (83201).* 208/237-7650; FAX 208/238-1355. 149 rms, 3 story. No elvtr. S $63; D $69; studio rms $78-$84; each addl $6; suites $110-$150; under 18 free. Crib free. Pet accepted. TV; cable (premium). Indoor pool; whirlpool. Restaurant 6 am-11 pm. Rm serv. Bar 3:30 pm-1 am. Ck-out noon. Coin lndry. Meeting rms. Business servs avail. Bellhops. Valet serv. Free airport transportation. Some refrigerators; microwaves avail. Cr cds: A, C, D, DS, MC, V.

D ✔ ⛫ ⊠ 🏋 SC

★ ★ **QUALITY INN POCATELLO PARK.** *1555 Pocatello Creek (83201),* at jct I-15 & I-86. 208/233-2200; FAX 208/234-4524. 152 rms, 2 story. S, D $69; suites $125; each addl $5; under 18 free. Crib free. Pet accepted, some restrictions; $10. TV; cable. Indoor pool; wading pool, whirlpool. Coffee in rms. Restaurant open 24 hrs. Rm serv. Bar. Ck-out noon. Coin lndry. Meeting rms. Business center. Valet serv. Free airport transportation. Exercise equipt; weight machine, bicycle, sauna. Microwaves avail. Some balconies. Cr cds: A, C, D, DS, MC, V.

D ✔ ⛫ ✕ ⊠ 🏋 SC ⛷

Priest Lake Area (A-1)

(See also Sandpoint)

Area code 208

Information Chamber of Commerce, PO Box 174, Coolin 83821; 208/443-3191.

(25 mi N of Priest River via ID 57)

Among the few remaining unspoiled playgrounds of the Pacific Northwest are lovely and spectacular Priest Lake and the Idaho Panhandle National Forest. North of the confluence of the Pend Oreille and Priest rivers, giant lake trout, big game, towering mountains, waterfalls, lakes and tall trees make this area one of the most attractive in the country. Mountain ranges and Pacific breezes keep the climate moderate.

This entire water and forest domain was explored by a Jesuit priest, Father Peter John DeSmet, also known as "great black robe" and the "first apostle of the Northwest." Priest Lake and Priest River were both named in his honor. A Ranger District office of the Idaho Panhandle National Forests-Kaniksu is located at Priest Lake.

What to See and Do

Albeni Falls Dam & Reservoir. Dam, 3 mi W of town of Priest River on US 2; overlook, free guided tours of powerhouse (Memorial Day-Labor Day, daily). Boat ramp, picnicking, swimming, showers, camping (fee) at Priest River Recreation Area (1 mi E on US 2), Riley Creek (8 mi E on US 2), and Springy Point (2 mi S of Sandpoint on US 95, then 3 mi W on Lakeshore Dr). Trestle Creek has boat launch, picnic facilities; Albeni Cove has boat ramps, swimming, camping (fee). Recreation areas (mid-Apr-mid-Sept). On Pend Oreille River. Phone 208/437-3133 or phone 208/437-5517 (campground reservation information).

Chimney Rock. Glacially formed tower of rock (elev 7,136 ft) provides challenging 200-ft climb. E of Priest Lake, reached via local road from US 2/95 at Samuels.

Other forests in the Panhandle are Coeur d'Alene (see COEUR D'ALENE) and St Joe (see ST MARIES).

Idaho Panhandle National Forests—Kaniksu. Surrounds Priest Lake and Lake Pend Oreille; other areas NE. Rich with huge trees, wildflowers, fishing streams. Boating, swimming, fishing in Pend Oreille and Priest lakes, big game hunting, cross-country skiing, snowmobiling trails, picnicking, 12 forest-run campgrounds on the west side of Priest Lake (may be fee); other state-run campgrounds in the area. Contact the Priest Lake Ranger District, HCR 5, Box 207, Priest River 83856, phone 208/443-2512; or the Sandpoint Ranger District, 1500 US 2, Sandpoint 83864, phone 208/263-5111; or the Supervisor, 1201 Ironwood Dr, Coeur d'Alene 83814, phone 208/765-7223. Within the forest is

Priest Lake. Lower Priest, the main lake, is 18$\frac{1}{2}$ mi long, about 4 mi wide and has a 63-mi shoreline. Upper Priest (inaccessible by road; best reached by boat) is 3$\frac{1}{4}$ mi long, 1 mi wide and has an 8-mi shoreline. The area is very popular for picnics, overnight cruises and camp-outs. There are three state-run campgrounds on the east side: Dickensheet, Indian Creek and Lionhead; the US Forest Service operates other campgrounds in the area, on the west side. Nearby is the Roosevelt Grove of ancient cedars with 800-year-old trees standing as tall as 150 ft. Granite Falls is within the grove. Priest Lake is famous for its giant-size lake trout (Mackinaw trout), and cutthroat trout. The main lake contains 6 islands ideal for picnicking and camping (10-day max). Recreation around the lake includes swimming, boating (ramp); cross-country skiing, snowmobiling, ice-skating, ice fishing, sledding. 22 mi N of town of Priest River via ID 57, then approx 6 mi E on East Shore Rd; or approx 6 mi farther on ID 57, then 1 mi E on Outlet Bay Rd. On the E side of the lake is

Priest Lake State Park. This park comprises three state-run campgrounds: **Dickensheet** unit is 1 mi off ID 57, on the Coolin Rd (46 acres; 11 campsites); **Indian Creek** unit is 11 mi N of Coolin, on the Eastshore Rd (park headquarters; 295 acres; 93 campsites, store, boating facilities, RV hookups, trails); and **Lionhead** unit is 23 mi N of Coolin, on the

Eastshore Rd (415 acres; 47 tent sites, group camp, boating facilities, trails). Reservations are available for Indian Creek campsites; reservations are required for the group camp at Lionhead. Phone 208/443-2200.

Priest River. Old logging roads parallel much of it. Only at north and south stretches is it easily reached from ID 57. Long stretches of white water provide adventure for canoe experts; riffles, big holes, smooth-flowing parts make it a tantalizing trout stream (fishing: June-Oct). Winds for 44 mi S of lake through wild, forested country.

Annual Events

Pacific Northwest Sled Dog Championship Races. On ID 57 at Priest Lake Airport, W shore. Last wkend Jan.

Spring Festival. Flotilla, fishing derby, auction, parade. Memorial Day wkend.

Resorts

★ **ELKIN'S.** (W Shore Priest Lake, Priest Lake 83848) W shore of Priest Lake. 208/443-2432. 30 air-cooled kit. cottages. July-Aug (1-wk min), Sept-June (2-day min): S, D $80-$235; wkly rates; higher rates hol wkends; lower rates rest of yr. Crib free. Pet accepted. Restaurant 8 am-9 pm; closed Mar & Apr. Box lunches, picnics. Bar. Ck-out 11 am, ck-in 4 pm. Gift shop. Grocery. Coin lndry 2 mi. Meeting rms. Game rm. Private beach. Boats. X-country ski on site. Picnic tables. Cr cds: MC, V.

★★ **GRANDVIEW.** (HCO-1, Box 48, Nordman 83848) W shore of Priest Lake, via ID 57 to Reeder Bay Rd. 208/443-2433; FAX 208/443-3033. 8 rms, 1-2 story. No A/C. June-mid-Sept: S, D $59-$75; suites $75-$125; cottages $69-$145; lower rates rest of yr. TV. Heated pool. Dining rm 8 am-3:30 pm, 6-9:30 pm (summer, off-season wkends). Box lunches. Picnics. Bar 10-1 am; entertainment. Ck-out 11 am. Grocery. Coin lndry. Meeting rms. Airport transportation. Private beach, boats, canoes, waterskiing. X-country ski on site. Sleighing. Lawn games. Game rm. Some fireplaces. Private patios, balconies. Cr cds: D, DS, MC, V.

★★ **HILL'S.** (HCR 5, Box 162A, Priest Lake 83856) W shore of Priest Lake via ID 57 to Luby Bay Rd. 208/443-2551; FAX 208/443-2363. 50 kit. chalets, cabins, 1-2 story. No A/C. Last wk June-Labor Day: $700-$1,750/wk; each addl $10; lower rates rest of yr. Crib $5. Pet accepted. Dining rm 8 am-9:30 pm. Box lunches. Bar 1 pm-1 am. Ck-out 11 am. Grocery. Coin lndry. Meeting rms. Business servs avail. Tennis. Golf privileges, putting green, driving range. Private beach, boats, rowboats, canoes, waterskiing. X-country ski on site. Sleighing, tobogganing, snowmobiles. Bicycles (rentals). Lawn games. Entertainment, dancing, movies. Game rm. Housekeeping units. Fireplaces. Balconies. Picnic tables, grills. Cr cds: DS, MC, V.

Rexburg (E-5)

(See also Ashton, Idaho Falls, St Anthony)

Founded 1883 **Pop** 14,302 **Elev** 4,865 ft **Area code** 208 **Zip** 83440
E-mail rexcc@srv.net **Web** www.srv.net/~rexcc/rexburg.html
Information Chamber of Commerce Tourist & Information Center, 420 W 4th South; 208/356-5700.

A Mormon-rooted community, Rexburg enjoys its position as a farm and trading center. Founded on instructions of the Mormon Church, the community was named for Thomas Ricks, but usage changed it to Rexburg.

What to See and Do

Idaho Centennial Carousel. Restored Spillman Engineering carousel. (June-Labor Day, daily) Porter Park. Phone 208/359-3020. ¢

Parks.

Beaver Dick. A 12-acre preserve on W bank of the North Fork of Snake River. Picnic facilities, primitive camping, fishing, boating, ramp. (Mar-Dec) 7 mi W on ID 33.

Twin Bridges. A 30-acre preserve on N bank of the South Fork of Snake River. Picnic facilities, camping, fishing, boating, ramp. (Apr-Nov) 13 mi SE on Archer-Lyman Rd.

Teton Flood Museum. Artifacts, photographs and films document the 1976 flood caused by the collapse of the Teton Dam, which left 11 persons dead and $1 billion in damage. Also various historical displays. (May-Aug, daily exc Sun; rest of yr, Mon-Fri, limited hrs; closed hols exc July 4) 51 N Center. Phone 208/356-9101. **Free.**

Annual Event

International Folkdance Festival. Dance teams from around the world, events. Last wk July-1st wkend Aug.

Motels

★★ **BEST WESTERN COTTONTREE INN.** 450 W Fourth St S. 208/356-4646; FAX 208/356-7461. 101 rms, 2 story. S $64; D $69-74; each addl $5; suite $195; under 18 free. Crib free. Pet accepted. TV; cable. Indoor pool; whirlpool. Restaurant adj 7 am-10 pm. Ck-out noon. Coin lndry. Meeting rms. Business servs avail. Health club privileges. Some refrigerators, microwaves. Balconies. Cr cds: A, C, D, DS, MC, V.

★★ **COMFORT INN.** 1513 W Main St. 208/359-1311; FAX 208/359-1387. 52 rms, 2 story. June-mid-Sept: S $50-$84; D $60-$84; suites $94; under 18 free; lower rates rest of yr. Crib $5. Pet accepted. TV; cable. Indoor pool; whirlpool. Complimentary continental bkfst. Ck-out 11 am. Meeting rms. Business servs avail. Exercise equipt; bicycle, treadmill. Refrigerator, microwave in suites. Cr cds: A, C, D, DS, JCB, MC, V.

✔★ **SUPER 8.** 215 W Main St. 208/356-8888; FAX 208/356-8896. 42 rms, 2 story. June-Sept: S $42.88; D $46.88-$50.88; each addl $4; under 12 free; lower rates rest of yr. Crib free. TV; cable. Complimentary continental bkfst. Restaurant nearby. Ck-out 11 am. Business servs avail. Cr cds: A, D, DS, MC, V.

Restaurant

✔★ **FRONTIER PIES.** 460 W 4th St S. 208/356-3600. Hrs: 6:30 am-10 pm; Fri, Sat to 11 pm. Closed Dec 25. Semi-a la carte: bkfst $2.95-$5.59, lunch $4.59-$7.29, dinner $4.99-$10.99. Child's meals. Specialties: Navajo taco, broiled chicken Hawaiian. Own soups, pies. Rustic decor; Old West antiques. Totally nonsmoking. Cr cds: D, DS, MC, V.

St Anthony (E-5)

(See also Ashton, Idaho Falls, Rexburg)

Pop 3,010 **Elev** 4,972 ft **Area code** 208 **Zip** 83445
Information South Fremont Chamber of Commerce, City Hall, 110 W Main St; 208/624-3494.

Seat of Fremont County, headquarters for the Targhee National Forest and a center of the seed potato industry, St Anthony is named for Anthony

Falls, Minnesota. Tourists make it a base for exploring Idaho's tiny (30 miles long, 1 mile wide) "sahara desert," the St Anthony Sand Dunes.

What to See and Do

Ft Henry Trading Post Site (1810). First fort on what early voyageurs called the "accursed mad river." 7 mi W along Henry's Fork of Snake River.

St Anthony Sand Dunes. 12 mi W. Phone 208/624-3494.

Annual Events

Cowboy Poet Festival. Entertainment, clogging demonstrations. Apr.

Fremont County Pioneer Days. Rodeo, parade, carnival. Late July.

Fremont County Fair. Fairgrounds. Features demolition derby. Aug.

St Maries (B-2)

(For accommodations see Coeur d'Alene)

Pop 2,442 **Elev** 2,216 ft **Area code** 208 **Zip** 83861

Information Chamber of Commerce, Box 162; 208/245-3563.

St Maries (St Marys) is a center for lumbering and the production of plywood, a crossroads for lake, rail and road transportation and the jumping-off place for exploring the shadowy St Joe River country. A Ranger District office of the Idaho Panhandle National Forests-St Joe is located in St Maries.

What to See and Do

Benewah, Round and Chatcolet lakes. Famous as one of state's best bass-fishing and duck-hunting areas. The three lakes became one lake with the construction of Post Falls Dam. Along St Joe River. Also here is

Heyburn State Park. More than 7,800 acres. Swimming beach; fishing; boating (ramps). Hiking and bridle trails; self-guided nature walks. Ice-skating, ice fishing. Picnicking, concession. Tent & trailer campsites (15-day max; hookups), dump station. Campfire and interpretive programs. Park (daily). Standard fees. 7 mi W on ID 5. Phone 208/686-1308.

Idaho Panhandle National Forests—St Joe. Hunting, fishing, hiking, camping, cabins, picnicking, summer and winter sports areas, cross-country skiing, snowmobiling trails; digging for garnets; scenic drives. Access from US 95 & I-90; other areas E on local roads. Contact the St Maries Ranger District, PO Box 407, phone 208/245-2531; or the Avery Ranger District, HC Box 1, Avery 83802, phone 208/245-4517; or the Supervisor, 1201 Ironwood Dr, Coeur d'Alene 83814, phone 208/765-7223.

Other forests in the Panhandle are Coeur d'Alene (see COEUR D'ALENE) and Kaniksu (see PRIEST LAKE AREA).

St Joe Baldy Mt. Lookout at top has view of Washington and Montana. 8 mi E on St Joe River Rd (Forest Hwy 50).

St Joe River. Called "the river through the lakes," one of the world's highest navigable rivers. Connects St Maries with Lake Coeur d'Alene. Just E on ID 5.

Annual Events

smART Festival. St Maries City Park. Paintings & crafts by local and regional artists featured in juried art show. Food; entertainment; swimming. Phone 208/245-3417. 3rd wkend July.

Paul Bunyan Days. Includes parade, fireworks, logging events, water show, carnival. Labor Day wkend.

Salmon (D-3)

Settled 1866 **Pop** 2,941 **Elev** 4,004 ft **Area code** 208 **Zip** 83467

Information Salmon Valley Chamber of Commerce, 200 Main St, Suite 1; 208/756-2100.

This town, at the junction of the Salmon and Lemhi rivers, serves as a doorway to the Salmon River country. It has towering mountains, lush farmland, timberland and rich mines. The Salmon River runs through the town on its way to the Columbia River and the Pacific Ocean. Fishing and boating are available along the Salmon and Lemhi rivers and in more than 250 lakes. The headquarters and two Ranger District offices of the Salmon National Forest are located here.

What to See and Do

Lemhi ghost town. The village, like the forest, county, mountain range, valley and river, is named for Lemhi, a character in *The Book of Mormon*. Mormons attempted to colonize here in 1855 and built a fort; but by 1858, Native Americans had driven them out. The walls of old Ft Lemhi still stand. (For information on other ghost towns in the area contact the Salmon Valley Chamber of Commerce.) 29 mi SE on ID 28.

River rafting, backpack, fishing and pack trips along the Lemhi, Salmon, Middle Fork and other rivers can be arranged. Contact the Chamber of Commerce for a list of outfitters in the area.

Salmon National Forest. Approx 1.8 million acres. Boat trips, hunting, fishing, picnicking, camping. Includes portion of the Frank Church-River of No Return Wilderness. N, E & W of town along US 93. For further information contact the Supervisor, PO Box 729; 208/756-2215.

Annual Events

High School Rodeo. 1st wkend June.

Little Britches Rodeo. 3rd wkend July.

The Great Salmon BalloonFest. Hot air balloon festival. Aug.

Lemhi County Fair & Rodeo. 3rd wk Aug.

Motel

✔★ ★ **STAGECOACH INN.** *201 US 93N. 208/756-4251.* 100 rms, 2-3 story. Mid-May-Nov: S $47-$69; D $55-$75; each addl $6; under 12 free; lower rates rest of yr. Crib $6. TV; cable. Heated pool. Continental bkfst. Restaurant nearby. Ck-out 11 am. Coin lndry. Meeting rms. Some balconies, patios. Overlooks Salmon River. Cr cds: A, C, D, MC, V.

Restaurant

★ **SALMON RIVER COFFEE SHOP.** *606 Main St. 208/756-3521.* Hrs: 5 am-11 pm. Closed Jan 1, Thanksgiving, Dec 25. Bar. Semi-a la carte: bkfst $3-$6.95, lunch from $3.75, dinner $5.95-$22. Child's meals. Specializes in steak, lobster, seafood. Salad bar. Entertainment exc Sun. Cr cds: A, D, MC, V.

Sandpoint (A-2)

(See also Priest Lake Area)

Pop 5,203 **Elev** 2,085 ft **Area code** 208 **Zip** 83864 **E-mail** chamber@ netw.com **Web** www.keokee.com/chamber/index.html

Information Chamber of Commerce, 100 US 95 N, PO Box 928; 208/263-2161or 800/800-2106.

At the point where the Pend Oreille River empties into Lake Pend Oreille (pon-da-RAY, from a Native American tribe given to wearing pendant ear ornaments), Sandpoint straddles two major railroads and three US highways. All of these bring a stream of tourists into town. In the surrounding area are dozens of smaller lakes and streams. A Ranger District office of the Idaho Panhandle National Forests-Coeur d'Alene (see COEUR D'ALENE) is located here.

What to See and Do

Bonner County Historical Society Museum. Exhibits depict history of Bonner County. Research library with newspaper collection dating from 1899. (Apr-Oct, Tues-Sat; rest of yr, Thurs; closed hols) In Lakeview Park, Ontario & Ella Sts. Phone 208/263-2344. ¢

Coldwater Creek on the Cedar St Bridge. Shopping mall built on a bridge over Sand Creek. Inspired by the Ponte Vecchio in Florence, Italy, the Coldwater Creek shops provide panoramic views of Lake Pend Oreille and nearby mountains. (Daily)

Lake Pend Oreille. Largest in Idaho, one of the largest natural lakes wholly within US; more than 43 mi long, 6 mi wide, with more than 111 mi of shoreline. Approx 14 varieties of game fish including famous Kamloops, largest rainbow trout in world (avg 16-26 lbs). Boating, swimming, water-skiing, camping, picnicking.

Lake loop drive. More than 100 mi of outstanding mountain scenery; fishing; picnicking.

Round Lake State Park. Approx 140 acres of coniferous woods. Swimming, skin diving; fishing; boating (ramp, no motors). Hiking; cross-country skiing, sledding, ice-skating, ice fishing, tobogganing, snowshoeing in winter; picnicking. Camping (15-day max; no hookups), dump station. Campfire programs. Park (daily). Standard fees. 10 mi S on US 95, then 2 mi W, near Sagle. Phone 208/263-3489.

Sandpoint Public Beach. Nearly 20 acres. Bathhouse, swimming, water-skiing, boat docks, ramps; picnic tables, fireplaces; volleyball, tennis courts; concession (seasonal). Park (daily). Foot of Bridge St, E edge of town. **Free.**

Skiing. Schweitzer Mountain Resort. 5 chairlifts, high-speed quad; school, rentals; lodging, restaurants, bars, cafeteria; nursery. Longest run 2.7 mi; vertical drop 2,400 ft. (Nov-Apr, daily) Summer chairlift rides (fee). 11 mi NW off US 2 & US 95, in Selkirk Mts of Idaho Panhandle Natl Forests. Phone 800/831-8810.

Annual Event

Winter Carnival. Two wkends of festivities including snow sculpture, snowshoe softball and other games, races, torchlight parade. Mid-Jan.

Motels

★ ★ ★ **BEST WESTERN CONNIE'S MOTOR INN.** *323 Cedar St, downtown.* 208/263-9581; FAX 208/263-3395. 53 rms, 3 story. S $72; D $80-$84; each addl $8; suites $100-$150; under 12 free; golf, ski plans. Crib $8. TV; cable (premium), VCR avail. Heated pool; whirlpool. Restaurant 6 am-10 pm; Fri, Sat to midnight. Rm serv 7 am-10 pm. Bar 11-1 am. Ck-out 1 pm. Meeting rm. Business servs avail. In-rm modem link. Valet serv. Downhill/x-country ski 9 mi. Game rm. Some bathrm phones, refrigerators. Balconies. Cr cds: A, C, D, DS, MC, V.

★ ★ **EDGEWATER.** *56 Bridge St, just E of US 95.* 208/263-3194; FAX 208/263-3194; res: 800/635-2534. 55 rms, 3 story. No elvtr. S $90; D $98; each addl $6; suites $125-$160; ski plans. Crib $5. TV; cable, VCR avail. Restaurant 6:30 am-10 pm; Sun to 9 pm. Rm serv. Bar. Ck-out noon. Meeting rms. Business servs avail. Downhill/x-country ski 11 mi. Whirlpool, sauna. Private patios, balconies. On Lake Pend Oreille; swimming beach. Cr cds: A, C, D, DS, ER, JCB, MC, V.

★ **LAKESIDE INN.** *106 Bridge St.* 208/263-3717; FAX 208/265-4781; res: 800/543-8126. 60 units, 2-3 story, 10 kits. No elvtr. July-Aug: S $68; D $68-$84; each addl $5; suites $125; kits. $105; under 12 free; ski, golf plans; higher rates major hols; lower rates rest of yr. Crib free. Pet accepted, some restrictions; $5/day. TV; cable. Complimentary continental bkfst. Restaurant nearby. Ck-out 11 am. Coin lndry. Free airport, RR station transportation. Whirlpool, sauna. Lawn games. Balconies. Picnic tables, grills. On Lake Pend Oreille. Cr cds: A, C, D, DS, MC, V.

✔★ ★ **QUALITY INN.** *807 N 5th Ave.* 208/263-2111; FAX 208/263-3289. 57 rms, 2 story. S $59-$88; D $65-$90; each addl $6; under 16 free; ski plan. Crib $5. TV; cable, VCR avail. Indoor pool; whirlpool. Restaurant 5:30 am-10 pm. Bar 11-2 am. Ck-out noon. Business servs avail. Coin lndry. Sundries. Downhill/x-country ski 11 mi. Cr cds: A, D, DS, MC, V.

Restaurants

★ ★ ★ **GARDEN.** *15 E Lake St.* 208/263-5187. Hrs: 11:30 am-3 pm, 5-10:30 pm; Sun 10:30 am-9:30 pm. Closed Thanksgiving. Bar 11-1 am; Sun (summer only) 10:30 am-9:30 pm. Semi-a la carte: lunch $5-$12, dinner $12-$24. Sun brunch $5.50-$12. Child's meals. Specializes in prime rib, seafood, pasta. Salad bar. Outdoor dining in summer. Overlooks Lake Pend Oreille. Docking facilities. Family-owned. Cr cds: A, C, D, DS, ER, JCB, MC, V.

★ **HYDRA.** *115 Lake St.* 208/263-7123. Hrs: 11:30 am-3 pm, 5-10 pm; Mon, Sat from 5 pm; Sun 10 am-9 pm; Sun brunch to 2 pm. Closed Thanksgiving, Dec 25. Bar 4-11 pm. Buffet lunch $5.89. Semi-a la carte: dinner $5.25-$16.95. Sun brunch $6.95. Specializes in beef, seafood, pasta. Salad bar. Eclectic decor. Cut-glass by local artist. Cr cds: A, C, D, DS, MC, V.

✔★ ★ **IVANO'S.** *124 Second Ave.* 208/263-0211. Hrs: 5-10 pm. Closed some major hols. Res accepted. Italian menu. Bar. Semi-a la carte: dinner $6.95-$15.95. Child's meals. Specializes in pasta, seafood, tortellini Ivano. Outdoor dining. Mediterranean decor. Cathedral ceiling in main dining rm. Cr cds: A, D, DS, JCB, MC, V.

Shoshone (F-3)

(For accommodations see Twin Falls; also see Jerome)

Founded 1882 **Pop** 1,249 **Elev** 3,970 ft **Area code** 208 **Zip** 83352 **E-mail** sholib@magiclink.com

Information City Hall, 207 S Rail St W, Box 208; 208/886-2030.

Shoshone (sho-SHOWN or sho-SHO-nee) is the seat of Lincoln County and the marketplace for a farming and livestock area fed by irrigation.

What to See and Do

Mary L. Gooding Memorial Park. Playground, pool (May-Aug, daily), picnic area along Little Wood River. (Daily) 300 N Rail St. Phone 208/886-2030.

✪ **Shoshone Indian Ice Caves.** Natural refrigerator, with temperatures ranging from 18°-33°F. Cave is 3 blks long, 30 ft wide and 40 ft high. On grounds are statue of Shoshone Chief Washakie and a museum of Native American artifacts; minerals, gems (free). 40-min guided tours (May-Sept, daily). 17 mi N on ID 75. Phone 208/886-2058. ¢¢

Annual Events

Manty Shaw Fiddlers' Jamboree. 2nd wkend July.

Arts in the Park. Arts & crafts fair. 2nd wkend July.

Lincoln County Fair. 3rd wk July.

Stanley (E-3)

Pop 71 **Elev** 6,260 ft **Area code** 208 **Zip** 83278

Information Chamber of Commerce, PO Box 8; 208/774-3411.

Situated on the Salmon River (the famous "river of no return"), Stanley is located at the center of the Sawtooth Wilderness, Sawtooth Valley and scenic Stanley Basin. A Ranger District office of the Sawtooth National Forest (see BELLEVUE, BURLEY) is located here.

What to See and Do

Salmon River. Rafting, kayaking; fishing; camping.

River Expeditions. Many outfitters offer wilderness float trips on the Middle Fork of the Salmon River. Along the river are Native American pictographs, caves, abandoned gold mines and abundant wildlife. Activities include boating, fishing, hiking, natural hot water springs and photography. For a list of outfitters contact the Chamber of Commerce or the Idaho Company Outfitters and Guides Assn, 208/734-8872.

Sawtooth National Recreation Area. Fishing, boating, waterskiing, hiking, biking, camping (fee). Many lakes are here, including Stanley, Redfish and Alturas. In Sawtooth National Forest. Contact Area Ranger, Star Rte, Ketchum 83340; 208/727-5000. (Also see SUN VALLEY AREA) In recreation area are

Redfish Lake Visitor Center. Historical, geological, naturalist displays and dioramas. Self-guiding trails. Campfire programs, guided tours. (Memorial Day-Labor Day, daily) 5 mi S on ID 75, then 2 mi SW. Phone 208/774-3376. **Free.**

Sawtooth Wilderness. Many lakes; wilderness hiking, backpacking and mountain climbing. For a list of outfitters, contact the Chamber of Commerce or phone Sawtooth National Recreation Area Headquarters, 208/726-7672.

Sawtooth Valley & Stanley Basin. Cross-country skiing, snowmobiling, mountain biking, backpacking, hunting, fishing. Dude ranches featuring pack trips; big-game guides. Contact Chamber of Commerce.

Annual Events

Sawtooth Mountain Mamas Arts & Crafts Fair. 3rd wkend July.

Sawtooth Quilt Festival. Community Bldg. 3rd wkend Sept.

Motel

★ ★ **MOUNTAIN VILLAGE LODGE.** *PO Box 150, Jct ID 75 & 21. 208/774-3661; FAX 208/774-3761; res: 800/843-5475.* 60 rms, 2 story. S from $60; D $65-$75; suites $85-$125; package plan. TV; cable (premium), VCR avail. Coffee in rms. Restaurant 7 am-11 pm. Bar 11-1 am; entertainment. Ck-out 11 am. Coin lndry. Meeting rms. Business servs avail. Airport transportation. Lawn games. Panoramic view of Sawtooth Mts. Near Salmon River. Cr cds: A, D, DS, MC, V.

Guest Ranch

★ ★ **IDAHO ROCKY MOUNTAIN RANCH.** *HC 64, Box 9934, On ID 75, approx 9 mi S. 208/774-3544; FAX 208/774-3477.* 4 rms in lodge, 9 cabins. No phones. June-Sept: MAP S $90-$180; D $126-$216; each addl $27-$64; wkly rates. Nov-Apr: kit. cabins $75-$135. Crib $10. Pool. Dining rm 7-10 am, 6:30-8:30 pm. Box lunches. Ck-out 11 am, ck-in 3 pm. Grocery store 9 mi. Meeting rm. Gift shop. X-country ski on site. Horse stables. Hiking. Bicycle rentals. Stone fireplace in cabins. On Salmon River. View of Sawtooth Mountains. Totally nonsmoking. Cr cds: DS, MC, V.

Sun Valley Area (E-3)

Elev 5,920 ft **Area code** 208 **E-mail** sunval@micron.net **Web** www.visit sunvalley.com

Information Sun Valley/Ketchum Chamber of Commerce, PO Box 2420, Sun Valley 83353; 208/726-3423 or 800/634-3347.

In a sun-drenched, bowl-shaped valley, this is one of the most famous resorts in the world. Developed by the Union Pacific Railroad, this area was established after an extensive survey of the West. Sheltered by surrounding ranges, it attracts both winter and summer visitors and offers nearly every imaginable recreational opportunity. Powder snow lasts until late spring, allowing long skiing seasons, and there is hunting, mountain biking and superb fly-fishing. Two Ranger District offices of the Sawtooth National Forest (see BELLEVUE, BURLEY) are located in Ketchum.

What to See and Do

Sawtooth National Recreation Area. Fishing, boating, waterskiing, hiking, camping (fee). Many lakes are here, including Stanley, Redfish and Alturas. NW via ID 75, in Sawtooth National Forest. Contact Area Ranger, Star Rte, Ketchum 83340; 208/726-7672. (Also see STANLEY) In recreation area on ID 75 is

Headquarters Visitor Information Center. Orientation exhibits, maps, brochures, interpretive material. Evening programs (summer). Center (daily; schedule may vary, phone ahead). Phone 208/727-5013. **Free.**

Sun Valley Resort. Year-round activities: Sports director, supervised recreation for children; bowling; three outdoor pools, two glass-enclosed, lifeguard; sauna, massage; indoor and outdoor ice-skating; movies, dancing; Sun Valley Center for the Arts and Humanities. Special activities. Contact Sun Valley Resort, 208/622-4111 or 208/622-2231 (sports center).

Winter: 17 ski lifts to slopes for every level of skier; ski school, rentals. Longest run 3 mi; vertical drop 3,400 ft. Ice-skating, sleigh rides and groomed cross-country trails. (Thanksgiving-Apr, daily)

Summer: Fishing, boating; tennis, school; 18-hole Robert Trent Jones golf course, pro; Olympic ice show; skeet and trap shooting; lawn games; 3 outdoor pools; horseback riding, school; mountain biking, whitewater river raft trips; hiking, pack trips; hay rides. Auto trips may be arranged to Redfish Lake near Stanley.

Annual Event

Wagon Days. Celebration of the area's mining history; large, non-motorized parade, band concerts, entertainment, arts & crafts fair, dramas. Labor Day wkend.

Motels

✔★ **AIRPORT INN.** *(820 Fourth Ave S, Hailey 83333)* 8 blks S on ID 75, near Hailey Airport. 208/788-2477; FAX 208/788-3195. 30 rms, 1-2 story, 4 kits. S $58; D $66; each addl $8; suites $75; under 12 free. Crib free. TV; cable, VCR avail. Restaurant nearby. Ck-out 11 am. Coin lndry.

Downhill ski 12 mi; x-country ski adj. Whirlpool. Some refrigerators, microwaves. Cr cds: A, C, D, DS, MC, V.

⊠ ✈ ⊠ ♨ SC

✔ ★ ★ **HEIDELBERG INN.** *(1908 Warm Springs Rd (PO Box 5704), Ketchum 83340) N on ID 75, then W on Warm Springs Rd.* 208/726-5361; FAX 208/726-2084; res: 800/284-4863. 30 rms, 2 story, 14 kits. S, D $80-$95; kit. units $80-$90; each addl $8. Crib free. Pet accepted; $5. TV; cable, VCR (movies $2). Heated pool; whirlpool. Complimentary continental bkfst. Complimentary coffee in rms. Restaurant nearby. Ck-out 11 am. Coin lndry. Downhill ski 1 mi; x-country ski adj. Sauna. Refrigerators, microwaves; some fireplaces. Picnic tables, grills. Cr cds: A, C, D, DS, MC, V.

D ✔ ⊠ ♨ ⊠ ♨ SC

★ **TAMARACK LODGE.** *(Sun Valley Rd & Walnut Ave, Sun Valley 83353) 3 blks E of ID 75.* 208/726-3344; FAX 208/726-3347; res: 800/521-5379. 26 rms, 3 story. No elvtr. Dec-Mar: S, D $89-$96; each addl $10; suites $119; under 13 free; lower rates rest of yr. Crib $5. TV; cable (premium). Indoor pool; whirlpool. Complimentary coffee in rms. Restaurant nearby. Ck-out 11 am. Downhill/x-country ski 1 mi. Refrigerators, microwaves, fireplaces. Cr cds: A, C, D, DS, MC, V.

⊠ ♨ ⊠ ♨ SC

Lodge

★ ★ **BEST WESTERN TYROLEAN.** *(Sun Valley 83353) 1 mi N on ID 75, then W on River Run Rd; near base of Mt Baldy and River Run Ski Lift.* 208/726-5336; FAX 208/726-2081. 56 rms, 3 story, 7 suites. No A/C. Mid-Dec-early Jan: S $100; D $110-$115; each addl $8; suites $129-$165; under 12 free; ski plan; lower rates rest of yr. Crib free. TV; cable. Pool; whirlpool. Complimentary continental bkfst. Restaurant nearby. Ck-out 11 am. Coin lndry. Meeting rms. Business servs avail. Downhill/x-country ski adj. Exercise equipt; bicycles, treadmill, sauna. Game rm. Microwaves avail. Cr cds: A, C, D, DS, MC, V.

⊠ ⊠ ♨ ⊠ ♨ SC

Motor Hotel

★ ★ **BEST WESTERN KENTWOOD LODGE.** *(180 S Main St, Ketchum 83340)* 208/726-4114; FAX 208/726-2417. 57 rms, 3 story. Feb-mid-Apr, mid-June-mid-Sept, mid-Dec-early Jan: S, D $145; each addl $10; suites, kit. units $145; under 13 free; 2-day min some wkends, 3-day min some hols; lower rates rest of yr. Crib $5. TV; cable. Indoor pool; whirlpool. Restaurant adj 6:30 am-10 pm. Ck-out 11 am. Coin lndry. Meeting rms. Business servs avail. Valet serv. Exercise equipt; weight machine, stair machine. Refrigerators; microwaves avail. Some balconies. Totally nonsmoking. Cr cds: A, D, DS, MC, V.

⊠ ♨ ⊠ ♨

Inns

★ ★ ★ **IDAHO COUNTRY.** *(134 Latigo Ln, Sun Valley 83353) 1/2 mi N on ID 75 right on Saddle Rd, turn left on Valleywood to Latigo Lane.* 208/726-1019; FAX 208/726-5718. 11 rms, 6 A/C, 2 story. Jan-Mar & June-Sept: S, D $125-$185; higher rates wk of Dec 25; lower rates rest of yr. TV; cable. Complimentary full bkfst; afternoon refreshments. Restaurant nearby. Ck-out 11 am, ck-in 3 pm. Downhill/x-country ski 1/2 mi. Whirlpool. Refrigerators. Balconies. Library, warming rm; individually decorated rms. Stone fireplace. View of Bald Mountain. Totally nonsmoking. Cr cds: A, MC, V.

⊠ ⊠ ♨

★ ★ ★ **RIVER STREET INN BED & BREAKFAST.** *(100 Rivers St W, Sun Valley 83353)* 208/726-3611; FAX 208/726-2439; res: 800/954-8585. 8 rms, 2 story. Dec-Mar, July-Sept: S $120-$175; D $130-$185; each addl $25; lower rates rest of yr. Pet accepted, some restrictions; $10. TV; cable (premium). Complimentary full bkfst; afternoon refreshments. Ck-out 11 am, ck-in 4 pm. Downhill/x-country ski 1/4 mi. Refrigerators.

Japanese soaking tubs in all rms. Totally nonsmoking. Cr cds: A, DS, MC, V.

✔ ⚡ ⊠ ⊠ ♨ SC

Resorts

★ ★ ★ **ELKHORN RESORT & GOLF CLUB.** *(Elkhorn Rd, Sun Valley 83354)* 208/622-4511; FAX 208/622-3261; res: 800/355-4676. 139 rms, 4 story; 48 condo units, 2 story. No A/C. Mid-Dec-Mar, June-Sept: S, D $119-$219; each addl $10; condos $120-$320; under 17 free; ski, golf plans; lower rates rest of yr. Crib free. Pet accepted, some restrictions. TV; cable, VCR. Pools; whirlpool, lifeguard. Supervised child's activities (June-Aug); ages 6-12. Dining rms 7 am-11 pm. Rm serv. Bars 11-1 am. Ck-out 10 am-noon, ck-in 4 pm. Meeting rms. Business servs avail. In-rm modem link. Valet serv. Shopping arcade. Free airport transportation. Tennis, pro. 18-hole golf, greens fee (incl cart) $76, pro, putting green, driving range, golf school. Downhill ski on site. Bicycles, bike trails. Lawn games. Entertainment. Music concerts in summer. Exercise equipt; weights, bicycles, sauna, steam rm. Massage. Fishing/hunting guides. Fly fishing lessons. Luxury level. Cr cds: A, D, DS, MC, V.

D ✔ ⚡ ⊠ 🏇 ⊠ ✈ 🏃 ⊠ ♨ SC

★ ★ ★ **SUN VALLEY.** *(Sun Valley Rd, Sun Valley 83353)* 208/622-4111; FAX 208/622-2030; res: 800/786-8259. Web www.sunvalley.com. 262 rms, 4 story; 193 condo units, 2-4 story. No A/C. Jan-Mar: S, D $100-$189; each addl $15; suites $349; condos (1-4-bedrm) $160-$389; under 12 free; lower rates rest of yr. Crib free. TV; cable. 3 pools, heated; wading pool, poolside serv; lifeguard. Supervised child's activities. Dining rms 7 am-10 pm (also see GRETCHEN'S). Bars noon-1 am. Ck-out 11 am, ck-in 4 pm. Grocery. Package store. Convention facilities. Business servs avail. Bellhops. Valet serv. Concierge. Barber, beauty shop. Free airport transportation. Sports dir. Tennis, pro. 18-hole golf, greens fee $83, pro, putting green, driving range. Paddle boats. Downhill/x-country ski on site. Sleigh rides. 2 ice-skating rinks; ice shows. Horseback riding. River rafting. Bicycles. Roller blades (rentals). Lawn games. Trap & skeet shooting. Entertainment, movies. Bowling. Game rm. Exercise equipt; bicycles, treadmill, sauna. Massage. Fishing/hunting guides. Refrigerator, microwave in condos; some fireplaces. Some private patios, balconies. Picnic tables. Cr cds: A, D, DS, MC, V.

D ✔ ⚡ ⊠ 🏇 🏃 ⊠ ✈ 🏃 ⊠ ♨

Restaurants

★ ★ **CHANDLER'S.** *(200 S Main St, Ketchum 83340)* 208/726-1776. Hrs: 6-10 pm. Closed Dec 25. Res accepted. No A/C. Wine, beer. Semi-a la carte: dinner $14-$29. Prix fixe: dinner $16.95. Child's meals. Specialties: fresh Hawaiian ahi, elk loin, Yankee pot roast. Outdoor dining. 1940s home has antique furnishings, open beamed ceilings. Totally nonsmoking. Cr cds: A, MC, V.

★ ★ ★ **EVERGREEN BISTRO.** *(171 First Ave, Ketchum)* 208/726-3888. Hrs: 6:30-10 pm. Closed May, Nov. Res accepted. French, Amer menu. Beer. Wine cellar. Semi-a la carte: dinner $16.95-$30. Specializes in venison, rack of lamb, fresh fish. Outdoor dining. In converted house; view of Mt Baldy. Totally nonsmoking. Cr cds: A, MC, V.

★ ★ ★ **GRETCHEN'S.** *(See Sun Valley Resort)* 208/622-2144. E-mail svcmktpr@sunvalley.com; web www.sunvalley.com. Hrs: 7 am-10 pm. Res accepted. Continental menu. Bar noon-1 am. Semi-a la carte: $5-$8, lunch $6.25-$9.75, dinner $14.50-$22. Child's meals. Specialties: hazelnut-crusted elk loin, spicy farfalle pasta with roasted roma tomatoes, raspberry chocolate mousse. Own baking. Outdoor dining. Cozy, country-French atmosphere. Totally nonsmoking. Cr cds: A, C, D, DS, MC, V.

D

★ ★ ★ **OTTER'S.** *(180 W Sixth St, Ketchum 83340)* 208/726-6837. Web www.otters.com. Hrs: 11:30 am-3 pm, 6:30-10:30 pm; Mon, Sun from 6:30 pm. Closed Thanksgiving, Dec 25; also Sun Mar-June, Sept-Dec. Res accepted. No A/C. Continental menu. Bar. Semi-a la carte: lunch $6-$14.95, dinner $13.95-$17.95. Prix fixe: dinner $17.95-$40. Specialties: wild caribou and pintelle pheasant, fresh foie gras. Own baking, desserts. Outdoor dining. Open, Mediterranean decor; picture windows offer view of mountain. Totally nonsmoking. Cr cds: A, C, D, DS, JCB, MC, V.

D

★ ★ **WARM SPRINGS RANCH.** *(1801 Warm Springs Rd, Ketchum)* 208/726-2609. Hrs: 6-10 pm. Res accepted. Bar 5 pm-1 am. Semi-a la carte: dinner $10.95-$20.95. Child's meals. Specializes in scones, seafood, barbecued ribs. Parking. Outdoor dining. Overlooks mountains & stocked, spring-fed ponds. Family-owned. Cr cds: A, MC, V.

★ ★ **THE WILD RADISH.** *(200 S Main St, Ketchum)* 208/726-8468. Hrs: noon-10 pm. Res accepted. No A/C. Continental menu. Wine, beer. Semi-a la carte: lunch $6.95-$14.50, dinner $16.50-$29.50. Specializes in wild game, fresh seafood, fowl. Parking. Outdoor dining. Country inn atmosphere. Totally nonsmoking. Cr cds: A, DS, MC, V.

Twin Falls (F-3)

(See also Buhl, Burley, Jerome, Shoshone)

Founded 1904 **Pop** 27,591 **Elev** 3,745 ft **Area code** 208 **Zip** 83301
E-mail tfidcham@cyberhighway.net **Web** www.cyberhighway.net/~tfidcham/
Information Chamber of Commerce, 858 Blue Lakes Blvd N; 208/733-3974 or 800/255-8946.

After rising "like magic" on the tide of irrigation that reached this valley early in the century, Twin Falls has become the major city of south central Idaho's "Magic Valley" region. Seat of agriculturally rich Twin Falls County, it is also a tourist center, boasting that visitors in the area can enjoy almost every known sport. The headquarters and a Ranger District office of the Sawtooth National Forest (see BELLEVUE, BURLEY, STANLEY) are located here.

What to See and Do

Fishing. In Snake River and numerous other rivers, lakes. Sturgeon of up to 100 pounds can be caught, but by law cannot be removed from the water. Twin Falls Chamber of Commerce can provide detailed information.

Herrett Center. Exhibits on archaeology of North, Central and South America; gallery of contemporary art; Faulkner Planetarium. (Tues-Sat; closed hols) 315 Falls Ave, on College of Southern Idaho campus. Phone 208/733-9554, ext 2655.

Perrine Memorial Bridge. Bridge, 486 ft high and 1,500 ft long, crosses the Snake River canyon. 1 1/2 mi N on US 93.

Sawtooth Twin Falls Ranger District. Camping (fee at some designated campgrounds), picnicking, fishing, hiking trails. Snowmobile trails, downhill & cross-country skiing. 9 mi E on US 30 to Hansen, then 28 mi S on local roads, in Sawtooth National Forest. Phone 208/737-3200.

Shoshone Falls. "Niagara of the West" drops 212 ft (52 ft more than Niagara Falls). During irrigation season, the flow is limited; it is best during spring and fall. 5 mi NE, on Snake River. Access to the falls is avail through

Shoshone Falls Park. Picnic tables, stoves, fireplace, trails, waterskiing. (Mar-Nov, daily) S bank of river. Phone 208/736-2265 or 208/736-2266. Per vehicle (mid-May-Aug) ¢

Twin Falls. 5 1/2 mi NE. These 132-ft falls are accessible by

Twin Falls Park. Picnic area with electric outlets, hot plates (free); boating (dock, ramp), fishing, waterskiing. S bank of river. Phone 208/423-4223. (Daily)

Annual Events

Western Days. 3-day event featuring shoot-out, barbecue contests, dances, parade. The dates may vary, phone 800/255-8946 for schedule; usually wkend following Memorial Day.

Twin Falls County Fair & Rodeo. County Fairgrounds, 6 mi W via US 30 in Filer. 1 wk starting the Wed before Labor Day.

Motels

★ ★ **AMERITEL INN.** *1377 Blue Lakes Blvd.* 208/736-8000; FAX 208/734-7777. 117 rms, 3 story. June-Aug: S, D $74.75; each addl $5; suites $110; kit. units $98.75; under 12 free; lower rates rest of yr. Crib $5. TV; cable (premium). Indoor pool; whirlpool. Complimentary continental bkfst. Restaurant adj 6 am-10 pm. Ck-out 11 am. Coin lndry. Meeting rms. Free airport transportation. Exercise equipt; weight machine, bicycles. Microwaves avail. Cr cds: A, D, DS, MC, V.

D ≊ ✗ ⊠ ⋒ SC

★ ★ **BEST WESTERN CANYON SPRINGS PARK HOTEL.** *1357 Blue Lakes Blvd N.* 208/734-5000. 112 rms, 2 story. S $69.75; D $75.75; each addl $6; under 12 free. Crib free. TV; cable (premium). Heated pool. Restaurant 6 am-10 pm; Fri, Sat to 11 pm. Rm serv. Bar 4 pm-1 am. Ck-out 1 pm. Meeting rms. Bellhops. Valet serv. Free airport transportation. Exercise equipt; bicycles, treadmill. Balconies. Cr cds: A, C, D, DS, MC, V.

D ≊ ✗ ⊠ ⋒ SC

✔ ★ ★ **COMFORT INN.** *1893 Canyon Springs Rd.* 208/734-7494. 52 rms, 2 story, 15 suites. S $52.99; D $59.99; each addl $7; suites $67.99; under 18 free. Crib free. Pet accepted. TV; cable (premium). Indoor pool; whirlpool. Complimentary continental bkfst. Ck-out 11 am. Health club privileges. Cr cds: A, D, DS, MC, V.

D ✦ ≊ ⊠ ⋒ SC

★ ★ **SHILO INN.** *1586 N Blue Lakes Blvd.* 208/733-7545; FAX 208/736-2019. 128 rms, 4 story. May-Sept: S, D $95-$99; each addl $10; kit. units $99-$125; under 12 free; family rates; wkly rates; lower rates rest of yr. Crib free. Pet accepted, some restrictions; $7. TV; cable (premium), VCR (movies). Complimentary continental bkfst. Complimentary coffee in rms. Restaurant adj 6 am-midnight. Ck-out noon. Meeting rms. Business servs avail. In-rm modem link. Bellhops. Sundries. Coin lndry. Exercise equipt; weight machine, stair machine, sauna. Indoor pool; whirlpool. Bathrm phones, refrigerators, microwaves, wet bars. Cr cds: A, C, D, DS, ER, JCB, MC, V.

D ✦ ≊ ✗ ⊠ ⋒ SC

Restaurant

★ ★ **JAKER'S.** *1598 Blue Lakes Blvd.* 208/733-8400. Hrs: 11:30 am-2 pm, 5-10 pm; Fri, Sat 5-10:30 pm; Sun 5-9 pm. Closed most major hols. Res accepted. Bar. Semi-a la carte: lunch $2.95-$9.95, dinner $10.95-$39.95. Child's meals. Specializes in prime rib, pasta, seafood. Outdoor dining. Bistro decor. Cr cds: A, DS, MC, V.

D ⌐

Wallace (B-2)

(See also Coeur d'Alene, Kellogg)

Founded 1884 **Pop** 1,010 **Elev** 2,744 ft **Area code** 208 **Zip** 83873
Information Chamber of Commerce, 10 River St, PO Box 1167; 208/753-7151.

Gold was discovered in streams near here in 1882; lead, zinc, silver and copper deposits were found in 1884. A Ranger District office of the Idaho Panhandle National Forests-Coeur d'Alene (see COEUR D'ALENE) is located in nearby Silverton.

What to See and Do

Auto tour. In Idaho Panhandle National Forests—Coeur d'Alene and St Joe—15-mi drive through spectacular scenery. Local roads follow Nine Mile Creek, Dobson Pass and Two Mile Creek to Osburn. This trip may be extended by traveling N & E out of Dobson Pass along Beaver and Trail creeks to Murray, then W to Prichard; then follow Coeur d'Alene River W & S to Kingston; return to Wallace on US 10, I-90.

Lookout Pass Ski Area. Chairlift, rope tow; patrol, school, rentals; cafeteria; bar (beer and wine only). Longest run 5,300 ft; vertical drop 850 ft. Half-day rate. (Mid-Nov-mid-Apr, Thurs-Sun) Cross-country skiing is also avail. Snowmobiling. 13 mi E on I-90, in Idaho Panhandle National Forests. For further information phone 208/744-1392. ¢¢¢¢

Northern Pacific Depot Railroad Museum (1901). Houses artifacts, photographs and memorabilia that portray railroad history of the Coeur d'Alene Mining District; display of railroad depot (ca 1910). (May-Oct, daily; rest of yr, Tues-Sat) 6th & Pine Sts. Phone 208/752-0111. ¢

Oasis Bordello Museum. Former bordello (ca 1895); moonshine still, display of evolution of mine lighting. (May-Oct, daily; closed hols) 605 Cedar St. Phone 208/753-0801. ¢¢

Sierra Silver Mine Tour. Offers 1¼-hr guided tour through a depleted silver mine. Demonstrations of mining methods, techniques and operation of modern day equipment. Departs every 30 min. (May-mid-Oct, daily) 420 5th St. Phone 208/752-5151. ¢¢¢

Wallace District Mining Museum. Material on the history of mining, slide show, old mining machinery. Information on mine tours and old mining towns in the area. (May-Sept, daily; rest of yr, Mon-Fri) 509 Bank St. Phone 208/556-1592. ¢

Motels

★ ★ ★ **BEST WESTERN-WALLACE INN.** *100 Front St, I-90 exit 61.* 208/752-1252; FAX 208/753-0981. 63 rms, 2 story. S $68.50; D $78.50; each addl $8; suites $225-$250; under 12 free. Crib free. TV; cable (premium). VCR avail. Indoor pool; whirlpool, poolside serv. Restaurant 7 am-9 pm. Rm serv. Bar. Ck-out noon. Meeting rms. Business servs avail. Gift shop. Bus depot transportation. Exercise equipt; weights, bicycles, sauna. Refrigerator, minibar in suites. Cr cds: A, C, D, DS, MC, V.

D ⊠ ⌇ ⌇ ⌇ SC

↙★ **STARDUST.** *410 Pine St.* 208/752-1213; FAX 208/753-0981; res: 800/643-2386. 42 rms, 22 A/C, 2 story. S $44.50; D $52.50; each addl $8; under 12 free. Pet accepted; $25. TV; cable (premium). Restaurant nearby. Ck-out noon. Meeting rms. Airport transportation. Sundries. Downhill ski 10 mi; x-country ski 11 mi. Cr cds: A, C, D, DS, MC, V.

↙ ⌇ ⌇ ⌇ SC

Weiser (D-1)

(For accommodations see Ontario, OR)

Founded 1888 **Pop** 4,571 **Elev** 2,117 ft **Area code** 208 **Zip** 83672
Information Chamber of Commerce, 8 E Idaho St; 208/549-0452.

Located at the confluence of the Weiser and Snake rivers, the town of Weiser (WEE-zer) is both a center for tourism for Hells Canyon National Recreation Area to the north and a center for trade and transportation for the vast orchards, onion, wheat and sugar beet fields of the fertile Weiser Valley to the east. Lumbering, mining, the manufacture of mobile homes and the raising of cattle also contribute to the town's economy. A Ranger District office of the Payette National Forest (see McCALL) is located in Weiser.

What to See and Do

Fiddlers Hall of Fame. Mementos of past fiddle contests, pictures of champion fiddlers, state winners; collection of old-time fiddles; state scrapbook on view. (Mon-Fri; also wkend during Fiddlers' Contest; closed hols) 10 E Idaho St. Phone 208/549-0450 or 208/549-0452. **Free.**

Hells Canyon National Recreation Area. Spanning the Idaho/Oregon border, this canyon, the deepest in North America, was created by the Snake River, which rushes nearly 8,000 feet below Seven Devils rim on the Idaho side. Three dams built by the Idaho Power Company have opened up areas that were once inaccessible and created man-made lakes that provide boating, fishing and waterskiing. Whitewater rafting and jet boating tours available below the dams, on the Snake River. Stretching north for 100 miles; access approx 55 mi NW via US 95 to Cambridge, then via ID 71.

Brownlee Dam. The southernmost dam of the three, at end of ID 71. This 395-ft rockfill dam creates Brownlee Lake, 57½ mi long, reaching to 10 mi N of Weiser. Woodhead Park, a short distance south, and McCormick Park, a short distance north, provide tent & trailer sites, showers; picnicking, boat ramps. ¢¢¢

Oxbow Dam. This 205-ft-high barrier makes a 12½-mi-long reservoir. Copperfield Park, just below the dam on the Oregon side, has trailer & tent spaces, showers and day-use picnicking; 9 mi N of dam on the Idaho side is Hells Canyon Park, offering tent & trailer sites, showers; picnicking, boat ramp. 12½ mi N of Brownlee Dam. ¢¢¢

Hells Canyon Dam. This structure (330 ft high) creates another water recreation area. The improved Deep Creek trail, Idaho side, provides angler and other recreational access to the Snake River below Hells Canyon Dam. 23 mi N of Oxbow Dam.

Snake River Heritage Center. Artifacts and memorabilia portray the history of Snake River Valley. (By appt only) 2295 Paddock Ave, in Hooker Hall. Phone 208/549-0205. ¢

Trips into Hells Canyon. Several companies offer river rafting, jet boat and pack trips into and around Hells Canyon National Recreation Area. For information on additional outfitters, contact the Chamber of Commerce.

Hells Canyon Adventures. Jet boat tours; rafting. Contact PO Box 159, Oxbow, OR 97840. Phone 503/785-3352 or 800/422-3568.

Hughes River Expeditions. Outfitters for whitewater and fishing trips on backcountry rivers of Idaho and eastern Oregon, including 3-, 4- and 5-day trips on the Snake River through Hells Canyon. (May-Oct, several dates) Advance reservations required. 26 mi N on US 95, at 95 First St in Cambridge. Phone 208/257-3477. ¢¢¢¢

Annual Event

National Oldtime Fiddlers' Contest. High School gym. One of the oldest such contests in the country, attracting some of the nation's finest fiddlers. Also parade, barbecue, arts & crafts. Phone 800/437-1280. Mon-Sat, 3rd full wk June.

Iowa

Population: 2,776,755
Land area: 55,965 square miles
Elevation: 480-1,670 feet
Highest point: Near Ocheyedan (Osceola County)
Entered Union: December 28, 1846 (29th state)
Capital: Des Moines
Motto: Our liberties we prize and our rights we will maintain
Nickname: The Hawkeye State
State flower: Wild rose
State bird: Eastern goldfinch
State tree: Oak
State fair: August 13-23, 1998, in Des Moines
Time zone: Central
Web: www.state.ia.us

Iowa, the heartland of American agriculture, is also a growing center of industry. Iowa is a leader in corn and soybean production, but Iowa industry generates about 3 ½ times the revenue of agriculture. The 3,600 manufacturing firms in the state produce more than 3,000 different products, ranging from motor homes to microwave ovens. Major appliances, farm implements and plastics are exported all over the world. Iowa is the only state bordered by two navigable rivers, with the Mississippi River forming its eastern boundary and the Missouri River most of its western boundary. The Sioux called Iowa the "beautiful land."

Iowa's countryside offers tourists a wide range of recreational activities, from boating and fishing on lakes, rivers and reservoirs to hiking and picnicking at the many state parks and forests. Iowa also offers medium-sized cities with cultural activities, including performing arts, historic sites and art museums. This is the land of Native American warrior Black Hawk and the birthplace of Buffalo Bill Cody, John Wayne, Herbert Hoover, Meredith Willson and Dr. James Van Allen.

Four glacial epochs and centuries of untouched wilderness fertilized the soil of Iowa before Marquette and Jolliet came in 1673. A favorite Native Amererican hunting ground, Iowa was part of the Louisiana Purchase. Lewis and Clark passed through in 1804 on their arduous trip to find out what the United States had bought. Treaties with the Native Americans in 1832, 1837 and 1842 opened the area to European settlers. Pioneer settlements were made in Lee County in 1820, at Burlington in 1832 and at Dubuque in 1833. The Territory of Iowa was created from the Territory of Wisconsin in 1838.

In its 300-mile east-west sweep and 210-mile north-south stretch, Iowa has nearly 56,000 acres of natural and man-made lakes; 19,000 miles of interior fishing streams and 72 state parks and recreation areas.

When to Go/Climate

Typical midwestern weather is the norm in Iowa. Summers are hot and humid, winters are cold and harsh. Long Indian summers can stretch into November, while spring is usually very short and rainy.

AVERAGE HIGH/LOW TEMPERATURES (°F)

DES MOINES

Jan 28/11	May 73/52	Sept 76/55
Feb 34/16	June 82/61	Oct 64/43
Mar 47/28	July 87/67	Nov 48/30
Apr 62/40	Aug 84/64	Dec 33/16

DUBUQUE

Jan 24/8	May 69/48	Sept 72/52
Feb 30/13	June 78/57	Oct 61/40
Mar 43/25	July 82/62	Nov 45/28
Apr 58/37	Aug 80/60	Dec 29/14

Parks and Recreation Finder

Directions to and information about the parks and recreation areas below are given under their respective town/city sections. Please refer to those sections for details.

Key to abbreviations: I.P. = Interstate Park; N.B.C. = National Battlefield & Cemetery; N.B.P. = National Battlefield Park; N.F. = National Forest; N.G. = National Grassland; N.H. = National Historical Park; N.H.S. = National Historic Site; N.M. = National Monument; N. Mem. = National Memorial; N.M.P. = National Military Park; N.P. = National Park; N.Pres. = National Preserve; N.R. = National Recreational Area; N.R.R. = National Recreational River; N.Res. = National Reserve; N.S. = National Seashore; N.S.R. = National Scenic River; N.S.T. = National Scenic Trail; N.V.M. = National Volcanic Monument; S.B. = State Beach; S.C.P. = State Conservation Park; S.G. = State Garden; S.H.A. = State Historic Area; S.H.P. = State Historic Park; S.N.A. = State Natural Area; S.P. = State Park; S.R. = State Reserve; S.R.A. = State Recreation Area; S.Res.P. = State Resort Park; S.R.P. = State Rustic Park.

NATIONAL PARK AND RECREATION AREAS

Place Name	Listed Under
Effigy Mounds N.M.	MARQUETTE
Herbert Hoover N.H.S.	IOWA CITY

STATE RECREATION AREAS

Place Name	Listed Under
Ambrose A. Call S.P.	ALGONA
Backbone S.P.	STRAWBERRY POINT
Beed's Lake S.P.	HAMPTON
Bellevue S.P.	DUBUQUE
Black Hawk S.P.	CARROLL
Clear Lake S.P.	CLEAR LAKE
Dolliver Memorial S.P.	FORT DODGE
Fort Defiance S.P.	ESTHERVILLE
Geode S.P.	BURLINGTON
George Wyth Memorial S.P.	CEDAR FALLS
Green Valley S.P.	CRESTON
Gull Point S.P.	OKOBOJI
Honey Creek S.P.	CENTERVILLE
Lacey-Keosauqua S.P.	FAIRFIELD
Lake Ahquabi S.P.	INDIANOLA
Lake Darling S.P.	WASHINGTON
Lake Keomah S.P.	OSKALOOSA
Lake Macbride S.P.	IOWA CITY
Lake Manawa S.P.	COUNCIL BLUFFS
Lake Wapello S.P.	OTTUMWA
Lake of Three Fires S.P.	CLARINDA
Ledges S.P.	BOONE
Lewis and Clark S.P.	ONAWA
Maquoketa Caves S.P.	MAQUOKETA
McIntosh Woods S.P.	CLEAR LAKE
Mini-Wakan S.P.	SPIRIT LAKE
Nine Eagles S.P.	OSCEOLA
Palisades-Kepler S.P.	CEDAR RAPIDS
Pikes Peak S.P.	MARQUETTE
Pikes Point S.P.	OKOBOJI
Pilot Knob S.P.	GARNER
Prairie Rose S.P.	AVOCA
Red Haw S.P.	CHARITON
Rice Lake S.P.	GARNER
Rock Creek S.P.	GRINNELL
Shimek State Forest	FORT MADISON
Stephens State Forest	CHARITON
Stone S.P.	SIOUX CITY
Twin Lakes S.P.	FORT DODGE
Viking Lake S.P.	RED OAK
Volga River S.R.A.	WEST UNION
Wapsipinicon S.P.	CEDAR RAPIDS
Wildcat Den S.P.	MUSCATINE
Wilson Island S.R.A.	MISSOURI VALLEY

Water-related activities, hiking, riding, various other sports, picnicking and visitor centers, as well as camping, are available in many of these areas. Swimming fees at supervised beaches (bathhouse included) vary. Camping (limited to 2 wks; no reservations accepted): $5-$7/night/site (electricity $2 additional; sewer & water $2 additional). Cabins (no bedding, linens): $15-$40/day or $80-$225/week; cot, where available, 50¢/cot/day; deposit $25. Pets on leash only. State properties open daily. At most parks, water facilities are not available mid-Oct-mid-Apr. Contact the Department of Natural Resources, Wallace State Office Building, Des Moines 50319; 515/281-5145.

CALENDAR HIGHLIGHTS

MARCH

St Patrick's Day Celebration (Emmetsburg). Parade, pageant, cultural exhibits. Irish stew dinner, dances, and a guest member of Irish Parliament. Phone 712/852-4326.

APRIL

Veishea Spring Festival (Ames). Iowa State campus. Parade, sports, theatrical events, academic open houses. Phone 515/294-1026.

MAY

Snake Alley Criterium Bicycle Races (Burlington). Olympic-style racing. Phone 319/752-0015.

JUNE

Glenn Miller Festival (Clarinda). Musical event in honor of Glenn Miller and his birthplace. Phone 712/542-2461.

My Waterloo Days Festival (Waterloo). Citywide festival features air show, balloon rallies, parade, laser and fireworks show, music, renaissance fair, food. Phone 319/233-8431.

Burlington Steamboat Days & the American Music Festival (Burlington). Downtown riverfront. Athletic competitions, fireworks, midway, parade, entertainment. Phone 319/754-4334.

JULY

Freedom Festival (Cedar Rapids). Eighty events for all ages held citywide, topped off by large fireworks display. Phone 319/363-7000.

AUGUST

All-Iowa Fair (Cedar Rapids). Hawkeye Downs. Stock car races, fine arts, exhibits, entertainment. Phone Cedar Rapids Area Convention and Visitors Bureau, 319/398-5000 or 800/735-5557.

Iowa State Fair (Des Moines). Fairgrounds. One of the oldest and largest in the country; includes 20 acres of farm machinery, fine arts, grandstand stage and track events, free entertainment, exhibits, demonstrations, contests; camping. Phone 515/262-3111.

Field of Dreams Festival (Dubuque). In Dyersville at movie site of Field of Dreams. Features all-star baseball players. Phone 319/875-6012 or 800/443-8981.

SEPTEMBER

Midwest Old Settlers and Threshers Reunion (Mount Pleasant). Iowa's largest working craft show, antique car show; steam and gas engines, vintage tractors; Midwest Village, log village, narrow-gauge steam railroad and electric trolley cars; entertainment. Phone 319/385-8937.

OCTOBER

Covered Bridge Festival (Winterset). Late 19th-centry crafts, entertainment; parade, bus tour of covered bridges. Phone 800/298-6119.

SKI AREA

Place Name	Listed Under
Sundown Mountain Ski Area	DUBUQUE

FISHING & HUNTING

Fishing for walleye, muskellunge, northern pike, perch, bluegill, smallmouth bass, catfish and bullhead is good in the natural lakes of northern Iowa. The south's man-made lakes are abundant with largemouth bass, catfish, crappie and bluegill. There are 87,000 farm ponds in the state, 50 spring-fed trout streams in the northeastern section and more than 56,000 acres of natural and man-made lakes. Public access to fishing water is furnished at more than 200 state-owned areas, 19,000 miles of meandering inland streams and 600 miles of boundary streams.

Ring-necked pheasant is a popular target, with all counties open for a 50-plus day season. Quail hunting, primarily in the southern half of the state, lasts for approximately 90 days. Ruffed grouse provide a challenge to hunters in northeastern hills while gray partridge offer good hunting opportunities in the north and north central counties. Raccoons, rabbits, fox and gray squirrels are numerous.

Nonresident season hunting license, $60.50; duck stamp, $5 more. Nonresident season fishing license, $22.50; 7-day license, $8.50; trout stamp, $10 more. Required for all hunters and fur harvesters: state habitat stamp, $5. Nonresident fur harvester license $175.50. Nonresident deer tag $110; nonresident turkey tag $55; both require habitat stamp. For full information contact the Department of Natural Resources, Wallace State Office Building, Des Moines 50319-0034; 515/281-5918.

Driving Information

Safety belts are mandatory for all persons in front seat of vehicle. Children under age 6 must be in an approved passenger restraint anywhere in vehicle; children ages 3-6 may use a regulation safety belt; children under age 3 must use an approved safety seat. For further information phone 515/281-3907.

INTERSTATE HIGHWAY SYSTEM

The following alphabetical listing of Iowa towns in *Mobil Travel Guide* shows that these cities are within 10 miles of the indicated Interstate highways. A highway map, however, should be checked for the nearest exit.

Highway Number	Cities/Towns within 10 miles
Interstate 29	Council Bluffs, Missouri Valley, Onawa, Sioux City.
Interstate 35	Ames, Clear Lake, Des Moines, Mason City, Osceola.
Interstate 80	Atlantic, Avoca, Council Bluffs, Davenport, Des Moines, Grinnell, Iowa City, Newton.

Additional Visitor Information

The Department of Economic Development, Iowa Division of Tourism, 200 E Grand Ave, Des Moines 50309, has further information, including an Iowa Travel Guide, Camping & Outdoor Guide, and Calendar of Events; phone 515/242-4705 or 800/345-IOWA.

Two periodicals worth looking at are *Annals of Iowa,* quarterly, State Historical Society of Iowa, 402 Iowa Ave, Iowa City 52240 and *The Iowan,* quarterly, Mid-America Publishing Corp, Box 130, Shenandoah 51601.

There are 20 welcome centers in Iowa; visitors will find information and brochures most helpful in planning stops at points of interest. They are located near the following cities: Amana, Bloomfield, Burlington, Clear Lake, Davis City, Des Moines, Dows, Dubuque, Elk Horn, Elkader, Emmetsburg, Lamoni, LeClaire, Missouri Valley, Sergeant Bluff, Sioux City, Underwood, Victor and Wilton.

Algona (B-4)

(See also Emmetsburg)

Settled 1854 **Pop** 6,015 **Elev** 1,200 ft **Area code** 515 **Zip** 50511
Information Chamber of Commerce, 123 E State St; 515/295-7201.

Originally known as Call's Grove, the town later chose its present name, a shortened form of "Algonquin." In 1857, a fort enclosed the town hall; after the frontier hostilities abated, this was torn down and the wood used for a plank road. On the wide bend of the east fork of the Des Moines River, Algona is the seat and crossroads city of Kossuth County.

What to See and Do

Ambrose A. Call State Park. These 130 acres of rolling timbered hills include hiking trails. Frisbee golf course. Picnicking; playground. Camping (no hookups); lodge. Standard hrs, fees. 1½ mi S on US 169, then W on paved road. Phone 515/295-3669.

Smith Lake Park. The 124 acres include 53-acre Smith Lake. Swimming; fishing, boating (electric motors only). Picnicking, playground, hiking trail, tree garden. Camping (fee; dump station addl). Standard hrs, fees. 3 mi N on US 169. Phone 515/295-2138.

Motel

✔★ **BURR OAK.** US 169 South, 3 mi SE on US 169. 515/295-7213; FAX 515/295-2979; res: 800/341-8000. 42 rms. S $29-$40; D $34-$45. Crib $5. TV; cable (premium). Complimentary continental bkfst. Restaurant adj 5-11 pm. Ck-out 10 am. Meeting rm. Cr cds: A, C, D, DS, MC, V.

D ⌨ 🐾 SC

Restaurant

★ ★ **SISTER SARAH'S.** US 18. 515/295-7757. Hrs: 11 am-2 pm, 5-9 pm; Fri, Sat to 10 pm. Closed Mon. Res accepted. Bar. Semi-a la carte: lunch $3.75-$6.25, dinner $5.95-$28.50. Child's meals. Specializes in chicken Kiev, prime rib, seafood. Salad bar. Outdoor dining. Rms vary from 1920s & 1950s to contemporary decor. Cr cds: MC, V.

D

Amana Colonies (D-7)

(See also Cedar Rapids, Iowa City)

Settled 1855 **Pop** (7 colonies) 1,640 **Elev** 715 ft **Area code** 319 **Zip** 52203 **E-mail** accvb@netins.net **Web** www.jeonet.com/amanas/
Information Amana Colonies Convention & Visitors Bureau, 39 38th Ave, Suite 100, Amana; 319/622-7622 or 800/245-5465.

A religiously motivated community, the Amana Colonies produce smoked meats, woolen goods, bakery products, furniture, ovens and radar ranges, refrigerators, food freezers and air conditioners. The history of the community goes back to the founding in Germany of the "Inspirationists" (1714), a Lutheran separatist group. Members migrated to America and settled near Buffalo, NY. Later they bought 25,000 acres of prairie land in Iowa and moved west. Their first Iowa village was called Amana, a Biblical name meaning "remain faithful." Five more villages were built (West, High, Middle, East and South Amana). The village of Homestead was purchased outright to acquire use of its railroad terminal.

At first the members of the Amana Colonies lived a simple communal life. Although they had individual houses, there were common kitchen and dining facilities. Goods and gains were shared equally. Farming was and still is a mainstay of the group.

The community finally yielded to the pressures of the 20th century. In 1932 common property was dissolved and redistributed on a stock corporation basis. The new corporation, encouraging individual skills and vigor, prospered mostly because of the quality work of its artisans. Today nearly every family owns its own house.

What to See and Do

✪ **Amana.** This community has a furniture factory that offers tours of the production area; a woolen mill with salesroom (daily); woodworking shops, meat shop, general store, brewery, wineries, restaurants and shops. The residence of the late Christian Metz, former leader of Amana Colonies, is in Amana. At jct US 151 & IA 220. Also here is

Museum of Amana History. Exhibits include schoolhouse, crafts and trades, lithographs, documents; audiovisual presentation of history of the Amanas. (Apr-Nov, Mon-Sat, also Sun afternoons) Phone 319/622-3567. ¢¢

East Amana. 1 mi NE of Amana on IA 220.

High Amana. Amana Arts Guild Center; old-fashioned general store. 2 mi W of Middle Amana on IA 220.

Homestead. Meat shop; winery. 5 mi E of South Amana on US 6.

Middle Amana. Restored original Amana kitchen, hearth-oven bakery; coopers shop; Amana Refrigeration, Inc; Amana lily lake. 2 mi W of Amana on IA 220.

Old Creamery Theatre Company. Professional theatre company performs variety of productions. (May-mid-Dec, Thurs-Sun; closed Thanksgiving) 39 38th Ave, Price Creek Stage. Phone 800/352-6262. ¢¢¢¢

South Amana. Winery, miniature-barn museum, furniture factory and refinishing shops; agricultural museum with displays of early farm equipment. 2 mi S of West Amana on IA 220.

West Amana. General store, basket and antique shops. 1 mi W of High Amana on IA 220.

Motels

★ ★ **BEST WESTERN QUIET HOUSE SUITES.** (1708 N Highland, Williamsburg 52361) 15 mi SW on I-80, exit 220 N. 319/668-9770; FAX 319/668-9777. 33 rms, 2 story, 7 suites. S $63-$125; D $73-$135; suites $89-$99; under 12 free; higher rates: wkends, hols. Crib free. Pet accepted; $15. TV; cable (premium). Complimentary continental bkfst. Complimentary coffee in rms. Meeting rms. Business servs avail. Exercise equipt; bicycle, treadmill. Indoor/outdoor pool; whirlpool. Cr cds: A, D, DS, MC, V.

D 🐾 🏊 ✈ ☀ 🔥 **SC**

✔ ★ **GUEST HOUSE MOTOR INN.** (4712 220th Trail, Amana) 319/622-3599. 38 rms, 2 story. Apr-Dec: S $36.90-$45.90; D $42.90-$47; each addl $3; under 12 free; lower rates rest of yr. Crib free. TV; cable (premium). Restaurant nearby. Ck-out 11 am. Cr cds: A, DS, MC, V.

🔥 **SC**

★ ★ ★ **HOLIDAY INN.** (Amana) At I-80 exit 225. 319/668-1175; FAX 319/668-2853. 155 rms, 2 story. S, D $84; under 19 free. Crib free. Pet accepted. TV; cable (premium). Indoor pool; wading pool, whirlpool, poolside serv. Playground. Complimentary coffee in rms. Restaurant 6 am-10 pm. Rm serv. Bar noon-11 pm. Ck-out 11 am. Coin lndry. Meeting rms. Business servs avail. Exercise equipt; bicycles, treadmills, sauna. Game rm. Little Amana complex adj; old-time general store & winery. Cr cds: A, C, D, DS, JCB, MC, V.

D 🐾 🏊 ✈ ☀ 🔥 **SC**

★ **RAMADA LIMITED.** (I-80 at IA 149, Williamsburg 52361) 319/668-1000. 40 rms, 2 story. S $42-$65; D $49-$75; each addl $7. Crib free. TV. Complimentary continental bkfst. Restaurant opp 5 am-midnight. Ck-out 11 am. Exercise equipt; bicycle, rower. Opp Tanger Factory Outlet Center. Cr cds: A, D, DS, MC, V.

D ✈ ☀ 🔥

★ **SUPER 8.** (2228 U Ave, Williamsburg 52361) I-80 exit 225. 319/668-2800. 63 rms, 2 story. May-Oct: S, D $49.88; each addl $6; under 12 free; lower rates rest of yr. Crib $3. Pet accepted, some restrictions; $6. TV; cable (premium). Complimentary continental bkfst. Restaurant adj 6 am-10 pm. Ck-out 11 am. Business servs avail. Cr cds: A, C, D, DS, ER, JCB, MC, V.

D 🐾 ☀ 🔥 **SC**

Inns

✔ ★ **DIE HEIMAT COUNTRY INN.** Homestead (52236), at jct US 6, 151. 319/622-3937. 19 rms, 2 story. S, D $45.95-$76.95; each addl $5; under 6, $3. Crib $3. Pet accepted, some restrictions; $10. TV; some B/W. Complimentary full bkfst. Ck-out 10:30 am. Some refrigerators. Restored inn (1858). Cr cds: DS, MC, V.

🐾 ☀ 🔥

★ **DUSK TO DAWN.** (2616 K St, Middle Amana 52307) 2 mi W on I-80 exit 225. 319/622-3029; res: 800/669-5773. 7 rms, 4 with shower only, 2 story. No rm phones. S, D $60-$70. Crib free (premium). Complimentary continental bkfst. Restaurant nearby. Ck-out 10:30 am, ck-in 2-6 pm. Heated pool; whirlpool. Microwaves avail. Picnic tables, grills. Built in 1868; original communal settlement house. Totally nonsmoking. Cr cds: A, DS, MC, V.

🏊 ☀ 🔥

Restaurants

★ ★ **AMANA BARN.** (4709 220th Trail, Amana) 3 blks E of US 151. 319/622-3214. Hrs: 11 am-9 pm; Sun 10 am-8 pm. Closed Jan 1, Dec 24, 25, 31. Res accepted. German, Amer menu. Bar. Semi-a la carte: lunch $5.25-$8.25, dinner $6.50-$15.95. Child's meals. Specializes in sauerbraten, schnitzel, local dishes. Family-style serv. Parking. Country decor. Cr cds: A, DS, MC, V.

D

✔ ★ ★ **BILL ZUBER'S DUGOUT.** Homestead, at jct US 6, 151. 319/622-3911. Hrs: 11 am-2 pm, 4:30-8 pm; Sun 11 am-7:30 pm. Closed Dec 24, 25. Res accepted. German, Amer menu. Serv bar. Semi-a la carte: lunch $5-$5.50, dinner $8-$13. Child's meals. Specializes in oven-baked steak, chicken. Own pies. Family-style serv. Parking. Baseball memorabilia. Restored century-old inn. Family-owned. Cr cds: A, DS, MC, V.

D

★ ★ **BRICK HAUS.** (728 47th Ave, Amana) E on IA 220, 3 blks E of US 151. 319/622-3278. Hrs: 7:30 am-8 pm. Closed Jan 1, Dec 25. Res accepted. German, Amer menu. Wine, beer. Complete meals: bkfst $6.35, lunch $5.95-6.95, dinner $9.95-$14.95. Child's meals. Specialties: Wienerschnitzel, Amana ham and bratwurst, smoked pork chops. Parking. Photos on wall detail history of village. Totally nonsmoking. Cr cds: A, MC, V.

D

★ ★ **COLONY VILLAGE.** Williamsburg, just S of I-80 exit 225. 319/668-1223. Hrs: 7 am-10 pm. Res accepted. German, Amer menu. Bar. Semi-a la carte: bkfst $2.89-$6.85, lunch $2.25-$7, dinner $8.95-$14.25. Child's meals. Specializes in homemade pie, cinnamon & pecan rolls. Entertainment Fri, Sat. Parking. Bavarian decor, beer garden. Family-owned. Cr cds: A, C, D, DS, MC, V.

D

✔ ★ **HOMESTEAD KITCHEN.** (3146 US 6 Trail, Homestead 52236) 3 mi S on US 6 at exit 225, at US 151. 319/622-3203. Hrs: 7:30 am-8 pm; Fri, Sat to 9 pm. Closed Jan 1, Thanksgiving, Dec 25. Res accepted. Wine, beer. Semi-a la carte: bkfst $3.25-$4.95, lunch $4.95-$5.50, dinner $4.95-$8.50. Child's meals. Specializes in hand-breaded tenderloins, homemade pies. Casual atmosphere. No cr cds accepted.

D 🍽

★ ★ **OX YOKE INN.** (4420 220th Trail, Amana) 10 mi N of I-80. 319/622-3441. Web www.jeonet.com.amanas/oxyoke. Hrs: 11 am-8 pm; Sun 9 am-7 pm; Sept-Apr 11 am-2 pm, 5-8 pm; Sun 9 am-7 pm; Sun brunch to noon; summer hrs vary. Closed Mon-Thurs Jan-Feb; Jan 1, Dec 24, 25, 31. Res accepted. German, Amer menu. Bar. Semi-a la carte: lunch, dinner $3.95-$17.95. Sun brunch $9.95. Child's meals. Specialties: Wienerschnitzel, sauerbraten, rhubarb custard pie. Family-style serv. Parking. Old German decor; display of antiques. Family-owned. Cr cds: A, D, DS, MC, V.

D

★ ★ **RONNEBURG.** (Main St, Amana) IA 220, E off US 151. 319/622-3641. Hrs: 11 am-8 pm. Closed Jan 1, Dec 24, 25, 31. Res accepted. German, Amer menu. Bar 9 am-10 pm. Semi-a la carte: lunch $2.50-$8.25, dinner $9.95-$19.95. Specialties: sauerbraten, Wienerschnitzel.

Family-style serv. Parking. Antiques. Family-owned. Cr cds: A, C, D, DS, MC, V.

Ames (C-5)

(See also Boone)

Settled 1864 **Pop** 47,198 **Elev** 921 ft **Area code** 515 **Zip** 50010 **E-mail** amescvb@netins.net **Web** www.netins.net/showcase/amescvb

Information Convention & Visitors Bureau, 213 S Duff Ave; 515/232-4032 or 800/288-7470.

Located near the geographical center of the state, Ames's economy beats to the pulse of Iowa State University. There are 38 small factories and a regional medical center complex but no major industrial activity. Ames has 500 clubs and organizations. A municipal band performs weekly during the summer. The town is named in honor of a Massachusetts congressman, Oakes Ames, who was financially interested in a local railroad project.

What to See and Do

Iowa Arboretum. Arboretum includes 340 acres of trees, shrubs and gardens. Trails, horticultural plantings, scenic overlooks, ravines, streams. Guided and self-guided tours; educational programs (fee). (Daily) 18 mi SW via UA 30, IA 17 & County E-57. Phone 515/795-3216. **Free.** Guided tours ¢

Iowa State University (1858). (25,250 students) One of the oldest land-grant universities in the US, ISU is known for its spacious, green central campus with sculptures and fountains by artist Christian Petersen and for its many historic buildings. The school is also the birthplace of the electronic digital computer, built by John V. Atanasoff in the basement of the Physics Bldg in the late 1930s. N of US 30. Phone 515/294-4777. Major places of interest are

Iowa State Center. Complex of four buildings includes auditorium, coliseum, two theaters; Brunnier Museum and Art Gallery (daily exc Mon; closed most hols). For information on theatrical and musical performances phone 515/294-3347.

Farm House (1860). Restored original residence on the Iowa State Agricultural College farm; period furnishings. (Early Apr-Dec, Sun, Tues & Thurs; rest of yr, by appt; closed some hols) Near Dairy Industry Building, off Union Dr. Phone 515/294-3342. **Free.**

Reiman Gardens. Peonies, irises, geraniums, many varieties of roses. Teaching garden on NE edge of campus. Phone 515/294-2710.

Campanile (1899). The 50-bell carillon is played during the academic year (Mon-Fri) and also played on special occasions. On central campus.

Grant Wood Murals. Considered among the best works of this Iowa artist, the nine murals were begun as a CWA project during the Great Depression. They depict various academic divisions of the school as well as the breaking of the sod by pioneer farmers. In the Parks Library, on Morrill Rd.

Christian Petersen Sculptures. Works, executed in 1930s and 1940s when Petersen was artist-in-residence at ISU, are on display at Memorial Union fountain, State Gym, Dairy Industry Bldg, MacKay Hall and several other locations.

Annual Event

Veishea Spring Festival. Iowa State campus. Parade, sports, theatrical events, academic open houses. Mid-late Apr.

Motels

★ ★ **BEST WESTERN STARLITE VILLAGE.** *I-35 & 13th St.* 515/232-9260. 131 rms, 3 story. S $45-$50; D $55-$60; each addl $6; higher rates special events. Crib $6. Pet accepted. TV; cable (premium),

VCR avail. Indoor pool; whirlpool, sauna. Restaurant 6 am-10 pm. Rm serv to 9 pm. Bar noon-2 am. Ck-out noon. Meeting rms. Valet serv. Game rm. Cr cds: A, C, D, DS, MC, V.

★ **COMFORT INN.** *1605 S Dayton.* 515/232-0689. 52 rms, 2 story, 6 suites. Sept-Nov: S $43.95; D $49.95; each addl $5; suites $50.95-$60.95; under 18 free; higher rates football season; lower rates rest of yr. Crib free. Pet accepted. TV; cable. Indoor pool; whirlpool. Complimentary continental bkfst. Restaurant adj open 24 hrs. Ck-out 11 am. Meeting rms. Business servs avail. Some refrigerators. Cr cds: A, C, D, DS, MC, V.

✔ ★ **HEARTLAND INN.** *I-35 & US 30, exit 111B.* 515/233-6060; FAX 515/233-1911; res: 800/334-3277. 91 rms, 2 story. S $45; D $62; each addl $7; under 16 free. Crib free. Pet accepted. TV; cable. Complimentary continental bkfst. Restaurant nearby. Ck-out noon. Whirlpool, sauna. Cr cds: A, C, D, DS, JCB, MC, V.

★ ★ ★ **HOLIDAY INN GATEWAY CENTER.** *US 30 and Iowa State Center (50014), 2 mi W on US 30 at ISU exit.* 515/292-8600; FAX 515/292-4446. 188 rms, 8 story. S $69-$87; D $79-$87; each addl $10; suites $150-$225; studio rms $69; under 18 free. Crib free. TV; cable (premium), VCR avail. Indoor pool; whirlpool, sauna. Restaurant 6:30 am-2 pm, 5-10 pm; Sun from 7 am. Rm serv. Bar 2 pm-midnight; Sun 4-10 pm. Ck-out noon. Meeting rms. Business center. In-rm modem link. Valet serv. Sundries. Free airport transportation. Cr cds: A, C, D, DS, JCB, MC, V.

★ ★ **RAMADA INN.** *1206 S Duff, I-35 exit 111B, just off ISU campus.* 515/232-3410; FAX 515/232-6036. 103 rms, 2 story. S $52; D $62; each addl $10; suites $80-$150; under 18 free. Crib free. TV; cable (premium), VCR avail. Pool. Restaurant 6:30 am-10 pm. Rm serv. Bar 4 pm-2 am. Ck-out noon. Meeting rms. Fireplace in lobby. Cr cds: A, C, D, DS, ER, MC, V.

★ **UNIVERSITY INN.** *316 S Duff, I-35 S Ames exit.* 515/232-0280; FAX 515/232-4578; res: 800/422-5250. 120 rms, 2 story. S $45-$90; D $49-$99; each addl $6-$10; under 12 free. Crib free. TV; cable (premium). Restaurant 5-10 pm. Rm serv. Bar 4 pm-2 am; entertainment. Ck-out noon. Meeting rms. Valet serv. Cr cds: A, C, D, DS, MC, V.

Motor Hotel

★ ★ **BUDGETEL.** *2500 Elwood Dr.* 515/296-2500; FAX 515/296-2500. 89 rms, 2 story. S $50; D $56; under 18 free. Crib free. Pet accepted. TV; cable (premium). Indoor pool; whirlpool. Complimentary continental bkfst. Restaurant nearby. Ck-out noon. Meeting rms. Some refrigerators. Cr cds: A, D, DS, MC, V.

Restaurants

★ ★ **BROILER.** *4 1/2 mi W on Lincoln Way.* 515/292-2516. Hrs: 5:30-9:30 pm; Sun 11:30 am-2 pm, 5-9 pm. Closed Jan 1, Thanksgiving, Dec 24-25. Res accepted. Bar. Semi-a la carte: lunch, dinner $7.95-$28.95. Child's meals. Specializes in seafood, steak. Family-owned. Cr cds: A, C, D, DS, MC, V.

★ ★ **ELWELL'S CHEF'S INN.** *6100 W Lincoln Way (50014).* 515/292-4454. Hrs: 5-10 pm; Fri, Sat to 11 pm; early-bird dinner Sun-Thurs 5-6:30 pm; Sun brunch 10 am-2 pm. Closed Dec 25. Res accepted. Bar. Semi-a la carte: dinner $7.95-$15.95. Sun brunch $9.95. Child's meals. Specializes in prime rib, seafood, steak. Multi-level dining areas. Cr cds: A, C, D, DS, MC, V.

✔★ **HICKORY PARK.** *123 S 16th. 515/232-8940.* Hrs: 11 am-9 pm; Fri, Sat to 10 pm. Closed Thanksgiving, Dec 25. Semi-a la carte: lunch $1.95-$4.95, dinner $1.95-$12. Child's meals. Specializes in barbecue. 1890s atmosphere. Family-owned. No cr cds accepted.

D ↴

★ **LUCULLANS.** *400 Main St. 515/232-8484.* Hrs: 11 am-10 pm; Fri, Sat to 11 pm; Sun to 9 pm. Closed Thanksgiving, Dec 24, 25. Res accepted. Italian menu. Bar. Semi-a la carte: lunch $4.95-$7.50, dinner $4.95-$13.85. Child's meals. Own bread. Contemporary decor; informal atmosphere. Cr cds: A, DS, MC, V.

Atlantic (D-3)

(See also Avoca, Walnut)

Pop 7,432 **Elev** 1,215 ft **Area code** 712 **Zip** 50022
Information Chamber of Commerce, 614 Chestnut; 712/243-3017.

What to See and Do

Danish Windmill. Built in Denmark (1848), this 60-ft-high working windmill was dismantled and shipped to Elk Horn where it was reassembled by community volunteers. Tours. (Daily; closed Jan 1, Dec 25) 15 mi N via IA 173; 7 mi N of I-80 exit 54 in Elk Horn. Phone 712/764-7472. ¢

Motels

✔★ **ECONO LODGE.** *US 71, ½ mi S of I-80 exit 60. 712/243-4067; FAX 712/243-1713.* 51 rms, 1-2 story. S $35-$37; D $39-$45; each addl $2. Crib $2. Pet accepted. TV; cable. Pool. Coffee in rms. Restaurant nearby. Ck-out 11 am. Meeting rm. Sundries. Cr cds: A, C, D, DS, MC, V.

D ✔ ⛱ ⊠ ⋈ SC

★ **SUPER 8.** *1902 E Seventh St, 8 blks E on US 6, 7 mi S of I-80 exit 60. 712/243-4723; FAX 712/243-2864.* 44 rms. S $39-$45; D $50-$59; each addl $2. Crib $2. TV; cable (premium). Complimentary continental bkfst. Coffee in rms. Restaurant 5-10 pm. Ck-out 11 am. Meeting rm. Business servs avail. In-rm modem link. Sundries. Whirlpool. Cr cds: A, C, D, DS, MC, V.

D ⊠ ⋈ SC

Inn

★ ★ ★ **CHESTNUT CHARM.** *1409 Chestnut St. 712/243-5652.* 5 rms, 1 with shower only, 1 guest house. Many rm phones. S, D, guest house $65-$250; each addl $10. Adults only. TV in many rms; cable (premium). Complimentary full bkfst. Ck-out 11 am, ck-in 4 pm. Concierge serv. Gift shop. Many in-rm whirlpools, refrigerators, microwaves, fireplaces. Victorian mansion built in 1898; antiques, gazebo. Totally non-smoking. Cr cds: MC, V.

D ⊠ ⋈

Avoca (D-2)

(See also Atlantic)

Pop 1,497 **Elev** 1,138 ft **Area code** 712 **Zip** 51521

What to See and Do

Prairie Rose State Park. More than 650 acres of wind-formed hills surround a 204-acre lake. Swimming; fishing; boating (ramp). Snowmobiling. Picnicking. Camping (electricity, dump station). Standard hrs, fees. 2 mi N

via US 59, then 6 mi E on I-80, exit 46, then 9 mi N on paved road. Phone 712/773-2701.

Motel

✔★ **CAPRI.** *US 59, ½ mi S of I-80. 712/343-6301.* 26 rms. S $35; D $41; each addl $5. Crib $5. Pet accepted. TV; cable. Complimentary coffee in lobby. Restaurant nearby. Ck-out 10:30 am. Cr cds: A, DS, MC, V.

✔ ⊠ ⋈

Bettendorf (D-9)

(See also Clinton, Davenport)

Pop 28,132 **Elev** 565 ft **Area code** 319 **Zip** 52722 **E-mail** cvb@quadcities.com **Web** quadcities.com/cvb
Information Quad Cities Convention & Visitors Bureau, 102 S Harrison St, Davenport 52801; 309/788-7800 or 800/747-7800.

Bettendorf began as a quiet rural village called Gilbert. Then, in 1903, the town's future changed with the arrival of the Bettendorf Axle and Wagon Company, which became the largest manufacturer of railroad cars west of the Mississippi. The growing city changed its name in honor of the company. Today, Bettendorf, on the Mississippi River, is part of the Quad Cities metropolitan area, that includes Davenport, Iowa, and Moline and Rock Island, Illinois.

What to See and Do

Buffalo Bill Cody Homestead. Restored boyhood home of Buffalo Bill Cody, built by his father in 1847. On grounds are buffalo, deer and farm animals. (Apr-Oct, daily; rest of yr, by appt) 3 mi N on US 67, then W on 280th/Bluff Rd near McCausland. Phone 319/225-2981. **Donation.**

Family Museum of Arts & Science. Hands-on exhibits; Rhythm Alley, Heartland, The Homestead, Kinder Garten; also traveling exhibit gallery, children's program area. (Daily exc Mon; closed most major hols) 2900 18th St. Phone 319/344-4106. ¢

Lady Luck Casino. Casino gambling; restaurant, gift shop. Valet parking. Riverfront, just E of I-74. For schedule and fee information phone 319/359-7280 or 800/724-5825.

Motels

★ ★ **COURTYARD BY MARRIOTT.** *895 Golden Valley Dr. 319/355-3999; FAX 319/355-0308.* 108 rms, 3 story. S, D $86; suites $109. Crib free. TV; cable (premium). Indoor pool; whirlpool. Complimentary coffee in rms. Restaurant 6-9:30 am; Sat, Sun 7-11 am. Rm serv. Bar 5-10 pm. Ck-out noon. Coin lndry. Meeting rm. Business servs avail. In-rm modem link. Valet serv. Sundries. Exercise equipt; weight machine, bicycles. Health club privileges. Some refrigerators; microwaves avail. Balconies. Cr cds: A, C, D, DS, MC, V.

D ⛱ 🏋 ⊠ ⋈ SC

✔★ **ECONO LODGE-QUAD CITIES.** *2205 Kimberly Rd. 319/355-6471; FAX 319/359-0559.* 67 rms. S, D $40-$58; each addl $4; under 18 free. Crib free. Pet accepted, some restrictions. TV; cable (premium), VCR avail. Pool. Playground. Complimentary continental bkfst. Restaurant 10 am-10 pm. Bar from 11 am. Ck-out noon. Meeting rm. Business servs avail. Cr cds: A, C, D, DS, MC, V.

D ✔ ⛱ ⊠ ⋈ SC

★ **HEARTLAND INN.** *815 Golden Valley Dr. 319/355-6336; FAX 319/355-0039; res: 800/334-3277.* 85 rms, 3 story. May-Aug: S, D $47-$66; each addl $7; suites $110-$140; under 16 free; lower rates rest of yr. Crib free. TV; cable, VCR avail. Pool. Complimentary continental bkfst. Ck-out 11 am. Meeting rms. Business servs avail. In-rm modem link.

Sundries. Valet serv. Sauna. Health club privileges. Microwaves avail. Cr cds: A, D, DS, MC, V.

D ≋ ⊠ ⋊ SC

★★ **HOLIDAY INN.** *909 Middle Rd. 319/355-4761; FAX 319/355-5572.* 157 rms, 2 story. S, D $65-$86; each addl $7; under 18 free. Crib free. TV; cable (premium), VCR avail. Heated pool. Restaurant 6 am-1:30 pm, 5-10 pm. Rm serv. Bar 4 pm-2 am. Ck-out noon. Coin lndry. Meeting rms. Business servs avail. In-rm modem link. Valet serv. Complimentary airport transportation. Exercise equipt; weight machine, bicycles. Cr cds: A, C, D, DS, JCB, MC, V.

D ≋ ⋇ ⊠ ⋊ SC

✔★★ **SIGNATURE INN.** *3020 Utica Ridge Rd, 2 mi E off I-74. 319/355-7575; FAX 319/355-7575, ext. 500.* 124 rms, 3 story. S, D $52-$67; each addl $7; suite $109; under 17 free. Crib free. TV; cable (premium), VCR avail (movies). Pool. Complimentary full bkfst. Ck-out noon. Business center. In-rm modem link. Free airport transportation. Exercise equipt; weight machine, stair machine. Health club privileges. Cr cds: A, C, D, DS, ER, MC, V.

D ≋ ⋇ ⊠ ⋊ SC 🏃

Hotel

★★★ **JUMER'S CASTLE LODGE.** *900 Spruce Hills Dr. 319/359-7141; FAX 319/359-7141; res: 800/285-8637.* 210 rms. S $78; D $87; each addl $9; suites $88-$142; under 18 free. Crib free. Pet accepted, some restrictions; $25 refundable. TV; cable (premium). 2 pools, 1 indoor; whirlpool. Restaurant (see JUMER'S). Bars 11-1 am; entertainment. Ck-out noon. Convention facilities. Business servs avail. Free airport, bus depot transportation. Putting green. Exercise equipt; weight machine, bicycles, sauna. Health club privileges. Rec rm. Lawn games. Bavarian architecture & decor; antiques, tapestries. Cr cds: A, D, DS, MC, V.

D ✔ ≋ ⋇ ⊠ ⋊ SC

Inn

★★★ **THE ABBEY HOTEL.** *1401 Central, 1/2 mi E on I-74, exit 4. 319/355-0291; res: 800/438-7535; FAX 319/355-7647.* 19 rms, 3 story. S $75; D $85; each addl $10; suite $125; under 12 free. Crib free. TV; cable (premium), VCR avail. Complimentary full bkfst. Rm serv 3-11 pm. Bar 5 pm-midnight. Ck-out noon, ck-in 2 pm. Meeting rms. Business servs avail. In-rm modem link. Free airport transportation. Exercise equipt; rowers, stair machine. Heated pool. Romanesque structure was once a Carmelite monastery. Totally nonsmoking. Cr cds: A, D, DS, MC, V.

D ≋ ⋇ ⊠ ⋊ SC

Restaurants

★★★ **JUMER'S.** *(See Jumer's Castle Lodge Hotel) 319/359-1607.* Hrs: 6 am-10 pm; Fri, Sat to 11 pm; Sun from 7 am; hols to 8 pm. Res accepted. German, Amer menu. Bar. Semi-a la carte: bkfst $2.25-$6.50, lunch $4.45-$8.45, dinner $7.95-$19.95. Child's meals. Specialties: Wienerschnitzel, sauerbraten, Kirschtorte. Own baking. Pianist. Bavarian decor, antiques. Cr cds: A, C, D, MC, V.

D ⌐

★★ **STUBBS EDDY.** *1716 State St. 319/355-0073.* Hrs: 5 pm-2 am. Closed Sun; major hols. Res accepted. Bar. Semi-a la carte: dinner $4.95-$38.95. Child's meals. Specializes in filet mignon, pasta, fresh seafood. Entertainment Tues, Thurs evenings. Cr cds: A, MC, V.

Boone (C-4)

(For accommodations see Ames)

Founded 1865 **Pop** 12,392 **Elev** 960 ft **Area code** 515 **Zip** 50036
Information Chamber of Commerce, 806 7th St; 515/432-3342 or 800/266-6312.

In the fertile Des Moines River Valley, Boone is a farming center with several factories. There are a number of summer camps for children in the surrounding area.

What to See and Do

Boone & Scenic Valley Railroad. The ride on this shortline railroad includes a scenic, 12-mi, round-trip tour (1 3/4 hr) in vintage 1920s cars pulled by a steam engine (wkends, hols; 3 trips daily) or diesel (wkdays; 1 trip daily); steam locomotive, made in China, is the only engine of its class in the US; train crosses the highest "single-track, interurban bridge" in US. Depot has snack bar and **Iowa Railroad Museum** with railroad history exhibits. (Memorial Day wkend-Oct, daily) 225 10th St. Phone 515/432-4249. ¢¢¢

Ledges State Park. More than 1,200 acres with foot trails, streams and 25-150-ft-high sandstone ledges. Fishing. Hiking. Snowmobiling. Picnicking. Camping (electric hookups, dump station). Standard fees. 6 mi S on IA 164. Phone 515/432-1852.

Mamie Doud Eisenhower Birthplace. One-story frame house restored to original Victorian style includes such period furnishings as the bed in which Mamie Eisenhower was born. Summer kitchen, library, museum. (June-Oct, daily; Apr-May, Tues-Sun afternoons; also by appt) 709 Carroll St. Phone 515/432-1896. ¢¢

Annual Event

Pufferbilly Days. Features train rides, model railroad display, handcar races, spike driving contest; antique car show; parade, entertainment, food, bike races. Wkend after Labor Day.

Burlington (E-8)

(See also Fort Madison)

Settled 1832 **Pop** 27,208 **Elev** 540 ft **Area code** 319 **Zip** 52601
Information Convention & Tourism Bureau, 807 Jefferson St, PO Box 6; 319/752-6365 or 800/82-RIVER.

Burlington, a river port, shopping, industrial and farm center, traces its history back to the days when it was called Flint Hills by Native Americans and served as neutral ground where tribes hunted flint for implements. Zebulon Pike raised the Stars & Stripes here in 1805, and a trading post was built in 1808. The city became capital of the Wisconsin Territory in 1837, then capital of the Iowa Territory from 1838-1840. Its retail trade draws shoppers from three states; factories turn out tractors, chemicals, electronic instruments, furniture and other products.

What to See and Do

Crapo and Dankwardt Parks. The parks (approx 175 acres) are situated along the Mississippi on the site where the American flag first flew over Iowa soil (1805); includes illuminated fountain, arboretum, formal flower garden. Swimming. Black Hawk Spring Indian trail; tennis, archery range, ice-skating. Picnicking; playground. (Daily) On Great River Rd at SE corner of city. Phone 319/753-8110 or 319/753-8117. **Free.**

Geode State Park. More than 1,600 heavily wooded acres along limestone bluffs rising out of 187-acre lake. Swimming, supervised beach; fishing; boating (ramps, rentals). Hiking trails. Snowmobiling. Picnicking.

Camping (electricity, dump station). Standard hrs, fees. 6 mi W on US 34, then 6 mi W on IA 79 & County J2O. Phone 319/392-4601.

Grandpa Bill's Farm. This 100-acre "country fun park" was created from an actual Iowa farm. Original buildings have been converted to house attractions: country barn theater features live musical shows and dances; play barn has play area, hay loft, educational exhibits; mini-farm contains examples of conventional farm buildings and animals. Hayrides, crafts fair. Restaurant. (June-late Aug, daily; May & late Aug-Oct, wkends only) 10 mi N on US 61 in Sperry. Phone 319/985-2262. ¢

Heritage Hill National Historic District. This 29-sq-blk area contains churches, mansions and houses in a wide variety of architectural styles, including a full range of Victorian buildings from the 1870s to the turn of the century. Walking tours, auto cassette tours and brochures avail. Contact the Convention & Tourism Bureau. N of downtown, between Washington & High Sts. Also here is

Snake Alley. The zigzagging brick-paved street, built in 1894, is, according to Ripley's Believe It or Not, the "crookedest street in the world." Between Washington & Columbia Sts. At top of street is

Phelps House (ca 1850). Mansard-roofed, Italianate, Victorian mansion with original furnishings used by three generations of one family; extensive collection of rare china; family portraits. Guided tours (by appt; fee). (May-Oct, Wed & Sun afternoons) 521 Columbia St. Phone 319/753-2449. ¢

Mosquito Park. Located on a bluff overlooking the city, the Mississippi and a vast stretch of Iowa and Illinois. 3rd & Franklin Sts.

The Apple Trees Historical Museum. The museum, a remaining wing of railroad magnate Charles E. Perkins's mansion, contains Victorian furnishings; antique tools, costumes, dolls, toys, buttons, glass, china; Native American artifacts; changing exhibits. Maintained by Des Moines County Historical Society. Guided tours (by appt; fee). (May-Oct, Wed & Sun afternoons) 1616 Dill St, in Perkins Park. Phone 319/753-2449. **Free.** The society also maintains

Hawkeye Log Cabin. Replica (1910) of pioneer cabin; antique furnishings and tools. Guided tours (by appt; fee). (May-Sept, Wed & Sun afternoons) On bluff in Crapo Park. Phone 319/753-2449. **Free.**

Annual Events

Snake Alley Criterium Bicycle Races. Olympic-style racing. Memorial Day wkend.

Burlington Steamboat Days & the American Music Festival. Downtown riverfront. Athletic competitions, fireworks, midway, parade, name entertainment. Phone 319/754-4334. 6 days ending Father's Day, mid-June.

Motels

✔★ **COMFORT INN.** 3051 Kirkwood. 319/753-0000; FAX 319/753-0000, ext. 301. 52 rms, 2 story. S $35-$50; D $45-$60; each addl $5; suites $99; under 18 free; higher rates: hol wkends, special events. Crib avail. Pet accepted. TV; cable (premium). Pool. Complimentary continental bkfst. Restaurant nearby. Ck-out 11 am. Business servs avail. In-rm modem link. Cr cds: A, C, D, DS, ER, JCB, MC, V.

D ✔ ≋ ⊠ 🔥 SC

★ **DAYS INN.** 1601 N Roosevelt Ave, at jct US 34, 61. 319/752-0000; FAX 319/754-1111. 43 rms. S $35-$45; D $45-$55; each addl $5; under 12 free. Crib free. Pet accepted. TV; cable (premium). Restaurant nearby. Ck-out 11 am. Meeting rm. Microwaves avail. Cr cds: A, C, D, DS, MC, V.

✔ ⊠ 🔥 SC

✔★ **SUPER 8.** 3001 Kirkwood. 319/752-9806; FAX 319/752-9806, ext. 404. 63 rms, 3 story. No elvtr. S $32.98-$60.98; D $39.73-$68.98; under 12 free. Crib $2.24. TV; cable (premium). Complimentary continental bkfst. Restaurant nearby. Ck-out 11 am. Sundries. Microwaves avail. Cr cds: A, C, D, DS, MC, V.

D ⊠ 🔥 SC

Motor Hotel

★ ★ **BEST WESTERN PZAZZ MOTOR INN.** 3001 Winegard Dr, just N of jct US 34, 61. 319/753-2223; FAX 319/753-2224. 151 rms, 3 story. S $59.75; D $67.75; each addl $4; suites $105; studio rms $55-$85; under 18 free. Crib free. Pet accepted. TV; cable (premium), VCR (movies). Indoor pool; whirlpool. Restaurant 6:30 am-10 pm. Bar 11:30-2 am; entertainment. Ck-out noon. Balconies. Coin lndry. Meeting rms. Business servs avail. In-rm modem link. Gift shop. Barber, beauty shop. Airport transportation. Game rm. Exercise equipt; rower, weight machine, sauna. Cr cds: A, C, D, DS, ER, MC, V.

D ✔ ≋ 🛩 ⊠ 🔥 SC

Carroll (C-3)

Pop 9,579 **Elev** 1,261 ft **Area code** 712 **Zip** 51401 **E-mail** cchamber @netins.net

Information Chamber of Commerce, 223 W 5th St, PO Box 307; 712/792-4383.

This town is named for Charles Carroll, a signer of the Declaration of Independence.

What to See and Do

Black Hawk State Park. Park consists of 86 acres along 925-acre Black Hawk Lake. Swimming; fishing; boating (ramps). Snowmobiling. Picnicking. Camping (electricity, dump station). Standard hrs, fees. 23 mi NW on US 71 in Lake View. Phone 712/657-8712.

Swan Lake Park. The 510 acres include 115-acre Swan Lake. Swimming, fishing. Nature trails, wildlife exhibit. Access to Sauk Rail Trail. Winter activities. Picnicking. Camping (fee). (Daily) 2 mi S, then ½ mi E. Phone 712/792-4614.

Motel

★ ★ ★ **CARROLLTON INN.** 1730 US 71 North, On US 71 N at jct US 30. 712/792-5600; FAX 712/792-5600, ext. 431; res: 800/798-3535. 89 rms, 2 story. S $45-$50; D $55-$60; each addl $5; suites $54-$90. Crib free. TV; cable (premium), VCR avail (movies). Indoor pool; whirlpool, sauna. Restaurant 6:30 am-10 pm. Rm serv. Bar 4 pm-2 am. Ck-out noon. Coin lndry. Meeting rms. Sundries. Beauty shop. Cr cds: A, C, D, DS, MC, V.

D ≋ ⊠ 🔥 SC

Restaurant

★ ★ **TONY'S.** At jct US 71 & US 30. 712/792-3792. Hrs: 7 am-10:30 pm. Closed Jan 1, Dec 25. Res accepted. Continental menu. Semi-a la carte: bkfst $3.45-$5.95, lunch $4.45-$7.95, dinner $5-$13. Sun brunch $6.95. Child's meals. Specializes in chicken, ribs, lasagna. Salad bar. Family-owned. Cr cds: A, D, DS, MC, V.

D

Cedar Falls (C-6)

(See also Waterloo, Waverly)

Settled 1845 **Pop** 34,298 **Elev** 900 ft **Area code** 319 **Zip** 50613 **E-mail** cf.tourism@cedarnet.org **Web** www.cedarnet.org/cf.tourism

Information Chamber of Commerce, Tourism & Visitors Bureau, PO Box 367; 319/266-3593.

Once one of the most important milling centers in the state, today Cedar Falls is a university town and home to a diverse industrial base.

What to See and Do

Black Hawk Park. Fishing, boating. Hiking; shooting and archery ranges; cross-country skiing, ice-skating, snowshoeing, ice-fishing. Picnicking. Camping (fee). (Daily) 3 mi N on US 218, then 1 mi W on Lone Tree Rd. Phone 319/266-6813.

Cedar Falls Historical Society Victorian Home Museum. Civil War-era Victorian house furnished in 1890s period style. **Carriage House Museum** contains library, archives, fashions, memorabilia of the first permanent settlement in Black Hawk County (1845). (Wed-Sun afternoons) 308 W 3rd. Phone 319/266-5149. **Free.**

George Wyth House. The residence of George Wyth, founder of the Viking Pump Company, was built in 1907; now furnished in art-deco style of 1920s; including pieces by Gilbert Rhode. Viking Pump Company museum on third floor. Tours (Sun afternoons, also by appt; closed Jan-Mar). 303 Franklin St. Phone 319/266-5149 or 319/277-8817. **Free.**

George Wyth Memorial State Park. The 494-acre park includes several lakes. Swimming; fishing; boating (ramp). Nature, hiking, bicycle trails. Snowmobiling. Picnicking. Camping (electricity, dump station). Standard hrs, fees. Between Cedar River & US 20. Phone 319/232-5505.

Ice House Museum. This round structure, 100 ft in diameter, was once used for storing up to 8,000 tons of ice from the Cedar River. The icehouse now displays antique tools for the harvesting, storing, selling and use of natural ice; also antique farm equipment; early American kitchen; military memorabilia. (May-Oct, Wed, Sat & Sun afternoons; closed some major hols) 1st & Franklin Sts, enter off Clay St. Phone 319/266-5149 or 319/277-8817. **Free.**

The Little Red School. Country school (1909) has been authentically furnished to reflect turn-of-the-century education. (May-Oct, Wed, Sat & Sun afternoons; closed some major hols) 1st & Clay Sts. Phone 319/266-5149 or 319/277-8817. **Free.**

University of Northern Iowa (1876). (13,150 students) Campanile in Italian Renaissance style, 100 ft high; chimes played daily. UNI-Dome, Iowa's first and only multipurpose domed coliseum. Also on campus is a museum (Mon-Fri; closed hols) with exhibits on geology and natural history. College St between 23rd St & University Ave. For campus tours phone 319/273-2281; for self-guided tour maps contact Office of Public Relations, 127 Gilchrist Hall; 319/273-2761.

> **Gallery of Art.** Permanent collection and changing exhibits. (Daily; closed school hols & in-between exhibits) 27th St & Hudson Rd in Kamerick Art Building-South. Phone 319/273-2077. **Free.**

Annual Event

Sturgis Falls Days Celebration. Overman & Island parks. Includes Dixieland jazz festival, parade, street fair, arts & crafts. Last full wkend June.

Seasonal Event

Band concerts. In Overman Park. Tues evenings, June-July.

Motels

☜★ **BEST WESTERN MIDWEST LODGE.** *4410 University Ave. 319/277-1550; FAX 319/277-8947.* 96 rms, 2 story. S $43-$55; D $54-$59; each addl $5; under 12 free. Crib free. TV; cable (premium), VCR avail (movies). Indoor pool; whirlpool, sauna. Complimentary continental bkfst. Complimentary coffee in rms. Restaurant nearby. Ck-out noon. Business servs avail. In-rm modem link. Sundries. Valet serv. Balconies. Cr cds: A, C, D, DS, MC, V.

D ⊠ ⊠ ⊠ SC

★ ★ **HOLIDAY INN.** *5826 University Ave. 319/277-2230; FAX 319/277-0364.* 182 rms, 2 story. S $59; D $74; each addl $10; suites $125-$150. Crib free. Pet accepted. TV; cable (premium). Heated pool; poolside serv. Complimentary coffee in rm. Restaurant 6 am-10 pm. Rm serv. Bar 4 pm-midnight. Ck-out noon. Coin lndry. Meeting rms. Business servs avail. In-rm modem link. Bellhops. Valet serv. Free airport transportation. Exercise equipt; bicycle, stair machine. Game rm. Cr cds: A, C, D, DS, JCB, MC, V.

D ⊠ ⊠ ⊠ ⊠ ⊠ SC

Restaurant

★ ★ **OLDE BROOM FACTORY.** *110 N Main St. 319/268-0877.* Hrs: 11 am-2:30 pm, 5-10 pm; Sat 11 am-2 pm, 4:30-11 pm; Sun 10 am-10 pm; Sun brunch to 2 pm. Closed most major hols. Res accepted. Continental menu. Bar 4 pm-midnight. A la carte entrees: lunch, dinner $6-$17. Sun brunch $8.95. Child's meals. Specializes in prime rib, desserts. Structure built 1862. Cr cds: A, C, D, DS, MC, V.

D SC ♥

Cedar Rapids (C-7)

(See also Amana Colonies)

Settled 1838 **Pop** 108,751 **Elev** 730 ft **Area code** 319 **E-mail** visitors@fyiowa.infi.net **Web** www.cedar-rapids.com/iowa/cvb

Information Cedar Rapids Area Convention & Visitors Bureau, 119 1st Ave SE, PO Box 5339, 52406-5339; 319/398-5009 or 800/735-5557.

Cedar Rapids, located at the rapids of the Cedar River, is the industrial leader of the state. More than $475 million worth of cereals, corn products, milk processing machinery, farm hardware, stock feeds and electronic material are exported to worldwide markets.

What to See and Do

Brucemore (1886). Queen Anne-style 21-rm mansion with formal gardens, lawns, orchard and pond; sunroom decorated by native artist Grant Wood. The estate serves as community cultural center. (Feb-Dec, Tues-Sat; closed major hols) 2160 Linden Dr SE. Phone 319/362-7375. ¢¢

Cedar Rapids Museum of Art. Extensive collection of work by Grant Wood, Marvin Cone and Mauricio Lasansky; changing exhibits; children's gallery. Gift shop. (Daily exc Mon; closed hols) 410 3rd Ave SE. Phone 319/366-7503. ¢¢

◪ **Czech Village.** Bakery, gift shops, restaurants, historic structures preserving Czech heritage. (See ANNUAL EVENTS) On 16th Ave SW near downtown. Phone 319/362-2846 or 319/362-8500 (tour info). In Village is

> **National Czech & Slovak Museum & Library.** Houses large collection of national costumes. Changing exhibits; restored immigrant home. Tours. (Tues-Sat, also Sun afternoons mid-May-Dec; closed hols) 30 16th Ave SW. Phone 319/362-8500. ¢¢

Five Seasons Center. This 10,000-seat entertainment center features sports events, concerts, exhibits, rodeos, ice shows, other events. 370 1st Ave NE. For schedule phone 319/398-5211.

Indian Creek Nature Center. On this 210-acre nature preserve is an observatory/museum, in a remodeled dairy barn, which offers changing exhibits. Hiking trails. (Daily; closed hols) 6665 Otis Rd SE. Phone 319/362-0664. ¢

Masonic Library (1955). Houses most complete Masonic collection in the US; also two museum rooms in this late- *moderne,* Vermont-marble structure with bas-relief decoration and stained-glass windows. Tours. (Daily, afternoons; closed hols) Grand Lodge Office Bldg, 813 1st Ave SE. Phone 319/365-1438.   **Free.**

Palisades-Kepler State Park. This 970-acre park includes limestone palisades that rise 75 ft above the Cedar River; timbered valleys, wildflowers. Fishing; boating (ramps). Nature, hiking trails. Snowmobiling. Picnicking. Lodge. Camping (electricity, dump station); cabins. Standard hrs, fees. 12 mi E via US 30. Phone 319/895-6039.

Paramount Theatre. Restored Theater (ca 1925). Stage productions, films; home of Cedar Rapids Symphony. 123 Third Ave SE. For schedule and fees phone 319/398-5211 or 319/366-8203 (Symphony).

Science Station. Science and technology museum features unusual hands-on exhibits including a working hot-air balloon and giant kaleidoscope. In historic fire station. (Daily exc Mon; closed most hols) 427 1st St SE. Phone 319/366-0968.   ¢¢

Wapsipinicon State Park. This 251-acre park is along the west bank of the Wapsipinicon River and includes high rock cliffs, open meadows, wooded hills, caves, wildflowers. Fishing; boating (ramp). 9-hole golf course. Hiking trails. Snowmobiling. Picnicking. Lodge. Camping (electric hookups). Standard hrs, fees. 27 mi NE, off US 151 in Anamosa. Phone 319/462-2761.

Annual Events

Houby Days. Czech Village. Features Czech fine arts, folk arts and customs, music, dancing, food; mushroom hunt contests, races. Wkend after Mother's Day.

Celebration of the Arts. Brucemore. Open-air festival celebrating all performing and visual arts. Father's Day.

Freedom Festival. Eighty events for all ages held citywide, topped off by large fireworks display. Wk preceding July 4.

All-Iowa Fair. Hawkeye Downs. Stock car races, fine arts, exhibits, name entertainment. Aug.

Motels

★ **COMFORT INN-NORTH.** *5055 Rockwell Dr (52402), I-380 exit 24A.* 319/393-8247. 59 rms, 2 story. May-Aug: S, D $50.95-$65.95; under 18 free; lower rates rest of yr. Crib free. Pet accepted, some restrictions. TV; cable (premium), VCR avail. Complimentary continental bkfst. Ck-out 11 am. Business servs avail. In-rm modem link. Whirlpool. Some refrigerators. Cr cds: A, C, D, DS, ER, JCB, MC, V.

[D] [icons] SC

★ ★ **COMFORT INN-SOUTH.** *390 33rd Ave SW (52404).* 319/363-7934. 60 rms, 3 story. S $43-$60; D $45-$65; each addl $5; suites $53-$65; under 18 free. Crib free. Pet accepted. TV; cable (premium). Complimentary continental bkfst. Restaurant nearby. Ck-out 11 am. Meeting rms. Cr cds: A, C, D, DS, ER, JCB, MC, V.

[D] [icons] SC

★ **DAYS INN-SOUTH.** *3245 Southgate Place SW (52404), SW off I-380 exit 17.* 319/365-4339. 40 rms, 2 story, 4 suites. S $42-$50; D $44-$52; each addl $5; suites $55-$65; under 18 free. Crib free. Pet accepted. TV; cable. Indoor pool; whirlpool. Complimentary continental bkfst. Restaurant nearby. Ck-out 11 am. Business servs avail. In-rm modem link. Some refrigerators. Cr cds: A, D, DS, ER, MC, V.

[D] [icons] SC

✔★ **ECONO LODGE.** *622 33rd Ave SW (52404), 2 blks W of I-380, 33rd St exit.* 319/363-8888. 50 rms, 2 story. S $38.95-$58.95; D $42.95-$58.95; each addl $5; suites $70-$125; under 18 free; higher rates: farm show, conventions. Crib free. Pet accepted. TV; cable. Indoor pool; whirlpool. Complimentary continental bkfst. Restaurant nearby. Ck-out 11 am. Coin lndry. Cr cds: A, C, D, DS, MC, V.

[D] [icons] SC

✔★ **EXEL INN.** *616 33rd Ave SW (52404).* 319/366-2475; FAX 319/366-5712. 103 rms, 2 story. S $32.99-$41.99; D $37.99-$47.99; each addl $4; under 18 free. Crib free. Pet accepted. TV; cable. Complimentary continental bkfst. Restaurant nearby. Ck-out noon. Guest lndry. Business servs avail. In-rm modem link. Cr cds: A, C, D, DS, MC, V.

[D] [icons] SC

★ ★ **FAIRFIELD INN BY MARRIOTT.** *3243 Southridge Dr SW (52404), I-380 exit 17.* 319/364-2000. 105 rms, 3 story. S $48.95; D $56.95; each addl $7; under 18 free. Crib free. TV; cable (premium). Heated pool. Continental bkfst. Ck-out noon. Coin lndry. Meeting rm. Business servs avail. In-rm modem link. Cr cds: A, C, D, DS, MC, V.

[D] [icons] SC

★ **HEARTLAND INN.** *3315 Southgate Court SW (52404).* 319/362-9012; FAX 319/362-9694; res: 800/334-3277. 117 units, 2 story, 30 suites. S $45-$60; D $54-$69; each addl $8; suites $68-$150; under 16 free; some lower rates avail. Crib free. TV. Complimentary bkfst. Restaurant adj open 24 hrs. Ck-out noon. Meeting rm. Sauna. Cr cds: A, C, D, DS, MC, V.

[D] [icons] SC

✔★ **RED ROOF INN.** *3325 Southgate Court (52404), I-380 exit 17 (33rd Ave).* 319/366-7523; FAX 319/366-7639. 108 rms, 2 story. S $29.99-$41.99; D $35.99-$53.99; each addl $8; under 18 free. Crib free. TV; cable (premium). Complimentary coffee. Restaurant opp open 24 hrs. Ck-out noon. Cr cds: A, C, D, DS, MC, V.

[D] [icons] SC

Motor Hotels

★ ★ **BEST WESTERN LONGBRANCH.** *90 Twixtown Rd NE (52402), just off jct IA 150, US 151.* 319/377-6386. 106 rms, 4 story. S $53.95-$59.95; D $61.95-$67.95; each addl $3; suites $85.95-$199.95; under 18 free; wknd rates. Crib $5. TV; cable (premium), VCR avail. Heated pool. Restaurant 6 am-10 pm. Rm serv. Bars 11 am-midnight; entertainment. Ck-out 1 pm. Meeting rms. Business servs avail. In-rm modem link. Bellhops. Valet serv. Free airport transportation. Health club privileges. Cr cds: A, C, D, DS, JCB, MC, V.

[D] [icons] SC

★ ★ **DAYS INN.** *2501 Williams Blvd SW (52404), at IA 151, 16th Ave.* 319/365-9441; FAX 319/365-0255. 184 rms, 2 story. S $62-$68; D $68-$74; each addl $6; under 19 free. Crib free. Pet accepted. TV; cable. Indoor pool; whirlpool, sauna. Restaurant 6 am-2 pm, 5-10 pm. Rm serv. Bar 4 pm-midnight; Sun to 10 pm. Ck-out noon. Coin lndry. Meeting rms. Business servs avail. In-rm modem link. Free airport transportation. Cr cds: A, C, D, DS, JCB, MC, V.

[D] [icons] SC

★ ★ ★ **FOUR POINTS BY SHERATON.** *525 33rd Ave SW (52404).* 319/366-8671; FAX 319/362-1420. 157 rms, 6 story. S $78-$88; D $88-$98; each addl $10; suites $185; under 18 free; wkend rates. Crib free. Pet accepted. TV; cable (premium). Indoor pool; whirlpool, poolside serv. Restaurant 6:30 am-10 pm; Sat 7 am-11 pm. Rm serv. Bar 11-2 am; Sun noon-10 pm; entertainment. Ck-out noon. Meeting rms. Business servs avail. In-rm modem link. Bellhops. Valet serv. Sundries. Free airport transportation. Exercise equipt; bicycles, treadmill, sauna. Game rm. Rec rm. Cr cds: A, C, D, DS, JCB, MC, V.

[D] [icons] SC

✔★ **VILLAGE INN.** *100 F Avenue NW (52405).* 319/366-5323; res: 800/858-5511. 86 rms, 4 story. S $42-$44; D $48-$50; each addl $2; under 12 free. Crib $5. Pet accepted; $5/day. TV; cable (premium). Restaurant 6-3 am; Sun to midnight. Rm serv. Bar 11-2 am; closed Sun. Ck-out noon. Meeting rms. Business servs avail. In-rm modem link. Valet serv. Cr cds: A, C, D, DS, JCB, MC, V.

[icons] SC

Hotels

★ ★ ★ **COLLINS PLAZA.** *1200 Collins Rd NE (52402). 319/393-6600; FAX 319/393-2308; res: 800/541-1067.* 221 units, 7 story, 85 suites. S, D $90.50-$98.50; each addl $8; suites $107.50-$125.50; under 18 free. Crib free. TV; cable. Indoor pool; whirlpool. Restaurants 6 am-11 pm. Bars 11-1 am; entertainment. Ck-out noon. Coin lndry. Meeting rms. Business center. In-rm modem link. Gift shop. Free airport, bus depot transportation. Exercise equipt; weight machine, bicycles, steam rm, sauna. Refrigerator, wet bar in suites. Cr cds: A, C, D, DS, JCB, MC, V.

★ ★ ★ **FIVE SEASONS.** *350 1st Ave NE (52401). 319/363-8161; FAX 319/363-3804.* 275 rms, 16 story. S $79-$105; D $89-$115; each addl $10; suites $175-$325; under 18 free; wknd rates. Crib free. Pet accepted. Parking $3. TV; cable. Indoor pool; whirlpool. Complimentary coffee in rms. Restaurant 6:30 am-11 pm. Rm serv 24 hrs. Bar. Ck-out noon. Convention facilities. Business center. In-rm modem link. Concierge. Free airport transportation. Exercise equipt; weights, bicycles, sauna. Game rm. Cr cds: A, C, D, DS, MC, V.

★ ★ **HAMPTON INN.** *3265 6th St SW (52404). 319/364-8144; FAX 319/399-1877.* 106 rms, 3 story. S, D $79-$99; suite $89-$99; under 18 free. Crib free. TV; cable (premium), VCR avail (movies). Indoor pool; whirlpool. Complimentary continental bkfst. Restaurant adj open 24 hrs. Bar 6-2 am. Ck-out noon. Meeting rms. Business servs avail. Valet serv. Coin lndry. Exercise equipt; bicycle, treadmill. Cr cds: A, C, D, DS, MC, V.

Restaurant

★ ★ **CHARLIES ON THE RIVER.** *415 1st St SE. 319/366-2412.* Hrs: 11 am-2 pm, 5-9:30 pm; Fri, Sat to 10 pm. Closed Sun. Res accepted. Bar. Semi-a la carte: lunch $4.50-$7, dinner $11-$29. Specializes in Cajun dishes, seafood, smoked meats. Cr cds: A, DS, MC, V.

Centerville (F-6)

Founded 1846 **Pop** 5,936 **Elev** 1,010 ft **Area code** 515 **Zip** 52544
Information Chamber of Commerce, 128 N 12th St; 515/437-4102.

Once an important ferry point for Chariton River traffic, Centerville today is an agricultural, industrial and retail center.

What to See and Do

Rathbun Lake. Offers swimming, bathhouse; fishing; boating (ramps, 2 marinas). Picnicking. Camping (electricity, dump station May-Sept; fee). 7 mi NW. Phone 515/647-2464. On N shore is

Honey Creek State Park. On 828 acres. Swimming; fishing; boating. Hiking trails; snowmobiling. Picnicking. Camping (electric hookups, dump station). Scenic overlook. Standard hrs, fees. 12 mi N on IA 5, then 9 1/2 mi W on IA 142, 3 mi SE on unnumbered road. Phone 515/724-3739.

Sharon Bluffs Park. More than 140 acres on the Chariton River; scenic view from high bluffs of clay and shale. Boating (ramp). Hiking trails. Picnicking, shelter. Camping (hookups, fee). (Daily) 3 mi E on IA 2, then 1 mi S. Phone 515/856-8528.

Annual Event

Croatian Fest. Courthouse lawn on city square. Ethnic festival featuring entertainment, dancing and food. Last Sat July.

Motel

✔ ★ **SUPER 8.** *1021 N 18th St, N on IA 5. 515/856-8888.* 41 rms, 2 story. S $38-$47; D $48-$65; each addl $4; suites $55-$85; under 12 free. Crib $5. TV; cable (premium). Complimentary continental bkfst. Restaurant opp 11 am-11 pm. Ck-out 11 am. Meeting rm. Business servs avail. Cr cds: A, C, D, DS, MC, V.

Restaurant

★ **GREEN CIRCLE.** *IA 5S. 515/437-4472.* Hrs: 11 am-2 pm, 4:30-9 pm; Mon, Sat from 4:30 pm; Sun 8 am-2 pm. Closed Dec 25. Res accepted. Bar. Semi-a la carte: lunch, dinner $4.75-$16.95. Specializes in steak, seafood, pasta. Family-owned. Cr cds: A, DS, MC, V.

Chariton (E-5)

(See also Osceola)

Pop 4,616 **Elev** 1,041 ft **Area code** 515 **Zip** 50049

Information Chariton Chamber and Development Corp, PO Box 488; 515/774-4059.

The site of this town was recorded as Chariton by Lewis and Clark after the French corrupted the Native American word "thier-aton," meaning "two rivers."

What to See and Do

John L. Lewis Museum of Mining and Labor. Exhibits; library; theater; mining tools collection. (Mid-Apr-mid-Oct, Tues-Sat; also by appt) 102 Division St, Lucas. Approx 10 mi W on US 34, jct US 65. Phone 515/766-6831. ¢

Lucas County Historical Museum. Restored and furnished 1907 home; rural Puckerbrush school and Otterbein church; John L. Lewis building with library, replica of mine, antique farm machinery. (Memorial Day-Oct, Sun & Wed) 123 17th St at Braden Ave. Phone 515/774-4464. **Free.**

Red Haw State Park. Approx 420 acres with 72-acre lake. Swimming beach; fishing; boating (electric motors only; ramps, rentals). Snowmobiling. Picnicking. Camping (electricity, dump station). Standard hrs, fees. 1 mi E on US 34. Phone 515/774-5632.

Stephens State Forest. Five units totaling 8,466 acres of evergreens and hardwoods; pond. Fishing; boating (electric motors only). Hiking, bridle trails. Snowmobiling. Picnicking. Primitive camping. Standard hrs, fees. 10 mi W on US 34 to Lucas, then 2 mi S on US 65, then W on county road. Phone 515/774-4559.

Wayne County Historical Museum. More than 80,000 artifacts from county's history; replicas of 17 buildings including doctor's office, bank, jail, toy shop and music room; Jesse James exhibit includes the safe he robbed in Corydon; bird and animal exhibits; old machinery and vehicles; genealogy section; Mormon exhibit; collection of 150 creche figures from Italy and Germany. (Mid-Apr-mid-Oct, daily) Approx 18 mi S via IA 14 to IA 2 in Corydon. Phone 515/872-2211. ¢¢

Charles City (B-6)

(See also Mason City, Waverly)

Settled 1852 **Pop** 7,878 **Elev** 1,000 ft **Area code** 515 **Zip** 50616

Information Chamber of Commerce and Area Development, 610 S Grand Ave; 515/228-4234.

One of the first gasoline tractor engines for agricultural and industrial use was produced here.

What to See and Do

Floyd County Historical Society Museum. Includes authentic 1873 drugstore, barber shop, model railroad display, military exhibits, Native American artifacts, doctor and dentist offices, farm equipment, blacksmith shop, country store, newspaper printshop. (May-Sept, daily exc Mon; rest of yr, Tues-Fri; also by appt) 500 Gilbert St on US 218 & 18. Phone 515/228-1099. ¢

Annual Event

Art-A-Fest. Central Park, Main St. Fine arts festival with art and craft displays, ethnic foods, music, drama, dance performances. 3rd wkend Aug.

Motel

★ **HARTWOOD INN.** *1312 Gilbert St. 515/228-4352; FAX 515/228-2672; res: 800/972-2335.* 35 rms, 1 & 2 story. S $33-$45; D $45-$65; each addl $5; under 16 free. Crib free. Pet accepted, some restrictions. TV; cable (premium). Complimentary coffee in rms. Restaurant nearby. Ck-out 11 am. Coin lndry. Cr cds: A, C, D, DS, MC, V.

D 🐾 ✈ 🏊 SC

Restaurant

✔★ **BROOKS.** *102 Cedar Mall. 515/228-7162.* Hrs: 6:30 am-10 pm. Closed Jan 1, Memorial Day, Dec 25. Res accepted. Bar from 4 pm. Semi-a la carte: bkfst $1-$5, lunch $1.50-$6, dinner $3.99-$16.99. Specializes in steak. Diner atmosphere. Cr cds: A, C, D, DS, MC, V.

Cherokee (B-2)

(See also Storm Lake)

Pop 6,026 **Elev** 1,200 ft **Area code** 712 **Zip** 51012 **E-mail** cofccherokee @ncn.net **Web** www.ncn.net/~cofccherokee

Information Chamber of Commerce, 228 W Main St; 712/225-6414.

Center of one of the heaviest cattle feeding and hog raising areas of Iowa, Cherokee is home to many processing and manufacturing plants. The Cherokee Community Center houses a symphony orchestra and an active community theater.

What to See and Do

City Parks. Wescott. Canoeing. Picnicking, playgrounds. Sand volleyball courts. S 2nd St on Little Sioux River. **Spring Lake.** Fishing. Cross-country skiing, ice-skating. Picnicking. Camping (hookups, dump station; fee). S 2nd St. **Gillette.** Swimming pool (Memorial Day-Aug, daily; fee). Tennis. W Bluff St. Phone 712/225-2715.

Sanford Museum and Planetarium. Natural history, science, historical and changing art exhibits. Classes by appt; planetarium programs (last

Sun of month; also by appt). (Daily; closed major hols) 117 E Willow St. Phone 712/225-3922. **Free.**

Annual Events

Cherokee Rodeo. PRCA sanctioned. Early June.

Cherokee County Fair. July.

Motels

★ ★ **BEST WESTERN LA GRANDE HACIENDA.** *1401 N 2nd St. 712/225-5701; FAX 712/225-3926.* 55 rms, 2 story. S $45-$50; D $54-$65; each addl $4; suites $70. TV, cable (premium). VCR avail (movies). Indoor pool; whirlpool. Complimentary bkfst. Restaurant 4-10 pm. Rm serv. Ck-out 11 am. Meeting rm. Business servs avail. In-rm modem link. Sundries. Cr cds: A, C, D, DS, ER, JCB, MC, V.

D 🏊 ✖ 🐾 SC

★ **SUPER 8.** *1400 N 2nd St. 712/225-4278; FAX 712/225-4678.* 34 rms, 2 story. S $38; D $48; suites $41-$47; under 12 free. Crib $5. TV. Complimentary coffee in lobby. Restaurant adj open 24 hrs. Ck-out 11 am. Exercise equipt; bicycles, stair machine. Cr cds: A, C, D, DS, MC, V.

D 🏋 ✈ 🐾 SC

Clarinda (F-3)

(See also Shenandoah)

Settled 1853 **Pop** 5,104 **Elev** 1,012 ft **Area code** 712 **Zip** 51632 **E-mail** cabi@clarinda.heartland.net

Information Association of Business & Industry, 200 S 15th St; 712/542-2166.

Clarinda is the birthplace of Big Band-era legend Glenn Miller. It's also where, at the turn of the century, rural school teacher Jessie Field Shambaugh started the Boys' Corn Clubs and Girls' Home Clubs, which later became the 4-H movement.

What to See and Do

Lake of Three Fires State Park. Park has 691 acres with 97-acre lake. Swimming; fishing; electric boating (ramps, rentals). Hiking, bridle trails. Snowmobiling. Picnicking. Camping (electricity, dump station), cabins. Standard hrs, fees. 18 mi E on IA 2 to Bedford, then 3 mi NE on IA 49. Phone 712/523-2700.

Nodaway Valley Historical Museum. Exhibits on history of Nodaway River area including agricultural displays, artifacts from early days of 4-H movement and Glenn Miller memorabilia. Visits to the nearby Glenn Miller Birthplace Home (by appt only; addl fee) can be arranged through the museum. (Tues-Sun afternoons) 1600 S 16th St. Phone 712/542-3073. ¢

Annual Events

Glenn Miller Festival. Honoring his music and birthplace. 2nd wkend June.

Page County Fair. Last wk July.

Southwest Iowa Band Jamboree. High school bands from 3 states participate. 1st Sat Oct.

Motel

★ **CELEBRITY INN.** *US 2 & 71. 712/542-5178.* 36 rms. S $32-$38; D $40-$48; under 16 free. Crib $4. TV; cable. Complimentary coffee. Restaurant opp 7 am-11 pm. Ck-out 11 am. Meeting rms. Cr cds: A, MC, V.

Restaurant

★ ★ **J. BRUNER'S.** *1100 E Washington. 712/542-3364.* Hrs: 5-10:30 .pm; Sun 11:30 am-2 pm. Closed Mon; most major hols. Bar 4:30-11:30 pm. Semi-a la carte: lunch, dinner $9-$35. Child's meals. Specializes in steak, seafood, onion rings. Country French decor. Cr cds: A, DS, MC, V.

Clear Lake (B-5)

(See also Garner, Mason City)

Settled 1851 **Pop** 8,183 **Elev** 1,236 ft **Area code** 515 **Zip** 50428

Information Chamber of Commerce, 205 Main Ave, PO Box 188; 515/357-2159.

Scene of a Native American uprising in 1854, Clear Lake rivaled Mason City (see) for honors as the county seat but lost out because it was not in the geographic center of the area. Taking its name from the nearby lake, Clear Lake is an ancient Native American fishing and hunting ground. Today it is a popular, modern resort town.

What to See and Do

State parks. Swimming; fishing; boating (ramps). Snowmobiling. Picnicking. Camping (electric hookups). Standard hrs, fees.

Clear Lake. Park has 102 acres with 3,684-acre lake. Picnicking. Also dump station. 2 mi S on IA 107. Phone 515/357-4212.

McIntosh Woods. Also nature trails in this 62-acre park. On N shore of lake, off US 18. Phone 515/829-3847.

⭐ **Surf Ballroom.** Site of Buddy Holly's last concert before Holly, Ritchie Valens and J.P. Richardson (the Big Bopper) died in local plane crash Feb 2, 1959. Ballroom features varied entertainment wkends; plaque and monument outside commemorate the musicians; museum of musical history. Tours avail. 460 North Shore Dr. Phone 515/357-6151.

Motels

✓★ **BUDGET INN.** *1306 N 25th St, 1 blk W of I-35 on US 18 exit 194. 515/357-8700; FAX 515/357-8811.* 60 rms, 2 story. S $36.95; D $42.95; each addl $4; under 16 free. Crib free. Pet accepted. TV; cable (premium). Pool. Playground. Restaurant adj open 24 hrs. Ck-out noon. Meeting rms. Sundries. Cr cds: A, C, D, DS, MC, V.

★ **HEARTLAND INN.** *1603 South Shore Dr, I-35 exit 193. 515/357-5123; FAX 515/357-2228; res: 800/334-3277.* 18 rms, 2 story. June-Aug: S, D $75-$125; children free; lower rates rest of yr. Crib free. TV; cable. Restaurant nearby. Ck-out 11 am. In-rm modem link. Some refrigerators. Some balconies. On lake; dock. Cr cds: A, C, D, DS, MC, V.

✓★ **SUPER 8.** *1 mi SE on I-35, 1 blk E of exit 193, near Mason City Municipal Airport. 515/357-7521; FAX 515/357-5999.* 60 rms, 3 story. No elvtr. S $35.88; D $39.88-$40.88; each addl $2. Crib $2. TV; cable. Complimentary continental bkfst. Restaurant adj open 24 hrs. Ck-out 11 am. Sundries. Cr cds: A, C, D, DS, MC, V.

Motor Hotel

★ ★ **BEST WESTERN HOLIDAY MOTOR LODGE.** *1 mi E on US 18, 1 blk W of I-35, near Mason City Municipal Airport. 515/357-5253; FAX 515/357-8153.* 144 rms, 5 story. S $47.95-$57.95; D $55.95-$59.95; each addl $8; suites $66.95-$116.90; under 12 free. Crib free. Pet accepted. TV; cable. Indoor pool; whirlpool, sauna, poolside serv. Complimentary bkfst. Restaurant 6 am-10 pm; dining rm from 5 pm. Rm serv. Bar 4 pm-2 am. Ck-out 11 am. Valet serv. Meeting rm. Sundries. Free airport transportation. Cr cds: A, C, D, DS, MC, V.

Clinton (D-9)

Founded 1855 **Pop** 29,201 **Elev** 600 ft **Area code** 319 **Zip** 52732

Information Convention & Visitors Bureau, 333 4th Ave S, PO Box 1024; 319/242-5702 or 800/828-5702.

Agriculture, industry and business are blended in this city of wide streets and modern buildings on the Mississippi River. First called New York, it was later renamed after DeWitt Clinton, former governor of New York. Once the largest lumber-producing city in the world, Clinton today is the home of a diverse group of industries. It is also the seat of a county famous for its prime beef production.

What to See and Do

Eagle Point Park. Flower gardens; picnicking (shelters), lodge; playground, observation tower; children's nature center; petting zoo. (Apr-mid-Nov, daily) On US 67 at N city limits, overlooking the Mississippi. Phone 319/243-1260. **Free.**

Riverview Park. Swimming pool (Memorial Day-Labor Day, daily; fee); marina, boat ramp; lighted tennis courts, fountain; playground, recreational trail, baseball stadium, horseshoes, picnicking; RV parking (fee). (Daily) 6th Ave N, on the Mississippi. Phone 319/243-1260. **Free.** Also here are

Lillian Russell Theatre. Aboard the paddlewheel showboat *The City of Clinton.* Musicals and comedies. (June-Aug) Phone 319/242-6760 for schedule and fee information.

Mississippi Belle II. Offers yr-round casino gambling along the Mississippi River. Entertainment. Concession. Showboat Landing. For schedule and fee information phone 319/243-9000 or 800/457-9975.

Annual Events

Civil War Reenactment. Eagle Point Park. Battle for Burnside Bridge; Military Ball with period music and costumes. May 8-10.

Riverboat Days. Pageant, events, tractor pulls, entertainment, shows, carnival. Early July.

Motels

★ ★ ★ **BEST WESTERN FRONTIER MOTOR INN.** *2300 Lincolnway, at jct US 30, 67W. 319/242-7112; FAX 319/242-7117.* 117 rms, 1-2 story. S $46-$66; D $54-$72; each addl $6; suites $89-$135; under 12 free. Crib $6. Pet accepted, some restrictions. TV; cable (premium). Indoor pool; whirlpool. Restaurant 6 am-9 pm. Rm serv. Bar 11:30-2 am; closed Sun. Ck-out noon. Meeting rms. Business servs avail. Valet serv. Sundries. Exercise equipt; bicycle, treadmill. X-country ski 5 mi. Some refrigerators. Cr cds: A, C, D, DS, MC, V.

★ ★ **RAMADA INN.** *1522 Lincoln Way. 319/243-8841; FAX 319/242-6202.* 103 rms, 2 story, 10 suites. S $54; D $60; each addl $6; suites $80-$90; under 18 free; package plans. Crib free. Pet accepted, some restrictions. TV; cable (premium), VCR avail. Complimentary coffee in lobby. Indoor pool. Rm serv. Bar 11-2 am. Ck-out noon. Meeting rms. Business servs avail. Game rm. Some refrigerators, microwaves. Cr cds: A, C, D, DS, MC, V.

✔★ **SUPER 8.** *1711 Lincoln Way. 319/242-8870; FAX 319/242-8870, ext. 177.* 63 rms, 3 story. No elvtr. S $43.98; D $52.98; under 12 free. Crib $2. TV, cable (premium). Complimentary coffee in lobby. Restaurant nearby. Ck-out 11 am. Business servs avail. Sundries. Cr cds: A, C, D, DS, MC, V.

★ **TRAVELODGE.** *302 Sixth Ave S, at 3rd St. 319/243-4730; FAX 319/243-4732.* 51 rms, 2 story. S $38; D $48; each addl $5; under 17 free. Crib $5. Pet accepted. Pool. Complimentary coffee. Restaurant adj 11 am-8 pm. Ck-out 11 am. Some refrigerators. Some private patios. Cr cds: A, C, D, DS, ER, JCB, MC, V.

Council Bluffs (E-2)

(See also Omaha, NE)

Settled 1824 **Pop** 54,315 **Elev** 986 ft **Area code** 712 **Web** www.councilbluffsiowa.com
Information Convention & Visitors Bureau, 7 N 6th St, PO Box 1565, 51502; 712/325-1000 or 800/228-6878.

Across the Missouri River from Omaha, Nebraska, and at an intersection for five railroad lines, Council Bluffs is a key trading center and busy manufacturing town. The city sits on bluffs above the river, but newer parts have spilled over onto the riverbanks. Lewis and Clark camped near here in 1804, as did generations of fur traders. First called Hart's Bluff, the community took the name Kanesville when Mormons settled here and built a thriving community. Population reached nearly 8,000 but dropped to 1,000 when the Mormons left en masse to join Brigham Young in Salt Lake City, Utah. The town was renamed Council Bluffs, as the whole bluff area along the Missouri had long been known. By 1870, eight railroads cut through Council Bluffs, indicating the direction of its future development. Today, the Loess Hills Scenic Byway (see MISSOURI VALLEY) passes through the area.

What to See and Do

Golden Spike. Erected in 1939, this 56-ft golden concrete spike commemorates the junction of the Union Pacific and Central Pacific railroads in Council Bluffs. 21st St & 9th Ave.

Historic General Dodge House (1869). Restored Victorian home built by Grenville M. Dodge, chief construction engineer for Union Pacific Railroad and general in Civil War. Guided tours (daily exc Mon; closed most major hols; also Jan). 605 3rd St. Phone 712/322-2406. ¢¢

Historic Pottawattamie County Jail (1885). This unique three-story rotary jail is sometimes referred to as the "human squirrel cage" or "lazy Susan jail." (Apr-Sept, or by appt; closed hols) 226 Pearl St. Phone 712/323-2509. ¢¢

Lake Manawa State Park. More than 1,500-acre park with 660-acre lake. "Dream Playground" designed by and for children. Swimming, supervised beach; fishing; boating (ramps, rentals). Hiking trails. Bicycle trails. Snowmobiling. Picnicking. Camping (electricity). Standard hrs, fees. 1 mi S on IA 192. Phone 712/366-0220.

Lewis and Clark Monument. Shaft of native stone on bluffs depicts Lewis and Clark holding council with Oto and Missouri. Rainbow Dr.

Lincoln Monument. Granite shaft marks spot from which Lincoln designated the town as the eastern terminus of the Union Pacific Railroad. Lafayette & Oakland Aves.

Mormon Trail Memorial. Huge boulder marks passage of Mormons out of city on trek to Utah. Bayliss Park, Pearl St & 1st Ave.

National Western Historical Trails Center. Explore preserved and restored sites along Lewis & Clark, Mormon Pioneer, California and Oregon trails. Discover history of Native American tribes and trails heritage in the region. Guided group tours (by appt; fee). (Daily; closed most major hols) Jct I-80 & S 24th St. Phone Convention & Visitors Bureau for tours and information. **Free.**

RailsWest Railroad Museum. Historic Rock Island depot (1899); railroad memorabilia, HO gauge model trains on display. (Memorial Day-Labor Day, daily exc Wed; rest of yr, by appt) 16th Ave & South Main St. Phone 712/323-5182 or 712/322-0612. ¢¢

Ruth Anne Dodge Memorial. Commissioned by the daughters of G.M. Dodge in memory of their mother, this bronze statue of an angel is the work of Daniel Chester French. N 2nd & Lafayette Aves.

Annual Event

Renaissance Faire of the Midlands. Renaissance period crafts, entertainment, concessions; jousting contests, street performers. Phone 402/330-8446 or 712/328-4992. June 12-14.

Motels

★ **BEST WESTERN-METRO.** *3537 W Broadway (51501).* 712/328-3171. 89 rms, 2 story, 43 suites. Feb-Nov: S $59-$99; D $69-$109; each addl $6; under 18 free; lower rates rest of yr. Crib avail. Pet accepted. TV; cable (premium). Complimentary continental bkfst. Complimentary coffee in rms. Restaurant 6 am-10 pm. Ck-out noon. Meeting rms. Business servs avail. In-rm modem link. Free airport transportation. Indoor pool. Game rm. Refrigerators; microwave in suites. Cr cds: A, C, D, DS, MC, V.

★ **ECONO LODGE.** *3208 S 7th St (51501).* 712/366-9699; FAX 712/366-6129. 60 rms, 3 story. No elvtr. May-Oct: S, D $42-$49; each addl $5; suites $90-$99; under 16 free; lower rates rest of yr. Crib $5. TV; cable (premium). Complimentary continental bkfst. Restaurant adj open 24 hrs. Ck-out noon. Coin lndry. Meeting rms. Business servs avail. Valet serv. Exercise equipt; bicycles, treadmill. Refrigerator in suites. Cr cds: A, C, D, DS, ER, MC, V.

★ **FAIRFIELD INN BY MARRIOTT.** *520 30th Ave (51501).* 712/366-1330. 62 rms, 3 story. May-Sept: S, D $59.95-$79.95; under 18 free; higher rates special events; lower rates rest of yr. Crib free. TV; cable (premium), VCR avail. Complimentary continental bkfst. Restaurant opp 6 am-10 pm. Ck-out noon. Meeting rms. Business servs avail. Indoor pool; whirlpool. Cr cds: A, D, DS, MC, V.

★ **HEARTLAND INN.** *1000 Woodbury Ave (51503), I-80 exit 5. 712/322-8400; FAX 712/322-4022.* 89 rms, 2 story. S $51-$61; D $59-$66; under 16 free. Crib avail. TV; cable (premium). Complimentary continental bkfst. Restaurant opp 6-3 am. Ck-out 11 am. Meeting rm. Business servs avail. Sauna. Whirlpool. Microwaves avail. Cr cds: A, C, D, DS, MC, V.

✔★★ **WESTERN INN.** *Madison Ave & I-80 (51503), exit 5. 712/322-4499; res: 800/322-1842.* 51 rms, 2 story. S $46; D $54; each addl $7; suites $69.95-$88; under 12 free. Crib free. TV; cable (premium). Indoor pool; whirlpool. Restaurant adj 6 am-midnight. Ck-out 11 am. Business servs avail. Cr cds: A, DS, MC, V.

Hotel

★ ★ ★ **AMERISTAR CASINO.** *2200 River Rd (51501).* 712/328-8888; FAX 712/328-8882. Web www.ameristars.com. 160 rms, 5 story. S, D, suites $65-$295; wkend plans; higher rates special events. Crib free. TV; cable, VCR avail. Restaurant open 24 hrs. Rm serv to 11 pm. Bar 11-2 am. Ck-out noon. Meeting rms. Business servs avail. Gift shop. Exercise equipt; stair machine, weight machine, sauna. Indoor/outdoor pool; whirlpool. Supervised child's activities; 6 wks-12 yrs. Game rm. Bathrm phones; some in-rm whirlpools. Cr cds: A, C, D, DS, MC, V.

Creston (E-4)

Founded 1869 **Pop** 7,911 **Elev** 1,314 ft **Area code** 515 **Zip** 50801
Information Chamber of Commerce, 116 W Adams, PO Box 471; 515/782-7021.

In the heart of Iowa's cattle country, Creston has long been a railroad town and trading mart for the surrounding farmlands.

What to See and Do

Green Valley State Park. The 991-acre park, amid rolling hills, has a 428-acre lake. Swimming; fishing; boating (ramps, rentals). Snowmobiling. Picnicking. Camping (electricity, dump station). Standard hrs, fees. 2 1/2 mi N off IA 25. Phone 515/782-5131.

Annual Event

Creston Hot-Air Balloon Days. Municipal Airport on S Cherry St Rd. Three balloon races; parade, marching band contest, art & book fairs. Sept 19-20.

Motels

✔ ★ **BERNING MOTOR INN.** *301 W Adams St.* 515/782-7001; FAX 515/782-7415. 48 rms, 2 story. S $28-$35; D $35-$40; each addl $5; under 10 free. Crib $1. TV; cable (premium). Restaurant 5:30 am-10:30 pm; Sun to 2 pm. Bar 11 am-midnight; Sun to 2 pm. Ck-out 11 am. Meeting rms. Cr cds: A, MC, V.

★ **SUPER 8.** *804 W Taylor St.* 515/782-6541. 83 rms, 2 story. S $38-$43; D $45-$50; each addl $2. Crib $2. TV; cable (premium). Complimentary coffee in lobby. Restaurant adj open 24 hrs. Ck-out 11 am. Business servs avail. In-rm modem link. Cr cds: A, D, DS, MC, V.

Davenport (D-9)

(See also Muscatine)

Founded 1808 **Pop** 95,333 **Elev** 589 ft **Area code** 319 **E-mail** cvb@quadcities.com **Web** quadcities.com
Information Quad Cities Convention & Visitors Bureau, 102 S Harrison St, 52801; 309/788-7800 or 800/747-7800.

Stretching five miles along the Mississippi River, Davenport is part of the Quad Cities metropolitan area, which also includes Bettendorf, Iowa, and Moline and Rock Island, Illinois. Principally a regional retail center, Davenport also produces machinery, agricultural goods and food products. Davenport's Palmer College of Chiropractic is the fountainhead of that practice in the US. The city is named for its founder, a former US Army officer who explored this bank of the river while stationed on Rock Island. The state's first railroad came here when tracks were put across the Mississippi at this point in 1854. In pre-Civil War days, Dred Scott claimed the town as his home, and John Brown provisioned here before his attack on Harpers Ferry.

What to See and Do

Casino Rock Island/Jumers Riverboat. Departs from Rock Island, IL. Phone 800/477-7747.

Davenport Museum of Art. Rotating displays from permanent collection of 19th- and 20th-century paintings, Mexican-colonial, Oriental, native Haitian art collections; works by regional artists Grant Wood and Thomas Hart Benton. (Daily exc Mon; closed most hols) 1737 W 12th St. Phone 319/326-7804. **Donation.**

Parks.

Fejervary Park. Swimming pool, picnic areas, playground (Apr-Oct). A zoo in the park features Monkey Island and North American hoofed animal exhibit (late May-early Sept, Wed-Sun). 1800 W 12th St. Phone 319/326-7812. **Free.**

Scott County Park. More than 1,000 acres with pioneer village, nature center. Swimming (fee), fishing. Ball fields. 18-hole golf. Skiing, tobogganing, ice-skating. Picnicking. Camping, trailer sites (fee; electricity addl). (Daily) 8 mi N on US 61, follow signs. Phone 319/381-1114.

President Riverboat Casino. Departs from River Drive, between Centennial and Government bridges. Phone 800/BOAT-711.

Putnam Museum of History & Natural Science. Permanent and changing exhibits of regional history, natural science and world cultures. (Tues-Sat, also Sun afternoons; closed major hols) 1717 W 12th St. Phone 319/324-1933. ¢¢

Walnut Grove Pioneer Village. Three-acre walk-through site contains 10 historic buildings moved from various locations in the county. Visitors can explore a blacksmith shop, schoolhouse, pioneer family home; also St Anne's Church. (Apr-Oct, daily) 8 mi N on US 61, Long Grove. Phone 319/285-9903. **Free.**

Annual Event

Bix Beiderbecke Jazz Festival. Riverfront at LeClaire Park. Honors Davenport-born musician. Contact PO Box 3688, 52808; 319/324-7170. Last full wkend July.

Motels

★ ★ ★ **BEST WESTERN STEEPLEGATE INN.** *100 W 76th St (52806).* 319/386-6900; FAX 319/388-9955. 121 rms, 2 story. S $67-$72; D $74-$80; each addl $6; suites $125-$150; under 12 free. Crib $4. Pet accepted; $3. TV; cable (premium). Indoor pool; whirlpool. Restaurant 6 am-9 pm; Fri, Sat to 10 pm. Rm serv. Bar 11-2 am; entertainment. Ck-out noon. Business servs avail. Valet serv. Free airport, bus depot transportation. Exercise equipt; bicycle, treadmill. Game rm. Some refrigerators, microwaves. Cr cds: A, C, D, DS, MC, V.

★ **COMFORT INN.** *7222 Northwest Blvd (52806), just S of I-80 at exit 292.* 319/391-8222; FAX 319/391-1595. 89 rms, 2 story. S $45.50; D $54.50; each addl $4. Pet accepted, some restrictions; $20 refundable & $2/day. TV; cable (premium), VCR avail. Complimentary continental bkfst. Restaurant adj 6 am-10 pm. Ck-out 11 am. Business servs avail. Exercise equipt; weight machine, stair machine. Microwaves avail. Cr cds: A, C, D, DS, ER, JCB, MC, V.

★ **DAYS INN.** *101 W 65th St (52806).* 319/388-9999. 64 rms, 2 story, 7 suites. Apr-Sept: S $40-$60; D $45-$70; each addl $5; suites $60-$109; under 13 free; lower rates rest of yr. Crib free. TV; cable (premium), VCR avail. Indoor pool; whirlpool. Complimentary continental bkfst. Restaurant nearby. Ck-out 11 am. Meeting rm. Business servs avail.

In-rm modem link. Exercise equipt; weights, bicycle, sauna. Game rm. Some refrigerators. Cr cds: A, C, D, DS, MC, V.

D ⊠ 🏃 ⊠ 🔥 SC

★ **DAYS INN.** *3202 E Kimberley Rd (52807), I-74 exit Spruce Hills Dr.* 319/355-1190. 65 rms, 2 story. Apr-Sept: S $40-$85; D $44-$85; under 13 free; lower rates rest of yr. Crib free. Pet accepted, some restrictions. TV; cable (premium). Indoor pool; whirlpool. Complimentary continental bkfst. Restaurant nearby. Ck-out 11 am. Meeting rms. Business servs avail. Valet serv. Game rm. Cr cds: A, D, DS, MC, V.

D ✊ ⊠ ⊠ 🔥 SC

✔ ★ **EXEL INN.** *6310 Brady St N (52806).* 319/386-6350; FAX 319/388-1548. 103 rms, 2 story. S $37.99; D $44.99; each addl $5; under 18 free. Crib free. Pet accepted. TV; cable. Complimentary continental bkfst. Ck-out noon. In-rm modem link. Valet serv. Cr cds: A, C, D, DS, MC, V.

D ✊ ⊠ ⊠ 🔥 SC

★ ★ **FAIRFIELD INN BY MARRIOTT.** *3206 E Kimberly Rd (52807).* 319/355-2264. 62 rms, 3 story. S, D $55.95-$63.95; each addl $6; under 18 free; higher rates Bix Jazz Festival; lower rates rest of yr. Crib free. TV; cable (premium). Indoor pool; whirlpool. Complimentary continental bkfst. Restaurant nearby. Ck-out 11 am. Meeting rms. Business servs avail. Sundries. Valet serv. Game rm. Refrigerator in suites. Cr cds: A, C, D, DS, MC, V.

D ⊠ ⊠ 🔥 SC

★ ★ **HAMPTON INN.** *3330 E Kimberly Rd (52807).* 319/359-3921; FAX 319/359-1912. 132 rms, 2 story. S $52-$59; D $54-$64; under 18 free. Crib free. Pet accepted, some restrictions. TV; cable (premium). Indoor pool. Complimentary continental bkfst. Ck-out noon. Business servs avail. In-rm modem link. Bellhops. Free airport transportation. Exercise equipt; bicycle, treadmill. Cr cds: A, C, D, DS, MC, V.

D ✊ ⊠ 🏃 ⊠ 🔥 SC

✔ ★ **HEARTLAND INN.** *6605 N Brady (52806).* 319/386-8336; FAX 319/386-6005; res: 800/334-3277. 86 rms, 3 story. S, D $47-$66; each addl $9; suites $110-$140. Crib free. Pet accepted. TV; cable (premium). Indoor pool. Complimentary continental bkfst. Restaurant adj 6 am-11 pm. Ck-out 11 am. Meeting rm. Business servs avail. Sundries. Rec rm. Cr cds: A, C, D, DS, MC, V.

D ✊ ⊠ ⊠ 🔥 SC

★ ★ **HOLIDAY INN.** *5202 Brady St (52806).* 319/391-1230; FAX 319/391-6715. 295 rms, 2-3 story. S $58-$75; D $65-$85; under 19 free. Crib free. TV; cable (premium). Indoor pool. Restaurant 6 am-1 pm, 5-9:30 pm. Rm serv from 7 am. Bar 4 pm-midnight. Ck-out noon. Coin lndry. Meeting rms. Business servs avail. Bellhops. Sundries. Gift shop. Free airport transportation. Exercise equipt; treadmill, stair machine. Miniature golf. Game rm. Cr cds: A, C, D, DS, JCB, MC, V.

D ⊠ 🏃 ⊠ 🔥 SC

★ **SUPER 8.** *410 E 65th St (52807).* 319/388-9810; FAX 319/388-9810, ext. 198. 61 rms, 2 story. Apr-Sept: S $39.88; D $46.88-$58.88; each addl $5; suites $50.88-$52.88; under 12 free; higher rates: jazz festival, special events; lower rates rest of yr. Crib free. Pet accepted. TV; cable (premium). Complimentary continental bkfst. Restaurant adj 11 am-10 pm; Sat, Sun from 8 am. Ck-out 11 am. Business servs avail. Microwaves avail. Cr cds: A, C, D, DS, MC, V.

D ✊ ⊠ 🔥 SC

Motor Hotel

★ ★ **BEST WESTERN RIVERVIEW INN.** *227 Le Claire St (52801).* 319/324-1921; FAX 319/324-9621. 150 rms, 6 story. S $55; D $59; each addl $6; studio rms $55-$80. Crib $5. TV; cable (premium). 2 pools, 1 indoor; whirlpool. Complimentary continental bkfst. Coffee in rms. Restaurant 6 am-2 pm, 5-10 pm. Rm serv. Bar 3 pm-1 am. Ck-out 11 am. Coin lndry. Meeting rms. Business center. In-rm modem link. Valet serv.

Sauna. Game rm. Rec rm. Refrigerators. Some rms with view of the Mississippi. Cr cds: A, C, D, DS, MC, V.

D ⊠ ⊠ ⊠ SC 🏃

Hotel

★ ★ **BLACKHAWK.** *200 E Third St (52801).* 319/328-6000; FAX 319/328-6047. 189 rms, 11 story. S $61-$69; D $69-$75; each addl $10; suites $79-$95; under 12 free. Crib free. TV; cable (premium). Restaurant 6 am-2 pm, 5-10 pm. Bar 11-2 am. Ck-out noon. Meeting rms. Business servs avail. Gift shops. Barber, beauty shop. Free airport transportation. Exercise equipt; weights, treadmill. Microwaves avail. Cr cds: A, C, D, DS, MC, V.

D 🏃 ⊠ 🔥 SC

Inn

★ ★ **FULTON'S LANDING.** *1206 E River Dr (52803).* 319/322-4069; FAX 319/322-8186. 5 rms, 2 story. S, D $60-$125. Crib $10. TV; VCR avail. Complimentary full bkfst. Complimentary coffee in rms. Ck-out noon. Antique furnishings; overlooks Mississippi. Cr cds: A, MC, V.

⊠ 🔥

Restaurants

★ ★ **CHRISTIE'S.** *2207 E 12th St, exit I-74, S on US 67 to the Village of East Davenport.* 319/323-2822. Hrs: 11 am-2 pm, 5-9 pm; Sun-Thurs from 5 pm. Closed Mon; major hols. Res accepted. French, continental menu. Serv bar. Semi-a la carte: dinner $15.95-$21.95. Specialties: Veal Marsala, filet mignon, lamb. Intimate dining in restored 1910 bungalow; some leaded-glass windows, antiques. Cr cds: A, C, D, DS, MC, V.

✔ ★ **GRAMMA'S KITCHEN.** *(I-80, Walcott) exit 284.* 319/284-5055. Hrs: 6 am-10 pm; Nov-Apr to 9 pm; Sun 7 am-10 pm. Closed Jan 1, Thanksgiving, Dec 25. Semi-a la carte: bkfst $2.60-$6.25, lunch $4.95-$6.95, dinner $5.99-$9.95. Specialties: homemade pot pies, chicken-fried steak, apple dumplings. Salad bar. Country decor; crafts, collectibles displayed. Gift shop. Cr cds: A, D, DS, MC, V.

D

✔ ★ **IOWA MACHINE SHED.** *7250 Northwest Blvd (52806).* 319/391-2427. Hrs: 6 am-10 pm; Sun 7 am-9 pm. Closed some major hols. Bar. Semi-a la carte: bkfst $2-$7, lunch $3.50-$10, dinner $5-$20. Child's meals. Specializes in stuffed pork loin, beef. Salad bar. Own desserts. "Down-on-the-farm" atmosphere; country artifacts. Cr cds: A, D, DS, MC, V.

D

★ ★ **THUNDER BAY GRILLE.** *6511 Brady St (52806).* 319/386-2722. Hrs: 11 am-10 pm; Fri to 11 pm; Sat 8 am-11 pm; Sun 8 am-9 pm; Sat, Sun brunch to 1:30 pm. Closed Jan 1, Thanksgiving, Dec 25. Res accepted. Bar. Semi-a la carte: lunch $4.99-$6.99, dinner $4.99-$19.95. Sat, Sun brunch $6.99. Child's meals. Specializes in fish, steak, seafood. Bi-level dining. Cr cds: A, DS, MC, V.

D

Decorah (A-7)

Pop 8,063 **Elev** 904 ft **Area code** 319 **Zip** 52101 **E-mail** decorah@salamander.com **Web** www.salamander.com/~decorah

Information Decorah Area Chamber of Commerce, 111 Winnebago St; 319/382-3990 or 800/463-4692.

A center of Norwegian culture in the US, Decorah is the seat of Winneshiek County, one of the state's most picturesque areas. Within a short distance are Siewers and Twin Springs and towering spires of limestone along the Upper Iowa River. The town is named for a Native American chief who aided settlers during the Black Hawk War.

What to See and Do

Antonin Dvorak Memorial. Tablet on huge boulder is monument to famed Czech composer who lived here one summer. Titles of some of his outstanding works are inscribed on base of monument. In Spillville.

Bily Clocks. Collection of elaborately-carved musical clocks with moving figures, some 9 ft tall. (May-Oct, daily; phone ahead for other dates) 9 mi S on US 52, then 4 mi W on IA 325 in Spillville. Phone 319/562-3569 or 319/562-3627. ¢¢

Fort Atkinson State Preserve. Fort built in 1840 as federal protection for the Winnebago from the Sac, Fox and Sioux. Restored buildings include barracks, blockhouse, magazine. Museum exhibits Native American and pioneer relics. (Mid-May-mid-Oct, daily) 16 mi SW via US 52, IA 24. Phone 319/425-4161. **Free.**

Seed Savers Heritage Farm. 173-acre farm features displays of endangered vegetables, apples, grapes and Ancient White Park Cattle. Preservation Gardens house 15,000 rare vegetable varieties; Cultural History Garden displays old-time flowers and vegetables. Historic Orchard has 650 19th-century apples and 160 hardy grapes. Meeting Center; gift shop. (Daily) 3076 N Winn Rd, 6 mi N of town off US 52. Phone 319/382-5990. ¢

Upper Iowa River. Popular for canoeing and tubing. Phone 800/463-4692 for canoe, tube rental information.

⭐ **Vesterheim, the Norwegian-American Museum.** Extensive exhibits relate history of Norwegians in America and Norway. Pioneer objects, handicrafts, ship gallery, arts displayed in complex of 13 historic buildings; restored mill. (Daily; closed some major hols) 502 W Water St. Phone 319/382-9681. ¢¢

Annual Event

Nordic Fest. Parades, dancing, pioneer tool display; demonstrations in cooking, needlework and rosemaling. Phone 800/382-FEST. Last full wkend July.

Motels

⭐ **HEARTLAND INN.** 705 Commerce Dr. 319/382-2269; FAX 319/382-4767. 59 rms, 2 story. S, D $45-$55; each addl $7; suites $65-$110; under 16 free. Crib free. TV; cable. Complimentary continental bkfst. Restaurant nearby. Ck-out 11 am. Meeting rms. Sundries. Valet serv. Exercise equipt; bicycles, stair machine, sauna. Cr cds: A, C, D, DS, MC, V.

D 🏃 ✈ 🐾 SC

✔⭐ **SUPER 8.** 810 IA 9 East, 1½ mi E on IA 9 at jct US 52. 319/382-8771. 60 rms, 2 story. S $36.88-$38.88; D $45.88-$47.88; each addl $4; suites $52.88-$70.88. Crib $2. Pet accepted. TV; cable (premium), VCR avail. Complimentary continental bkfst. Restaurant nearby. Ck-out 11 am. Coin lndry. Meeting rm. Business servs avail. In-rm modem link. Cr cds: A, C, D, DS, MC, V.

D ✔ ✈ 🐾 SC

Restaurant

✔⭐ **STONE HEARTH INN.** 811 Commerce Dr (IA 9 & US 52). 319/382-4614. Hrs: 11 am-9:30 pm; Fri, Sat to 11 pm; Sun brunch 10:30 am-2 pm. Closed most major hols. Res accepted. Bar. Semi-a la carte: lunch $3.50-$5.50, dinner $5.95-$16.95. Sun brunch $6.95. Child's meals. Specializes in prime rib. Casual decor. Cr cds: A, DS, MC, V.

Denison (C-2)

Founded 1855 **Pop** 6,604 **Elev** 1,280 ft **Area code** 712 **Zip** 51442 **E-mail** chamber@denisonia.frontiercomm.net **Web** elwood.pionet.net /~crawdvia/

Information Chamber of Commerce, 109 N 14th St; 712/263-5621.

J.W. Denison, an agent for the Providence Western Land Co and a Baptist minister, came to this area in 1855 and gave the new town his name. The following year the town survived raids by Native Americans. In 1933, Denison survived martial law, brought about when farmers nearly rioted during land foreclosures triggered by the Great Depression. Denison is the seat of Crawford County.

What to See and Do

Yellow Smoke Park. A 320-acre recreation area with swimming beach; fishing; boating (no power boats). Hiking. Winter sports. Picknicking. Camping (fee). (Daily) 1 mi E on US 30, then ½ mi N on county road. Phone 712/263-2070. **Free.**

Annual Event

Donna Reed Festival for the Performing Arts. Special workshops in the performing arts conducted by professionals from Hollywood and around the nation. Parade. Golf tourney. 10K run. Saturday night gala. Street fair. Phone 712/263-3334. Late June.

Motel

✔⭐ **BEST WESTERN DENISON'S INN.** 502 Boyer Valley Rd. 712/263-5081; FAX 712/263-2898. 40 rms, 2 story. S $30-$34; D $38-$46. Crib $4. TV; cable. Continental bkfst. Restaurant nearby. Ck-out 11 am. Cr cds: A, C, D, DS, MC, V.

✈ 🐾 SC

Restaurant

✔⭐ **CRONK'S.** 812 4th Ave S (US 30 & 59). 712/263-4191. Hrs: 6 am-10 pm; Fri, Sat to 11 pm; Sun 11:30 am-2 pm, 5-9 pm. Closed Dec 25. Res accepted. Bar to midnight. Semi-a la carte: bkfst $1.95-$4.95, lunch $1.95-$5.95, dinner $1.95-$9.95. Sun brunch $6.95. Specializes in steak. Salad bar. Casual decor. Cr cds: A, MC, V.

D

Des Moines (D-5)

(See also Indianola)

Founded 1843 **Pop** 193,187 **Elev** 803 ft **Area code** 515 **Web** www.desmoinesia.com

Information Greater Des Moines Convention & Visitors Bureau, Two Ruan Center, Suite 222, 601 Locust St, 50309; 515/286-4960 or 800/451-2625.

Des Moines (De-MOYN) is the capital and largest city in the state. This metropolis is the industrial, retail, financial and political hub of Iowa. A military garrison established Fort Des Moines at a point on the Raccoon and Des Moines rivers in 1843. Two years later the territory was opened to settlers, and the town of Fort Des Moines was chosen as the county seat. The word "fort" was abandoned when the community became a city in 1857; the next year it became the state capital. Today more than 60 insurance companies have their home offices here.

Transportation

Des Moines Intl Airport: Information 515/256-5100; lost and found 515/256-5050; weather 515/270-2614; cash machines, Terminal Bldg.

Car Rental Agencies: See IMPORTANT TOLL-FREE NUMBERS.

Public Transportation: Buses (Metropolitan Transit Authority), phone 515/283-8100.

What to See and Do

Adventureland Park. Amusement park with more than 100 rides, shows and attractions. Features the Dragon, double-looping roller coaster, Tornado roller coaster, Outlaw roller coaster; Raging River, whitewater rapids; live musical entertainment. (June-Aug, daily; May & Sept, wkends) NE on US 65 at jct I-80. Phone 515/266-2121. Admission includes all rides and shows. ¢¢¢¢

Aquarium Center. More than 300 species of exotic fish, sea horses and sharks. (Daily; closed major hols) 501 E 30th St. Phone 515/263-0612. ¢

Blank Park Zoo. Animal and bird areas designed for close viewing; Australian and African walk-through displays; farm animal contact area; camel rides and Old West train ride; concession. (May-mid-Oct, daily) 7401 SW 9th St. Phone 515/285-4722 or 515/237-1386. ¢¢

Botanical Center. Displays of nearly 1,500 species from all over the world; seasonal floral displays. (Daily; closed Jan 1, Thanksgiving, Dec 25) 909 E River Dr. Phone 515/242-2934. ¢

Civic Center. Varied musical and theatrical entertainment, symphony concerts and ballet performances all yr. Free tours by appt. 221 Walnut St. For performance schedule, fees phone 515/243-1120 (recording), 515/243-1109 (box office) or 515/243-0766.

Des Moines Art Center. Exhibits of 19th- and 20th-century paintings and sculptures in striking contemporary building, original building by Eliel Saarinen, additions by Meier and Pei; changing exhibits; library, museum shop, restaurant. Free admission mornings & Thurs. (Daily exc Mon; closed Jan 1, Dec 25 & 31) 4700 Grand Ave, in Greenwood Park. Phone 515/277-4405. ¢

Drake University (1881). (6,500 students) Six colleges and schools. Many buildings designed by distinguished architects, including Eliel and Eero Saarinen, Harry Weese & Associates, Brooks, Borg & Skiles, Ludwig Mies van der Rohe. Campus tours. (See ANNUAL EVENTS) University Ave & 25th St. Phone 515/271-2011.

Francesca's House (1870). Victorian farmhouse used in the film *The Bridges of Madison County*. (May-Oct, daily) 15 mi SW off I-35, exit 65 about 4 mi W. Phone 515/981-5268. ¢¢

Heritage Village. Century-old barn, exposition hall (1886) with display of early farm machinery; authentically furnished country school; replicas of 1834 church, Ft Madison blockhouse, turn-of-the-century pharmacy, general store, telephone building, totem pole; state fair museum, barber shop

and railroad station. Tours (mid-Apr-mid-Oct, by appt). State fairgrounds, 12 blks E of I-235 on E University. Phone 515/262-3111. ¢   During state fair   **Free.**

Hoyt Sherman Place (1877). Once home of General Sherman's brother. Now features the city's oldest art gallery, including artifacts, antique furniture and art collection. Tours (by appt; fee). Theater (1,400 seats) added in 1922. (Mon-Fri) 1501 Woodland Ave. Phone 515/243-0913.

★ **Living History Farms.** Complex has 4 farms and town on 600 acres: Native American settlement of 1700 includes gardens, shelters, crafts of Ioway tribe; pioneer farm of 1850 features log cabin and outbuildings, demonstrations of early farming methods; horse-powered farm of 1900 depicts farm and household chores typical of period; crop center emphasizes modern agriculture and crops. The 1875 town of Walnut Hill includes Victorian mansion; schoolhouse; pottery, blacksmith and carpentry shops; veterinary infirmary; church, law, bank, newspaper and doctor's offices; general store. (May-late Oct, daily) W via I-35, I-80 exit 125, to Hickman Rd (US 6). Phone 515/278-2400. ¢¢¢

Polk County Heritage Gallery. Formerly the city's main post office (1908), the building's lobby was restored to its original beaux-arts classical architecture. The gallery houses changing art exhibits and historical material, including brass writing desks and gas lamps. (Mon-Fri; closed between exhibits) 2nd Ave & Walnut. Phone 515/286-3215. **Free.**

Prairie Meadows Racetrack & Casino. Facility features live Thoroughbred and Quarter Horse racing (May-Aug); simulcasting of Thoroughbred and greyhound racing (daily); 24-hr casino with over 1,000 slots (daily). 10 mi E on I-80, exit 142. Phone 800/325-9015. **Free.**

Salisbury House. A 42-rm replica of King's House in Salisbury, England, on 11 acres of woodland. Houses authentic furnishings of Tudor age; classic paintings and sculpture; tapestries; 80 Oriental rugs; stained-glass windows; huge fireplaces; collector's library contains a leaf from the Gutenberg Bible. Guided tours only (phone for schedule). (Mon-Fri; closed major hols, also Dec 25-Jan 1) 4025 Tonawanda Dr. Phone 515/279-9711. Tour ¢¢

Science Center of Iowa. Natural and physical science exhibits, live demonstrations; Digistar planetarium shows; laser shows (addl fee). (Daily; closed Thanksgiving, Dec 25) 4500 Grand Ave, in Greenwood Park. Phone 515/274-4138. ¢¢

State Capitol (1871). Towering central dome covered with 23-carat gold leaf; four smaller domes have golden seam marks. State offices and Supreme Court on first floor. House and Senate chamber, law library on second floor. Paintings, mosaics, collection of war flags. Building (daily). E 9th St & Grand Ave. For tour information phone 515/281-5591. **Free.**

State of Iowa Historical Building. Modern cultural center houses state historical museum; displays portray Iowa history and heritage. Library contains county, state and family history materials, rare books and manuscripts about Iowa, census records and newspapers. Museum (daily exc Mon). 600 E Locust, Capitol Complex. Phone 515/281-5111. **Free.**

★ **Terrace Hill** (1869). Extravagant Italianate/Second Empire mansion, now residence of Iowa governors, is situated on commanding knoll above downtown. Restored house is outstanding example of Victorian residential architecture. Tours include 1st & 2nd floors, carriage house and gardens. (Tues-Sat; closed hols, also Jan) 2300 Grand Ave. Phone 515/281-3604. ¢¢

White Water University. Water park featuring wave pool, slides, tubing, hot tub; children's pool; picnicking, refreshments. (Memorial Day-Labor Day, daily) Miniature golf, go-karts (also open wkends spring & fall; addl fee). 5401 E University, E on I-235, then 3½ mi E on E University. Phone 515/265-4904. ¢¢¢¢-¢¢¢¢¢

Annual Events

Drake Relays. Drake University. One of the most prestigious intercollegiate track and field events in the country; more than 5,000 athletes compete. Phone 515/271-2115. Apr 24-25.

Art in the Park. Fairgrounds. Phone 515/277-4405. 1st wkend June.

Iowa State Fair. Fairgrounds, E 30th & University Ave. One of the oldest and largest in country; includes 20 acres of farm machinery, fine arts, giant midway, grandstand stage and track events, free entertainment, exhibits, demonstrations, contests; camping. Phone 515/262-3111. Aug 13-23.

Doors to the Past. Walking tour of 6-10 historic houses in Sherman Hill area. Phone 515/284-5717. Last 2 wkends Sept.

Additional Visitor Information

The Greater Des Moines Convention & Visitors Bureau, Two Ruan Center, Suite 222, 601 Locust St, 50309, has tourist guidebooks, maps and brochures as well as a guide to events; phone 515/286-4960 or 800/451-2625. There is a visitor information center located at the Des Moines Intl Airport, Fleur Dr, phone 515/287-4396 (daily exc Sat).

City Neighborhoods

Many of the restaurants, unrated dining establishments and some lodgings listed under Des Moines include neighborhoods as well as exact street addresses. Geographic descriptions of the Downtown and Sherman Hill are given, followed by a table of restaurants arranged by neighborhood.

Downtown: South of I-235, east of the Des Moines River, north of Court Ave and Cherry St and west of W 15th St. **North of Downtown:** North of I-235. **South of Downtown:** South of Court Ave. **East of Downtown:** East of 14th St. **West of Downtown:** West of Des Moines River.

Sherman Hill: West of Downtown; south of I-235, west of 15th St, north of High St and east of Harding Rd.

DES MOINES RESTAURANTS BY NEIGHBORHOOD AREAS

(For full description, see alphabetical listings under Restaurants)

DOWNTOWN
Nacho Mammas. 216 Court Ave
Spaghetti Works. 310 Court Ave

NORTH OF DOWNTOWN
Christopher's. 2816 Beaver Ave
House of Hunan. 6810 Douglas Ave

EAST OF DOWNTOWN
A Taste of Thailand. 215 E Walnut St

WEST OF DOWNTOWN
Jesse's Embers. 3301 Ingersoll

Note: When a listing is located in a town that does not have its own city heading, it will appear under the city nearest to its location. In these cases, the address and town appear in parenthesis immediately following the name of the establishment.

Motels

(Rates may be higher during state fair)

★ ★ ★ **ADVENTURELAND INN.** *(50316). 8 mi E on I-80, exit 142 at US 65, east of downtown.* 515/265-7321; FAX 515/265-3506. 130 rms, 2 story. June-Aug: S $70-$90; D $80-$100; each addl $5; suites $140-$155; under 12 free; lower rates rest of yr. Crib free. TV; cable (premium). Indoor pool; poolside serv. Playground. Restaurant 6:30 am-9 pm. Rm serv. Bar 4 pm-midnight; entertainment. Ck-out 11 am. Meeting rms. Business servs avail. Sundries. Gift shop. Game rm. Some private patios, balconies. Amusement park adj. Cr cds: A, C, D, DS, MC, V.

D ≃ ✻ ⋈ 🔥

✔★ ★ **BEST INNS OF AMERICA.** *(5050 Merle Hay Rd, Johnston 50131) Just N of I-35, I-80 exit 131.* 515/270-1111; res: 800/BEST-INN. 92 rms, 2 story, 14 suites. S $49.88; D $52.88-$62.88; each addl $10; suites $67-$77; under 18 free. Crib free. Pet accepted. TV; cable (premium), VCR avail (movies $3). Indoor pool; whirlpool. Complimentary continental bkfst. Restaurant opp 6 am-midnight. Ck-out 1 pm. Meeting rms. Business servs avail. Health club privileges. Microwaves avail. Cr cds: A, C, D, DS, MC, V.

D ✔ ≃ ⋈ 🔥 SC

★ ★ **BEST WESTERN AIRPORT INN.** *1810 Army Post Rd (50315), near Intl Airport, south of downtown.* 515/287-6464; FAX 515/287-5818. 145 rms. S $62; D $72; each addl $5; suites $99; under 17 free. Crib free. Pet accepted. TV; cable, VCR avail (movies). Indoor pool; poolside serv. Complimentary continental bkfst. Restaurant 11 am-2 pm, 5-9 pm. Rm serv. Bar 4 pm-1 am. Ck-out noon. Coin lndry. Meeting rms. Business servs avail. Bellhops. Valet serv. Free airport transportation. Cr cds: A, D, DS, MC, V.

D ✔ ≃ ✈ ⋈ 🔥 SC

★ ★ **BEST WESTERN STARLITE VILLAGE.** *(133 SE Delaware, Ankeny 50021) 14 mi N on I-35, exit 92.* 515/964-1717; FAX 515/964-8781. 116 rms, 2 story. June-Aug: S $48-$53; D $53-$62; each addl $5; kits. $120; under 12 free; wkly rates; lower rates rest of yr. Crib $3. Pet accepted, some restrictions. TV; cable. Indoor pool; whirlpool. Restaurant 6 am-10 pm. Rm serv. Bar 1 pm-2 am; Sun to 10 pm. Meeting rms. Business servs avail. Sundries. Microwaves avail. Cr cds: A, D, DS, MC, V.

D ✔ ≃ ⋈ 🔥 SC

✔★ **COMFORT INN.** *5231 Fleur Dr (50321), near Intl Airport, south of downtown.* 515/287-3434. 55 rms, 3 story, 16 suites. No elvtr. May-Aug: S $49-$64; D $59-$79; each addl $5; suites $59-$95; under 18 free; higher rates special events; lower rates rest of yr. Pet accepted, some restrictions. TV; cable (premium). Indoor pool; whirlpool. Complimentary continental bkfst. Restaurant nearby. Ck-out 11 am. Meeting rm. Business servs avail. In-rm modem link. Sundries. Free airport transportation. Refrigerator in suites. Cr cds: A, D, DS, MC, V.

D ✔ ≃ ✈ ⋈ 🔥 SC

★ ★ **COMFORT SUITES.** *(11167 Hickman Rd, Urbandale 50322) I-80/35 exit 125, then 1 blk E on Hickman Rd.* 515/276-1126. 101 rms, 2 story. S $79-$169; D $89-$179; each addl $10; under 18 free; higher rates special events. Crib free. TV; cable (premium). Heated pool; whirlpool. Complimentary continental bkfst. Complimentary coffee in rms. Restaurant adj 6 am-10 pm. Bar. Ck-out noon. Meeting rms. Business servs avail. Bellhops. Sundries. Exercise equipt; stair machine, bicycles. Game rm. Refrigerators. Living History Farms adj. Cr cds: A, C, D, DS, ER, JCB, MC, V.

D ≃ 🏃 ⋈ 🔥 SC

✔★ **COUNTRY INN.** *(3225 Adventureland Dr, Altoona 50009) Exit 142 off I-80.* 515/967-5252; res: 800/383-6545. 110 rms, 2 story. S $45.50-$57.50; D $62.50-$66.50; suites $80.50; under 14 free. Crib $3. Pet accepted; $6. TV; cable (premium). Indoor pool; whirlpool. Complimentary coffee in lobby. Restaurant adj open 24 hrs. Ck-out 11 am. Meeting rm. Business servs avail. Cr cds: A, D, DS, MC, V.

D ✔ ≃ ⋈ 🔥 SC

✔★ **ECONO LODGE.** *5626 Douglas Ave (50310), north of downtown.* 515/278-1601; FAX 515/278-1602. 48 rms, 2 story. S $31.95-$52; D $35.95-$60; each addl $5; under 18 free. Crib free. TV; cable (premium). Complimentary continental bkfst. Restaurant nearby. Ck-out 11 am. Business servs avail. Microwaves avail. Cr cds: A, C, D, DS, MC, V.

D ⋈ 🔥 SC

★ ★ **EXECUTIVE INN.** *(3530 Westown Pkwy, West Des Moines 50266) 7 mi W on I-35, exit 35th St.* 515/225-1144; FAX 515/225-6463; res: 800/998-9669. 100 rms, 2 story. S $49; D $54; each addl $5; suites $75-$150; under 12 free. Crib $6. TV; cable (premium), VCR avail (movies). Indoor/outdoor pool; whirlpool. Complimentary continental bkfst. Restaurant 11 am-11 pm; Sun from 8:30 am. Rm serv. Bar 4 pm-midnight. Ck-out 11 am. Meeting rms. Business servs avail. Sundries. Exercise equipt; bicycle, treadmill, sauna. Refrigerators; microwaves avail. Balconies. Cr cds: A, C, D, DS, JCB, MC, V.

≃ 🏃 ⋈ 🔥 SC

★ **FAIRFIELD INN BY MARRIOTT.** *1600 114th St (50325), I-80 exit University Ave E, west of downtown.* 515/226-1600. 135 rms, 3 story. S, D $42-$69; each addl $7; under 18 free. Crib free. TV; cable (premium). Pool. Complimentary continental bkfst. Restaurant nearby.

Ck-out noon. Business servs avail. Health club privileges. Cr cds: A, D, DS, JCB, MC, V.

[D] [≈] [⋈] [☀] [SC]

★ ★ HAMPTON INN. 5001 Fleur Dr (50321), near Intl Airport, south of downtown. 515/287-7300; FAX 515/287-6343. 122 rms, 4 story. S $64; D $74; under 18 free. Crib free. TV; cable. Pool. Complimentary continental bkfst. Restaurant nearby. Ck-out 11 am. Meeting rm. Business servs avail. In-rm modem link. Bellhops. Valet serv. Sundries. Free airport transportation. Exercise equipt; bicycles, treadmill. Cr cds: A, C, D, DS, MC, V.

[D] [≈] [✕] [✈] [⋈] [☀] [SC]

✔ ★ HEARTLAND INN. 11414 Forest Ave (50325), I-80/35 exit 124, west of downtown. 515/226-0414; FAX 515/226-9769. 87 rms, 2 story. S $48-$58; D $56-$66; each addl $5; under 16 free. Crib free. Pet accepted, some restrictions; $10. TV; cable (premium). Complimentary continental bkfst. Restaurant nearby. Ck-out 11 am. Business servs avail. Sauna. Health club privileges. Whirlpool. Microwaves avail. Cr cds: A, D, DS, MC, V.

[D] [♥] [≈] [☀] [SC]

★ ★ HOLIDAY INN EXPRESS AT DRAKE. 1140 24th St (50311), north of downtown. 515/255-4000; FAX 515/255-1192. 52 rms, 2 story. S $55; D $60; each addl $5; under 19 free. Crib free. TV; cable (premium). Complimentary continental bkfst. Restaurant adj 7 am-11 pm; Sun to 10 pm. Ck-out noon. Meeting rms. Business servs avail. Sundries. Health club privileges. Microwaves avail. Cr cds: A, C, D, DS, JCB, MC, V.

[D] [≈] [☀] [SC]

★ ★ INN AT MERLE HAY. (5055 Merle Hay Rd, Johnston 50131) 2 mi W on I-35/80 exit 131. 515/276-5411; FAX 515/276-0696; res: 800/643-1197. 146 rms. S $50-$80; D $55-$90; suites $119-$149; under 16 free. Crib $5. Pet accepted; $40 ($30 refundable). TV; cable (premium). Indoor pool; whirlpool. Complimentary coffee in rms. Restaurant 6:30 am-11 pm. Bar. Ck-out noon. Meeting rms. Business servs avail. Bellhops. Free airport, bus depot transportation. Microwaves avail. Cr cds: A, D, DS, ER, MC, V.

[D] [♥] [≈] [⋈] [☀] [SC]

★ INN AT UNIVERSITY. (11001 University Ave, Clive 50325) 515/225-2222; FAX 515/224-9816; res: 800/369-7476. 104 rms, 2 story. S $49.50-$65; D $68-$78; each addl $5; under 17 free. Pet accepted; $50 refundable. TV; cable. Heated pool; whirlpool. Restaurant nearby. Bar 4:30 pm-2 am. Ck-out noon. Meeting rms. Business servs avail. Sundries. Free airport transportation. Exercise equipt; weight machine, stair machine. Microwaves avail. Cr cds: A, C, D, DS, MC, V.

[D] [♥] [≈] [✕] [✈] [⋈] [☀] [SC]

★ ★ RESIDENCE INN BY MARRIOTT. (11428 Forest Ave, Clive 50325) I-35/80 exit University Ave, N on 114th St, then W on Forest Ave. 515/223-7700; FAX 515/223-7222. 112 kit. suites, 2 story. S $74-$99; D $84-$110; wkly, monthly rates. Crib free. Pet accepted; $50. TV; cable (premium). Pool; whirlpool. Complimentary continental bkfst. Complimentary coffee in rms. Restaurant nearby. Ck-out noon. Coin lndry. Meeting rms. Business servs avail. In-rm modem link. Valet serv. Sundries. Exercise equipt; stair machine, bicycles. Health club privileges. Microwaves. Balconies. Picnic tables, grills. Cr cds: A, C, D, DS, JCB, MC, V.

[D] [♥] [≈] [✕] [✈] [⋈] [☀] [SC]

✔ ★ RODEWAY INN. 4995 Merle Hay Rd (50322), just off I-35, I-80 exit 131, north of downtown. 515/278-2381; FAX 515/278-9760. 120 rms, 2 story. S $35-$80; D $41-$86; each addl $6; suites $90-$225; under 18 free. Crib free. TV; cable (premium). Indoor/outdoor pool; whirlpool. Complimentary continental bkfst. Restaurant 6 am-11 pm; Fri, Sat open 24 hrs. Bar. Ck-out noon. Coin lndry. Meeting rms. Business servs avail. Sauna. Microwaves avail. Cr cds: A, C, D, DS, ER, JCB, MC, V.

[D] [≈] [☀] [⋈] [☀] [SC]

Motor Hotels

★ ★ BEST WESTERN EXECUTIVE CENTER. 11040 Hickman Rd (50325), at jct US 6, I-35, I-80 exit 125, north of downtown. 515/278-5575; FAX 515/278-4078. 161 rms, 6 story. S $84; D $89; each addl $5; under 17 free. Crib free. Pet accepted. TV; cable (premium). Indoor pool; wading pool, whirlpool. Restaurant 6:30 am-2 pm, 5-10:30 pm. Rm serv. Bar 4 pm-midnight. Ck-out noon. Coin lndry. Meeting rms. Business servs avail. In-rm modem link. Valet serv. Free airport transportation. Sauna. Health club privileges. Cr cds: A, C, D, DS, JCB, MC, V.

[D] [♥] [≈] [⋈] [☀] [SC]

★ ★ ★ HOLIDAY INN-AIRPORT. 6111 Fleur Dr (50321), near Intl Airport, south of downtown. 515/287-2400; FAX 515/287-4811. 227 rms, 3 story. S, D $95. TV; cable (premium), VCR avail. Indoor pool; whirlpool. Restaurant 6 am-10 pm. Rm serv. Bar 11-1 am. Ck-out noon. Meeting rms. Business center. In-rm modem link. Bellhops. Valet serv. Sundries. Free airport transportation. Indoor putting green. Exercise equipt; weight machines, bicycles. Microwaves avail. Cr cds: A, C, D, DS, ER, JCB, MC, V.

[D] [≈] [✕] [✈] [⋈] [☀] [SC] [⛷]

Hotels

★ ★ ★ EMBASSY SUITES-ON THE RIVER. 101 E Locust St (50309), on the Des Moines River, downtown. 515/244-1700; FAX 515/244-2537. 234 suites, 8 story. S, D $134; each addl $15; under 18 free; special wkend plans. Crib free. Parking $3; garage $7. TV; cable (premium), VCR avail. Indoor pool; whirlpool. Complimentary full bkfst. Complimentary coffee in rms. Restaurant 11 am-2 pm, 5-10 pm. Rm serv to midnight. Bar to 2 am; entertainment. Ck-out noon. Coin lndry. Meeting rms. Business servs avail. Gift shop. Free airport, bus depot transportation. Exercise equipt; weight machine, bicycles, sauna. Refrigerators, microwaves, wet bars. Cr cds: A, D, DS, MC, V.

[D] [≈] [✕] [⋈] [☀] [SC]

★ ★ ★ FORT DES MOINES. 1000 Walnut St (50309), downtown. 515/243-1161; FAX 515/243-4317; res: 800/532-1466. E-mail hotelfdm@radiks.net; web www.hotelfortdm.com. 242 rms, 11 story, 56 suites. S, D $59-$119; suites $75-$250; under 18 free; wkend rates. Pet accepted. TV; cable. Pool; whirlpool. Restaurant 6:30 am-10:30 pm. Bar 11-2 am. Ck-out noon. Meeting rms. In-rm modem link. Gift shop. Free airport transportation. Exercise equipt; weight machines, bicycles. Refrigerator in some suites. Cr cds: A, C, D, DS, MC, V.

[D] [♥] [≈] [✕] [⋈] [☀] [SC]

★ ★ HOLIDAY INN-DOWNTOWN. 1050 6th Ave (50314), north of downtown. 515/283-0151. 253 rms, 12 story. S, D $89; each addl $10; suites $225; under 19 free. Crib free. TV; cable (premium), VCR avail. Indoor pool. Restaurant 6 am-2 pm, 5-10 pm. Bar noon-2 am. Meeting rms. Business servs avail. Gift shop. Airport transportation. Cr cds: A, C, D, DS, JCB, MC, V.

[D] [≈] [⋈] [☀] [SC]

✔ ★ KIRKWOOD CIVIC CENTER. 400 Walnut St (50309), downtown. 515/244-9191; FAX 515/282-7004; res: 800/798-9191. 150 rms, 12 story. S, D $49-$89; suites $99-$200; under 14 free. Crib free. TV; cable. Restaurant 6 am-2 pm. Ck-out noon. Health club privileges. Some in-rm whirlpools. Cr cds: A, D, DS, MC, V.

[☀] [SC]

★ ★ ★ MARRIOTT. 700 Grand (50309), downtown. 515/245-5500; FAX 515/245-5567. 415 rms, 33 story. S, D $70-$140; suites $125-$600; under 18 free; wkend rates. Crib free. Pet accepted, some restrictions. Covered parking $10/day, valet $10/day. TV; cable (premium), VCR avail. Indoor pool; whirlpool, poolside serv. Restaurants 6:30 am-11 pm. Bar. Ck-out noon. Convention facilities. Business servs avail. Free airport transportation. Barber, beauty shop. Exercise equipt; weights, bicycles, sauna. Some bathrm phones. Luxury level. Cr cds: A, C, D, DS, ER, JCB, MC, V.

[D] [♥] [≈] [✕] [⋈] [☀] [SC]

★ ★ **SAVERY.** *401 Locust St (50309), downtown. 515/244-2151; FAX 515/244-1408; res: 800/798-2151.* 221 units, 12 story, 20 kits. S, D $95-$125; each addl $10; suites $225-$500. Crib $10. Pet accepted, some restrictions. TV; cable. Indoor pool. Restaurants 6:30 am-2 pm, 5-8 pm. Rm serv 6:30 am-10 pm. Bar 11-1 am; entertainment. Ck-out noon. Meeting rms. Beauty shop. Free airport, bus depot transportation. Valet parking. Exercise equipt; weight machines, bicycles, sauna. Built 1919. Cr cds: A, C, D, DS, ER, MC, V.

D ✔ ☜ 🏋 🏃 ☜ ⊠ SC

★ ★ **WILDWOOD LODGE.** *(11431 Forest Ave, Clive 50325) 515/222-9876; res: 800/728-1223.* 104 rms, 3 story. S $80-$100; D $90-$110. Crib free. TV; cable (premium), VCR avail. Indoor pool; whirlpool. Complimentary continental bkfst. Restaurant nearby. Bar 10 am-11 pm. Ck-out noon. Meeting rms. Business servs avail. In-rm modem link. Gift shop. Exercise equipt; bicycle, treadmill. Microwaves avail. Cr cds: A, D, DS, ER, JCB, MC, V.

D ☜ 🏃 ⊠ SC

Restaurants

★ ★ **CHINA PALACE.** *(2800 University Ave, West Des Moines)* In Clock Tower Square. 515/225-2800. Hrs: 11:30 am-10 pm; Fri, Sat to 11 pm; Sun brunch to 2:30 pm. Res accepted. Chinese menu. Bar. A la carte entrees: lunch $4.25-$6, dinner $5.95-$12.95. Sun brunch $10.95. Specializes in Szechwan, Mandarin, Hunan dishes. Parking. Formal atmosphere. Cr cds: A, C, D, DS, MC, V.

D

★ ★ **CHINA WOK.** *(1960 Grand Ave, Suite 23, West Des Moines 50317)* In Normandy Plaza shopping ctr. 515/223-8408. Hrs: 11:30 am-10 pm; Fri, Sat to 11 pm; Sun brunch 11 am-2:30 pm. Closed Thanksgiving. Res accepted. Chinese menu. Bar. Semi-a la carte: lunch $3.85-$4.95, dinner $5.95-$11.95. Sun brunch $8.95. Specialties: China Wok delicacy, Neptune catch in a bird's nest, General Tso's chicken. Parking. Dining rm features Oriental art, figurines, fans, porcelain. Cr cds: A, C, D, DS, MC, V.

D ⊡

★ ★ **CHRISTOPHER'S.** *2816 Beaver Ave, north of downtown. 515/274-3694.* E-mail avrij@dux.com. Hrs: 5-10:30 pm; Fri, Sat to 11:30 pm. Closed Sun; major hols. Res accepted. Italian, Amer menu. Bar 3 pm-2 am; Sat from 2 pm. Semi-a la carte: dinner $7-$18.95. Child's meals. Specializes in prime rib, steak, seafood. Own pasta. Parking. Family-owned. Cr cds: A, DS, MC, V.

D

✔ ★ **HOUSE OF HUNAN.** *6810 Douglas Ave, north of downtown. 515/276-5556.* Hrs: 11:30 am-10 pm; Fri, Sat to 11 pm. Res accepted wkends. Chinese menu. Bar. A la carte entrees: lunch $3.50-$5.95, dinner $5.50-$11.95. Buffet: lunch (Sun) $8.95. Parking. Oriental decor. Cr cds: A, D, DS, MC, V.

D SC

✔ ★ **IOWA MACHINE SHED.** *(11151 Hickman Rd, Urbandale 50322)* I-80/35 exit 125, then 1 blk E on Hickman Rd. 515/270-6818. Hrs: 6 am-10 pm; Sun 7 am-9 pm. Closed Jan 1, Thanksgiving, Dec 25. Bar. Complete meals: bkfst $3.25-$7.50, lunch $4.95-$11.95, dinner $6.99-$20. Semi-a la carte: lunch, dinner $3.75-$7.50. Child's meals. Specializes in roast pork loin, stuffed pork chops, barbecued ribs. Parking. Family atmosphere. Farm implements on display. Cr cds: A, D, DS, MC, V.

D

★ **JESSE'S EMBERS.** *3301 Ingersoll, west of downtown. 515/255-6011.* Hrs: 11:30 am-2 pm, 5-10:30 pm; Sat 5-11 pm. Closed Sun; major hols. Bar. Semi-a la carte: lunch $4.50-$11.95, dinner $6.95-$34. Specializes in steak, seafood, ribs. Parking. Family-owned. Cr cds: A, MC, V.

⊡

★ **MAXIE'S.** *(1311 Grand Ave, West Des Moines) 515/223-1463.* Hrs: 11 am-2 pm, 5-10 pm; Fri, Sat 5-11 pm. Closed Sun; major hols. Res accepted. Bar. Semi-a la carte: lunch $3.95-$5.25, dinner $5.50-$20. Child's meals. Specializes in chicken, ribs, steak. Parking. Cr cds: A, C, D, DS, MC, V.

D

✔ ★ **NACHO MAMMAS.** *216 Court Ave (50309), downtown. 515/280-6262.* Hrs: 11 am-10 pm; Fri, Sat to 11 pm; Sun noon-9 pm. Closed Easter, Thanksgiving, Dec 25. Res accepted. Mexican, Southwestern menu. Bar. Semi-a la carte: lunch $3.95-$6.50, dinner $6.99-$10.99. Child's meals. Specializes in tortillas. Sidewalk patio dining. Cr cds: A, D, MC, V.

D

★ **OHANA STEAKHOUSE.** *(2900 University Ave, West Des Moines 50265)* at jct 28th St, in Clocktower Square shopping center. 515/225-3325. Hrs: 5-9 pm; Fri, Sat to 10:30 pm. Closed Mon; some major hols. Res accepted. Japanese menu. Bar. Complete meals: dinner $10-$16.50. Child's meals. Specializes in chicken, steak, seafood. Tableside preparation. Japanese rock garden. Cr cds: A, C, DS, MC, V.

D

✔ ★ **SPAGHETTI WORKS.** *310 Court Ave, downtown. 515/243-2195.* Hrs: 11:15 am-10:15 pm; Fri to 11 pm; Sat, Sun from noon. Closed some major hols. Italian, Amer menu. Bar. Semi-a la carte: lunch $3.29-$6.99, dinner $3.99-$7.95. Child's meals. Specializes in spaghetti. Salad bar. Own sauces. Big band music Mon (fall & winter); comedy Fri, Sat. Outdoor dining. Cr cds: A, C, D, MC, V.

D ⊡

✔ ★ **A TASTE OF THAILAND.** *215 E Walnut St, east of downtown. 515/282-0044.* Hrs: 11 am-2 pm, 5-9 pm; Fri, Sat to 10 pm. Closed Sun; major hols. Res accepted. Thai menu. Wine, beer. Semi-a la carte: lunch $4.25, dinner $4.95-$10.50. Parking. Specializes in vegetarian dishes. Cr cds: A, C, D, DS, JCB, MC, V.

D ⊡

★ ★ ★ **TROSTEL'S GREENBRIAR.** *(5810 Merle Hay Rd, Johnston 50131)* I-80 exit 131, then 1½ mi N on Merle Hay Rd. 515/253-0124. Hrs: 11:30 am-2 pm, 5-10 pm; Sat 5-10:30 pm; early-bird dinner Mon-Thurs 5-6:30 pm. Closed Sun; major hols. Semi-a la carte: lunch $4.95-$7.95, dinner $8.95-$19.95. Child's meals. Specializes in prime rib, rack of lamb, fresh seafood. Patio dining. Cr cds: A, DS, MC, V.

D

★ **WATERFRONT SEAFOOD MARKET.** *(2900 University Ave, West Des Moines)* W on University Ave, in Clocktower Square shopping center. 515/223-5106. Hrs: 11 am-2:30 pm, 5-10 pm; Fri, Sat 11 am-11 pm. Closed Sun; major hols. Bar. Semi-a la carte: lunch $5-$9, dinner $9-$25. Child's meals. Specializes in clam chowder, fresh seafood. Oyster bar. Cr cds: A, DS, MC, V.

D SC

★ ★ **WEEPING RADISH.** *(3309 Ute Ave, Waukee 50263)* I-80 exit 117. 515/987-1652. Hrs: 4:30-10 pm; Fri, Sat to 10 pm; Sun brunch 10:30 am-2 pm. Closed Mon; most major hols. Res accepted. Amer menu. Bar. Semi-a la carte: dinner $7.95-$14.95. Specializes in steak, seafood. Outdoor dining. Casual decor. Cr cds: C, D, MC, V.

D ⊡

Unrated Dining Spot

MUSTARDS. *(6612 University Ave, Windsor Heights)* 5 mi W on University Ave. 515/274-9307. Hrs: 11 am-10 pm; Fri, Sat to 11 pm. Closed some major hols. Beer. Semi-a la carte: lunch, dinner $4-$15. Specializes in barbecued ribs. Parking. Cr cds: DS, MC, V.

D

Dubuque (C-8)

Settled 1833 **Pop** 57,546 **Elev** 650 ft **Area code** 319 **Zip** 52001 **E-mail** chamber@mwci.net **Web** www.dubuque.org

Information Convention and Visitors Bureau, 770 Town Clock Plaza, PO Box 705, 52004-0705; 319/557-9200 or 800/798-8844.

Facing both Wisconsin and Illinois across the broad Mississippi River, Dubuque became the first known European settlement in Iowa when Julien Dubuque, a French Canadian, came from Quebec in 1788 and leased land from the Native Americans to mine lead. After his death, Native Americans barred settlement until 1833 when the territory was opened under a treaty with Chief Black Hawk. Once a boisterous river and mining town, Dubuque had the first bank and the first newspaper in what is now Iowa. Dubuque now prospers as a center of more than 300 industries, including publishing, software development and manufacturing.

What to See and Do

Bellevue State Park. Approx 540 acres on a high bluff; river view. Native American mounds, rugged woodlands. Hiking trails. Snowmobiling. Picnicking. Camping (electricity, dump station). Nature center. Standard hrs, fees. 26 mi S on US 52, 67, near Bellevue. Phone 319/872-3243 or 319/872-4019.

Cathedral Square. Surrounding square are stylized figures of a lead miner, farmer, farmer's wife, priest and river hand; opposite square is architecturally and historically significant St Raphael's Cathedral. 2nd & Bluff St.

Clarke College (1843). (1,000 students) Music performance hall, art gallery, library and chapel open from 56-ft-high glass atrium plaza. Tours (by appt). 1550 Clarke Dr at W Locust St. Phone 319/588-6318.

Crystal Lake Cave. Network of passageways carved by underground streams; surrounding lake with glittering stalactites and stalagmites. Guided tours (Memorial Day-late Oct, daily; May, Sat & Sun). 3 mi S off US 52. Phone 319/556-6451 or 319/872-4111. ¢¢¢

Diamond Jo Casino. Casino gambling on river. 3rd St Ice Harbor. Phone 319/583-7005 or 800/LUCKY-JO.

Dubuque Arboretum and Botanical Gardens. Features annual and perennial gardens, rose, water, formal gardens; ornamental trees, woodland and prairie wildflower walk. (Daily) 3800 Arboretum Dr. Phone 319/556-2100. **Free.**

Dubuque County Courthouse. This gold-domed courthouse is on the National Historic Register of Places. Guided tours. (Daily; closed most major hols) 720 Central Ave. Phone 319/557-1851. **Free.** Adj is

   Dubuque Museum of Art/Old County Jail. Museum is housed in the old jail; gallery is an example of Egyptian Revival archtechture. (Tues-Fri, also wkend afternoons) 36 E Eighth St. Phone 319/557-1851. ¢-¢¢¢

Eagle Point Park. On a high bluff above the Mississippi, the 164-acre park overlooks three states. A WPA project, the park's Prairie school pavillions and naturalistic landscaping were designed by Alfred Caldwell, who studied under Frank Lloyd Wright. Floral displays. Tennis. Picnicking (shelters), playgrounds. (Mid-May-mid-Oct, daily) Off Shiras Ave, NE corner of city. Phone 319/589-4263. Per vehicle ¢

Fenelon Place Elevator. One of world's shortest, steepest incline railways; connects Fenelon Place with 4th St, providing three-state view. In operation since 1882. (Apr-Nov, daily) 512 Fenelon Place. Phone 319/582-6496. ¢

☆ *Field of Dreams* **Movie Site.** Background set of movie *Field of Dreams*, including baseball diamond. (Daily) Gift shop (early Apr-early Nov, daily). 25 mi W on US 20, on Lansing Rd in Dyersville. Phone 319/875-2311. **Free.**

Five Flags Theater (1910). Designed by Rapp and Rapp, premier theater architects of their day, the Five Flags was modeled after Parisian music halls. Tours (by appt). (Daily) Fourth & Main Sts. Phone 319/589-4254.

General Zebulon Pike Lock and Dam. Steady stream of barges and other river traffic moves through lock. Can be seen from Eagle Point Park.

Grand Opera House. Century-old opera house offers a variety of entertainment throughout the yr. 135 8th St. Phone 319/588-1305.

Heritage Trail. Trail provides 26 mi of scenic hiking, biking and cross-country skiing on old railroad along rugged Little Maquoketa River valley. Level, surfaced trail crosses from wooded, hilly, "driftless" area to rolling prairie near Dyersville. Self-guided tour identifies railroad landmarks, including water-powered mill sites. (Daily) 2 mi N on US 52. Phone 319/556-6745. ¢

Iowa Welcome Center. 3rd St, Ice Harbor. Phone 319/556-4372 or 800/798-8844. **Free.**

Julien Dubuque Monument. Tower built in 1897 at site of Dubuque's mine and the spot where Native Americans buried him in 1810. Provides excellent view of Mississippi River. On 18 acres. ¹/₂ mi from end of Julien Dubuque Dr.

Loras College (1839). (1,900 students) Liberal arts. On campus is Heitkamp Planetarium (academic yr, Fri evenings; also by appt; free). Wahlert Memorial Library has collection of 2,200 rare books, many printed before 1500. 1450 Alta Vista St. For tours phone 319/588-7100.

Mathias Ham House Historic Site (1857). Italianate villa/Victorian mansion (32 rms) with cupola, offering spectacular views of Mississippi River. Built by lead miner Mathias Ham. Also Iowa's oldest log cabin and one-room schoolhouse. (June-Oct, daily) 2241 Lincoln Ave, below Eagle Point Park. Phone 319/583-2812 or 319/557-9545. ¢¢

Mines of Spain Recreation Area. 1,380-acre park features nature trails, limestone quarry, wetlands, prairie. (Daily) 8999 Bellevue Heights. Phone 319/556-0620.

☆ **Mississippi River Museum.** Complex of six Dubuque County Historical Society museums, all emphasizing the city's river history. (Daily) Ice Harbor, downtown. Phone 319/557-9545. ¢¢¢ Two-day pass includes

   National Rivers Hall Of Fame. Museum celebrating nation's river heroes—Samuel Clemens, Lewis and Clark, Robert Fulton and others.

   Woodward Riverboat Museum. Dramatizes 300 yrs of Mississippi River history: Native Americans, explorers, lead miners, boat builders and steamboat captains; lead mines; pilothouse & log raft displays.

   River of Dreams. Interactive film. (15 min) on history of Mississippi River. (Daily) Shown in Iowa Welcome Center.

   Sidewheeler *William M. Black.* One of the last steam-powered sidewheelers. Tour main deck, boiler and hurricane decks, pilothouse with speaking tubes and brass gauges and engine room. (May-Oct only)

   Paddlewheel towboat *Logsdon.* One of the last wooden-hulled paddlewheel towboats on inland waterways; first operated in 1940.

   Boatyard. Exhibits and replicas of small craft that plied the Mississippi; boat building and restoration demonstrations.

   Dubuque Heritage Center. Changing exhibits on riverboating and other local history.

Old Shot Tower (1856). Tower, 140 ft high, produced 3 tons of shot daily during Civil War; lead melted on ninth floor was dropped through screens into water at bottom as finished shot. River & Tower Sts.

Redstone Inn (1894). Red sandstone Queen Anne/Victorian mansion built by a prominent Dubuque industrialist as a wedding present for his daughter. Overnight stays avail (see INN), restaurant; open all yr. 504 Bluff St. Phone 319/582-1894.

Rustic Hills Carriage Tours. Half-hr narrated tours; horse-drawn carriage. Sleigh and hay rides. (Daily) 4th & Bluff Sts. Phone 319/556-6341. ¢¢¢

Spirit of Dubuque. Sightseeing and dinner cruises (1¹/₂-hr) on Mississippi River aboard paddlewheeler (May-Oct). 3rd St Ice Harbor, in the Port of Dubuque. Phone 319/583-8093 or 800/747-8093. Cruises ¢¢¢-¢¢¢¢

Storybook Hill Children's Zoo. Recreation area and petting zoo; playground; concession; train ride. (Memorial Day-Labor Day, daily) N Cascade Rd (Fremont Rd Extension). Phone 319/588-2195.

Sundown Mountain Ski Area. 5 chairlifts, rope tow; patrol, school, rentals; snowmaking; cafeteria, concession, bar. 22 runs; longest run ¹/₂ mi;

vertical drop 475 ft. (Day after Thanksgiving-mid-Mar, daily; closed Dec 25) Cross-country skiing. 17017 Asbury Rd. Phone 319/556-6676 or 888/SUNDOWN (exc Dubuque). ¢¢¢¢

Trolleys of Dubuque, Inc. One-hr narrated tours explore history of town, offer panoramic views of Dubuque, Mississippi River, Wisconsin and Illinois. (Apr-Oct, daily) Depart from Iowa Welcome Center, 3rd St Ice Harbor. Phone 319/582-0077 or 800/408-0077. ¢¢¢

University of Dubuque (1852). (1,200 students) Liberal arts; theological seminary. Historic Alumni Hall (1907), a replica of a 15th-century English structure, features changing art exhibits; Blades Hall has impressive stained-glass windows; Steffens Arcade serves as doorway to the campus. Carillon on campus plays concerts. Tours (Mon-Fri, by appt). 2000 University Ave. Phone 319/589-3000 or 319/589-3200.

Annual Events

Dubuque Catfish Festival. Catfish tournament; carnival; music; boat show; food & entertainment. 4th wkend June.

Music on the March. Midwest drum and bugle corps competition. Ten corps; youth competition. Phone 319/582-4872. July 6.

Dubuque County Fair. Dubuque County Fairgrounds. Phone 319/588-1406. July 22-27.

Field of Dreams Festival. In Dyersville at movie site of *Field of Dreams*. Features all-star baseball players. Phone 319/875-6012 or 800/443-8981. 3rd wkend Aug.

Motels

★ ★ **BEST WESTERN DUBUQUE INN.** *3434 Dodge St (US 20), on US 20.* 319/556-7760; FAX 319/556-4003. 155 rms, 3 story. S $49.50-$75.50; D $69-$89; each addl $4; suites $125-$150; under 18 free; package plans. Crib free. TV; cable (premium). Indoor pool; whirlpool. Complimentary coffee in rms. Restaurant 6 am-2 pm, 4:30-10 pm. Rm serv. Bar. Ck-out 11 am. Meeting rms. Business servs avail. In-rm modem link. Valet serv. Free airport transportation. Downhill/x-country ski 5 mi. Game rm. Sauna. Some refrigerators, microwaves. Cr cds: A, C, D, DS, MC, V.

★ ★ **BEST WESTERN MIDWAY.** *3100 Dodge (52003), 2½ mi W on US 20.* 319/557-8000; FAX 319/557-7692. 151 rms, 4 story. June-Oct: S $63-$67; D $74-$82; each addl $5; suites $125-$150; under 18 free; wkend rates; lower rates rest of yr. Crib $3. Pet accepted, some restrictions. TV; cable, VCR (movies). Complimentary bkfst buffet Mon-Fri. Complimentary coffee in rms. Restaurant 6:30 am-10 pm; Sat from 7 am; Sun 7 am-1 pm, 5-9 pm. Rm serv. Bar 11 am-midnight; wkends to 2 am. Ck-out 11 am. Meeting rms. Business servs avail. In-rm modem link. Bellhops. Free airport transportation. Exercise equipt; bicycle, treadmill, sauna. Indoor pool; whirlpool. Game rm. Refrigerator, wet bar in suites. Picnic tables. Cr cds: A, C, D, DS, MC, V.

★ ★ **COMFORT INN.** *4055 Dodge St.* 319/556-3006. 52 rms, 3 story, 14 suites. May-Oct: S, D $59-$79; each addl $5; suites $69-$89; under 18 free; lower rates rest of yr. Crib free. Pet accepted. TV; cable (premium). Indoor pool; whirlpool. Complimentary continental bkfst. Ck-out 11 am. Meeting rms. Business servs avail. In-rm modem link. Sundries. Downhill ski 6 mi; x-country ski 5 mi. Refrigerator, microwave in suites. Cr cds: A, C, D, DS, ER, JCB, MC, V.

★ ★ **DAYS INN.** *1111 Dodge St.* 319/583-3297; FAX 319/583-5900. 154 rms, 2 story. S $45-$69; D $55-$69; under 18 free. Crib free. Pet accepted. TV; cable (premium), VCR avail. Pool. Complimentary continental bkfst. Restaurant 11 am-10 pm. Bar to midnight. Ck-out 11 am. Meeting rms. Business servs avail. Bellhops. Valet serv. Sundries. Free airport transportation. Exercise equipt; bicycles, weight machine. Refrigerators, microwaves in suites. Picnic tables. Cr cds: A, C, D, DS, JCB, MC, V.

✔★ ★ **HEARTLAND INN.** *4025 McDonald Dr (52003), off US 20 (Dodge St).* 319/582-3752; FAX 319/582-0113; res: 800/334-3277, ext. 12. 88 rms, 2 story. S $51-$57; D $57-$63; each addl $6; under 16 free; ski plans. Crib free. Pet accepted, some restrictions. TV; cable (premium). Indoor pool; whirlpool. Complimentary continental bkfst. Ck-out 11 am. Meeting rm. Business servs avail. Downhill/x-country ski 5 mi. Sauna. Health club privileges. Cr cds: A, C, D, DS, MC, V.

★ ★ **HEARTLAND INN.** *2090 Southpark Court (52003), US 61/151 S to Twin Valley Dr, then W.* 319/556-6555; FAX 319/556-0542; res: 800/334-3277, ext. 13. 59 rms, 2 story, 6 suites. S $44-$58; D $52-$66; each addl $5; suites $75-$115; under 16 free. Crib free. Pet accepted, some restrictions. TV; cable (premium). Indoor pool. Complimentary continental bkfst. Restaurant nearby. Ck-out 11 am. Business servs avail. In-rm modem link. Downhill ski/x-country ski 12 mi. Exercise equipt; weight machine, bicycle. Some microwaves. Cr cds: A, C, D, DS, MC, V.

✔★ **SUPER 8.** *2730 Dodge St (52003), on US 20.* 319/582-8898. 61 rms, 3 story. No elvtr. S $42.88-$48.88; D $50.88-$57.88; each addl $4; under 12 free. Crib $3. Pet accepted, some restrictions. TV; cable (premium). Complimentary continental bkfst. Restaurant nearby. Ck-out 11 am. Business servs avail. Downhill ski 7 mi. Cr cds: A, C, D, DS, MC, V.

★ ★ **TIMMERMAN'S LODGE.** *(7777 Timmerman Dr, East Dubuque IL 61025) 1 mi E on US 20.* 815/747-3181; FAX 815/747-6556; res: 800/336-3181. 74 rms, 3 story. S $49-$85; D $64-$85; each addl $5; suites $149; under 18 free. Crib $4. Pet accepted. TV; cable, VCR (movies). Indoor pool; whirlpool. Restaurant 7 am-2 pm. Rm serv. Bar. Ck-out noon. Coin lndry. Meeting rm. Business servs avail. In-rm modem link. Sundries. Downhill ski 10 mi; x-country ski ¼ mi. Sauna. Game rm. Rec rm. Private patios, balconies. Cr cds: A, DS, MC, V.

Motor Hotels

★ ★ **HOLIDAY INN.** *450 Main St.* 319/556-2000; FAX 319/556-2303. 193 rms, 5 story. May-Oct: S, D $59-$117; suites $120-$148; under 18 free; lower rates rest of yr. Crib free. Pet accepted, some restrictions; $75. TV; cable (premium), VCR avail. Indoor pool. Restaurant 6:30 am-10 pm. Rm serv. Bar. Ck-out noon. Meeting rms. Business center. Free airport transportation. Exercise equipt; weight machine, stair machine. Some refrigerators, microwaves. Cr cds: A, C, D, DS, MC, V.

✔★ ★ **JULIEN INN.** *200 Main St.* 319/556-4200; FAX 319/582-5023. 145 rms, 8 story. Apr-Oct: S $29.50-$54; D $39-$59; each addl $6; suites $75-$125; under 12 free; lower rates rest of yr. Crib free. TV; cable. Complimentary coffee in lobby. Restaurant 7 am-10 pm. Bar 11-2 am. Ck-out 11 am. Meeting rms. Business servs avail. Bellhops. Free airport transportation. Exercise equipt; bicycle, treadmills. Cr cds: A, C, D, DS, MC, V.

Inn

★ ★ **REDSTONE.** *504 Bluff St.* 319/582-1894; FAX 319/582-1893. 15 units, 3 story. S $60-$75; D $75-$98; each addl $10; suites $115-$175. TV; cable. Complimentary continental bkfst. Ck-out noon, ck-in 3 pm. Business servs avail. In-rm modem link. Whirlpool in some rms. Victorian mansion (1894) built by prominent Dubuque industrialist; fireplaces, antiques. Totally nonsmoking. Cr cds: A, MC, V.

Restaurants

★ **MARIO'S.** *1298 Main St. 319/556-9424.* Hrs: 11 am-11 pm; Sun 4-10:30 pm. Closed major hols. Res accepted. Italian, Amer menu. Bar. Semi-a la carte: lunch $2.75-$4.75, dinner $2.75-$16.95. Specializes in pasta, pizza, steak. Casual atmosphere, contemporary decor. Cr cds: A, C, D, MC, V.

★ ★ **PASTA O'SHEA'S.** *Ninth & Bluff Sts. 319/582-7057.* Hrs: 11:30 am-2 pm, 5-9 pm; Fri, Sat to 10 pm. Closed some major hols. Res accepted; required Fri, Sat. Italian, Amer menu. Bar. Semi-a la carte: lunch $4.95-$8.95, dinner $9.50-$16.95. Child's meals. Specialties: chicken parmigiana, pasta O'Shea's, pepper steak. Child's meals. Contemporary decor with art-deco touches. Cr cds: A, MC, V.

★ **YEN CHING.** *926 Main St. 319/556-2574.* Hrs: 11 am-2 pm, 5-9:30 pm. Closed Sun; Thanksgiving, Dec 25, also wk of July 4. Res accepted. Mandarin, Hunan menu. Semi-a la carte: lunch $4.50-$6, dinner $7-$10. Specializes in twice-cooked pork, cashewed chicken, Szechuan spicy shrimp. Traditional Chinese decor. Cr cds: A, C, D, DS, MC, V.

Emmetsburg (B-3)

(See also Spencer, West Bend)

Settled 1858 **Pop** 3,940 **Elev** 1,234 ft **Area code** 712 **Zip** 50536
Information Chamber of Commerce, 1013 Broadway; 712/852-2283.

In the Des Moines River valley, flanked by Kearney Park, Emmetsburg is the seat of Palo Alto County. A colony of Irish families built the first settlement here and named the community in honor of Irish patriot Robert Emmet. A statue of Emmet stands in the courthouse square. The town is Dublin, Ireland's official "Sister City."

What to See and Do

Kearney Park. 45 acres on Five Island Lake, which covers 945 acres. Boating; fishing. Golf. Picknicking. Camping (fee). NW edge of town. Phone 712/852-4030.

Annual Event

St Patrick's Day Celebration. Features a guest member of Irish Parliament. Parade, pageant, cultural exhibits. Irish stew dinner, dances. Phone 712/852-4326. 3 days around Mar 17.

Motel

✔★ **SUBURBAN.** *RR 1, 1½ mi W on US 18, IA 4. 712/852-2626; FAX 712/852-2821.* 27 rms. S $29-$34; D $39-$44; each addl $3. Crib $3. TV; cable. Coffee in lobby. Restaurant nearby. Ck-out 11 am. Sundries. Cr cds: A, DS, MC, V.

Inn

✔★ **QUEEN MARIE VICTORIAN BED & BREAKFAST.** *707 Harrison St. 712/852-4700; FAX 712/852-3090; res: 800/238-9485.* 5 rms, 2 share bath. No rm phones. S, D $45-$55. TV; cable (premium). Complimentary full bkfst. Restaurant nearby. Ck-out 11 am, ck-in 3-7 pm. Built 1890 by local lumber baron. Totally nonsmoking. Cr cds: MC, V.

Estherville (A-3)

(For accommodations see Okoboji, Spirit Lake)

Settled 1857 **Pop** 6,720 **Elev** 1,298 ft **Area code** 712 **Zip** 51334 **E-mail** echamber@ncn.net **Web** www.ncn.net/~echamber
Information Chamber of Commerce, PO Box 435; 712/362-3541.

What to See and Do

Fort Defiance State Park. Memorial to fort erected during Civil War to protect settlers from attacks by Native Americans. 181 acres; picnic area surrounded by wooded hills, wildflowers. Bridle, hiking trails. Snowmobiling. Picnicking, lodge. Primitive camping. Standard hrs, fees. 1 mi W on IA 9, then 1½ mi S on County N 26. Phone 712/362-2078.

Annual Event

Winter Sports Festival. Ice & snow sculptures, skiing, skating; art, quilt shows; dance, concert. Phone 712/362-3541. 1st wkend Feb.

Fairfield (E-7)

(See also Mount Pleasant, Ottumwa)

Settled 1839 **Pop** 9,768 **Elev** 778 ft **Area code** 515 **Zip** 52556

What to See and Do

✪ **Bentonsport-National Historic District.** Preserved 1840s village with 13 original buildings; Mason House Inn (1846) with original furnishings offers lodging and tours (fee); churches, stately brick houses; antique & craftshops; lodging. Canoeing. Special events. Village (Apr-Nov, daily). 20 mi S on IA 1, then 5 mi E on County J40, in Keosauqua. Phone 319/592-3133.

Jefferson County Park. This 175-acre area is mostly oak and hickory timberland, which provides an excellent wildlife habitat; three ponds stocked with bass, bluegill and catfish. Hiking, bicycle trails. Cross-country skiing. Picnicking, playground. Camping (fee; electricity addl). ½ mi SW on County H33 (Libertyville Rd). Phone 515/472-4421. **Free.**

Lacey-Keosauqua State Park. Approx 1,500 acres includes Ely's Ford, famous Mormon crossing. Heavily wooded; scenic views; 61-acre lake. Swimming, supervised beach; fishing; boating (ramp, rentals). Hiking trails. Snowmobiling. Picnicking, lodge. Camping (electricity, dump station), cabins. Standard hrs, fees. 23 mi S on IA 1, near Keosauqua. Phone 319/293-3502.

Old Settlers Park. An 11-acre park; Bonnifield Cabin (1838); grave of first settler. B St, N edge of town.

Motels

★ ★ **BEST WESTERN.** *2220 W Burlington, on US 34. 515/472-2200; FAX 515/472-7642.* 52 rms, 2 story. S $55-$64; D $62-$71; each addl $8; under 18 free. Crib free. Pet accepted, some restrictions. TV. Indoor pool; whirlpool. Complimentary continental bkfst. Restaurant 11 am-2 pm, 5-9 pm. Ck-out noon. Meeting rms. Cr cds: A, C, D, DS, ER, JCB, MC, V.

★ ★ **ECONOMY INN.** *2701 W Burlington, 1½ mi W on US 34. 515/472-4161.* 42 rms, 1-2 story. S $35; D $36-$45; each addl $5; Crib $3. Pet accepted, some restrictions. TV; cable. Restaurant opp 6 am-11 pm. Ck-out 11 am. Meeting rm. Cr cds: A, DS, MC, V.

Fort Dodge (C-4)

(See also Humboldt, Webster City)

Founded 1853 **Pop** 25,894 **Elev** 1,030 ft **Area code** 515 **Zip** 50501
E-mail cofc@dodgenet.com

Information Chamber of Commerce, 1406 Central Ave, PO Box T; 515/955-5500 or 800/765-1438.

Astride the Des Moines River, atop a gypsum bed that covers nearly 30 square miles, and nestled amid fertile farms, Fort Dodge has every ingredient for prosperity. Major industries are veterinary pharmaceuticals, gypsum products, pet food and aluminum cans.

Fort Dodge was established to protect settlers. Its commander, Major William Williams, was given a large tract of land as part of his compensation, and here the town was laid out. Fort Dodge was an innocent party to a scientific hoax when a huge slab of gypsum cut here was freighted to Chicago and carved into the celebrated Cardiff Giant, falsely claimed to be a petrified prehistoric man (now at the Farmer's Museum, Cooperstown, NY).

What to See and Do

Blanden Memorial Art Museum. American and European paintings and sculpture; Asian paintings and decorative arts; African, Pre-Columbian art, graphic art; photography; changing exhibits. (Daily exc Mon) 920 3rd Ave S. Phone 515/573-2316.   **Free.**

⭐ **Fort Dodge Historical Museum, Fort Museum and Frontier Village.** Replica of 1862 fort houses museum, trading post, blacksmith shop, general store, log home, drugstore, cabinet shop, newspaper office, church, jail and one-room school. A replica of the "Cardiff Giant" is on display at the Fort Museum. (May-Oct, daily; rest of yr, by appt) At jct US 20 Business, Museum Rd. Phone 515/573-4231.   ¢¢

John F. Kennedy Memorial Park. Swimming, fishing, boating (ramp; no motors). Picnicking, shelter; "children's forest," playground; golfing. Tent & trailer sites (mid-Apr-Oct; fee). (Daily) 5 mi N on County P56. Phone 515/576-4258.   **Free.**

Kalsow Prairie. Approx 160 acres preserving untouched Iowa prairie. 15 mi W on IA 7 to Manson, then 2 mi N on county road.

Site of Old Fort Dodge. Boulder with bronze tablet marks spot where fort stood. 1st Ave N & N 4th St.

State parks.

Twin Lakes. Approx 15 acres adj N Twin Lake. Swimming; fishing; boating (ramps). Picnicking. Standard hrs, fees. 26 mi W on IA 7, then 3 mi S on IA 4, then E on IA 124. Phone 712/657-8712.

Dolliver Memorial. This 572-acre park features deep ravines, 75-ft limestone walls, Native American mounds and scenic overlook. Fishing; boating (ramp). Hiking trails. Picnicking. Camping (electricity, dump station). Cabins, lodges. Standard hrs, fees. 8 mi S on US 169, then 5 mi E on IA 50, then 1 mi N. Phone 515/359-2539.

Motels

✔⭐⭐ **BEST WESTERN STARLITE VILLAGE.** *2 mi NW at jct US 169, IA 7.* 515/573-7177; FAX 515/573-3999. 120 rms, 1-2 story. S $40-$46; D $54-$60; each addl $5. TV; cable. Indoor pool; whirlpool, poolside serv. Restaurant 6 am-2 pm, 5-10 pm. Rm serv. Bar 11-2 am. Ck-out noon. Meeting rms. Valet serv. Game rm. Cr cds: A, C, D, DS, MC, V.

D ⛱ ⊠ 🐾 SC

⭐ **COMFORT INN.** *2938 5th Ave S.* 515/573-3731; FAX 515/573-3751. 48 rms, 2 story. S $45-$110; D $47-$110; each addl $6; under 18 free. Crib free. TV; cable. Indoor pool; whirlpool. Complimentary continental bkfst. Restaurant adj open 24 hrs. Ck-out 11 am. Some refrigerators. Cr cds: A, D, DS, JCB, MC, V.

D ⛱ ⊠ 🐾 SC

⭐⭐ **HOLIDAY INN.** *2001 US 169S, at jct US 20.* 515/955-3621; FAX 515/955-3643. 102 rms, 2 story. S $49-$58; D $57-$61; under 19 free. Crib free. TV. Heated pool; wading pool. Playground. Restaurant 6 am-10 pm, Sun 7 am-3 pm. Rm serv. Bar 11-1 am; Sun 3-8 pm. Ck-out 1 pm. Meeting rms. Cr cds: A, C, D, DS, JCB, MC, V.

D ⛱ ⊠ 🐾 SC

Fort Madison (F-8)

(See also Burlington, Keokuk)

Settled 1808 **Pop** 11,618 **Elev** 536 ft **Area code** 319 **Zip** 52627

Information Riverbend Regional Convention & Visitors Bureau, 933 Ave H, PO Box 425; 319/372-5472 or 800/210-TOUR.

Fort Madison began as the first military outpost (1808-1813) on the upper Mississippi River. Settlers established the town in the early 1830s; steamboats and logging were important early industries. Fort Madison entered an era of prosperity when the Sante Fe Railroad arrived in the 1880s. Today, the manufacture of pens and paints is important to the economy. Fort Madison is also home to the state's only maximum-security prison.

What to See and Do

Lee County Courthouse (1841). Oldest courthouse in continuous use in the state. (Mon-Fri; closed hols) 701 Ave F. Phone 319/372-3523.   **Free.**

Riverview Park. Approx 35 landscaped acres. Marina; flower garden; picnicking. Reflective pool and fountain. (May-Sept, daily) Between river and business section at E end of town. Phone 319/372-7700.   ¢¢ Also here is

Old Fort Madison. Full-scale replica of fort that existed from 1808-1813. Complete living history experience includes uniformed soldiers loading and firing muskets. (Memorial Day-Aug, daily; May, Sept, Oct, wkends) Phone 319/372-6318 or -7700.   ¢¢

Rodeo Park. 234 acres. Picnicking; camping (Apr-Oct, fee); nature trails. (Daily) 1 mi N on IA 88. Phone 319/372-7700.   **Free.**

Sante Fe Depot Historic Museum and Complex. Local historical displays, farm machinery, old fire engine; replica of old icehouse; prison and railroad displays. (Apr-Sept, daily) 9th & Ave H. Phone 319/372-7661.   ¢

Santa Fe Railway Bridge. The largest double-track, double-decked railroad swing-span bridge in the world. E edge of town.

Shimek State Forest. Park has 7,940 acres with 20-acre lake. Fishing; boating (electric motors only). Hunting. Hiking, bridle trails. Snowmobiling. Picnicking. Primitive camping. Standard hrs, fees. 25 mi W on IA 2, E of Farmington. Phone 319/878-3811.

Annual Event

Tri-State Rodeo. Rodeo Arena, N on County X32, at Old Denmark Rd. Rated one of top 10 PRCA rodeos in US. Preceded by wk of festivities. Phone 319/372-2550 or 800/369-3211. Thurs-Sat following Labor Day.

Motel

✔⭐ **MADISON INN.** *3440 Avenue L.* 319/372-7740; res: 800/728-7316. 20 rms. S, D $38-$47; each addl $5; higher rates Tri-State Rodeo. Pet accepted, some restrictions; $2. TV; cable (premium). Complimentary coffee in rms. Restaurant adj 6 pm-midnight. Ck-out 11 am. Business servs avail. In-rm modem link. Cr cds: A, C, D, DS, MC, V.

D 🐾 ⊠ 🐾 SC

Inn

⭐⭐⭐ **KINGSLEY.** *707 Avenue H.* 319/372-7074; FAX 319/372-7096; res: 800/441-2327. Web www.abba.com. 14 rms, 3 story. Apr-Oct:

S, D $70-$115; package plans; lower rates rest of yr. Children over 12 yrs. TV; cable (premium). Complimentary full bkfst. Restaurant adj 11 am-11 pm; Fri, Sat to midnight. Ck-out 11 am, ck-in 3 pm. Gift shop. Health club privileges. Microwaves avail. Some balconies. Restored historic building (1860s); antiques. Opp Mississippi River. Cr cds: A, C, D, DS, MC, V.

D ⛵ 🔥 SC

Garner (B-5)

(For accommodations see Clear Lake, Mason City)

Pop 2,916 **Elev** 1,216 ft **Area code** 515 **Zip** 50438

What to See and Do

Pilot Knob State Park. Glacial formation rising to one of highest points in state. More than 700 heavily wooded acres with 15-acre lake. Fishing; boating (electric motors only). Bridle, hiking trails. Snowmobiling. Picnicking. Observation tower. Camping (electricity, dump station). Standard hrs, fees. 3 mi W via US 18, then 10 mi N on US 69, then 6 mi E on IA 9, then 1 mi S on IA 332 near Forest City. Phone 515/581-4835.

Rice Lake State Park. Park has 47 acres on 612-acre lake. Fishing. Picnicking. 3 mi W via US 18, then 24 mi NE on US 69, then S on unnumbered road. Phone 515/581-4835.

Grinnell (D-6)

(See also Marshalltown, Newton)

Founded 1854 **Pop** 8,902 **Elev** 1,016 ft **Area code** 515 **Zip** 50112
Information Chamber of Commerce, 1010 Main St, PO Box 538; 515/236-6555.

When Horace Greeley said, "Go west, young man, go west and grow up with the country!" he was talking to Josiah Bushnell Grinnell, who took the advice, went west to a bit of prairie between the Iowa and Skunk rivers and established the town of Grinnell. Today, Grinnell is a thriving college town prospering on the fruits of the surrounding farmland and its more than 20 factories and processing plants.

What to See and Do

Brenton National Bank - Poweshiek County (1914). The second in the series of "jewel box" banks that architect Louis Henri Sullivan designed late in his career. This unique structure, one of the more important designs in the series, has been restored within the confines of a working bank environment. (Mon-Fri) Downtown, on corner opposite town square.

Grinnell College (1846). (1,243 students) Considered one of top coeducational, liberal arts colleges in US. Tours (by appt). On US 6, NE of business district. Phone 515/269-3400.

Grinnell Historical Museum. Historical furnishings; relics, documents of J.B. Grinnell and aviator Billy Robinson in late Victorian house. (June-Aug, Tues-Sun afternoons; rest of yr, Sat afternoons) 1125 Broad St. Phone 515/236-3252. **Donation.**

Rock Creek State Park. More than 1,260 acres on 602-acre lake. Swimming; fishing; boating (ramp, rentals). Hiking trails. Snowmobiling. Picnicking. Camping (electricity, dump station). Standard hrs, fees. 7 mi W on US 6, then 3 mi N on IA 224. Phone 515/236-3722.

Motels

★ **DAYS INN.** *IA 146, I-80 exit 182. 515/236-6710; FAX 515/236-5783.* 41 rms, 2 story. S $49; D $65; under 12 free. Pet accepted;

$5. TV; cable. Indoor pool. Complimentary continental bkfst. Ck-out 11 am. Cr cds: A, C, D, DS, MC, V.

D ⛵ 🏊 ⛵ 🔥 SC

✔ ★ **SUPER 8.** *exit 182, I-80 & IA 146. 515/236-7888.* 53 rms, 2 story. S $42.88; D $52.88; each addl $3; under 12 free; higher rates: special events, wkends. Crib $4. Pet accepted, some restrictions. TV; cable (premium). Complimentary continental bkfst. Restaurant opp 6:30 am-9 pm. Ck-out 11 am. Cr cds: A, C, D, DS, MC, V.

D ⛵ ⛵ 🔥 SC

Restaurants

★ ★ **KELCY'S.** *812 6th Ave. 515/236-3132.* Hrs: 11 am-1:30 pm, 5:30-10 pm. Closed Sun; major hols. Res accepted. Bar. Semi-a la carte: lunch $3.20-$5.75, dinner $6.95-$15.95. Child's meals. Specializes in steak, prime rib. Casual elegance. Cr cds: MC, V.

✔ ★ **LONGHORN.** *1011 Main St. 515/236-4144.* Hrs: 6 am-9 pm; Sun to 2 pm. Res accepted. Bar. Semi-a la carte: bkfst $1.25-$5.25, lunch $1.50-$6.40, dinner $3.50-$11.95. Specializes in steak, seafood. Western decor. Cr cds: MC, V.

Hampton (B-5)

Founded 1856 **Pop** 4,133 **Elev** 1,145 ft **Area code** 515 **Zip** 50441
Information Chamber of Commerce, 5 First St SW; phone 515/456-5668.

What to See and Do

Beed's Lake State Park. Park of 319 acres; dam creates 100-acre lake. Swimming, beach; fishing; boating (ramps). Hiking. Snowmobiling. Picnicking. Camping (electricity, dump station). Standard hrs, fees. 3 mi NW near jct US 65, IA 3. Phone 515/456-2047.

Motel

✔ ★ **GOLD KEY.** *US 65, Rte 2, 2 mi N on US 65. 515/456-2566.* 20 rms. S $26-$30; D $31-$40; each addl $3-$5. Crib free. Pet accepted. TV; cable. Restaurant adj 6:30 am-10:30 pm. Sundries. Ck-out 11 am. Cr cds: A, D, DS, MC, V.

⛵ 🔥

Humboldt (B-4)

(See also Fort Dodge)

Pop 4,438 **Elev** 1,089 ft **Area code** 515 **Zip** 50548
Information Humboldt/Dakota City Chamber of Commerce, 29 S 5th St, PO Box 247; 515/332-1481.

A small religious sect, led by the Rev. S.H. Taft, came to this site on the West Fork of the Des Moines River and founded the community of Springvale, later renamed Humboldt in honor of the German scientist.

What to See and Do

Frank A. Gotch Park. A 67-acre park at the confluence of the east and west forks of the Des Moines River. Fishing; boating. Picnicking, camping (fee). 3 mi SE off US 169. Phone 515/332-4087.

Humboldt County Historical Museum. Housed in eight buildings; Mill Farm House (1879), a handmade two-story brick house with summer kitchen, enclosed summer porch, Victorian furnishings, doll and toy collections; Red Barn exhibits include Native American artifacts, farm equipment, tools, carpenter and blacksmith shops and old-time post office; Willow School (1883), restored as a one-room 1890s schoolhouse. Also an authentically furnished log cabin, kettle shed, jail (ca 1907) and chicken house (ca 1875). (May-Sept, daily exc Wed) E edge of Dakota City, S of IA 3 and County P 56. Phone 515/332-5280. ¢

Joe Sheldon Park. An 81-acre park with camping (fee); fishing; boating (ramp); picnicking. Phone 515/332-4087. 2 mi W of US 169, S of IA 3.

Motels

✔★ **BROADWAY INN.** *812 N 13th St (US 169).* 515/332-3545. 38 rms, 13 with shower only, 2 story. S $25-$32; D $28-$40; each addl $2; under 16 free. TV; cable. Complimentary continental bkfst. Restaurant nearby. Ck-out 11 am. Cr cds: A, DS, MC, V.

★ **CORNER INN.** *US 169 & IA 3.* 515/332-1672. 22 rms, 1 story. S $29-$30; D $35-$39; each addl $6. Pet accepted. TV; cable. Restaurant opp 6 am-midnight. Ck-out 11 am. Cr cds: MC, V.

Indianola (E-5)

(See also Des Moines, Winterset)

Pop 11,340 **Elev** 970 ft **Area code** 515 **Zip** 50125 **E-mail** linda@chamber.indianola.ia.us **Web** www.indianola.ia.us/chamber
Information Chamber of Commerce, 515 N Jefferson, Suite D; 515/961-6269.

What to See and Do

Lake Ahquabi State Park. More than 770 acres with 114-acre lake. Swimming, supervised beach; fishing; boating (ramps, rentals). Hiking trail. Snowmobiling. Picnicking. Lodge. Camping (electricity, dump station). Standard hrs, fees. 5 mi S off US 69. Phone 515/961-7101.

National Balloon Museum. Ballooning artifacts and history spanning more than 200 yrs. (Daily; closed most major hols) N edge of town on US 65/69. Phone 515/961-3714. **Free.**

Simpson College (1860). (1,700 students) On campus are George Washington Carver Science Bldg, Dunn Library with historic exhibit, Blank Performing Arts Center and Amy Robertson Music Center. Tours. N Buxton St & W Clinton Ave. Phone 515/961-6251.

Annual Event

National Balloon Classic. 2 mi E on IA 92. Phone 515/961-8415. Late July or early Aug.

Seasonal Event

Des Moines Metro Opera Summer Festival. Blank Performing Arts Center, Simpson College. Three operas performed in repertory by the Des Moines Metro Opera Company. For schedule, reservations phone 515/961-6221. Mid-June-mid-July.

Motel

✔★ ★ **APPLE TREE INN.** *1215 N Jefferson St, at US 65/69.* 515/961-0551; FAX 515/961-0555; res: 800/961-0551. 60 rms, 2 story. S $45; D $50; each addl $3; suites $55; under 10 free. Crib $3. TV; cable (premium). Complimentary coffee in lobby. Restaurant adj 6 am-11 pm.

Ck-out noon. Meeting rm. Business servs avail. Cr cds: A, C, D, DS, MC, V.

Iowa City (D-7)

(See also Amana Colonies, Cedar Rapids)

Founded 1839 **Pop** 59,738 **Elev** 698 ft **Area code** 319 **E-mail** cvb@icccvb.org **Web** www.icccvb.org
Information Iowa City/Coralville Convention & Visitors Bureau, 408 First Ave, Riverview Square, Coralville 52241; 319/337-6592 or 800/283-6592.

Fondly referred to as "the river city," Iowa City is the home of the University of Iowa and the state's first capitol. Founded to become Iowa's territorial capital, Iowa City boomed as a backwoods metropolis with the Territorial Legislative Assembly meeting here for the first time in 1841. A Doric stone capitol was erected, but with the shift of population the legislators moved to Des Moines in 1857. As a conciliatory gesture to Iowa City they selected it as the site of the new university. The "Old Capitol" and 10 acres of land were given for use by the university.

The university is the major enterprise, but the community is also important as one of the top medical centers in the country, the key city of hog, cattle and grain-raising in Johnson County and an industrial center.

What to See and Do

Coralville Lake. A 4,900-acre lake; swimming; boating (marinas, ramps); off-road biking; fishing, hunting. Picnicking. Improved camping (8 areas, 7 with fees). The flooding that occurred during the summer of 1993 eroded a 15-ft-deep channel exposing the underlying bedrock. Now called Devonian Fossil Gorge, it offers a rare opportunity to view Iowa's geological past. An Army Corps of Engineers project. (Daily) 3½ mi N of I-80. Phone 319/338-3543.

Herbert Hoover National Historic Site. The 187-acre park includes restored house in which President Hoover was born; Quaker meetinghouse where he worshiped as a boy; school; blacksmith shop; graves of President and Lou Henry Hoover. (Daily; buildings closed Jan 1, Thanksgiving, Dec 25) 10 mi E on I-80 exit 254 to West Branch. Phone 319/643-2541. ¢ Also in park is

Herbert Hoover Presidential Library-Museum (1962). Administered by the National Archives and Records Administration. Features a museum with recreated historic settings in China, Belgium, Washington and other places prominent in Hoover's 50 yrs of public service. Changing exhibits, film. Research library (by appt). (Daily; closed Jan 1, Thanksgiving, Dec 25) Phone 319/643-5301. ¢

⭐ **Kalona Historical Village.** Amish traditions and lifestyle are preserved in village containing the Wahl Museum, the Mennonite Museum & Archives and an implement building; restored 110-yr-old depot, log house (1842), one-room school, country store, outdoor bake oven, Victorian house, working windmill, post office (1880) and church (1869). (Daily exc Sun) Approx 18 mi SW via IA 1 in Kalona. Phone 319/656-3232. ¢¢

Lake Macbride State Park. More than 2,150 acres with 812-acre lake. Swimming, bathhouse, supervised beach; fishing; boating (ramps, rentals). Hiking. Snowmobile trails. Picnicking, concession. Improved & primitive camping (electricity, dump station; fee). Standard hrs, fees. 11 mi N on IA 1, then 4 mi W on IA 382 in Solon. Phone 319/644-2200.

Plum Grove (1844). Residence of territory's first governor, Robert Lucas; restored and furnished. (Mid-Apr-mid-Oct, Wed-Sun) 1030 Carroll St. Phone 319/337-6846 or 319/644-2200. ¢

University of Iowa (1847). (28,000 students) More than 90 major buildings on 1,900 acres; 10 colleges, 6 schools, 82 departments. In the central section of city on both sides of Iowa River. University Relations office at 5 Old Capitol; phone 319/335-3500. On campus are

Old Capitol. First capitol of state; restored to original appearance of 1840s-1850s. (Daily; closed hols) Clinton St & Iowa Ave, on E campus. **Free.**

Medical Museum. Photographs, artifacts and hands-on displays focusing on history of medicine and patient care in Iowa. Changing exhibits. (Mon-Fri; also Sat & Sun afternoons; closed Jan 1, Thanksgiving wkend, Dec 25) On W campus at The University of Iowa Hospitals & Clinics, Patient and Visitor Activities Center, eighth floor. Phone 319/356-7106. **Free.**

Museum of Natural History. Habitat dioramas; mounted mammals, fish, reptiles, birds. (Daily; closed hols) In Macbride Hall, Jefferson & Capitol Sts, on east campus. **Free.** Also here is

Iowa Hall. An exhibit gallery showing the state's geological, cultural and environmental history. **Free.**

Museum of Art. Paintings, prints, lithographs; sculpture; silver; African art. (Daily exc Mon; closed hols) W bank of Iowa River, near jct of Riverside Dr & River St. **Free.**

Carver-Hawkeye Arena. Seats 15,500. Big 10 basketball games, wrestling meets, gymnastics, volleyball; also concerts and special events. On Elliott Dr, between Hawkins Dr & Newton Rd.

Annual Events

Iowa Arts Festival. Celebration of the arts. Phone 319/337-9637. Mid-June.

Kalona Fall Festival. At Kalona Historical Village. Amish food, crafts and displays. Last wkend Sept.

Motels

(Rates may be higher football wkends)

★ ★ **BEST WESTERN WESTFIELD INN.** *(1895 27th Ave, Coralville 52241) I-80 & IA 965 exit 240.* 319/354-7770. 155 rms, 2 story. S $57-$65; D $65-$73; each addl $8; under 17 free; wkly, monthly rates. Pet accepted. TV; cable (premium). Indoor pool; whirlpool. Complimentary continental bkfst. Restaurant 6:30 am-2 pm, 5-10 pm. Rm serv. Bar 4 pm-midnight. Ck-out 11 am. Meeting rms. Business servs avail. Airport transportation. Exercise equipt; treadmill, stair machine, sauna. Putting green. Game rm. Rec rm. Microwaves avail. Cr cds: A, C, D, DS, MC, V.

D ⬦ ≋ ✗ ⬟ ⬛ SC

★ ★ **CLARION.** *(1220 First Ave, Coralville 52241) 3 mi NW on I-80 exit 242.* 319/351-5049; *FAX 319/354-4214; res: 800/962-0110.* 96 rms, 4 story. No elvtr. S, D $59-$69; under 18 free. Crib free. Indoor pool. TV; cable (premium). Complimentary continental bkfst. Restaurant 11 am-2 pm, 5-10 pm; Fri, Sat to 11 pm. Ck-out noon. Meeting rms. Business servs avail. Exercise equipt; bicycle, stair machines. Cr cds: A, D, DS, MC, V.

D ≋ ✗ ⬟ ⬛

★ ★ **HAMPTON INN.** *(1200 First Ave, Coralville 52241) W on I-80, exit 237.* 319/351-6600; *FAX 319/351-3928.* 115 rms, 4 story. S, D $59-$69; under 10 free. TV; cable (premium). Complimentary continental bkfst. Restaurant 5-10 pm. Ck-out noon. Meeting rms. Business center. In-rm modem link. Free airport transportation. Exercise equipt; bicycle, treadmill. Indoor pool; whirlpool. Some refrigerators, microwaves. Cr cds: A, D, DS, MC, V.

D ≋ ✗ ⬟ ⬛ SC ⬥

★ **HEARTLAND INN.** *(87 Second St, Coralville 52241) 1 mi W off I-80 exit 242, at jct 1st Ave & US 6, near University Hospital.* 319/351-8132; *FAX 319/351-2916.* 171 rms, 3 story. S $52.50-$61.50; D $60.50-$69.50; each addl $8; suites $80-$225; under 16 free; hospital rates. Crib free. TV; cable (premium), VCR avail. Complimentary continental bkfst. Restaurant adj 10 am-10 pm. Ck-out 11 am. Business servs avail. In-rm modem link. Exercise equipt; stair machine, bicycle, sauna. Cr cds: A, C, D, DS, MC, V.

D ✗ ⬟ ⬛ SC

★ **PRESIDENTIAL MOTOR INN.** *(711 S Downey Rd, West Branch 52358) I-80 exit 254.* 319/643-2526. 38 rms, 2 story. S $36-$44; D $55-$65; each addl $12; wkly rates. Crib $3. Pet accepted, some restrictions. TV; cable (premium). Complimentary coffee in lobby. Ck-out 11 am. Coin lndry. Refrigerators; microwaves avail. Cr cds: A, D, DS, MC, V.

D ⬦ ≋ ⬛

✔ ★ **SUPER 8.** *(611 1st Ave, Coralville 52241) I-80 exit 242.* 319/337-8388; *FAX 319/337-4327.* 87 rms, 2 story. S $47.98; D $56.98; each addl $3. Crib $2. TV; cable (premium). Complimentary continental bkfst. Restaurant nearby. Ck-out 11 am. Business servs avail. Sundries. Microwaves avail. Cr cds: A, C, D, DS, MC, V.

D ≋ ⬛ SC

Motor Hotel

★ ★ ★ **HOLIDAY INN.** *210 S Dubuque St (52240).* 319/337-4058; *FAX 319/337-9045.* E-mail holiday@ia.net. 236 rms, 9 story. S $79; D $89; each addl $10; suites $145-$160; under 19 free. Pet accepted, some restrictions. TV; cable (premium). Indoor pool; whirlpool. Restaurant 6 am-2 pm, 5-10 pm. Rm serv. Bar 4 pm-1 am. Ck-out noon. Meeting rms. Business servs avail. Bellhops. Beauty shop. Airport transportation. Exercise equipt; bicycles, treadmills, sauna. Game rm. Refrigerators. Cr cds: A, C, D, DS, MC, V.

D ⬦ ≋ ✗ ⬟ ⬛ SC

Restaurants

★ ★ **IOWA RIVER POWER COMPANY.** *(501 First Ave, Coralville) I-80 exit 242.* 319/351-1904. Hrs: 11:30 am-2 pm, 5-9:30 pm; Fri to 10:30 pm; Sat 5-10:30 pm; Sun 4-9:30 pm; Sun brunch 10 am-2 pm. Closed Dec 25. Res accepted. Bar. Semi-a la carte: lunch $6-$7.50, dinner $10.95-$28.95. Sun brunch $8.95. Child's meals. Specializes in prime rib, fowl, seafood. Salad bar. Multi-tiered dining in former power generating building. Overlooks river. Cr cds: A, C, D, MC, V.

D

★ ★ **JIMMY'S BISTRO.** *325 E Washington (52240).* 319/337-2378. E-mail jimocooks@aol.com. Hrs: 11 am-10 pm; Sat, Sun from 8 am. Closed Thanksgiving, Dec 25. Res accepted. Bar. Contemporary Southwestern menu. Semi-a la carte: lunch, dinner $2.99-$13.99. Specializes in lambchops, portabello spinach potato lasagna, swordfish. Outdoor dining. Cr cds: A, MC, V.

D

★ **LB STEAK HOUSE.** *(102 W Main St, West Branch 52358)* I-80 exit 254. 319/643-5420. Hrs: 5-10 pm; Sun to 9 pm. Closed Mon; Thanksgiving, Dec 24, 25. Res accepted. Bar. Semi-a la carte: dinner $8.95-$14.50. Sun brunch $6.95. Child's meals. Salad bar. 10 x 4 brick charcoal grill where customers grill own steak. Cr cds: A, D, MC, V.

D

★ **MONDO'S.** *212 S Clinton (52240).* 319/337-6787. Hrs: 11 am-10 pm; Fri, Sat to 11 pm; Sun brunch from 9:30 am. Closed Thanksgiving, Dec 25. Bar. Semi-a la carte: lunch, dinner $5.99-$10.99. Sun brunch $4.99-$7.99. Child's meals. Specializes in pizza, burritos, hot oatmeal pie. Informal atmosphere. Cr cds: A, D, MC, V.

D

Keokuk (F-8)

(See also Fort Madison)

Settled 1820 **Pop** 12,451 **Elev** 550 ft **Area code** 319 **Zip** 52632 **E-mail** keochcom@inter1.net **Web** www.inter1.net
Information Keokuk Area Convention & Tourism Bureau, Pierce Bldg, 401 Main St; 319/524-5599 or 800/383-1219.

At the foot of the Des Moines rapids on the Mississippi, Keokuk served as a gateway to the West and North and a manufacturing center for the pioneer frontier. The town was named for a Native American chief and developed as a fur-trading center. Manufacturing and agricultural industries are its mainstays now.

What to See and Do

Keokuk Dam (1910-1913). Union Electric Company Hydroelectric Power Plant with a mi-long dam across the Mississippi River to Hamilton, IL. Offers half-hr tours (Memorial Day-Labor Day, daily; rest of yr, by appt; lobby open Mon-Fri; closed hols). Lock 19, operated by Army Corps of Engineers, has observation platform. End of N Water St at riverfront. Phone 319/524-4091 or 319/524-9660. **Free.**

Keokuk River Museum. In Sternwheel towboat *George M. Verity,* houses historical items of upper Mississippi River valley. (Apr-Oct, daily) Victory Park, foot of Johnson St. Phone 319/524-4765. ¢

National Cemetery. Unknown Soldier monument, Civil War graves. S 18th & Ridge Sts.

Rand Park. Statue and grave of Chief Keokuk. Flower gardens, picnic area. (Daily) Orleans Ave between N 14th & N 17th Sts.

Samuel F. Miller House and Museum. Restored home of US Supreme Court Justice appointed by Abraham Lincoln. (Fri & Sat afternoons) 318 N 5th St. Phone 319/524-7283. ¢

Annual Events

Bald Eagle Appreciation Days. Jan 16-18.

Civil War Reenactment. April 23-26.

Motels

★ ★ **HOLIDAY INN EXPRESS.** *Fourth & Main Sts, on US 136.* 319/524-8000; FAX 319/524-4114. 80 rms, 5 story. S $59; D $67; each addl $8. Crib free. TV; cable (premium). Pool; whirlpool. Complimentary continental bkfst. Ck-out noon. Meeting rms. Business servs avail. In-rm modem link. Exercise equipt; weight machine, treadmill, sauna. Game rm. Cr cds: A, C, D, DS, MC, V.

[D] [≈] [⊀] [⊁] [⊁] [SC]

✔★ **SUPER 8.** *3511 Main St.* 319/524-3888. 62 rms, 2 story. S $43.98; D $52.98; suites $56.98. Crib $2. TV; cable. Restaurant adj 11 am-9 pm. Ck-out 11 am. Business servs avail. Microwaves avail. Cr cds: A, C, D, DS, MC, V.

[D] [⊁] [⊁] [SC]

Le Mars (B-1)

(See also Sioux City)

Settled 1869 **Pop** 8,454 **Elev** 1,231 ft **Area code** 712 **Zip** 51031
Information Chamber of Commerce, 50 Central Ave SE; 712/546-8821.

A young English gentleman learned of the opportunities in this part of Iowa, formed a land company and induced a colony of Englishmen to settle here.

A training farm, cricket and polo fields and a tavern called "The House of Lords" soon blossomed. Le Mars was well-known in Great Britain and was advertised there as a training ground for second sons in the areas of farming and stock-raising. However, as the young Englishmen preferred horse racing, pubs and sports to working the soil, the Germans, Irish, Luxembourgers and Scandinavians took over the serious business of farming.

Today, Le Mars is the financial, educational and recreational center for the area. And as home to Wells Dairy, Inc, it has earned the name "Ice Cream Capital of the World."

What to See and Do

Plymouth County Historical Museum. More than 100 antique musical instruments; antique farm machinery, tools and furnishings; Native American artifacts; restored log cabin; four 1900 period rms. (Daily exc Mon; closed hols) 355 1st Ave SW. Phone 712/546-7002. **Free.**

Westmar University (1890). (780 students) The Charles A. Mock Library houses an art gallery (daily). Also on campus is the Danner Arboretum, a botanical laboratory that encompasses the campus. 3rd Ave SE. Phone 712/546-7081.

Annual Events

Ice Cream Days. Citywide event includes Art in the Park, children's learning fair, parade, street dance, fireworks. July 4th wkend.

Plymouth County Fair. Pioneer village and historic round barn; exhibits, arts & crafts; entertainment. Last wk July.

Motels

✔★ **AMBER INN.** *1 mi S on US 75.* 712/546-7066; FAX 712/548-4058; res: 800/338-0298. 73 rms. S $28-$32; D $30-$35; each addl $2. Crib $2. Pet accepted. TV; cable. Continental breakfast. Restaurant nearby. Ck-out 11 am. Meeting rm. Business servs avail. Cr cds: A, C, DS, MC, V.

[D] [✔] [⊁] [⊁]

★ **SUPER 8.** *1201 Hawkeye Ave SW.* 712/546-8800. 61 rms, 3 story. S $36.88; D $41.88; suites $49.88-$63.88. Crib $3. TV. Complimentary bkfst. Restaurant nearby. Ck-out 11 am. Meeting rms. Business servs avail. Whirlpool. Cr cds: A, D, DS, MC, V.

[D] [⊁] [⊁] [SC]

Maquoketa (C-8)

Founded 1838 **Pop** 6,111 **Elev** 700 ft **Area code** 319 **Zip** 52060
Information Chamber of Commerce, 112 N Main St; 319/652-4602.

From 1840-1870, this town was a stopping point for wagon trains before they ferried across the Maquoketa River heading west. Today, Maquoketa is a beef and dairy production center and the home of several diversified industries.

What to See and Do

Costello's Old Mill Gallery. Restored stone mill with waterwheel, built in 1867; inside constructed entirely of oak. Art gallery. (Apr-Dec, daily; rest of yr, Wed-Sun) 1 mi E on IA 64. Phone 319/652-3351. **Free.**

Jackson County Historical Museum. Replicas of general store and one-room country school; 19th-century bedrm, living rm and kitchen; old fire equipment, log cabin, buggies; barn with antique machinery, blacksmith shop; church; medical center; entertainment center, tent show; toy shop; wildlife display. Changing exhibits; exhibits by local artists. (Mar-Dec, Tues-Sun; closed hols) E Quarry St at Fairgrounds. Phone 319/652-5020. **Free.**

Maquoketa Caves State Park. Park of 272 acres. Large limestone caves; natural bridge rises 50 ft above valley floor; 17-ton rock balanced on cliff. Hiking trail. Picnicking. Camping. Standard hrs, fees. 7 mi NW on IA 428. Phone 319/652-5833.

Annual Event

Octoberfest of Bands. 40 marching bands; parade, field marching competitions. Phone 319/652-4602 or contact Chamber of Commerce. 1st Sat Oct.

Motel

✔★ **KEY.** 119 McKinsey Ave, 1 blk E of US 64/61 Bypass on McKinsey Dr. 319/652-5131; res: 800/622-3285. 30 rms, 2 story. S, D $30-$40; each addl $5. Crib free. Pet accepted. TV; cable. Restaurant adj 6 am-10 pm. Ck-out 11 am. Cr cds: A, C, D, DS, MC, V.

Inn

★ ★ **SQUIERS MANOR.** 418 W Pleasant St, US 61 exit Platt St, E to Prospect St, 1 blk S. 319/652-6961. 8 rms, 2 with shower only, 3 story, 3 suites. No rm phones. S, D $75-$100; each addl $15; suites $150-$185. Crib free. TV. Complimentary full bkfst. Restaurant nearby. Ck-out 11 am, ck-in 4 pm. Downhill/x-country ski 12 mi. Many in-rm whirlpools; fireplace in suites. First Maquoketa residence with utilities. Built in 1882; antiques. Cr cds: A, MC, V.

Marquette (B-8)

Settled 1779 **Pop** 479 **Elev** 627 ft **Area code** 319 **Zip** 52158
Information Chamber of Commerce, PO Box 105, 52157; 319/873-3735 or 319/873-2050.

First known as North McGregor, this town was later renamed for Father Jacques Marquette; he and Louis Jolliet were the first to see Iowa territory from the mouth of the Wisconsin River in 1673. Within a 15-mile radius of the town are hundreds of effigy mounds, fortifications and earthworks.

What to See and Do

⊠ **Effigy Mounds National Monument.** Preserves traces of indigenous civilization from 2,500 yrs ago. Mounds built in shapes of animals, birds, other forms. Area divided by Yellow River; Great Bear Mound is the largest known bear effigy in state, 70 ft across shoulders, 137 ft long, 5 ft high. Footpath leads from headquarters to Fire Point Mound Group, to scenic viewpoints overlooking Mississippi and Yellow rivers. Guided walks (Memorial Day-Labor Day, daily). Visitor center has museum, 15-min film. (Daily; closed Dec 25) 3 mi N on IA 76. Phone 319/873-3491. ¢

Pikes Peak State Park. Park of 970 acres on bluffs overlooking Mississippi River. Native American mounds, colored sandstone outcroppings, woods and wild flowers. Trail leads across rugged terrain to Bridal Veil Falls. Hiking. Picnicking. Camping (electricity, dump station). Observation point. Boardwalks. Views of river. Standard hrs, fees. 5 mi SE on IA 340. Phone 319/873-2341.

Spook Cave and Campground. Guided 35-min tour of underground cavern via power boat. Campground has swimming beach; lake fishing; hiking trails; picnic areas. (May-Oct, daily) 5 mi SW on US 18, then 2 mi N on unnumbered road, near McGregor. Phone 319/873-2144. Cave tour ¢¢¢

Motels

★ **HOLIDAY SHORES.** (US 18 Business, McGregor 52157) 319/873-3449. 33 rms, 2-3 story. No elvtr. S, D $45-$80. Crib $4. TV; cable. Indoor pool; whirlpool. Restaurant nearby. Ck-out 10:30 am. Game rm. Balconies. Overlooks Mississippi River. Cr cds: MC, V.

✔★ **PORT OF MARQUETTE.** US 18, at Marquette Bridge. 319/873-3477; FAX 319/873-3479. 24 rms, 3 story. No elvtr. S $70; D $74. TV; cable. Complimentary continental bkfst. Ck-out 10 am. Business servs avail. Balconies. On bluff overlooking Mississippi River. Cr cds: DS, MC, V.

Marshalltown (C-6)

(See also Grinnell)

Founded 1853 **Pop** 25,178 **Elev** 938 ft **Area code** 515 **Zip** 50158 **E-mail** npalks@marshalltown.org **Web** www.marshalltown.org/cvb.html
Information Convention & Visitors Bureau, 709 S Center St, PO Box 1000; 515/753-6645 or 800/697-3155.

The business center of Marshall County prides itself on its symbols of the "good life" in the Midwest—the historic courthouse, pleasant parks and numerous churches. Perhaps its most famous son is "Cap" Anson, son of the founder, who is enshrined in the Baseball Hall of Fame, Cooperstown, New York.

What to See and Do

Fisher Community Center Art Gallery. Art collection includes paintings by Sisley, Utrillo and Cassatt. (Daily; closed most hols) Contact Convention & Visitors Bureau. 709 S Center St. **Free.**

Riverview Park. Swimming pool (June-Aug, daily). Camping. Picnicking, playground, ballfields. Park (Apr-Oct, daily). Some fees. N 3rd Ave & Woodland. Phone 515/754-5715.

Glick-Sower Historical Homestead. Contains original furnishings of post-Civil War era; also furnished one-room country school with world maps of 1880. (Apr-Oct, Sat; groups by appt yr-round) 2nd Ave & State St. Phone 515/752-6664. **Free.**

Motels

★ ★ **BEST WESTERN REGENCY INN.** 3303 S Center, at jct US 30, IA 14. 515/752-6321; FAX 515/752-4412. 161 rms, 2 story. S $52-$82; D $59-$89; each addl $7; under 18 free. Crib free. TV; cable. Indoor pool; whirlpool. Restaurant 6:30 am-9 pm; Sat, Sun from 7 am. Rm serv. Bar 4 pm-2 am. Ck-out noon. Meeting rms. Bellhops. Valet serv. Sundries. Free airport transportation. Cr cds: A, C, D, DS, MC, V.

★ **COMFORT INN.** 2613 S Center St. 515/752-6000; FAX 515/752-8762. 62 rms, 2 story. June-Aug: S, D $45.95-$75.95; suites $139.95; under 18 free; lower rates rest of yr. Crib free. Pet accepted; $10. TV; cable (premium). Indoor pool; whirlpool. Complimentary continental bkfst. Restaurant nearby. Ck-out noon. Business servs avail. Cr cds: A, D, DS, MC, V.

★ **DAYS INN.** 403 E Church St. 515/753-7777. 28 units, 2 story. S $32.90-$35.90; D $39.90-$46.90; each addl $5; suites $41.90-$46.90; under 12 free. Crib free. TV; cable. Complimentary continental bkfst. Ck-out noon. Cr cds: A, C, D, DS, MC, V.

✔★ **SUPER 8.** *Jct US 30 & IA 14. 515/753-8181.* 61 rms, 2 story. S $34.88-$37.88; D $39.88; under 12 free. Crib $2. TV; cable. Complimentary coffee in lobby. Restaurant adj open 24 hrs. Ck-out 11 am. Cr cds: A, C, D, DS, MC, V.

Mason City (B-5)

(See also Clear Lake)

Settled 1853 **Pop** 29,040 **Elev** 1,138 ft **Area code** 515 **Zip** 50401 **E-mail** masoncty@mach3ww.com **Web** www.netconx.net/masoncitycvb

Information Convention & Visitors Bureau, 15 W State St, PO Box 1128, 50402-1128; 800/423-5724.

A trading, manufacturing, farming and transportation hub, Mason City is a major producer of cement; it also processes meat and dairy products. A Native American uprising slowed growth of the city after the first settlement, but pioneers, many of whom were Masons, gradually returned. The town was first known as Shibboleth, later as Masonic Grove. This is the seat of Cerro Gordo County and was the inspiration for the classic musical, *The Music Man.*

What to See and Do

Charles H. MacNider Museum. Art Center features changing and permanent exhibits with emphasis on American art; gallery featuring "Bil Baird: World of Puppets," films, music, lectures, classes. (Daily exc Mon; closed legal hols) 303 2nd St SE. Phone 515/421-3666. **Free.** Just E of the museum is

 Meredith Willson Footbridge. Formerly called the Willow Creek Bridge, featured in the movie, *The Music Man.*

Frank Lloyd Wright Stockman House (1908). Only Prairie School-style house in Iowa designed by Frank Lloyd Wright; one of few houses built by Wright during this period to address middle-class housing needs. Tours. (June-Aug, Thurs-Sat, also Sun afternoons; Sept-Oct, wkends) 530 First St NE. Phone 515/423-1923. ¢¢

Kinney Pioneer Museum. Local history, pioneer, military exhibits; antique cars; original log cabin (ca 1854); one-room schoolhouse; old farm machinery, railroad caboose; artifacts, fossils. (May-Sept, Wed-Sun) 7 mi W on US 18, at entrance to Municipal Airport. Phone 515/423-1258 or 515/357-2980. ¢

Lime Creek Nature Center. On limestone bluffs in the Lime Creek Conservation Area, center includes plant, bird, mammal, insect and fish displays. Five trails wind throughout 400 acres of forest, field, prairie, pond and river. (Daily; closed major hols) 3501 Lime Creek Rd. Phone 515/423-5309. **Free.**

Margaret M. MacNider/East Park. Winnebago River divides this park into two areas. Swimming pool; fishing. Hiking trails. Picnicking facilities, playground. Improved camping (fees). (Apr-Oct, daily) 841 Birch Dr at Kentucky Ave NE. Phone 515/421-3673.

Meredith Willson Boyhood Home. Birthplace of author of *The Music Man.* (May-Oct, Fri-Sun afternoons) 314 S Pennsylvania Ave. Phone 515/423-3534. ¢¢

Van Horn's Antique Truck Museum. Features large collection of some of the oldest and most unusual trucks in the nation. Also on display is a scale model circus. (Late May-mid-Sept, daily) 2 mi N on US 65. Phone 515/423-0550 or 515/423-9066 (off season). ¢¢

Annual Event

North Iowa Fair. Fairgrounds, US 18 W. Nine-county area fair; carnival; food, wine and livestock exhibits; crafts; concessions; entertainment. Mid-Aug.

Motels

 ★ **COMFORT INN.** *410 5th St SW. 515/423-4444; FAX 515/424-5358.* 60 rms, 3 story. S $55-$67; D $52-$70; each addl $6; suites $85-$107; under 16 free. Crib free. TV; cable (premium). Indoor pool; whirlpool. Complimentary continental bkfst. Restaurant nearby. Ck-out noon. Refrigerator in suites. Cr cds: A, C, D, DS, ER, JCB, MC, V.

 ★ **DAYS INN.** *2301 4th St SW. 515/424-0210; FAX 515/424-0210, ext. 133.* 58 rms, 2 story. S $32-$44; D $42-$59; each addl $6; under 18 free. Crib free. Pet accepted. TV; cable. Complimentary continental bkfst. Ck-out noon. Business servs avail. Cr cds: A, C, D, DS, MC, V.

Missouri Valley (D-2)

(For accommodations see Council Bluffs; also see Blair, NE)

Settled 1858 **Pop** 2,888 **Elev** 1,019 ft **Area code** 712 **Zip** 51555 **E-mail** chambermv@aol.com **Web** www.missourivalley.com

Information Chamber of Commerce, 400 E Erie, PO Box 130; 712/642-2553.

A town rich in Native American history, this was the site of the first settler's cabin in the Missouri Valley along the Willow River.

What to See and Do

DeSoto National Wildlife Refuge. Partly in Nebraska and partly in Iowa, this approx 7,800-acre refuge surrounds DeSoto Lake, once a bend in the Missouri River. In spring and fall thousands of geese and ducks may be found here. Self-guided auto tours (mid-Oct-mid-Nov). Excavation site of the *Bertrand,* a steamboat sunk in 1865. Visitor center (daily; closed major hols). houses steamboat's artifacts and wildlife exhibits. Fishing, hunting; boating. Nature trails. Picnicking. 6 mi W on US 30. Phone 712/642-4121 or 712/642-2772. Per vehicle ¢¢

Harrison County Historical Village/Welcome Center. Includes a two-story log display building. The village consists of a school (1868), log cabin (1853), harness shop, print shop and chapel. Contains relics of pioneer period. Museum (mid-Apr-mid-Nov, daily). Welcome center (daily; closed major hols) 3 mi NE on US 30. Phone 712/642-2114. ¢

Loess Hills Scenic Byway. This 220-mi paved byway takes travelers through the Loess Hills region of Western Iowa, traversing 7 counties and revealing beautiful geologic formations along the way. Byway runs from Akron, SD to Franklin, MD. For map and information, contact Welcome Center, RR #3 Box 130A; 712/642-2114. **Free.**

Wilson Island State Recreation Area. More than 550 acres. Fishing; hunting; boating (ramps). Hiking; cross-country skiing, snowmobiling. Picnicking, playground. Camping (electricity addl; dump station). Standard hrs, fees. US 30 to I-29 S, exit Loveland, then 7 mi W on IA 362. Phone 712/642-2069.

Mount Pleasant (E-7)

(See also Fairfield)

Settled 1834 **Pop** 8,027 **Elev** 725 ft **Area code** 319 **Zip** 52641
Information Henry County Tourism Assn, 502 W Washington; 319/385-2460 or 800/421-4282.

The first courthouse in Iowa was constructed here. One of the first roads in the state was a plank road between Burlington and Mount Pleasant.

What to See and Do

Iowa Wesleyan College (1842). (550 students) Harlan-Lincoln Museum is on campus (open by appt at IWC Chadwick Library). 601 N Main St. Phone 319/385-6215 or 319/385-8021.   **Free.**

✪ **Midwest Old Settlers and Threshers Heritage Museum.** Houses one of nation's largest collections of steam engines, steam-powered farm machines; agricultural artifacts; turn-of-the-century farmhouse and barn; women's exhibit. **Museum of Repertoire Americana** has memorabilia of early tent, folk and repertoire theater (Sept-May, Mon-Fri; rest of yr, daily exc Mon; fee). Camping (fee). (Memorial Day-Labor Day, daily; mid-Apr-Memorial Day & after Labor Day-Oct, Mon-Fri) S of town. Phone 319/385-8937.   ¢¢

Oakland Mills Park. Approx 104 wooded acres with picnic area overlooking Skunk River. Fishing; boating. Hiking trails. Camping (electrical hookups; fee). 4 mi S, off US 34. Phone 319/986-5067.   **Free.**

Annual Event

Midwest Old Settlers and Threshers Reunion. Iowa's largest working craft show, antique car show; steam and gas engines, vintage tractors; Midwest Village, log village, narrow-gauge steam railroad and electric trolley cars; entertainment. Phone 319/385-8937. Five days ending Labor Day.

Motels

★ **HEARTLAND INN.** US 218 N, on Frontage Rd. 319/385-2102; FAX 319/385-3223. 59 rms, 2 story. S $42-$51; D $56-$61; each addl $8; under 16 free. Crib free. Pet accepted. TV; cable (premium). Complimentary continental bkfst. Restaurant adj 11 am-9 pm. Ck-out 11 am. Business servs avail. Sauna. Whirlpool. Cr cds: A, C, D, DS, MC, V.

D ✇ ⇘ 🐾 SC

✔ ★ **SUPER 8.** US Hwy 218N. 319/385-8888. 55 rms, 2 story. S $39.88-$41.88; D $47.88-$51.88; each addl $3; under 12 free. Crib $2. TV; cable (premium). Complimentary continental bkfst. Restaurant opp 11 am-9:30 pm. Ck-out 11 am. Meeting rms. Business servs avail. Microwaves avail. Cr cds: A, C, D, DS, MC, V.

D ⇘ 🐾 SC

Muscatine (D-8)

(See also Davenport)

Founded 1836 **Pop** 22,881 **Elev** 550 ft **Area code** 319 **Zip** 52761 **E-mail** visitorinfo@muscatine.com **Web** www.muscatine.com

Information Convention & Visitors Bureau, 319 E 2nd St, PO Box 297; 319/263-8895 or 800/25-PEARL.

Famous Muscatine cantaloupes and watermelons, as well as plastics, grain handling, food processing and manufacturing, are the major industries of this city. Samuel Clemens, who once lived here, declared Muscatine's summer sunsets unsurpassed.

What to See and Do

Mark Twain Overlook. Three acres with panoramic view of Mississippi River Valley, boat harbor and downtown Muscatine; picnicking. Lombard & 2nd Sts.

Muscatine Art Center. Consists of the Laura Musser Museum and the Stanley Gallery. Museum is housed in an Edwardian mansion; changing art exhibits, special events, Estey player pipe organ with 731 pipes, antiques and historical displays; Oriental carpets, furniture, paintings, drawings, prints, sculpture, graphics in permanent collection. (Daily exc Mon; closed hols) 1314 Mulberry Ave. Phone 319/263-8282.   **Free.**

Pearl Button Museum. Dedicated to pearl button industry. Exhibits on making buttons from Mississippi River mussel shells. (Sat) Iowa Ave & 2nd St.   **Free.**

Saulsbury Bridge Recreation Area. Approx 675 acres. Fishing, canoeing. Picnicking, playground. Nature trails and center; cross-country skiing. Camping (hookups mid-Apr-mid-Oct only; fee). Park (daily). W on IA 22. Phone 319/649-3379 or 319/264-5922.   **Free.**

Shady Creek Recreation Area. 15 acres. Boat ramp. Picnicking, playground, shelter. Improved camping (May-Oct; fee). Park (daily). 7 mi E on IA 22, on Mississippi River. Phone 319/263-7913.   ¢¢¢

Wildcat Den State Park. A 321-acre park with historic mid-19th-century gristmill, one-room schoolhouse, Pine Creek Bridge; scenic overlook. Hiking trails. Picnicking. Primitive camping. Standard hrs, fees. 12 mi E on IA 22. Phone 319/263-4337.

Motels

✔ ★ **ECONO LODGE FANTASUITE HOTEL.** 2402 Park Ave. 319/264-3337; FAX 319/263-0413; res: 800/234-7829. 91 rms, 2 story. S $39.95-$59; D $49.95-$69; each addl $6; suites $99-$179; under 18 free; wkend rates. Crib free. TV; cable (premium). Indoor pool. Restaurant 5-9 pm. Rm serv. Bar 4:30-11 pm; Fri, Sat to midnight. Ck-out noon. Coin lndry. Meeting rm. Business servs avail. Cr cds: A, C, D, DS, MC, V.

≋ ⇘ 🐾 SC

★ ★ ★ **HOLIDAY INN.** 2915 N US 61, at IA 38. 319/264-5550; FAX 319/264-0451. 112 rms, 3 story. S $69; D $69-$79; each addl $6. Crib free. TV; cable (premium). Indoor pool; wading pool, whirlpool. Restaurant 6 am-2 pm, 5-10 pm. Rm serv. Bar 5 pm-midnight. Coin lndry. Ck-out noon. Meeting rms. Business center. In-rm modem link. Exercise equipt; weight machine, stair machine, sauna. Health club privileges. Rec rm. Some refrigerators. Cr cds: A, C, D, DS, ER, JCB, MC, V.

D ≋ 🏋 ⚡ ⇘ 🐾 SC ↟

Newton (D-5)

(See also Grinnell)

Pop 14,789 **Elev** 950 ft **Area code** 515 **Zip** 50208
Information Visitor & Conference Bureau, 113 1st Ave W; 515/792-0299.

The washing machine industry was born here in 1898, and the Maytag Company continues to make Newton the "home laundry appliance center of the world."

What to See and Do

Fred Maytag Park. Donated by founder of Maytag Co. Tennis, picnicking, playground; amphitheater, log cabin, concession. Pool & water slide (June-Aug, daily; fee). Park (daily). W 3rd St S. Phone 515/792-1470.   **Free.**

Jasper County Historical Museum. Local historical displays include bas-relief sculpture of natural history of the county, Victorian home, schoolroom, chapel, tool and farm equipment collections, sound film of early county scenes. Also the Maytag historical display of washing machines. (May-Sept, afternoons) 1700 S 15th Ave W. Phone 515/792-9118.   ¢

Trainland, USA. Toy train museum exhibits depict development of the railroad across the US in three eras: frontier, steam and diesel; original railroad memorabilia and toy trains dating from 1916 to the present. (Memorial Day-Labor Day, daily; rest of Sept, wkends) 12 mi W via I-80, then 2½ mi N on IA 117, in Colfax. Phone 515/674-3813.   ¢¢

Motels

★ **BEST WESTERN NEWTON INN.** IA 14 at I-80 exit 164. 515/792-4200; FAX 515/792-0108. 118 rms, 2 story. S $39-$53; D $45-$75; each addl $6; under 12 free; higher rates Knoxville racing season.

Crib $3. Pet accepted. TV; cable (premium), VCR avail. Indoor pool; whirlpool. Complimentary full bkfst. Restaurant 6 am-1 pm, 5:30-10 pm. Bar 5:30 pm-1 am. Ck-out noon. Meeting rms. Business servs avail. Putting green. Exercise equipt; bicycles, treadmill, sauna. Game rm. Cr cds: A, C, D, DS, MC, V.

✔★ **DAYS INN.** *1065 W 19th St S, 2 mi S on IA 14 at I-80 exit 164.* 515/792-2330; FAX 515/792-1045. 59 rms, 2 story. S $43-$48; D $49-$54; each addl $5. Crib free. Pet accepted. TV; cable (premium), VCR avail. Complimentary continental bkfst. Restaurant adj open 24 hrs. Ck-out 11 am. Business servs avail. Cr cds: A, C, D, DS, JCB, MC, V.

★ **SUPER 8.** *1635 S 12th Ave W, I-80 exit 164.* 515/792-8868. 43 rms, 2 story. S $37.88-$54.88; D $47.88-$60.88; under 12 free; higher rates: Knoxville National Race, wkends. Crib $4. TV; cable (premium). Complimentary continental bkfst. Restaurant adj 6-10 am. Ck-out 11 am. Meeting rms. Business servs avail. Cr cds: A, C, D, DS, ER, JCB, MC, V.

Inn

★★★ **LA CORSETTE MAISON.** *629 1st Ave E (US 6), 7 blks E of city square.* 515/792-6833; FAX 515/292-6597. 7 units, 2 story, 2 suites. S, D $80-$185; suites $80-$175; kit. unit $80; higher rates special events. TV in some rms. Complimentary full bkfst. Restaurant (see LA CORSETTE MAISON INN). Ck-out 11:45 am, ck-in 4-6 pm. Business servs avail. 1909 mission-style mansion with all original woodwork; art nouveau stained-glass windows; some original brass light fixtures and furnishings. Unique decor in each rm. Totally nonsmoking. Cr cds: A, MC, V.

Restaurant

★★★ **LA CORSETTE MAISON INN.** *(See La Corsette Maison Inn)* 515/792-6833. Hrs: One sitting per day, usually at 7 pm; phone for schedule. Closed Sun-Tues. Res required 24-48 hrs in advance. French, continental menu. Complete meals: dinner $29.50-$35.50. Specialties: roasted beef tenderloin, medallions of Iowa pork, La Corsett French bread. Gourmet dining in 1909 mission-style mansion; original dining rm furnishings; 3 sets of floral patterned leaded glass French doors lead to enclosed, mosiac-tiled atrium. Totally nonsmoking. Cr cds: A, MC, V.

Okoboji (A-3)

(See also Spencer, Spirit Lake)

Founded 1855 **Pop** 775 **Elev** 1,450 ft **Area code** 712 **Zip** 51355 **E-mail** okobojicofc@ncn.net **Web** www.okoboji.com

Information Iowa Great Lakes Area Chamber of Commerce, US 71, Lakes Center Mall, Box 9, Arnolds Park 51331; 712/332-2107 or 800/839-9987.

Lake Okoboji and the surrounding area are among the most popular resort areas in Iowa.

What to See and Do

Boji Bay. Family water park features water slides, wave pool, tube rides, sand volleyball courts, arcades and games. Concessions. Gift shop. (Memorial Day-Labor Day) Jct US 71 & IA 86, N of town. Phone 712/338-2473. ¢¢¢¢

Gardner Cabin (1856). Restored; period furnishings; displays on pioneer life and history of the region. (Memorial Day-Labor Day, afternoons) 3 mi SW on US 71 in Arnolds Park. Phone 712/332-7248. **Free.**

Higgins Museum. Displays notes and artifacts of the National Banks. (Memorial-Labor Day, daily exc Mon; May & Sept, wkends also) 1507 Sanborn Ave. Phone 712/332-5859. **Free.**

State parks. Swimming; fishing; boating. Snowmobiling. Picnicking. Standard fees. On 3,847-acre West Okoboji Lake. Phone 712/337-3211.

Gull Point. Has 165 acres. Also boating. Hiking trails. Picnicking, lodge. Camping (electricity, dump station). Approx 6 mi SW off US 71.

Pikes Point. Has 15 acres. Picnicking. Approx 3 mi W.

Seasonal Event

Okoboji Summer Theater. 1 mi N on US 71. New play each week; operated by Stephens College of Columbia, MO. Daily exc Mon. Also children's theater. For reservations, schedule phone 712/332-7773. Mid-June-mid-Aug.

Motels

★ **COUNTRY CLUB.** *Airport Rd, 1 blk W on US 71.* 712/332-5617; FAX 712/332-7705; res: 800/831-5615. 53 rms. Memorial Day-late Sept: S, D $80-$150; lower rates rest of yr. Crib $5. Pet accepted. TV; cable (premium). Heated pool. Restaurant nearby. Ck-out 10 am. Business servs avail. Picnic tables, grills. Cr cds: A, D, DS, MC, V.

★★ **FILLENWARTH BEACH.** *Arnolds Park (51331), 1 blk W on US 71.* 712/332-5646. 93 kit. units in motel, cottages, 1-3 story. No elvtr. Late June-late Aug: apts for 2-8, $500-$1,380/wk; daily rates; lower rates Apr-mid-June, Sept. Closed rest of yr. Crib free. Pet accepted. TV; cable, VCR. Indoor/outdoor pool. Playground. Supervised child's activities (late May-early Sept). Restaurant opp 6 am-midnight. Ck-out noon. Business servs avail. Free airport, bus depot transportation. Sports dir in season. Tennis. Rec rm. Private beach. Waterskiing, instruction. Boat dock, canoes, boats. Free sail and cruiser boat rides. Balconies. Picnic tables, grills. On West Okoboji Lake. No cr cds accepted.

✔★ **FOUR SEASONS RESORT.** *(US 71, Arnolds Park 51331)* 1/2 mi S on US 71. 712/332-2103; res: 800/876-2103. 32 units, 1-2 story. S, D, suites $45-$145. Pet accepted. Restaurant 9 am-11 pm. Bar to 2 am. Ck-out 11 am. Many private patios, balconies. Picnic tables, grills. On West Okoboji Lake. Cr cds: A, MC, V.

★★★ **THE INN.** *1 1/4 mi NW, 1/2 mi W of US 71.* 712/332-2113; FAX 712/332-2714; res: 800/831-5092. 130 1-2 rm studio units, 1-2 story. June-Aug: S, D $100-$170; lower rates May & Sept. Closed rest of yr. Crib $10. TV; cable. 2 pools, 1 indoor; poolside serv. Playground. Free supervised child's activities (Memorial Day-Labor Day); ages 4 & up. Restaurant 7 am-10 pm. Rm serv. Bar 11-2 am; entertainment Tues-Sat. Ck-out noon. Meeting rms. Business servs avail. Concierge. Sundries. Gift shop. Tennis. 9-hole golf, putting green, driving range. Soc dir. Lawn games. Boating; rentals, docks. Refrigerators. Spacious grounds on West Okoboji Lake. Cr cds: A, DS, MC, V.

★★★ **VILLAGE EAST.** *1/2 mi N on US 71.* 712/332-2161; FAX 712/332-7727; res: 800/727-4561. 99 rms, 2 story. Late May-Sept: S $139; each addl $10; lower rates rest of yr. Pet accepted. TV; cable. 2 pools; whirlpool. Restaurant 6 am-10 pm. Rm serv. Bar. Ck-out 11 am. Meeting rms. Business servs avail. Beauty shop. Indoor & outdoor tennis. 18-hole golf, greens fee $39. X-country ski on site. Exercise rm; instructor, weight machines, bicycles, sauna. Rec rm. Private patios, balconies. Lake opp. Cr cds: A, C, D, DS, ER, MC, V.

Onawa (C-1)

Pop 2,936 **Elev** 1,052 ft **Area code** 712 **Zip** 51040

What to See and Do

Lewis and Clark State Park. Park of 176 acres on 250-acre lake. Swimming; fishing; boating (ramp). Hiking trails. Snowmobiling. Picnicking. Replica of Lewis & Clark keelboat *Discovery.* Camping (electricity, dump station). Standard hrs, fees. 3 mi NW via IA 175, 324. Phone 712/423-2829.

Motel

✔★ **SUPER 8.** *2 mi W at jct IA 175, I-29. 712/423-2101; FAX 712/423-3480.* 80 rms. S $40-$65; D $45-$65; each addl $3. Pet accepted. TV; cable. Restaurant nearby. Ck-out 11 am. Picnic table. Cr cds: A, D, DS, MC, V.

D ✔ ⊠ 🛇 SC

Osceola (E-4)

(See also Chariton)

Settled 1850 **Pop** 4,164 **Elev** 1,139 ft **Area code** 515 **Zip** 50213
Information Chamber of Commerce, 100 S Fillmore St, PO Box 1; 515/342-4200.

The seat of Clarke County is named for a Seminole warrior; a 30-foot figure of Oseola, carved from a cedar tree trunk, stands on the west side of the city. The town was settled by pioneers from Indiana and Ohio.

What to See and Do

Nine Eagles State Park. Timbered 1,119-acre park with 67-acre lake. Swimming, supervised beach; fishing; electric boating (ramps, rentals). Hiking. Snowmobiling. Picnicking. Camping (electricity, dump station). Standard hrs, fees. 29 mi S on US 69 to Davis City, then 6 mi SE on county road. Phone 515/442-2855.

Motel

✔★ **BLUE HAVEN.** *325 S Main St. 515/342-2115; res: 800/333-3180.* 24 rms, 1-2 story. S $33-$43; D $41-$49; each addl $4; higher rates hunting seasons. Crib free. Pet accepted. TV; cable (premium). Restaurant nearby. Ck-out 11 am. Cr cds: A, DS, MC, V.

✔ ⊠ 🛇 SC

Oskaloosa (E-6)

(See also Ottumwa, Pella)

Settled 1843 **Pop** 10,632 **Elev** 845 ft **Area code** 515 **Zip** 52577 **E-mail** oskycofc@kdsi.net **Web** www.oskaloosa.ia.us
Information Chamber of Commerce, 124 N Market St; 515/673-2591.

Native American tribes lived here when the site was picked for the county seat, and the name of a Native American maiden ("last of the beautiful") was chosen as the name of the new community. Oskaloosa has a thriving retail trade and is the home of several manufacturers. It is also a center of production of corn, hay, hogs, cattle and soybeans.

What to See and Do

Lake Keomah State Park. More than 370 acres with 84-acre lake. Swimming, supervised beach; fishing; electric boating (ramps, rentals). Hiking trails. Snowmobiling. Picnicking, lodge. Camping (electricity, dump station). Standard hrs, fees. 5 mi E off IA 92. Phone 515/673-6975.

Nelson Pioneer Farm & Craft Museum. Family farm of 1800s includes house, barn, one-room schoolhouse, log cabin, quilt collection, Friends Meeting House; post office and country store (1900); museum with historical exhibits; mule cemetery. (Mid-May-mid-Oct, daily exc Mon) 2 mi NE of Penn College on Glendale Rd. Phone 515/672-2989. ¢

Annual Events

Art On The Square. Arts & crafts demonstrations and workshops; children's activities. June 14.

Southern Iowa Fair. Late July.

Motels

★ **RED CARPET INN.** *2278 US 63N, 2 mi N on US 63. 515/673-8641; FAX 515/673-4111.* 41 rms, 2 story. S $30-$35; D $38-$45; each addl $5. Pet accepted. TV; cable (premium). Complimentary continental bkfst. Coffee in rms. Cr cds: A, DS, MC, V.

✔ ⊠ 🛇

★ **RODEWAY INN MAHASKA.** *1315 A Avenue East. 515/673-8351.* 42 rms, 1-2 story. S $35-$50; D $45-$60; each addl $3. Crib $2. TV; cable (premium). Playground. Coffee in rms. Restaurant nearby. Ck-out 11 am. Meeting rm. Business servs avail. Picnic table. Cr cds: A, C, D, DS, MC, V.

D ⊠ 🛇 SC

★ **SUPER 8.** *306 S 17th St. 515/673-8481.* 51 rms, 2 story, 4 suites. S $46.62; D $56.16; each addl $3; under 12 free. Crib $2. TV; cable (premium). Complimentary coffee in lobby. Restaurant nearby. Ck-out 11 am. Business servs avail. Cr cds: A, C, D, DS, MC, V.

D ⊠ 🛇 SC

Ottumwa (E-6)

(See also Oskaloosa)

Settled 1843 **Pop** 24,488 **Elev** 650 ft **Area code** 515 **Zip** 52501
Information Ottumwa Area Convention & Visitors Bureau, 217 E Main St, PO Box 308; 515/682-3465.

A major Iowa trade center, Ottumwa is an industrial and agricultural city. The city was born in a land rush as settlers staked out this site on both sides of the Des Moines River. The name Ottumwa comes from a Native American word meaning "swift rapids" and later "perseverance." Historical marker east of town marks the site of the 1842 Indian Council, which resulted in the purchase of much of Iowa from the Sac and Fox.

What to See and Do

John Deere Ottumwa Works. Hay, forage implements; 90-min guided tour (Mon-Fri; no tours last wk July, Aug, Dec 25-Jan 2). Over 12 yrs only; no sandals or tennis shoes. 928 E Vine St. Phone 515/683-2394 one day in advance. **Free.**

Lake Wapello State Park. A 1,168-acre park with 289-acre lake. Swimming beach; fishing; boating (ramp). Hiking trails. Snowmobiling. Picnicking. Camping (electricity, dump station), cabins. Standard hrs, fees. 16 mi S on US 63, then 10 mi W on IA 273 near Drakesville. Phone 515/722-3371.

Ottumwa Park. A 365-acre recreation area in center of city includes camping (fee), fishing, tennis, horseshoes. (Apr-mid-Oct, daily) At jct US 34, 63. Phone 515/682-1307.

The Beach—Ottumwa. Water recreation park featuring 22,000-sq-ft wave pool, 340-ft body slide, 200-ft speed slide and 4-acre lagoon with kayak and paddleboats. Children's activity pool. Sand volleyball courts. Concessions. Some indoor recreational facilities operational year-round (phone for schedule). Outdoor attractions (Memorial Day-Labor Day, daily). At jct US 63 & 34. Phone 515/682-7873. ¢¢¢

Annual Event

Ottumwa Pro Balloon Races. Ottumwa Park. Balloon flights, races; concessions, fireworks. Phone 515/684-8838. Mid-July.

Motels

★ ★ **FAIRFIELD INN BY MARRIOTT.** *2813 N Court St, on US 63N. 515/682-0000.* 63 rms, 3 story. Mar-Oct: S $39.95-$47.95; D $47.95-$54.95; under 18 free; higher rates special events. Crib free. TV; cable. Indoor pool; whirlpool. Complimentary continental bkfst. Restaurant nearby. Ck-out noon. Coin lndry. Meeting rms. Health club privileges. Some refrigerators; microwaves avail. Cr cds: A, D, DS, MC, V.

✔★ **HEARTLAND INN.** *125 W Joseph (US 63 N). 515/682-8526; FAX 515/682-7124.* 89 units. S $42; D $50-$57; each addl $8; under 17 free. Crib free. Pet accepted. TV; cable (premium). Pool; whirlpool. Complimentary continental bkfst. Restaurant nearby. Ck-out noon. Coin lndry. Meeting rm. Business servs avail. Sauna. Cr cds: A, C, D, DS, MC, V.

★ **SUPER 8.** *2823 North Court, 3 mi N on US 63, N edge of town. 515/684-5055; FAX 515/682-6622.* 62 rms, 2 story. S $42.88; D $54.88; suites $68.88-$78.88; under 13 free. Crib $4.90. TV; cable (premium). Indoor pool; whirlpool. Complimentary continental bkfst. Restaurant nearby. Ck-out 11 am. Coin lndry. Meeting rm. Sauna. Cr cds: A, D, DS, MC, V.

Restaurant

★ **FISHERMAN'S BAY.** *221 N Wapello St, NW on US 63 to Wapello St. 515/682-6325.* Hrs: 11 am-9 pm; Fri, Sat to 10 pm. Closed Dec 25. Res accepted. Bar. Semi-a la carte: lunch $2.95-$7, dinner $7.95-$18. Child's meals. Specializes in seafood, french fries. Salad bar. Casual dining; nautical decor. Cr cds: A, DS, MC, V.

Pella (D-6)

(See also Oskaloosa)

Settled 1847 **Pop** 9,270 **Elev** 878 ft **Area code** 515 **Zip** 50219
Information Chamber of Commerce, 518 Franklin St; 515/628-2626.

Dutch refugees from religious intolerance first settled Pella, and the town retains many Dutch customs. Dutch influence can be seen in the architectural design of the business district and in the many tulip gardens in the area. Pella was the boyhood home of Wyatt Earp. It is the headquarters of the Pella Corp, a major manufacturer of prefabricated windows.

What to See and Do

Central College (1853). (1,700 students) Liberal arts. Mills Gallery with changing exhibits. Tours. 812 University St. Phone 515/628-9000.

Klokkenspel at Franklin Place. A 147-bell carillon in the Franklin Place Arch with figurines representing Pella's early history, town founders, Wyatt Earp and others; Sinterklaas and his faithful companion, Black Piet, during the Christmas season. Courtyard on S side of arch has scenes of Holland in Dutch tiles. Concerts (5 times daily). 1/2 blk E of town square. **Free.**

 Pella Historical Village Museum. Restoration project of 21 buildings housing exhibits and antiques; pottery and blacksmith shops, pioneer log cabin, Wyatt Earp Boyhood Home, Heritage Hall, Dutch museum and bakery; gristmill in garden. (Apr-Dec, daily exc Sun; rest of yr, Mon-Fri; closed hols exc during summer) 507 Franklin St. Phone 515/628-4311. ¢¢

Red Rock Lake. A 19,000-acre lake formed by Army Corps of Engineers dam impounding Des Moines River. Swimming, boating, fishing. Picnicking. Approx 400 developed campsites (mid-Apr-mid-Oct; fee). 4 1/2 mi SW. Phone 515/828-7522.

Scholte House. Oldest permanent dwelling in Pella built by town founder H.P. Scholte; many original furnishings and possessions, collection of old world French & Italian furniture; gardens with more than 25,000 tulips. (Mon-Sat afternoons; also by appt; closed Easter & Dec 25) 728 Washington. Phone 515/628-3684 or 515/628-2409. ¢¢

Annual Event

Tulip Time Festival. Citizens dress in Dutch costumes; scrubbing the streets is a colorful and traditional feature; Dutch dancers; stage performances, parades. Phone 515/628-4311. Mid-May.

Motel

★ ★ ★ **STRAWTOWN INN.** *1111 Washington St. 515/628-4043; FAX 515/628-3055.* 17 rms, 2 story. S $72.50-$82.50; D $70-$85; suites $107-$130. Crib $5. TV; cable. Complimentary full bkfst. Restaurant (see STRAWTOWN INN). Ck-out 11:30 am. Elegant lodgings with a distinctly Dutch theme; many antiques. Totally nonsmoking. Cr cds: A, D, DS, MC, V.

Restaurant

★ ★ **STRAWTOWN INN.** *(See Strawtown Inn Motel) 515/628-4043.* Hrs: 11:30 am-2 pm, 5-9 pm; Fri, Sat to 10 pm. Closed Sun; major hols. Res accepted. Bar. Semi-a la carte: lunch $3.95-$9.50, dinner $5.50-$22. Child's meals. Specializes in stuffed pork chops, chicken breast supreme, Dutch spiced beef. Dutch theme; wooden floors, lace curtains. Cr cds: A, D, DS, MC, V.

Pocahontas (B-3)

(See also Humboldt, Storm Lake)

Pop 2,085 **Elev** 1,227 ft **Area code** 712 **Zip** 50574

Named in honor of the famous daughter of Powhatan, this town, in pheasant-hunting country, is also the seat of Pocahontas County.

Motel

★ **CHIEF.** *At jct IA 3. 712/335-3395.* 34 rms, 1-2 story, 4 kits. S $22.80-$25.65; D $32.30; each addl $5. Crib free. TV; cable. Complimentary continental bkfst. Restaurant nearby. Ck-out 11 am. Sundries. Cr cds: A, C, D, DS, MC, V.

Red Oak (E-2)

Pop 6,264 **Elev** 1,077 ft **Area code** 712 **Zip** 51566

What to See and Do

Viking Lake State Park. More than 950 acres on 137-acre lake. Swimming; fishing; boating (ramp, rentals). Hiking trail. Snowmobiling. Picnicking. Camping (electricity, dump station). Standard hrs, fees. 12 mi E off US 34. Phone 712/829-2235.

Motel

✔★ **RED COACH INN.** *US 34 N, 1 mi NE on US 34. 712/623-4864; FAX 712/623-2389; res: 800/544-6002.* 74 rms, 2 story. S $38; D $45; each addl $5; studio rm $38-$48. Crib free. TV; cable (premium), VCR avail. Heated pool. Restaurant 6:30 am-10 pm. Rm serv. Bar 4 pm-2 am. Ck-out noon. Meeting rms. Business servs avail. Valet serv. Cr cds: A, C, D, DS, MC, V.

D ◻ ◻ ◻ SC

Sheldon (A-2)

Pop 4,937 **Elev** 1,420 ft **Area code** 712 **Zip** 51201

Motel

✔★ **IRON HORSE INN.** *1111 S IA 60. 712/324-5353.* 33 rms, 2 story. S $32.07; D $42.45; under 10 free. TV; cable. Complimentary continental bkfst. Restaurant 11 am-midnight. Bar. Ck-out 11 am. Cr cds: A, D, DS, MC, V.

D ◻

Shenandoah (F-2)

(See also Clarinda, Red Oak)

Founded 1870 **Pop** 5,572 **Elev** 981 ft **Area code** 712 **Zip** 51601
Information Chamber of Commerce, 614 W Sheridan, PO Box 38; 712/246-3260.

Mormons settled here, moving in from Manti (Fisher's Grove). Other early settlers fought with General Sheridan in the Shenandoah Valley of Virginia and brought the name back with them. The town is now the home of three large seed and nursery companies.

Motels

★ **DAYS INN.** *108 N Fremont St. 712/246-5733; FAX 712/246-2230.* 33 rms, 2 story. S $40; D $46; each addl $6; suite $55; under 12 free. Crib free. TV; cable. Complimentary continental bkfst. Restaurant nearby. Ck-out 11 am. Refrigerators. Cr cds: A, D, DS, MC, V.

D ◻ ◻ SC

✔★ **TALL CORN.** *1503 Sheridan Ave, at US 59. 712/246-1550; FAX 712/246-4773.* 65 rms, 1-2 story. S $37; D $47; each addl $3; family rates. Crib $5. Pet accepted. TV; cable (premium). Indoor pool. Restaurant

6 am-9 pm. Rm serv. Bar 5 pm-1 am. Ck-out 11 am. Meeting rms. Business servs avail. Airport transportation. Cr cds: A, C, D, DS, MC, V.

D ◻ ◻ ◻ ◻ SC

Sioux City (C-1)

Settled 1854 **Pop** 80,505 **Elev** 1,117 ft **Area code** 712 **E-mail** ccat@pionet.net **Web** www.siouxlan.com
Information Sioux City Convention Center/Tourism Bureau, 801 4th St, PO Box 3183, 51102; 712/279-4800 or 800/593-2228.

At the heart of a tri-state region bordered by the Sioux and Missouri rivers, Sioux City has historically been a hub for shipping, transportation and agriculture. The Lewis and Clark expedition followed the Missouri River; the only fatality of that historic march is commemorated here with the Sergeant Floyd Monument, the first registered historic landmark in the US.

Today, the Missouri River is important to the city from a recreational standpoint. A developed riverfront with parks, a dance pavilion and riverboat casinos greets visitors. Sioux City's claim to be the cultural and recreational mecca of the Great Plains is further supported by its many parks and playgrounds, a symphony orchestra, theaters, an art center, and the excitement of Thoroughbred horse racing within minutes of downtown.

What to See and Do

Belle of Sioux City. Tri-level riverboat casino. (May-Oct, daily) 100 Larsen Park Dr. Phone 712/255-0080 or 800/424-0080.

Morningside College (1894). (1,400 students) Liberal arts. Fine Arts Building contains lobby art gallery. Tours. 1501 Morningside Ave. Phone 712/274-5000 or 712/274-5111 (tours).

Sergeant Floyd Monument. First registered national historic landmark in the US. The 100-ft obelisk marks burial place of Sgt Charles Floyd, the only casualty of the Lewis and Clark expedition. Glenn Ave & US 75, on E bank of Missouri River.

Sergeant Floyd Welcome Center and Museum. Former Missouri River inspection ship now houses museum, information center and gift shop. (Daily) Exit 149 off I-29, Hamilton Blvd to S Larsen Park Rd. Phone 712/279-4840. **Free.**

Sioux City Art Center. Contemporary Upper Midwestern art. Three-story glass atrium. Permanent collection; special programs. (Tues-Sat, also Sun afternoon; closed hols) At Third & Nebraska Sts. Phone 712/279-6272. **Free.**

Sioux City Public Museum. Exhibits show life in pioneer and Civil War days; geological, archaeological and Native American materials. Located in Romanesque 23-rm mansion. (Daily; closed some hols) 2901 Jackson St. Phone 712/279-6174. **Free.**

Stone State Park. 1,069 acres. Park overlooks the Missouri and Big Sioux river valleys; view of three states from Dakota Point Lookout near Big Sioux River. Fishing. Bridle, hiking trails. Snowmobiling. Picnicking. Camping. Standard hrs, fees. 10-acre **Loess Ridge Nature Center** is on grounds (daily exc Mon; closed hols). Off IA 12 or Memorial Dr, in NW part of city. Phone 712/255-4698 or 712/258-0838 (Nature Center only).

Trinity Heights. A 30-ft stainless steel statue of the Immaculate Heart of Mary, Queen of Peace. Life-size carving of the Last Supper. (Daily) 33rd & Floyd Blvd. Phone 712/239-8670. ¢¢

Woodbury County Courthouse (1916-1918). Courthouse was the largest structure ever completed in architectural style of Chicago's prairie school. Designed by Purcell and Elmslie, who were long-time associates of Louis Sullivan, the building, a city block long, is constructed of Roman brick, ornamented with massive pieces of Sullivanesque terra cotta, stained glass and relief sculpture by Alfonso Ianelli, who also worked with Frank Lloyd Wright. Both exterior and highly detailed interior are in near-pristine condition; courtrooms still contain original architect-designed furniture, lighting fixtures. (Mon-Fri) Between 7th & Douglas Sts.

Annual Events

Saturday in the Park. Day-long music festival. July 4.

River-Cade Festival. Features fireworks, antique show, entertainment, midway, baseball, bowling, "fun-run." Phone 712/277-4226. Last wk July.

Motels

★ ★ **BEST WESTERN REGENCY EXECUTIVE.** *2nd & Nebraska (51101), business exit 147B.* 712/277-1550; FAX 712/277-1120. 114 rms, 2 story. S $50-$63; D $58-$69; each addl $10; suites $113-$173; under 18 free. Pet accepted, some restrictions. TV; cable. Heated pool. Bar 5-8 pm. Ck-out noon. Coin lndry. Meeting rms. Business servs avail. Free airport transportation. Cr cds: A, C, D, DS, JCB, MC, V.

D ✔ ≈ ✗ 🖈 SC

★ **COMFORT INN.** *4202 S Lakeport St (51106), I-29 exit 144.* 712/274-1300. 70 rms, 2 story. S $60; D $65; suites $90-$100; under 18 free. Crib free. TV. Indoor pool; whirlpool. Complimentary continental bkfst. Restaurant nearby. Ck-out 11 am. Meeting rms. Business servs avail. In-rm modem link. Cr cds: A, C, D, DS, ER, JCB, MC, V.

D ≈ ✗ 🖈 SC

★ **HOLIDAY INN EXPRESS.** *4230 S Lakeport St (51106), I-29 exit 144A.* 712/274-1400; FAX 712/276-2136. 58 rms, 2 story. S $55-$70; D $60-$80; under 18 free. Crib free. TV; cable, VCR avail (movies free). Complimentary continental bkfst. Restaurant nearby. Ck-out 11 am. Meeting rms. Business servs avail. In-rm modem link. Exercise equipt; bicycles, stair machine. Whirlpool. Cr cds: A, C, D, DS, ER, JCB, MC, V.

D ✗ ✗ 🖈 SC

✔★ **PALMER HOUSE.** *3440 E Gordon Dr (51106).* 712/276-4221; FAX 712/276-9535; res: 800/833-4221. 63 rms, 1-2 story. S $37; D $47.75; Pet accepted. TV; cable. Complimentary continental bkfst. Restaurant adj open 24 hrs. Ck-out 11 am. Business servs avail. Cr cds: A, D, DS, MC, V.

D ✔ ✗ 🖈 SC

★ **SUPER 8.** *4307 Stone Ave (51106).* 712/274-1520. 60 rms, 2 story. Mid-May-mid-Oct: S $37.98; D $46.98; each addl $5. Crib. Pet accepted. TV; cable. Continental bkfst. Restaurant 5-10 pm. Ck-out 11 am. Cr cds: A, C, D, DS, MC, V.

D ✔ ✗ 🖈 SC

Hotel

★ ★ **HILTON INN.** *707 4th St (51101).* 712/277-4101; FAX 712/277-3168. 193 units, 12 story. S $70-$80; D $80-$90; each addl $10; suites $125-$500; family rates; wkend rates. Crib free. TV; cable (premium), VCR avail. Indoor pool. Restaurant 6 am-10 pm; Sat, Sun from 6:30 am. Bar 4 pm-2 am. Ck-out noon. Meeting rms. Business servs avail. In-rm modem link. Free airport transportation. Exercise equipt; stair machine, treadmill, sauna. Cr cds: A, C, D, DS, MC, V.

≈ ✗ ✗ 🖈 SC

Restaurants

✔★ **GREEN GABLES.** *Pierce at 18th St.* 712/258-4246. Hrs: 11 am-11 pm; Fri, Sat to midnight. Closed Dec 25. Res accepted. Beer, wine. Semi-a la carte: lunch $3-$7.95, dinner $5.25-$11.50. Child's meals. Specializes in chicken, barbecued ribs, steak. Family-owned. Cr cds: A, D, MC, V.

✔★ **HUNAN PALACE.** *4280 Sergeant Rd, in Mayfair Shopping Mall.* 712/274-2336. Hrs: 11:30 am-2:30 pm; 4:30-9:30 pm; Fri, Sat to 10:30 pm. Closed Thanksgiving, Dec 25. Res accepted. Chinese menu. Bar. A la carte entrees: lunch $3.25-$4.95, dinner $5.75-$9.75. Specializes

in seafood, duck, Szechwan dishes. Several dining areas. Cr cds: A, DS, MC, V.

D

Spencer (B-3)

(See also Okoboji, Spirit Lake)

Founded 1859 **Pop** 11,066 **Elev** 1,321 ft **Area code** 712 **Zip** 51301 **E-mail** saabi@nwiowa.com

Information Spencer Area Association of Business and Industry, 122 W 5th St, PO Box 7937; 712/262-5680.

In 1859, George E. Spencer gave his name to this city. In 1878, the first railroad was built through the black, fertile prairie, and in less than a year the settlement known as Spencer grew from 300 to a bustling town of 1,000. Its growth has continued, and due to its location in the middle of a large agricultural area, the town is now a prosperous business center serving the surrounding farm communities.

What to See and Do

East Leach Park Campground. Campground with tent and trailer sites (dump station); fishing; playground. Campground (mid-Apr-mid-Oct, daily). 305 4th St SE. Phone 712/264-7265. Camping ¢¢¢

Oneota State Park. Park has 160 wooded acres overlooking scenic Little Sioux River valley. Hiking. Picnicking. 16 mi S on US 71, then 10 mi W on IA 10 in Peterson. Phone 712/337-3211.

Annual Events

Flagfest Summer Festival. Art festival, craft fair, parade, air show, dance, talent contest, entertainment. Phone 712/262-5680. June 5-7.

Clay County Fair. 9 days early Sept.

Motels

✔★ **IRON HORSE.** *1 mi S at jct US 18.* 712/262-3720; FAX 712/262-4538; res: 800/242-5115. 94 rms, 2 story. S $31-$36; D $41-$44; under 12 free. TV; cable. Complimentary coffee. Restaurant nearby. Ck-out 11 am. Valet serv. Cr cds: A, C, D, DS, MC, V.

✗ 🖈 SC

★ **PLAZA 1.** *Jct Hwy 18 & 71 S, 1 mi S at jct US 18, US 71.* 712/262-6100; FAX 712/262-5742; res: 800/369-3891. 58 rms, 2 story. S $33; D $41; each addl $4; suites $38-$50; under 12 free. Crib free. TV; cable. Complimentary coffee in rms. Restaurant adj 6 am-11 pm. Ck-out 11 am. Meeting rm. Business servs avail. Valet serv. Cr cds: A, C, D, DS, MC, V.

D ✗ 🖈

★ **SUPER 8.** *209 11th St (51304), jct US 18 & 71.* 712/262-8500. 31 rms, 2 story. S $33.20-$39.88; D $41.30. Crib $3. TV; cable. Complimentary coffee in lobby. Restaurant adj 6 am-10 pm. Ck-out 11 am. Cr cds: A, C, D, DS, MC, V.

D 🖈 SC

Motor Hotel

✔★ **THE HOTEL.** *605 Grand Ave.* 712/262-2010; FAX 712/262-5610. 41 rms, 39 shower only, 4 story. S, D $33-$53; each addl $4; under 12 free; wkly rates; higher rates county fair. TV; cable. Restaurant 5:30 am-9 pm; Sun 6:30 am-8 pm. Rm serv. Bar 11-2 am. Ck-out 11 am. Meeting rms. Business servs avail. Valet serv. Free airport transportation. Some refrigerators, wet bars. Cr cds: A, C, D, DS, MC, V.

🔥

Unrated Dining Spot

STUB'S RANCH KITCHEN. *2 mi SW on US 71. 712/262-2154.* Hrs: 11:30 am-1:30 pm, 5:30-8:30 pm; Sun 11 am-8 pm. Closed Dec 24 eve-Dec 25. Res accepted Mon-Sat. Wine, beer. Buffet: lunch $3.75, dinner $7. Specializes in roast sirloin, baked ham, barbecued ribs. Salad bar. Western decor, fireplace. No cr cds accepted.

Spirit Lake (A-3)

(For accommodations see Okoboji, Spencer; also see Estherville)

Settled 1856 **Pop** 3,871 **Elev** 1,450 ft **Area code** 712 **Zip** 51360 **E-mail** okobojicofc@ncn.net **Web** www.okoboji.com

Information Iowa Great Lakes Area Chamber of Commerce, US 71, Lakes Center Mall, Box 9, Arnolds Park 51331; 712/332-2107 or 800/839-9987.

Spirit Lake serves tourists in the resort region and the farming community flanking it. This area was a popular Native American meeting ground, visited by French explorers about 1700. The so-called Indian Massacre of Spirit Lake actually took place on the shores of three lakes—Spirit, East and West Okoboji. This is the scene of McKinlay Kantor's book *Spirit Lake*.

What to See and Do

Mini-Wakan State Park. 20 acres. Swimming; fishing; boating (ramp). Snowmobiling. Picnicking. Off IA 276, on N shore of Spirit Lake. Phone 712/337-3211.

Spirit Lake. 4,169 acres; largest glacier-carved lake in state. Swimming, fishing, boating (ramp). Camping (fee). Access area at Marble Beach, 3 mi NW on IA 276.

Storm Lake (B-3)

(See also Cherokee)

Pop 8,769 **Elev** 1,435 ft **Area code** 712 **Zip** 50588 **E-mail** slc@nwiowa.com **Web** nwiowa/stormlake

Information Chamber of Commerce, 119 W 6th, PO Box 584; 712/732-3780.

A college town—Buena Vista University is located here—and county seat on the north shore of Storm Lake, this community is also a meat and poultry center for the surrounding farms.

What to See and Do

Buena Vista County Historical Museum. Exhibits of early county history; changing displays; genealogy library. Changing exhibits and video presentations on early county history. (Mon-Fri mornings) 200 E 5th St, annex at 214 W 5th St. Phone 712/732-4955. **Donation.**

Living Heritage Tree Museum. Seedlings and cuttings of more than 30 noteworthy trees, including the Charter Oak Tree and the NASA seedling sent into space with Apollo 14. Descriptive plaques; pamphlets avail at City Hall. Illuminated at night. (Daily) In Sunset Park, W Lakeshore Dr. **Free.**

Storm Lake. Fourth-largest natural lake in Iowa with more than a 3,000-acre water surface, Storm Lake offers swimming on the north, east and south shores; fishing for bullhead, walleye, crappie, catfish, northern and bass. Along shore are 135 acres of state and municipal parks with boating

(docks, ramps). Golf. Camping at Sunrise Campground (Apr-Oct, daily; hookups; fee). Phone 712/732-8023.

Annual Events

Star-Spangled Spectacular. North side of lake. July 4.

Balloon Days. Airport. Hot air balloon races, fireworks, parade, amusement rides, food. 3 days Labor Day wkend.

Seasonal Event

Santa's Castle. More than 70 detailed animated characters, some dating to the early 1900s. Daily. Thanksgiving-Dec 25.

Motels

★ **LAMPLIGHTER.** *1504 N Lake Ave. 712/732-2505; FAX 712/732-7056; res: 800/383-7666.* 50 rms, 2 story. S $28.50; D $36.50; each addl $3. TV; cable (premium). Pool. Complimentary coffee in lobby. Restaurant adj. Ck-out 11 am. Meeting rm. In-rm modem link. Cr cds: A, C, D, DS, MC, V.

🏊 ⚡ 🔥 SC

★ **SAIL-INN.** *1015 E Lakeshore Dr. 712/732-1160; FAX 712/732-9441.* 44 rms, 2 story. S, D $24.95-$54.95. Crib $1. TV; cable. Complimentary continental bkfst. Restaurant nearby. Ck-out 11 am. Coin laundry. Business servs avail. In-rm modem link. Some refrigerators. Cr cds: A, DS, MC, V.

D ⚡ 🔥

Strawberry Point (B-7)

(For accommodations see Dubuque)

Pop 1,357 **Elev** 1,200 ft **Area code** 319 **Zip** 52076

This town took its name from the wild strawberries that once grew nearby.

What to See and Do

State parks.

Backbone. Approx 1,780 acres with limestone bluffs rising 140 ft from Maquoketa River, scenic overlook and 100-acre lake. Swimming, supervised beach; fishing on stocked trout stream; boating (ramps, rentals). Hiking trails. Snowmobiling. Improved & primitive camping (electricity, dump station), cabins. Civilian Conservation Corps museum. Standard hrs, fees. 4 mi SW on IA 410. Phone 319/924-2527.

Brush Creek Canyon. More than 210 acres featuring gorge with steep limestone walls that cut through 100 ft of bedrock; diversity of wildlife; state preserve. Hiking trails. Picnicking. 6 mi W on IA 3, then 5 mi N on IA 187 to Arlington, then 2 mi N. Phone 319/425-4161.

Wilder Memorial Museum. More than 850 dolls and 3 dollhouses; many rms furnished in style of late 1800s; art glassware, porcelain; oil paintings; rare Queen Anne doll; model of Iowa farm; display of Norwegian rosemaling; spinning wheels; Victorian lamps. (Schedule varies, call for appt) 123 W Mission St. Phone 319/933-4615. ¢¢

Washington (E-7)

(For accommodations see Iowa City)

Pop 7,074 **Elev** 762 ft **Area code** 319 **Zip** 52353

What to See and Do

Lake Darling State Park. A 1,387-acre park with 299-acre lake. Swimming, supervised beach; fishing; boating (ramps, rentals). Hiking trail. Snowmobiling. Picnicking. Camping (electricity, dump station). Standard hrs, fees. 12 mi SW on IA 1, then 3 mi W on IA 78, near Brighton. Phone 319/694-2323.

Waterloo (C-6)

(See also Cedar Falls)

Settled 1845 **Pop** 66,467 **Elev** 867 ft **Area code** 319 **E-mail** julie@waterloocvb.org **Web** www.waterloocvb.org

Information Convention & Visitors Bureau, 215 E 4th St, PO Box 1587, 50704; 319/233-8350 or 800/728-8431.

One of the largest tractor production facilities in the world is located here and contributes to the area's production of more than $1 billion worth of goods per year. On both banks of the wide Cedar River, Waterloo has established park and picnic areas, docks and boating facilities along the shoreline.

What to See and Do

Grout Museum of History and Science. Permanent and changing exhibits on regional history and science; Discovery Zone offers many hands-on activities. Pioneer Hall, photo history area, industrial hall; genealogy library. Planetarium shows. (Tues-Sat; closed hols). W Park Ave & South St, on US 218. Phone 319/234-6357. ¢¢

John Deere Waterloo Works. Guided 2 1/2-hr tours of farm tractor facility (Mon-Fri; closed most major hols; also 2 wks late July-early Aug). Over 12 yrs only; low-heeled shoes advised; no open-toed sandals. Also tours of John Deere Component Works and John Deere Engine Works. Res advised. 3500 E Donald St. Phone 319/292-7801 or 319/292-7697. **Free.**

Rensselaer Russell House Museum (1861). Guided tours of restored Victorian mansion; period furnishings. (June-Aug, Tues-Fri, also Sat afternoons; Apr-May & Sept-Oct, Tues-Sat afternoons) 520 W 3rd St. Phone 319/233-0262 (seasonal). ¢

Waterloo Museum of Art. Permanent collections include Haitian, American and regional art; Grant Wood drawings. Changing exhibits. Gift shop offers works by Midwest artists. (Daily; closed Jan 1, Thanksgiving, Dec 25) 225 Commercial St. Phone 319/291-4491. **Free.**

Waterloo Community Playhouse. Since 1916; offers 7 productions yrly including comedies, dramas, mysteries and classics. 225 Commercial St. For schedule phone 319/235-0367 or 319/291-4494. ¢¢¢¢

Annual Events

My Waterloo Days Festival. Citywide festival features air show, balloon rallies, parade, laser & fireworks show, music, renaissance fair, food. Phone 319/233-8431. 10 days beginning Fri after Memorial Day.

National Cattle Congress. Cattle Congress Grounds, off Ansborough Ave. Cattle, horse and agricultural exhibits; entertainment; carnival, saddle horse show. Phone 319/234-7515. Late Sept.

Motels

✔★ **EXEL INN.** 3350 University Ave (50701). 319/235-2165; FAX 319/235-7175. 104 rms, 2 story. S $29.99; D $39.99; each addl $4; under 17 free. Pet accepted. TV; cable. Complimentary continental bkfst. Restaurant nearby. Ck-out noon. Coin lndry. In-rm modem link. Game rm. Cr cds: A, C, D, DS, MC, V.

[🐾] [⊠] [🏂] [SC]

★ **FAIRFIELD INN BY MARRIOTT.** 2011 La Porte Rd (50702), Crossroads Shopping Center. 319/234-5452. 57 rms, 3 story. S $48.95; D $48.95-$53.95; under 18 free. Crib free. Pet accepted, some restrictions. TV; cable. Indoor pool; whirlpool. Complimentary continental bkfst. Restaurant opp open 24 hrs. Ck-out 11 am. Cr cds: A, D, DS, MC, V.

[D] [🐾] [≋] [⊠] [🏂] [SC]

★★ **HEARTLAND INN.** 1809 LaPorte Rd (50702). 319/235-4461; FAX 319/235-0907; res: 800/334-3277. 118 rms, 2 story. S $45-$57; D $53-$65; each addl $5; suites $120-$150. Crib free. Pet accepted; $10. TV; cable. Complimentary bkfst. Restaurant nearby. Ck-out noon. Meeting rm. Business servs avail. In-rm modem link. Exercise equipt; bicycle, stair machine, sauna. Cr cds: A, C, D, DS, MC, V.

[D] [🐾] [🏊] [⊠] [🏂] [SC]

★ **HEARTLAND INN.** 3052 Marnie Ave (50701). 319/232-7467; FAX 319/232-0403; res: 800/334-3277, ext. 11. 56 rms, 2 story. S $42-$51; D $49-$58; suites $115-$130; under 17 free. Crib free. Pet accepted; $10. TV; cable. Complimentary bkfst. Restaurant adj 6 am-10 pm. Ck-out noon. Meeting rms. Business servs avail. Cr cds: A, C, D, DS, MC, V.

[D] [🐾] [⊠] [🏂] [SC]

✔★ **SUPER 8.** 1825 Laporte Rd (50702), in Crossroads Shopping Center. 319/233-1800. 62 rms, 3 story. S $42.95; D $47.95; under 16 free. Crib free. Pet accepted, some restrictions. TV; cable. Complimentary continental bkfst. Restaurant opp open 24 hrs. Ck-out 11 am. Sundries. Cr cds: A, D, DS, MC, V.

[D] [🐾] [⊠] [🏂] [SC]

Hotels

★★ **BEST WESTERN STARLITE VILLAGE.** 214 Washington St (50701). 319/235-0321; FAX 319/235-6343. 219 rms, 11 story. S, D $52-$59; each addl $7; suites $95-$150; under 12 free. Crib free. Pet accepted. TV; cable. Indoor pool. Restaurant 6:30 am-2 pm, 5-9 pm; Sun 7 am-2 pm. Bar 4 pm-2 am. Ck-out noon. Meeting rms. Business servs avail. In-rm modem link. Airport, RR station, bus depot transportation. Cr cds: A, C, D, DS, MC, V.

[D] [🐾] [≋] [⊠] [🏂] [SC]

★★ **HOLIDAY INN-CONVENTION CENTER.** 4th & Commercial (50704). 319/233-7560; FAX 319/236-9590. 229 rms, 10 story. S $58-$66; D $60-$67; under 18 free. Crib free. Pet accepted. TV; cable. Indoor pool; whirlpool, poolside serv. Restaurant 6 am-2 pm; dining rm 5-10 pm. Bar 11-2 am; entertainment. Ck-out noon. Meeting rms. In-rm modem link. Airport transportation. Some refrigerators. Atrium lobby. Cr cds: A, C, D, DS, JCB, MC, V.

[D] [🐾] [≋] [⊠] [🏂] [SC]

Waverly (B-6)

(For accommodations see Cedar Falls, Waterloo)

Pop 8,539 **Elev** 919 ft **Area code** 319 **Zip** 50677
Information Chamber of Commerce, 118 W Bremer Ave; 319/352-4526.

Astride the Cedar River, Waverly serves a rich farm area as a major retail and industrial center.

What to See and Do

Iowa Star Clipper Dinner Train. Scenic round-trip, four-course dining excursions (3 hrs) through Cedar River Valley in 1950s-era dining cars. (All-yr, days vary) Departs from Waverly depot for afternoon or evening trips. For res phone 319/352-5467 or 800/525-4773. ¢¢¢¢¢

Wartburg College (1852). (1,450 students) Liberal arts. The Becker Hall of Science has collection of New Guinea artifacts (daily; closed Sun in June-Aug, hols). Also Schield International Museum (fee), a planetarium and art gallery. The Wartburg College Lageschulte Prairie is 3 mi NE. (Sept-May, Mon-Fri; closed hols) 9th St NW & Bremer Ave. Phone 319/352-8200.

Webster City (C-4)

(See also Fort Dodge)

Settled 1850 **Pop** 7,894 **Elev** 1,050 ft **Area code** 515 **Zip** 50595 **E-mail** wcabi@ncn.net **Web** www.ncn.net/~wcabi/
Information Area Association of Business & Industry, 628 2nd St, PO Box 310; 515/832-2564.

What to See and Do

Country Relics Little Village & Homestead. Reproduction of turn-of-the-century, Midwestern town features 1/2- to 2/3-scale model buildings; includes steeple church, one-room schoolhouse, general store and railway depot. Also on display are tractors and memorabilia relating early history of International Harvester. Gift shop. (May-Oct, daily) Approx 10 mi S on IA 17; just N of Stanhope. Phone 515/826-3491. ¢¢

Depot Museum Complex. Log cabin, original courthouse, other historic buildings. (May-Sept, daily) Ohio & Superior Sts. Phone 515/832-1424. **Free.**

Motels

★ **BEST WESTERN NORSEMAN INN.** (I-35 exit 144, Williams 50271) 15 mi E on Old US 20 to I-35. 515/854-2281; FAX 515/854-2447. 33 rms. S $36; D $48; each addl $6. Crib $6. Pet accepted. TV; cable. Complimentary continental bkfst. Restaurant nearby. Bar. Ck-out noon. Cr cds: A, C, D, DS, MC, V.

D 🐾 🛰 🐕 SC

✔★ **EXECUTIVE INN.** 1700 Superior St. 515/832-3631; FAX 515/832-6830; res: 800/322-3631. 39 rms, 2 story. S $35.88-$43.88; D $38.88-$45.88. Crib $3. TV; cable. Indoor pool; sauna. Complimentary continental bkfst. Restaurant nearby. Ck-out 11 am. Meeting rm. Business servs avail. Cr cds: A, C, D, DS, MC, V.

D 🛰 🛰 🐕 SC

West Bend (B-4)

(See also Algona, Emmetsburg)

Founded 1880 **Pop** 862 **Elev** 1,203 ft **Area code** 515 **Zip** 50597
Information Chamber of Commerce, PO Box 366; 515/887-4721.

The large bend in the West Fork of the Des Moines River gives this town its name.

What to See and Do

Grotto of the Redemption. Begun in 1912 by Rev. P.M. Dobberstein, the grotto, which covers entire city block, tells the story of fall and redemption of man. Constructed of ornamental stones from many states and countries, the shrine is reputed to be the largest collection of shells, minerals, fossils and other petrified material in the world. Illuminated at night. Camping (hookups, dump station). (Daily; guided tours June-mid-Oct; also by appt) 2 blks off IA 15 at N end of town. Phone 515/887-2371. **Donation.**

West Union (B-7)

Pop 2,490 **Elev** 1,107 ft **Area code** 319 **Zip** 52175
Information Chamber of Commerce, 101 N Vine St, PO Box 71; 319/422-3070.

What to See and Do

Montauk (1874). Former home of William Larrabee, Iowa's 12th governor. Original furnishings; art objects; personal memorabilia; 40-acre grounds. Tours (late May-Oct, daily; mid-Mar-Apr, by appt). 9 mi NE on US 18, near Clermont. Phone 319/423-7173. ¢¢

Volga River State Recreation Area. A 5,500-acre wooded area with lake; boating; fishing. Hunting. Hiking, horseback riding. Cross-country skiing, snowmobiling. Camping. Standard hrs, fees. 6 mi S via IA 150. Phone 319/425-4161.

Motel

✔★ **LILAC.** 310 US 150 N, just N of jct US 18, 150. 319/422-3861. 27 rms. S $29-$34; D $37-$40; under 12 free. TV; cable. Restaurant nearby. Ck-out 11 am. In-rm modem link. Cr cds: A, D, DS, MC, V.

🛰 🔥

Winterset (E-4)

(See also Indianola)

Settled 1846 **Pop** 4,196 **Elev** 1,100 ft **Area code** 515 **Zip** 50273 **Web** www.madisoncounty.com
Information Chamber of Commerce, 73 Jefferson; 515/462-1185.

What to See and Do

✪ **Covered bridges.** Six remain in Madison County; for leaflet, map and information on guided tours contact Chamber of Commerce.

John Wayne Birthplace. House where the actor was born May 26, 1907; front parlor and kitchen restored to era when he lived here; other rooms contain memorabilia. Visitor center. (Daily; closed Jan 1, Thanksgiving, Dec 25) 224 S 2nd St. Phone 515/462-1044. ¢

Madison County Museum & Complex. Twelve buildings and restored Bevington Mansion (1856). Fossils, Native American artifacts, memorabilia; old barn with live poultry display, log cabin school, log post office, 1881 church, general store, train depot. (May-Oct, daily; also by appt) 815 S 2nd Ave. Phone 515/462-2134. All buildings ¢¢

Annual Events

National Skillet-Throwing Contest. 15 mi SW via US 169 & Co G61 in Macksburg. Contestants throw skillets at stuffed dummies. 2nd full wkend June.

South River Festival. S via Co P71 & Co G68 to Truro. Features National Dry-land Canoe Race, in which canoes race down Main St using brooms for paddles. Phone 515/765-4586. Aug.

Madison County Fair. Fairgrounds. Aug.

Covered Bridge Festival. Late 19th-century crafts, entertainment; parade, bus tour of two covered bridges. 2nd full wkend Oct.

Motel

 ✔★ VILLAGE VIEW MOTEL. *711 E IA 92. 515/462-1218; FAX 515/462-1231; res: 800/862-1218.* 16 rms, 1 story. S $31.95-$41.95; D $41.95-$51.95; under 12 free. Crib free. Pet accepted. TV; cable (premium), VCR avail. Complimentary coffee in lobby. Restaurant nearby. Ck-out 11 am. Rec rm. Cr cds: A, C, D, DS, MC, V.

D ✔ ⊠ 🐾 SC

Minnesota

Population: 4,375,099
Land area: 79,548 square miles
Elevation: 602-2,301 feet
Highest point: Eagle Mt (Cook County)
Entered Union: May 11, 1858 (32nd state)
Capital: St Paul
Motto: Star of the North
Nickname: Gopher State, North Star State
State flower: Pink and white ladyslipper
State bird: Common loon
State tree: Norway pine
State fair: August 27-September 7, 1998, in St Paul
Time zone: Central
Web: www.explore.state.mn.us

Mother of the Mississippi, dotted by more than 4,000 square miles of water surface, Minnesota is not the "land of 10,000 lakes" as it so widely advertises—a recount indicates that the figure is closer to 12,000. Natives of the state may tell you that the lakes were stamped out by the hoofs of Paul Bunyan's giant blue ox, "Babe"; geologists say they were created by retreating glaciers during the Ice Age. They are certainly the Minnesota vacationland's prize attraction.

Although Minnesota borders on Canada and is 1,000 miles from either ocean, it is nevertheless a seaboard state, thanks to the St Lawrence Seaway, which makes Duluth, on Lake Superior, an international port and the world's largest inland freshwater port.

Dense forests, vast grainfields, rich pastures, a large open-pit iron mine, wilderness parks, outstanding hospitals and universities, high technology corporations and a thriving arts community—these are facets of this richly endowed state.

This is the get-away-from-it-all state: you can fish in a lake, canoe along the Canadian border or search out the Northwest Angle, which is so isolated that until recently it could be reached only by boat or plane. In winter you can ice fish, snowmobile or ski the hundreds of miles of downhill and cross-country areas. If you are not the outdoor type, there are spectator sports, nightlife, shopping, music, theater and sightseeing in the Twin Cities (Minneapolis/St Paul).

Explored by Native Americans, fur traders and missionaries since the dawn of its known history, Minnesota surged ahead on the economic tides of lumber, grain and ore. The state has 92,000 farms covering 30 million acres; its agricultural production ranks high in sugar beets, butter, turkeys, sweet corn, soybeans, sunflowers, spring wheat, hogs and peas. Manufacturing is important to Minnesota's economy. It also is a wholesale transportation hub and financial and retailing center of the Upper Midwest.

The flags of four nations have flown over Minnesota as it passed through Spanish, French and British rule, finally to become part of the United States in segments in 1784, 1803 and 1818. A territory in 1849, Minnesota was admitted as a state less than a decade later. The Dakota (Sioux) War was a turning point in the state's history, claiming the lives of 400 settlers and an unknown number of Native Americans in 1862. It marked the end of Sioux control in the domain they called "the land of the sky-tinted waters." The vast forests poured out seemingly unending streams of lumber and the people spun legends of Paul Bunyan, an enduring part of American folklore. With the first shipment of iron ore in 1884, Minnesota was on its way to a mine-farm-factory future.

When to Go/Climate

This state of lakes and prairieland offers warm summers, cool falls, wet springs, and cold winters.

AVERAGE HIGH/LOW TEMPERATURES (°F)

INTERNATIONAL FALLS

Jan 12/-10	**May** 65/40	**Sept** 64/43
Feb 19/-4	**June** 73/50	**Oct** 52/33
Mar 33/11	**July** 79/55	**Nov** 33/17
Apr 50/28	**Aug** 76/52	**Dec** 17/-2

MINNEAPOLIS/ST PAUL

Jan 21/3	**May** 69/48	**Sept** 71/50
Feb 27/9	**June** 79/58	**Oct** 59/39
Mar 39/23	**July** 84/63	**Nov** 41/25
Apr 57/36	**Aug** 81/60	**Dec** 26/10

Parks and Recreation Finder

Directions to and information about the parks and recreation areas below are given under their respective town/city sections. Please refer to those sections for details.

Key to abbreviations: I.P. = Interstate Park; N.B.C. = National Battlefield & Cemetery; N.B.P. = National Battlefield Park; N.F. = National Forest; N.G. = National Grassland; N.H. = National Historical Park; N.H.S. =

CALENDAR HIGHLIGHTS

JANUARY

John Beargrease Sled Dog Marathon (Duluth). Approximately 500-mile, 5-day marathon from Duluth to Grand Portage and back. About 20 to 25 mushers compete. Phone 218/722-7631.

Winter Carnival (St Paul). Citywide happening, with ice and snow carving; parades, sports events, parties, pageants. Phone 612/223-4700.

JUNE

Judy Garland Festival (Grand Rapids). Museum. Discussions and presentations on Judy Garland's life and accomplishments. Viewing of *The Wizard of Oz*, children's activities, gala dinner. Phone 218/327-9276 or 800/664-JUDY.

Vikingland Drum Corps Classic (Alexandria). National drum and bugle corps performs in the state's only field show competition. Phone Chamber of Commerce, 320/763-3161 or 800/245-2539.

JULY

Laura Ingalls Wilder Pageant (Tracy). Celebration of the life of Laura Ingalls Wilder, author of the *Little House* books. Phone 507/859-2174.

Paul Bunyon Water Carnival (Bemidji). Water show, parade, fireworks. Phone Chamber of Commerce, 218/751-3541 or 800/458-2223, ext 100.

Lumberjack Days (Cloquet). Citywide program features concert; antique car show; airplane, helicopter, hot-air balloon rides. Phone 218/879-1551.

Minneapolis Aquatennial (Minneapolis). Parades, aquatic events, sports events, entertainment. Phone 612/377-4621.

Heritagefest (New Ulm). Old World-style celebration highlighting German traditions and culture through music, food, arts and crafts. Features entertainers from around the area and from Europe. Phone 507/354-8850.

AUGUST

WE Country Music Fest (Detroit Lakes). Soo Pass Ranch. Three-day event featuring many top country musicians and groups. Phone 218/847-1681.

Bayfront Blues Festival (Duluth). Three days of nonstop blues performances. Phone 715/392-1857.

Minnesota State Fair (St Paul). Fairgrounds. Horse show, kids' days, all-star revue; more than one million visitors each year; 300 acres of attractions. Phone 612/642-2200.

National Historic Site; N.M. = National Monument; N.Mem. = National Memorial; N.M.P. = National Military Park; N.P. = National Park; N.Pres. = National Preserve; N.R. = National Recreational Area; N.R.R. = National Recreational River; N.Res. = National Reserve; N.S. = National Seashore; N.S.R. = National Scenic River; N.S.T. = National Scenic Trail; N.V.M. = National Volcanic Monument; S.B. = State Beach; S.C.P. = State Conservation Park; S.G. = State Garden; S.H.A. = State Historic Area; S.H.P. = State Historic Park; S.N.A. = State Natural Area; S.P. = State Park; S.R. = State Reserve; S.R.A. = State Recreation Area; S.Res.P. = State Resort Park; S.R.P. = State Rustic Park.

NATIONAL PARK RECREATION AREAS

Place Name	Listed Under
Chippewa N.F.	GRAND RAPIDS
Grand Portage N.M.	GRAND PORTAGE
Pipestone N.M.	same
St Croix and the Lower St Croix N.S.R.	TAYLORS FALLS
Superior N.F.	same
Voyageurs N.P.	INTERNATIONAL FALLS

STATE RECREATION AREAS

Place Name	Listed Under
Blue Mounds S.P.	LUVERNE
Camden S.P.	MARSHALL
Charles A. Lindbergh S.P.	LITTLE FALLS
Flandrau S.P.	NEW ULM
Forestville S.P.	SPRING VALLEY
Ft Ridgely S.P.	NEW ULM
Fort Snelling S.P.	ST PAUL
Gooseberry Falls S.P.	TWO HARBORS
Hayes Lake S.P.	ROSEAU
Interstate S.P.	TAYLORS FALLS
Itasca S.P.	same
Jay Cooke S.P.	DULUTH
Kilen Woods S.P.	JACKSON
Lac qui Parle S.P.	GRANITE FALLS
Lake Bemidji S.P.	BEMIDJI
Lake Carlos S.P.	ALEXANDRIA
Lake Shetek S.P.	TRACY
McCarthy Beach S.P.	HIBBING
Mille Lacs Kathio S.P.	ONAMIA
Minneopa S.P.	MANKATO
Myre-Big Island S.P.	ALBERT LEA
Nerstrand Woods S.P.	NORTHFIELD
Savanna Portage S.P.	AITKIN
Scenic S.P.	GRAND RAPIDS
Sibley S.P.	WILLMAR
Soudan Underground Mine S.P.	TOWER
Split Rock Creek S.P.	PIPESTONE
Split Rock Lighthouse S.P.	TWO HARBORS
St Croix S.P.	HINCKLEY
Whitewater S.P.	ROCHESTER
Wild River S.P.	TAYLORS FALLS
William O'Brien S.P.	STILLWATER
Zippel Bay S.P.	BAUDETTE

Water-related activities, hiking, riding, various other sports, picnicking and visitor centers, as well as camping, are available in many of these areas. A $20 annual permit is required for vehicles entering a state park: good for a calendar year. A daily permit, $4, is also available. Permits may be purchased at parks. Camping $8-$12/night is limited to 2 weeks in any one park, and reservations are accepted in all parks. In state forests, camping, backpack or canoe-in sites are $7/night. There are small fees for other services. Fees subject to change. Parks are open year-round; however summer facilities vary in their opening and closing dates. All state parks are game refuges; hunting is prohibited. Pets are allowed on leash only. For further information contact Information Center, Minnesota Dept of Natural Resources, 500 Lafayette Rd, St Paul 55155; 612/296-6157 or 800/766-6000 (MN).

SKI AREAS

Place Name	Listed Under
Afton Alps Ski Area	HASTINGS
Buck Hill Ski Area	MINNEAPOLIS
Detroit Mt Ski Area	DETROIT LAKES
Hyland Hills Ski Area	MINNEAPOLIS
Lutsen Mountains Ski Area	LUTSEN
Mt Frontenac Ski Area	RED WING
Mt Kato Ski Area	MANKATO
Powder Ridge Ski Area	ST CLOUD
Quadna Mt Resort Ski Area	GRAND RAPIDS
Spirit Mountain Ski Area	DULUTH

Welch Village Ski Area   RED WING
Wild Mt Ski Area   TAYLORS FALLS

FISHING & HUNTING

There's every kind of freshwater fishing here. Many of the lakes have more than 50 pounds of game fish per acre; the total catch in the state is as high as 20 million pounds a year. Dip a line for walleye, large or smallmouth bass, crappie, northern pike, muskellunge, brook, brown, rainbow, lake trout or panfish.

Nonresident fishing license: $27.50; nonresident family license: $37.50; nonresident 24-hr license: $7.50; nonresident 3-day license: $16; nonresident 7-day license: $19; trout stamp: $5. Nonresident small game license: $61. Fees subject to change. For a more complete summary of hunting, fishing and trapping regulations contact Dept of Natural Resources, 500 Lafayette Rd, St Paul 55155-4040; 612/296-6157 or 800/766-6000 (MN).

Driving Information

Safety belts are mandatory for all persons in front seat of a vehicle. Children under 12 years must be restrained anywhere in vehicle: ages 4-11 must use a regulation safety belt; under age 4 must be in a federally approved safety seat. For further information phone 612/282-6558.

INTERSTATE HIGHWAY SYSTEM

The following alphabetical listing of Minnesota towns in *Mobil Travel Guide* shows that these cities are within 10 miles of the indicated Interstate highways. A highway map, however, should be checked for the nearest exit.

Highway Number	Cities/Towns within 10 miles
Interstate 35	Albert Lea, Bloomington, Cloquet, Duluth, Faribault, Hinckley, Lakeville, Minneapolis, Northfield, Owatonna, St Paul.
Interstate 90	Albert Lea, Austin, Blue Earth, Fairmont, Jackson, Luverne, Rochester, Winona.
Interstate 94	Alexandria, Anoka, Bloomington, Elk River, Fergus Falls, Minneapolis, Moorhead, St Cloud, St Paul, Sauk Centre.

Additional Visitor Information

Minnesota travel information is available free from the Minnesota Travel Information Center, 100 Metro Square, 121 7th Place East, St Paul 55101. Phone 612/296-5029 or 800/657-3700, for information on special events, recreational activities and places of interest. Also available are: *1998 Minnesota Guide; Minnesota Explorer,* a free seasonal newspaper with events and attraction information, including a calendar of events for each season; canoeing, hiking, backpacking, biking, and fishing brochures; a state map and directories to restaurants, accommodations and campgrounds, as well as regional and community tourism publications.

There are twelve travel information centers at entry points and along several traffic corridors of Minnesota; visitors will find the information provided at these stops very helpful in planning their trip through the area. Their locations are as follows: northbound I-35 at Iowa border; US 53, 10 mi south of Eveleth; I-90 at South Dakota border near Beaver Creek; I-90 at Wisconsin border near La Crescent; US 2, 10 mi east of North Dakota border near Fisher; US 61, 5 mi south of Canadian border near Grand Portage (May-Oct); US 53 in International Falls; I-94 at North Dakota border in Moorhead; I-94 at Wisconsin border near Lakeland; I-35 and US 2W in Duluth; US 59 & MN 60, 5 mi N of Iowa border near Worthington; US 10 south of St Cloud.

Aitkin (D-3)

(See also Brainerd, Deerwood, Onamia)

Pop 1,698 **Elev** 1,201 ft **Area code** 218 **Zip** 56431
Information Aitkin Area Chamber of Commerce, PO Box 127; 218/927-2316.

Once the bed of Lake Aitkin, and since drained by the deep channel of the Mississippi, the city now produces wild rice and other crops. Fishing enthusiasts, bound for one of the hundreds of lakes in Aitkin County, often stop off here.

What to See and Do

Mille Lacs Lake. 14 mi S on US 169. (See ONAMIA)

Rice Lake National Wildlife Refuge. An 18,127-acre refuge that includes 4,500-acre Rice Lake; migration and nesting area for ducks and Canada geese along Mississippi Flyway. Walking and auto trails; fishing. Headquarters (Mon-Fri; closed hols). Area (daily). 23 mi E on MN 210, then 5 mi S, off MN 65 near McGregor. Phone 218/768-2402. **Free.**

Savanna Portage State Park. A 15,818-acre wilderness area built around historic portage linking Mississippi River and Lake Superior. Swimming; fishing; boating (electric motors only; rentals), canoeing; hiking; cross-country skiing, snowmobiling; picnicking; camping. Standard fees. 8 mi NE on US 169, then 14 mi E on US 210 to McGregor, then 7 mi N on MN 65, 10 mi NE on County 14. Phone 218/426-3271.

Annual Events

Riverboat Heritage Days. 3rd wkend in July.

Fish House Parade. Fri after Thanksgiving.

Motel

 RIPPLE RIVER. *701 S Minnesota Ave, ¹/₂ mi S on US 169.* 218/927-3734; FAX 218/927-3540; res: 800/258-3734. 28 rms. S $35-$75; D $42-$85; each addl $6. Pet accepted. TV; cable. Complimentary coffee in lobby. Restaurant nearby. Ck-out 11 am. Business servs avail. X-country ski ¹/₄ mi. Some refrigerators, microwaves. On 7 acres. Cr cds: DS, MC, V.

Albert Lea (H-4)

(See Austin, also Blue Earth)

Settled 1855 **Pop** 18,310 **Elev** 1,299 ft **Area code** 507 **Zip** 56007 **Web** www.albertlea.org/cvb
Information Convention & Visitors Bureau, 202 N Broadway; 507/373-3938 or 800/345-8414.

An important agriculture, manufacturing and distribution center, Albert Lea bears the name of the officer who surveyed the area. Albert Lea is the seat of Freeborn County.

What to See and Do

Fountain Lake. Numerous parks offer picnicking, hiking, fishing, swimming, boating. NW part of city. Phone 507/377-4370.

Freeborn County Historical Museum, Library and Village. Restored buildings include schoolhouse, general store, sheriff's office and jail, blacksmith and wagon shops, post office, train depot, church and log cabin. Museum has displays of tools, household items, firefighting equipment, toys, musical instruments. Library specializes in Freeborn County history and genealogy. (Apr-mid-Dec, daily exc Mon) 1031 N Bridge Ave. Phone 507/373-8003. ¢¢

Myre-Big Island State Park. 1,600 acres. Prairie pothole landscape includes rare white pelicans; hundreds of wildflowers; Native American displays; hiking, cross-country skiing; camping. Interpretive center. Standard fees. 3 mi E at jct I-35 & I-90. Phone 507/373-3403.

Story Lady Doll & Toy Museum. Collection of 400 storybook dolls on display. Every other month, museum exhibits unique dolls from area collectors. Gift shop has antique, designer and ethnic dolls. (Apr-Dec, daily exc Mon; closed hols) 131 N Broadway Ave. 507/377-1820. ¢

Annual Events

Freeborn County Fair. Fairgrounds. Just N of city limits on Bridge St. Entertainment; livestock exhibits; midway. Phone 507/373-6965. 5 days late July or early Aug.

Big Island Rendezvous & Festival. Bancroft Bay Park. Reenactment of the fur trade period; bluegrass music; ethnic food. Phone 507/373-3938 or 800/658-2526. 1st wkend Oct.

Motels

✔★ **BEL AIRE.** *700 US 69S, 1 blk S of jct 16 & MN 13.* 507/373-3983; FAX 507/373-5161; res: 800/373-4073. 46 rms, 1 story. S $28-$34; D $34-$45; each addl $4; under 14 free. Crib free. Pet accepted. TV; cable. Pool. Playground. Complimentary continental bkfst. Restaurant nearby. Ck-out 11 am. Cr cds: DS, MC, V.

★ ★ **BEST WESTERN ALBERT LEA INN.** *2301 E Main St.* 507/373-8291; FAX 507/373-4043. 124 rms, 3 story. S $46-$56; D $59-$69; each addl $5; under 18 free. Crib free. Pet accepted. TV. Indoor pool; wading pool, whirlpool. Restaurant 6:30 am-9:30 pm. Bar 5 pm-midnight, closed Sun; entertainment wkends. Ck-out 11 am. Coin lndry. Meeting rms. Business servs avail. Sundries. X-country ski 1 mi. Exercise equipt; bicycle, stair machine, sauna. Game rm. Cr cds: A, C, D, DS, MC, V.

⊡ ✔ 🏊 ✕ 🏋 🚭 SC

★ ★ **DAYS INN.** *2306 E Main St.* 507/373-6471; FAX 507/373-7517. 129 rms, 2 story. S, D $59-$75; each addl $5; under 18 free. Crib free. Pet accepted. TV. Indoor pool. Restaurant 6:30 am-9 pm. Bar 4 pm-12:30 am. Ck-out 11 am. Coin lndry. Meeting rms. Business servs avail. In-rm modem link. Sundries. X-country ski 1 mi. Cr cds: A, C, D, DS, ER, JCB, MC, V.

⊡ ✔ 🏊 🏊 🚭 SC

✔★ **SUPER 8.** *2019 E Main St.* 507/377-0591. 60 rms, 3 story. No elvtr. S $36.88; D $47.88; each addl $4. Crib $2. Pet accepted. TV; cable, VCR avail (movies $5). Complimentary coffee Mon-Fri. Restaurants adj. Ck-out 11 am. Business servs avail. Sundries. X-country ski 1 mi. Snowmobile trail adj. Cr cds: A, C, D, DS, MC, V.

⊡ ✔ 🏊 🏊 🚭 SC

Alexandria (E-2)

(See also Glenwood, Sauk Centre)

Settled 1866 **Pop** 7,838 **Elev** 1,400 ft **Area code** 320 **Zip** 56308

Information Chamber of Commerce, 206 Broadway; 320/763-3161 or 800/245-ALEX.

Easy access to hundreds of fish-filled lakes attracts a steady stream of tourists. The city has a manufacturing and trade industry base. Red River fur traders first explored this area, followed by settlers, one of whom gave the city his name.

What to See and Do

Lake Carlos State Park. A 1,261-acre park. Swimming, fishing, boat ramp; hiking, bridle trails; ski trails, snowmobiling; picnicking; camping. Sandy shoreline. Standard fees. 8 mi N on MN 29, then 2 mi W on County 38. Phone 320/852-7200.

Runestone Museum. Runic inscriptions on graywacke stone carry a 1362 date, supporting belief of exploration of North America long before Columbus discovered the New World. Found at the roots of a tree in 1898, authenticity of the stone has been the subject of great controversy. Also restored log cabins, farm artifacts, horse-drawn machinery, schoolhouse. (Mon-Sat, also Sun afternoons) Children with adult only. 206 Broadway. Phone 320/763-3160. ¢¢

Annual Events

Vikingland Drum Corps Classic. National drum and bugle corps performs in state's only field show competition. Last Sat June.

Vikingland Band Festival. Twenty select high school marching bands compete in state's largest summer marching band competition. Last Sun June.

Motels

✔★ **AMERICINN.** *4520 S MN 29.* 320/763-6808. 53 rms, 2 story. Memorial Day-Labor Day: S $46.90; D $60.90; each addl $6; under 12 free; lower rates rest of yr. Crib free. Pet accepted. TV; cable (premium). Complimentary continental bkfst. Restaurant adj 6 am-11 pm. Ck-out 11 am. Business servs avail. Indoor pool; whirlpool. Cr cds: A, C, D, DS, MC, V.

⊡ ✔ 🏊 🏊 🚭 SC

★ ★ **COMFORT INN.** *507 50th Ave W.* 320/762-5161; FAX 320/762-5337. 48 rms, 2 story. May-Aug: S $45.90-$66.90; D $56.90-$66.90; each addl $5; under 18 free; lower rates rest of yr. Crib avail. TV; cable (premium). Indoor pool; whirlpool. Complimentary continental bkfst. Restaurant nearby. Ck-out 11 am. Meeting rms. Business servs avail. In-rm modem link. Downhill ski 10 mi; x-country ski 1 mi. Cr cds: A, C, D, DS, ER, JCB, MC, V.

⊡ 🏊 🏊 🏊 🚭 SC

✔★ **DAYS INN.** *4810 MN 29S, 3 mi S at I-94.* 320/762-1171; FAX 320/762-1171, ext. 234. 59 rms, 2 story. S $42-$45; D $47-$50; each addl $6; under 18 free. Crib free. TV; cable (premium). Complimentary continental bkfst. Restaurant adj open 24 hrs. Ck-out 11 am. Business servs avail. Sundries. Cr cds: A, C, D, DS, MC, V.

🏊 🚭 SC

★ ★ **HOLIDAY INN.** *MN 29 & I-94.* 320/763-6577; FAX 320/763-2092. 149 rms, 2 story. S, D $64-$79; under 18 free. Crib free. TV; cable (premium), VCR (movies). Indoor pool; wading pool, whirlpool. Restaurant 6 am-10 pm. Rm serv. Bar 4 pm-1 am; entertainment exc Sun. Ck-out noon. Coin lndry. Meeting rms. Business servs avail. In-rm modem link. Valet serv. Sundries. Sauna. Rec rm. Cr cds: A, C, D, DS, ER, JCB, MC, V.

⊡ 🏊 🏊 🚭 SC

✔★ **SUPER 8.** *4620 MN 29S.* 320/763-6552. 57 rms, 2 story. May-Sept: S $38.88-$44.88; D $43.88-$49.88; each addl $3-$10; under 12 free; lower rates rest of yr. Crib $2. TV; cable (premium). Restaurant nearby. Ck-out 11 am. Business servs avail. Game rm. Cr cds: A, C, D, DS, MC, V.

⊡ 🏊 🚭 SC

Resort

★ ★ ★ **RADISSON ARROWWOOD.** *2100 Arrowwood Lane, 3¼ mi NW on County 22.* 320/762-1124; FAX 320/762-0133. E-mail resort @rea-arp.com. 200 rms, 5 story, 24 suites. June-Sept: S, D $115-$150; each addl $15; suites $160-$274; family, wkly rates; golf plans; lower rates rest of yr. TV; cable (premium), VCR avail (movies). 2 pools, 1 indoor; whirlpool, poolside serv. Playground. Supervised child's activities (June-Sept). Dining rm 6:30 am-10 pm. Box lunches. Snack bar. Rm serv. Bars 11-1 am; entertainment exc Sun. Ck-out noon, ck-in after 4 pm. Convention facilities. Business servs avail. In-rm modem link. Free airport, bus depot transportation. Tennis. 18-hole golf, greens fee $28. Exercise equipt; weight machines, stair machines, sauna. Private beach. Waterskiing. Boats, launching ramp, dockage, motors, rowboats, canoes, sailboats, paddlebikes. Downhill ski 20 mi; x-country ski adj. Tobogganing, snowmobiles, sleighrides. Ice-skating. Bicycles. Hayrides. Nature trails. Soc dir. Rec rm. Game rm. Some refrigerators; microwaves avail. Balconies. Picnic tables. Cr cds: A, C, D, DS, ER, MC, V.

Anoka (F-4)

(For accommodations see Minneapolis, St Paul)

Settled 1844 **Pop** 17,192 **Elev** 870 ft **Area code** 612
Information Anoka Area Chamber of Commerce, 222 E Main St, Suite 108, 55303; 612/421-7130.

Once rivaling Minneapolis as the metropolitan center of the state, Anoka continues as a thriving industrial city at the confluence of the Mississippi and Rum rivers. A city of parks and playgrounds, Anoka is minutes away from ten well-stocked lakes.

What to See and Do

Father Hennepin Stone. Inscription reads "Father Louis Hennepin—1680"; possibly carved by the Franciscan explorer. Near mouth of Rum River.

Jonathan Emerson Monument. Old settler inscribed 2,500 words from the Bible and personal philosophy on monument, erected it and died a year later. City Cemetery.

Annual Event

Anoka County Suburban Fair. NTPA Tractor/truck pull, PRCA rodeo, demolition derbies, free entertainment, beer garden. Exhibits and an "old farm place." Phone 612/427-4070. Early Aug.

Restaurants

★ ★ **SEASONS.** *(MN 242 & Foley Blvd, Coon Rapids) on Bunker Hills Golf Course.* 612/755-4444. Hrs: 11:30 am-2 pm, 5-9 pm; Sun brunch 10 am-1 pm. Res accepted. Continental menu. Bar. Semi-a la carte: lunch $4.25-$7.25, dinner $8.25-$19.95. Sun brunch $9.95. Child's meals. Specializes in steak, seafood, pasta. Overlooks golf course. Cr cds: A, C, D, DS, MC, V.

[D]

✔★ ★ **VINEYARD.** *1125 W Main St, Jct MN 10W & Thurston.* 612/427-0959. Hrs: 11 am-10 pm; Sat from 4 pm; Sun from noon. Closed Thanksgiving, Dec 25. Bar. Semi-a la carte: lunch $4.95-$10.90, dinner $9.95-$16.95. Child's meals. Specializes in homemade soup, seafood, steak. Cr cds: A, DS, MC, V.

[D]

Austin (H-4)

(See also Albert Lea, Owatonna)

Founded 1856 **Pop** 21,907 **Elev** 1,198 ft **Area code** 507 **Zip** 55912
Information Convention & Visitors Bureau, 1301 NW 18 Ave, Suite 118, PO Box 613; 507/437-4563 or 800/444-5713.

Named for a pioneer settler, Austin became the county seat after two of its citizens stole the county records from another contender. The act aroused the voters, who cast their ballots for Austin. The Hormel Institute here, a unit of the Graduate School of the University of Minnesota, does research on fats and oils and their effect on heart disease. Austin's meat and food processing plants are an important industry; livestock, grain and vegetables from a 100-mile radius are delivered here.

What to See and Do

Austin Fine Arts Center. Features local artists. (Fri-Sun) Oak Park Mall. Phone 507/433-8451. **Free.**

J.C. Hormel Nature Center. Located on the former estate of Jay Hormel, the center includes interpretive building (Mon-Sat, also Sun afternoons; closed major hols); footpaths; woods, pond, streams, meadows; also cross-country skiing in winter, canoeing in summer. (Daily) 1/4 mi N off I-90, at 1304 NE 21st St. Phone 507/437-7519. **Free.**

Mower County Historical Center. Restored buildings include original Hormel building, log cabin, church, depot, country school; also steam locomotive, firefighting equipment and horse-drawn carriages; Native American artifacts; telephone museum; guide service (summer only). (June-Aug, daily; rest of yr, by appt) 12th St & 6th Ave SW, at County Fairgrounds. Phone 507/437-6082. **Donation.**

Annual Events

SpamTown USA Festival/Spam Jam. 1st wkend July.

Mower County Fair. Fairgrounds, 12th St & 4th Ave SW. Mid-Aug.

National Barrow Show. Fairgrounds. 2nd wk Sept.

Motor Hotel

★ ★ **HOLIDAY INN.** *1701 4th St NW.* 507/433-1000; FAX 507/433-8749. 121 rms, 2 story. S $59-$79; D $69-$89; each addl $10; suites $88-$150; under 19 free. Crib avail. Pet accepted. TV; cable (premium). Indoor pool; wading pool; poolside serv. Complimentary coffee in lobby. Restaurant 6 am-10 pm. Rm serv. Bar 11-1 am; entertainment Mon-Sat. Ck-out 11 am. Coin lndry. Meeting rms. Business servs avail. In-rm modem link. Airport, RR station transportation. Exercise equipt; weights, bicycles, whirlpool, sauna. Game rm. Refrigerator in suites. Cr cds: A, C, D, DS, JCB, MC, V.

[D] [SC]

Restaurant

★ **OAK LEAF.** *208 S Main St.* 507/437-8555. Hrs: 6 am-10 pm. Closed Dec 25. Res accepted. Semi-a la carte: bkfst $2-$6, lunch $3-$7, dinner $6-$22. Child's meals. Specializes in steak, seafood, homemade pies. Small art gallery. Cr cds: MC, V.

Baudette (B-3)

Pop 1,146 **Elev** 1,086 ft **Area code** 218 **Zip** 56623 **E-mail** lakwoods @baudette.means.net **Web** www.lakeofthewoodsmn.com

Information Lake of the Woods Area Tourism Bureau, PO Box 518; 218/634-1174 or 800/382-FISH.

On the Rainy River, Baudette is the gateway to the waters and thousands of islands of the Lake of the Woods area. Across from Ontario, it is an important trade and commerce center for a farm area producing seed potatoes, flax, alfalfa, clover and small grain crops. It is a port of entry, with a toll-free bridge to Canada. (For Border Crossing Regulations, see MAKING THE MOST OF YOUR TRIP.)

What to See and Do

Lake of the Woods County Museum. Museum of local history. (May-Sept, Tues-Sat) 8th Ave SE. Phone 218/634-1200. **Free.**

Lake of the Woods. This lake is partly in the US, partly in Canada. Noted for fishing, sandy beaches and scenic beauty; more than 2,000 sq mi in area, with 14,000 charted islands and 65,000 mi of shoreline. Famous for walleyed pike. Maps of driving tours through lush forests & wildlife areas are avail from the Tourism Bureau. 12 mi N on MN 172. Also here is

Zippel Bay State Park. A 2,946-acre park. Swimming; fishing; boating (ramps). Hiking, snowmobiling. Picnicking. Camping. Beach area. Standard fees. 1 mi W on MN 11 to MN 172, 12 mi N to County 8, then 9 mi W. Phone 218/783-6252.

Northwest Angle/Islands. A Minnesota peninsula connected to Canada and separated by Lake of the Woods. Fishing. Lodging.

Rainy River. Fishing, boating. Begins 70 mi E, flows NW into Lake of the Woods.

Red Lake Wildlife Management Area & Norris Camp. 285,000 acres. Songbirds, bald eagles, moose, wolf, bear, grouse, deer and waterfowl; hunting permitted in season; blueberry picking; camping (permit required). Norris Camp is an historic CCC camp from the 1930s. Phone 218/783-6861. **Free.**

Motel

✔★ **WALLEYE INN.** 1½ mi W on MN 11. 218/634-1550. 39 rms, 2 story. S $34.50; D $44.90-$51.90; each addl $5; suites $59-$90; under 6 free. Crib $4. TV; cable (premium). Complimentary continental bkfst. Restaurant nearby. Ck-out 11 am. Business servs avail. Microwaves avail. Cr cds: MC, V.

Cottage Colony

★ **SPORTSMAN'S LODGE.** Rte 1, Box 167, 12 mi NW on MN 172. 218/634-1342; res: 800/862-8602. E-mail northern@means.net. 29 rms in 3-story lodge, 20 kit. cabins (1-3 bedrm). S $45-$49; D $65-$69; suites $75-$100; cabins for 2-10, $66-$199. TV; cable. Indoor pool; whirlpool. Dining rm 6-10 pm. Box lunches, snacks. Bar 8-1 am. Ck-out 11 am, ck-in 2 pm. Grocery 1 mi. Coin lndry 1 mi. Meeting rms. Business servs avail. Gift shop. Waterskiing. Boats; motors; boat dockage, charter fishing trips. X-country ski 4 mi. Snowmobile trails. Entertainment. Rec rm. Hunting in season. Freezers. Microwaves avail in cabins. Picnic tables, grill. Cr cds: A, DS, MC, V.

Bemidji (C-2)

Settled 1894 **Pop** 11,245 **Elev** 1,350 ft **Area code** 218 **E-mail** cbemidji @mail.paulbunyan.net **Web** www.paulbunyan.net/bemidji/chamber/

Information Chamber of Commerce, PO Box 850; 56619-0850; 218/751-3541 or 800/458-2223, ext 100.

Northland vacations support this city in a lake and forest area at the foot of Lake Bemidji (beh-MID-jee). Many logging and Native American trails, wooded shorelines and scenic rivers are just a few minutes away. Bemidji started as a trading post, became a lumber boomtown, a dairy and farming center and is now enjoying the bounty of a new cycle of forest harvests. Once strictly a summer vacation area, Bemidji is host to winter sports enthusiasts, spring anglers, fall hunters and nature lovers.

What to See and Do

Bemidji State University (1919). (5,400 students) Renowned for peat research, music programs, environmental studies, accounting, industrial technology. Guided tours. Overlooking Diamond Point and Lake Bemidji. Phone 218/755-2040 for appt and calendar of campus events.

Bemidji Tourist Information Center. Houses collection of Paul Bunyan tools and artifacts with amusing descriptions. Fireplace of the States has stones from every state (exc Alaska and Hawaii) and most Canadian provinces. (Memorial Day-Labor Day, daily; rest of yr, Mon-Fri) MN 197 (Paul Bunyan Dr). **Free.** Adj is

Paul Bunyan and Blue Ox. Giant replicas of Paul Bunyan and "Babe," the Blue Ox; one of the most photographed statues in America.

Lake Bemidji State Park. A 1,688-acre park. Swimming, picnicking, fishing, hiking in a virgin pine forest. Boating (ramp, rentals); cross-country skiing; camping; biking. Naturalist programs. Visitor center. Standard fees. 6 mi NE off US 71. Phone 218/755-3843.

Annual Events

Paul Bunyan Water Carnival. Water show, parade, fireworks. July 4 wkend.

Beltrami County Fair. Agricultural exhibits, carnival rides, nightly entertainment. July or Aug.

Seasonal Event

Paul Bunyan Playhouse. Downtown. Plays and musicals; professional casts. Wed-Sun. Res advised. Phone 218/751-7270. Mid-June-mid-Aug.

Motels

★ **AMERICINN.** 1200 Paul Bunyan Dr NW (56601), near Municipal Airport. 218/751-3000. 62 rms, 2 story. June-Aug: S $47.90-$67.90; D $53.90-$73.90; each addl $6; suites $63.90-$98.90; under 12 free; ski plan; lower rates rest of yr. Crib free. TV; cable (premium). Indoor pool; whirlpool, sauna. Complimentary continental bkfst. Restaurant adj open 24 hrs. Ck-out 11 am. Coin lndry. In-rm modem link. Downhill/x-country ski 18 mi. Some in-rm whirlpools, refrigerators. Cr cds: A, C, D, DS, MC, V.

★ **BEST WESTERN.** 2420 Paul Bunyan Dr NW (56601), 2½ mi NW at jct US 2 & 71N, near Municipal Airport. 218/751-0390; FAX 218/751-2887. 60 rms, 2 story. July-Labor Day: S $39-$55; D $40-$75; each addl $6; under 18 free; lower rates rest of year. Crib free. TV; cable, VCR avail (movies). Indoor pool; whirlpool. Complimentary continental bkfst. Restaurant adj open 24 hrs. Ck-out noon. Business servs avail. Downhill ski 12 mi; x-country ski 4 mi. Cr cds: A, C, D, DS, MC, V.

★ ★ **COMFORT INN.** *US 2W (56601), near Municipal Airport.* *218/751-7700.* 61 rms, 2 story, 18 suites. Mid-June-early Sept: S $49; D $59; each addl $5; suites $59-$89; under 19 free; lower rates rest of yr. Crib free. TV; cable, VCR avail (movies). Indoor pool; whirlpool, sauna. Complimentary continental bkfst. Restaurant adj 6 am-10 pm. Ck-out noon. Business servs avail. In-rm modem link. Valet serv. Sundries. Airport transportation. Refrigerator in suites; whirlpool in some suites. Cr cds: A, C, D, DS, JCB, MC, V.

D ≈ ✕ ⊠ ⚲ SC

★ ★ ★ **NORTHERN INN.** *US 2W (56601), near Municipal Airport.* *218/751-9500.* 123 rms, 2 story. Mid-May-Oct: S $59-$69; D $69-$79; each addl $10; suites $130; family rates; lower rates rest of yr. Crib free. Pet accepted. TV; cable, VCR avail (movies). Indoor pool; whirlpool, poolside serv. Restaurant 6 am-10 pm; Fri, Sat to 11 pm. Rm serv. Bar 3 pm-1 am; Sat, Sun from noon. Ck-out noon. Coin lndry. Meeting rms. Business servs avail. In-rm modem link. Valet serv. Sundries. Beauty shop. Free airport, bus depot transportation. Indoor putting green. Downhill ski 10 mi; x-country ski 4 mi. Exercise equipt; weight machine, stair machine, sauna. Game rm. Rec rm. Cr cds: A, C, D, DS, JCB, MC, V.

D ✔ ➤ ≈ ✕ ✈ ⊠ ⚲ SC

✔★ **SUPER 8.** *1815 Paul Bunyan Dr NW (56601). 218/751-8481; FAX 218/751-8870.* 101 rms, 2 story. S $37.98-$42.98; D $44.98-$59.98; each addl $5; suites $64.88; under 12 free. Crib free. TV; cable (premium). Complimentary continental bkfst. Restaurant nearby. Ck-out 11 am. Business servs avail. Downhill ski 15 mi; x-country ski 3 blks. Whirlpool, sauna. Cr cds: A, C, D, DS, MC, V.

D ➤ ⊠ ⚲ SC

Resort

★ ★ ★ **RUTTGER'S BIRCHMONT LODGE.** *530 Birchmont Beach Rd NE (56601), 4 mi N on Bemidji Ave (County 21). 218/751-1630; 800 888/788-8437.* 28 rms in 3-story lodge, 29 cottages (1-4 bedrm), 11 kits. Some A/C. No elvtr. Late June-mid-Aug: S $66-$69; D $78-$148; MAP avail; family rates; package plans; lower rates rest of yr. Fewer units late Sept-early May. Crib $4. Pet accepted. TV; cable. 2 pools, 1 indoor; whirlpool, poolside serv. Free supervised child's activities (June-Labor Day). Dining rm (seasonal) 7:30-10:30 am, 11:30-2 pm, 5:30-8:30 pm. Bar (seasonal) noon-1 am. Ck-out 11:30 am, ck-in after 4:30 pm. Coin lndry. Grocery, package store 4 mi. Meeting rms. Business servs avail. In-rm modem link. Airport, bus depot transportation. Sports dir. Tennis. 18-hole golf privileges, greens fee $28. Private beach. Waterskiing instruction. Boats, motors, sailboats, boat launch, dockage. Downhill ski 15 mi; x-country ski on site. Indoor, outdoor games. Soc dir. Movies. Exercise rm; instructor, weights, bicycles, sauna. Some refrigerators; fireplace in most cabins. Screened porches. Cr cds: A, DS, MC, V.

D ✔ ➤ ≈ ⚹ ✕ ≈ ⚲ SC

Cottage Colony

★ ★ ★ **FINN 'N FEATHER.** *Rte 3, Box 870 (56601), 1½ mi S on US 2, 71, then 10 mi E on County 8. 218/335-6598.* 19 kit. cottages (2-4 bedrm). No A/C. Mid-June-Labor Day, wkly: $600-$1,400 for 2-6 persons; MAP avail mid-May-mid-June; lower rates mid-May-mid-June, Labor Day-mid-Oct. Closed rest of yr. Crib avail. Heated pool; whirlpool. Supervised child's activities (June-Aug); ages 3-10. Box lunches, snacks. Ck-out 9 am, ck-in 4 pm. Coin lndry. Grocery, package store 1 mi. Tennis. 18-hole golf privileges. Private beach. Boats, motors, canoes, pontoon boat. Lawn games. Movies. Game rm. Rec rm. Some fireplaces. Many screened porches. Picnic tables, grills. Sand beach on Lake Andrusia. Cr cds: MC, V.

 ➤ ⚹ ⚲ ≈

Bloomington (F-4)

(See also Minneapolis)

Pop 86,335 **Elev** 830 ft **Area code** 612
Information Convention and Visitors Bureau, 1550 E 79th St, #450, 55420; 612/858-8500 or 800/346-4289.

Bloomington, located south of Minneapolis, is one of the state's largest cities.

What to See and Do

★ **Mall of America.** A retail/family entertainment complex with more than 400 stores and restaurants. Features Knott's Camp Snoopy, a 7-acre indoor theme park with rides and entertainment; LEGO Imagination Center with giant LEGO models and play areas; Golf Mountain miniature golf course; 14-screen movie complex; walk-through aquarium. (Daily) Separate fees for activities. I-494 exit 24th Ave S, bounded by 81st St, Killebrew Dr, MN 77 & 24th Ave S. Phone 612/883-8800.

Minnesota Valley National Wildlife Refuge. One of the only urban wildlife refuges in the nation. A 34-mi corridor of marsh and forest that is home to coyotes, badgers and bald eagles, the refuge offers miles of trails for hiking, biking, horseback riding and skiing. (Daily) 3815 E 80th St. Phone 612/335-2323.

Minnesota Zoo. Simulated natural habitats house 450 species of animals and 2,000 varieties of plants. Includes Minnesota, tropics, ocean and Discovery Trails sections; 1¼-mi monorail. (Daily; closed Dec 25) E on I-494, then S on MN 77 in Apple Valley. Phone 612/432-9000. ¢¢¢

Valleyfair. A 68-acre family amusement park bordering the Minnesota River. More than 50 rides and attractions, including 4 roller coasters, 3 water rides, antique carousel and special rides for children. Entertainment: IMAX Theater plus musical shows. (Memorial Day-Labor Day, daily; May & Sept, some wknds) 7 mi S on I-35W, then 9 mi W on MN 101 in Shakopee. Phone 612/445-6500 or 612/445-7600. Admission includes all rides, attractions and waterpark. ¢¢¢¢¢

Annual Event

Renaissance Festival. Re-creation of 16th-century Renaissance village celebrating a harvest holiday. Entertainment, ethnic foods, 250 arts & crafts shops, games, equestrian events. Phone 612/445-7361. 7 wknds beginning mid-Aug.

Motels

★ ★ ★ **BEST WESTERN THUNDERBIRD.** *2201 E 78th St (55425). 612/854-3411; FAX 612/854-1183.* 263 rms, 2 story. S $85-$110; D $91-$110; each addl $6; suites $135-$370; under 13 free. Crib free. Pet accepted. TV; cable. 2 pools, 1 indoor; whirlpool. Restaurant 6:30 am-10:30 pm. Rm serv to 11 am. Bar 4-11:30 pm; entertainment. Ck-out 11 am. Meeting rms. Business servs avail. Valet serv. Sundries. Gift shop. Free airport transportation. Downhill ski 10 mi; x-country ski 1 mi. Exercise equipt; weights, bicycles, sauna. Game rm. Refrigerators, microwaves avail. Cr cds: A, C, D, DS, ER, JCB, MC, V.

D ✔ ➤ ≈ ✕ ⊠ ⚲ SC

✔★ **BUDGETEL INN.** *7815 Nicollet Ave S (55420). 612/881-7311; FAX 612/881-0604.* 190 rms, 2 story. S $55.95; D $63.95; under 18 free. Crib free. Pet accepted, some restrictions. TV; cable (premium). Complimentary continental bkfst. Restaurant nearby. Ck-out noon. Meeting rms. Business servs avail. In-rm modem link. Downhill ski 10 mi; x-country ski ½ mi. Cr cds: A, C, D, DS, MC, V.

D ✔ ➤ ⊠ ⚲ SC

★ ★ **DAYS INN-AIRPORT.** *1901 Killebrew Dr (55420), near Minneapolis/St Paul Intl Airport. 612/854-8400; FAX 612/854-3615.* 207 rms, 2 story. May-Oct: S $110; D $120-$130; under 17 free; lower rates rest of yr. Crib avail. TV; cable (premium). Heated pool; whirlpool. Complimentary coffee in lobby. Restaurant nearby. Ck-out 11 am. Meeting rms. Free airport transportation. Downhill ski 12 mi; x-country 1 mi. Sauna. Game rm. Some balconies. Cr cds: A, C, D, DS, MC, V.

[D] [⊷] [≋] [✈] [⊣] [🔥]

★ EXEL INN. 2701 E 78th St (55425), near Minneapolis/St Paul Intl Airport. 612/854-7200; FAX 612/854-8652. 203 rms, 2 story. S $50-$70; D $60-$75; under 18 free. Crib free. TV; cable (premium), VCR avail. Complimentary continental bkfst. Restaurant nearby. Ck-out noon. Business servs avail. In-rm modem link. Sundries. Free airport transportation. Downhill ski 10 mi; x-country ski 2 mi. Exercise equipt; bicycles, treadmill. Microwaves avail. Cr cds: A, C, D, DS, MC, V.

[D] [⊷] [🏃] [✈] [⊣] [🔥] [SC]

★★ HAMPTON INN. 4201 W 80th St (55437), near Minneapolis/St Paul Intl Airport. 612/835-6643; FAX 612/835-7217. 135 rms, 4 story. S $64-$104; D $74-$114; each addl $10; suites $89-$119; under 18 free. Crib free. TV; cable (premium). Complimentary continental bkfst. Restaurant adj open 24 hrs. Ck-out noon. Meeting rms. Business servs avail. In-rm modem link. Valet serv. Free airport transportation. Downhill/x-country ski 2 mi. Health club privileges. Private balconies. Cr cds: A, C, D, DS, ER, JCB, MC, V.

[D] [⊷] [✈] [⊣] [🔥] [SC]

★★ HAMPTON INN. (7740 Flying Cloud Dr, Eden Prairie 55344) NW on I-494 to exit 11A. 612/942-9000; FAX 612/942-0725. 122 rms, 3 story. S $69-$79; D $75-$79; under 18 free. Crib free. TV; cable (premium). Complimentary continental bkfst. Restaurant nearby. Ck-out noon. Meeting rms. Business servs avail. In-rm modem link. Downhill ski 6 mi; x-country ski 1 mi. Cr cds: A, C, D, DS, MC, V.

[D] [⊷] [⊣] [🔥] [SC]

★ HOLIDAY INN EXPRESS-AIRPORT. 814 E 79th St (55420). 612/854-5558; FAX 612/854-4623. 142 rms, 4 story. S $74-$90; D $79-$95; each addl $10; suites $90; under 18 free. Crib free. TV; cable (premium). Complimentary continental bkfst. Restaurant open 24 hrs. Ck-out noon. Business servs avail. In-rm modem link. Free airport transportation. Downhill ski 15 mi; x-country ski 2 mi. Refrigerator in suites. Cr cds: A, C, D, DS, ER, JCB, MC, V.

[D] [⊷] [⊣] [🔥] [SC]

★★ QUALITY INN & SUITES-BURNSVILLE. (250 N River Ridge Circle, Burnsville 55337) S on I-35. 612/890-9550; FAX 612/890-5161. 94 rms, 2 story, 30 suites. May-Oct: S $69; D $79; each addl $8; suites $99-$280; under 18 free; lower rates rest of yr. TV; cable (premium), VCR avail (movies). Indoor/outdoor pool; whirlpool. Bar. Ck-out noon. Meeting rms. Business servs avail. Balconies. Suites decorated in different themes. Cr cds: A, C, D, DS, MC, V.

[D] [≋] [⊣] [🔥] [SC]

★★ RESIDENCE INN BY MARRIOTT. (7780 Flying Cloud Dr, Eden Prairie 55344) W on I-494. 612/829-0033; FAX 612/829-1935. 126 kit. suites, 1-2 story. S, D $129-$195; under 18 free. Pet accepted, some restrictions; $50. TV; cable (premium), VCR (movies $3.50). Heated pool; whirlpool. Complimentary bkfst buffet. Ck-out noon. Coin lndry. Meeting rms. Business servs avail. In-rm modem link. Valet serv. Airport transportation avail. Downhill ski 10 mi; x-country ski 1 mi. Exercise equipt; stair machine, weights. Refrigerators. Private patios, balconies. Cr cds: A, C, D, DS, JCB, MC, V.

[D] [⊶] [⊷] [≋] [🏃] [⊣] [🔥] [SC]

✔★ SELECT INN. 7851 Normandale Blvd (55435). 612/835-7400; FAX 612/835-4124; res: 800/641-1000. 148 rms, 2 story. S $46.90; D $55.90; each addl $4; under 13 free. Crib $3. Pet accepted; $25. TV; cable. Indoor pool. Complimentary continental bkfst. Restaurant nearby. Ck-out 11 am. Coin lndry. Meeting rms. Business servs avail. Free airport transportation. Downhill ski 5 mi. Exercise equipt; weights, treadmill. Cr cds: A, C, D, DS, MC, V.

[D] [⊶] [⊷] [≋] [🏃] [⊣] [🔥] [SC]

✔★ SUPER 8. (11500 W 78th St, Eden Prairie 55344) W on I-494 to US 169. 612/829-0888; FAX 612/829-0854. 61 rms, 3 story. No elvtr. S $50.88; D $60.88; each addl $6; under 12 free. Crib free. TV; cable (premium). Complimentary continental bkfst. Ck-out 11 am. Coin lndry. Business servs avail. X-country ski. Cr cds: A, C, D, DS, MC, V.

[D] [⊷] [⊣] [🔥] [SC]

Motor Hotels

★★ COMFORT INN. 1321 E 78th St (55425). 612/854-3400; FAX 612/854-2234. 272 rms, 5 story. S, D $69-$89; each addl $7; suites $145; under 17 free. Crib free. TV; cable (premium). Indoor pool. Coffee in rms. Restaurant 6-11 am, 5-10 pm; Sat 7 am-midnight; Sun 8 am-10 pm. Bar 11-1 am. Ck-out 11 am. Meeting rms. Business servs avail. Valet serv. Sundries. Free airport transportation. Downhill ski 10 mi; x-country ski 1 mi. Exercise equipt; weights, bicycles. Cr cds: A, C, D, DS, ER, JCB, MC, V.

[D] [⊷] [≋] [🏃] [⊣] [🔥] [SC]

★★ COUNTRY INN AND SUITES. 2221 Killebrew Dr (55425). 612/854-5555; FAX 612/854-5564. 234 rms, 6 story. S $95-$165; D $109-$165; each addl $10; suites $109-$165; under 19 free. Crib free. TV; cable (premium). Indoor pool; whirlpool; poolside serv. Complimentary continental bkfst. Restaurant adj 11 am-midnight. Ck-out noon. Meeting rms. Business servs avail. Free airport transportation. Downhill ski 14 mi; x-country 1 mi. Exercise equipt; weights, treadmills. Some refrigerators; microwaves avail. Cr cds: A, C, D, DS, MC, V.

[D] [⊷] [≋] [🏃] [⊣] [🔥] [SC]

★★ FAIRFIELD INN BY MARRIOTT. 2401 E 80th St (55425). 612/858-8475; FAX 612/858-8475. 134 rms, 4 story. May-Oct: S, D $79-$140; under 18 free; lower rates rest of yr. Crib avail. Pet accepted. TV; cable (premium). Indoor pool; whirlpool. Complimentary continental bkfst. Restaurant adj 6 am-11 pm. Ck-out noon. Meeting rms. Business servs avail. Downhill ski 15 mi; x-country ski 1 mi. Rec rm. Some refrigerators. Cr cds: A, C, D, DS, JCB, MC, V.

[D] [⊶] [⊷] [≋] [⊣] [🔥]

✔★ HOLIDAY INN CENTRAL. 1201 W 94th St (55431). 612/884-8211; FAX 612/881-5574. 171 rms, 4 story. S, D $89-$104; under 19 free. Crib avail. TV; cable. Indoor pool; whirlpool; poolside serv. Restaurant 6:30 am-10 pm. Rm serv. Bar. Ck-out 11 am. Coin lndry. Meeting rms. Business servs avail. In-rm modem link. Sundries. Free airport transportation. Downhill ski 6 mi. Exercise equipt; bicycles, treadmill, sauna. Game rm. Refrigerators avail. Cr cds: A, C, D, DS, JCB, MC, V.

[D] [⊷] [≋] [🏃] [⊣] [🔥] [SC]

★★★ MARRIOTT. 2020 E 79th St (55425), at jct 24th Ave & I-494, near Minneapolis/St Paul Intl Airport. 612/854-7441; FAX 612/854-7671. Web www.marriott.com. 478 rms, 2-5 story. S $99-$175; D $109-$170; under 18 free; wkend rates. Crib free. TV; cable (premium), VCR. Indoor pool; whirlpool. Restaurant 6 am-10 pm; Sat, Sun 7 am-11 pm. Rm serv. Bar 11-1 am. Ck-out noon. Meeting rms. Business center. In-rm modem link. Gift shop. Free airport transportation. Exercise equipt; bicycles, stair machine. Game rm. Luxury level. Cr cds: A, C, D, DS, ER, JCB, MC, V.

[D] [≋] [🏃] [✈] [⊣] [🔥] [SC] [⛷]

★★★ SHERATON-AIRPORT. 2500 E 79th St (55425), near Minneapolis/St Paul Intl Airport. 612/854-1771; FAX 612/854-5898. 250 rms, 2-4 story. S, D $110-$120; suites $140-$160; each addl $10; under 18 free. Crib free. TV; cable (premium), VCR avail. Indoor pool; whirlpool. Restaurant 6 am-10:30 pm; Sat, Sun from 7 am. Rm serv. Bar 11:30-1 am. Ck-out noon. Meeting rms. Business servs avail. Valet serv. Sundries. Free airport transportation. Downhill ski 10 mi; x-country ski 2 mi. Exercise equipt; weights, bicycles. Microwaves avail. Near Mall of America. Cr cds: A, C, D, DS, ER, JCB, MC, V.

[D] [⊷] [≋] [🏃] [✈] [⊣] [🔥] [SC]

★★ WYNDHAM GARDEN. 4460 W 78th St Circle (55435), near Minneapolis/St Paul Intl Airport. 612/831-3131; FAX 612/831-6372. 209 rms, 8 story. S $79-$125; D $89-$135; each addl $10; suites $99-

$145; under 19 free; wkend rates. Crib free. TV; cable (premium). Indoor pool; whirlpool. Coffee in rms. Restaurant 7 am-10 pm. Rm serv from 5 pm. Bar. Ck-out noon. Meeting rms. Business servs avail. In-rm modem link. Valet serv. Sundries. Free airport transportation. Exercise equipt; weights, stair machine. Downhill/x-country ski 2 mi. Wet bar in suites. Cr cds: A, C, D, DS, ER, JCB, MC, V.

[D] [symbols] SC

Hotels

✔★ ★ **BEST WESTERN BRADBURY SUITES.** *7770 Johnson Ave (55435).* 612/893-9999; FAX 612/893-1316. 164 rms, 6 story. S $69.95-$79.95; D $90.95; each addl $5; under 16 free. Crib free. TV; cable (premium), VCR. Complimentary bkfst buffet. Restaurant adj. Ck-out noon. Meeting rms. Business servs avail. In-rm modem link. Airport transportation. Downhill/x-country ski 1 mi. Health club privileges. Refrigerators. Cr cds: A, C, D, DS, MC, V.

[D] [symbols] SC

✔★ ★ **BEST WESTERN HOTEL SEVILLE.** *8151 Bridge Rd (55437).* 612/830-1300; FAX 612/830-1535. Web www.bestwestern.com. 252 rms, 18 story. S, D $79.95-$89.95; under 16 free; wkend rates. Crib free. TV. Indoor pool; whirlpool. Restaurant 6 am-1:30 pm, 5:30-9:30 pm; wkend hrs vary. Bar. Ck-out 11 am. Convention facilities. Business servs avail. In-rm modem link. Free airport transportation. Downhill ski 5 mi; x-country ski 1 mi. Sauna. Health club privileges. Game rm. Balconies. Cr cds: A, C, D, DS, JCB, MC, V.

[D] [symbols] SC

★ ★ ★ **DOUBLETREE GRAND HOTEL-MALL OF AMERICA.** *7901 24th Ave S (55425), just off I-494 exit 24th Ave, opp Mall of America, near Minneapolis/St Paul Intl Airport.* 612/854-2244; FAX 612/854-4421. 321 rms, 15 story. S, D $135-$155; each addl $20; suites $225-$400; wkend rates. TV; cable (premium), VCR. Indoor pool; whirlpool, poolside serv. Restaurant 6 am-10 pm. Rm serv 24 hrs. Bar from 11 am. Ck-out noon. Business center. In-rm modem link. Gift shop. Free airport transportation. Exercise equipt; weights, stair machine, sauna. Some private patios, balconies. Luxury level. Cr cds: A, C, D, DS, ER, MC, V.

[D] [symbols] SC

★ ★ **DOUBLETREE GUEST SUITES.** *2800 W 80th (55431), near Minneapolis/St Paul Intl Airport.* 612/884-4811; FAX 612/884-8137. Web www.doubletreehotels.com. 219 rms, 8 story. S, D $110-$179; each addl $10; under 12 free. Crib free. TV; cable (premium). Indoor pool; whirlpool. Restaurant 11:30 am-10 pm. Bar to 1 am. Ck-out noon. Coin lndry. Meeting rms. Business servs avail. In-rm modem link. Free airport transportation. Downhill ski 8 mi; x-country ski 1 mi. Exercise equipt; weights, stair machines, sauna, steam rm. Game rm. Refrigerators, microwaves. Private patios, balconies. Cr cds: A, C, D, DS, JCB, MC, V.

[D] [symbols] SC

★ ★ **EMBASSY SUITES-AIRPORT.** *7901 34th Ave S (55425), near Minneapolis/St Paul Intl Airport.* 612/854-1000; FAX 612/854-6557. 310 rms, 10 story. S, D $129-$159; each addl $10; under 18 free. Crib free. TV; cable (premium). Indoor pool; whirlpool. Complimentary full bkfst. Restaurant 11 am-10 pm. Bar to 1 am. Ck-out noon. Meeting rms. Business servs avail. In-rm modem link. Gift shop. Free airport transportation. Downhill ski 15 mi; x-country ski 2 mi. Exercise equipt; weight machine, treadmills, sauna. Microwaves. Private balconies. All rms open to courtyard atrium. Cr cds: A, C, D, DS, ER, JCB, MC, V.

[D] [symbols]

★ ★ **HAWTHORN SUITES.** *(3400 Edinborough Way, Edina 55435) ½ mi E of jct MN 100 & I-494.* 612/893-9300; FAX 612/893-9885. 141 kit. suites, 7 story. S, D $135-$145; under 18 free; wkend rates. Crib free. TV; cable (premium), VCR (movies $6). Indoor pool. Playground. Complimentary full bkfst. Complimentary coffee in rms. Restaurant nearby. No rm serv. Ck-out noon. Coin lndry. Meeting rms. Business servs avail. In-rm modem link. Sundries. Airport transportation. Downhill ski 7 mi;

x-country ski 1 mi. Health club privileges. Microwaves. Cr cds: A, C, D, DS, MC, V.

[D] [symbols] SC

★ ★ ★ **HOLIDAY INN SELECT-INTERNATIONAL AIRPORT.** *3 Apple Tree Square (55425), I-494 exit 34th Ave, opp river, near Minneapolis/St Paul Intl Airport.* 612/854-9000. 430 rms, 13 story. S, D $97-$169; each addl $10; suites $103-$250; under 19 free; wkend plans. Crib free. TV; cable (premium), VCR avail. Indoor pool; whirlpool, poolside serv. Restaurant 6 am-11 pm. Bar 11-1 am. Ck-out noon. Convention facilities. Business servs avail. In-rm modem link. Free covered parking. Free airport transportation. Downhill/x-country ski 10 mi. Exercise rm; instructor, weights, bicycles, sauna. Massage. Some refrigerators. Cr cds: A, C, D, DS, ER, JCB, MC, V.

[D] [symbols] SC

★ ★ ★ **HOTEL SOFITEL.** *5601 W 78th St (55439), at jct MN 100 & I-494.* 612/835-1900; FAX 612/835-2696; res: 800/876-6303 (exc MN). 282 rms, 6 story. S $149-$167; D $164-$181; each addl $15; suites $185-$275; wkend rates. Crib free. TV; cable (premium), VCR avail. Indoor pool. Restaurants 6:30-1 am (also see LA TERRASSE, Unrated Dining). Bars 11-1 am; Sun 10 am-midnight. Ck-out noon. Convention facilities. Business center. In-rm modem link. Concierge. Valet parking. Airport transportation. Downhill/x-country ski 1 mi. Exercise equipt; weights, bicycles. Massage. Cr cds: A, C, D, MC, V.

[D] [symbols]

★ ★ ★ **RADISSON-SOUTH.** *7800 Normandale Blvd (55439), jct I-94 & MN 100.* 612/835-7800; FAX 612/893-8419. Web www.radisson .com. 580 rms, 22 story. S, D $139-$159; each addl $15; suites $250-$450; under 18 free; cabanas $125-$135; wkend rates. Crib free. TV; VCR avail. Indoor pool; whirlpool. Coffee in rms. Restaurant 6:30 am-10 pm. Bar 11-1 am. Ck-out noon. Convention facilities. Business servs avail. In-rm modem link. Shopping arcade. Airport transportation avail. Downhill/x-country ski 2 mi. Exercise equipt; weights, bicycle, sauna. Luxury level. Cr cds: A, C, D, DS, ER, JCB, MC, V.

[D] [symbols] SC

Restaurants

✔★ ★ **ASIA GRILLE.** *(549 Prairie Center Dr, Eden Prairie 55344)* 612/944-4095. Hrs: 11 am-10 pm; Fri, Sat to 11 pm. Closed most major hols. Asian menu. Bar. Semi-a la carte: lunch $6.95-$9.95, dinner $6.95-$14.95. Specialties: spit-roasted garlic chicken, Asian pork with mushrooms. Contemporary decor. Cr cds: A, C, D, DS, MC, V.

[D]

✔★ ★ **ASIA GRILLE.** *(14023 Aldrich Ave S, Burnsville 55337) S on US 35W.* 612/898-3303. Hrs: 11:30 am-10 pm; Fri, Sat to 11 pm; Sun, Mon to 9 pm. Closed Memorial Day, Thanksgiving, Dec 25. Res accepted. Chinese menu. Bar. Semi-a la carte: lunch $5-$7, dinner $7-$12. Specialties: Asian tacos, soy-garlic rotisserie chicken. Own noodles. Outdoor dining. Casual, Asian decor. Cr cds: A, D, DS, MC, V.

[D] [symbol]

★ **DAVID FONG'S.** *9392 Lyndale S (55420).* 612/888-9294. Hrs: 11 am-9 pm; Thurs-Sat to 10 pm. Closed Sun; most major hols. Res accepted. Chinese menu. Bar to 1 am. Semi-a la carte: lunch, dinner $10.75-$21.95. Child's meals. Oriental decor. Cr cds: A, C, D, MC, V.

★ ★ **KINCAID'S.** *8400 Normandale Lake Blvd.* 612/921-2255. Hrs: 11 am-2:30 pm, 5-10 pm; Sat 4:30-11 pm; Sun 5-9 pm; Sun brunch 10 am-2 pm. Closed July 4, Thanksgiving, Dec 25. Res accepted. Bar to midnight. Semi-a la carte: lunch $5.95-$14.95, dinner $14.95-$26.95. Sun brunch $8.95-$16.95. Child's meals. Specialties: mesquite-grilled king salmon, rock salt prime rib. Own baking, desserts. Parking. Outdoor dining. In 5-story atrium; overlooks Lake Normandale. Cr cds: A, C, D, DS, MC, V.

✔★ **TEJAS.** *3910 W 50th St (55424).* 612/926-0800. Hrs: 11:30 am-10 pm; Fri, Sat to 10:30 pm; Sun 11 am-9 pm. Res accepted. Southwestern menu. Wine, beer. A la carte entrees: lunch $5.25-$8.50, dinner

$7-$17. Specialties: smoked chicken nachos, braised lamb shank. Patio dining in summer. Totally nonsmoking. Cr cds: A, C, D, DS, MC, V.

Unrated Dining Spots

DA AFGHAN. *929 W 80th St. 612/888-5824.* Hrs: 4:30-9:30 pm; Thur, Fri 11 am-1:30 pm, 4:30-9:30 pm; Sat 4-9 pm. Closed July 4. Res accepted. Middle Eastern, Greek menu. Wine, beer. Semi-a la carte: lunch $4.95-$9.95, dinner $8.95-$16. Child's meals. Specializes in lamb, chicken, vegetarian dishes. Parking. Cr cds: A, MC, V.

LA TERRASSE. *(See Hotel Sofitel) 612/835-1900.* Hrs: 11 am-midnight; Fri-Sat to 1 am; Sun 10:30 am-midnight; Sun brunch to 2:30 pm. French menu. Bar to 1 am. Semi-a la carte: lunch, dinner $5.75-$11.50. Sun brunch $8.50. Specializes in onion soup, seasonal French dishes. Valet parking. Outdoor dining. Cr cds: A, C, D, MC, V.

PLANET HOLLYWOOD. *S-402 (55425), Mall of America. 612/854-7827.* Hrs: 11-1 am; Sun to midnight. Closed Thanksgiving, Dec 25. Bar. Semi-a la carte: lunch, dinner $6.50-$17.95. Specialties: chicken tenders, fajitas. Authentic Hollywood memorabilia displayed. Gift shop. Cr cds: A, C, D, DS, JCB, MC, V.

RAINFOREST CAFE. *S-102 (55425), Mall of America. 612/854-7500.* Hrs: 11 am-10 pm; Sat 10 am-11 pm; Sun to 9 pm. Closed Thanksgiving, Dec 25. Bar. Semi-a la carte: lunch, dinner $8.95-$15.95. Child's meals. Specialties: rasta pasta, pita quesadillas. Rainforest atmosphere with flashing lighting, roaring thunder. Cr cds: A, C, D, DS, JCB, MC, V.

Blue Earth (H-3)

(See also Albert Lea, Fairmont)

Pop 3,745 **Elev** 1,093 ft **Area code** 507 **Zip** 56013
Information Chamber of Commerce, 119 N Main, Suite 1-2; 507/526-2916

The city gets its name from the Blue Earth River, which circles the town. The river was given the Native American name "Mahkota" (meaning blue earth) for a blue-black clay found in the high river banks. The town is the birthplace of the ice cream sandwich, and a 55½-foot statue of the Jolly Green Giant stands in Green Giant Park.

What to See and Do

Faribault County Historical Society (Wakefield House). Maintained as a pioneer home with furnishings depicting life between 1875-1900 (Tues-Sat afternoons; also by appt). Also 1870 rural school, an original log house, an Episcopal Church (1872) and the Etta C. Ross Museum (limited hrs). 405 E 6th St. Phone 507/526-5421. **Free.**

The Woodland School and Krosch Log House. The Woodland School (ca 1870) is furnished as were one-room schools in the early 20th century. The Krosch Log House (ca 1860) was once home to a family of 11 children. Inquire for tours. Located at Faribault County Fairgrounds, N Main St, jct I-90 & US 169. Phone 507/526-5421.

Annual Events

Faribault County Fair. Fairgrounds. Carnival, 4-H exhibits, entertainment. Phone 507/854-3374. 3rd wk July.

Upper Midwest Woodcarvers and Quilters Expo. Phone 507/526-2916. Last full wkend Aug.

Motel

✔★ SUPER 8. *1120 N Grove, jct US 169 & I-90. 507/526-7376; FAX 507/526-2246.* 40 rms. S $38.88; D $45.88; each addl $4; under 12 free. Crib $2. TV; cable (premium), VCR avail. Restaurant adj 6 am-10 pm. Ck-out 11 am. Meeting rms. Business servs avail. Gift shop. Whirlpool. Cr cds: A, C, D, DS, MC, V.

Brainerd (E-3)

(See also Aitkin, Deerwood, Little Falls, Onamia)

Founded 1870 **Pop** 12,353 **Elev** 1,231 ft **Area code** 218 **Zip** 56401 **Web** www.brainerd.com
Information Brainerd Lakes Area Chamber of Commerce, 124 N 6th St, PO Box 356; 218/829-2838 or 800/450-2838.

Brainerd calls itself the "hometown of Paul Bunyan" and is the center of lore and legend about the giant lumberjack and his blue ox, Babe. On the Mississippi River at the geographical center of the state, the city was once part of a dense forest used by the Chippewa as a hunting ground and blueberry field. Created by the Northern Pacific Railroad, Brainerd was named for the wife of a railroad official. There are 465 pine-studded, sandy-bottomed lakes within a 25-mile radius and over 100 lodging choices. Golfing fishing, canoeing, swimming and water sports are available in the summer, skiing and snowmobiling in the winter.

What to See and Do

Crow Wing County Historical Society Museum. Restored sheriff's residence and remodeled jail features exhibits on domestic life, logging, mining and the railroad. Research library. (Daily exc Sun; closed hols) 320 Laurel St, adj to Courthouse. Phone 218/829-3268. **¢¢**

Paul Bunyan Amusement Center. A 26-ft animated Paul Bunyan, 15-ft Babe, the blue ox; 27 rides in amusement park, lumbering exhibits, trained animals, picnic grounds. 21-hole miniature golf. (Memorial Day-Labor Day, daily) 1 mi W at jct MN 210, 371. Phone 218/829-6342 (summer only). **¢¢¢**

Recreational Areas. Swimming at hundreds of lakes in the area. Also boating, canoe routes, fishing, waterskiing, playground, golf courses, picnicking, hiking, biking, camping; snowmobile & ski trails. Phone Chamber of Commerce.

Annual Events

Icefest. Ice sculptures, carving. Bands, races, dance, golf. Usually wkend Jan.

Crow Wing County Fair. Amusement rides; livestock; entertainment. 5 days early Aug.

Seasonal Event

Brainerd International Raceway. 7 mi N on MN 371. Motor racing events. Phone 218/829-9836. Mid-Apr-early Oct.

Motels

✔★★ AMERICINN-BAXTER. *(600 Dellwood Dr, Baxter 56425) ½ mi N of jct MN 210 & MN 371. 218/829-3080; FAX 218/829-9715; res: 800/634-3444.* 60 rms, 2 story. Memorial Day-Oct: S $49.90-$59; D $57.90-$69; each addl $6; suites $72.90-$99.90; under 13 free; higher rates racing events; lower rates rest of yr. Crib free. TV; cable (premium). Indoor pool; whirlpool. Complimentary continental bkfst. Restaurant adj 10 am-10 pm. Ck-out noon. Coin lndry. Business servs avail. Sundries. Valet serv. Downhill ski 11 mi; x-country ski 1 mi. Some refrigerators, in-rm whirlpools. Microwaves in suites. Cr cds: A, D, DS, MC, V.

[D] [symbols] SC

★ ★ **BEST WESTERN PAUL BUNYAN INN.** *1800 Fairview Dr N (56425), 2 mi W at jct MN 210 & MN 371.* 218/829-3571. Web www.best western.com/best.html. 34 rms, 10 suites. Memorial Day wkend-Labor Day: S, D $55-$70; suites $85-$110; lower rates rest of yr. Crib $2. TV; cable (premium). Indoor pool; whirlpool. Complimentary continental bkfst. Coffee in rms. Restaurant adj open 24 hrs. Ck-out noon. Business servs avail. Sundries. Downhill ski 15 mi; x-country ski 1 mi. Sauna. Microwaves in suites. Picnic tables. Paul Bunyan Amusement Center adj. Cr cds: A, C, D, DS, ER, JCB, MC, V.

[D] [symbols] SC

★ ★ **COUNTRY INN.** *(1220 Dellwood Dr N, Baxter 56425) 1 mi N on MN 371.* 218/828-2161; FAX 218/825-8419. 68 rms, 2 story. Mid-May-Sept: S, D $68-$78; suites $99-$107; under 18 free; higher rates auto races; lower rates rest of yr. Crib free. Pet accepted. TV; cable (premium), VCR avail (movies). Complimentary continental bkfst. Complimentary coffee in rms. Ck-out noon. Meeting rms. Business servs avail. In-rm modem link. Valet serv. Coin lndry. X-country ski 1½ mi. Health club privileges. Indoor pool; whirlpool, sauna. Refrigerators, microwaves; many wet bars; some in-rm whirlpools. Cr cds: A, D, DS, MC, V.

[D] [symbols] SC

★ **DAYS INN.** *1630 Fairview Rd, 2 mi W of town at jct MN 210, MN 371.* 218/829-0391; FAX 218/828-0749. 59 rms, 2 story. May-Sept: S $48-$57; D $54-$66; each addl $6; higher rates special events; lower rates rest of yr. Crib free. Pet accepted, some restrictions. TV; cable (premium). Complimentary continental bkfst. Restaurant adj open 24 hrs. Ck-out 11 am. Business servs avail. Downhill ski 15 mi; x-country ski 1 mi. Cr cds: A, C, D, DS, MC, V.

[D] [symbols] SC

★ ★ **DAYS INN-NISSWA.** *(45 N Smiley Rd, Nisswa 56468) 13 mi N on MN 371.* 218/963-3500; FAX 218/963-4936. 46 rms, 2 story. Mid-May-Sept: S $51.90-$61.90; D $54.90-$71.90; each addl $5; under 12 free; higher rates special events; lower rates rest of yr. Crib free. Pet accepted; $25 deposit. TV; cable, VCR avail (movies). Indoor pool; whirlpool. Complimentary continental bkfst. Restaurant nearby. Ck-out 11 am. Coin lndry. Downhill ski 15 mi; x-country ski 3 blks. Cr cds: A, C, D, DS, MC, V.

[D] [symbols] SC

★ ★ **HOLIDAY INN.** *MN 371S, 1 mi S on MN 371.* 218/829-1441; FAX 218/829-1444. 150 rms, 2 story. Mid-May-early Sept: S, D $65-$89; under 18 free; lower rates rest of yr. Crib free. Pet accepted. TV; cable. Indoor pool; whirlpool, poolside serv. Restaurant 6 am-2 pm, 5-10 pm. Rm serv. Bar 3 pm-1 am. Ck-out noon. Coin lndry. Meeting rms. Business servs avail. In-rm modem link. Bellhops. Valet serv. Free airport, bus depot transportation. Tennis. Downhill ski 7 mi; x-country ski 3 mi. Sauna. Rec rm. Cr cds: A, C, D, DS, JCB, MC, V.

[D] [symbols] SC

★ **SUPER 8.** *(MN 371N, Baxter 56425) 3 blks N of jct MN 210 & MN 371N.* 218/828-4288. 62 rms, 2 story. S $48; D $56. Crib avail. TV; cable (premium). Continental bkfst. Restaurant nearby. Ck-out 11 am. Guest lndry. Business servs avail. Sundries. Downhill ski 13 mi; x-country ski 1 mi. Game rm. Cr cds: A, D, DS, MC, V.

[D] [symbols] SC

Resorts

★ ★ **BREEZY POINT.** *18 mi N on US 371, then 5 mi E on County 11, on Big Pelican Lake.* 218/562-7811; FAX 218/562-4510; res: 800/432-3777. Web www.breezypt.com. 40 kit. units in lodge, 1-2 story; 50 motel rms; 29 units in marina inn, 2 story; 132 kit. units in 11 condominium bldgs; 10 units in Fawcett House, 2 story. Memorial Day-Labor Day, MAP: $76.95-$135.95/person; EP: D $61.50-$500; family rates; mid-wk & wkend packages; lower rates rest of yr. Crib avail. TV; cable (premium), VCR

avail. 5 pools, 2 indoor; whirlpools. Playground. Supervised child's activities (Memorial Day-Labor Day). Dining rm 7 am-10:30 pm. Box lunches, snack bar. Bars 11:30-1 am. Ck-out noon, ck-in 5 pm. Package store. Meeting rms. Business servs avail. Tennis, pro. 36-hole golf, greens fee $27-$37. Private beach; water sports. Marina; boats, motors; guided tours. Downhill ski 20 mi; x-country ski on site. Exercise equipt; bicycles, stair machine, sauna. Ice skating. Lawn games. Entertainment. Rec rm. Game rm. Refrigerator in motel rms. 2,600-ft airstrip. Cr cds: A, D, DS, MC, V.

[D] [symbols]

★ ★ ★ **CRAGUN'S LODGE, SPA, RESORT & CONFERENCE CENTER.** *2001 Pine Beach Rd, 4³/4 mi N on MN 371, then 6 mi W on County 77.* 218/829-3591; FAX 218/829-9188; res: 800/272-4867. E-mail info@craguns.com; web www.craguns.com. 285 rms, 1-2 story. 50 kits., 105 lakeview units. July-Aug & wkends: S, D $110-$190; family, wkly rates; package plans; MAP avail; lower rates rest of yr. Serv charge 15%. Crib avail. TV. 2 pools, 1 indoor; whirlpools. Free supervised child's activities (mid-June-mid-Sept); ages 4-12. Dining rm 6:30-8 pm. Restaurant 5:30-9 pm (summer). Snack bar. Barbecues. Bar 5 pm-1 am; entertainment. Ck-out noon, ck-in 5 pm. Coin lndry. Grocery 1 mi. Deli. Meeting rms. Business servs avail. Airport, bus depot transportation. 8 tennis courts, 2 indoor, 6 lighted. Golf privileges. Downhill ski 9 mi; x-country ski on site (equipt & rentals). Private beaches. Boats, motors, canoes, sailboats, pontoon boats. Lake excursions. Exercise equipt; weight machines, bicycles, saunas. Snowmobile trails. Many refrigerators, microwaves, fireplaces. Balconies. Cr cds: A, C, DS, MC, V.

[D] [symbols] SC

★ ★ ★ **GRAND VIEW LODGE.** *(S 134 Nokomis, Nisswa 56468) 14 mi N on MN 371, then 1 mi W on County 77.* 218/963-2234; FAX 218/963-2269; res: 800/432-3788. E-mail vacation@grandviewlodge.com; web www.grandviewlodge.com. 12 rms in 1-2 story lodge, 65 units in 45 cottages, 30 kits. Mid-June-mid-Aug, MAP: S, D $205-$290; AP, EP avail; family, wkly rates; lower rates rest of yr. Serv charge 15%, no tipping. Crib avail. TV; cable, VCR avail. Heated pool; whirlpool, poolside serv. Free supervised child's activities (Memorial Day-Labor Day, daily exc Sun); ages 3-12. Dining rm 7-10 am, noon-1 pm, 6-9 pm. Box lunches. Bar 11:30-1 am. Ck-out 12:30 pm, ck-in 4:30 pm. Meeting rms. Business servs avail. Airport, bus depot transportation. Sports dir. Tennis, pro. 54-hole golf privileges, driving range, putting green. X-country ski on site. Private beach. Waterskiing. Boats, motors, canoes, paddle boats, kayaks, pontoon boat. Water sports. Bicycles. Lawn games. Soc dir; entertainment exc Sun. Rec rm. Game rm. Refrigerators; some fireplaces. Some private patios, decks (all cottages). Overlooks Gull Lake. Garden walk. Cr cds: A, DS, MC, V.

[D] [symbols]

★ ★ ★ **MADDEN'S ON GULL LAKE.** *8001 Pine Beach Peninsula, 4³/4 mi N on MN 371, then 7³/4 mi W on County 77 at Pine Beach.* 218/829-2811; FAX 218/829-6583; res: 800/642-5363. E-mail info@maddens .com; web www.maddens.com. 41 rms in 3-story lodge; 24 units in three 2-story villas; 16 units in three 2-story bay view buildings; 86 units in 74 cottages. July-late Aug, MAP: $97.50-$135/person; EP: S, D $79-$271; each addl $25; family, wkly rates; wkly & package plans off-season; lower rates mid-Apr-June, late Aug-mid-Oct. Closed rest of yr. Crib avail. TV; cable, VCR avail. 5 pools, 3 indoor; whirlpools, poolside serv. Playground. Supervised child's activities (July-mid-Aug); ages 4-12. Dining rm (July-Aug) 8 am-6 pm. Pizzeria 5:30 pm-1 am. Bar 11-1 am; entertainment. Ck-out 1 pm, ck-in 4:30 pm. Coin lndry. Convention facilities. Business servs avail. In-rm modem link. Grocery, package store. Shopping arcade. Airport, bus depot transportation. Tennis. 63-hole golf, greens fee $23, putting green, driving range. Exercise equipt; weights, bicycles, saunas. Private beaches. Boats; motors, sailboats, kayaks, water bikes, pontoon boats, rowboats, speedboats. Marina, dockage, launching facilities. Bicycles. Lawn games. Movies. Rec rm. Game rm. Sun deck. Refrigerators; many fireplaces. Private patios. On Gull Lake. 2,600-ft airstrip ¹/2 mi. Cr cds: MC, V.

[D] [symbols]

Restaurants

★ ★ **BAR HARBOR SUPPER CLUB.** *6512 Interlachen Rd-Lakeshore, 14³/₄ mi N on MN 371, then 3 mi W on County 77. 218/963-2568.* Hrs: noon-1 am; Sun from 10 am. Closed Dec 24-25. Bar. Semi-a la carte: lunch, dinner $8.95-$24.95. Sun brunch $8.50. Child's meals. Specializes in charcoal-broiled steak, lobster, barbecued ribs. Entertainment Wed-Sun. Outdoor dining. Overlooks Gull Lake; dockage. Family-owned. Cr cds: A, D, DS, MC, V.

★ ★ **IVEN'S ON THE BAY.** *5195 MN 371 N, 7 mi N on MN 371. 218/829-9872.* Web www.brainerd.com/ivens. Hrs: 5-9:30 pm; Fri, Sat to 10:30 pm; Sun brunch 9:30 am-1:30 pm. Closed some major hols. Res accepted. Bar. Semi-a la carte: dinner $10.95-$18.95. Sun brunch $5.95-$9.95. Child's meals. Specializes in fresh seafood, pasta. Outdoor dining. Contemporary nautical decor; lakeside dining. Cr cds: A, D, MC, V.

★ ★ **QUARTERDECK ON GULL.** *(1588 Quarterdeck Rd W, Nisswa 56468) 218/963-7537.* E-mail quarterdeck@braineronline.com; web www.quarterdeckongulllake.com. Hrs: 11 am-10 pm; Sat, Sun from 9 am; Sun brunch to 3 pm. Closed Dec 24 evening, Dec 25. Res accepted. Italian, Amer menu. Bar to 1 am; Sun to midnight. Semi-a la carte: bkfst $3.95-$7.95, lunch $3.95-$7.95, dinner $7.95-$22.95. Buffet: lunch $5.95. Sun brunch $9.95. Child's meals. Specializes in steak, ribs, seafood. Entertainment Tues-Sun. Outdoor dining. Nautical decor. Scenic view; overlooks Gull Lake. Cr cds: A, C, D, DS, MC, V.

Cloquet (D-4)

(See also Duluth)

Pop 10,885 **Elev** 1,204 ft **Area code** 218 **Zip** 55720

Annual Event

Lumberjack Days. Citywide program features concert; antique car show; airplane, helicopter, hot-air balloon rides. Phone 218/879-1551. Mid-July.

Motel

✔★ **AMERICINN.** *MN 33 & Big Lake Rd, N of I-35 Cloquet exit. 218/879-1231; FAX 218/879-2237; res: 800/634-3444.* 51 rms, 2 story. S $41.90-$80.90; D $46.90-$80.90; each addl $4. Crib free. Pet accepted. TV; cable (premium). Indoor pool; whirlpool. Complimentary continental bkfst. Restaurant adj open 24 hrs. Ck-out 11 am. Meeting rm. Business servs avail. Sauna. Many refrigerators. Cr cds: A, D, DS, MC, V.

Cook (C-4)

Pop 680 **Elev** 1,306 ft **Area code** 218 **Zip** 55723

Almost at the center of the "arrowhead country," Cook provides access to outdoor vacations, serves the logging industry and is the western gateway to Superior National Forest (see). A Ranger District office of the forest is located here.

What to See and Do

Lakes. Fishing in this area is excellent for northern pike, panfish, crappie and walleye.

Pelican Lake. 54 mi of shoreline, 50 islands, sandy beaches; fishing for northern pike and panfish. 21 mi N on US 53.

Lake Vermilion. 5¹/₂ mi NE via County 24 or County 78. (See TOWER)

Elbow Lake. 2,000 acres, 12 islands. 10 mi N on County 24.

Motel

✔★ **NORTH COUNTRY INN.** *(4483 US 53, Orr 55771) N on US 53. 218/757-3778.* 12 rms. May-Sept: S $38.90; D $43.90-$45.90; each addl $6; under 12 free; lower rates rest of yr. Crib free. Pet accepted. TV; cable (premium), VCR avail. Complimentary coffee in lobby. Restaurant nearby. Ck-out 11 am. Picnic tables. Cr cds: A, DS, MC, V.

Cottage Colony

★ ★ ★ **LUDLOW'S ISLAND LODGE.** *on private island in Lake Vermilion; 3 mi N on County 24, then 3 mi E on County 78, then 2 mi E on County 540, then call for boat via private line. 218/666-5407; FAX 218/666-2488.* E-mail info@ludlowsresort.com; web www.ludlowsresort.com. 18 kit. cabins (1-5 bedrm), some 2 story. No A/C. Mid-June-Aug (boat incl), wkly: D $1,400-$2,000; each addl $30-$150; lower rates mid-May-mid-June, Sept-early Oct. Closed rest of yr. Crib avail. TV in some cabins; VCR avail (movies). Playground. Free supervised child's activities (June-Aug). Ck-out Sat 9 am, ck-in Sat 5 pm. Grocery. Coin lndry. Meeting rm. Business center. Airport transportation. Tennis. Golf privileges. Exercise equipt; weight machine, treadmill, sauna. Private beach; waterskiing (equipt). Boats, motors; rowboats; sailboats; kayaks, pontoon boats; paddleboats. Covered dockage; launching facilities. Fishing guides, fish clean & store. Racquetball. Rec rm. Lawn games. Exercise, nature trails. Fireplaces, microwaves; some whirlpools. Private decks; some screened porches. Grills. Secluded cabins on 4 acres. Cr cds: A, MC, V.

Crane Lake (B-4)

(See also Cook)

Pop 350 (est) **Elev** 1160 ft **Area code** 218 **Zip** 55725

A natural entry to the Voyageur Country, Crane Lake, in Superior National Forest (see), is bounded on the north by the Canadian Quetico Provincial Park. (For Border Crossing Regulations, see MAKING THE MOST OF YOUR TRIP.)

Cottage Colony

★ ★ ★ **NELSON'S RESORT.** *7632 Nelson Rd. 218/993-2295; FAX 218/993-2242; res: 800/433-0743.* 28 cabins, 16 kits. No A/C. Mid-May-late Sept, AP: D $105/person; MAP: D $90/person; family rates. Closed rest of yr. Crib avail. TV in lodge. Playground. Dining rm 7 am-8 pm. Box lunches. Bar 5 pm-1 am. Ck-out 11 am, ck-in 3 pm. Grocery. Coin lndry. Gift shop. Meeting rm. Business servs avail. Airport, bus depot transportation. Waterskiing. Boats, motors, canoes; launching ramp, docks, canoe trips. Nature trails; naturalist program. Guide serv. Bicycle rentals. Lawn games. Rec rm. Sauna. Fish cleaning, storage facilities. Some microwaves, fireplaces. Spacious grounds; private sand beach. Cr cds: DS, MC, V.

Crookston (C-1)

(See also Thief River Falls; also see Grand Forks, ND)

Settled 1872 **Pop** 8,119 **Elev** 890 ft **Area code** 218 **Zip** 56716

Information Crookston Area Chamber of Commerce, 1915 University Ave, Suite 2; 218/281-4320 or 800/809-5997.

Crookston is the major city of the broad and level Red River valley carved by glacial Lake Agassiz. A branch of the University of Minnesota is located here.

What to See and Do

Central Park. Playground, picnicking, boat ramp, fishing, canoeing; tent, trailer & RV camping (mid-May-Oct 1, fee), showers. Indoor swimming pool adj. Civic arena, roller skating (May-Oct), ice-skating (Nov-Mar), indoor tennis (Apr-Oct). N Ash St, on Red Lake River. Phone 218/281-1232. Camping ¢¢¢

Polk County Historical Museum. Houses several rooms depicting early days of America including an original log cabin, one-room schoolhouse and a building with antique machinery. Also on the premises are a chapel and miniature train exhibit. (Mid-May-mid-Sept, daily; rest of yr, by appt) US 2E. Phone 218/281-1038. **Donation.**

Annual Event

Ox Cart Days. Phone 800/809-5997. 3rd wkend Aug.

Motel

✔★★ **NORTHLAND INN.** *US 2, 75N. 218/281-5210; res: 800/423-7541.* 74 rms, 2 story. S $45.95; D $52.95; each addl $6. Crib free. TV; cable (premium). Indoor pool; whirlpool. Restaurant 6:30 am-2 pm, 5-9:30 pm; Fri, Sat to 10 pm. Bar 4 pm-1 am. Ck-out noon. Meeting rms. Business servs avail. In-rm modem link. Sundries. Game rm. Cr cds: A, C, D, DS, MC, V.

Crosslake (D-3)

(See also Aitkin, Brainerd, Pine River)

Pop 1,132 **Elev** 1,240 ft **Area code** 218 **Zip** 56442

Cottage Colony

★★★ **BOYD LODGE.** *HC 83 Box 667, 2 mi N on County 66, then 4½ mi W on County 16, on Big Whitefish Lake. 218/543-4125.* 35 kit. cottages (1-5 bedrm), 1-3 story. Jan-Mar, May-Labor Day, wkly for 2-6: $700-$1,600; family rates; package plans; lower rates rest of yr. No maid serv. Crib free. TV; cable. 2 pools; wading pool, 2 whirlpools, 2 saunas. Playground. Free supervised child's activities (June-Aug). Snack bar. Ck-out 9:30 am, ck-in 3 pm. Coin lndry. Business servs avail. Grocery, package store 4 mi. Meeting rm. Free airport transportation. Tennis. 9-hole golf privileges, greens fee $26. Private beach; launching ramp. Boats, motors, canoes, pontoon boat, water bikes avail. X-country ski on site. Snowmobile trails. Lawn games. Soc dir. Rec rm. Fireplaces. Deck on cottages. Marina with lifts. Picnic tables, grills. 200 acres. Cr cds: MC, V.

Deer River (C-3)

(For accommodations see Grand Rapids, Hibbing)

Pop 838 **Elev** 1,291 ft **Area code** 218 **Zip** 56636

A harvesting point for lumber products of Chippewa National Forest, Deer River also serves nearby farms and hunting and fishing camps. A Ranger District office of the Chippewa National Forest (see GRAND RAPIDS) is located here.

What to See and Do

Chippewa National Forest. At W edge of city, access on MN 46. (See GRAND RAPIDS)

Cut Foot Sioux Lakes. Fishing, hunting, camping. Turtle and Snake Indian Mound along shore. 15 mi NW on both sides of MN 46.

Deerwood (D-3)

(See also Aitkin, Brainerd, Crosslake)

Pop 524 **Elev** 1,079 ft **Area code** 218 **Zip** 56444

Motel

★★ **COUNTRY INN BY CARLSON.** *115 E Front St. 218/534-3101; FAX 218/534-3685; res: 800/456-4000.* 38 rms, 2 story. Late May-Aug: S, D $65-$85; each addl $6; under 18 free; lower rates rest of yr. Crib free. Pet accepted, some restrictions. TV; cable (premium), VCR avail (movies). Indoor pool; whirlpool. Complimentary continental bkfst. Complimentary coffee in rms. Restaurant nearby. Ck-out 11 am. Coin lndry. X-country ski 1 mi. Sauna. Game rm. Some refrigerators, wet bars. Cr cds: A, D, DS, MC, V.

Resort

★★★ **RUTTGER'S BAY LAKE LODGE.** *5 mi S on MN 6. 218/678-2885; FAX 218/678-2864; res: 800/450-4545.* 30 rms in lodges, 37 cottages (1-3 bedrm), 1-2 story, 88 town houses, 2 story. MAP, July-Aug: for 2-6, $102-$134/person; EP: $118-$316/day; wkly, family rates; hol, wkday, package plans; lower rates rest of yr. Crib free. TV; cable, VCR avail (movies). 3 pools, 1 indoor; whirlpools. Free supervised child's activities (MAP guests July-Labor Day); ages 4-12. Dining rm (public by res) 8-9:30 am, noon-1:30 pm, 6-8 pm. Snack bar. Bar noon-midnight. Ck-out noon, ck-in 5 pm. Coin lndry. Meeting rms. Business servs avail. Gift shop. Tackle shop. 27-hole golf, pro, putting green, pro shop. Exercise equipt; bicycles, treadmills, saunas. Private beach. Waterskiing instruction. Boats, launching ramp, motors; canoes, sailboat, kayaks, paddleboat. Lawn games. Soc dir (July-Aug); naturalist, trails, entertainment; movies. Rec rm. Game rm. Some fireplaces in kit. units. Lodge overlooks lake. Cr cds: DS, MC, V.

Detroit Lakes (D-2)

(See also Moorhead, Park Rapids)

Pop 6,635 **Elev** 1,365 ft **Area code** 218 **Zip** 56501 **Web** www.detlakes .k12.mn.us

Information Detroit Lakes Regional Chamber of Commerce, PO Box 348, 56502; 218/847-9202 or 800/542-3992.

A French missionary visiting this spot more than 200 years ago commented on the beautiful *détroit* (strait), and this came to be the name of the town. "Lakes" was added to promote the 412 lakes found within 25 miles. Tourism and agriculture are major sources of income.

What to See and Do

Becker County Historical Society Museum. Exhibits pertaining to history of county. (Memorial Day-Labor Day, daily; rest of yr, Mon-Fri; closed hols) Corner of Summit & W Front. Phone 218/847-2938. **Free.**

Detroit Mt Ski Area. Double and triple chairlifts, 2 T-bars, 4 rope tows; patrol, school, rentals, snowmaking; cafeteria; bar. (Mid-Nov-late Mar, Thurs-Sun) 2 mi E, off MN 34. Phone 218/847-1661. ¢¢¢¢

Parks. Contact Chamber of Commerce for information.

    Detroit Lakes City Park. Picnic tables, grills, shelters; tennis courts, shuffleboard, ball diamonds; playground, boat rentals, fishing. 1-mi-long beach, bathhouse. Motorboat sightseeing services nearby. Shops. (June-Labor Day, daily) Washington Ave & W Lake Dr. **Free.**

    Legion Park. Overnight camping (tent & trailer; fee), lifeguard (mid-June-Aug), bathhouse, beach. West Lake Dr. **Free.**

Tamarac National Wildlife Refuge. 43,000 acres. 21 lakes, abundant wild rice; trumpeter swans, grouse, beaver, deer; flyway sanctuary for thousands of songbirds, ducks, geese; picnicking, fishing. (Daily) Visitor center (Memorial Day-Labor Day, daily; rest of yr, Mon-Fri; closed hols). 8 mi E on MN 34, then 9 mi N on County 29. Phone 218/847-2641. **Free.**

Annual Events

White Earth Powwow. Celebrates the treaty between the Sioux and Chippewa. Phone 800/542-3992. Mid-June.

Northwest Water Carnival. Detroit Lake, throughout city. Includes water show, races, fishing derby, parade, flea markets. Mid-July.

WE Country Music Fest. Soo Pass Ranch, 3 mi S on MN 59. 3-day event featuring many top country musicians and groups. Phone 218/847-1681. 1st wkend Aug.

Becker County Fair. Exhibits, rides, carnival, demolition derby, fiddler's contest. Late Aug.

Motels

    ★ ★ **BEST WESTERN HOLLAND HOUSE & SUITES.** *615 US 10E.* 218/847-4483; FAX 218/847-1770. 56 rms, 1-2 story. D $59-$89; each addl $6; suites $75-$125. Crib free. TV; cable (premium), VCR avail. Indoor pool; whirlpool, wading pool, sauna. Complimentary continental bkfst. Coffee in rms. Restaurant adj. Ck-out 11 am. Coin lndry. Meeting rms. Business servs avail. In-rm modem link. Downhill ski 2 mi. Refrigerators; some bathrm phones, in-rm whirlpools. Cr cds: A, C, D, DS, ER, JCB, MC, V.

⊡ ⬚ ⬚ ⬚ ⬚ SC

    ✔ ★ **SUPER 8.** *400 Morrow Ave.* 218/847-1651. 39 rms, 2 story. S $37.88-$43.88; D $42.88-$52.88; each addl $4; under 13 free. Crib free. TV; cable. Complimentary coffee in lobby. Restaurant adj open 24 hrs. Ck-out 11 am. Business servs avail. Downhill/x-country ski 5 mi. Cr cds: A, C, D, DS, MC, V.

⊡ ⬚ ⬚ ⬚ SC

Motor Hotel

    ★ ★ ★ **HOLIDAY INN.** *US 10E, 1½ mi E on US 10.* 218/847-2121; FAX 218/847-2121, ext. 142. 103 rms, 4 story. Late May-Labor Day: S, D $79-$89; family rates; lower rates rest of yr. Crib free. TV; cable, VCR avail (movies). Indoor pool; whirlpool, sauna. Restaurant 6:30 am-10 pm. Rm serv. Bar 11-1 am; entertainment. Ck-out noon. Coin lndry. Meeting rms. Business servs avail. In-rm modem link. Valet serv. Sundries. Downhill ski 2 mi; x-country ski on site. Rec rm. Paddle boat rentals. Some minibars. Some poolside rms. Lakeside rms with private balconies. On lake; 500-ft private beach, dockage. Cr cds: A, C, D, DS, JCB, MC, V.

⊡ ⬚ ⬚ ⬚ ⬚ ⬚

Resort

    ★ ★ ★ **FAIR HILLS.** *Rte 1, 11 mi SW on US 59, then 3 mi W on County 20.* 218/532-2222. 18 rms in lodge, 76 cottages (1-4 rm), 10 kit. cabins on private lake. Late June-mid-Aug, AP: wkly, S, D $575 each; kit. cabins; EP: wkly $515-$1,410; family rates; varied lower rates mid-May-late June, mid-Aug-late Sept. Closed rest of yr. Serv charge 15%. Crib avail. Heated pool; wading pool, whirlpool. Free supervised child's activities (mid-June-mid Aug); ages 4-14. Dining rm (public by res) 8-9 am, noon-1 pm, 6-7 pm. Box lunches, snacks. Ck-out noon, ck-in 4 pm. Coin lndry. Business servs avail. Airport, bus depot transportation. Rec dirs. Tennis. 27-hole golf. Private beach. Waterskiing, instruction; boats, motors, canoes, sailboats, water bikes, windsurfing; launching ramp, dockage. Indoor, outdoor games. Soc dir; entertainment, bingo. Some fireplaces. Picnic tables, grills. On Pelican Lake. Cr cds: A, DS, MC, V.

⊡ ⬚ ⬚ ⬚ ⬚ ⬚ ⬚ ⬚

Restaurants

    ★ ★ **FIRESIDE.** *1462 E Shore Dr (56502), 2 mi E on US 10, then 4 blks S on County 53 (East Shore Dr).* 218/847-8192. Hrs: 5:30-10:30 pm; days vary off-season. Closed late Nov-Mar. Semi-a la carte: dinner $7.95-$15. Child's meals. Specializes in charcoal-grilled steak, barbecued ribs, seafood. Open charcoal grill. Fireplace. Overlooks Big Detroit Lake. Family-owned. Cr cds: A, D, DS, MC, V.

⊡

    ✔ ★ **LAKESIDE.** *200 W Lake Dr (56502).* 218/847-7887. Hrs: 5-10 pm; Fri, Sat to 11 pm; Sun brunch 10 am-1 pm. Closed most major hols. Res accepted. Bar. Semi-a la carte: dinner $9.50-$16.25. Sun brunch $7.95. Child's meals. Specializes in tableside cooking. Outdoor dining. Rustic decor. Former hotel built in 1891. Cr cds: MC, V.

⊡

Duluth (D-5)

Founded 1856 **Pop** 85,493 **Elev** 620 ft **Area code** 218

Information Convention & Visitors Bureau, 100 Lake Place Dr, 55802; 218/722-4011 or 800/4-DULUTH.

At the western tip of Lake Superior, Duluth is a world port, thanks to the St Lawrence Seaway. Ships of many countries fly their flags at its 49 miles of docks. This gives the products of Minnesota and the Northwestern states better access to the markets of the world and helps stimulate development of new industries converting raw materials to finished goods. One of the foremost grain-exporting ports in the nation, Duluth-Superior harbor also handles iron ore, coal, limestone, petroleum products, cement, molasses, salt, grain, soybean oil, soybeans, wood pulp, paper and chemicals. The twin ports are the westernmost water terminus for goods consigned to the Northwest.

High bluffs rise from the lakeshore, protecting the harbor from the elements. Minnesota Point, a sandbar extending seven miles from Minnesota to the Wisconsin shore, protects the inner harbor.

There are two ways for ships to enter the Duluth-Superior Harbor: one by way of the Superior side, called the Superior Entry, and the other, the Duluth Ship Canal, with an aerial lift bridge located a few blocks south of downtown Duluth. The distance between the two is about eight miles.

As the state's gateway to the sea, Duluth is a business, industrial, cultural, recreational and vacation center. The great Minnesota north woods begin almost at the city's boundaries. From here the North Shore Drive (see GRAND MARAIS) follows Lake Superior into Canada; other highways fan out to the lake country, the great forests and south to the Twin Cities. The headquarters of the Superior National Forest (see) is located here.

Long a fur trading post, Duluth is the city of early voyageurs, Chippewa, and French and British explorers. The first major shipment from the twin ports of Duluth and Superior was 60 canoe loads of furs in 1660. Modern commerce started in 1855 following construction of the lock at Sault Ste Marie, Michigan, eastern entrance to Lake Superior. The French explorer, Daniel Greysolon, Sieur Du Lhut, landed here in 1679. The city takes its name from him.

What to See and Do

Aerial Lift Bridge (138 ft high, 336 ft long, 900 tons in weight). Connects mainland with Minnesota Point, lifting 138 ft in less than a minute to let ships through. Foot of Lake Ave.

Canal Park Marine Museum. Ship models, relics of shipwrecks, reconstructed ship cabins; exhibits related to maritime history of Lake Superior and Duluth harbor & the Corps of Engineers. Vessel schedules and close-up views of passing ship traffic. (Apr-mid-Dec, daily; rest of yr, Fri-Sun; closed Jan 1, Thanksgiving, Dec 25) Canal Park Dr next to Aerial Bridge. Phone 218/727-2497.   **Free.**

Enger Tower. Tower providing best view of Duluth-Superior; dedicated in 1939 by Norway's King Olav V, then Crown Prince; dwarf conifer & Japanese gardens, picnic tables on grounds. On Skyline Dr at 18th Ave W. **Free.**

Fitger's On The Lake. Historic renovated brewery transformed into more than 25 specialty shops and restaurants on the shore of Lake Superior. Summer courtyard activities. (Daily; closed Jan 1, Easter, Thanksgiving, Dec 25) 600 E Superior St. Phone 218/722-8826.   **Free.**   From here take the

Duluth Lakewalk. Walk along Lake Superior to the Aerial Lift Bridge; statues, kiosks; horse & buggy rides. Phone 800/4-DULUTH.

Glensheen (ca 1905-1908). Historic 22-acre Great Lake estate, on W shore of Lake Superior; owned by University of Minnesota. Tours. Grounds (daily). Mansion (May-Oct, daily exc Wed; rest of yr, limited hrs; closed Jan 1, Easter, Thanksgiving, Dec 25). 3300 London Rd. Phone 218/724-8863 (recording) or 218/724-8864.   ¢¢¢

Karpeles Manuscript Library Museum. Holds original drafts of *US Bill of Rights, Emancipation Proclamation,* Handels' *Messiah* and others. (June-Aug, daily; rest of yr, Tues-Sun) 902 E 1st St. Phone 218/728-0630.   **Free.**

Jay Cooke State Park. Located on 8,813 acres of rugged country; fishing; cross-country skiing, snowmobiling; picnicking; camping (electric hookups, dump station); visitor center. Standard fees. SW via MN 23, 210, adjoining gorge of St Louis River. Phone 218/384-4610.

Recreation areas.

Park Point Recreation Center. 200-acre playground; picnicking; boat ramp; swimming facilities, lifeguard. (June-Labor Day, daily) At tip of Minnesota Point.   **Free.**

Leif Erikson Park. Statue of Norwegian explorer and half-size replica of boat he sailed to America in A.D. 997. Rose Garden. (May-mid-Sept, daily) 11th Ave E & London Rd.   **Free.**

Lake Superior Zoological Gardens. 12-acre zoo with more than 80 exhibits; picnicking. (Daily) 72nd & Grand Aves W, on MN 23.   ¢¢¢

S/S *William A. Irvin* . Guided tours of this former flagship of United States Steel's Great Lakes Fleet that journeyed inland waters from 1938-1978.

Explore the decks and compartments of this restored 610-ft ore carrier, including the engine rm, the elaborate guest staterooms, galley, pilothouse, observation lounge, elegant dining rm. Free parking. (May-mid-Oct) 350 Harbor Dr; on the waterfront, adj to Duluth Convention Center. For schedule information phone 218/722-5573 or -7876.   ¢¢

Scenic North Shore Drive. MN 61 from Duluth to Canada along Lake Superior.

Sightseeing.

Duluth-Superior Excursions. Two-hr tour of Duluth-Superior Harbor and Lake Superior on the *Vista King, and Star.* (Mid-May-mid-Oct, daily) Also dinner and dance cruises. Foot of 5th Ave W & waterfront. Phone 218/722-6218.   ¢¢¢

North Shore Scenic Railroad. Narrated sightseeing trips along 28 mi of Lake Superior's scenic North Shore, from Duluth to Two Harbors. Other excursions avail: Duluth to Lester River, Two Harbors to Tom's Logging Camp, Pizza Train. Trips range from 1 1/2-6 hrs. (Apr-Oct, daily) Departs from the Depot, 506 W Michigan St. Phone 218/722-1381 or 800/423-1273.   ¢¢¢

Site of Fond du Lac. Originally a Native American village, later a trading post; school, mission established here in 1834. On St Louis River.

Skyline Parkway Drive. 27-mi scenic road along bluffs of city constructed during 1930s; view from 600 ft overlooks harbor, lake, bay and river.

Spirit Mountain Ski Area. 2 quad, 2 triple, double chairlifts; patrol, school, rentals, snowmaking; bar, cafeteria; children's center. Longest run 5,400 ft; vertical drop 700 ft. (Nov-Mar, daily) Half-day rates. Snowboarding; tubing. Cross-country trails (Dec-Apr, daily). 10 mi S on I-35, exit 249. Phone 218/628-2891 or 800/642-6377.   ¢¢¢¢

⭐ **The Depot, St Louis County Heritage and Arts Center.** Building was originally Union Depot (1890); houses three museums, a visual arts institute and four performing arts organizations. (Daily; closed major hols) 506 W Michigan St. Phone 218/727-8025.   ¢¢   Admission includes

Depot Square (lower level). Reproduction of 1910 Duluth street scene, with ice cream parlor, storefronts, gift shops, trolley rides.

Duluth Children's Museum. Natural, world and cultural history; featuring giant walk-through tree in the habitat exhibit.

St Louis County Historical Society. Settlement of northern Minnesota; logging, mining, railroading and pioneer life exhibits.

Lake Superior Museum of Transportation. Extensive displays of historic railroad equipment and memorabilia. Trolley car rides and periodical excursions, some using steam locomotives.

University of Minnesota, Duluth (1902). (7,800 students) 10 University Dr. Phone 218/726-8000. On campus are

Tweed Museum of Art. Exhibits of 19th- and 20th-century paintings; contemporary works. (Daily exc Mon; closed hols) **Donation.**

Marshall W. Alworth Planetarium. Shows (Wed; closed hols). Phone 218/726-7129.   **Free.**

Annual Events

John Beargrease Sled Dog Marathon. Phone 218/722-7631. Mid-Jan.

International Folk Festival. Leif Erikson Park. Folk music, dancing, crafts, foods. Phone 218/722-8563 or -7425. 1st Sat Aug.

Bayfront Blues Festival. Phone 715/392-1857. 2nd wkend Aug.

Motels

✔★ **ALLYNDALE.** *510 N 66th Ave W (55807), I-35N exit 251A or I-35S exit 252, near Spirit Mountain Recreation Area.* 218/628-1061; *res: 800/806-1061.* 21 rms. Mid-Apr-mid-Oct: S $38; D $43-$48; each addl $5; lower rates rest of yr. Crib $5. Pet accepted, some restrictions; $5. TV; cable. Playground. Complimentary coffee. Restaurant nearby. Ck-out 11 am. Downhill/x-country ski 1 1/2 mi. Refrigerators, microwaves. Picnic tables. Cr cds: A, C, D, DS, MC, V.

✔ ⚫ 🏂 🏊 ⚫

★ ★ **BEST WESTERN EDGEWATER EAST & WEST.** *2400 London Rd (55812). 218/728-3601; FAX 218/728-3727; res: 800/777-7925.* 283 rms, 2-5 story. June-mid-Oct: D $64-$115; each addl $6; suites $98-$169; under 18 free; ski plans; lower rates rest of yr. Crib $2. Pet accepted, some restrictions. TV; cable (premium). Indoor pool; whirlpool. Playground. Complimentary continental bkfst. Restaurant adj. Ck-out noon. Meeting rm. Business servs avail. Valet serv. Miniature golf. Downhill ski 7 mi; x-country ski 1 mi. Sauna. Game rm. Lawn games. Refrigerators. Many rms with balcony, view of Lake Superior. Cr cds: A, C, D, DS, ER, JCB, MC, V.

D ✔ ⚞ ≋ ⊠ ☇ SC

★ ★ **COMFORT INN.** *3900 W Superior St (55807). 218/628-1464.* 81 rms, 2 story, 10 kit. units. May-Oct: S $61; D $72; each addl $5; suites $108; kit. units (no equipt) $82; under 18 free; lower rates rest of yr (exc wkends). Crib free. TV; cable (premium). Indoor pool; whirlpool. Complimentary continental bkfst. Restaurant adj open 24 hrs. Ck-out 11 am. Coin lndry. Meeting rm. Business servs avail. Sauna. Microwaves avail. Cr cds: A, C, D, DS, MC, V.

D ≋ ⊠ ☇ SC

★ ★ **COMFORT SUITES.** *408 Canal Park Dr (55802). 218/727-1378; FAX 218/727-1947.* 82 rms, 3 story. Early June-Sept: S, D $105-$115; suites $155; under 18 free; higher rates special events; lower rates rest of yr. Crib free. TV; cable (premium). Indoor pool; whirlpools. Complimentary continental bkfst. Restaurant adj 8 am-11 pm. Ck-out 11 am. Coin lndry. Meeting rm. Business servs avail. In-rm modem link. Bellhops (in season). Downhill/x-country ski 5 mi. Refrigerators; some in-rm whirlpools. Cr cds: A, D, DS, JCB, MC, V.

D ⚞ ≋ ⊼ ⊠ ☇ SC

★ **DAYS INN.** *909 Cottonwood Ave (55811), opp Hill Mall. 218/727-3110; FAX 218/727-3110, ext. 301.* 86 rms, 2-3 story. No elvtr. June-mid-Oct: S $59-$82; D $68-$82; each addl $6; higher rates special events; lower rates rest of yr. Crib free. TV; cable (premium), VCR avail. Complimentary continental bkfst. Restaurant opp open 24 hrs. Ck-out noon. Business servs avail. Cr cds: A, C, D, DS, JCB, MC, V.

D ✔ ⊠ ☇ SC

★ **SUPER 8.** *4100 W Superior St (55807), I-35 exit 253B. 218/628-2241.* Web www.super8motels.com. 59 rms, 2 story. Late May-early Sept: S $55; D $64; each addl $3; under 12 free; higher rates special events; lower rates rest of yr. Crib free. TV; cable (premium). Complimentary continental bkfst. Restaurant opp open 24 hrs. Ck-out 11 am. Coin lndry. Business servs avail. Downhill/x-country ski 5 mi. Sauna. Whirlpool. Cr cds: A, C, D, DS, ER, MC, V.

D ⚞ ⊠ ☇ SC

Hotels

★ ★ ★ **FITGER'S INN.** *600 E Superior St (55802). 218/722-8826; res: 800/726-2982.* E-mail fitgers@fitgers.com; web www.fitgers.com. 60 rms, 5 story, 18 suites. May-Oct: S, D $90-$120; suites $145-$245; under 17 free; lower rates rest of yr. Pet accepted, some restrictions. TV; cable (premium), VCR avail. Restaurant (see AUGUSTINO'S). Rm serv. Bar 11 am-11 pm; entertainment wkends. Ck-out noon. Meeting rms. Business servs avail. In-rm modem link. Shopping arcade. Exercise equipt; stair machine, ski machine. Some in-rm whirlpools, fireplaces. Most rms overlook Lake Superior. Part of renovated 1858 brewery; shops, theater adj. Cr cds: A, C, D, DS, MC, V.

D ✔ ⊼ ⊠ ≋

★ ★ ★ **HOLIDAY INN.** *200 W First St (55802). 218/722-1202; FAX 218/722-0233; res: 800/477-7089.* E-mail holidayinn@duluth.com; web www.duluth.com/holidayinn. 353 rms, 16 story, 56 suites. S, D $69-$106; each addl $10; suites $89-$195; ski, package plans. Crib free. TV; cable. Indoor pools; whirlpools. Restaurant 6:30 am-11 pm. Bar 11-1 am. Ck-out noon. Meeting rms. In-rm modem link. Free garage parking. Downhill/x-country ski 12 mi. Exercise equipt; bicycles, treadmills, saunas.

Health club privileges. Refrigerators; microwave, wet bar in suites. Adj large shopping complex. Cr cds: A, C, D, DS, MC, V.

D ⚞ ≋ ⊼ ⊠ ☇ SC

★ ★ ★ **RADISSON.** *505 W Superior St (55802), NE of I-35 Superior St exit. 218/727-8981; FAX 218/727-0162.* Web www.radisson.com. 268 rms, 15 story. June-mid-Oct: S $80-$110; D $80-$110; each addl $10; suites $135-$250; under 18 free; seasonal package plans; lower rates rest of yr. Crib free. Pet accepted. TV; cable, VCR avail. Indoor pool; whirlpool, poolside serv. Restaurant (see TOP OF THE HARBOR). Bar 11:30-1 am; closed Sun. Ck-out noon. Meeting rms. Business servs avail. Downhill/x-country ski 10 mi. Sauna. Health club privileges. Cr cds: A, C, D, DS, ER, JCB, MC, V.

D ✔ ⚞ ⊠ ☇ SC

Restaurants

★ ★ **AUGUSTINO'S.** *(See Fitger's Inn Hotel) 218/722-2787.* E-mail fitgers@fitgers.com; web www.fitgers.com. Hrs: 7 am-10 pm; Fri, Sat to 11 pm; Sun 8 am-10 pm; Sun brunch 10 am-2 pm. Closed Dec 25. Res accepted. Bar 11 am-11 pm. Semi-a la carte: bkfst $4-$6.50, dinner $10-$24. Sun brunch $12. Specialties: certified Angus beef, walleye Augustino, herb-encrusted salmon. Jazz Sun brunch. Valet parking. Outdoor dining. In renovated brewery; overlooks Lake Superior. Cr cds: A, C, D, DS, MC, V.

D

✔ ★ **GRANDMA'S CANAL PARK.** *522 Lake Ave S (55802), at foot of aerial bridge. 218/727-4192.* Hrs: 11 am-10:30 pm; Sun to 10 pm. Closed some major hols. Res accepted. Bar to 1 am. Semi-a la carte: lunch $4.50-$8.99, dinner $6.99-$18.99. Child's meals. Specializes in sandwiches, pasta. Under Aerial Lift Bridge at entrance to harbor. Early 1900s building; antiques. Cr cds: A, D, DS, MC, V.

D SC ♥

★ ★ **PICKWICK.** *508 E Superior St. 218/727-8901.* Hrs: 11 am-11 pm. Closed Sun; major hols. Bar 8-1 am. Semi-a la carte: lunch $6.25-$8.50, dinner $9.95-$20.95. Child's meals. Specializes in charcoal-broiled steak, seafood. Open-hearth grill. View of Lake Superior; pub atmosphere. Family-owned. Cr cds: A, C, D, DS, MC, V.

SC

★ ★ **TOP OF THE HARBOR.** *(See Radisson Hotel) 218/727-8981.* Hrs: 6:30 am-2 pm, 4:30-10 pm; Fri, Sat 5-11 pm; early-bird dinner Thurs-Sun 4:30-6 pm; Sun brunch 9 am-2 pm (hrs vary with season). Res accepted. Serv bar. Semi-a la carte: bkfst $4.25-$9.95, lunch $4.95-$8.95, dinner $9.95-$19.95. Sun brunch $9.95. Child's meals. Specializes in steak, Lake Superior whitefish, salmon, trout. Salad bar (lunch only). Panoramic view of city, Duluth Harbor, Lake Superior from 16th-floor revolving restaurant. Cr cds: A, D, DS, MC, V.

D SC

Elk River (F-3)

(See also Anoka, Minneapolis, St Cloud, St Paul)

Pop 11,143 **Elev** 924 ft **Area code** 612 **Zip** 55330

Information Elk River Area Chamber of Commerce, 509 US 10; 612/441-3110.

What to See and Do

Oliver H. Kelley Farm. Birthplace of National Grange and organized agriculture. Now a living history farm of the mid-19th century (May-Oct, daily). Visitor center only (Nov-mid-Apr, Sat-Sun; closed major hols; free). 2 mi SE on US 10, 52. Phone 612/441-6896. ¢¢

Sherburne National Wildlife Refuge. Wildlife observation; interpretive hiking and cross-country skiing trails in season; hunting, fishing; canoeing. Includes a self-guided auto tour route (wkends & hols). 13 mi N on MN 169, then 5 mi W on County 9. Phone 612/389-3323. **Free.**

Motels

★ ★ **AMERICINN.** 17432 US 10. 612/441-8554; res: 800/634-3444. 42 rms, 2 story. S $49.90-$56.90; D $56.90-$92.90; under 12 free. Crib free. Pet accepted, some restrictions; $5. TV; cable, VCR (movies). Indoor pool; whirlpool. Complimentary continental bkfst. Restaurant opp 6 am-11 pm. Ck-out 11 am. Meeting rms. X-country ski 3 blks. Sauna. Mississippi River 1 blk. Cr cds: A, C, D, DS, MC, V.

✔★ **RED CARPET INN.** 17291 US 10 NW. 612/441-2424; FAX 612/241-9720. 43 rms, 1-2 story. S $32-$38; D $42-$52; each addl $4; suites $60-$80. Crib $2. TV; cable (premium). Heated pool. Complimentary continental bkfst. Restaurant 11 am-10 pm. Ck-out 11 am. Meeting rms. Sundries. Cr cds: A, C, D, DS, MC, V.

Ely (C-5)

(See also Tower)

Settled 1883 **Pop** 3,968 **Elev** 1,473 ft **Area code** 218 **Zip** 55731 **E-mail** fun@ely.org **Web** www.ely.org

Information Chamber of Commerce, 1600 E Sheridan St; 800/777-7281.

A vacation and resort community, Ely is also gateway to one of the finest canoeing areas, Boundary Waters Canoe Area Wilderness, and is in the heart of the Superior National Forest (see). A Ranger District office of this forest is located here. From the Laurentian Divide, south of here, all waters flow north to the Arctic.

What to See and Do

Canoe trips. Canoes, equipment, supplies. Guides available. Phone Chamber of Commerce for information.

Canoe Country Outfitters. Offers complete and partial ultra-light outfitting for trips to BWCAW & Quetico Park. Boat fishing trips and fly-in canoe trips; also camping, cabins on Moose Lake. (May-Oct, daily) 629 E Sheridan St. Phone 218/365-4046.

Tom and Woods' Moose Lake Wilderness Canoe Trips. Family, wkly rates. Specializes in ultra-lightweight canoe trips. (May-Sept) 20 mi NE on Moose Lake. Phone 800/322-5837.

International Wolf Center. Houses wolf pack; exhibits. (May-mid-Oct, daily; rest of yr, Fri-Sun) E on MN 169. Phone 800/ELY-WOLF.

Native American Pictographs. Cliff paintings can be seen on Hegman Lake. These are simple exhibits of art painted by tribes who inhabited the region long ago. 7 mi N via MN 88 & 116 (Echo Trail).

Greenstone outcropping. Only surface ellipsoidal greenstone in US, judged to be more than 2 billion yrs old. 13th Ave E & Main St.

Superior-Quetico Wilderness. Superior in the US, Quetico in Canada. (See SUPERIOR NATIONAL FOREST)

Vermilion Interpretive Center. Offers a presentation of local history through photos, tapes, film, artifacts and displays; focuses on the heritage of the local people and land. (Apr-Oct, daily) 1900 E Camp St. Phone 218/365-3226. ¢

Annual Events

Voyageur Winter Festival. 10 days beginning 1st Sat Feb.

Blueberry/Art Festival. Last wkend July.

Motels

✔★ **BUDGET HOST.** 1047 E Sheridan St. 218/365-3237; FAX 218/365-3099. E-mail pat@ely-motels.com; web www.ely-motels.com. 17 rms. S $44.95; D $54.95-$59.95; each addl $5-$8; family rates. Crib free. Pet accepted; $10/day. TV; cable (premium). Complimentary coffee in rms. Restaurant nearby. Ck-out 10 am. Business servs avail. Free airport transportation. X-country ski ½ mi. Sauna. Cr cds: A, C, D, DS, MC, V.

✔★ **SUPER 8.** 1605 E Sheridan St, 1 mi E on US 169. 218/365-2873; FAX 218/365-5632. 30 rms, 2 story. S $45; D $55; each addl $5; kit. unit $85; under 12 free. Crib free. TV; cable. Complimentary coffee in lobby. Ck-out 11 am. Business servs avail. X-country ski 1 mi. Whirlpool, sauna. Cr cds: A, C, D, DS, JCB, MC, V.

✔★ **WESTGATE.** 110 N 2nd Ave W. 218/365-4513; FAX 218/365-5364; res: 800/806-4979. 17 units, 2 story. S $40-$45; D $55; each addl $5; under 5 free. Crib free. TV; cable, VCR avail (movies $2). Complimentary continental bkfst. Restaurant nearby. Ck-out 10:30 am. Business servs avail. Free airport transportation. Downhill ski 20 mi; x-country ski 1 mi. Cr cds: A, C, D, DS, MC, V.

Cottage Colonies

★ **OLSON BAY RESORT.** 2279 Grant McMahan Blvd. 218/365-4876; FAX 218/365-3431; res: 800/777-4419. E-mail olsonbay @northernnet.com. 7 kit. cottages. EP, May-Sept: $450-$700/wk. Closed rest of yr. Crib free. TV; VCR avail. Playground. Free supervised child's activities (mid-June-mid-Aug); ages 2 & up. Dining rm 5-9 pm; Fri, Sat to 11 pm. Bar. Ck-out 9 am, ck-in 2 pm. Grocery, coin lndry, package store 8 mi. Free airport, bus depot transportation. Swimming beach. Boats. Hiking. Sauna. Fish guides, clean & store. Lawn games. Microwaves. Picnic tables, grills. On lake. Cr cds: DS, MC, V.

★ ★ **TIMBER BAY LODGE & HOUSEBOATS.** (Babbitt 55706) 15 mi S on County 21, then 3 mi E on County 70; 2 mi NE of Babbitt, in Superior Natl Forest. 218/827-3682; res: 800/846-6821. E-mail timber @uslink.net; web www.timberbay.com. 12 kit. cabins (1-3-bedrm), 12 houseboats. No A/C. Mid-June-mid-Aug: houseboats for 2-10, $150-$300/day (3-day min); cabins: $650-$1,075/wk; daily rates; lower rates mid-May-mid-June, mid-Aug-Sept. Closed rest of yr. Pet accepted; $6/day, $30/wk. No maid serv. TV in cabins. Free supervised child's activities (mid-June-mid-Aug). Ck-out 10 am, ck-in 3 pm. Grocery, coin lndry, package store 2 mi. Golf privileges. Private beach. Boats, motors, canoes, kayaks, marina. Naturalist program. Lawn games. Rec rm. Game rm. Microwaves in cabins. Cabins with fireplaces & decks. On Birch Lake, among tall pines. Cr cds: DS, MC, V.

Eveleth (C-4)

(See also Cook, Hibbing, Tower, Virginia)

Founded 1893 **Pop** 4,064 **Elev** 1,610 ft **Area code** 218 **Zip** 55734

Information Eveleth Area Chamber of Commerce, PO Box 556; 218/744-1940.

Site of a large taconite operation, mines within a 50-mile radius produce a large amount of the nation's requirements of iron ore. Located about 1 mile west of town on County Highway 101, Leonidas Overlook provides a panoramic view of the taconite operations and Minntac Mine.

What to See and Do

US Hockey Hall of Fame. Museum honoring American players and the sport; theater. (Mid-May-Dec, daily; rest of yr, Mon-Tues; closed some major hols) 801 Hat Trick Ave (US 53). Phone 218/744-5167 or 800/443-7825. ¢¢

Motels

★ ★ ★ **HOLIDAY INN.** *On Hat Trick Ave (US 53), adj to US Hockey Hall of Fame. 218/744-2703; FAX 218/744-5865.* 145 rms, 2 story. S, D $59-$92; under 19 free. Crib free. Pet accepted. TV; cable (premium). Indoor pool. Restaurant 6 am-10 pm. Rm serv. Bar 4 pm-1 am. Ck-out noon. Coin lndry. Meeting rms. Business servs avail. Sundries. Gift shop. Sauna. Rec rm. Some refrigerators, microwaves. Cr cds: A, C, D, DS, JCB, MC, V.

✔★ **SLOVENE.** *US 53 at Jones St, 1 blk S of US Hockey Hall of Fame. 218/744-3427; res: 800/628-2526.* 21 rms. S $31; D $45; each addl $3. Crib free. TV; cable. Complimentary coffee in lobby. Restaurant nearby. Downhill/x-country ski 10 mi. Sauna. Whirlpool. Cr cds: A, DS, MC, V.

✔★ **SUPER 8.** *1080 Industrial Park Dr. 218/744-1661; FAX 218/744-4343.* 54 rms, 2 story. Mid-May-late Oct: S $55.88; D $59.88-$64.88; each addl $5; under 12 free; ski, golf plans; lower rates rest of yr. Crib $1. TV; cable (premium). Complimentary continental bkfst. Complimentary coffee in rms. Restaurant opp 6 am-10 pm. Ck-out 11 am. Meeting rms. Business servs avail. Coin lndry. Downhill ski 20 mi; x-country ski 10 mi. Indoor pool; whirlpool, sauna. Game rm. Cr cds: A, C, D, DS, MC, V.

Fairmont (H-3)

(See also Blue Earth, Jackson)

Pop 11,265 **Elev** 1,185 ft **Area code** 507 **Zip** 56031 **Web** www.oweb .com/fairmont

Information Fairmont Area Chamber of Commerce, PO Box 826; 507/235-5547.

Fairmont, the seat of Martin County, is 10 miles north of the Iowa line, at the junction of I-90 and MN 15. It is situated on a north-south chain of lakes; fishing and water sports are popular pastimes. A group of English farmers, who arrived in the 1870s and were known as the "Fairmont sportsmen," introduced fox hunting into southern Minnesota.

What to See and Do

Fairmont Opera House. Built in 1901, historic theater has been completely restored. Guided tours. Fees for productions vary. (Mon-Fri, also by appt; closed hols) 45 Downtown Plaza. Phone 507/238-4900 or 800/657-3280. **Free.**

Pioneer Museum. Operated by Martin County Historical Society; pioneer memorabilia, Native American artifacts. (May-Sept, Mon-Sat; rest of yr, by appt) Under 12 yrs with adult only. 304 E Blue Earth Ave. Phone 507/235-5178. **Free.**

Motels

✔★ **BUDGET INN.** *1122 N State St, 1½ mi NE on MN 15. 507/235-3373; FAX 507/235-3286.* 43 rms. S $26-$42; D $35-$49. Crib free. TV; cable. Indoor pool; whirpool, sauna. Complimentary coffee in

lobby. Restaurant nearby. Ck-out 11 am. Meeting rm. X-country ski 2 mi. Cr cds: A, C, D, DS, MC, V.

★ ★ ★ **HOLIDAY INN.** *MN 15 & I-90, exit 102. 507/238-4771; FAX 507/238-9371.* 105 rms, 2 story. S $62-$79; D $72-$89; under 18 free. TV; cable. Indoor pool; wading pool, whirlpool, sauna, poolside serv. Restaurant 6 am-10 pm. Rm serv. Bar 11-1 am. Ck-out noon. Coin lndry. Meeting rms. Business servs avail. In-rm modem link. Sundries. Free airport transportation. X-country ski 2 mi. Balconies. Cr cds: A, C, D, DS, JCB, MC, V.

✔★ **SUPER 8.** *MN 15 & I-90, exit 102. 507/238-9444; FAX 507/238-9371.* 47 rms, 2 story. S, D $44.98-$53.98; each addl $5; under 12 free. Crib $5. Pet accepted. TV; cable. Continental bkfst. Restaurant opp 6 am-10 pm. Ck-out noon. Business servs avail. Free airport transportation. Cr cds: A, C, D, DS, MC, V.

Restaurant

✔★ **THE RANCH.** *1330 N State St. 507/235-3044.* Hrs: 6 am-10 pm; Fri, Sat to 11 pm. Closed Dec 25. Res accepted. Bar. Semi-a la carte: bkfst $2.50-$4, lunch $3.50-$6, dinner $6.75-$10.95. Child's meals. Specializes in steak, seafood, salad. Salad bar. Casual, family-style dining. Cr cds: MC, V.

Faribault (G-4)

(See also Lakeville, Le Sueur, Mankato, Northfield, Owatonna, St Peter)

Settled 1826 **Pop** 17,085 **Elev** 971 ft **Area code** 507 **Zip** 55021 **E-mail** fbltcofc@polaristel.net **Web** www.polaristel.net/faribault

Information Faribault Area Chamber of Commerce, 530 Wilson Ave, PO Box 434; 507/334-4381 or 800/658-2354.

In 1826, Alexander Faribault, a French-Canadian fur trader, built the largest of his six trading posts here. Faribault now is known for Faribo wool blankets and Tilt-A-Whirl amusement rides. The town, seat of Rice County, is surrounded by 20 area lakes and 3,000 acres of parkland. Faribault is also home to several historic landmarks, including the Cathedral of Our Merciful Saviour, built in 1869, and the limestone buildings of Shattuck-St Mary's Schools founded in 1858.

What to See and Do

Alexander Faribault House (1853). House of the fur trader for whom the town was named. Period furnishings; museum of Native American artifacts and historical items. (By appt) 12 NE 1st Ave. Phone 507/334-7913. ¢

Faribault Woolen Mill Co. Wool blankets, items made in century-old mill on the Cannon River. Factory store, mill seconds. Check in at store for 45-min guided tour (Mon-Fri; closed 1st 2 wks July). Store (daily; closed some major hols). 1500 NW 2nd Ave. Phone 507/334-1644. **Free.**

Rice County Historical Society Museum. Slide show; video presentation; Native American and pioneer artifacts; turn-of-the-century Main St; works of local artists. Nearby are log cabin, church, one-room schoolhouse and 2 steel annexes. (May-Sept, daily; rest of yr, Mon-Fri) 1814 NW 2nd Ave, adj to county fairgrounds. Phone 507/332-2121. ¢

River Bend Nature Center. 646 acres of mixed habitat including woodlands, prairie, ponds and rivers. 10 mi of trails (cross-country in winter) meander through the area. (Daily) SE via MN 60, on Rustad Rd. Phone 507/332-7151. **Free.**

Motels

✔★ ★ **BEST WESTERN GALAXIE.** *1401 W MN 60. 507/334-5508; FAX 507/334-2165.* 59 rms, 2 story. S $39-$56; D $42-$56; each addl $3. Crib $2. TV; cable (premium). Indoor pool; whirlpool, sauna. Complimentary continental bkfst. Restaurant adj 6 am-11 pm. Rm serv. Ck-out 11 am. Meeting rms. Business servs avail. In-rm modem link. Cr cds: A, C, D, DS, JCB, MC, V.

★ ★ **SELECT INN.** *4040 W MN 60. 507/334-2051.* 67 rms, 2 story. S $35; D $42-$58; each addl $5; under 13 free. Crib $3. TV; cable (premium), VCR (movies). Indoor pool. Restaurant adj open 24 hrs. Ck-out 11 am. Meeting rms. Business servs avail. Cr cds: A, D, DS, MC, V.

Restaurant

★ ★ **LAVENDER INN.** *2424 N Lyndale Ave. 507/334-3500.* Hrs: 11 am-10 pm. Closed Jan 1, Thanksgiving, Dec 24 eve, Dec 25. Res accepted. Bar. Semi-a la carte: lunch $6-$10, dinner $9-$25. Child's meals. Specializes in steak, broasted chicken, seafood. Art display. Family-owned. Cr cds: A, C, D, DS, MC, V. ¢

Fergus Falls (E-1)

Settled 1857 **Pop** 12,362 **Elev** 1,196 ft **Area code** 218 **Zip** 56537
Information Chamber of Commerce, 202 S Court St; 218/736-6951.

Fergus Falls was named in honor of James Fergus, who financed Joseph Whitford, a frontiersman who led an expedition here in 1857. The town is the seat of Otter Tail County, which has 1,029 lakes. The city has a remarkable park and recreation system.

What to See and Do

Otter Tail County Historical Society Museum. Modern facility featuring dioramas and changing exhibits interpreting regional history; also library, archives and genealogical materials. (Daily; closed some major hols) 1110 W Lincoln Ave. Phone 218/736-6038. ¢

Recreation areas. Pebble Lake City Park. Picnicking, swimming, beach. 18-hole golf (Apr-Sept, daily; fee). Park (early June-late Aug, daily). **DeLagoon Park.** Picnicking, swimming, beach, fishing, boating (ramp); camping (fee). Park (mid-May-Oct, daily). SE on US 59. Phone 218/739-3205.

Motels

✔★ **COMFORT INN.** *425 Western Ave. 218/736-5787.* 35 rms, 2 story. May-Oct: S $44; D $49; each addl $5; suites $99; under 19 free; lower rates rest of yr. Crib free. TV; cable (premium), VCR avail (movies). Complimentary continental bkfst. Restaurant nearby. Ck-out 11 am. Business servs avail. Valet serv. Coin lndry. X-country ski 15 mi. Some refrigerators. Cr cds: A, C, D, DS, MC, V.

✔★ **DAYS INN.** *MN 210 W. 218/739-3311.* 57 rms, 2 story. S $36.90-$38.90; D $40.90-$46.90; each addl $5; under 12 free. Crib free. TV; cable. Indoor pool; whirlpool. Complimentary continental bkfst 4-9 am. Restaurant adj 6 am-midnight. Ck-out 11 am. Business servs avail. Sundries. Downhill/x-country ski 2 mi. Cr cds: A, C, D, DS, MC, V.

★ **SUPER 8.** *I-94 at MN 210. 218/739-3261.* 32 rms, 2 story. S $37.88-$43.88; D $46.88-$49.88; each addl $5. Crib $2. TV; cable (premium). Complimentary coffee. Restaurant adj open 6 am-midnight. Ck-out 11 am. Business servs avail. Cr cds: A, C, D, DS, MC, V.

Restaurant

★ ★ **MABEL MURPHY'S.** *At jct I-94 & MN 210. 218/739-4406.* Hrs: 11 am-2 pm, 5-10 pm; Sun 5-9 pm. Bar 11-1 am. Semi-a la carte: lunch $4.25-$6.95, dinner $8.95-$24.95. Child's meals. Specializes in seafood, prime rib, pastas. Salad bar. Own desserts. Country inn decor; fireplaces, antiques. Cr cds: A, D, DS, MC, V.

Glenwood (E-2)

(See also Alexandria, Morris, Sauk Centre)

Pop 2,573 **Elev** 1,350 ft **Area code** 320 **Zip** 56334
Information Glenwood Area Chamber of Commerce, 200 N Franklin St; 320/634-3636 or 800/304-5666.

What to See and Do

Chalet Campsite. Boating (launch), swimming beach, bicycling, picnicking, playground, tennis court, camping (fee), rest rms, showers. (Mid-May-Sept, daily) 1/2 mi S on MN 104. Phone 320/634-5433.

Department of Natural Resources, Area Fisheries Headquarters. Trout in display ponds (Mon-Fri; closed hols). Grounds (daily). 1 1/2 mi W on N Lakeshore Dr, MN 28, 29. **Free.**

Pope County Historical Museum. Helbing Gallery of Native American arts & crafts; country store, school & church; exhibits of local history, farm machinery and artifacts; furnished log cabin (1880). (Memorial Day-Labor Day, daily; rest of yr, Mon-Fri) 1/2 mi S on MN 104. Phone 320/634-3293. ¢¢

Annual Events

Scout Fishing Derby. 1st wkend Feb.

Terrace Mill Heritage Festival. Phone 320/278-3289. Last wkend June.

Waterama. Water carnival; contests, parade. Last full wkend July.

Pope County Fair. 1st wk Aug.

Terrence Mill Fiddlers' Contest. Phone 320/278-3289. 1st Sun Oct.

Motels

✔★ **HI-VIEW.** *MN 55, 1 mi NE, between MN 28 & 29. 320/634-4541.* 12 rms. S $26; D $40; each addl $3. Crib free. Pet accepted. TV; cable (premium). Playground. Restaurant nearby. Ck-out 11 am. Sundries. Picnic tables, grill. Overlooks city, Lake Minnewaska. Cr cds: DS, MC, V.

★ **SCOTWOOD.** *US 28 & 55, 1/2 mi E. 320/634-5105.* 46 rms, 2 story. S $35.90-$42.90; D $42.90-$45.90; each addl $5. Crib $5. TV; cable (premium). Indoor pool; whirlpool. Complimentary continental bkfst. Restaurant nearby. Ck-out 11 am. Game rm. Cr cds: A, DS, MC, V.

Resort

★ ★ ★ **PETERS' SUNSET BEACH.** *2500 S Lakeshore Dr, 2 1/2 mi S on MN 104 to Pezhekee Rd, then 1 1/2 mi W, on Lake Minnewaska. 320/634-4501.* E-mail golfpsb @runestone.net; web www.digitmaster.com/resorts/peters. 24 lodge rms, 20 kit. cottages. Some rm phones. Mid-June-mid-Aug: cottages for 1-9, $123-$259; MAP, family rates; golf plans; 2-4 day min stay: hols; some wkends; lower rates May-mid-June, mid-Aug-Oct.

Closed rest of yr. Crib $8. TV; VCR avail (movies). Dining rm (public by res) 7:30-9:30 am, 7-8:30 pm. Snack bar. Ck-out 12:30 pm, ck-in 4:30 pm. Business servs avail. Grocery. Coin lndry. Package store 3 mi. Tennis. 18-hole golf, greens fee $28, putting green. Private beach. Boats, motors, rowboats; launching ramp. Bicycles. Saunas. Cr cds: MC, V.

Restaurant

★ ★ **MINNEWASKA HOUSE SUPPER CLUB.** *MN 28, 4 mi SW.* 320/634-4566. Hrs: 11 am-2 pm, 5-10 pm; Sun 5-9 pm. Closed most hols. Res accepted. Bar to 1 am. Semi-a la carte: lunch $4.95-$12.50, dinner $8.50-$29.50. Specializes in steak. Entertainment. Open charcoal grill. Cr cds: A, MC, V.

Grand Marais (C-6)

(See also Grand Portage, Lutsen)

Pop 1,171 **Elev** 688 ft **Area code** 218 **Zip** 55604

This municipality, on the rocky north shore of Lake Superior, is the major community in the northeast point of Minnesota. The area resembles the tip of an arrow and is known as the "arrowhead country." The cool climate and pollen-free air, as well as lake and stream fishing, abundant wildlife, water sports, camping and stretches of wilderness, make this a leading resort area. A Ranger District office of the Superior National Forest (see) is located here.

What to See and Do

Canoe trips. Canoes, equipment, guides. For map, folder, names of outfitters contact Tip of the Arrowhead Assn, PO Box 1048; 218/387-2524 or 800/622-4014.

Grand Portage National Monument. 38 mi NE on MN 61. (See GRAND PORTAGE)

Gunflint Trail. Penetrates into area of hundreds of lakes where camping, picnicking, fishing, canoeing are available. Starting at NW edge of town, the road goes N & W 58 mi to Saganaga Lake on the Canadian border.

North Shore Drive. MN 61 along Lake Superior from Duluth to Pigeon River (150 mi); considered one of the most scenic shore drives in the US.

Annual Events

Fisherman's Picnic. Parade, rides, dancing, queen's coronation; food. 1st wk Aug.

Cook County Fair. 5 blks N on MN 61. Late Aug.

Motels

★ ★ **BEST WESTERN SUPERIOR INN & SUITES.** *1st Ave E, 1 blk E, just off US 61.* 218/387-2240; FAX 218/387-2244; res: 800/842-8439. Web www.bestwestern.com. 50 rms, 2-3 story. June-Oct: D $79-$109; suites $89-$149; lower rates rest of yr. Crib free. Pet accepted. TV; cable (premium), VCR avail (movies). Complimentary continental bkfst. Coffee in rms. Restaurant nearby. Ck-out 11 am. Coin lndry. Business servs avail. Downhill ski 18 mi; x-country ski ½ mi. Snowmobiling. Whirlpool. Refrigerators; some bathrm phones, whirlpools, fireplaces. Balconies. Private beach on lake. View of Lake Superior. Cr cds: A, C, D, DS, ER, MC, V.

★ ★ **EAST BAY.** 218/387-2800; res: 800/414-2807; FAX 218/387-2801. 36 rms, 2-3 story, 4 suites. No A/C. Mid-May-Oct: S, D $51-$92.50; suites $125-$150; under 12 free; lower rates rest of yr. Crib

free. Pet accepted. TV; cable. Restaurant 7 am-2 pm, 5-9 pm. Rm serv. Bar 11 am-9 pm; entertainment. Ck-out 11 am. Downhill ski 18 mi; x-country ski 5 mi. Massage. Whirlpool. Many refrigerators. Some in-rm whirlpools, refrigerators. Microwave, wet bar, fireplace in suites. On lake. Cr cds: A, DS, MC, V.

★ ★ **ECONO LODGE.** *US 61E (55604-0667), 2 blks E on US 61.* 218/387-2500; FAX 218/387-2647. E-mail gmhotel@worldnet.att.net. 52 rms. Mid-June-mid-Oct, mid-Dec-mid-Mar: S $46-$79; D $49-$89; suites $65-$136; package plans avail; lower rates rest of yr. Pet accepted, some restrictions. TV; cable (premium). Indoor pool; whirlpool. Complimentary continental bkfst. Restaurant nearby. Ck-out 11 am. Guest lndry. Meeting rm. Business servs avail. In-rm modem link. Downhill ski 18 mi; x-country ski 1 mi. Snowmobiling. Refrigerators; some in-rm whirlpools. Cr cds: A, C, D, DS, MC, V.

★ **SHORELINE.** *20 S Broadway (55604-0667), 2 blks S of US 61.* 218/387-2633; FAX 218/387-2499; res: 800/247-6020 (MN). E-mail gmhotel@worldnet.att.com. 30 rms, 2 story. No A/C. Mid-June-mid-Oct, mid-Dec-mid-Mar: S $39-$74; D $40-$84; each addl $8; package plans; lower rates rest of yr. Crib free. Complimentary continental bkfst. Restaurant nearby. Ck-out 11 am. Business servs avail. In-rm modem link. Gift shop. Downhill ski 18 mi; x-country ski 1 mi. Snowmobiling. Refrigerators. Beach on Lake Superior. Cr cds: A, C, D, DS, MC, V.

✔★ **SUPER 8.** *US 61W (55604-0667), 1 mi SW on US 61.* 218/387-2448; FAX 218/387-9859; res: 800/247-6020 (MN). E-mail gmhotel@worldnet.att.com. 35 rms. Mid-June-mid-Oct & mid-Dec-mid-Mar: S $45-$72; D $69-$79; each addl $8; package plans; lower rates rest of yr. Crib free. Pet accepted, some restrictions. TV; cable (premium). Complimentary continental bkfst. Restaurant nearby. Ck-out 11 am. Guest lndry. Business servs avail. In-rm modem link. Downhill ski 18 mi; x-country ski 2 mi. Snowmobiling. Sauna. Whirlpool. Refrigerators. Cr cds: A, C, D, DS, MC, V.

Lodge

★ ★ **NANIBOUJOU LODGE.** *20 Naniboujou Trail, 15 mi NE on US 61.* 218/387-2688. E-mail naniboujou@compuserve.com; web ourworld.compuserve.com/homepages/naniboujou. 24 rms, 2 story. No A/C. No rm phones. Mid-May-late Oct: S $59-$89; D $69-$89; each addl $10; under 3 free; lower rates rest of yr. Winter hrs wkends only. Crib $10. Restaurant 8 am-10:30 am, 11:30 am-2:30 pm, 5:30-8:30 pm. Ck-out 10:30 am. Business servs avail. X-country ski on site. Some fireplaces. On lake/river. Totally nonsmoking. Cr cds: DS, MC, V.

Resorts

★ ★ **BEARSKIN LODGE.** *124 E Bearskin Rd, 26 mi NW on Gunflint Trail then 1 mi NE on E Bearskin Rd.* 218/388-2292; FAX 218/388-4410; res: 800/338-4170. E-mail stay@bearskin.com; web www.bearskin.com. 4 kit. units (1-3 bedrm) in 2-story lodge, 11 kit. cottages (2-3 bedrm). No A/C. Lodge: D $140; each addl $34; kit. cottages: D $115-$198; each addl $34; package plans. Crib avail. Playground. Free supervised child's activities (June 1-Sept 1); ages 3-13 yrs. Dining rm (res required) 6 pm. Box lunches. Wine, beer. Ck-out 10 am, ck-in 4 pm. Coin lndry. Business servs avail. Grocery. Package store 5 mi. Private swimming beach. Boats, motors, canoes. X-country ski on site. Hiking trails. Mountain bikes. Nature program. Sauna, whirlpool. Fishing guides. Microwaves, fireplaces. Some balconies, screened porches. Picnic tables, grills. Private docks. Cr cds: DS, MC, V.

★ **BORDERLAND LODGE.** *194 N Gunflint Lake. 218/388-2233; FAX 218/388-9476; res: 800/451-1667.* E-mail borderland@boreal.org. 9 kit. units, 2 story, 7 kit. cottages. May-Sept, mid-Dec-mid-Mar: S, D, kit. cottages $490-$900/wk; daily rates avail; ski plans; lower rates Oct-mid-Dec. Closed rest of yr. Crib free. Playground. Dining rm 7-9 am, 6:30-8 pm. Box lunches. Ck-out 10 am, ck-in 2 pm. Coin lndry 3 mi. Package store 16 mi. Gift shop. Swimming beach. Boats. X-country ski on site. Hiking. Mountain bikes (rentals). Sauna. Fishing guides. Microwaves; some fireplaces. Picnic tables, grills. On peninsula; overlooks Gunflint Lake. Cr cds: MC, V.

★ **CLEARWATER LODGE.** *5 Old Rail Ln, 28 mi NW on Gunflint Trail, 4 mi NE on Clearwater Lake Rd. 218/388-2254; res: 800/527-0554.* E-mail clearwater@canoe-bwca.com; web www.canoe-bwca.com. 6 kit. log cabins (2-3 bedrm); 5 rms in lodge, 2 story. No A/C. Mid-May-mid-Oct, cabins: D $715-$750/wk; each addl $60-$100; lodge rms: D $65-$95; family rates; lower rates. Closed rest of yr. Pet accepted. Playground. Box lunches. Ck-out 10 am, ck-in 2 pm. Grocery 6 mi. Coin lndry 8 mi. Sand beach. Private docks; boats, motors, kayaks, canoe outfitting (with bunkhouses). Hiking trails. Nature program. Mountain bikes. Sauna. Microwaves, fireplaces. Some porches. Picnic tables, grills. Cr cds: DS, MC, V.

★ **NOR'WESTER LODGE.** *7778 Gunflint Trail, 30 mi NW. 218/388-2252; res: 800/992-4386.* 10 kit. cottages (1-4 bedrm), 1-2 levels. No A/C. EP, wkly: D $774-$1,134; each addl $120-$180; under 3 free; spring, fall rates. Crib avail. Pet accepted; $40/wk. TV; cable in lodge, VCR avail (movies). Playground. Ck-out 10 am, ck-in 3 pm. Grocery. Coin lndry. Package store 1 mi. Gift shop. Private sand beach. Waterskiing. Pontoon boat, motors, canoes & outfitting serv; boat launch. X-country ski 4 mi. Snowmobile trails. Hunting. Lawn games. Sauna. Fishing guide. Trophy display in lodge. Fireplaces, microwaves. Picnic tables, grills. Private docks. Cr cds: DS, MC, V.

★ ★ **ROCKWOOD LODGE.** *625 Gunflint Trail, 34 mi NW on Gunflint Trail, on Poplar Lake. 218/388-2242; res: 800/942-2922.* E-mail rockwood@boreal.org; web www.boreal.org/rockwood. 9 kit. cottages (1-3 bedrm). No A/C. 2-8 persons, EP, wkly: D $650-$1,400; AP, dinner plan avail; daily, family rates. Crib avail. Playground. Dining rm (guests only). Box lunches. Bar. Ck-out 10:30 am, ck-in 2 pm. Business servs avail. Grocery 2 mi. Coin lndry 2 mi. Private & children's beaches. Boats, motors, canoes. Canoe outfitting (with bunkhouses). Hiking trail. Lawn games. Saunas. Fishing/hunting guides. Microwaves; many fireplaces. Cr cds: A, DS, MC, V.

Restaurants

✔★ **ANGRY TROUT CAFE.** *US 61, 3 blks W on US 61, W side of harbor. 218/387-1265.* Hrs: 11 am-9 pm. Closed late Oct-Apr. No A/C. Wine, beer. Semi-a la carte: lunch $3.95-$7.95, dinner $13.50-$16.95. Specializes in grilled lake trout, organic salads. Outdoor dining. Solarium overlooking Lake Superior; bldg and its furnishings all handcrafted. Totally nonsmoking. Cr cds: MC, V.

D

★ ★ **BIRCH TERRACE.** *W Sixth Ave, 1/2 mi W on US 61. 218/387-2215.* Hrs: 5-11 pm. Res accepted. No A/C. Bar 4 pm-1 am. Semi-a la carte: dinner $8.95-$16.95. Child's meals. Specializes in fresh Lake Superior trout, ribs, steak. Northwoods mansion built in 1898; fireplaces. Native American burial grounds in front yard. Overlooks Lake Superior. Family-owned. Cr cds: DS, MC, V.

D

Grand Portage (C-6)

(For accommodations see Grand Marais)

Pop 250 (est) **Elev** 610 ft **Area code** 218 **Zip** 55605

What to See and Do

Grand Portage National Monument. Once this area was a rendezvous point and central supply depot for fur traders operating between Montreal and Lake Athabasca. Partially reconstructed headquarters of the North West Company includes stockade, great hall, kitchen and warehouse. Buildings and grounds (mid-May-mid-Oct, daily). S of MN 61, 5 mi from Canadian border. Phone 218/475-2202. ¢

The Grand Portage begins at the stockade and runs 8 1/2 mi NW from Lake Superior to Pigeon River. Primitive camping at Ft Charlotte (accessible only by hiking the Grand Portage or by canoe). Trail (all-yr). **Free.**

From Grand Portage there is passenger ferry service to Isle Royale National Park within Michigan state waters (mid-May-late Oct). Phone 715/392-2100. ¢¢¢¢

Grand Rapids (C-3)

(See also Deer River, Hibbing)

Settled 1877 **Pop** 7,976 **Elev** 1,290 ft **Area code** 218 **Zip** 55744 **E-mail** info@chamber.grand-rapids.mn.us **Web** www.chamber.grand-rapids.mn.us

Information Grand Rapids Area Chamber of Commerce, The Depot, 1 NW 3rd St; 218/326-6619 or 800/472-6366.

At the head of navigation on the Mississippi River, Grand Rapids was named for nearby waters. For years it served as a center for logging. Paper production and tourism are the principal industries today. Seat of Itasca County, Grand Rapids serves as a diverse regional center at the western end of the Mesabi Iron Range. A number of open pit mines nearby have observation stands for the public. The forested area surrounding the town includes more than a thousand lakes. Four of them—Crystal, Hale, Forest and McKinney—are within the city limits.

What to See and Do

Canoeing. On Mississippi River, N on Bigfork waters to Rainy Lake, Lake of the Woods; also to Lake Itasca and on many nearby rivers.

Central School. Heritage center housing historical museum, Judy Garland museum, antiques, shops and a restaurant. (Daily) 10 NW 5th St. Phone 218/327-1843.

Chippewa National Forest. 661,400 acres of timbered land; 1,321 lakes, with 699 larger than 10 acres; swimming, boating, canoeing, hiking, hunting, fishing, picnicking, camping (fee); winter sports. Bald eagle viewing; several historic sites. Between Grand Rapids & Bemidji on US 2. Phone 218/335-8600.

Forest History Center. Center includes a museum building, re-created 1900 logging camp and log drive wanigan maintained by Minnesota Historical Society as part of an interpretive program. Early Forest Service cabin & fire tower, modern pine plantation, living history exhibits; nature trails. (Mid-May-mid-Oct, daily). 3 mi SW via S US 169. Phone 218/327-4482. ¢¢

Judy Garland Museum. Childhood home of actress. (Tues-Sat, also Sun afternoon) 2727 US 169 S. Phone 218/327-9276. ¢

Pokegama Dam. Camping on 16 trailer sites (hookups, dump station; 14-day max); picnicking, fishing. 2 mi W on US 2. Phone 218/326-6128. Camping per night ¢¢¢¢

Quadna Mt Resort Ski Area. Quad chairlift, 2 T-bars, rope tow; patrol, school, rentals, snowmaking; motel, lodge & restaurant. Cross-country trails. (Thanksgiving-mid-Mar, Thurs-Sun) Also golf, outdoor tennis, horse-back riding, lake activities in summer. 18 mi S on US 169, 1 mi S of Hill City. Phone 218/697-8444. ¢¢¢¢-¢¢¢¢¢

Scenic State Park. Primitive area of 3,000 acres with seven lakes. Swimming; fishing; boating (ramp, rentals), hiking; cross-country skiing, snowmobiling; picnicking; camping (electrical hookups); lodging; interpretive programs. Standard fees. 12 mi N on US 169, then 32 mi N on County 7. Phone 218/743-3362.

Annual Events

Judy Garland Festival. Museum. Phone 218/327-9276. Late June.

Mississippi Melodie Showboat. 16th Ave W, on Mississippi River. Amateur musical variety show. Phone 800/722-7814. 3 wkends July.

North Star Stampede. 3-day rodeo. Phone 218/743-3893. Late July.

Tall Timber Days and US Chainsaw Carving Championships. Downtown. Phone 800/472-6366. Early Aug.

Itasca County Fair. Fairgrounds, on Crystal Lake. Mid-Aug.

Motels

★ ★ **AMERICINN.** *1812 Pokegama Ave S. 218/326-8999; FAX 218/326-9190.* 43 rms, 2 story. Mid-June-Labor Day: S, D $55.90-$60.90; each addl $6; under 17 free; lower rates rest of yr. Crib free. TV; cable (premium). Indoor pool; whirlpool, sauna. Complimentary continental bkfst. Restaurant nearby. Ck-out 11 am. Business servs avail. Downhill/x-country ski 18 mi. Cr cds: A, C, D, DS, MC, V.

D ✈ ≋ ≋ 🔥 SC

✔★ ★ **BEST WESTERN RAINBOW INN.** *1300 E US 169, 1 mi E, near Itasca County Airport. 218/326-9655; FAX 218/326-9651.* 80 rms, 2 story. S $45-$60; D $52-$70; each addl $8; suites $75-$90; under 12 free. Crib free. TV; cable. Indoor pool; whirlpool, sauna. Restaurant 6 am-2 pm, 5-9 pm. Rm serv. Bar 3 pm-1 am; entertainment Fri, Sat. Ck-out noon. Meeting rms. Business center. Airport transportation. Downhill/x-country ski 10 mi. Cr cds: A, C, D, DS, MC, V.

≋ ≋ ✈ 🔥 SC 🚶

★ ★ **COUNTRY INN.** *2601 US 169S. 218/327-4960; FAX 218/327-4964.* June-Aug: S $55-$65; D $63-$73; each addl $5; under 18 free; lower rates rest of yr. Crib free. Pet accepted, some restrictions. TV; cable (premium). Indoor pool; whirlpool. Complimentary continental bkfst. Restaurant adj 6:30 am-10 pm. Ck-out noon. Downhill ski 10 mi; x-country 2 mi. Some refrigerators. Cr cds: A, C, D, DS, MC, V.

D ✈ ✈ ≋ 🔥 SC

★ **DAYS INN.** *311 E US 2, at US 169. 218/326-3457; FAX 218/326-3795.* 34 rms, 2 story. Mid-Apr-late Sept: S, D $50-$69; each addl $4; under 12 free; lower rates rest of yr. Crib free. Pet accepted. TV; cable, VCR avail (movies $1). Playground. Complimentary coffee in lobby. Restaurant adj open 24 hrs. Ck-out 11 am. Business servs avail. Free airport, bus depot transportation. Grill. Cr cds: A, D, DS, MC, V.

✔ 🔥 SC

★ ★ **SAWMILL INN.** *2301 S Pokegama Ave, 1¹/₂ mi S on US 169, near Itasca County Airport. 218/326-8501; FAX 218/326-1039; res: 800/235-6455 (MN).* 124 rms, 2 story. S $51-$72; D $61-$72; each addl $4; suites $84-$105; under 12 free. Crib free. Pet accepted. TV; cable. Indoor pool; whirlpool, sauna, poolside serv. Restaurant 6:30 am-10 pm; Fri, Sat to 11 pm. Rm serv. Bar 11-1 am. Ck-out noon. Coin lndry. Meeting rms. Business servs avail. Sundries. Free airport, bus depot transportation. Downhill/x-country ski 18 mi. Game rm. Cr cds: A, C, D, DS, MC, V.

D ✈ ≋ ✈ 🔥 SC

✔★ **SUPER 8.** *1902 S Pokegama Ave, Hwy 169S, near Itasca County Airport. 218/327-1108.* 58 rms, 2 story. S $46; D $46-$54. Crib $2. TV; cable (premium). Complimentary continental bkfst. Restaurant nearby. Ck-out 11 am. Guest lndry. Business servs avail. In-rm modem link.

Downhill/x-country ski 18 mi. Shopping nearby. Cr cds: A, C, D, DS, MC, V.

D ✈ ≋ 🔥 SC

Granite Falls (F-2)

(See also Marshall, Redwood Falls)

Pop 3,083 **Elev** 920 ft **Area code** 320 **Zip** 56241
Information Chamber of Commerce, 155 7th Ave, PO Box 220; 320/564-4039.

What to See and Do

Lac qui Parle State Park. Approx 529 acres. On Lac qui Parle and Minnesota rivers. Dense timber. Swimming; fishing; boating (ramps); hiking, riding; cross-country skiing; picnicking; camping. Standard fees. (Daily) 14 mi NW on US 212, 8 mi NW on US 59, then 4¹/₂ mi W on County 13. Phone 320/752-4736.

Olof Swensson Farm Museum. A 22-rm brick family-built farmhouse, barn and family burial plot on a 17-acre plot. Olof Swensson ran unsuccessfully for governor of Minnesota, but the title was given to him by the community out of respect and admiration. (Memorial Day-Labor Day, Sun) 4 mi N on County 5, then 2¹/₂ mi W on County 15. Phone 320/269-7636. ¢¢

Upper Sioux Agency State Park. 1,280 acres. Boating (ramps, canoe campsites). Bridle trails. Snowmobiling. Picnicking. Primitive camping. Visitor center. Standard fees. 8 mi SE on MN 67. Phone 320/564-4777.

Yellow Medicine County Museum. Depicts life in the county and state dating from the 1800s. 2 authentic log cabins & bandstand on site. Also here is an exposed rock outcropping estimated to be 3.8 billion yrs old. (Mid-May-mid-Oct, daily exc Mon; mid-Apr-mid-May, Tues-Fri) ¹/₂ mi from center of town via MN 67. Phone 320/564-4479. **Free.**

Motels

✔★ **SCENIC VALLEY.** *168 E US 212, ¹/₂ mi SE on US 212, MN 23. 320/564-4711.* 16 rms. S $27.50; D $30.55-$35.50. TV; cable. Complimentary coffee in rms. Restaurant nearby. Ck-out 11 am. X-country ski 1 mi. Cr cds: MC, V.

✈ ≋ 🔥

★ **VIKING SUNDANCE INN.** *US 212W, at jct MN 67 & MN 23. 320/564-2411.* 20 rms. S $28; D $31-$42; each addl $3. Crib $3. Pet accepted. TV; cable, VCR avail (movies). Ck-out 11 am. Cr cds: A, DS, MC, V.

✔ ≋ 🔥 SC

Hastings (F-4)

(See also Minneapolis, Northfield, Red Wing, St Paul)

Settled 1850 **Pop** 15,445 **Elev** 726 ft **Area code** 612 **Zip** 55033
Information Hastings Area Chamber of Commerce & Tourism Bureau, 119 W 2nd St, Suite 201; 612/437-6775 or 888/612-6122.

Diversified farming and industry are the mainstays of this community, founded by a trader who felt the area was a good town site.

What to See and Do

Afton Alps. 3 triple, 15 double chairlifts, 2 rope tows; patrol, school, rentals; snowmaking; store, cafeteria, snack bar; bar. Longest run 3,000 ft;

vertical drop 330 ft. (Nov-Mar, daily) 10 mi N via US 61, MN 95. Phone 612/436-5245 or 800/328-1328. ¢¢¢¢

Alexis Bailly Vineyard. First vineyard to make wine with 100% Minnesota-grown grapes. Wine tastings (June-Oct, Fri-Sun). Group tours (by appt). 18200 Kirby Ave. Phone 612/437-1413. **Free.**

Carpenter St Croix Valley Nature Center. Environmental education center with more than 15 mi of hiking trails and 1 mi of shoreline on the St Croix River. Various seasonal programs and activities (some fees). (Daily; closed major hols) 12805 St Croix Trail, 2 mi N via US 61, then 3 mi E via US 10. Phone 612/437-4359. ¢

Hiawatha Valley Highway. US 61 extends 116 mi SE from Hastings to La Crescent, following the bluff-banked Mississippi through the Hiawatha Valley, an area rich in Native American and steamboat lore.

Historic Walking Tour. A self-guided tour featuring the historic buildings of Hastings, including the LeDuc-Simmons Mansion & Norrish "Octagon House." Tour booklets with background detail and map are available at the Chamber of Commerce. Guided tours by appt.

Ramsey Mill. Remains of first flour mill in state, built by Governor Alexander Ramsey in 1857. On MN 291 on the Vermillion River.

Treasure Island Casino & Bingo. 24-hr casino offers blackjack, slots, bingo and pull-tabs. Buffet, sports bar. Marina. Comedy shows (Tues night). (Daily) 5734 Sturgeon Lake Rd. S on US 61, 316 to Welch, follow signs. Phone 800/222-7077.

Annual Event

Rivertown Days. Gala community-wide festival. Riverfront activities; exhibits & tours; sporting events; fireworks. July 17-19.

Motels

★ **AMERICINN.** 2400 Vermillion St. 612/437-8877; FAX 612/437-8184; res: 800/634-3444. 27 rms, 2 story. S $42.90-$79.90; D $48.90-$85.90; each addl $6; under 12 free. Crib free. TV; cable (premium), VCR avail. Complimentary continental bkfst. Restaurant nearby. Ck-out 11 am. Meeting rms. Business servs avail. Downhill ski 11 mi; x-country ski 1 mi. Cr cds: A, C, D, DS, MC, V.

[D] [≉] [⊠] [⅄] [SC]

✔ ★ **HASTINGS INN.** 1520 Vermillion St. 612/437-3155; FAX 612/437-3530. 43 rms. S $28-$44; D $35-$59.95; each addl $5; family units to 8, $75-$79. TV; cable. Indoor pool; sauna. Complimentary coffee 7-9 am. Restaurant nearby. Ck-out 11 am. In-rm modem link. Sundries. Downhill ski 11 mi; x-country ski 1 mi. Game rm. Sun deck. Cr cds: A, C, D, DS, MC, V.

[≉] [⊠] [⅄] [⅄] [SC]

✔ ★ **SUPER 8.** 2450 Vermillion St, at jct US 61 & MN 316. 612/438-8888; FAX 612/438-8888, ext. 100. 50 rms. Apr-Sept: S $43.88-$46.88; D $49.88-$56.88; each addl $6; lower rates rest of yr. Crib $3. TV; cable. Complimentary continental bkfst. Restaurant nearby. Ck-out 11 am. Cr cds: A, C, D, DS, JCB, MC, V.

[D] [⊠] [⅄] [SC]

Inn

★ ★ ★ **THORWOOD.** 315 Pine. 612/437-3297; res: 800/992-4667. 15 rms, 3 story. S, D $87-$217; each addl $15; under 12 free. TV avail; VCR. Complimentary full bkfst. Ck-out noon, ck-in 4 pm. Business servs avail. In-rm modem link. Downhill ski 6 mi; x-country ski 3 mi. Some in-rm whirlpools. Historic houses built 1880; antiques, feather comforters, marble fireplaces. Dinner avail with notice. Cr cds: A, DS, MC, V.

[D] [≉] [⊠] [⅄]

Restaurant

★ ★ **MISSISSIPPI BELLE.** 101 E 2nd St, under bridge, just off US 61. 612/437-4814. Hrs: 11 am-2:30 pm, 4:30-9 pm; Fri, Sat to 10 pm; Sun to 8 pm. Closed Mon. Res accepted. Semi-a la carte: lunch $6.35-$7.50, dinner $10.95-$41. Child's meals. Specializes in baked seafood au gratin, fresh seafood, steak. Dining in the tradition of the riverboat era (1855-1875); riverboat steel engravings. Cr cds: A, D, DS, MC, V.

Hibbing (C-4)

(See also Cook, Deer River, Eveleth, Grand Rapids, Virginia)

Founded 1893 **Pop** 18,046 **Elev** 1,489 ft **Area code** 218 **Zip** 55746

Information Chamber of Commerce, 211 E Howard St, PO Box 727; 218/262-3895.

Here is the world's largest open-pit iron mine, which produced one-quarter of the ore mined in the country during World War II. Hibbing calls itself the "iron ore capital of the world." On the Mesabi (Native American for "sleeping giant") Iron Range, Hibbing mines and processes taconite, yielding a rich iron concentrate. Frank Hibbing, the founder of the town, built the first hotel, sawmill and bank building. In 1918, when the Hull-Rust pit encroached on the heart of town, the community was moved on wheels two miles south. The move was not completed until 1957. A local bus line, begun here in 1914 with an open touring car, is now the nationwide Greyhound Bus system. Hibbing was the boyhood home of singer-guitarist Bob Dylan.

What to See and Do

Bus tour. Four-hr bus tour of town & nearby taconite plant. Includes stops at Hull-Rust Mine, Paulucci Space Theatre, high school. (Mid-June-mid-Aug, Mon-Fri) For information phone 218/262-3895. ¢¢

Hull-Rust Mahoning Mine. Observation building provides view of "Grand Canyon of Minnesota," mining area extending 3 mi. Individual mines have merged through the yrs into single pit producing hundreds of millions of tons. Deepest part of pit, on east side, dips 535 ft into earth. Observation building; self-guided walking tours. (Mid-May-Sept, daily) Contact the Chamber of Commerce for further information. N of town. **Free.**

⊠ **Ironworld USA.** Displays and audiovisual presentations interpret culture and history of the iron mining industry and its people. Ethnic craft demonstrations and food specialties; entertainment; scenic train rides; outdoor amphitheater. (Apr-Oct, daily) (See ANNUAL EVENTS) 5 mi NE on US 169 in Chisholm. Phone 218/254-3321 or 800/372-6437. ¢¢¢

McCarthy Beach State Park. Approx 2,566 acres. Virgin pine, 2 lakes. Swimming, fishing, boating (ramp, rentals); cross-country skiing; hiking; snowmobiling; camping; naturalist (summer). Standard fees. 20 mi NW on County 5. Phone 218/254-2411. Per vehicle ¢¢

Minnesota Museum of Mining. Records the past 70 yrs of iron mining; equipment, exhibits, models; jet and rotary drills, steam engine, ore cars & railroad caboose, 120-ton Euclid & fire trucks; first Greyhound bus. (Mid-May-mid-Sept, daily) Self-guided tours. Picnicking. Memorial Park Complex. 6 mi NE via MN 73, on W Lake St in Chisholm. Phone 218/254-5543. ¢¢

Paulucci Space Theatre. General interest programs from astronomy to dinosaurs, using stars, slides, special effects and hemispheric film projection; multimedia theater with tilted-dome screen; display area; gift shop. Shows (June-Aug, daily; hrs vary, phone ahead; rest of yr, wkends only). E 23rd St & US 169 Business. Phone 218/262-6720. ¢¢

Annual Events

Last Chance Curling Bonspiel. Memorial Building. International curling competition on 14 sheets of ice. Early Apr.

Minnesota Ethnic Days. Ironworld USA. A series of celebrations of ethnic heritage. Entertainment, history, crafts and food. Each day devoted to different nationality. July.

St Louis County Fair. Fairgrounds, 12th Ave. Cattle and rock exhibits, auto races, carnival midway. Early Aug.

Motels

★ **DAYS INN.** *1520 E MN 37, Jct US 169 & MN 37. 218/263-8306.* 60 rms, 2 story. S $40.95-$45.95; D $43.95-$50; each addl $3. Crib free. Pet accepted, some restrictions. TV; cable (premium), VCR avail (movies). Complimentary continental bkfst. Ck-out 11 am. Business servs avail. Cr cds: A, C, D, DS, MC, V.

★ **SUPER 8.** *1411 E 40th St, jct US 169 & MN 37. 218/263-8982.* 49 rms, 2 story. Apr-Sept: S $36.79-$40.88; D $47.59-$52.88; each addl $3; under 13 free; wkly rates; higher rates special events; lower rates rest of yr. Crib free. Pet accepted, some restrictions; $25 deposit. TV; cable (premium), VCR avail. Complimentary coffee in lobby. Restaurant opp 6 am-11 pm. Ck-out 11 am. Meeting rms. Business servs avail. X-country ski 2 mi. Cr cds: A, C, D, DS, MC, V.

Hinckley (E-4)

(See also Mora)

Pop 946 **Elev** 1,030 ft **Area code** 612 **Zip** 55037

What to See and Do

Hinckley Fire Museum. Old Northern Pacific Railroad Depot houses museum that depicts the disastrous forest fire that swept across Hinckley in 1894. Mural, video tape, diorama, reconstructed living quarters. (May-Oct, daily) 106 US 61. Phone 612/384-7338. ¢¢

North West Company Fur Post. A reconstruction of an 1800 fur trade outpost, based on archaeological findings and other research; picnic area. (May-Labor Day, Tues-Sat & Sun afternoons) 2 mi W of I-35 Pine City exit. Phone 612/629-6356. **Free.**

St Croix State Park. A 34,037-acre park. Swimming (lake), fishing, boating (Memorial Day-Labor Day, rentals); hiking, riding trails, cross-country skiing, snowmobiling; picnicking, 6-mi blacktop wooded bike trail, camping (electric, dump station). Standard fees. 15 mi E on MN 48, then S. Phone 612/384-6591. Per vehicle ¢¢

Motels

★ **BEST WESTERN GOLD PINE MOTOR INN.** *at jct MN 48 & I-35. 612/384-6112.* 50 rms, 1-2 story. May-Nov: S $55-$75; D $66-$81; each addl $6; suites $89-$119; under 18 free; lower rates rest of yr. Crib $2. TV; cable (premium), VCR avail. Complimentary coffee in rms. Restaurant nearby. Ck-out 11 am. Business servs avail. X-country ski 15 mi. Game rm. Some refrigerators; microwaves avail. Cr cds: A, C, D, DS, MC, V.

★★ **DAYS INN.** *104 Grindstone Court, I-35 exit 183, at MN 48. 612/384-7751.* 69 rms, 2 story. S $44-$75; D $49-$85; each addl $5; suites $90-$135; under 18 free. Crib free. Pet accepted; $5. TV; cable, VCR avail. Indoor pool; whirlpool. Complimentary continental bkfst. Complimentary coffee in rms. Restaurant adj open 24 hrs. Ck-out 11 am. Coin lndry. Business servs avail. X-country ski 10 mi. Sauna. Some refrigerators; microwaves avail. Cr cds: A, C, D, DS, MC, V.

★★ **ECONO LODGE.** *502 Weber Ave, jct I-35, MN 48. 320/384-7451; res: 800/894-7451 (MN).* 29 rms, 2 story. S $48-$64; D $54-$70; each addl $6; under 17 free. Crib free. TV; cable. Complimentary continental bkfst. Restaurant adj open 24 hrs. Ck-out 11 am. X-country ski 15 mi. Sauna. Whirlpool. Large fieldstone fireplace in lobby. Cr cds: A, C, D, MC, V.

★★ **HOLIDAY INN EXPRESS.** *604 Weber Ave, I-35 exit 183. 320/384-7171; FAX 320/384-7735.* 101 rms, 2 story. May-Sept: D $69-$89; each addl $10; whirlpool rms $85-$129; under 19 free; lower rates rest of yr. Crib free. Pet accepted. TV; cable. Indoor pool; whirlpool. Complimentary continental bkfst. Coffee in rms. Ck-out noon. X-country ski 10 mi. Sauna. Microwaves avail. Cr cds: A, C, D, DS, MC, V.

★ **SUPER 8.** *(2811 MN 23, Finlayson 55735) 10 mi N on I-35 exit 195. 320/245-5284; FAX 320/245-2233.* 30 rms, 2 story. S $44.88-$56.88; D $48.88-$56.88; each addl $4; under 12 free. Crib free. Pet accepted. TV; cable (premium). Complimentary continental bkfst. Restaurant opp 6 am-10 pm. Ck-out 11 am. Coin lndry. Business servs avail. X-country ski opp. Whirlpool. Game rm. Cr cds: A, C, D, DS, MC, V.

Motor Hotel

★★ **GRAND HINCKLEY INN.** *111 Lady Luck Dr, 1 mi E of I-35 on MN 48. 320/384-7622; res: 800/468-3517; FAX 320/384-7610.* 154 rms, 2 story, 16 suites. Mid-May-Sept: S, D $94; each addl $5; suites $104-$159; under 18 free; golf plans; lower rates rest of yr. Crib free. TV; cable. Complimentary continental bkfst. Complimentary coffee in rms. Restaurant adj open 24 hrs. Ck-out 11 am. Meeting rms. Business servs avail. In-rm modem link. Bellhops. Sundries. Gift shop. Coin lndry. X-country ski 10 mi. Exercise equipt; weight machine, bicycle, sauna. Indoor pool; whirlpool. Game rm. Some bathrm phones, in-rm whirlpools; refrigerator, microwave, wet bar in suites. Cr cds: A, D, DS, MC, V.

Restaurants

✔★★ **CASSIDY'S.** *RR 2, I-35 exit Hinckley. 612/384-6129.* Hrs: 6 am-10 pm; Sat bkfst buffet 7-10:45 am. Res accepted. Wine, beer. Semi-a la carte: bkfst .99-$7.95, lunch $4-$8.95, dinner $5.50-$11.95. Buffet (Sat): bkfst $5.95. Child's meals. Specializes in barbecued ribs, pressure-fried chicken, steak. Salad bar. Own baking, soups. Cr cds: DS, MC, V.

✔★ **TOBIE'S.** *I-35, exit Hinckley. 320/384-6174.* Hrs: Coffee shop open 24 hrs. Closed Dec 25. Res accepted. Bar 11-1 am. Semi-a la carte: bkfst $2-$6, lunch $3-$6, dinner $5-$12. Specializes in prime rib, salads, pastries. Entertainment Thurs-Sun. Bistro atmosphere. Bakery on premises. Family-owned. Cr cds: A, C, D, MC, V.

International Falls (B-4)

Pop 8,325 **Elev** 1,124 ft **Area code** 218 **Zip** 56649 **E-mail** intlfall@intlfalls.org **Web** www.intlfalls.org

Information International Falls Area Chamber of Commerce, 301 2nd Ave; 218/283-9400 or 800/325-5766.

In addition to tourism, converting trees and wood chips into paper is big business here. The town takes its name from a 35-foot drop of the Rainy River, now concealed by a reservoir above a dam that harnesses the water power. International Falls is a port of entry to Canada by way of Fort

Frances, ON, Canada. (For border crossing regulations, see MAKING THE MOST OF YOUR TRIP.)

What to See and Do

Boise Cascade Paper Mill. No cameras allowed. No children under 10 yrs. Proper footwear required. Tours (June-Aug, Mon-Fri; closed hols). Res advised. 2nd St. Phone 218/285-5511. **Free.**

Fishing. Rainy Lake. E along international boundary. Walleye, sand pike, muskie, crappie, perch, bass. **Rainy River.** W along international boundary. Walleye, sand pike, sturgeon, northern pike.

Grand Mound History Center. Several ancient Native American burial mounds exist in this area, the largest being the Grand Mound, which has never been excavated. Interpretive Center offers audiovisual program, sound system exhibit and 1/4-mi trail to mound site. (May-Aug, daily; rest of yr, wkends; also by appt) 17 mi W via MN 11. Phone 218/285-3332. **Free.**

International Falls City Beach. Sandy beach for swimming; picnic grounds, play equipment. 3 1/2 mi E on MN 11.

Smokey the Bear Statue. Giant symbol of the campaign against forest fires. In park is a giant thermometer, standing 22 ft tall; it electronically records the temperature. Municipal Park. NW edge of business district. Also in the park is

Koochiching County Historical Museum. Exhibits, manuscripts, pictures, articles used by early settlers in area. (Mid-May-mid-Sept, daily; research center Mon & Tues rest of yr) Phone 218/283-4316. ¢¢ Located in the same bldg and included in admission is

Bronko Nagurski Museum. Highlighting the life and career of football hero Bronko Nagurski; features exhibits, diorama, audiovisual program, photographs and archives.

✠ **Voyageurs National Park.** Approx 219,000 acres of forested lake country along the northern Minnesota border. Fishing, boating, camping, naturalist-guided activities, hiking trails. Off US 53 or E on MN 11. Phone 800/325-5766. **Free.**

Motels

★ **DAYS INN.** 2331 US 53S. 218/283-9441. 58 rms, 2 story. S $46-$58; D $60-$70; under 18 free. Crib free. Pet accepted, some restrictions. TV; cable (premium). Complimentary continental bkfst. Restaurant adj open 24 hrs. Ck-out noon. Business servs avail. Exercise equipt; bicycle, treadmill, sauna. Whirlpool. Cr cds: A, C, D, DS, JCB, MC, V.

⟋ ✕ ⟍ ⟍ SC

★★★ **HOLIDAY INN.** 1500 Hwy 71. 218/283-4451; FAX 218/283-3774. 126 rms, 2 story. S, D $69-$109; suites $85-$135; family rates. Crib free. Pet accepted. TV; cable (premium). Indoor pool; wading pool, whirlpool. Restaurant 6 am-10 pm. Rm serv. Bar. Ck-out noon. Coin lndry. Meeting rms. Business servs avail. In-rm modem link. Bellhops. Sundries. Free airport transportation. Sauna. Health club privileges. Some refrigerators; microwaves avail. View of Rainy River. Cr cds: A, C, D, DS, JCB, MC, V.

D ⟋ ⟍ ⟍ ⟍ SC

✔★ **SUPER 8.** 2326 US 53S. 218/283-8811; FAX 218/283-8880. 53 rms, 2 story, 7 suites. Mid-May-Sept: S $41.88; D $49.88; each addl $6; suites $69.44; under 12 free; lower rates rest of yr. Crib free. TV; cable (premium). Complimentary coffee in lobby. Restaurant nearby. Ck-out 11 am. Coin lndry. Business servs avail. In-rm modem link. Refrigerator, whirlpool, minibar in suites; some microwaves. Cr cds: A, C, D, DS, MC, V.

D ⟍ ⟍ SC

Cottage Colonies

★ **ISLAND VIEW LODGE & MOTEL.** 1817 MN 11E, 12 mi E on MN 11, on Rainy Lake. 218/286-3511; res: 800/777-7856. E-mail

jbischol@northernnet.com; web www.northernnet.com/islandview/. 9 A/C rms in 2-story lodge, 12 kit. cottages (1-6 bedrm), 5 A/C. S, D $65-$70; each addl $11; cottages (3-day min) 1-6 bedrm, $115-$250/day. Pet accepted, some restrictions. TV in lodge rms, some cabins. Dining rm 6:30 am-2 pm, 5-10 pm. Box lunches, snack bar. Bar noon-1 am. Ck-out 10 am, ck-in 3 pm. Grocery, coin lndry 12 mi. Package store. Free airport transportation. Private beach; dockage, boats, motors, guides. Snowmobiling. National park tours. Jukebox dancing. Rec rm. Picnic table, grills. Cr cds: DS, MC, V.

 D ⟋ ⟍ ⟍ ⟍

★ **NORTHERNAIRE FLOATING LODGES.** 2690 County Rd 94, at Jackfish Bay, 7 mi E on MN 11, then 2 mi N on County 94, on Rainy Lake. 218/286-5221. E-mail nflhboat@northernnet.com; web www.northern net.com/nflhboat. 15 power-driven floating kit. lodges on pontoon boats. No A/C. Mid-May-mid-Oct (3-day min): for 2-10, $795-$2,100/wk; package plans avail; daily rates. Res, deposit required. Closed rest of yr. Pet accepted, some restrictions. Ck-out noon. Grocery. Waterskiing, motors. Hunting; guides, cooks. Unique houseboat living. Cr cds: MC, V.

⟋ ⟋

Restaurant

★★ **SPOT FIREHOUSE.** 1801 Second Ave W, 1 mi S on US 53. 218/283-2440. Hrs: 5-11 pm. Closed Sun; major hols. Res accepted. Bar. Semi-a la carte: dinner $5.95-$17.95. Child's meals. Specializes in barbecued ribs, char-broiled steak, prime rib. Salad bar. Firefighter theme and memorabilia. Family-owned. Cr cds: A, C, D, DS, MC, V.

D

Itasca State Park (C-2)

(See also Bemidji, Park Rapids)

(28 mi N of Park Rapids on US 71)

In the deep forests that cover most of the 32,000 acres of this park, there is a small stream just 15 steps across; this is the headwaters of the Mississippi River at its source, Lake Itasca. The name of the park and the lake itself is a contraction of the Latin *veritas caput,* meaning "true head." The lake is the largest of more than 100 that sparkle amid the virgin woodlands. The park offers swimming, boating (ramp, rentals), snowmobiling, cross-country skiing, fishing, biking (rentals), hiking. There are cabins, camping and picnic grounds and a lodge that offers food service (see RESORT). In the summer there are daily boat cruises aboard the *Chester Charles,* from Douglas Lodge Pier to the headwaters of the Mississippi River (fee). A lookout tower, Aiton Heights, in the southeastern part of the park just off the 10-mile wilderness drive, provides a bird's eye view of the park. Native American burial mounds and a pioneer cabin are some of the many historical sites preserved at Itasca. The University of Minnesota's forestry school and biological station operates here during the summer.

Naturalist program provides self-guided and guided hikes, auto tours, boat launch tours, campfire programs and evening movies on history and features of the area. Exhibits show many animals and plants native to the state, as well as park history. Inquire at the entrance gates for details. Standard entrance fees.

(For further information contact Superintendent, HC05, Box 4, Lake Itasca, 56460; 218/266-2114.)

Resort

✔★ **DOUGLAS LODGE.** (Park Rd, Lake Itasca 56460) 2 mi W of jct 71, MN 200 (in center of park). 218/266-2100; res: 800/246-2267. 28 rms in lodge, annexes, 19 A/C, 1 with shower only, 2 story, 22 cabins (1-3 bedrm), 6 with kit., central shower area. Memorial Day wkend-mid-Oct, lodge, annexes: S $34-$36; D $40-$44; each addl $10; cabins $68-$120;

kit. cabins $70. Closed rest of yr. Crib avail. Playground. Dining rm 8 am-8 pm. Picnic lunches. Ck-out 11 am, ck-in 4 pm. Grocery 2 mi. Coin lndry 8 mi. Meeting rms. Business servs avail. Sand beach 3 mi; boats, canoes; launch tours. Hiking trails & naturalist program. Bicycles. Some cabins with fireplace, screened porch. State park sticker required for entry to park & lodge. Cr cds: A, DS, MC, V.

Jackson (H-2)

(See also Fairmont)

Founded 1856 **Pop** 3,559 **Elev** 1,312 ft **Area code** 507 **Zip** 56143
Information Chamber of Commerce, 1000 US 71 N; 507/847-3867.

A peaceful community on the banks of the Des Moines River, Jackson processes the farm produce of the fertile river valley and also manufactures industrial farm equipment. Thirteen blocks of Jackson's business district are on the National Registry of Historic Places.

What to See and Do

Ft Belmont. Museum with antique automobiles; log chapel, sodhouse, waterwheel-operated flour mill and other buildings; Native American artifacts. Museum (Memorial Day-Labor Day, daily). 2 mi S of jct US 71 & I-90. Phone 507/847-5840. ¢¢

Kilen Woods State Park. 219 acres of forested hills in Des Moines Valley. Fishing, hiking, snowmobiling, picnicking, camping (hookups, dump station); visitor center. Standard fees. 4 mi N on US 71, then 5 mi W. Phone 507/662-6258.

Monument to Slain Settlers. Marks scene of attack by the Sioux in 1857. Ashley Park, State St & Riverside Dr.

Annual Events

County Fair. Late July, early Aug.

Town & Country Day Celebration. Main St. 3rd Sat July.

Motels

★ ★ **BEST WESTERN COUNTRY MANOR INN.** *I-90 & US 71.* 507/847-3110. 42 rms. S $40-$48; D $50-$62; each addl $4. Crib free. TV; cable. Indoor pool; wading pool, whirlpool, sauna. Restaurant 6 am-10 pm. Bar 11-12:30 am. Ck-out noon. Meeting rms. Business servs avail. In-rm modem link. Sundries. Cr cds: A, C, D, DS, MC, V.

✔★ **BUDGET HOST PRAIRIE WINDS.** *950 N US 71, ½ mi S of I-90 on US 71.* 507/847-2020. 24 rms. S $31-$36; D $43-$54; each addl $4. Crib $4. TV; cable. Coffee in rms. Restaurant nearby. Ck-out 10 am. In-rm modem link. Sundries. X-country ski 2 mi. Golf opp. Cr cds: A, C, D, DS, MC, V.

Lakeville (G-4)

(See also Faribault, Hastings, Minneapolis, Northfield, Red Wing, St Paul)

Pop 24,854 **Elev** 974 ft **Area code** 612 **Zip** 55044

Motels

★ **FRIENDLY HOST LAKEVILLE.** *17296 I-35 (17296), at jct MN 50.* 612/435-7191. 48 rms. S $35-$55; D $45-$70; each addl $5; kit. units $5 addl. Crib $4. TV; cable, VCR avail (movies). Indoor pool; whirlpool. Complimentary coffee in lobby. Restaurant nearby. Ck-out 11 am. Sundries. Downhill/x-country ski 1 mi. Game rm. Cr cds: A, D, DS, MC, V.

✔★ **MOTEL 6.** *11274 210th St (11274).* 612/469-1900; FAX 612/469-5359. 84 rms, 2 story. S $30-$34; D $36-$42; under 17 free. Crib free. Pet accepted. Complimentary coffee in lobby. Restaurant opp 7 am-11 pm. Ck-out noon. Downhill ski 5 mi; x-country ski 2 mi. Cr cds: A, C, D, DS, MC, V.

Inn

★ ★ ★ **SCHUMACHER'S NEW PRAGUE HOTEL.** *(212 W Main St, New Prague 56071)* Approx 15 mi S on I-35, W on MN 19. 612/758-2133; FAX 612/758-2400. 11 rms, 2 story. S, D $107-$165. Restaurant (see SCHUMACHER'S). Bar to 11 pm; Fri, Sat to midnight. Ck-out 11:30 am, ck-in 3 pm. Business servs avail. Valet serv. Gift shop. X-country ski 1 mi. Built in 1898. Decor resembles country inns, hotels in Bavaria, southern Bohemia and Austria. Cr cds: A, D, DS, MC, V.

Restaurant

★ ★ ★ **SCHUMACHER'S.** *(See Schumacher's New Prague Hotel Inn)* 612/758-2133. Hrs: 7 am-9 pm; Fri, Sat to 10 pm. Res accepted. Continental menu. Bar. Wine list. Semi-a la carte: bkfst $3-$10, lunch $5-$19, dinner $19-$27. Specializes in veal, game dishes. Own baking. Decor resembles country inns in Bavaria, Austria and southern Bohemia. Cr cds: A, DS, MC, V.

Le Sueur (G-3)

(For accommodations see Faribault, Mankato; also see St Peter)

Pop 3,714 **Elev** 800 ft **Area code** 507 **Zip** 56058
Information Chamber of Commerce, 500 N Main St, Suite 106; 507/665-2501.

This town on the Minnesota River was named for Pierre Charles Le Sueur, who explored the river valley at the end of the 17th century. The Green Giant Company, one of the world's largest packers of peas and corn, was founded here and merged with Pillsbury in 1980. Home office of Le Sueur Incorporated and plant sites for ADC Telcommunications, UNIMIN and Le Sueur Cheese are located here.

What to See and Do

W.W. Mayo House (1859). Home of founder of Mayo Clinic; restored to 1859-1864 period when Dr. Mayo carried on a typical frontier medical practice from his office on the 2nd floor. Adj park is location of Paul Granland's bronze sculpture *The Mothers Louise.* (June-Aug, daily exc

Mon; May & Sept-Oct, wkends & hols only) 118 N Main St. Phone 507/665-3250. ¢

Litchfield (F-3)

(See also Minneapolis, Willmar)

Pop 6,041 **Elev** 1,132 ft **Area code** 612 **Zip** 55355

What to See and Do

Meeker County Historical Society Museum. The museum stands behind the Grand Army of the Republic Hall (see). Includes a log cabin, old barn display, blacksmith shop, general store and Native American display. Original newspapers, furniture and uniforms are also exhibited. (Tues-Sun afternoons; also by appt; closed major hols exc Memorial Day) 308 N Marshall Ave. Phone 612/693-8911. **Donation.**

Grand Army of the Republic Hall. Built in 1885, the hall has two rms in original condition. Commemorates the members of the GAR (Grand Army of the Republic).

Motels

✔★ **LAKE RIPLEY RESORT.** *1205 S Sibley Ave. 612/693-3227.* 17 rms. S $23-$29; D $29-$36.95; each addl $4; under 8 free. Crib free. TV; cable (premium). Complimentary coffee in rms. Restaurant nearby. Ck-out 11 am. Cr cds: A, DS, MC, V.

★ **SCOTWOOD.** *1017 E Frontage Rd. 612/693-2496; res: 800/225-5489.* 35 rms, 2 story. S $38.95-$41.50; D $42.95-$45.75; each addl $5. Crib free. Pet accepted, some restrictions. TV; cable (premium). Complimentary continental bkfst. Restaurant nearby. Ck-out 11 am. Sundries. Cr cds: A, C, D, DS, MC, V.

Little Falls (E-3)

(See also Brainerd, Onamia, St Cloud)

Pop 7,232 **Elev** 1,120 ft **Area code** 320 **Zip** 56345 **E-mail** chamber @upstel.net **Web** www.upstel.net/~falls/tour7.html
Information Chamber of Commerce, 200 First St NW; 320/632-5155.

This town gets its name from the rapids of the Mississippi River. The seat of Morrison County, it is a paper milling town and a center of the small boat industry.

What to See and Do

Charles A. Lindbergh House. Home of Charles A. Lindbergh, Sr, former US congressman, and Charles A. Lindbergh, Jr, famous aviator. Homestead restored to its 1906-1920 appearance with much original furniture; history center has exhibits, audiovisual program. (May-Labor Day, daily) 1200 Lindbergh Dr S, S edge of town, on W bank of Mississippi River. Phone 320/632-3154. ¢¢ Adj is

Charles A. Lindbergh State Park. 294 acres. Hiking; cross-country skiing; picnicking; camping (hookups, dump station). Standard fees. Phone 320/632-9050.

Charles A. Weyerhaeuser Memorial Museum. Museum and resource center for Morrison County and regional history. (May-Sept, Tues-Sun; rest of yr, Tues-Sun; closed some hols) 2 mi SW of town via Lindbergh Dr S. Phone 320/632-4007. **Free.**

Minnesota Military Museum. Located in a former regimental headquarters, the museum documents US military history as experienced by Minnesotans, from frontier garrisons to the Persian Gulf. Exhibits; military decorations; tanks and aircraft. (Sept-Apr, Thurs & Fri; late May-late Aug, Wed-Sun) Camp Ripley, 7 mi N on MN 371, W on MN 115. Phone 320/632-7374. **Free.**

Primeval Pine Grove Municipal Park. Picnicking, playground, zoo with native animals (all yr); stand of virgin pine. (May-Sept, daily) W on MN 27. Phone 320/632-2341. **Free.**

Motels

✔★ **PINE EDGE.** *308 First St SE. 320/632-6681; res: 800/344-6681; FAX 320/632-4332.* 56 rms, 1-2 story. S $35-$40; D $40-$50; each addl $5; suites $60-$95; under 12 free. Crib $5. Pet accepted. TV; cable (premium). Heated pool. Playground. Restaurant 7 am-9 pm. Rm serv. Bar 11:30 am-midnight. Ck-out 11 am. Business servs avail. On river; built in 1923; hosted Charles Lindbergh after historic trans-Atlantic flight. Cr cds: A, C, D, DS, MC, V.

★ **SUPER 8.** *300 12th St NE, just off I-371, US 10. 320/632-2351.* 51 rms, 2 story. S $38.88; D $48.88-$52.88. Crib free. TV; cable. Coffee in rms. Restaurant nearby. Ck-out 11 am. Sundries. Refrigerators avail. Cr cds: A, C, D, DS, MC, V.

Lutsen (C-6)

(See also Grand Marais)

Pop 290 (est) **Elev** 671 ft **Area code** 218 **Zip** 55612

What to See and Do

Lutsen Mountains Ski Area. 4 double chairlifts, T-bar; school, rentals; snowmaking; lodge (see RESORTS), cafeteria, bar. Longest run 1¼ mi; vertical drop 800 ft. Gondola. (Mid-Nov-May, daily) 1½ mi SW on MN 61, then 1½ mi N. Phone 218/663-7281. ¢¢¢¢ Also here are

Alpine Slide. Chairlift takes riders up mountain to slide; riders control sled on ½-mi track down mountain. (June-mid-Oct) Concession & picnic area. Phone 218/663-7281. ¢¢- ¢¢¢¢

Gondola Skyride. 2-mi round trip sightseeing ride to the highest point on the North Shore. Particularly scenic view in fall. (June-mid-Oct) Phone 218/663-7281. ¢¢

Motels

★★ **BEST WESTERN CLIFF DWELLER.** *6452 US 61 (55615), 3½ mi SW. 218/663-7273.* E-mail gmhotel@worldnet.att.com. 22 rms, 2 story. Mid-June-mid-Oct, mid-Dec-mid-Mar: S $49-$69; D $59-$79; each addl $8; package plans; lower rates rest of yr. Crib free. Pet accepted, some restrictions. TV; cable (premium). Restaurant (late June-Sept) 7 am-9 pm. Ck-out 11 am. Business servs avail. In-rm modem link. Downhill ski 3 mi; x-country ski adj. 18-hole golf privileges. Balconies. On lake; scenic view. Cr cds: A, C, D, DS, MC, V.

★★★ **BLUEFIN BAY.** *(US 61S, Tofte 55615) 218/663-7296; FAX 218/663-7130; res: 800/258-3346.* E-mail bluefin@boreal.org; web www.bluefinbay.com. 72 units, 2 story, 56 kits. No A/C. Late Dec-Mar, June-Oct: S, D, kit. units $69-$345; each addl $10; under 12 free; ski plans; higher rates; ski wkends, hols; lower rates rest of yr. Crib free. Pet accepted. TV; cable, VCR avail (movies). 2 pools, 1 indoor; whirlpool. Supervised child's activities. Complimentary coffee in rms. Restaurant 7:30 am-10 pm. Bar 3 pm-1 am. Ck-out noon. Coin lndry. Meeting rms.

Business servs avail. Gift shop. Tennis. 18-hole golf privileges. Downhill ski 9 mi; x-country ski opp. Exercise equipt; weight machine, bicycles, sauna. Massage. Game rm. Lawn games. Many in-rm whirlpools, fireplaces; microwaves avail. Balconies. Grills. On Lake Superior. Cr cds: DS, JCB, MC, V.

★ ★ **HOLIDAY INN EXPRESS.** *(Tofte 55615) S on US 61. 218/663-7899; FAX 218/663-7387.* 52 rms, 2 story. Late Dec-Mar, mid-June-mid-Oct: S, D $75-$130; suite, kit. unit $170-$230; under 19 free; ski, golf plans; wkends (2-day min); lower rates rest of yr. Crib free. Pet accepted. TV; cable. Complimentary continental bkfst. Restaurant nearby. Ck-out noon. Meeting rms. Business servs avail. Downhill ski 7 mi; x-country ski on site. Indoor pool; whirlpool, sauna. Many refrigerators, microwaves; some in-rm whirlpools. Picnic tables. Opp lake. Cr cds: A, D, DS, MC, V.

★ **THE MOUNTAIN INN.** *Ski Hill Rd, 1¹/₂ mi W off US 61. 218/663-7244; res: 800/686-4669; FAX 218/387-2446.* 30 rms, 2 story. Jan-Mar, July-mid-Oct: S, D $99-$119; each addl $8; under 18 free; wkend rates; ski, golf plans; hols (2-day min); lower rates rest of yr. Crib free. Pet accepted, some restrictions. TV; cable (premium), VCR avail. Complimentary continental bkfst. Restaurant opp 7 am-11 pm. Ck-out noon. Business servs avail. 18-hole golf privileges, greens fee $23, pro, putting green, driving range. Downhill ski 1 blk; x-country ski on site. Sauna, whirlpool. Many refrigerators, microwaves, wet bars. Picnic tables. Opp lake. Cr cds: A, D, DS, MC, V.

Resorts

★ ★ **CASCADE LODGE.** *3719 W US 61, 9 mi NE on US 61, in Cascade River State Park. 218/387-1112; FAX 218/387-1113; res: 800/322-9543 (MN).* E-mail cascade@cascadelodgemn.com; web www.cascadelodgemn.com. 12 rms in 2-story lodge, 11 cabins, 4 motel units (1-2 bedrm), 8 kits. No A/C. Late June-mid-Oct & late Dec-late Mar: Lodge D $65-$105; each addl $10-$12; cabins, kit. units $100-$175; motel units D $66-$105; family rates; package plans. Crib $5. TV; VCR avail (movies). Playground. Dining rm 7:30 am-8 pm. Box lunches. Ck-out 11 am, ck-in after 1 pm. Grocery, coin lndry, package store 10 mi. Meeting rms. Business servs avail. Downhill ski 11 mi; x-country ski adj. Bicycles. Canoes. Hiking trails. Indoor, outdoor games. Rec rm. Many refrigerators; some in-rm whirlpools, fireplaces. Picnic tables, grill. Overlooks Lake Superior. Lodge rms totally nonsmoking. Cr cds: A, DS, MC, V.

★ ★ **LUTSEN.** *1¹/₂ mi SW on US 61. 218/663-7212; res: 800/258-8736.* E-mail lutsen@lutsenresort.com; web www.lutsenresort.com. 49 rms in 2 lodges; 6 cabins; 51 kit. units in townhome villas (2¹/₂ mi S of lodge on lake). No A/C. Lodge: S $33-$125; D $38-$135; cabins: S, D $125-$249; villas for 2-8 (2-day min): S $80-$159; D $95-$219; each addl $10; under 12 free; honeymoon rates. Crib avail. Pet accepted, some restrictions. TV; cable, VCR avail. Indoor pool; whirlpool. Playground. Dining rm 7:30 am-2 pm, 5:30-9 pm. Box lunches. Bar 4 pm-1 am, wkends from noon. Ck-out 11 am; ck-in after 4 pm. Grocery 1¹/₂ mi. Meeting rms. Coin lndry 20 mi. Tennis. 9-hole golf course. Downhill ski 1¹/₂ mi; x-country ski adj. Sauna. Lawn games. Rec rm; indoor games. Fireplace, balcony in villas. Sun deck. On Lake Superior. Cr cds: A, D, DS, MC, V.

★ ★ ★ **THE VILLAGE INN & RESORT.** *371 Ski Hill Rd, 1¹/₂ mi NW of US 61. 218/663-7241; res: 800/642-6036; FAX 218/663-7920.* E-mail info@villageinnresort.com; web www.villageinnresort.com. 99 units in 15 bldgs, 1-3 story. Feb-Mar: S, D $100-$600; kit. units $180-$600; wkly, wkend, hol rates; ski, golf plans; wkends Feb-Mar (3-day min), also wkends mid-July-Labor Day (2-day min); lower rates rest of yr. Crib free. TV; cable, VCR avail (movies). Complimentary coffee in lobby. Restaurant 7-1 am. Box lunches, snack bar, picnics. Rm serv. Bar 11-1 am. Ck-out 11 am, ck-in 4:30 pm. Grocery 2¹/₂ mi. Coin lndry 18 mi. Package store 2¹/₂ mi. Meeting rms. Business servs avail. Sports dir. Tennis. 18-hole golf

privileges, greens fee $39, pro, putting green, driving range. Downhill/x-country ski on site. Rental equipt avail. Sleighing. Hiking. Horse stables. Bicycle rentals. Social dir. Game rm. Exercise equipt; bicycle, stair machine, sauna. Spa. Fishing/hunting guides. 2 pools, 1 indoor. Playground. Supervised child's activities; ages 4-12. Many refrigerators, microwaves, fireplaces. Many balconies. Picnic tables, grills. Cr cds: MC, V.

Luverne (H-1)

(See also Pipestone; also see Sioux Falls, SD)

Pop 4,382 **Elev** 1,450 ft **Area code** 507 **Zip** 56156

What to See and Do

Blue Mounds State Park. A 2,028-acre park. Main feature is Blue Mound, 1¹/₂-mi-long quartzite bluff. According to legend, Native Americans drove herds of buffalo off this bluff. Buffalo can still be observed in park. Swimming, fishing, boating; snowmobiling; picnicking; camping; visitor center. Standard fees. 5 mi N of I-90 on US 75, 1 mi E on County 20. Phone 507/283-4892. Per vehicle ¢¢

Motel

✔★ **SUPER 8.** *I-90 & US 75. 507/283-9541.* 36 rms, 2 story. S $40.88-$54.88; D $45.88-$64.88; each addl $5. Crib free. Pet accepted. TV; cable (premium). Ck-out 11 am. Cr cds: A, C, D, DS, MC, V.

Mankato (G-3)

(See also Faribault, Le Sueur, New Ulm, St Peter)

Founded 1852 **Pop** 31,477 **Elev** 785 ft **Area code** 507
Information Chamber & Convention Bureau, PO Box 999, 56002; 507/345-4519.

In a wooded valley where the Minnesota and Blue Earth rivers join, Mankato (Native American for "blue earth") takes its name from the blue clay that lines the riverbanks. Settled by Eastern professional men, farmers and Scandinavian and German immigrants, Mankato today enjoys an economy based on farming, retailing, manufacturing and distributing.

What to See and Do

Hubbard House (1871). Historic Victorian home with cherry woodwork, three marble fireplaces, silk wall coverings, signed Tiffany lampshade; carriage house; Victorian gardens. 606 S Broad St. Phone 507/345-4154 or 507/345-5566. ¢¢

Land of Memories. Picnicking, camping (hookups, dump station, rest rms), fishing, boating (launch), nature trails. S via US 169, then E at municipal campground unit. Camping ¢¢¢

Minneopa State Park. A 1,145-acre park. Scenic falls and gorge; historic mill site; fishing, hiking, picnicking, camping. Standard fees. 3 mi W off US 60. Phone 507/389-5464. Adj is

Minneopa-Williams Outdoor Learning Center. Wide variety of native animals and vegetation; information stations; outdoor classrm. (Daily) Phone 507/625-3281. **Free.**

Mt Kato Ski Area. 5 quad, 3 double chairlifts; patrol, school, rental; snowmaking; cafeteria; bar. (Nov-Apr, daily) 1 mi S on MN 66. Phone 507/625-3363. Lifts ¢¢¢¢

Sibley Park. Fishing, picnicking; river walk, playground, zoo (daily); rest rms; beautiful gardens, scenic view of rivers. End of Park Lane. **Free.**

Tourtelotte Park. Picnicking, playground. Swimming pool (early June-Labor Day, daily; fee), wading pool. N end of Broad St, on Mabel St. **¢**

Motels

✔★ **BUDGETEL INN.** *111 W Lind Court (56001). 507/345-8800; FAX 507/345-8921.* 66 rms, 2 story. S $35.95-$39.95; D $44.95-$49.95; under 18 free. Crib free. Pet accepted, some restrictions. TV; cable. Continental bkfst. Coffee in rms. Restaurant adj 7 am-11 pm. Ck-out noon. Business servs avail. Valet serv. Sundries. Downhill ski 6 mi; x-country ski 2 mi. Whirlpool, sauna. Cr cds: A, C, D, DS, MC, V.

D ✔ ⚡ ⊠ 👿 SC

★ **DAYS INN.** *1285 Range St (56001). 507/387-3332.* 50 rms, 2 story. S $37.95-$59.95; D $42.95-$69.95; suites $65-$125; under 18 free. Crib free. Pet accepted. TV; cable. Indoor pool; whirlpool. Complimentary continental bkfst. Restaurant nearby. Ck-out 11 am. Business servs avail. In-rm modem link. Downhill/x-country ski 5 mi. Cr cds: A, C, D, DS, MC, V.

D ✔ ⚡ ⊠ 👿 SC

✔★ **RIVERFRONT INN.** *1727 N Riverfront Dr (56001). 507/388-1638; FAX 507/388-6111.* 19 rms. S $30-$59; D $39-$79; each addl $7. Crib free. Pet accepted, some restrictions. TV; cable, VCR avail (movies). Complimentary coffee in rms. Restaurant nearby. Ck-out 11 am. Business servs avail. In-rm modem link. Downhill ski 5 mi; x-country ski 1 mi. Refrigerators. Cr cds: A, C, D, DS, MC, V.

D ✔ ⚡ ⊠ 👿 SC

★ **SUPER 8.** *Jct US 169N & 14 (56001). 507/387-4041; FAX 507/387-4107.* 61 rms, 3 story. S $37.88-$40.88; D $43.88-$49.88. Crib $1. TV; cable. Complimentary coffee in lobby. Restaurant adj open 24 hrs. Ck-out 11 am. Business servs avail. In-rm modem link. Downhill ski 5 mi; x-country ski 2 mi. Whirlpool. Cr cds: A, C, D, DS, MC, V.

D ⚡ ⊠ 👿 SC

Motor Hotels

★ ★ **BEST WESTERN GARDEN INN.** *(1111 Range St, N Mankato 56003) 1 mi N on US 169. 507/625-9333.* 147 rms, 2 story. S $45-$65; D $60-$80; each addl $6; under 18 free. Crib free. TV; cable, VCR avail (movies). Indoor pool; whirlpool, sauna. Coffee in rms. Restaurant 6 am-9 pm. Rm serv. Bar. Ck-out noon. Coin lndry. Meeting rms. Business servs avail. Sundries. Free airport transportation. Downhill ski 6 mi; x-country ski 1 mi. Rec rm. Cr cds: A, C, D, DS, MC, V.

D ⚡ ⊠ 👿 SC

★ ★ ★ **HOLIDAY INN-DOWNTOWN.** *101 Main St (56002). 507/345-1234.* 151 rms, 4 story. S $59-$69; D $69-$79; each addl $6; suites $89; under 19 free. Crib free. TV; cable. Indoor pool; whirlpool, poolside serv. Restaurant 7 am-10 pm. Rm serv. Bar 3 pm-1 am. Ck-out noon. Coin lndry. Meeting rms. Business servs avail. In-rm modem link. Valet serv. Sundries. Putting green. Downhill ski 4 mi; x-country ski 1 mi. Exercise equipt; weights, bicycles. Rec rm. Civic Center nearby. Cr cds: A, C, D, DS, JCB, MC, V.

D ⚡ ⊠ 🏃 ⊠ 👿 SC

Marshall (G-2)

(See also Granite Falls, Redwood Falls, Tracy)

Pop 12,023 **Elev** 1,170 ft **Area code** 507 **Zip** 56258 **E-mail** chamber @starpoint.net **Web** www.marshall-mn.org

Information Marshall Area Chamber of Commerce, 1210 E College Dr, PO Box 352B; 507/532-4484.

Crossroads of five highways, Marshall is a major industrial and retail center for the southwest part of Minnesota.

What to See and Do

Camden State Park. Approx 1,500 acres in forested Redwood River Valley. Swimming, fishing; hiking, riding, cross-country skiing, snowmobiling; picnicking, camping; visitor center. Standard fees. 10 mi S, off MN 23. Phone 507/865-4530.

Southwest State University (1963). (3,000 students) Liberal arts & technical programs. Planetarium (fee), museum & greenhouse (daily; closed hols; free). 1501 State St. For information phone 507/537-6255.

Annual Event

International Rolle Bolle Tournament. 150 teams compete for prize money. Mid-Aug.

Motels

★ **COMFORT INN.** *1511 E College Dr, at jct MN 23 & MN 19. 507/532-3070.* 49 rms, 2 story. S $48-$100; D $54-$100; each addl $6; under 18 free. Crib $2. Pet accepted. TV; cable (premium), VCR avail (movies). Complimentary continental bkfst. Restaurant nearby. Ck-out 11 am. Meeting rm. Business servs avail. In-rm modem link. Whirlpool. Cr cds: A, C, D, DS, ER, JCB, MC, V.

D ⚡ ⊠ 👿 SC

★ **SUPER 8.** *1106 E Main St, ¾ mi S on US 59, 2 blks S of US 23. 507/537-1461.* 50 rms, 2 story. S $42.88-$45.88; D $50.88; each addl $5. Crib free. Pet accepted. TV; cable (premium). Restaurant adj 6 am-10 pm. Ck-out 11 am. Coin lndry. Meeting rm. Business servs avail. X-country ski 1 mi. Cr cds: A, C, D, DS, MC, V.

D ✔ ⚡ ⊠ 👿 SC

✔★ ★ **TRAVELER'S LODGE.** *1425 E College Dr (MN 19), SW State University adj. 507/532-5721; FAX 507/532-4911; res: 800/532-5721.* 90 rms, 1-2 story. S, D $34-$42; each addl $4; under 12 free. Crib free. Pet accepted. TV; cable (premium), VCR avail (movies $3.50). Complimentary continental bkfst. Restaurant adj open 24 hrs. Ck-out noon. Meeting rm. Business servs avail. Sundries. Free airport transportation. X-country ski 1 mi. Cr cds: A, C, D, DS, MC, V.

✔ ⚡ ⊠ 👿 SC

Motor Hotel

★ ★ ★ **BEST WESTERN MARSHALL INN.** *E College Dr, SW State University opp. 507/532-3221; FAX 507/532-4089.* 100 rms, 2 story. S $43.95-$60.95; D $53.95-$60.95; suites $79.95-$84.95; under 17 free. Crib free. Pet accepted. TV; cable. Indoor pool; whirlpool, sauna, poolside serv. Restaurant 6:30 am-2 pm, 5-9:30 pm; wkend hrs vary. Rm serv. Bar noon-11:30 pm. Ck-out noon. Meeting rms. Business servs avail. In-rm modem link. Sundries. Free airport, bus depot transportation. X-country ski 1 mi. Cr cds: A, C, D, DS, MC, V.

D ✔ ⚡ ⊠ ⊠ 👿 SC

Minneapolis (F-4)

(See also Bloomington, St Paul)

Settled 1847 **Pop** 368,383 **Elev** 687-980 ft **Area code** 612

Information Greater Minneapolis Convention & Visitors Assn, 4000 Multifoods Tower, 33 S 6th St, 55402; 612/661-4700 or 800/445-7412.

Across the Mississippi from Minnesota's capital, St Paul, is this handsome city with skyscrapers, lovely parks and teeming industries. Minneapolis still has a frontier vigor; it is growing and brimming with confidence in itself and its future. Clean and modern, a north-country fountainhead of culture, Minneapolis is also a university town, a river town and a lake town.

A surprising array of nightlife, a revitalized downtown with many fine stores, a rich, year-round sports program, a symphony orchestra and theaters provide an excellent opportunity to enjoy the niceties of city life. Minneapolis has one of the largest universities in the country on one campus and more than 400 churches and synagogues. Hunting and fishing, which are among the state's major tourist attractions, are within easy access. The Minneapolis park system, with over a hundred parks, has been judged one of the best in the country. The city has also been a consistent winner of traffic safety awards.

Capital of upper Midwest agriculture, with one of the largest cash grain markets in the world, Minneapolis is the processing and distribution center for a large sector of America's cattle lands and grainfields. Several of the largest milling companies in the world have their headquarters here. Graphic arts, electronics, medical technology, machinery, lumber, paper and chemicals are also major industries.

Minneapolis was born when two mills were built to cut lumber and grind flour for the men of a nearby fort. Despite the fact that these were reservation lands and army troops tore down cabins almost as soon as settlers raised them, the community of St Anthony developed at St Anthony Falls around the twin mills. In 1885, the boundaries of the reservation were changed, and the squatters' claims became valid. The swiftly-growing community took the new name of Minneapolis (*Minne*, a Sioux word for water, and *polis*, Greek for city).

Transportation

Car Rental Agencies: See IMPORTANT TOLL-FREE NUMBERS.

Public Transportation: Buses (Metropolitan Transit Commission), phone 612/349-7000.

Rail Passenger Service: Amtrak 800/872-7245.

Airport Information

Minneapolis/St Paul Intl Airport: Information 612/726-5555; 612/726-5141 (lost and found); 612/452-2323 (weather); cash machines, Main Terminal, between entrances to Blue & Green Concourses..

What to See and Do

American Swedish Institute. Museum housed in turn-of-the-century 33-rm mansion; features hand-carved woodwork, porcelainized tile stoves, sculpted ceilings, plus Swedish fine art and artifacts. (Daily exc Mon; closed hols) 2600 Park Ave S. Phone 612/871-4907. ¢¢

Basilica of St Mary. Renaissance architecture patterned after Basilica of St John Lateran in Rome. (Daily) Hennepin Ave & 16th St.

Eloise Butler Wildflower Garden and Bird Sanctuary. Horseshoe-shaped glen contains natural bog, swamp; habitat for prairie and woodland flowers and birds. Guided tours; phone for schedule. (Apr-Oct, daily) Wirth Park, S of MN 55 (Olson Memorial Hwy) on Theodore Wirth Pkwy. Phone 612/348-5702 or 612/348-4448. **Free.**

Fort Snelling State Park. (See ST PAUL)

Guthrie Theater. Produces classic plays in repertory. (June-Feb, nightly exc Mon; matinees Wed, Sat & Sun) Vineland Pl, 1 blk S of jct I-94 & I-394. Phone 612/377-2224.

Hennepin History Museum. Permanent and temporary exhibits on the history of Minneapolis and Hennepin County. Includes collection of textiles, costumes, toys, and material unique to central Minnesota. Research library & archive. (Daily exc Mon; closed hols) 2303 3rd Ave S. Phone 612/870-1329. ¢

Hubert H. Humphrey Metrodome. Sports stadium. Home of Minnesota Twins (baseball), Vikings (football) and University of Minnesota football. (Mon-Fri & special events) 900 S 5th St. For tour information phone 612/332-0386. Tours ¢¢

Lyndale Park. Garden displays of roses, bulbs, other annuals and perennials; exotic and native trees; rock garden; 2 decorative fountains; bird sanctuary. Apr-Sept is best time to visit. (Daily) Off E Lake Harriet Pkwy & Roseway Rd, on NE shore of Lake Harriet. **Free.**

Minneapolis City Hall (1891). Father of Waters statue in rotunda, carved of largest single block of marble produced from quarries of Carrara, Italy. Self-guided tours. (Mon-Fri; closed hols) 5th St & 3rd Ave S. Phone 612/673-2491. **Free.**

Minneapolis College of Art and Design (1886). (650 students) 4-yr college of fine arts, media arts & design. MCAD Gallery (daily; closed hols). 2501 Stevens Ave S. Gallery **Free.**

Minneapolis Grain Exchange. Visit cash grain market and futures market. Tours (Tues-Thurs). Visitors' balcony; res required (mornings; closed hols). 400 S 4th St. Phone 612/338-6212. **Free.**

Minneapolis Institute of Arts. Masterpieces from every age and culture. A collection of more than 80,000 objects covering American and European painting, sculpture, decorative arts; period rms, prints and drawings, textiles, photography; American, African, Oceanic, ancient and Oriental objects. Lectures, classes, films (fee), special events (fee), monthly expertise clinic; restaurants. (Tues-Sat, also Sun afternoons; closed July 4, Thanksgiving, Dec 25) 2400 3rd Ave S. Phone 612/870-3131. **Free.**

Minneapolis Planetarium. More than 2,000 stars, the visible planets, the sun, moon and a multitude of other celestial phenomena are projected onto the 40-ft dome of the planetarium; astronomically-oriented multi-media presentations. Laser light show (evenings). (Closed major hols) 300 Nicollet Mall, at Public Library. Phone 612/372-6644 for schedule of shows. ¢¢

Minnehaha Park. Minnehaha Falls, immortalized as the "laughing water" of Longfellow's epic poem *Song of Hiawatha*; statue of Hiawatha and Minnehaha; picnicking; Stevens House, first frame house built west of the Mississippi. Park (May-mid-Oct, daily). Minnehaha Pkwy & Hiawatha Ave S, along the Mississippi. Phone 612/661-4806 or 612/661-8942. **Free.**

Minnesota Transportation Museum. Display museum and restoration shop; 2-mi rides in early 1900s electric streetcars along reconstructed Como-Harriet line (Memorial Day wkend-Labor Day, daily; after Labor Day-Oct, wkends). W 42nd St & Queen Ave S. Phone 612/228-0263. Streetcar ¢

⭐ **Nicollet Mall.** The world-famous shopping promenade with a variety of shops, restaurants, museums, art galleries; also entertainment ranging from an art show to symphony orchestra performances (see SEASONAL EVENTS). No traffic is allowed on this avenue except for buses and cabs. Beautifully designed with spacious walkways, fountains, shade trees, flowers and a skyway system, it is certainly worth a visit. Downtown. Also here is

IDS Tower. 775 ft, 57 stories; one of the tallest buildings between Chicago and the West Coast. 80 S 8th St.

Professional sports.

American League baseball (Minnesota Twins). Hubert H. Humphrey Metrodome, 501 Chicago Ave S. Phone 612/375-1366.

NBA (Minnesota Timberwolves). Target Center, 600 First Ave N. Phone 612/673-1600.

NFL (Minnesota Vikings). Hubert H. Humphrey Metrodome, 501 Chicago Ave S. Phone 612/828-6500.

Queen of the Lakes **Cruise.** Excursions (30-min) on stern-wheeler replica. (Memorial Day-Labor Day, daily; leaves every 45 min; open hols) Departs from Lake Harriet. Phone 612/348-4825 for schedule. ¢¢

Skiing.

Buck Hill. Quad, 3 double chairlifts, J-bar, 3 rope tows; snowmaking; patrol, school, rentals; restaurant, bar, cafeteria. (Thanksgiving-Mar, daily) 15400 Buck Hill Rd, 14 mi S on I-35W or I-35E, in Burnsville. Phone 612/435-7174. ¢¢¢¢¢

Hyland Hills. 3 triple chairlifts, 4 tows; patrol, school, rentals; snowmaking; cafeteria, snack bar; nursery. Longest run 2,000 ft; vertical drop 175 ft. (Thanksgiving-mid-Mar, daily; closed Dec 25) Cross-country trails. Chalet Rd, 2 mi SW off I-494. Phone 612/835-4250, 835-4604 (recording). ¢¢¢¢¢

St Anthony Falls. Head of the navigable Mississippi, site of village of St Anthony. A public vantage point at the upper locks and dam provides a view of the falls and of the operation of the locks. Also includes a renovated warehouse with shops & restaurants. Main St SE & Central Ave.

Tours.

River City Trolley. A 40-min loop traverses the core of downtown, passing through the Mississippi Mile, St Anthony Falls and the Warehouse District. On-board narration; runs approx every 20 mins. (Daily, also Fri & Sat evenings) Phone 612/204-0000. ¢

Gray Line bus tours. Tours of the Twin Cities area (summer). Contact 835 Decatur Ave N, 55427; 612/591-0999.

MetroConnections. Stops include Minnehaha Falls, Mall of America and Minnesota History Center. (June-Aug, daily; Sept-Oct, Fri-Sun) Phone 612/333-8687 or 800/747-8687. ¢¢¢¢

University of Minnesota-Twin Cities (1851). (39,315 students) One of the largest single campuses in US. Several art galleries & museums on campus. Tours. On E & W banks of Mississippi, University Ave SE. Phone 612/626-8687. On campus are

Frederick R. Weisman Art Museum. Striking exterior is oddly-shaped stainless steel designed by Frank Gehry. Inside are collections of early 20th-century and contemporary American art, Asian ceramics and Native American Mimbres pottery. Special exhibits. Group tours (by appt, phone 612/625-9656 3 wks in advance). Museum store. (Daily exc Mon; closed hols) 333 East River Rd. Phone 612/625-9494. **Free.**

Bell Museum of Natural History. Dioramas show Minnesota birds and mammals in natural settings; special traveling exhibits; exhibits on art, photography and natural history research change frequently. Touch and See Room encourages hands-on exploration and comparison of natural objects. (Daily exc Mon; closed Thanksgiving, Dec 25) Free admission Thurs. 17th & University Ave SE. For information on tours, family programs and field trips phone 612/624-7083. ¢¢

Walker Art Center. Permanent collection of 20th-century painting, sculpture, prints and photographs; also changing exhibits, performances, concerts, films, lectures. (Daily exc Mon) Vineland Pl. Phone 612/375-7577. ¢¢   Opp is

Minneapolis Sculpture Garden. 10-acre urban garden featuring more than 40 sculptures by leading American and international artists; glass conservatory. (Daily) **Free.**

Annual Event

Minneapolis Aquatennial. Parades, aquatic events, sports events, entertainment. Phone 612/377-4621. Mid-July.

Seasonal Events

Showboat. On Univ of Minnesota campus, on Mississippi River. During the 1800s, melodramas, comedies and light opera were presented on riverboats; University Theater productions preserve this tradition aboard an authentic, air-conditioned stern-wheeler moored on the river. Daily exc Mon. Phone 612/625-4001 for schedule and ticket information. July-Aug.

Sommerfest. Orchestra Hall, 1111 Nicollet Mall. Summer concert series of Minnesota Orchestra (see) with Viennese flavor; food booths. Phone 612/371-5656. July-Aug.

Minnesota Orchestra. Orchestra Hall, 1111 Nicollet Mall. Box office phone 612/371-5656. Mid-Sept-June.

University Theatre. 120 Rarig Center, 330 21st Ave S, on Univ of Minnesota campus. Student-professional productions of musicals, comedies & dramas in 4-theatre complex. Phone 612/625-4001. Early Oct-late May.

Additional Visitor Information

For further information contact the Greater Minneapolis Convention & Visitors Association, 4000 Multifoods Tower, 33 S 6th St, 55402, phone 612/661-4700 or 800/445-7412. The Minneapolis Park and Recreation Board, 310 4th Ave S, 55415, phone 612/661-4800, provides city park information.

City Neighborhoods

Many of the restaurants, unrated dining establishments and some lodgings listed under Minneapolis include neighborhoods as well as exact street addresses. Geographic descriptions of Downtown and Nicollet Ave Mall Area are given, followed by a table of restaurants arranged by neighborhood.

Downtown: South of 3rd St and the Mississippi River, west of I-35W, north of 16th St and east of US 12 and Spruce Place. **North of Downtown:** North of Mississippi River. **South of Downtown:** South of 16th St.

Nicollet Ave Mall Area: Downtown area from 16th St, along Nicollet Ave to Washington Ave.

MINNEAPOLIS RESTAURANTS BY NEIGHBORHOOD AREAS
(For full description, see alphabetical listings under Restaurants)

DOWNTOWN
510. 510 Groveland Ave
Backstage at Bravo. 900 Hennepin Ave
Buca Little Italy. 1204 Harmon Place
Cafe Brenda. 300 First Ave N
Cafe Un Deux Trois. 114 S Ninth St
Chez Bananas. 129 N Fourth St
D'Amico Cucina. 100 N Sixth St
Gardens of Salonica. 19 5th St NE
J.D. Hoyt's. 301 Washington Ave N
Linguini & Bob. 100 N Sixth St
Loring Cafe. 1624 Harmon Place
Meadows (Radisson Metrodome Hotel). 615 Washington Ave SE
Murray's. 26 S Sixth St
New French Cafe & Bar. 128 N Fourth St
Origami. 30 N First St
Palomino. 825 Hennepin Ave
Pickled Parrot. 26 N Fifth St
Ruth's Chris Steak House. 920 Second Ave S
Sawatdee. 607 Washington Ave S
Shuang Cheng. 1320 SE Fourth St
Song Thanh. 418 13th Ave SE
Table of Contents. 1310 Hennepin Ave
Whitney Grille (Whitney Hotel). 150 Portland Ave

NORTH OF DOWNTOWN
Emily's Lebanese Deli. 641 University Ave NE
Giorgio. 2451 Hennepin Ave
Jax Cafe. 1928 University Ave NE
Kikugawa. 43 SE Main St
Nye's Polonnaise. 112 E Hennepin Ave
Pracna on Main. 117 Main St
Sidney's Pizza Cafe. 2120 Hennepin Ave
Sophia. 65 SE Main St

SOUTH OF DOWNTOWN
Black Forest Inn. 1 E 26th St
Campiello. 1320 W Lake St
Caravelle. 2529 Nicollet Ave S
Christos. 2632 Nicollet Ave S
Figlio. 3001 Hennepin Ave S
It's Greek to Me. 626 W Lake St

Lowry's. 1934 Hennepin Ave S
Lucia's. 1432 W 31st St
Mud Pie. 2549 Lyndale Ave S
New French Bistrot. 1300 Lagoon Ave

NICOLLET AVE MALL AREA
1313 Nicollet (Regal Minneapolis Hotel). 1313 Nicollet Mall
Goodfellow's. 40 S 7th St
Ichiban Japanese Steak House. 1333 Nicollet Mall Ave
Jerusalem's. 1518 Nicollet Ave
The King & I. 1034 Nicollet Ave
Manny's (Hyatt Regency Hotel). 1300 Nicollet Mall
Market Bar-B-Que. 1414 Nicollet Ave S
Morton's of Chicago. 555 Nicollet Mall
Ping's. 1401 Nicollet Ave S
Pronto (Hyatt Regency Hotel). 1300 Nicollet Mall

Note: When a listing is located in a town that does not have its own city heading, it will appear under the city nearest to its location. In these cases, the address and town appear in parenthesis immediately following the name of the establishment.

Motels

★ **AMERICINN OF ROGERS.** *(Jct I-94 & MN 101, Rogers 55374)* 612/428-4346; res: 800/634-3444. 35 rms, 2 story. S $39.90-$48.90; D $46.90-$57.90; each addl $5; whirlpool rms $89.90-$109.90; under 12 free. Crib free. Pet accepted. TV; cable (premium), VCR. Complimentary continental bkfst. Restaurant adj open 24 hrs. Ck-out 11 am. Business servs avail. Cr cds: A, C, D, DS, MC, V.

★ **AQUA CITY.** *5739 Lyndale Ave S (55419), south of downtown.* 612/861-6061; res: 800/861-6061. 37 rms, 1-2 story, 8 kit. units. S $35-$42; D $45-$50; each addl $5; under 5 free. Crib $5. TV; cable (premium). Complimentary coffee. Restaurant nearby. Ck-out 11 am. X-country ski ½ mi. Game rm. Cr cds: A, C, D, DS, MC, V.

★★ **BEST WESTERN KELLY INN.** *(2705 Annapolis, Plymouth 55441)* 612/553-1600; FAX 612/553-9108. 150 rms, 4 story. S $69-$200; D $75-$200; each addl $8; suites $91-$200; under 13 free. Crib $8. TV; cable. Indoor pool; whirlpool. Complimentary coffee in rms. Restaurant 7 am-midnight. Rm serv. Bar 11-1 am. Ck-out 11 am. Meeting rms. Business servs avail. Downhill ski 20 mi; x-country ski 1 mi. Exercise equipt; bicycles, treadmill, sauna. Some refrigerators. Some balconies. Cr cds: A, C, D, DS, MC, V.

✔★ **BUDGETEL INN.** *(6415 James Circle, Brooklyn Center 55430)* 18 mi N on I-694, change at Shingle Creek Pkwy. 612/561-8400; FAX 612/560-3189. 99 rms, 3 story. S $43.95-$66.95; D $51.95-$74.95. Crib free. TV; cable (premium). Complimentary continental bkfst. Complimentary coffee in rms. Restaurant nearby. Ck-out noon. Meeting rm. Business servs avail. In-rm modem link. Valet serv. X-country ski ½ mi. Cr cds: A, C, D, DS, MC, V.

★★ **CHANHASSEN INN.** *(531 W 79th St, Chanhassen 55317)* 3 mi S on MN 101. 612/934-7373; res: 800/242-6466. 74 rms, 2 story. S $45-$50; D $51-$55; each addl $4; under 17 free. Crib free. TV; cable. Complimentary continental bkfst. Ck-out noon. Business servs avail. In-rm modem link. X-country ski 1 mi. Cr cds: A, C, D, DS, MC, V.

★★ **COMFORT INN.** *(1600 James Circle N, Brooklyn Center 55430)* N on US 52. 612/560-7464. 60 rms, 3 story. June-Sept: S $74.95-$79.95; D $79.95-$84.95; each addl $5; under 19 free; lower rates rest of yr. TV; cable (premium). Complimentary continental bkfst. Restaurant adj

6 am-11 pm. Ck-out 11 am. Meeting rms. Business servs avail. Game rm. Some refrigerators, microwaves. Cr cds: A, C, D, DS, MC, V.

★ **DAYS INN UNIVERSITY.** *2407 University Ave SE (55414), east of downtown.* 612/623-3999; FAX 612/331-2152. 131 rms, 6 story. S $73-$99; D $79-$99; each addl $10; under 18 free. Crib free. TV; cable. Complimentary continental bkfst. Restaurant nearby. Ck-out 11 am. Coin lndry. Meeting rms. Business servs avail. In-rm modem link. Downhill ski 10 mi; x-country ski 1 mi. Some refrigerators. Cr cds: A, C, D, DS, JCB, MC, V.

✔★ **ECONO LODGE.** *2500 University Ave SE (55414), east of downtown.* 612/331-6000; FAX 612/331-6821. 80 rms, 2 story. May-Sept: S $55-$65; D $61-$71; each addl $6; under 18 free; lower rates rest of yr. Crib free. TV; cable (premium). Complimentary coffee in rms. Restaurant nearby. Ck-out 11 am. Business servs avail. In-rm modem link. Pool. Cr cds: A, C, D, DS, JCB, MC, V.

★★ **HAMPTON INN.** *10420 Wayzata Blvd (55343), west of downtown.* 612/541-1094; FAX 612/541-1905. 127 rms, 4 story. S, D $74-$84; under 18 free. Crib free. TV; cable (premium). Complimentary continental bkfst. Restaurant nearby. Ck-out noon. Meeting rms. Business servs avail. In-rm modem link. Downhill ski 25 mi; x-country ski 1 mi. Cr cds: A, C, D, DS, MC, V.

✔★ **METRO INN.** *5637 Lyndale Ave S (55419), south of downtown.* 612/861-6011; FAX 612/869-1041. 35 rms. Apr-Oct: S $35-$44; D $42-$52; each addl $6; lower rates rest of yr. Crib $4-$5. Pet accepted, some restrictions; $3. TV; cable (premium). Ck-out 11 am. X-country ski ½ mi. Cr cds: A, C, D, DS, MC, V.

✔★★ **MOUNDS VIEW INN.** *(2149 Program Ave, Mounds View 55112)* Jct I-35W & US 10. 612/786-9151; FAX 612/786-2845; res: 800/777-7863. 70 rms, 2 story. S $35.95-$49.95; D $43.95-$61.95; each addl $5; under 15 free; higher rates special events. Crib $3. TV; cable (premium), VCR (movies). Complimentary continental bkfst. Restaurant adj open 24 hrs. Bar. Ck-out 11 am. Coin lndry. Meeting rms. Business servs avail. Sundries. X-country ski 3 mi. Cr cds: A, C, D, DS, MC, V.

★★ **REGENCY PLAZA-TARGET CENTER.** *41 N 10th St (55403), 3 blks W of Nicollet Mall, downtown.* 612/339-9311; FAX 612/339-4765. 192 rms, 3 story. S, D $59-$109; each addl $6; suites $85-$110; under 18 free; wknd rates. Crib free. TV; cable, VCR avail. Indoor pool; whirlpool, poolside serv. Restaurant 6:30 am-2 pm, 4-11 pm; Sat, Sun from 7:30 am. Rm serv. Bar 4 pm-1 am; entertainment exc Sun. Ck-out noon. Coin lndry. Meeting rms. Business servs avail. In-rm modem link. Bellhops. Sundries. X-country ski 1 mi. Cr cds: A, C, D, DS, MC, V.

✔★ **SUPER 8.** *(6445 James Circle, Brooklyn Center 55430)* jct I-94, I-694 & Shingle Creek Pkwy interchange exit 34. 612/566-9810; FAX 612/566-8680. 102 rms, 2 story. S $51.98; D $56.98-$61.98; each addl $5; under 12 free. Crib free. TV; cable (premium). Complimentary continental bkfst. Restaurant adj. Ck-out 11 am. Business servs avail. Cr cds: A, C, D, DS, MC, V.

Motor Hotels

★★ **BEST WESTERN KELLY INN.** *(5201 Central Ave NE, Fridley 55421)* 612/571-9440; FAX 612/571-1720. 95 rms, 2 story. S, D $64-$72; each addl $8; suites $105-$185; under 18 free. Crib free. Pet accepted. TV; cable (premium). Indoor pool; whirlpool. Restaurant 6 am-9 pm. Rm serv. Ck-out 11 am. Meeting rms. Business servs avail. Exercise equipt; weight machine, bicycles, sauna. Game rm. Some refrigerators. Cr cds: A, D, DS, MC, V.

🄳 ⚲ ≋ 🕺 ⅍ 🔥 SC

✔★★★ **BEST WESTERN NORMANDY INN.** *405 S Eighth St (55404), downtown.* 612/370-1400; FAX 612/370-0351. 159 rms, 4 story. S $74.50-$104.50; D $82-$108.50; each addl $7.50; under 18 free. Crib free. TV; cable (premium). Indoor pool; whirlpool, poolside serv. Complimentary continental bkfst. Bar 4:30-11 pm. Ck-out noon. Meeting rms. Business servs avail. In-rm modem link. Valet serv. Sundries. Exercise equipt; bicycles, treadmill, sauna. Cr cds: A, C, D, DS, ER, MC, V.

🄳 ≋ 🕺 ⅍ 🔥 SC

★★ **RAMADA INN.** *2540 N Cleveland Ave (55113).* 612/636-4567; FAX 612/636-7110. 256 rms, 4 story. June-Labor Day: S, D $89; each addl $10; under 19 free; lower rates rest of yr. Crib free. TV; cable. Indoor pool; wading pool, whirlpool. Complimentary coffee in rms. Restaurant 6:30 am-10 pm. Rm serv. Bar 3 pm-1 am. Ck-out noon. Meeting rms. Business servs avail. Valet serv. Coin lndry. Exercise equipt; bicycle, treadmill, sauna. Game rm. Some refrigerators. Cr cds: A, C, D, DS, ER, JCB, MC, V.

🄳 ≋ 🕺 ⅍ 🔥 SC

★★ **RAMADA PLAZA HOTEL.** *(12201 Ridgedale Dr, Minnetonka 55305) W on Wayzata Blvd, behind Ridgedale Shopping Center.* 612/593-0000; FAX 612/544-2090. 222 rms, 4 story. S $119; D $129; each addl $10; suites $150; under 18 free; wknd rates. Crib free. TV; cable (premium). Indoor pool; poolside serv. Coffee in rms. Restaurant 6:30 am-10 pm. Rm serv 6:30-10 pm. Bar 4 pm-1 am. Ck-out noon. Meeting rms. Business servs avail. In-rm modem link. Gift shop. X-country ski 2 mi. Exercise equipt; bicycles, stair machines. Some private patios, balconies. Cr cds: A, C, D, DS, ER, JCB, MC, V.

🄳 ⚲ ≋ 🕺 ⅍ 🔥 SC

Hotels

★★★ **DOUBLETREE.** *1101 LaSalle Ave (55403), downtown.* 612/332-6800; FAX 612/332-8246. 230 suites, 12 story. S $175; each addl $10; under 17 free; wknd rates. Covered parking $9. Crib free. TV; cable (premium), VCR avail. Restaurant 6:30 am-midnight. Bar 11-1 am. Ck-out 11 am. Meeting rms. Business servs avail. In-rm modem link. Exercise equipt; weights, bicycles, sauna. X-country ski 1 mi. Refrigerators, microwaves. Cr cds: A, C, D, DS, JCB, MC, V.

🄳 ⚲ 🕺 ⅍ 🔥 SC

★★★ **EMBASSY SUITES-DOWNTOWN.** *425 S Seventh St (55415), downtown.* 612/333-3111; FAX 612/333-7984. 217 suites, 6 story. S $155-$165; D $165-$185; each addl $10; under 13 free; wknd rates. Crib free. TV; cable (premium). Indoor pool; whirlpool. Complimentary full bkfst. Restaurant 11 am-2:30 pm, 5-10 pm; Fri, Sat 5-11 pm. Bar 11-1 am. Ck-out noon. Meeting rms. Business servs avail. In-rm modem link. X-country ski 1 mi. Exercise equipt; weight machine, bicycles, sauna, steam rm. Refrigerators, microwaves. Cr cds: A, C, D, DS, ER, JCB, MC, V.

🄳 ⚲ ≋ 🕺 ⅍ 🔥 SC

★★★ **HILTON & TOWERS.** *1001 Marquette Ave S (55403).* 612/376-1000; FAX 612/397-4875. 814 rms, 25 story. S $140-$215; D $160-$235; each addl $20; suites $700-$1,000; under 18 free. Crib avail. Valet parking $15; garage $9.75. TV; cable (premium), VCR avail. Heated pool; whirlpool, poolside serv. Restaurant 6:30 am-11 pm. Bar 11-1 am. Ck-out noon. Convention facilities. Business servs avail. In-rm modem link. Concierge. Sundries. Shopping arcade. X-country ski 1 mi. Exercise equipt; bicycle, treadmill, sauna. Some refrigerators. Cr cds: A, C, D, DS, ER, JCB, MC, V.

🄳 ⚲ ≋ 🕺 ⅍ 🔥

★★★ **HOLIDAY INN CROWNE PLAZA NORTHSTAR.** *618 Second Ave S (55402), above 6-story Northstar Parking Ramp, downtown.* 612/338-2288; FAX 612/338-2288, ext. 318. 226 rms, 17 story. June-Sept: S $159.50-$174.50; each addl $15; suites $250-$500; under 17 free;

wknd rates; lower rates rest of yr. Crib free. Garage parking $11.50. TV; cable, VCR avail (movies). Restaurants 6:30 am-11:30 pm. Bar 11-1 am. Ck-out 1 pm. Meeting rms. Business servs avail. In-rm modem link. Barber, beauty shop. X-country ski 1 mi. Exercise equipt; bicycles, rowers. Luxury level. Cr cds: A, C, D, DS, MC, V.

🄳 ⚲ 🕺 ⅍ 🔥 SC

✔★★★ **HOLIDAY INN-METRODOME.** *1500 Washington Ave S (55454), south of downtown.* 612/333-4646; FAX 612/333-7910. 265 rms, 14 story. S, D $134.50; each addl $10; suites $149.50; under 18 free. Crib free. Garage $8. TV; cable (premium), VCR avail. Indoor pool. Coffee in rms. Restaurant 6:30 am-11 pm. Bar 11-1 am; pianist. Ck-out noon. Meeting rms. Business servs avail. In-rm modem link. Gift shop. Airport transportation. Exercise equipt; weights, bicycles. Cr cds: A, C, D, DS, JCB, MC, V.

🄳 ≋ 🕺 ⅍ 🔥 SC

★★★ **HYATT REGENCY.** *1300 Nicollet Mall (55403), in Nicollet Ave Mall Area.* 612/370-1234; FAX 612/370-1463. 533 rms, 21 suites, 24 story. S $199; D $224; each addl $25; suites $290-$800; under 18 free. Crib free. Parking $9.75. TV; VCR avail (movies). Indoor pool. Restaurants 6:30-1 am; Sun 7 am-11 pm (also see MANNY'S and PRONTO). Bar 11-1 am. Ck-out noon. Convention facilities. Business servs avail. In-rm modem link. Concierge. Shopping arcade. Barber, beauty shop. Airport transportation. Indoor tennis privileges. X-country ski 1 mi. Health club privileges. Luxury level. Cr cds: A, C, D, DS, ER, JCB, MC, V.

🄳 ⚲ 🏃 ≋ ⅍ 🔥 SC

★★★ **THE MARQUETTE.** *710 Marquette Ave (55402), in IDS Tower, downtown.* 612/333-4545; res: 800/328-4782; FAX 612/376-7419. 278 rms, 19 story. S $228; D $248; each addl $15; suites $349-$810; family rates; wknd packages. Crib free. Garage parking $12; wknds $6. TV; cable (premium), VCR avail. Restaurant 6:30 am-10:30 pm. Bar 11:30-1 am. Ck-out noon. Convention facilities. Business center. In-rm modem link. X-country ski 1 mi. Exercise equipt; weight machines, treadmills. Steam bath in suites. Luxury level. Cr cds: A, C, D, DS, ER, JCB, MC, V.

🄳 ⚲ 🕺 ⅍ ≋ 🏃

★★★ **MARRIOTT-CITY CENTER.** *30 S Seventh St (55402), downtown.* 612/349-4000; FAX 612/332-7165. 583 rms, 31 story. S $169; D $189; each addl $10; suites $250-$650; under 18 free; wknd rates. Crib free. Valet parking $17. TV; cable (premium), VCR avail (movies). Restaurants 6:30 am-11 pm. Bar 11-1 am. Ck-out noon. Convention facilities. Business center. In-rm modem link. Shopping arcade. X-country ski 1 mi. Exercise rm; instructor, weights, treadmills, sauna. Massage. Health club privileges. Whirlpool. Some bathrm phones. Luxury level. Cr cds: A, C, D, DS, ER, JCB, MC, V.

🄳 ⚲ 🕺 ⅍ 🔥 SC 🏃

★★★ **NORTHLAND INN.** *(7025 Northland Dr, Brooklyn Park 55428)* 612/536-8300; FAX 612/533-6607; res: 800/441-6422. 231 rms, 6 story. S, D $125-$195; under 12 free. Crib free. TV; cable (premium), VCR avail. Indoor pool; whirlpool, poolside serv. Restaurant 6:30 am-10 pm. Bar to 1 am. Ck-out noon. Meeting rms. Business servs avail. In-rm modem link. Concierge. Sundries. Gift shop. Valet serv. Downhill ski 20 mi; x-country 1 mi. Exercise equipt; weight machine, bicycles. Game rm. Refrigerators avail. Cr cds: A, C, D, DS, JCB, MC, V.

🄳 ⚲ ≋ 🕺 ⅍ 🔥

★★★ **RADISSON HOTEL & CONFERENCE CENTER.** *(3131 Campus Dr, Plymouth 55441) jct I-494, MN 55, on Northwest Business Campus.* 612/559-6600; FAX 612/559-1053. 243 rms, 6 story. S, D $124; each addl $10; suites $159-$249; under 18 free. Crib free. TV; cable (premium), VCR avail. Indoor pool; whirlpool, poolside serv. Restaurant 6:30 am-10 pm. Bar 11-1 am. Ck-out noon. Meeting rms. Business servs avail. In-rm modem link. Gift shop. Lighted tennis. Downhill ski 20 mi; x-country ski 2 mi. Exercise rm; instructor, weight machines, bicycles, sauna. Racquetball. Rec rm. Refrigerators. On wooded site. Cr cds: A, C, D, DS, ER, JCB, MC, V.

🄳 ⚲ 🏃 ≋ 🕺 🏃 ⅍ 🔥 SC

★ ★ ★ **RADISSON-METRODOME.** *615 Washington Ave SE (55414). 612/379-8888; FAX 612/379-8436.* 304 rms, 8 story. S $102; D $112; each addl $10; suites $135-$325; under 18 free. Crib avail. Pet accepted. Valet parking $9.50; garage $6.50. TV; cable, VCR avail. Pool privileges. Complimentary coffee in rms. Restaurants 6:30 am-10:30 pm (also see MEADOWS). Bar to 1 am. Ck-out noon. Meeting rms. Business servs avail. In-rm modem link. Gift shop. Downhill ski 20 mi; x-country ski 1 mi. Exercise equipt; bicycle, weights. Health club privileges. Some refrigerators. Cr cds: A, C, D, DS, ER, JCB, MC, V.

★ ★ ★ **RADISSON PLAZA.** *35 S Seventh St (55402), downtown. 612/339-4900; FAX 612/337-9766.* 357 rms, 17 story. S, D $178-$258; each addl $10; suites $310-$410; under 18 free. Crib free. Parking $10. TV; cable (premium), VCR avail. Restaurant 6 am-11 pm. Rm serv 24 hrs. Bar 11-1 am; entertainment. Ck-out noon. Meeting rms. Business servs avail. In-rm modem link. Concierge. Shopping arcade. X-country ski 1 mi. Exercise rm; instructor, weights, bicycles, sauna. Whirlpool. Atrium lobby; fountain, marble columns. Luxury level. Cr cds: A, C, D, DS, ER, JCB, MC, V.

★ ★ ★ **REGAL MINNEAPOLIS.** *1313 Nicollet Mall (55403), in Nicollet Ave Mall Area. 612/332-6000; FAX 612/359-2160; res: 800/522-8856.* 325 rms, 14 story. S $175; D $195; suites $190-$250. Crib free. Pet accepted. TV; cable (premium). Indoor pool. Restaurant (see 1313 NICOLLET). Bars 11-1 am. Ck-out noon. Coin lndry. Convention facilities. Business servs avail. In-rm modem link. Gift shop. Airport transportation avail. X-country ski 1 mi. Exercise equipt; weight machine, bicycle, sauna. Cr cds: A, C, D, DS, ER, JCB, MC, V.

★ ★ ★ **SHERATON-METRODOME.** *1330 Industrial Blvd (55413), north of downtown. 612/331-1900; FAX 612/331-6827.* 252 rms, 8 story. S $105-$145; D, studio rms $115-$195; each addl $10; suites $150-$280; wkend packages. Crib free. TV; cable (premium). Indoor pool; whirlpool, poolside serv. Coffee in rms. Restaurant 6:30 am-10:30 pm; Sat, Sun 7:30-11 pm. Bar 11-1 am; entertainment exc Sun. Ck-out 11 am. Meeting rms. Business servs avail. In-rm modem link. Free airport transportation. X-country ski 1 mi. Exercise equipt; bicycles, treadmill, sauna. Luxury level. Cr cds: A, C, D, DS, ER, JCB, MC, V.

★ ★ ★ **SHERATON-PARK PLACE.** *1500 Park Place Blvd (55416), north of downtown. 612/542-8600; FAX 612/542-8068.* 298 rms, 15 story. S, D $99-$129; each addl $20; suites $129-$169; under 18 free; wkend rates. Crib free. TV; cable (premium), VCR avail. Indoor pool; whirlpool, poolside serv. Restaurant 6:30 am-midnight. Rm serv 24 hrs. Bar 11-1 am. Ck-out noon. Convention facilities. Business servs avail. In-rm modem link. Airport transportation. X-country ski 2 mi. Exercise equipt; weights, bicycles, sauna. Game rm. Cr cds: A, C, D, DS, ER, JCB, MC, V.

★ ★ ★ **WHITNEY.** *150 Portland Ave (55401), downtown. 612/339-9300; FAX 612/339-1333; res: 800/248-1879.* 97 rms, 8 story, 40 suites. S, D $160-$170; suites 195-$1,600; under 10 free. Crib free. Parking $6. TV; cable (premium), VCR avail. Restaurant (see WHITNEY GRILLE). Rm serv 24 hrs. Bar 11:30-1 am; pianist. Ck-out noon. Meeting rms. Business servs avail. In-rm modem link. Concierge. Airport transportation. Bathrm phones, refrigerators. Bi-level suites with honor bar. Elegantly renovated hotel located on the banks of the Mississippi River; outdoor plaza with fountain. Cr cds: A, C, D, DS, ER, JCB, MC, V.

Inns

★ ★ ★ **INN ON THE FARM.** *(6150 Summit Dr N, Brooklyn Center 55430) 612/569-6330; res: 800/428-8382.* 10 rms, 2 story. S, D $100-$130. TV. Complimentary full bkfst; afternoon refreshments. Restaurant

nearby. Ck-out 11 am, ck-in 4 pm. Business servs avail. X-country ski ½ mi. Built in the 1880s; furnished with antiques. Cr cds: A, C, D, DS, MC, V.

★ ★ **NICOLLET ISLAND INN.** *95 Merriam St (55401), east of downtown. 612/331-1800; FAX 612/331-6528.* 24 rms, 2 story. S, D $115-$254; under 12 free. TV; cable (premium). Complimentary continental bkfst. Restaurant 6 am-10 pm. Rm serv. Ck-out 1 pm, ck-in 3 pm. Business servs avail. In-rm modem link. Downhill ski 20 mi; x-country ski 10 mi. Built in 1893. Cr cds: A, C, D, DS, MC, V.

Restaurants

★ ★ **1313 NICOLLET.** *(See Regal Minneapolis Hotel) 612/332-6000.* Hrs: 6:30 am-2 pm, 5-10 pm. Res accepted. Bar to 1 am. Semi-a la carte: bkfst $6.25-$7.50, lunch $6.25-$8.50, dinner $7.50-$16.95. Child's meals. Specializes in pasta, steak. Contemporary decor. Cr cds: A, C, D, DS, ER, JCB, MC, V.

★ ★ ★ **510.** *510 Groveland Ave, downtown. 612/874-6440.* Hrs: 5:30-10 pm. Closed Sun. Res accepted. French, Amer menu. Wine cellar. Semi-a la carte: dinner $12-$22. Complete meals: dinner $19. Specializes in rack of lamb, seafood. Own baking. Cr cds: A, C, D, DS, MC, V.

★ ★ **AUGUST MOON.** *(5340 Watzata Blvd, Golden Valley) Approx 3 mi W on MN 55. 612/544-7017.* Hrs: 11 am-9 pm; Fri to 10 pm; Sat 4-10 pm; Sun 4-9 pm. Closed Dec 25. New Asian menu. Wine, beer. Semi-a la carte: lunch $5-$11.95, dinner $8-$15. Specialties: Cal-Asian crab cakes, tandoori chicken. Parking. Oriental artwork. Cr cds: A, C, D, MC, V.

★ ★ **BACKSTAGE AT BRAVO.** *900 Hennepin Ave (55403), downtown. 612/338-0062.* Hrs: 11:30 am-2:30 pm, 5-11:30 pm; Fri to 12:30 am; Sat to midnight. Closed Thanksgiving, Dec 24, 25. Res accepted. Continental menu. Bar. Semi-a la carte: lunch $5.95-$18.50, dinner $12.50-$25. Specializes in fresh oysters, steak. Own pasta. Valet parking (dinner). Contemporary decor with rooftop dining. Cr cds: A, C, D, DS, MC, V.

✔ ★ ★ **BLACK FOREST INN.** *1 E 26th St, at Nicollet, south of downtown. 612/872-0812.* Hrs: 11-1 am; Sun noon-midnight. German menu. Semi-a la carte: lunch $3.50-$8, dinner $5.50-$15. Specialties: sauerbraten, Wienerschnitzel, bratwurst. Outdoor dining. German decor. Family-owned. Cr cds: A, C, D, DS, MC, V.

✔ ★ ★ **BUCA LITTLE ITALY.** *1204 Harmon Place (55403), downtown. 612/638-2225.* Hrs: 5-10 pm; Fri, Sat to 11 pm. Closed Thanksgiving, Dec 24, 25. Italian menu. Bar to midnight. Semi-a la carte: dinner $8.95-$22.95. Specialties: chicken marsala, ravioli with meat sauce. Pictures of Italian celebrities along walls. Cr cds: A, C, D, MC, V.

✔ ★ ★ **CAFE BRENDA.** *300 First Ave N, downtown. 612/342-9230.* Hrs: 11:30 am-2 pm, 5:30-9 pm; Fri to 10 pm; Sat 5:30-10 pm. Closed Sun; most major hols. Res accepted. Vegetarian, seafood menu. Bar. Semi-a la carte: lunch $6-$10, dinner $9-$16. Specializes in fresh broiled rainbow trout, organic chicken enchiladas. Parking (dinner). Totally nonsmoking. Cr cds: A, C, D, MC, V.

★ ★ **CAFE UN DEUX TROIS.** *114 S Ninth St (55402), downtown. 612/673-0686.* Hrs: 11:30 am-10 pm; Fri, Sat to 11 pm. Closed Sun; most major hols. Res accepted. French bistro menu. Bar. Semi-a la carte: lunch $7.95-$17.50, dinner $12.95-$19.50. Specialties: poulet rôti, roast Long Island duck. Own pasta. Free valet parking (dinner). Eclectic, bistro atmosphere with murals, mirrors on walls. Cr cds: A, C, D, MC, V.

★ **CAMPIELLO.** *1320 W Lake St (55408), 5 mi S on Lake St, south of downtown.* 612/825-2222. Hrs: 5-10 pm; Thurs to 10:30 pm; Fri, Sat to 11 pm; Sun 10:30 am-3 pm (brunch), 5-10:30 pm. Closed Dec 25. Res accepted. Italian menu. Bar to midnight. Semi-a la carte: dinner $8.95-$17.95. Sun brunch $8.95-$13.95. Specialties: balsamic-glazed short ribs, wood-oven pizzas. Own pasta. Valet parking. Outdoor dining. Upscale atmosphere with high ceilings, chandeliers. Cr cds: A, C, D, DS, MC, V.

✔★ **CARAVELLE.** *2529 Nicollet Ave S, south of downtown.* 612/871-3226. Hrs: 11 am-9 pm; Sat from noon; Sun noon-7 pm. Closed July 4, Thanksgiving, Dec 25. Res accepted. Chinese menu. Semi-a la carte: lunch, dinner $5.95-$8.95. Buffet: lunch $5.50, dinner $5.95. Specializes in shrimp, scallops. Parking. Outdoor dining. Oriental decor. Cr cds: MC, V.

★ **CHEZ BANANAS.** *129 N Fourth St, downtown.* 612/340-0032. Hrs: 11:30 am-10 pm; Fri to 11 pm; Sat, Sun 5-11 pm. Closed some major hols. Res accepted Sun-Thurs. Caribbean menu. Bar. Semi-a la carte: lunch $4.50-$9, dinner $6.50-$15. Specializes in mustard pepper chicken, Caribbean barbecue. Informal & fun atmosphere; inflatable animals hanging from ceiling, toys at tables. Cr cds: A, MC, V.

✔★ **CHRISTOS.** *2632 Nicollet Ave S, south of downtown.* 612/871-2111. Hrs: 11 am-10 pm; Fri to 10:30 pm; Sat noon-10:30 pm; Sun noon-9 pm. Closed most major hols. Res accepted. Greek menu. Wine, beer. Semi-a la carte: lunch $4.50-$7.50, dinner $7.95-$12.95. Specialties: spanakópita, moussaka, shish kebab. Cr cds: A, C, D, DS, MC, V.

★ ★ ★ **D'AMICO CUCINA.** *100 N Sixth St, downtown.* 612/338-2401. Hrs: 5:30-10 pm; Fri, Sat to 11 pm; Sun 5-9 pm. Closed major hols. Res accepted. Italian menu. Bar. Semi-a la carte: dinner $21-$29.50. Specializes in Modern Italian cuisine. Piano, bass Fri, Sat. Restored warehouse. Cr cds: A, C, D, DS, MC, V.

★ **FIGLIO.** *3001 Hennepin Ave S, Calhoun Square, south of downtown.* 612/822-1688. Hrs: 11:30-1 am; Fri, Sat to 2 am. Res accepted. Italian menu. Bar. Semi-a la carte: lunch, dinner $6.50-$16.95. Specializes in pasta, pizza, sandwiches. Outdoor dining. Art-deco decor; neon lighting. Cr cds: A, C, D, DS, MC, V.

✔★ **GARDENS OF SALONICA.** *19 5th St NE (55413), downtown.* 612/378-0611. Hrs: 11 am-9 pm; Fri, Sat to 10 pm. Closed Sun; Thanksgiving, Dec 25. Greek menu. Bar. Semi-a la carte: lunch, dinner $5-$10. Specializes in boughatsa, lamb dishes. Own pasta. Casual dining; Greek decor. No cr cds accepted.

✔★ ★ **GIORGIO.** *2451 Hennepin Ave (55408), north of downtown.* 612/374-5131. Hrs: 11:30 am-2:30 pm, 5-11 pm; Sun 5-11 pm. Closed Thanksgiving, Dec 24, 25. Res accepted wkdays. Italian menu. Wine, beer. Semi-a la carte: lunch $2.95-$10.95, dinner $2.95-$16.50. Specialties: marinated leg of lamb, calamari steak. Outdoor dining. Italian decor. Cr cds: D, MC, V.

★ ★ ★ **GOODFELLOW'S.** *40 S 7th St, in Nicollet Ave Mall Area.* 612/332-4800. Hrs: 11:30 am-2 pm, 5:30-9 pm; Fri to 10 pm; Sat 5:30-10 pm. Closed Sun; major hols. Res accepted. Bar. Wine list. Semi-a la carte: lunch $6-$13, dinner $20-$31. Specialties: grilled salmon, hickory-grilled Wisconsin veal chop. Beamed ceiling. Cr cds: A, C, D, DS, MC, V.

★ ★ **ICHIBAN JAPANESE STEAK HOUSE.** *1333 Nicollet Mall Ave, in Nicollet Ave Mall Area.* 612/339-0540. Hrs: 4:30-9:30 pm; Fri, Sat to 10 pm. Closed Thanksgiving, Dec 24. Res accepted. Japanese menu.

Bar. Semi-a la carte: dinner $13.95-$29.50. Specializes in sushi, tempura. Tableside cooking. Japanese decor. Cr cds: A, C, D, DS, MC, V.

✔★ **IT'S GREEK TO ME.** *626 W Lake St, south of downtown.* 612/825-9922. Hrs: 11 am-11 pm. Closed major hols. Greek menu. Bar. Semi-a la carte: lunch, dinner $7.75-$13.95. Specialties: lamb kebab, pastitsio. Parking. Cr cds: MC, V.

★ ★ **J.D. HOYT'S.** *301 Washington Ave N, downtown.* 612/338-1560. Hrs: 7-1 am; Sat from 7:30 am; Sun 10 am-midnight; Sun brunch 10 am-2 pm. Closed some major hols. Res accepted. Bar. Semi-a la carte: bkfst $1.99-$7, lunch $7.50-$9.95, dinner $8-$27.95. Sun brunch $9.95. Specializes in pork chops, charcoal-grilled steak. Valet parking. Casual dining; roadhouse atmosphere. Cr cds: A, C, D, DS, MC, V.

★ ★ ★ **JAX CAFE.** *1928 University Ave NE, north of downtown.* 612/789-7297. Hrs: 11 am-10:30 pm; Sun to 9 pm; Sun brunch 10 am-1:30 pm. Closed major hols. Res accepted. Wine list. Semi-a la carte: lunch $6.95-$12.95, dinner $14-$25. Sun brunch $14.50. Specializes in prime rib, seafood, rainbow trout (in season). Pianist Thurs-Sun. Parking. Overlooks trout pond; waterwheel. Fireplace. Family-owned. Cr cds: A, C, D, DS, MC, V.

✔★ **JERUSALEM'S.** *1518 Nicollet Ave (55403), in Nicollet Ave Mall Area.* 612/871-8883. Hrs: 11 am-10 pm; Fri to 11 pm; Sat, Sun noon-10 pm. Closed Thanksgiving, Dec 25. Res accepted. Middle Eastern menu. Bar. Semi-a la carte: lunch $4.25-$8.25, dinner $9.95-$15.95. Specializes in vegetarian combination. Middle Eastern tapestries on walls. Cr cds: D, DS, MC, V.

★ **KIKUGAWA.** *43 SE Main St, Riverplace, north of downtown.* 612/378-3006. Hrs: 11:30 am-2 pm, 5-10 pm; Sat noon-2 pm, 5-11 pm; Sun noon-2:30 pm, 4:30-9:30 pm. Closed Jan 1, Thanksgiving, Dec 25. Res accepted. Japanese menu. Bar. Semi-a la carte: lunch $4.95-$10, dinner $9.50-$26.50. Specialties: sukiyaki, sushi bar. Parking. Modern Japanese decor. Overlooks Mississippi River. Cr cds: A, C, D, DS, JCB, MC, V.

✔★ **THE KING & I.** *1034 Nicollet Ave, in Nicollet Ave Mall Area.* 612/332-6928. Hrs: 11 am-10 pm; Sat from 5 pm. Closed Sun. Res accepted. Thai menu. Wine, beer. Semi-a la carte: lunch, dinner $7.25-$17.95. Specialties: pad Thai, king's spring roll, tom yum goong. Informal dining. Cr cds: A, C, D, DS, MC, V.

★ ★ **LINGUINI & BOB.** *100 N Sixth St, downtown.* 612/332-1600. Hrs: 5-9:30 pm; Fri, Sat to 11 pm. Closed Sun; most major hols. Res accepted. Italian menu. Bar. Semi-a la carte: dinner $8.95-$17.95. Specializes in spicy shrimp, pasta. 2nd floor overlooks Butler Square. Cr cds: A, C, D, MC, V.

★ ★ ★ **LORD FLETCHER'S OF THE LAKE.** *(3746 Sunset Dr, Spring Park) 18 mi W on US 12, 6 mi S on County 15W, then ½ mi N on County 19 to signs, on Lake Minnetonka.* 612/471-8513. Hrs: 11:30 am-2:30 pm, 5-10 pm; Sun 4:30-9:30 pm; Sun brunch 11 am-2 pm. Closed Jan 1, Dec 24 evening-25. Res accepted. English, Amer menu. Bar. Wine list. Semi-a la carte: lunch $6.25-$11.50, dinner $12.95-$22.95. Sun brunch $10.95. Specializes in beef, fish, prime rib. Outdoor dining. Mesquite charcoal grill. Old English decor; fireplaces, wine kegs, antiques. Boat dockage. Cr cds: A, C, D, DS, MC, V.

★ **LOWRY'S.** *1934 Hennepin Ave S, south of downtown.* 612/871-0806. Hrs: 11 am-10 pm; Fri to 11 pm; Sat 10 am-11 pm; Sun 10 am-9 pm; Sun brunch 10 am-2 pm. Closed Thanksgiving, Dec 25. Res accepted. Wine, beer. Semi-a la carte: lunch $5-$9, dinner $7-$18. Sun brunch $6-$12. Specializes in risotto, polenta. Parking. Cr cds: A, MC, V.

⊡

★ ★ **LUCIA'S.** *1432 W 31st St, south of downtown.* 612/825-1572. Hrs: 11:30 am-2:30 pm, 5:30-9:30 pm; Fri, Sat to 10 pm; Sun 10 am-2 pm, 5:30-9 pm; Sat, Sun brunch 10 am-2 pm. Closed Mon; most major hols. Res accepted. Contemporary American menu. Bar. Semi-a la carte: lunch $5.50-$8.95, dinner $8.95-$16.95. Sat, Sun brunch $5.95-$8.95. Specialties: polenta, crostini. Parking. Outdoor dining. Menu changes wkly. Cr cds: MC, V.

★ ★ **MANNY'S.** *(See Hyatt Regency Hotel)* 612/339-9900. Hrs: 5:30-10 pm; Sun to 9 pm. Closed major hols. Res accepted. Bar. A la carte entrees: $20-$40. Specializes in steak, lobster. Contemporary decor. Cr cds: A, C, D, DS, MC, V.

⊡

✔★ ★ **THE MARSH.** *(15000 Minnetonka Blvd, Minnetonka 55345)* 15 mi W on Hwy 5. 612/935-2202. Hrs: 7 am-9 pm; Sat 8 am-8:30 pm; Sun 8 am-5 pm; Sun brunch 11 am-2 pm. Closed Thanksgiving, Dec 25. Res accepted. Bar. Semi-a la carte: lunch $3.50-$8.50, dinner $8-$15. Sun brunch $8.50. Child's meals. Specialties: portobello mushroom melt, fish of the day. Own baking, pasta. Outdoor dining. Adj large fitness facility; menu changes daily, features healthy choices. Cr cds: A, MC, V.

D ♥

★ ★ **MEADOWS.** *(See Radisson Metrodome Hotel)* 612/379-8888. Hrs: 5:30-10 pm. Closed Sun; most major hols. Res accepted. Continental menu. Bar 4 pm-1 am. Semi-a la carte: dinner $18.95-$30.95. Specializes in wild game, walleye. Own pasta. Pianist Fri, Sat. Valet parking. Elegant, semi-formal atmosphere; brass ceiling fans, high-backed chairs. Cr cds: A, C, D, DS, ER, JCB, MC, V.

D ⊡

★ ★ **MORTON'S OF CHICAGO.** *555 Nicollet Mall (55402), in Nicollet Ave Mall Area.* 612/673-9700. Hrs: 11:30 am-2:30 pm, 5:30-11 pm; Sat 5:30-11 pm; Sun 5-10 pm. Closed most major hols. Continental menu. Bar. Semi-a la carte: lunch $9.95-$29.95, dinner $29.95-$59.95. Specializes in steak, lobster. Contemporary decor. Cr cds: A, C, D, JCB, MC, V.

⊡

★ ★ **MURRAY'S.** *26 S Sixth St, downtown.* 612/339-0909. Hrs: 11 am-10:30 pm; Fri to 11 pm; Sat 4-11 pm; Sun 4-10 pm. Res accepted. Bar. Wine list. Semi-a la carte: lunch $5.25-$12.25, dinner $19.50-$32.50. Tea time: 2-3:30 pm Mon-Fri. Specialty: silver butter knife steak for 2. Own baking. Entertainment Thurs-Sat. Family-owned. Cr cds: A, C, D, DS, JCB, MC, V.

D

★ ★ **NEW FRENCH BISTROT.** *1300 Lagoon Ave (55408), south of downtown.* 612/825-2525. Hrs: 11 am-10 pm; Fri, Sat to 11 pm; Sun 9 am-2 pm (brunch). Closed Thanksgiving, Dec 25. Res accepted. French menu. Bar. Semi-a la carte: lunch $6.50-$13, dinner $8-$21. Sun brunch $6.50-$13. Specializes in fresh seafood. Outdoor dining. Modern decor; large windows, high ceiling. Cr cds: A, C, D, MC, V.

D ⊡

★ ★ **NEW FRENCH CAFE & BAR.** *128 N Fourth St, downtown.* 612/338-3790. Hrs: 7 am-2 pm, 5:30-10 pm; Fri to 11 pm; Sat 5:30-11 pm; Sun 5-9 pm; Sat, Sun brunch 8 am-2 pm. Res accepted. Country & contemporary French menu. Bar 11-1 am, Sun from 6 pm. Semi-a la carte: bkfst $3.95-$7.95, lunch $6.95-$11, dinner $16.95-$23. Prix fixe dinner: $18. Sat, Sun brunch $3.50-$10.75. Specializes in duck, seafood. Outdoor dining (bar). Remodeled building (1900); French bistro theme. Cr cds: A, C, D, MC, V.

⊡

✔★ ★ **NYE'S POLONNAISE.** *112 E Hennepin Ave (55414), north of downtown.* 612/379-2021. Hrs: 11 am-11 pm; Sun 5-10 pm. Closed Dec 25. Res accepted. Polish, Amer menu. Bar to 1 am. Semi-a la carte: lunch

$4.95-$7.95, dinner $11.95-$17.95. Specializes in prime rib, pierogi. Polka Thurs-Sat. Casual decor. Cr cds: A, C, D, DS, MC, V.

★ **ORIGAMI.** *30 N First St, downtown.* 612/333-8430. Hrs: 11 am-2 pm, 5-9:30 pm; Fri, Sat to 11 pm, Sun 5-9 pm. Closed most major hols. Japanese menu. Bar. Semi-a la carte: lunch $5-$12, dinner $7-$25. Specialties: sushi bar, sashimi. Parking. Outdoor dining. Cr cds: A, C, D, DS, MC, V.

★ ★ ★ **PALOMINO.** *825 Hennepin Ave (55402), downtown.* 612/339-3800. Hrs: 11:15 am-2:30 pm, 5-10 pm; Fri, Sat to 11 pm; Sun 5-10 pm. Closed most major hols. Res accepted. Mediterranean menu. Bar to 1 am. Semi-a la carte: lunch $4.50-$16.95, dinner $6.95-$25.95. Specialties: spit-roasted garlic chicken, hardwood grilled salmon. Contemporary decor. Cr cds: A, C, D, DS, MC, V.

D

✔★ **PICKLED PARROT.** *26 N Fifth St, downtown.* 612/332-0673. Hrs: 11-1 am; Sun 10 am-10 pm; Sun brunch 10 am-2 pm. Closed Jan 1, Dec 24, 25. Res accepted. Bar. Semi-a la carte: lunch $7.95-$13, dinner $12.95-$22.50. Sun brunch $12.95. Specialties: barbecued ribs, pork sandwich, Southern dishes. Colorful decor. Cr cds: A, C, D, DS, MC, V.

⊡

✔★ ★ **PING'S.** *1401 Nicollet Ave S, in Nicollet Ave Mall Area.* 612/874-9404. Hrs: 11 am-10 pm; Fri to midnight; Sat noon-midnight; Sun noon-9 pm. Closed Easter, Thanksgiving, Dec 24, 25. Res accepted. Chinese menu. Bar. Lunch buffet $6.95. Semi-a la carte: dinner $9-$14. Specialties: Peking duck, Ping's wings, Szechwan trio. Valet parking. Cr cds: A, C, D, DS, MC, V.

⊡

★ **PRACNA ON MAIN.** *117 Main St, under 3rd Ave Bridge on Mississippi River, north of downtown.* 612/379-3200. Hrs: 11:30 am-10 pm. Bar to 1 am. Semi-a la carte: lunch $6-$10, dinner $12-$17.95. Outdoor dining. Warehouse (1890); turn-of-the-century decor. Overlooks Mississippi River. Cr cds: A, C, D, DS, MC, V.

★ ★ **PRONTO.** *(See Hyatt Regency Hotel)* 612/333-4414. Hrs: 11:30 am-2 pm, 5-10 pm; Fri, Sat to 11 pm; Sun 5-9 pm. Closed Thanksgiving, Dec 25. Res accepted. Italian menu. Bar. Semi-a la carte: lunch $10-$15, dinner $20-$30. Specializes in fresh fish, provimi veal. Own pasta. On 2nd floor; large windows overlook Nicollet Ave. Cr cds: A, D, DS, MC, V.

D ⊡

★ ★ ★ **RUTH'S CHRIS STEAK HOUSE.** *920 Second Ave S (55402), downtown.* 612/672-9000. Hrs: 5-10:30 pm. Closed Thanksgiving, Dec 25. Res accepted. Bar. Semi-a la carte: dinner $35-$45. Specializes in steak. Elegant decor. Cr cds: A, C, D, JCB, MC, V.

✔★ ★ **SANTORINI.** *(9920 Wayzata Blvd, St Louis Park 55426)* 612/546-6722. Hrs: 11 am-3 pm, 5-10 pm; Fri, Sat to 11 pm. Sun brunch 10:30 am-2:30 pm. Closed Memorial Day, July 4. Res accepted. Mediterranean menu. Bar to 1 am. Semi-a la carte: lunch $4.50-$9.50, dinner $4.50-$13. Sun brunch $15.95. Specialties: saganaki, souvlaki, moussaka. Mediterranean decor. Cr cds: A, C, D, DS, MC, V.

⊡

✔★ **SAWATDEE.** *607 Washington Ave S, downtown.* 612/338-6451. Web www.sawatdee.com. Hrs: 11 am-10 pm; Fri, Sat to 11 pm. Res accepted. Thai menu. Bar. A la carte entrees: lunch $8.25-$14.95. Buffet: lunch $7.95. Specialties: Pad Thai, Bangkok seafood special. Parking. Cr cds: A, C, D, DS, MC, V.

⊡

✔★ ★ **SHUANG CHENG.** *1320 SE Fourth St (55414), downtown.* 612/378-0208. Hrs: 10 am-10 pm; Fri, Sat 11 am-11 pm; Sun 4-10 pm. Chinese menu. Semi-a la carte: lunch $3.55-$4.75, dinner $4.50-$10.95. Specializes in seafood, pork, chicken. Casual decor. Cr cds: A, C, D, DS, MC, V.

↙★ SIDNEY'S PIZZA CAFE. *2120 Hennepin Ave (55405), north of downtown.* 612/870-7000. Hrs: 7 am-11 pm; Fri to midnight; Sat 10 am-midnight; Sun 10 am-11 pm. Closed Dec 24, 25. Italian, Amer menu. Wine, beer. Semi-a la carte: bkfst $4.95-$9.95, lunch, dinner $4.95-$9.95. Specializes in pizza, pasta. Outdoor dining. Casual decor. Cr cds: A, C, D, DS, MC, V.

⌐⌐

★ SONG THANH. *418 13th Ave SE (55414), downtown, near Univ of Minnesota campus.* 612/379-3121. Hrs: 11 am-10 pm; Fri to 11 pm. Res accepted. Vietnamese menu. Semi-a la carte: lunch $3.95-$6.95, dinner $4.95-$24.95. Specialties: flaming game hen, lemon grass chicken. Own noodles. Casual dining in colorful Vietnamese atmosphere. Cr cds: A, C, D, DS, MC, V.

D

★★ SOPHIA. *65 SE Main St, north of downtown.* 612/379-1111. Hrs: 11 am-3 pm, 5-9:45 pm; Fri, Sat to 11:45 pm; Sun 11 am-3 pm. Closed Jan 1, Dec 25. Res accepted. French, continental menu. Bar. Semi-a la carte: lunch $5.95-$10.95, dinner $11.95-$19.95. Specializes in Norwegian salmon, steaks. Pianist Tues-Sat. Outdoor dining. Many of the ingredients are provided through the restaurant's own ranch. Overlooks river. Cr cds: A, C, D, MC, V.

D ⌐⌐

★ TABLE OF CONTENTS. *1310 Hennepin Ave (55403), downtown.* 612/339-1133. Hrs: 11:30 am-2 pm, 5-10 pm; Fri, Sat to 11 pm; Sun 10 am-3 pm, 5-9 pm. Closed most major hols. Res accepted. Contemporary Amer menu. Bar. Semi-a la carte: lunch $7.50-$12.50, dinner $12.50-$22.95. Sun brunch $4.95-$11.95. Specializes in grilled fish, grilled beef tenderloin. Contemporary decor. Cr cds: A, C, D, DS, MC, V.

⌐⌐

★★★ WHITNEY GRILLE. *(See Whitney Hotel)* 612/372-6405. Hrs: 6:30 am-10:30 pm; Sun 10 am-3 pm. Closed Dec 25. Res accepted. Bar to midnight. Semi-a la carte: bkfst $6-$10, lunch $7-$13, dinner $19-$29. Sun brunch $19.95. Specialty: Minnesota walleye. Entertainment Fri, Sat. Outdoor dining. Formal decor. Totally nonsmoking. Cr cds: A, C, D, DS, ER, JCB, MC, V.

D

Unrated Dining Spots

EMILY'S LEBANESE DELI. *641 University Ave NE, north of downtown.* 612/379-4069. Hrs: 9 am-9 pm; Fri, Sat to 10 pm. Closed Tues; Easter, Thanksgiving, Dec 25. Lebanese menu. Semi-a la carte: lunch, dinner $4.50-$7.50. Specialties: spinach pie, tabooleh salad. Parking. No cr cds accepted.

⌐⌐

LINCOLN DEL. *(4100 W Lake St, St Louis Park) Approx 3 mi S on MN 100.* 612/927-9738. Hrs: 7 am-11 pm; Fri, Sat to 1 am; Sun 8 am-11 pm. Closed Dec 25. Semi-a la carte: bkfst $2-$5, lunch $4-$8, dinner $6-$11. Specializes in corned beef. Parking. New York-style deli. Cr cds: A, D, MC, V.

SC ⌐⌐

LORING CAFE. *1624 Harmon Place, adj Loring Playhouse Theatre, downtown.* 612/332-1617. Hrs: 11:30 am-3:30 pm, 5:30-11 pm; Fri, Sat 11:30 am-3 pm, 4 pm-midnight; Sun 11:30 am-3 pm, 5:30-11 pm. Closed Dec 24, 25. Res accepted. Bar. Semi-a la carte: lunch $9-$15, dinner $12-$25. Specialties: shrimp with pears, manicotti with lamb & cheese. Entertainment. Outdoor dining. Restored 1918 building. Eclectic decor. Cr cds: MC, V.

MARKET BAR-B-QUE. *1414 Nicollet Ave S, in Nicollet Ave Mall Area.* 612/872-1111. Hrs: 11:30-2:30 am; Sun noon-midnight. Bar. Semi-a la carte: lunch $5-$9, dinner $9-$15.95. Specializes in barbe-cued chicken, ribs, pork. Valet parking. 1930s cafe atmosphere. Cr cds: A, C, D, DS, MC, V.

D ⌐⌐

MUD PIE. *2549 Lyndale Ave S (55405), south of downtown.* 612/872-9435. Hrs: 11 am-10 pm; Sat, Sun from 8 am. Closed major hols. Vegetarian menu. Wine, beer. Semi-a la carte: bkfst $2-$4.50, lunch $4-$12, dinner $7-$15. Outdoor dining. Cr cds: A, D, DS, MC, V.

D

Moorhead (D-1)

(See also Detroit Lakes; also see Fargo, ND)

Founded 1871 **Pop** 32,295 **Elev** 903 ft **Area code** 218 **Zip** 56560

Information Moorhead Area Chamber of Commerce, 725 Center Ave, PO Box 719, 56561-0719; 218/236-6200.

Along with the neighboring city to the west, Fargo, ND, Moorhead is considered an agricultural capital. A shipping and processing center for agricultural products, the town is also a retailing and distribution point. The biggest industries are sugar refining and grain malting. Millions of pounds of sugar are produced annually from beets raised in and near Clay County. Moorhead is the home of Moorhead State University, Concordia College and Northwest Technical College-Moorhead.

What to See and Do

Comstock Historic House (1882). Eleven-rm home of Solomon Comstock, the founder of Moorhead State University, and his daughter Ada Louise Comstock, who was the first full-time president of Radcliffe College (1923-1943). House has period furniture, historical artifacts. Guided tours. (June-Sept, Sat & Sun) 506 8th St S. Phone 218/233-0848 or 218/233-1772. ¢

Heritage-Hjemkomst Interpretive Center. Home of the *Hjemkomst,* a replica Viking ship that sailed to Norway in 1982; also home of Clay County Museum. (Mon-Sat, also Sun afternoons; closed some major hols) 202 1st Ave N. Phone 218/233-5604. ¢¢

Regional Science Center-Planetarium. Offers variety of astronomy programs. (Sept-May, Sun-Mon; summer, Thurs) Moorhead State University campus, 11th St & 8th Ave S. Phone 218/236-3982. ¢¢

Viking Mooring Stones. These stones are believed to be evidence of the presence of Viking explorers in the area (1362). Stones are approx 6 by 4 by 5 ft, embedded above the highest water-line level and at the foot of nearby hills. Fishermen now use them as piers to moor their boats. 21 mi E of town in Hawley.

Annual Event

Scandinavian Hjemkomst Festival. June 27-30.

Motel

★ SUPER 8. *3621 8th St S, US 75S, ¼ mi S of I-94.* 218/233-8880. 61 rms, 2 story. S $31.88; D $36.88-$40.88; under 13 free. Crib $2. TV; cable. Complimentary continental bkfst. Restaurant nearby. Ck-out 11 am. Coin lndry. Business servs avail. Game rm. Cr cds: A, C, D, DS, MC, V.

D ⌐ ⌐ SC

Restaurant

★★ TREE TOP. *403 Center Ave, 7th floor of Metropolitan Federal Bldg.* 218/233-1393. Hrs: 11 am-2 pm, 5-10 pm; Sat from 5 pm. Closed Sun; most major hols. Res accepted. Continental menu. Bar. Semi-a la carte: lunch $5.75-$7.25, dinner $9.95-$18.95. Specialties: pork chop fettucine, filet mignon flambé. Pianist wkend evenings. Panoramic view of Red River Valley. Cr cds: A, D, DS, MC, V.

Mora (E-4)

(See also Hinckley)

Pop 2,905 **Elev** 1,010 ft **Area code** 612 **Zip** 55051
Information Mora Area Chamber of Commerce, Tourist Information Center, 114 Union St S; 800/291-5729.

In its early lumbering days, Mora was a boomtown. Mora's name led to its sister city affiliation with Mora, Sweden.

What to See and Do

Fishing. Snake River. Runs along N, S & W perimeters of city. Canoeing. **Fish Lake.** 5 mi S off MN 65. **Ann Lake.** 8 mi NW, off MN 47. **Knife Lake.** 8 mi N on MN 65.

Kanabec History Center. Exhibits, gift shop, picnic area, hiking and ski trails; research information. (Daily; closed Jan 1, Thanksgiving, Dec 24-25) W Forest Ave. Phone 612/679-1665. ¢

Annual Events

Vasaloppet-Cross-Country Ski Race. 2nd Sun Feb.
Canoe Race. 1st Sat May.

Motel

✔★ **MOTEL MORA.** *301 S MN 65, on MN 23/65. 320/679-3262; FAX 320/679-5135; res: 800/657-0167.* 23 rms. S $29-$42; D $36-$42; each addl $5; kit. units $29-$42. Crib $5. Pet accepted, some restrictions; $5. TV; cable (premium). Complimentary coffee in rms. Restaurant nearby. Ck-out 11 am. Business servs avail. In-rm modem link. X-country ski 1 mi. Picnic tables. Sun deck. Many refrigerators; microwaves avail. Cr cds: A, C, D, DS, MC, V.

Morris (E-1)

(See also Glenwood)

Pop 5,613 **Elev** 1,140 ft **Area code** 320 **Zip** 56267 **Web** www.infolink .morris.mn.us/users/chamber/welcome.html
Information Morris Area Chamber of Commerce & Agriculture, 507 Atlantic Ave; 320/589-1242.

Morris is the seat of Stevens County and provides a regional shopping center for west central Minnesota. The surrounding area offers good fishing and hunting and is known for wildfowl, especially pheasants. The Wetland Management office is located here and manages seven counties along with 43,000 acres of waterfowl protection areas.

What to See and Do

Pomme de Terre City Park. A 363-acre public recreational area along Pomme de Terre River; picnicking, canoeing, fishing; camping (hookups; fee), nature & bicycle trail; swimming beach; sand volleyball court; concession. (Apr-Oct, daily) 2³⁄₄ mi E on County 10. **Free.**

University of Minnesota, Morris (1960). (2,000 students) Humanities Fine Arts Center Gallery presents changing contemporary exhibits (Oct-

mid-June, Mon-Fri) and performing arts series (Oct-April). Tours. 4th & College Sts. For information phone 320/589-6050.

Annual Event

Prairie Pioneer Days. Arts & crafts, parade, bike ride, games & activities for children. 2nd wkend July.

Motels

★ **MORRIS.** *207 S MN 9, ³⁄₄ mi S on MN 9. 320/589-1212.* 14 rms. S $23; D $26.50-$32; each addl $2.50. TV; cable (premium). Complimentary coffee in rms. Ck-out 11 am. Cr cds: DS, MC, V.

★ ★ **PRAIRIE INN.** *200 MN 28E, 2 mi N on MN 28. 320/589-3030; res: 800/535-3035.* 90 rms, 2 story. S, D $34-$84; under 17 free. Crib free. Pet accepted, some restrictions. TV; cable (premium). Indoor pool; wading pool, whirlpool, poolside serv. Complimentary continental bkfst. Restaurant 6:30 am-10 pm. Bar 4 pm-1 am. Ck-out 11 am, Sun noon. Meeting rms. Business servs avail. Sauna. Game rm. Cr cds: A, C, D, DS, MC, V.

New Ulm (G-3)

(See also Mankato, Redwood Falls, St Peter)

Founded 1854 **Pop** 13,132 **Elev** 896 ft **Area code** 507 **Zip** 56073 **E-mail** nuchamber@ic.new-ulm.mn.us **Web** www.ic.new-ulm.mn.us
Information New Ulm Convention & Visitors Bureau, 1 N Minnesota, Box 862; 507/354-4217 or 888/4NEWULM.

Settled by German immigrants who borrowed the name of their home city, New Ulm is one of the few planned communities in the state. After more than a century, it still retains the order and cleanliness of the original settlement. The city today is in the center of a prosperous agricultural and dairy area and has developed a substantial business community. There is a visitor center at 1 N Minnesota St (May-Oct, daily; Nov-Apr, daily exc Sun).

What to See and Do

Brown County Historical Museum. Former post office. Historical exhibits on Native Americans and pioneers; artwork; research library with 4,000 family files. (Mon-Fri, also Sat & Sun afternoons; closed hols) Center St & Broadway. Phone 507/354-2016. ¢

Harkin Store. General store built by Alexander Harkin in 1870 in the small town of West Newton. The town died when it was bypassed by the railroad, but the store stayed open as a convenience until 1901, when rural free delivery closed the post office. The store has been restored to its original appearance and still has many original items on the shelves. Special programs in summer months. (Summer, daily exc Mon; May-Sept, wkends) 8 mi NW of town via County 21. Phone 507/354-2016 or 507/354-8666. ¢

Hermann's Monument. Erected by a fraternal order, monument recalls Hermann the Cheruscan, a German hero of A.D. 9. Towering 102 ft, monument has winding stairway to platform with view of city and Minnesota Valley. (June-Labor Day, daily) Picnic area. On the bluff W of city in Hermann Heights Park. Phone 507/359-8344. ¢

Schell Garden and Deer Park. Garden with deer and peacocks (all yr). Brewery tours, museum, gift shop. (Memorial Day-Labor Day; daily) S on MN 15, then W on 18th St; on Schell Brewery grounds. Phone 507/354-5528. Tours ¢

State parks.

Flandrau. Comprised of 801 acres on Cottonwood River. Swimming; cross-country skiing (rentals); camping; hiking. Standard fees. Located at the city limits, on S Summit Ave; 1 mi S on MN 15, then W. Phone 507/354-3519.

Ft Ridgely. A 584-acre park. Fort partly restored; interpretive center (May-Labor Day, daily). 9-hole golf course (fee); cross-country skiing; camping; hiking; annual historical festival. Standard fees. 14 mi W on US 14, then 12 mi N on MN 4. Phone 507/426-7840.

The Glockenspiel. A 45-ft-high musical clock tower with performing animated figures; carillon with 37 bells. Performances (3 times daily). 4th N & Minnesota Sts. Phone 507/354-4217 for schedule.

Annual Events

Fasching. Traditional German winter festival. Includes German food, music; costume ball. Phone 507/354-8850. Feb 21.

Blues Fest. Fairgrounds. June.

Heritagefest. Old World-style celebration highlighting German traditions and culture through music, foods, arts & crafts. Features entertainers from around the area and from Europe. Phone 507/354-8850. July 10-12 & July 17-19.

Brown County Fair. Fairgrounds. Aug.

Motels

★ **BUDGET HOLIDAY.** *1316 N Broadway. 507/354-4145; FAX 507/354-4146.* 45 rms. S $26.95-$32.95; D $29.95-$34.95; each addl $5. Crib $5. Pet accepted. TV; cable (premium). Restaurant nearby. Ck-out 11 am. Business servs avail. X-country ski 2 mi. Cr cds: A, C, D, DS, MC, V.

✔★ **COLONIAL INN.** *1315 N Broadway. 507/354-3128.* 24 rms (10 with shower only). S $24-$28; D $32-$50. Crib free. TV; cable (premium). Complimentary coffee in lobby. Restaurant nearby. Ck-out 11 am. X-country ski 1 mi. Cr cds: A, DS, MC, V.

★ ★ **HOLIDAY INN.** *2101 S Broadway. 507/359-2941; FAX 507/354-7147.* 126 rms, 2 story. S, D $69-$89; each addl $10; suites $89-$129; under 19 free. Crib free. TV; cable (premium). Indoor pool; whirlpool, sauna. Restaurant 6:30 am-2 pm, 5-10 pm. Rm serv. Bar 11-1 am; entertainment. Ck-out noon. Meeting rms. Business center. In-rm modem link. Valet serv. X-country ski 2 mi. Game rm. Cr cds: A, C, D, DS, JCB, MC, V.

Restaurants

✔★ **DJ's.** *1200 N Broadway. 507/354-3843.* Hrs: 6 am-9 pm; Sat, Sun from 7 am. Closed Dec 24 (eve) & 25. German, Amer menu. Semi-a la carte: bkfst $1.59-$4.99, lunch $3.15-$4.99, dinner $5.25-$11.95. Specializes in broasted chicken, bratwurst with sauerkraut. Informal atmosphere. No cr cds accepted.

★ ★ **VEIGEL'S KAISERHOFF.** *221 N Minnesota St. 507/359-2071.* Hrs: 11 am-10:30 pm; Sun 11 am-10 pm. Closed Dec 24, 25. Res accepted. Bar to 1 am. Semi-a la carte: lunch $4-$8, dinner $9-$18. Child's meals. Specializes in barbecued ribs. Bavarian decor. Family-owned. Cr cds: A, DS, MC, V.

Northfield (G-4)

(See also Faribault, Hastings, Lakeville, Minneapolis, Owatonna, Red Wing, St Paul)

Founded 1855 **Pop** 14,684 **Elev** 919 ft **Area code** 507 **Zip** 55057

Information Northfield Area Chamber of Commerce, 500 Water St S, PO Box 198; 507/645-5604.

This bustling, historic river town, located 30 miles south of the Twin Cities, offers a captivating blend of the old and new. Its history is one of the most dramatic of any Midwestern community. Each year on the weekend after Labor Day, thousands flock here to share in the retelling of the defeat of Jesse James and his gang, who, on September 7, 1876, were foiled in their attempt to raid the Northfield Bank in what proved to be one of the last chapters in the brutal saga of the Old West.

This history has been preserved in the Northfield Bank Museum at 408 Division St, keystone of the city's unique historical downtown district. The well-preserved storefronts house boutiques, antique stores and other interesting shops.

What to See and Do

Carleton College (1866). (1,800 students) Liberal arts college. Arboretum (455 acres) has hiking and jogging trails along Cannon River. Also here is a 35-acre prairie maintained by college. Tours of arboretum and prairie with advance notice. Summer theater programs. NE edge of town on MN 19. Phone 507/646-4000.

Nerstrand Woods State Park. More than 1,280 acres, heavily wooded; hiking, cross-country skiing, snowmobiling; picnicking, camping (dump station). Standard fees. 12 mi SE, off MN 246. Phone 507/334-8848.

Northfield Arts Guild. Exhibits of local & regional fine arts housed in historic YMCA Building (1885); juried handcrafted items. (Daily exc Sun; closed holidays) Downtown. Phone 507/645-8877. **Free.**

St Olaf College (1874). (3,000 students) Famous for its choir, band and orchestra, which tour nationally and abroad. Steensland Art Gallery (daily). Home of national offices and archives of Norwegian-American Historical Association. 1 mi W of business district. Phone 507/646-2222.

Annual Event

Defeat of Jesse James Days. Raid reenactment, parade, outdoor arts fair, rodeo. 4 days beginning wkend after Labor Day.

Motels

✔★ **COLLEGE CITY.** *MN 3N. 507/645-4426; res: 800/775-0455.* 24 rms. S $24-$27; D $29-$39; Crib free. TV, cable. Complimentary coffee 7 am-noon. Ck-out 11 am. Sundries. X-country ski 1 mi. Cr cds: A, DS, MC, V.

★ ★ **COUNTRY INN.** *300 MN 3S. 507/645-2286; FAX 612/645-2958.* 54 rms, 2 story. S $47-$82; D $53-$88; each addl $6; suites $82-$88; under 18 free. Crib free. TV; cable (premium). Indoor pool; whirlpool. Complimentary continental bkfst. Restaurant nearby. Ck-out noon. Coin lndry. Downhill ski 20 mi; x-country ski 1 mi. Some refrigerators. Cr cds: A, C, D, DS, MC, V.

★ **SUPER 8.** *1420 Riverview Dr. 507/663-0371; FAX 509/663-0185.* 40 rms, 2 story. S $39.88; D $47.88. Crib $3. TV. Restaurant adj. Ck-out 11 am. Business servs avail. X-country ski 1 mi. Cr cds: A, C, D, DS, MC, V.

Inn

★ ★ **ARCHER HOUSE.** *212 Division St. 507/645-5661; FAX 507/645-4295; res: 800/247-2235.* 36 rms, 3 story. D $45-$150. Crib avail. TV; cable (premium), VCR avail. Dining rm 6:30 am-10 pm. Rm serv. Ck-out noon, ck-in 3 pm. Downhill ski 20 mi; x-country ski 1 mi. On river. Built 1877; antiques, country decor. Cr cds: A, MC, V.

Onamia (E-3)

(See also Aitkin, Brainerd, Little Falls)

Pop 676 **Elev** 1,264 ft **Area code** 612 **Zip** 56359

What to See and Do

Fort Mille Lacs Village. Recreational complex includes tame animal park; paddleboats (addl fee); Native American museum; art gallery; picnic area. Three gift shops; country store with smoked fish, cheese and ice cream parlor. (May-Oct, daily) 6 mi N via US 169, then 1 mi S on County Rd, on SW shore of Mille Lacs Lake. Phone 612/532-3651. **Free.**

Mille Lacs Kathio State Park. 10,577 acres surrounding main outlet of Mille Lacs Lake. Evidence of Native American habitation and culture dating back over 4,000 yrs. Here in 1679, Daniel Greysolon, Sieur Du Lhut, claimed the upper Mississippi region for France. Swimming, fishing, boating (rentals); hiking, riding trails; cross-country skiing (rentals), snowmobiling; picnicking; camping (dump station). Interpretive center. Standard fees. 8 mi NW on US 169, then 1 mi S on County Road 26. Phone 612/532-3523. Per vehicle **¢¢**

Mille Lacs Lake. 150 mi of shoreline; one of the largest and loveliest in the state. Near lakeshore are nearly 1,000 Native American mounds. Fishing, boating, camping. 4 mi N on US 169. Phone 218/829-2838.

Resort

★ ★ ★ **IZATYS GOLF & YACHT CLUB.** *40005 85th Ave (40005), 3 mi E on MN 27, then 1 mi N on Izatys Rd, on Mille Lacs Lake. 320/532-3101; FAX 320/532-3208; res: 800/533-1728.* 28 rms in lodge, 2 story, 59 townhouses for 2-8. D $65-$125; townhouses $115-$389 (2-day min wkends); family, mid-wk rates; golf plan. Crib avail. TV; cable, VCR avail (movies). 2 pools, 1 indoor; whirlpool. Free supervised child's activities (Memorial Day-Labor Day); ages 4-10 yrs. Coffee in rms. Dining rm 7 am-10 pm. Box lunches, snacks, barbecues. Bar 11-1 am. Ck-out noon, ck-in 4 pm. Meeting rms. Business servs avail. Tennis. 18-hole golf, greens fee $25-$55, pro. Sauna. Motors, pontoons, launch serv, boat marina. Jet ski rentals. X-country ski on site. Snowmobiling. Lawn games. Game rm. Fishing guides. Fireplaces; microwaves in townhouses. Private patios. Balconies. Cr cds: A, D, DS, MC, V.

Owatonna (G-4)

(See also Austin, Faribault, Northfield, Rochester)

Settled 1854 **Pop** 19,386 **Elev** 1,154 ft **Area code** 507 **Zip** 55060
Information Convention & Visitors Bureau, 320 Hoffman Dr, PO Box 331; 507/451-7970 or 800/423-6466.

Legend has it that the city was named after a beautiful but frail Native American princess named Owatonna. It is said that her father, Chief Wabena, had heard about the healing water called "minnewaucan." When the waters' curing powers restored his daughter's health, he moved his entire village to the site now known as Mineral Springs Park. A statue of Princess Owatonna stands in the park and watches over the springs that are still providing cold, fresh mineral water.

What to See and Do

Norwest Bank Owatonna, NA Building. Completed in 1908 as the National Farmers Bank, this nationally acclaimed architectural treasure was designed by one of America's outstanding architects, Louis H. Sullivan. The cube-like exterior, with huge arched stained-glass windows by Louis Millet, quickly earned the building widespread recognition as, according to one historian, "a jewel box set down in a prairie town." 101 N Cedar Ave, at Broadway. Phone 507/451-5670.

Owatonna Arts Center. Housed in a historic Romanesque structure. Permanent collection includes 100-piece collection of garments from around the world, and 14-ft stained-glass panels featured in the Performing Arts Hall. Outdoor sculpture garden has works by Minnesota artists John Rood, Richard and Donald Hammel, Paul Grandlund and Charles Gagnon. Changing gallery shows every month. (Daily exc Mon; closed hols) 435 Dunnell Dr, West Hills Complex. Phone 507/451-0533. **Donation.**

Village of Yesteryear. Eleven restored pioneer buildings from mid-1800s include church, two log cabins, schoolhouse, large family home, old fire department and country store; depot, farm machinery bldg, blacksmith shop; museum; period furnishings, memorabilia and a C-52 locomotive caboose (1905). (May-Oct, afternoons) 1448 Austin Rd. Phone 507/451-1420. **¢**

Motels

✔★ **BUDGET HOST INN.** *745 State Ave, 1 blk E of I-35 at exit 42B. 507/451-8712; FAX 507/451-4456.* 27 rms, 2 story. S $29.90-$38.90; D $32.90-$48.90; each addl $5. Crib $5. TV; cable. Coffee in lobby. Restaurant adj. Ck-out 11 am. Meeting rm. X-country ski 1 mi. Cr cds: A, DS, MC, V.

★ **DAYS INN.** *205 N Oak St, at Vine St. 507/451-4620.* 48 rms, 2 story. S $32-$69; D $38-$75; each addl $6; family rates. Crib free. TV; cable (premium), VCR avail. Bar 5 pm-1 am; entertainment. Ck-out 11 am. Meeting rms. Business servs avail. X-country ski 1 mi. Cr cds: A, C, D, DS, MC, V.

★ ★ **RAMADA INN.** *1212 I-35N. 507/455-0606; FAX 507/455-3731.* 117 rms, 2 story. S $47-$57; D $54-$64; each addl $5. Crib free. TV; cable. Indoor pool; whirlpool, sauna. Restaurant 6 am-2 pm, 5-9 pm. Rm serv. Bar 4 pm-1 am. Ck-out noon. Coin lndry. Business servs avail. Sundries. Free airport transportation. X-country ski 1 mi. Cr cds: A, D, DS, MC, V.

★ **SUPER 8.** *I-35 & US 14W, exit 42B. 507/451-0380; FAX 507/451-0380, ext. 236.* 60 rms, 2 story. S $40-$45; D $52-$60; each addl $3-$5. Crib $3. TV; VCR (movies). Complimentary coffee in lobby. Restaurant adj open 24 hrs. Ck-out 11 am. Business servs avail. Sundries. X-country ski 1 mi. Cr cds: A, C, D, DS, MC, V.

Park Rapids (D-2)

(See also Detroit Lakes, Walker)

Founded 1880 **Pop** 2,863 **Elev** 1,440 ft **Area code** 218 **Zip** 56470
Information Chamber of Commerce, PO Box 249; 800/247-0054.

This resort center is surrounded by 400 lakes, nearly as many streams and beautiful woods. There are more than 200 resorts within 20 miles. Fishing is excellent for bass, walleye, northern pike, muskie and trout.

What to See and Do

Aqua Park. Freshwater fish in 7,000-gallon tank aquarium. Deer and wildlife park, trout fishing, game birds, petting area. (May-Sept, daily) E MN 34. Phone 218/732-4442. ¢¢

Itasca State Park (see). 28 mi N on US 71.

Rapid River Logging Camp. Authentic logging camp with nature trail; antiques; serves lumberjack meals; logging demonstrations (Tues & Fri). See sluiceway in the river. (Memorial Day wkend-Labor Day wkend, daily) 3 mi N via US 71, 2½ mi E on County 18 and follow signs. Phone 218/732-3444. **Free.**

Smoky Hills Artisan Community. North country's artists and craftsmen produce and sell their wares in a miniature village. Nature trails. Live music; scenic lookout tower. Restaurant. (Memorial Day wkend-Labor Day, daily) 10 mi W on MN 34. Phone 218/573-3300. ¢¢

Motel

✔★ **SUPER 8.** MN 34E. 218/732-9704. 62 rms, 2 story. S $37.88-$52.88; D $47.88-$52.88; each addl $5; under 13 free. Crib $2. TV; cable. Complimentary continental bkfst. Restaurant nearby. Ck-out 11 am. Guest lndry. Business servs avail. In-rm modem link. Whirlpool, sauna. Rec rm. Cr cds: A, C, D, DS, JCB, MC, V.

[D] [≈] [⚄] [SC]

Resort

★★ **VACATIONAIRE.** Island Lake Dr, Island Lake Dr, 9½ mi N on US 71, then ¾ mi NE on County 89, on Island Lake. 218/732-5270. 12 A/C lodge rms, 4 kits, 1-2 story; 16 kit. cottages (1-4 bedrm). S $32; D $50; suites for 2-6, $60-$100; cottages for 2-8 (2-day min) $75-$225 each; each addl $10; EP; family, wkly rates. Crib avail. TV. Indoor pool; sauna. Playground. Dining rm 5-10 pm. Bar 8-1 am. Ck-out 10 am, ck-in 4 pm. Coin lndry (summer only). Business servs avail. Grocery, package store 9 mi. Tennis. Private beach; launching ramp, dock. Boats, motors, canoe, sailboat, pontoon boat, water bike. X-country ski on site. Skating. Snowmobile trails. Occasional entertainment. Rec rm. Fireplace. 373 acres. Cr cds: A, DS, MC, V.

[⛵] [≈] [⛷] [≈] [🔥] [⚄]

Cottage Colonies

★★ **BROOKSIDE RESORT.** Two Inlets Lake Rd, 11 mi N on US 71, then 2¼ mi W on County 41, then 1½ mi S on County 50, on Two Inlets Lake. 218/732-4093; res: 800/247-1615. 28 kit. cottages (2-4 bedrm). Mid-July-mid-Aug, wkly (with boat): kit. cottages for 4-8, $1,000-$1,400; each addl $100; lower rates late May-mid-July, mid-Aug-Sept. Closed rest of yr. No maid serv. Crib avail. TV in lodge. Indoor/outdoor pool; sauna. Supervised child's activities (May-Aug); ages 2-16. Snack bar. Ck-out Sat, 9:30 am, ck-in Sat, 4:30 pm. Coin lndry. Business servs avail. Grocery 2½ mi. Package store 16 mi. Airport, bus depot transportation. Tennis. Golf, greens fee $6, putting green. Miniature golf. Private beach; waterskiing. Boats, motors, canoes, pontoon boats, sailboats; dock, launching ramps. Hayrides. Lawn games. Movies. Library. Some fireplaces. Picnic tables, grills. Cr cds: MC, V.

[⛵] [🕴] [⛷] [≈] [≈] [🔥] [⚄]

★★ **EVERGREEN LODGE.** Big Sand Lake Rd, 2 mi E on MN 34, then 5 mi N on County 4, then ½ mi E, on Big Sand Lake. 218/732-4766; FAX 218/732-0762. 19 kit. cabins (2-4 bedrm) (no towels, maid serv). July-early Aug: wkly (with boat) for 1-4, $575-$735; 1-6, $720-$875; 1-8, $690-$965; each addl $40; under 2 free; lower rates mid-May-June, early Aug-Labor Day. Closed rest of yr. Playground. Free supervised child's activities (June-Aug). Ck-out 9:30 am, ck-in 3 pm. Grocery, coin lndry, package store 7 mi. Free airport transportation. Tennis. Par-3 golf, greens fee $6. Private beach. Motorboats, canoes, sailboats, pontoon

boat; launching ramp. Lawn games. Rec rm. Sauna. Picnic tables, grills. No cr cds accepted.

[⛵] [🕴] [⛷] [≈] [≈] [🔥] [⚄]

★★ **SUNSET LODGE.** Potato Lake Rd, 2 mi E on MN 34, then 5½ mi N on County 4, then ½ mi W on County 40, on Potato Lake. 218/732-4671. 11 kit. cottages (2-4 bedrm) (no towels, maid serv). Late June-mid-Aug: wkly (with boat) for 1-4, $540; 1-6, $720; 1-8, $895; each addl $10/day; varied lower rates mid-May-late June & mid-Aug-mid Nov (2-day min). Closed rest of yr. Crib avail. TV. Playground. Ck-out Sat, 10 am, ck-in 4 pm. Grocery 4 mi. Coin lndry. Package store 8 mi. Airport transportation. Tennis. 18-hole golf privileges, greens fee. Private beach. Boats, canoes, sailboats, water bikes; launching ramp. Lawn games. Rec rm. Picnic tables, grills. No cr cds accepted.

[⛵] [🕴] [⛷] [≈] [≈] [🔥] [⚄]

Pine River (D-3)

(See also Brainerd, Crosslake, Walker)

Pop 871 **Elev** 1,290 ft **Area code** 218 **Zip** 56474

Resorts

★★★ **DRIFTWOOD.** Whitefish and Hay Lakes, 4½ mi NE of Jenkins on County 15. 218/568-4221. 27 cottages (1-4 bedrm), 8 kits. AP, July-mid-Aug, wkly: $546 each; MAP avail; family rates; daily rates avail; lower rates mid-May-June, mid-Aug-late Sept. Closed rest of yr. Crib avail. Heated pool; wading pool. Free supervised child's activities (mid-May-Sept); ages 2-13. Dining rm 8-9:30 am, noon-1 pm, 6-7:30 pm. Box lunches, snacks. Barbecues, outdoor buffet Mon. Ck-out noon, ck-in 4 pm. Business servs avail. Grocery, package store 4½ mi. Coin lndry. Rec dir. Tennis, pro. 9-hole golf, putting greens. Private sand beach. Canoes, rowboats, sailboats, motors; launching facilities. Pony rides. Bicycles. Indoor, outdoor games. Rec hall. Nature trails. Entertainment; movies, dancing. Refrigerators. Minnesota resort museum. 55 acres. Sternwheel paddleboat cruises avail. Cr cds: A, MC, V.

[D] [⛵] [🕴] [⛷] [≈] [≈] [🔥] [⚄]

★★ **McGUIRE'S PINEY RIDGE.** Wildemere Dr, 6½ mi NE of Jenkins on County 15. 218/587-2296. 12 cottages (1-4 bedrm), 8 with kit. 14 deluxe condo kit. units. Mid-June-late Aug, wkly: $700-$1,575 (2-6 persons); MAP, wkend plans; lower rates May-mid-June, late Aug-late Sept. Closed rest of yr. Crib avail. Pool; sauna. Free supervised child's activities (mid-June-Labor Day). Dining rm 8-10 am, 11:30-3 pm, 5-10 pm. Box lunches, snack bar. Private club 8-11 pm. Ck-out 10 am, ck-in 4 pm. Grocery, package store 6½ mi. Coin lndry. Business servs avail. Airport, bus depot transportation. Tennis. 18-hole golf, pro shop. Miniature golf. Private beach. Dockage, boats, motors, canoes. Lawn games. Soc dir. Movies. Rec rm. Refrigerators; fireplaces. Picnic tables, grills. Cr cds: DS, MC, V.

[D] [⛵] [🕴] [⛷] [≈] [≈] [🔥] [⚄]

Pipestone (G-1)

(See also Luverne; also see Sioux Falls, SD)

Settled 1874 **Pop** 4,554 **Elev** 1,738 ft **Area code** 507 **Zip** 56164 **E-mail** pipecham@rconnect.com **Web** www.pipestone.mn.us

Information Chamber of Commerce, 117 8th Ave SE, PO Box 8; 507/825-3316.

County seat and center of a fertile farming area, Pipestone is host to visitors en route to Pipestone National Monument (see). Some of the red Sioux quartzite from the quarries shows up in Pipestone's public buildings.

George Catlin, famous painter of Native Americans, was the first white man to report on the area.

What to See and Do

Pipestone County Museum. Prehistory, early settlement, pioneer exhibits; research library. Tours. (Daily, closed most hols) ¢

Split Rock Creek State Park. 238 acres. Swimming; fishing (accessible to the disabled); boating (rentals). Hiking; cross-country skiing; picnicking; camping (dump station). Standard fees. 6 mi SW on MN 23, then 1 mi S on County 20. Phone 507/348-7908 or 800/766-6000.

Annual Events

Watertower Festival. Courthouse lawn. Large art & craft show; parade. Last Fri & Sat June.

Song of Hiawatha Pageant. Just S of Pipestone National Monument entrance. Outdoor performance. All seats reserved; ticket office opens 1 pm on show dates, phone 507/825-3316 or contact the Chamber of Commerce. Last 2 wkends July & 1st wkend Aug.

Motels

✔★ ARROW. 600 8th Ave NE, on US 75. 507/825-3331; res: 800/815-3331. 17 rms. S $21-$23.50; D $27.50-$41.50; each addl $4. Crib. TV; cable (premium). Playground. Pool. Complimentary continental bkfst. Restaurant opp 6 am-9 pm. Ck-out 11 am. Meeting rms. Gift shop. Shaded lawn. Cr cds: A, DS, MC, V.

★ SUPER 8. 605 8th Ave SE (US 75), MN 23, 30. 507/825-4217; FAX 507/825-4219. 39 rms, 2 story. S $40.88-$72.88; D $45.88-$72.88; each addl $4; under 12 free. Crib $1. TV; cable (premium). Restaurant adj 6 am-10 pm. Ck-out 11 am. Business servs avail. Some in-rm whirlpools. Cr cds: A, C, D, DS, MC, V.

D ⬚ ⬚ SC

Hotel

★★ DAY'S INN HISTORIC CALUMET. 104 W Main St. 507/825-5871; FAX 507/825-4578. 38 rms, 4 story. S, D $46-$65; each addl $4; under 12 free. Crib free. TV; cable (premium), VCR avail (movies). Complimentary continental bkfst. Restaurant 6:30 am-9 pm. Bar 4 pm-1 am. Ck-out 11 am. Meeting rms. Business servs avail. In-rm modem link. Gift shop. Cr cds: A, C, D, DS, JCB, MC, V.

D ⬚ ⬚ SC

Restaurant

★ LANGE'S CAFE. 110 8th Ave SE (US 75), at MN #30. 507/825-4488. Open 24 hrs. Res accepted. Semi-a la carte: bkfst $1.29-$6.95, lunch $3.25-$6.95, dinner $4.25-$13.95. Specializes in roast beef, homemade pastries. Casual, family-style dining. Family-owned. Cr cds: MC, V.

Pipestone National Monument (G-1)

(For accommodations see Pipestone; also see Sioux Falls, SD)

(On US 75, MN 23, 30, adj to north boundary of Pipestone)

The ancient pipestone in the quarries of this 283-acre area is found in few other places. The Native Americans quarried this reddish stone and carved it into ceremonial pipes. Pipestone deposits, named catlinite for George Catlin, who first described the stone, run about a foot thick, though most usable sections are about two inches thick. Principal features of the monument are **Winnewissa Falls,** flowing over quartzite outcroppings; **Three Maidens,** group of glacial boulders near quarries; **Leaping Rock,** used by Native Americans as a test of strength of young men who attemped to leap from the top of quartzite ridge to its crest, 11 feet away; **Nicollet Marker,** inscription on boulder recalls visit here in 1838 of Joseph Nicollet's exploring party. He carved his name and initials of members of his party, including Lt John C. Frémont.

Established as a national monument in 1937, Pipestone protects the remaining red stone and preserves it for use by Native Americans of all tribes. The visitor center has exhibits, slides, pipe-making demonstrations and a self-guided tour booklet for the circle trail and other information; also here is Upper Midwest Indian Cultural Center with craft displays. (Daily; visitor center closed Jan 1, Dec 25) Phone 507/825-5464. ¢

Ray (B-4)

(For accommodations see International Falls)

Pop 60 (est) **Elev** 1,155 ft **Area code** 218 **Zip** 56669
Information Kabetogama Lake Assn, Inc, 9707 Gamma Rd; 218/875-2621 or 800/524-9085.

Ray is a trade center for the Kabetogama Lake resort area.

What to See and Do

Kabetogama Lake. 22 mi long, 6 mi wide, with hundreds of miles of rugged shoreline, numerous islands, secluded bays for fishing, sand beaches, woodland trails, snowmobiling, cross-country skiing, hunting for partridge, deer, bear; many resorts. 7 mi NE off US 53.

Voyageurs National Park. Off US 53 on county roads. (See INTERNATIONAL FALLS)

Red Wing (G-4)

(See also Hastings, Lakeville, Northfield, St Paul)

Founded 1836 **Pop** 15,134 **Elev** 720 ft **Area code** 612 **Zip** 55066 **E-mail** visitorinfo@redwing.org **Web** www.redwing.org
Information Visitors and Convention Bureau, 418 Levee St; 612/385-5934 or 800/498-3444.

Established as a missionary society outpost, this community bears the name of one of the great Dakota chiefs, Koo-Poo-Hoo-Sha (Wing of the Wild Swan Dyed Scarlet). Red Wing industries produce leather, shoes, precision instruments, malt, flour, linseed oil, diplomas, rubber and wood products.

What to See and Do

Goodhue County Historical Museum. One of state's most comprehensive museums. Permanent exhibits relate local and regional history from glacial age to present. Extensive collection of Red Wing pottery; artifacts from Prairie Island Native American community. (Daily exc Mon; closed hols) 1166 Oak St. Phone 612/388-6024. ¢

Picnicking. Soldiers' Memorial Park/East End Recreation Area. Skyline Dr. On plateau overlooking city and river; 476 acres; 5 mi of hiking/cross-country ski trails. **Colvill Park.** On Mississippi. Also pool (June-Aug, fee), playground; boat launching, marina. **Bay Point Park.** On Mississippi. Showers, boat launching, marina, picnicking, vita course, playground, walking trail. (May-Oct, daily)

Hiking. 1½-mi hiking trail to top of Mt LaGrange (Barn Bluff) with scenic overlook of Mississippi River. Cannon Valley Trail provides 25 mi of improved trail following Cannon Bottom River to Cannon Falls.   **Free.**

Biking. Wheel passes needed for biking. For further information, contact the Cannon Valley Trail office, 507/263-3954.

Skiing.

Cannon Valley Trail. 20-mi cross-country skiing trail connects Cannon Falls, Welch, and Red Wing. Phone 612/296-6157 or 800/766-6000 (MN) or 612/258-4141 (snow conditions).   ¢¢¢

Mt Frontenac. 2 chairlifts, T-bar, 2 rope tows; patrol, school, rentals; snowmaking; cafeteria. (Nov-mid-Mar, Wed-Sun; closed Dec 25) Also 18-hole golf course (mid-Apr-Oct; fee). 9 mi S on US 61. Phone 612/388-5826.   ¢¢¢¢¢

Welch Village. 2 quad, 5 double, triple chairlifts, Mitey-mite; patrol, rentals; snowmaking; cafeteria. Longest run 4,000 ft; vertical drop 350 ft. (Nov-Mar, daily; closed Dec 25) 12 mi NW on US 61, then 3 mi S on County 7 to Welch. Phone 800/421-0699.   ¢¢¢¢

Trolley Tour. San Francisco-style cable car tour through Red Wing. Schedule varies; phone Visitors and Convention Bureau for information. ¢¢

Annual Events

River City Days. 1st wkend Aug.

Fall Festival of the Arts. 2nd wkend Oct.

Motels

★ ★ **BEST WESTERN QUIET HOUSE SUITES.** *752 Withers Harbor Dr. 612/388-1577; FAX 612/388-1150.* 51 rms, 2 story. S $69-$152; D $79-$162; under 5 free. Pet accepted. TV; cable. Indoor/outdoor pool; whirlpool. Complimentary coffee. Restaurant nearby. Ck-out 11 am. In-rm modem link. Exercise equipt; weights, stair machine. Some refrigerators. Balconies. Cr cds: A, C, D, DS, ER, MC, V.

D ✔ 🏊 ✕ 🐾 ≈ 🔥 SC

★ ★ **DAYS INN.** *955 E 7th St, US 61 & 63 S. 612/388-3568; FAX 612/385-1901.* 48 rms. S, D $40.50-$80.50; each addl $5; under 13 free. Pet accepted. TV; cable. Indoor pool; whirlpool. Complimentary coffee in rms. Complimentary continental bkfst. Restaurant nearby. Ck-out 11 am. Business servs avail. Downhill ski 7 mi; x-country ski 1 mi. Municipal park, marinas opp. Cr cds: A, C, D, DS, JCB, MC, V.

D ✔ 🏊 ≈ 🔥 SC

✔★ **RODEWAY INN.** *235 Withers Harbor Dr. 612/388-1502; FAX 612/388-1501.* 39 rms, 2 story. S $39-$57; D $49-$67; each addl $5; suites $59-$130. Crib $5. TV; cable (premium), VCR avail (movies). Indoor pool; whirlpool. Restaurant adj 6 am-midnight. Ck-out 11 am. Business servs avail. Downhill ski 12 mi; x-country ski 1 mi. Casino 10 mi. Cr cds: A, C, D, DS, MC, V.

D 🏊 ≈ 🔥 SC

★ **SUPER 8.** *232 Withers Harbor Dr. 612/388-0491; FAX 612/388-1066.* 60 rms, 2 story. June-Dec: S $42.88-$49.88; D $52.88-$64.88; higher rates Sat; lower rates rest of yr. Crib $3. TV; cable (premium), VCR avail, (movies). Indoor pool. Complimentary continental bkfst in lobby. Restaurant adj 6 am-11 pm. Ck-out 11 am. Business servs avail. Downhill ski 12 mi. Casino 10 mi. Cr cds: A, C, D, DS, JCB, MC, V.

D 🏊 ≈ 🔥 SC

Hotel

★ ★ ★ **ST JAMES.** *406 Main St. 612/388-2846; FAX 612/388-5226; res: 800/252-1875.* 60 rms, 2-5 story. S, D $100-$155; under 18 free. TV; cable (premium), VCR avail. Restaurant 6:30 am-9:30 pm. Bars 11-12:30 am; entertainment Fri, Sat. Meeting rms. Business servs avail. In-rm modem link. Shopping arcade. Beauty shop. Free covered parking. Airport transportation. Downhill/x-country ski 10 mi. Some whirlpools. Built

in 1875; each rm completely different; furnished with antiques. Overlooks Mississippi. Cr cds: A, C, D, DS, MC, V.

D 🏊 ≈ 🔥

Inns

★ ★ **GOLDEN LANTERN.** *721 E Ave. 612/388-3315.* 5 rms, 2 story. No rm phones. S, D $89-$125. Children over 12 yrs only. Complimentary full bkfst. Restaurant nearby. Ck-out 11 am, ck-in 4-5:30 pm. Downhill ski 8 mi; x-country ski 1 mi. Tudor brick house built in 1932. Totally nonsmoking. Cr cds: MC, V.

🏊 ≈ 🔥

★ ★ **PRATT TABER INN.** *706 W 4th St. 612/388-5945.* 5 rms, 2 story. No rm phones. S, D $89-$110. Children over 10 yrs only. TV; VCR in parlor. Complimentary continental bkfst. Restaurant nearby. Ck-out noon, ck-in 4 pm. Downhill ski 12 mi; x-country ski 1 mi. Italianate-style brick house built in 1876 furnished with antiques. Totally nonsmoking. No cr cds accepted.

🏊 ≈ 🔥

Restaurants

★ **LIBERTY'S.** *303 W 3rd. 612/388-8877.* Hrs: 8 am-11 pm; Fri, Sat to 1 am. Sun brunch 9:30 am-2 pm. Closed most major hols. Res accepted. Continental menu. Bar to 1 am. Semi-a la carte: bkfst $1.95-$6.50, lunch $3-$7, dinner $3-$14.95. Sun brunch $8.25. Specializes in ribs, burgers. Entertainment Fri, Sat. Casual decor. Cr cds: A, C, D, DS, MC, V.

✔★ **NYBO'S LANDING.** *233 Withers Harbor Dr, ½ mi N, off US 61. 612/388-3597.* Hrs: 7 am-midnight; Fri fish fry 4:30-10 pm. Bar. Semi-a la carte: bkfst $1.75-$4.25, lunch $3-$7.95, dinner $6-$13. Fri fish fry $6.95. Buffet: Sat dinner $7.95, Sun bkfst $4.95. Specializes in butter-baked chicken, smoked ribs. Cr cds: A, DS, MC, V.

D SC

Redwood Falls (G-2)

(See also Granite Falls, Marshall, New Ulm)

Pop 4,859 **Elev** 1,044 ft **Area code** 507 **Zip** 56283

Information Redwood Area Chamber and Tourism, 610 E Bridge St; 507/637-2828.

What to See and Do

Lower Sioux Agency and History Center. Exhibits trace history of the Dakota in Minnesota from the mid-17th century through the present. (May-Oct, daily; rest of yr, by appt; closed Jan 1, Easter, Thanksgiving, Dec 25) 9 mi E via MN 19, County 2. Phone 507/697-6321.   **Free.**

Ramsey Park. A 200-acre park of rugged woodland carved by Redwood River & Ramsey Creek. Includes picnicking, trail riding, cross-country ski trail, hiking; golf; camping. Small zoo, playground & other recreational equipment for children, 30-ft waterfall. W edge of town, off MN 19.

Annual Event

Minnesota Inventors Congress. Redwood Valley School. Exhibit of inventions by adult and student inventors; seminars. Food; arts & crafts; parade; also resource center. Phone 507/637-2344. 3 days 2nd full wkend June.

Motel

✔★ **REDWOOD INN.** *1303 E Bridge St. 507/637-3521; FAX 507/637-2507; res: 800/801-3521.* 60 rms, 1-2 story. S $39.50; D $49.50; each addl $5. Crib free. TV; cable (premium). Complimentary continental bkfst. Bar. Ck-out 11 am. Meeting rms. Business servs avail. Sundries. Cr cds: A, D, DS, MC, V.

🔲 🔥 SC

Rochester (G-4)

(See also Owatonna, Spring Valley)

Settled 1854 **Pop** 70,745 **Elev** 1,297 ft **Area code** 507
Information Convention & Visitors Bureau, 150 S Broadway, Suite A, 55904; 507/288-4331 or 800/634-8277.

The world-famous Mayo Clinic has made what was once a crossroads campground for immigrant wagon trains a city of doctors, hospitals and lodging places. Each year, thousands of people come here in search of medical aid. One of the first dairy farms in the state began here, and Rochester still remains a central point of this industry. Canned goods, fabricated metals and electronic data processing equipment are among its industrial products.

What to See and Do

Mayo Clinic. Over 30 buildings now accommodate the famous group practice of medicine that grew from the work of Dr. William Worrall Mayo and his sons, Dr. William James Mayo and Dr. Charles Horace Mayo. There are now 1,041 doctors at the clinic, as well as 935 residents in training in virtually every medical and surgical specialty. The Plummer Building (1928), 14 stories, includes medical library and historical exhibit. The Conrad N. Hilton and Guggenheim buildings (1974) house clinical and research laboratories. The 19-story Mayo Building (1955, 1967) covers an entire block. It houses facilities for diagnosis and treatment. Clinic tours (Mon-Fri; closed hols). 200 1st St SW. Phone 507/284-9258. **Free.**

The Rochester Carillon is in the tower of the Plummer Bldg. Concerts (schedule varies). **Free.**

Mayowood. Home of Drs. C.H. and C.W. Mayo, historic 55-rm country mansion on 15 acres; period antiques, works of art. For reservations and schedule phone 507/282-9447 or 507/287-8691 (recording). ¢¢¢

Olmsted County History Center and Museum. Changing historical exhibits (daily; closed hols); research library (Mon-Fri; closed hols). Corner of County Rds 22 & 25. Phone 507/282-9447. ¢

Plummer House of the Arts. Former estate of Dr. Henry S. Plummer, a 35-yr member of the Mayo Clinic. 11-acres remain, with formal gardens, quarry, water tower. 5-story house is English Tudor mansion (ca 1920) with original furnishings and slate roof. Tours (June-Aug, Wed afternoons, also 1st & 3rd Sun afternoons). Entrance is at corner of 12th Ave & 9th St. Phone 507/281-6160. ¢

Whitewater State Park. A 1,822-acre park. Limestone formations in a hardwood forest. Swimming, fishing; hiking, cross-country skiing; picnicking; primitive camping. Interpretive center. Standard fees. 20 mi E on US 14, then 7 mi N on MN 74. Phone 507/932-3007.

Motels

✔★ **AMERICINN OF STEWARTVILLE.** *(1700 2nd Ave NW, Stewartville 55976) 1 mi S of I-90 on MN 63. 507/533-4747.* 29 rms. S $40-$45; D $45-$50; each addl $6; under 12 free. Crib free. Pet accepted. TV; cable. Complimentary continental bkfst. Restaurant nearby. Ck-out 11 am. Business servs avail. Cr cds: A, C, D, DS, MC, V.

🔲 💳 🔲 🔥 SC

★ **BEST WESTERN.** *20 5th Ave NW (55901). 507/289-3987; FAX 507/289-3987, ext. 130.* 91 rms, 3 story. S, D $56; each addl $5; under 18 free. Crib free. Pet accepted. TV; cable (premium). Indoor pool. Complimentary coffee in lobby. Restaurant nearby. Ck-out noon. X-country ski 1 mi. Cr cds: A, C, D, DS, MC, V.

🔲 💳 🔲 🔲 🔲 🔥 SC

★★ **BEST WESTERN-APACHE.** *1517 16th St SW (55902). 507/289-8866; FAX 507/289-8866, ext. 312.* 151 rms, 3 story. S $51.95-$99.95; D $61.95-$109.95; each addl $5; suites $85-$159; under 18 free; wkend rates. Pet accepted. TV; cable (premium), VCR avail. Indoor pool; whirlpool. Complimentary bkfst. Restaurant 6:30 am-10 pm. Rm serv. Bar 5 pm-1 am. Ck-out noon. Meeting rms. Business servs avail. In-rm modem link. Valet serv. Sundries. Free airport transportation. X-country ski 2 mi. Game rm. Tropical atrium. Cr cds: A, C, D, DS, MC, V.

🔲 💳 🔲 🔲 🔲 🔥 SC

★ **BLONDELL'S CROWN SQUARE.** *1406 2nd St SW (55902). 507/282-9444; FAX 507/282-8683; res: 800/441-5209.* 60 rms, 3 story, 7 suites. S $42-$50; D $47-$55; each addl $5; suites $85-$94; kit. units $42-$50; under 12 free. Crib free. Pet accepted. TV; cable (premium). Restaurant 6 am-10 pm. Rm serv. Bar 11-1:30 am. Ck-out 1 pm. Meeting rms. Business servs avail. Gift shop. X-country ski 1 mi. Cr cds: A, MC, V.

🔲 💳 🔲 🔲 🔥 SC

★ **DAYS INN.** *6 First Ave NW (55901). 507/282-3801.* 71 rms, 5 story. S $43-$75; D $49-$75; each addl $6; under 17 free. Crib free. Pet accepted. TV; cable. Restaurant 6 am-8 pm. Ck-out noon. Coin lndry. Some refrigerators. Cr cds: A, C, D, DS, MC, V.

💳 🔲 🔥 SC

★ **DAYS INN-SOUTH.** *111 28th St (55901). 507/286-1001.* 130 rms. S $46-$62; D $52-$62; each addl $5; under 18 free. Crib free. Pet accepted. TV; cable (premium). Complimentary continental bkfst. Restaurant nearby. Ck-out noon. Business servs avail. Free airport transportation. X-country ski 2 mi. Cr cds: A, C, D, DS, ER, JCB, MC, V.

🔲 💳 🔲 🔲 🔲 🔥 SC

★ **DAYS INN-WEST.** *435 16th Ave NW (55901), US 52 exit 5th St. 507/288-9090; FAX 507/288-9090, ext. 502.* 120 rms, 3 story, 20 kit. units. S $45-$66; D $50-$70; each addl $6; under 18 free. Crib free. Pet accepted. TV; cable (premium). Heated pool. Restaurant 6:30 am-8 pm. Ck-out noon. Coin lndry. Meeting rms. Valet serv. Sundries. X-country ski 1 mi. Cr cds: A, C, D, DS, MC, V.

🔲 💳 🔲 🔲 🔲 🔥 SC

✔★ **ECONO LODGE.** *519 3rd Ave SW (55902), near clinic. 507/288-1855; FAX 507/288-1855, ext. 300.* 62 rms, 2 story, 6 kits. S, D $43-$46; each addl $5; kit. units $45; under 19 free. Crib free. TV; cable. Complimentary coffee in rms. Restaurant nearby. Ck-out noon. Coin lndry. X-country ski 1 mi. City park opp. Cr cds: A, C, D, DS, MC, V.

🔲 🔲 🔥 SC

★ **FIKSDAL HOTEL AND SUITES.** *1215 2nd St SW (55902), US 52 exit 2nd St, opp St Mary's Hospital. 507/288-2671; FAX 507/366-3451.* 55 rms, 6 story. S $43.90-$45.90; D $48.90-$50.90; each addl $5. Crib free. TV; cable. Complimentary continental bkfst. Restaurant adj 6 am-10 pm. Ck-out 11 am. Business servs avail. Airport transportation. X-country ski 1 mi. Sun deck. Cr cds: A, DS, MC, V.

🔲 🔲 🔲 🔥 SC

✔★ **GAS LIGHT INN.** *1601 2nd St SW (55902), near St Mary's Hospital. 507/289-1824; FAX 507/289-3611; res: 800/658-7016.* 25 rms, 2 story. S $33-$45; D $43-$50; each addl $5; under 12 free. Crib free. TV; cable. Complimentary coffee in rms. Restaurant adj open 24 hrs. Ck-out noon. Coin lndry. Business servs avail. In-rm modem link. Sundries. X-country ski 1 mi. Refrigerators. Balconies. Cr cds: A, C, D, DS, MC, V.

🔲 🔥 SC

★ ★ **HAMPTON INN.** *1755 S Broadway (55904). 507/287-9050; FAX 507/287-9139.* 105 rms, 3 story. S $59-$99; D $69-$109; under 18 free. Crib free. TV; cable (premium). Indoor pool; whirlpool. Complimentary continental bkfst. Restaurant nearby. Ck-out noon. Meeting rm. Business servs avail. Valet serv. Coin lndry. X-country ski 1 mi. Exercise equipt; bicycle, rower. Refrigerator avail. Cr cds: A, C, D, DS, MC, V.

D ⛵ ≋ ✕ ⋈ 🔥 SC

★ ★ **HOLIDAY INN-SOUTH.** *1630 S Broadway (55904). 507/288-1844; FAX 507/288-1844, ext. 440.* 200 rms, 2 story, 7 kits. S, D $59-$69; each addl $7; kit. units $79-$119. Crib free. Pet accepted. TV; cable. Indoor pool. Restaurant 6 am-10 pm; Fri, Sat to 11 pm. Rm serv. Bar 11:30-1 am. Ck-out 2 pm, Sat noon. Coin lndry. Meeting rms. Business servs avail. Valet serv. Sundries. Free airport, bus depot transportation. Rec rm. Cr cds: A, C, D, DS, JCB, MC, V.

D ⛵ ≋ ⋈ 🔥 SC

★ **KNIGHTS INN.** *106 21st St SE (55904). 507/282-1756.* 80 rms, 2 story. S $32.40-$36.40; D $36-$40; under 18 free. Crib free. TV; cable (premium). Complimentary continental bkfst. Restaurant nearby. Ck-out noon. Business servs avail. X-country ski 2 mi. Some refrigerators, wet bars. Cr cds: A, C, D, DS, MC, V.

D ≋ ⋈ 🔥 SC

✔★ **LANGDON'S UPTOWN.** *526 3rd Ave SW (55902), near clinic. 507/282-7425.* 38 rms, 2 story. S $23-$27; D $25-$31; each addl $2. TV; cable. Complimentary coffee in rms. Restaurant nearby. Ck-out 11 am. Refrigerators. City pool, park opp. Cr cds: A, MC, V.

🔥

★ ★ **RAMADA INN.** *1625 S Broadway (55901). 507/281-2211; FAX 507/288-8979.* 165 rms, 5 story. S, D $64; each addl $10; under 17 free. Crib free. TV; cable (premium). Indoor pool; whirlpool, sauna. Restaurant 6 am-10 pm. Rm serv. Bar 4-midnight. Ck-out noon. Coin lndry. Meeting rms. Business servs avail. In-rm modem link. Valet serv. Airport transportation. X-country ski 1 mi. Some private patios. Cr cds: A, C, D, DS, JCB, MC, V.

D ≋ ≋ ⋈ 🔥 SC

★ **RED CARPET INN.** *2214 S Broadway (55904). 507/282-7448.* 47 rms, 2 story, 6 kits. S $36.45; D $40.45-$42.45; each addl $5; kit. units $28.95-$31.95; under 12 free; wkend rates. Crib free. Pet accepted. TV; cable. Indoor pool. Complimentary coffee in lobby. Restaurant nearby. Ck-out noon. Coin lndry. Meeting rm. Business servs avail. Sundries. X-country ski 1 mi. Cr cds: A, DS, MC, V.

D ⛵ ≋ ≋ ⋈ 🔥 SC

★ **SUPER 8.** *1230 S Broadway (55904). 507/288-8288; FAX 507/288-8288, ext. 350.* 89 rms. S $49.88-$52.88; D $54.88-$60; each addl $5; under 18 free. Crib free. Pet accepted. TV; cable. Restaurant adj open 24 hrs. Ck-out noon. In-rm modem link. X-country ski adj. Cr cds: A, DS, MC, V.

D ⛵ ≋ ⋈ 🔥 SC

★ **THRIFTLODGE.** *1837 S Broadway (55904). 507/288-2031.* 27 rms. S, D $33-$50; each addl $5. Crib free. Pet accepted. TV; cable. Complimentary coffee in lobby. Restaurant nearby. Ck-out noon. X-country ski 1 mi. Cr cds: A, C, D, DS, MC, V.

⛵ ≋ ⋈ 🔥 SC

✔★ **VILLAGE LODGE.** *116 SW 5th St (55901), near Mayo Clinic. 507/289-1628.* 59 rms, 2 story. S, D $29-$39; under 18 free. Crib free. TV; cable. Indoor pool; sauna. Complimentary continental bkfst. Ck-out noon. Coin lndry. Sundries. X-country ski 2 mi. Some refrigerators. Cr cds: A, C, D, DS, MC, V.

≋ ≋ ⋈ 🔥 SC

Motor Hotels

★ ★ **KAHLER INN AND SUITES.** *9 NW 3rd Ave (55901). 507/289-8646; FAX 507/282-4478.* 266 rms, 9 story. S $71.95-$102.95; D $81.95-$112.95; each addl $10; under 18 free. Pet accepted. TV; cable (premium). Indoor pool; whirlpool. Complimentary continental bkfst. Restaurant 6 am-9 pm. Bar 3-9 pm. Ck-out 2 pm. Meeting rm. Business servs avail. In-rm modem link. Sundries. Grocery store. Valet serv. Coin lndry. X-country ski 1 mi. Exercise equipt; bicycle, treadmil, sauna. Rec rm. Some refrigerators. Cr cds: A, C, D, DS, MC, V.

D ⛵ ≋ ≋ ✕ ⋈ 🔥 SC

★ **QUALITY INN & SUITES.** *1620 1st Ave SE (55904). 507/282-8091.* 40 suites, 2 story. S, D $69-$74; each addl $7; under 18 free. Crib free. Pet accepted. TV; cable (premium). Complimentary continental bkfst. Complimentary coffee in rms. Restaurant nearby. Ck-out noon. Coin lndry. Business servs avail. In-rm modem link. Airport transportation. Cr cds: A, C, D, DS, MC, V.

D ⛵ ≋ 🔥 SC

Hotels

★ ★ **BEST WESTERN SOLDIERS FIELD.** *401 6th St SW (55902). 507/288-2677; FAX 507/282-2042.* 228 rms, 8 story, 100 kit. suites. S, D, kit. suites $80; each addl $5; under 12 free. Crib free. TV; cable. Indoor pool; wading pool, whirlpool. Restaurant 6 am-10 pm. Bar 11 am-midnight; entertainment. Ck-out noon. Coin lndry. Meeting rms. Business servs avail. Gift shop. Free airport, bus depot transportation. X-country ski 1 blk. Exercise equipt; weights, bicycles. Game rm. Rec rm. Some refrigerators. Cr cds: A, C, D, DS, MC, V.

D ≋ ≋ ✕ ⋈ 🔥 SC

★ ★ **HOLIDAY INN-DOWNTOWN.** *220 S Broadway (55904), Hwy 63. 507/288-3231; FAX 507/288-6602.* 170 rms, 8 story. S, D $64-$94; each addl $10; suites $84-$252; under 18 free. Crib free. TV; cable (premium). Restaurant 6:30 am-2 pm, 5:30-10 pm; Sat, Sun from 7 am. Bars 5 pm-midnight. Meeting rms. Business servs avail. In-rm modem link. X-country ski 2 mi. Cr cds: A, C, D, DS, JCB, MC, V.

D ≋ ⋈ 🔥 SC

★ ★ ★ **KAHLER.** *20 2nd Ave SW (55902). 507/282-2581; FAX 507/285-2775; res: 800/533-1655.* 700 rms, 11 story. S $55-$140; D $65-$150; each addl $10; suites $350-$1,500; under 18 free. Crib free. Pet accepted. TV; cable. Indoor pool; whirlpool, poolside serv. Restaurant 6:30 am-11 pm, 5:30-9 pm. Bars 11-12:45 am; entertainment exc Sun. Ck-out 2 pm. Meeting rms. Business servs avail. In-rm modem link. Concierge. Drugstore. Barber, beauty shop. Airport transportation. X-country ski 2 mi. Exercise equipt; weights, bicycles, sauna. Game rm. Refrigerators. Original section English Tudor; vaulted ceilings, paneling. Walkway to clinic. Cr cds: A, C, D, DS, MC, V.

D ⛵ ≋ ≋ ✕ ⋈ 🔥 SC

★ ★ ★ **KAHLER PLAZA.** *101 1st Ave SW (55902). 507/280-6000; FAX 506/280-8531; res: 800/533-1655.* 194 rms, 9 story. S, D $129; each addl $10; suites $220-$1,700; under 18 free. Crib free. TV; cable. Indoor pool; whirlpool. Restaurant 6:30 am-10 pm. Bar 11 am-11 pm; entertainment. Ck-out 2 pm. Meeting rms. Business servs avail. In-rm modem link. Concierge. Gift shop. Drugstore. Barber, beauty shop. Exercise equipt; bicycles, treadmill, sauna. Game rm. Refrigerators; some bathrm phones, minibars. Mayo Medical Complex adj. Luxury level. Cr cds: A, C, D, DS, MC, V.

D ≋ ≋ ✕ ⋈ 🔥

★ ★ ★ **RADISSON PLAZA.** *150 S Broadway (55904). 507/281-8000; FAX 507/281-4280.* 212 rms, 11 story, 19 suites. S $86-$129; D $96-$139; suites $139-$295. Crib free. TV; cable (premium). Indoor pool; whirlpool. Restaurant 6:30 am-midnight. Bar 11-1 am. Ck-out noon. Coin lndry. Meeting rms. Business servs avail. In-rm modem link. Concierge.

Gift shop. X-country ski 1 mi. Exercise equipt; weights, bicycles, sauna. Refrigerator in suites. Cr cds: A, C, D, DS, ER, JCB, MC, V.

Restaurants

✔★ **AVIARY.** *4320 N US 52. 507/281-5141.* Hrs: 11-1 am. Closed most major hols. Res accepted. Bar. Semi-a la carte: lunch $5-$7, dinner $8-$12. Specialties: blackened steak sandwich, garlic shrimp fettucine. Parking. Many trees, plants. Cr cds: A, C, D, DS, MC, V.

★★ **BROADSTREET CAFE.** *300 1st Ave NW (55904). 507/281-2451.* Hrs: 11 am-9:30 pm; Sat, Sun 5-9:30 pm. Closed Easter, Thanksgiving, Dec 25. Res accepted. Mediterranean menu. Bar. Semi-a la carte: lunch $7-$10, dinner $19-$23. Specialties: boursin chicken breast, Canadian walleye. Former warehouse. Casual decor. Cr cds: A, C, D, MC, V.

★★ **CHARDONNAY.** *723 2nd St SW (55902). 507/252-1310.* Hrs: 11 am-2 pm, 5:30-9:30 pm; Sat from 5:30 pm. Closed Sun; major hols. Res accepted. French, Amer menu. Wine, beer. Semi-a la carte: lunch $6.50-$10, dinner $16-$24. Specialties: breast of duck with foie gras Hollandaise. Parking. 4 dining rms in remodeled house. Cr cds: A, C, D, DS, MC, V.

★★ **HENRY WELLINGTON.** *216 1st Ave SW. 507/289-1949.* Hrs: 11 am-midnight; Sat 4 pm-midnight; Sun 4-11 pm. Closed July 4, Thanksgiving, Dec 24, 25. Bar. Semi-a la carte: lunch $5-$7, dinner $9-$18. Specialties: filet Wellington, clam chowder. Outdoor dining. Antique decor. Cr cds: A, C, D, MC, V.

★★ **HUBBELL HOUSE.** *(MN 57, Mantorville 55955) 13 mi W on US 14, then 3 mi N on MN 57. 507/635-2331.* Hrs: 11:30 am-2 pm, 5-10 pm; Sun 11:30 am-9:30 pm; early-bird dinner Tues-Fri 5-6 pm. Closed Mon; Jan 1, Thanksgiving, Dec 24-25. Res accepted; required wkends. Bar to 1 am. Semi-a la carte: lunch $5-$7.95, dinner $9.95-$19.95. Child's meals. Specializes in steak, barbecued ribs, seafood. Parking. Country inn built in 1854; antiques. Family-owned. Cr cds: A, C, D, DS, MC, V.

★ **JOHN BARLEYCORN.** *2780 S Broadway. 507/285-0178.* Hrs: 11 am-2 pm, 5-10 pm; Sat, Sun from 5 pm. Closed Dec 24, 25. Res accepted. Bar. Semi-a la carte: lunch $4.25-$7.25, dinner $5.95-$23.95. Specializes in prime rib, barbecue ribs. Salad bar. Parking. Atmosphere of 1890s dining halls; Western decor. Cr cds: A, C, D, DS, MC, V.

★★★ **MICHAEL'S PAPPAGEORGE TAVERNA.** *15 S Broadway. 507/288-2020.* Hrs: 11 am-11 pm; early-bird dinner Mon-Thurs 3-5 pm, Fri & Sat to 5:30 pm. Closed Sun; most hols. Res accepted. Bar 11-midnight. Semi-a la carte: lunch $6-$8, dinner $8-$21.95. Child's meals. Specializes in Greek, Amer dishes. Own baking. Parking. Art display. Family-owned. Cr cds: A, C, D, DS, MC, V.

★★ **SANDY POINT.** *18 Sandy Point Court NE, 10 mi N on County Rd 12. 507/367-4983.* Hrs: 4:30-10 pm; Fri to 11 pm; Sat noon-11 pm; Sun 11:30 am-10 pm. Closed Dec 25. Bar. Semi-a la carte: lunch, dinner $9.95-$19.95. Child's meals. Specializes in seafood, steak. Parking. Overlooks river. Cr cds: A, C, D, DS, MC, V.

Roseau (B-2)

(For accommodations see Baudette)

Pop 2,396 **Elev** 1,048 ft **Area code** 218 **Zip** 56751

What to See and Do

Hayes Lake State Park. A 2,950-acre park. Swimming, fishing, hiking, cross-country skiing, snowmobiling, picnicking, camping (dump station). Standard hrs, fees. 15 mi S on MN 89, then 9 mi E on County 4. Phone 218/425-7504.

Pioneer Farm and Village. Restored buildings include log barn, museum, church, parish hall, equipped printery, log house, school, store, blacksmith shop and post office. Picnicking. (Mid-May-mid-Sept; schedule varies) 2 1/2 mi W via MN 11. Phone 218/463-2187 or -2690. **Free.**

Roseau City Park. Forty-acre park with canoeing, hiking and picnicking. Camping (electric and water hook-ups, dump station). 11th Ave SE.

Roseau County Historical Museum and Interpretive Center. Natural history, collection of mounted birds and eggs; Native American artifacts and pioneer history. (Tues-Sat; closed hols) 110 2nd Ave NE. Phone 218/463-1918. ¢

Roseau River Wildlife Management Area. More than 2,000 ducks raised here annually on 65,000 acres. Bird-watching area, canoeing on river, hunting during season, with license. 20 mi W & N via MN 11, 89 & County Rd 3. Phone 218/463-1557. **Free.**

St Cloud (F-3)

(See also Elk River, Little Falls)

Founded 1856 **Pop** 48,812 **Elev** 1,041 ft **Area code** 320
Information St Cloud Area Covention & Visitors Bureau, 30 S 6th Ave, PO Box 487, 56302; 320/251-2940 or 800/264-2940.

Its central location makes the city of St Cloud a convention hub and retail center for the area. The granite quarried here is prized throughout the United States. St Cloud also processes dairy products of the region. This Mississippi River community's architecture reflects the German and New England roots of its early settlers.

What to See and Do

City recreation areas. Riverside Park, Monument to Zebulon Pike who discovered and named the nearby Beaver Islands in 1805 during exploration of the Mississippi. Shelter; flower gardens; wading pool, tennis, picnicking, lighted cross-country skiing. 1725 Kilian Blvd. **Wilson Park,** picnicking; boat landing, tennis. 625 Riverside Dr NE. **Lake George Eastman Park,** Swimming (early June-mid-Aug, daily; fee); skating (late Dec-early Feb, daily; free); paddleboats (fee), fishing, picnicking. 9th Ave & Division. **Municipal Athletic Center,** Indoor ice skating (mid-June-mid-May, phone 612/255-7223 for fee and schedule information). 5001 8th St N. **Whitney Memorial Park,** Walking trails, softball & soccer. Northway Dr. **Heritage Park,** Nature trails, skating, cross-country skiing, earth-covered shelter; nearby is an interpretive heritage museum (Memorial Day-Labor Day, daily; rest of yr, daily exc Mon; closed hols; fee) with replica of working granite quarry and historical scenes of central Minnesota. 33rd Ave S. For further information about St Cloud's parks phone 320/255-7256.

College of St Benedict (1887). (1,742 women) On campus is the $6-million Ardolf Science Center. Guided tours. Art exhibits, concerts, plays, lectures and films in Benedicta Arts Center. 7 mi W on I-94 in St Joseph. Phone 320/363-5777 or -5308 for schedules. Also here is

St Benedict's Convent (1857). Community of more than 400 Benedictine women. Tours of historic Sacred Heart Chapel (1913), and archives.

Gift and crafts shop; Monastic Gardens. NW via I-94, in St Joseph at 104 Chapel Lane. For further information phone 320/363-7100. **Free.**

Powder Ridge Ski Area. 3 chairlifts, J-bar, rope tow; patrol, school, rentals; snowmaking; bar, cafeteria. (Nov-Apr, daily) 15 runs. 16 mi S on MN 15. Phone 320/398-7200 or 800/348-7734 (MN). ¢¢¢¢

Saint John's University and Abbey, Preparatory School (1857). (1,771 university students) Impressive modern abbey, university, church and nine other buildings designed by the late Marcel Breuer; 2,450 acres of woodlands and lakes. 13 mi W on I-94 in Collegeville. Phone 320/363-2573.

St Cloud State University (1869). (16,500 students) Marked historical sites; anthropology museum, planetarium, art gallery (Mon-Fri; closed hols & school breaks). 4th Ave S, overlooking Mississippi River. Phone 320/255-3151.

Stearns County Heritage Center. Located in a 100-acre park, the center showcases cultural and historical aspects of past and present life in central Minnesota; contains replica of working granite quarry; agricultural and automobile displays; research center & archives. (Daily exc Mon; June-Aug, daily; closed hols) 235 S 33rd Ave. Phone 320/253-8424. ¢¢

Annual Events

Mississippi Music Fest. Riverside Park. May.

Wheels, Wings & Water Festival. Mid-July.

Motels

✔★ **BUDGETEL INN.** 70 S 37th Ave (56301). 320/253-4444; FAX 320/259-7809. 91 units, 2 story. Mid-June-early Sept: S $39.95-$42.95; D $44.95-$49.95; each addl $7; under 18 free; lower rates rest of yr. Crib free. Pet accepted, some restrictions. TV; cable (premium). Restaurant nearby. Ck-out noon. Sauna. Whirlpool. Cr cds: A, C, D, DS, MC, V.

D ✔ ⊠ ≋ ⚙ SC

★ **COMFORT INN.** 4040 S Second St (56302). 320/251-1500. 63 rms, 2 story. S, D $45.95-$66.95; each addl $6; under 18 free. Crib $7. TV; cable (premium). Complimentary continental bkfst. Restaurant nearby. Ck-out 11 am. Coin lndry. Meeting rms. Business servs avail. Sundries. Exercise equipt; bicycles, rowers, sauna. Cr cds: A, C, D, DS, ER, JCB, MC, V.

D ✈ ⚙ SC

★ **DAYS INN-EAST.** 420 SE US 10, jct MN 23. 320/253-0500. 78 rms, 2 story. S $38.95-$56.95; D $45.95-$59.95; each addl $7; under 18 free. Crib free. Pet accepted. TV; cable (premium). Indoor pool; whirlpool. Complimentary continental bkfst. Ck-out 11 am. Business servs avail. Sundries. Downhill ski 10 mi; x-country ski 1 mi. Cr cds: A, C, D, DS, MC, V.

D ✔ ⊠ ≋ ⊠ ⚙ SC

★ **FAIRFIELD INN BY MARRIOTT.** 4120 Second St S (56301). 320/654-1881. 57 rms, 3 story. S $46.95-$64.95; D $49.95-$69.95; each addl $6; under 19 free. Crib free. TV; cable (premium). Indoor pool; whirlpool. Complimentary continental bkfst. Restaurant adj open 24 hrs. Ck-out 11 am. Meeting rms. Business servs avail. In-rm modem link. Downhill ski 18 mi; x-country ski 1 mi. Game rm. Some refrigerators. Cr cds: A, D, DS, MC, V.

D ⊠ ≋ ⊠ ⚙ SC

✔★ **MOTEL 6.** (815 S 1st St, S Waite Park 56387) On MN 23, 3¾ mi NE of I-94. 320/253-7070; FAX 320/253-0436. 94 rms, 2 story. S $29.99-$39.99; D $35.95-$45.99; under 18 free. Crib free. TV; cable (premium). Restaurant nearby. Ck-out noon. Business servs avail. In-rm modem link. Downhill ski 10 mi. Cr cds: A, C, D, DS, MC, V.

D ⊠ ⊠ ⚙ SC

★ **SUPER 8.** 50 Park Ave S (56301). 320/253-5530; FAX 320/253-5292. 68 rms, 2 story. S $34.88-$45.88; D $42.88-$58.88; each addl $5; under 13 free. Crib free. TV; cable (premium).

Complimentary continental bkfst. Restaurant adj open 24 hrs. Ck-out 11 am. Meeting rms. Business servs avail. Downhill ski 8 mi; x-country ski 1 mi. Cr cds: A, C, D, DS, MC, V.

D ✔ ⊠ ⊠ ⚙ SC

✔★ **TRAVEL HOUSE.** 3820 Roosevelt Rd (56301), County Rd 75 & I-94. 320/253-3338. 28 rms, 2 story. S, D $26.95-$51.95; each addl $3. TV. Continental bkfst. Bar noon-1 am. Ck-out 11 am. Refrigerators. Cr cds: A, C, D, DS, MC, V.

D ⊠ ⚙ SC

Motor Hotels

★★ **BEST WESTERN AMERICANNA INN.** 520 S US 10 (56304), S of jct US 10 & MN 23. 320/252-8700. 64 rms, 2 story. S $42.95-$60.95; D $59.95-$68.95; each addl $5; suites for 2-6, $74.95-$99.95; under 19 free. Crib $2. Pet accepted, some restrictions. TV; cable (premium). Indoor pool; whirlpool. Complimentary coffee in rms. Restaurant 11 am-10 pm; Sun to 9 pm. Rm serv. Bar 10:30-1 am; entertainment. Ck-out 11 am. Meeting rms. Business servs avail. In-rm modem link. Valet serv. Sundries. Sauna. Game rm. Cr cds: A, C, D, DS, ER, JCB, MC, V.

D ✔ ≋ ⊠ ⚙ SC

★★ **BEST WESTERN KELLY INN.** 1 Sunwood Dr (56301). 320/253-0606; FAX 320/202-0505. 230 rms, 6 story. S $58-$81; D $65-$79; each addl $6; suites $95-$175; under 18 free. Crib free. Pet accepted, some restrictions. TV; cable (premium), VCR avail (movies). Indoor pool; wading pool, whirlpool. Restaurant 6:30 am-10 pm. Bar 11-1 am; Sun to midnight. Ck-out 11 am. Coin lndry. Meeting rms. Business servs avail. In-rm modem link. Valet serv. Sundries. Gift shop. Sauna. Game rm. Poolside rms. Cr cds: A, C, D, DS, ER, MC, V.

D ✔ ≋ ⊠ ⚙ SC

★★ **HOLIDAY INN.** (56302). 37th Ave & W Division St. 320/253-9000; FAX 320/253-5998. 257 rms, 3 story. S, D $59-$112; suites $89-$169; under 19 free. Crib free. TV; cable (premium). 5 indoor pools; wading pool, whirlpool, poolside serv. Restaurant 6 am-2 pm, 5-10 pm; Sun from 7 am. Bar 11-1 am. Ck-out 11 am. Meeting rms. Business servs avail. Sundries. X-country ski 1 mi. Exercise equipt; weights, bicycles, sauna. Balconies. Cr cds: A, C, D, DS, JCB, MC, V.

D ✈ ≋ ⚶ ⊠ ⚙ SC

Restaurant

★★ **D.B. SEARLE'S.** 18 S Fifth Ave (56301). 320/253-0655. Hrs: 11 am-10 pm; Fri, Sat to 11 pm; Sun 3-10 pm. Closed some hols. Res accepted. Bar to 1 am; Sun 3 pm-midnight. Semi-a la carte: lunch $6.49-$7.39, dinner $9.39-$19.69. Specializes in French onion soup, stuffed popovers. Built 1886. Cr cds: A, MC, V.

St Paul (F-4)

(See also Hastings, Minneapolis, Stillwater)

Settled 1840 **Pop** 272,235 **Elev** 874 ft **Area code** 612

Information Convention and Visitors Bureau, 102 Norwest Center, 55 E Fifth St, 55101-1713; 612/297-6985 or 800/627-6101.

Distribution center for the great Northwest and dignified capital of Minnesota, stately St Paul had its humble beginnings in a settlement known as "Pig's Eye." At the great bend of the Mississippi and tangent to the point where the waters of the Mississippi and Minnesota rivers meet, St Paul and its twin city, Minneapolis, form a mighty northern metropolis. Together they are a center for computers, electronics, medical technology, printing and publishing. In many ways they complement each other, yet they are also friendly rivals. Fiercely proud of their professional athletes (the baseball Minnesota Twins, the football Minnesota Vikings, and the basketball Minnesota Timberwolves), the partisans of both cities troop to the Hubert H. Humphrey Metrodome Stadium in Minneapolis (see), as well as other arenas in the area, to watch their heroes in action.

A terraced city of diversified industry and lovely homes, St Paul boasts 30 lakes within a 30-minute drive, as well as more than 90 parks. St Paul is home to 3M Companies and other major corporations.

The junction of the Mississippi and Minnesota rivers was chosen in 1807 as the site for a fort that later became known as Fort Snelling. Squatters soon settled on the reservation lands nearby, only to be expelled in 1840 with one group moving a few miles east and a French-Canadian trader, Pierre Parrant, settling at the landing near Fort Snelling. Parrant was nicknamed "Pig's Eye," and the settlement that developed at the landing took this name.

When Father Lucien Galtier built a log cabin chapel there in 1841, he prevailed on the settlers to rename their community for Saint Paul. A Mississippi steamboat terminus since 1823, St Paul prospered on river trade, furs, pioneer traffic and agricultural commerce. Incorporated as a town in 1849, it was host to the first legislature of the Minnesota Territory and has been the capital ever since.

A number of institutions of higher education are located in St Paul, including University of Minnesota—Twin Cities Campus, University of St Thomas, College of St Catherine, Macalester College, Hamline University, Concordia College, Bethel College and William Mitchell College of Law.

Transportation

Car Rental Agencies: See IMPORTANT TOLL-FREE NUMBERS.

Public Transportation: Buses (Metropolitan Council Transit Operations) phone 612/373-3333.

Rail Passenger Service: Amtrak 612/644-1127 or 800/872-7245.

Airport Information

Minneapolis/St Paul Intl Airport: Information 612/726-5555; 612/726-5141 (lost and found); 612/452-2323 (weather); cash machines, Main terminal between Blue & Green Concourses.

What to See and Do

Alexander Ramsey House (1872). Home of Minnesota's first territorial governor; original furnishings. Guided tours; res suggested. (Apr-Dec, limited hrs; closed Thanksgiving, Dec 25) 265 S Exchange St. Phone 612/296-8760. ¢¢

Capitol City Trolley. Downtown. (Mon-Sat, also Sun afternoon) Phone 612/223-5600. ¢

Cathedral of St Paul (Roman Catholic) (1915). Dome 175 ft high; central rose window. (Daily) 239 Selby Ave. Phone 612/228-1766.

City Hall and Court House (1932). Prominent example of Art Deco, with Carl Milles' 60-ton, 36-ft-tall onyx *Vision of Peace* statue in the lobby. 15 W Kellogg Blvd. Phone 612/266-8023.

Fort Snelling State Park. A 4,000-acre park at confluence of the Minnesota and Mississippi rivers. Swimming, fishing, boating; hiking, biking, cross-country skiing; picnicking; visitor center. Standard fees. At jct MN 5 & Post Rd, just S of Main Terminal exit. Phone 612/725-2390. Includes

Historic Fort Snelling. Stone frontier fortress restored to its appearance of the 1820s; daily drills and cannon firings; craft demonstrations (June-Aug, daily; May & Sept-Oct, wkends only). Visitor Center with films, exhibits. (May-Oct, daily) Phone 612/725-2413. ¢¢

Gray Line bus tours. Greyhound Bus Depot. (See MINNEAPOLIS)

James J. Hill House (1891). Showplace of city when built for famous railroad magnate. Res suggested. (Wed-Sat; closed hols) 240 Summit Ave. Phone 612/297-2555. ¢¢

Landmark Center. Restored Federal Courts Building constructed in 1902; currently center for cultural programs and gangster history tours. Houses 4 courtrooms and 4-story indoor courtyard (the Cortile). Includes restaurant, archive gallery, auditorium, Schubert Club Keyboard Instrument Collection (Mon-Fri), and the Minnesota Museum of American Art. (Daily;

closed hols) 45-min tours (Thurs & Sun; also by appt); self-guided tours (daily). 75 W 5th St. Phone 612/292-3233 or -3230 (tours).   **Free.**

Luther Northwestern Theological Seminary (1869). (780 students) On campus is the Old Muskego Church (1844), first church built by Norse immigrants in America; moved to present site in 1904. Tours. 2481 Como Ave. Phone 612/641-3456.

Minnesota Children's Museum. Hands-on learning exhibits for children up to 12 yrs old; museum store stocked with unique puzzles, maps, toys, games, books. Self-guiding. (June-Aug & school hols, daily; rest of yr, daily exc Mon) 7th St & Wabasha. Phone 612/225-6000.   ¢¢

Minnesota History Center. Home to the Historical Society, the center houses a museum with interactive exhibits, extensive genealogical collection; special events, gift shop, restaurant. (Daily; hrs may vary, phone ahead) 345 Kellogg Blvd W, just S of State Capitol. Phone 612/296-6126 or 800/657-3773 (exc Twin Cities).   **Free.**

Minnesota Museum of American Art—Landmark Center. Changing exhibits and gallery of contemporary Midwest artists and new art forms. Also Museum School and store. (Daily exc Mon; closed hols) Fifth at Market St. Phone 612/292-4355. **Donation.**

Norwest Center Skyway. Created out of the 2nd level of Norwest Center's 5-story parking garage. The center includes shops and restaurants. (Daily; closed major hols) 56 E 6th St, located in the center of downtown.

Parks.

Town Square Park. Glass-enclosed indoor park includes waterfalls, streams, pools and greenery, giving it a tropical atmosphere. (Daily; closed some major hols) 7th & Cedar Sts, downtown. Phone 612/266-6400.

Como Park. A 448-acre park with 70-acre lake. Conservatory features authentic Japanese garden and tea house; "Gates Ajar" floral display, zoo. (Daily) Amusement area (Memorial Day-Labor Day, daily) with children's rides (fee). 18-hole golf course (fee). Midway & Lexington Pkwys. Phone 612/266-6400, 612/489-1740 (Conservatory), 612/488-5571 (Zoo).

Mounds Park. More than 25 acres of park containing prehistoric Native American burial mounds. 18 mounds existed on this site in 1856, 6 remain. Picnic facilities, ball field, view of Mississippi River. Mounds Blvd & Burns Ave, in Dayton's Bluff section. Phone 612/266-6400.

Sibley Historic Site. (1835). Home of General Henry Sibley, first governor, now preserved as museum. On same grounds is Faribault House Museum (1837), home of pioneer fur trader Jean Baptiste Faribault, a museum of the Native American and fur trade era. (May-Oct, daily exc Mon) 55 D St in Mendota, 1/2 mi N of MN 55 on Sibley Memorial Hwy. Phone 612/452-1596. ¢¢

⭐ **Sightseeing cruises.** Authentic Mississippi River sternwheelers *Harriet Bishop, Josiah Snelling* and *Jonathan Padelford* make 1 3/4-hr narrated trips to Historic Fort Snelling. Side-wheeler *Anson Northrup* makes trip through lock at St Anthony Falls. Dinner, brunch cruises also avail. (Memorial Day-Labor Day, daily; May & Sept, wkends) Harriet Island Park, W of Wabasha bridge. Phone 612/227-1100. Sightseeing cruises   ¢¢¢

State Capitol (1896-1905). Designed in the Italian Renaissance style by Cass Gilbert, and decorated with murals, sculpture, stencils and marble, the Capitol opened in 1905. 45-min guided tours leave on the hr; last tour leaves 1 hr before closing (group res required). (Daily; closed some major hols) 75 Constitution Ave. Phone 612/296-2881.   **Free.**

The Science Museum of Minnesota. Technology, anthropology, paleontology, geography and biology exhibits; William L. McKnight 3M Omnitheater. (Daily; Labor Day-Dec 25, daily exc Mon) 30 E 10th St. Phone 612/221-9444. ¢¢¢   Also here is

Great American History Theatre. Original works with American and Midwestern themes. (Sept-May, Thurs-Sun) Phone 612/292-4323.

University of Minnesota, Twin Cities Campus (1851). (39,315 students) Campus tours; animal barn tours (for small children). Phone 612/626-8687. Near campus is

Gibbs Farm Museum (1854). Restored furnished farmhouse depicting life on an urban fringe farm at the turn of the century. Includes 2 barns and a one-room schoolhouse. Interpretations, demonstrations, summer schoolhouse program. (May-Oct, Tues-Fri, also Sat & Sun afternoons) 2097 W Larpenteur Ave, Falcon Heights. Phone 612/646-8629. ¢¢

Annual Events

Winter Carnival. Throughout city. One of the leading winter festivals in America; ice and snow carving; parades, sports events, parties, pageants. Phone 612/223-4700. Last wkend Jan-1st wkend Feb.

Minnesota State Fair. Fairgrounds, 1265 Snelling Ave. Midway, thrill show, horse show, kids' days, all-star revue; more than one million visitors each year; 300 acres of attractions. Phone 612/642-2200. Late Aug-early Sept.

City Neighborhoods

Many of the restaurants, unrated dining establishments and some lodgings listed under St Paul include neighborhoods as well as exact street addresses. Geographic descriptions of these areas are given, followed by a table of restaurants arranged by neighborhood.

Downtown: South of 11th St, west of Jackson St, north of Kellogg Blvd and east of St Peter St. **North of Downtown:** North of I-94. **West of Downtown:** West of St Peter St.

Summit Hill: Adj to Rice Park; south of I-94, west of Kellogg Blvd, north of Summit Ave and east of Snelling Ave.

Rice Park: Adj to Downtown; south of 11th St, west of St Peter St and north and east of Kellogg Blvd.

ST PAUL RESTAURANTS BY NEIGHBORHOOD AREAS
(For full description, see alphabetical listings under Restaurants)

DOWNTOWN
Gallivan's. 354 Wabasha St
Leeann Chin Chinese Cuisine. 214 E 4th St
Mancini's Char House. 531 W Seventh St
No Wake Cafe. Pier One
The Saint Paul Grill (The Saint Paul Hotel). 350 Market St
Sakura. 34 W 6th St
Sawatdee. 289 E Fifth St

NORTH OF DOWNTOWN
Dakota Bar & Grill. 1021 E Bandana
Muffuletta in the Park. 2260 Como Ave
Toby's on the Lake. 249 Geneva Ave N

WEST OF DOWNTOWN
Buca Little Italy. 2728 Gannon Rd
Caravan Serai. 2175 Ford Pkwy
Cecil's Delicatessen, Bakery & Restaurant. 651 S Cleveland
Forepaugh's. 276 S Exchange St
Old City Cafe. 1571 Grand Ave
Ristorante Luci. 470 Cleveland Ave S
Table of Contents. 1648 Grand Ave
Tulips. 452 Selby Ave
W.A. Frost & Company. 374 Selby Ave

SUMMIT HILL
Ciatti's. 850 Grand Ave
Dixie's. 695 Grand Ave
Green Mill Inn. 57 S Hamline Ave
Lexington. 1096 Grand Ave

Note: When a listing is located in a town that does not have its own city heading, it will appear under the city nearest to its location. In these cases, the address and town appear in parenthesis immediately following the name of the establishment.

Motels

★ ★ **BEST WESTERN DROVER'S INN.** *(701 S Concord St, South St Paul 55075)* At jct I-494 & Concord St. 612/455-3600; FAX 612/455-0282. 85 rms, 4 story. S, D $70-$90; each addl $10; under 19 free. Crib free. TV; cable (premium). VCR avail. Indoor pool; whirlpool. Coffee in rms. Restaurant 6:30 am-2 pm, 5-9 pm; Sun 8 am-1 pm. Rm serv. Bar 2 pm-1 am; closed Sun. Ck-out noon. Meeting rms. Business servs avail. Valet serv. Sundries. Free airport transportation. Microwaves avail. Cr cds: A, C, D, DS, MC, V.

D ≈ 🛏 🛇 🐾

★ ★ **BEST WESTERN MAPLEWOOD INN.** *1780 E County Road D (55109), adj to Maplewood Mall, north of downtown.* 612/770-2811; FAX 612/770-2811, ext. 184. 118 rms, 2 story. S $58-$108; D $62-$108; each addl $4; under 18 free. Crib free. Pet accepted; $5 deposit. TV; cable (premium). Indoor pool; whirlpool. Coffee in rms. Restaurant 6:30 am-2 pm, 5-10 pm. Rm serv. Bar 4 pm-1 am; entertainment Fri, Sat. Ck-out noon. Coin lndry. Meeting rms. Business servs avail. In-rm modem link. Valet serv. Sundries. Sauna. Health club privileges. Game rm. Microwaves avail. Cr cds: A, C, D, DS, ER, JCB, MC, V.

D 🐾 ✦ ≈ 🛇 🛏 SC

★ ★ **COUNTRY INN BY CARLSON.** *(6003 Hudson Rd, Woodbury 55125)* 4 mi E on I-94, exit Century Ave (MN 120). 612/739-7300; FAX 612/731-4007; res: 800/456-4000. Web www.countryinns-suites.com. 158 rms, 2 story. S, D $81-$99; each addl $8; under 19 free. Crib free. TV; cable (premium). Indoor pool; whirlpool. Complimentary continental bkfst. Complimentary coffee in rms. Restaurant 11 am-10 pm; Fri, Sat to midnight. Rm serv. Bar from 11 am. Ck-out noon. Coin lndry. Meeting rms. Business servs avail. In-rm modem link. Concierge. Valet serv. Downhill ski 12 mi, x-country ski 11 mi. Exercise equipt; weight machine, treadmill, sauna. Game rm. Many refrigerators. Cr cds: A, C, D, DS, MC, V.

D 🐾 ✦ ≈ 🏋 🛇 🛏 SC

✔★ **EXEL INN.** *1739 Old Hudson Rd (55106).* 612/771-5566; FAX 612/771-1262. 100 rms, 3 story. S $38.99-$53.99; D $43.99-$58.99; each addl $5; under 18 free; ski, wkly plans; higher rates special events. Crib free. Pet accepted. TV; cable (premium). Complimentary continental bkfst. Restaurant adj open 24 hrs. Ck-out noon. Coin lndry. Business servs avail. In-rm modem link. Downhill ski 15 mi; x-country ski 2 mi. Game rm. Refrigerators; microwaves avail. Cr cds: A, C, D, DS, MC, V.

D 🐾 ✦ 🛇 🛏 SC

★ ★ **HAMPTON INN-NORTH.** *(1000 Gramsie Rd, Shoreview 55126)* 612/482-0402; FAX 612/482-8917. 120 rms, 2 story. S, D $69-$89; under 16 free. Crib free. TV; cable (premium). Indoor pool; whirlpool. Complimentary continental bkfst. Restaurant 11 am-11 pm. Rm serv. Bar to 1 am. Ck-out 11 am. Meeting rms. Business servs avail. In-rm modem link. Coin lndry. Exercise equipt; bicycle, stair machine. Cr cds: A, C, D, DS, MC, V.

≈ 🏋 🛇 🛏 SC

★ ★ **HOLIDAY INN EXPRESS.** *1010 Bandana Blvd W (55108), north of downtown.* 612/647-1637; FAX 612/647-0244. 109 rms, 2 story. S, D $81-$101; suites $101-$131. Crib free. TV; cable (premium). Indoor pool; wading pool, whirlpool. Complimentary continental bkfst. Ck-out noon. Meeting rms. Business servs avail. In-rm modem link. Downhill ski 15 mi; x-country ski 1 mi. Sauna. Some refrigerators. Motel built within exterior structure of old railroad repair building; old track runs through lobby. Shopping center adj; connected by skywalk. Cr cds: A, C, D, DS, ER, MC, V.

D 🐾 ≈ 🛇 🛏 SC

✔★ **RED ROOF INN.** *(1806 Wooddale Dr, Woodbury 55125)* I-494 at Valley Creek Rd. 612/738-7160; FAX 612/738-1869. 108 rms, 2 story. S $33.99-$58.99; D $46.99-$68.99; each addl $8; under 18 free. Crib free. Pet accepted. TV; cable (premium). Complimentary coffee.

Restaurant nearby. Ck-out noon. Business servs avail. In-rm modem link. Downhill ski 15 mi; x-country ski 3 mi. Cr cds: A, C, D, DS, MC, V.

D ⚡ 🏊 🦅 🔥

★ **SUPER 8.** (285 N Century Ave, Maplewood 55119) 612/738-1600; FAX 612/738-9405. 112 rms, 4 story. Late May-early Sept: S $48.88-$55.88; D $55.88-$60.88; each addl $5; under 12 free; lower rates rest of yr. Crib free. Pet accepted; $50. TV; cable (premium). Complimentary continental bkfst. Restaurant adj. Ck-out 11 am. Coin lndry. Business servs avail. In-rm modem link. Sundries. Airport transportation. Downhill ski 15 mi; x-country ski 2 mi. Health club privileges. Microwaves avail. Picnic tables. On lake. Cr cds: A, C, D, DS, MC, V.

D ⚡ 🏊 🦅 🔥 🐾 SC

Motor Hotels

★ **BEST WESTERN KELLY INN.** 161 St Anthony Blvd (55103), I-94 exit Marion St, west of downtown. 612/227-8711; FAX 612/227-1698. 126 rms, 7 story. S $74-$89; D $79-$99; each addl $8; suites $115-$185; under 15 free; higher rates special events. Crib free. Pet accepted. TV; cable. Indoor pool; wading pool, whirlpool. Restaurant 6:30 am-9 pm. Rm serv. Bar 11-1 am; Sat 4 pm-midnight; Sun 4-10 pm. Meeting rms. Business servs avail. In-rm modem link. Sundries. Valet serv. Downhill ski 20 mi; x-country ski 4 mi. Sauna. Game rm. Microwaves in suites. Cr cds: A, C, D, DS, MC, V.

D ⚡ 🏊 🦅 🔥 🐾 SC

★ **DAYS INN-CIVIC CENTER.** 175 W Seventh St (55102), at Kellogg, opp St Paul Civic Center, downtown. 612/292-8929; FAX 612/292-1749. E-mail daysinnmn@aol.com. 203 rms, 8 story. S $60-$75; D $68-$83; each addl $8; suites $115-$155; under 18 free; wknd rates; higher rates state tournament wknds. Crib free. Pet accepted. TV; cable (premium). Restaurant 6 am-midnight. Bar 4 pm-1 am. Ck-out 11 am. Meeting rms. Business servs avail. In-rm modem link. Valet serv. Downhill ski 20 mi; x-country ski 4 mi. Health club privileges. Some refrigerators; microwaves avail. Cr cds: A, C, D, DS, ER, JCB, MC, V.

D ⚡ 🏊 🦅 🔥 🐾 SC

★★★ **HOLIDAY INN.** 1201 W County Rd E (55112). 612/636-4123; FAX 612/636-2526. Web www.traveler.net/ht10/custom/1910.html. 156 rms, 4 story. S, D $89-$130; each addl $10; suites $99-$149; under 19 free. Crib free. TV; cable (premium). Indoor pool; whirlpool. Complimentary full bkfst. Coffee in rms. Restaurant 6:30 am-10 pm. Bar to 1 am. Ck-out noon. Meeting rms. Business servs avail. Valet serv. Coin lndry. Exercise equipt; bicycles, treadmill. Some refrigerators. Cr cds: A, C, D, DS, MC, V.

D 🏊 🏃 🦅 🐾 SC

★★★ **HOLIDAY INN-EAST.** 2201 Burns Ave (55119), I-94 & McKnight Rd, east of downtown. 612/731-2220; FAX 612/731-0243. 192 rms, 8 story. S, D $86-$96; under 19 free; wknd rates. Crib free. TV; cable (premium). Indoor pool; whirlpool. Restaurant 6 am-2 pm, 5-10 pm; Sat, Sun from 7 am. Rm serv. Bar 4 pm-1 am. Ck-out noon. Coin lndry. Meeting rms. Business servs avail. In-rm modem link. Bellhops. Valet serv. Sundries. Gift shop. Downhill ski 10 mi; x-country ski ½ mi. Exercise equipt; weight machine, bicycles, sauna. Game rm. Some bathroom phones. Luxury level. Cr cds: A, C, D, DS, JCB, MC, V.

D 🏃 🏊 🏃 🦅 🐾 SC

★★★ **SHERATON-MIDWAY.** 400 Hamline Ave N (55104), west of downtown. 612/642-1234; FAX 612/642-1126. 197 rms, 4 story. S $95-$125; D $102-$125; each addl $10; under 18 free; wknd rates. Crib free. TV; cable (premium). Indoor pool; whirlpool. Complimentary coffee in rms. Restaurant 6:30 am-10:30 pm. Rm serv. Bar 11 am-midnight, Sun from noon. Ck-out noon. Meeting rms. Business servs avail. In-rm modem link. Bellhops. Downhill ski 15 mi; x-country ski 7 mi. Exercise equipt; weights, bicycles. Health club privileges. Cr cds: A, C, D, DS, MC, V.

D 🏃 🏊 🏃 🦅 🐾 SC

Hotels

★★★ **EMBASSY SUITES.** 175 E 10th St (55101), downtown. 612/224-5400; FAX 612/224-0957. Web www.embassy-suites.com. 210 suites, 8 story. S $129; D $139; each addl $10; under 12 free; wkend, hol rates. Crib free. TV; cable (premium). Indoor pool; whirlpool. Complimentary full bkfst. Coffee in rms. Restaurant 11 am-10 pm. Bar to 1 am. Ck-out noon. Coin lndry. Meeting rms. Business servs avail. In-rm modem link. Gift shop. Free airport transportation. Exercise equipt; weight machine, bicycles, sauna, steam rm. Refrigerators, microwaves, wet bars. Atrium with pond, waterfalls, fountains, ducks; many plants and trees. Cr cds: A, C, D, DS, ER, JCB, MC, V.

D 🏊 🏃 🦅 🔥 SC

★★★ **HOLIDAY INN SELECT-MINNEAPOLIS AIRPORT/EAGAN.** (2700 Pilot Knob Rd, Eagan 55121) SW on I-494. 612/454-3434; FAX 612/454-4904. 187 rms, 6 story. S, D $79-$109; suites $129-$149; under 20 free. Crib free. TV; cable (premium). Indoor pool; whirlpool. Coffee in rms. Restaurant 7 am-11 pm. Bar. Ck-out noon. Coin lndry. Meeting rms. Business servs avail. In-rm modem link. Free airport transportation. Exercise equipt; stair machine, bicycles, sauna. Health club privileges. Cr cds: A, C, D, DS, JCB, MC, V.

D 🏊 🏃 🦅 🔥 SC

★★★ **RADISSON.** 11 E Kellogg Blvd (55101), downtown. 612/292-1900; FAX 612/224-8999. Web www.radisson.com. 475 rms, 22 story. S $110; D $140; each addl $10; under 18 free; package plans. Crib free. Pet accepted, some restrictions. Garage parking $11. TV; cable (premium), VCR avail. Indoor pool. Restaurant 6:30 am-10:30 pm; Fri, Sat to 11:30 pm. Bars 11:30-1 am. Ck-out noon. Convention facilities. Business servs avail. In-rm modem link. Concierge. Downhill ski 15 mi; x-country ski 4 mi. Exercise equipt; weight machine, stair machine. Health club privileges. Some refrigerators, microwaves. Indoor skyway to major stores, businesses. Luxury level. Cr cds: A, C, D, DS, ER, MC, V.

D ⚡ 🏊 🏃 🦅 🐾 SC

★★★★ **THE SAINT PAUL.** 350 Market St (55102), downtown. 612/292-9292; FAX 612/228-9506; res: 800/292-9292. This stately, stone hotel overlooks Rice Park and the center of St Paul. Rooms are done in a pleasing, traditional decor. Business services and health club privileges are available; exercise equipment will be delivered to your room on request. 254 rms, 12 story. S, D $149-$164; each addl $15; suites $425-$650; under 19 free; wkend rates; package plans. Crib free. Garage $10.95. TV; cable, VCR avail. Restaurant (see THE SAINT PAUL GRILL). Bar 11-1 am. Ck-out noon. Convention facilities. Business center. In-rm modem link. Concierge. Downhill ski 15 mi; x-country ski 4 mi. Exercise equipt; bicycles, stair machine; equipt delivered to rms on request. Health club privileges. Connected to downtown skyway system. Cr cds: A, C, D, DS, MC, V.

D 🦅 🏃 🦅 🐾 SC ⛷

Restaurants

✔★ **BUCA LITTLE ITALY.** 2728 Gannon Rd (55116), west of downtown. 612/772-4388. Hrs: 5-10 pm; Fri to 11 pm; Sat 4-11 pm; Sun 4-10 pm. Closed Thanksgiving, Dec 24, 25. Italian menu. Bar. A la carte entrees: dinner $13-$17. Specializes in pasta, seafood. Outdoor dining. Italian decor. Cr cds: A, D, MC, V.

D

✔★★ **CARAVAN SERAI.** 2175 Ford Pkwy, west of downtown. 612/690-1935. Hrs: 11 am-2 pm, 5-9:30 pm; Mon from 5 pm; Fri to 10:30 pm; Sat 5-10:30 pm; Sun 4:30-9:30 pm; early-bird dinner Sun-Thurs 5-6 pm. Closed most major hols. Res accepted. Afghani, Northern Indian menu. Wine, beer. Semi-a la carte: lunch $3.25-$6.25, dinner $8.95-$16.95. Child's meals. Specialties: tandoori chicken, vegetarian combination platter. Guitarist, Egyptian dancers Tues, Thurs-Sat. Hand-crafted tapestries, floor seating. Cr cds: A, C, D, MC, V.

🦅

★ ★ **CIATTI'S.** *850 Grand Ave, in Summit Hill.* 612/292-9942. Hrs: 11 am-10 pm; Fri, Sat to 11 pm; Sun from 2:30 pm; Sun brunch 10 am-2 pm. Closed Thanksgiving, Dec 24, 25. Italian menu. Res accepted. Bar to 1 am. Semi-a la carte: lunch $6.95-$9.95, dinner $7.95-$14.95. Sun brunch $6.95-$11.95. Child's meals. Specializes in northern Italian dishes. Own sauces. Cr cds: A, D, DS, MC, V.

★ ★ **DAKOTA BAR & GRILL.** *1021 E Bandana, north of downtown.* 612/642-1442. E-mail dakotajazz@aol.com. Hrs: 5:30-10:30 pm; Fri, Sat to 11:30 pm; Sun to 9:30 pm; Sun brunch 11 am-2:30 pm. Closed most major hols. Res accepted. Bar 4 pm-midnight; Fri, Sat to 1 am. Semi-a la carte: dinner $13-$26.95. Sun brunch $9.95-$18.95. Child's meals. Specializes in regional and seasonal dishes. Jazz evenings. Parking. Outdoor dining. Located in restored railroad building in historic Bandana Square. Modern decor. Cr cds: A, C, D, DS, MC, V.

★ **DIXIE'S.** *695 Grand Ave (55105), in Summit Hill.* 612/222-7345. E-mail dixies@iaxs.net; web www.iaxs.net/~dixies. Hrs: 11 am-midnight; Sun 2:30-11 pm; Sun brunch 10 am-2 pm. Closed Thanksgiving. Res accepted. Southern, Cajun menu. Bar to 1 am; Sun to midnight. Semi-a la carte: lunch $4.50-$9.95, dinner $4.95-$15.95. Sun brunch $10.95. Specialties; hickory-smoked ribs, Key lime pie. Parking. Informal dining. Cr cds: A, D, DS, MC, V.

★ ★ **FOREPAUGH'S.** *276 S Exchange St, west of downtown.* 612/224-5606. Hrs: 11:30 am-2, 5:30-9:30 pm; Sat from 5:30 pm; Sun 5-8:30 pm; Sun brunch 10:30 am-1:30 pm. Closed some hols. Res accepted. French menu. Bar to 1 am; Sun to midnight. Semi-a la carte: lunch $7.50-$9.95, dinner $11.95-$18.75. Sun brunch $12.50. Child's meals. Specialties: shrimp scampi, twin tournedos, veal calvados. Valet parking. Outdoor dining. Restored mansion (1870); 9 dining rms. Cr cds: A, D, MC, V.

★ **GALLIVAN'S.** *354 Wabasha St, downtown.* 612/227-6688. Hrs: 11 am-10 pm; Fri, Sat to 11 pm; Sun 4-8 pm. Closed major hols. Res accepted. Bar to 1 am. Semi-a la carte: lunch $3.95-$8.45, dinner $9.95-$21.95. Specializes in steak, prime rib, seafood. Entertainment Fri, Sat. Cr cds: A, C, D, DS, MC, V.

★ ★ **KOZLAK'S ROYAL OAK.** *(4785 Hodgson Rd, Shoreview 55126) 3 mi N of I-694 on MN 49.* 612/484-8484. Hrs: 11 am-2:30 pm, 4-9:30 pm; Fri to 10:30 pm; Sat 4-10:30 pm; Sun 10 am-1:30 pm (brunch), 4-8:30 pm; early-bird dinner Sun-Fri to 5:45 pm. Closed most major hols. Res accepted. Bar to midnight; Fri, Sat to 1 am. Semi-a la carte: lunch $5.50-$12, dinner $15.50-$27. Sun brunch $9.95-$16.95. Child's meals. Specialties: steer tenderloin filet, duckling, salmon. Salad bar. Own baking. Strolling jazz musicians Sun brunch. Outdoor dining. Elegant decor with arched windows, etched glass; dining rm overlooks garden that changes seasonally. Family-owned. Cr cds: A, C, D, DS, MC, V.

★ ★ **LAKE ELMO INN.** *(3442 Lake Elmo Ave, Lake Elmo 55042) 12 mi E on I-94 to I-694, 2 mi N to MN 5, then 4 mi E.* 612/777-8495. Hrs:11 am-2, 5-10 pm; Sun 10 am-2 pm, 4:30-8:30 pm. Closed some major hols. Res accepted. Continental menu. Bar to midnight. Wine list. Semi-a la carte: lunch $6-$8.95, dinner $14-$18. Sun brunch $13.95. Child's meals. Specializes in rack of lamb, roast duckling. Outdoor dining. Casual elegance in restored inn & stagecoach stop (1881). Cr cds: A, C, D, DS, MC, V.

✔★ ★ **LEEANN CHIN CHINESE CUISINE.** *214 E 4th St (55101), downtown.* 612/224-8814. Hrs: 11 am-2:30 pm, 5-9 pm; Fri, Sat to 10 pm. Closed major hols. Res accepted. Chinese menu. Serv bar. Buffet: lunch $7.95, dinner $13.95. Child's meals. Specializes in Cantonese, mandarin and Szechwan dishes. Contemporary decor. Totally nonsmoking. Cr cds: A, D, DS, MC, V.

★ ★ ★ **LEXINGTON.** *1096 Grand Ave, at Lexington Pkwy, in Summit Hill.* 612/222-5878. Hrs: 11 am-10 pm; Fri, Sat to 11 pm; Sun 4-9 pm; Sun brunch 10 am-3 pm. Closed Dec 24 evening, 25, July 4. Res accepted. Bar. Semi-a la carte: lunch $6.95-$11.95, dinner $9.95-$27. Sun brunch $4.95-$11.95. Child's meals. Specializes in prime rib, fresh walleye. Parking. French Provincial decor. Cr cds: A, C, D, DS, MC, V.

★ **LINDEY'S.** *(3600 Snelling Ave N, Arden Hills 55112)* 612/633-9813. Hrs: 5-10:30 pm; Fri, Sat to 11:30 pm. Closed Sun; major hols. Bar. Semi-a la carte: dinner $13.65-$19.85. Child's meals. Specializes in steak. Rustic, Northwoods lodge atmosphere. No cr cds accepted.

★ **MANCINI'S CHAR HOUSE.** *531 W Seventh St, downtown.* 612/224-7345. Hrs: 5-11 pm; Fri, Sat to 12:30 am. Closed major hols. Bar to 1 am. Semi-a la carte: dinner $10-$29. Specializes in steak, lobster. Entertainment Wed-Sat. Parking. Open charcoal hearths; 2 fireplaces. Family-owned. Cr cds: A, C, D, MC, V.

★ ★ **MUFFULETTA IN THE PARK.** *2260 Como Ave, north of downtown.* 612/644-9116. Hrs: 11 am-2:30 pm, 5-9:30 pm; Fri, Sat to 10 pm; Sun 10 am-2 pm, 5-8 pm. Closed some major hols. Res accepted. Continental menu. Wine, beer. Semi-a la carte: lunch $5.95-$9.95, dinner $7.95-$15.95. Sun brunch $5.25-$9.95. Specializes in pasta, fresh fish. Own soup, dressings. Parking. Outdoor dining. Cafe decor. Totally nonsmoking. Cr cds: A, D, DS, MC, V.

✔★ ★ **RISTORANTE LUCI.** *470 Cleveland Ave S (55105), west of downtown.* 612/699-8258. Hrs: 5-9:30 pm; Fri, Sat to 10:30 pm; Sun 4:30-9 pm. Closed major hols. Res accepted. Italian menu. Wine, beer. Semi-a la carte: dinner $7.75-$18.95. Child's meals. Specializes in pasta, seafood. Italian decor. Totally nonsmoking. Cr cds: MC, V.

★ ★ ★ **THE SAINT PAUL GRILL.** *(See The Saint Paul Hotel)* 612/224-7455. Hrs: 11:30 am-midnight; Sun brunch 11 am-2 pm. Res accepted. Bar to 1 am; Sun to midnight. Wine list. Semi-a la carte: lunch $6-$12, dinner $9-$26. Sun brunch $9-$15. Child's meals. Specializes in fresh fish, regional cuisine. Valet parking. Elegant dining rm in historic hotel offers panoramic view of Rice Park. Cr cds: A, C, D, DS, MC, V.

✔★ **SAKURA.** *34 W 6th St (55102), downtown.* 612/224-0185. Hrs: 11:30 am-2:30 pm, 5-10:30 pm; Fri, Sat to 11 pm; Sun to 9:30 pm. Closed Jan 1, Thanksgiving, Dec 25. Res accepted. Japanese menu. Bar. Semi-a la carte: lunch $6-$10, dinner $10-$15. Specializes in sushi, sashimi, teriyaki. Validated parking. Contemporary Japanese decor; sushi bar. Cr cds: A, D, DS, JCB, MC, V.

★ **SAWATDEE.** *289 E Fifth St (55101), downtown.* 612/222-5859. Web www.sawatdee.com. Hrs: 11 am-10 pm; Fri, Sat to 11 pm. Closed most major hols. Res accepted. Thai menu. Bar. Semi-a la carte: lunch, dinner $6-$8. Buffet: lunch $5.95. Specializes in noodle dishes, curry dishes. Thai decor. Cr cds: A, D, DS, MC, V.

★ **TABLE OF CONTENTS.** *1648 Grand Ave (55105), west of downtown.* 612/699-6595. Hrs: 11:30 am-2, 5:30-9:30 pm; Fri, Sat to 10:30 pm; Sun 10 am-2 pm, 5-9 pm. Closed most major hols. Res accepted. Contemporary Amer menu. Wine, beer. Semi-a la carte: lunch $5.95-$11.95, dinner $10.95-$19.95. Sun brunch $5.25-$9.75. Specializes in pasta, seafood. Contemporary decor. Adj bookstore. Cr cds: A, D, DS, MC, V.

★ ★ **TOBY'S ON THE LAKE.** *249 Geneva Ave N, on Tanners Lake, north of downtown.* 612/739-1600. Hrs: 11 am-2:30 pm, 5-10 pm; Sat 11 am-11 pm; Sun 11 am-9 pm; Sun brunch to 2 pm. Closed Dec 25.

Res accepted. Bar. Semi-a la carte: lunch $5.95-$11.95, dinner $9.95-$19.95. Sun brunch $5.95-$8.50. Child's meals. Specializes in prime rib, fresh seafood. Parking. Outdoor dining. Olde English atmosphere. Overlooks Tanners Lake. Cr cds: A, C, D, DS, MC, V.

D ⌐⌐

✔★ **TULIPS.** 452 Selby Ave (55102), Cathedral Hill area, west of downtown. 612/221-1061. Hrs: 11:30 am-3 pm, 5-10 pm; Fri, Sat to 11 pm; Sun brunch to 2:30 pm. Closed most major hols. Res accepted. French menu. Wine, beer. Semi-a la carte: lunch $6-$12, dinner $10-$20. Sun brunch $6-$15. Specialties: sea scallops, herbed walnut walleye, filet mignon with béarnaise sauce. Outdoor dining. Country French decor; intimate dining. Cr cds: D, MC, V.

D ⌐⌐

★ ★ **VENETIAN INN.** (2814 Rice St, Little Canada) S of I-694 Rice St exit. 612/484-7215. Hrs: 11 am-10 pm; Fri, Sat to 11 pm. Closed Sun; most major hols. Res accepted. Italian, Amer menu. Bar to 1 am. Semi-a la carte: lunch $6.50-$8.50, dinner $7.95-$17.95. Complete meals: Sicilian dinner (for 2 or more) $22.50. Child's meals. Specializes in steak, barbecued ribs, lasagne. Theatre entertainment Fri, Sat. Parking. Family-owned. Cr cds: A, C, D, DS, MC, V.

D ⌐⌐

★ ★ **W.A. FROST & COMPANY.** 374 Selby Ave (55102), west of downtown. 612/224-5715. E-mail wafrost@popp.ix.netcom.com. Hrs: 11-11 am; Sun 10:30 am-midnight. Closed some major hols. Res accepted. Bar. Semi-a la carte: lunch $7-$11, dinner $6.95-$22. Sun brunch $5-$10. Child's meals. Specialties: Nantucket chicken, chocolate silk pie. Parking. Outdoor dining in garden area. Three dining rms; Victorian-style decor. Renovated pharmacy (1887). Totally nonsmoking. Cr cds: A, C, D, DS, MC, V.

D

Unrated Dining Spots

CECIL'S DELICATESSEN, BAKERY & RESTAURANT. 651 S Cleveland, west of downtown. 612/698-0334. Hrs: 9 am-8 pm. Semi-a la carte: bkfst $1.75-$4.50, lunch, dinner $3-$6.50. Specializes in corned beef, pastrami sandwiches, homemade desserts. Own baking, soups. Parking. Family-owned. Cr cds: MC, V.

GREEN MILL INN. 57 S Hamline Ave, in Summit Hill. 612/698-0353. Hrs: 11 am-11 pm; Fri, Sat to midnight. Closed Dec 24 eve-Dec 25. Italian, Amer menu. Wine, beer. Semi-a la carte: lunch, dinner $2.95-$10.75. Specializes in deep dish pizza, sandwiches. Own soups, chili. Cr cds: A, D, MC, V.

D ⌐⌐

NO WAKE CAFE. Pier One (55107), Harriet Island, downtown. 612/292-1411. Hrs: 8 am-2 pm; Thur also 5-9 pm; Fri, Sat also 5-10 pm; Sun 8 am-noon. Closed Mon; most major hols; also Jan-Feb. Wine, beer. Semi-a la carte: bkfst $4-$6, lunch $3.50-$7, dinner $9-$15. Specialties: Tuscan tenderloin, almond crusted walleye. Vintage towboat on Mississippi River. Cr cds: MC, V.

OLD CITY CAFE. 1571 Grand Ave (55105), west of downtown. 612/699-5347. Hrs: 11 am-9 pm; Fri to 2 pm; Sun from 10 am. Closed Sat; major Jewish hols. Wine, beer. A la carte entrees: bkfst $1.25-$4.95, lunch $1.50-$4.95, dinner $3.50-$8.50. Specializes in kosher deli fare, Middle Eastern salads, falafel. Informal neighborhood deli with Middle Eastern decor. No cr cds accepted.

D SC ⌐⌐

St Peter (G-3)

(For accommodations see Faribault, Mankato, New Ulm; also see Le Sueur)

Founded 1853 **Pop** 9,421 **Elev** 770 ft **Area code** 507 **Zip** 56082 **Web** tourism.st-peter.mn.us

Information St Peter Area Chamber of Commerce, 101 S Front St; 507/931-3400 or 800/473-3404.

What to See and Do

Eugene Saint Julien Cox House (1871). Fully restored home is best example of Gothic Italianate architecture in the state. Built by town's first mayor; late-Victorian furnishings. Guided tours. (June-Aug, Wed-Sun; May & Sept, Sat & Sun afternoons) 500 N Washington Ave. Phone 507/931-2160. ¢¢

Gustavus Adolphus College (1862). (2,300 students) On campus are Old Main (dedicated 1876); Alfred Nobel Hall of Science and Gallery; Lund Center for Physical Education; Folke Bernadotte Memorial Library; Linnaeus Arboretum; Schaefer Fine Arts Gallery; Christ Chapel, featuring door and narthex art by noted sculptor Paul Granlund. At various other locations on campus are sculptures by Granlund, sculptor in residence, including one depicting Joseph Nicollét, mid-19th-century French explorer & cartographer of the Minnesota River Valley. Campus tours. In Oct, the college hosts the nationally known Nobel Conference, which has been held annually since 1965. 800 W College Ave. Phone 507/933-8000.

Treaty Site History Center. County historical items relating to Dakota people, explorers, settlers, traders and cartographers and their impact on the 1851 Treaty of Traverse des Sioux. Archives. Museum shop. (Daily; closed major hols) 1851 N Minnesota Ave. Phone 507/931-2160. ¢¢

Sauk Centre (E-2)

(See also Alexandria, Glenwood)

Pop 3,581 **Elev** 1,246 ft **Area code** 320 **Zip** 56378 **Web** www.sauk centre.com

Information Sauk Centre Area Chamber of Commerce, PO Box 222; 320/352-5201.

This is "Gopher Prairie," the boyhood home of Sinclair Lewis and the setting for Main Street, as well as many of his other novels. The town is at the southern tip of Big Sauk Lake.

What to See and Do

Sinclair Lewis Boyhood Home. Restored home of America's first Nobel prize-winning novelist. Original furnishings; family memorabilia. (Memorial Day-Labor Day, daily; rest of yr, by appt) 812 Sinclair Lewis Ave. Phone 320/352-5201. ¢¢

Sinclair Lewis Interpretive Center. Exhibits include original manuscripts, photographs, letters; 15-min video on the author's life; research library. (Mon-Fri; Memorial Day-Labor Day, Sat & Sun) At jct I-94, US 71. Phone 320/352-5201. **Free.**

Annual Event

Sinclair Lewis Days. 3rd wkend July.

Motels

✔★ **ECONO LODGE.** I-94 & US 71. 320/352-6581; FAX 320/352-6584. 38 rms, 2 story. S $40-$50; D $50-$65; each addl $5; under 12 free. Crib $2.50. Pet accepted, some restrictions. TV; cable (premium).

Indoor pool. Ck-out 11 am. Business servs avail. Cr cds: A, C, D, DS, JCB, MC, V.

★ **HILLCREST.** *965 S Main St. 320/352-2215; res: 800/858-6333.* 21 rms. S $24; D $26-$32; each addl $4. TV; cable (premium). Restaurant nearby. Ck-out 11 am. Cr cds: A, DS, MC, V.

Spring Valley (H-4)

(For accommodations see Austin, Rochester)

Pop 2,461 **Elev** 1,279 ft **Area code** 507 **Zip** 55975

As the name suggests, there are many large springs in this area. Geologists find the underground rivers, caves and limestone outcroppings here of particular interest.

What to See and Do

Forestville State Park. A 2,691-acre park in Root River valley with historic townsite. Fishing; hiking; bridle trails. Cross-country skiing, snowmobiling; picnicking; camping. Standard fees. 6 mi E on MN 16, 4 mi S on County 5, then 2 mi E on County 12. Phone 507/352-5111. Per vehicle ¢¢ Also in park is

   Mystery Cave. Eighty-min guided tours; 48°F in cave. (Memorial Day-Labor Day, daily) Picnicking. Vehicle permit required (addl fee). Phone 507/352-5111. ¢¢¢

Historic buildings.

   Washburn-Zittleman House. (1866). Two-story frame house with period furnishings, quilts; farm equipment, one-room school, toys. (Memorial Day-Labor Day, daily; also Oct by appt) 220 W Courtland St. Phone 507/346-7659. ¢

   Methodist Church (1878). Victorian Gothic architecture; 23 stained-glass windows. Laura Ingalls Wilder site. Lower-level displays include country store, history rm; military & business displays. (June-Aug, daily; Sept-Oct, Sun; also by appt) 221 W Courtland St. Phone 507/346-7659. ¢¢

Stillwater (F-4)

(See also St Paul, Taylors Falls)

Settled 1839 **Pop** 13,882 **Elev** 700 ft **Area code** 612 **Zip** 55082
Information Chamber of Commerce, 423 S Main St, Brick Alley Bldg; 612/439-7700.

Center of the logging industry in pioneer days, Stillwater became a busy river town, host to the men who rode the logs downriver and the lumbermen who cleared the forests.

What to See and Do

St Croix Scenic Highway. MN 95 runs 50 mi from Afton to Taylors Falls (see) along the "Rhine of America," the St Croix River.

Washington County Historical Museum. Former warden's house at old prison site; mementos of lumbering days (1846-1910); pioneer kitchen, furniture. (May-Oct, Tues, Thurs, Sat & Sun; also by appt) 602 N Main St. Phone 612/439-5956. ¢

William O'Brien State Park. A 1,273-acre park. Swimming, fishing, boating (ramp); hiking, cross-country skiing, picnicking, camping (hookups, dump station). Standard fees. 16 mi N on MN 95. Phone 612/433-0500.

Annual Events

Rivertown Art Fair. Lowell Park. 3rd wkend May.

Lumberjack Days. Last wkend July.

Motels

★★ **BEST WESTERN STILLWATER INN.** *1750 Frontage Rd W, near St Croix Mall.* 612/430-1300; FAX 612/430-0596. 60 rms, 2 story. Mid-May-mid-Oct:S $55-$69; D $61-$75; each addl $4; under 18 free; lower rates rest of yr. Crib free. Pet accepted. TV; cable (premium). Complimentary continental bkfst. Restaurant nearby. Ck-out 11 am. Business servs avail. In-rm modem link. Downhill ski 20 mi; x-country ski 2 mi. Exercise equipt; bicycles, treadmill. Whirlpool. Picnic table. Cr cds: A, D, DS, MC, V.

★★ **COUNTRY INN & SUITES.** *2200 W Frontage Rd, 2 mi W on MN 36.* 612/430-2699; FAX 612/430-1233. 52 rms, 2 story, 20 suites. S, D $69-$79; each addl $6; suites $78-$129; under 18 free. Crib free. TV; cable (premium). Complimentary continental bkfst. Complimentary coffee in rms. Restaurant nearby. Ck-out noon. Meeting rms. Business servs avail. In-rm modem link. Valet serv. Coin lndry. Downhill ski 15 mi; x-country ski 2 mi. Exercise equipt; treadmill, stair machine. Indoor pool; whirlpool. Game rm. Some in-rm whirlpools; refrigerator, microwave in suites. Cr cds: A, D, DS, MC, V.

✔★ **SUPER 8.** *2190 W Frontage Rd.* 612/430-3990. 49 rms, 2 story. S $42.88-$59.88; D $52.88-$69.88; each addl $7; under 12 free. Crib free. TV; cable (premium). Complimentary continental bkfst. Restaurant adj open 24 hrs. Ck-out 11 am. Coin lndry. Business servs avail. Downhill ski 15 mi; x-country ski 2 mi. Near St Croix River. Cr cds: A, C, D, DS, MC, V.

Hotel

★★★ **LUMBER BARON'S.** *101 Water St S.* 612/439-6000; FAX 612/430-9393. 42 rms, 3 story. S, D $139-$199; each addl $15; under 5 free. Crib free. TV. Complimentary full bkfst. Restaurant 7 am-3 pm, 5-11 pm. Bar 11-1 am. Ck-out 11 am. Meeting rms. Business servs avail. Fireplaces, in-rm whirlpools. Cr cds: A, C, D, DS, MC, V.

Inns

★★★ **AFTON HOUSE.** *(3291 S St Croix Trail, Afton 55001) 1 blk from St Croix River.* 612/436-8883. E-mail kat@presenter.com; web www.presenter/~kat. 16 rms, 2 story. D $60-$140; AP avail; mid-wk rates. Crib free. TV; VCR avail. Restaurant (see AFTON HOUSE). Rm serv. Ck-out 11 am, ck-in 2 pm. Business servs avail. Airport transportation. Downhill/x-country ski 2 mi. Some in-rm whirlpools, fireplaces. Some balconies. Historic inn (1867); antiques. River cruises avail. Cr cds: A, DS, MC, V.

★★ **JAMES A MULVEY INN.** *622 W Churchill St.* 612/430-8008; res: 800/820-8008. Web www.cotn.com/bb. 7 rms, 2 story. No rm phones. June-Oct: S, D $99-$159; lower rates rest of yr. Children over 12 yrs only. Complimentary full bkfst; afternoon refreshments. Restaurant nearby. Ck-out noon, ck-in 4 pm. Downhill ski 15 mi; x-country ski 3 mi. Lawn games. Fireplaces, in-rm whirlpools. Victorian house built in 1878 furnished with antiques. Totally nonsmoking. Cr cds: DS, MC, V.

★★★ **LOWELL.** *102 N 2nd St.* 612/439-1100; FAX 612/439-4686. Web www.lowellinn.com. 21 rms, some with shower only, 3 story. D $69-$179; higher rates Fri, Sat (MAP). TV. Bkfst 8-10:30 am. Restaurant (see LOWELL INN). Bar 11:30 am-2:30 pm, 5:30 pm-1 am; Sun, hols noon-11 pm. Ck-out noon. Business servs avail. Downhill ski 15 mi; x-country ski 9 mi. Antique furnishings. Cr cds: MC, V.

★ ★ **THE RIVERTOWN.** *306 W Olive. 612/430-2955.* 8 rms, 3 story. No elvtr. No rm phones. S, D $79-$169; 2-day min hols. Complimentary full bkfst; afternoon refreshments. Restaurant nearby. Ck-out 11:30 am, ck-in 4 pm. Some fireplaces, in-rm whirlpools. Victorian house built in 1882 furnished with antiques. Totally nonsmoking. Cr cds: A, C, D, DS, MC, V.

Restaurants

★ ★ ★ **AFTON HOUSE.** *(See Afton House Inn)* 612/436-8883. E-mail kat@presenter.com; web www.presenter.com/~bb. Hrs: 11:30 am-10 pm; Sat to 11 pm; Sun 10 am-9 pm; Sun brunch to 2 pm. Closed Dec 24; also Mon, Jan-Apr. Res accepted. Bar to 1 am. Semi-a la carte: lunch $5.95-$9.95, dinner $13.95-$20.95. Sun brunch 12.95. Child's meals. Specializes in seafood. Entertainment Fri-Sat. Parking. Renovated inn (1867); nautical decor. Dockage on St Croix River. Tableside preparation. Cr cds: A, DS, MC, V.

★ ★ ★ **BAYPORT AMERICAN COOKERY.** *(328 Fifth Ave N, Bayport 55003)* 612/430-1066. Sitting: 6:30 pm; Fri, Sat 7:30 pm. Closed Sun, Mon; major hols. Res required. Contemporary Amer menu. Wine, beer. Prix fixe: dinner $29.95. Child's meals. Specializes in regional ingredients. Contemporary decor with local artwork displayed. Totally nonsmoking. Cr cds: A, D, DS, MC, V.

✔★ **CRABTREE'S KITCHEN.** *(19713 Quinnell Ave N, Marine on St Croix) 12 mi N on MN 95, 1 1/2 mi S of jct MN 97.* 612/433-2455. Hrs: 11 am-8:30 pm; Sat, Sun from 8:30 am. Closed Mon; Dec 24, 25. Res accepted hols. Beer, wine. Semi-a la carte: lunch $3.50-$7.50, dinner $4.50-$9.95. Family-style bkfst wkends: $5.95-$6.50. Child's meals. Specializes in roasted chicken, beef, pork. Own desserts. Parking. Outdoor dining. Winter sleigh rides. Antiques; country atmosphere. Cr cds: DS, MC, V.

✔★ **ESTEBAN'S.** *423 S Main St.* 612/430-1543. Hrs: 11 am-10 pm; Fri, Sat to 11 pm. Closed Dec 24, 25. Mexican, Amer menu. Bar. Semi-a la carte: lunch, dinner $5-$15. Child's meals. Specializes in fajitas, fried ice cream. Parking. Mexican/Southwest decor. Cr cds: A, C, D, DS, MC, V.

★ **GASTHAUS BAVARIAN HUNTER.** *8390 Lofton Ave N.* 612/439-7128. Hrs: 11 am-9 pm; Fri to 10 pm; Sat noon-10 pm; Sun noon-8 pm. Closed some major hols. Res accepted. German menu. Bar. Semi-a la carte: lunch $4-$7, dinner $9-$17. Sun lunch buffet: $11.95. Child's meals. Specializes in schnitzel, pork hock. Accordianist Fri evening & Sun afternoon. Parking. Outdoor dining in beer garden. Authentic Bavarian decor. Family-owned. Cr cds: A, MC, V.

★ ★ **HARVEST INN.** *114 Chestnut St, 2 blks W of Main St.* 612/430-8111. Hrs: 11:30 am-2 pm, 5:30-9:30 pm; Sat from 5:30 pm; early-bird dinner Mon-Fri to 6:15 pm. Closed Sun; most major hols. Res accepted. Continental menu. Wine, beer. A la carte entrees: lunch $7.95-$9.95, dinner $15.95-$17.95. Child's meals. Specialties: frutti di mare, steak au poivre, chicken marsala. Own baking. Street parking. Outdoor dining. Restored Victorian home (1848) is oldest surviving wood-frame structure in city; antique interior; intimate dining. Totally nonsmoking. Cr cds: A, DS, MC, V.

★ ★ ★ **LOWELL INN.** *(See Lowell Inn)* 612/439-1100. Web www.lowellinn.com. Hrs: 8 am-10 pm. Closed Thanksgiving, Dec 24, 25. Res accepted. Swiss, Amer menu. Bar to 1 am; Sun, hols to 11 pm. Semi-a la carte: bkfst $4.35-$8.95, lunch $11.75-$20.75, dinner $20.95-$35.95. Serv charge 20%. Child's meals. Specializes in fresh brook trout in season

(select your own from pool). Prix fixe: dinner $60 (Swiss fondue Bourguignonne). Own baking. Parking. Elegant furnishings; wood carvings, paintings. Antique silverware, china. Formal dining. Family-owned. Cr cds: MC, V.

✔★ ★ **VITTORIO'S.** *402 S Main St.* 612/439-3588. Hrs: 11 am-10 pm; Fri, Sat to 11 pm. Closed Thanksgiving, Dec 24 evening, 25. Res accepted. Italian menu. Bar. Semi-a la carte: lunch $4.50-$8.75, dinner $5.95-$19.95. Child's meals. Specializes in canelloni, antipasto salad. Parking. Outdoor dining. Unique dining experience in caves used as "brewery" from 1870s through prohibition. Family-owned. Cr cds: A, C, D, DS, MC, V.

Superior National Forest (C-5)

(For accommodations see Crane Lake, Ely, Grand Marais, Virginia; also see Tower)

(On N side of Lake Superior, W to Virginia, N to Canadian border, E to Grand Marais)

With more than 2,000 beautiful clear lakes, rugged shorelines, picturesque islands and deep woods, this is a magnificent portion of Minnesota's famous northern area.

The Boundary Waters Canoe Area Wilderness, part of the forest, is perhaps the finest canoe country in the United States (travel permits required for each party, $9 for advance reservations, phone 800/745-3399). Scenic water routes through wilderness near the international border offer opportunities for adventure. Adjacent Quetico Provincial Park is similar, but guns are prohibited. Entry through Canadian Customs (see Border Crossing Regulations in MAKING THE MOST OF YOUR TRIP) and Park Rangers' Ports of Entry.

Boating, swimming, water sports; fishing and hunting under Minnesota game and fish regulations; winter sports; camping (fee); picnicking and scenic drives along Honeymoon, Gunflint, Echo and Sawbill trails.

For further information contact Forest Supervisor, 8901 Grand Avenue Pl, Duluth 55808; 218/626-4300.

Taylors Falls (F-4)

(For accommodations see St Paul, Stillwater)

Settled 1838 **Pop** 694 **Elev** 900 ft **Area code** 612 **Zip** 55084 **E-mail** wildmt@visi.com **Web** www.visi.com/~wildmt

Information Taylors Falls Chamber of Commerce, PO Box 235; 612/465-6315, 612/257-3550 (Twin Cities) or 800/447-4958, outside MN.

What to See and Do

Boat Excursions. Taylors Falls Scenic Boat Tour. Base of bridge, downtown. (Early May-mid-Oct, daily); 30-min, 3-mi trip through St Croix Dalles; also 1 1/3-hr, 7-mi trip on *Taylors Falls Queen* or *Princess*. Scenic, brunch, luncheon and dinner cruises; fall color cruises. Also Taylors Falls one-way canoe rentals, trips (with shuttle) (May-mid-Oct, daily). For schedule and fee information phone 612/465-6315, 612/257-3550 or 800/447-4958. Also, Taylors Falls Adventurers, 612/465-6501 or 800/996-4448.

St Croix and Lower St Croix National Scenic Riverway. From its origins in northern Wisconsin the St Croix flows southward to form part of the Minnesota-Wisconsin border before joining the Mississippi near Point Douglas. 2 segments of the river, totaling more than 250 mi, have been designated National Scenic Riverways and are administered by the National Park Service. Information headquarters (mid-May-Oct, daily; rest of yr, Mon-Fri); 3 information stations (Memorial Day-Labor Day, daily). For information contact PO Box 708; 612/483-3284. **Free.**

State parks.

Interstate. A 295-acre park. Geologic formations. Boating (ramp), canoe rentals, fishing, hiking, picnicking, camping (electric hookups, dump station). Excursion boat (fee). Standard fees. 1 mi S on MN 8. Phone 612/465-5711.

Wild River. 6,706 acres in the St Croix River Valley. Fishing, canoeing (rentals); 35 mi of trails for hiking, cross-country skiing and 20 mi of horseback riding trails; picnicking; primitive and modern camping (electric hookups, dump station). Interpretive center & Trail Center (daily). Standard hrs, fees. 10 mi NW via MN 95, then 3 mi N on County 12. Phone 612/583-2125.

W.H.C. Folsom House (1855). Federal/Greek-revival mansion reflects New England heritage of early settlers; many original furnishings. (Memorial Day wkend-mid-Oct, daily) 120 Government Rd. Phone 612/465-3125. ¢¢

Wild Mt Ski Area. 4 quad chairlifts, 2 rope tows; patrol, school, rentals; snowmaking; cafeteria. Longest run 5,000 ft; vertical drop 300 ft. (Nov-Mar, daily) 7 mi N on County 16. Phone 612/465-6315. ¢¢¢¢¢ Also here is

Water Park. Also chairlift rides and alpine slide (late May-early Sept). Area (Memorial Day-Labor Day, daily; rest of yr, wkends only). Phone 612/465-6315 or 612/257-3550 for more information. ¢¢¢¢¢

Thief River Falls (B-1)

(See also Crookston)

Pop 8,010 **Elev** 1,133 ft **Area code** 218 **Zip** 56701

What to See and Do

Agassiz National Wildlife Refuge. Approx 61,500 acres of forest, water and marshland. A haven for 280 species of migratory and upland game birds; 41 species of resident mammals. Observation tower; refuge headquarters (Mon-Fri; closed hols); auto tour route (daily, exc winter). No camping. 23 mi NE via MN 32 to County 7E. Phone 218/449-4115. **Free.**

Motels

✔★ ★ **BEST WESTERN INN.** *1060 MN 32S, ½ mi S.* 218/681-7555. 78 rms. S, studio rms $44-$50; D $56-$62; each addl $4; under 18 free. Crib free. TV; cable (premium), VCR avail. Indoor pool; whirlpool. Supervised child's activities; ages 1-17. Complimentary coffee in rms. Restaurant 6 am-10 pm. Rm serv. Bar 3 pm-1 am; entertainment. Ck-out noon. Meeting rms. Business servs avail. In-rm modem link. Sundries. Free airport transportation. X-country ski 3 mi. Exercise equipt; bicycles. Game rm. Refrigerators. Cr cds: A, C, D, DS, MC, V.

[D] [≈] [≋] [🖈] [🐾] [SC]

★ **C'MON INN.** *1586 US 59S.* 218/681-3000; FAX 218/681-3060; res: 800/950-8111. 44 rms, 2 story. S $42.90-$48.90; D $49.90-$65.90; each addl $7; suites $74.90-$79.90; under 13 free. Crib free. Pet accepted, some restrictions. TV; cable. Indoor pool; whirlpool. Complimentary continental bkfst. Restaurant nearby. Ck-out noon. Meeting rms. Business servs avail. In-rm modem link. Game rm. Balconies. Cr cds: A, DS, MC, V.

[D] [✦] [≋] [🐾] [SC]

✔★ **SUPER 8.** *US 59S, 1½ mi SE.* 218/681-6205; FAX 218/681-7519. 46 rms. S $40-$45; D $48-$58; each addl $4; under 16 free. Crib free. TV; cable (premium). Complimentary continental bkfst. Restaurant adj 6:30 am-11 pm. Ck-out 11 am. Business servs avail. Cr cds: A, D, DS, MC, V.

[D] [≧] [🐾] [SC]

Tower (C-4)

(For accommodations see Cook, Crane Lake, Ely, Virginia)

Founded 1882 **Pop** 502 **Elev** 1,400 ft **Area code** 218 **Zip** 55790

Oldest mining town in northern Minnesota, Tower today serves as a shopping center for Lake Vermilion, Superior National Forest (see) and the "arrowhead country."

What to See and Do

Lake Vermilion. 40 mi long, 1,250 mi of wooded shoreline, 365 islands varying in size from specklike rocks to Pine Island, which is 9 mi long and has its own lake in its interior. Fishing for walleye, northern pike, bass, panfish. Swimming, boating, water sports; hunting for duck, deer and small game in fall; snowmobiling & cross-country skiing; camping & lodging. Primarily located in Superior National Forest (see). Phone 218/753-2301 for more information.

Soudan Underground Mine State Park. 1,300 acres include site of the Soudan Mine, the state's first underground iron mine (52°F; 2,400 ft) in operation 1882-1962. Self-guided tour of open pits, engine house, crusher building, drill shop, interpretive center; one-hr guided underground mine tour includes train ride (fees). Hiking trails. Picnic area. (Memorial Day-Labor Day, daily) Standard fees. 2 mi E on MN 169, in Soudan. Phone 218/753-2245. Per vehicle ¢¢

Steam locomotive and coach. Locomotive (1910) served Duluth & Iron Range Railroad. Coach is now a museum housing early logging, mining and Native American displays. (Memorial Day-Labor Day, daily; early spring & late fall by appt) On grounds is a tourist information center. W end Main St, near jct MN 135, 169. Phone 218/753-2301. **Donation.**

Tracy (G-2)

(For accommodations see Marshall, Pipestone, Redwood Falls)

Pop 2,059 **Elev** 1,395 ft **Area code** 507 **Zip** 56175

Information Chamber of Commerce, Prairie Pavilion, 372 Morgan St; 507/629-4021.

What to See and Do

Lake Shetek State Park. 1,011 acres on one of largest lakes in SW Minnesota. Monument to settlers who were victims of the Dakota Conflict in 1862; restored pioneer cabin. Swimming, fishing, boating (ramp, rentals); hiking, snowmobiling, picnicking, camping. Standard fees. Naturalist (late May-early Sept). 14 mi S on County 11 & 38. Phone 507/763-3256.

Laura Ingalls Wilder Museum & Tourist Center. This tribute to Laura Wilder is located in an old railroad depot. The depression in the ground where the dugout used to be, and the rock and spring mentioned in *On the Banks of Plum Creek* are all 1½ mi N of Walnut Grove; fee per vehicle at farm site. (May-Oct, daily; rest of yr, by appt) 7 mi E on US 14, in Walnut Grove at 330 8th St. Phone 507/859-2358. **Free.**

Annual Event

Laura Ingalls Wilder Pageant. 7 mi E on US 14, 1 mi W of Walnut Grove. Story of the Ingalls family of Walnut Grove in the 1870s. Daughter was Laura Ingalls Wilder, author of the *Little House* books. Phone 507/859-2174. July.

Two Harbors (D-5)

(For accommodations see Duluth)

Founded 1884 **Pop** 3,651 **Elev** 699 ft **Area code** 218 **Zip** 55616
Information Two Harbors Area Chamber of Commerce, 721 7th St; 800/777-7384.

Two Harbors was given its start when the Duluth & Iron Range Railroad reached Lake Superior at Agate Bay. Ore docks were constructed immediately and the city became an important ore shipping terminal. Today it is a bustling harbor community nestled between the twin harbors of Agate Bay and Burlington Bay.

What to See and Do

Depot Museum. Historic depot (1907) highlights the geological history and the discovery and mining of iron ore. Mallet locomotive (1941), world's most powerful steam engine, on display. (Mid-May-Oct, daily; winter, wkends) In depot of Duluth & Iron Range Railroad, foot of Waterfront Dr. Phone 218/834-4898. ¢

Gooseberry Falls State Park. A 1,662-acre park. Fishing, hiking, cross-country skiing, snowmobiling, picnicking, camping (dump station). State park vehicle permit required. Standard fees. 14 mi NE on MN 61. Phone 218/834-3855.

Lighthouse Point & Harbor Museum. Displays tell the story of iron ore shipping and the development of the first iron ore port in the state. A renovated pilot house from an ore boat is located on the site. Tours of operating lighthouse. (May-Nov 1, daily) Off MN 61, on Waterfront Dr at Lighthouse Point. Phone 218/834-4898. ¢

Split Rock Lighthouse State Park. 1,987 acres. Lighthouse served as guiding sentinel for N shore of Lake Superior from 1910-1969. Also in the park is a historic complex (fee) which includes fog-signal building, keeper's dwellings, several outbuildings and the ruins of a tramway (mid-May-mid-Oct, daily). Waterfalls. Picnicking. cart-in camping (fee) on Lake Superior, access to Superior Hiking Trail. State park vehicle permit required. Standard hrs, fees. 20 mi NE on MN 61. Phone 218/226-6377 (park) or -6372 (historic site). Per vehicle ¢¢

Motel

★ ★ **COUNTRY INN BY CARLSON.** *1204 Seventh Ave, on US 61. 218/834-5557; FAX 218/834-3777; res: 800/456-4000.* 46 rms, 2 story. Mid-May-mid-Oct: S, D $59-$109; each addl $5; under 18 free; higher rates special events; lower rates rest of yr. Crib free. Pet accepted, some restrictions; $5/day. TV; cable (premium), VCR avail (movies). Indoor pool; whirlpool. Complimentary continental bkfst. Complimentary coffee in rms. Restaurant adj 6 am-11 pm. Ck-out 11 am. Coin lndry. Business servs avail. X-country ski 1 mi. Sauna. Some refrigerators, microwaves, wet bars. Near Lake Superior. Cr cds: A, C, D, DS, MC, V.

Resort

★ ★ ★ **SUPERIOR SHORES.** *10 Superior Shores Dr, just off US 61. 218/834-5671; FAX 218/834-5677; res: 800/242-1988.* E-mail sup shores@norshor.dst.mn.us.; web www.superiorshores.com. 104 rms in 3-story lodge, 42 kit. units in 3-story townhouses. Mid-June-mid Oct: S, D $69-$269; under 18 free; wkly rates; 2-day min wkends; 3-day min hols; lower rates rest of yr. Pet accepted. TV; cable, VCR (movies). 3 pools, 1 indoor; whirlpool. Restaurant 7 am-9 pm. Bar 11-1 am. Ck-out 11 am, ck-in by arrangement. Gift shop. Meeting rms. Business servs avail. Tennis. X-country ski opp. Sauna. Snowmobiles. Hiking trails. Game rm. Many refrigerators, microwaves. Balconies. Picnic tables, grills. On Lake Superior. Cr cds: A, DS, MC, V.

Virginia (C-4)

(See also Cook, Eveleth, Hibbing, Tower)

Founded 1892 **Pop** 9,410 **Elev** 1,437 ft **Area code** 218 **Zip** 55792
Information Virginia Area Chamber of Commerce, 403 1st St N, PO Box 1072; 218/741-2717.

Born of lumbering, Virginia is nurtured by mining and vacationing. Great open iron ore pits mark the surrounding green countryside—man-made canyons are right at the city limits. Vacationers come to Virginia en route to the Boundary Waters Canoe Area Wilderness, Superior National Forest and Voyagers National Park. A Ranger District office of the Superior National Forest (see) is located nearby.

What to See and Do

Mine View in the Sky. Observation building gives view of a Mesabi Range open-pit mine 650 ft below. (May-Sept daily) S edge of town on US 53. Phone 218/741-2717. **Free.**

World's Largest Floating Loon. Listed in the *Guinness Book of World Records,* this 20-ft long, 10-ft high, 7¹/₂-ft wide, fiberglass loon swims on Silver Lake (located in the heart of the city) during the summer months.

Motels

★ **LAKESHORE MOTOR INN.** *404 N 6th Ave. 218/741-3360; res: 800/569-8131.* 16 rms, 2 story. Mid-May-Aug: S $34; D $42-$46; each addl $4; family rates; lower rates rest of yr. Crib avail. Pet accepted. TV; cable. Complimentary coffee in rms. Restaurant nearby. Ck-out 11 am. Gift shop. Downhill ski 18 mi; x-country ski 4 mi. Cr cds: A, C, D, DS, MC, V.

✔ ★ **SKI VIEW.** *903 N 17th St. 218/741-8918.* 59 rms, 2 story. S $28-$30; D $38-$40; each addl $4. Crib $5. Pet accepted. TV; cable (premium). Complimentary continental bkfst. Complimentary coffee in rms. Restaurant nearby. Ck-out 11 am. Downhill/x-country ski 20 mi. Snowmobile trails adj. Sauna. Microwaves avail. Cr cds: A, C, D, DS, MC, V.

Walker (D-3)

(See also Bemidji, Park Rapids, Pine River)

Pop 950 **Elev** 1,336 ft **Area code** 218 **Zip** 56484
Information Chamber of Commerce, PO Box 1089; 218/547-1313 or 800/833-1118.

At the foot of Chippewa National Forest and Leech Lake, Walker serves tourists heading for adventures among woods and waters. Snowmobiling and cross-country skiing are popular sports here. The town is named for a pioneer lumberman and landowner. A Ranger District office of the Chippewa National Forest (see GRAND RAPIDS) is located here.

What to See and Do

Leech Lake. 3rd-largest in state; fishing & swimming. MN 200/371.

Motel

★ ★ **AMERICINN.** *MN 371, at jct MN 34. 218/547-2200; res: 800/634-3444.* 37 rms, 2 story. S $43.90-$56.90; D $59.90-$65.90; each addl $6; suites $64.90-$96.90; under 12 free. Crib free. TV; cable, VCR avail (movies). Indoor pool; whirlpool, sauna. Complimentary continental bkfst. Restaurant adj 7 am-9 pm. Ck-out 11 am. X-country ski 10 mi. Some refrigerators, wet bars. Cr cds: A, C, D, DS, MC, V.

Cottage Colony

★ **BIG ROCK.** *Leech Lake, 5 mi SE on MN 200, then 2 mi N on Onigum Rd (County 13), then 2^1/$_2$ mi E. 218/547-7106; res: 800/827-7106.* 20 kit. cottages (1-3 bedrm). June-Aug, wkly: D $400; each addl $75; 4-6 persons $590-$815; lower rates rest of yr. No maid serv. Crib avail. TV; cable. Heated pool; whirlpool. Playground. Snack bar 7 am-11 pm. Ck-out 9 am, ck-in 4 pm Sat. Grocery. Coin lndry, package store 5 mi. Free airport, bus depot transportation. Tennis. Private sand beach. Boat harbors. Boats, motors, canoes, paddleboat, boat ramp, dockage. X-country ski 10 mi. Snowmobile trails. Indoor, outdoor games. Rec rm. Picnic tables, grills. Screened porches, patios. Cr cds: DS, MC, V.

Willmar (F-2)

(See also Granite Falls, Litchfield)

Founded 1869 **Pop** 17,531 **Elev** 1,130 ft **Area code** 320 **Zip** 56201

Information Willmar Area Chamber of Commerce, PO Box 287; 320/235-0300 or 800/845-TRIP.

What to See and Do

Kandiyohi County Historical Society Museum. Steam locomotive, country schoolhouse, restored house (1893); historical exhibits, agriculture building, research library. (Memorial Day-Labor Day, daily; rest of yr, daily exc Sat; also by appt; closed major hols) 1 mi N on US 71 Business. Phone 320/235-1881. **Free.**

Sibley State Park. A 2,300-acre park; was a favorite hunting ground of first governor of state, for whom park is named. Swimming, fishing, boating (ramps, rentals); horseback riding, hiking; cross-country skiing, snowmobiling; camping (dump station); nature center. Standard fees. 15 mi N on US 71. Phone 320/354-2055.

Motels

★ **AMERICINN.** *2404 E US 12. 320/231-1962; res: 800/634-3444.* 30 rms, 2 story. S, D $51.14-$64.84; each addl $6; under 13 free. Crib free. TV; cable (premium). Indoor pool; whirlpool. Complimentary continental bkfst. Restaurant adj open 24 hrs. Ck-out 11 am. Meeting rms. Business servs avail. X-country ski 1 mi. Cr cds: A, C, D, DS, MC, V.

✓★ **DAYS INN.** *1200 E US 12. 320/231-1275.* 59 rms, 2 story. S $38.99-$51.99; D $44.99-$57.99; each addl $6; under 18 free. Crib free. Pet accepted. TV; cable (premium). Complimentary continental bkfst. Restaurant nearby. Ck-out 11 am. Exercise equipt; bicycle, treadmill, sauna. Whirlpool. Cr cds: A, C, D, DS, MC, V.

✓★ **SUPER 8.** *2655 1st St S. 320/235-7260; FAX 320/235-5580.* 60 rms, 3 story. No elvtr. S $37.88-$40.38; D $42.58-$45.88; each addl $5; under 12 free. Crib free. Pet accepted. TV; cable (premium). Complimentary coffee in lobby. Restaurant nearby. Ck-out 11 am. Business servs avail. Cr cds: A, DS, MC, V.

Motor Hotel

★ ★ ★ **HOLIDAY INN.** *2100 E US 12. 320/235-6060; FAX 320/235-4731.* 98 rms, 2 story. S $63-$69; D $73-$79; each addl $10; under 18 free. Crib free. Pet accepted. TV; cable (premium). Complimentary coffee in lobby. Restaurant 6 am-10 pm. Rm serv. Bar 4 pm-1 am. Ck-out noon. Business servs avail. In-rm modem link. Indoor pool; wading pool, whirlpool, poolside serv. Some balconies. Cr cds: A, C, D, DS, JCB, MC, V.

Winona (G-5)

(See also Rochester)

Settled 1851 **Pop** 25,399 **Elev** 666 ft **Area code** 507 **Zip** 55987 **E-mail** altwncvb@luminet.net **Web** visitwinona.com

Information Convention & Visitors Bureau, 67 Main St, PO Box 870, phone 507/452-2272 or 800/657-4972; or the Visitors Center, Huff St & US 61, phone 507/452-2278, open Mar-Nov, daily.

New Englanders and Germans came to this site on the west bank of the Mississippi and built an industrial city graced with three colleges. An early lumbering town, Winona today is one of the state's leading business and industrial centers and home of Winona State University.

What to See and Do

Fishing. Whitman Dam & Locks #5. 12 mi N on US 61. **Dresbach Dam & Locks #7.** 15 mi S on US 61. **Lake Winona.** S side of town. Float and boat fishing.

Julius C. Wilkie Steamboat Center. Replica and exhibits. (June-Oct, Tues-Sun) Levee Park. Phone 507/454-1254. ¢

Prairie Island Park. Camping (Apr-Oct), picnicking, water, rest rms, fireplaces. Fishing (all-yr). Some fees. Prairie Island Rd, 3 mi N off US 61.

Upper Mississippi River National Wildlife & Fish Refuge. From Wabasha, MN, extending 261 mi to Rock Island, IL, the refuge encompasses 200,000 acres of wooded islands, marshes, sloughs and backwaters. Abounds in fish, wildlife & plants. (Daily) Twenty percent of the refuge is closed for hunting and trapping until after duck-hunting season. Boat is required for access to most parts of refuge. 51 E 4th St. Phone 507/452-4232 (Mon-Fri).

Winona County Historical Society Museum. Country store, kitchen; blacksmith, barber shops; Native American artifacts; logging and lumbering exhibits; early vehicles and fire fighting equipment. (Daily; closed some major hols) 160 Johnson St. Phone 507/454-2723. ¢¢ The society also maintains

Bunnell House (ca 1850). Unusual mid-19th-century "Steamboat Gothic" architecture; period furnishings. (Memorial Day-Labor Day, Wed-Sun; Labor Day-2nd wknd Oct, wkends only; rest of yr, by appt) ¢¢ Also here is Carriage House Museum Shop (same schedule). 5 mi S on US 14, 61 in Homer.

Winona Island Princess Cruises. Departs from Levee Park; one- to two-hour cruises on the Mississippi with scenic views. Res required for dinner. (May-Oct, daily) 356 E Sarnia. Phone 507/457-0979. ¢¢¢¢-¢¢¢¢¢

Annual Events

Winona Steamboat Days. Wk of July 4.

Victorian Fair. Living history; costumed guides; boat rides. Sept. 26-27.

Wildlife Weekend Art Show. Oct 23-25.

Motels

★ ★ **BEST WESTERN RIVERPORT INN.** *900 Bruski Dr. 507/452-0606; FAX 507/457-6489.* 106 rms, 3 story. May-Oct: S $52-$89; D $62-$89; each addl $10; suites $52-$89; under 13 free; lower rates rest of yr. Crib free. Pet accepted; $10. TV; cable (premium), VCR avail. Indoor pool; whirlpool. Complimentary continental bkfst. Restaurant 11 am-10 pm. Rm serv. Bar 11-1 am. Ck-out noon. Meeting rms. Gift shop. Downhill ski 8 mi; x-country ski 1 mi. Game rm. Some refrigerators. Cr cds: A, C, D, DS, MC, V.

★ **DAYS INN.** *420 Cottonwood Dr. 507/454-6930; FAX 507/454-7917.* 58 rms, 2 story. S $42-$56; D $43-$62; each addl $6; under 18 free. Crib free. TV; cable. Complimentary continental bkfst. Restaurant nearby. Ck-out 11 am. X-country ski 1 mi. Cr cds: A, C, D, DS, MC, V.

★ ★ **HOLIDAY INN.** *956 Mankato Ave. 507/454-4390; FAX 507/452-2187.* 112 rms, 2 story. S $50-$60; D $60-$70; each addl $10; family rates. Crib free. TV; cable. Indoor pool; whirlpool. Complimentary coffee in rms. Restaurant open 24 hrs. Rm serv. Bar 4 pm-1 am, Sun from 11 am. Ck-out 11 am. Meeting rms. Valet serv. Sundries. X-country ski 1 mi. Cr cds: A, C, D, DS, MC, V.

✔★ **STERLING.** *1450 Gilmore. 507/454-1120; res: 800/452-1235.* 32 rms. S $25-$38; D $30-$49; each addl $4; family rates. Crib free. TV; cable (premium). Restaurant adj open 24 hrs. Ck-out 11 am. X-country ski 1 mi. Cr cds: A, C, D, DS, MC, V.

✔★ **SUPER 8.** *1025 Sugarloaf Rd. 507/454-6066.* 61 rms, 3 story. No elvtr. S, D $44.88-$48.88; each addl $5; family rates. Crib $2. TV; cable. Complimentary continental bkfst. Restaurant nearby. Ck-out 11 am. X-country ski 1 mi. Cr cds: A, C, D, DS, MC, V.

Restaurant

★ ★ **HOT FISH SHOP.** *965 S Mankato Ave, at foot of Sugar Loaf Hill. 507/452-5002.* Hrs: 6 am-10 pm; Sun to 8 pm. Closed Mon; Thanksgiving, Dec 24-25; also 1st 2 wks in Jan. Res accepted. Bar. Semi-a la carte: bkfst $2.95-$4.95, lunch $6.95-$15.50, dinner $10-$18.95. Child's meals. Specializes in seafood, steak. Entertainment. Family-owned. Cr cds: A, C, D, MC, V.

Montana

Population: 799,065
Land area: 145,392 square miles
Elevation: 1,800-12,799 feet
Highest point: Granite Peak (Park County)
Entered Union: November 8, 1889 (41st state)
Capital: Helena
Motto: Oro y Plata ("Gold and Silver" in Spanish)
Nickname: The Treasure State, Big Sky Country
State flower: Bitterroot
State bird: Western meadowlark
State tree: Ponderosa pine
State fair: July 25-August 2, 1998, in Great Falls
Time zone: Mountain
Web: www.travel.mt.gov

This magnificent state took its name from the Spanish *montaña* —meaning mountainous. The altitude of about half the state is more than 5,000 feet, and the sprawling ranges of the Continental Divide rise more than two miles into air so clear photographers must use filters to avoid overexposure. The names of many towns, though, indicate that Montana has more than mountains. Grassrange, Roundup and Buffalo tell of vast prairie regions, where tawny oceans of wheat stretch to the horizon and a cattle ranch may be 30 miles from front gate to front porch. Big Timber and Highwood suggest Montana's 22 million acres of forests; Goldcreek and Silver Gate speak of the roaring mining days (the roaring is mostly over, but you can still pan for gold in almost any stream); and Jim Bridger reminds us of the greatest mountain man of them all. Of special interest to the vacationing visitor are Antelope, Lame Deer and Trout creeks, which indicate hunting and fishing *par excellence.*

First glimpsed by French traders Louis and François Verendrye in 1743, Montana remained unexplored and largely unknown until Lewis and Clark crossed the region in 1805. Two years later, Manuel Lisa's trading post at the mouth of the Big Horn ushered in a half century of hunting and trapping.

The Treasure State's natural resources are enormous. Its hydroelectric potential is the greatest in the world—annual flow of the four major rivers is enough to cover the whole state with six inches of water. The 25 major dams include Fort Peck, one of the world's largest hydraulic earthfill dams. Near Great Falls, one of the world's largest freshwater springs pours out nearly 400 million gallons of water every day. In more than 1,500 lakes and 16,000 miles of fishing streams the water is so clear you may wonder if it's there at all.

For a hundred years the state has produced gold and silver, with Virginia City (complete with Robbers' Roost situated within convenient raiding distance) probably the most famous mining town. Montana produces about $1 billion worth of minerals a year. Leading resources are coal, copper, natural gas, silver, platinum and palladium. Montana also produces more gem sapphires than any other state. Farms and ranches totaling 67 million acres add $2 billion a year to the state's economy.

Along with the bounty of its resources, Montana's history has given us Custer's Last Stand (June 25, 1876), the last spike in the Northern Pacific Railroad (September 8, 1883), the country's first Congresswoman (Jeannette Rankin of Missoula, in 1916), the Dempsey-Gibbons fight (July 4, 1923) and a state constitution originally prefaced by the Magna Carta, the Declaration of Independence, the Articles of Confederation and the United States Constitution.

If you come in winter, bring your mittens. Temperatures can drop below zero, but the climate is milder than perceived because of the state's location in the interior of the continent. Snowmobiling, downhill and cross-country skiing are popular sports here. Summer days are warm, dry and sunny.

When to Go/Climate

Montana's weather is changeable and temperatures are cold for much longer than they are warm. To the east of the divide, weather is more extreme than in the west, due to winds blowing unhindered across the plains. There is heavy snowfall in the mountains and summer doesn't really begin until July. Summer is tourist season; early fall is less crowded and temperatures are still good for outdoor adventures.

AVERAGE HIGH/LOW TEMPERATURES (°F)

BILLINGS

Jan 32/14	**May** 67/43	**Sept** 72/47
Feb 39/19	**June** 78/52	**Oct** 61/38
Mar 46/25	**July** 87/58	**Nov** 45/26
Apr 57/34	**Aug** 85/57	**Dec** 34/17

MISSOULA

Jan 30/15	**May** 66/38	**Sept** 71/40
Feb 37/21	**June** 74/46	**Oct** 57/31
Mar 47/25	**July** 83/50	**Nov** 41/24
Apr 58/31	**Aug** 82/50	**Dec** 30/16

CALENDAR HIGHLIGHTS

JANUARY

Montana Pro Rodeo Circuit Finals (Great Falls). Four Seasons Arena. Best riders in the state compete for a chance to reach the nationals. Phone 406/727-8900.

FEBRUARY

Chocolate Festival (Anaconda). Chocolate baking contest with winners sold at charity bake sale. Free chocolates at local merchants. Various "sweetheart" activities throughout town. Phone Chamber of Commerce, 406/563-2400.

JULY

Top of the World Bar (Red Lodge). Citizens of Red Lodge welcome travelers with free beverages served from bar carved from snow bank atop 11,000-foot Beartooth Pass. Phone Chamber of Commerce, 406/446-1718.

Wild Horse Stampede (Wolf Point). One of Montana's best and oldest rodeos. Phone Chamber of Commerce & Agriculture, 406/653-2012.

State Fair (Great Falls). Fairgrounds. Rodeo, livestock exhibits, horse racing, petting zoo, commercial exhibits, entertainment, carnival. Phone 406/727-8900.

AUGUST

Western Montana Fair (Missoula). Fairgrounds. Live horse racing, three-night rodeo, nightly fireworks. Carnival, livestock, commercial exhibits. Musical performance, demolition derby, blacksmith competition. Phone 406/721-FAIR.

Montana Cowboy Poetry Gathering (Lewistown). Modern-day cowboys and admirers of Western folklore relate life "down on the range" through original poetry. Phone 406/538-5436.

OCTOBER

Bridger Raptor Festival (Bozeman). Bridger Bowl ridge area. View birds of prey, including the largest concentration of migrating Golden Eagles in the contiguous 48 states, on their trip south. Phone 406/587-6752.

Parks and Recreation Finder

Directions to and information about the parks and recreation areas below are given under their respective town/city sections. Please refer to those sections for details.

Key to abbreviations: I.P. = Interstate Park; N.B.C. = National Battlefield & Cemetery; N.B.P. = National Battlefield Park; N.G. = National Grassland; N.H. = National Historical Park; N.H.S. = National Historic Site; N.M. = National Monument; N.Mem. = National Memorial; N.M.P. = National Military Park; N.P. = National Park; N.Pres. = National Preserve; N.Res. = National Recreational Area; N.R.R. = National Recreational River; N.Res. = National Reserve; N.S. = National Seashore; N.S.R. = National Scenic River; N.S.T. = National Scenic Trail; N.V.M. = National Volcanic Monument; S.B. = State Beach; S.C.P. = State Conservation Park; S.G. = State Garden; S.H.A. = State Historic Area; S.H.P. = State Historic Park; S.N.A. = State Natural Area; S.P. = State Park; S.R. = State Reserve; S.R.A. = State Recreation Area; S.Res.P. = State Resort Park; S.R.P. = State Rustic Park.

NATIONAL PARK AND RECREATION AREAS

Place Name	Listed Under
Beaverhead N.F.	DILLON
Bear's Paw Battleground	CHINOOK
Big Hole National Battlefield	same
Bitterroot N.F.	HAMILTON
Custer N.F.	HARDIN
Deerlodge N.F.	BUTTE
Flathead N.F.	KALISPELL
Fort Union Trading Post N.H.S.	SIDNEY
Gallatin N.F.	BOZEMAN
Glacier N.P.	same
Grant-Kohrs Ranch N.H.S.	DEER LODGE
Helena N.F.	HELENA
Kootenai N.F.	LIBBY
Lewis and Clark N.F.	GREAT FALLS
Little Bighorn Battlefield N.M.	same
Lolo N.F.	MISSOULA

The national forests of Montana are part of the more than 25,000,000 acres that make up the Northern Region of the Forest Service. The terrain runs from rugged mountains to rolling hills, from lodgepole pine and Douglas fir to grass. The highest point in the region is Granite Peak in the Beartooth Mts, 12,799 feet. Recreation opportunities abound: hiking, rock hounding, fishing, boating, mountain camping, hunting, and horseback riding. For further information contact the Forest Service, Northern Region, Federal Bldg, PO Box 7669, Missoula 59807; 406/329-3511. For reporting forest fires, phone 406/329-3857.

STATE RECREATION AREAS

Place Name	Listed Under
Bannack S.P.	DILLON
Canyon Ferry S.P.	HELENA
Deadman's Basin S.P.	HARLOWTON
Flathead Lake S.P. (Big Arm, Elmo and Finley Point units)	POLSON
Flathead Lake S.P. (Wayfarers and Yellow Bay units)	BIGFORK
Hell Creek S.P.	GLASGOW
Lewis and Clark Caverns S.P.	THREE FORKS
Lost Creek S.P.	ANACONDA
Makoshika S.P.	GLENDIVE
Missouri River Headwaters S.P.	THREE FORKS
Painted Rocks S.P.	HAMILTON
Pictograph Cave S.P.	BILLINGS
Whitefish S.P.	WHITEFISH

Water-related activities, hiking, riding, various other sports, picnicking and visitor centers, as well as camping, are available in many of these areas. Parks are open approx May-Sept. Day-use fee, $3 per vehicle, 50¢ per walk-in visitor. Camping (limited to 14 days), $7-$9/site/night. Additional fees may be charged at some areas for other activities. Pets on leash only. For information on state parks write Parks Division, Montana Dept of Fish, Wildlife & Parks, 1420 E Sixth Ave, Helena 59620; 406/444-3750.

SKI AREAS

Place Name	Listed Under
Big Mt Ski & Summer Resort	WHITEFISH
Big Sky Ski and Summer Resort	BIG SKY
Bridger Bowl Ski Area	BOZEMAN
Discovery Basin Ski Area	ANACONDA
Lost Trail Powder Mt Ski Area	HAMILTON
Marshall Mt Ski Area	MISSOULA
Montana Snowbowl Ski Area	MISSOULA
Maverick Mt Ski Area	DILLON
Red Lodge Mt Ski Area	RED LODGE
Showdown Ski Area	WHITE SULPHUR SPRINGS
Turner Mt Ski Area	LIBBY

FISHING & HUNTING

Game fish include all species of trout as well as salmon, whitefish, grayling, sauger, walleye, paddlefish, sturgeon, pike, burbot, channel catfish and bass. Nonresident fishing license: annual, $45; two-day consecutive license, $10; non-fee permit needed in Glacier or Yellowstone National Parks.

Big game includes moose, elk, deer, antelope, bighorn sheep, mountain goat, mountain lion and black bear; game birds include both mountain and prairie species. Nonresident hunting license: game birds, $55; big game combination: birds, one elk, one deer and fishing license, $475; deer combination: birds, one deer and fishing license, $245. Licenses for moose, sheep, goat, antelope are awarded through special drawings. License for mountain lion must be applied for by August 31.

A $5 conservation license is a prerequisite to hunting or fishing license. For detailed information write Montana Dept of Fish, Wildlife and Parks, 1420 E Sixth Ave, PO Box 200701, Helena 59620; 406/444-2950.

Driving Information

Safety belts are mandatory for all persons anywhere in vehicle. Children under 4 years or under 40 pounds in weight must be in an approved safety seat anywhere in vehicle. For information phone 406/444-3412.

INTERSTATE HIGHWAY SYSTEM

The following alphabetical listing of Montana towns in *Mobil Travel Guide* shows that these cities are within 10 miles of the indicated Interstate highways. A highway map, however, should be checked for the nearest exit.

Highway Number	Cities/Towns within 10 miles
Interstate 15	Butte, Dillon, Great Falls, Helena.
Interstate 90	Anaconda, Big Timber, Billings, Bozeman, Butte, Deer Lodge, Hardin, Livingston, Missoula, Three Forks.
Interstate 94	Billings, Glendive, Miles City.

Additional Visitor Information

Several pamphlets and brochures, which comprise a "Vacation Planning Guide," list points of interest, motels, campgrounds, museums, events and attractions. They may be obtained from Travel Montana PO Box 7549, Missoula, 59807-7549; 800/VISIT-MT.

Three periodicals are recommended to the Montana visitor. They are: *Montana: Magazine of Western History,* quarterly, Montana Historical Society, 225 N Roberts St, Helena 59620; *Montana Magazine Inc,* bimonthly, 3020 Bozeman, Helena 59624; *Montana Outdoors,* bimonthly, Dept of Fish, Wildlife & Parks, 1420 E Sixth St, Helena 59620.

Anaconda (D-3)

(See also Butte, Deer Lodge)

Founded 1883 **Pop** 10,278 **Elev** 5,265 ft **Area code** 406 **Zip** 59711
Information Chamber of Commerce, 306 E Park St; 406/563-2400.

Chosen by Marcus Daly, a copper king, as the site for a copper smelter, the city was first dubbed with the tongue-twisting name of Copperopolis, but was later renamed. In 1894, the "war of the copper kings" was waged between Daly and W.A. Clark over the location of the state capital. Clark's Helena won by a small margin. After his rival's death, the world's largest copper smelter was built, standing 585 feet 1.5 inches.

What to See and to Do

Anaconda's Old Works. 18-hole Jack Nicklaus signature golf course located on developed grounds of former copper smelters. Also features fully accessible trail that skirts the foundations of the old works and allows interpretation of town's smelting heritage (free). Clubhouse, dining room; pro shop. (Late May-Oct, daily, weather permitting) 1205 Pizzini Way. Phone 406/563-5989. ¢¢¢¢¢

Big Hole Basin. Fishing, hunting; raft races; lodge, skiing. 25 mi SW on MT 274.

Big Hole National Battlefield (see). 22 mi SW on MT 274, then 40 mi SW on MT 43.

Copper Village Museum and Arts Center. Local and traveling art exhibitions; theater, music, films; museum of local pioneer and industrial history. (Summer, daily; rest of yr, Tues-Sat; closed hols) 401 E Commercial St. Phone 406/563-2422. **Free.**

Georgetown Lake. Waterskiing, boating, fishing, swimming, camping, picnicking, wilderness area; skiing, snowmobiling. 15 mi W on Pintler Scenic Route (MT 1).

Ghost towns & Sapphire mines. Near Georgetown Lake on Pintler Scenic Route (MT 1). Inquire at local chambers or visitor centers.

Lost Creek State Park. Lost Creek Falls is feature of a deep canyon carved through mountains of limestone. Hiking. Picnicking, grills. Camping. Interpretive display. Standard fees. 1 1/2 mi E on MT 1, then 2 mi N on MT 273, then 6 mi W on unnumbered road. Phone 406/542-5500.

Skiing. Discovery Basin. 3 double chairlifts, 2 beginner lifts, snowmaking; patrol, school, rentals; restaurant, bar. Longest run 2 mi; vertical drop 1,480 ft. (Thanksgiving-Easter, daily) Cross-country trail. 18 mi NW on MT 1. Phone 406/563-2184. ¢¢¢¢

⊠ Visitor Center. Display of smelter works photographs; outdoor railroad exhibit; self-guided walking tours; historic bus tours (Memorial Day-Labor Day, daily); video presentation (20 min) showing area attractions; tourist information for both city and state. (Summer, daily; rest of yr, Mon-Fri) 306 E Park St. Bus tours ¢¢

Annual Event

Chocolate Festival. Chocolate baking contest with winners sold at charity bake sale. Free chocolates at local merchants. Various "sweetheart" activities throughout town. Wkend before Feb 14.

Motels

✔★ MARCUS DALY. *119 W Park St. 406/563-3411; FAX 406/563-2268; res: 800/535-6528 (MT).* 19 rms, 10 A/C, 2 story. June-Aug: S $36; D $45; each addl $5; wkly rates; ski plan; lower rates rest of yr. Crib free. TV; cable. Complimentary coffee in lobby. Restaurant nearby. Ck-out 11 am. Free airport transportation. Cr cds: A, C, D, DS, MC, V.

⊠ 🐾

★ VAGABOND. *1421 E Park. 406/563-5251; FAX 406/563-3356.* 19 rms. S, D $45-$52. Crib $6. TV; cable. Restaurant opp open 24 hrs. Ck-out 11 am. Downhill/x-country ski 16 mi. Health club nearby. Cr cds: MC, V.

🐾 ⊠ 🐾

Resort

★ ★ FAIRMONT HOT SPRINGS RESORT. *1500 Fairmont Rd, 4 mi S of I-90 exit 211. 406/797-3241; FAX 406/797-3337; res: 800/332-3272 (exc MT), 800/332-3272 (MT).* 135 rms, 3 story. June-Sept: S, D $91-$100; each addl $10; suites, kit. units $97-$277; under 12 free; ski plan; lower rates rest of yr. Crib free. TV; cable, VCR avail (movies). 4 pools, 2 indoor; lifeguard. Restaurants 6:30 am-10 pm. Rm serv. Bar to 1:30 am; entertainment Tues-Sat. Ck-out 11 am. Ck-in 3 pm. Meeting rms. Business servs avail. Gift shop. Airport transportation. Tennis. 18-hole golf, greens fee $30, driving range. Bicycle rentals. Exercise equipt; weights, bicycles. Game rm. Lawn games. Hayrides. Private patios, balconies. Cr cds: A, C, D, DS, MC, V.

🏊 🧖 🏃 🏊 🎿 🏌 🚣 🐾 SC

Restaurant

★ ★ BARCLAY II. *1300 E Commercial, 1 mi E on US 10A. 406/563-5541.* Hrs: 5-10 pm; Sun 4-9:30 pm. Closed Mon, some major hols. Bar. Complete meals: dinner $9-$25. Specialties: tenderloin steak, halibut, breaded veal. Cr cds: DS, MC, V.

Bigfork (B-3)

(See also Kalispell, Polson)

Pop 1,080 (est) **Elev** 2,968 ft **Area code** 406 **Zip** 59911

Surrounded by lakes, a river and a dam, Bigfork's businesses are electric power and catering to tourists who visit the east shore of Flathead Lake (see POLSON). A Ranger District office of the Flathead National Forest (see KALISPELL) is located here.

What to See and Do

Bigfork Art & Cultural Center. Exhibits of artists and crafters of northwestern Montana; gift shop. (Apr-Dec, Wed-Sat) 525 Electric Ave. Phone 406/837-6927. **Free.**

Flathead Lake Biological Station, University of Montana. Laboratories for teaching and research in natural sciences; museum; self-guided nature trips. (Mon-Fri) MT 35, milepost 17 1/2, midway between Bigfork & Polson. Phone 406/982-3301. **Free.**

Flathead Lake State Park. On Flathead Lake (see POLSON). At all units: swimming; fishing; boating (ramp). Picnicking. Camping (no hookups). Standard fees.

Wayfarers Unit. Hiking trails. Camping (dump station, patrons only). Off MT 35. Phone 406/837-4196 (summer) or 406/752-5501.

Yellow Bay Unit. Joint state/tribal fishing license required. No RVs or trailers permitted. 10 mi S on MT 35. Phone 406/752-5501.

Swan Lake. About 10 mi long. Swimming, waterskiing; fishing, boating. 14 mi SE on MT 83.

Seasonal Event

Bigfork Summer Playhouse. 526 Electric Ave. Broadway musicals. Nightly exc Sun. For res contact PO Box 456; 406/837-4886. May-Labor Day.

Motel

★ **TIMBERS.** *8540 MT 35, at jct MT 35 & MT 209.* 406/837-6200; FAX 406/837-6203; res: 800/821-4546. 40 rms, 1-2 story. Mid-June-mid-Sept: S $58; D $58-$68; each addl $5; lower rates rest of yr. Crib $5. Pet accepted; $50 deposit & $5/day. TV; cable. Heated pool; whirlpool. Complimentary coffee in rms. Restaurant nearby. Ck-out 11 am. X-country ski 7 mi. Sauna. Cr cds: A, DS, MC, V.

Inns

★ **COYOTE ROADHOUSE INN & RIVERSIDE CABINS.** *(602 Three Eagle Lane, Ferndale)* 4 mi E on MT 209. 406/837-4250; FAX 406/837-0048. E-mail coyote@cyberport.net; web www.glaciercountry.com/coyote. 8 rms, 2 with shower only, 2 story. No A/C. No rm phones. June-Sept: S $90; D $110-$150; lower rates Apr-May, Oct. Closed rest of yr. Complimentary full bkfst. Ck-out 11 am, ck-in 3 pm. On Swan River. Many antiques. Totally nonsmoking. Cr cds: MC, V.

★ ★ **O'DUACHAIN COUNTRY INN.** *675 Ferndale Dr, 3 1/2 mi E off MT 209.* 406/837-6851; res: 800/837-7460; FAX 406/837-0778. E-mail knollmc@aol.com. 5 rms, all share bath, 3 story, 1 guest house. No A/C. No rm phones. June-Sept: S, D, guest house $95-$110; each addl $15; under 5 free; lower rates rest of yr. Crib free. Pet accepted, some restric-

tions. TV in common rm; cable (premium), VCR avail. Complimentary full bkfst. Ck-out 11 am, ck-in 2 pm. Luggage handling. Whirlpool. Authentic log home. Totally nonsmoking. Cr cds: A, DS, MC, V.

Resort

★ **MARINA CAY.** *180 Vista Lane.* 406/837-5861; FAX 406/837-1118; res: 800/433-6516. Web www.montanaweb.com/marina cay/. 119 rms, 3 story. Mid-June-Sept: S, D $77.50; studio rms $104.50-$125.50; suites $175.50-$289.50; lower rates rest of yr. Crib $10. TV; cable, VCR avail. Heated pool; whirlpool, poolside serv. Dining rm 7 am-9:30 pm. Bar. Ck-out 11 am, ck-in 3 pm. Meeting rms. Business servs avail. X-country ski 6 mi. Rental boats, canoes, water cycles. Fishing trips, whitewater rafting. Refrigerators, fireplaces; microwaves avail. Some private patios, balconies. Picnic table, grill. On Bigfork Bay of Flathead Lake. Cr cds: A, C, D, DS, MC, V.

Guest Ranch

★ ★ ★ **FLATHEAD LAKE LODGE.** *1/2 mi SW of MT 35.* 406/837-4391; FAX 406/837-3815. E-mail fll@digisys.net. The 2,000 acres of this rustic lakeside ranch with a huge stone fireplace is redolent of the feel for Big Sky country. 19 rms in 2-story lodge, 22 cottages. No A/C. AP, mid-June-Sept, wkly: S, D $1,750; 13-19 yrs $1,310; 6-12 yrs $1,090; 3-5 yrs $795; under 3 yrs $96. Closed rest of yr. Crib free. Heated pool. Free supervised child's activities (June-Sept); ages 6-teens. Dining rm 8 am-6:30 pm. Patio barbecues. Ck-out 11 am, ck-in 1 pm. Grocery, package store 1 mi. Coin lndry. Business servs avail. Valet serv. Gift shop. Airport, RR station transportation. Tennis. Private beach; boats, motors, canoes, sailboats, raft trips, waterskiing, instruction. Lake cruises. Fly-fishing instruction. Whitewater rafting. Soc dir. Indoor, outdoor games. Rec rm. Many private patios, balconies. Picnic tables, grills. Cr cds: A, MC, V.

Restaurants

✔ ★ ★ **BIGFORK INN.** *604 Electric Ave, on grounds of Bigfork Inn Hotel.* 406/837-6680. Hrs: 5-10 pm. Closed Thanksgiving, Dec 25. Res accepted. Bar to midnight. Semi-a la carte: dinner $12-$28. Child's meals. Specializes in fresh seafood, chicken, emu steaks. Entertainment Fri, Sat. Outdoor dining. Swiss chalet country inn. Cr cds: A, DS, MC, V.

★ ★ **COYOTE ROADHOUSE.** *(600 Three Eagle Lane, Ferndale)* E on MT 209. 406/837-1233. Hrs: 5:30-8:30 pm. Closed Mon, Tues. Res accepted. No A/C. Continental menu. Bar. Semi-a la carte: dinner $17-$20. Child's meals. Specialties: scampi etouffee, veal saltimbocca, char-grilled Mayan pork tenderloin. Own desserts. Outdoor dining. Secluded country dining with view of Swan River; flower gardens. Totally nonsmoking. Cr cds: MC, V.

D SC

★ ★ **SHOWTHYME.** *548 Electric Ave.* 406/837-0707. Hrs: 5-10 pm; May-Sept 11:30 am-2:30 pm, 5-10 pm. Closed Sun; Dec 25. A la carte entrees: dinner $10-$16.95. Child's meals. Specializes in fresh seafood, duck, lamb. Outdoor dining. In old bank building (1910). Cr cds: A, DS, MC, V.

★ ★ **TUSCANY'S.** *331 Bridge St.* 406/837-6065. Hrs: 5-10 pm. Closed Thanksgiving, Dec 25. Res accepted. No A/C. Italian menu. Beer, wine. Semi-a la carte: dinner $9.95-$24.95. Child's meals. Specialties: veal piccata, linguine al whiskey, chicken sorentino. Outdoor dining. Warm country inn atmosphere. Totally nonsmoking. Cr cds: A, DS, MC, V.

Big Hole National Battlefield (D-3)

(10 mi W of Wisdom on MT 43 or 16 mi E of Lost Trail Pass on MT 43, off MT 93, near Idaho border.)

Fleeing the US Army from what is now Idaho and Oregon, five "nontreaty" bands of Nez Perce were attacked here before dawn by US troops and citizen volunteers on August 9, 1877. More than 655 acres of the battlefield are preserved today. The Nez Perce escaped, but were pursued by the army to what is now called Bears' Paw Battleground (see CHINOOK), where Chief Joseph and the surviving Nez Perce surrendered after a six-day battle. Ironically, the tribe had previously been on good terms with the settlers until a treaty, forced on them in 1863, diminished the land originally granted to them in 1855. Those left out refused to recognize the 1863 treaty.

Three self-guided trails lead through the Siege Area, the Nez Perce Camp and the Howitzer Capture Site. Wildlife roam the area; fishing is permitted with a license. Visitor Center Museum exhibits firearms and relics of the period (summer, daily; winter, daily exc Sun; closed Jan 1, Thanksgiving, Dec 25). Interpretive walks presented daily in summer. Some access roads are closed in winter. For further information contact PO Box 237, Wisdom 59761; 406/689-3155. Per vehicle (Memorial Day-Labor Day) ¢¢

Big Sky (Gallatin Co) (E-5)

(See also Bozeman)

Pop 450 (est) **Elev** 5,934 ft **Area code** 406 **Zip** 59716 **E-mail** bigskymail@mcn.net **Web** www.bigskyresort.com

Information Sky of Montana Resort, PO Box 160001; 406/995-5000 or 800/548-4487.

Located 45 miles southwest of Bozeman in Gallatin National Forest, Big Sky is a resort community developed by the late newscaster and commentator, Chet Huntley. Golf, tennis, skiing, fishing, whitewater rafting and horseback riding are among the many activities available in the area.

What to See and Do

Big Sky Ski and Summer Resort. Quad, 3 high-speed quads, 3 triple, 3 double chairlifts, 3 surface tows; patrol, school, rentals; bar, concession area, cafeteria; nursery. Longest run 3 mi; vertical drop 4,180 ft. (Mid-Nov-mid-Apr, daily) 50 mi of cross-country trails. Gondola. Tram. Also summer activities. Phone 406/995-5000 or 800/548-4486. ¢¢¢¢

River trips. Yellowstone Raft Co. Half- and full-day whitewater raft trips on Gallatin and Madison rivers. No experience necessary. Paddle or oar powered rafts. For reservations contact PO Box 160262; phone 406/995-4613 or 800/348-4376. ¢¢¢¢

Motel

★ ★ ★ **BEST WESTERN-BUCK'S T-4 LODGE.** PO Box 160279, 1¹/₂ mi S of US 191 Big Sky exit. 406/995-4111; FAX 406/995-2191. 75 rms, 2¹/₂ story. No A/C. Late May-early Apr: S $59-$87; D $69-$99; each addl $6; under 12 free; ski plan; higher rates late Dec. Closed rest of yr. Crib $5. TV; cable, VCR avail (movies $3). Complimentary coffee in rms. Restaurant 7-11 am, 4-10 pm. Bar 5 pm-2 am. Ck-out 11 am. Coin lndry. Gift shop. Meeting rms. Business servs avail. Downhill/x-country ski 9 mi. Whirlpools. Game rm. Cr cds: A, C, D, DS, MC, V.

Lodge

★ ★ ★ **RIVER ROCK.** *(3080 Pine Dr, Big Sky)* 406/995-2295; FAX 406/995-2727; res: 800/995-9966. 29 rms, 2 story. Mid-Nov-mid-Apr: S $100-$140; D $110-$155; each addl $15; suite $200-$250; under 12 free; lower rates rest of yr. Crib $15. TV; cable, VCR (movies). Complimentary continental bkfst. Restaurant nearby. Ck-out 10:30 am. Meeting rms. Business servs avail. Bellhops. Concierge. Sundries. Free airport transportation. Downhill/x-country ski 6 mi. Exercise equipt; bicycle, treadmill. Refrigerator. Totally nonsmoking. Cr cds: A, C, D, DS, MC, V.

Resort

★ ★ ★ **BIG SKY RESORT.** Box 160001, 9 mi W of US 191. 406/995-5000; FAX 406/995-5001; res: 800/548-4486. 298 rms. Some A/C. Thanksgiving-mid-Apr: S, D $137-$176; each addl $20; ski plan; higher rates late Dec; lower rates rest of yr. Crib $10. TV; cable. 2 heated pools; whirlpool. Playground. Coffee in rms. Dining rm 6-10 am, 6-9 pm. Box lunches. Picnics. Rm serv. Bar 4 pm-2 am; entertainment. Ck-out noon, ck-in 5 pm. Coin lndry. Convention facilities. Business center. Concierge. Shopping arcade. Airport transportation. Tennis. 18-hole golf, pro, putting green, driving range. Exercise equipt; weights, bicycles, sauna, steam rm. Downhill/x-country ski on site. Ski storage, school. Ski and sports shops. Refrigerators. Picnic tables. Established by famed newscaster Chet Huntley. Cr cds: A, C, D, DS, MC, V.

Guest Ranches

★ ★ ★ **LONE MOUNTAIN RANCH.** Box 160069, 4¹/₂ mi W on US 191, then 1 mi N. 406/995-4644; FAX 406/995-4670; res: 800/514-4644. 30 cabins. No A/C. AP, Dec-Apr, June-Oct: S $1,600/wk; D $2,600/wk; each addl $970/wk. Closed rest of yr. Crib free. Playground. Supervised child's activities (June-Labor Day). Restaurant (see LONE MOUNTAIN RANCH DINING ROOM). Bar 3:30 pm-midnight. Ck-out 11 am, ck-in 2 pm. Coin lndry. Meeting rms. Gift shop. Airport transportation. Downhill ski 6 mi; x-country ski on site. Ski rentals, lessons. Sleigh ride dinners. Lawn games. Soc dir; entertainment. Rec rm. Whirlpool. Fishing guides. Fireplaces. Private patios. Picnic tables. Rustic setting. Cr cds: DS, MC, V.

★ ★ **NINE QUARTER CIRCLE RANCH.** *(5000 Taylor Fork Rd, Gallatin Gateway 59730)* 14 mi S to Taylors Fork, then 5 mi W. 406/995-4276. 15 cabins (1-bedrm), 8 cabins (2-bedrm). No A/C. AP, mid-June-mid-Sept: S $1,075/wk; D $1,980/wk; family rates. Closed rest of yr. Crib free. Pool. Playground. Free supervised child's activities (mid-June-mid-Sept). Dining rm sittings: 7 am, noon, 6:30 pm. Ck-out varies, ck-in noon. Coin lndry. Meeting rms. Airport transportation. Lawn games. Some fireplaces. 4,000-ft landing strip. No cr cds accepted.

Restaurants

★ **EDELWEISS.** *(Big Sky Spur Road, Big Sky)* 406/995-4665. Hrs: 11:30 am-10 pm; winter from 6 pm. Closed Apr-May & Oct-Nov. Res accepted. German, Amer menu. Bar. Semi-a la carte: lunch $4.50-$8, dinner $14-$22. Child's meals. Specializes in Wienerschnitzel, rack of lamb. Original Austrian wood carvings. World Cup ski trophies on display. Cr cds: A, DS, MC, V.

✔ ★ ★ **FIRST PLACE.** Meadow Village, 1³/₄ mi W of US 191 Big Sky exit. 406/995-4244. Hrs: 6-10 pm. Closed last 2 wks May. Res accepted. No A/C. Bar 5 pm-2 am. Semi-a la carte: dinner $11.50-$20.75.

Child's meals. Specializes in fresh fish, game birds. Scenic mountain view. Cr cds: A, DS, MC, V.

★ ★ ★ **LONE MOUNTAIN RANCH DINING ROOM.** *(See Lone Mountain Ranch Guest Ranch)* 406/995-2782. Hrs: 7-9 am, 11:30 am-2 pm, 6-8:30 pm. Closed Memorial Day, Thanksgiving. Res accepted; required dinner. No A/C. Continental menu. Bar noon-midnight. Buffet: bkfst $5.95, lunch $8.95. Prix fixe: dinner $36. Specialties: symphony of lamb, beef tenderloin tournedos. Outdoor dining. Western ranch atmosphere. Totally nonsmoking. Cr cds: DS, MC, V.

Big Timber (D-6)

(See also Bozeman, Livingston)

Pop 1,557 **Elev** 4,081 ft **Area code** 406 **Zip** 59011

Some of the tall cottonwoods that gave this settlement its name and the grasses that endowed the county with the name Sweet Grass remain. Livestock ranches make Big Timber their selling and shopping center. This is also a popular dude ranch area, with good hunting and fishing facilities. The Yellowstone and Boulder rivers provide good trout fishing. The first dude ranch in the state was started here around 1911. Natural bridge and falls area is located approximately 25 miles south of town.

A Ranger District office of the Gallatin National Forest (see BOZEMAN) is located here.

Annual Event

NRA/MRA Rodeo. Phone 406/252-1122. Late June-early July.

Motels

★ **C.M. RUSSELL LODGE.** *Hwy 10W, 1/2 mi E of I-90 exit 367.* 406/932-5245; FAX 406/932-5243. 42 rms, 2 story. S $36; D $39-$48; each addl $6; suites $60-$86. Crib free. TV; cable. Restaurant 6 am-10 pm. Bar from 5 pm. Ck-out 11 am. Coin lndry. Sundries. Gift shop. Totally nonsmoking. Cr cds: A, D, DS, MC, V.

★ **SUPER 8.** *I-90 exit 367.* 406/932-8888; FAX 406/932-4103. 39 rms, 2 story. May-Sept: S $46.88; D $50.88-$55.88; each addl $4; lower rates rest of yr. Crib free. Pet accepted; $15 deposit. TV; cable. Complimentary continental bkfst. Restaurant adj 6 am-10 pm. Ck-out 11 am. Coin lndry. Cr cds: A, D, DS, JCB, MC, V.

Restaurant

★ ★ **THE GRAND.** *139 McLeod St.* 406/932-4459. Hrs: 5-10 pm; Sun brunch 11 am-2 pm. Res accepted. Bar 11-1 am. Semi-a la carte: dinner $9.90-$24. Sun brunch $8.95. Child's meals. Specializes in pan-roasted salmon, rack of lamb, tenderloin. 1890 hotel dining rm. Cr cds: DS, MC, V.

Billings (D-7)

(See also Hardin)

Founded 1882 **Pop** 81,151 **Elev** 3,124 ft **Area code** 406

Information Billings Area Chamber of Commerce, 815 S 27th St, PO Box 31177, 59107; 406/245-4111 or 800/735-2635.

On the west bank of the Yellowstone River, Billings, seat of Yellowstone County, was built by the Northern Pacific Railway and took the name of railroad President Frederick K. Billings. Today, it is the center of a vast trade region. Billings is a major distribution point for Montana's and Wyoming's vast strip-mining operations. Industries include agriculture, tourism and oil trade. Billings offers excellent medical facilities and is a regional convention center. It is also the headquarters of the Custer National Forest (see HARDIN).

What to See and Do

Boothill Cemetery. Final resting place of Billings' gunmen and lawmen who died with their boots on. E end of Chief Black Otter Trail.

Chief Black Otter Trail. Drive above city, past Boothill Cemetery, up Kelly Mt and down along edge of sheer cliff. Excellent view of Billings. Starts at E end of city.

Geyser Park. 18-hole mini golf course; water bumper boats, Lazer-Tag, Go-Karts and track; concessions. (May-Oct, daily; closed hols) 4910 Southgate Dr. Phone 406/254-2510. ¢¢¢

Oscar's Dreamland Yesteryear Museum. The dream of Oscar O. Cooke: 15 acres containing what is considered the world's largest private collection of farm artifacts; tractors, threshers, steam engines, plows; antique cars, covered wagons; more than 5,000 antiques; 1900s pioneer town. (May-mid-Oct, daily) 7 mi SW via I-90 to King Ave exit and S Frontage to Shiloh underpass. Phone 406/656-0966. ¢¢

Peter Yegen, Jr—Yellowstone County Museum. Native American artifacts, antique steam locomotive, horse-drawn vehicles; dioramas depict homesteading days and Native American sacrificial ceremony; vast display of valuable guns, saddles, precious stones. Breathtaking view of Yellowstone Valley and the mountains. (Daily exc Sat; closed hols) At Logan Field Airport, on MT 3. For tour information phone 406/256-6811. **Donation.**

Pictograph Cave State Park. Inhabited 4,500 yrs ago; pictographs on walls. Picnicking. (Mid-Apr-mid-Oct) I-90 at Lockwood exit, 6 mi S on county road. Phone 406/252-4654. Per vehicle ¢¢

Range Rider of the Yellowstone. Life-size bronze statue of cowboy and his mount; posed for by William S. Hart, an early silent film cowboy star. Near airport, off Chief Black Otter Trail.

Rocky Mt College (1878). (850 students) First college in Montana. Sandstone buildings are some of Billings's oldest permanent structures. 1511 Poly Dr. For tours phone 406/657-1000.

Western Heritage Center. Featuring rotating exhibits relating to the history of the Yellowstone Valley from prehistoric to modern times. (Daily exc Mon; closed major hols) 2822 Montana Ave. Phone 406/256-6809. **Donation.**

Yellowstone Art Center. Contemporary and historic art exhibitions, lectures, chamber concerts, films. (Daily exc Mon; closed Jan) 401 N 27th St. Phone 406/256-6804. **Free.**

ZooMontana. The state's only wildlife park features homestead petting zoo. (Mid-Apr-mid-Oct, daily; rest of yr, wkends, weather permitting) 2100 S Shiloh Rd. Phone 406/652-8100. ¢¢

Annual Events

Peaks to Prairies Triathlon. Apr.

Montana Fair. MetraPark. Phone 406/256-2400. Mid-Aug.

Northern International Livestock Exposition. Oct.

Motels

★ ★ **BEST WESTERN.** *5610 S Frontage Rd (59101), I-90 exit 446.* 406/248-9800; FAX 406/248-2500. 80 rms, 3 story, 12 suites. June-Aug: S $54-$58; D $66-$76; each addl $4; suites $78-$110; under 18 free; lower rates rest of yr. Crib free. Pet accepted, some restrictions. TV; cable (premium). Indoor pool; whirlpool. Complimentary continental bkfst. Restaurant adj open 24 hrs. Ck-out noon. Coin lndry. Meeting rms. Business servs avail. Valet serv. Sauna. Cr cds: A, C, D, DS, ER, MC, V.

[D] [☞] [≋] [⊠] [🔥] [SC]

★ ★ **BEST WESTERN PONDEROSA INN.** *2511 First Ave N (59103), I-90 exit 27th St S, near Logan Field Airport.* 406/259-5511; FAX 406/245-8004. 130 rms, 2 story. S $50-$60; D $60-$70; each addl $5. Crib free. Pet accepted, some restrictions. TV; cable (premium). Pool. Complimentary coffee in rms. Restaurant open 24 hrs. Bar 3 pm-2 am; closed Sun. Ck-out 11 am. Coin lndry. Meeting rm. Business servs avail. Valet serv. Free airport transportation. Exercise equipt; rowing machine, bicycles, sauna. Cr cds: A, C, D, DS, ER, JCB, MC, V.

[☞] [≋] [🏃] [✈] [⊠] [SC]

✔ ★ **BILLINGS INN.** *880 N 29th St (59101), I-90 exit 27th St, then 2 mi N, near Logan Field Airport.* 406/252-6800; FAX 406/252-6800; res: 800/231-7782. E-mail tbi@wtp.net. 60 rms, 4 story. S $42.50; D $46.50-$52; each addl $5; under 12 free. Crib $5. Pet accepted, some restrictions; $5. TV; cable. Complimentary continental bkfst. Ck-out 11 am. Coin lndry. Valet serv. Sundries. Airport transportation. Some refrigerators, microwaves. Cr cds: A, C, D, DS, MC, V.

[D] [☞] [✈] [⊠] [🔥] [SC]

★ **C'MON INN.** *2020 Overland Ave (59102).* 406/655-1100; FAX 406/652-7672; res: 800/655-1170. 80 rms, 2 story, 8 suites. May-Aug: S $58.95; D $64.95-$75.95; each addl $6; suites $103; under 13 free; lower rates rest of yr. Crib free. TV; cable (premium). Indoor pool; wading pool, whirlpool. Complimentary continental bkfst. Restaurant nearby. Ck-out noon. Meeting rms. Business servs avail. Exercise equipt; bicycles, treadmill. Valet serv. Game rm. Minibars; refrigerator in suites. Cr cds: A, DS, MC, V.

[D] [≋] [🏃] [⊠] [🔥] [SC]

★ ★ **COMFORT INN.** *2030 Overland Ave (59102).* 406/652-5200. 60 rms, 2 story. June-mid-Sept: S $64.95; D $76.95; each addl $5; suites $84-$90; under 18 free; lower rates rest of yr. Crib free. Pet accepted, some restrictions. TV; cable (premium). Indoor pool; whirlpool. Complimentary continental bkfst. Ck-out 11 am. Business servs avail. Game rm. Some refrigerators. Cr cds: A, C, D, DS, ER, JCB, MC, V.

[D] [☞] [≋] [⊠] [🔥] [SC]

✔ ★ **DAYS INN.** *843 Parkway Lane (59101).* 406/252-4007; FAX 406/252-4007, ext. 301. 63 rms. S $65; D $55-$80; each addl $5; under 12 free. Crib free. Pet accepted, some restrictions. TV; cable, VCR avail (movies). Complimentary continental bkfst. Restaurant nearby. Ck-out noon. Coin lndry. Whirlpool. Cr cds: A, D, DS, JCB, MC, V.

[☞] [⊠] [🔥] [SC]

★ ★ **FAIRFIELD INN BY MARRIOTT.** *2026 Overland Ave (59102).* 406/652-5330; FAX 406/652-5330. 63 rms, 3 story. June-mid-Sept: S $62.95; D $72.95; each addl $5; under 18 free; lower rates rest of yr. Crib free. TV; cable. Indoor pool; whirlpool. Complimentary continental bkfst. Restaurant nearby. Ck-out noon. Meeting rms. Business servs avail. Game rm. Some refrigerators. Cr cds: A, C, D, DS, MC, V.

[D] [≋] [⊠] [🔥] [SC]

✔ ★ **HILLTOP INN.** *1116 N 28th St (59101).* 406/245-5000; FAX 406/245-7851; res: 800/878-9282. E-mail hilltop@wtp.net. 45 rms, 3 story. S $42.50; D $46.50; each addl $5; under 12 free. Crib $5. Pet accepted. TV; cable. Complimentary continental bkfst. Restaurant nearby. Ck-out 11 am. Sundries. Valet serv. Coin lndry. Some refrigerators, microwaves. Cr cds: A, D, DS, MC, V.

[D] [☞] [⊠] [🔥] [SC]

★ **HOWARD JOHNSON EXPRESS.** *1001 S 27th St (59101).* 406/248-4656; FAX 406/248-7268; res: 800/654-2000. 173 rms, 3 story. June-Sept: S $64; D $68; each addl $4; under 18 free. Crib free. TV; cable. Complimentary continental bkfst. Ck-out noon. Coin lndry. Meeting rms. Business servs avail. Bellhops. Valet serv. Free airport transportation. Cr cds: A, C, D, DS, JCB, MC, V.

[D] [⊠] [🏔] [🔥] [SC]

★ ★ **QUALITY INN HOMESTEAD.** *2036 Overland Ave (59102).* 406/652-1320; FAX 406/652-1320. 119 rms, 2 story. S, D $56-$75; each addl $5; suites $62-$80; under 18 free. Crib free. Pet accepted; $25 deposit. TV; cable (premium), VCR avail (movies). Indoor pool; whirlpool. Complimentary full bkfst; afternoon refreshments. Restaurant nearby. Ck-out noon. Coin lndry. Bellhops. Valet serv. Free airport transportation. Golf privileges. Sauna. Health club privileges. Some refrigerators. Cr cds: A, C, D, DS, ER, JCB, MC, V.

[D] [☞] [🏃] [≋] [⊠] [🔥] [SC]

★ **RAMADA LIMITED.** *1345 Mullowney Lane (59101), at jct I-90 & King Ave exit.* 406/252-2584; FAX 406/252-2584, ext. 308. 116 rms, 2 story. S $58-$68; D $63-$68; each addl $5; under 18 free. Crib free. Pet accepted, some restrictions. TV; cable (premium). Pool. Playground. Complimentary continental bkfst. Restaurant nearby. Ck-out noon. Business servs avail. Exercise equipt; weight machine, treadmill. Cr cds: A, D, DS, MC, V.

[D] [☞] [≋] [🏃] [⊠] [🔥] [SC]

★ ★ **SLEEP INN.** *4904 Southgate Dr (59101), at I-90 exit 447.* 406/254-0013; FAX 406/254-9878. 75 rms, shower only, 2 story. S $51; D $58-$63; each addl $5; under 18 free. Crib free. TV; cable (premium). Complimentary continental bkfst. Restaurant nearby. Ck-out 11 am. Cr cds: A, D, DS, JCB, MC, V.

[D] [⊠] [🔥] [SC]

✔ ★ **SUPER 8 LODGE.** *5400 Southgate Dr (59102), at I-90 exit 446.* 406/248-8842; FAX 406/248-8842. 115 rms, 2 story. S $50.88; D $55.88-$59.88; each addl $5; suites $72.11; under 12 free. Crib free. Pet accepted, some restrictions; $20. TV; cable (premium), VCR avail (movies). Restaurant nearby. Ck-out 11 am. Cr cds: A, C, D, DS, MC, V.

[D] [☞] [⊠] [🔥] [SC]

Hotels

★ ★ ★ **RADISSON NORTHERN.** *Broadway & First Ave N (59101), downtown.* 406/245-5121; FAX 406/259-9862. Web www.radisson.com. 160 rms, 10 story. S, D $112; each addl $10; under 18 free. Crib free. Pet accepted, some restrictions. TV; cable (premium). Restaurant 6:30 am-10 pm. Bar 11-1 am. Ck-out noon, ck-in 3 pm. Meeting rms. Business servs avail. Gift shop. Free covered parking. Airport transportation. Exercise equipt; weight machine, bicycles. Some refrigerators. Cr cds: A, C, D, DS, ER, JCB, MC, V.

[D] [☞] [🏃] [⊠] [🔥] [SC]

★ ★ ★ **SHERATON.** *27 N 27th St (59101), near Logan Field Airport.* 406/252-7400; FAX 406/252-2401. 282 rms, 23 story. S $90; D $100; each addl $10; suites $140-$190; under 18 free. Crib free. Pet accepted, some restrictions. TV; cable (premium). Indoor pool; wading pool, whirlpool. Coffee in rms. Restaurant 6:30 am-10 pm. Bar 11-2 am. Ck-out noon. Convention facilities. Business servs avail. Gift shop. Airport transportation. Exercise rm; instructor, weight machines, bicycles, sauna. Game rm. Some refrigerators. Cr cds: A, C, D, DS, ER, MC, V.

[D] [☞] [≋] [🏃] [✈] [⊠] [🔥] [SC]

Restaurants

✔ ★ **BRUNO'S.** *1002 First Ave N (59102).* 406/248-4146. Hrs: 11 am-10 pm; Sat from 5 pm. Closed Sun; most major hols. Res accepted. Italian menu. Bar. Semi-a la carte: lunch $4.95-$6.25, dinner $4.95-$9.95.

Child's meals. Specializes in fresh pasta, pizza. Parking. Cozy atmosphere; many antiques. Cr cds: DS, MC, V.

★ ★ **GEORGE HENRY'S.** 404 N 30th St. 406/245-4570. Hrs: 11 am-2 pm, 5:30-9 pm; Sat from 5:30 pm. Closed Sun; major hols. Res accepted. Continental menu. Beer, wine. Semi-a la carte: lunch $4.50-$7.25, dinner $8.95-$18.95. Child's meals. Specializes in chicken, steaks, seafood. Own desserts. Parking. Built 1882; former boardinghouse and tearoom; some original fixtures. Totally nonsmoking. Cr cds: A, MC, V.

✔★ ★ **GREAT WALL.** 1309 Grand Ave. 406/245-8601. Hrs: 11 am-9:30 pm; Fri, Sat to 10 pm. Closed Thanksgiving, Dec 25. Res accepted. Chinese menu. Wine, beer. Semi-a la carte: lunch $5.25-$8.25, dinner $5.75-$15.95. Child's meals. Specialties: marinated crisp duck, Taiwanese seafood in bird's nest, hot amazing chicken. Parking. Cr cds: A, DS, MC, V.

★ ★ **JULIANO'S.** 2912 Seventh Ave N. 406/248-6400. E-mail shunzo@aol.com. Hrs: 11:30 am-2 pm, 5:30-9 pm; Wed-Sat from 5:30 pm. Closed Sun; Thanksgiving, Dec 25. Res accepted. Continental menu. Bar. Wine list. Semi-a la carte: lunch $5.95-$7.95, dinner $13.95-$21.95. Specializes in fresh seafood, peppered Montana ostrich, Jamaican spit-roasted chicken. Own baking. Parking. Outdoor dining. Converted Victorian home (1902); turn-of-the-century decor. Totally nonsmoking. Cr cds: A, DS, MC, V.

✔★ ★ **MATTHEW'S TASTE OF ITALY.** 1233 N 27th (59101). 406/254-8530. Hrs: 11 am-10 pm; Sat, Sun from noon. Closed Thanksgiving, Dec 25. Res accepted. Italian menu. Bar. Semi-a la carte: lunch $4.95-$9.95, dinner $7.95-$16.95. Child's meals. Specialties: scallopini di pollo, pasta con pollo al sugo bianco. Italian bistro decor. Cr cds: A, DS, MC, V.

★ ★ **REX.** 2401 Montana Ave. 406/245-7477. E-mail chef@imt.net. Hrs: 5:30-10:30 pm. Closed Thanksgiving, Dec 25. Res accepted. Bar 4 pm-2 am; Sat, Sun from 5 pm. Semi-a la carte: dinner $12.95-$27.95. Specializes in hand-cut steak, prime rib, fresh seafood. In National Historic District. Totally nonsmoking. Cr cds: A, D, DS, MC, V.

★ ★ **WALKERS GRILL.** 301 N 27th St. 406/245-9291. Hrs: 5:30-10:30 pm. Closed Sun; some major hols. Res accepted. Bar from 4 pm. Semi-a la carte: dinner $7.50-$18.95. Child's meals. Specializes in dry-aged beef, fresh fish. Parking. Bistro atmosphere. Cr cds: A, DS, MC, V.

Bozeman (D-5)

(See also Livingston, Three Forks, White Sulphur Springs)

Settled 1864 **Pop** 22,660 **Elev** 4,810 ft **Area code** 406 **E-mail** bchamber@avicom.net **Web** www.avicom.net/bozchmbr/
Information Chamber of Commerce, 1205 E Main, PO Box B, 59771; 406/586-5421 or 800/228-4224.

Blazing a trail from Wyoming, John M. Bozeman led a train of immigrants who settled here and named the town for their leader. The first settlements in the Gallatin Valley were agricultural, but were economically surpassed by the mines nearby. Today, small grain farming, livestock, dairying, tourism and the state university are important sources of income. The city is the marketplace for the cattle-producing Gallatin Valley.

What to See and Do

Bicycling and hiking. Backcountry Tours. Trips through Oregon, Yellowstone, Utah, Grand Tetons, Canadian Rockies and other areas. Phone 406/586-3556. ¢¢¢¢

Bridger Bowl Ski Area. Quad, 5 double chairlifts, ski school, patrol, rentals; half-day rates; lodge, cafeteria, bar. Longest run 2¹/₂ mi; vertical drop 2,000 ft. (Mid-Dec-Apr, daily) 16 mi NE via MT 86, in Gallatin National Forest. Phone 406/587-2111 or 800/223-9609. ¢¢¢¢

Gallatin National Forest. 1,735,412 acres. Mountain peaks, pine and fir forest, winter sports, pack trips, picnicking, camping, fishing, hunting; 574,788-acre Absaroka-Beartooth Wilderness south of Livingston, 253,000-acre Lee Metcalf Wilderness, Gallatin Gateway to Yellowstone. Forest rangers provide interpretive programs in summer at the Madison River Canyon Earthquake Area (see WEST YELLOWSTONE); exhibits. N & S of town. For information contact Supervisor, 10 E Babcock St, PO Box 130, 59771; 406/587-6701. A Ranger District office is located here.

Montana State University (1893). (11,000 students) 11th Ave, College St, 7th Ave & Lincoln St, at S edge of town. On campus are

Museum of the Rockies. Pioneer, Native American exhibits; dinosaurs; art and science displays. Taylor Planetarium. (Daily; closed major hols) S 7th Ave & Kagy Blvd S. Phone 406/994-2251. ¢¢¢

Fieldhouse. Circular building with portable stage. Scene of concerts, sports events, rodeos. Capacity 9,500. (Mon-Fri) 11th Ave & Grant St.

Annual Events

Montana Winter Fair. 3rd wk Jan.

Gallatin County Fair. Last full wkend July.

Sweet Pea Festival. 1st full wkend Aug.

Bridger Raptor Festival. Bridger Bowl ridge area. View birds of prey, including the largest concentration of migrating Golden Eagles in the contiguous 48 states, on their trip south. Usually 1st 2 wks Oct.

Motels

★ ★ **COMFORT INN.** 1370 N 7th Ave (59715), I-90 exit 306. 406/587-2322; FAX 406/587-2423. 87 rms, 3 story. May-Sept: S $60-$69; D $65-$77; each addl $4; suites $69-$99; under 18 free; lower rates rest of yr. Crib $5. TV; cable (premium). Indoor pool; whirlpool. Complimentary continental bkfst. Restaurant opp 6:30 am-11 pm. Ck-out 11 am. Coin lndry. Meeting rm. Business servs avail. In-rm modem link. Exercise equipt; bicycles, treadmill, sauna. Cr cds: A, C, D, DS, JCB, MC, V.

D ≈ ᴛ ⊠ ⋈ SC

✔★ **DAYS INN.** 1321 N 7th Ave (59715). 406/587-5251. 79 rms, 2 story. S $56; D $72-$76; each addl $5; under 12 free. Crib free. Pet accepted; $25 deposit. TV; cable (premium), VCR avail (movies). Complimentary continental bkfst. Restaurant adj 6 am-10 pm. Ck-out noon. Business servs avail. Downhill/x-country ski 17 mi. Whirlpool, sauna. Cr cds: A, C, D, DS, MC, V.

D ✦ ≈ ⊠ ⋈ SC

★ ★ **FAIRFIELD INN BY MARRIOTT.** 828 Wheat Dr (59715), I-90 7th Ave exit. 406/587-2222. 57 rms, 3 story. June-Aug: S $68.95; D $70.95-$75.95; each addl $6; under 18 free; lower rates rest of yr. Crib free. TV; cable (premium). Indoor pool; whirlpool. Complimentary continental bkfst. Restaurant opp open 24 hrs. Ck-out noon. Business servs avail. Valet serv. Sundries. Downhill/x-country ski 16 mi. Game rm. Refrigerator in suites. Cr cds: A, C, D, DS, MC, V.

D ≈ ⊠ ⋈ SC

★ ★ **HOLIDAY INN.** 5 Baxter Lane (59715), 1¹/₂ mi NW on N 7th St, S of I-90, N 7th Ave exit. 406/587-4561; FAX 406/587-4413. 178 rms, 2 story. S, D $74-$95; under 18 free. Crib free. Pet accepted. TV; cable. Indoor pool; whirlpool. Restaurant 6 am-2 pm, 5-10 pm. Rm serv. Bar 2 pm-midnight. Ck-out noon. Coin lndry. Meeting rms. Business servs avail. Bellhops. Valet serv. Free airport, bus depot transportation. Downhill/x-country ski 16 mi. Lawn games. Exercise equipt; weights, bicycles. Rec rm. Some refrigerators. Picnic tables. Cr cds: A, C, D, DS, MC, V.

D ✦ ≈ ᴛ ⊠ ⋈ SC

★ **HOMESTEAD INN.** (6261 Jackrabbit Ln, Belgrade 59714) 406/388-0800; FAX 406/388-0804; res: 800/542-6791. 67 rms, 3 story.

June-Aug: S, D $54.95-$64.95; under 12 free; lower rates rest of yr. Crib free. Pet accepted. TV; cable (premium). Complimentary coffee in lobby. Restaurant adj open 24 hrs. Ck-out 11 am. Totally nonsmoking. Cr cds: A, D, DS, MC, V.

[D] [♿] [⊠] [🔥] [SC]

★ **PRIME RATE.** *805 Wheat Dr (59715), I-90 7th Ave exit. 406/587-2100; res: 800/800-7089.* 42 rms, 3 story. No elvtr. June-Aug: S $40; D $46-$60; each addl $4; under 12 free; lower rates rest of yr. Crib $3. TV; cable. Complimentary continental bkfst. Ck-out 11 am. Whirlpool, sauna. Cr cds: A, C, D, DS, MC, V.

[⊠] [🔥] [SC]

★ **RAMADA LIMITED.** *2020 Wheat Dr (59715). 406/585-2626; FAX 585/-2727.* 50 rms, shower only, 2 story. June-Aug: S $49-$79; D $49-$109; suites $69-$119; lower rates rest of yr. Crib free. Pet accepted. TV; cable. Indoor pool. Complimentary continental bkfst. Restaurant nearby. Ck-out noon. Valet serv. Downhill/x-country ski 16 mi. Cr cds: A, C, D, DS, MC, V.

[♿] [⊠] [≋] [⊠] [🔥] [SC]

★ **ROYAL 7.** *310 N 7th Ave (59715), on business loop from I-90, exit 306W. 406/587-3103; res: 800/587-3103.* 47 units. S $39.75-$42.75; D $48.75-$58.75; kit. unit $63.75. Crib $4. Pet accepted. TV; cable (premium). Playground. Restaurant adj 7 am-10 pm. Ck-out noon. Business servs avail. Downhill/x-country ski 16 mi. Whirlpool. Picnic tables. Cr cds: A, D, DS, MC, V.

[♿] [≋] [⊠] [🔥]

★ **SLEEP INN.** *817 Wheat Dr (59715). 406/585-7888; FAX 406/585-8842.* 56 rms, showers only, 2 story. June-mid-Sept: S $65-$85; D $75-$90; each addl $5; suites $89-$99; under 18 free; lower rates rest of yr. Crib free. TV; cable, VCR avail. Indoor pool; whirlpool, sauna. Complimentary continental bkfst. Restaurant nearby. Ck-out 11 am. Downhill/x-country ski 16 mi. Game rm. Some refrigerators. Cr cds: A, C, D, DS, MC, V.

[D] [≋] [≋] [⊠] [🔥] [SC]

★ **WESTERN HERITAGE.** *1200 E Main (59715). 406/586-8534; FAX 406/587-8729; res: 800/877-1094.* 38 rms, 3 story. June-Sept: S $53-$73; D $58-$83; each addl $7; suites $95-$150; studio rms $95; under 13 free; ski plan; higher rates Sweet Pea Festival; lower rates rest of yr. Crib $7.50. Pet accepted. TV; cable (premium). Complimentary continental bkfst. Restaurant adj 6 am-10:30 pm. Ck-out 11 am. Coin lndry. Meeting rms. Business servs avail. Valet serv. Sundries. Downhill/x-country ski 16 mi. Exercise equipt; treadmill, bicycles, whirlpool, steam rm. Some in-rm whirlpools. Cr cds: A, C, D, DS, MC, V.

[D] [♿] [≋] [🍴] [⊠] [🔥] [SC]

Inns

★ ★ **GALLATIN GATEWAY.** *US 191 (59730). 406/763-4672; res: 800/676-3522.* 35 rms, 2 story. Some A/C. June-Sept: S $85; D $95; each addl $10; suites $125; under 12 free; lower rates rest of yr. Crib $5. TV; cable (premium). Heated pool; whirlpool. Complimentary continental bkfst. Restaurant (see GALLATIN GATEWAY INN). Bar 5 pm-midnight. Concierge serv. Airport transportation. Tennis. Lawn games. Mountain bike rentals. On river. Restored railroad hotel (1927); many antiques. Cr cds: A, DS, MC, V.

[D] [♿] [🏂] [≋] [⊠] [🔥]

★ ★ **LINDLEY HOUSE.** *202 Lindley Place (59715). 406/587-8403; FAX 406/582-8112; res: 800/787-8404.* 8 rms, 2 share baths, 4 with shower only, 4 story. No A/C. No elvtr. Some rm phones. Mid-May-Oct: S, D $75-$130; each addl $20; suites $175-$250; lower rates rest of yr. Children over 10 only. TV; cable (premium). Complimentary full bkfst. Restaurant nearby. Ck-out 11 am, ck-in 3-5 pm. Victorian house built in 1889 furnished with antiques. Totally nonsmoking. Cr cds: MC, V.

[⊠] [🔥]

★ ★ **TORCH & TOES.** *309 S 3rd Ave (59715). 406/586-7285; FAX 406/585-2749; res: 800/446-2138 (exc MT).* 4 rms in 2 bldgs, 2 story. No A/C. No rm phones. S, D $70-$90; each addl $10; under 5 free; wkly rates. Crib free. TV in sitting rm. Complimentary full bkfst. Restaurant nearby. Ck-out 11 am, ck-in 4-6 pm. Colonial revival-style house (1906); large front porch with swing; antiques, library. Totally nonsmoking. Cr cds: MC, V.

[⊠] [🔥] [SC]

★ ★ **VOSS.** *319 S Willson (59715). 406/587-0982; FAX 406/585-2964.* 6 rms, 2 A/C, 2 story. S $70-$80; D $80-$95; each addl $10. TV in sitting rm. Complimentary full bkfst. Ck-out noon, ck-in 2 pm. Downhill/x-country ski 16 mi. Built 1883; Victorian decor, antiques; brass and iron beds. Totally nonsmoking. Cr cds: A, MC, V.

[🏂] [⊠] [🔥]

Restaurants

★ ★ **THE BAXTER.** *105 W Main St (59715). 406/586-1314.* Hrs: 5:30-10 pm. Closed some major hols. Res accepted. Italian menu. Bar 11 am-midnight. A la carte entrees: dinner $12.75-$17.95. Child's meals. Specialties: slow-roasted prime rib, tortellini with smoked chicken, crab ravioli. Own baking. In old Baxter Hotel (1929). Cr cds: A, DS, MC, V.

★ ★ ★ **GALLATIN GATEWAY INN.** *(See Gallatin Gateway Inn) 406/763-4672.* Hrs: 6-9:30 pm; Sun brunch 10 am-2 pm. Res accepted. Continental menu. Bar to midnight. Wine list. Semi-a la carte: dinner $14-$30. Sun brunch $7.50. Child's meals. Specializes in prime rib, pasta, salmon. Spanish decor. Cr cds: A, DS, MC, V.

[D]

★ ★ **JOHN BOZEMAN BISTRO.** *242 E Main St (59715). 406/587-4100.* Hrs: 11 am-3 pm, 5-9:30 pm; Sun 8 am-1 pm. Closed Mon; most major hols. Res accepted. Continental menu. Wine, beer. Semi-a la carte: bkfst $4.95-$7.75, lunch $2.95-$8.95, dinner $9.95-$17.95. Child's meals. Specializes in fresh seafood, Montana steaks, fresh sushi. Parking. Eclectic decor; original art. Totally nonsmoking. Cr cds: A, DS, MC, V.

★ ★ **SPANISH PEAKS BREWERY & ITALIAN CAFE.** *120 N 19th St (59715). 406/585-2296.* Hrs: 11:30 am-10:30 pm. Res accepted. Italian menu. Bar to 1 am. Semi-a la carte: lunch $5.95-$7.95, dinner $7.95-$18.95. Specializes in homemade pasta, wood-fired pizza. Parking. Own beer brewed on site. Contemporary decor. Cr cds: DS, MC, V.

Unrated Dining Spots

LEAF & BEAN COFFEE HOUSE. *35 W Main St (59715). 406/587-1580.* Hrs: 6:30 am-10 pm; wkends to 11 pm. Closed Thanksgiving, Dec 25. No A/C. Pastries/desserts $1-$3. Selection of specialty coffees, teas and desserts. Entertainment Fri, Sat. Totally nonsmoking. Cr cds: MC, V.

MACKENZIE RIVER PIZZA. *232 E Main St (59715). 406/587-0055.* Hrs: 11:30 am-10 pm; Sun from 5 pm. Closed some major hols. Semi-a la carte: lunch, dinner $4.95-$16.75. Specializes in gourmet pizza. Cr cds: A, DS, MC, V.

[D]

Browning (A-3)

(For accommodations see East Glacier Area under Glacier National Park)

Pop 1,170 **Elev** 4,362 ft **Area code** 406 **Zip** 59417

Eastern gateway to Glacier National Park (see), Browning is the capital of the Blackfeet Nation. The town was named for a US Commissioner of Indian Affairs. The reservation itself covers 2,348,000 acres.

What to See and Do

Museum of Montana Wildlife and Hall of Bronze. Miniature dioramas, mounted specimens; paintings, sculpture. (May-Sept, daily) Just E of Museum of the Plains Indian on US 2, 89. Phone 406/338-5425. ¢

Museum of the Plains Indian. Collection of Blackfeet and Northern Plains Native American tribal artifacts plus history of tribes of the northern Great Plains. Administered by Dept of Interior, Indian Arts and Crafts Board. (June-Sept, daily; rest of yr, Mon-Fri; closed Jan 1, Thanksgiving, Dec 25) W at jct US 2, 89; 13 mi from Glacier National Park. Phone 406/338-2230. **Free.**

Annual Event

North American Native American Days Powwow. Blackfeet Reservation. Phone 406/338-7276. Mid-July.

Butte (D-4)

(See also Anaconda, Three Forks)

Settled 1864 **Pop** 33,336 **Elev** 5,549 ft **Area code** 406 **Zip** 59701 **Web** www.butteinfo.org
Information Butte-Silver Bow Chamber of Commerce, 1000 George; 800/735-6814.

Settled more than 100 years ago, Butte, atop the "richest hill on earth," harvests treasures of copper along with by-product gold, silver and other metals from 1,000 acres of mines. Although mined for more than a century, this treasure chest seems to be inexhaustible. Butte's famous old properties continue to produce high-grade ores. Modern mining techniques have exposed vast new low-grade mineral resources.

Butte was born as a bonanza silver camp. When the silver ores became lower grade at comparatively shallow depths, copper ores were discovered. Although development of the copper mines was a slow process, culminating in the "war of the copper kings," fortunes were made and lost and battles were fought in court for control of ore on surface and underground.

The brawny, colorful mining-camp days of Butte are over. Although copper mining still plays an important role in the Butte economy, it is also a retailing, distribution and diversified industrial center. A Ranger District office of the Deerlodge National Forest is located here.

What to See and Do

Arts Chateau (1898). Originally home of Charles Clark, now a heritage museum and arts center. Stairway leads from first floor galleries to fourth floor ballroom. Stained-glass windows, intricate moldings. (Daily exc Mon) 321 W Broadway. Phone 406/723-7600. ¢¢

Copper King Mansion (ca 1888). Restored 32-rm home of Senator W.A. Clark, prominent political figure of Montana's early mining days; of particular interest are frescoed ceilings and walls, stained-glass windows, nine hand-carved fireplaces, antique pipe organ; silver and crystal collections. (May-Sept, daily) 219 W Granite St. Phone 406/782-7580. ¢¢

Deerlodge National Forest. 1,176,452 acres include 158,516-acre Anaconda-Pintler Wilderness, alpine lakes, ghost towns. Fishing, hunting.

Bridle trails. Winter sports. Picknicking. Camping. Sections surround town, reached by I-90, I-15, MT 2, MT 1 (Pintler scenic route). Contact Forest Supervisor, 400 N Main St, PO Box 400; 406/496-3400.

Montana Tech of the University of Montana. (1893). (1,900 students) Mineral energy-oriented college near mining operations. On W Park St. Phone 406/496-4266. On campus is

Mineral Museum. Mineral display; some fossils; specimens from collection of 15,100 rotate periodically; special fluorescent & Montana minerals. Guided tours. (Mon-Fri; also by appt; closed hols) Phone 406/496-4414. **Free.**

Old No. 1. Tour of city aboard replica of early-day streetcar departs from Chamber of Commerce office. (June-Labor Day, Mon-Fri; closed July 4) For reservations phone 406/494-5595. ¢¢

Our Lady of the Rockies. 90-ft likeness of Mary, Mother of Jesus, sits atop Continental Divide overlooking town. Trips to mountaintop avail in summer, phone 406/494-2656 for res (fee). Phone 406/782-1221 for more information.

World Museum of Mining and 1899 Mining Camp. Outdoor and indoor displays of mining mementos; turn-of-the-century mining camp, Hell Roarin' Gulch. Picnic area. (Memorial Day-Labor Day, daily; rest of yr, daily exc Mon) W Park St. Phone 406/723-7211. ¢

Annual Event

Vigilante Rodeo. July.

Motels

★ ★ **BEST WESTERN COPPER KING PARK HOTEL.** *4655 Harrison Ave S, S of I-90, Harrison Ave exit, near Bert Mooney Airport.* 406/494-6666; FAX 406/494-3274. 150 rms, 2 story. S, D $76-$92; each addl $8; under 18 free. Crib free. Pet accepted. TV; cable. Indoor pool. Coffee in rms. Restaurants 6 am-9 pm. Rm serv. Bar 11-2 am; entertainment Fri, Sat. Ck-out 11 am. Coin lndry. Meeting rms. Business servs avail. Bellhops. Free airport transportation. Indoor tennis. Exercise equipt; weight machine, bicycles, sauna. Private patios. Cr cds: A, C, D, DS, MC, V.

[D] [✦] [🏃] [≋] [🛪] [✈] [⊠] [🔥] [SC]

★ **COMFORT INN.** *2777 Harrison Ave, near Bert Mooney Airport.* 406/494-8850; FAX 406/494-2801. 150 rms, 3 story. No elvtr. Mid-May-Sept: S $58.99; D $63.99; each addl $10; suites $80-$125; under 18 free; lower rates rest of yr. Pet accepted; $5. TV; cable (premium), VCR avail (movies). Complimentary continental bkfst. Restaurant nearby. Ck-out 11 am. Coin lndry. Meeting rms. Business servs avail. Airport transportation. Exercise equipt; weight machines, bicycles, whirlpool, sauna. Cr cds: A, C, D, DS, MC, V.

[D] [✦] [🛪] [✈] [⊠] [🔥] [SC]

✔★ **SUPER 8.** *2929 Harrison Ave.* 406/494-6000; FAX 406/494-6000. 104 rms, 3 story. No elvtr. Mid-May-mid-Sept: S $50.88; D $54.88-$58.88; each addl $4; suites $70.88; under 12 free; lower rates rest of yr. Crib free. TV; cable, VCR avail (movies). Complimentary continental bkfst. Restaurant opp 6 am-11 pm. Ck-out 11 am. Cr cds: A, C, D, DS, MC, V.

[D] [⊠] [🔥] [SC]

Restaurants

★ ★ ★ **LYDIA'S.** *4915 Harrison Ave, 3 blks S of airport turnoff.* 406/494-2000. Hrs: 5:30-10:30 pm. Closed major hols. Italian, Amer menu. Complete meals: dinner $9.25-$18.50. Child's meals. Specializes in tenderloin steaks, homemade ravioli, seafood. Victorian decor; stained-glass windows. Family-owned. Cr cds: A, DS, MC, V.

[D]

✔★ **SPAGHETTINI'S.** *748 Utah Ave.* 406/782-8855. Hrs: 11 am-2 pm, 5-10 pm. Closed Sun; most major hols. Res accepted. Italian menu. Wine, beer. Semi-a la carte: lunch $4-$5, dinner $7-$13. Specializes in seafood, chicken. Outdoor dining. Former 1890s warehouse with Italian decor. No cr cds accepted.

★ ★ **UPTOWN CAFÉ.** *47 E Broadway. 406/723-4735.* Hrs: 11 am-2 pm, 5-10 pm; Mon to 2 pm. Closed Sun; major hols. Res accepted. Wine, beer. Buffet: lunch $5. Complete meals: dinner $6.95-$29. Specializes in beef, fresh seafood. Own desserts. Monthly art display. Cr cds: A, DS, MC, V.

SC

Chinook (A-6)

(See also Havre)

Pop 1,512 **Elev** 2,438 ft **Area code** 406 **Zip** 59523
Information Chamber of Commerce, PO Box 744; 406/357-2100.

Gas wells, farming and grazing are the main concerns of this town, which takes its name from the much-desired January and February winds that melt the snow, exposing grass for cattle.

What to See and Do

Bear's Paw Battleground. Scene of final battle and surrender of Chief Joseph of the Nez Perce following trek N from the Big Hole River, ending Montana's Native American wars in 1877. It was here that Chief Joseph spoke the eloquent words "From where the sun now stands, I will fight no more forever." This is the newest addition to the Nez Perce National Historic Park system. Picnicking. (See BIG HOLE NATIONAL BATTLEFIELD) 16 mi S on MT Sec 240.

Blaine County Museum. Local historical exhibits. (June-Aug, Tues-Sat & Sun afternoons; rest of yr, Mon-Fri) 501 Indiana. Phone 406/357-2590. **Free.**

Annual Event

Blaine County Fair. July.

Motel

✔★ **BEAR PAW COURT.** *W 2nd St. 406/357-2221; 800 888/357-2224.* 16 rms. S $35; D $42-$48; each addl $5. Crib $2. TV; cable. Complimentary coffee in most rms. Restaurant nearby. Ck-out 11 am. Cr cds: DS, MC, V.

Columbia Falls (A-2)

(See also Kalispell, Whitefish)

Pop 2,942 **Elev** 3,087 ft **Area code** 406 **Zip** 59912
Information Chamber of Commerce, PO Box 312; 406/892-2072.

A gateway to Glacier National Park (see), and the Northfork of the Flathead River, this is an area of superb hunting and fishing. Here also is the *Hungry Horse News*, Montana's only Pulitzer Prize-winning newspaper.

What to See and Do

Big Sky Water Slide. Nine water slides, inner tube river run, hot tubs. Picnicking, concessions. (Memorial Day-Labor Day, daily) Jct US 2, MT 206; 1 mi SE via US 2. Phone 406/892-5025. ¢¢¢¢

Glacier Maze. A two-level, three-dimensional maze with passages more than 1 mi long; also 18-hole miniature golf course. Picnicking, conces-

sions. (May-Labor Day, daily) 10 mi NE on US 2E. Phone 406/387-5902. ¢¢

Lodge

★ ★ **MOUNTAIN TIMBERS.** *5385 Rabe Rd (59936), 10 mi N on MT486 to Blankenship Rd, turn E and continue for 2 mi to "Y" intersection, then S 1 mi. 406/387-5830; FAX 406/387-5835; res: 800/841-3835.* 7 rms. 3 share bath. No A/C. No rm phones. S, D $55-$125. Complimentary full bkfst. Ck-out 11 am, ck-in 3-6 pm. Meeting rm. X-country ski on site. Whirlpool. Game rm. Balconies. Picnic tables, grills. Modern, Western decor. Rustic log lodge in wooded area overlooking Rocky Mts. Totally nonsmoking. Cr cds: A, MC, V.

Inns

★ ★ ★ **BAD ROCK COUNTRY BED & BREAKFAST.** *480 Bad Rock Dr, 2½ mi S of MT 206. 406/892-2829; res: 800/422-3666; FAX 406/892-2930.* E-mail jalper@digisys.net; web www.wtp.net/go/badrock. 8 rms, 5 A/C, 5 with shower only, 2 share bath, 1-2 story. June-Sept: S $100-$126; D $110-$136; each addl $20; lower rates rest of yr. TV in common rm; cable, VCR avail. Complimentary full bkfst. Ck-out 11 am, ck-in 3 pm. Business servs avail. Luggage handling. Free airport, RR station transportation. X-country ski 20 mi. Whirlpool. Game rm. Some fireplaces. Old West atmosphere. Totally nonsmoking. Cr cds: A, D, DS, MC, V.

★ ★ **PLUM CREEK HOUSE.** *985 Vans Ave. 406/892-1816; FAX 406/892-1876; res: 800/682-1429.* 6 rms, 2 with shower only. No A/C. June-mid-Sept: S $95-$105; D $105-$115; each addl $15; under 12 free; wkly rates; lower rates rest of yr. Children over 8 yrs only. TV; cable, VCR (free movies). Pool, whirlpool. Complimentary full bkfst. Complimentary coffee in rms. Ck-out 11 am, ck-in 3 pm. On bluff overlooking Flathead River. Built 1957 as home for timber mill owner; many antiques. Totally nonsmoking. Cr cds: A, D, DS, MC, V.

Resort

★ ★ ★ **MEADOW LAKE.** *100 St Andrews Dr. 406/892-7601; FAX 406/892-0330; res: 800/321-4653.* E-mail mdwlake@meadowlake.com; web www.meadowlake.com. 114 units, 24 inn rms, 1-3 story, 60 condos, 30 townhouses. June-Sept: D $134; each addl $15; condos $184-$273; townhouses $304-$443; lower rates rest of yr. Crib $5. Pet accepted, some restrictions. TV; cable (premium), VCR (movies). 2 pools, 1 indoor; wading pool, whirlpools. Playground. Supervised child's activities. Restaurant 7 am-10 pm. Ck-out 10 am, ck-in 4 pm. Meeting rms. Business servs avail. Free airport, RR station transportation. Tennis. 18-hole golf, greens fee $38, pro, putting green, driving range. Downhill ski 18 mi; x-country ski on site. Ice skating. Rec rm. Exercise equipt; weight machine, treadmill. Some woodburning fireplaces. Balconies. Cr cds: A, D, DS, MC, V.

Cooke City (E-6)

(See also Red Lodge; also see Cody, WY)

Settled 1873 **Pop** 100 (est) **Elev** 7,651 ft **Area code** 406 **Zip** 59020
Information Chamber of Commerce, PO Box 1071; 406/838-2272.

Once the center of a gold rush area in which $1 million was panned from the rushing streams, Cooke City today is busy serving tourists on their way to Yellowstone National Park (see WYOMING). Available locally are jeep, horse and snowmobile trips.

What to See and Do

Grasshopper Glacier. One of the largest icefields in US; so named because of the millions of grasshoppers frozen in its 80-ft ice cliff. Accessible only by trail, the last 2 mi reached only by foot; be prepared for adverse weather. Grasshoppers are visible only during brief time periods; glacial ice must be exposed by snow melt, which generally does not occur until mid-Aug, while new snow begins to accumulate late Aug. 14 mi NE on mountain trail in the Absaroka-Beartooth Wilderness, Custer National Forest (see HARDIN).

Motels

✔★ HIGH COUNTRY. *US 212. 406/838-2272.* 15 rms, 1-2 story, 4 kits. No A/C. S $40; D $40-$58; each addl $5; kit. units $52-$65. Crib $2. Pet accepted. TV. Restaurant nearby. Ck-out 10 am. X-country ski 1 mi. Some refrigerators. Cabins avail. Cr cds: A, D, DS, MC, V.

✔★ HOOSIER'S. *US 212. 406/838-2241.* 12 rms, 1-2 story. No A/C. S, D $55-$60; each addl $5. TV; cable (premium). Restaurant nearby. Bar 6 pm-2 am. Ck-out 10 am. Totally nonsmoking. Cr cds: DS, MC, V.

Restaurant

★ LOG CABIN CAFE. *(US 212, Silver Gate) 3 mi W on US 212. 406/838-2367.* Hrs: 7 am-10 pm. Closed Sept-May. Semi-a la carte: bkfst $1.75-$6.95, lunch $1.75-$7.95, dinner $7.95-$19.95. Specializes in rainbow trout, steak. Own desserts. Rustic, Western log cabin (1938). View of mountains. Totally nonsmoking. Cr cds: MC, V.

Deer Lodge (C-3)

(See also Anaconda, Helena)

Settled 1862 **Pop** 3,378 **Elev** 4,521 ft **Area code** 406 **Zip** 59722

Information Powell County Chamber of Commerce, 1171 S Main St; 406/846-2094.

Near Montana's first important gold discovery at Gold Creek, this town was first a trapping and trading center, later an important stage and travel station between the early gold camps. Remnants of old mining camps are a few miles from town.

What to See and Do

Deerlodge National Forest. (See BUTTE) A Ranger District office is located here. Self-guided auto tour (inquire locally). W & E of town.

Frontier Montana. Museum houses western memorabilia including weapons, clothing, bar. (Memorial Day-Labor Day) 1106 Main St. Phone 406/846-3111 or -3114. ¢¢¢

Grant-Kohrs Ranch National Historic Site. Preserved in its pioneer state, this was once headquarters for over a million acres of ranchland. The house was called the "finest home in Montana Territory." Original furniture, horse-drawn vehicles and buildings provide an authentic look into history. Visitors may tour the house, barns and bunkhouse. In season, see blacksmith and ranch hands at work, 19th-century style. (Daily; closed Jan 1, Thanksgiving, Dec 25) N edge of town. Phone 406/846-2070. Per person ¢; Per vehicle ¢¢

Montana Territorial Prison. Montana prison from 1871 to 1979. A sandstone wall, built in 1893, surrounds the five acre complex. The 1912 castlelike cell block remains intact and offers the visiting public a rare view of early prison life. Montana Law Enforcement Museum on grounds. (Daily) 1106 Main St. Phone 406/846-3111. ¢¢

Powell County Museum. Displays reflecting the history of Powell county and SW Montana. (June-Labor Day, daily) 1193 Main St. Phone 406/846-3111. **Free.**

Towe Ford Museum. Collection of antique Ford cars. 100 on display, dating from 1903. Picnic area. (Daily) 1106 Main St. Phone 406/846-3111. ¢¢

Yesterday's Playthings. Extensive doll collection from different time periods and cultures. Antique toys. (Mid-May-mid-Sept, daily) 1017 Main St. Phone 406/846-1480. ¢¢

Annual Events

Territorial Days. 2nd wkend June.

Tri-County Fair and Rodeo. 3rd wkend Aug.

Motel

✔★ SUPER 8. *1150 N Main St. 406/846-2370; FAX 406/846-2373.* 54 rms, 2 story. June-Aug: S $46.68; D $51.88-$55.88; each addl $5; suites $63.88; under 5 free; lower rates rest of yr. Crib free. Pet accepted. TV; cable, VCR avail (movies $3). Complimentary coffee in lobby. Restaurant adj open 24 hrs. Ck-out 11 am. Meeting rms. Cr cds: A, C, D, DS, MC, V.

Dillon (E-4)

Founded 1880 **Pop** 3,991 **Elev** 5,096 ft **Area code** 406 **Zip** 59725 **E-mail** chamber@bmt.net

Information Tourist Information Center or the Chamber of Commerce, both located at 125 S Montana, PO Box 425; 406/683-5511.

Named after a president of the Union Pacific Railroad, Dillon is in an area rich in gold-camp lore. Its farms and ranches produce more than 200,000 tons of hay each year. Livestock raising is also important.

What to See and Do

Bannack State Park. First territorial capital, now ghost town. Created by big gold strike on Grasshopper Creek (1862). Fishing. Picnicking. Camping (no hookups). Standard fees. 5 mi S on I-15, then 21 mi W on MT 278, then 4 mi S on county road. Phone 406/834-3413.

Beaverhead County Museum. Geological displays, mining, livestock and commercial artifacts, pioneer housewares, outdoor interpretive area. (Daily; closed hols) 15 S Montana St. Phone 406/683-5027. **Free.**

Beaverhead National Forest. More than 2 million acres. Rugged mountains, alpine lakes, hot springs. Fishing, hunting. Skiing, snowmobiling. Picnicking. Camping (standard fees). E & W off US 91, I-15. For information contact Supervisor, 420 Barrett St; 406/683-3900. A Ranger District office also is located here.

Maverick Mt Ski Area. Double chairlift, pony lift; school, rentals, patrol; half-day rates; cafeteria and bar. Longest run 2 1/4 mi; vertical drop 2,100 ft. (Thanksgiving-Easter, Thurs-Sun; closed Dec 25) Cross-country trails. 40 mi NW on MT 278. Phone 406/834-3454. ¢¢¢¢

Annual Events

Bannack Days. Bannack State Park. Reliving of Gold Rush days in Bannack. Gold panning; demonstrations. 3rd wkend July.

Beaverhead County Fair. 5 days before Labor Day.

Motels

★ **BEST WESTERN PARADISE INN.** *650 N Montana St. 406/683-4214; FAX 406/683-4216.* 65 rms, 2 story. Mid-May-Oct: S $50; D $54-$56; each addl $2; suites $70-$80; some lower rates rest of yr. Crib $6. TV; cable. Heated pool; whirlpool. Restaurant 6 am-10 pm; summer to 11 pm. Bar 3 pm-2 am. Ck-out 11 am. Business servs avail. Cr cds: A, C, D, DS, ER, MC, V.

⊠ ⊁ 👋 SC

★ **COMFORT INN-DILLON.** *Box 666, 450 N Interchange, ¹/₂ blk from I-15 exit 63. 406/683-6831; FAX 406/683-2021.* 48 rms, 2 story. July-mid-Sept: S $47.99-$58.99; D $51.99-$62.99; each addl $4; under 12 free; lower rates rest of yr. Crib $3. Pet accepted. TV; cable (premium), VCR avail (movies $6). Indoor pool. Restaurant nearby. Bar. Ck-out 11 am. Coin lndry. Sundries. Cr cds: A, D, DS, MC, V.

👉 ⊠ ⊁ 👋 SC

★ **SUPER 8.** *550 N Montana St. 406/683-4288.* 46 rms, 3 story. No elvtr. May-Aug: S $45.88; D $53.88-$57.88; each addl $5; under 12 free; lower rates rest of yr. Crib free. Pet accepted. TV; cable. Restaurant opp open 24 hrs. Ck-out 11 am. Cr cds: A, C, D, DS, MC, V.

D 👉 ⊁ 👋 SC

Ennis (E-4)

(See also Three Forks, Virginia City)

Settled 1864 **Pop** 773 **Elev** 4,939 ft **Area code** 406 **Zip** 59729

Surrounded by three Rocky Mountain ranges in the Madison River Valley and encircled by cattle ranches, Ennis has good trout fishing and big-game hunting. Beartrap Canyon offers whitewater floats. Swimming, boating, snowmobiling and Nordic skiing are popular. A Ranger District office of the Beaverhead National Forest (see DILLON) is located here.

What to See and Do

National Fish Hatchery. Raises rainbow trout. (Daily) 12 mi S off US 287. Phone 406/682-4847. **Free.**

Motels

★ ★ **EL WESTERN.** *Box 487, ¹/₂ mi S on US 287. 406/682-4217; FAX 406/682-5207; res: 800/831-2773.* 28 units, 18 kits. No A/C. May-mid-Oct: S, D $65-$90; each addl $5-$10; kit. units $85-$300. Closed rest of yr. Crib $5. Pet accepted. TV; cable (premium). Restaurant nearby. Ck-out 11 am. Patios. Some fireplaces. Western decor. Cr cds: DS, MC, V.

👉 👋

✔★ **FAN MOUNTAIN INN.** *204 N Main. 406/682-5200.* 28 rms, 2 story. S $37.50; D $48-$54; each addl $5; suite $75. Pet accepted; $5. TV; cable (premium), VCR avail (movies). Complimentary coffee in lobby. Restaurant nearby. Ck-out 11 am. Meeting rm. Cr cds: A, C, D, DS, MC, V.

D 👉 ⊁ 👋

★ **RAINBOW VALLEY.** *Box 26, ¹/₂ mi S on US 287. 406/682-4264; FAX 406/682-5012; res: 800/452-8254.* 24 rms, 6 kits. June-Nov: S $50; D $65; each addl $5-$15; kit. units $52-$95; lower rates rest of yr. TV; cable (premium). Heated pool. Restaurant nearby. Ck-out noon. Coin lndry. River float trips. Refrigerators avail. Picnic tables. Grills. Cr cds: A, C, D, DS, MC, V.

D ⊠ 👋

Fort Benton (B-5)

(For accommodations see Great Falls)

Founded 1846 **Pop** 1,660 **Elev** 2,632 ft **Area code** 406 **Zip** 59442
Information City Clerk, PO Box 8; 406/622-5494.

Established as a fur-trading post and named in honor of Senator Thomas Hart Benton of Missouri, this famous frontier outpost at the head of navigation on the Missouri River became a strategic commercial stronghold. Supplies were received here and shipped overland to trappers and miners throughout Montana. The seat of Chouteau County and one of the oldest communities in the state, it continues as a trading center. The Lewis and Clark State Memorial in Fort Benton Park honors the surveyors who opened the area for trade and commerce.

What to See and Do

Museum of the Northern Great Plains. Agricultural and homestead history displays. (Memorial Day-Labor Day, daily) 20th & Washington. Phone 406/622-5494. ¢¢

Museum of the Upper Missouri River. Displays of steamboats, freighting, stagecoaches, fur and Canadian trade. (Mid-May-mid-Sept, daily) 18th & Front Sts. Phone 406/622-5494. ¢¢

Ruins of Old Fort Benton (1847). One building and parts of another remain of old trading post and blockhouse. On riverfront, near Main St.

Annual Events

Summer Celebration. Last wkend June.

Chouteau County Fair. Late Aug.

Gardiner (E-5)

Founded 1883 **Pop** 600 (est) **Elev** 5,314 ft **Area code** 406 **Zip** 59030

Gardiner was established as the original entrance to Yellowstone Park. Named for a trapper who worked this area, Gardiner is the only gateway open throughout the year to Yellowstone National Park (see WYOMING). A Ranger District office of the Gallatin National Forest (see BOZEMAN) is located here.

What to See and Do

Rafting. Yellowstone Raft Co. Half- and full-day whitewater raft trips on the Yellowstone, Gallatin and Madison rivers. Departures from Gardiner and Big Sky (see). Reservations recommended. Phone 406/848-7777 or 800/858-7781. ¢¢¢¢

Annual Event

Gardiner Rodeo. NRA sanctioned rodeo. Phone 406/848-7971. June.

Motels

★ **ABSAROKA.** *US 89 at Yellowstone River Bridge. 406/848-7414; FAX 406/848-7560; res: 800/755-7414.* 41 rms, 2 story, 8 kit. units. June-mid-Sept: S, D $80-$90; each addl $5; kit. units $90-$100; under 12 free; lower rates rest of yr. Crib $5. TV; cable. Complimentary coffee in lobby. Restaurant nearby. Ck-out 11 am. Balconies overlooking Yellowstone River. Cr cds: A, C, D, DS, MC, V.

D 👉 ⊠ 👋

★ ★ **BEST WESTERN BY MAMMOTH HOT SPRINGS.** *US 89, ¹/₂ mi N on US 89, at N entrance to Yellowstone Park. 406/848-7311; FAX*

406/848-7120. 85 rms, 2 story, 4 kits. June-Sept: S, D $89-$104; each addl $5; kit. units $145-$165; under 13 free; lower rates rest of yr. Crib $5. Pet accepted. TV; cable, VCR avail (movies). Indoor pool; whirlpool. Restaurant adj. Meeting rm. Business servs avail. Sauna. Some in-rm whirlpools, microwaves, refrigerators. Some balconies. On the Yellowstone River. Cr cds: A, D, DS, MC, V.

★ ★ **COMFORT INN.** *107 Hellroaring Rd, on US 89. 406/848-7536; FAX 406/848-7536.* 80 rms, 3 story. Mid-June-mid-Aug: S $109; D $119; each addl $8; suites $129-$149; under 16 free; lower rates rest of yr. Closed March, Dec. TV; cable. Complimentary continental bkfst. Ck-out 10 am. Coin lndry. Business servs avail. Whirlpools. Cr cds: A, D, DS, JCB, MC, V.

★ **SUPER 8.** *Hwy 89 S, 1/4 mi N on US 89. 406/848-7401; FAX 406/848-9401.* Web super8gomontana.com. 65 rms, 2 story. Mid-June-mid-Sept: S, D $85; suites $120-$150; each addl $5; lower rates rest of yr. Crib $5. Pet accepted, some restrictions; $5. TV; cable (premium). Indoor pool. Complimentary continental bkfst. Restaurant nearby. Ck-out 10 am. Opp river. Cr cds: A, C, D, DS, MC, V.

✔★ **WESTERNAIRE.** *US 89, 1 mi N. 406/848-7397.* 11 rms. No A/C. June-Sept: S, D $65-$70; each addl $5; lower rates rest of yr. TV; cable. Restaurant nearby. Ck-out 10 am. Cr cds: MC, V.

★ ★ **YELLOWSTONE VILLAGE INN.** *US 89, 3/4 mi N, at Yellowstone Park north entrance. 406/848-7417; FAX 406/848-7418; res: 800/228-8158.* E-mail yellowstoneinn@gomontana.com; web www.gomontana.com/yellowstoneinn.html. 43 rms, 3 condos, 2 story. June-Sept: S, D $79-$89; condos $125-$150; each addl $5; lower rates rest of yr. Crib free. TV; cable (premium). Indoor pool. Complimentary coffee in lobby. Restaurant nearby. Ck-out 11 am. Coin lndry. Business servs avail. Sauna. Microwaves avail. Cr cds: A, DS, MC, V.

Restaurant

★ ★ **YELLOWSTONE MINE.** *US 89, 1/2 mi N, near N entrance to park. 406/848-7336.* Hrs: 6-11:30 am, 5-10 pm. Bar 11:30-2 am. Semi-a la carte: bkfst $2.50-$5.50, dinner $6.95-$19.95. Child's meals. Specializes in prime rib, seafood, stuffed chicken. Old West mining decor. Totally nonsmoking. Cr cds: A, C, D, DS, MC, V.

Glacier National Park (A-3)

Big, rugged and primitive, Glacier National Park is nature's unspoiled domain. Human civilization is reduced to insignificance by the wild grandeur of these million acres. It's the place for a snowball fight in mid-summer, for glacial solitude, for fishing, for alpine flowers, lonely and remote campgrounds along fir-fringed lakes. The park is also a living textbook in geology.

Declared a national park on May 11, 1910, these 1,013,595 acres of spectacular scenery are preserved year after year much as they were when Meriwether Lewis saw them in the distance in 1806. The US and Canada share these treasures of nature; the 204 square miles of Canada that are linked to Glacier are known as the Waterton-Glacier International Peace Park. Glacier National Park contains 50 glaciers, among the few in the US, some of which are comparatively accessible. There are more than 200 lakes and 1,200 varieties of plants, 60 species of animals—from mice to moose—and 246 varieties of birds.

Visitors here can choose a variety of activities during their stay; they can enjoy the scenery from the shadow of a hotel or chalet, share the camaraderie of a community campground or seek solitude in the wilderness. The delights of Glacier, however, should be savored cautiously. Rangers recommend that visitors stay on the trails and never hike alone. The behavior of wild animals can be unpredictable.

This is a land where winter does not beat a full retreat until mid-June, and sometimes returns in mid-September. The summer season extends between those periods, but until July, high snowbanks line the roads and the mountains are capped with snow. Late June is a time of cascading waterfalls and profuse wildflowers. In the fall, the dense forests are a blaze of colors set against a background of snow-covered peaks. Winter brings deep-snow peace, which only the most hardy invade for cross-country skiing or photography.

Spectacular views of the park may be seen from your car, particularly when crossing the Continental Divide on the Going-to-the-Sun Road; it is 50 miles long and one of the most magnificent drives in the world (approx mid-June-mid-October). As of January, 1994, vehicles in excess of 21 feet in length (including combinations of units) and 8 feet in width (including mirrors) are prohibited on the Going-to-the-Sun Road between Avalanche and Sun Point. Vehicles exceeding these restrictions may use US 2, or may be parked at Avalanche or Sun Point parking areas. The road continuously winds up and down in tight curves and requires caution. This unforgettable ride links the east and west sides of the park, passing over Logan Pass (a visitor center with exhibits is here; June-September, daily; closed rest of yr) for a 100-mile view from an elevation of 6,680 ft. It connects with US 89 at St Mary (here is a visitor center with exhibits, programs; June-September, daily) and with US 2 at West Glacier. US 89 on the east side of the park is the Blackfeet Highway, extending from Browning to Canada. The road to Many Glacier Valley branches from US 89, 9 miles north of St Mary. The road to Two Medicine Lake leaves MT 49, 4 miles north of East Glacier Park. Chief Mt International Highway (MT 17) leads to Waterton Lakes National Park in Canada (see).

Most of the park, however, including the glaciers, is accessible only by trail. There are 732 maintained miles of trails penetrating to remote wilderness areas. By foot or on horseback, magnificent and isolated parts of Glacier await discovery.

There are eight major and five primitive campgrounds. The camping limit is 7 days. A fee is charged for auto sites mid-May-late September. Hikers, however, must get a non-fee backcountry camping permit and camp at designated sites (a total of 61) in the back country.

Place-name signs and roadside exhibits mark the major roads from late May-September 15. Also, ranger-naturalists conduct daily walks and campfire programs that are both rewarding and scenic. Park-wide guided hikes for day and overnight trips available through Glacier Wilderness Guides, PO Box 535, West Glacier 59936. All-expense tours available through Glacier Park, Inc, Dial Tower, Dial Corporate Ctr, Phoenix, AZ 85077 (October-mid-May); or East Glacier Park 59434 (rest of yr). Saddle horses available through Mule Shoe Outfitters, LLC, PO Box 174, Kila 59920; also at Many Glacier, Lake McDonald Lodge and Apgar Village Lodge. Launch service operates on Two Medicine, Swiftcurrent, Josephine, St Mary and McDonald lakes through Glacier Park Boat Co, PO Box 5262, Kalispell 59903; and between the townsite in Waterton Lakes National Park, Canada, and the head of Waterton Lake in Glacier National Park through Waterton Shoreline Cruises, PO Box 126, Waterton, Alberta, Canada TOK 2M0 (June-August).

Contact the Superintendent, Glacier National Park, West Glacier 59936; 406/888-7800, for detailed information. Golden Eagle Passport accepted (see MAKING THE MOST OF YOUR TRIP). Seven-day pass: per vehicle ¢¢; per person ¢¢

What to See and Do

Avalanche Creek. Flows through deep gorge filled with spray. 2-mi hike to Avalanche Lake Basin with waterfalls, 2,000-ft-high cliffs.

Belly River Country. Trails, lake fishing, glacial valleys.

Cut Bank. A primitive, densely wooded valley. At head of valley is 8,011-ft Triple Divide Peak. Hiking.

Flattop Mt. Between the Lewis Range and the Livingston Range; meadows and groves of trees contrast with dense forest growth elsewhere.

Granite Park. Much of this area is a mass of lava; trails, glacial valleys, alpine flowers. Accessible only by foot or horseback.

⚠ Lake McDonald. Largest in park: 10 mi long, 1 mi wide; heavily forested shores with peaks rising 6,000 ft above lake. Trail to Sperry Glacier. 1-hr boat tours, horseback riding trips leave from Lake McDonald Lodge (mid-June-mid-Sept, daily).

Many Glacier Area. Fishing, boating (trips), hiking, riding; trails to Morning Eagle Falls, Cracker Lake, Grinnell Glacier and Lake, Iceberg Lake. Footpaths go around Swiftcurrent and Josephine lakes and to Appekunny Falls and Cirque. Self-guided trail from hotel.

Red Eagle Lake. Located in a glacially carved basin with dramatic falls and gorge.

River Rafting. Four companies offer several half- to 6-day trips on the Middle and North forks of the Flathead River. Guided fishing trips, combination trips. For information & reservations contact:

Glacier Raft Co. Phone 406/888-5454 or 800/332-9995. ¢¢¢¢¢

Great Northern Whitewater. Phone 406/387-5340 or 800/735-7897 (res). ¢¢¢¢¢

Northwest Voyageurs. Phone 406/387-9453 or 800/826-2724. ¢¢¢¢¢

Montana Raft Company & Glacier Wilderness Guides. Phone 406/387-5555 or 800/521-RAFT. ¢¢¢¢¢

Sperry and Grinnell Glaciers. Largest in the park. Inquire about trips to Grinell.

St Mary Lake. Emerald green, with peaks on three sides. Fishing, boating, hiking. 1¹/₂-hr boat tours leave from Rising Sun Boat Landing (mid-June-mid-Sept, daily). Self-guided trail from Sun Point.

Two Medicine Valley. Deep valleys, towering peaks surround mountain lake. Brook, rainbow trout; trails for hiking; boating; camping.

(Many of the following accommodations are in the park, run by Glacier Park, Inc under concession from the Dept of the Interior; they are included for the convenience of those who wish to stay in the park proper. Reservations strongly advised for accommodations in this area; phone 602/207-6000.)

East Glacier Area (A-3)

Area code 406 **Zip** 59434

Motels

★ **JACOBSON'S COTTAGES.** *(MT 49, East Glacier 33950)* ¹/₂ *mi N.* 406/226-4422. 12 cottages, 1 kit. No A/C. No rm phones. Mid-May-Oct: S $50; D $50-$56; each addl $3; kit. cottage $65; under 6 free. Closed rest of yr. Crib free. Pet accepted, some restrictions. TV; cable. Restaurant adj 6:30 am-10:30 pm. Ck-out 11 am. Picnic table. Cr cds: A, DS, MC, V.

★★ **MOUNTAIN PINE.** *(MT 49, East Glacier 33950)* ¹/₂ *mi N of US 2.* 406/226-4403; FAX 406/226-9290. 26 rms. No A/C. Mid-June-mid-Sept: S $51; D $56; each addl $3; family units $98-$110; log house $175; lower rates May-mid-June, late Sept. Closed rest of yr. Crib free. TV; cable. Restaurant nearby. Ck-out 11 am. Free RR station transportation. Picnic tables. Cr cds: A, D, DS, MC, V.

✔★ **SWIFTCURRENT MOTOR INN.** *(13 mi W of Babb,* ³/₄ *mi SW of Swiftcurrent Lake, East Glacier 33950)* 602/207-6000; FAX 602/207-5589. 88 units, 26 cottages. No A/C. Mid-June-mid-Sept: S $29-

$75; D $35-$81; each addl $10. Closed rest of yr. Restaurant 7 am-9:30 pm. Ck-out 11 am. Coin lndry. Sundries. Trail center for hikers. Cr cds: A, DS, MC, V.

Lodge

★★ **ST MARY LODGE & RESORT.** *(US 89, St Mary 59417)* at Going To The Sun Rd. 406/732-4431; res: 800/368-3689; FAX 406/732-9265. 76 rms, 62 with shower only, 34 with AC, 1-2 story. Mid-June-mid-Sept: S, D $89-$100; each addl $10; suites $160-$250; kits. $130-$150; under 12 free; lower rates May-mid-June & mid-Sept-early Oct. Closed rest of yr. Crib $3. Pet accepted; $50. Restaurant (see SNOW GOOSE GRILL). Bar noon-1 am; entertainment exc Sun. Ck-out 11 am, ck-in 4 pm. Coin lndry. Gift shop. Some balconies. Views of St Mary Lake & Glacier Park. Totally nonsmoking. Cr cds: A, DS, MC, V.

Hotel

★ **MANY GLACIER.** *12 mi W of Babb off US 89.* 602/207-6000; FAX 602/207-5589. 210 rms, 5 story. No A/C. No elvtr. Early June-mid-Sept: S $91-$174; D $97-$174; each addl $10; suites $163-$174; under 12 free. Closed rest of yr. Crib free. Restaurant 6:30 am-9:30 pm. Bar 11:30 am-midnight; entertainment. Ck-out 11 am. Gift shop. Hiking. Overlooks Swiftcurrent Lake. A Glacier Park, Inc hotel. Cr cds: DS, MC, V.

Restaurants

✔★★ **GLACIER VILLAGE.** *Jct US 2 & MT 49, town center.* 406/226-4464. Hrs: 6 am-10 pm. Closed late Sept-early May. Res accepted. Wine, beer. Semi-a la carte: bkfst $2.25-$5.95, lunch $4.50-$6.25, dinner $5.95-$10.95. Specializes in broiler items, seafood, roast turkey. Own bread, desserts. Family-owned. Cr cds: MC, V.

★★ **SNOW GOOSE GRILLE.** *(See St Mary Lodge & Resort Lodge)* 406/732-4431. Hrs: 7 am-10 pm. Closed Oct-mid-May. Bar. Semi-a la carte: bkfst $3.75-$7.50, lunch $4.95-$8.95, dinner $9.95-$18.95. Child's meals. Specialties: sourdough scones, range-fed buffalo, locally caught whitefish. Family-owned. Totally nonsmoking. Cr cds: A, DS, MC, V.

West Glacier Area (A-3)

Area code 406 **Zip** 59936

Hotel

★ **LAKE McDONALD LODGE.** *(Going-to-the-Sun Rd, West Glacier 33960)* 12 mi NE on Lake McDonald. 602/207-6000; FAX 406/888-5681. 32 rms in lodge, 38 cabins, 30 motel rms, 1-2 story. No A/C. Early June-late Sept: lodge: S $115; D $121; each addl $10; under 12 free; cabins: S $65-$113; D $71-$119; each addl $10; motel: S $78; D $83; each addl $10. Closed rest of yr. Crib free. Restaurant. Bar 11 am-midnight. Ck-out 11 am. Gift shop. Boating; launch cruises. Hiking. Camp store. Rustic hunting lodge amid giant cedars. Lodge totally nonsmoking. Cr cds: DS, MC, V.

Inn

★ ★ **IZAAK WALTON.** *Essex (59916), Essex exit off US 2, half-way between East and West Glacier.* 406/888-5700; FAX 406/888-5200. E-mail izaakw@digisys.net; web www.vtown.com/izaakw. 33 rms, 3 story. No A/C. No rm phones. S, D $95; each addl $5; suites $146; caboose kit. cottages (3-day min) $475; wkly rates; package plans. Crib free. Dining rm 7 am-8 pm. Bar. Ck-out 11 am, ck-in 3 pm. Coin lndry. Meeting rm. Business servs avail. X-country ski on site; rentals. Sauna. Game rm. Rec rm (movies). Lawn games. Bicycle rentals. Picnic tables. Old railroad hotel (1939); restored sleeper cars avail for rental (3-day min). Adj to Glacier National Park. Totally nonsmoking. Cr cds: MC, V.

Glasgow (B-8)

Founded 1887 **Pop** 3,572 **Elev** 2,090 ft **Area code** 406 **Zip** 59230

Information Glasgow Area Chamber of Commerce & Agriculture, 740 US 2E, PO Box 832; 406/228-2222.

Glasgow has had four booms in its history. The first was opening of land to white settlement in 1888, the second when another 18,000,000 acres were opened around 1910. In the 1930s, Glasgow was headquarters for the 10,000 construction workers on Ft Peck Dam. Glasgow AFB made its home 18 miles northeast of town from 1954 to 1968; the flight facilities are now owned by Boeing and the residential area is being developed into a military retirement community. Wheat and livestock are raised in Valley County.

What to See and Do

Ft Peck Dam and Lake. Built by Army Corps of Engineers. Largest hydraulic earthfill dam in the world, forming huge reservoir with 1,600-mi lakeshore. Dam rises 280 1/2 ft above Missouri River; total length 21,026 ft; road follows crest of the dam, leading to mile-long concrete spillway. Information center; museum. Guided tours of power plant (Memorial Day-Labor Day, daily; rest of yr, by appt). Self-guided nature trail. There are several recreation areas with fishing, camping (fee), trailer sites, boating (ramps), concession. 20 mi SE on MT 24. **Free.**

Hell Creek State Park. Swimming; fishing; boating (ramp, rentals). Picnicking. Camping (no hookups). Standard fees. 50 mi S on MT 24, then 6 mi W on county road. Phone 406/232-4365.

Pioneer Museum. Displays of Native American artifacts; photos of pioneers and events of their time; pioneer farm machinery. Also fossils and aviation display. (Memorial Day-Labor Day, daily) 1/2 mi W on US 2. Phone 406/228-8692. **Free.**

Annual Events

Longest Dam Run. Kiwanis Park, ft of Ft Peck Dam. 5K & 10K run/walk crosses 1.8 mi of Dam. Refreshments, prizes. Phone 406/228-2222. June 20.

Montana Governor's Cup Walleye Tournament. Ft Peck Lake. Phone 406/228-2222. July 9-11.

Northeast Montana Fair & Rodeo. Fairgrounds at W edge of city. Exhibits, midway, rodeo, nightly shows. 3 days early Aug.

Seasonal Event

Ft Peck Summer Theater. 17 mi SE on MT 24 in Ft Peck. Professional cast performs musicals, comedies. Fri-Sun. Historical landmark. Phone 406/228-9219. Late June-late Aug.

Motel

✔ ★ **COTTONWOOD INN.** *Hwy 2E, 1 mi E on US 2, near City-County Airport.* 406/228-8213; FAX 406/228-8248; res: 800/321-8213. 92 rms, 2 story. S $48; D $55-$60; each addl $5; studio rms $75-$80; under 12 free. Pet accepted, some restrictions. TV; cable (premium). Indoor pool; whirlpool. Restaurant 6 am-10 pm. Rm serv. Bar 11-2 am. Ck-out 11 am. Coin lndry. Business servs avail. Valet serv. Airport, RR station transportation. Exercise equipt; weight machine, bicycles, sauna. Some refrigerators. Cr cds: A, C, D, DS, MC, V.

Restaurant

★ ★ **SAM'S SUPPER CLUB.** *307 Klein (US 2).* 406/228-4614. Hrs: 11 am-2 pm, 5-10:30 pm; Sat from 4 pm. Closed Sun, Mon; July 4, Thanksgiving, Dec 25. Res accepted. Bar to 2 am. Semi-a la carte: lunch $2-$6.75, dinner $6-$19.50. Child's meals. Specializes in char-broiled steak, walleye pike, fresh pasta. Cr cds: MC, V.

Glendive (C-10)

Settled 1864 **Pop** 4,802 **Elev** 2,078 ft **Area code** 406 **Zip** 59330 **E-mail** chamber@inetco.net **Web** www.inetco.net/chamber

Information Chamber of Commerce & Agriculture, PO Box 930; 406/365-5601.

Glendive is the shipping center for the crops of Dawson County. It also serves the oil wells, railroad yards and natural gas fields that ring the city.

What to See and Do

Fishing. The unusual spatula-nosed paddlefish (*Polyodon spathula*) is found here in the Yellowstone River. Fishing for this rare, prehistoric species is permitted mid-May-June only.

Frontier Gateway Museum. Collection depicts Glendive and early Dawson County; "Main Street 1881" exhibit in basement; one-room schoolhouse, blacksmith shop, display of early farm machinery on grounds and five other buildings in complex. (June-Aug, daily) Belle Prairie Frontage Rd, 1 mi E off I-94, exit 215. Phone 406/365-8168. **Free.**

Hunt moss agates. Along Yellowstone River.

Makoshika (Ma-KO-she-ka) **State Park.** Spectacular badlands scenery; fossils. The eroded sandstone cliffs are particularly striking at sunrise and sunset. Visitor Center. Hiking. Picnicking. Camping (no hookups). Standard fees. 1/4 mi SE on Snyder Ave. Phone 406/365-8596.

Annual Event

Dawson County Fair & Rodeo. 4 days mid-Aug.

Motel

✔ ★ **DAYS INN.** *2000 N Merrill.* 406/365-6011; FAX 406/365-2876. 59 rms, 2 story. S $37; D $44-$47; each addl $5; under 12 free; lower rates winter. Crib free. TV; cable (premium). Complimentary continental bkfst. Restaurant adj 6 am-10 pm. Ck-out 11 am. Cr cds: A, C, D, DS, MC, V.

Great Falls (B-5)

(See also Fort Benton)

Founded 1884 **Pop** 55,097 **Elev** 3,333 ft **Area code** 406

Information Chamber of Commerce, 710 1st Ave N, PO Box 2127, 59403; 406/761-4434.

Great Falls's growth has been powered by thriving diversified industry, agriculture and livestock, construction and activity at nearby Malmstrom AFB. The city takes its name from the falls of the Missouri River, a source of electric power.

What to See and Do

C.M. Russell Museum Complex & Original Log Cabin Studio. Charles Russell paintings, bronzes, original models and illustrated letters; exhibits of Russell's contemporaries. Browning Firearms Collection. (Daily; winter, daily exc Mon) 400 13th St N. Phone 406/727-8787. ¢¢

Giant Springs State Park and State Trout Hatchery. One of the largest freshwater springs in the world produces nearly 390 million gallons of water every 24 hrs. The hatchery next to the springs raises trout. Picnic grounds. (Daily) 4 mi NE on Missouri River Dr. Phone 406/454-5840. ¢¢

Lewis and Clark National Forest. More than 1.8 million acres of canyons, mountains, meadows and wilderness. Parts of the Scapegoat Wilderness and the Bob Marshall Wilderness (384,407 acres), with the 15-mi-long, 1,000-ft-high Chinese Wall, are here. Activities include scenic drives, stream and lake fishing, big-game hunting, hiking, camping (fee); picnicking, winter sports. E on US 87, 89, MT 200. For information contact Supervisor, 1101 15th St N, PO Box 869, 59403; 406/791-7700.

Malmstrom AFB. Home of the 43rd Air Refueling Wing and center of one of the largest intercontinental ballistic missile complexes in the world. Museum featuring historical military displays. Tours by appt. 2 mi E. Phone 406/731-4046. **Free.**

Paris Gibson Square. "Tea Room and Sales Emporium"; historical site designed as art pavilion; exhibitions and gathering spot. Tours (by appt; free). (Summer, daily) 1400 1st Ave N. Phone 406/727-8255.

University of Great Falls (1932). (1,200 students) A 40-acre campus. Chapel sculpture and stained-glass windows designed and produced at college. The pool in McLaughlin Memorial Center is open to public (inquire for days, hrs, fees). 1301 20th St S. Phone 406/761-8210.

Annual Events

Montana Pro Rodeo Circuit Finals. Four Seasons Arena. Phone 406/727-8900. Mid-Jan.

State Fair. Fairgrounds. Rodeo, livestock exhibits, horse racing, petting zoo, commercial exhibits, entertainment, carnival. Phone 406/727-8900. July 25-Aug 2.

Motels

✔★ **BUDGET INN.** *2 Treasure State Dr (59404), W of I-15 10th Ave exit S, near Intl Airport.* 406/453-1602; res: 800/362-4842. 60 rms, 2 story. S $46; D $52; each addl $4; under 16 free; lower rates winter. Crib free. Pet accepted, some restrictions. TV; cable. Complimentary continental bkfst. Coffee in rms. Restaurant adj 6 am-11 pm. Ck-out noon. Airport transportation. Valet serv. Health club privileges. Cr cds: A, D, DS, MC, V.

D ✔ ✈ ⟲ 🔥 SC

★ **COMFORT INN.** *1120 Ninth St S (59403).* 406/454-2727. 64 rms, 3 story. S, D $69.95; each addl $5; suites $79.95; under 18 free. Crib free. Pet accepted; $5. TV; cable (premium). Indoor pool; whirlpool. Complimentary continental bkfst. Restaurant nearby. Ck-out 11 am. Business servs avail. Health club privileges. Cr cds: A, D, DS, MC, V.

D ✔ ⟲ ⟲ 🔥 SC

✔★ **DAYS INN.** *101 14th Ave NW (59404).* 406/727-6565; FAX 406/727-6308. 62 rms, 2 story. June-Sept: S $54; D $59; each addl $5; under 13 free. Crib free. TV; cable. Complimentary continental bkfst. Ck-out 11 am. Coin lndry. Cr cds: A, C, D, DS, JCB, MC, V.

D ⟲ ⟲ 🔥 SC

★★ **FAIRFIELD INN BY MARRIOTT.** *1000 Ninth Ave S (59405), opp Holiday Village Shopping Center.* 406/454-3000. 63 rms, 3 story, 16 suites. S $69.95; D $74.95; each addl $5; suites $79.95; under 18 free. Crib free. TV; cable. Indoor pool; whirlpool. Complimentary continental bkfst. Restaurant opp open 24 hrs. Ck-out 11 am. Valet serv. Game rm. Refrigerator, microwave in suites. Cr cds: A, D, DS, MC, V.

D ⟲ ⟲ 🔥 SC

★ **TOWNHOUSE INN.** *1411 10th Ave S (59405).* 406/761-4600; FAX 406/761-7603; res: 800/442-4667. 109 rms, 2 story, May-Sept: S $65; D $70; each addl $5; under 13 free; lower rates rest of yr. Crib free. Pet accepted; $5. TV; cable (premium). Indoor pool; whirlpool. Restaurant 7 am-10 pm. Rm serv. Bar. Ck-out 11 am. Coin lndry. Meeting rms. Business servs avail. Bellhops. Sundries. Valet serv. Free airport transportation. Sauna. Game rm. Cr cds: A, D, DS, MC, V.

✔ ⟲ ⟲ 🔥 SC

Motor Hotel

★★ **BEST WESTERN HERITAGE INN.** *1700 Fox Farm Rd (59404), I-15 exit 10th Ave S.* 406/761-1900; FAX 406/761-0136; res: 800/548-0361. 239 rms, 2 story. S $79; D $87; each addl $6; suites $85-$125; under 18 free. Crib free. Pet accepted, some restrictions. TV; cable. Indoor pool; whirlpool. Coffee in rms. Restaurant 6 am-11 pm. Rm serv. Bar 9-2 am. Ck-out noon. Business servs avail. Coin lndry. Bellhops. Valet serv. Gift shop. Free airport, bus depot transportation. Exercise equipt; treadmill, stair machine, sauna. Microwaves avail. Cr cds: A, D, DS, MC, V.

D ✔ ⟲ 🏋 ⟲ 🔥 SC

Hotel

★★★ **HOLIDAY INN.** *400 10th Ave S (59405).* 406/727-7200. 169 rms, 7 story. S, D $75; suites $145. Crib free. Pet accepted, some restrictions. TV; cable (premium). Indoor pool; whirlpool. Coffee in rms. Restaurant 6 am-11 pm. Bar noon-2 am. Ck-out noon. Meeting rms. Business servs avail. Free airport, bus depot transportation. Sauna. Health club privileges. Cr cds: A, C, D, DS, ER, JCB, MC, V.

D ✔ ⟲ ⟲ 🔥 SC

Restaurants

★★ **BORRIE'S.** *(Box B, 1800 Smelter Ave, Black Eagle) 3 mi N on 15th St, then E on Smelter Ave just after crossing Missouri River.* 406/761-0300. Hrs: 5-10 pm; Fri to 11 pm; Sat 4-11 pm; Sun from 3 pm. Closed some major hols. Res accepted. Italian, Amer menu. Bar. Semi-a la carte: dinner $5-$22. Child's meals. Specializes in ravioli, rigatoni, steak. Family-owned. Cr cds: DS, MC, V.

⟲

★ **EDDIE'S SUPPER CLUB.** *38th & 2nd Ave N.* 406/453-1616. Hrs: 9:30 am-11 pm; Fri, Sat to midnight. Italian, Amer menu. Bar. Semi-a la carte: lunch $3-$7, dinner $9.95-$20.95. Specializes in campfire steak, hamburgers. Entertainment Fri, Sat. Cr cds: DS, MC, V.

⟲

★★ **JAKER'S STEAK, RIBS & FISH HOUSE.** *1500 10th Ave S.* 406/727-1033. Hrs: 11:30 am-10 pm; Fri to 11 pm; Sat 4-11 pm; Sun from 4 pm. Closed Dec 25. Res accepted. Semi-a la carte: lunch $4.95-$7.95, dinner $6.45-$19.95. Child's meals. Specializes in prime rib, baby-back ribs, seafood. Cr cds: A, DS, MC, V.

D ⟲

Hamilton (D-2)

(See also Missoula)

Pop 2,737 **Elev** 3,572 ft **Area code** 406 **Zip** 59840 **E-mail** localinfo@brchamber.com **Web** www.brchamber.com

Information Bitterroot Valley Chamber of Commerce, 105 E Main; 406/363-2400.

Hamilton is the county seat and main shopping center for Ravalli County and headquarters for the Bitterroot National Forest.

What to See and Do

Big Hole National Battlefield (see). S on US 93.

Bitterroot National Forest (1,579,533 acres). Lake and stream fishing, big-game hunting; Anaconda-Pintler Wilderness, Selway-Bitterroot Wilderness, and River of No Return Wilderness. Mountain lakes, hot springs. Scenic drives in Bitterroot Valley; Skalkaho Falls. Hiking and riding trails, winter sports, camp and picnic sites. Inquire locally for wilderness pack trips. Fees may be charged at recreation sites. Surrounding Hamilton with access by US 93, MT 38. Contact Supervisor, 1801 N 1st St; 406/363-7161.

Daly Mansion (ca 1890). This 42-rm mansion was the home of Marcus Daly, an Irish immigrant who became one of Montana's "copper kings" through the copper mines near Butte. Seven Italian marble fireplaces, original furniture, transplanted exotic trees, "dollhouse" built for Daly children. Tours (May-Sept, daily; rest of yr, by appt). 2 mi NE on County 269. Phone 406/363-6004. ¢¢

Ft Owen State Park. Restoration of Montana's first white settlement, more a trading post than a fort. Day use only. 20 mi N, off US 93 to Stevensville, then 5 mi E on MT 269. **Free.**

Painted Rocks State Park. Swimming; fishing; boating (ramp). Picnicking. Camping (no hookups). Standard fees. 20 mi S on US 93, then 23 mi SW on MT 473, in the Bitterroot Mts. Phone 406/542-5500.

Skiing. Lost Trail Powder Mt. 2 chairlifts, 2 rope tows; patrol, ski school, rentals, concession area. Vertical drop 1,100 ft. (Dec-Apr, Thurs-Sun, hols) Cross-country trails. 50 mi S on US 93. Phone 406/821-3211. ¢¢¢¢

St Mary's Mission (1841). Picturesque log church and residence; one of the oldest churches in Northwest (present structure built in 1866); also old pharmacy (1868). Restored and furnished to period. Pioneer relics, Chief Victor's house and cemetery. Site is first in religion, education, agriculture, music in Montana. Gift shop. Guided tours. Park, picnicking. (Mid-Apr-mid-Oct, daily) 20 mi N off US 93; W end of 4th St in Stevensville. Phone 406/777-5734. ¢

Annual Events

Good Nations Powwow. July.

Ravalli County Fair, Rodeo & Horse Races. Late Aug.

McIntosh Apple Days. Oct.

Motels

✔★ ★ **BEST WESTERN HAMILTON INN.** 409 S 1st St. 406/363-2142. 36 rms, 2 story. May-Sept: S $53; D $58-$63; each addl $5; lower rates rest of yr. Crib free. TV; cable (premium). Restaurant nearby. Ck-out 11 am. Outdoor whirlpool. Cr cds: A, C, D, DS, MC, V.

D ◹ ☒ 🖐 SC

★ **COMFORT INN.** 1113 N 1st St, 1 mi N on US 93. 406/363-6600; FAX 406/363-5644. 64 rms, 2 story. May-Sept: S $55; D $62-$64; each addl $5; under 18 free; lower rates rest of yr. Crib $4. Pet accepted. TV; cable (premium), VCR avail (movies). Complimentary coffee in lobby.

Restaurant adj 8 am-10 pm. Rm serv. Ck-out 11 am. Meeting rm. Business servs avail. Coin lndry. Whirlpool, sauna. Cr cds: A, D, DS, MC, V.

Inn

★ **DEER CROSSING.** 396 Hayes Creek Rd. 406/363-2232; res: 800/763-2232. 4 rms, 1 story. No A/C. No rm phones. S, D $75-$100; each addl $10; under 12 free. Complimentary continental bkfst. Ck-out 11 am, ck-in 3-6 pm. Luggage handling. Lawn games. Western ranch furnished with antiques. Totally nonsmoking. Cr cds: MC, V.

🖐 ☒ 🖐

Guest Ranch

★ ★ ★ **TRIPLE CREEK RANCH.** (5551 W Fork Stage Rte, Darby 59829) Approx 23 mi S on US 93, W on County Rd 473 for approx 5 mi. 406/821-4664; FAX 406/821-4666. 18 cabins, 3 with shower only, 10 kit. cabins. AP: S $425-$945; D, kit. cabins $475-$995; each addl $150. Children over 16 yrs only. TV; cable (premium), VCR (movies). Pool; poolside serv. Complimentary coffee in lobby. Restaurant 8-10:30 am, noon-2 pm, 6-8:30 pm. Rm serv. Box lunches, picnics. Bar 6-11 pm; entertainment Wed, Sat, Sun. Ck-out noon, ck-in 3 pm. Bellhops. Concierge. Gift shop. Meeting rms. Business servs avail. In-rm modem link. Free airport transportation. Sports dir. Tennis. Putting green. X-country ski on site. Horse stables. Snowmobiles. Hiking. Lawn games. Soc dir. Massage. Refrigerators. Picnic tables. Cr cds: A, DS, MC, V.

🖐 🖐 🖐 🖐 🖐 🖐

Hardin (D-7)

(See also Billings)

Pop 2,940 **Elev** 2,902 ft **Area code** 406 **Zip** 59034
Information Chamber of Commerce, 21 E 4th St; 406/665-1672.

Hardin became the seat of Big Horn County after the area was opened to white settlers in 1906. It is the trading center for ranchers, farmers, and Native Americans from the Crow Reservation.

What to See and Do

Bighorn Canyon National Recreation Area. 43 mi S on MT 313. (See LOVELL, WY)

Custer National Forest. Approx 1.2 million acres in Montana and South Dakota; Little Missouri Grasslands, an additional 1.2 million acres in North Dakota, is also included. Rolling pine hills and grasslands; picnicking; saddle and pack trips; big game hunting; camping. E via US 212; includes Beartooth Hwy, a Natl Forest Scenic Byway (see RED LODGE). Headquarters: 2602 1st Ave N, Billings 59103; 406/657-6361.

Little Bighorn Battlefield National Monument (see). 13 mi SE off I-90.

Annual Events

Little Big Horn Days. Custer's last stand reenactment. Military Ball, rodeo, street dance, bed races, children's games. 3rd wkend June.

Crow Fair. Crow Reservation, S on MT 313. Features largest all-Native American rodeo in the country. Aug.

Motels

✔★ **AMERICAN INN.** 1324 N Crawford, at I-90 City Center exit. 406/665-1870; FAX 406/665-1615; res: 800/582-8094. 42 rms, 2 story. May-Oct: S $45; D $56-$63; each addl $5; lower rates rest of yr. Crib $2. TV; cable. Pool; whirlpool. Playground. Restaurant opp 7 am-10 pm.

Ck-out 11 am. Coin lndry. Exercise equipt; bicycle, rower. Game rm. Cr cds: A, C, D, DS, MC, V.

[D] [≈] [✕] [⊀] [🐾] [SC]

★ **SUPER 8.** *201 14th St. 406/665-1700.* 53 rms, 2 story. May-Sept: S $44.88; D $46.88-$50.88; each addl $4; under 12 free; higher rates special events; lower rates rest of yr. Crib $2. Pet accepted. TV; cable. Complimentary continental bkfst. Ck-out 11 am. Coin lndry. Meeting rms. Cr cds: A, C, D, DS, MC, V.

[D] [↩] [⊀] [🐾] [SC]

Harlowton (C-6)

Pop 1,049 **Elev** 4,167 ft **Area code** 406 **Zip** 59036
Information Chamber of Commerce, PO Box 694; 406/632-4694.

A Ranger District office of the Lewis and Clark National Forest (see GREAT FALLS) is located here.

What to See and Do

Deadman's Basin State Park. Swimming; fishing; boating. Picnicking. Standard fees. 23 mi E on US 12 to milepost 120, then 1 mi N on county road.

Fishing, camping. Martinsdale, Harris and North Fork lakes. W on US 12. **Lebo Lake.** 9 mi W on US 12 to Twodot, then 7 mi S on County 296.

Annual Event

Rodeo. Chief Joseph Park. NRA approved; parade, concessions, campgrounds. July 2-4.

Havre (A-6)

(See also Chinook)

Founded 1887 **Pop** 10,201 **Elev** 2,494 ft **Area code** 406 **Zip** 59501 **Web** www.nmclites.edu/havre
Information Chamber of Commerce, 518 1st St, PO Box 308, 406/265-4383.

Center of a cattle and wheat-producing area, Havre (HAVE-er) is an important retail and wholesale distribution point for northern Montana. It is one of the oldest and largest division points on the Burlington Northern (formerly Great Northern) Railway.

What to See and Do

Beaver Creek Park. 10,000 acres. Swimming; fishing; boating. Skiing, cross-country skiing, snowmobiling. Camping (fee). **Fresno Lake.** Waterskiing, boating, camping. 15 mi NW. About 10 mi S, in Bear Paw Mts. Phone 406/395-4565. **Free.**

Fort Assinniboine. Built in 1879-1883 and used as a military fort until 1911. In 1913 it became an agricultural experiment station. Some original buildings still stand. Tours (May-Sept). 6 mi SW on US 87. Phone 406/265-4383. ¢¢

H. Earl Clack Memorial Museum. Regional history. (Memorial Day-Labor Day, daily; rest of yr, by appt) 306 3rd Ave, in Havre Heritage Center. Phone 406/265-4000. **Free.** Museum manages

Wahkpa Chu'gn. Archealogical excavation of prehistoric bison jump site. Also campground (fee). Tours (Memorial Day-Labor Day, daily exc Mon). ½ mi W on US 2. Phone 406/265-6417 or -7550. ¢¢

Havre Beneath the Streets. Tour an "underground mall" where many of the first businesses in the town were established. Includes turn-of-the-century Sporting Eagle Saloon; Holland and Son Mercantile; Wah Sing Laundry; even an Opium den. Tours take approx 1 hr. Res required. (Daily) 100 3rd Ave. Phone 406/265-8888 for schedule and reservations. ¢¢

Annual Events

Rocky Boy Powwow. 1st wkend Aug.

Great Northern Fair. Phone 406/265-7121. 2nd wk Aug.

Havre Festival Days. 3rd wkend Sept.

Motel

★ **TOWNHOUSE INN.** *629 W First St. 406/265-6711; FAX 406/265-6213; res: 800/422-4667.* 104 rms, 1-2 story. S $58; D $62-$66; each addl $4; suites $88-$170. Crib free. Pet accepted, some restrictions; $4. TV; cable (premium). Indoor pool; whirlpool. Restaurant opp open 24 hrs. Bar 8-12:30 am. Ck-out noon. Coin lndry. Meeting rm. Free airport, RR station, bus depot transportation. Cr cds: A, C, D, DS, MC, V.

[↩] [≈] [⊀] [🐾] [SC]

Helena (C-4)

(See also Deer Lodge, White Sulphur Springs)

Settled 1864 **Pop** 24,569 **Elev** 4,157 ft **Area code** 406 **Zip** 59601
Information Helena Area Chamber of Commerce, 225 Cruse Ave, Suite A; 406/442-4120 or 800/7-HELENA, outside MT.

Montana's state capital and fourth-largest city, Helena was the site of one of the state's largest gold rushes. In 1864, a party of discouraged prospectors decided to explore a gulch—now Helena's Main St—as their "last chance." This gulch and the area surrounding it produced more than $20 million in gold. A hundred cabins soon appeared. The mining camp, known as "Last Chance," was renamed Helena, after a town in Minnesota. Besides being the governmental center for Montana, today's Helena hosts agricultural and industrial business, including an important smelting and ore refining plant in East Helena.

What to See and Do

Canyon Ferry State Park (Chinamans Unit). There are numerous recreation sites around this reservoir, which was created in 1954 by the construction of the Canyon Ferry Dam. Swimming, waterskiing; fishing; boating. Picnicking. Camping (no hookups). Standard fees. 10 mi E on US 12/287, then 6 mi N on MT 284. Phone 406/444-4475.

Cathedral of St Helena. Gothic cathedral with 230-ft spires and 68 stained-glass windows made in Germany. Modeled after cathedral in Cologne. (Daily) Lawrence & Warren Aves.

Frontier Town. Rustic pioneer village shaped with solid rock and built with giant logs. 75-mi view of the Continental Divide. Restaurant, bar. (Mother's Day-early Oct, daily) 15 mi W on US 12, atop MacDonald Pass. Phone 406/442-4560. **Free.**

Gates of the Mountains. 12-mi, 2-hr Missouri River cruise explores deep gorge in Helena National Forest, discovered and named by Lewis & Clark. Views of cliffs, canyons, wildlife and wilderness. (Memorial Day wkend-mid-Sept, daily) Launching facilities (Apr-Nov). 16 mi N, off I-15. Phone 406/458-5241. ¢¢¢

Gold Collection. Collection includes nuggets, wire and leaf gold, gold dust and coins. (Mon-Fri; closed hols) Norwest Bank Helena, 350 N Last Chance Gulch. Phone 406/447-2000. **Free.**

Helena National Forest. Approx 975,000 acres include part of the Scapegoat Wilderness and the Gates of the Mountains Wilderness, camp and picnic sites. Scenic drives, fishing, hunting for deer and elk. Adj to Helena, accessible from US 12, 91, 287, I-15, MT 200. For information contact Forest Supervisor, 2880 Skyway Dr, 59601; 406/449-5201.

Holter Museum of Art. Changing exhibits featuring paintings, sculpture, photography, ceramics, weaving. (Daily exc Mon; closed major hols) 12 E Lawrence. Phone 406/442-6400. **Donation.**

⭐ **Last Chance Tour Train.** Departs from historical museum. Covered trains tour the city's major points of interest, including Last Chance Gulch. (Mid-May-Sept, daily) Contact Chamber of Commerce. **¢¢**

Montana Historical Society Museum. History of Montana in Montana Homeland exhibit; notable collection of Charles M. Russell's art, Haynes Gallery on Montana Photography; military history rm; changing exhibits. Montana Historical Library is on 2nd flr. (Memorial Day-Labor Day, daily; rest of yr, daily exc Sun; closed Jan 1, Thanksgiving, Dec 25) 225 N Roberts St. Phone 406/444-2694. **Free.**

Original Governor's Mansion (1888). Restored 22-rm brick house used as governor's residence 1913-1959. 304 N Ewing St. Phone 406/444-4710.

Pioneer Cabin (1864). Depicts frontier life (1863-1883); many authentic furnishings. (Memorial Day-Labor Day, Mon-Fri; rest of yr, by appt) 280 S Park Ave. Phone 406/443-7641, 406/265-5205 off season. **Donation.**

Reeder's Alley. This area previously housed miners, muleskinners and Chinese laundry workers, now houses specialty shops and a restaurant. Near S end of Last Chance Gulch.

State Capitol. Neoclassic structure faced with Montana granite and sandstone, topped with a copper dome. Murals by Charles M. Russell, E.S. Paxson and other artists on display inside. (Daily; guided tours mid-June-Labor Day) Bounded by Lockey & Roberts Sts, 6th & Montana Aves. Phone 406/444-4789. **Free.**

Annual Events

"Race to the Sky" Dog Sled Races. Feb.

Governor's Cup Marathon. Early June.

Montana Traditional Jazz Festival. Mid-June.

Last Chance Stampede & Fair. Lewis & Clark County Fairgrounds. Rodeo. July.

Western Rendezvous of Art. Early Aug.

Seasonal Event

Eagle Watch. Bald eagles migrate to nearby Missouri River to feed on salmon. Mid-Nov-mid-Dec.

Motels

⭐ **ALADDIN MOTOR INN.** *2101 11th Ave.* 406/443-2300; FAX 406/442-7057; res: 800/541-2743 (MT). 72 rms, 3 story. S $50; D $55-$70; each addl $5. Crib $5. TV; cable (premium), VCR avail (movies $6). Indoor pool; whirlpool, sauna. Coffee in rms. Bar 4-10 pm. Ck-out noon. Meeting rms. Business servs avail. Free airport, bus depot transportation. Some bathrm phones, refrigerators, fireplaces. Cr cds: A, D, DS, MC, V.

⭐⭐ **BEST WESTERN COLONIAL PARK INN.** *2301 Colonial Dr.* 406/443-2100; FAX 406/442-0301. 149 rms, 2 story. S $72-90; D $79-$102; each addl $7; under 18 free. Crib free. TV; cable (premium). 2 heated pools, 1 indoor; poolside serv. Restaurant 6 am-10 pm. Rm serv. Bar 4 pm-1:30 am. Ck-out 1 pm. Coin lndry. Meeting rms. Business servs avail. Bellhops. Valet serv. Gift shop. Barber, beauty shop. Free airport transportation. Some bathrm phones, in-rm whirlpools. Cr cds: A, C, D, DS, MC, V.

⭐ **COMFORT INN.** *750 Fee St.* 406/443-1000. 56 rms, 2 story, 14 suites. June-Aug: S $59.95; D $79.95; each addl $5; suites $69-$79; under 18 free; lower rates rest of yr. Crib free. Pet accepted. TV; cable (premium). Indoor pool; whirlpool. Complimentary continental bkfst.

Restaurant opp open 24 hrs. Ck-out 11 am. Ck-in 2 pm. Business servs avail. Cr cds: A, C, D, DS, ER, JCB, MC, V.

⭐⭐ **HOLIDAY INN EXPRESS.** *701 Washington St.* 406/449-4000; FAX 406/449-4522. 75 rms. Mid-June-mid-Sept: S, D $66; suites $84-$93; under 19 free; lower rates rest of yr. Crib free. TV; cable (premium). Complimentary continental bkfst. Restaurant nearby. Ck-out noon. Meeting rms. Business servs avail. Exercise equipt; weight machines, bicycles. Some refrigerators. Totally nonsmoking. Cr cds: A, D, DS, MC, V.

⭐ ⭐ **JORGENSON'S HOLIDAY.** *1714 11th Ave, 3 blks W of I-15 Capital exit.* 406/442-1770; FAX 406/449-0155; res: 800/272-1770 (MT). 117 rms, 3 story. June-Sept: S $42.95-$62.95; D $48.95-$81.95; each addl $5; suites $79.95-$103.95; under 10 free; lower rates rest of yr. Crib $3. TV; cable (premium). Indoor pool. Complimentary coffee in lobby. Restaurant 6:30 am-10 pm. Bar 11:30 am-11 pm. Ck-out noon. Meeting rms. Business servs avail. Free airport transportation. Many bathrm phones; refrigerator in suites. Cr cds: A, D, DS, MC, V.

⭐ **SHILO INN.** *2020 Prospect Ave, W of I-15 on US 12, Capitol exit.* 406/442-0320; FAX 406/449-4426. 47 rms, 3 story, 3 kits. No elvtr. S,D $75; each addl $9; kit. units $85. Crib free. Pet accepted. TV; cable (premium); VCR (movies $5). Indoor pool; whirlpool, sauna, steam rm. Complimentary continental bkfst. Restaurant adj open 24 hrs. Ck-out noon. Coin lndry. Meeting rm. Valet serv. Free airport, bus depot transportation. Bathrm phones, refrigerators. Cr cds: A, C, D, DS, ER, JCB, MC, V.

⭐ **SUPER 8.** *2200 11th Ave.* 406/443-2450; FAX 406/443-2450. 102 rms, 3 story. No elvtr. S $49.88; D $57.88-$62.88; each addl $5. Crib free. TV; cable. Restaurant adj 11 am-10 pm. Ck-out 11 am. Cr cds: A, C, D, DS, MC, V.

Hotel

⭐ ⭐ **PARK PLAZA.** *22 N Last Chance Gulch.* 406/443-2200; FAX 406/442-4030; res: 800/332-2290 (MT). 71 rms, 7 story. S $60; D $66; each addl $6; under 12 free. Crib $5. Pet accepted. TV; cable. Restaurant 6:30 am-9 pm. Bar 11-2 am. Ck-out 3 pm. Meeting rms. Business servs avail. Airport transportation. Cr cds: A, C, D, DS, ER, MC, V.

Inns

⭐⭐ **BARRISTER.** *416 N Ewing St.* 406/443-7330; FAX 406/442-7964. 5 rms, 2 story. No rm phones. S $80; D $80-$100; each addl $15; under 10 free. Pet accepted. TV; cable, VCR avail. Complimentary full bkfst. Restaurant nearby. Ck-out 10:30 am, ck-in 4-7 pm. Luggage handling. Business servs avail. Free airport transportation. Built in 1880; furnished with antiques. Totally nonsmoking. Cr cds: A, MC, V.

⭐⭐⭐ **THE SANDERS.** *328 N Ewing.* 406/442-3309; FAX 406/443-2361. 7 rms, 2 story. S $75; D $90-$110; each addl $20. TV. Complimentary full bkfst; afternoon refreshments. Restaurant nearby. Ck-out 11 am, ck-in 4-7 pm. Built 1875 by Senator Wilbur Fisk Sanders. Many original furnishings. Totally nonsmoking. Cr cds: A, DS, MC, V.

Restaurants

⭐ ⭐ **ON BROADWAY.** *106 Broadway.* 406/443-1929. Hrs: 5:30-9:30 pm. Fri, Sat to 10 pm. Closed Sun; major hols. Wine, beer. Semi-a la carte: dinner $8.75-$16. Specialties: oven-roasted fresh salmon, chicken in mornay sauce, fresh East Coast mussels. In 1889 grocery store. Cr cds: A, MC, V.

★ ★ **STONEHOUSE.** *120 Reeder's Alley. 406/449-2552.* Hrs: 11:30 am-2 pm, 5:30-9 pm; Fri, Sat 11:30 am-2 pm, 5-10 pm; Sun from 5 pm. Closed some major hols. Res accepted. Wine, beer. Semi-a la carte: lunch $4.95-$7, dinner $10.95-$16.95. Child's meals. Specializes in wild game, sautéed salmon. Turn-of-the-century house. Totally nonsmoking. Cr cds: A, DS, MC, V.

SC

★ **WINDBAG GRILL.** *19 S Last Chance Gulch. 406/443-9669.* Hrs: 11 am-2:30 pm, 5-9:30 pm; Sun 5-9 pm (June-Sept); Closed Sun (Oct-May); some major hols. Bar. Semi-a la carte: lunch $5-$6.75, dinner $5-$17.95. Specializes in Northwestern seafood, prime rib. In former bordello; antique bar. Cr cds: A, DS, MC, V.

Kalispell (B-2)

(See also Bigfork, Columbia Falls, Whitefish)

Founded 1891 **Pop** 11,917 **Elev** 2,955 ft **Area code** 406 **Zip** 59901
E-mail fcva@fcva.org **Web** www.fcva.org/flathead
Information Flathead Convention & Visitor Bureau, 15 Depot Park; 406/756-9091 or 800/543-3105.

Center of a mountain vacationland, Kalispell is the convention center of the Flathead Valley. Seed potatoes and sweet cherries are grown and processed in great quantities. Recreational activities abound in the area.

What to See and Do

Conrad Mansion (1895). A 23-rm Norman-style mansion, authentically furnished and restored. Tours (mid-May-mid-Oct, daily). 6 blks E of Main St on 4th St E. Phone 406/755-2166. ¢¢

Flathead Lake. 9 mi S on US 93. (See POLSON)

Flathead National Forest. 2.3 million acres; includes part of 1,009,356-acre Bob Marshall Wilderness; 286,700-acre Great Bear Wilderness and the 73,573-acre Mission Mts Wilderness; 15,368-acre Jewel Basin hiking area and the 219-mi Flathead National Wild & Scenic river system. Spectacular geological formations; glaciers, wild areas. Swimming; fishing, boating, canoeing; riding; picnicking; camping (June-Sept; fee); hunting, outfitters and guides; winter sports; recreation resorts; scenic drives. Near US 2, 93, adj to W & S sides of Glacier Natl Park. Contact Supervisor, 1935 3rd Ave E; 406/755-5401.

Glacier National Park (see).

Hockaday Center for the Arts. Changing exhibits; sales gallery. (Tues-Sat; closed hols) 3rd St & 2nd Ave E. Phone 406/755-5268. ¢

Lawrence Park. Preserved in natural state. Picnic, playground facilities. E off N Main St. **Free.**

Woodland Park. 37 acres. Flower and rock gardens; bird exhibit; mile-long lagoon; skating rink (winter); picnicking, kitchen; playground; pool, wading pool (fees). (Daily) 8 blks E of Main St on 2nd St E. **Free.**

Annual Events

Agriculture-Farm Show. 2 days mid-Feb.

Youth Horse Show. May.

Flathead Music Festival. July.

Quarter Horse Show. July.

Northwest Montana Fair & Rodeo. Flathead County Fairgrounds. Mid-Aug.

Glacier Jazz Stampede. Oct.

Motels

★ **DAYS INN.** *1550 US 93 N. 406/756-3222; FAX 406/756-3277.* 53 rms, 2 story. Mid-May-Sept: S $59-$69; D $64-$74; each addl $5; suites $75-$85; under 12 free; lower rates rest of yr. Crib free. TV; cable (premium). Complimentary continental bkfst. Restaurant nearby. Ck-out 11 am. Meeting rm. Cr cds: A, C, D, DS, JCB, MC, V.

★ ★ **HAMPTON INN.** *1140 US 2 W. 406/755-7900; FAX 406/755-5056.* 120 rms, 3 story. June-Sept: S $78; D $88; suites $155-$205; under 19 free; lower rates rest of yr. Crib free. Pet accepted. TV; cable (premium), VCR. Complimentary continental bkfst. Complimentary coffee in rms. Restaurant adj 7 am-10 pm. Ck-out noon. Meeting rms. Business center. Bellhops. Valet serv. Sundries. Gift shop. Coin lndry. Free airport transportation. Downhill/x-country ski 16 mi. Exercise equipt; bicycles, treadmill. Indoor pool; whirlpool. Rec rm. Refrigerators; in-rm whirlpool, microwave, wet bar, fireplace in suites. Cr cds: A, D, DS, MC, V.

Motor Hotels

★ ★ **BEST WESTERN OUTLAW INN.** *1701 US 93S. 406/755-6100; FAX 406/756-8994.* 220 rms, 3 story. S $82-$135; D $92-$175; each addl $10; under 12 free; package plans. Crib $7. Pet accepted; $10. TV; cable (premium). 2 indoor pools; wading pool, whirlpool. Playground. Coffee in rms. Restaurant 6 am-10 pm. Rm serv. Bar 11-2 am. Ck-out 11 am. Coin lndry. Meeting rms. Business servs avail. Bellhops. Valet serv. Sundries. Gift shop. Barber, beauty shop. Tennis. Exercise equipt; weight machine, bicycle, sauna. Game rm. Microwaves avail. Some balconies. Casino. Western art gallery. Cr cds: A, C, D, DS, ER, JCB, MC, V.

★ ★ ★ **CAVANAUGH'S.** *20 N Main St. 406/752-6660; FAX 406/752-6628; res: 800/843-4667.* Web www.cavanaughs.com. 132 rms, 3 story, 14 suites. Mid-May-Sept: S $98; D $105; each addl $12; suites $120-$190; kit. units $150, under 18 free; ski, golf plans; lower rates rest of yr. Crib free. Pet accepted, some restrictions. TV; cable. Indoor pool; whirlpools. Coffee in rms. Restaurant 6:30 am-10 pm. Rm serv. Bar 4 pm-2 am; entertainment Fri, Sat. Ck-out noon. Meeting rms. Business servs avail. Bellhops. Shopping arcade. Barber, beauty shop. Downhill ski 20 mi; x-country ski 15 mi. Exercise equipt; rower, stair machine, sauna. Casino. Adj to 50-store indoor shopping mall. Cr cds: A, C, D, DS, ER, MC, V.

Hotel

★ **KALISPELL GRAND.** *100 Main St. 406/755-8100; FAX 406/752-8012.* E-mail grand@vtown.com; web www.vtown.com/grand. 40 rms, 38 with shower only, 3 story. No elvtr. June-Aug: S $65; D $75; each addl $7; suites $79-$115; under 12 free. Crib free. Pet accepted, some restrictions. TV; cable. Complimentary continental bkfst. Bar 8-2 am; entertainment Thurs-Sat. Ck-out 11 am. Business servs avail. Exercise equipt; weight machine, treadmill. Casino. Cr cds: A, D, DS, MC, V.

Inns

★ ★ ★ **ANGEL POINT.** *(829 Angel Point Rd, Lakeside 59922)* 14 mi S on US 93. 406/844-2204; res: 800/214-2204. 2 kit. suites. No A/C. June-Sept (3-day min): S, D $110-$125; each addl $40; lower rates rest of yr. Complimentary full bkfst. Ck-out 11 am, ck-in 3 pm. X-country ski 7 mi. Lawn games. Refrigerators. Balconies. Picnic tables, grill. Gazebo. Secluded, elegant lodging on lake; antiques, original art. Totally nonsmoking. No cr cds accepted.

★ ★ **LOGAN HOUSE.** *528 Woodland Ave. 406/755-5588; res: 800/615-5588; FAX 406/755-5589.* Web www.cyberport.net/ads/logan /loganl.html. 4 rms, 1 with shower only, 2 story. No A/C. No rm phones. July-Aug: S $85; D $110; each addl $10; under 10 free; wkly rates; lower rates rest of yr. TV in common rm; cable. Complimentary full bkfst; afternoon refreshments. Complimentary coffee in rms. Ck-out 10:30 am, ck-in 3-7 pm. Luggage handling. Downhill/x-country ski 15 mi. Game rm. Built in 1908; turn-of-the-century home with period antiques and furnishings. Totally nonsmoking. Cr cds: DS, MC, V.

Restaurants

★ ★ **1ST AVENUE WEST.** *139 1st Ave W. 406/755-4441.* Hrs: 11 am-3 pm, 5:30-10 pm; Sat, Sun from 5:30 pm. Closed Thanksgiving, Dec 25. Res accepted. Bar to 1 am. Semi-a la carte: lunch $3.95-$7.95, dinner $4.95-$16.95. Child's meals. Specializes in grilled fresh seafood, pasta, filet mignon. Outdoor dining. Casual, bistro atmosphere. Cr cds: A, MC, V.

✔★ ★ **ROCCO'S.** *3796 US 2E, 7 1/2 mi N. 406/756-5834.* Hrs: 5-10 pm. Closed Dec 25. Res accepted. Italian, Amer menu. Bar. Semi-a la carte: dinner $9.25-$17.95. Child's meals. Specialties: fettucine pescatora, beefsteak Florentine, scampi alfredo. Aviation theme. Rustic decor. Cr cds: A, D, DS, MC, V.

Lewistown (C-6)

Founded 1881 **Pop** 6,051 **Elev** 3,963 ft **Area code** 406 **Zip** 59457
Information Chamber of Commerce, PO Box 818; 406/538-5436.

At the geographic center of the state, amid some of Montana's finest farming and ranching country, Lewistown is a farm trade community. The area is famous for hard, premium wheat and high-grade registered cattle. Originally a small trading post on the Carroll Trail, it was first called "Reed's Fort," and later renamed to honor a Major Lewis who established a fort two miles south in 1876.

What to See and Do

Big Spring Creek. One of the top rainbow trout streams in the country. Picnic grounds. Running N and S.

Charles M. Russell National Wildlife Refuge. Missouri River "Breaks" and prairie lands; wildlife includes pronghorn, elk, mule and whitetail deer; bighorn sheep, sage and sharptail grouse. Refuge (daily, 24 hrs). Lewistown headquarters (Mon-Fri; closed hols). 70 mi NE via US 191 or MT 200. Phone 406/538-8706. **Free.**

Ft Maginnis. Ruins of 1880 frontier post. 15 mi E on US 87, then 10 mi N.

Historical points of 19th-century gold mining. Maiden. 10 mi N on US 191, then 6 mi E. **Kendall.** 16 mi N on US 191, then 6 mi W on gravel road. **Giltedge.** 14 mi E on US 87, then 6 mi NW.

Annual Events

Central Montana Horse Show, Fair, Rodeo. Fergus County Fairgrounds. Last full wk in July.

Montana Cowboy Poetry Gathering. Modern-day cowboys and admirers of Western folklore relate life "down on the range" through original poetry. 3rd wkend Aug.

Seasonal Events

Drag Races. Quarter-mile races. NHRA sanctioned. Late May-late Sept.

Charlie Russell Chew-Choo. 3 1/2-hr dinner train runs through rugged beauty of Central Montana. Sat. June-Sept.

Motel

✔★ **SUPER 8.** *102 Wendell Ave. 406/538-2581; FAX 406/538-2702.* 44 rms, 2 story. June-Sept: S $42.88; D $45.88-$48.88; each addl $4; under 12 free; lower rates rest of yr. Crib free. TV; cable (premium). Complimentary coffee in lobby. Restaurant opp 7 am-10 pm. Ck-out 11 am. Coin lndry. Cr cds: A, D, DS, MC, V.

D ☒ ☒ SC

Restaurant

✔★ **WHOLE FAMDAMILY.** *206 W Main St, on US 87. 406/538-5161.* Hrs: 11 am-8 pm; Sat to 5 pm. Closed Sun; major hols. Res accepted. Wine, beer. Semi-a la carte: lunch $4-$7, dinner $5.95-$6.50. Child's meals. International specials each day. Own desserts. Decorated with family portraits. Totally nonsmoking. Cr cds: A, DS, MC, V.

Libby (A-1)

(For accommodations see Kalispell; also see Bonners Ferry, ID, Sandpoint, ID)

Settled 1863 **Pop** 2,532 **Elev** 2,086 ft **Area code** 406 **Zip** 59923 **E-mail** libbyacc@libby.org **Web** www.libby.org/libbyacc
Information Chamber of Commerce, 905 W 9th St, PO Box 704; 406/293-4167.

Nestled in the Cabinet Mts, Libby, formerly a gold town, is now busy processing logs. It is headquarters for Kootenai National Forest and has three Ranger District offices.

What to See and Do

Camping. Libby Creek. 12 mi SE on US 2. **Lions Springs.** 32 mi SE on US 2. **Carrigan.** 12 mi N on Pipe Creek Rd. (June-mid-Sept; fees) Phone 406/293-4141.

Heritage Museum. Located in 12-sided log building and features various exhibits on area pioneers; animal exhibits; art gallery; exhibits by the Forest Service, mining interests, the lumber industry. (June-Aug, Mon-Sat, also Sun afternoons) 1 1/4 mi S via US 2. Phone 406/293-7521. **Donation.**

Kootenai National Forest. More than 2.2 million acres. Includes 94,272-acre Cabinet Mts Wilderness. Scenic drives along Yaak River, Lake Koocanusa Reservoir, Fisher River, Bull River; Giant Cedars Nature Trail. Fishing. Boating, canoeing. Hiking trails. Cross-country skiing. Picknicking. Camping. Surrounds Libby, accessible on US 2, MT 37. For information contact Supervisor, 506 US 2W; 406/293-6211. In the forest is

Turner Mt Ski Area. T-bar, rope tow; patrol, school; snack bar. (Late Dec-early Jan, daily; rest of Dec, early Jan-Mar, Sat & Sun) 23 mi NW on Pipe Creek Hwy. ¢¢¢¢

Libby Dam. Lake Koocanusa extends 90 mi upstream. A US Army Corps of Engineers project. Fishing; boating (dock). Picnicking. (Daily) Visitor center; tours of dam and powerhouse (hrly); viewpoints (Memorial Day-Labor Day, daily). 17 mi NE on MT 37. Phone 406/293-5577. **Free.**

Annual Events

Logger Days. Adult & child logging contests. Carnival, parade, karaoke contest. Vendors, food. Early July.

Nordicfest. Scandinavian festival, parade, dances, food, melodrama. 3rd wkend Sept.

Little Bighorn Battlefield National Monument (D-8)

(For accommodations see Billings, Hardin)

(2 mi SE of Crow Agency. Entrance 1 mi E of I-90 on US 212.)

Scene of Custer's "last stand," this monument memorializes one of the last armed clashes between Northern Plains tribes, fighting to preserve their traditional way of life, and the forces of the United States, charged with safeguarding westward expansion. Here, on June 25, 1876, Lieutenant Colonel George A. Custer and approximately 263 men of the US Army 7th Cavalry and attached personnel were killed in a battle against an overwhelming force of Lakota and Cheyenne warriors. Also here are a national cemetery, established in 1879, and the Reno-Benteen Battlefield, five miles southeast, where the remainder of the 7th Cavalry withstood until late on June 26. Headstones show where the soldiers fell and a large obelisk marks the mass grave of the 7th Cavalry. A visitor center contains a bookstore and museum with dioramas and exhibits (daily; closed Jan 1, Thanksgiving, Dec 25). National Park Service personnel provide interpretive programs (Memorial Day-Labor Day) and guided tours of Custer National Cemetery. Grounds (daily). For further information contact PO Box 39, Crow Agency 59022; 406/638-2621. ¢-¢¢

Livingston (D-5)

(See also Big Timber, Bozeman)

Settled 1882 **Pop** 6,701 **Elev** 4,503 ft **Area code** 406 **Zip** 59047 **E-mail** lacc@avicom.net **Web** www.avicom.net/livingstoncham

Information Chamber of Commerce, 208 W Park; 406/222-0850.

Railroading has been a key to the town's history and economy since railroad surveyors first named it Clark City; later the present name was adopted to honor a director of the Northern Pacific Railway. Today, agriculture, ranching and tourism are the chief industries. Farm products from Paradise and Shields valleys also pass through the town. Trout fishing is excellent in the Yellowstone River. A Ranger District office of the Gallatin National Forest (see BOZEMAN) is located here.

What to See and Do

Depot Center. Changing exhibits & cultural art shows. Gift shop. (Mid-May-mid-Oct, Mon-Sat, also Sun afternoons) Park & 2nd Sts. Phone 406/222-2300. ¢

Emigrant Gulch. Gold was discovered here in 1862. Chico and Yellowstone City boomed busily but briefly—the gold supply was limited and the Crow were aggressive. Both are ghost towns now. 37 mi S, off US 89.

Park County Museum. "House of Memories"; pioneer tools, library, old newspapers, sheep wagon, stagecoach, Native American & archaeological exhibits. Northern Pacific Railroad Room. (June-Labor Day, afternoons; rest of yr, by appt) 118 W Chinook. Phone 406/222-4184. ¢-¢¢

Annual Event

Round-up Rodeo. Fairgrounds. July 2-4.

Motels

★ **BEST WESTERN YELLOWSTONE INN.** *1515 W Park St.* *406/222-6110; FAX 406/222-3976.* 99 rms, 3 story. Mid-May-mid-Sept: S, D $69-$89; each addl $5; kit. unit $139; under 13 free; wkly rates; lower rates rest of yr. Crib free. Pet accepted; $5. TV; cable. Complimentary coffee in lobby. Restaurant 6 am-10 pm. Bar noon-2 am. Ck-out noon. Meeting rms. Business servs avail. Bellhops. Sundries. Barber, beauty shop. Indoor pool. Game rm. Cr cds: A, C, D, DS, MC, V.

⊗ ⊠ ≈ ≋ 🛇 SC

★ ★ **COMFORT INN.** *114 Loves Ln, I-90, exit 333. 406/222-4400; FAX 406/222-7658.* 49 rms, 2 story. July-Aug: S $74.95; D $79.95-$84.95; each addl $5; suites $96.95-$106.95; under 18 free; lower rates rest of yr. Crib free. TV; cable (premium). Complimentary continental bkfst. Retaurant nearby. Ck-out 11 am. Meeting rm. Bellhops. Sundries. Coin lndry. Indoor pool; whirlpool. Game rm. Regerigerator, wet bar in suites. Cr cds: A, C, D, DS, MC, V.

D ⊗ ≈ ≋ 🛇 SC

★ **PARADISE INN.** *I-90 & MT 89, exit 333. 406/222-6320; FAX 406/222-2481; res: 800/437-6291.* 43 rms. Mid-May-Sept: S, D $79-$89; each addl $5; suites $99-$129; lower rates rest of yr. Crib $5. Pet accepted. TV; cable (premium). Indoor pool. Restaurant 6 am-10:30 pm. Bar 12:30 pm-2 am. Ck-out 11 am. Cr cds: A, MC, V.

D ⊬ ≈ ≋ 🛇

✔★ **SUPER 8.** *105 Centennial Dr, I-90 exit 333. 406/222-7711.* 36 rms. June-Sept: S $51.88; D $55.88-$59.88; each addl $4; under 12 free; lower rates rest of yr. Crib free. TV; cable (premium). Complimentary coffee in lobby. Restaurant adj 6 am-11 pm. Ck-out 11 am. Coin lndry. Cr cds: A, D, DS, MC, V.

≋ 🛇

Lodge

★ ★ **CHICO HOT SPRINGS.** *(Pray 59065) approx 25 mi S on US 89 to Emigrant, then E on MT 540. 406/333-4933; FAX 406/333-4694; res: 800/468-9232.* 49 lodge rms, 3 story, 29 motel units, 16 cottages. No A/C. Some rm phones. June-Sept: (lodge) S, D $85; (motel) S, D $105; cabins $75-$85; chalets (1-5 bedrm) $129-$300; under 7 free; lower rates rest of yr. Crib free. Pet accepted; $5. Heated pool. Supervised child's activities (summer only). Dining rm 7-11 am, 5:30-10 pm. Box lunches. Bar 11-2 am; entertainment Fri, Sat. Ck-out 11 am, ck-in 3 pm. Grocery. Coin lndry 5 mi. Meeting rms. Business servs avail. Gift shop. Exercise equipt; bicycles, treadmill. X-country ski 3 mi. Hiking. Bicycle rentals. Lawn games. Fishing/hunting guides. Massage. Some refrigerators. Picnic tables. Rustic surroundings; secluded in Paradise Valley. Cr cds: A, DS, MC, V.

⊗ ⊬ 🏋 ≋ ≈ 🍴 ≋ 🛇

Guest Ranch

★ ★ ★ **MOUNTAIN SKY.** *(Bozeman 59715) 35 mi S of Livingston; off US 89, turn at Big Creek Rd. 406/333-4911; FAX 406/587-3977 (winter); res: 800/548-3392.* E-mail mountainsky@mcn.net; web www.mtnsky.com. 27 cabins, 1-3 bedrm. No rm phones. AP, June-Sept: S, D $1,925-$2,345/wk; family rates; 50% deposit required to confirm res. Closed rest of yr. Heated pool; whirlpool. Playground. Free supervised child's activities (mid-June-Aug). Coffee in rms. Ck-out 10 am, ck-in 3 pm. Guest lndry. Meeting rms. Business servs avail. Airport transportation. Tennis, pro. Sauna. Float trips. Lawn games. Hiking. Soc dir; entertainment. Rec rm. Refrigerators. 30 mi N of Yellowstone Natl Park. Cr cds: MC, V.

⊬ 🏋 ≋ ≈ ≋ 🛇

Restaurants

★ ★ ★ **LIVINGSTON BAR & GRILLE.** *130 N Main St. 406/222-7909.* Hrs: 11:30 am-2 pm, 5:30-10 pm; Sun to 9 pm. Closed Thanksgiving, Dec 25. Res accepted. Continental menu. Bar. Wine list. Semi-a la carte: lunch $4.75-$11.50, dinner $18-$20. Child's meals. Specialties: baked poussin, fresh grouper, New York strip steak. Own baking. Street parking. Turn-of-the-century bldg has 100-yr-old mahogany bar; overlooks downtown. Cr cds: A, DS, MC, V.

D

★ ★ **UNCLE LOOIE'S.** *119 W Park St. 406/222-7177.* Hrs: 11:30 am-2:30 pm, 5:30-10 pm; Sat, Sun from 5:30 pm. Closed Thanksgiving, Dec 25. Res accepted. Italian, Continental menu. Bar. Semi-a la carte: lunch $5.95-$10.95, dinner $7.95-$21.95. Buffet: lunch $5.95. Child's meals. Specializes in pasta, beef, seafood. Italian, Mediterranean theme. Totally nonsmoking. Cr cds: A, DS, MC, V.

D

Malta (A-7)

Pop 2,340 **Elev** 2,255 ft **Area code** 406 **Zip** 59538

Information Malta Area Chamber of Commerce, PO Box 1420; 406/654-1776 or 800/704-1776.

What to See and Do

Bowdoin National Wildlife Refuge. Approx 15,500 acres provide excellent nesting, resting and feeding grounds for migratory waterfowl. The refuge also supports whitetailed deer and pronghorns. Use of the self-guided drive-through trail is recommended. (Daily; weather permitting) 7 mi E via Old US 2. Phone 406/654-2863. **Free.**

Phillips County Museum. Features Native American, homestead and dinosaur exhibits. (Mid-May-Labor Day, Tues-Sat) US 2 E. Phone 406/654-1037. ¢¢

Motel

✔★ **MALTANA.** *138 First Ave W. 406/654-2610; FAX 406/654-1663.* 19 rms. S $34; D $39-$42; each addl $3. Crib $3. TV; cable. Complimentary coffee in rms. Restaurant nearby. Ck-out 11 am. Airport, RR station transportation. Cr cds: A, C, D, DS, MC, V.

Miles City (C-9)

Pop 8,461 **Elev** 2,358 ft **Area code** 406 **Zip** 59301 **E-mail** mcchamber@servco.com **Web** www.servco.com/mcchamber

Information Chamber of Commerce, 901 Main St; 406/232-2890.

This trade, industrial and energy-concerned city is also a livestock and agricultural center. Seat of Custer County, the city is named for a US infantry general. Here are the Livestock Auction Saleyards where about 25 percent of Montana's livestock is processed.

What to See and Do

Custer County Art Center. Housed in former holding tanks of old Miles City Water Works, overlooking the Yellowstone River. Contemporary art exhibits. Gift shop. (Tues-Sun afternoons; closed hols) Water Plant Rd, W via US 10, 12. Phone 406/232-0635. **Free.**

Range Riders Museum and Pioneer Memorial Hall. Exhibits and memorabilia of the days of the open range. Bert Clark gun collection one of the largest in the Northwest. (Apr-Oct) W end of Main St. Phone 406/232-6146. ¢¢

Annual Events

Bucking Horse Sale. Fairgrounds. Exit 135 off I-94. Born in 1951, it grew out of the Miles City Roundup. Features Wild Horse Stampede, bronc and bull riding, and the sale of both bucking horses and bulls. 3rd wkend May.

Ballon Roundup. 4th wkend June.

Eastern Montana Fair. Fairgrounds. Exit 135 off I-94. 4 days late Aug.

Motels

★ **BEST WESTERN WAR BONNET INN.** *1015 S Haynes, just off I-90 exit 138. 406/232-4560; FAX 406/232-0363.* 54 rms, 2 story. May-Sept: S $66; D $71; each addl $6; suites $100; under 12 free; higher rates Bucking Horse Sale; lower rates rest of yr. Crib $6. Pet accepted. TV; cable. Indoor pool; whirlpool, sauna. Complimentary continental bkfst. Ck-out noon. Meeting rms. Cr cds: A, C, D, DS, JCB, MC, V.

✔★ ★ **COMFORT INN.** *1615 S Haynes Ave. 406/232-3141.* 49 rms, 2 story. May-Aug: S $49.95; D $54.95-$59.95; each addl $5; under 18 free; higher rates Bucking Horse Sale; lower rates rest of yr. Crib free. TV; cable (premium). Indoor pool; whirlpool. Complimentary continental bkfst. Ck-out 11 am. Coin lndry. Meeting rms. Business servs avail. Cr cds: A, D, DS, MC, V.

D

Missoula (C-3)

(See also Hamilton)

Settled 1860 **Pop** 42,918 **Elev** 3,200 ft **Area code** 406

Information Chamber of Commerce, 825 E Front, PO Box 7577, 59807; 406/543-6623.

Since the days of the Lewis and Clark Expedition, Missoula has been a trading and transportation crossroads. It is a lumber and paper manufacturing center, the hub of large reserves of timber, the regional headquarters of the US Forest Service and Montana State Forest Service.

What to See and Do

✪ **Aerial Fire Depot.** Forest Service headquarters for aerial attack on forest fires in western US. Smokejumpers trained and based here during summer. 7 mi W on US 10, I-90, 1/2 mi W of Johnson Bell Airport. Phone 406/329-4900.

Visitor Center. Fire management exhibits, guided tour of parachute loft and training facilities; films, information on recreational facilities in 13 national forests in region. (Memorial Day-Labor Day, daily; rest of yr, by appt) Phone 406/329-4934. **Donation.**

Smokejumper Center. Training and dispatching center for airborne fire crews; parachute and fire training. **Free.**

Northern Forest Fire Laboratory. Conducts research in fire prevention and control and the beneficial uses of fire in forest management. Tours by appt. Phone 406/329-4934.

Historical Museum at Ft Missoula. Established to interpret the history of Missoula County, forest management and timber production in western Montana. The museum features indoor galleries with permanent and changing exhibits; outdoor area includes ten historic structures, four are restored. Located in the core of what was originally Ft Missoula (1877-1947). Several original buildings remain. Other areas include railroad and military history. (Daily exc Mon; closed most hols) 5 mi S from I-90 via Reserve St to South Ave, then 1 mi W. Phone 406/728-3476. **Free.**

Lolo National Forest. Foot trails to 100 lakes and peaks, camping (mid-May-Sept, full service campgrounds, some free); picnicking, fishing, hunting, winter sports, scenic drives through 2,062,545 acres. Includes Welcome Creek Wilderness and Rattlesnake National Recreation Area and Wilderness, part of Scapegoat Wilderness, and Selway-Bitterroot Wilderness. The Pattee Canyon Recreation Area is 5 mi from town. Historic Lolo Trail and Lewis & Clark Hwy (US 12) over Bitterroot Mts take visitors along route of famed exploration. Surrounds Missoula, accessible on US 10, 12, 93, MT 200, 83, I-90. Contact Supervisor, Ft Missoula, Bldg 24, 59801; 406/329-3750. A Ranger District office is also located here.

Missoula Museum of the Arts. Art of the western states. Changing exhibits. Educational programs. Museum shop. (Daily exc Sun, afternoons) 335 N Pattee. Phone 406/728-0447. **Free.**

Missoula Public Library. Outstanding collection of historical works on Montana and the Northwest and genealogical materials. 301 E Main St. Phone 406/721-2665.

Paxson Paintings. Eight murals depicting Montana's history by one of the West's outstanding artists. (Mon-Fri; closed hols) County Courthouse, 200 W Broadway between Orange & Higgins Sts. Phone 406/721-5700, ext 3200. **Free.**

Skiing.

Montana Snowbowl. 2 double chairlifts, T-bar, rope tow; patrol, school, rentals; cafeteria, bar. Longest run 3 mi; vertical drop 2,600 ft. (Late Nov-Apr, daily exc Tues) Lifts fee; tow free. Summer chairlift. Hiking trails; mountain biking. (July-Aug, Fri-Sun) 3 mi NW on I-90 (Reserve St exit), then 9 mi N on Giant Creek Rd to Snow Bowl Rd. Phone 406/549-9777. Summer ¢¢¢; Winter ¢¢¢¢¢

Marshall Mt Ski Area. Triple chairlift, T-bar, rope tow; school, patrol, rentals, snowmaking; half-day rates; cafeteria, snack bar. Longest run 2 mi; vertical drop 1,500 ft. (Dec-Mar, daily exc Mon) 7 mi NE via I-90, E Missoula exit. Phone 406/258-6000. ¢¢¢¢¢

St Francis Xavier Church (1889). Steeple highlights this structure built the same year Montana became a state. (Daily) 420 W Pine St. Phone 406/542-0321.

University of Montana (1893). (10,000 students) At the foot of Mt Sentinel. University Center Gallery and Gallery of Visual Arts. University & Arthur Aves. Campus tours; for res phone 406/243-2522.

Annual Events

International Wildlife Film Festival. Downtown. Phone 406/728-9380. Early Apr.

Western Montana Quarter Horse Show. Fairgrounds. Early July.

Western Montana Fair. Fairgrounds. Mid-Aug.

Motels

★ **4 B'S INN-NORTH.** 4953 N Reserve St (59802), I-90 exit 101. 406/542-7550; FAX 406/721-5931; res: 800/272-9500 (exc MT). 67 rms, 3 story. Mid-May-mid-Sept: S $50.95; D $61.50; suites $71.50; under 12 free. Crib $5. Pet accepted. TV; cable. Complimentary coffee in lobby. Restaurant adj open 24 hrs. Ck-out 11 am. Coin lndry. Whirlpool. Refrigerator in suites. Cr cds: A, C, D, DS, MC, V.

[D] [✆] [≈] [⚞] [🔥] [SC]

✔★ **4 B'S INN-SOUTH.** 3803 Brooks St (59801). 406/251-2665; FAX 406/251-5733; res: 800/272-9500. 91 rms, 3 story. Mid-May-mid-Sept: S $50.95; D $61.50; each addl $5; lower rates rest of yr. Crib $5. TV; cable (premium). Restaurant adj open 24 hrs. Ck-out 11 am. Coin lndry. Meeting rms. Business servs avail. Whirlpool. Cr cds: A, D, DS, MC, V.

[D] [≈] [⚞] [🔥] [SC]

★ **DAYS INN.** 8600 Truckstop Rd (59802), 6 mi W on I-90 exit 96. 406/721-9776; FAX 406/721-9781. 69 rms, 2 story. June-Sept: S $56; D $66-$71; under 12 free; lower rates rest of yr. Crib free. TV; cable, VCR avail (movies). Complimentary continental bkfst. Restaurant adj open 24 hrs. Ck-out 11 am. Coin lndry. Free airport transportation. Whirlpool. Sundries. Cr cds: A, C, D, DS, JCB, MC, V.

[D] [≈] [⚞] [🔥] [SC]

★★ **HAMPTON INN.** 4805 N Reserve St (59802). 406/549-1800; FAX 406/549-1737. 60 rms, 4 story. S $66-$69; D $76-$79; under 18 free. Crib free. Pet accepted. TV; cable (premium). Indoor pool; whirlpool. Complimentary continental bkfst. Restaurant nearby. Ck-out noon. Meeting rms. Business servs avail. Bellhops. Valet serv. Free airport

transportation. Exercise equipt; bicycles, treadmill. Cr cds: A, C, D, DS, MC, V.

[D] [✆] [≈] [✕] [⚞] [🔥] [SC]

★ **ORANGE STREET BUDGET MOTOR INN.** 801 N Orange St (59802). 406/721-3610; FAX 406/721-8875; res: 800/328-0801. 81 rms, 3 story. May-Sept: S $51; D $53-$58; each addl $5; lower rates rest of yr. Crib $3. Pet accepted. TV; cable (premium), VCR avail (movies). Complimentary continental bkfst. Restaurant nearby. Ck-out 11 am. Meeting rms. Business servs avail. Free airport transportation. Exercise equipt; bicycles, rower. Cr cds: A, C, D, DS, MC, V.

[✆] [✕] [⚞] [🔥] [SC]

★ **RED LION.** 700 W Broadway (59802), ½ mi S of I-90 Orange St exit. 406/728-3300; FAX 406/728-4441. 76 rms, 2 story. S $69; D $79-$84; each addl $10; under 18 free. Crib free. Pet accepted; $5. TV; cable (premium). Heated pool. Complimentary coffee in rms. Restaurant adj 6:30 am-10 pm. Ck-out noon. Meeting rm. Business servs avail. In-rm modem link. Valet serv. Sundries. Free airport, bus depot transportation. Downhill/x-country ski 20 mi. Cr cds: A, C, D, DS, MC, V.

[✆] [≈] [≈] [⚞] [🔥] [SC]

✔★ **SUPER 8.** 3901 S Brooks (59801). 406/251-2255; FAX 406/251-2989. 104 rms, 3 story. No elvtr. S $43.88; D $47.88-$52.88; each addl $4; ski plan. Crib $3. TV; cable. Complimentary continental bkfst. Restaurant nearby. Ck-out 11 am. Downhill/x-country ski 20 mi. Cr cds: A, C, D, DS, JCB, MC, V.

[≈] [⚞] [🔥] [SC]

✔★ **SUPER 8.** 4703 N Reserve St (59804). 406/549-1199; FAX 406/549-0677. 58 rms, 2 story. May-Sept: S $49.88; D $53.88-$56.88; each addl $5; under 13 free; lower rates rest of yr. Crib $3. TV; cable (premium). Complimentary continental bkfst. Restaurant nearby. Ck-out 11 am. Sundries. Coin lndry. Free airport transportation. Cr cds: A, C, D, DS, MC, V.

[D] [≈] [⚞] [🔥] [SC]

★ **TRAVELODGE.** 420 W Broadway (59802), ½ mi S of I-90 Orange St exit. 406/728-4500; FAX 406/543-8118. 60 rms, 3 story, no ground floor rms. Mid-May-mid-Sept: S $48-$52; D $54-$58; each addl $3; suites $64-$78; under 17 free; lower rates rest of yr. Crib free. TV; cable (premium). Restaurant 6:30 am-9:30 pm. Ck-out noon. Sundries. Downhill/x-country ski 10 mi. Balconies. Cr cds: A, C, D, DS, MC, V.

[D] [≈] [⚞] [🔥] [SC]

✔★ **VAL-U INN.** 3001 Brooks St (59801). 406/721-9600; FAX 406/721-7208; res: 800/443-7777 (MT). 84 rms, 3 story. S $44-$48; D $55-$66; each addl $4; suites $90; under 12 free. Crib free. TV; cable (premium), VCR avail (movies). Complimentary continental bkfst. Restaurant nearby. Ck-out noon. Coin lndry. Meeting rm. Business servs avail. Airport transportation. Downhill/x-country ski 11 mi. Whirlpool, sauna. Cr cds: A, C, D, DS, MC, V.

[≈] [⚞] [⚞] [🔥] [SC]

Motor Hotels

★★★ **HOLIDAY INN-PARKSIDE.** 200 S Pattee St (59802). 406/721-8550; FAX 406/721-7427. 200 rms, 4 story. S, D $85-$95; suites $125-$150; under 18 free. Pet accepted. TV; cable. Indoor pool; whirlpool. Restaurant 6:30 am-2 pm, 5:30-10:30 pm. Rm serv. Bar 2 pm-2 am; entertainment Fri, Sat. Ck-out noon. Meeting rms. Business servs avail. Bellhops. Gift shop. Free airport transportation. Downhill ski 12 mi; x-country ski 5 mi. Exercise equipt; weights, bicycles, sauna. Balconies. Open atrium, outside patio dining. On Clark Fork River and park. Cr cds: A, C, D, DS, ER, JCB, MC, V.

[D] [✆] [≈] [≈] [✕] [⚞] [🔥] [SC]

★★★ **RED LION VILLAGE INN.** 100 Madison St (59802), ¼ mi SW of I-90 Van Buren exit. 406/728-3100; FAX 406/728-2530. 171 rms, 3 story. S $73-$85; D $83-$95; each addl $10; suites $125-$285; under 18 free. Crib free. Pet accepted. TV; cable, VCR avail. Heated pool; whirlpool.

Coffee in rms. Restaurant 6 am-10 pm. Rm serv. Bar 11-2 am. Ck-out noon. Meeting rms. Business servs avail. In-rm modem link. Bellhops. Gift shop. Beauty shop. Free airport transportation. Downhill/x-country ski 12 mi. Exercise equipt; stair machine, treadmill. Some refrigerators. Balconies. On Clark Fork River. Cr cds: A, C, D, DS, ER, MC, V.

Inn

★ ★ **GOLDSMITH'S BED & BREAKFAST.** *809 E Front St (59802), I-90 Van Buren St exit.* 406/721-6732. 7 rms, 2 story. May-Sept: S $79; D $89; suite $110; under 10 free; lower rates rest of yr. Crib free. TV; cable. Complimentary full bkfst. Restaurant nearby. Ck-out & ck-in 11 am. Picnic tables. Built 1911; Victorian decor; antiques. On Clark Fork river. Totally nonsmoking. Cr cds: A, D, MC, V.

Restaurants

★ ★ **DEPOT.** *201 W Railroad St, S of I-90 Orange St exit.* 406/728-7007. Hrs: 5:30-10:30 pm; Fri, Sat to 11 pm. Closed Thanksgiving, Dec 25. Res accepted. Bar 4 pm-2 am; Sun from 5 pm. Semi-a la carte: dinner $9.95-$16.95. Specializes in fresh seafood, prime rib, handcut steak. Salad bar. Parking. Outdoor dining. Cr cds: A, C, D, DS, MC, V.

✔ ★ **GOLDSMITH'S.** *809 E Front St (59802), at "U" Footbridge.* 406/721-6732. Hrs: 7 am-11 pm. Closed Dec 25. Semi-a la carte: bkfst $3-$5, lunch $3.50-$6, dinner $4-$8. Child's meals. Specializes in breakfast burritos, char-broiled chicken sandwiches, homemade New York-style bagels. Own ice cream. Outdoor dining. Totally nonsmoking. Cr cds: A, D, MC, V.

★ **HEIDELHAUS.** *2620 Brooks St, opp Southgate Mall.* 406/543-3200. Hrs: 6 am-11 pm. Closed Dec 25. German, Amer menu. Bar. Semi-a la carte: bkfst $1.99-$5, lunch $3-$6, dinner $5.95-$19.95. Child's meals. Salad bar. Parking. Bavarian decor; greenhouse. Cr cds: A, DS, MC, V.

✔ ★ **ORIGINAL MONTANA PIE COMPANY.** *910 Brooks St.* 406/728-7437. Hrs: 7 am-10 pm; Fri, Sat to 11 pm. Closed Dec 25. Semi-a la carte: bkfst $2.75-$6.50, lunch $4.75-$6.50, dinner $6-$10. Child's meals. Specializes in chicken pot pies, chicken-fried steak, homemade soups and pies. Own desserts. Parking. Rustic decor. Antiques. Totally nonsmoking. Cr cds: A, DS, MC, V.

★ **THE SHACK.** *222 W Main St (59802).* 406/549-9903. Hrs: 7 am-9:30 pm. Closed July 4, Dec 25. Res accepted. Bar. Semi-a la carte: bkfst $2.50-$8.50, lunch $4.95-$7.50, dinner $5.50-$14.95. Child's meals. Specializes in beef, rainbow trout. Outdoor dining. Large antique bar. Family-owned. Totally nonsmoking. Cr cds: MC, V.

✔ ★ ★ **ZIMORINO'S.** *424 N Higgins St (59802).* 406/549-7434. Hrs: 5-10 pm. Closed most major hols. Italian menu. Bar. Semi-a la carte: dinner $8-$15. Child's meals. Specializes in pizza, chicken parmigiana, manicotti. Italian bistro decor. Totally nonsmoking. Cr cds: MC, V.

Polson (B-2)

(For accommodations see Bigfork)

Pop 3,283 **Elev** 2,931 ft **Area code** 406 **Zip** 59860

Information Chamber of Commerce, 7 Third Ave W, PO Box 667; 406/883-5969.

At the south edge of Flathead Lake, Polson is the trade center for a productive farming area and a provisioning point for mountain trips. According to legend, Paul Bunyan dug the channel from Flathead Lake to Flathead River.

What to See and Do

Flathead Lake Cruise. *Port Polson Princess* departs from Kwatapnuk Resort for sightseeing around Flathead Lake. View the Narrows, Bird Island and Wildhorse Island. (June-Sept, daily) Reservations recommended. Phone 406/883-2448. ¢¢¢¢- ¢¢¢¢

Flathead Lake State Park. 28 mi long, 15 mi wide, average depth 220 ft; formed by glacial action. Fishing best in early spring, late fall; swimming, boating, waterskiing. There are six state park units surrounding the lake (also see BIGFORK).

Big Arm Unit. Also fishing (joint state/tribal license required). Camping (no hookups, dump station). 13 mi N, along W shore on US 93.

Elmo Unit. 16 mi N on US 93.

Finley Point Unit. 12 mi N off MT 35.

National Bison Range. Visitor center, exhibits, nature trails; picnic grounds near headquarters. Bison, antelope, bighorn sheep, deer, elk, and other big game species roam over 18,500 acres of fenced-in range. A 19-mi self-guided tour route rises 2,000 ft over Mission Valley (mid-May-mid-Oct, daily). Motorcycles and bicycles are not permitted on the drives. 32 mi S on US 93, then 13 mi SW on US 212 to main entrance in Moiese. **Free.**

Ninepipe and Pablo National Wildlife Refuges. More than 180 species of birds have been observed on these waterfowl refuges, including ducks, geese, grebes, great blue herons and cormorants. Fishing permitted at certain times and areas in accordance with tribal and state regulations. Joint state/tribal recreation permit and fishing stamp required. Portions of (or all) refuges may be closed during waterfowl season and nesting period. Visitors may obtain more information, including regulations, from Refuge Manager at National Bison Range, 132 Bison Range Rd, Moiese 59824. Pablo is 7 mi S on US 93; Ninepipe is 18 mi S on US 93. Phone 406/644-2211.

Polson-Flathead Historical Museum. Native American artifacts, farm and household items from the opening of the Flathead Reservation in 1910; home of Rudolph, a Scotch-Highland steer, who appeared in over 136 parades in 5 states and Canada; wildlife display and old stagecoach. (Summer, daily) 8th Ave & Main St. Phone 406/883-3049. **Donation.**

River Rafting. Glacier Raft Company offers half-day whitewater trips on Lower Flathead River, leaving from Port Polson, S end of Flathead Lake, Main St & US 93. For information, res phone 406/883-5838 (Polson office in-season) or 406/888-5454 (West Glacier office off-season). ¢¢¢¢

Lodge

★ **BEST WESTERN KWATAQNUK RESORT AT FLATHEAD BAY.** *303 US 93E.* 406/883-3636; FAX 406/883-5392. 112 rms, 3 story. Mid-June-mid-Sept: S $92-$113; D $102-$123; each addl $10; suites $179; under 12 free; lower rates rest of yr. Crib free. TV; cable (premium), VCR avail. 2 pools, 1 indoor; whirlpool. Coffee in rms. Restaurant 6 am-11 pm. Rm serv. Ck-out 11 am. Meeting rms. Business servs avail. Bellhops. Sundries. Gift shop. Game rm. Many balconies. On Flathead Lake; swimming, boat cruises (fee). Cr cds: A, C, D, DS, MC, V.

Red Lodge (E-6)

(See also Cooke City; also see Cody, WY)

Pop 1,958 **Elev** 5,553 ft **Area code** 406 **Zip** 59068 **E-mail** redlodge@wtp.net **Web** www.wtp.net/redlodge

Information Chamber of Commerce, PO Box 988; 406/446-1718.

The seat of Carbon County and a busy resort town, Red Lodge was, according to legend, named for a Native American band whose tepees were painted red. It is a most magnificent approach to Yellowstone National Park (see WYOMING) and gateway to the half-million-acre Beartooth-Absaroka Wilderness Area. A Ranger District office of the Custer National Forest (see HARDIN) is located here.

What to See and Do

Beartooth Highway (National Forest Scenic Byway). US 212 travels 64 mi over an 11,000-ft pass in the Beartooth Mts to the NE entrance of Yellowstone National Park. Includes Rock Creek Vista Point; Granite Peak, highest point in Montana (12,799 ft); a 345,000-acre portion of the Absaroka-Beartooth Wilderness; Grasshoper Glacier (see COOKE CITY); and 900-ft Woodbine Falls. The area is characterized by alpine plateaus, rugged peaks, and hundreds of lakes. Offers winter sports and trout fishing. Views of glaciers, lakes, fields of alpine flowers, peaks and canyons. There are no service areas or gas stations on the 64-mi (2¹/2-hr) stretch between Red Lodge and Cooke City. Beartooth Hwy is closed each winter between Red Lodge and Cooke City (closing dates depend on snow conditions) and is open approx June-Sept.

Red Lodge Mt Ski Area. Triple, 2 high-speed detachable quads, 4 double chairlifts, mitey-mite; patrol, school, rentals; snowmaking; restaurant, cafeteria, bar. Longest run 2¹/2 mi; vertical drop 2,016 ft. (Thanksgiving-Easter, daily) 6 mi W off US 212, in Custer National Forest. Phone 406/446-2610. ¢¢¢¢¢

Annual Events

Winter Carnival. Ski races, snow sculpting, entertainment. Mar.

Music Festival. Features performances by faculty members from schools throughout the country. June.

International Ski Race Camp. Summer ski racing instruction. June-July.

Top of the World Bar. 30 mi SW via US 212. Citizens of Red Lodge welcome travelers with free beverages served from bar carved from snow bank atop 11,000-ft Beartooth Pass. July.

Festival of Nations. Exhibits, nightly entertainment reflecting several European cultures. Art demonstrations and displays. Early-mid-Aug.

Motels

★ ★ **BEST WESTERN LU PINE INN.** *702 S Hauser.* 406/446-1321; FAX 406/446-1465. 46 rms, 2 story. S $62; D $72; kit. unit $4 addl; under 12 free; higher rates special events; lower rates May & Labor Day-Thanksgiving. Crib free. Pet accepted, some restrictions. TV; cable (premium). Indoor pool; whirlpool. Playground. Restaurant nearby. Ck-out noon. Coin lndry. Meeting rms. Business servs avail. Sundries. Downhill/x-country ski 6 mi. Exercise equipt; bicycles, stair machine, sauna. Game rm. Some in-rm whirlpools. Some balconies. Cr cds: A, C, D, DS, MC, V.

[D] [icons] SC

★ ★ **COMFORT INN.** *612 N Broadway.* 406/446-4469. 55 rms, 2 story. July-Aug: S, D $79; each addl $10; suites $89-$99; under 18 free; ski plans; lower rates rest of yr. Crib free. Pet accepted; $25 deposit. TV; cable, VCR avail. Complimentary continental bkfst. Ck-out 11 am. Meeting rms. Business servs avail. Downhill/x-country ski 6 mi. Indoor pool; whirlpool. Cr cds: A, D, DS, JCB, MC, V.

[D] [icons] SC

✔ ★ **SUPER 8.** *1223 S Broadway.* 406/446-2288; FAX 406/446-3162. 50 rms, 2 story. S $59.88; D $59.88-$89.88. Crib free. Pet accepted, some restrictions. TV; cable (premium). Indoor pool; whirlpool. Complimentary continental bkfst. Ck-out 11 am. Coin lndry. Meeting rm. Downhill/x-country ski 5 mi. Game rm. Some refrigerators, in-rm whirlpools; microwaves avail. Some rms with view of mountains. Cr cds: A, C, D, DS, MC, V.

[D] [icons] SC

Hotel

★ ★ **THE POLLARD.** *2 N Broadway.* 406/446-0001; FAX 406/446-0002; res: 800/765-5273. Web www.pollardhotel.com. 36 rms, 5 with shower only, 3 story, 4 suites. Mid-June-mid-Sept, mid-Dec-mid-Apr: S, D $85-$110; each addl $20; suites $170-$185; ski plan; lower rates rest of yr. Crib free. TV; cable. Complimentary full bkfst. Restaurant (see GREENLEE'S AT THE POLLARD). No rm serv. Ck-out noon. Meeting rms. Business servs avail. Concierge. Gift shop. Downhill/x-country ski 6 mi. Exercise rm; instructor, weight machines, treadmill, sauna. Whirlpool. Some in-rm whirlpools. Restored hotel built 1893. Totally nonsmoking. Cr cds: A, DS, MC, V.

[D] [icons]

Resort

★ ★ ★ **ROCK CREEK.** *HC 49 Box 3500, 5 mi S on US 212.* 406/446-1111; FAX 406/446-3688. E-mail rcresort@wtp.net. 90 rms, 2-3 story, 39 kits. A/C. S $86; D $86-$92; kit. units $98-$275. Crib free. TV; cable (premium). VCR avail. Indoor pool; whirlpool. Playground. Dining rm 7 am-2 pm. Ck-out 11 am, ck-in 3 pm. Coin lndry. Meeting rms. Business servs avail. Gift shop. Tennis. Downhill ski 11 mi. Exercise equipt; weights, stair machine. Lawn games. Some in-rm whirlpools; microwaves avail. Balconies. Cr cds: A, D, DS, MC, V.

[D] [icons]

Restaurants

★ ★ ★ **GREENLEE'S AT THE POLLARD.** *(See The Pollard Hotel)* 406/446-0001. Hrs: 7 am-1:30 pm, 6-9 pm. Res accepted. French, Amer menu. Bar. Wine cellar. Semi-a la carte: bkfst $3.50-$5.75, lunch $5.50-$7.50, dinner $12.95-$18.50. Child's meals. Specialties: rosemary shrimp, Montana ostrich, sage-smoked chicken. Own desserts. Victorian hotel dining rm; original art. Totally nonsmoking. Cr cds: A, DS, MC, V.

★ ★ **OLD PINEY DELL.** *On grounds of Rock Creek Resort.* 406/446-1196. Hrs: 5-10 pm; Sun 3-9 pm; Sun brunch 7:30 am-1 pm. Res accepted. No A/C. Continental menu. Bar. Semi-a la carte: dinner $13.50-$22. Sun brunch $12.95. Child's meals. Specializes in steak, seafood, chicken. View of Beartooth Mountains. Family-owned. Cr cds: A, D, DS, MC, V.

Sidney (B-10)

Pop 5,217 **Elev** 1,931 ft **Area code** 406 **Zip** 59270

Information Chamber of Commerce, 909 S Central; 406/482-1916.

Irrigation in Richland County produces bountiful crops of sugar beets and wheat, which are marketed at Sidney, the county seat. Oil fields, open-pit coal mining and livestock feeding contribute to the town's economy.

What to See and Do

Blue Rock Products Co-Pepsi Cola Bottling Plant. Guided tours of the mixing and bottling process of the Pepsi Cola soft drink. (Mon-Fri) 501 9th Ave NE. For res phone 406/482-3403. **Free.**

Fort Union Trading Post National Historic Site. 22 mi N via MT 200 to Fairview, N 18 mi on Williams County 58. (See WILLISTON, ND)

MonDak Heritage Center. Seventeen-unit street scene displaying historical artifacts of the area; changing art exhibits; historical and art library. (Mon-Fri, also Sat & Sun afternoons in summer; rest of yr, Tues-Sun afternoons; closed hols) 120 3rd Ave SE. Phone 406/482-3500. **Free.**

Annual Events

Peter Paddlefish Day. The sighting of Peter on his spawning run up the Yellowstone River indicates a normal run-off on the Yellowstone and a normal season. Phone 406/482-1916. Last Sat Apr.

Sunrise Festival of the Arts. Central Park. 2nd Sat July.

Richland County Fair and Rodeo. Exhibits, livestock shows, petting zoo, carnival, PRCA rodeos, country western show. Phone 406/482-2801. Early Aug.

Restaurant

★ **SOUTH 40.** *207 2nd Ave NW. 406/482-4999.* Hrs: 11 am-10:30 pm; Sun to 10 pm. Closed Dec 25. Bar 9-2 am. Res accepted. Semi-a la carte: lunch $2.45-$6.95, dinner $6.95-$25.95. Child's meals. Specializes in homemade soups, prime rib, Mexican dishes. Salad bar. Cr cds: A, C, D, MC, V.

Three Forks (D-4)

(See also Bozeman, Butte, Ennis)

Pop 1,203 **Elev** 4,080 ft **Area code** 406 **Zip** 59752

In 1805, Lewis and Clark discovered the source of the Missouri River, beginning of the world's largest river chain, at the confluence of the Jefferson, Madison and Gallatin rivers here. Native Americans resisted settlement of the valley, a favorite bison hunting ground, but before long it became a trading post headquarters for hunters and trappers.

What to See and Do

Lewis and Clark Caverns State Park. Underground wonderland of colorful rock formations; 3/4-mi lighted path; 55°F. Two-hr (2-mi) guided tour (May-Sept, daily) Picnicking. Camping (no hookups, dump station). Visitor center. Standard fees. 19 mi W on MT 2, milepost 271. Phone 406/287-3541. Tour ¢¢¢

Madison Buffalo Jump State Monument. Native American hunting technique of herding charging buffalo over cliffs is illustrated. Hiking. Picnicking. Day use only. E on I-90, then 7 mi S on Buffalo Jump Rd. ¢¢

Missouri River Headwaters State Park. Where Lewis and Clark discovered the source of the Missouri. Fishing; boating (ramp). Picnicking. Camping (no hookups, dump station). Standard fees. 3 mi E on I-90, then E on MT Secondary 205, then 3 mi N on MT Secondary 286. Phone 406/994-4042.

Motel

✔★ **FORT THREE FORKS.** *10776 US 287, I-90 exit 274. 406/285-3233; FAX 406/285-3787; res: 800/477-5690.* 24 rms, 2 story. June-Sept: S $38; D $48-$52; each addl $4; suites $75; under 12 free; lower rates rest of yr. Crib $5. Pet accepted; $5. TV; cable. Complimentary continental bkfst. Restaurant adj 6 am-8 pm. Ck-out 11 am. Coin lndry. Meeting rm. Business servs avail. Cr cds: A, C, D, DS, MC, V.

Inn

★ ★ **SACAJAWEA.** *5 N Main St, 5 N Main St. 406/285-6515; FAX 406/285-4210; res: 800/821-7326.* 33 rms, 3 story. June-Sept: S $69; D $69-$99; each addl $10; under 12 free; wkly rates; fishing plan; lower rates rest of yr. Crib free. Pet accepted; $5. TV; cable. Restaurant (see SACAJAWEA INN). Rm serv. Ck-out 11 am, ck-in 3 pm. Meeting rm. Business servs avail. Restored grand old railroad hotel (1910). Cr cds: A, DS, MC, V.

Restaurant

★ ★ **SACAJAWEA INN.** *(See Sacajawea Inn) 406/285-6515.* Hrs: 5-9 pm; Sun brunch 9 am-2 pm. Closed Dec 25. Res accepted. Continental menu. Semi-a la carte: dinner $11.95-$17.25. Sun brunch $4.50-$14. Child's meals. Specializes in prime rib, Montana beef, pasta. Outdoor dining. Totally nonsmoking. Cr cds: A, DS, MC, V.

Virginia City (E-4)

(For accommodations see Ennis)

Settled 1863 **Pop** 142 **Elev** 5,822 ft **Area code** 406 **Zip** 59755

Information Bovey Restoration, PO Box 338, phone 406/843-5377 or 800/648-7588; Chamber of Commerce, phone 800/829-2969.

On May 26, 1863, gold was found in Alder Gulch. The old days of the rough 'n' tough West are rekindled in this restored gold boomtown, once the capital of the territory. Alder Gulch (Virginia and Nevada cities) sprouted when six men who had escaped from Native Americans discovered history's richest placer deposit. Ten thousand gold miners arrived within a month, followed by bands of desperadoes; 190 murders were committed in seven months. Vigilantes hunted down 21 road agents and discovered that the sheriff was the leader of the criminals. Nearly $300 million in gold was washed from Alder Gulch, but the area faded as the diggings became less productive and Nevada City became a ghost town. In 1946 a restoration program began, which has brought back much of the early mining-town atmosphere.

What to See and Do

Boot Hill. Graves of five criminals hanged by the vigilantes.

Restored buildings include the offices of the Montana *Post,* first newspaper in the state; the Gilbert Brewery, dressmaker's shop, Wells Fargo Express office, livery stable, barbershop, blacksmith shop, general store, many others. Phone 406/843-5377 or 800/648-7588. Includes

Gilbert's Brewery. Virginia City's first brewery was built in 1864. The main building has been restored and original brewery is still inside. Musical variety shows (mid-June-mid-Sept, nightly exc Tues). E Cover St. Phone 406/843-5377. ¢¢¢

Nevada City Depot. Houses steam railroad museum (fee) of early-day engines and cars. Train ride to Virginia City. (Early June-Labor Day, daily; fee)

Nevada City. Authentic buildings including early mining camp stores, homes, school, offices. Music Hall has large collection of mechanical musical machines. (Memorial Day-mid-Sept, daily) 1 1/2 mi W on MT 287. **Free.**

Robbers' Roost. Old-time stage station often used by outlaws. 15 mi W on MT 287.

St Paul's Episcopal Church (Elling Memorial) (1902). Built on site of 1867 building; oldest Protestant congregation in state. Tiffany windows. Idaho St.

Thompson-Hickman Memorial Museum. Relics of the gold camps. (May-Sept, daily) Wallace St. **Donation.**

Virginia City-Madison County Historical Museum. Traces western Montana history. (Early June-Labor Day, daily) Wallace St. ¢¢

Seasonal Event

Classic melodramas. In Old Opera House, foot of Wallace St. Virginia City Players present 19th-century entertainment. Tues-Sun. Res required. Phone 406/843-5377. Early June-Labor Day.

West Yellowstone (E-5)

Pop 913 **Elev** 6,666 ft **Area code** 406 **Zip** 59758 **E-mail** wycc @wyellowstone.com

Information Chamber of Commerce, 30 Yellowstone Ave, PO Box 458; 406/646-7701.

At the west entrance to Yellowstone National Park (see WYOMING), this town serves as a hub for incoming tourists. Not too long ago, West Yellowstone was abandoned and snowbound in the winter; today winter sports and attractions allow the town to serve visitors all year. A Ranger District office of the Gallatin National Forest (see BOZEMAN) is located here.

What to See and Do

Interagency Aerial Fire Control Center. A US Forest Service facility. Guided tour by smokejumpers who explain firefighting techniques. (Late June-Labor Day, daily) 2 mi N on US 191. Phone 406/646-7691. **Free.**

Madison River Canyon Earthquake Area. Includes Quake Lake, formed by earthquake of Aug 17, 1959. This area, with its slides and faults, is a graphic demonstration of earthquake damage. Camping (mid-June-mid-Sept; Beaver Creek Campground, fee/night). Visitor Center (on US 287, 22 mi W of US 191) with talks, exhibits; list of self-guided tours (Memorial Day-Labor Day, daily). Road through area (all yr) 8 mi N on US 191, then 3 mi W on US 287, in Gallatin National Forest (see BOZEMAN). For details inquire at the Chamber of Commerce or at the US Forest Service Office on US 191/287 N of town; or contact PO Box 520, phone 406/646-7369. **Free.**

National Geographic Theatre. Six-story-high screen shows "Yellowstone," a film interpreting the history, wildlife, geothermal activity and grandeur of America's first national park. Exhibits include wildlife photography, props used in film, and "Effects of the Yellowstone Hot Spot." (Daily, shows hourly) 101 S Canyon St. Phone 406/646-4100. ¢¢¢

Sightseeing tours.

Buffalo Bus Lines. Phone 406/646-9564 or 800/426-7669.

Gray Line bus tours. For information phone 800/523-3102.

Amfac Parks & Resorts, Inc offers guided snowcoach tours and cross-country ski trips through Yellowstone National Park (see WYOMING) departing from West Yellowstone and other locations surrounding the park (mid-Dec-early Mar). Summer season offers full-day bus tours, boat tours and horseback rides in the park (June-Aug). Res recommended. Phone 307/344-7311.

Annual Events

Great American Ski Chase. Mar.

World Snowmobile Expo. 3rd wkend Mar.

Seasonal Event

Playmill Theater. 29 Madison Ave. Musical comedies and melodramas. Daily exc Sun. Phone 406/646-7757. Memorial Day-Labor Day.

Motels

★ ★ **COMFORT INN.** *638 Madison Ave. 406/646-4212.* 78 rms, 3 story, 7 suites. June-Sept: S, D $129; each addl $8; suites $169; under 18 free; lower rates rest of yr. Crib avail. TV; cable (premium). Complimentary continental bkfst. Ck-out 10 am. Meeting rms. Business servs avail. Bellhops. Sundries. Coin lndry. Exercise equipt; bicycle, stair machine. Indoor pool; whirlpool. Microwave, wet bar in suites. Cr cds: A, C, D, DS, MC, V.

D ≈ ✗ ⊠ 🔥 SC

★ **DAYS INN.** *118 Electric St. 406/646-7656; FAX 406/646-7965.* 45 rms, 2 story. June-Oct, Dec-mid-Mar: S, D $89; each addl $5; suites $152; kit. unit $152; under 13 free; lower rates rest of yr. Crib free. TV; cable (premium). Indoor pool; whirlpool. Complimentary continental bkfst. Restaurant adj 7 am-10 pm. Ck-out 11 am. Business servs avail. Sauna. Some refrigerators. Cr cds: A, D, DS, MC, V.

≈ ⊠ 🔥 SC

★ ★ **HAMPTON INN & SUITES.** *250 S Canyon St. 406/646-0000; FAX 406/646-9260.* 102 rms, 3 story, 16 suites. June-Sept: S, D $129; each addl $10; suites $190; under 18 free; higher rates special events; lower rates rest of yr. Crib free. TV; cable (premium). VCR avail. Complimentary continental bkfst. Complimentary coffee in rms. Restaurant nearby. Ck-out 11 am. Meeting rm. Business servs avail. Bellhops. Sundries. Coin lndry. Free garage parking. X-country ski 3 blks. Indoor pool; whirlpool, sauna. Refrigerator, microwave, wet bar in suites. Cr cds: A, C, D, DS, MC, V.

D ≈ ≈ ⊠ 🔥 SC

★ ★ **KELLY INN.** *104 S Canyon St. 406/646-4544; res: 800/259-4672; FAX 406/646-9838.* 78 rms, 3 story. June-Sept: S, D $105-$120; each addl $8; under 12 free; lower rates rest of yr. Crib free. Pet accepted. TV; cable. Complimentary continental bkfst. Restaurant nearby. Ck-out 11 am. Business servs avail. Coin lndry. X-country ski 3 blks. Indoor pool; whirlpool. Many refrigerators, microwaves. Cr cds: A, D, DS, MC, V.

D ✦ ≈ ⊠ 🔥 SC

★ **STAGE COACH INN.** *209 Madison Ave, at Dunraven Ave. 406/646-7381; FAX 406/646-9575; res: 800/842-2882.* 80 rms, 1-2 story. Early June-mid-Sept: S $115; D $115-$121; each addl $6; under 12 free; lower rates rest of yr. Crib free. TV; cable. Restaurant 6:30 am-10 pm. Bar noon-1 am; entertainment Tues-Sat (in season). Ck-out 11 am. Coin lndry. Meeting rms. Gift shop. X-country ski 1/4 mi. Sauna. Whirlpools. Snowmobiling. Cr cds: A, C, D, DS, MC, V.

D ≈ ⊠ 🔥 SC

★ **SUPER 8.** *1545 Targhee Pass Hwy, approx 7 mi S on US 20. 406/646-9584; FAX 406/646-7404.* 44 rms, 2 story. Memorial Day-Labor Day: S, D $77; each addl $5; under 13 free; lower rates rest of yr. Crib $5. TV; cable (premium). Playground. Restaurant 7-11 am, 5-9:30 pm. Ck-out 11 am. Coin lndry. Sauna. Whirlpool. Cr cds: A, C, D, DS, MC, V.

D ⚡ ⊠ 🔥 SC

Motor Hotel

★ ★ **HOLIDAY INN.** *315 Yellowstone Ave, 3 blks W of park entrance. 406/646-7365; FAX 406/646-4433.* E-mail wyconference-hotel@wyellowstone.com. 123 rms, 3 story. Mid-June-Sept: S, D $129-$200; each addl $8; under 12 free; lower rates rest of yr. Crib free. TV; cable. Indoor pool; whirlpool. Complimentary coffee in rms. Restaurant 6:30 am-10 pm. Bar 11-2 am. Ck-out 11 am. Coin lndry. Meeting rms. Business servs avail. Bellhops. Valet serv. Gift shop. Exercise equipt; treadmill, rowers, sauna. Refrigerators, microwaves; some in-rm whirlpools. Cr cds: A, C, D, DS, MC, V.

D ≈ ✗ ⊠ 🔥 SC

Restaurant

✔★ ★ **THREE BEAR.** *205 Yellowstone. 406/646-7811.* Hrs: 7-11 am, 5-10 pm. Closed Dec 25; mid-Mar-early-May, mid-Oct-mid-Dec. No A/C. Bar 4 pm-midnight. Semi-a la carte: bkfst $2.95-$8.75, dinner $9.25-$18. Child's meals. Specializes in seafood, hand-cut steaks, pasta. Family-owned. Totally nonsmoking. Cr cds: D, DS, MC, V.

D

Whitefish (A-2)

(See also Columbia Falls, Kalispell)

Pop 4,368 **Elev** 3,036 ft **Area code** 406 **Zip** 59937
Information Chamber of Commerce, PO Box 1120; 406/862-3501.

On the shore of Whitefish Lake, this community prospers from tourism and railroading. The town is headquarters for a four-state summer vacation area and is a winter ski center. A growing forest products industry and the railroad constitute the other side of Whitefish's economy. A Ranger District office of the Flathead National Forest (see KALISPELL) is located here.

What to See and Do

Big Mt Ski & Summer Resort. Double, 4 triple, 2 quad chairlifts, T-bar, platter lift, patrol; school, rentals; hotels, restaurants, bars, cafeteria, concession area; sleigh rides; nursery. Longest run 2½ mi; vertical drop 2,100 ft. (Thanksgiving-mid-Apr, daily) Cross-country trails. Gondola (also operates in summer) provides views of Rockies, Flathead Valley; travels 6,800 ft to summit of Big Mt. Summer activites (mid-May-early Oct): gondola rides overlooking Glacier National Park (see), horseback riding, hiking, mountain biking, tennis; outdoor theater, events. 8 mi N on County 487 in Flathead National Forest (see KALISPELL); shuttle bus trips daily in winter. Phone 800/858-5439. Winter ¢¢¢¢; Summer ¢¢¢

Hungry Horse Dam and Power Plant One of world's largest concrete dams (564 ft), set in a wooded canyon near Glacier National Park. The 2,115-ft-long crest is crossed by a 30-ft-wide roadway. The reservoir is approximately 34 mi long and 3½ mi at its widest point. Self-guided tours, pictorial and interactive displays; video (mid-May-late Sept, daily). Several recreation and camping sites of the Flathead National Forest (see KALISPELL) are on the reservoir. 13 mi SE via US 93, MT 40, US 2 to Hungry Horse, then 4 mi SE on unnumbered road. **Free.**

✪ **Whitefish Lake.** Seven mi long, two mi wide. Studded with resorts, particularly on E shore; swimming, waterskiing; fishing; sailing; picnicking. On lake is

Whitefish State Park. Swimming; fishing; boating (ramp). Picnicking. Camping (no hookups). Standard fees. ½ mi W on US 93, milepost 129, then 1 mi N. Phone 406/862-3991 (summer) or 406/752-5501.

Annual Event

Winter Carnival. 1st wkend Feb.

Motels

★ ★ **BEST WESTERN ROCKY MOUNTAIN LODGE.** *6510 US 93S. 406/862-2569; FAX 406/862-1154.* E-mail bwrml@fcva.org; web www.fcva.org/rckymtn. 79 rms, 3 story. July-Aug: S $109; D $109-$119; each addl $10; suites $149; under 12 free; ski, golf plans; lower rates rest of yr. Crib free. TV; cable. Heated pool; whirlpool. Complimentary continental bkfst. Restaurant nearby. Ck-out 11 am. Coin lndry. Meeting rms. Downhill ski 8 mi; x-country ski 1 mi. Exercise equipt; weight machine, bicycles. Some in-rm whirlpools, fireplaces; microwaves avail. Cr cds: A, D, DS, ER, JCB, MC, V.

D ⊠ ≈ 🎿 🏌 🐾 SC

★ ★ **QUALITY INN PINE LODGE.** *920 Spokane Ave. 406/862-7600; FAX 406/862-7616.* 76 rms, 4 story, 25 suites. June-Sept: S $80-$100; D $80-$110; suites $125-$195; under 18 free; ski plan; lower rates rest of yr. Crib $5. Pet accepted, some restrictions. TV; cable. Indoor pool; whirlpool. Complimentary continental bkfst. Ck-out 11 am. Coin lndry. Meeting rms. Business servs avail. Valet serv. Free airport transportation. Exercise equipt; weights, bicycles. Game rm. Refrigerators, microwaves in suites. Cr cds: A, C, D, DS, JCB, MC, V.

D 🐾 ≈ 🎿 🏌 🐾 SC

★ **SUPER 8.** *800 Spokane Ave. 406/862-8255.* 40 rms, 3 story. No elvtr. July-Aug: S, D $74.88-$79.88; each addl $5; lower rates rest of yr. Crib free. Pet accepted, some restrictions; $5. TV; cable (premium). Complimentary coffee in lobby. Ck-out 11 am. Free RR transportation. Whirlpool. Grill. Cr cds: A, D, DS, MC, V.

D 🐾 ≈ 🐾 SC

Lodge

★ ★ **KANDAHAR.** *8 mi N on Big Mountain Rd, at Big Mountain Village. 406/862-6098; FAX 406/862-6095; res: 800/862-6094.* E-mail kandahar@vtown.com; web www.vtown.com/kandahar. 48 rms, 3 story, 16 kit. units. No A/C. No elvtr. Mid-Nov-mid-Apr: S $127; D $139; each addl $10; kit. $151-$185; under 12 free; higher rates wk of Dec 25, last 2 wks of Feb; lower rates rest of yr. Crib free. TV; cable. Restaurant 7 am-9:30 pm. Bar 4 pm-midnight. Ck-out 11 am. Coin lndry. Meeting rms. Business servs avail. Downhill/x-country ski on site. Sauna. Massage. Whirlpool. Microwaves avail. European-style alpine ski lodge. Cr cds: A, DS, MC, V.

🎿 ≈ 🐾 SC

Inn

★ ★ **GOOD MEDICINE LODGE.** *537 Wisconsin Ave. 406/862-5488; FAX 406/862-5489; res: 800/860-5488.* E-mail goodrx@digisys.net; web www.wtp.net/go/goodrx. 9 rms, 2 with shower only, 2 story. Some A/C. Mid-May-mid-Oct: S $85; D $95-$105; each addl $30; suites $125-$190; under 11 free; ski plan; lower rates mid-Dec-mid-Apr. Closed rest of yr. Complimentary full bkfst. Restaurant nearby. Ck-out 11 am, ck-in 3 pm. Lawn games. Some balconies. Rustic mountain decor. Totally nonsmoking. Cr cds: A, DS, MC, V.

D ≈ 🐾 SC

Resort

★ ★ **GROUSE MOUNTAIN LODGE.** *2 Fairway Dr, on Whitefish Lake Golf Course. 406/862-3000; FAX 406/862-0326; res: 800/321-8822.* E-mail gmlodge@digisys.net. 144 rms, 3 story, 10 kits. June-Sept: S, D $125; each addl $10; suites $155; kit. units $185; under 12 free; ski, golf, rafting plans; lower rates rest of yr. Crib free. TV; cable (premium). Indoor pool; whirlpools. Dining rm 7 am-2 pm, 5-10 pm. Box lunches. Rm serv. Bar 11-2 am; entertainment Tues-Sat. Ck-out 11 am, ck-in 4 pm. Grocery 1 mi. Coin lndry. Package store ½ mi. Meeting rms. Business servs avail. Bellhops. Airport, RR station, ski area transportation. Tennis. 36-hole golf, greens fee $38, pro, putting green, driving range. Downhill ski 8 mi; x-country ski adj. Sauna. Game rm. Some refrigerators, in-rm whirlpools. Some balconies. Rustic, elegant lodge. Cr cds: A, D, DS, MC, V.

D 🐾 🛗 🐾 🏌 ≈ 🐾 SC

Restaurant

★ ★ **FENDERS.** *US 93S, 7 mi S. 406/752-3000.* Hrs: 11 am-3 pm, 5-10 pm. Res accepted. Bar. Semi-a la carte: lunch $4.95-$7.95, dinner $9.95-$19.95. Child's meals. Specializes in prime rib, seafood. Many collectibles, old cars. Totally nonsmoking. Cr cds: A, MC, V.

White Sulphur Springs (C-5)

(For accommodations see Bozeman, Helena)

Pop 963 **Elev** 5,100 ft **Area code** 406 **Zip** 59645

Mineral springs as well as fine hunting and fishing make this a popular summer and fall resort town. It lies in a mile-high valley ringed by mountains—the Castles, Crazies and Big and Little Belts. Agates may still be found in the area. A Ranger District office of the Lewis and Clark National Forest (see GREAT FALLS) is located here.

What to See and Do

Showdown Ski Area. 2 chairlifts, Pomalift, free beginners tow; patrol, school, rentals; cafeteria, bar; day care. Longest run 2 mi; vertical drop 1,400 ft. (Late Nov-mid-Apr, Wed-Sun) 29 mi N on US 89, in Lewis & Clark National Forest. Phone 406/236-5522. ¢¢¢¢

Wolf Point (B-9)

Pop 2,880 **Elev** 1,997 ft **Area code** 406 **Zip** 59201

Information Chamber of Commerce & Agriculture, 201 4th St S, PO Box 237; 406/653-2012.

During the winters of the 1870s, trappers poisoned wolves and hauled the frozen carcasses to this point on the Missouri River for spring shipment to St Louis. Wolf Point is the seat of Roosevelt County and a trading point for oil, wheat and cattle. Hunting for antelope, deer and sharp-tailed and sage grouse is popular here.

Annual Events

Wild Horse Stampede. One of Montana's best and oldest rodeos. Contact Chamber of Commerce & Agriculture for information. 2nd wkend July.

Wadopana Powwow. Phone 406/653-3742. 1st wkend Aug.

Nebraska

Population: 1,578,385
Land area: 77,355 square miles
Elevation: 840-5,426 feet
Highest point: Near Bushnell (Kimball County)
Entered Union: March 1, 1867 (37th state)
Capital: Lincoln
Motto: Equality before the law
Nickname: Cornhusker State
State flower: Goldenrod
State bird: Western meadowlark
State tree: Cottonwood
State fair: August 28-September 7, 1998, in Lincoln
Time zone: Central and Mountain
Web: www.ded.state.ne.us/tourism.html

In little more than a century, Nebraska—part of what was once called the "great American desert"—has grown from Native American-fighting, buffalo-slaughtering prairie to a farming, ranching and manufacturing mainstay of America, with an ample variety of recreational and cultural opportunities.

Spaniards visited the region first, but it was on the basis of explorations by Father Marquette and Louis Jolliet in 1673 that French voyageurs, fur traders and missionaries swept over the land and France claimed it. Nevertheless, it was recognized as Spanish land until 1800, when it became a plaything of European politics and was sold by Napoleon to the United States as part of the Louisiana Purchase in 1803. Famous pathfinders like John C. Frémont, Kit Carson and the men who trapped for John Jacob Astor thought it a land unfit for cultivation.

Nebraska was the path for many westward-bound travelers. Native Americans, fur trappers and explorers, pioneers, the Pony Express, the Mormon and Oregon trails, the Overland Freight Company and the railroads all made their way through the state, following the natural path of the Platte River. In 1854, Nebraska became a US territory along with Kansas. Febold Feboldson, the Paul Bunyan of the Great Plains, is said to be responsible for the perfectly straight southern boundary line with Kansas. According to the legend, he bred bees with eagles for 15 years, until he had an eagle-sized bee. He then hitched the critter to a plow and made a beeline between the two states.

Within 13 years after being named a territory, statehood was approved by Congress; the town of Lincoln won the fight for the state capital over Omaha, and the Homestead Act opened the way for settlement. The Pawnee were often friendly with settlers, but were devastated by the smallpox, cholera and tuberculosis the settlers brought with them. Wars with the Native Americans ended by 1890; by then the land was teeming with farms and ranches, railroads were creating new towns for repairs and supplies and the twin aids of irrigation and better stock pushed up farm profits.

Farming is big business in southern and eastern Nebraska. With continually improving crop returns, Nebraska has few equals in total output of farm production. It is a leading producer of wild hay, beans, grain sorghum, sugar beets, wheat, soybeans, rye, corn and alfalfa. Good grazing land can be found in the north central and northwest parts of the state. America's largest formation of stabilized sand dunes is located in the Sandhills, heart of Nebraska's nearly $5-billion cattle industry. Real cowboy country, the ranches of the Sandhills have given starts to many professional rodeo stars.

The fine highway system makes it a pleasure to drive in the state. Several villages and towns settled by Old World immigrants still celebrate their ethnic heritage in folk festivals each year. Native Americans on the Santee, Winnebago and Omaha reservations also keep their customs at annual powwows. Besides pioneer and Native American history, Nebraska offers a wealth of state parks and recreation areas. The angler has many well-stocked fishing streams and lakes from which to choose. For hunters, game birds, waterfowl and deer are abundant, and seasons are long.

When to Go/Climate

Nebraska experiences the typically extreme temperatures of the Plains states. Winters are icy cold, summers stifling hot. The state is dry and prone to droughts; tornadoes are a summer reality. Fall and spring are good times to visit.

AVERAGE HIGH/LOW TEMPERATURES (°F)

OMAHA

Jan 30/11	**May** 73/52	**Sept** 75/55
Feb 35/17	**June** 82/61	**Oct** 64/43
Mar 48/28	**July** 87/67	**Nov** 48/30
Apr 62/40	**Aug** 84/64	**Dec** 33/16

SCOTTSBLUFF

Jan 38/12	**May** 71/42	**Sept** 77/46
Feb 44/17	**June** 82/53	**Oct** 66/34
Mar 50/22	**July** 90/59	**Nov** 50/22
Apr 61/32	**Aug** 87/56	**Dec** 40/13

CALENDAR HIGHLIGHTS

MAY

Willa Cather Spring Conference (Hastings). Willa Cather State Historic Site. Features a different Cather novel each year. Discussion groups, banquet, entertainment. Tour of "Cather Country." Phone 402/746-2653.

JUNE

NCAA College Baseball World Series (Omaha). Rosenblatt Stadium. Phone 402/444-4750.

Cottonwood Prairie Festival (Hastings). Brickyard Park. Music, crafts, foods. Phone 800/967-2189.

"NEBRASKAland DAYS" Celebration (North Platte). Parades, entertainment, food and the famous PRCA Rodeo. Phone 308/532-7948.

JULY

Oregon Trail Days (Gering). Parades, chili cook-off, contests, square dancing, barbecue, music festival. Phone Scottsbluff-Gering United Chamber of Commerce, 308/632-2133.

Central Nebraska Ethnic Festival (Grand Island). Music, dance, ethnic meals, dramatic presentations. Phone 308/385-5455, ext 230.

July Jamm 98 (Lincoln). Art show, music festival. Phone 402/434-6900.

AUGUST

Nebraska State Fair (Lincoln). State Fair Park. Phone 402/474-5371.

SEPTEMBER

River City Round-up (Omaha). Fairgrounds. Celebration of agriculture and western heritage includes parade, barbecues, trail rides. Phone 402/554-9610.

DECEMBER

The Light of the World **Christmas Pageant** (Minden). Kearney County Courthouse, Town Square. A town tradition for many years; highlight of outdoor pageant is illumination of courthouse dome by 10,000 lights. Phone the Chamber of Commerce, 308/832-1811.

Parks and Recreation Finder

Directions to and information about the parks and recreation areas below are given under their respective town/city sections. Please refer to those sections for details.

Key to abbreviations: I.P. = Interstate Park; N.B.C. = National Battlefield & Cemetery; N.B.P. = National Battlefield Park; N.F. = National Forest; N.G. = National Grassland; N.H. = National Historical Park; N.H.S. = National Historic Site; N.M. = National Monument; N.Mem. = National Memorial; N.M.P. = National Military Park; N.P. = National Park; N.Pres. = National Preserve; N.R. = National Recreational Area; N.R.R. = National Recreational River; N.Res. = National Reserve; N.S. = National Seashore; N.S.R. = National Scenic River; N.S.T. = National Scenic Trail; N.V.M. = National Volcanic Monument; S.B. = State Beach; S.C.P. = State Conservation Park; S.G. = State Garden; S.H.A. = State Historic Area; S.H.P. = State Historic Park; S.N.A. = State Natural Area; S.P. = State Park; S.R. = State Reserve; S.R.A. = State Recreation Area; S.Res.P. = State Resort Park; S.R.P. = State Rustic Park.

NATIONAL PARK AND RECREATION AREAS

Place Name	Listed Under
Agate Fossil Beds N.M.	SCOTTSBLUFF
Chimney Rock N.H.S.	same
Homestead N.M.	same
Nebraska N.F.	CHADRON, THEDFORD, VALENTINE
Oglala N.G.	CRAWFORD
Scotts Bluff N.M.	same

STATE RECREATION AREAS

Place Name	Listed Under
Alexandria Lakes S.R.A.	FAIRBURY
Arnold Lake S.R.A.	NORTH PLATTE
Atkinson Lake S.R.A.	O'NEILL
Bluestem Lake S.R.A.	LINCOLN
Branced Oak Lake S.R.A.	LINCOLN
Bridgeport S.R.A.	BRIDGEPORT
Brownville S.R.A.	AUBURN
Chadron S.P.	CHADRON
Conestoga Lake S.R.A.	LINCOLN
Crystal Lake S.R.A.	HASTINGS
Eugene T. Mahoney S.P.	LINCOLN
Fort Kearny S.H.P.	KEARNEY
Fort Robinson S.P.	CRAWFORD
Fremont S.R.A.	FREMONT
Gallagher Canyon S.R.A.	COZAD
Indian Cave S.P.	AUBURN
Johnson Lake S.R.A.	LEXINGTON
Lake Maloney S.R.A.	NORTH PLATTE
Lake McConaughy S.R.A.	OGALLALA
Lake Minatare S.R.A.	SCOTTSBLUFF
Lake Ogallala S.R.A.	OGALLALA
Lewis and Clark Lake S.R.A.	CROFTON
Louisville S.R.A.	OMAHA
Medicine Creek Reservoir S.R.A.	McCOOK
Merritt Reservoir S.R.A.	VALENTINE
Mormon Island S.R.A.	GRAND ISLAND
Pawnee Lake S.R.A.	LINCOLN
Pibel Lake S.R.A.	O'NEILL
Platte River S.P.	OMAHA
Ponca S.P.	SOUTH SIOUX CITY
Red Willow Reservoir S.R.A.	McCOOK
Rock Creek Station S.H.P.	FAIRBURY
Schramm Park S.R.A.	OMAHA
Swanson Reservoir S.R.A.	McCOOK
Two Rivers S.R.A.	OMAHA
Verdon Lake S.R.A.	AUBURN
Victoria Springs S.R.A.	BROKEN BOW
Walgren Lake S.R.A.	CHADRON
Wildcat Hills S.R.A.	SCOTTSBLUFF

Water-related activities, hiking, riding, various other sports, picnicking and visitor centers, as well as camping, are available in many of these areas. The state maintains 87 areas, including state parks, recreation areas and historical parks; park-user permit required ($2.50/day, $14/yr). Seven areas have cabins ($30-$210/night). Camping ($3-$13/site/night, plus $3 for electricity, at some parks), 14-day limit at most sites. Some facilities are open May-Sept only. Pets on leash only; health certificate required for pets of out-of-state owners. All mechanically powered boats must be registered. Cross-country skiing is a popular winter sport in the larger state parks. For detailed information contact Game and Parks Commission, Division of State Parks, PO Box 30370, Lincoln 68503; 402/471-0641.

FISHING & HUNTING

Nonresident fishing permit: annual $35; 3-day $10.75; aquatic habitat stamp for all fishing permits $5. Nonresident small game hunting permit:

$55; deer permit, $150; antelope permit, $112; wild turkey $56; habitat stamp for game birds and animals and fur-bearing animals $10.

Nebraska has 11,000 miles of streams and more than 3,300 lakes with trout, northern pike, walleye, sauger, white bass, striped bass, large and small mouth bass, catfish, bluegill and crappie. Pheasant, quail, prairie chicken, wild turkey, sharp-tailed grouse, cottontail rabbits, squirrel, ducks, geese, antelope and deer are available here also.

For details, write the Game and Parks Commission, PO Box 30370, Lincoln 68503-0370; 402/471-0641.

Driving Information

Safety belts are mandatory for all persons in the front seat of any 1973 or newer vehicle. Children under 5 years must be in an approved passenger restraint anywhere in vehicle: ages 4-5 may use a regulation safety belt; under age 4 must use an approved safety seat. For further information phone 402/471-2515.

INTERSTATE HIGHWAY SYSTEM

The following alphabetical listing of Nebraska towns in *Mobil Travel Guide* shows that these cities are within 10 miles of the indicated Interstate highways. A highway map, however, should be checked for the nearest exit.

Highway Number	Cities/Towns within 10 miles
Interstate 80	Cozad, Gothenburg, Grand Island, Kearney, Kimball, Lexington, Lincoln, North Platte, Ogallala, Omaha, Sidney, York.

Additional Visitor Information

The Department of Economic Development, Travel and Tourism Division, PO Box 94666, 700 S 16th, Lincoln 68509, phone 800/228-4307, supplies visitor information about the state; events, parks, hiking, biking, camping, and boating are some of the topics featured. *NEBRASKAland,* published monthly, is available from the Game and Parks Commission, PO Box 30370, Lincoln 68503.

To aid the traveler, visitor centers are located at Melia Hill, off I-80 between Omaha & Lincoln (daily) and at the Nebraska/Omaha Travel Information Center at 10th St & Deer Park Blvd (intersection of I-80 and 13th St) in Omaha (May-Oct, daily). There are also 25 information centers at rest areas along I-80 (June-Aug).

Auburn (E-10)

(See also Nebraska City)

Pop 3,443 **Elev** 994 ft **Area code** 402 **Zip** 68305 **Web** www.ci.auburnne.us/

Information Chamber of Commerce, 1211 J St; 402/274-3521.

What to See and Do

Brownville State Recreation Area. Approx 20 acres. Fishing; boat ramps. Picnicking. Camping. Entry permit required. In Brownville. Phone 402/883-2575. Per vehicle ¢¢

Brownville. Restored riverboat town of the 1800s. 9 mi E on US 136. Over 30 buildings, many of which are open to the public, include

Captain Bailey Museum. (June-Aug, daily; May, Sept-Oct, wkends only) ¢

Land Office. Reproduction of the land office where Daniel Freeman filed for the first homestead in the US; houses Tourist Center and Brownville Historical Society Headquarters. **Free.**

Village Theater. Nebraska's oldest repertory theater; plays produced by Nebraska Wesleyan University in converted church; eight wks beginning last Sat June. Phone 402/825-4121. ¢¢¢

Carson House. Original 1864-1872 furnishings. (Memorial Day-Labor Day, daily; Apr, May, Sept & Oct, wkends) ¢

Depot (museum). (May-Aug, daily) **Free.**

Old Dental Office. (May-Aug, daily) **Free.**

Agriculture Museum. (May-Aug, daily) **Free.**

Schoolhouse Art Gallery. (May-Sept, Sat & Sun) **Free.**

Spirit of Brownville. Cruises (2 hrs) on Missouri River. (July-mid-Aug, Thurs-Sun) Departs from Brownville State Recreation Area. Phone 402/825-6441 or 402/292-2628. Afternoon cruise ¢¢¢

Missouri River History Museum. Contains exhibits on river history. (May-mid-Sept, daily) Aboard the *Captain Meriwether Lewis,* former Corps of Engineers dredge, which has been dry-docked and restored. Phone 402/825-3341. ¢

Indian Cave State Park. On approx 3,400 acres, including oak-covered Missouri River bluffs and the old St Deroin townsite, which has been partially reconstructed; living history demonstrations. Fishing. Hiking trails (20 mi), horseback riding. Cross-country skiing, sledding. Picnicking. Primitive and improved camping (fee, dump station). Also here are ancient petroglyphs in Indian Cave; scenic overlooks of the river. Redbud trees bloom in profusion during spring. 9 mi E on US 136, then 14 mi S on NE 67 then E on NE 64. Phone 402/883-2575. Per vehicle ¢¢

Nemaha Valley Museum. Exhibits trace history of Nemaha County; period rms; farm equipment. (Tues-Sat afternoons) 1423 19th St. Phone 402/274-3203. **Free.**

Verdon Lake State Recreation Area. Approx 30 acres on 33-acre lake. Fishing. Picnicking. Camping. Entry permit required. 17 mi S via US 73, 75, then E on US 73. Phone 402/883-2575. Per vehicle ¢¢

Annual Events

Spring Festival with Antique Flea Market. Brownville. Phone 402/825-6001. Memorial Day wkend.

Tour of Homes. Brownville. Phone 402/825-6001. June, Nov-Dec.

Nemaha County Fair. Auburn fairgrounds. Early Aug.

Motels

★ **AUBURN INN.** *517 J St, on US 75/73N. 402/274-3143; FAX 402/274-4404; res: 800/272-3143.* 36 rms. S $32; D $38-$45; each addl $5. Pet accepted, some restrictions. TV; cable (premium). Coffee in rms. Restaurant opp 6 am-10 pm. Ck-out 11 am. Refrigerators, microwaves. Cr cds: A, C, D, DS, MC, V.

✔★ **PALMER HOUSE.** *1918 J St, on US 75/73N. 402/274-3193; FAX 402/274-4165; res: 800/272-3193.* 22 rms, 8 suites. S $30; D $42; each addl $3; suites from $49. TV; cable (premium). Complimentary coffee in lobby. Restaurant nearby. Ck-out 11 am. Refrigerators. Cr cds: A, C, D, DS, MC, V.

Restaurant

✔★ **WHEELER INN.** *US 75. 402/274-4931.* Hrs: 5-10 pm. Closed most major hols. Res accepted. Bar to 1 am. A la carte entrees: dinner $6-$34.50. Specializes in prime rib, fried chicken, scampi. Salad bar. Casual country atmosphere. Cr cds: D, DS, MC, V.

Beatrice (E-9)

(See also Fairbury, Lincoln)

Founded 1857 **Pop** 12,354 **Elev** 1,284 ft **Area code** 402 **Zip** 68310
E-mail lsmith@beatrice-ne.com **Web** www.beatrice-ne.com
Information Chamber of Commerce, 226 S 6th St; 402/223-2338 or 800/755-7745.

Beatrice (be-AT-riss), a prosperous farm and industrial community, was named for the daughter of Judge John Kinney, a member of the Nebraska Association that founded this settlement on the Blue River. Hollywood stars Harold Lloyd and Robert Taylor grew up in Beatrice.

What to See and Do

Gage County Historical Museum. Local historical artifacts housed in former Burlington Northern Depot (1906). History and artifacts of all towns of the county displayed. Artifacts of industry, medicine, agriculture, railroads and rural life. Special exhibits (fee). Tours by appt. (June-Labor Day, daily exc Mon; rest of yr, Tues-Fri, also Sun afternoons; closed most major hols) 2nd & Court Sts. Phone 402/228-1679.   **Free.**

Homestead National Monument (see). 4 mi NW, just off NE 4.

Annual Events

Homestead Days. Four-day event with pioneer theme. Demonstrations, parade. Last full wkend June.

Gage County Fair. Fairgrounds, W Scott St. Last wk July.

Motels

★ ★ **BEATRICE INN.** *3500 N 6th St.* 402/223-4074; FAX 402/223-4074, ext. 300; res: 800/232-8742. 63 rms, 2 story. May-Dec: S $35.75-$42.75; D $41.75-$48.50; each addl $3; under 12 free; lower rates rest of yr. Crib $4. Pet accepted, some restrictions. TV; cable (premium). Heated pool. Restaurant 6 am-9 pm; Sun to 8 pm. Bar 5 pm-1 am. Ck-out 11 am. Coin lndry. Meeting rms. Sundries. Cr cds: A, C, D, DS, MC, V.

⮐ ⚲ ⊠ 🔥 SC

⮐★ **HOLIDAY VILLA.** *1820 N 6th St.* 402/223-4036; FAX 402/228-3875. 46 rms, 1-2 story, 8 kits. S $26-$29; D $34-$40; each addl $4; kit. units $42; under 10 free. Crib free. Pet accepted, some restrictions. TV; cable. Playground. Complimentary coffee in lobby. Ck-out 11 am. Meeting rms. Cr cds: A, D, DS, MC, V.

⮐ ⊠ 🔥 SC

★ **VICTORIAN INN.** *1903 N 6th.* 402/228-5955. 31 rms, 2 story. S $29.95; D $36.95-$39.95; each addl $3. Pet accepted. TV; cable (premium), VCR avail. Complimentary continental bkfst. Ck-out 11 am. Cr cds: A, C, D, DS, MC, V.

D ⮐ 🔥 SC

Blair (C-9)

(See also Fremont, Omaha)

Founded 1869 **Pop** 6,860 **Elev** 1,075 ft **Area code** 402 **Zip** 68008
E-mail pplugge@huntel.net **Web** www.washcone@huntel.net
Information Chamber of Commerce, 1526 Washington St; 402/533-4455.

What to See and Do

Dana College (1884). (500 students) Liberal arts school founded by Danish pioneers; campus includes Danish immigrant archives, gas lamps from Copenhagen and Hans Christian Andersen beech trees. Heritage and Lauritz Melchior memorial rms in library include complete collections of Royal Copenhagen and Bing & Grondahl Christmas plates (after Labor Day-mid-May, daily; early June-early Aug, Mon-Fri; closed hols). 1/2 mi W, 2848 College Dr. Phone 402/426-7216. On campus is

Tower of the Four Winds. Set on a hill overlooking Blair, the 44-ft tower displays a mosaic interpretation of a vision seen by Black Elk, an Oglala Sioux prophet and medicine man.

De Soto National Wildlife Refuge. 4 mi E on US 30. (See MISSOURI VALLEY, IA)

Fort Atkinson State Historical Park. Ongoing reconstruction of military post established in 1820 (16 yrs after Lewis and Clark recommended the site) to protect the fur trade and secure the Louisiana Purchase; museum (late May-early Sept, daily). Park (daily). Watch reconstruction of old barracks. 1 mi E of US 75 & Ft Calhoun. Phone 402/468-5611.   ¢¢

Annual Events

"Gateway to the West" Days. Carnival, parade, street dance. Mid-June.

Sights & Sounds of Christmas. Dana College. Danish, German, French, American and other ethnic Christmas customs, foods, traditions; smorgasbord (res); concert in a setting of hundreds of poinsettias and evergreen trees, dramatic presentations. Phone 402/426-7216 (after Oct 1). Early Dec.

Motel

⮐★ **RATH INN.** *US 30W.* 402/426-2340; FAX 402/426-8703. 32 rms, 2 story. S $32.99; D $41.98; each addl $5; suites $43.96. Pet accepted. TV; cable (premium). Heated pool. Continental bkfst. Restaurant adj 6 am-11 pm. Ck-out 11 am. Refrigerator in suites. Cr cds: A, D, DS, MC, V.

 ⮐ ⚲ ⊠ 🔥

Bridgeport (C-2)

(For accommodations see Scottsbluff)

Founded 1900 **Pop** 1,581 **Elev** 3,666 ft **Area code** 308 **Zip** 69336

What to See and Do

Bridgeport State Recreation Area. Approx 190 acres of sand pit lakes on North Platte River. Swimming; fishing; boating (ramp). Hiking. Picnicking. Camping (dump station). W edge of town on US 26. Per vehicle   ¢

Chimney Rock National Historic Site (see). 13 mi W off US 26, NE 92.

Oregon Trail Wagon Train. Re-creation of an 1840s wagon train, with authentic covered wagons. Chuck wagon cookouts, canoeing, camping and one- to six-day wagon trips. Fees charged for meals, rentals and activities; res necessary for evening events. (May-Sept) 12 mi W via US 26, NE 92. Phone 308/586-1850.

Broken Bow (C-6)

Founded 1882 **Pop** 3,778 **Elev** 2,475 ft **Area code** 308 **Zip** 68822

What to See and Do

Victoria Springs State Recreation Area. Approx 60 acres; mineral springs. Fishing; nonpower boating (rentals). Hiking. Picnicking. Camping (fee), shelters, rental cabins. Standard fees. 21 mi NW on NE 2, then 7 mi E on Secondary NE 21A. Phone 308/749-2235.

Motels

★ **GATEWAY.** *1 mi E on NE 2, 70, 92.* 308/872-2478. 23 rms. S $25; D $34. Crib $1. Pet accepted, some restrictions. TV; cable (premium). Restaurant nearby. Ck-out 11 am. Sauna. Cr cds: A, C, D, DS, MC, V.

★ **SUPER 8.** *215 East South E St.* 308/872-6428; FAX 308/872-5031. 32 rms, 2 story. Apr-Sept: S $35.88; D $44.88; lower rates rest of yr. Crib $3. TV; cable (premium). Restaurant adj 6 am-11 pm. Ck-out 11 am. Meeting rm. Coin lndry. Exercise equipt; weights, weight machine, whirlpool. Cr cds: A, C, D, DS, JCB, MC, V.

✔★ **WAGON WHEEL.** *W on NE 2, 92, jct NE 70.* 308/872-2433. 15 rms. S $22-$25; D $26-$34; each addl $3. Crib $4. TV; cable (premium). Heated pool. Ck-out 10:30 am. Cr cds: A, D, DS, MC, V.

★ **WM PENN LODGE.** *853 E South St, E on NE 2.* 308/872-2412. 28 rms. S $24-$30; D $28-$40; each addl $3. Crib $5. Pet accepted. TV; cable (premium). Restaurant opp 6 am-11 pm. Ck-out 10 am. Refrigerators. Cr cds: A, DS, MC, V.

Chadron (A-2)

(See also Crawford)

Founded 1885 **Pop** 5,588 **Elev** 3,380 ft **Area code** 308 **Zip** 69337 **Web** www.prairieweb.com/chadron

Information Chamber of Commerce, 706 W Third, PO Box 646; 308/432-4401 or 800/603-2937.

Starting point of a sensational 1,000-mile horse race to Chicago in 1893, Chadron saw nine men leave in competition for a $1,000 prize. Doc Middleton, former outlaw, was one of the starters, but John Berry beat him to the door of Buffalo Bill's Wild West Show in 13 days and 16 hours. The headquarters and a Ranger District office of the Nebraska National Forest and headquarters of the Oglala National Grasslands are located here.

What to See and Do

Chadron State College (1911). (3,600 students) Tours. Planetarium, museum open to public by appt. 1000 Main St. Phone 308/432-6000.

Chadron State Park. Approx 950 acres; scenic pine ridge, lagoon, creek. Swimming pool (daily; fee); fishing; paddleboats (rentals). Hiking, horseback riding. Cross-country skiing. Picnicking, playground. Camping (dump station, hookups, standard fees), cabins. Scenic drives. 9 mi S on US 385. Phone 308/432-6167. Per vehicle ¢¢

Museum of the Fur Trade. Displays depict history of the North American fur trade 1500-1900; fine gun collection; Native American exhibits. Restored trading post (1833) and storehouse used by James Bordeaux, a French trader; garden of primitive crops. (June-Sept, daily; rest of yr, by appt) 3 1/2 mi E on US 20. Phone 308/432-3843. ¢

Nebraska National Forest. Fishing, hunting. Picnicking. Camping. S off US 20. Phone 308/432-0300 or 308/432-4475. (See THEDFORD and Samuel R. McKelvie National Forest, VALENTINE)

Walgren Lake State Recreation Area. Approx 80 acres on 50-acre lake. According to legend, a Loch Ness-type creature inhabits the Sandhills Lake here. Fishing; boating (nonpower or electric). Picnicking. Camping. Standard hrs, fees. 20 mi SE via US 20, then 2 mi S via NE 87.

Annual Events

Ride the Ridge. 12-mi trail ride through scenic Pine Ridge. Catered meal and ranch rodeo at end of ride. Phone 308/432-4475. July.

Fur Trade Days. 3 days early July.

Dawes County Fair. 5 days early Aug.

Motels

★ ★ **BEST WESTERN WEST HILLS INN.** *Jct US 385 & 10th St, 1 mi SW, 6 blks S of US 20.* 308/432-3305; FAX 308/432-5990. 67 rms, 2 story. S $55; D $65; each addl $5; suites $65-$105. Crib free. Pet accepted. TV; cable (premium). Indoor pool (heated); whirlpool. Complimentary continental bkfst. Coffee in rms. Restaurant nearby. Ck-out 11 am. Coin lndry. Meeting rms. Exercise equipt; weights, treadmill. Game rm. Some refrigerators, in-rm whirlpools. Cr cds: A, C, D, DS, MC, V.

★ **ECONOMY 9.** *1201 W US 20.* 308/432-3119; FAX 308/432-3119. 21 rms. Mid-May-Sept: S $45; D $52.99-$62.99; under 12 free; higher rates: rodeo, college graduation, fur trade days; lower rates rest of yr. Crib $2. Pet accepted. TV; cable (premium). Complimentary coffee in lobby. Restaurant opp 6 am-9 pm. Ck-out 10:30 am. Whirlpool. Cr cds: A, C, D, DS, MC, V.

✔★ **SUPER 8.** *5 blks W on US 20.* 308/432-4471; FAX 308/432-3991. 45 rms, 2 story. June-Sept: S $40.88; D $50.88-$54.88; each addl $2; lower rates rest of yr. Crib $3. TV; cable (premium). Indoor pool; whirlpool. Restaurant adj 6 am-9:30 pm. Ck-out 11 am. Coin lndry. Cr cds: A, D, DS, MC, V.

Chimney Rock National Historic Site (C-2)

(For accommodations see Scottsbluff; also see Bridgeport, Gering)

(13 mi W of Bridgeport off US 26, NE 92)

A landmark of the Oregon Trail, Chimney Rock rises almost 500 feet above the south bank of the North Platte River. Starting as a cone-shaped mound, it becomes a narrow 150-foot column towering above the landscape. For early travelers, many of whom sketched and described it in their journals, Chimney Rock marked the end of the prairies. It became a National Historic Site in 1956. Visitor center (fee). Phone 308/586-2581.

Columbus (C-8)

Founded 1856 **Pop** 19,480 **Elev** 1,449 ft **Area code** 402 **Zip** 68602 **E-mail** chamber@megavision.com

Information Chamber of Commerce, 764 33rd Ave, Box 515; 402/564-2769.

Named by its founders for Ohio's capital, Columbus has become a center of industry, agriculture and statewide electrical power.

What to See and Do

Parks. Pawnee Park. Swimming pool. Ball fields, tennis. Picnicking facilities, playground on 130 acres along Loup River. Quincentenary Belltower dedicated to Columbus's voyage to the new world. S on US 30, 81. Phone 402/564-0914. **Lake North & Loup Park.** Swimming, waterskiing; fishing;

boating (ramps, docks). Picnicking. Camping. 4 mi N on Monastery Rd. Phone 402/564-3171. **Free.**

Platte County Historical Society. Exhibits on local history; period school-room, barbershop; research library; cultural center. (Apr-mid-Oct, Wed-Sun) 29th Ave & 16th St. Phone 402/564-7960 or 402/564-0043. **Free.**

Annual Events

Platte County Fair. Agricultural Park, E edge of town. Phone 402/563-4901. Mid-July.

Columbus Days. Phone 402/564-2769. Late Aug.

Seasonal Event

Horse racing. Agricultural Park. Parimutuel betting. Mid-Aug-mid-Sept.

Motels

★ **ECO-LUX INN.** 3803 23rd St (68601), jct NE 81 & US 30. 402/564-9955; FAX 402/564-9436. 39 rms, 2 story. S $36-$39; D $43-$45; Crib $2. TV; cable (premium). Restaurant adj 6-2:30 am. Ck-out 11 am. Meeting rm. Coin lndry. Cr cds: A, C, D, DS, JCB, MC, V.

✔★ **GEMBOL'S.** 3220 8th St (68601). 402/564-2729; res: 800/288-3658. 21 rms. S $24-$28; D $28-$34; each addl $4. Crib $4. TV; cable (premium). Restaurant nearby. Ck-out 11 am. City park, pool 1 blk. Cr cds: A, C, D, DS, MC, V.

★ **JOHNNIE'S.** (222 W 16th St, Schuyler 68661) 16 mi E on US 30. 402/352-5454; FAX 402/352-5456. 31 rms. S $27; D $33; each addl $4. Crib $4. TV; cable (premium). Restaurant nearby. Ck-out 11 am. Cr cds: A, C, D, DS, MC, V.

★ ★ **NEW WORLD INN.** (68601). 1 mi SW on US 30, 81, near Municipal Airport. 402/564-1492; res: 800/433-1492. 154 rms, 2 story. S $46-$54; D $49-$56; each addl $5; suites $100; under 19 free. Crib free. TV; cable. Indoor pool; whirlpool, poolside serv. Restaurant 6 am-2 pm, 5-10 pm. Rm serv. Bar 4 pm-1 am; entertainment Tues, Wed, Fri, Sat. Ck-out noon. Coin lndry. Meeting rms. Business servs avail. Sundries. Free airport transportation. Indoor courtyard. Cr cds: A, C, D, DS, MC, V.

★ **SUPER 8.** 3324 20th St (68601). 402/563-3456. 64 rms, 2 story. S $43.98; D $52.98; each addl $3. Crib free. TV; cable (premium). Complimentary coffee in lobby. Restaurant nearby. Ck-out 11 am. Business servs avail. Cr cds: A, C, D, DS, MC, V.

Cozad (D-5)

(See also Gothenburg, Lexington)

Pop 3,823 **Elev** 2,490 ft **Area code** 308 **Zip** 69130
Information Chamber of Commerce, 211 W 8th St, PO Box 14; 308/784-3930.

Cozad is headquarters for a number of industries, as well as a shipping and agricultural center known for the production of alfalfa.

What to See and Do

Gallagher Canyon State Recreation Area. Approx 20 acres of park surround 400 acres of water. Fishing; boating (ramp). Hiking. Picnicking. Camping. Standard hrs, fees. 8 mi S on NE 21.

Robert Henri Museum and Historical Walkway. Museum occupies the childhood home of artist Robert Henri, founder of the Ash Can School and former hotel built by Henri's father. Other historic buildings along walkway are an original Pony Express station, a pioneer school and an early 20th-century church. (Memorial Day-Sept, Mon-Sat, also by appt) 218 E 8th St. Phone 308/784-4154. ¢

Motel

★ **BUDGET HOST CIRCLE "S".** 440 S Meridian, at I-80. 308/784-2290; FAX 308/784-3917. 49 rms, 2 story. S $30; D $38; each addl $4. Crib $3. Pet accepted. TV; cable (premium). Heated pool. Restaurant 6 am-10 pm. Ck-out 11 am. Cr cds: A, DS, MC, V.

Restaurant

✔★ **PLAINSMAN.** 128 E 8th. 308/784-2080. Hrs: 6 am-2 pm; Mon, Sat to 1 pm; Sun 11 am-1 pm. Closed most major hols. Semi-a la carte: bkfst $1.25-$3.50, lunch $2-$3.85. Child's meals. Specializes in broasted chicken. Salad bar. Country motif. No cr cds accepted.

Crawford (A-2)

(See also Chadron)

Founded 1885 **Pop** 1,115 **Elev** 3,673 ft **Area code** 308 **Zip** 69339

What to See and Do

⭐ **Fort Robinson State Park.** Approx 22,000 acres of pine-covered hills; rocky buttes. Fort established in 1874 in the midst of Native American fighting (the Sioux leader, Crazy Horse, was killed here). Swimming pool (fee); fishing. Hiking, horseback riding. Cross-country skiing. Picnicking, restaurant, lodge (see MOTEL). Camping (dump station), cabins. Post Playhouse; stagecoach and jeep rides (daily, summer); cookouts. Displays herds of buffalo. Park entry permit required. 3 mi W on US 20. Phone 308/665-2660. Also here are

Fort Robinson Museum. Main museum located in former headquarters building (1905); authentic costumes and weapons of Native Americans and soldiers. Other exhibit buildings include 1874 guardhouse, 1904 harness repair, 1906 blacksmith and 1900 wheelwright shops, 1887 adobe officer quarters and 1908 veterinary hospital. Site of Red Cloud Indian Agency (1873-1877). Guided tours (Memorial Day-Labor Day). Museum (Memorial Day-Labor Day, daily; Apr-May & Sept-Oct, Sat & Sun). Maintained by State Historical Society. Phone 308/665-2919. ¢

Trailside Museum. Exhibits of natural history from Fort Robinson area. Museum also offers natural history tours of the area and daily science field trips to Toadstool Park and fossil sites (fee). (Memorial Day-Labor Day, daily; May, Wed-Sun) Operated by University of Nebraska State Museum. Phone 308/665-2929. **Donation.**

Nebraska National Forest. 8 mi S on NE 2 (see CHADRON).

Oglala National Grassland. Nearly 95,000 acres of prairie grasses in the badlands of northwestern Nebraska, popular for hunting (in season), hiking and backpacking. 10 mi N via NE 2, 71. Phone 308/432-4475.

Motel

✔★ **FORT ROBINSON LODGE.** Box 392, 3 mi W on US 20, in Ft Robinson State Park. 308/665-2900; FAX 308/665-2906. 22 rms in inn, 1-2 story; 24 kit. cabins (2-5 bedrm), 7 kit. units (6-9 bedrm). No A/C in cabins. No rm phones. Mid-Apr-late Nov: S, D $26; cabins $52-$151. Closed rest of yr. Crib $5. Indoor pool. Playground. Restaurant 6:30 am-8 pm (Memorial Day-Labor Day). Ck-out 11 am. Sundries. Tennis. Access to facilities of state park. Cr cds: MC, V.

Crofton (A-8)

(For accommodations see Vermillion & Yankton, SD)

Pop 820 **Elev** 1,440 ft **Area code** 402 **Zip** 68730

What to See and Do

Lewis and Clark Lake State Recreation Area. Approx 1,300 acres with 7,982-acre lake. Six separate recreation areas on Lewis & Clark Trail. Swimming; fishing; boating (ramps). Picnicking. Tent & trailer camping (dump station). 9 mi N via NE 121. Phone 605/668-2985.

Fairbury (E-8)

(See also Beatrice)

Pop 4,335 **Elev** 1,317 ft **Area code** 402 **Zip** 68352
Information Chamber of Commerce, 515 4th St, PO Box 274; 402/729-3000.

What to See and Do

Alexandria Lakes State Recreation Area. Approx 50 acres with 46 acres of water. Swimming; fishing; boating (no motors). Picnicking, concession. Camping (dump station). Standard hrs, fees. 12 mi W via US 136, then 3 1/2 mi N on NE 53.

Rock Creek Station State Historical Park. Located on site of Pony Express station and Oregon Trail ruts. Reconstructed post office and ranch buildings, covered wagon rides, picnic area and visitors center with interpretive material and slide presentation. Hiking, nature trails. Picnicking, playground. Camping. (Daily) 5 1/2 mi E, 1 mi S on marked country rds. Phone 402/729-5777. Per vehicle ¢¢

Annual Event

Germanfest. Parade, crafts, dances. Phone 402/729-3000. 2nd full wknd Sept.

Motel

★ **CAPRI.** *Jct US 136 & NE 15. 402/729-3317; res: 800/932-0589.* 36 rms. S $28; D $34; each addl $2. Crib $5. TV; cable (premium). Complimentary coffee in lobby. Restaurant nearby. Ck-out 11 am. Cr cds: A, DS, MC, V.

Fremont (C-9)

(See also Omaha)

Founded 1856 **Pop** 23,680 **Elev** 1,198 ft **Area code** 402 **E-mail** judy@teknetwork.com **Web** www.teknetwork.com/dccvb
Information Fremont Area Chamber & Dodge County Convention & Visitors Bureau, 92 W 5th St, PO Box 182, 68026-0182; 402/721-2641.

This town was named for John C. Frémont, Union general in the Civil War, who ran for president of the United States. In the town's early days the crops were so bad that lots sold for 75¢ each. Finally, travelers on the Overland Trail brought in enough trade that the town began to prosper and grow. Midland Lutheran College gives a collegiate atmosphere to an otherwise industrial town, chiefly involved in food processing and retail trade.

What to See and Do

Fremont State Recreation Area. Approx 660 acres with 22 lakes. Swimming; fishing; boating (ramp, rentals). Picnicking, concession. Tent & trailer sites (dump station). Standard fees. (Apr-mid-Oct) 3 mi W on US 30. Phone 402/727-3290. Per vehicle ¢¢

Fremont and Elkhorn Valley Railroad. Train rides to Nickerson and Hooper aboard vintage rail cars. Res recommended. (Schedule varies) 1835 N Somers Ave. Phone 402/727-0615. ¢¢¢-¢¢¢¢¢ Also boarding here is

> **Fremont Dinner Train.** Two restored 1940s rail cars make 30-mi round trips through Elkhorn Valley. Dinner and varied entertainment. (Fri-Sun, also some hols) For res phone 402/727-8321 or 800/942-RAIL. ¢¢¢¢

Louis E. May Historical Museum (1874). A 25-rm house of Fremont's first mayor; oak and mahogany paneling, art glass windows, rooms furnished in late 19th-century style. (Apr-Dec, Wed-Sun afternoons; closed Jan 1, Thanksgiving, Dec 25) 1643 N Nye Ave. Phone 402/721-4515. ¢¢

Annual Events

Old Settlers Celebration and Parade. 18 mi W via US 30, in North Bend. Festivities include parade, carnival, ice cream social. Late June.

John C. Frémont Days. Balloon race, train rides, historical re-enactments, barbecue. Phone 402/727-9428. Mid-July.

Bull Riding Classic and Dance. Christensen Field. Phone 402/721-2641. Mid-Oct.

Motels

↙★ **BUDGET HOST MODERN-AIRE.** *1435 E 23rd St (68025). 402/721-5656.* 35 rms. S $35.95; D $45.95; each addl $4. Crib $3. TV; cable (premium). Coffee in lobby. Restaurant opp 6 am-11 pm. Bar 5 pm-1 am. Ck-out 11 am. Cr cds: A, DS, MC, V.

★ ★ **COMFORT INN.** *1649 E 23rd St (68025). 402/721-1109.* 48 rms, 2 story. June-Sept: S $47.95-$52.95; D $50.95-$55.95; each addl $5; suites $59.95-$64.95; under 16 free; higher rates special events. Crib free. Pet accepted, some restrictions. TV; cable (premium). Indoor pool; whirlpool. Complimentary continental bkfst. Restaurant adj 6 am-midnight. Ck-out 11 am. Business servs avail. Refrigerator in suites; microwaves avail. Cr cds: A, D, DS, MC, V.

★ ★ **HOLIDAY LODGE.** *1220 E 23rd St (68025), at jct US 30 & Old US 275. 402/727-1110; FAX 402/727-4579; res: 800/743-7666.* 100 rms, 2 story. S $42-$45; D $49-$63. Crib free. Pet accepted. TV; cable (premium). Indoor pool; whirlpool. Restaurant 6 am-9:30 pm. Bar 3 pm-1 am. Ck-out noon. Meeting rms. Business servs avail. Exercise equipt; treadmill, rowers. Cr cds: A, C, D, DS, MC, V.

D ⚑ ≈ ✕ ⬚ 🐾 SC

★ **SUPER 8.** *1250 E 23rd St (68025). 402/727-4445.* 43 rms, 2 story. S $39.88; D $50.88; each addl $5; under 12 free. Crib free. TV; cable (premium). Complimentary coffee. Restaurant nearby. Cr cds: A, C, D, DS, MC, V.

D ⊠ 🐾 SC

Restaurants

★ **KC'S.** *631 N Park (68025). 402/721-3353.* Hrs: 11 am-2 pm, 5-9:30 pm. Closed Sun, Mon; most major hols. Res accepted. Bar. Semi-a la carte: lunch $2.85-$6.50, dinner $5.95-$11.95. Child's meals. Specializes in prime rib, quiche, broccoli salad. Old cooler used as salad bar. Many antiques. Cr cds: A, MC, V.

D SC

✔★ **KINDLER CAFE.** *353 W 23rd (68025). 402/721-9865.* Hrs: 11 am-2 pm, 5-10 pm; Sun 5-9 pm. Closed major hols. Bar to 1 am. Semi-a la carte: lunch $4.95, dinner $6.25-$12.95. Child's meals. Specializes in chicken, steak. Family-owned. No cr cds accepted.

D

Gering (C-1)

(For accommodations see Scottsbluff)

Pop 7,946 **Elev** 3,914 ft **Area code** 308 **Zip** 69341 **Web** www.scb_ger@prairieweb.com/scb_gering_ucc/
Information Scottsbluff-Gering United Chamber of Commerce, 1517 Broadway, Scottsbluff 69361; 308/632-2133.

What to See and Do

North Platte Valley Museum. Sod house (1889), log house (1890), items and literature of local historical interest. (May-Sept, daily; rest of yr, by appt) 11th & J Sts. Phone 308/436-5411. ¢

Scotts Bluff National Monument (see). 3 mi W on NE 92.

Annual Events

Sugar Valley Rally. Gathering of antique automobiles; precision driving contest. Early June.

Oregon Trail Days. Parades, chili cook-off, contests, square dancing, barbecue, music festival. Four days mid-July.

Gothenburg (D-5)

(For accommodations see Cozad, North Platte)

Pop 3,232 **Elev** 2,567 ft **Area code** 308 **Zip** 69138 **E-mail** gothenburg@navix.net **Web** www.ci.gothne.us/
Information Chamber of Commerce, PO Box 263; 308/537-3505 or 800/482-5520.

What to See and Do

Pony Express Station (1854). Pony Express station 1860-1861; later a stop for the Overland Stage; memorabilia, artifacts. (May-Sept, daily) Ehmen Park. Phone 308/537-3505.   **Free.**

Annual Events

Pony Express Rodeo. Carnival, barbeque, "mutton busting." July 3-4.

Harvest Festival. Art show, parade, contests, antique farm machinery. Late Sept-early Oct.

Grand Island (D-7)

(See also Hastings)

Founded 1857 **Pop** 39,386 **Elev** 1,870 ft **Area code** 308 **E-mail** cvb@gionline.net **Web** www.cnweb.com/grandisland
Information Grand Island/Hall County Convention & Visitors Bureau, PO Box 1486, 68802; 308/382-4400 or 800/658-3178.

Named by French trappers for a large island in the Platte River, the town was moved five miles north in 1869 to its present location on the Union Pacific Railroad, which dominated Grand Island's early existence. Traditionally a trade center for a rich irrigated agriculture and livestock region, the city now has diversified industry, including meat and food processing, agricultural and irrigation equipment and mobile homes.

What to See and Do

Crane Meadows Nature Center. Educational center features exhibits and programs about Platte River habitat. Five miles of public nature trails. (Daily; closed hols) S side of exit 305 on I-80. Phone 308/382-1820.   ¢¢

Fonner Park. Thoroughbred racing. Parimutuel betting. (Mid-Feb-late Dec) 700 E Stolley Park Rd, N of I-80. Phone 308/382-4515.   ¢

Heritage Zoo. The zoo (7½ acres) features more than 200 native Nebraska and exotic animals; train; special exhibits, events. (Daily) Stolley Park. Phone 308/385-5416.   ¢¢

Island Oasis Water Park. 6-acre park has 4 water slides, wave pool, children's pool, Lazy River. Also sand volleyball; concessions. (Memorial Day-Labor Day, daily) 321 Fonner Rd, exit 312 off I-80. Phone 308/385-5381.   ¢¢

Mormon Island State Recreation Area. Approx 90 acres; 61 water acres on Mormon Trail. Swimming; fishing; boating (non-power or electric). Picnicking. Tent & trailer sites (standard fees, dump station). 10 mi S via US 34, 281. Phone 308/385-6211.

⚅ **Stuhr Museum of the Prairie Pioneer.** Museum, on 200 acres situated on island surrounded by man-made lake, was designed by Edward Durell Stone. (Daily; closed Jan 1, Thanksgiving, Dec 25) 4 mi N of I-80 at jct US 281 & US 34. Phone 308/385-5316.   ¢¢   Included are

Railroad Town. Turn-of-the-century outdoor museum contains 60 original buildings, including 3 houses; cottage where Henry Fonda was born; schoolhouse, newspaper office, bank, post office, hotel, country church, depot and railstock; blacksmith, shoe and barber shops. (May-mid-Oct, daily)

Gus Fonner Memorial Rotunda. Native American and Old West collections of Gus Fonner. (Daily)

Antique Auto and Farm Machinery Exhibit. Over 200 items on display, including many steam tractors. (May-mid-Oct, daily)

Annual Events

Central Nebraska Ethnic Festival. Music, dance, ethnic meals, dramatic presentations. Phone 308/385-5455, ext 230. 4th wkend July.

Husker Harvest Days. Cornhusker Army Ammunition Plant, US 30 W. Agricultural exhibits, techniques and equipment used in irrigation. Phone 308/382-9210. Mid-Sept.

Harvest of Harmony Festival & Parade. Band & queen competitions. 1st Sat Oct.

Seasonal Event

"Wings Over the Platte" Celebration. Each spring, more than 500,000 sandhill cranes, as well as ducks, geese, hawks and eagles, pause at the Mormon Island Preserve on the Platte River before continuing north to the nesting destinations in Canada, Alaska and Siberia. Guided tours (res necessary) take visitors to carefully concealed blind, where they may observe the birds feeding and resting. For information contact Visitors Bureau, 308/382-4400 or 800/658-3178. Seven wks Mar, Apr.

Motels

★ **DAYS INN.** *2620 N Diers Ave (68803).* 308/384-8624; FAX 308/384-1626. 62 rms, 2 story. S $37.30; D $41.60-$49.25; each addl $5; under 12 free. Crib free. TV; cable (premium). Complimentary continental bkfst. Restaurant nearby. Ck-out 11 am. Coin lndry. Business servs avail. Whirlpool, sauna. Cr cds: A, D, DS, MC, V.

✔★ **OAK GROVE INN.** *3205 S Locust (68801).* 308/384-1333. 60 rms, 2 story. Mid-Feb-Sept: S $27.75; D $33.75; each addl $3; suites $38; under 18 free; lower rates rest of yr. Crib free. TV; cable. Complimentary coffee in lobby. Restaurant nearby. Ck-out 11 am. Cr cds: A, C, D, DS, MC, V.

★ **SUPER 8.** *2603 S Locust (68801).* 308/384-4380; FAX 308/384-5015. 80 rms, 2 story. S $36.88; D $41.88; each addl $2; suites $50.88-$60.88; under 12 free. Crib free. TV; cable. Indoor pool; whirlpool. Complimentary continental bkfst. Restaurant opp 6 am-midnight. Ck-out 11 am. Cr cds: A, C, D, DS, MC, V.

Motor Hotels

★ ★ **BEST WESTERN RIVERSIDE INN.** *3333 Ramada Rd (68801),* at S Locust St. 308/384-5150; FAX 308/384-6551. 183 rms, 2 story. S $46; D $51; suites $78; under 18 free. Crib free. Pet accepted. TV; cable (premium). Heated pool; whirlpool, sauna. Complimentary continental bkfst. Restaurant 6 am-1:30 pm, 5-9 pm. Rm serv. Bar 4 pm-1 am. Ck-out noon. Coin lndry. Meeting rms. Business servs avail. Sundries. Cr cds: A, C, D, DS, MC, V.

★ ★ **HOLIDAY INN-MIDTOWN.** *2503 S Locust St (68801).* 308/384-1330; FAX 308/382-4615. 206 rms, 2 story. S $61-$69; D $66-$74; suites $95; under 18 free. Crib free. Pet accepted. TV; cable (premium). Heated pool; wading pool, whirlpool, poolside serv. Restaurant 6 am-10 pm. Rm serv. Bar 3 pm-1 am. Ck-out noon. Coin lndry. Meeting rms. Cr cds: A, C, D, DS, JCB, MC, V.

Restaurants

✔★ ★ **DOS HERMANOS.** *Stolley Park & Webb Rd.* 308/382-1080. Hrs: 11 am-10 pm; Sun 5-9 pm. Closed most major hols. Res accepted. Mexican menu. Bar. Semi-a la carte: lunch $3.95-$5.95, dinner $4.35-$8.95. Child's meals. Specializes in fajitas, chimichangas. Dining rm with Mexican tiles, furnishings, fountain. Cr cds: A, DS, MC, V.

★ ★ **DREISBACH'S.** *1137 S Locust St (68801).* 308/382-5450. Hrs: 11 am-1:30 pm, 4:30-10 pm; Sat from 4:30 pm; Sun, Mon 11 am-1:30 pm, 4:30-9 pm; early-bird dinner Mon-Fri 4:30-6:30 pm. Closed some major hols. Res required. Bar. Semi-a la carte: lunch $2.95-$6.95, dinner $3.95-$20.95. Lunch buffet: (Sun) $6.95. Child's meals. Specializes in dry-aged beef, chicken, rabbit. Family-owned. Cr cds: A, C, D, DS, MC, V.

✔★ **HUNAN.** *B49 N Webb Rd.* 308/384-6964. Hrs: 11:30 am-9:30 pm; wkends to 10:30 pm. Closed Jan 1, Dec 25. Res accepted. Chinese menu. Bar. Semi-a la carte: lunch $3.25-$4.75, dinner $4.95-$8.95. Specialties: crispy shrimp, Hunan flower steak, princess chicken. Cr cds: MC, V.

Unrated Dining Spot

PICCADILLY DINNER THEATRE. *118 W 3rd.* 308/381-0383. Hrs: Wed-Sat refreshments from 6 pm, buffet 6:30-7:30 pm, show 8 pm; Sun matinee buffet 11:30 am-12:30 pm, show 1 pm, refreshments 5 pm, buffet 5:30-6:30 pm, show 7 pm. Closed Mon, Tues. Res required. Bar. Buffet: lunch $15, dinner $16-$19. Specializes in prime roast beef, hickory smoked ham. Outdoor dining. Several dining areas; performances after buffet. No cr cds accepted.

Hastings (D-7)

(See also Grand Island)

Founded 1872 **Pop** 22,837 **Elev** 1,931 ft **Area code** 402 **Zip** 68901
Information Convention & Visitors Bureau, PO Box 941, 68902; 402/461-2370 or 800/967-2189.

Hastings came into being almost overnight when two railroad lines crossed. Within eight years of its founding, its population swelled to almost 3,000. After 75 years as a depot and supply center, the town turned out large quantities of ammunition during World War II and the Korean Conflict.

What to See and Do

Crosier Asmat Museum. Collection of art and artifacts from the Asmat people of Irian Jaya, Indonesia. Many fine examples of the woodcarvings for which these people are famous. (Daily; by appt) 223 E 14th St. Phone 402/463-3188. **Free.**

Crystal Lake State Recreation Area. Approx 30 acres surrounding 30-acre lake. Swimming; fishing; boating (non-power or electric). Picnicking. Camping, trailer pads. Standard hrs, fees. 10 mi S on US 281.

Hastings Museum. Includes natural science, pioneer history, Native American lore, bird displays; guns, antique cars, horse-drawn vehicles; sod house, country store, coin rm. (Daily; closed Jan 1, Thanksgiving, Dec 24 eve-Dec 25) J.M. McDonald Planetarium, sky shows (daily). Lied IMAX Theatre (fee). 1330 N Burlington Ave. Phone 402/461-2399. **¢¢**

Lake Hastings. Waterskiing; fishing; boating. Picnicking. (May-Sept, daily) 1 mi N off US 281.

Willa Cather State Historic Site. Author's letters, first editions, photos; Cather family memorabilia; art gallery; research library; bookstore. (Daily; closed most major hols) Other buildings include Cather childhood home, Red Cloud depot, St Juliana Falconieri Catholic Church, Grace Episcopal Church and *My Antonia* farmhouse. Tours of properties (5 times daily). (See ANNUAL EVENTS) 38 mi S via US 281 on Webster St, in Red Cloud (branch museum of Nebraska State Historical Society). Phone 402/746-2653. **¢**

Annual Events

Willa Cather Spring Conference. Willa Cather State Historic Site. Features different Cather novel each year. Discussion groups, banquet, entertainment. Tour of "Cather Country." Phone 402/746-2653. 1st wkend May.

Cottonwood Prairie Festival. Brickyard Park. Music, crafts, foods. Phone 800/967-2189. Mid-June.

Oregon Trail PRCA Rodeo. Labor Day wkend.

Motels

★ ★ **HOLIDAY INN.** *2205 Osbone Dr, W 22nd St, 1½ mi N on US 34/281.* 402/463-6721. 100 rms, 2 story. S $50-$60; D $55-$65; each addl $7; suites $75; under 19 free. Crib free. TV; cable (premium). Indoor pool; whirlpool, sauna. Restaurant 6:30 am-10 pm. Rm serv. Bar 4 pm-1 am. Ck-out 11 am. Meeting rms. Business servs avail. In-rm modem link. Sundries. Cr cds: A, C, D, DS, MC, V.

D ≈ ⇲ 🐾 SC

★ **SUPER 8.** *2200 N Kansas, US 281 N.* 402/463-8888; FAX 402/463-8899. 50 rms, 2 story. May-Sept: S $37.88-$42.88, D $44.88-$48.88; lower rates rest of yr. Crib free. Pet accepted. TV; cable (premium). Restaurant adj 6 am-10 pm. Ck-out 11 am. Cr cds: A, D, DS, MC.

D 🐾 🐾

★ **USA INNS.** *2424 E Osborne Dr, US 281N & US 6 Bypass.* 402/463-1422; FAX 402/463-2956. 62 rms, 2 story. S $37.50; D $46.50; each addl $2. Crib free. Pet accepted, some restrictions. TV; cable (premium), VCR avail. Complimentary coffee. Ck-out 11 am. Some refrigerators. Cr cds: A, D, DS, MC, V.

D 🐾 ⇲ 🐾 SC

★ **X-L.** *1400 W "J" St, US 34, 281, near Municipal Airport.* 402/463-3148. 41 rms, 2 kit. units. S $28.75-$32.75; D $36.75; each addl $5; kit. units $2 addl. Crib $5. TV; cable. Heated pool; whirlpool. Continental bkfst. Complimentary coffee in rms. Restaurant nearby. Ck-out 11 am. Refrigerators. Cr cds: A, D, DS, MC, V.

≈ ⇲ 🐾

Restaurants

✔★ **BERNARDO'S STEAK HOUSE.** *1109 S Baltimore.* 402/463-4666. Hrs: 11 am-1:30 pm, 5-11 pm; Sat 5 pm-midnight; Sun 5-10 pm. Closed some major hols. Res accepted Sun-Fri. Bar. Semi-a la carte: lunch $3.75-$6.25, dinner $6-$14. Child's meals. Specializes in steak, prime rib. Family-owned. Cr cds: A, DS, MC, V.

SC

★ ★ **TAYLOR'S STEAKHOUSE.** *1609 N Kansas.* 402/462-8000. Hrs: 11 am-1:30 pm, 4:30-10 pm; Fri, Sat to 10:30 pm; Sun 4:30-9 pm; Sun brunch 11 am-2 pm. Closed Jan 1, Dec 25. Res accepted. Bar. Semi-a la carte: lunch $3.95-$6.95, dinner $5.95-$30. Sun brunch $6.50. Child's meals. Specializes in prime rib, aged beef, freshwater fish. Fireplace. Cr cds: A, MC, V.

D SC

Homestead National Monument (E-9)

(4 mi NW of Beatrice, just off NE 4)

This is one of the first sites claimed under terms of the Homestead Act of 1862. A quarter section, 160 acres, went for a nominal fee to citizens who lived and worked on it for five years; eventually, grants equaling the combined states of Texas and Louisiana were made. Set aside in 1939, the site is a memorial to the pioneer spirit that began cultivation of the West.

At the Brownville Land Office, Daniel Freeman filed Application No. 1 under the act for this land, built a log cabin and later a brick house. A surviving homesteader's cabin similar to Freeman's has been moved to the grounds and furnished as an exhibit. Visitors may take a self-guided tour (2½ miles) of the area. Many other historical items are on display in the Visitor Center museum. Freeman school, one-quarter mile west of the Visitor Center, is a one-room brick schoolhouse restored to turn-of-the-

century appearance; it commemorates the role of education in frontier society. The homestead story is explained in detail. Camping nearby. (Daily; closed Jan 1, Dec 25) Phone 402/223-3514. **Free.**

Kearney (D-6)

(See also Grand Island, Lexington, Minden)

Founded 1873 **Pop** 24,396 **Elev** 2,153ft **Area code** 308 **Zip** 68847
Information Visitors Bureau, PO Box 607; 308/237-3101 or 800/652-9435.

Kearney (CAR-nee), named for the frontier outpost Fort Kearny, had hopes of being the capital of Nebraska because of its central location in the state—and even entertained the thought of being capital of the US. Today its economy is based on agriculture and diversified industry.

What to See and Do

Fort Kearny State Historical Park. The first Fort Kearny was erected at Nebraska City in 1846; it was moved here in 1848 to protect the Oregon Trail. In park are restored 1864 stockade, sod blacksmith-carpenter shop, museum and interpretive center (Memorial Day-Labor Day, daily). Swimming; fishing; electric boating. Hiking and bicycling on nature trail (approx 1.5 mi) along Platte River. Picnicking. Campground (standard fees; dump station). 4 mi S on NE 10, 3 mi W on link 50A. Phone 308/865-5305. Per vehicle ¢¢

★ **Harold Warp Pioneer Village.** 12 mi S via NE 10. (See MINDEN)

Museum of Nebraska Art. Collection of paintings, sculptures, drawings and prints created by Nebraskans or with Nebraska as the subject. (Tues-Sat, also Sun afternoons; closed major hols) 24th & Central. Phone 308/865-8559. **Free.**

Trails and Rails Museum. Restored 1898 depot, 1880s freighters' hotel, 1871 country schoolhouse; displays of pioneer trails and rails, exhibits in baggage rm; steam engine, flat car, caboose. (Memorial Day-Labor Day, daily; rest of yr, by appt) 710 W 11th St. Phone 308/234-3041. **Free.**

University of Nebraska at Kearney (1905). (10,000 students) Offers undergraduate, graduate and specialist degrees. Two art galleries, planetarium; theater productions, concerts; campus tours. 905 W 25th St. Phone 308/865-8441. Also here is

George W. Frank House (1889). Three-story mansion with Tiffany window; turn-of-century showplace and center of city's social life. (June-Aug, daily exc Mon) Phone 308/865-8284. ¢

Motels

★ ★ ★ **BEST WESTERN TEL-STAR.** *1010 3rd Ave.* 308/237-5185; FAX 308/234-1002. 69 rms, 2 story. June-Aug: S $49; D $62; each addl $5; under 12 free; lower rates rest of yr. Crib free. Pet accepted. TV; cable (premium), VCR avail (movies). Heated pool; wading pool, whirlpool, sauna. Complimentary full bkfst. Restaurant 5-9 pm. Rm serv. Ck-out noon. Meeting rms. Business servs avail. Exercise equipt; weights, treadmill, rower. Cr cds: A, C, D, DS, MC, V.

🐾 ≈ 🏃 ⇲ 🐾 SC

✔★ **BUDGET.** *411 S 2nd Ave.* 308/237-5991. 68 rms, 2 story. June-Labor Day: S, D $34-$56.50; each addl $4; lower rates rest of yr. Crib free. TV; cable (premium). Indoor pool; sauna. Complimentary coffee in lobby. Restaurant adj open 24 hrs. Ck-out 11 am. Coin lndry. Meeting rms. Game rm. Cr cds: A, D, DS, MC, V.

≈ ⇲ 🐾 SC

★ ★ **BUDGET HOST WESTERN INN.** *1401 2nd Ave.* 308/237-3153; FAX 308/234-6073. 34 rms, 2 story. June-Aug: S $38; D $47; each addl $5; under 12 free; lower rates rest of yr. Crib free. TV; cable (premium). Heated pool. Restaurant 6:30 am-9 pm. Bar from 10 am. Ck-out 11 am. Cr cds: A, DS, MC, V.

★ **WESTERN INN SOUTH.** *510 3rd Ave. 308/234-1876; FAX 308/237-0543.* 45 rms. June-Aug: S $45; D $48-$59; each addl $5; under 12 free; lower rates rest of yr. Crib $3. TV; cable (premium). Indoor pool; whirlpool, sauna. Continental bkfst. Restaurant nearby. Ck-out 11 am. Cr cds: A, C, D, DS, MC, V.

Motor Hotels

✔★ ★ **FORT KEARNY INN.** *I-80 exit 272. 308/234-2541; FAX 308/237-4512; res: 800/652-7245.* 106 rms, 3 story. S $38; D $45; each addl $7; suites $75; under 12 free. Crib free. TV; cable (premium). Heated pool. Restaurant 6 am-10 pm. Bar 4 pm-1 am. Ck-out noon. Coin lndry. Meeting rms. Sundries. Cr cds: A, C, DS, MC, V.

★ ★ **HOLIDAY INN.** *301 S 2nd Ave. 308/237-3141; FAX 308/234-4675.* 210 rms, 2 story. S, D $69-$79; suites $80-$150; under 20 free. Crib free. Pet accepted. TV; cable (premium). Indoor pool; wading pool, whirlpool, sauna, poolside serv. Restaurant 6 am-10 pm. Rm serv. Bar 3 pm-1 am; entertainment exc Sun. Ck-out noon. Coin lndry. Meeting rms. Business servs avail. Sundries. Gift shop. Private patios, balconies. Cr cds: A, C, D, DS, JCB, MC, V.

★ ★ ★ **RAMADA INN.** *S 2nd Ave, 1 blk N of I-80 exit 272. 308/237-5971; FAX 308/236-7549.* 155 rms, 2 story. S $65; D $80; suites $110; under 18 free. Crib free. Pet accepted. TV; cable (premium). Indoor pool; whirlpool. Restaurant 6 am-9 pm. Rm serv. Bar 11-1 am; Sun 6-9 pm. Ck-out 11 am. Coin lndry. Meeting rms. Business servs avail. In-rm modem link. Gift shop. Game rm. Cr cds: A, C, D, DS, MC, V.

Restaurants

★ ★ **ALLEY ROSE.** *2013 Central Ave. 308/234-1261.* Hrs: 11 am-10 pm. Closed Memorial Day, Labor Day, Dec 25; also Sun Labor Day-Memorial Day. Res accepted. Bar Fri, Sat to 1 am. Semi-a la carte: lunch $2.99-$6.29, dinner $3.99-$28.99. Child's meals. Specializes in prime rib, chicken. Salad bar. Piano player wkends. Many antiques, fireplace. Cr cds: A, DS, MC, V.

★ ★ **GRANDPA'S STEAK HOUSE.** *2 mi S on NE 10, 44; ¼ mi S of I-80. 308/237-2882.* Hrs: 5-11 pm; Sun 11:30 am-2 pm. Closed major hols. Bar. Semi-a la carte: dinner $6-$17. Buffet: lunch (Sun) $7.25. Child's meals. Specializes in seafood, prime rib, steak. Salad bar. Fireplace. Cr cds: A, C, D, DS, MC, V.

Kimball (C-1)

(For accommodations see Sidney)

Pop 2,574 **Elev** 4,709 ft **Area code** 308 **Zip** 69145 **E-mail** kbccc@megavision.com **Web** www.ci.kimball.ne.us
Information Chamber of Commerce, 119 E 2nd St; 308/235-3782.

What to See and Do

Recreation. Oliver Reservoir. Swimming, waterskiing; fishing; boating. Camping. 8 mi W on US 30. **Gotte Park.** Swimming pool. Tennis. Picnicking, playground. In park is Titan I missile. E on US 30.

Lexington (D-5)

(See also Cozad, Gothenburg, Kearney)

Founded 1872 **Pop** 6,601 **Elev** 2,390 ft **Area code** 308 **Zip** 68850 **E-mail** lexcoc@krun.com
Information Lexington Area Chamber of Commerce, 200 W Pacific, PO Box 97; 308/324-5504 or 888/966-0564.

Originally a frontier trading post and settlement along the Oregon Trail, Plum Creek was established in 1872. Completion of the Union Pacific Railroad brought more settlers to this farmland; it was at this time that the name was changed to Lexington. The economy of Lexington has been boosted by the addition of agricultural equipment, machine manufacturing and beef processing to its already prosperous farming and cattle operations.

What to See and Do

Dawson County Historical Museum. Exhibits include Dawson County history gallery, furnished rural schoolhouse (1888), 1885 Union Pacific depot, 1903 locomotive, farm equipment and 1919 experimental biplane. Collection also includes quilts and prehistoric Native American artifacts. Art gallery and archives. (Mon-Sat, also Sun afternoons; closed Jan 1, Thanksgiving, Dec 25) 805 N Taft St. Phone 308/324-5340. ¢

Johnson Lake State Recreation Area. Approx 80 acres on 2,061-acre lake. Swimming; fishing; boating (ramps). Picnicking. Tent & trailer sites (standard fees, dump station). 7 mi S on US 283. Phone 308/785-2685. Per vehicle ¢¢

Annual Events

Johnson Lake Open Regatta. At Johnson Lake. June 20-21.

Dawson County Fair. Aug 11-15.

Motels

✔★ **BUDGET HOST-MINUTE MAN.** *801 S Bridge St. 308/324-5544.* 36 rms. S $30-$34; D $32-$36; each addl $4. Crib free. TV; cable (premium). Heated pool. Complimentary coffee in lobby. Restaurant adj 6 am-11 pm. Ck-out 11 am. Cr cds: A, C, D, DS, MC, V.

★ ★ **ECONO LODGE.** *1½ mi S on US 283 at I-80. 308/324-5601; FAX 308/324-4284.* 50 rms, 2 story. May-Nov: S $29.95-$31.95; D $33.95-$37.95; each addl $5; kit. units $5 addl; lower rates rest of yr. Crib free. Pet accepted. TV; cable (premium). Heated pool. Complimentary continental bkfst. Ck-out noon. Lndry facilities. Meeting rm. Cr cds: A, C, D, DS, ER, JCB, MC, V.

★ **SUPER 8.** *Rte 2, Box 149U, near jct I-80, US 283. 308/324-7434; FAX 308/324-4433.* 47 rms, 2 story. S $34.09; D $40.39; each addl $3; under 6 free. Crib $2. TV; cable (premium). Complimentary coffee in lobby. Restaurant adj open 24 hrs. Cr cds: A, C, D, DS, MC, V.

[D] [≈] [✕] [🐾] [SC]

✔★ **TODDLE INN.** *2701 Plum Creek Pkwy, 1³/₄ mi N on US 283, at jct I-80, Lexington exit. 308/324-5595.* 25 rms, 2 story. May-Sept: S $32.95-$37.95; D $42.95-$48.95; lower rates rest of yr. Crib free. TV; cable. Heated pool. Complimentary coffee in lobby. Ck-out 11 am. Cr cds: A, DS, MC, V.

[≈] [✕] [🐾] [SC]

Lincoln (D-9)

(See also Nebraska City, Omaha)

Settled 1856 **Pop** 191,972 **Elev** 1,176 ft **Area code** 402 **E-mail** info@lincoln.org **Web** www.lincoln.org/cvb

Information Convention & Visitors Bureau, 1221 N St, Suite 320 PO Box 83737, 68501; 402/434-5348 or 800/423-8212.

Second-largest city in Nebraska, Lincoln feuded with Omaha, the territorial seat of government, for the honor of being capital of the new state. When the argument was settled in Lincoln's favor in 1867, books, documents and office furniture were moved in covered wagons late one night to escape the armed band of Omaha boosters. At that time, only 30 people lived in the new capital, but a year later there were 500, and in 1870, 2,500. As a young lawyer in the 1890s, William Jennings Bryan went to Congress from Lincoln; in 1896, 1900 and 1908 he ran unsuccessfully for president. General John J. Pershing taught military science at the University of Nebraska. Business and many cultural activities revolve around state government and the university. Lincoln is also a major grain market, as well as a manufacturing, insurance, finance, printing and trade center.

The unicameral form of government in Nebraska, which was set up by an amendment to the state constitution in 1934 (mostly by the efforts of Nebraska's famous senator, George W. Norris), is of great interest to students of political science. It works efficiently and avoids delays and deadlocks common to two-house legislatures.

What to See and Do

American Historical Society of Germans from Russia. Located here are the society's headquarters, archives, library, special displays and museum; also chapel, summer kitchen replicas. (Mon-Fri, also Sat mornings; closed major hols) 631 D St. Phone 402/474-3363. **Free.**

Bluestem Lake State Recreation Area. Approx 400 acres on 325-acre lake. Swimming; fishing; boating. Picnicking. Camping (dump station). 13 mi SW via US 77, NE 33. Phone 402/471-5566.

Branched Oak Lake State Recreation Area. Approx 1,150 acres on 1,800-acre lake. Swimming; fishing; boating (ramps). Picnicking, concession. Camping (dump station). Standard fees. 12 mi NW via US 34, NE 79. Phone 402/783-3400.

City parks.

Antelope Park. Nine-hole junior golf course (fee) at Normal and South Sts. Sunken Garden and Test Rose Garden at 27th & D Sts. 23rd & N Sts to 33rd & Sheridan Sts.

Holmes Park. Approx 550 acres with large lake. Fishing; boating (no motors). Golf course (fee), ball fields. Ice-skating. Picnicking, playground. Hyde Memorial Observatory (Sat evenings). Park (daily). 70th & Van Dorn Sts. **Free.**

Pioneers Park. Hiking, bike trails, bridle path; golf course (fee). Picnicking, playgrounds. Nature preserve & center, outdoor amphitheater. (Daily) ¹/₂ mi S of jct Coddington Ave & Van Dorn St. **Free.**

Conestoga Lake State Recreation Area. Approx 450 acres on 230-acre lake. Fishing; boating (ramps). Picnicking. Camping (dump station). 6 mi W on US 6, then 3 mi S off NE 55A. Phone 402/471-5566.

Eugene T. Mahoney State Park. More than 570 acres with 2 lakes. Swimming pool, waterslide (Memorial Day-Labor Day, daily); fishing; paddleboats. Hiking, horseback riding; miniature golf, driving range, tennis courts. Picnicking, lodging, restaurant. Camping, cabins. Greenhouse, conservatory. 25 mi NE on I-80, exit 426. Phone 402/944-2523. Per vehicle ¢¢

Folsom Children's Zoo. Exotic animals, contact areas, botanical gardens. (May-Labor Day, daily) Train and pony rides (fee). 1222 S 27th St. Phone 402/475-6741. ¢¢

Lincoln Children's Museum. A variety of cultural and scientific exhibits invite exploration and involve the senses. (June-Aug, daily; rest of yr, daily exc Wed) 121 S 13th St. Phone 402/477-0128. ¢¢

Museum of Nebraska History. History of Nebraska summarized in exhibits covering events from prehistoric times through the 1950s. Native American Gallery, period rms. (Daily; closed most major hols) 15th & P Sts. Phone 402/471-4754. Reference library and archives are located at 15th & R Sts, phone 402/471-3270. **Free.**

National Museum of Roller Skating. Skates, costumes and photographs documenting the sport and industry from 1700 to the present; also archives dealing with world and national competitions since 1910. The only museum in the world devoted solely to roller skating. (Mon-Fri; closed major hols) 4730 South St. Phone 402/483-7551. **Free.**

Nebraska Wesleyan University (1887). (1,600 students) Liberal arts school founded by the United Methodist Church. On campus is Elder Art Gallery (late Aug-mid-May, daily exc Mon). Also here is the Old Main Building (1888) and the Nebraska United Methodist Historical Center, containing archives. 50th & St Paul Sts. Phone 402/466-2371.

Pawnee Lake State Recreation Area. Approx 1,800 acres on 740-acre lake. Blue rock area. Swimming; fishing; boating (ramps). Picnicking, concession. Camping (dump station). Standard fees. 6 mi W on US 6, then 3 mi N on NE 55A. Phone 402/471-5566.

State Capitol. Designed by Bertram Goodhue, the most dominant feature of the building is the central tower, which rises 400 ft. Ground was broken in 1922 for this third capitol building at Lincoln; it was completed 10 yrs later. Sculpture by Lee Lawrie includes reliefs and friezes depicting the history of law and justice, great philosophers, symbols of the state and a bronze statue of the Sower (32 ft) atop the tower dome. The great hall, rotunda and legislative chambers are decorated in tile and marble murals, tapestries and wood inlaid panels. Hrly guided tours (daily; closed major hols). 1445 K St. Phone 402/471-0448. Nearby are

Lincoln Monument (1912). This standing figure of Lincoln was designed by sculptor Daniel Chester French, who also produced the seated Lincoln statue for Henry Bacon's Lincoln Memorial in Washington, DC. Architectural setting by Bacon.

Executive Mansion (1957). Georgian-colonial architecture. Guided tours. (Thurs afternoons; closed hols) 1425 H St. Phone 402/471-3466. **Free.**

Statehood Memorial—Thomas P. Kennard House (1869). Restored residence of Nebraska's first secretary of state. (Daily exc Mon; closed most major hols) 1627 H St. Phone 402/471-4764. **Free.**

Union College (1891). (700 students) Tours of campus. 3800 S 48th St, between Bancroft & Prescott Sts. Phone 402/488-2331 or 402/486-2504. On campus is

College View Seventh-day Adventist Church. Church noted for its stained-glass windows and Rieger pipe organ. For tours phone 402/486-2880 or -2504.

University of Nebraska (1869). (24,620 students) The university has research-extension divisions throughout the state. 14th & R Sts; E campus at 33rd & Holdrege. Phone 402/472-7211. On grounds are

University of Nebraska State Museum. Displays of fossils (dinosaurs and mounted elephants), rocks and minerals, ancient life, Nebraska plants and animals. Native American exhibits; changing exhibits. (Mon-Sat & Sun afternoons; closed Jan 1, Thanksgiving, Dec 25) **Encounter**

Center (daily). **Ralph Mueller Planetarium** (daily; fee). 14th & U Sts. Phone 402/472-2642 (museum), 402/472-2641 (planetarium). ¢

Sheldon Memorial Art Gallery and Sculpture Garden. Designed by Philip Johnson. Fine collection of 20th-century American art; changing exhibitions; film theater. (Daily exc Mon; closed hols) 12th & R Sts. Phone 402/472-2461.

Great Plains Art Collection. Works by Remington, Russell and other masters are among the nearly 700 pieces of this collection. Also featured are 4,000 volumes of Great Plains and Western Americana. (Daily; closed major hols & between academic semesters) 205 Love Library, 13th & R Sts. Phone 402/472-6220. **Free.**

Annual Events

Camp Creek Antique Machinery & Threshing Association Festival. 12 mi NE via US 6, in Waverly. Antique tractor pull; parades of antique farm machinery, cars and horse-drawn equipment; demonstrations of farm tasks and crafts. Phone 402/421-6442. Mid-July.

July Jamm 98. Art show, music festival. Downtown. Late July.

National Czech Festival. 20 mi SW via US 77, NE 41, 103, in Wilber. Czechoslovakian food, parades, polkas, contests and pageant. Phone 402/821-2732. Early Aug.

Nebraska State Fair. State Fair Park, 1800 State Fair Park Dr. Contact the State Fair, PO Box 81223, 68501; 402/474-5371. Aug 28-Sept 7.

Seasonal Event

Horse racing. State Fair Park, 1800 State Fair Park Dr. Thoroughbred racing. Phone 402/474-5371. Mid-June.

Motels

(Rates may be higher state fair week)

★ ★ **BEST WESTERN VILLAGER MOTOR INN.** 5200 O St (68510). 402/464-9111; FAX 402/467-0505. 186 rms, 2 story. S, D $60-$70; each addl $6; suites $150; under 18 free. Crib free. Pet accepted, some restrictions. TV; cable (premium), VCR avail. Pool; whirlpool. Restaurant 6 am-10 pm; Fri, Sat to 11 pm. Rm serv. Bar 3:30 pm-1 am. Ck-out noon. Coin Indry. Meeting rms. Bellhops. Valet serv. Cr cds: A, C, D, DS, MC, V.

⊠ ≋ ⊠ 🐾 SC

✔★ **BUDGET HOST GREAT PLAINS.** 2732 O St (68510). 402/476-3253; FAX 402/476-7540. 42 rms, 2 story, 6 kits. S $34-$38; D $42-$46; each addl $5; kit. units $34-$48; under 12 free; wkly rates. Crib free. TV; cable (premium). Coffee in rms. Restaurant nearby. Ck-out noon. Refrigerators. Cr cds: A, C, D, DS, ER, MC, V.

≋ 🐾 SC

★ **COMFORT INN.** 2940 NW 12th St (68521), near Municipal Airport. 402/475-2200. 67 rms, 2 story. May-Oct: S $45-$50; D $48-$55; each addl $5; under 18 free; higher rates university football season; lower rates rest of yr. Crib free. Pet accepted. TV; cable (premium). Complimentary continental bkfst. Restaurant adj open 24 hrs. Ck-out 11 am. Meeting rms. Business servs avail. Whirlpool. Game rm. Microwaves avail. Cr cds: A, C, D, DS, ER, JCB, MC, V.

D ≋ ⊠ 🐾 SC

✔★ **DAYS INN.** 2920 NW 12th St (68521), at Cornhusker Blvd. 402/475-3616; FAX 402/475-4356. 84 rms, 2 story. S $35-$48; D $45-$60; each addl $5; under 12 free. Crib free. TV; cable (premium). Complimentary continental bkfst. Restaurant adj open 24 hrs. Ck-out noon. Cr cds: A, C, D, DS, MC, V.

D ⊠ 🐾 SC

✔★ **FAIRFIELD INN BY MARRIOTT.** 4221 Industrial Ave (68504), 4 mi N on I-80, exit 403. 402/476-6000. 63 rms, 3 story. June-Sept: S $49.95-$59.95; D $59.95-$69.95; under 18 free; lower rates rest of yr. Crib free. TV; cable (premium). Complimentary coffee in lobby. Restau-

rant opp 11 am-11 pm. Meeting rms. Indoor pool; whirlpool. Cr cds: A, C, D, MC, V.

D ≋ ⊠ 🐾 SC

★ ★ **HAMPTON INN.** 1301 W Bond Circle (68521). 402/474-2080; FAX 402/474-3401. 111 rms, 3 story. S $55-$65; D $65-$75; suites $75-$150; under 18 free. Crib free. TV; cable (premium). Heated pool. Complimentary continental bkfst. Restaurant nearby. Ck-out noon. Meeting rms. Business servs avail. In-rm modem link. Microwaves avail. Private patios, balconies. Cr cds: A, C, D, DS, ER, MC, V.

D ≋ ⊠ 🐾 SC

★ **HARVESTER.** 1511 Center Park Rd (68512). 402/423-3131; res: 800/500-1366; FAX 402/423-3155. 80 rms, 28 with shower only, 2 story. S $45; D $60; under 12 free. Crib free. TV; cable (premium). Complimentary continental bkfst. Complimentary coffee in rms. Restaurant adj 6:30 am-8 pm. Meeting rms. Pool. Cr cds: A, C, D, DS, MC, V.

≋ ⊠ 🐾 SC

★ **QUALITY INN-NORTHEAST.** 5250 Cornhusker Hwy (68504). 402/464-3171; FAX 402/464-7439. 147 rms, 2 story. S $51; D $77; each addl $8-$15; under 18 free. TV; cable (premium). Indoor pool. Restaurant 6:30 am-2 pm, 5-10 pm. Rm serv. Bar 5 pm-1 am. Ck-out noon. Coin Indry. Meeting rms. Exercise equipt; bicycle, treadmill. Game rm. Cr cds: A, C, D, DS, JCB, MC, V.

D ≋ 🏃 ⊠ 🐾 SC

★ ★ **RESIDENCE INN BY MARRIOTT.** 200 S 68th · Place (68510). 402/483-4900; FAX 402/483-4464. 120 kit. suites, 2 story. S, D $98-$150; under 16. Crib free. Pet accepted; $100 ($50 refundable). TV; cable (premium), VCR avail. Heated pool; whirlpool. Complimentary full bkfst. Complimentary coffee in rms. Ck-out noon. Coin Indry. Meeting rms. Business servs avail. Valet serv. Sundries. Lighted tennis. Exercise equipt; weights, bicycles. Health club privileges. Microwaves. Balconies. Picnic tables, grills. Cr cds: A, C, D, DS, JCB, MC, V.

D 🐾 🏃 ≋ 🍴 ⊠ 🐾 SC

✔★ **TRAVELODGE.** 2901 NW 12th St (68521), near Municipal Airport. 402/474-5252; FAX 402/474-5259. 40 rms, 2 story, 5 suites. June-Aug: S $39.99; D $47.95; each addl $4; suites $40-$90; under 18 free; lower rates rest of yr. Crib free. TV; cable. Complimentary coffee in lobby. Restaurant adj open 24 hrs. Ck-out noon. Cr cds: A, C, D, DS, MC, V.

D ⊠ 🐾 SC

Hotels

★ ★ ★ **CORNHUSKER.** 333 S 13th St (68508). 402/474-7474; FAX 402/474-1847; res: 800/793-7474. Web www.thecornhusker.com. 290 rms, 10 story. S $124-$140; D $140-$155; each addl $15; suites $175-$450; under 18 free; wkend rates. Crib free. TV; cable (premium), VCR avail. Indoor pool. Restaurants 6:30 am-10 pm. Rm serv 24 hrs. Bar 4 pm-1 am. Ck-out noon. Convention facilities. Business servs avail. Gift shop. Valet parking. Free airport transportation. Exercise equipt; weights, bicycle. Health club privileges. Cr cds: A, C, D, DS, MC, V.

D ≋ 🍴 ⊠ 🐾 SC

★ ★ **RAMADA.** 141 N Ninth St (68508). 402/475-4011; FAX 402/475-9011. 233 rms, 16 story. S $75-$95; D $85-$105; each addl $10; suites $135-$240; family, wkend rates. Crib free. TV; cable (premium). Indoor pool; whirlpool, poolside serv. Coffee in rms. Restaurant 6:30 am-10 pm. Bar 11-1 am. Ck-out noon. Meeting rms. In-rm modem link. Gift shop. Free garage parking. Game rm. Cr cds: A, C, D, DS, MC, V.

D ≋ ⊠ 🐾 SC

Inn

★ **THE ROGERS HOUSE.** 2145 B St (68502). 402/476-6961; FAX 402/476-6473. 12 rms, 4 with shower only, 2 story. Many rm phones. S, D $65-$120. Children over 10 yrs only. Complimentary full bkfst. Ck-out

11 am, ck-in 4 pm. Built in 1914; historical landmark. Totally nonsmoking. Cr cds: A, DS, MC, V.

⊠ 🖑 SC

Restaurants

★ ★ **BILLY'S.** *1301 13th St, at H St. 402/474-0084.* Hrs: 11 am-2 pm, 5-10 pm, Sat from 5 pm. Closed Sun; most major hols. Res accepted. Continental menu. Bar. Semi-a la carte: lunch $5.25-$7.25, dinner $10.95-$17.95. Child's meals. Specializes in fresh fish, beef, veal. In historic house; antiques. Each of 3 dining rms pays tribute to a famous Nebraskan. Cr cds: A, C, D, DS, MC, V.

D

★ **JABRISCO.** *700 P St (68508). 402/474-7272.* Hrs: 11 am-10:30 pm. Closed most major hols. Continental menu. Bar. Semi-a la carte: lunch $2.95-$8.95, dinner $2.95-$11.95. Specialties in pasta, chicken, pizza. Cr cds: A, D, DS, MC, V.

D

McCook (E-5)

Founded 1882 **Pop** 8,112 **Elev** 2,576 ft **Area code** 308 **Zip** 69001 **E-mail** mccookchamber@navix.net **Web** www.ci.mccook.ne.us **Information** Chamber of Commerce, PO Box 337; 308/345-3200 or 800/657-2179.

McCook began as the small settlement of Fairview. The Lincoln Land Company and the Burlington & Missouri Railroad gave the town its name and ensured its growth. It is now a trading center in the middle of a vast reclamation, irrigation and oil production area.

What to See and Do

George W. Norris House. (Branch museum of Nebraska State Historical Society) Restored house of former senator (1861-1944); original furnishings; museum depicts events in his life. (Wed-Sat; also Tues & Sun afternoons; closed some major hols) 706 Norris Ave. Phone 308/345-8484. ¢

Medicine Creek Reservoir State Recreation Area. Approx 1,200 acres on 1,768-acre reservoir. Swimming; fishing; boating (ramps, rentals). Picnicking, concession. Tent & trailer camping (dump station, standard fees). 23 mi NE via US 6, 34, then 7 mi N on unnumbered road.

Museum of the High Plains. Pioneer & Native American artifacts; World War II prisoner of war paintings; apothecary shop; fossils; flour mill; oil industry exhibit; special exhibits. (Tues-Sun afternoons; closed major hols) 423 Norris Ave. Phone 308/345-3661. **Free.**

Red Willow Reservoir State Recreation Area. Approx 1,300 acres on 1,628-acre reservoir. Swimming; fishing; boating (ramps). Picnicking, concession. Tent & trailer camping (dump station, standard fees). 11 mi N on US 83. Phone 308/345-6507.

Swanson Reservoir State Recreation Area. Approx 1,100 acres on 4,973-acre reservoir. Swimming; fishing; boating (ramps). Picnicking, concession. Tent & trailer camping (dump station, standard fees). 23 mi W on US 34.

Annual Events

Sailing Regatta. Early July.

Red Willow County Fair & Rodeo. Fairgrounds, M St & 5th St W. Late July.

Heritage Days. Entertainment, parade, arts & crafts fair, carnival. Last wkend Sept.

Motels

★ ★ **BEST WESTERN CHIEF.** *612 West B St, Near Municipal Airport. 308/345-3700; FAX 308/345-7182.* 111 rms, 1-2 story. May-Dec: S $48; D $56; each addl $4; suites $72-$80; higher rates: pheasant season, first wk Nov; lower rates rest of yr. Crib $5. Pet accepted. TV; cable (premium). Indoor pool; whirlpool, poolside serv. Restaurant 6:30 am-10 pm. Ck-out 11 am. Meeting rm. Business servs avail. Cr cds: A, C, D, DS, MC, V.

D 🖛 ⊠ 🖑 SC

✔★ **SUPER 8.** *1103 East B Street. 308/345-1141; FAX 308/345-1144.* 40 rms. S $33.88; D $40.88; each addl $2; under 12 free. Crib $3. Pet accepted. TV; cable (premium). Complimentary coffee in rms. Ck-out 11 am. Cr cds: A, C, D, DS, MC, V.

D 🖛 ⊠ 🖑 SC

Minden (D-6)

(See also Kearney)

Founded 1878 **Pop** 2,749 **Elev** 2,172 ft **Area code** 308 **Zip** 68959 **Web** www.webworksltd.com/webpub/minden/minden.html **Information** Chamber of Commerce, 325 N Colorado Ave, PO Box 375; 308/832-1811.

What to See and Do

☒ **Harold Warp Pioneer Village.** Large collection of Americana that follows man's progress since 1830. Three city blks and over 30 buildings, including original sod house, schoolhouse and pony express station, chronologically represent the country's pioneer heritage. More than 50,000 historic items, including farm implements, 100 vintage tractors, locomotives, 350 antique autos and 22 historic flying machines. Restaurant; lodging (see MOTEL). Camping. (Daily) Jct US 6, 34 & NE 10. Phone 308/832-1181 or 800/445-4447. ¢¢

Annual Event

The Light of the World **Christmas Pageant.** Kearney County Courthouse, Town Square. A town tradition for many yrs; highlight of outdoor pageant is illumination of courthouse dome by 10,000 lights. Contact the Chamber of Commerce for details. Sat after Thanksgiving & 1st 2 Sun Dec.

Motel

✔★ **HAROLD WARP PIONEER VILLAGE.** *Rte 1, Box 68, 1/2 mi N on US 6/34. 308/832-2750; FAX 308/832-2750, ext. 312; res: 800/445-4447 (exc NE).* 90 rms. May-Oct: S $34-$38; D $38-$42; each addl $4; under 5 free; lower rates rest of yr. Crib $2. TV. Restaurant 6 am-9 pm; winter 7 am-8 pm. Ck-out 11 am. Campground. Harold Warp Pioneer Village adj. Cr cds: DS, MC, V.

D ⊠ 🖑

Nebraska City (D-10)

(See also Auburn, Lincoln)

Founded 1855 **Pop** 6,547 **Elev** 1,029 ft **Area code** 402 **Zip** 68410
E-mail necity@nebraskacity.com **Web** www.nebraskacity.com
Information Chamber of Commerce, 806 First Ave; 402/873-3000 or 800/514-9113.

Nebraska City began as a trading post but grew larger and wilder as the Missouri River and overland traffic brought bullwhackers, muleskinners and riverboat men with bowie knives and pistols in their belts. Located on the Missouri River, Nebraska City ships grain and agricultural products worldwide.

What to See and Do

Arbor Lodge State Historical Park. More than 60 acres of wooded grounds surround 52-rm, neo-colonial mansion of J. Sterling Morton (originator of Arbor Day and secretary of agriculture under Grover Cleveland) and summer residence of son Joy Morton (founder of Morton Salt Co). Picnicking. (See ANNUAL EVENTS) Mansion (Mar-Dec, daily). Park grounds (daily). 1 mi W on 2nd Ave. Phone 402/873-7222. ¢¢

John Brown's Cave. Original log cabin and cave where slaves were hid before and after the Civil War. (Apr-Nov, daily) 1900 4th Corso (Highway 2). Phone 402/873-3115. ¢¢

River Country Nature Center. Mounted animals native to Nebraska, 80-ft panoramic mural of the state; library, gift shop. (Late Apr-Oct, Sun; rest of yr, by appt) 110 N 6th St. Phone 402/873-5491. **Free.**

Wildwood Park. Picnicking, playground. W on 4th Corso, then N. In park is

Wildwood Historic Home (1869). A 10-rm house with mid-Victorian furnishings; formal parlor; antique lamps and fixtures. Original brick barn is now art gallery. (Apr-Nov; Tues-Sat, also Sun afternoons) Steinhart Park Rd. Phone 402/873-6340. ¢

Annual Events

Arbor Day Celebration. Tree-planting ceremonies in Arbor Lodge State Historical Park; parade, arts festival, fly-in, breakfast. Last wkend Apr.

Applejack Festival. Celebration of the apple harvest. Parade, antique & craft show, classic car show, football game. 3rd wkend Sept.

Motel

✔★ **APPLE INN.** *502 S 11th St, at jct US 75 & NE 2 Business. 402/873-5959; FAX 402/873-6640; res: 800/659-4446.* 65 rms, 1-2 story. S $35.95; D $44.95; each addl $5. TV; cable (premium). Pool. Complimentary continental bkfst. Restaurant nearby. Coin lndry. Ck-out 11 am. Business servs avail. Some refrigerators. Cr cds: A, C, D, DS, MC, V.

Inn

★ **WHISPERING PINES.** *2018 Sixth Ave, 10 blks W & 10 blks N of jct US 75 & 2 Business. 402/873-5850; res: 800/632-8477.* 5 air-cooled rms, 3 share bath, 1 with shower only, 2 story. 2 rm phones. S, D $50-$75; under 3 free. TV in some rms. Complimentary full bkfst. Ck-out 10:30 am, ck-in 5 pm. Whirlpool. Picnic tables, grills. Built in 1883; country atmosphere. Family-owned for 100 yrs. Totally nonsmoking. Cr cds: DS, MC, V.

Restaurant

★★ **EMBERS STEAKHOUSE.** *Jct US 75 & NE 2. 402/873-6416.* Hrs: 11 am-10 pm; Sun to 8:30 pm. Closed Jan 1, Dec 25. Bar. Semi-a la carte: lunch $3.50-$12.95, dinner $7.95-$17.95. Child's meals. Specializes in prime rib, fried chicken, steak. Contemporary decor. Cr cds: A, DS, MC, V.

Norfolk (B-8)

(See also Wayne)

Founded 1866 **Pop** 21,476 **Elev** 1,527 ft **Area code** 402 **Zip** 68701
E-mail mcvb@ncfcomm.com **Web** www.norfolk.ne.us
Information Madison County Convention & Visitors Bureau, PO Box 386, 68702-0386; 402/371-2932 or 888/371-2932.

German families from Wisconsin were the first to till the rich soil around Norfolk. The town's livestock business and expanding industries have brought prosperity, making Norfolk the chief marketplace of northeastern Nebraska.

What to See and Do

Neligh Mills. Complete 19th-century flour mill; milling exhibits. Maintained by the Nebraska State Historical Society. (May-Sept, daily; rest of yr, by appt) W off US 275 at Wylie Dr & N St, in Neligh. Phone 402/887-4303. ¢

Skyview Lake. Fishing; boating (no motors), canoeing. Picnicking. 1 mi W on Maple Ave.

The Cowboy Trail. 321-mi trail follows former Chicago & North Western railroad line from Norfolk to Chadron, NE. Includes 13,878 ft of hand-railed bridges. Trail is suitable for hiking and mountain biking, with horseback riding allowed alongside the trail. Phone local Chamber of Commerce for more information.

Annual Event

LaVitsef Celebration. Fall festival featuring entertainment, parade, softball tournaments. Last wkend Sept.

Motels

✔★ **ECO-LUX INN.** *1909 Krenzien Dr. 402/371-7157.* 44 rms, 2 story. S $34; D $42-$48; each addl $4; under 12 free. Crib free. TV; cable (premium). Complimentary continental bkfst. Restaurant adj 7 am-midnight. Ck-out 11 am. Cr cds: A, C, D, DS, MC, V.

★★ **NORFOLK COUNTRY INN.** *13th St, at Omaha Ave. 402/371-4430; FAX 402/371-6373; res: 800/233-0733.* 127 rms, 2 story. S $38-$46; D $44-$55; each addl $6; under 16 free. Crib free. TV; cable (premium). Pool; poolside serv. Restaurant 6 am-2 pm, 5-10 pm. Bar 11-1 am. Ck-out noon. Meeting rms. Cr cds: A, C, D, DS, MC, V.

★★ **RAMADA INN.** *1227 Omaha Ave. 402/371-7000.* 98 rms, 2 story. S, D $45-$55; each addl $7; suites $75; under 12 free. Crib free. TV; cable (premium). Indoor pool. Playground. Restaurant 6 am-2 pm, 5-10 pm. Rm serv. Bar 4 pm-1 am. Ck-out 11 am. Meeting rms. Business servs avail. Sundries. Cr cds: A, C, D, DS, JCB, MC, V.

✔★ **SUPER 8.** *1223 Omaha Ave, at jct US 81 & 275 Business. 402/379-2220; FAX 402/379-3817.* 66 rms, 2 story. S $42.98; D $51.98;

each addl $3. Crib $2. TV; cable (premium). Restaurant adj 6 am-11 pm. Ck-out 11 am. Business servs avail. Cr cds: A, C, D, DS, MC, V.

[D] [⊠] [🐾] [SC]

Restaurants

★ ★ **BRASS LANTERN.** *1018 S 9th St. 402/371-2500.* Hrs: 11 am-2 pm, 5-10 pm; Sat 5-11 pm; early-bird dinner Mon-Sat 5-7 pm. Bar. Semi-a la carte: lunch $3-$5, dinner $5-$20. Child's meals. Specializes in steak, seafood, prime rib. Salad bar. Family-owned. Cr cds: A, C, D, DS, MC, V.

★ **GRANARY.** *922 E 13th St. 402/371-5334.* Hrs: 11 am-9:30 pm; Thurs-Sat to 10:30 pm. Closed Sun; most major hols. Bar. Semi-a la carte: lunch $4.25, dinner $4.25-$6.45. Child's meals. Specializes in fried chicken. Country kitchen antiques. Family-owned. No cr cds accepted.

★ ★ **PRENGER'S.** *116 E Norfolk. 402/379-1900.* Hrs: 11 am-10 pm; Sun to 2 pm. Closed most major hols. Res accepted. Bar to midnight. Semi-a la carte: lunch $4.25-$8.95, dinner $4.50-$13.95. Child's meals. Specializes in steak, seafood. Old World atmosphere; dark wood, brass railing. Family-owned. Cr cds: A, DS, MC, V.

[D]

✔★ ★ ★ **UPTOWN.** *326 Norfolk Ave. 402/371-7171.* Hrs: 10 am-2 pm, 5-10 pm; Sat 8 am-2 pm, 5-11 pm. Res accepted. Bar. Wine list. Semi-a la carte: bkfst $1.50-$4.25, lunch $3-$5, dinner $8-$12. Specializes in seafood, prime rib, beef Wellington. Johnny Carson started his first radio show in upstairs ballroom. Cr cds: A, C, DS, MC, V.

[D]

North Platte (D-4)

Founded 1866 **Pop** 22,605 **Elev** 2,800 ft **Area code** 308 **Zip** 69101
Information North Platte/Lincoln County Convention & Visitors Bureau, 502 S Dewey, PO Box 1207; 308/532-4729 or 800-955-4528.

North Platte, Buffalo Bill Cody's home town, is the retail railroad and agricultural hub of west central Nebraska. Cattle, hogs, corn, wheat, alfalfa and hay are the principal crops.

What to See and Do

Buffalo Bill Ranch State Historical Park. Remaining of William F. Cody's ranch are the 18-rm house, barn and many outbuildings. Interpretive film; display of buffalo. (Apr-late Oct, daily) 1 mi N on Buffalo Bill Ave. Phone 308/535-8035. Per vehicle ¢¢

Cody Park. Heated swimming pool (June-Aug; fee). Tennis, softball, children's circus rides (fee). Picnicking, playgrounds. Camping (fee). Wildlife refuge. Railroad display and museum. (Daily) 3 mi N on US 83. Phone 308/534-7611. **Free.**

Fort McPherson National Cemetery. Soldiers and scouts of Native American and later wars buried here. 14 mi E on I-80 to Maxwell, then 3 mi S on county road.

Lincoln County Historical Museum. Several authentically furnished rooms and exhibits, including a World War II canteen, depict the life and history of Lincoln County. In back is re-creation of railroad village with restored depot, house, church, schoolhouse, log house, barn. (Memorial Day-Labor Day, daily; rest of yr, by appt) 2403 N Buffalo Bill Ave. Phone 308/534-5640. **Donation.**

State recreation areas.

Lake Maloney. Approx 1,100 acres on 1,000-acre lake. Swimming; fishing; boating (ramps). Picnicking. Camping (dump station). Standard hrs, fees. 6 mi S on US 83.

Arnold Lake. Approx 15 acres with 22-acre lake on upper reaches of the Loup River. Fishing; Non-power or electric boating. Picnicking. Camping. Standard hrs, fees. 37 mi NE via NE 70, 92 near Arnold.

Annual Event

"NEBRASKAland DAYS" Celebration. Parades, entertainment, food and the famous PRCA Rodeo. Phone 308/532-7948. Mid-late June.

Motels

★ **1ST INTERSTATE INN.** *on US 83 at jct I-80. 308/532-6980; res: 800/992-9026 (exc NE), 800/682-0021 (NE).* 29 rms. Mid-May-mid-Sept: S $34.95; D $40.95; each addl $2; under 12 free; lower rates rest of yr. Crib $3. Pet accepted. TV; cable (premium). Coffee in lobby. Restaurant nearby. Ck-out 11 am. Some refrigerators. Cr cds: A, C, D, DS, JCB, MC, V.

[✔] [⊠] [🐾] [SC]

★ **BEST WESTERN CHALET LODGE.** *920 N Jeffers, at US 30, 83. 308/532-2313.* 38 rms, 2 story. June-Aug: S,D $51-$69; each addl $3; under 12 free; lower rates rest of yr. Crib $2. TV; cable (premium). Heated pool. Complimentary coffee in rms. Restaurant nearby. Ck-out 11 am. Many refrigerators. Cr cds: A, C, D, DS, MC, V.

[⊠] [⊠] [🐾] [SC]

★ **BLUE SPRUCE.** *821 S Dewey St. 308/534-2600; res: 800/434-2602.* 14 rms. June-mid-Sept: S $24-$31; D $31-$39; each addl $2; lower rates rest of yr. Crib $2. Pet accepted, some restrictions. TV; cable (premium). Complimentary coffee. Restaurant nearby. Ck-out 11 am. Cr cds: A, DS, MC, V.

[✔] [⊠] [🐾] [SC]

★ **COUNTRY INN.** *321 S Dewey, I-80 exit 177. 308/532-8130; FAX 308/532-8138; res: 800/532-8130.* 40 rms, 2 story. Mid-May-Aug: S, D $29-$49; lower rates rest of yr. Crib $3. TV; cable (premium). Pool; whirlpool. Restaurant nearby. Cr cds: A, DS, MC, V.

[D] [⊠] [🐾] [SC]

★ ★ **HAMPTON INN.** *200 Platte Oasis Pkwy, I-80 & NE 83. 308/534-6000; FAX 308/534-3415.* 111 rms, 4 story. June-Sept: S $64; D $70; lower rates rest of yr. Crib free. TV; cable (premium), VCR avail. Indoor pool; whirlpool. Complimentary continental bkfst. Restaurant nearby. Ck-out noon. Business servs avail. Cr cds: A, C, D, DS, MC, V.

[D] [⊠] [⊠] [🐾] [SC]

★ **NORTH PLATTE RECREATION.** *at jct US 83 & I-80. 308/534-3120; FAX 308/532-3065.* 80 rms, 2 story. S $49.95-$52.95; D $52.95-$62.95; each addl $4; under 12 free. Crib free. TV; cable (premium). Heated pool. Complimentary coffee in lobby. Restaurant adj 11 am-9:30 pm; wkends to 10:30 pm. Bar 4 pm-1 am. Ck-out 11 am. Coin lndry. Sundries. Gift shop. Cr cds: A, C, D, DS, MC, V.

[⊠] [⊠] [🐾] [SC]

★ **SANDS MOTOR INN.** *501 Halligan Dr. 308/532-0151; FAX 308/532-6299.* 81 rms, 2 story. May-Sept: S $39-$49; D $52; each addl $6; under 12 free; lower rates rest of yr. Crib $5. TV; cable (premium). Heated pool. Restaurant open 24 hrs. Ck-out 11 am. Meeting rm. Cr cds: A, D, DS, ER, JCB, MC, V.

[D] [⊠] [⊠] [🐾]

✔★ **STANFORD.** *1400 E 4th St. 308/532-9380; res: 800/743-4934.* 32 rms. June-Aug: S $34.95; D $38.95; each addl $4; lower rates rest of yr. Crib $3. TV; cable. Complimentary coffee in lobby. Ck-out 11 am. Cr cds: A, DS, MC, V.

[⊠] [🐾] [SC]

✔★ **SUPER 8.** *220 Eugene Ave, at jct US 83 & I-80. 308/532-4224.* 113 rms, 2 story. S $34.88; D $39.88-$41.88; each addl $4; under 12 free. Crib $3. TV; cable (premium). Complimentary continental bkfst.

Restaurant nearby. Ck-out 11 am. Coin lndry. Exercise equipt; weight machine, bicycles. Cr cds: A, D, DS, MC, V.

Motor Hotel

★ ★ STOCKMAN INN. *1402 S Jeffers. 308/534-3630; FAX 308/534-0110; res: 800/624-4643 (exc NE), 800/237-2222 (NE).* 150 rms, 2 story. S $45-$50; D $50-$55; each addl $5; higher rates May-Sept. Crib free. Pet accepted, some restrictions. TV; cable (premium). Heated pool. Restaurant 6 am-10 pm. Rm serv. Bar 4 pm-1 am; entertainment exc Sun. Ck-out 11 am. Meeting rms. Business servs avail. Cr cds: A, C, D, DS, MC, V.

Restaurant

✔★ GOLDEN DRAGON. *120 W Leota. 308/532-5588.* Hrs: 11 am-2:30 pm, 4:30-9:30 pm; Fri, Sat to 10 pm. Closed some major hols. Chinese menu. Wine, beer. Semi-a la carte: lunch $3.60-$5; dinner $6-$15. Cr cds: A, DS, MC, V.

Ogallala (D-3)

Founded 1868 **Pop** 5,095 **Elev** 3,223 ft **Area code** 308 **Zip** 69153
Information Chamber of Commerce, 204 E A St, PO Box 628; 308/284-4066 or 800/658-4390.

Developed as a shipping point on the Union Pacific Railroad for the great western cattle herds, Ogallala was the goal of the cattle-driving cowboys who rode day and night with their "eyelids pasted open with tobacco." Many of them are buried in a genuine Boot Hill Cemetery, between 11th and 12th Sts, on a 100-foot rise above the South Platte River, where there have been no burials since the 1880s.

What to See and Do

Ash Hollow State Historical Park. Approx 1,000 acres on the Oregon Trail. The hills, cave and spring of Ash Hollow have sheltered man from prehistoric times through the pioneer days. Hiking. Picnicking. Interpretive center, restored school. 29 mi NW on US 26. Phone 308/778-5651. Per vehicle ¢¢

Crescent Lake National Wildlife Refuge. A nesting and migratory bird refuge comprising more than 45,000 acres with numerous pothole lakes. Birds found in the refuge include Canada geese, great blue herons, American bitterns, prairie chickens, prairie falcons and long-billed curlews. Fishing. Nature trail (1½ mi). Refuge office (Mon-Fri). 43 mi NW on US 26 to Oshkosh, then 28 mi N on unnumbered, partially paved road. Phone 308/762-4893. **Free.**

Front Street. Cowboy museum (free), general store, saloon, arcade, restaurant. Shows in Crystal Palace (summer, nightly; fee). (Daily) 519 E First St (E NE 30). Phone 308/284-4066.

Lake McConaughy State Recreation Area. Approx 5,500 acres on Nebraska's largest lake (35,700 acres). Swimming; fishing; boating (ramps, rentals). Picnicking, concession. Camping (dump station). 9 mi N on NE 61. Phone 308/284-3542. Per vehicle ¢¢

Lake Ogallala State Recreation Area. Approx 300 acres on 320-acre lake. Swimming; fishing; boating (ramps, rentals). Picnicking. Camping (dump station nearby at Martin Bay). Standard fees. 9 mi N on NE 61, below Kingsley Dam. Phone 308/284-3542. Per vehicle ¢¢

Mansion on the Hill. This 1890s mansion contains period furniture, pioneer household items. (Memorial Day-Labor Day, daily, afternoons) Contact the Chamber of Commerce for further information. 1004 N Spruce St. **Free.**

Annual Events

Keith County Fair & Round-Up Rodeo. Early Aug.
Governor's Cup Sailboat Regatta. Labor Day wkend.

Motel

★ COMFORT INN. *110 Pony Express Rd, I-80 exit 126. 308/284-4028.* 49 rms, 2 story. June-Aug: S $46.95; D $51.95-$56.95; each addl $5; suites $64.95-$84.95; under 19 free; lower rates rest of yr. Crib free. TV; cable. Indoor pool; whirlpool. Complimentary coffee in rms. Complimentary continental bkfst. Restaurant nearby. Ck-out 11 am. Coin lndry. Meeting rms. Exercise equipt; bicycles, stair machine. Cr cds: A, D, DS, MC, V.

Motor Hotels

✔★ BEST WESTERN STAGECOACH INN. *201 Stagecoach Trail, at jct NE 61 & I-80. 308/284-3656; FAX 308/284-6734.* 100 rms, 2 story. May-Sept: S $57-$67; D $62-$67; each addl $5; under 12 free; lower rates rest of yr. Crib free. Pet accepted. TV; cable, VCR (movies). Indoor/outdoor pool; wading pool, whirlpool. Playground. Restaurant 6 am-9 pm. Bar 5-10 pm. Ck-out 11 am. Coin lndry. Meeting rms. Business center. In-rm modem link. Free airport transportation. Cr cds: A, C, D, DS, MC, V.

★ ★ RAMADA LIMITED. *201 Chuckwagon Rd, at jct NE 61, I-80. 308/284-3623; FAX 308/284-4949.* 152 rms, 2 story. S, D $66; each addl $7; under 18 free. Pet accepted. TV; cable. Heated pool; wading pool, poolside serv. Continental bkfst. Restaurant 6 am-10 pm. Rm serv. Bar 5 pm-1 am. Ck-out noon. Ck-in 3 pm. Coin lndry. Meeting rms. Business servs avail. Free airport transportation. Game rm. Cr cds: A, C, D, DS, MC, V.

Restaurant

★ ★ HILL TOP INN. *197 Kingsley Dr, 8 mi N on NE 61. 308/284-4534.* Hrs: 5-10 pm. Closed Thanksgiving, Dec 25; also Jan-Mar. Bar. Semi-a la carte: dinner $7.95-$15.95. Child's meals. Specializes in steak, seafood. Hill-top view of Kingsley Dam, Lake McConaughy. Family-owned. Cr cds: A, DS, MC, V.

Omaha (C-10)

(See also Blair, Lincoln; also see Council Bluffs, IA)

Founded 1854 **Pop** 335,795 **Elev** 1,040 ft **Area code** 402 **E-mail** gocvb@aol.com **Web** www.visitomaha.org
Information Greater Omaha Convention & Visitors Bureau, 6800 Mercy Rd, Suite 202, 68106-2627; 402/444-4660 or 800/332-1819.

The largest city in Nebraska, Omaha is named for the Native American people who lived here until they signed a treaty with the federal government on June 24, 1854. Opportunists across the Missouri River in Council Bluffs, Iowa, who had been waiting for the new territory to open, then rushed to stake out property, triggering a real estate boom. Omaha also saw the trial of Standing Bear, chief of the Ponca Tribe, which established the precedent that Native Americans were human beings and entitled to constitutional rights and protections.

During early boom times, steamboats docked in Omaha daily, bringing gold-seekers and emigrants to be outfitted for the long journey west. Local merchants further prospered when Omaha was named the eastern terminus for the Union Pacific. The first rail was laid in 1865. Public buildings rose on the prairie; schools, plants and stockyards flourished in the '70s and '80s. Fighting tornadoes, grasshopper plagues, floods and drought, the people built one of the farm belt's great commercial and industrial cities.

Today, Omaha continues to be a major transportation and agribusiness center, but it is also a recognized leader in telecommunications, insurance and manufacturing as well as the home of five Fortune 500 companies. Omaha is also the headquarters of STRATCOM, the Strategic Air Command, one of the vital links in the national defense chain.

Visitors are not in Omaha long before hearing the term "AKsarben." It is, in fact, only Nebraska spelled backward and the name of a civic organization.

Transportation

Eppley Airfield: Information, lost and found, 402/422-6817; 402/422-6800; weather, 402/392-1111; cash machines, Terminal Building.

Car Rental Agencies: See IMPORTANT TOLL-FREE NUMBERS.

Public Transportation: Buses (Metro Area Transit), phone 402/341-0800.

Rail Passenger Service: Amtrak 800/872-7245.

What to See and Do

AKsarben Field and Coliseum. Site of Omaha Lancers (hockey), Omaha Racers (basketball), stock shows, a rodeo, and a variety of fairs, festivals and family entertainment. 6800 Mercy Rd. Phone 402/444-4000. (See ANNUAL EVENTS)

Belle Riverboat. An old-time riverboat offering sightseeing, dinner and dance cruises on the Missouri River. Res recommended. (Memorial Day-Labor Day, daily exc Mon) Departs Miller's Landing, off Abbott Dr. Phone 402/342-3553. Sightseeing cruise ¢¢¢

Boys Town. A community for abandoned, abused, neglected and handicapped boys and girls. Founded in 1917 by Father Flanagan, Boys Town now has six direct care programs: a residential care facility for 550 boys and girls on the Boys Town campus; a national diagnostic, treatment and research institute for children with hearing, speech and learning disorders; an urban high school for troubled youths who may have difficulty in traditional school settings; Boys Town mini-campuses around the nation; a national training program for other child care facilities; and a family-based program. Boys Town provides services to more than 17,000 youths annually. Tours of Father Flanagan museum and the Hall of History. Visitor center (daily; closed most major hols). 138th & W Dodge Rd. Phone 402/498-1140. **Free.**

City parks.

> **Heartland of America Park.** Bounded by Missouri River on the E, 8th St on the W and Douglas St on the N. A 31-acre site features picnic facilities, arbors and waterfalls. The park's 15-acre lake has a computer-driven fountain that has a colored light show at night. Excursion boat rides on The General Marion (Memorial Day-Labor Day, Wed-Sun, afternoons & evenings; fee). **Gene Leahy Mall,** bounded by Douglas & Farnam, 10th & 14th Sts. **N.P. Dodge Memorial Park,** John Pershing Dr, 7 mi N. Fishing; boating (ramp, marina). Tennis, lighted ball fields. Picnicking, playground. Camping (fee). Inquire about facilities for the disabled. **Elmwood Park,** Dodge & 60th Sts. Swimming pool. Golf course. Picnicking. **Memorial Park,** Dodge & 63rd Sts, across street from Elmwood Park. World War II memorial, rose garden, walking and jogging paths.

Fontenelle Forest Nature Center. Approx 1,250 acres of forest; 17 mi of foot trails through forest marsh, lake, prairie, floodplain environments; indoor animal exhibits; guided walks, lectures, films. (Daily; closed Jan 1, Thanksgiving, Dec 25) 7 mi S via US 75, in Bellevue, 1111 N Bellevue Blvd. Phone 402/731-3140. ¢¢

Fun Plex. Nebraska's largest waterpark includes waterslides, wave-making pool, bumper cars, go-karts. (Memorial Day-Labor Day, daily) 72nd & Q, I-80 72nd St exit. Phone 402/331-8436. ¢¢¢¢¢

General Crook House. Built in 1878 to serve as the residence of the commander of the Department of the Platte. Originally called Quarters I, Fort Omaha, the house soon came to be known by the name of its first occupant, General George Crook. Italianate architecture; many antiques from the Victorian era; Victorian garden in summer. Guided tours (by appt). (Tues-Fri, also Sun afternoons; closed major hols) 30th & Fort Sts. Phone 402/455-9990. ¢¢

Gerald Ford Birth Site. Model of original house, White House memorabilia; park, gardens, Betty Ford Memorial Rose Garden. (Daily) 32nd & Woolworth Ave. **Free.**

Great Plains Black Museum. Housed in a building designed in 1907 by prominent Nebraska architect Thomas R. Kimball, the museum preserves the history of black Americans and their part in the heritage of Omaha and Nebraska since the territorial period of the 1850s. Included are rare photographs, relics, historical displays; films. (Mon-Fri) 2213 Lake St. Phone 402/345-2212. ¢

Henry Doorly Zoo. More than 18,500 animals, many quite rare, are on display in 110-acre park. Exhibits include aquarium, indoor rainforest, walk-through aviary, white tigers and polar bears. Steam train rides (Memorial Day-Labor Day, daily). IMAX 3-D theater (daily; fee). Restaurant. Picnic areas. (Daily; closed Jan 1, Thanksgiving, Dec 25) 3701 S 10th St, I-80 13th St South exit. Phone 402/733-8401(zoo) or 402/330-IMAX (theater). ¢¢¢

Historic Bellevue. Restored buildings include old church (1856), the first church in the Nebraska territory; old depot (1869), contains period artifacts; settlers' log cabin (ca. 1830); and Fontenelle Bank (1856). Sarpy County Historical Museum, 2402 SAC Place, has displays concerning the history of the county and changing exhibits (daily; closed Jan 1, Thanksgiving, Dec 25). 9 mi S via US 75. Phone 402/293-3080. Museum ¢

Joslyn Art Museum (1931). Museum building of art-deco design with collections of art, ancient through modern, including European and American paintings, sculpture; art of the Western frontier, Native American art; traveling exhibitions. Guided tours, lectures, workshops, films, gallery talks, concerts. A 30,000-volume art reference library; museum shop. (Daily exc Mon; closed major hols) 2200 Dodge St. Phone 402/342-3300. ¢¢

Louisville State Recreation Area. Approx 192 acres with 50 acres of water area. Swimming; fishing; boating (no motors). Picnicking, concession. Camping (standard fees, dump station). 25 mi SW via I-80, NE 50. Phone 402/234-6855.

Mormon Trail Center at Winter Quarters. The winter of 1846-1847 took the lives of more than 600 Mormon emigrants who camped near here. A monument commemorates their hardship. Films and pioneer exhibits in visitor center. 32nd & State Sts. Phone 402/453-9372.

Old Market. Art galleries, antique shops, restaurants. Revitalization of old warehouse district; some of Omaha's oldest commercial buildings line the market's brick-paved streets. Center at 11th & Howard Sts extending E to 10th St & W to 13th. Phone 402/341-7151.

Omaha Childrens Museum. A private, nonprofit institution that emphasizes self-directed exploration and play for children and families, the museum offers a constantly changing series of hands-on exhibits in science, the arts and humanities, health and creative play. (Daily exc Mon; closed hols) 500 S 20th St. Phone 402/342-6164 or -6163 (recording). ¢¢

Platte River State Park. An innovative 413-acre park offering a wide variety of activities and lodging facilities. Located on rolling bluffs overlooking the Platte River. Swimming pool; paddleboats. Hiking, horseback riding; tennis courts, archery range, recreational fields. Cross-country skiing. Picnicking, concession, restaurant. Camper cabins & housekeeping cabins. Arts & crafts building; observation tower; free use of recreational equipment. 17 mi SW on I-80, then 14 mi S on NE 50 to NE Spur 13E, then W. Phone 402/234-2217.

Schramm Park State Recreation Area. Approx 330 acres along the north bank of the Platte River. A day-use area offering hiking and nature trails, picnicking and several other activities. In the park are geological displays, fish hatchery ponds and the Gretna Fish Hatchery Museum, which utilizes displays and audiovisual presentations to tell the story of fish and fishery management in Nebraska. Museum (Memorial Day-Labor Day, daily; Apr-late May & after Labor Day-Nov, daily exc Tues; rest of yr, Wed-Sun;

closed some hols). Park (daily). I-80 exit 432, then 6 mi S on NE 31. Phone 402/332-3887 or -3901. Entry permit ¢¢ Also located here is

AK-Sar-Ben Aquarium, a modern facility featuring aquariums that display more than 50 species of fish native to Nebraska, a terrarium, World Herald Auditorium, a natural history classroom and orientation and display areas. (Seasons same as Gretna Fish Hatchery Museum) Phone 402/332-3901. ¢

Strategic Air Command Museum. Past, present aircraft and missiles used by SAC. (Daily; closed Jan 1, Thanksgiving, Dec 25) 2510 SAC Pl, in Bellevue, 12 mi S via US 75. Phone 402/292-2001. ¢¢

Trolley. Trackless *Ollie the Trolley* provides transportation along Douglas and Farnam Sts to the Old Market, Gene Leahy Mall and 16th Street Mall. Stops posted along route. (Daily) Phone 402/597-3596. ¢

Two Rivers State Recreation Area. More than 600 acres with water area of 320 acres. Swimming; trout fishing (fee); boating. Picnicking, concession. Camping (standard fees, dump station), trailer pads (fee), rental cabins (converted Union Pacific Railroad cabooses; late Apr-Oct). 23 mi W off US 275, NE 92. Phone 402/359-5165. Per vehicle ¢

University of Nebraska at Omaha (1908). (16,000 students) 60th & Dodge Sts. For tours contact Admissions office, phone 402/554-2393. On campus is

Kountze Planetarium. Planetarium shows display galaxies, stars, planets and other celestial phenomena. Observatory (first Fri, Sat each month). Shows (limited hrs; fee). 60th & Dodge Sts, on first floor of Durham Science Center. For schedule phone 402/554-2219. ¢¢

Western Heritage Museum. Restored art deco railroad depot is now a history museum. Exhibits on Omaha history from 1880 to 1954; Byron Reed coin collection. (Daily exc Mon; closed major hols) In Omaha Union Station, 801 S 10th St. Phone 402/444-5071. ¢¢

Annual Events

NCAA College Baseball World Series. Rosenblatt Stadium, 13th St & Bert Murphy Dr. Phone 402/444-4750. Early June.

Summer Arts Festival. Downtown. Phone 402/333-2442. Last wkend June.

River City Round-up. Fairgrounds. Celebration of agriculture and western heritage includes parade, barbecues, trail rides. Phone 402/554-9610. Late Sept.

Christmas at Union Station. For details, contact Western Heritage Museum. Dec.

City Neighborhoods

Many of the restaurants, unrated dining establishments and some lodgings listed under Omaha include neighborhoods as well as exact street addresses. Geographic descriptions of Downtown and Old Market are given, followed by a table of restaurants arranged by neighborhood.

Downtown: Area south of Capitol St, west of the Missouri River, north of Leavenworth St and east of 24th St. **South of Downtown:** South of Leavenworth St. **West of Downtown:** West of 25th St.

Old Market: Area of downtown south of Harney St, west of 10th St, north of Jackson St and east of 13th St.

OMAHA RESTAURANTS BY NEIGHBORHOOD AREAS
(For full description, see alphabetical listings under Restaurants)

DOWNTOWN
Le Cafe de Paris. 1128 S 6th St
Maxine's (Red Lion Inn Hotel). 1616 Dodge St

SOUTH OF DOWNTOWN
Bohemian Cafe. 1406 S 13th St
Imperial Palace. 11201 Davenport St
Johnny's Cafe. 4702 S 27th St

WEST OF DOWNTOWN
Aquarium. 1850 S 72nd St
Chu's Chop Suey. 6455 Center St
Gallagher's. 10730 Pacific
Gorat's Steak House. 4917 Center St
Grandmother's. 8989 W Dodge St
La Strada 72. 3125 S 72nd St

OLD MARKET
Butsy Le Doux's. 1014 Howard St
French Cafe. 1017 Howard St
Garden Cafe. 1212 Harney
Indian Oven. 1010 Howard St
Neon Goose. 1012 S 10th St
Trini's. 1020 Howard St
V. Mertz. 1022 Howard St

Note: When a listing is located in a town that does not have its own city heading, it will appear under the city nearest to its location. In these cases, the address and town appear in parenthesis immediately following the name of the establishment.

Motels

★ ★ **BUDGETEL INN.** *10760 M Street (68127), south of downtown.* 402/592-5200; FAX 402/592-1416. 96 rms, 2 story. S $42.95; D $49.95; suites $49.95-$51.95; under 19 free; wkend, special events rates. Crib free. Pet accepted. TV; cable (premium). Complimentary continental bkfst. Complimentary coffee in rms. Restaurant nearby. Ck-out noon. Business servs avail. In-rm modem link. Cr cds: A, C, D, DS, MC, V.

D ⮌ ⊠ ⊠ ⊠ SC

✔ ★ **ECONO LODGE.** *I-80 & 84th St (68124), west of downtown.* 402/391-4321. 81 rms, 2 story. S $34.95; D $39.95; each addl $4; suites $59.95-$78.95; under 12 free. TV; cable (premium), VCR avail (movies $2). Restaurant adj open 24 hrs. Ck-out 11 am. Meeting rms. Cr cds: A, D, MC, V.

D ⊠ ⊠ ⊠ SC

★ ★ **HAMPTON INN.** *9720 W Dodge Rd (68114).* 402/391-5300; FAX 402/391-8995. 129 rms, 4 story. S $60-$75; D $65-$81; suites $90-$170; under 18 free. Crib free. TV; cable (premium), VCR avail. Complimentary continental bkfst. Restaurant adj open 24 hrs. Ck-out noon. Meeting rms. Business servs avail. In-rm modem link. Sundries. Valet serv. Cr cds: A, C, D, DS, MC, V.

D ⊠ ⊠ ⊠ SC

★ ★ **HAMPTON INN.** *10728 L Street (68127), south of downtown.* 402/593-2380; FAX 402/593-0859. 133 rms, 4 story. S $56-$62; D $61-$68; under 18 free. Crib free. Pet accepted. TV; cable, VCR avail (movies). Pool. Complimentary continental bkfst. Restaurant nearby. Meeting rms. Business servs avail. In-rm modem link. Cr cds: A, C, D, DS, MC, V.

D ⮌ ⊠ ⊠ ⊠ SC

★ ★ **LA QUINTA.** *3330 N 104th Ave (68134), north of downtown.* 402/493-1900; FAX 402/496-0757. 130 rms, 2 story. S $56; D $54-$61; 1st addl $5; suites $68-$80; under 18 free. Crib free. Pet accepted, some restrictions. TV; cable (premium). Heated pool. Continental bkfst in lobby. Restaurant adj open 24 hrs. Ck-out noon. Coin lndry. Meeting rms. In-rm modem link. Sundries. Cr cds: A, C, D, DS, MC, V.

D ⮌ ⊠ ⊠ ⊠ SC

✔ ★ **PARK INN INTERNATIONAL.** *9305 S 145th St (68138), south of downtown.* 402/895-2555; FAX 402/895-1565. 56 rms, 3 story. No elvtr. S $41.50; D $46.50; each addl $5; suites $85; under 16 free. Crib free. Pet accepted; $25. TV; cable (premium), VCR avail (movies). Complimentary coffee in lobby. Bar 1 pm-1 am. Ck-out 11 am. Coin lndry. Whirlpool. Cr cds: A, C, D, DS, ER, JCB, MC, V.

D ⮌ ⊠ ⊠ ⊠ SC

★ **QUALITY INN.** *78th & Dodge Sts (68114), west of downtown.* 402/393-5500; FAX 402/393-2240. 330 rms, 2 story. May-Aug: S $50-$55; D $56-$61; each addl $5; suites $90-$150; under 12 free; package plans. Crib free. TV; cable. Indoor pool; whirlpool. Complimentary coffee in rms. Restaurant 6:30-12:30 am. Rm serv. Bars 10-1 am. Ck-out noon. Coin lndry. Meeting rms. In-rm modem link. Valet serv. Sundries. Beauty shop. Free airport transportation. Exercise equipt; weights, stair machine, sauna. Some refrigerators. Some private patios, balconies. Cr cds: A, C, D, DS, JCB, MC, V.

⊡ ⩲ ⌇ ⊠ ⩗ SC

★★ **QUALITY INN CROWN COURT.** *NE 370 & Hillcrest (68005), south of downtown.* 402/292-3800. 127 rms, 2 story. S $46.99; D $51.99; each addl $5; under 18 free. Crib free. TV; cable. Indoor pool; wading pool, whirlpool, poolside serv. Complimentary full bkfst. Restaurant 6 am-9 pm. Rm serv. Bar 3 pm-1 am. Ck-out noon. Coin lndry. Meeting rms. Business servs avail. Game rm. Some refrigerators. Balconies. Cr cds: A, C, D, DS, ER, JCB, MC, V.

⊡ ⩲ ⊠ ⩗ SC

★★ **RESIDENCE INN BY MARRIOTT.** *6990 Dodge St (68132), east of downtown.* 402/553-8898. 80 kit. suites. S $120; D $150. Crib free. Pet accepted, some restrictions; $25. TV; cable (premium), VCR avail (movies). Heated pool; whirlpool. Complimentary continental bkfst. Ck-out noon. Business servs avail. In-rm modem link. Tennis. Health club privileges. Fireplaces. Balconies. Cr cds: A, C, D, DS, JCB, MC, V.

⊡ ⧓ ⌇ ⩲ ⊠ ⩗ SC

✔★★ **SAVANNAH SUITES.** *4809 S 107 Ave (68127).* 402/592-8000; FAX 402/592-8000; res: 800/937-8483. 34 rms, 2 story. S, D $55; each addl $2; under 12 free. Crib free. TV; cable, VCR avail (movies). Complimentary continental bkfst. Restaurant nearby. Ck-out noon. Meeting rm. Refrigerators. Cr cds: A, C, D, DS, MC, V.

⊡ ⊠ ⩗ SC

★ **SLEEP INN.** *2525 Abbott Dr (68110), near Eppley Field Airport, north of downtown.* 402/342-2525; FAX 402/342-2525, ext. 303. 93 rms, shower only, 2 story, 12 suites. S $41.99-$46.99; D $51.99-$61.99; each addl $5; suites $51.95; under 18 free; wkend rates. Crib free. TV; cable. Complimentary continental bkfst. Ck-out noon. Meeting rms. In-rm modem link. Free airport transportation. Cr cds: A, C, D, DS, ER, JCB, MC, V.

⊡ ⌇ ⊠ ⩗ SC

✔★ **SUPER 8.** *10829 M St (68137), south of downtown.* 402/339-2250; FAX 402/339-6922. 118 rms, 3 story. No elvtr. S $40.88; D $49.88; each addl $3; under 13 free. Crib $2. TV; cable (premium). Complimentary continental bkfst. Ck-out 11 am. Meeting rm. Sundries. Cr cds: A, C, D, DS, MC, V.

⊡ ⊠ ⩗ SC

★ **SUPER 8.** *(303 Fort Crook Rd, Bellevue 68005) 10 mi S on NE 75.* 402/291-1518; FAX 402/292-1726. 40 rms, 2 story. S $33-$39; D $42-$52; each addl $4. Crib $6. TV; cable (premium). Complimentary continental bkfst. Restaurant adj open 24 hrs. Ck-out 11 am. Business servs avail. In-rm modem link. Cr cds: A, C, D, DS, ER, JCB, MC, V.

⊡ ⊠ ⩗ SC

Motor Hotels

★★★ **BEST WESTERN OMAHA INN.** *4706 S 108th St (68137), west of downtown.* 402/339-7400; FAX 402/339-5155. 102 rms, 7 story. May-Sept: S $56-$64; D $64-$74; under 12 free; wkend rates; lower rates rest of yr. Crib free. TV; cable (premium), VCR avail (movies). Indoor pool; whirlpool. Complimentary continental bkfst. Bar 5 pm-1 am. Ck-out noon. Meeting rms. Business servs avail. In-rm modem link. Exercise equipt; weights, bicycles, sauna. Rec rm. Some refrigerators. Cr cds: A, C, D, DS, MC, V.

⩲ ⌇ ⊠ ⩗ SC

★★★ **BEST WESTERN-CENTRAL.** *3650 S 72nd St (68124), I-80 exit 449, west of downtown.* 402/397-3700; FAX 402/397-8362. 213 rms, 5 story. June-Aug: S $59-$69; D $69-$89; each addl $6; suites $85-$150; under 18 free; wkend rates; lower rates rest of yr. Pet accepted, some restrictions. TV; cable (premium). Indoor pool; whirlpool, sauna. Restaurant 6:30 am-10 pm. Rm serv. Bar 4 pm-1 am. Ck-out noon. Coin lndry. Meeting rms. Business servs avail. In-rm modem link. Bellhops. Airport transportation. Game rm. Refrigerator in suites. Cr cds: A, C, D, DS, ER, JCB, MC, V.

⊡ ⧓ ⩲ ⊠ ⩗ SC

★★★ **CLARION CARLISLE HOTEL.** *10909 M Street (68137), west of downtown.* 402/331-8220; FAX 402/331-8729. 139 rms, 2-3 story. S, D $69-$99; suites $175; under 18 free. Crib free. Pet accepted, some restrictions; $30. TV; cable. Indoor pool; whirlpool. Complimentary continental bkfst. Coffee in rms. Restaurant 6:30-10:30 am, noon-2 pm, 5-10 pm. Rm serv. Bar 4:30 pm-midnight. Ck-out noon. Coin lndry. Meeting rms. Business center. In-rm modem link. Bellhops. Valet serv. Free airport transportation. Cr cds: A, C, D, DS, ER, JCB, MC, V.

⊡ ⧓ ⩲ ⊠ ⩗ SC ⌘

✔★★ **HOLIDAY INN EXPRESS.** *3001 Chicago (68131), north of downtown.* 402/345-2222; FAX 402/345-2501. 123 rms, 6 story. S $61-$64; D $67; each addl $6; suites $100-$140; under 18 free. Crib free. TV; cable (premium). Complimentary continental bkfst. Restaurant nearby. Ck-out noon. Coin lndry. Meeting rms. Business servs avail. In-rm modem link. Valet serv. Free airport transportation. Exercise equipt; weight machine, bicycle, whirlpool, sauna. Refrigerators. Cr cds: A, C, D, DS, MC, V.

⊡ ⌇ ⊠ ⩗ SC

★★ **SHERATON INN.** *4888 S 118th St (68137), west of downtown.* 402/895-1000; FAX 402/895-9247. 168 rms, 6 story. S $74; D $84; under 17 free. Crib free. Pet accepted, some restrictions. TV; cable (premium). Indoor pool; wading pool, whirlpool, sauna. Restaurant 6:30 am-10 pm. Rm serv. Bar 11-1 am. Ck-out noon. Coin lndry. Meeting rm. Business servs avail. Valet serv. Sundries. Free airport transportation. Game rm. Sun deck. Cr cds: A, C, D, DS, JCB, MC, V.

⊡ ⧓ ⩲ ⊠ ⩗ SC

Hotels

★★★ **DOUBLETREE GUEST SUITES.** *7270 Cedar St (68124), west of downtown.* 402/397-5141; FAX 402/397-3266. 189 kit. suites, 6 story. S $109; D $119; each addl $10; under 16 free; wkend rates. Crib free. TV; cable (premium), VCR avail (movies). Indoor pool; whirlpool. Complimentary bkfst. Restaurant 7 am-2 pm, 5-10 pm; Fri, Sat to 11 pm. Coin lndry. Meeting rms. Business servs avail. In-rm modem link. Gift shop. Free airport transportation. Exercise equipt; weights, stair machine, sauna. Indoor tropical courtyard. Cr cds: A, C, D, DS, MC, V.

⊡ ⩲ ⌇ ⊠ ⩗ SC

★★★ **MARRIOTT.** *10220 Regency Circle (68114), west of downtown.* 402/399-9000; FAX 402/399-0223. 301 rms, 4-6 story. S, D $180; suites $250; under 18 free; long-wkend rates. Crib free. Pet accepted, some restrictions. TV; cable, VCR avail. Indoor/outdoor pool; whirlpool, poolside serv, lifeguard. Restaurants 6:30 am-11 pm. Bar 4 pm-1 am. Ck-out noon. Convention facilities. Business servs avail. In-rm modem link. Shopping arcade. Exercise equipt; weights, bicycles, sauna, steam rm. Private patios, balconies. Luxury level. Cr cds: A, C, D, DS, ER, JCB, MC, V.

⊡ ⧓ ⩲ ⌇ ⊠ ⩗ SC

★★★ **RADISSON.** *1504 Harney St (68102), downtown.* 402/342-1500; FAX 402/342-5317. 89 rms, 11 story. Apr-Oct: S, D $115; each addl $15; suites $145-$275; under 18 free; wkend rates. Crib free. Garage $4. TV; cable (premium). Complimentary bkfst. Rm serv 24 hrs. Bar. Ck-out noon. Meeting rms. Business servs avail. In-rm modem link. Free airport, RR station, bus depot transportation. Exercise equipt; weights, bicycles, whirlpool, sauna. Cr cds: A, C, D, DS, ER, MC, V.

⊡ ⌇ ⊠ ⩗ SC

✔★ ★ **RAMADA-CENTRAL.** *7007 Grover St (68106), south of downtown.* 402/397-7030; FAX 402/397-8449. 215 rms, 9 story. S, D $79-$89; each addl $10; suites $135-$145; under 18 free; wkend rates. Crib free. Pet accepted. TV; cable (premium). Indoor pool; whirlpool, sauna. Playground. Restaurant 6 am-10 pm; Sat, Sun from 7 am. Bar 5 pm-1 am. Ck-out noon. Meeting rms. Business servs avail. In-rm modem link. Gift shop. Free airport transportation. Cr cds: A, C, D, DS, MC, V.

★ ★ ★ **RED LION INN.** *1616 Dodge St (68102), downtown.* 402/346-7600; FAX 402/346-5722. 413 rms, 19 story. S $148; D $163; each addl $15; suites $150-$450; under 18 free; wkend rates. Crib free. TV; cable (premium). Coffee in rms. Restaurant 6 am-midnight (also see MAXINE'S). Bar 11-1 am; entertainment exc Sun. Ck-out noon. Meeting rms. Business center. In-rm modem link. Gift shop. Barber, beauty shop. Free airport transportation. Exercise equipt; weights, bicycles, sauna, steam rm. Some refrigerators. Cr cds: A, C, D, DS, ER, JCB, MC, V.

Restaurants

★ ★ ★ **AQUARIUM.** *1850 S 72nd St, west of downtown.* 402/392-0777. Hrs: 5 pm-closing. Closed Sun; major hols. Res accepted; required wknds. Continental menu. Bar. Wine list. Semi-a la carte: dinner $12.95-$89.95. Child's meals. Specializes in seafood. Pianist Fri, Sat. Parking. Aquariums with exotic fish. Cr cds: A, C, D, DS, MC, V.

✔★ **BOHEMIAN CAFE.** *1406 S 13th St, south of downtown.* 402/342-9838. Hrs: 11 am-9 pm; Fri, Sat to 10 pm. Closed Dec 25. Res accepted. Czechoslovakian, Amer menu. Semi-a la carte: lunch $4.25, dinner $5.95-$10.95. Specialties: jägerschnitzel, hasenpfeffer, roast pork. Accordian player Fri, Sat. European atmosphere; Czechoslovakian prints. Cr cds: DS, MC, V.

★ ★ **BUTSY LE DOUX'S.** *1014 Howard St, in Old Market.* 402/346-5100. Hrs: 11:30 am-10 pm; Fri, Sat to 11 pm. Closed Sun; most major hols. Cajun menu. Bar. Semi-a la carte: lunch $3.50-$7.25, dinner $7.25-$15.95. Specialties: Bayou boiled crawfish, blackened fish, VooDoo stew. Entertainment Fri & Sat evenings in summer. Parking. Outdoor dining. Collection of Salvador Dali paintings. Cr cds: A, C, D, MC, V.

★ **CHU'S CHOP SUEY.** *6455 Center St, west of downtown.* 402/553-6454. Hrs: 11 am-9 pm; Fri, Sat to 10 pm; Sun, hols from noon. Closed Tues; Jan 1, Thanksgiving, Dec 24, 25. Res accepted. Chinese menu. Bar. Semi-a la carte: lunch $4.25-$4.95, dinner $5.25-$14.75. Child's meals. Specializes in chicken subgum, sweet & sour pork. Parking. Family-owned. Cr cds: A, C, D, DS, MC, V.

★ ★ ★ **FRENCH CAFE.** *1017 Howard St, in Old Market.* 402/341-3547. Hrs: 11 am-2 pm, 5:30-10 pm, Fri, Sat to 11 pm; Sat, Sun brunch 10:30 am-2 pm. Res accepted. French, Amer menu. Bar. Wine list. Semi-a la carte: lunch $5.95-$8.75, dinner $16.95-$25. Specializes in fresh fish, pasta. Own pastries. Cr cds: A, C, D, DS, MC, V.

★ **GALLAGHER'S.** *10730 Pacific, in Shaker Place Shopping Ctr, west of downtown.* 402/393-1421. Hrs: 11 am-10 pm; Fri, Sat to 11 pm. Closed Thanksgiving, Dec 25. Bar. Res accepted. A la carte entrees: lunch $5.25-$7.95. Semi-a la carte: dinner $6.95-$15.95. Child's meals. Specialties: chicken ranchero, turkey Raphael. Cr cds: A, C, D, DS, MC, V.

★ **GARDEN CAFE.** *1212 Harney, in Old Market.* 402/422-1574. Hrs: 6 am-10 pm. Closed Dec 25. Wine, beer. Semi-a la carte: bkfst $2.99-$5.99, lunch $3.99-$7.99, dinner $5.99-$14.99. Child's meals. Own

desserts. Parking. Cafe-style dining. Totally nonsmoking. Cr cds: A, D, DS, MC, V.

★ ★ **GORAT'S STEAK HOUSE.** *4917 Center St, west of downtown.* 402/551-3733. Hrs: 11 am-2 pm, 5-10:30 pm; Mon 5-10 pm; Fri, Sat to midnight. Closed Sun; major hols. Res accepted; required Fri, Sat. Bar. Semi-a la carte: lunch $3.50-$6.25, dinner $6.25-$29. Child's meals. Specializes in steak, seafood, Italian dishes. Piano bar; entertainment Fri, Sat. Parking. Fireplace. Cr cds: A, MC, V.

✔★ **GRANDMOTHER'S.** *8989 W Dodge St, west of downtown.* 402/391-8889. Hrs: 11 am-11 pm; Fri, Sat to midnight; Sun 10 am-11 pm. Closed Thanksgiving, Dec 25. Bar. Semi-a la carte: lunch, dinner $4.25-$11.99. Buffet (Sun): $7.99. Child's meals. Specialites: taco salad, quiche. Parking. Rustic, early-American decor. Cr cds: A, C, D, DS, MC, V.

✔★ ★ ★ **IMPERIAL PALACE.** *11201 Davenport St, south of downtown.* 402/330-3888. Hrs: 11:30 am-2:30 pm, 5-9:30 pm; Fri to 10:30 pm; Sat 5-10:30 pm; Sun noon-9 pm. Closed major hols. Chinese menu. Bar. Wine list. A la carte entrees: lunch $4.35-$5.95, dinner $6.50-$12.95. Specializes in Peking duck, Szechwan dishes, family dinners. Parking. Chinese artwork and decor. Cr cds: A, MC, V.

★ ★ **INDIAN OVEN.** *1010 Howard St, in Old Market.* 402/342-4856. Hrs: 11:30 am-2 pm, 5:30-10 pm; Fri, Sat to 11 pm; Sun 5:30-10 pm. Closed Mon; Thanksgiving, Dec 25. Res accepted; required Fri, Sat. Northern Indian menu. Bar. A la carte entrees: lunch $5.50-$6.75, dinner $12-$15. Specializes in chicken, lamb, fish. Parking. Outdoor dining. East Indian decor. Cr cds: A, C, D, DS, MC, V.

★ **JOHNNY'S CAFE.** *4702 S 27th St, south of downtown.* 402/731-4774. Hrs: 11 am-2 pm, 5-10 pm; Fri, Sat to 10:30 pm. Closed Sun; some hols. Res accepted; required hols. Bar. Semi-a la carte: lunch $5-$8.65, dinner $9-$20. Child's meals. Specializes in steak, prime rib, fresh seafood. Parking. Western decor. Family-owned. Cr cds: A, D, DS, MC, V.

★ ★ ★ **LA STRADA 72.** *3125 S 72nd St, west of downtown.* 402/397-8389. Hrs: 11 am-2 pm, 5:30-10 pm; Fri, Sat 5:30-11 pm. Closed Sun; major hols. Res accepted. Italian menu. Bar to midnight. Wine list. Semi-a la carte: lunch $6-$8, dinner $10-$30. Specializes in veal, pasta, fresh seafood. Own pastries. Parking. Outdoor dining. European bistro decor. Cr cds: A, D, MC, V.

★ ★ ★ **LE CAFE DE PARIS.** *1128 S 6th St, downtown.* 402/344-0227. Hrs: 6-10:30 pm. Closed Sun; major hols. Res required. French menu. Bar. Wine cellar. A la carte entrees: dinner $16-$36. Specializes in fresh fish, veal, seasonal fowl. Own breads. Parking. Intimate atmosphere. Chef-owned. Jacket. No cr cds accepted.

★ ★ ★ **MAXINE'S.** *(See Red Lion Inn Hotel)* 402/346-7600. Hrs: 11 am-2 pm, 5-10 pm; Fri, Sat 5-11 pm; Sun 9:30 am-2 pm, 5-9 pm; Sun brunch to 2 pm. Res accepted. Bar. Semi-a la carte: lunch $6.95, dinner $16-$24. Sun brunch $12.95. Specializes in steak, fresh seafood. Own pastries. Parking. Panoramic view of city from 19th floor. Cr cds: A, C, D, DS, ER, MC, V.

★ ★ **NEON GOOSE.** *1012 S 10th St, in Old Market.* 402/341-2063. Hrs: 11 am-10 pm; Fri, Sat to 11 pm; Sun 4-10 pm. Closed Mon; major hols. Continental menu. Piano bar. Semi-a la carte: lunch $4-$7.95, dinner $7.25-$17.95. Sun brunch $3.65-$6.95. Specializes in omelets, quiche, fresh fish. Own baking. Parking. Outdoor dining. In early 1900s building; antique furniture. Cr cds: A, C, D, DS, MC, V.

[D]

✔★ **TRINI'S.** *1020 Howard St, in Old Market. 402/346-8400.* Hrs: 11:30 am-10 pm; Fri, Sat to 11 pm. Closed Sun; some major hols. Mexican menu. Bar. Semi-a la carte: lunch $3.95-$6.95, dinner $4.95-$7.95. Specializes in seafood, enchiladas, fajitas. Parking. Cr cds: A, C, D, MC, V.

[D]

★ ★ ★ **V. MERTZ.** *1022 Howard St, in Old Market. 402/345-8980.* Hrs: 11:30 am-2 pm, 6-10 pm; Fri, Sat to 11 pm. Res accepted. Continental menu. Bar. Semi-a la carte: lunch $6.95-$9.50, dinner $21.95-$29.95. Specializes in fresh fish, pepper steak. Parking. Cr cds: A, C, D, DS, MC, V.

[D]

O'Neill (B-7)

Settled 1874 **Pop** 3,852 **Elev** 2,000 ft **Area code** 402 **Zip** 68763 **E-mail** oneill@inetnebr.com **Web** www.inetnebr.com/~oneill

Information Chamber of Commerce, 315 E Douglas; 402/336-3007.

General John J. O'Neill founded this Irish colony along the Elkhorn River in the north central portion of the state. His colorful career included fighting, as a captain of black troops, for the North in the Civil War and attacking Canada in the armed Fenian invasion of Irish patriots. O'Neill is known as the Irish capital of Nebraska and holds an annual St Patrick's Day celebration.

What to See and Do

Atkinson Lake State Recreation Area. Approx 53 acres on the Elkhorn River. Fishing; boating (non-power or electric). Picnicking. Camping. Standard hrs, fees. 18 mi W on US 20, near Atkinson.

Pibel Lake State Recreation Area. Approx 40 acres with a 24-acre lake. Fishing; boating (non-power or electric). Picnicking. Camping. Standard hrs, fees. 51 mi S on US 281, near Bartlett.

Motels

★ **CAPRI.** *1/2 mi E on US 20, 275. 402/336-2762; FAX 402/336-4365; res: 800/341-8000.* 26 rms. S $29-$38; D $38-$45; each addl $2. Crib free. Pet accepted. TV; cable (premium). Playground. Complimentary coffee in lobby. Restaurant nearby. Ck-out 11 am. Free airport transportation. Picnic tables, grill. Cr cds: A, C, D, DS, MC, V.

✔ ➡ 🐾

✔★ **ELMS.** *1 mi E on US 20, 275. 402/336-3800; res: 800/526-9052.* 21 rms. S $25; D $30-$38; each addl $3. Crib $2. Pet accepted. TV; cable (premium). Playground. Restaurant opp 7 am-11 pm. Ck-out 11 am. Cr cds: A, DS, MC, V.

✔ ➡ 🐾 SC

★ **GOLDEN HOTEL.** *406 E Douglas, jct US 20, 281. 402/336-4436; FAX 402/336-3549; res: 800/658-3148.* 27 rms, 3 story. S $27; D $32; each addl $5. Crib free. Pet accepted, some restrictions. TV; cable (premium), VCR (movies). Complimentary continental bkfst. Restaurant adj 6 am-10 pm. Ck-out 11 am. Valet serv. Restored hotel built 1913. Cr cds: A, DS, MC, V.

[D] ✔ 🐾

★ **INNKEEPER INN.** *725 E Douglas. 402/336-1640.* 45 rms, 1-2 story. S $30-$34; D $35-$39; each addl $5. Crib $5. TV; cable. Heated pool. Complimentary continental bkfst. Restaurant 11 am-2 pm, 5:30-10

pm; Sun 10 am-2 pm. Bar 5:30-11 pm. Ck-out 11 am. Meeting rms. Cr cds: A, C, D, DS, MC, V.

➡ 🐾 SC

Scottsbluff (C-1)

(See also Gering)

Pop 13,711 **Elev** 3,885 ft **Area code** 308 **Zip** 69361 **Web** www.scb_ger@prairieweb.com/scb_gering_ucc/

Information Scottsbluff-Gering United Chamber of Commerce, 1517 Broadway; 308/632-2133.

Scottsbluff is the trading center for a large area of western Nebraska and eastern Wyoming.

What to See and Do

Agate Fossil Beds National Monument. An approx 2,700-acre area under development; two self-guided nature trails; visitor center with exhibits of the fossil story of mammals that roamed the area 19-21 million yrs ago; also exhibits of Plains Native Americans. Visitor center (daily; closed Dec 25). Park (all yr). 9 mi NW on US 26 to Mitchell, then 34 mi N on NE 29. Phone 308/668-2210. For further information contact the Superintendent, PO Box 27, Gering 69341; 308/436-4340. Per vehicle ¢¢

Lake Minatare State Recreation Area. Approx 800 acres on 2,158-acre lake. Swimming; fishing; boating (ramps). Hiking. Picnicking, concession. Camping (dump station). (Mid-Jan-Sept) 10 mi E on US 26, then 10 mi N on unnumbered road. Phone 308/783-2911.

Riverside Zoo. More than 70 species of both native and exotic animals in a lush park setting. Walk-through aviary, white tiger, moose woods. (Oct-Apr, daily, weather permitting). 1600 S Beltline West, W of NE 71. Phone 308/630-6236. ¢¢

Scotts Bluff National Monument (see). 3 mi S on NE 71 to Gering, then 3 mi W on NE 92.

West Nebraska Arts Center. Changing gallery shows in all media throughout the yr showcasing the finest artists in the region. (Dec 25-Jan 1) 106 E 18th St. Phone 308/632-2226. **Donation.**

Wildcat Hills State Recreation Area Reserve & Nature Center. Approx 650 acres in unusual, rugged terrain of the high country of western Nebraska. Buffalo and elk in natural scenic habitat. Shelter houses. Hiking. Picnicking. Camping. 13 mi S on NE 71. Phone 308/436-2383.

Motels

★ **CANDLELIGHT INN.** *1822 E 20th Pl. 308/635-3751; FAX 308/635-1105; res: 800/424-2305.* 56 rms, 2 story. S $55; D $60; each addl $6. Crib $5. TV; cable (premium). Heated pool. Complimentary continental bkfst. Restaurant adj 6 am-11 pm. Bar 4 pm-midnight. Ck-out 11 am. Airport transportation. Exercise equipt; weights, treadmill. Some refrigerators. Cr cds: A, C, D, DS, MC, V.

➡ 🏋 ➡ 🐾 SC

★ ★ **COMFORT INN.** *2018 Delta Dr. 308/632-7510; FAX 308/632-8495.* 46 rms, 2 story, 4 suites. June-Aug: S $44.95; D $49.95-$54.95; each addl $5; suites $71.95; under 18 free. Crib free. TV; cable (premium). Indoor pool; whirlpool. Complimentary continental bkfst. Ck-out 11 am. Coin lndry. Meeting rms. Refrigerator in suites. Cr cds: A, D, DS, ER, MC, V.

[D] ➡ ➡ 🐾 SC

Scotts Bluff National Monument (C-1)

(For accommodations see Scottsbluff; also see Gering)

(3 mi W of Gering on NE 92)

This 800-foot bluff in western Nebraska was a landmark to pioneers who traveled the California/Oregon Trail by wagon trains. Historians often speak of this natural promontory in the North Platte Valley, which was originally named me-a-pa-te, "hill that is hard to go around," by the Plains Native Americans. Many people, including fur traders, Mormons and gold seekers, came this way. Westward-bound pioneers, Pony Express riders and the first transcontinental telegraph all passed through Mitchell Pass (within Monument boundaries) in order to skirt this pine-studded bluff. The Oregon Trail Museum at the monument's visitor center (daily; closed Dec 25) depicts the story of westward migration along the trail; artwork by the famous pioneer artist and photographer William Henry Jackson is on permanent display. Check with the Oregon Trail Museum for a schedule of special events. A paved road and hiking trail provide access to the summit for a view of the North Platte Valley and other landmarks, such as Chimney Rock (see). The summit road is open to traffic daily. Visitors also may walk along the old Oregon Trail, remnants of which still exist within the park. Covering five square miles, Scotts Bluff became a national monument in 1919. (Daily) For further information contact PO Box 27, Gering 69341-0027; 308/436-4340. Per vehicle ¢¢

Sidney (D-2)

Founded 1867 **Pop** 5,959 **Elev** 4,085 ft **Area code** 308 **Zip** 69162
Information Cheyenne County Visitor's Committee, 740 Illinois St; 800/421-4769.

In 1867, Sidney was established as a division point on the Union Pacific Railroad. Fort Sidney was established shortly thereafter, providing military protection for railroad workers and immigrants. Many relics of the Fort Sidney era remain and have been restored. Sidney, the seat of Cheyenne County, is also a peaceful farm, trading and industrial center.

What to See and Do

Cabela's. Corporate headquarters for one of world's largest outdoor gear outfitters. 73,000-sq-ft bldg displays over 60,000 products; also over 500 wildlife mounts. Other attractions in showroom are an 8,000-gallon aquarium; art gallery; gun library; restaurant; and "Royal Challenge," a twice-lifesize bronze sculpture of 2 battling elk. (Daily) I-80, exit 59. Phone 308/254-5505.

Fort Sidney Post Commander's Home (1871). One of the original buildings of old Fort Sidney; used in the 19th century to protect railroad workers during the Native American wars; authentically restored. (Memorial Day-Labor Day, daily, afternoons) 1108 6th Ave. Phone 308/254-2150. **Free.** Other restored buildings in the Fort Sidney complex include

Double Set Officer's Quarters Museum. Built in 1884 as quarters for married officers. (Daily, afternoons) 6th & Jackson. Phone 308/254-2150. **Free.**

Powder House. Can be viewed only from the outside. 1033 Fifth Ave.

Annual Events

County Fair & NSRA Rodeo. Late July-early Aug.

Oktoberfest. 1st wkend Oct.

Motels

★ **COMFORT INN.** *730 E Jennifer Lane, I-80 exit 59.* 308/254-5011; FAX 308/254-5122. 94 rms, 2 story. June-Oct: S $47-$50; D $50-$58; each addl $4; under 18 free; lower rates rest of yr. Crib $3. TV; cable. Complimentary continental bkfst. Restaurant nearby. Ck-out 11 am. Coin lndry. Whirlpool. Cr cds: A, D, DS, JCB, MC, V.

D 🐾 🏊 🐾 SC

✓★ **DAYS INN.** *3042 Silverberg Dr.* 308/254-2121. 47 rms, 2 story. June-Sept: S $46-$50; D $51-$55; each addl $5; suites $73-$80; under 12 free; lower rates rest of yr. Crib free. TV; cable (premium). Indoor pool; whirlpool. Complimentary continental bkfst. Complimentary coffee in rms. Restaurant adj 6:30 am-10 pm. Ck-out 11 am. Coin lndry. Business servs avail. In-rm modem link. Valet serv. Sundries. Exercise equipt; bicycles, rowers. Refrigerator in suites. Cr cds: A, C, D, DS, MC, V.

D 🏊 🏋 🐾 🐾 SC

South Sioux City (B-9)

(See also Sioux City, IA)

Pop 9,677 **Elev** 1,096 ft **Area code** 402 **Zip** 68776
Information Visitors Bureau, 2700 Dakota Ave; 800/793-6327.

What to See and Do

Ponca State Park. Approx 850 acres. Panoramic views of the Missouri River Valley. Swimming pool (fee); fishing; boating (ramps). Hiking, horseback riding. Cross-country skiing. Picnicking. Camping (14-day max, standard fees; dump station, trailer pads), cabins (mid-Apr-mid-Nov), primitive camping during off-season. 18 mi NW off NE 12, on Missouri River. Phone 402/755-2284.

Annual Event

Waterfest Weekend. On the bank of the Missouri River. Balloon races, Mighty MO 5k run/walk, waterskiing expo, athletic tournaments. Phone 800/793-6327. Last wkend June.

Seasonal Event

Horse racing. Atokad Park, 2½ mi SW. Thoroughbred racing; parimutuel betting. For information phone 402/494-3611. Early Sept-late Oct.

Motels

✓★ **ECONO LODGE.** *4402 S Dakota Ave.* 402/494-4114. 60 rms, 2 story. S $40; D $52-$62; each addl $5; under 12 free. Crib free. TV; cable. Complimentary continental bkfst. Restaurant nearby. Ck-out 11 am. Coin lndry. Business servs avail. Whirlpool. Cr cds: A, D, DS, MC, V.

D 🐾 🐾 SC

★ **PARK PLAZA.** *1201 1st Ave.* 402/494-2021; FAX 402/494-5998; res: 800/341-8000. 52 rms. S $35-$45; D $43-$53; each addl $3. Crib $5. TV; cable. Pool. Restaurant 6 am-9 pm. Bar from 11 am. Ck-out 11 am. Cr cds: A, C, D, DS, MC, V.

🏊 🐾 🐾 SC

✓★ **TRAVELODGE.** *400 Dakota Ave.* 402/494-3046; FAX 402/494-8299. 61 rms, 2 story. S $40; D $48-$60; each addl $4. Pet accepted. TV; cable (premium). Complimentary continental bkfst. Restaurant nearby. Ck-out 11 am. Business servs avail. Airport transportation. Cr cds: A, D, DS, MC, V.

D 🐾 🐾 🐾 SC

Motor Hotel

★ ★ ★ **MARINA INN.** *4th & B Streets, I-29 exit 148. 402/494-4000; FAX 402/494-2550; res: 800/798-7980.* 182 rms, 5 story. S $65-$77; D $75-$87; each addl $10; under 18 free. Crib free. Pet accepted. TV; cable, VCR avail. Indoor pool; whirlpool. Restaurant 6:30 am-10 pm. Rm serv. Bars 11-1 am. Ck-out 11 am. Meeting rms. Free airport transportation. Some private patios. On Missouri River. Cr cds: A, D, DS, MC, V.

D 🐾 ⚲ 🔥 SC

Thedford (B-5)

Pop 243 **Elev** 2,848 ft **Area code** 308 **Zip** 69106

What to See and Do

Nebraska National Forest. Site of the Bessey Nursery (1902), oldest Forest Service tree nursery in the US. Swimming pool (fee). Hiking; tennis. Picnicking. Camping (some fees). 15 mi E on NE 2. Bessey Ranger District office is 2 mi W of Halsey; phone 308/533-2257. (Also see CHADRON and Samuel R. McKelvie Natl Forest, VALENTINE)

Valentine (A-5)

(See also Mission, SD)

Settled 1882 **Pop** 2,826 **Elev** 2,579 ft **Area code** 402 **Zip** 69201 **Web** www.valentine_ne.com

Information Chamber of Commerce, PO Box 201; 402/376-2969 or 800/658-4024.

Valentine, the seat of Cherry County, depends on cattle raising for its economy.

What to See and Do

Cherry County Historical Museum. Items and exhibits related to the history of Cherry County; 1882 log cabin; newspapers dating back to 1883; genealogy library. (May-Sept, daily) S Main St & US 20. Phone 402/376-2015. **Donation.**

Fishing. Bass, crappie, perch, northern pike in numerous lakes S of town, including

Big Alkali Lake Wildlife Area. Swimming; hunting; boating. Picnicking. Camping. 17 mi S on US 83, then 3 mi W on NE 16B.

Valentine National Wildlife Refuge. Eight fishing lakes, waterfowl, upland game bird and deer hunting. Nature study, bird watching. (Daily, daylight hrs) 17 mi S on US 83, then 13 mi W on NE 16B. Phone 402/376-3789. **Free.**

Fort Niobrara National Wildlife Refuge. Visitor center with exhibits. Nature study, canoeing, wildlife observation, picnicking. Also here are Fort Falls Nature Trail, Fort Niobrara Wilderness Area, a prairie dog town and herds of buffalo, Texas longhorns and elk. (Memorial Day-Labor Day, daily; rest of yr, Mon-Fri) 5 mi E on NE 12. Phone 402/376-3789. **Free.**

Samuel R. McKelvie National Forest. Hunting. Hiking. Picnicking. Camping. Part of the Bessey Ranger District of the Nebraska National Forest (see CHADRON and THEDFORD). 30 mi W on US 20, then 19 mi S on NE 97. For information contact PO Box 38, Halsey 69142; 308/533-2257. In the forest are Merritt Reservoir is

Merritt Reservoir State Recreation Area. Approx 6,000 acres with a 2,906-acre reservoir in sandhill area. Swimming; fishing; boating (ramps). Picnicking, concession. Camping (dump station). Wildlife refuges nearby. Standard hrs, fees. 25 mi SW on NE 97.

Sawyer's Sandhills Museum. Pioneer and Native American artifacts, antique autos. (Memorial Day-Labor Day, daily; rest of yr, by appt) On US 20, 4 blks W of US 83. Phone 402/376-3293. ¢

Annual Events

Cherry County Fair. Cherry County Fairgrounds. Midway, rodeo, agricultural & crafts exhibits; races; concessions. Aug.

Old West Days & Poetry Gathering. Poetry, music and fun celebrating Old West heritage. Sept.

Motels

★ **DUNES.** *US 20E, E US 20. 402/376-3131.* 24 rms. May-mid-Sept: S $30; D $36-$38; each addl $3; lower rates rest of yr. Crib $2. TV; cable. Restaurant nearby. Ck-out 11 am. Cr cds: A, DS, MC, V.

🐾 ★ **RAINE.** *W US 20. 402/376-2030; res: 800/999-3066.* 34 rms. May-Oct: S $36; D $36-$42; each addl $2. Crib $2. Pet accepted. TV; cable. Coffee in rms. Restaurant nearby. Ck-out 11 am. Free airport transportation. Cr cds: A, C, D, DS, MC, V.

🐾 ⚲ 🔥

★ **TRADE WINDS LODGE.** *US 20E & 83. 402/376-1600; res: 800/341-8000.* 32 rms. May-Sept: S $27-$40; D $42-$50; each addl $2; lower rates rest of yr. Crib free. Pet accepted. TV; cable. Heated pool. Complimentary coffee. Ck-out 11 am. Free airport transportation. Cr cds: A, C, D, DS, MC, V.

🐾 ⚲ 🔥 SC

Restaurant

🐾 ★ **HOME CAFE.** *109 W US 20. 402/376-3222.* Hrs: 6 am-10 pm; Sun brunch 11 am-2 pm. Res accepted. Bar. Semi-a la carte: bkfst $2.65-$4.35, lunch $3.50-$5.25, dinner $5.25-$10. Sun brunch $6. Child's meals. Specializes in T-bone, rib-eye & Swiss steaks. Informal, family-style dining. Family-owned. Cr cds: MC, V.

Wayne (B-8)

(See also Norfolk)

Founded 1881 **Pop** 5,142 **Elev** 1,500 ft **Area code** 402 **Zip** 68787

Information Wayne Area Chamber of Commerce, 108 W 3rd St; 402/375-2240.

Laid out when the railroad connecting St Paul to Sioux City was being built, the town was named after General "Mad Anthony" Wayne.

What to See and Do

Wayne State College (1910). (4,000 students) Liberal arts, business and teacher education. Tours. 200 E 10th. Phone 402/375-7000.

Fred G. Dale Planetarium. Features dome-shaped screen, dozens of auxiliary and special effects projectors, and unique sound system. (Oct-Apr, by appt; closed hols) Phone 402/375-7329. **Free.**

Annual Events

Chicken Show. Music contests, parade, omelet feed, chicken dinner feed, egg games, chicken arts & crafts, antique show & sale. 2nd Sat July.

Wayne County Fair. 1/2 mi W on NE 35. 4-H exhibits, agricultural displays, carnival, nightly entertainment, free barbecue. Aug.

Motel

✔★ **K-D INN.** *311 E 7th St. 402/375-1770; FAX 402/256-3442.* 21 rms, 2 story. S $29; D $35-$40. Crib $2. TV; cable (premium). Complimentary coffee in rms. Continental bkfst. Restaurant nearby. Ck-out 11 am. Cr cds: A, DS, MC, V.

West Point (C-9)

Founded 1857 **Pop** 3,250 **Elev** 1,335 ft **Area code** 402 **Zip** 68788

Named by early settlers who considered it the western extremity of settlement, West Point was originally a mill town.

What to See and Do

John G. Neihardt Center. Contains memorabilia of Nebraska's late poet laureate; restored one-rm study; Sioux Prayer Garden symbolizes Sioux Hoop of the World. (Daily; closed Jan 1, Thanksgiving, Dec 25) 11 mi N on NE 9, then 8 mi E on NE 51, at Elm & Washington Sts in Bancroft. Phone 402/648-3388. **Free.**

Motel

✔★ **POINTER'S INN.** *534 S Lincoln St, on US 275 at NE 9, 32. 402/372-2491.* 28 rms. S $23-$30; D $36-$38; each addl $3. TV; cable. Restaurant 6 am-9:30 pm. Bar 4:30 pm-1 am. Ck-out 10 am. Cr cds: MC, V.

York (D-8)

(See also Grand Island, Lincoln)

Founded 1869 **Pop** 7,884 **Elev** 1,609 ft **Area code** 402 **Zip** 68467

What to See and Do

Anna Bemis Palmer Museum. Items and displays relating to the history of the city, York County and the state of Nebraska. (Daily; closed hols) 211 E 7th St. Phone 402/363-2630. **Free.**

Motels

★ **BEST WESTERN PALMER INN.** *2426 S Lincoln Ave, on US 81. 402/362-5585; FAX 402/362-6053.* 41 rms. S $36-$40; D $47-$50; each addl $4; under 12 free. Crib $3. TV; cable (premium). Heated pool. Playground. Restaurant adj. Ck-out 11 am. Coin lndry. Cr cds: A, C, D, DS, MC, V.

★ **DAYS INN.** *3710 S Lincoln, US 81 & I-80. 402/362-6355; FAX 402/362-2827.* 39 rms, 2 story. Apr-Sept: S $42-$48; D $55; lower rates rest of yr. Crib free. TV; cable (premium). Indoor pool; whirlpool. Complimentary continental bkfst. Restaurant adj 6 am-11 pm. Ck-out 11 am. Cr cds: A, D, DS, MC, V.

★ **WAYFARER.** *Henderson (68371), 4 mi S via US 81 to I-80, at jct I-80 & S-93A. 402/723-5856; res: 800/543-0577.* 34 rms. June-mid-Sept: S $28; D $34; each addl $4; lower rates rest of yr. Crib $3. TV. Heated pool. Playground. Restaurant open 24 hrs. Ck-out 11 am. Coin lndry. Cr cds: A, C, D, MC, V.

✔★★ **YORK INN.** *4619 S Lincoln Ave. 402/362-6661; FAX 402/362-3727.* 120 rms, 2 story. S $34.50; D $39.50; each addl $5; under 18 free. Crib free. TV; cable (premium). Pool. Complimentary bkfst. Restaurant 6 am-11 pm; Fri, Sat to 2 am. Rm serv avail. Bar 4 pm-1 am. Ck-out 11 am. Meeting rms. Cr cds: A, C, D, DS, ER, JCB, MC, V.

★ **YORKSHIRE.** *Rte 3, Box 19B, 1/2 mi N of I-80 at US 81. 402/362-6633; FAX 402/362-5197; res: 800/341-8000.* 29 rms, 3 story. S $30-$33; D $34-$38; each addl $4; suites $45-$50. Crib $4. TV; cable (premium). Playground. Coffee in lobby. Restaurant adj 6 am-11 pm. Ck-out 11 am. Cr cds: A, C, D, DS, MC, V.

Restaurant

✔★★ **CHANCES "R".** *124 W 5th. 402/362-7755.* Hrs: 6-1 am; Sun 8 am-midnight; Sun brunch 10 am-2 pm. Closed Jan 1 & Dec 24 evenings, Dec 25. Res accepted. Bar. Semi-a la carte: bkfst $1.75-$5.95, lunch $4.75-$5.75, dinner $6.25-$15.45. Sun brunch $10.45. Child's meals. Specializes in pan-fried chicken, charcoal steak, prime rib. Salad bar. Turn-of-the-century decor; many antiques. Family-owned. Cr cds: DS, MC, V.

North Dakota

Population: 638,800
Land area: 69,299 square miles
Elevation: 750-3,506 feet
Highest point: White Butte (Slope County)
Entered Union: November 2, 1889 (39th state, same day as South Dakota)
Capital: Bismarck
Motto: Liberty and Union, Now and Forever, One and Inseparable
Nickname: Flickertail State, Sioux State, Peace Garden State
State flower: Wild prairie rose
State bird: Western meadowlark
State tree: American elm
State fair: July 24-August 1, 1998, in Minot
Time zone: Central and Mountain
Web: www.ndtourism.com

I n Bismarck stands a heroic statuary group, *Pioneer Family*, by Avard Fairbanks; behind it, gleaming white against the sky, towers the famous skyscraper capitol. One symbolizes the North Dakota of wagon trains and General Custer. The other symbolizes the North Dakota that has emerged in recent years—a land where a thousand oil wells have sprouted, dams have harnessed erratic rivers, vast lignite resources have been developed and industry is absorbing surplus farm labor created by mechanization.

At various times Spain, France and England claimed what is now North Dakota as part of their empires. French Canadian fur trappers were the first Europeans to explore the land. With the Louisiana Purchase, Lewis and Clark crossed Dakota, establishing Fort Mandan. The first settlement was established in 1812 at Pembina by settlers from the Earl of Selkirk's colony in Manitoba. The first military post at Fort Abercrombie served as a gateway into the area for settlers. The Dakota Territory was organized March 2, 1861, but cultivation of the land was interrupted by pitched battles with Native Americans during much of the 19th century.

This is a fascinating land of prairies, rich river valleys, small cities, huge ranches and vast stretches of wheat. Bordering Canada for 320 miles to the north, it shares straight-line borders with Montana to the west and South Dakota to the south. The Red River of the North forms its eastern boundary with Minnesota. The Garrison Dam (see) has changed much of the internal geography of the state's western areas, converting the Missouri River, known as "Big Muddy," into a broad waterway with splendid recreation areas bordering the reservoir, Lake Sakakawea. In addition, the Oahe Dam in South Dakota impounds Lake Oahe, which stretches north almost to Bismarck. To the southwest stretch the Badlands in all their natural grandeur, amid the open range about which Theodore Roosevelt wrote so eloquently in his *Ranch Life and the Hunting Trail*.

North Dakota's wealth is still in its soil—agriculture, crude oil and lignite (a brown variety of very soft coal). It is estimated that 1/3 of the state is under oil and gas lease, and it ranks high in the nation for the production of oil; the largest deposits of lignite coal in the world are here. The same land through which Custer's men rode with range grass growing up to their stirrups now makes North Dakota the nation's number one cash grain

state. North Dakota leads the nation in the production of barley, durum, spring wheat, pinto beans, oats and flaxseed. Nearly 2,000,000 head of cattle and more than 165,000 sheep are produced on North Dakota grass.

While the rural areas comprise the economic backbone of North Dakota, attractions attributed to a "big city" can be found. In July of 1981, blackjack became a legal form of gambling, causing a number of casinos to open statewide. High stakes games and slot machines can be found in casinos operated by Native Americans on four reservations. Parimutuel horse-racing was legalized in 1987. All gambling profits, above expenses, go to nonprofit and charitable organizations.

This is the state in which to trace 19th-century frontier history, to explore the International Peace Garden (see BOTTINEAU), to stand at the center of the continent, to watch Native American dances and outdoor dramas, to fish in the 180-mile-long Lake Sakakawea or just to watch the ten million migratory waterfowl that soar across the sky each spring and fall.

When to Go/Climate

North Dakota winters are long and merciless, with bitter cold temperatures and insistent winds. Spring is cool and rainy; summers are hot and sunny. Summer hailstorms and thunderstorms are not uncommon in the Badlands.

AVERAGE HIGH/LOW TEMPERATURES (°F)

BISMARCK

Jan 20/-2	**May** 68/42	**Sept** 71/43
Feb 26/5	**June** 77/52	**Oct** 59/33
Mar 39/18	**July** 84/56	**Nov** 39/18
Apr 55/31	**Aug** 83/54	**Dec** 25/3

FARGO

Jan 15/-4	**May** 69/44	**Sept** 69/46
Feb 21/3	**June** 77/54	**Oct** 57/35
Mar 35/17	**July** 83/59	**Nov** 37/19
Apr 54/32	**Aug** 81/57	**Dec** 20/3

CALENDAR HIGHLIGHTS

JUNE

Expo '98 (Bismarck). Civic Center. Carnival, livestock exhibits, food, music. Phone 701/222-6487.

Buffalo Trails Day (Williston). Parade, chuck wagon breakfast, old-time music, contests, games. Phone 701/859-4361.

Grand Forks County Fair (Grand Forks). County fairgrounds. Phone 701/772-3421.

Fort Seward Wagon Train (Jamestown). A one-week wagon train experience. Wagons are pulled by draft horses or mules; train stops along the way at historical sites. Participants dress and camp in the manner of the pioneers. Phone 701/252-6844.

AUGUST

North Dakota State Fair (Minot). State Fairgrounds. 4-H, livestock, commercial exhibits; horse and tractor pulls, carnival, machinery show, concerts, auto races, demolition derby. Phone 701/852-FAIR.

Pioneer Days (Fargo). Bonanzaville, USA. Celebration of area pioneer heritage. People in period costume, parades, arts and crafts. Phone 701/282-2822.

SEPTEMBER

United Tribes Powwow (Bismarck). One of the largest in the nation, featuring Native American dancing and singing, events, food, games, crafts and contests. Phone 701/255-3285.

Parks and Recreation Finder

Directions to and information about the parks and recreation areas below are given under their respective town/city sections. Please refer to those sections for details.

Key to abbreviations: I.P. = Interstate Park; N.B.C. = National Battlefield & Cemetery; N.B.P. = National Battlefield Park; N.F. = National Forest; N.G. = National Grassland; N.H. = National Historical Park; N.H.S. = National Historic Site; N.M. = National Monument; N.Mem. = National Memorial; N.M.P. = National Military Park; N.P. = National Park; N.Pres. = National Preserve; N.R. = National Recreational Area; N.R.R. = National Recreational River; N.Res. = National Reserve; N.S. = National Seashore; N.S.R. = National Scenic River; N.S.T. = National Scenic Trail; N.V.M. = National Volcanic Monument; S.B. = State Beach; S.C.P. = State Conservation Park; S.G. = State Garden; S.H.A. = State Historic Area; S.H.P. = State Historic Park; S.N.A. = State Natural Area; S.P. = State Park; S.R. = State Reserve; S.R.A. = State Recreation Area; S.Res.P. = State Resort Park; S.R.P. = State Rustic Park.

NATIONAL PARK AND RECREATION AREAS

Place Name	Listed Under
Fort Union Trading Post N.H.S.	WILLISTON
Knife River Indian Villages N.H.S.	GARRISON DAM
Theodore Roosevelt N.P.	same

STATE RECREATION AREAS

Place Name	Listed Under
Fort Abraham Lincoln S.P.	MANDAN
Lake Metigoshe S.P.	BOTTINEAU
Lake Sakakawea S.P.	GARRISON DAM
Lewis and Clark S.P.	WILLISTON
Turtle River S.P.	GRAND FORKS

Water-related activities, hiking, riding, various other sports, picnicking and visitor centers, as well as camping, are available in many of these areas. Camping facilities ($11-$13/night with electricity; $8-$10/night, no electricity; $3 less with annual permit) at state parks. All motor vehicles entering a state park must obtain a motor vehicle permit: annual $20; daily $3. Pets on leash only. The North Dakota Tourism Department, 604 E Boulevard Ave, Bismarck 58505, offers information on facilities at national, state and local parks and recreation areas; phone 800/HELLO-ND.

SKI AREAS

Place Name	Listed Under
Bottineau Winter Park Ski Area	BOTTINEAU
Huff Hills Ski Area	MANDAN

FISHING & HUNTING

Species found in the state are trout, pike, sauger, walleye, bass, salmon, panfish, catfish and muskie. Fishing season is year-round in many waters. Obtain state's fishing regulations for details. Nonresident license, $25; seven-day nonresident license, $15; three-day nonresident license, $10.

The pothole and slough regions of central North Dakota annually harbor up to four million ducks; waterfowl hunting is tops. Pheasants, sharptails, Hungarian partridge and deer are also found here. Nonresident small game license $83; with waterfowl $93.

For further information contact the State Game and Fish Department, 100 N Bismarck Expressway, Bismarck 58501-5095; 701/328-6300.

Driving Information

Children 10 years and under must be in an approved passenger restraint anywhere in vehicle: children ages 3-10 must be properly secured in an approved safety seat or buckled in a safety belt; children under age 3 must be properly secured in an approved safety seat. For further information phone 701/328-2455.

INTERSTATE HIGHWAY SYSTEM

The following alphabetical listing of North Dakota towns in *Mobil Travel Guide* shows that these cities are within 10 miles of the indicated Interstate highways. A highway map, however, should be checked for the nearest exit.

Highway Number	Cities/Towns within 10 miles
Interstate 29	Fargo, Grafton, Grand Forks, Wahpeton.
Interstate 94	Bismarck, Dickinson, Fargo, Jamestown, Mandan, Medora, Valley City.

Additional Visitor Information

North Dakota Tourism Department, Capitol Grounds, Bismarck 58505; phone 800/435-5663, has helpful travel information. *North Dakota Horizons*, published four times yearly, is available from the Greater North Dakota Assn, 2000 Shafer St, Bismarck 58501.

Seven state-owned tourist information centers are open Memorial Day-Labor Day. These centers are: Beach Tourist Information Center, located in the truck regulatory weigh station, eastbound lane of I-94 in Beach; Bowman Information Center, located on US 12W; Fargo Information Center, located at I-94, 45th St exit; Oriska Information Center, located at Oriska Rest Area, 12 miles east of Valley City on eastbound and westbound lanes of I-94; Hankinson Information Center, located at Lake Agassiz Rest Area, 2 miles south of Hankinson on northbound lane of I-29, 12 miles south of Wahpeton; Pembina Information Center, located on ND 59, in Pembina, adj to I-29, in tower building with observation deck; Williston Information Center, located at US 2 and 6th Ave W.

Bismarck (C-3)

(See also Mandan)

Settled 1873 **Pop** 49,256 **Elev** 1,680 ft **Area code** 701 **E-mail** visitnd @bismarck-mandancvb.org **Web** bismarck-mandancvb.org

Information Bismarck-Mandan Convention & Visitors Bureau, 107 W Main St, PO Box 2274, 58502; 701/222-4308 or 800/767-3555.

Lewis and Clark camped near here in 1804, and Jim Bridger, Prince Maximilian of Wied, Sitting Bull, General Sully, General Sibley, Theodore Roosevelt and the Marquis de Mores all figured in Bismarck's history. On the east bank of the Missouri, near the geographic center of the state and within 150 miles of the geographic center of the continent, the city flourished as a steamboat port called "the crossing." As the terminus of the Northern Pacific Railway, it gained new importance and was named for the Chancellor of Germany to attract German capital to invest in building transcontinental railroads. General Custer came to Bismarck to take command of the newly constructed Fort Abraham Lincoln nearby and in 1876 rode out to his fatal rendezvous with Sitting Bull. In 1883, Bismarck became the capital of the Dakota Territory and in 1889, the seat of the new state.

What to See and Do

Camp Hancock State Historic Site. This site preserves part of a military camp established in 1872 to provide protection for workers then building the Northern Pacific Railroad. Site includes headquarters building, now wood sheathed; an early Northern Pacific Railroad locomotive and one of Bismarck's oldest churches, which was moved to the site and restored. (Mid-May-mid-Sept, Wed-Sun) Main & 1st Sts. Phone 701/328-2666. **Free.**

Double Ditch Indian Village. State historic site contains the ruins of large Mandan Native American earth lodge village inhabited from 1675-1780; earth lodge and two surrounding fortifications are clearly discernible. (Daily) 9½ mi NW via ND 1804. Phone 701/328-2666.   **Free.**

Lewis & Clark **Riverboat.** Daily cruises to Ft Abraham Lincoln State Park; also dinner, family, pizza & moonlight cruises. (Memorial Day-Labor Day, daily) North River Rd at Riverboat Junction. Phone 701/255-4233. 1½- or 2-hr cruise   ¢¢¢¢

McDowell Recreation Area. Swimming beach; boating (no motors; ramp, dock; canoe, paddle and sailboat rentals). Walking trails. Picnicking (shelters by res); playground. Alcoholic beverage permit required. (May-Sept, daily) 6 mi E on ND 10. Phone 701/255-7385.

Riverside-Sertoma Park. Playground; amusement park with miniature golf, children's rides. (Late Apr-Labor Day wkend, daily; some fees). Along Missouri River at W Bowen Ave & Riverside Park Rd. Phone 701/255-1107.   ¢¢   Adj is

Dakota Zoo. More than 600 mammals, birds and reptiles on 80 acres. Miniature train ride (fee); concessions. (Early May-Sept, daily) Phone 701/223-7543.   ¢¢

⊠ **State Capitol** (1933-1934). "Skyscraper of the Prairies," 18 stories high, topped with an observation tower. White limestone shaft houses offices of officials and departments; three-story circular wing serves as forum for legislature. Unique and distinctive interiors with exotic wood paneling, stone and metals. Tours (daily; closed some major hols) N 6th St. Phone 701/328-2480.   **Free.**   Also on grounds are

North Dakota Heritage Center. Permanent and changing exhibits on history and settlement of northern Great Plains. State archives and research library. Gift shop. (Daily, limited hrs Sun; closed some major hols) Phone 701/224-2666.   **Free.**

The Pioneer Family. Statue by Avard Fairbanks.

Statue of Sakakawea. Memorial to the Native American woman who guided Lewis and Clark. A few blocks south is

Former Governors' Mansion State Historic Site (1884). Restored three-story Victorian mansion occupied 1893-1960. Interpretive exhibits;

governors' portraits. (Mid-May-mid-Sept, Wed-Sun afternoons, also by appt) Corner of 4th St & Ave B. Phone 701/328-2666.   **Free.**

Annual Events

Expo '98. Civic Center. Carnival, livestock exhibits, food, music. Phone 701/222-6487. Early June.

United Tribes Powwow. One of the largest in the nation, featuring Native American dancing and singing, events, food, games, crafts and contests. Phone 701/255-3285. Sept 3-6.

Folkfest. Downtown. Sept 10-13.

Motels

★ **BEST WESTERN DOUBLEWOOD INN.** *1400 E Interchange Ave (58501), just S of jct US 83, I-94 exit 159.* 701/258-7000; FAX 701/258-2001. 143 rms, 2 story. S $59; D $69; each addl $5; suites $69-$79; under 18 free. Crib free. Pet accepted. TV; cable, VCR avail. Indoor pool; whirlpool, sauna, poolside serv. Restaurant 6:30 am-2 pm, 5-10 pm. Rm serv. Bar 11-1 am. Ck-out noon. Meeting rms. Bellhops. Valet serv. Sundries. Free airport, bus depot transportation. Some refrigerators. Cr cds: A, C, D, DS, ER, MC, V.

D ⟆ ≋ ⩙ ⫪ SC

✔★ **COMFORT INN.** *1030 Interstate Ave (58502).* 701/223-1911; FAX 701/223-1911. 148 rms, 3 story. No elvtr. S $36; D $42-$51; suites $60; under 16 free. Crib $3. TV; cable. Indoor pool; whirlpool. Complimentary continental bkfst. Ck-out noon. Meeting rms. Free airport transportation. Game rm. Cr cds: A, C, D, DS, ER, MC, V.

≋ ⩙ ⫪ SC

✔★ **DAYS INN.** *1300 E Capitol Ave (58501), at US 83.* 701/223-9151; FAX 701/223-9423. 110 rms, 2 story. S $37; D $43-$58; each addl $6. Crib free. TV; cable, in-rm movies avail. Indoor pool; whirlpool, sauna. Complimentary continental bkfst. Restaurant nearby. Ck-out noon. Meeting rms. Cr cds: A, C, D, DS, MC, V.

D ≋ ⩙ ⫪ SC

★ ★ **FAIRFIELD INN BY MARRIOTT-NORTH.** *1120 Century Ave E (58501).* 701/223-9077; FAX 701/223-9077. 63 rms, 16 suites. S $49.95; D $55.95; each addl $5; suites $65.95; under 18 free; higher rates mid-Mar & June-Sept. Crib free. TV; cable (premium). Indoor pool; whirlpool. Complimentary continental bkfst. Ck-out noon. Meeting rms. Sundries. Game rm. Refrigerator in suites. Cr cds: A, D, DS, MC, V.

D ≋ ⩙ ⩙ SC

✔★ ★ **FAIRFIELD INN BY MARRIOTT-SOUTH.** *135 Ivy Ave (58504), near Municipal Airport.* 701/223-9293; FAX 701/223-9293. 63 rms, 3 story. S $60.95; D $65.95; each addl $5; suites $75-$85; under 18 free; higher rates special events. Crib free. Indoor pool; whirlpool. Complimentary continental bkfst. Restaurant adj 6 am-10 pm. Ck-out noon. Game rm. Some refrigerators. Cr cds: A, C, D, DS, MC, V.

D ≋ ⩙ ⩙ SC

★ ★ **KELLY INN.** *1800 N 12th St (58501), I-94 exit 159.* 701/223-8001; res: 800/635-3559. 101 rms, 2 story. S $42-$46; D $48-$53; each addl $5; suites $65-$95; under 18 free. Crib free. Pet accepted. TV; VCR avail (movies). Indoor pool; whirlpool, sauna. Restaurant 6:30 am-2 pm, 5-9 pm. Rm serv. Bar 11 am-1:30 pm, 4 pm-1 am. Ck-out noon. Meeting rms. Business servs avail. Valet serv. Free airport transportation. Game rm. Cr cds: A, C, D, DS, ER, MC, V.

D ⟆ ≋ ⩙ ⫪ SC

★ **SUPER 8.** *1124 E Capitol Ave (58501).* 701/255-1314; FAX 701/255-1314. 60 rms, 3 story. S $36.88; D $43.88-$47.88; each addl $5. Crib free. Pet accepted. TV; cable, in-rm movies avail. Complimentary coffee. Restaurant nearby. Ck-out 11 am. Cr cds: A, C, D, DS, MC, V.

⟆ ⩙ ⩙ SC

Motor Hotels

✓★ **EXPRESSWAY INN.** *200 Expressway (58504), opp Kirkwood Mall.* 701/222-2900; FAX 701/222-2900; res: 800/456-6388. 163 rms, 5 story. S $32.95; D $49.95; each addl $4; suites $65; under 14 free. Crib free. TV; cable (premium), VCR avail. Pool. Playground. Complimentary continental bkfst. Restaurant nearby. Ck-out noon. Coin lndry. Meeting rms. Business servs avail. Free airport transportation. Game rm. Cr cds: A, C, D, DS, MC, V.

★ ★ ★ **RADISSON INN.** *800 S 3rd St (58504), near Municipal Airport.* 701/258-7700; FAX 701/224-8212. 306 rms, 3 story. S $70-$80; D $75-$85; each addl $10; suites $130-$185; under 18 free. Crib free. TV; cable. Indoor pool; wading pool, whirlpool. Restaurant 6 am-10:30 pm; Sat, Sun from 7 am. Rm serv. Bar 11-1 am. Ck-out noon. Ck-in 3 pm. Meeting rms. Business servs avail. In-rm modem link. Bellhops. Valet serv. Sundries. Gift shop. Free airport transportation. Exercise equipt; weights, bicycles, sauna. Game rm. Rec rm. Casino. Some refrigerators. Many private patios, balconies. Shopping mall opp. Cr cds: A, C, D, DS, ER, MC, V.

Hotel

★ ★ ★ **HOLIDAY INN.** *605 E Broadway (58501).* 701/255-6000; FAX 701/223-0400. 215 rms, 9 story. S $65-$70; D $71-$78; each addl $7; suites $89-$108; under 19 free; wkend rates. Crib free. Pet accepted. TV; cable, VCR avail. Indoor pool; whirlpool, poolside serv. Restaurant 6 am-10:30 pm. Bar 11:30-1 am. Ck-out noon. Meeting rms. Business servs avail. Beauty shop. Free airport transportation. Exercise equipt; treadmill, stair machine, sauna. Game rm. Refrigerators in suites. Cr cds: A, C, D, DS, ER, JCB, MC, V.

Restaurants

★ ★ **CASPAR'S EAST 40.** *1401 Interchange Ave.* 701/258-7222. Hrs: 11:30 am-9:30 pm. Closed Sun; major hols. Res accepted. Continental menu. Bar to 1 am. Semi-a la carte: lunch $3.95-$9.50, dinner $8.95-$16.50. Child's meals. Specializes in prime rib, steak, seafood. Salad bar. Antique decor; fireplaces. Cr cds: A, C, D, DS, MC, V.

★ ★ **PEACOCK ALLEY.** *422 E Main St.* 701/255-7917. Hrs: 11 am-2 pm, 5:30-10 pm; Mon to 9 pm; Sun brunch 9 am-1 pm. Closed some major holidays. Res accepted. Continental menu. Bar to 1 am; closed Sun. Semi-a la carte: lunch $4.25-$7.25, dinner $9.95-$25.50. Sun brunch $4.95. Child's meals. Specialties: pasta primavera, sliced tenderloin. Turn-of-the-century decor; located in historic former hotel (1915). Cr cds: A, D, MC, V.

Bottineau (A-4)

Founded 1883 **Pop** 2,598 **Elev** 1,635 ft **Area code** 701 **Zip** 58318

Information Greater Bottineau Area Chamber of Commerce, 103 E 11th St; 701/228-3849 or 800/735-6932 .

What to See and Do

Bottineau Winter Park Ski Area. 2 rope tows, 2 T-bars, hand tow; patrol, school, rentals, snowmaking; snack bar. Longest run 1,200 ft; vertical drop 200 ft. (Mid-Nov-mid-Mar, Thurs-Sun) 11 mi NW via county roads in the Turtle Mountains. Phone 701/263-4556. ¢¢¢¢

⭐ **International Peace Garden.** This 2,339-acre landscaped park symbolizes lasting friendship between the two nations. Formal gardens, floral clock, arboretum, peace chapel, bell tower, pavilion, Masonic Auditorium, Peace Tower. Picnicking, lodge. Camping (May-mid-Oct). Grounds (daily, weather permitting). Astride Canadian border, 18 mi E on ND 5 to Dunseith, then 13 mi N on US 281, ND 3. Phone 701/263-4390 or 204/534-2510 (CAN). Per vehicle ¢¢¢

J. Clark Salyer National Wildlife Refuge. Long, narrow, irregularly shaped 58,693-acre refuge stretching from Canadian border to point about 25 mi S of Bottineau. Fishing, hunting, picnicking, bird-watching, photography permitted on some parts of refuge during specified periods. Self-guided auto tour (May-Oct); also canoe trail on Souris River. Details at headquarters, 2 mi N of Upham (daily; office closed wkends, hols). 12 mi W on ND 5, then 14 mi N on ND 14. Contact Refuge for road conditions. Phone 701/768-2548. **Free.**

Lake Metigoshe State Park. One of the largest, most attractive lakes in state amid heavily wooded hills of Turtle Mts. Wildlife. Swimming beach, bathhouses; fishing; boating (ramp). Hiking (guides). Cross-country skiing, snowmobiling. Picnicking, playground. Primitive and improved camping. Amphitheater programs. Standard fees. 12 mi N on Lake Rd, 2 mi E of Bottineau Fairgrounds. Phone 701/263-4651. Per vehicle ¢¢

Turtle Mt Provincial Park. NE on county roads. (See TURTLE MT PROVINCIAL PARK, MANITOBA, CANADA)

Seasonal Events

International Music Camp. International Peace Garden. Music, dance, drama, art; Sat concerts with guest conductors; old-time fiddlers' contest. 7 wks early June-July.

Sports Camp. Sponsored by the Canadian Legion. Equestrian events, volleyball, wilderness adventure, judo, sailing, weights, gymnastics, basketball, track, soccer, football, lacrosse. Late July-Aug.

Motels

✓★ **NORWAY HOUSE.** *ND 5E.* 701/228-3737. 46 rms. S $29-$33; D $35-$37; each addl $2. Crib $2. TV; cable. Restaurant 7 am-2 pm, 5-10 pm. Rm serv. Bar 4 pm-1 am. Ck-out 11 am. Meeting rm. Free airport transportation. Downhill/x-country skiing 12 mi. Cr cds: DS, MC, V.

★ **TURTLE MOUNTAIN LODGE.** *1 Hahn's Bay Rd, 12 mi N on RR 1.* 701/263-4206; res: 800/546-5047. 24 rms, 2 story, some kits. S $29.50-$34; D $49.50-$58; each addl $2. Pet accepted. TV; cable. Indoor pool; whirlpool. Restaurant 7 am-10 pm. Bar 4 pm-midnight; entertainment Fri, Sat. Ck-out noon. Meeting rms. Business servs avail. Downhill/x-country ski 5 mi. On Lake Metigoshe. Cr cds: A, DS, MC, V.

Bowman (D-1)

Pop 1,741 **Elev** 2,960 ft **Area code** 701 **Zip** 58623

What to See and Do

Bowman-Haley Lake. Rolled earth-fill dam 74 ft high, 5,730 ft long. Two-mi-long reservoir; fishing for panfish; boating (ramp). Picnicking, concession. 21 mi SE via US 12 or US 85. Phone 701/252-7666. **Free.**

Butte View State Park. Picnicking. Camping (electric hookups, dump station). (Mid-May-mid-Sept, daily) Standard fees. 1 mi E on US 12. Phone 701/859-3071.

Carrington (C-4)

Founded 1882 **Pop** 2,267 **Elev** 1,587 ft **Area code** 701 **Zip** 58421

What to See and Do

Arrowwood Lake Area. James River flows through Arrowwood Lake, Mud Lake and Jim Lake in a 30-mi interconnecting chain of waterways to Jamestown (see). 14 mi S on US 281, then 6 mi E on gravel road. Along E & W shores is

Arrowwood National Wildlife Refuge. Hunting. Picnicking. Self-guided auto tour, wildlife observation. (May-Sept, daily) Headquarters are 6 mi E of Edmunds on gravel road. Phone 701/285-3341.   **Free.**

Garrison Diversion Conservancy District. "Nerve center" for the multi-purpose 130,000-acre irrigation Garrison Diversion Unit. Project tours with advance notice. (Mon-Fri) 1 mi N on US 281. Phone 701/652-3194.

Annual Events

Harvest Festival. Entertainment, dance, crafts. Sept.

Steam Threshers Show. Rodeo grounds in New Rockford, 15 mi N on US 281. Threshing grain with steam engines, lumber sawing, antique tractor display, fiddlers jamboree, other activities. 3rd wkend Sept.

Motels

★ ★ CHIEFTAIN. *60 4th St (US 281).* 701/652-3131; FAX 701/652-2151. 51 rms, 2 story. S $28.95-$40.95; D $36.95-$45.95; each addl $5; suites $40.95-$65; under 12 free. Crib avail. TV; cable (premium), VCR avail. Restaurant 6 am-midnight. Rm serv 9 am-10 pm. Bar 11-1 am. Ck-out 11 am. Meeting rms. Business servs avail. In-rm modem link. Casino. Native American artifacts on display. Cr cds: A, C, D, DS, MC, V.

D ⊠ 🖚 SC

✔★ SUPER 8. *US 281.* 701/652-3982; FAX 701/652-3984. 40 rms, 2 story. S $28.95-$36.95; D $36.95-$40.95; each addl $5; suites $40.95-$75.95; under 12 free. Crib $5. TV; cable. Complimentary continental bkfst. Restaurant opp 6 am-midnight. Ck-out 11 am. Coin lndry. Business servs avail. In-rm modem link. Sundries. Cr cds: A, C, D, DS, MC, V.

D ⊠ 🖚 SC

Devils Lake (B-5)

Settled 1882 **Pop** 7,782 **Elev** 1,473 ft **Area code** 701 **Zip** 58301
Information Devils Lake Area Chamber of Commerce, PO Box 879; 701/662-4903 or 800/233-8048.

Located near the shore of Devils Lake, the city is in the heart of some of the best fishing in the North. The opening of the federal land office here in 1883 sparked growth of the city.

What to See and Do

Devils Lake Area Welcome Center. Tourist information. (Daily) 1½ mi E on US 2. Phone 701/662-4903 or 800/233-8048.   **Free.**

Devils Lake. According to legend, victorious Sioux, returning from battle in canoes, were drowned in the lake during a storm. The Sioux then named the area "Bad Spirit Lake." Fishing, hunting; boating. Golfing. Biking. Snowmobiling. Picnicking. Camping (fee). 6 mi S.

⭐ **Fort Totten State Historic Site** (1867). Built to protect overland route to Montana; last outpost before 300 mi of wilderness. One of the best preserved military forts west of the Mississippi; 16 original buildings.

Pioneer Daughters Museum; interpretive center, commissary display; videotape program of site history. Summer theater (see SEASONAL EVENT). Self-guided tours. (Memorial Day-Labor Day, daily; rest of yr, by appt) 13 mi SW on ND 57. Phone 701/766-4441.   ¢¢

Sullys Hill National Game Preserve. More than 1,600 scenic acres of which 700 acres is a big-game enclosure populated by bison, deer, elk, prairie dogs, turkeys; 4-mi self-guided auto tour. (May-Oct, daily) Nature trail. Observation towers. 12 mi SW on ND 57, on Devils Lake, 1 mi E of Fort Totten. Phone 701/766-4272.   **Free.**

Seasonal Event

Fort Totten Little Theater. Fort Totten Historic Site. Adaptive use of historic auditorium (1904). Broadway musical productions. (Wed, Thurs, Sat, Sun) Phone 701/662-8888. July.

Motels

✔★ COMFORT INN. *215 US 2E.* 701/662-6760. 60 rms, 2 story. S $39.95-$49.95; D $49.95-$59.95; each addl $5; under 18 free. Crib free. Pet accepted. TV; cable. Indoor pool; whirlpool. Coffee in rms. Complimentary continental bkfst. Restaurant opp 6 am-11 pm. Ck-out 11 am. Business servs avail. Sundries. Game rm. Refrigerators avail. Cr cds: A, C, D, DS, JCB, MC, V.

D ⊯ 🖚 ⊠ 🖚 SC

★ DAYS INN. *ND 20S.* 701/662-5381; FAX 701/662-3578. 45 rms, 2 story. S $39-$44; D $49-$54; each addl $5; under 12 free. Crib free. Pet accepted; $3. TV; cable. Complimentary continental bkfst. Restaurant nearby. Ck-out 11 am. Business servs avail. Some refrigerators. Cr cds: A, C, D, DS, MC, V.

D ⊯ ⊠ 🖚 SC

★ SUPER 8. *US 2, just E of town.* 701/662-8656. 39 rms, 1-2 story. S $29.88; D $39.88-$49.88. Crib free. TV; cable (premium), VCR avail. Complimentary continental bkfst. Restaurant opp open 24 hrs. Ck out 11 am. Business servs avail. In-rm modem link. Sundries. Cr cds: A, C, D, DS, JCB, MC, V.

D ⊠ 🖚 SC

Dickinson (C-2)

(See also Medora)

Settled 1880 **Pop** 16,097 **Elev** 2,420 ft **Area code** 701 **Zip** 58601

A marketing and trading base for a three-state sector, Dickinson has two of the regions largest livestock commission rings, a steel prefabrication plant, furniture manufacturing and other industries. Dickinson State University (1918) is located at the western part of town. A Ranger District office of the Custer National Forest (see HARDIN, MT) is located in Dickinson.

What to See and Do

Joachim Regional Museum. Art gallery; dinosaur exhibit. (May-Sept, daily) 1266 Sims St. Phone 701/225-4409.   ¢

Patterson Reservoir. Part of Missouri River Valley reclamation project. Swimming (June-Aug, daily); fishing; boating. Volleyball, horseshoes. Picnicking. Camping (fee). Park (Apr-Sept, daily). 3 mi W on US 10, then 1 mi S. Phone 701/225-2074. Per vehicle   ¢

Annual Event

Roughrider Days Celebration. Rodeo, parade, tractor pulls, street dance, demolition derby, races, carnival. Early July.

Motels

✔★ **COMFORT INN.** *493 Elk Dr, off I-94. 701/264-7300; FAX 701/264-7300.* 115 rms, 2 story. June-mid-Sept: S $31-$33; D $40-$44; each addl $3; suites $50.50; under 18 free; higher rates special events; lower rates rest of yr. Crib $2. Pet accepted. TV; cable. Pool; whirlpool. Complimentary continental bkfst. Ck-out 11 am. Coin lndry. Free airport transportation. Cr cds: A, C, D, DS, ER, MC, V.

★ ★ **HOSPITALITY INN.** *N on ND 22, 2 blks N of I-94. 701/227-1853; FAX 701/225-0090; res: 800/422-0949 (ND).* 149 rms, 2-3 story. S $50-$60; D $60-$70; each addl $7; suites $65-$110; under 18 free. Crib free. TV; cable. Heated pool; whirlpool, sauna, poolside serv. Restaurant 6 am-10 pm. Rm serv. Bar 11:30-1 am. Ck-out noon. Coin lndry. Meeting rms. Business servs avail. Bellhops. Free airport, bus depot transportation. Rec rm. Casino. Some private patios, balconies. Cr cds: A, C, D, DS, MC, V.

D ≋ ⇗ 🔥 SC

Fargo (C-6)

Founded 1872 **Pop** 74,111 **Elev** 900 ft **Area code** 701

Information Fargo-Moorhead Convention & Visitors Bureau, 2001 44th St SW, 58103; 701/282-3653 or 800/235-7654 .

Fargo, largest city in North Dakota, is the leading retail and wholesale center of the rich Red River Valley and one of the leading commercial centers in the Northwest. Farm products and byproducts keep many factories busy. The city is named for William G. Fargo of Wells-Fargo Express Company. It is also the home town of baseball great Roger Maris; a display museum filled with his personal memorabilia is located in West Acres Mall.

With blackjack legal in North Dakota, Fargo has taken the lead in promoting its gaming tables. There are approximately 30 casinos in the city, making it a major tourist attraction for the three-state region, including Minnesota and South Dakota. Charities and nonprofit organizations run the casinos and collect all profits above expenses.

What to See and Do

🟫 **Bonanzaville, USA.** More than 45 buildings reconstruct the 19th-century farm era. Hemp Antique Vehicle Museum, 1884 locomotive, train depot, model railroad, pioneer farm homes, church, school, log cabins, sod house, home of Kodak film inventor, general stores, farm machinery buildings, operating farmsteads, doll house, Plains Indian Museum and more. (See ANNUAL EVENTS) Village & museums (May-late Oct, daily; rest of yr, Mon-Fri). 4½ mi W of I-29 on Main Ave or via I-94, exit 343 (US 10W). Phone 701/282-2822. Museum only ¢¢; Village & museum combination (exc during special events) ¢¢¢

Children's Museum at Yunker Farm. Hands-on exhibits include legoland, infant-toddler play center, puppet theater. Also outdoor playground; picnic shelters. (Summer, daily; rest of yr, daily exc Mon) 1201 28th Ave N. Phone 701/232-6102. ¢¢

Fargo Theatre (1937). Classic and first-run films; stage productions; Wurlitzer organ concerts (wkends) in streamlined *moderne* theater. 314 Broadway. For schedule phone 701/235-4152.

Fargo-Moorhead Community Theatre. Units for the hearing impaired available. 333 S Fourth St. For schedule and tickets call 701/235-6778.

North Dakota State University (1890). (9,534 students) Herbarium and wildlife museum in Stevens Hall; North Dakota Institute for Regional Studies at NDSU Library (Mon-Fri exc hols). Campus tours. N University Dr & 12th Ave N. Phone 701/231-8643.

Annual Events

Red River Valley Fair. 5 mi W on I-94, exit 85, in West Fargo. Pioneer village, livestock exhibits. Late June.

Pioneer Days. Bonanzaville, USA. Celebration of area pioneer heritage. People in period costume, parades, arts & crafts. 3rd wkend Aug.

Motels

✔★ ★ **AMERICINN.** *1423 35th St SW (58103). 701/234-9946; FAX 701/234-9946.* 43 rms, 2 story. May-Sept: S $47.90-$64.90; D $53.90-$109.90; each addl $4; under 18 free; lower rates rest of yr. Crib free. Pet accepted. TV; cable (premium), VCR avail (movies). Indoor pool; whirlpool, sauna. Complimentary continental bkfst. Restaurant nearby. Ck-out 11 am. Business servs avail. Valet serv. Coin lndry. Some refrigerators. Cr cds: A, C, D, DS, MC, V.

D ✔ ≋ ⇗ 🔥 SC

★ ★ **BEST WESTERN KELLY INN.** *3800 Main Ave (58103), I-29 exit 65. 701/282-2143; FAX 701/281-0243.* 133 rms, 2 story, 13 suites. Apr-Sept: S $52; D $62; each addl $5; suites $100-$150; under 16 free; lower rates rest of yr. Crib free. TV; cable (premium), VCR avail. 2 pools; 1 indoor; whirlpool, sauna. Restaurant 6:30 am-midnight. Bar 11-1 am. Ck-out 11 am. Coin lndry. Meeting rms. Business servs avail. Valet serv. Sundries. Free airport, RR station, bus depot transportation. Wet bar in suites. Some patios. Cr cds: A, C, D, DS, ER, MC, V.

D ≋ ⇗ 🔥 SC

✔★ ★ **COMFORT INN.** *1407 35th St S (58103). 701/280-9666; FAX 701/235-1174.* 66 rms, 2 story. June-Sept: S $49.95-$59.95; D $59.95; each addl $5; suites $54.95-$64.95; family rates; higher rates special events; lower rates rest of yr. Crib free. Pet accepted. TV; cable. Indoor pool; whirlpool. Complimentary continental bkfst. Restaurant nearby. Ck-out 11 am. Business servs avail. Game rm. Refrigerators in suites. Cr cds: A, C, D, DS, ER, MC, V.

D ✔ ≋ ⇗ 🔥 SC

★ ★ **COMFORT INN-WEST.** *3825 9th Ave S (58103), I-29 exit 64. 701/282-9596.* 56 rms, 2 story, 14 suites. S $40-$60; D $44-$70; each addl $5; suites $66-$76; under 18 free. Crib free. Pet accepted. TV; cable. Indoor pool; whirlpool. Complimentary continental bkfst. Restaurant nearby. Ck-out 11 am. Business servs avail. In-rm modem link. Sundries. Game rm. Refrigerator in suites. Cr cds: A, C, D, DS, ER, JCB, MC, V.

D ✔ ≋ ⇗ 🔥 SC

★ ★ **COMFORT SUITES.** *1415 35th St S (58103), I-29 exit 13th Ave. 701/237-5911.* 66 rms, 2 story. June-Aug: S $58.95-$73.95; D $63.95-$78.95; each addl $5; under 18 free; higher rates special events; lower rates rest of yr. Crib free. Pet accepted; $5. TV; cable. Indoor pool; whirlpool. Complimentary continental bkfst. Restaurant nearby. Ck-out 11 am. Business servs avail. In-rm modem link. Valet serv. Game rm. Refrigerators. Cr cds: A, C, D, DS, ER, JCB, MC, V.

D ✔ ≋ ⇗ 🔥 SC

★ ★ **COUNTRY SUITES BY CARLSON.** *3316 13th Ave S (58013), I-29 exit 64. 701/234-0565; FAX 701/234-0565, ext. 408; res: 800/456-4000.* 99 rms, 3 story, 42 suites. S $65-$71; D $68-$74; suites $75-$139; under 18 free. Crib free. Pet accepted. TV; cable. Indoor pool; whirlpool. Complimentary continental bkfst. Coffee in rms. Restaurant adj 6 am-11 pm. Bar 4:30 pm-1 am. Ck-out noon. Meeting rms. Business servs avail. In-rm modem link. Valet serv. Sundries. Free airport transportation. Exercise equipt; weight machine, bicycles. Game rm. Refrigerators, wet bars. Cr cds: A, C, D, DS, MC, V.

D ✔ ≋ 🏋 ⇗ 🔥 SC

✔★ **ECONO LODGE.** *1401 35th St S (58103). 701/232-3412.* 44 rms, 2 story. S $28.96-$33.96; D $38.96-$44.96; each addl $5; under 16 free. Crib free. Pet accepted. TV; cable. Complimentary continental bkfst. Restaurant adj open 24 hrs. Ck-out 11 am. Business servs avail. In-rm modem link. Cr cds: A, C, D, DS, ER, JCB, MC, V.

D ✔ ≋ ⋈ 🔥 SC

★ ★ **FAIRFIELD INN BY MARRIOTT.** *3902 9th Ave (58103). 701/281-0494.* 63 rms, 3 story. Mid-May-mid-Sept: S $47.95-$53.95; D $53.95-$59.95; each addl $6; suites $54.95-$69.95; under 18 free; lower rates rest of yr. Crib free. TV; cable. Indoor pool; whirlpool. Complimentary continental bkfst. Ck-out noon. Business servs avail. In-rm modem link. Sundries. Game rm. Refrigerators in suites. Cr cds: A, C, D, DS, ER, JCB, MC, V.

D ≋ ⋈ 🔥 SC

★ ★ **HAMPTON INN.** *3431 14th Ave SW (58103). 701/235-5566; FAX 701/235-5566.* 75 rms, 2 story. S $48-$58; D $52-$68; under 18 free. Crib free. TV; cable (premium), VCR avail (movies). Indoor pool; whirlpool. Complimentary continenal bkfst. Restaurant nearby. Ck-out 11 am. Business servs avail. Valet serv. Exercise equipt; bicycle, treadmill. Game rm. Some refrigerators. Cr cds: A, C, D, DS, MC, V.

D ≋ ⋇ ⋈ 🔥 SC

✔ ★ **HOLIDAY INN EXPRESS.** *1040 40th St S (58103). 701/282-2000; FAX 701/282-4721.* 77 rms, 4 story. S, D $45-$59; under 18 free. Crib free. Pet accepted. TV; cable. Indoor pool; whirlpool. Complimentary continental bkfst. Restaurant adj 6 am-11 pm. Ck-out noon. Business servs avail. Sundries. Valet serv. Coin lndry. Game rm. Cr cds: A, C, D, DS, JCB, MC, V.

D ✔ ≋ ⋈ 🔥 SC

★ ★ **KELLY INN-13TH AVENUE.** *4207 13th Ave SW (58103). 701/277-8821; FAX 701/277-0208.* 59 rms, 2 story. S $46; D $51; each addl $5; suites $80-$100; under 18 free. Crib free. Pet accepted. TV; cable (premium). Indoor pool; whirlpool, sauna. Complimentary continental bkfst. Restaurant adj 6 am-11 pm. Ck-out 11 am. Business servs avail. Valet serv. Coin lndry. Game rm. Some refrigerators. Cr cds: A, C, D, DS, ER, MC, V.

D ✔ ≋ ⋈ 🔥 SC

★ **RED ROOF INN.** *901 38th St SW (58103). 701/282-9100.* 99 rms, 2 story. S $31.90-$37.90; D $45.90-$57.90; each addl $6; under 18 free. Crib free. TV; cable, VCR avail (movies). Complimentary continental bkfst. Restaurant nearby. Ck-out 11 am. Business servs avail. Sundries. Cr cds: A, C, D, DS, MC, V.

D ⋈ 🔥 SC

✔ ★ **SLEEP INN.** *1921 44th St SW (58103). 701/281-8240; FAX 701/281-2041.* 61 rms, shower only, 2 story. Mid-May-Sept: S $43.95-$49.95; D $49.95-$55.95; each addl $4; under 18 free; lower rates rest of yr. Crib $6. Pet accepted. TV; cable (premium). Complimentary continental bkfst. Restaurant opp open 24 hrs. Ck-out 11 am. Business servs avail. Valet serv. Free airport transportation. Exercise equipt; bicycle, weight machine. Cr cds: A, C, D, DS, MC, V.

D ✔ ⋇ ⋈ 🔥 SC

★ **SUPER 8.** *3518 Interstate Blvd (58103). 701/232-9202; FAX 701/232-4543.* 61 rms, 1-2 story, 25 suites. S $32.88-$40.88; D $42.88-$60.88; suites $45-$95; each addl $2-$5. Crib $2. Pet accepted. TV; cable (premium). Indoor pool; whirlpool. Complimentary continental bkfst. Restaurant nearby. Ck-out 11 am. Coin lndry. Business servs avail. Some in-rm whirlpools. Cr cds: A, C, D, DS, MC, V.

D ✔ ≋ ⋈ 🔥 SC

Motor Hotels

★ ★ **BEST WESTERN DOUBLEWOOD INN.** *3333 13th Ave S (58108). 701/235-3333; FAX 701/280-9482.* 174 rms, 3 story. S $60-$74; D $70-$84; each addl $5; suites $95-$200; under 18 free; wkend rates. Crib free. TV; cable (premium). Heated pool; whirlpool, sauna, poolside serv. Coffee in rms. Restaurant 6:30 am-10 pm. Rm serv. Bar 11-1 am. Ck-out noon. Meeting rms. Business servs avail. In-rm modem link. Bellhops. Valet serv. Barber, beauty shop. Free airport, RR station, bus depot

transportation. X-country ski 4 mi. Health club privileges. Casino. Refrigerators. Balconies. Cr cds: A, C, D, DS, MC, V.

D ⋇ ≋ ⋈ 🔥 SC

★ ★ **HOLIDAY INN.** *(58106). at I-29 13th Ave S exit. 701/282-2700; FAX 701/281-1240.* 309 rms, 2-7 story. S, D $64-$99; suites $95-$145; under 19 free; wkend rates; package plans. Crib free. Pet accepted. TV; cable (premium). Indoor pool; wading pool, whirlpool, poolside serv. Restaurant 6 am-11 pm; Sat from 7 am; Sun 7 am-10 pm. Rm serv. Bar 11-1 am; Sat from 10 am; Sun 7 am-10 pm; entertainment. Ck-out noon. Convention facilities. Business servs avail. In-rm modem link. Bellhops. Valet serv. Concierge. Sundries. Free airport, RR station, bus depot transportation. Exercise equipt; weight machines, bicycles, sauna. Rec rm. Casino. Cr cds: A, C, D, DS, JCB, MC, V.

D ✔ ≋ ⋇ ⋈ 🔥 SC

Hotel

★ ★ **RADISSON.** *201 5th St N (58102). 701/232-7363; FAX 701/298-9134.* 151 rms, 18 story. S $86-$99; D $90-$106; suites $125-$175; under 18 free; wkend rates; package plans. Crib free. TV; cable. Restaurant 6:30 am-10:30 pm. Bar 11-1 am. Ck-out noon. Meeting rms. Business servs avail. In-rm modem link. Free airport transportation. Exercise equipt; weight machines, bicycle, whirlpool, sauna. Game rm. Rec rm. Minibars. Cr cds: A, C, D, DS, ER, JCB, MC, V.

D ⋇ ⋈ 🔥 SC

Restaurants

★ ★ **THE GRAINERY.** *In West Acres Shopping Center, at I-29 13th Ave S exit. 701/282-6262.* Hrs: 11 am-10 pm; Fri, Sat to 11 pm; Sun 11 am-4 pm; Buffet to 2 pm. Closed Easter, Thanksgiving, Dec 25. Res accepted. Bar to 1 am; Sun noon-6 pm. Semi-a la carte: lunch $4.25-$7.95, dinner $5.75-$18.95. Buffet lunch $6.95-$7.50. Child's meals. Specialties: beer cheese soup, prime rib, broiled shrimp. Salad bar. Theodore Roosevelt memorabilia. Cr cds: A, C, D, DS, MC, V.

✔ ★ ★ **MEXICAN VILLAGE.** *814 Main Ave. 701/293-0120.* Hrs: 11 am-11 pm; Fri, Sat to midnight; Sun to 10 pm. Closed Easter, Thanksgiving, Dec 25. Res accepted. Mexican menu. Serv bar. Semi-a la carte: lunch $4-$5, dinner $5-$8. Specializes in burritos, fajitas. Cr cds: A, D, DS, MC, V.

D

★ **OLD BROADWAY.** *22 Broadway, at Northern Pacific Ave. 701/237-6161.* Hrs: 11 am-10 pm. Closed Sun; Dec 25. Res accepted. Bar to 1 am. Semi-a la carte: lunch $3-$7, dinner $6.95-$12.95. Child's meals. Specializes in steak, smoked ribs, pasta. Salad bar. Entertainment. Renovated dry goods store. Turn-of-the-century decor; antiques. Blackjack casino. Cr cds: A, C, D, DS, MC, V.

D

Garrison Dam (C-3)

Area code 701

(58 mi N of Bismarck on US 83, then 11 mi W on ND 200)

Garrison Project represents one of the key projects of the Missouri River Basin constructed by the US Army Corps of Engineers. The project cost nearly $300 million. Flood control, power generation, irrigation, navigation, recreation and fish & wildlife are the project purposes. Garrison Dam is one of the largest rolled earthfill dams in the world. It cuts more than two miles across the Missouri River and rises 210 feet above the river channel with ND 200 carried on its crest. Behind the dam, Lake Sakakawea stretches approximately 180 miles. Beaches, fishing and boating (ramps) are available on the 1,300-mile shoreline. There are also picnic areas and camping facilities (early May-mid-Oct; fee) and resorts. Displays in powerhouse lobby. (Memorial Day-Labor Day, daily; rest of yr, Mon-Fri) Guided tours (Memorial Day-Labor Day, daily; rest of yr, by appt). Phone 701/654-7441.

What to See and Do

Garrison Dam National Fish Hatchery. Produces northern pike, paddle-fish, walleye, rainbow trout and chinook salmon for waters in northern Great Plains; visitor center. (Mid-Apr-mid-Oct, daily) Phone 701/654-7451. **Free.**

Lake Sakakawea State Park. Swimming (beach); fishing for pike, walleye, sauger and catfish; boating (ramp, rentals, marina). Hiking. Cross-country skiing, snowmobiling, ice-fishing. Picnicking, playground, concession. Tent & trailer facilities. Summer interpretive programs, sailing regattas. Standard fees. On the S shore of 180-mi long lake. Phone 701/487-3315. Per vehicle ¢¢

Audubon National Wildlife Refuge. Wildlife observation and 8-mi auto trail. (Daily) 16 mi SE of Garrison via ND 37 to US 83. Phone 701/442-5474. **Free.**

Knife River Indian Villages National Historic Site. Three visible Mandan and Hidatsa earth lodge village sites. Ranger-guided tours to village sites, self-guided trails, canoe and cross-country ski trails. Visitor Center; museum exhibits, demonstrations, orientation film. (Daily) 19 mi S of Garrison Dam via ND 200, 1/4 mi N of Stanton via County 37. Phone 701/745-3309. **Free.**

Grafton (B-6)

(See also Grand Forks)

Pop 4,840 **Elev** 825 ft **Area code** 701 **Zip** 58237
Information Chamber of Commerce, PO Box 632; 701/352-0781.

The seat of Walsh County and a transportation and farming junction, Grafton bears the name of the New Hampshire county where the pioneer settlers of this area began their westward trek.

What to See and Do

Heritage Village. Includes furnished farmhouse; country church; depot with caboose; taxidermy shop and working carousel. (May-Sept, Sun; also by appt) Just W of downtown on ND 17. Phone 701/352-3280. **Donation.**

Homme Dam Recreation Area. In wooded valley of Park River, well-stocked for fishing. Boating (docks, ramps). Winter sports. Picnicking. Camping (fee). (Apr-Nov, daily) 19 mi W on ND 17. ¢

Motel

✔★ **SUPER 8.** *948 W 12th St.* 701/352-0888. 32 rms, 2 story. S $31.88; D $38.88-$41.88; each addl $4. Crib free. TV; cable. Complimentary coffee. Restaurant nearby. Ck-out 11 am. Business servs avail. Cr cds: A, C, D, DS, MC, V.

D ⊠ ✕ 🐾 SC

Grand Forks (B-6)

Settled 1871 **Pop** 49,425 **Elev** 834 ft **Area code** 701
Information Convention & Visitors Bureau, 4251 Gateway Dr, 58203; 701/746-0444 or 800/866-4566.

Grand Forks stands at the point where the Red River of the North and Red Lake River form a fork. Socially, culturally and commercially the town is closely allied with its cousin city across the river, East Grand Forks, Minnesota. First a French fur trading post, Grand Forks later developed as a frontier river town. The arrival of the railroad and cultivation of the farmland nearby brought about another change in its personality. The University of North Dakota plays a dominant role in the city's culture and economy. Grand Forks AFB is 14 miles west on US 2.

Note: The city may still be recovering from severe flooding that occurred in 1997. Contact Convention & Visitors Bureau for updated information.

What to See and Do

Grand Forks County Historical Society. Society maintains **Campbell House**, historic pioneer cabin of agricultural innovator Tom Campbell. Original log cabin portion dates from 1879. Also on grounds are log post office (1870), one-room schoolhouse and Myra Carriage Museum. **Myra Museum** houses collection of late 19th- and early 20th-century artifacts from surrounding area. (May-Oct, daily) 2405 Belmont Rd. Phone 701/775-2216. ¢¢

Turtle River State Park. This 784-acre park is named for Bell's Terrapins (mud turtles). Swimming pool. Hiking. Cross-country skiing, chalet warming house; snowmobiling, ice-skating, other winter recreation (mid-Dec-mid-Mar; fees). Picnicking, playground. Camping, trailer facilities. Standard fees. 22 mi W on US 2. Phone 701/594-4445.

University of North Dakota (1883). (12,430 students) *Eternal Flame of Knowledge,* an immense steel-girded sphere, commemorates Old Main and past presidents. J. Lloyd Stone Alumni Center, historic turn-of-the-century mansion; Center for Aerospace Sciences Atmospherium; North Dakota Museum of Art; Chester Fritz Library houses artwork. Tours. W end of University Ave. Phone 701/777-3304.

Waterworld. Water slides, tube slide, body slide, baby slide. Miniature golf. Picnic area. (June-Aug, daily) 3651 S Washington St. Phone 701/746-2795. ¢¢

Annual Events

State Hockey Tournament. Engelstad Arena, University of North Dakota. Late Feb.

Native American Annual Time Out and Wacipi. University of North Dakota Indian Association. Late Mar, early Apr.

Grand Forks County Fair. County fairgrounds. July.

Summerthing. University Park. Arts festivals. June & July.

Potato Bowl Week. Queen pageant, parade, football game, other events. Mid-Sept.

Motels

✔★★ **C'MON INN.** *3051 32nd Ave S (58201).* 701/775-3320; FAX 701/780-8141; res: 800/255-2323. 80 rms, 2 story. S $40.70-$48.70; D $46.70-$67.90; each addl $6; suites $83.90-$91.90; under 13 free. Crib free. TV; cable (premium), VCR (movies). Indoor pool; wading pool, whirlpool. Complimentary continental bkfst. Restaurant opp 6 am-11 pm. Ck-out noon. Meeting rms. Business servs avail. Sundries. Valet serv. X-country ski 2 mi. Exercise equipt; bicycle, treadmill. Game rm. Some refrigerators. Cr cds: A, DS, MC, V.

D 🏊 ⋈ ✕ ⋈ 🐾 SC

★★ **COMFORT INN.** *3251 30th Ave S (58201), adj to Columbia Mall.* 701/775-7503. 67 rms, 2 story. June-Aug: S $43.95-$54.95; D $43.95-$65.95; each addl $6; suites $55.95-$65.95; under 19 free; lower rates rest of yr. Crib free. Pet accepted. TV; cable. Indoor pool; whirlpool. Complimentary continental bkfst. Restaurant nearby. Ck-out 11 am. Business servs avail. Game rm. Refrigerator in suites. Cr cds: A, C, D, DS, ER, JCB, MC, V.

D 🐾 ⋈ ⋈ 🐾 SC

★★ **COUNTRY INN & SUITES BY CARLSON.** *3350 32nd Ave S (58201), I-29 exit 138.* 701/775-5000; FAX 701/775-9073; res: 800/456-4000. 89 rms, 3 story, 45 suites. S $40.95-$56.95; D $46.95-$62.95; each addl $6; under 18 free. Crib free. TV; VCR (movies free). Indoor pool; whirlpool, sauna. Complimentary continental bkfst. Ck-out 11 am. Coin lndry. Business servs avail. Valet serv. Refrigerators, minibars. Cr cds: A, C, D, DS, MC, V.

[D] [≈] [⇘] [⚡] [SC]

✔ ★ **DAYS INN.** 3101 34th St S (58201), at Columbia Mall. 701/775-0060. 52 rms, 2 story. June-Aug: S, D $50.95-$68.95; each addl $6; suites $55.95-$73.95; under 16 free; lower rates rest of yr. Crib free. TV; cable. Indoor pool; whirlpool. Complimentary continental bkfst. Ck-out 11 am. Business servs avail. Game rm. Refrigerator in suites. Cr cds: A, C, D, DS, MC, V.

[D] [≈] [⇘] [⚡] [SC]

✔ ★ **ECONO LODGE.** 900 N 43rd St (58203), jct US 2 & I-29. 701/746-6666. 44 rms, 2 story, 6 suites. Apr-Oct: S $34-$47; D $38-$52; each addl $5; under 18 free; lower rates rest of yr. Crib $3. TV; cable (premium). Complimentary continental bkfst. Restaurant nearby. Ck-out 11 am. Business servs avail. In-rm modem link. Refrigerator, wet bar in suites. Cr cds: A, C, D, DS, ER, JCB, MC, V.

[D] [⇘] [⚡] [SC]

★ ★ **FAIRFIELD INN BY MARRIOTT.** 3051 34th St S (58201), I-29 exit 138. 701/775-7910. 62 rms, 3 story. S $45.95-$53.95; D $51.95-$59.95; each addl $6; under 18 free. Crib free. TV; cable. Indoor pool; whirlpool. Complimentary continental bkfst. Ck-out noon. Business servs avail. In-rm modem link. Sundries. Valet serv. Game rm. Cr cds: A, D, DS, MC, V.

[D] [≈] [⇘] [⚡] [SC]

★ ★ ★ **HOLIDAY INN.** 1210 N 43rd St (58203). 701/772-7131; FAX 701/780-9112. 150 rms, 2 story. S, D $64; under 19 free. Crib free. TV; cable (premium), VCR avail (movies). Indoor pool; wading pool, whirlpool. Restaurant 6:30 am-2 pm, 5-10 pm. Rm serv. Bar 2 pm-1 am. Ck-out noon. Coin lndry. Meeting rms. Business servs avail. In-rm modem link. Bellhops. Valet serv. Sundries. Free airport, RR station, bus depot transportation. Putting green. Exercise equipt; bicycles, treadmill, sauna. Game rm. Casino. Cr cds: A, C, D, DS, JCB, MC, V.

[D] [≈] [🏃] [🏋] [⇘] [⚡] [SC]

★ ★ ★ **RAMADA INN.** (58208). at jct US 2, I-29. 701/775-3951; FAX 701/775-9774. 100 rms, 2 story. S $56-$66; D $66-$78; each addl $7; under 18 free. Crib free. TV; cable (premium), VCR avail. Indoor pool; wading pool, whirlpool, sauna, poolside serv. Restaurant 6:30 am-10 pm. Rm serv. Bar 2 pm-1 am. Ck-out noon. Coin lndry. Meeting rms. Business servs avail. In-rm modem link. Bellhops. Valet serv. Free airport, RR station, bus depot transportation. Rec rm. Casino. Cr cds: A, C, D, DS, JCB, MC, V.

[D] [≈] [⇘] [⚡] [SC]

✔ ★ **ROADKING INN.** 1015 N 43rd St (58203), at jct US 2, I-29 exit 141. 701/775-0691; FAX 701/775-9964; res: 800/950-0691. 98 rms, 2 story. S $27.95-$42.95; D $36.95-$42.95; each addl $5; under 12 free. Crib free. TV; cable. Complimentary continental bkfst; afternoon refreshments. Restaurant nearby. Ck-out noon. Coin lndry. Business servs avail. Valet serv. Health club privileges. Cr cds: A, C, D, DS, MC, V.

[⇘] [⚡] [SC]

★ ★ **ROADKING INN-COLUMBIA MALL.** 3300 30th Ave S (58201). 701/746-1391; FAX 701/746-8586; res: 800/707-1391. 85 rms, 2 story. S $39-$53; D $47-$63; each addl $6; suites $84-$92; under 12 free. Crib free. TV; cable (premium). Indoor pool; wading pool, whirlpool. Complimentary continental bkfst. Restaurant nearby. Ck-out noon. Coin lndry. Meeting rm. Business servs avail. In-rm modem link. Valet serv. Health club privileges. Game rm. Whirlpool in suites. Cr cds: A, DS, MC, V.

[D] [≈] [⇘] [⚡] [SC]

✔ ★ **SELECT INN.** 1000 N 42nd St (58203), at jct I-29, US 2. 701/775-0555; res: 800/641-1000. 120 rms. S $27.95-$35.95; D $36.95-$45.95; each addl $4; under 13 free. Crib free. Pet accepted. TV; cable (premium), VCR avail (movies). Complimentary continental bkfst. Restau-

rant nearby. Ck-out noon. Coin lndry. Business servs avail. Valet serv. Cr cds: A, D, DS, MC, V.

[✔] [⇘] [⚡]

★ **SUPER 8.** 1122 N 43rd St (58203). 701/775-8138. 33 rms, 2 story. S $38.88-$48.88; D $43.88-$63.88; each addl $6; under 12 free. Crib free. TV; cable. Restaurant nearby. Ck-out 11 am. Business servs avail. Cr cds: A, C, D, DS, MC, V.

[D] [⇘] [⚡] [SC]

Motor Hotels

✔ ★ **BEST WESTERN FABULOUS WESTWARD HO.** ND 2 (58206), 1/2 mi W on US 2. 701/775-5341; FAX 701/775-3703. 108 rms, 1-2 story. S $40; D $45-$49; each addl $5; suites $80; under 12 free. Crib free. Pet accepted. TV; cable, VCR avail (movies). Heated pool; sauna. Restaurant 6:30 am-10 pm; Sun 8 am-10 pm. Bars 11 am; entertainment Wed-Sat evenings. Ck-out noon. Meeting rms. Business servs avail. In-rm modem link. Bathrm phones. Picnic tables. Old West motif; model Western village. Casino. Cr cds: A, C, D, DS, ER, MC, V.

[✔] [≈] [⇘] [⚡] [SC]

★ ★ **BEST WESTERN TOWN HOUSE.** 710 1st Ave N (58203). 701/746-5411; FAX 701/746-1407. 113 units, 2 story. S $50-$60; D $60-$70; each addl $5; suites $90-$125; under 18 free. Crib free. TV; cable, VCR avail (movies). Indoor pool; whirlpool, sauna. Restaurant 6:30 am-2 pm, 5-10 pm; Sun 7 am-1:30 pm, 6-8 pm. Rm serv. Bar 4:30 pm-1 am. Ck-out noon. Meeting rms. Business servs avail. Valet serv. Airport, RR station, bus depot transportation. Indoor miniature golf. Game rm. Cr cds: A, C, D, DS, ER, MC, V.

[D] [≈] [⇘] [⚡] [SC]

Restaurants

★ ★ **G.F. GOODRIBS.** 4223 12th Ave N. 701/746-7115. Hrs: 11 am-10 pm; Fri, Sat to 11 pm; Sun 10:30 am-9 pm; early-bird dinner 4-6 pm; Sun brunch to 2 pm. Closed Dec 24, 25. Res accepted. Bar to 1 am; Sun from noon. Semi-a la carte: lunch $4-$6, dinner $9-$15. Sun brunch $6.39. Child's meals. Specializes in ribs, steak, seafood. Cr cds: A, D, DS, MC, V.

[SC]

★ ★ ★ **SANDERS 1907.** 312 Kittson Ave. 701/746-8970. Hrs: 5:30-9:30 pm. Closed Sun, Mon; Jan 1, Dec 24, 25; also 1st wk of July. Res accepted. Bar to midnight. A la carte entrees: dinner $10-$24. Specialties: roast caraway duck, Swiss Eiger beef (prime rib). Bistro atmosphere; eclectic decor. Cr cds: A, D, MC, V.

Jamestown (C-5)

(See also Carrington, Valley City)

Settled 1872 **Pop** 15,571 **Elev** 1,410 ft **Area code** 701 **Zip** 58401

Information Jamestown Promotion and Tourism Center, 212 Third Ave NE; 701/252-4835 or 800/22-BISON.

Settlers and businessmen, in the wake of soldiers and railroad workers, established Jamestown as a transportation center guarded by Fort Seward. When farmers discovered they could pay for their rich land with two years' crops, the area developed as a prosperous diversified agricultural sector. The James River, known as the longest unnavigable river in the world, flows through the town. On the northeastern edge of town is Jamestown College (1883).

What to See and Do

Fort Seward Historic Site and Interpretive Center. Built on the original site of Fort Seward, the center preserves the early military history of the region with a collection of historical documents and artifacts. There is also a picnic area on the grounds. (Apr-Oct, daily) US 281 & 8th St NW. Phone 701/252-8421. **Free.**

Frontier Village. Large statue of bison; restored school, church, log cabin, railroad depot, old shops, art exhibits, trading post, jail. Entertainment. (May-Sept, daily) Also **National Buffalo Museum** (All yr; fee) On I-94, SE edge of town. Phone 701/252-6307. **Free.**

Whitestone Hill Battlefield State Historic Site. Most probably triggered by the 1862 Sioux uprising in Minnesota, the Sept 1863 Battle of Whitestone Hill marked the beginning of a war between the US Cavalry and the Plains Sioux that lasted for more than 20 yrs. Granite monument of bugler, graves of soldiers; small museum. Picnicking, playgrounds. (Mid-May-mid-Sept, Thurs-Mon) 37 mi S on US 281, then 15 mi W on ND 13 to Kulm, then 15 mi S on ND 56, then E on unimproved road. **Free.**

Annual Events

Fort Seward Wagon Train. A one-wk wagon train experience. Wagons are pulled by draft horses or mules; train stops along the way at historical sites. Participants dress and camp in the manner of the pioneers. For information phone 701/252-6844. 1 wk late June.

Stutsman County Fair. Late June or early July.

Motels

✔★ ★ **COMFORT INN.** 811 20th St SW, at jct I-94 & US 281. 701/252-7125. 52 rms, 2 story, 8 suites. S $49.95; D $55.95; each addl $5; suites $61.95; under 18 free; wkly rates; higher rates: county fair, stockcar stampede. Crib free. Pet accepted. TV; cable. Indoor pool; whirlpool. Complimentary continental bkfst. Restaurant adj 6 am-10 pm. Ck-out 11 am. Business servs avail. Game rm. Refrigerator in suites. Cr cds: A, C, D, DS, ER, JCB, MC, V.

D ✚ ≈ ⊠ 🗶 SC

★ ★ **DAKOTA INN.** at jct I-94, US 281S. 701/252-3611; FAX 701/251-1212; res: 800/726-7924. 120 rms, 2 story. S $40-$50; D $45-$60; each addl $5; under 16 free. Crib $5. Pet accepted. TV; cable. Indoor pool; whirlpool. Restaurant 7 am-10 pm. Rm serv. Bar 3 pm-1 am; entertainment Fri, Sat. Ck-out 11 am. Meeting rms. Business servs avail. Bellhops. Valet serv. Free airport, bus depot transportation. Game rm. Lawn games. Cr cds: A, C, D, DS, MC, V.

✚ ≈ ⊠ 🗶 SC

★ ★ **GLADSTONE SELECT HOTEL.** 111 2nd St NE. 701/252-0700; res: 800/641-1000. 117 rms, 2 story. S, D $39-$63; each addl $4; under 13 free. Crib $3. TV; cable, VCR avail (movies). Indoor pool; whirlpool. Restaurant 6:30 am-10 pm. Rm serv. Bar. Ck-out 11 am. Meeting rms. Business servs avail. Valet serv. Free airport, bus depot transportation. Casino. Cr cds: A, C, D, DS, MC, V.

D ≈ ⊠ 🗶 SC

✔★ **INTERSTATE.** 2 mi S on US 281, 1/4 mi S of I-94 exit 59. 701/252-4715; FAX 701/251-1647. 62 rms, 2 story. S $38-$47; D $47-$54. Crib $2. TV; cable. Complimentary coffee in lobby. Ck-out 11 am. Business servs avail. Cr cds: A, D, DS, MC, V.

D ⊠ 🗶

Kenmare (A-2)

(For accommodations see Minot)

Settled 1897 **Pop** 1,214 **Elev** 1,850 ft **Area code** 701 **Zip** 58746

In the center of a rich farming area that produces durum wheat and sunflowers, Kenmare also enjoys the beauties of nature from its hillside location overlooking Middle Des Lacs Lake. At one time, grain was shipped down the lake by steamboat from the Canadian border area for shipment by rail to US markets.

What to See and Do

Des Lacs National Wildlife Refuge. Rings Upper, Middle and Lower Des Lacs Lakes, a 30-mi finger of water pointing down from Canadian border. A 6-mi stretch of the Upper Lake has a picnic site (Memorial Day-Labor Day, daily). The Taskers Coulee Recreational Area (3 mi SW of town) offers picnicking, bird-watching (Memorial Day-Labor Day, daily). Refuge headquarters is 1/2-mi W of town (Mon-Fri; closed hols). **Free.**

Lake Darling. 6 mi N on US 52, then 18 mi E on ND 5, then S. (See Upper Souris National Wildlife Refuge in MINOT.)

Mandan (C-3)

(See also Bismarck)

Settled 1881 **Pop** 15,177 **Elev** 1,651 ft **Area code** 701 **Zip** 58554 **E-mail** visitnd@bismarck-mandancvb.org **Web** bismarck-mandancvb.org

Information Bismarck-Mandan Convention & Visitor Bureau, PO Box 2274, Bismarck 58502; 701/222-4308 or 800/767-3555.

The Mandan originally farmed this area, and today the agricultural tradition persists in the dairy and dry farms that surround the city. Lignite, a soft coal, is mined in this region. Mandan has been an important railroad city since the tracks crossed the Missouri River the year the city was founded.

What to See and Do

Cross Ranch Nature Preserve. The Nature Conservancy. This 6,000-acre nature preserve has mixed grass prairies, Missouri River flood-plain forest, upland woody draws. Bison herd. Hiking, self-guided nature trails. (Daily) 30 mi N via ND H1806 (gravel). Phone 701/794-8741. **Free.**

★ **Fort Abraham Lincoln State Park.** Historic site marks fort which Custer commanded prior to his "last stand." Reconstructed fort buildings (tours Memorial Day-Labor Day) and Mandan earth lodge village. Fishing. Hiking. Cross-country skiing, snowmobiling. Picnicking, playground, concession. Camping. Visitor center, Amphitheater, museum, summer interpretive program. 4 mi S on ND 1806. Phone 701/663-9571. ¢¢

Huff Hills Ski Area. 2 double chairlifts; rope tow, T-bar. Rentals (snowboard & ski). Beginner lessons. Chalet. Longest run 2, 640 ft; vertical drop 430 ft. (Mid-Nov-Mar, Thurs-Sun) 15 mi S on ND 1806. Phone 701/663-6421 (during season). ¢¢¢¢

Annual Event

Jaycees Rodeo Days. Rodeo, parade, midway, arts & crafts. Early July.

Seasonal Event

Stock Car Racing. Dacotah Speedway. 3/8-mi dirt, high-banked, oval track. Fri. Phone 701/663-6843. Mid-May-1st wkend Sept.

Motor Hotel

★ ★ **BEST WESTERN SEVEN SEAS MOTOR INN.** 2611 Old Red Trail, 1/2 mi N at I-94 exit 152. 701/663-7401; FAX 701/663-0025. 103 rms, 3 story. S $51; D $61; each addl $5; suites $100; under 18 free. Crib free. TV; cable. Indoor pool; whirlpool. Complimentary coffee. Restaurant 6:30 am-10:30 pm. Bar 11-1 am; entertainment. Ck-out noon. Ck-in 3 pm. Meeting rms. Business servs avail. Valet serv. Sundries. Free airport transportation. Cr cds: A, C, D, DS, ER, MC, V.

≈ ⊠ 🗶 SC

Unrated Dining Spot

CAPTAIN MERIWETHERS LANDING & PASTA CO. 1700 River Rd. 701/224-0455. Hrs: 5-10 pm. Closed Thanksgiving, Dec 25. Bar. Semi-a la carte: dinner $4.95-$14.95. Child's meals. Specializes in steak, seafood, barbecue. Entertainment (summer). Outdoor dining. On Missouri River. Cr cds: DS, MC, V.

Medora (C-1)

(See also Dickinson)

Founded 1883 **Pop** 101 **Elev** 2,271 ft **Area code** 701 **Zip** 58645

This village is a living museum of two of the most colorful characters found on the raw badlands frontier: young, bespectacled Theodore Roosevelt and the hot-blooded, visionary Marquis de Mores. The Marquis, a wealthy Frenchman, established the town and named it for his wife, daughter of a New York banker. He built a packing plant and icehouses, then planned to slaughter cattle on the range and ship them to metropolitan markets in refrigerated railroad cars. The plan fizzled, but not before the mustachioed Frenchman left his stamp on the community. Roosevelt came here in 1883 and won respect as part-owner of the Maltese Cross and Elkhorn ranches and as organizer and first president of the Little Missouri Stockmen's Association.

What to See and Do

 Chateau de Mores State Historic Site. The site commemorates the life of Antoine de Vallombrosa, the Marquis de Mores. The Marquis busied himself with many undertakings, such as a stagecoach line, an experiment with refrigerated railroad cars and a beef packing plant. Remaining are the ruins of a packing plant; a 26-rm, two-story frame mansion filled with French furnishings; also library, servants' quarters, relic room displaying the Marquis' saddles, guns, boots, coats, and other possessions. An interpretive center is on the grounds. The site is not heated. Picnicking avail. Guided tours (mid-May-mid-Sept, daily; rest of yr, by appt; closed Jan 1, Thanksgiving, Dec 25). 1 mi W, off US 10, I-94. Phone 701/623-4355. Site **Free**; Tour ¢

Historic buildings. Rough Riders Hotel (1884) provided the name of T.R.'s regiment in the Spanish-American War; remodeled. **St Mary's Catholic Church** (1884), built by the Marquis. **Joe Ferris Store** (1885), owned by Roosevelt partner; remodeled (1965). On or near US 10, I-94.

Theodore Roosevelt National Park-South Unit (see).

Motel

★ **BAD LANDS.** *On I-94 Business.* 701/623-4422; *FAX* 701/623-4494; *res:* 800/663-6721. 116 rms. Memorial Day-Labor Day: S $59; D $70; each addl $3; under 6 free; lower rates May-Memorial Day, Labor Day-Sept. Closed rest of yr. Crib free. TV; cable. Heated pool; wading pool. Restaurant nearby. Ck-out 11 am. Business servs avail. Miniature golf. Cr cds: A, DS, MC, V.

Hotel

★ **ROUGH RIDERS.** *2 blks N of I-94 Business.* 701/623-4433; *res:* 800/633-6721. 9 rms, 1 cabin. S $59; D $70. TV; cable. Pool privileges. Restaurant 7 am-9 pm. Wine, beer. Ck-out 11 am. Meeting rm. Business servs avail. Restored hotel (1880s). Cr cds: A, DS, MC, V.

Minot (B-3)

Settled 1886 **Pop** 34,544 **Elev** 1,580 ft **Area code** 701 **Zip** 58701

Information Convention & Visitors Bureau, PO Box 2066, 58702; 701/857-8206 or 800/264-2626.

Minot's advance from tepee and tar paper to a supersonic-age city has been so vigorous that it lays claim to being the "Magic City." Where buffalo bones were once stacked by "plainscombers" stands a city rich with agriculture, lignite coal reserves, oil pools, industries and railroad yards on both sides of the Mouse River. Minot is the commercial center of a radius that sweeps into Canada. Minot State University is located here.

What to See and Do

Minot AFB. SAC Base for B-52 bombers, KC-135 tankers, UH-1 helicopters and Minuteman III missiles. Also T-38 training aircraft. 13 mi N on US 83. For tour information contact Base Public Affairs, 701/723-2889. **Free.**

Oak Park. Heated swimming pool, wading pool, bathhouse, lifeguards (fee; schedule same as Roosevelt Park). Exercise trail; picnicking, playground, fireplaces. Park (daily). 4th Ave NW between 10th & 16th Sts NW. **Free.**

Roosevelt Park and Zoo. Includes 90 acres of formal lawns and sunken gardens. On the grounds are a swimming pool, water slide, and bathhouse; lifeguards on duty (late May-early Sept, daily; fee). Also in the park are picnic facilities, playgrounds, tennis courts, mini train (fee); carousel (fee), a bandshell and a 28-acre zoo (May-Sept, daily; fee). Park (daily). 1215 Burdick Expy E. Phone 701/857-4166.

Upper Souris National Wildlife Refuge. Lake Darling, a 20-mi lake within the refuge is home to more than 290 species of birds. Ice fishing and open water fishing for walleye, northern pike, smallmouth bass and perch in designated areas; boat and bank fishing in summer. Canoe areas; picnic facilities; 3-mi auto tour route; hiking trails. Refuge headquarters are 7 mi N of Foxholm. 18 mi NW on US 52 to Foxholm, then continue 7 mi N, or travel 15 mi N on US 83, then 12 mi W on County 6. For more information contact Upper Souris National Wildlife Refuge, RR 1, Box 163, Foxholm 58738; 701/468-5467. **Free.**

Ward County Historical Society Museum and Pioneer Village. First county courthouse, early schoolhouse, depot, blacksmith shop, pioneer cabin, church and 10-rm house, barbershop, dental parlor; museum with antiques. (May-Sept, limited hrs; also by appt) State Fairgrounds. Phone 701/839-0785. **Free.**

Annual Events

North Dakota State Fair. State Fairgrounds. 4-H, livestock, commercial exhibits; horse and tractor pulls, carnival, machinery show, concerts, auto races, demolition derby. Phone 701/852-FAIR. July 24-Aug 1.

Norsk Hostfest. All Seasons Arena. Norwegian folk festival. Oct 13-17.

Motels

★ ★ **BEST WESTERN SAFARI INN.** *1510 26th Ave SW.* 701/852-4300; *FAX* 701/838-1234. 100 rms, 2 story. S $49-$59; D $59-$69; each addl $6; suites $69-$85; under 18 free; higher rates special events. Crib avail. Pet accepted. TV; cable (premium), VCR (movies). Indoor pool; whirlpool. Complimentary continental bkfst. Bar 5 pm-1 am. Ck-out 11 am. Meeting rm. Business servs avail. Game rm. Cr cds: A, D, DS, ER, MC, V.

★ ★ **COMFORT INN.** *1515 22nd Ave SW, adj to Dakota Square Mall.* 701/852-2201; *FAX* 701/852-2201. 142 rms, 3 story. S $39.95; D $44.95-$49.95; each addl $5; under 18 free. Crib free. Pet accepted. TV; cable. Indoor pool; whirlpool. Complimentary continental bkfst. Restaurant adj 6-1 am. Ck-out noon. Meeting rms. Business servs avail. Valet serv. Sundries. Game rm. Cr cds: A, C, D, DS, ER, JCB, MC, V.

✔★ **DAKOTA INN.** *Bypass US 2. 701/838-2700; FAX 701/839-7792; res: 800/862-5003.* 129 rms, 3 story. S $29.95; D $39.95-$48.95; each addl $3. Crib free. Pet accepted. TV; cable. Indoor pool; whirlpool. Complimentary continental bkfst. Restaurant adj 6 am-10 pm. Ck-out noon. Coin lndry. Sundries. Game rm. Cr cds: A, D, DS, MC, V.

✔📶≋🖧🐾SC

✔★ **DAYS INN.** *2100 4th St SW. 701/852-3646; FAX 701/852-0501.* 82 rms, 2 story. S $38-$42; D $44-$59; each addl $3; under 18 free. Crib free. Pet accepted. TV; cable, VCR avail. Indoor pool; whirlpool, sauna. Complimentary continental bkfst. Ck-out noon. Business servs avail. Cr cds: A, C, D, DS, MC, V.

📶✔≋🖧🐾SC

★★ **FAIRFIELD INN BY MARRIOTT.** *900 24th Ave SW. 701/838-2424; FAX 701/838-2424.* 62 rms, 3 story. May-Aug: S $44.95; D $50.95; each addl $6; suites $60.95; under 18 free; higher rates Norsk Hostfest; lower rates rest of yr. Crib free. TV; cable (premium). Indoor pool; whirlpool. Complimentary continental bkfst. Restaurant nearby. Ck-out noon. Meeting rms. Business servs avail. Sundries. Game rm. Cr cds: A, D, DS, MC, V.

📶✔≋🖧🐾SC

✔★ **SUPER 8.** *1315 N Broadway (US 83). 701/852-1817; FAX 701/852-1817.* 60 rms, 3 story. No elvtr. S $33.88-$36.88; D $40.88-$45.88; each addl $5; under 12 free; higher rates: state fair, Norsk Hostfest. Crib free. Pet accepted. TV; cable (premium). Complimentary coffee. Restaurant nearby. Ck-out 11 am. Coin lndry. Cr cds: A, C, D, DS, MC, V.

✔≋🖧🐾SC

Hotel

★★★ **HOLIDAY INN RIVERSIDE INN.** *2200 Burdick Expy E, 1 mi E on US 2. 701/852-2504; FAX 701/852-2630.* 173 rms. S $42-$53; D $55-$59; each addl $5; suites $88-$150; under 18 free; higher rates special events. Crib free. TV; cable. Heated pool; whirlpool, sauna, poolside serv. Complimentary coffee in rms. Restaurant 6-1 am. Bar 4:30 pm-1 am. Ck-out noon. Meeting rms. Business servs avail. Gift shop. Barber, beauty shop. Airport, RR station, bus depot transportation. Golf privileges. Game rm. Balconies. Cr cds: A, C, D, DS, JCB, MC, V.

📶🏃≋🖧🐾SC

Restaurant

★★ **FIELD & STREAM SUPPER CLUB.** *2 mi N of airport on US 83. 701/852-3663.* Hrs: 5-9:30 pm. Closed Sun; major hols. Res accepted. Semi-a la carte: dinner $8.95-$25.95. Child's meals. Specializes in prime rib, steak, seafood. Cr cds: A, C, D, DS, MC, V.

Rugby (B-4)

(For accommodations see Minot)

Founded 1886 **Pop** 2,909 **Elev** 1,545 ft **Area code** 701 **Zip** 58368

The geographical center of North America has been located by the US Geological Survey as one-half mile south of Rugby. The location is marked by a monument.

What to See and Do

Geographical Museum and Pioneer Village. A rather unusual museum featuring 27 buildings from Pierce County and the surrounding area. Each building is furnished with materials from the period when it was in use. Gun collections, displays of farm implements, dolls and glass items. (May-Sept, daily) US 2 E. Phone 701/776-6414. ¢¢

Theodore Roosevelt National Park (C-1)

(For accommodations see Medora)

The 70,447 scenic acres of spectacular badlands that compose this park are the state's foremost tourist attraction. This national park is a monument to Theodore Roosevelt, who, in addition to all of his other vigorous pursuits, was the nation's champion of conservation of natural resources. Roosevelt, who came to the badlands in September 1883, to hunt buffalo and other big game, became interested in the open-range cattle industry and purchased interest in the Maltese Cross Ranch near Medora (see). He returned the next year and established another ranch, the Elkhorn, about 35 miles north of Medora. The demands of his political career and losses in cattle production eventually forced him to abandon his ranching ventures.

The park preserves the landscape as Roosevelt knew it. General Sully, during his campaign against the Sioux in 1864, described it as "hell with the fires out . . . grand, dismal and majestic." Wind and water have carved, from a thick series of flat-lying sedimentary rocks, curiously sculptured formations, tablelands, buttes, canyons and rugged hills. Exposed in eroded hillsides are thick, dark layers of lignite coal that sometimes are fired by lightning and burn slowly for many years, often baking adjacent clay layers into a red, brick-like substance called scoria, or clinker.

Many forms of wildlife inhabit the area. Elk and bison have been reintroduced here and may be seen by visitors. There are several large prairie dog towns; mule and white-tailed deer are abundant; wild horses can be seen in the South Unit; and the area is rich in bird life including hawks, falcons, eagles and other more common species.

The park is divided into three units: the South Unit is accessible from I-94 at Medora, where there is a visitor center (daily) and Roosevelt's Maltese Cross cabin; the Elkhorn Ranch Site on the Little Missouri River can be reached only by rough dirt roads, and visitors should first obtain current information from rangers at the Medora Visitor Center, phone 701/623-4466, before attempting the trip; the North Unit is accessible from US 85, near Watford City, and this unit also has a visitor center. An additional visitor center is located at Painted Canyon Scenic Overlook on I-94 (Apr-Oct, daily). There are self-guided trails, picnic areas, camping (standard fees, daily), and evening campfire programs in both the North and South Units (June-mid-Sept). The park is open all year (fee). The visitor centers are closed Jan 1, Thanksgiving, Dec 25. Golden Eagle and Golden Age passports are accepted (see MAKING THE MOST OF YOUR TRIP).

Valley City (C-5)

(See also Jamestown)

Settled 1872 **Pop** 7,163 **Elev** 1,222 ft **Area code** 701 **Zip** 58072
Information Valley City Area Chamber of Commerce, 205 NE 2nd St, PO Box 724; 701/845-1891.

The railroad and the first settlers arrived here simultaneously to establish a community then known as Worthington. Later, as the seat of Barnes County, the town in the deeply forested Sheyenne River Valley changed to its present name. The grainfields and dairy farms of the surrounding area provide the basis of its economy.

What to See and Do

Baldhill Dam and Lake Ashtabula. Impounds Sheyenne River and Baldhill Creek in water supply project, creating 27-mi-long Lake Ashtabula; 8 recreational areas. Swimming, water-skiing, fishing, boating (ramps). Picnicking (shelters), concessions. Camping (hookups; fee). Fish hatchery. (May-Oct) 11 mi NW on county road. Phone 701/845-2970.

Clausen Springs Park. A 400-acre park with a 50-acre lake. Fishing; canoes, boating (electric motors only). Nature trails, bicycling. Picnicking, playground. Camping, tent & trailer sites (electric hookups, fee). (May-Oct, daily) 4 mi W on I-94, then 16 mi S on ND 1, then 1 mi E, 1/2 mi S following signs.

Little Yellowstone Park. Picnicking; camping (electric hookups, fee) in sheltered portion of rugged Sheyenne River Valley; fireplaces, shelters, rustic bridges. (May-Oct, daily) 4 mi W on I-94, then 19 mi S on ND 1, then 6 mi E off ND 46.

Valley City State University (1890). (1,100 students) Teacher education, business, industrial technology, liberal arts. Planetarium on campus; phone 701/845-7452. Campus tours. S side of town. Phone 701/845-7101.

Motel

★ **SUPER 8.** 822 11th St SW, at I-94 exit 292. 701/845-1140. 30 rms, 2 story. S $31.95; D $37.95; each addl $3. Crib free. TV; cable, VCR avail (movies). Complimentary coffee in lobby. Restaurant adj. Ck-out 11 am. Business servs avail. Cr cds: A, C, D, DS, MC, V.

⊠ 🖧 SC

Wahpeton (D-6)

(See also Fargo)

Settled 1871 **Pop** 8,751 **Elev** 963 ft **Area code** 701 **Zip** 58075 **E-mail** wahped@wahpeton.polaristel.net **Web** members.aol.com/chahinkapa
Information Visitors Center, 120 N 4th St; 701/642-8559 or 800/892-6673.

Thickly growing trees at this point, where the waters of the Bois de Sioux and Otter Tail rivers integrate to become the Red River of the North, gave the city its Native American name—"dwellers among the leaves." At the mouth of the north-flowing Red River and the hub of a series of highways, Wahpeton is the marketplace for a large segment of the southeast corner of the state.

What to See and Do

Chahinkapa Park. Chahinkapa Zoo includes petting zoo; many North American animals, several exotic displays, nature center. Restored 1926 *Prairie Rose Carousel* (Memorial Day-Labor Day; fee). Swimming, water slide (fee), trails, basketball, tennis, 18-hole golf, softball; picnicking; camping (fee). 1st St & 7th Ave N, on banks of Red River of the North. Phone 701/642-2811. ¢¢

⭐ **Fort Abercrombie State Historic Site.** First federal military post in state, rebuilt on authentic lines; blockhouses, guardhouse, stockade. Built on the west bank of the Red River, the fort regulated fur trade, kept peace between Chippewa and Sioux, served as gateway through which wagon trains, stagecoaches and Army units moved west. Established in 1858, abandoned in 1859, reoccupied in 1860 and moved to present site; repelled a six-week siege in 1862, abandoned in 1877. Museum interprets history of the fort; displays of relics and early settlers' possessions (mid-May-mid-Sept, daily; fee). Picnicking. 20 mi N, 1/2 mi E off US 81, in Abercrombie. Phone 701/224-2666. **Free.**

Kidder Recreation Area. Fishing, boating (docks, ramp), picnicking. 4th St & 19th Ave N. Phone 701/642-2811. **Free.**

Richland County Historical Museum. Pioneer artifacts trace county's history; display of Rosemeade pottery. (Apr-Nov, limited hrs) 2nd St & 7th Ave N. Phone 701/642-3075. **Free.**

Annual Event

Carousel Days. 2nd wkend June.

Motel

★ **SUPER 8.** 995 21st Ave N. 701/642-8731; FAX 701/642-8733. 58 rms, 2 story. S $40.88; D $44.88-$47.88; each addl $3; under 18 free. Crib free. TV; cable. Heated indoor pool; whirlpool. Complimentary continental bkfst. Restaurant 6 am-10 pm; Sun 7 am-2 pm. Rm serv. Bar 3 pm-1 am. Ck-out 11 am. Meeting rms. Business servs avail. In-rm modem link. X-country ski 1 1/2 mi. Casino. Cr cds: A, C, D, DS, MC, V.

D 🖈 ≈ ⊠ 🖧 SC

Williston (B-1)

Settled 1870 **Pop** 13,131 **Elev** 1,880 ft **Area code** 701 **Zip** 58801
Information Convention & Visitors Bureau, 10 Main St; 701/774-9041 or 800/615-9041.

A ravaged dust-bowl city in the 1930s, Williston is a sprightly community thriving on circumstances that have changed its economic personality. At one time, Williston was completely dependent on the grain harvests, which in turn were subject to the caprice of the weather. Today, grain and cattle continue as the chief concerns of the area, but the waters of the Garrison Dam project ease the drought threat. Since the discovery of oil in the early 1950s, the refining of high grade petroleum has had a major effect on the local economy. Today, Williston is the trading center for some 90,000 people.

What to See and Do

Buffalo Trails Museum. Seven-building complex with dioramas of Native American and pioneer life; fossils; interior of homesteader's shack; regional historical exhibits. (June-Aug, daily; Sept-Oct, Sun only; other days & May by appt) 6 mi N on US 2, 85, then 13 mi E on County Rd 6 in Epping. Phone 701/859-4361. ¢

Fort Buford State Historic Site. Established near the confluence of the Missouri and Yellowstone rivers in 1866, Fort Buford served primarily as the distribution point for government annuities to peaceful natives in the vicinity. During the war with the Sioux (1870s and 1880s), the post became a major supply depot for military field operations. The fort is perhaps best remembered as the site of the surrender of Sitting Bull in 1881. Original features still existing on the site include a stone powder magazine, the post cemetery and a large officers' quarters, which now houses a museum. Picnicking. (Mid-May-mid-Sept, daily; rest of yr, by appt) 7 mi W on US 2, then 17 mi SW on ND 1804. Phone 701/572-9034. ¢

Fort Union Trading Post National Historic Site. American Fur Company built this fort in 1829 at the confluence of the Yellowstone and Missouri rivers. During the next three decades it was one of the most important trading depots on the western frontier. In 1867, the government bought the fort, dismantled it and used the materials to build Fort Buford 2 mi away. Much of the fort has recently been reconstructed. A National Park Service visitor center is located in the Bourgeois House. Guided tours and interpretive programs (summer). Site (daily). 7 mi W on US 2, then SW on ND 1804W. For details contact Superintendent, Fort Union Trading Post NHS, Buford Rte; 701/572-9083. **Free.**

Lewis and Clark State Park. Situated on an upper bay of Lake Sakakawea and surrounded by beautiful scenery. Swimming; fishing. Hiking. Cross-country skiing and snowmobiling. Picnicking, playground. Camping. Amphitheater; summer interpretive program. Standard fees. 19 mi SE off ND 1804. Phone 701/859-3071.

Lewis and Clark Trail Museum. Diorama of Ft Mandan; rms furnished as pioneer home, country store, blacksmith, shoe and saddle shops, post office; farm machinery. (Memorial Day-Labor Day, daily) 19 mi S on US 85 in Alexander. Phone 701/828-3595. ¢

Spring Lake Park. Landscaped park area, lagoons. Picnicking. (Daily) 3 mi N on US 2, 85. **Free.**

Annual Events

Buffalo Trails Day. Parade, chuck wagon breakfast, old-time music, contests, games. June.

Fort Union Trading Post Rendezvous. Mid-June.

Fort Buford 6th Infantry State Historical Encampment. Re-enactment of Indian Wars frontier army exercises. July.

Oregon

Population: 2,842,321
Land area: 97,060 square miles
Elevation: 0-11,239 feet
Highest point: Mt Hood (Between Clackamas, Hood River Counties)
Entered Union: February 14, 1859 (33rd state)
Capital: Salem
Motto: The Union
Nickname: Beaver State
State flower: Oregon grape
State bird: Western meadowlark
State tree: Douglas fir
State fair: August 27-September 7, 1998, in Salem
Time zone: Mountain and Pacific
Web: www.traveloregon.com

This is the end of the famous Oregon Trail, over which came scores of pioneers in covered wagons. The state abounds in the romance of the country's westward expansion. Meriwether Lewis and William Clark, sent by President Thomas Jefferson to explore the vast area bought in the Louisiana Purchase, ended their explorations here. This was also the scene of John Jacob Astor's fortune-making fur trade and that of Hudson's Bay Company, which hoped to keep the area for England, as well as gold rushes and the traffic of stately clippers of the China trade.

English Captain James Cook saw the coast in 1778. Others had seen it before him and others after him, but it remained for Lewis and Clark to discover what a prize Oregon was. On their return to St Louis in 1806 they spread the word. In 1811, Astor's Pacific Fur Company built its post at Astoria, only to be frightened into selling to the British North West Company during the War of 1812. (In 1818 it again became US territory.) Other fur traders, missionaries, salmon fishermen and travelers followed them, but the Oregon country was far away and hard to reach. The first true settlers did not make their way there until 1839, four years before a great wagon train blazed the Oregon Trail.

Cattle and sheep were driven up from California and land was cleared for farms. Oregon was settled not by people hungry for gold but by pioneers looking for good land that could support them. The Native Americans resented the early settlers and fought them until 1880. The Oregon Territory, established in 1848, received a flood of immigrants; they continued to arrive after statehood was proclaimed under President James Buchanan 11 years later.

The rich forests grew rapidly in the moist climate west of the mountains called the Cascades, and lumber was an early product of this frontier. The streams were full of fish, the woods offered nuts and berries, and the lush, green scenery lifted hearts and hopes at the end of the weary journey. The rivers—Columbia, Willamette, Rogue and many others—offered transportation to the sea. Steamboats plied the Willamette and Columbia as early as 1850. The first full ship's cargo of wheat went from Portland to Liverpool in 1868, and when the railroad reached Portland in 1883, the world began receiving the fish, grain, lumber and livestock that Oregon was ready to deliver.

Vast rivers provide more than transportation. Dammed, they are the source of abundant electric power and water to irrigate farms east of the Cascades. Timber is still important; a quarter of Oregon is national forest land. Sustained yield practices by the big lumber companies ensure a continuing supply.

One of the most beautiful drives in Oregon extends from Portland (see) to The Dalles (see) along the Columbia River. Here is the spectacular Columbia Gorge, designated a National Scenic Area, where waterfalls, streams and mountains abound. The area offers many recreational activities such as camping—the Cascade Locks Marina Park lies 4 mi E of the Bonneville Dam (see HOOD RIVER), skiing (see MOUNT HOOD NATIONAL FOREST), snowmobiling, and hiking.

Whether one's taste is for an ocean beach, a ski slope, a mountain lake or ranch life with riding and rodeos, the visitor who loves the outdoors or the American West loves Oregon. Each year, millions of tourists enjoy the state's magnificent coastline, blue lakes, mountains and forests.

When to Go/Climate

Temperatures along the Pacific coast are mild, while Portland and the Willamette Valley experience more extreme weather conditions. Heavy snow falls in the Cascades and to the east there's a high desert area that experiences typical desert heat and dry conditions.

AVERAGE HIGH/LOW TEMPERATURES (°F)
BURNS

Jan 34/13	May 66/36	Sept 74/36
Feb 40/19	June 74/42	Oct 62/28
Mar 48/25	July 85/47	Nov 45/22
Apr 57/29	Aug 83/45	Dec 35/15

PORTLAND

Jan 45/34	May 67/47	Sept 75/52
Feb 51/36	June 74/53	Oct 64/45
Mar 56/39	July 80/57	Nov 53/40
Apr 61/41	Aug 80/57	Dec 46/35

Parks and Recreation Finder

Directions to and information about the parks and recreation areas below are given under their respective town/city sections. Please refer to those sections for details.

Key to abbreviations: I.P. = Interstate Park; N.B.C. = National Battlefield & Cemetery; N.B.P. = National Battlefield Park; N.F. = National Forest; N.G. = National Grassland; N.H. = National Historical Park; N.H.S. = National Historic Site; N.M. = National Monument; N.Mem. = National Memorial; N.M.P. = National Military Park; N.P. = National Park; N.Pres. = National Preserve; N.R. = National Recreational Area; N.R.R. = National Recreational River; N.Res. = National Reserve; N.S. = National Seashore; N.S.R. = National Scenic River; N.S.T. = National Scenic Trail; N.V.M. = National Volcanic Monument; S.B. = State Beach; S.C.P. = State Conservation Park; S.G. = State Garden; S.H.A. = State Historic Area; S.H.P. = State Historic Park; S.N.A. = State Natural Area; S.P. = State Park; S.R. = State Reserve; S.R.A. = State Recreation Area; S.Res.P. = State Resort Park; S.R.P. = State Rustic Park.

NATIONAL PARK AND RECREATION AREAS

Place Name	Listed Under
Crater Lake N.P.	same
Deschutes N.F.	BEND
Fort Clatsop N.Mem.	same
Fremont N.F.	LAKEVIEW
Hells Canyon N.R.	JOSEPH
John Day Fossil Beds N.M.	JOHN DAY
Malheur N.F.	JOHN DAY
Mount Hood N.F.	same
Newberry N.V.M.	BEND
Ochoco N.F.	PRINEVILLE
Oregon Caves N.M.	same
Oregon Dunes N.R.	REEDSPORT
Rogue River N.F.	MEDFORD
Siskiyou N.F.	GRANTS PASS
Siuslaw N.F.	CORVALLIS
Umatilla N.F.	PENDLETON
Umpqua N.F.	ROSEBURG
Wallowa-Whitman N.F.	BAKER CITY
Willamette N.F.	EUGENE
Winema N.F.	KLAMATH FALLS

STATE RECREATION AREAS

Place Name	Listed Under
Armitage S.P.	EUGENE
Bandon S.P.	BANDON
Bullards Beach S.P.	BANDON
Benson S.P.	PORTLAND
Beverly Beach S.P.	NEWPORT
Cape Arago S.P.	COOS BAY
Cape Blanco S.P.	PORT ORFORD
Cape Lookout S.P.	TILLAMOOK
Carl G. Washburne Memorial S.P.	FLORENCE
Catherine Creek S.P.	LA GRANDE
Champoeg S.P.	NEWBERG
Collier Memorial S.P.	KLAMATH FALLS
Dabney S.P.	PORTLAND
Devil's Lake S.P.	LINCOLN CITY
Ecola S.P.	CANNON BEACH
Emigrant Springs S.P.	PENDLETON
Farewell Bend S.P.	ONTARIO
Fogarty Creek S.P.	DEPOE BAY
Ft Stevens S.P.	ASTORIA
Harris Beach S.P.	BROOKINGS
Hat Rock S.P.	UMATILLA
Hilgard Junction S.P.	LA GRANDE
Humbug Mt S.P.	PORT ORFORD

CALENDAR HIGHLIGHTS

MAY

Maritime Week (Astoria). Week-long celebration of Astoria's maritime heritage includes Coast Guard demonstrations, ship model competition, Lower Columbia "row in." Phone 503/325-2323.

Boatnik Festival (Grants Pass). Riverside Park. Parade, concessions, carnival rides, boat races; entertainment. A 25-mile white-water hydroboat race from Riverside Park to Hellgate Canyon and back. Square dance festival at Josephine County Fairgrounds. Phone 541/476-0667.

JUNE

Return of the Sternwheeler Days (Hood River). Celebration of the sternwheeler Columbia Gorge's return to home port for the summer. Wine and cheese tasting, crafts, food. Phone 541/386-2000 or 800/366-3530.

Sandcastle Contest (Cannon Beach). Nationally known event features sand sculptures on beach. Phone 503/436-2623.

Portland Rose Festival (Portland). Held for more than 80 years, this festival includes the Grand Floral Parade (reservations required for indoor parade seats) and two other parades; band competition; rose show; championship auto racing; hot-air balloons; air show; carnival; Navy ships. Phone 503/227-2681.

Scandinavian Midsummer Festival (Astoria). Parade, folk dancing, display booths, arts and crafts demonstrations, Scandinavian food. Phone Astoria Warrenton Chamber of Commerce, 503/325-6311 or 800/875-6807.

Bach Festival (Eugene). Numerous concerts by regional and international artists; master classes; family activities. Phone 541/346-5666.

JULY

Oregon Coast Music Festival (Coos Bay). Variety of musical presentations ranging from jazz and dance to chamber and symphonic music. Phone 541/267-0938.

Da Vinci Days (Corvallis). Festival celebrating the relationship between art, science and technology. Phone 541/757-6363.

Salem Art Fair & Festival (Salem). Bush's Pasture Park. Arts and crafts booths and demonstrations, children's art activities and parade, ethnic folk arts, performing arts, street painting, 5K run, food; tours of historic Bush House. Phone 503/581-2228.

AUGUST

Oregon State Fair (Salem). Fairgrounds. Horse racing, wine competition and tastings, agricultural exhibits, horse show, livestock, food, carnival, entertainment. Phone 503/378-3247.

SEPTEMBER

Pendleton Round-up (Pendleton). Stadium. Rodeo and pageantry of Old West, annually since 1910. Gathering of Native Americans, PRCA working cowboys and thousands of visitors. Phone 800/457-6336.

Jackson F. Kimball S.P.	KLAMATH FALLS
Jessie M. Honeyman Memorial S.P.	FLORENCE
Joseph P. Stewart S.P.	MEDFORD
Lake Owyhee S.P.	ONTARIO
LaPine S.P.	BEND
Lewis and Clark S.P.	PORTLAND
Loeb S.P.	BROOKINGS
Mayer S.P.	THE DALLES
Milo McIver S.P.	OREGON CITY
Neptune S.P.	YACHATS
Ochoco Lake S.P.	PRINEVILLE
Ona Beach S.P.	NEWPORT
Ontario S.P.	ONTARIO
Oswald West S.P.	CANNON BEACH
Rooster Rock S.P.	PORTLAND
Saddle Mt S.P.	SEASIDE
Samuel H. Boardman S.P.	BROOKINGS
Shore Acres S.P.	COOS BAY
Silver Falls S.P.	SILVERTON
South Beach S.P.	NEWPORT
Sunset Bay S.P.	COOS BAY
The Cove Palisades S.P.	MADRAS
Tou Velle S.P.	MEDFORD
Tumalo S.P.	BEND
Ukiah-Dale Forest S.P.	PENDLETON
Umpqua Lighthouse S.P.	REEDSPORT
Unity Lake S.P.	BAKER CITY
Valley of the Rogue S.P.	GRANTS PASS
Wallowa Lake S.P.	JOSEPH
William M. Tugman S.P.	REEDSPORT
Yachats S.P.	YACHATS
Yaquina Bay S.P.	NEWPORT

Water-related activities, hiking, riding, various other sports, picnicking and visitor centers, as well as camping, are available in many of these areas. Some camping facilities in state parks stay open year-round, while others remain open as long as weather permits, often Mar-Nov. All campgrounds are open mid-Apr-late Oct. Campers are limited to 10 days in any 14-day period from May 15-Sept 14; and 14 days out of 18 the rest of the year. Discount rates are available at some campgrounds Oct-mid-May. Summer fees per night: primitive campsite $10-$13; tent sites $14-$16; electrical sites $15-$18; full hookup sites $16-$19; extra vehicle $7; firewood is available (fee varies). Campsites may be reserved at 26 state parks throughout the year with a $6 fee plus first night's camping rate. A day-use fee of $3 is charged for each motor vehicle entering 24 state parks. For more information, contact Oregon Parks & Recreation Department, 1115 Commercial St NE, Salem 97310. For campsite reservations phone 800/452-5687; for information phone 800/551-6949.

SKI AREAS

Place Name	Listed Under
Anthony Lakes Ski Area	BAKER CITY
Mt Ashland Ski Area	ASHLAND
Mt Bachelor Ski Area	BEND
Mt Hood Meadows Ski Area	MOUNT HOOD NATIONAL FOREST
Spout Springs Ski Area	LA GRANDE
Timberline Lodge	MOUNT HOOD NATIONAL FOREST
Williamette Pass Ski Area	EUGENE

FISHING & HUNTING

Nonresident fishing license, annual $40.50; 7-day license $30.50; salmon and steelhead tag $10.50; halibut tag $6; annual sturgeon tag $6; 1-day license, including either sturgeon or salmon/steelhead combination, $6.75.

Nonresident hunting license, annual $53. Special tags required in addition to license for big game. All licenses include agent-writing fee.

Oregon has 15,000 miles of streams, hundreds of lakes, and surf and deep-sea fishing. Fishing is good for Chinook and coho salmon, steelhead, rainbow and cutthroat trout, striped bass, perch, crappies, bluegill, catfish and many other varieties. The hunter will find mule and blacktail deer, elk, ring-necked pheasant, Hungarian and chukar partridge, quail, blue and ruffed grouse, band-tailed pigeons, mourning doves, waterfowl, jackrabbits, coyote, fox and bear.

For synopses of the latest angling and big-game regulations, contact Oregon Dept of Fish and Wildlife, PO Box 59, Portland 97207; 503/872-5275.

Driving Information

Safety belts are mandatory for all persons anywhere in vehicle. Under age 4 (or 40 lbs) must use an approved safety seat. For further information phone 503/986-4190 or 800/922-2022 (OR).

INTERSTATE HIGHWAY SYSTEM

The following alphabetical listing of Oregon towns in *Mobil Travel Guide* shows that these cities are within 10 miles of the indicated Interstate highways. A highway map, however, should be checked for the nearest exit.

Highway Number	Cities/Towns within 10 miles
Interstate 5	Albany, Ashland, Beaverton, Corvallis, Cottage Grove, Eugene, Grants Pass, Jacksonville, Medford, Oregon City, Portland, Roseburg, Salem.
Interstate 84	Baker City, Beaverton, Biggs, Hermiston, Hood River, La Grande, Ontario, Oregon City, Pendleton, Portland, The Dalles, Umatilla.

Additional Visitor Information

The Oregon Department of Economic Development, Tourism Commission, 775 Summer St NE, Salem 97310; 800/547-7842, will provide visitors with an Oregon travel guide and other informative brochures on request.

There are nine staffed state welcome centers in Oregon (Apr-Oct). They are: Astoria (downtown); Brookings (OR-CA border, S on US 101); Lakeview (downtown); Siskiyou (OR-CA border, S on I-5); Ontario (OR-ID border, E on I-84); Seaside (at Chamber of Commerce on US 101); Umatilla (on Brownell Blvd); Jantzen Beach-Portland (I-5 exit 308); Klamath Falls (OR-CA border, S on US 97).

Albany (C-4)

(See also Corvallis, Salem, Sweet Home)

Founded 1848 **Pop** 29,462 **Elev** 212 ft **Area code** 541 **Zip** 97321 **Web** www.albanyvisitors.com

Information Visitors Association, 300 SW 2nd Ave, PO Box 965; 541/928-0911 or 800/526-2256.

Gateway to Oregon's covered bridge country, Albany was founded by Walter and Thomas Monteith and named for their former home, Albany, New York. The city boasts the largest collection of Victorian homes in the state. Albany is neatly laid out from the Willamette River to the foothills of the Cascades. The Calapooia River joins the Willamette here. The seat of Linn County, Albany has diversified industry ranging from agriculture, timber and wood products to rare metals.

What to See and Do

Flinn's Heritage Tours. Twenty different narrated tours take visitors through historic areas in the Mid Williamette Valley. Tours range from 45 min-6 hrs; feature covered bridges of Linn County, Albany's historic districts, ghost towns, 100-yr-old apple orchard, or historic homes. (Daily; closed Dec 25) 222 First Ave W. For res and information phone 541/928-5008 or 800/636-5008. ¢¢¢-¢¢¢¢¢ Also here is

Flinn's Tea Time. Themed teas served by costumed wait-staff in Flinn's Tea Parlour. Three courses feature 10-15 items made from homemade or historic recipes and served on antique china. Enjoy O'Flinn's Irish Tea Party, Dear Mother's Tea Time and Victorian Tea Time, among others. Res required. (Feb-Aug, Sat & some hols) For schedule and res phone 541/928-5008 or 800/636-5008. ¢¢¢¢

Annual Events

World Championship Timber Carnival. Timber Linn Park, E edge of town. July 4 wkend.

Historic Interior Homes Tours. Phone 541/928-0911 or 800/526-2256. Summer & late Dec.

Great Balloon Escape. Last wkend July.

Veteran's Day Parade. One of the nation's largest. Nov 11.

Motels

★ ★ **BEST WESTERN PONY SOLDIER MOTOR INN.** 315 Airport Rd SE, off I-5 exits 234A(N), 234(S). 541/928-6322; FAX 541/928-8124. 72 rms, 2 story. S, D $76-$85; each addl $5; under 12 free. Crib $3. TV; cable. Pool; whirlpool. Complimentary continental bkfst. Restaurant nearby. Ck-out noon. Free guest lndry. Exercise equipt; weights, bicycles. Refrigerators; microwaves avail. Cr cds: A, C, D, DS, ER, JCB, MC, V.

D ⌨ ✕ ⚓ ☜ SC

★ ★ **COMFORT INN.** 251 Airport Rd SE. 541/928-0921; FAX 541/928-8055. 50 rms, 3 story. Apr-Aug: S $60-$75; D $67-$82; each addl $7; suites $150; kit. units $70-$107; under 18 free; wkly, monthly rates; higher rates special events; lower rates rest of yr. Crib free. Pet accepted. TV; cable. Indoor pool; whirlpool. Complimentary continental bkfst. Restaurant opp 5 am-11 pm. Ck-out noon. Coin lndry. Meeting rms. Business servs avail. Gift shop. Exercise equipt; stair machine, weights, sauna. Refrigerators avail. Cr cds: A, C, D, DS, JCB, MC, V.

D ⌨ ⚓ ✕ ☜ SC

✔★ **MOTEL ORLEANS.** 1212 SE Price Rd, off I-5 exit 233. 541/926-0170; res: 800/626-1900; FAX 541/967-3283. 78 rms, 2 story. S $35-$44; D $41-$50; each addl $5; suites $50-$60. Crib $5. TV. Heated pool. Ck-out 11 am. Coin lndry. Meeting rms. Cr cds: A, D, DS, MC, V.

⚓ ☜ SC

Ashland (F-4)

(See also Jacksonville, Medford)

Founded 1852 **Pop** 16,234 **Elev** 1,951 ft **Area code** 541 **Zip** 97520
Information Chamber of Commerce, 110 E Main St, PO Box 1360; 541/482-3486.

When the pioneers climbed over the Siskiyou Mts and saw the green expanse of the Rogue River Valley ahead of them, many decided to go no further. Later, when mineral springs were found, their Lithia water was piped in and now gushes from fountains on this city's plaza. Tourism, education and small industry support the town. Southern Oregon State College (1926) makes this a regional education center. Rogue River National Forest (see MEDFORD) is on three sides; a Ranger District office is located here.

What to See and Do

Lithia Park. Has 100 acres of woodlands and ponds. Nature trails; tennis. Picnicking, sand volleyball. Rose and Japanese gardens. Concerts. (Daily) Adj to City Plaza. Phone 541/488-5340. **Free.**

Mt Ashland Ski Area. Area has 2 triple, 2 double chairlifts; patrol, school, rentals; cafeteria, bar. Longest run 1 mi; vertical drop 1,150 ft. (Thanksgiving-Apr) 9 mi S on I-5, then 9 mi W on access road. Phone 541/482-2897 or 541/482-2754 (snow conditions). ¢¢¢¢ Wkends & hols ¢¢¢¢¢

Pacific Northwest Museum of Natural History. Hands-on exhibits, interactive video, live animal shows. (Daily; closed Thanksgiving, Dec 25) 1500 E Main St. Phone 541/488-1084. ¢¢¢

Seasonal Events

Oregon Cabaret Theatre. 1st & Hargadine Sts. Musicals, reviews and comedies in dinner club setting. Schedule varies. Phone 541/488-2902. Feb-Dec.

Oregon Shakespeare Festival. Elizabethan Theater (outdoor); Angus Bowmer Theater (indoor); Black Swan Theater (indoor). Series of 12 classic and contemporary plays. Daily exc Mon. Wheelchair seating by advance arrangement. Phone 541/482-4331. Mid-Feb-Oct.

Motels

(Rates are generally higher during Shakespeare Festival)

★ ★ **BEST WESTERN BARD'S INN.** 132 N Main St. 541/482-0049; FAX 541/488-3259. 92 rms, 2-3 story. June-Oct: S $92-$115; D $106-$128; each addl $10; lower rates rest of yr. Crib $10. Pet accepted; $10. TV; cable (premium). Pool; whirlpool. Ck-out 11 am. Business servs avail. Airport transportation. Downhill/x-country ski 15 mi. Refrigerators. Near Shakespeare Festival theater. Cr cds: A, C, D, DS, MC, V.

D ⌨ ⚓ ⚓ ☜ ⚓

★ **CEDARWOOD INN.** 1801 Siskiyou Blvd. 541/488-2000; res: 800/547-4141; FAX 541/482-2000. 59 rms, 14 with shower only, 2-3 story, 24 kit. units. Mid-May-mid-Oct: S $68; D $72; each addl $6; kit. units $78-$125; under 2 free; ski plans; lower rates rest of yr. Crib $6. Pet accepted, some restrictions. TV; cable, VCR avail (movies). Complimentary coffee in rms. Restaurant nearby. Bar. Ck-out 11 am. Business servs avail. Downhill/x-country ski 15 mi. 2 pools, 1 indoor; whirlpool. Microwaves avail. Picnic tables, grills. Cr cds: A, D, DS, MC, V.

D ⌨ ⚓ ⚓ ☜ SC

✔★ **KNIGHTS INN.** 2359 OR 66, at I-5 exit 14. 541/482-5111; res: 800/547-4566. 40 rms, 1-2 story. June-Sept: S $38-$51; D $42-$62; each addl $6; ski plans; lower rates rest of yr. Crib $6. Pet accepted, some restrictions; $6. TV; cable. Heated pool; whirlpool. Complimentary coffee in lobby. Restaurant 7 am-10 pm. Bar 11 am-midnight. Ck-out 11 am. Downhill ski 15 mi. Cr cds: A, D, DS, MC, V.

D ⌨ ⚓ ⚓ ☜ ⚓

★ ★ **QUALITY INN FLAGSHIP.** 2520 Ashland St. 541/488-2330; FAX 541/482-1068. E-mail fsi@cdsnet.net; web www.flagship inn.com. 60 rms, 2 story, 5 kit. units. Mid-May-Sept: S $60.75-$93.75; D $65.75-$93.75; each addl $6; kit. units $93.75-$103.75; lower rates rest of yr. Crib $6. Pet accepted, some restrictions; $6. TV; cable, VCR (movies). Heated pool. Complimentary continental bkfst. Restaurant adj open 24 hrs. Ck-out 1 pm. Business servs avail. Airport transportation. Downhill/x-country ski 13 mi. Microwaves in suites. Cr cds: A, C, D, DS, ER, JCB, MC, V.

D ⌨ ⚓ ⚓ ☜ ⚓ SC

✔★ **RODEWAY INN.** 1193 Siskiyou Blvd. 541/482-2641; FAX 541/488-1650. 64 rms, 1-3 story. S $72-$80; D $72-$82; each addl $6. Crib $6. Pet accepted, some restrictions; $6. TV; cable (premium). Heated pool. Coffee in rms. Restaurant adj. Ck-out 11 am. Business servs avail. Downhill/x-country ski 18 mi. Microwaves avail. College opp. Cr cds: A, C, D, DS, MC, V.

D ⌨ ⚓ ⚓ ⚓

★ **STRATFORD INN.** 555 Siskiyou Blvd. 541/488-2151; FAX 541/482-0479; res: 800/547-4741. 55 rms, 3 story, 6 kits. June-Sept: S $94; D $995; each addl $5; kit. units $105-$135; lower rates rest of yr. Crib free. TV; cable (premium). Indoor pool; whirlpool. Complimentary continental bkfst. Restaurant nearby. Ck-out 11 am. Downhill/x-country ski 18 mi. Refrigerators; some microwaves. Locker rm for skis and bicycles. Cr cds: A, C, D, DS, MC, V.

D ⚡ ≋ 🔥 SC

Motor Hotel

★ ★ ★ **WINDMILL'S ASHLAND HILLS INN & SUITES.** 2525 Ashland St, just E of I-5 exit 14. 541/482-8310; FAX 541/488-1783; res: 800/547-4747. 230 rms, 3 story. June-Sept: S, D $94-$125; each addl $6-$11; suites $142-$260; under 18 free; lower rates rest of yr. Crib $3.50. Pet accepted. TV; cable. Heated pool. Complimentary bkfst. Restaurant 6:30 am-9 pm. Rm serv. Bar. Ck-out 11 am. Meeting rms. Business servs avail. Bellhops. Valet serv. Sundries. Beauty shop. Airport transportation. Tennis. Downhill/x-country ski 13 mi. Exercise equipt; weight machine, bicycles. Some refrigerators; microwaves avail. Balconies. Cr cds: A, C, D, DS, MC, V.

D ⚡ 🏊 🎣 🏋 ✕ ≋ 🔥 SC

Hotel

★ **MARK ANTONY.** 212 E Main St. 541/482-1721. 79 rms, 9 story. June-Oct: S, D $65-$105; each addl $5. Pet accepted, some restrictions. Heated pool. Complimentary continental bkfst. Restaurant 7 am-11 pm. Bar. Ck-out noon. Meeting rms. Business servs avail. Airport transportation. Downhill/x-country ski 20 mi. Microwaves avail. Built 1925; some antiques. Cr cds: A, C, D, DS, ER, MC, V.

⚡ ≋ 🔥 SC

Inns

★ ★ ★ **CHANTICLEER.** 120 Gresham St. 541/482-1919; res: 800/898-1950. Web www.virtualcities.com/ons. 6 rms, 3 story. June-Oct: S, D $125-$160; each addl $25; lower rates rest of yr. Complimentary full bkfst; afternoon refreshments. Restaurant nearby. Ck-out 11 am, ck-in 3-6 pm. Free local airport, bus depot transportation. Downhill/x-country ski 14 mi. Lawn games. Antiques, comforters. Country French inn; river rock fireplace. Patio. Cr cds: A, MC, V.

🎣 ≋ 🔥 SC

★ ★ ★ **COUNTRY WILLOWS.** 1313 Clay St. 541/488-1590; res: 800/945-5697; FAX 541/488-1611. E-mail willows@willowsinn.com; web www.willowsinn.com. 9 rms, 3 with shower only, 2 story, 4 suites. Apr-Oct: S $85-$120; D $90-$125; each addl $30; suites $135-$185; lower rates rest of yr. Children over 12 yrs only. TV in common rm; cable (premium). Complimentary full bkfst. Complimentary coffee in rms. Ck-out 11 am, ck-in 3-5 pm. Business servs avail. In-rm modem link. Luggage handling. Concierge serv. Gift shop. Downhill/x-country ski 14 mi. Heated pool; whirlpool. Some refrigerators, microwaves, wet bars, fireplaces. Many balconies. Opp river. Built in 1896; country inn atmosphere and decor. Totally nonsmoking. Cr cds: A, DS, MC, V.

D 🎣 ≋ 🔥

★ ★ **McCALL HOUSE.** 153 Oak St. 541/482-9296; res: 800/808-9749; FAX 541/482-2125. E-mail mccall@mccallhouse.com; web www.mccallhouse.com. 9 rms, 2 story. Rm phones avail. June-Oct: S, D $115-$170; each addl $30; varied lower rates rest of yr. Children over 12 yrs only. Complimentary full bkfst. Restaurant nearby. Ck-out 11 am, ck-in 3-6 pm. Former residence (1883) of Civil War veteran and mayor of Ashland. Totally nonsmoking. Cr cds: MC, V.

🎣 🔥

★ ★ **MORICAL HOUSE.** 668 N Main St, 1 mi N on I-5, exit 19. 541/483-2254; res: 800/208-0960; FAX 541/482-1775. E-mail morical-hse@aol.com. 7 rms, 3 story. Mid-May-mid-Oct: S $110; D $160; each addl $25; wkends (2-day min); lower rates rest of yr. Children over 12 yrs only. Complimentary full bkfst. Restaurant nearby. Ck-out 11 am, ck-in 4-7 pm. Business servs avail. In-rm modem link. Concierge serv. Gift shop. Downhill/x-country ski 5 mi. Some in-rm whirlpools, refrigerators, microwaves, wet bars, fireplaces. Picnic tables. Restored farmhouse built in 1882; antiques, stained-glass windows. Totally nonsmoking. Cr cds: A, DS, MC, V.

D 🎣 ≋ 🔥

★ ★ ★ **MT ASHLAND.** 550 Mt Ashland Rd, W of I-5 exit 6. 541/482-8707; res: 800/830-8707; FAX 541/482-8707. E-mail mtashinn@teleport.com; web www.mtashlandinn.com. 5 air-cooled rms, 3 story. 3 suites. No rm phones. S $90; D $95; each addl $30; suites $115-$180; ski plan. Children over 10 yrs only. Complimentary full bkfst. Ck-out 11 am, ck-in 3-5 pm. Business servs avail. Downhill/x-country ski 3 mi. Sauna. Whirlpool. Some microwaves. Cedar log lodge; handmade furnishings, antiques. View of Mt Shasta. Totally nonsmoking. Cr cds: A, DS, MC, V.

🎣 ≋ 🔥

★ ★ **OAK HILL.** 2190 Siskiyou Blvd. 541/482-1554; FAX 541/482-1378; res: 800/888-7434. E-mail oakhill@mind.net; web www.expedia.msn.com. 6 rms, 2 story. No rm phones. June-Sept: S $95; D $105; each addl $25; ski plan. Children over 12 yrs only. Complimentary full bkfst; afternoon refreshments. Ck-out 11 am, ck-in 3-6 pm. Luggage handling. Downhill/x-country ski 15 mi. Bicycles. Built 1910 as farmhouse. Many antiques. Totally nonsmoking. Cr cds: MC, V.

🎣 ≋ 🔥

★ ★ **PEDIGRIFT HOUSE.** 407 Scenic Dr. 541/482-1888; res: 800/262-4073; FAX 541/482-8867. Web www.opendoor.com/pedigrift. 4 rms, 2 story. May-mid-Oct: S, D $120; each addl $15; lower rates rest of yr. Children over 12 yrs only. TV. Complimentary full bkfst; afternoon refreshments. Restaurant nearby. Ck-out 11 am, ck-in 3-6 pm. Concierge serv. Downhill/x-country ski 14 mi. Picnic tables. Built in 1888; restored Queen Anne Victorian. Totally nonsmoking. Cr cds: MC, V.

🎣 ≋ 🔥

★ ★ ★ **ROMEO.** 295 Idaho St. 541/488-0884; FAX 541/488-0817; res: 800/915-8899. 6 rms, 2 story. S, D $95-$180; each addl $30. Children over 12 yrs only. Heated pool; whirlpool. Complimentary full bkfst. Ck-out 11 am, ck-in 3 pm. Downhill ski 14 mi; x-country ski 15 mi. Private patios. Cape Cod-style house; fireplaces, hand-stitched Amish quilts; gardens. Totally nonsmoking. Cr cds: MC, V.

🎣 ≋ 🔥

★ ★ ★ **WINCHESTER.** 35 S Second St. 541/488-1113; FAX 541/488-4604; res: 800/972-4991. E-mail ashlandinn@aol.com; web www.mind.net/winchesterinn. 18 rms, 3 story. June-Oct: S $105-$135; D $110-$140; suites $135-$200; each addl $30; under 6 free; some wkend rates off-season; lower rates rest of yr. Complimentary full bkfst; afternoon refreshments. Restaurant (see WINCHESTER COUNTRY INN). Ck-out 11 am, ck-in 3 pm. Downhill/x-country ski 15 mi. Some whirlpools, fireplaces in suites. Some balconies. Patio tables. Restored Victorian house (1886) once served as the area's first hospital. Individually decorated rms; period furnishings. Gazebo, flower gardens. Cr cds: A, DS, MC, V.

D 🎣 ≋ 🔥 SC

★ ★ **WOODS HOUSE.** 333 N Main St. 541/488-1598; FAX 541/482-8027; res: 800/435-8260. E-mail woodshse@mind.net; web www.mind.net/woodshouse. 6 rms, 2 story. No rm phones. June-Oct: S $105-$115; D $110-$120; each addl $35; lower rates rest of yr. Children over 7 yrs only. Complimentary full bkfst. Restaurant nearby. Ck-out 11 am, ck-in 2 pm. Airport transportation. Downhill/x-country ski 15 mi. Rms in original Ashland house (1908); antiques; terraced gardens. Totally nonsmoking. Cr cds: MC, V.

🎣 ≋ 🔥

Restaurants

✔★ **ASHLAND BAKERY & CAFE.** *38 E Main St. 541/482-2117.* Hrs: 7 am-9 pm; Fri, Sat to 10 pm. Closed Thanksgiving, Dec 25. Wine, beer. Semi-a la carte: bkfst $3.25-$9.75, lunch $2.75-$9.75, dinner $2.75-$10.75. Specializes in baked goods, vegetarian dishes. Totally nonsmoking. Cr cds: MC, V.

D

★ ★ **CHATEAULIN.** *50-52 E Main St. 541/482-2264.* Hrs: 5-9:30 pm. Closed Thanksgiving, Dec 24-25. Res accepted. French menu. Bar. Semi-a la carte: dinner $9-$27. Child's meals. Specializes in fresh seafood, lamb, roast duckling. Totally nonsmoking. Cr cds: A, DS, MC, V.

D

★ **MACARONI'S.** *58 E Main St. 541/488-3359.* Hrs: 5-9 pm; Fri, Sat to 10 pm. Closed Jan 1, Thanksgiving, Dec 25. Italian menu. Bar. Semi-a la carte: dinner $9.50-$15.95. Specializes in pizza, pasta, Caesar salad. Cr cds: DS, MC, V.

D

★ ★ **WINCHESTER COUNTRY INN.** *(See Winchester Inn)* *541/488-1115.* E-mail ashlandinn@aol.com; web www.mind.net/winchesterinn. Hrs: 5:30-9 pm; Nov-May 5:30-8:30 pm; Sun brunch 9:30 am-1 pm. Continental menu. Serv bar. Semi-a la carte: dinner $14.95-$22.95. Sun brunch $7.95-$10.95. Specializes in fresh salmon, Teng Dah beef, lamb. Outdoor dining. Built 1886. Cr cds: A, DS, MC, V.

Astoria (A-3)

(See also Cannon Beach, Seaside)

Settled 1811 **Pop** 10,069 **Elev** 18 ft **Area code** 503 **Zip** 97103 **E-mail** awacc@seasure.com **Web** www.el.com/to/astoria

Information Chamber of Commerce, 111 W Marine Dr, PO Box 176; 503/325-6311 or 800/875-6807.

John Jacob Astor's partners sailed around Cape Horn and picked this point of land ten miles from the Pacific, overlooking the mouth of the Columbia River, for a fur-trading post. The post eventually lost its importance, but the location and the natural resources attracted immigrants, and the town continued to grow. A four-mile-long bridge crosses the mouth of the Columbia.

What to See and Do

Astoria Column (1926). A 125-ft tower commemorates first settlement; observation deck at top. (Daily) Information booth (Memorial Day-Labor Day, daily). Follow scenic drive signs to Coxcomb Hill. **Free.**

Columbia River Maritime Museum. Rare maritime artifacts and memorabilia of Columbia River, its tributaries and the NW coast. *Columbia,* Lightship 604 at moorage in Maritime Park. Fishing industry, discovery & exploration, steamship, shipwreck, navigation and steamboat exhibits. Coast Guard and Navy exhibits. (Daily; closed Thanksgiving, Dec 25) 17th & Marine Dr. Phone 503/325-2323. ¢¢

Flavel House (1883-1887). Built by Captain George Flavel, pilot and shipping man; outstanding example of Queen Anne architecture. Restored Victorian home houses antique furnishings and fine art; collection of 19th- and 20th-century toys. (Daily; closed major hols) Admission includes Heritage Museum at 16th & Duane and/or the Uppertown Firefighters' Museum at 30th & Marine Dr. 441 8th St. Phone 503/325-2203. ¢¢

⭐ **Ft Clatsop National Memorial** (see). 6 mi SW on US 101A.

Ft Stevens State Park. A 3,763-acre park adj old Civil War fort. Wreck of the *Peter Iredale* (1906) is on the ocean shore. Ft Stevens is the only military post in the lower 48 states to be fired upon by foreign forces since 1812. On June 21, 1942, a Japanese submarine fired several shells from its five-inch gun; only one hit land while the others fell short. Visitor center and self-guided tour at the Old Ft Stevens Military Complex. Ocean beach, lake swimming; fishing, clamming on beach; boating (dock, ramp). Bicycling. Picnicking at Coffenbury Lake. Improved tent & trailer sites (daily; standard fees, dump station) 5 mi W on US 101, then 5 mi N on unnumbered road. Phone 503/861-1671.

Annual Events

Astoria-Warrenton Crab & Seafood Festival. Hammond Mooring Basin on Columbia River. Crab feast, Oregon wines, food & craft booths. Carnival, water taxi, crabbing & fishing boats. Last wkend Apr.

Maritime Week. Wk-long celebration of Astoria's maritime heritage includes Coast Guard demonstrations, ship model competition, Lower Columbia "row in." Phone 503/325-2323. Mid-May.

Scandinavian Midsummer Festival. Parade, folk dancing, display booths, arts & crafts demonstrations, Scandinavian food. Mid-June.

Astoria Regatta. Parade, arts festival, public dinner, barbecue, boating competition. Mid-Aug.

Great Columbia Crossing Bridge Run. One of the most unusual and scenic runs; 8-mi course begins at Chinook, WA and ends at Astoria port docks. Mid-Oct.

Motels

✔★ **ASTORIA DUNES.** *288 W Marine Dr, foot of Astoria Megler Bridge.* 503/325-7111; FAX 503/325-0804; res: 800/441-3319. 58 rms, 18 A/C, 2-3 story. No elvtr. June-Sept: S $48-$80; D $60-$75; each addl $6; lower rates rest of yr. TV; cable (premium). Indoor pool; whirlpool. Complimentary coffee. Restaurant nearby. Ck-out 11 am. Coin lndry. Business servs avail. Some refrigerators. Opp river. Cr cds: A, C, D, DS, MC, V.

D ⛱ 🏊 ⚒ 🐾

★ **BAYSHORE MOTOR INN.** *555 Hamburg.* 503/325-2205; FAX 503/325-5550; res: 800/621-0641. 76 rms, 4 story. Some A/C. June-Oct: S $55-$80; D $65-$85; each addl $7; under 10 free; lower rates rest of yr. Crib avail. Pet accepted, some restrictions; $5. TV; cable. Indoor pool; whirlpool, sauna. Complimentary coffee. Ck-out 11 am. Coin lndry. Meeting rm. Business servs avail. In-rm modem link. Sundries. Some refrigerators. On river. Cr cds: A, C, D, DS, MC, V.

D 🐾 ⛱ 🏊 ⚒ SC

★ ★ **CREST.** *5366 Leif Erickson Dr.* 503/325-3141; res: 800/421-3141. 40 rms, 1-2 story. No A/C. Mid-May-mid-Oct: S, D $48.50-$82.50; each addl $7; under 10 free; lower rates rest of yr. Crib free. Pet accepted. TV; cable (premium). Continental bkfst 8-10 am. Complimentary coffee in rms. Ck-out noon. Coin lndry. Business servs avail. Whirlpool. Some refrigerators. Balconies. On high bluff overlooking Columbia River. Cr cds: A, C, D, DS, MC, V.

D 🐾 ⚒ 🏊

★ ★ **RED LION INN.** *400 Industry St, just W of bridge, on US 101.* 503/325-7373; FAX 503/325-8727. 124 rms, 2 story. No A/C. May-early Oct: S $65-$88; D $79-$92; each addl $15; under 18 free; lower rates rest of yr. Crib free. Pet accepted, some restrictions; $10. TV; cable. Restaurant 6 am-10 pm. Rm serv. Bar 11-2 am; entertainment exc Sun, Mon. Ck-out noon. Meeting rms. Business servs avail. Free airport, bus depot transportation. Private patios, balconies. Overlooks harbor; on Columbia River. Cr cds: A, C, D, DS, ER, JCB, MC, V.

🐾 ⚒ 🏊 SC

★ ★ **SHILO INN.** *(1609 E Harbor Dr, Warrenton 97146) 2 mi S on US 101, near airport.* 503/861-2181; FAX 503/861-2980. 62 rms, 4 story, 11 kit. units. May-Sept: S, D $79-$135; each addl $10; kit. units $109-$159; under 12 free; lower rates rest of yr. Crib free. Pet accepted; $7. TV; cable (premium), VCR (movies). Indoor pool; whirlpool. Restaurant 7 am-10:30 pm. Rm serv. Bar. Ck-out noon. Coin lndry. Meeting rms. Business servs avail. Sundries. Free airport transportation. Exercise equipt; weight machine, bicycle, sauna. Refrigerators. Cr cds: A, C, D, DS, ER, JCB, MC, V.

D ✐ ⚲ ✗ ✈ ⚲ ⚓ SC

Inns

★ **COLUMBIA RIVER INN.** 1681 Franklin Ave. 503/325-5044; res: 800/953-5044. 4 rms, 3 story. No rm phones. S, D $75-$125; each addl $10. Children over 6 only. Complimentary full bkfst. Complimentary coffee in rms. Restaurant nearby. Ck-out 11 am, ck-in 3-6 pm. Gift shop. Free airport, bus depot transportation. Refrigerators. Victorian house (ca 1870); many antiques. Cr cds: MC, V.

⚲ ⚓

★ **FRANKLIN ST STATION.** 1140 Franklin St. 503/325-4314; res: 800/448-1098. 5 rms, 3 story, 2 suites. No A/C. No rm phones. Mid-May-mid-Oct: S $63-$110; D, suites, kit. unit $68-$115; each addl $10; lower rates rest of yr. 2 cable TVs, 1 with VCR. Complimentary full bkfst; afternoon refreshments. Ck-out 11 am, ck-in 3 pm. Some refrigerators. Balconies. Victorian house built in 1900. Totally nonsmoking. Cr cds: A, DS, MC, V.

⚲

✔ ★ **ROSEBRIAR HOTEL.** 636 14th St. 503/325-7427; FAX 503/325-6937; res: 800/487-0224. 10 rms, 2 story. No A/C. S, D $65-$139; each addl $10. Complimentary bkfst. Restaurant nearby. Ck-out 11 am, ck-in 3 pm. Business servs avail. Some fireplaces. Built in 1902 as a residence; was also used as a convent. Many antiques. Overlooks town and river. Cr cds: MC, V.

⚲ ⚓

Restaurants

★ ★ **PIER 11 FEED STORE.** 77 11th St. 503/325-0279. Hrs: 7 am-10 pm; winter to 9 pm. Closed Thanksgiving, Dec 25. Res accepted. Bar to midnight wkends. Semi-a la carte: bkfst $2.25-$5.75, lunch $5-$9, dinner $8-$24.50. Specializes in seafood, steak. Salad bar. Old feed store on pier (late 1800s); natural beamed ceilings. View of Columbia River. Cr cds: DS, MC, V.

D

★ ★ **SHIP INN.** One 2nd St. 503/325-0033. Hrs: 11:30 am-9:30 pm. Closed major hols. Bar. Semi-a la carte: lunch, dinner $5-$12. Complete meals: lunch, dinner $8.50-$16.50. Specializes in Cornish and chicken pasties, seafood. Salad bar. View of Columbia River. Cr cds: DS, MC, V.

D

Baker City (C-9)

(See also La Grande)

Pop 9,140 **Elev** 3,443 ft **Area code** 541 **Zip** 97814
Information Baker County Visitor & Convention Bureau, 490 Campbell St; 541/523-3356 or 800/523-1235.

The Baker City Historic District includes more than 100 commercial and residential buildings, many built from stone quarried in town at the same place where gold was found. A 15-block area, from the Powder River to 4th St and from Estes to Campbell Sts, has many structures built between 1890 and 1910 that are being restored. Baker City, on the "old Oregon trail," is also the home of the Armstrong Gold Nugget found June 19, 1913, by George Armstrong. It weighs more than 80 ounces. A Ranger District office and the office of the supervisor of the Wallowa-Whitman National Forest is located here.

What to See and Do

Eastern Oregon Museum. Large collection of relics and implements used in the development of the West; turn-of-the-century logging and mining tools; period rms; doll collection; children's antique furniture. On grounds is 1884 railroad depot. (Mid-Apr-mid-Oct, daily) 9 mi NW on old US 30. Phone 541/856-3233. **Donation.**

Hells Canyon Tours. One-six-day float trips; horseback & rafting combinations. Guides, oar-powered or paddle rafts, camping equipment, meals provided. (May-Sept) Also two-hr, three-hr and all day (includes lunch) canyon tours by jet boat. E on OR 86 to Oxbow then N to Hells Canyon Dam. Phone 541/785-3352 or 800/422-3568. ¢¢¢¢

Horse-Drawn Trolley Tours. Narrated tours covering pioneer, gold rush and Oregon Trail histories. (June-Sept, Fri & Sat) Phone 800/523-1235. ¢¢¢

National Historic Oregon Trail Interpretive Center. Exhibits, living history presentations, multi-media displays. (Daily; closed Jan 1, Dec 25) 5 mi E on OR 86, at summit of Flagstaff Hill. Phone 800/523-1235. ¢¢¢

Oregon Trail Regional Museum. Houses one of the most outstanding collections of rocks, minerals and semiprecious stones in the West. Also, an elaborate sea-life display; wildlife display; period clothing and artifacts of early Baker County. (May-late Oct, daily) 2490 Grove St. Phone 800/523-1235. ¢

Sumpter Valley Railroad. Restored gear-driven Heisler steam locomotive and two observation cars travel 7 mi on narrow-gauge track through a wildlife game habitat area where beaver, muskrat, geese, waterfowl, herons and other animals may be seen. Also passes through the Sumpter mining district, location of the Sumpter Dredge which brought up more than $10 million in gold between 1913 and 1954 from as far down as 20 ft. (May-Sept, Sat, Sun, hols) 30 mi SW on OR 7. Phone 800/523-1235. ¢¢¢

Unity Lake State Park. A 39-acre park with swimming; fishing, boat ramp on Unity Lake. Picnicking. Tent & improved-site camping. Standard fees. 45 mi SW on OR 245, near jct US 26. Phone 541/575-2773.

Wallowa-Whitman National Forest. Reached via OR 7, 26, 86, 203, 82, I-84. More than two million acres with 14,000-acre North Fork John Day Wilderness; 7,000-acre Monument Rock Wilderness; 358,461-acre Eagle Cap Wilderness; 215,500-acre Hells Canyon Wilderness. Snowcapped peaks, Minam River; alpine meadows, rare wild flowers; national scenic byway, scenic drive Hells Canyon Overlook, which overlooks deepest canyon in North America—Hells Canyon National Recreation Area (see JOSEPH); Buckhorn Lookout; Anthony Lake and Phillips Lake. Stream and lake trout fishing, elk, deer and bear hunting; float and jet boat trips; saddle and pack trips. Picnic area. Camping. Sections W, NE and S. For further information contact Supervisor, PO Box 907; 541/523-6391. In forest is

Anthony Lakes Ski Area. Double chairlift, pomalift; patrol, school, rentals; nursery; day lodge, cafeteria, concession area, bar. Longest run more than 1 mi; vertical drop 860 ft. (Mid-Nov-mid-Apr, Thurs-Sun) Cross-country trails. Fishing, hiking, cabin rentals, store (summer). 35 mi NW, off I-84 at North Powder. Phone 800/523-1235. ¢¢¢¢

Annual Event

Miner's Jubilee. 3rd wkend July.

Motels

★ ★ ★ **BEST WESTERN SUNRIDGE INN.** 1 Sunridge Lane. 541/523-6444; FAX 541/523-6446; res: 800/233-2368. 156 rms, 2 story. S $54-$64; D $58-$68; each addl $4; suites $150-$175. Crib $5. TV; cable (premium), VCR avail. Heated pool; whirlpool. Restaurant 5:30 am-midnight. Ck-out noon. Meeting rms. Business servs avail. In-rm modem link. Sundries. Free airport transportation. Private patios, balconies. Cr cds: A, C, D, DS, ER, MC, V.

D ⚲ ⚲ ⚓ SC

✔ ★ ★ **EL DORADO.** 695 E Campbell St, at I-84 N City Center exit. 541/523-6494; FAX 541/523-6494; res: 800/537-5756. 56 rms, 2 story. S, D $43-$50; family rates. Crib $3. Pet accepted; $2/day. TV; cable,

VCR avail. Indoor pool; whirlpool. Restaurant open 24 hrs. Ck-out noon. Business servs avail. Cr cds: A, C, D, DS, MC, V.

★ **QUALITY INN.** *810 Campbell St. 541/523-2242; FAX 541/523-2242, ext. 400.* 54 rms, 2 story. Mid-May-mid-Sept: S $43-$47; D $46-$51; each addl $5; under 19 free; lower rates rest of yr. Crib $3. Pet accepted; $2/day. TV; cable. Pool privileges. Complimentary continental bkfst, coffee. Restaurant nearby. Ck-out noon. Meeting rms. Some refrigerators. Cr cds: A, C, D, DS, ER, JCB, MC, V.

✔★ **SUPER 8.** *250 Campbell St. 541/523-8282; FAX 541/523-9137.* 72 rms, 2 story, 2 kit. units. Apr-Sept: S $41.88; D $58.88; each addl $5; kit. units $71.88; under 13 free; lower rates rest of yr. Crib $4. TV; cable (premium), VCR avail (movies). Indoor pool. Complimentary coffee in lobby. Restaurant nearby. Ck-out 11 am. Coin lndry. Business servs avail. Refrigerators. Cr cds: A, C, D, DS, JCB, MC, V.

Bandon (E-2)

(See also Coos Bay, North Bend, Port Orford)

Pop 2,215 **Elev** 67 ft **Area code** 503 **Zip** 97411

Information Chamber of Commerce, PO Box 1515; 503/347-9616.

A fine beach, known for its picturesque beauty, legendary rocks and a harbor at the mouth of the Coquille River attract many tourists to Bandon. From November through March, the town is known for its short-lived storms followed by sunshine, and even has a group called the Storm Watchers. Popular seashore activities include beachcombing, hiking, fishing from the south jetty and crabbing from the docks. Summer and early autumn bring the salmon run in the Coquille River. Rockhounds search for agate, jasper and petrified wood.

What to See and Do

Bandon Museum. Exhibits on maritime activities of early Bandon and Coquille River; coastal shipwrecks, Coast Guard operations; extensive collection of Native American artifacts; old photos. (Schedule varies) US 101 & Filmore Ave. Phone 503/347-2164. ¢

Bandon State Park. An 879-acre park on coastal dune area with access to beach; fishing. Picnicking. 4 mi S on US 101, then 1 mi W on Bradley Lake Rd. Phone 503/347-3501.

Bullards Beach State Park. A 1,266-acre park with 4 mi of ocean beach. Fishing; boating (dock, ramp with access to Coquille River). Picnicking. Improved trailer campsites (dump station). Coquille Lighthouse (1896); interpretive plaques (daily). Standard fees. 2 mi N on US 101. Phone 503/347-3501.

West Coast Game Park. A 21-acre park with more than 450 exotic animals and birds. Visitors meet and walk with free-roaming wildlife. Animal keepers demonstrate the personalities of many large predators residing at the park. (Mar-Nov, daily; rest of yr, wkends & hols) 7 mi S on US 101. Phone 503/347-3106. ¢¢¢

Annual Events

Seafood and Wine Festival. Memorial Day wkend.

Cranberry Festival. Parade, barbecue, square dances, harvest ball, sports events. Late Sept.

Motels

★ **HARBOR VIEW.** *355 US 101. 541/347-4417; FAX 541/347-3616; res: 800/526-0209.* 59 rms, 3 story. No elvtr. Mid-June-late Sept: S $69-$82; D $74-$82; each addl $5; cottage $104-$130; lower rates

rest of yr. Crib $3. TV; cable (premium). Complimentary continental bkfst. Restaurant nearby. Ck-out noon. Refrigerators. Many balconies. On Coquille River. Cr cds: A, C, D, DS, MC, V.

★ **SUNSET.** *1755 Beach Loop Rd, ¹/₂ mi W of US 101. 541/347-2453; FAX 541/347-3636; res: 800/842-2407.* E-mail sunset@harborside.com; web www.harborside.com/home/s/sunset/sunset.htm. 58 rms, 1-3 story, 8 kits. S, D $45-$105; suites $110-$215; kit. units $66-$120; cottages w/kits $125-$215. Crib free. Pet accepted, some restrictions; $5/day. TV; cable. Restaurant 11 am-3 pm, 5-9 pm. Ck-out 11 am. Coin lndry. Business servs avail. Free airport transportation. Whirlpool. Ocean view; beach access. Cr cds: A, D, DS, MC, V.

Restaurants

★★ **BANDON BOATWORKS.** *275 Lincoln Ave SW, near South Jetty Rd. 541/347-2111.* Hrs: 11:30 am-2:30 pm, 5-9 pm; Sun noon-8:30 pm. Closed Dec 25. Res accepted. Wine, beer. Semi-a la carte: lunch $5-$8, dinner $9-$21.95. Child's meals. Specializes in seafood, steak, chicken. Salad bar. View of jetty, lighthouse. Totally nonsmoking. Cr cds: A, DS, MC, V.

★★★ **LORD BENNETT'S.** *1695 Beach Loop Dr. 541/347-3663.* Hrs: 11 am-3 pm, 5-10 pm; Sun brunch to 2 pm. Closed Dec 25. Res accepted. Serv bar. Semi-a la carte: lunch $4.50-$8.25, dinner $10-$17. Sun brunch $4.50-$7.75. Child's meals. Specializes in fresh seafood. Overlooks ocean. Cr cds: A, DS, MC, V.

★★ **WHEELHOUSE.** *125 Chicago Ave, at Old Town Mall. 541/347-9331.* Hrs: 11:30 am-9 pm; June-Sept to 10 pm. Closed Dec 25. Bar to 11 pm. Semi-a la carte: lunch $5-$10, dinner $8-$20. Specializes in seafood, local lamb. In restored fish warehouse. View of boat harbor & fishing boats. Cr cds: A, MC, V.

Beaverton (B-4)

(See also Forest Grove, Hillsboro, Oregon City, Portland)

Pop 53,310 **Elev** 189 ft **Area code** 503 **Zip** 97005

Information Beaverton Area Chamber of Commerce, 4800 SW Griffith Dr, Suite 100; 503/644-0123.

Motels

★★★ **COURTYARD BY MARRIOTT.** *8500 SW Nimbus Dr (97008). 503/641-3200; FAX 503/641-1287.* 149 rms, 3 story. S $95-$105; D $110-$120; each addl $10; suites $110-$120; under 12 free. Crib free. TV; cable (premium). Indoor pool; whirlpool. Complimentary coffee in rms. Bkfst avail. Bar 4-11 pm. Ck-out 1 pm. Coin lndry. Meeting rms. Business servs avail. Valet serv. Sundries. Exercise equipt; weight machine, bicycles. Refrigerator in suites. Balconies. Cr cds: A, C, D, DS, MC, V.

★★ **PEPPER TREE MOTOR INN.** *10720 SW Allen Blvd. 503/641-7477; res: 800/453-6219.* 73 rms, 2 story. S $64.95; D $74.95-$94.95. TV; cable (premium), VCR avail (movies). Heated pool; whirlpool. Complimentary continental bkfst. Coffee in rms. Restaurant adj 6:30 am-10 pm. Ck-out 11 am. Coin lndry. Business servs avail. Valet serv. Exercise equipt; weights, bicycles. Refrigerators. Cr cds: A, D, DS, MC, V.

Motor Hotels

★ ★ ★ **GREENWOOD INN.** *10700 SW Allen Blvd. 503/643-7444; FAX 503/626-4553; res: 800/289-1300.* 250 rms, 2 story, 24 kits. S $91-$115; D $106-$130; each addl $15; kit. suites $170-$400; under 12 free; wknd rates. Crib free. Pet accepted; $10. TV; cable (premium). Pools; whirlpool. Complimentary coffee in rms. Restaurant (see PAVILLION). Rm serv. Bar 11-2 am; entertainment exc Sun. Ck-out 1 pm. Meeting rms. Business servs avail. Sundries. Gift shop. Exercise equipt; weights, bicycles, sauna. Some refrigerators. Cr cds: A, C, D, DS, MC, V.

[D] [symbols] [SC]

★ **RAMADA INN.** *13455 SW Canyon Rd. 503/643-9100; FAX 503/643-0514.* 142 rms, 3 story, 18 kits. S, D $125-$135; each addl $10; kit. units $130-$150; under 18 free. Crib free. TV; cable (premium). Heated pool. Complimentary continental bkfst. Coffee in rms. Restaurant adj open 24 hrs. Ck-out noon. Business servs avail. Exercise equipt; weight machine, bicycle. Cr cds: A, C, D, DS, ER, JCB, MC, V.

[D] [symbols] [SC]

Restaurants

★ ★ **KOJI OSAKAYA.** *11995 SW Beaverton-Hillsdale Hwy. 503/646-5697.* Hrs: 11:30 am-2 pm, 5-10 pm; Fri to 11 pm; Sat noon-2:30 pm, 5-11 pm. Closed most major hols. Japanese menu. Bar. Semi-a la carte: lunch $4.50-$10.95, dinner $4.50-$18.95. Specializes in sushi, Japanese-style noodles. Japanese decor. Cr cds: A, JCB, MC, V.

[D]

★ ★ ★ **PAVILLION.** *(See Greenwood Inn Motor Hotel) 503/626-4550.* Hrs: 6:30 am-10 pm; Fri to 11 pm; Sun 7 am-11 pm; Sun 7 am-10 pm; early bird 4-6 pm. Res accepted. Northwestern menu. Bar. Semi-a la carte: bkfst $4-$9.25, lunch $5.95-$9.50, dinner $12-$20. Sun brunch $19.95. Child's meals. Specializes in salmon, prime rib. Entertainment Fri, Sat. Outdoor dining. Casual decor. Cr cds: A, C, D, DS, MC, V.

[D]

★ ★ **SAYLER'S OLD COUNTRY KITCHEN.** *4655 SW Griffith Dr. 503/644-1492.* Hrs: 4-11 pm; Fri to midnight; Sat 3 pm-midnight; Sun noon-11 pm. Closed July 4, Thanksgiving, Dec 24, 25. Bar from 2:30 pm. Semi-a la carte: dinner $8.95-$21.95. Child's meals. Specializes in steak, prime rib, chicken, seafood. Family-owned. Cr cds: A, DS, MC, V.

[D] [symbol]

Bend (D-5)

(See also Prineville, Redmond)

Settled 1900 **Pop** 20,469 **Elev** 3,628 ft **Area code** 541 **E-mail** bend@empnet.com **Web** www.empnet.com/bchamber
Information Chamber of Commerce, 63085 N US 97, 97701; 541/382-3221 or 800/905-2363.

The early town was named Farewell Bend after a beautiful wooded area on a sweeping curve of the Deschutes River, where pioneer travelers had their last view of the river. The Post Office Department shortened it, but there was good reason for this nostalgic name. As westward-bound settlers approached, they found the first lush, green forests and good water they had seen in Oregon.

Tourists are attracted year-round to the region by its streams and lakes, mountains, great pine forests, ski slopes and golf courses. There is also much of interest to the geologist and rockhound in this area. Movie and television producers take advantage of the wild western scenery.

Two Ranger District offices of the Deschutes National Forest are located here.

What to See and Do

✪ **Driving Tour In Deschutes National Forest.** An 89-mi paved loop (Century Drive, Cascade Lakes Hwy) provides a clear view of Three Sisters peaks, passes many mountain lakes and streams. Go W on Franklin Ave past Drake Park, follow the signs. Continue S past Mt Bachelor, Elk Lake, Lava Lakes and Cultus Lake. After passing Crane Prairie Reservoir, turn left (E) on Forest Rd 42 to US 97, then left (N) for return to Bend.

Also in the forest are Newberry National Volcanic Monument, the Lava Cast Forest and Lava Butte Geological Area, Mt Bachelor Ski Area, Crane Prairie Osprey Management Area, as well as Mt Jefferson, Diamond Peak, Three Sisters and Mt Washington wildernesses. Fishing, hiking, camping, picnicking and rafting are popular. The forest includes 1.6 million acres with headquarters in Bend. 10 mi S of Bend, at the base of Lava Butte, is Lava Lands Visitor Center, operated by the US Forest Service, with dioramas and exhibits on history and geology of volcanic area. For further information contact Supervisor, 1645 US 20E, 97701; 541/388-2715.

Lava Butte and Lava River Cave. Lava Butte is an extinct volcanic cone. Paved road to top provides view of Cascades; interpretive trails through pine forest and lava flow. One mi S, Lava River Cave offers a lava tube 1.2 mi long; ramps and easy walking. 11 mi S on US 97. Visitor center has audiovisual shows (May-Sept, daily), phone 541/593-2421. ¢

Mt Bachelor Ski Area. Panoramic, scenic view of forests, lakes and Cascade Range. Facilities at base of 6,000 ft; 6,000 acres. 10 chairlifts; patrol, school, rentals; cafeterias, concession areas, bars, lodges; day care. Longest run 2 mi; vertical drop 3,100 ft. (Mid-Nov-early July, daily) 56 mi of cross-country trails. Half-day rates. 22 mi SW on Century Dr. Phone 541/382-2442 or 541/382-2607; for res phone 800/829-2442. ¢¢¢¢¢

Newberry National Volcanic Monument. Wide range of volcanic features and deposits similar to Mt Etna; obsidian flow, pumice deposits. On same road are East and Paulina lakes. There is a view of entire area from Paulina Peak. Both lakes have excellent fishing; boat landings. Hiking. Picnicking (stoves, fireplaces); resorts. Tent & trailer sites. 24 mi S on US 97, then 14 mi E on Forest Road 21, in Deschutes National Forest. Phone 541/388-2715. Camping ¢¢¢

Pine Mt Observatory. University of Oregon astronomical research facility. Visitors may view stars, planets and galaxies through telescopes. (May-Oct, Fri & Sat) 26 mi SE near Millican, via US 20, then 9 mi S on marked road. Phone 541/382-8331 for appt. **Donation.**

State parks and recreation areas.

Pilot Butte. A 101-acre park noted for a lone cinder cone rising 511 feet above the city. Summit affords an excellent view of the Cascade Range. No water, no camping. 1 mi E on US 20. Phone 541/388-6055.

Tumalo. A 320-acre park situated along the banks of the Deschutes River; swimming nearby. Fishing. Hiking. Picnicking. Tent & trailer campsites; solar-heated showers. Standard fees. 5½ mi NW off US 20. Phone 541/382-3586 or 541/388-6055.

LaPine. A 2,333-acre park on Deschutes River in Ponderosa pine forest. Scenic views. Swimming, bathhouse; fishing; boating. Picnicking. Improved trailer campsites (dump station). Standard fees. 22 mi S on US 97, then 4 mi W. Phone 541/388-6055.

The High Desert Museum. Regional museum with indoor/outdoor exhibits featuring live animals and cultural history of Intermountain Northwest aridlands; hands-on activities; on-going presentations. Galleries house wildlife, Western art & Native American artifacts; landscape photography; walk-through dioramas depicting opening of American West. Desertarium showcases seldom-seen bats, burrowing owls, amphibians and reptiles. Visitor center. (Daily; closed Jan 1, Thanksgiving, Dec 25) 6 mi S on US 97. Phone 541/382-4754. ¢¢¢

Tumalo Falls. A 97-ft waterfall deep in pine forest devastated by 1979 fire. W via Franklin Ave & Galveston Ave, 12 mi beyond city limits, then 2 mi via unsurfaced forest road.

Whitewater Rafting. Sun Country Tours. Choose from 2-hr or all-day trips. Also canoeing and special programs. (May-Sept) Phone 541/382-6277 for more information. ¢¢¢¢¢

Motels

★ ★ **BEST WESTERN ENTRADA LODGE.** *19221 Century Dr (97702).* 541/382-4080. 79 rms. S, D $49-$89; each addl $5; ski plans; some higher rates major hols. Crib $5. Pet accepted; $5/day. TV; cable. Pool; whirlpool. Complimentary continental bkfst. Ck-out noon. Meeting rm. Business servs avail. In-rm modem link. Downhill/x-country ski 17 mi. On 31 acres. Whitewater rafting. Cr cds: A, D, DS, MC, V.

[D] [icons] SC

✔ ★ **CIMARRON MOTOR INN.** *201 NE Third St (97701).* 541/382-8282; FAX 541/388-6833; res: 800/304-4050. 60 rms, 2 story. S $44; D $49-$61; each addl $5. Pet accepted, some restrictions; $5. TV; cable (premium). Heated pool. Complimentary continental bkfst. Restaurant nearby. Ck-out noon. Business servs avail. Downhill/x-country ski 20 mi. Some microwaves. Cr cds: A, D, DS, MC, V.

[icons] SC

★ ★ **HAMPTON INN.** *15 NE Butler Market Rd (97701).* 541/388-4114; FAX 541/389-3261. 99 rms, 2 story. S, D $71-$95; under 18 free. Crib free. Pet accepted. TV; cable (premium). Heated pool; whirlpool. Complimentary continental bkfst. Ck-out noon. Business servs avail. In-rm modem link. Cr cds: A, C, D, DS, MC, V.

[D] [icons] SC

★ ★ **MT BACHELOR VILLAGE RESORT.** *19717 Mt Bachelor Dr (97702).* 541/389-5900; FAX 541/388-7820; res: 800/452-9846. E-mail mbvr@enpnet.com; web www.enpnet.com/mbr. 130 condominiums, some A/C, 2 story. Condos $97-$329; ski, golf plans. Crib $5. TV; cable. Heated pool; whirlpools. Complimentary coffee in lobby. Restaurant 11:30 am-10 pm. Ck-out noon. Coin lndry. Meeting rm. Business center. Downhill ski 18 mi; x-country ski 14 mi. Health club privileges. Refrigerators, fireplaces; some microwaves. Private patios, balconies. Picnic tables. Woodland setting along Deschutes River. Cr cds: A, MC, V.

[icons]

★ ★ **RED LION-NORTH.** *1415 NE Third St (97701).* 541/382-7011; FAX 541/382-7934. 75 rms, 2 story. S, D $79; each addl $10; under 18 free. Crib free. Pet accepted. TV; cable (premium). Heated pool; whirlpool. Restaurant 6 am-10 pm. Rm serv. Ck-out noon. Meeting rms. Business servs avail. In-rm modem link. Sundries. Saunas. Cr cds: A, C, D, DS, ER, MC, V.

[D] [icons] SC

✔ ★ ★ **RIVERHOUSE MOTOR INN.** *3075 N US 97 (97701).* 541/389-3111; FAX 541/389-0870; res: 800/547-3928 (exc OR), 800/452-6878 (OR). 220 rms, 2 story, 29 suites, 39 kits. S $55-$68; D $65-$74; each addl $6; suites $85-$175; kit. units $75-$105; under 6 free; ski, golf plans. Crib $10. Pet accepted. TV; cable (premium), VCR (movies). 2 heated pools, 1 indoor; poolside serv. Coffee in rms. Restaurant 6 am-10 pm. Rm serv. Ck-out noon. Coin lndry. Meeting rms. Business servs avail. In-rm modem link. Bellhops. Sundries. Ski area transportation. 18-hole golf, greens fee $33, pro, putting green, driving range. Exercise equipt; stair machine, rower. Some microwaves. Balconies. On the Deschutes River. Cr cds: A, C, D, DS, MC, V.

[D] [icons]

★ ★ ★ **SHILO INN SUITES HOTEL.** *3105 O.B. Riley Rd (97701),* opp Bend River Mall. 541/389-9600; FAX 541/382-4130. 151 rms, 2 story, 54 kit. units. S, D $89-$165; each addl $10; suites $165; kit. units $105-$135; under 12 free. Crib free. Pet accepted; $7. TV; cable (premium), VCR avail. 2 pools, 1 indoor; whirlpools. Complimentary bkfst buffet. Restaurant adj 7 am-10 pm. Bar. Ck-out noon. Coin lndry. Meeting rms. Business servs avail. Sundries. Free airport transportation. Downhill ski 20 mi; x-country ski 15 mi. Exercise equipt; weight machine, bicycles, sauna. Bathrm phones, refrigerators, microwaves; some wet bars. Some balconies. On Deschutes River. Cr cds: A, C, D, DS, ER, JCB, MC, V.

[D] [icons] SC

Resorts

★ ★ **BLACK BUTTE RANCH.** *(Black Butte 97759)* 30 mi NW via US 20. 541/595-6211; FAX 541/595-2077; res: 800/452-7455. 132 condo and house units (1-4 bedrm), 69 with kit. Condo units $85-$178; houses $130-$280; golf, ski plans. Crib $5. TV; VCR (movies $3-$5). 4 heated pools; wading pool, lifeguard. Supervised child's activities (June-Labor Day). Dining rm 8 am-3 pm, 5-9 pm. Snack bar. Bar 11 am-10 pm. Ck-out 11 am, ck-in 4 pm. Meeting rms. Business servs avail. Grocery. Sports dir. Lighted tennis, pro. Two 18-hole golf courses, pro, greens fee $55, putting green, driving range. Downhill/x-country ski 15 mi; x-country rental equipt. Exercise equipt; treadmill, stair machine. Massage. Game rm. Bicycles. Many microwaves, fireplaces. Private patios. On 1,830 wooded acres. Cr cds: A, D, DS, MC, V.

[D] [icons]

★ ★ ★ **INN OF THE SEVENTH MOUNTAIN.** *18575 SW Century Dr (97702),* 7 mi W. 541/382-8711; FAX 541/382-3517. E-mail reservations@7thmtn.com; web www.7thmtn.com. 300 rms, 3 story, 200 kits. No elvtr. Dec-Mar, June-Aug: S $69-$115; D $89-$155; kit. units $89-$109; kit. suites $169-$269; ski, golf package plans; higher rates: Christmas hols, Presidents' Day; lower rates rest of yr. Crib $3. TV; cable, VCR avail (movies). 2 outdoor pools, 2 heated; wading pool, whirlpools, poolside serv, lifeguard (summer). Supervised child's activities (June-Sept); ages 4-11. Dining rms 7 am-10 pm. Box lunches. Bar 4 pm-1 am. Ck-out noon. Coin lndry. Meeting rms. Business servs avail. Grocery. Sports dir. Tennis, pro. Canoeing, rafting trips. Downhill/x-country ski 14 mi. Outdoor ice/roller rink; horse-drawn sleigh rides. Snowmobile, bike tours. Bicycles. Lawn games. Sauna. Movies. Rec rm. Some refrigerators, microwaves, fireplaces. Private patios. Picnic tables, grills. Cr cds: A, C, D, DS, MC, V.

[D] [icons]

★ ★ ★ **SUNRIVER RESORT.** *(1 Center Dr, Sunriver 97707)* 15 mi S of Bend, 2 mi W of US 97. 541/593-1000; FAX 541/593-5458; res: 800/547-3922. Web www.sunriver~resort.com. 211 units (1-3 bedrm) in 2 story lodge units, 77 kits., 230 houses (1-4 bedrm). Mid-June-Sept: S, D $130-$139; kit. suites $190; houses (up to 8 persons) $165-$325; higher rates hols; lower rates rest of yr. TV; cable (premium), VCR avail (movies $3). 3 pools; 3 wading pools, outdoor whirlpools, lifeguard. Playground. Supervised child's activities (June-Sept); ages 3-14. Dining rms 7 am-10 pm (also see MEADOWS). Ck-out 11 am, ck-in 4 pm. Coin lndry. Meeting rms. Business center. Gift shop. Grocery. Barber, beauty shop. Airport transportation. Ski bus. Sports dir. 28 tennis courts. Three 18-hole golf courses, 6 pros, putting greens, driving ranges, pro shops. Canoes; whitewater rafting. Downhill ski 18 mi; x-country ski on site. Skating rink, equipt (fee). Racquetball. Bicycles; 30 mi of bike trails. Nature center. Stables. Indoor, outdoor games. Game rm (fee). Entertainment. Massage. Health club privileges. Fishing guide service. 5,500-ft airstrip. Marina. Houses with full amenities & private patios. Some microwaves. Balconies. Picnic tables. 3,300 acres on Deschutes River. Cr cds: A, C, D, DS, MC, V.

[D] [icons] SC

Guest Ranch

★ ★ **ROCK SPRINGS.** *64201 Tyler Rd (97701),* 9 mi NW of Bend off US 20. 541/382-1957; FAX 541/382-7774; res: 800/225-3833. E-mail info@rocksprings.com; web www.rocksprings.com. 26 cottages. S $1,430/wk; family rates; AP late June-Aug; MAP Thanksgiving. TV in sitting rm. Heated pool; whirlpool. Free supervised child's activities (late June-Aug); ages 3-16. Dining rm (sittings) 8-9 am, noon-1 pm, 6:30-7:30 pm. Box lunches. Picnics. Ck-out 11 am, ck-in 4:30 pm. Grocery 3 mi. Guest lndry. Meeting rm. Business servs avail. Free airport transportation. Lighted tennis, pro. Downhill/X-country ski 20 mi. Exercise equipt; weight machine, bicycle. Massage. Lawn games. Western trail rides. Game rm. Fish pond. Refrigerators, fireplaces. Picnic tables. Cr cds: A, C, D, DS, MC, V.

[D] [icons]

Restaurants

★ ★ ★ **ERNESTO'S ITALIAN RESTAURANT.** *1203 NE 3rd St, on US 97.* 541/389-7274. Hrs: 4:30-9:30 pm; Fri, Sat to 10 pm. Italian menu. Bar. Semi-a la carte: dinner $7.95-$15.50. Child's meals. Specializes in pizza, calzone. Parking. Housed in former church. Cr cds: A, DS, MC, V.

SC

★ ★ ★ **MEADOWS.** *(See Sunriver Resort)* 541/593-1000. True to its name, this restaurant has tables with meadow views, as well as views of Mount Bachelor. Handwoven hangings and pine walls lend warmth to an otherwise formal dining room. Northwest High Desert menu. Own pastries, desserts. Hrs: 5:30-10 pm. Res accepted. Bar noon-2 am. Extensive wine list. A la carte entrees: dinner $11-$25. Totally nonsmoking. Cr cds: A, C, D, DS, MC, V.

D

★ ★ **PINE TAVERN.** *967 NW Brooks (97701), on Mirror Pond, downtown.* 541/382-5581. Hrs: 11:30 am-9:30 pm; Sun from 5:30 pm. Res accepted. Bar. Semi-a la carte: lunch $5.95-$8.95, dinner $10.50-$17.50. Child's meals. Specializes in fresh trout, prime rib, seafood. Salad bar (lunch). Garden dining. 100-ft pine tree in dining rm. Overlooks Deschutes River, garden. Totally nonsmoking. Cr cds: A, D, DS, MC, V.

D

✔★ **ROSZAK'S FISH HOUSE.** *1230 NE 3rd St (97701).* 541/382-3173. Hrs: 11:30 am-2:30 pm, 4-10 pm; Sat, Sun from 4 pm. Closed Memorial Day, Labor Day. Res accepted. Bar. Semi-a la carte: lunch $5.50-$8.95, dinner $8.95-$22.95. Child's meals. Specializes in prime rib, seafood. Parking. Totally nonsmoking. Cr cds: A, DS, MC, V.

D

✔★ **TONY'S.** *415 NE 3rd St (97701).* 541/389-5858. Hrs: 6 am-9:30 pm. Closed Easter, Dec 25. Res accepted. Italian, Amer menu. Bar 3-10 pm. Semi-a la carte: bkfst $2.75-$6.95, lunch $2.95-$5.95, dinner $6.95-$12.95. Child's meals. Specializes in pizza. Parking. Early Amer building; original paintings, fireplace. Family-owned. Cr cds: DS, MC, V.

D SC

Unrated Dining Spot

WESTSIDE BAKERY & CAFE. *1005 NW Galveston Ave (97701).* 541/382-3426. Hrs: 7 am-3 pm; Sun to 2 pm. Closed Thanksgiving, Dec 25. Semi-a la carte: bkfst, lunch $5-$8. Child's meals. Specializes in baked goods, omelettes. Parking. 3 dining rms; many antiques & toys. Cr cds: DS, MC, V.

D

Biggs (A-6)

(See also The Dalles)

Pop 30 (est) **Elev** 173 ft **Area code** 503 **Zip** 97065

What to See and Do

John Day Locks and Dam. A $487-million unit in the US Army Corps of Engineers Columbia River Basin project. Visitors may view turbine generators from powerhouse observation rm; fish-viewing stations. Self-guided tours (daily; guided tours by appt; closed hols). 5 mi E off I-84N. Phone 503/296-1181. **Free.** The dam creates

Lake Umatilla. A 100-mi reservoir. The eastern part of lake is a national wildlife management area for the preservation of game waterfowl and fish.

Motel

★ ★ **BEST WESTERN RIVIERA.** *91484 Biggs & Rufus Hwy, 1 blk W of US 97, 1 blk S of I-84N, exit 104).* 541/739-2501; FAX 503/739-2091. 40 rms, 1-2 story. S $49; D $56; each addl $5; suites $75-$85. Crib $5. TV. Pool. Complimentary continental bkfst. Restaurant adj 6 am-10 pm. Ck-out noon. Business servs avail. Cr cds: A, C, D, DS, MC, V.

≋ ≋ 🐾 SC

Brookings (F-2)

(See also Coos Bay, Gold Beach)

Pop 4,400 **Elev** 130 ft **Area code** 541 **Zip** 97415
Information Brookings-Harbor Chamber of Commerce and Information Center, 16330 Lower Harbor Rd, PO Box 940; 800/535-9469.

Beachcombers, whale watchers and fisherman find this coastal city a haven for their activities. A commercial and sportfishing center, Brookings lies in an area that produces a high percentage of the nation's Easter lily bulbs. A Ranger District office of the Siskiyou National Forest (see GRANTS PASS) is located here.

What to See and Do

Azalea Park. A 36-acre city park with 5 varieties of large native azaleas, some blooming twice a yr (see ANNUAL EVENT). Observation point. Hiking. Picnicking. Just E off US 101.

State parks.

Harris Beach. A 171-acre park with scenic rock cliffs along ocean. Ocean beach; fishing. Hiking trails, observation point. Picnicking. Improved tent & trailer campsites (dump station). Standard fees. 2 mi N on US 101. Phone 541/469-2021.

Samuel H. Boardman. A 1,473-acre park with observation points along 11 mi of spectacular coastline. Fishing, clamming. Hiking. Picnicking. 4 mi N on US 101. Phone 541/469-2021.

Loeb. A 320-acre park on the Chetco River with an area of beautiful old myrtle trees; also redwoods. Swimming; fishing. Picnicking. Improved camping. Standard fees. 10 mi NE off US 101. Phone 541/469-2021.

Annual Event

Azalea Festival. Azalea Park. Parade, seafood, art exhibits, street fair, crafts fair, music. Memorial Day wkend.

Motel

✔★ **SPINDRIFT MOTOR INN.** *1215 Chetco Ave (US 101).* 541/469-5345; FAX 541/469-5213; res: 800/292-1171. 35 rms, 2 story. Mid-May-Sept: S $44-$49; D $52-$59; each addl $5; lower rates rest of yr. Crib $5. TV; cable (premium). Complimentary coffee in lobby. Restaurant opp 7 am-10 pm. Ck-out 11 am. Business servs avail. Refrigerators. Cr cds: A, C, D, DS, MC, V.

≋ 🐾 SC

Burns (D-8)

Pop 2,913 **Elev** 4,170 ft **Area code** 541 **Zip** 97720 **Web** www.el.com/to/burns
Information Harney County Chamber of Commerce, 18 West D St; 541/573-2636.

This remote trading center and county seat serves a livestock-raising and forage production area bigger than many eastern states. Tecton Laminates plant produces three million cubic feet of laminated veneer lumber annually. Ranger District offices of the Malheur National Forest (see JOHN DAY) and Ochoco National Forest (see PRINEVILLE) are located here.

What to See and Do

Harney County Historical Museum. Displays include arrowheads, quilts, wildlife, artifacts, furniture, clothing, cut glass, old-fashioned kitchen, Pete French's safe and spurs. The Hayes Rm contains a bedrm and dining rm furnished in antiques. Also old wagons, tools and machinery. (May-Oct, Tues-Sat; closed July 4) 18 West D St. Phone Chamber of Commerce, 541/573-2636. ¢

Malheur National Wildlife Refuge. Established in 1908 by Theodore Roosevelt, the 185,000-acre refuge was set aside primarily as a nesting area for migratory birds. It is also an important fall and spring gathering point for waterfowl migrating between the northern breeding grounds and the California wintering grounds. More than 30 species of birds and 50 species of mammals have been recorded on the refuge. Headquarters has museum. (Daily) 32 mi S on OR 205. Refuge Manager, phone 541/493-2612. **Free.**

Annual Events

John Scharff Migratory Bird Festival. Includes bird-watching & historical tours, films, arts & crafts. 1st wknd Apr.

Tu-Kwa-Hone'. Burns High School. Sobriety powwow. 2nd wknd June.

Steens Mountain Rim Run. In Frenchglen, approx 48 mi S on OR 205. Six-mi run at high elevation, pit barbecue, all-night street dance, team-roping, horse cutting. 1st wknd Aug.

Harney County Fair, Rodeo & Race Meet. Includes rodeo and parimutuel racing. Wed-Sun after Labor Day.

Motels

✔★ **BEST WESTERN PONDEROSA.** *577 W Monroe. 541/573-2047; FAX 541/573-3828.* 52 rms, 2 story. S $36-$50; D $42-$55; each addl $5. Pet accepted. TV; cable (premium), VCR avail. Pool. Complimentary coffee in lobby. Restaurant nearby. Ck-out 11 am. Business servs avail. Free airport transportation. Cr cds: A, C, D, DS, MC, V.

✔★ **SILVER SPUR.** *789 N Broadway. 541/573-2077; FAX 541/573-3921.* 26 rms, 2 story. S $34.65; D $44. TV; cable (premium). Complimentary continental bkfst. Ck-out 11:30 am. Free airport transportation. Health club privileges. Cr cds: A, C, D, DS, MC, V.

Restaurant

★★ **PINE ROOM CAFE.** *543 W Monroe, jct US 20, 395. 541/573-6631.* Hrs: 5-10 pm; winter to 9 pm. Closed Sun, Mon; major hols. Res accepted. Bar 4 pm-2:30 am. Semi-a la carte: dinner $8.45-$15.25. Child's meals. Specialties: chicken liver Bordelaise, stuffed prawns Mornay. Pictures of Harney County by local artist. Family-owned. Cr cds: MC, V.

Cannon Beach (A-3)

(See also Astoria, Seaside)

Pop 1,221 **Elev** 25 ft **Area code** 503 **Zip** 97110
Information Visitor Information Center, 207 N Spruce, PO Box 64; 503/436-2623.

The cannon and capstan from the schooner USS *Shark,* which was washed ashore near here in 1846, are now on a small monument four miles south of this resort town. Swimming (lifeguard on duty in summer), surfing and surf fishing can be enjoyed here and the seven-mile stretch of wide beach is wonderful for walking. Among the large rocks offshore is the 235-foot Haystack Rock, third-largest monolith in the world.

What to See and Do

Ecola State Park. End of the trail for Lewis and Clark expedition. A 1,303-acre park with 6 mi of ocean frontage; sea lion and bird rookeries on rocks and offshore islands; Tillamook Lighthouse. Beaches; fishing. Hiking (on the Oregon Coast Trail). Picnicking at Ecola Point. Whale-watching at observation point. 2 mi N off US 101.

Fort Clatsop National Memorial (see). Approx 15 mi N off US 101A.

Oswald West State Park. A 2,474-acre park with outstanding coastal headland; towering cliffs; low dunes; rain forest with massive spruce and cedar trees; road winds 700 ft above sea level and 1,000 ft below peak of Neahkahnie Mt. Surfing (at nearby Short Sands Beach); fishing. Hiking trails (on the Oregon Coast Trail). Picnicking. Primitive campgrounds accessible only by 1/4-mi foot trail. 10 mi S on US 101, walk last 1/4 mi.

Annual Event

Sandcastle Contest. Nationally known event features sand sculptures on beach. June 7.

Motels

★★★ **CANNON BEACH HOTEL.** *1116 S Hemlock. 503/436-1392; FAX 503/436-2101.* 26 rms, 2 story. No A/C. June-Oct: S, D $49-$159; each addl $10; lower rates rest of yr. TV; cable, VCR avail. Complimentary continental bkfst. Restaurant 8 am-10 pm. Ck-out 11 am. Business servs avail. Totally nonsmoking. Cr cds: A, C, D, DS, MC, V.

★★ **SCHOONER'S COVE.** *188 N Larch. 503/436-2300; FAX 503/436-2156; res: 800/843-0128.* 30 kit. units, 2 story, 12 kit. suites. No A/C. Mid-June-Labor Day: S, D $89-$149; each addl $5; kit. suites $119-$149; lower rates rest of yr. Crib $4. TV; cable (premium), VCR. Restaurant nearby. Ck-out 11 am. Coin lndry. Meeting rms. Whirlpool. Fireplaces. Balconies. Picnic tables, grills. On beach. Cr cds: A, C, D, DS, MC, V.

★★★ **SURFSAND RESORT.** *S on Hemlock St, at Gower St. 503/436-2274; FAX 503/436-9116; res: 800/547-6100.* 86 rms, 2 story, 38 kits. No A/C. June-mid-Oct: S, D $124-$165; suites, kit. units $149-$219; lower rates rest of yr. Crib $5. Pet accepted; $5/day. TV; cable (premium), VCR (movies $3). Indoor pool; whirlpool. Coffee in rms. Restaurant 8 am-midnight. Bar to 1 am. Ck-out noon. Lndry facilities. Meeting rms. Free airport transportation. Gift shop. Refrigerators, fireplaces. Balconies. On ocean, beach. View of Haystack Rock. Cr cds: A, C, D, DS, MC, V.

★★ **TOLOVANA INN.** *(Tolovana Park 97145) 1 1/2 mi S; 1/4 mi W of US 101. 503/436-2211; FAX 503/436-0134; res: 800/333-8890.* 180 rms, 3 story, 96 kits. No A/C. No elvtr. S, D $68-$145; suites $154-$225; kit. units $145-$225; studio rms $131-$145. Crib free. Pet accepted; $7. TV; cable, VCR avail (movies). Indoor pool; whirlpool. Ck-out 11 am. Coin lndry. Meeting rms. Business servs avail. Game rm. Refrigerators. Some fireplaces. Private patios, balconies. Overlooks Haystack Rock. Cr cds: A, DS, MC, V.

Motor Hotel

★ ★ ★ **HALLMARK RESORT.** *1400 S Hemlock. 503/436-1566; FAX 503/436-0324; 800 888/448-4449.* 132 rms, 3 story, 63 kits., 5 cottages. July-Sept: S, D $99-$189; suites $125-$229; kit. units $125-$229; cottages $265-$425; lower rates rest of yr. Crib free. Pet accepted; $8/day. TV; cable (premium), VCR avail (movies). Indoor pool; wading pool; whirlpool. Complimentary coffee. Restaurant adj 8 am-9 pm. Ck-out noon, ck-in 4 pm. Coin lndry. Meeting rms. Business servs avail. Gift shop. Free local airport, bus depot transportation. Exercise equipt; weight machine, bicycles, sauna. Refrigerators. Some fireplaces, in-rm whirlpools. Balconies. On beach. Cr cds: A, C, D, DS, JCB, MC, V.

Inn

★ **GREY WHALE.** *164 Kenai. 503/436-2848.* 5 rms, shower only, 3 kit. units. No A/C. Mid-June-mid-Sept: S, D $74-$94; each addl $10; wkly rates; lower rates rest of yr. TV; cable, VCR. Complimentary coffee in rms. Ck-out 11 am, ck-in 3 pm. Totally nonsmoking. Cr cds: MC, V.

Restaurant

★ ★ **DOOGER'S.** *1371 S Hemlock. 503/436-2225.* Hrs: 8 am-10 pm. Closed Thanksgiving, Dec 24, 25; also 2 wks Jan. Bar. Semi-a la carte: bkfst $2.75-$8.95, lunch $2.75-$9.50, dinner $7.95-$34.95. Child's meals. Specializes in steak, seafood. Totally nonsmoking. Cr cds: A, MC, V.

Cave Junction (F-3)

(For accommodations see Grants Pass)

Pop 1,126 **Elev** 1,295 ft **Area code** 541 **Zip** 97523

Information Illinois Valley Chamber of Commerce, 201 Caves Hwy, PO Box 312; 541/592-3326.

A Ranger District office of the Siskiyou National Forest (see GRANTS PASS) is located here.

What to See and Do

Kerbyville Museum. Home (ca 1870) furnished in the period; outdoor display of farm, logging and mining tools; Native American artifacts; rock display; log schoolhouse, blacksmith shop, general store. Picnic tables. (May-Sept, daily) 2 mi N on US 199 in Kerby. Phone 541/592-2076 or 541/592-4478. ¢

Oregon Caves National Monument (see). 20 mi E on OR 46.

Annual Events

Annual Moon Tree Country Run. Siskiyou Smoke Jump Base. Phone 541/596-2621. Mid-June.

Wild Blackberry Festival. Blackberry foods, cooking, games, crafts and music. Mid-Aug.

Lodge

★ ★ **OREGON CAVES.** *20000 Caves Hwy. 541/592-3400; FAX 541/592-6654.* E-mail mike@crater-lake.com; web www.crater-lake.com /caves/. 22 rms, 3 story, 3 suites. No A/C. No rm phones. S, D $89; each addl $10; suites $109; under 6 free. Closed Nov-Apr. Crib $10. Restaurants from 9 am. Rm serv. Ck-out 11 am. Meeting rms. Business center. Bellhops. Sundries. Gift shop. X-country ski on-site. Picnic tables, grills. Totally nonsmoking. Cr cds: MC, V.

Coos Bay (D-3)

(See also Bandon, Brookings, North Bend, Reedsport)

Founded 1854 **Pop** 15,076 **Elev** 11 ft **Area code** 541 **Zip** 97420 **E-mail** bacc@ucinet.com **Web** www.ucinet.com/~bacc

Information Bay Area Chamber of Commerce, 50 E Central, PO Box 210; 541/269-0215 or 800/824-8486.

Coos Bay, one of the world's largest shipping ports for forest products, is also a deep-sea fishing haven. Dairy herds graze in the surrounding area, providing milk for the production of butter and cheddar cheese. Local cranberry bogs supply fruit for processing.

What to See and Do

Charleston Marina Complex. Charter boats; launching & moorage facilities (fee); car & boat-trailer parking (free); dry boat storage, travel park; motel; marine fuel dock; tackle shops; restaurants. Office (Mon-Fri). 9 mi SW in Charleston. Phone 541/888-2548.

South Slough National Estuarine Research Reserve. A 4,400-acre area reserved for the study of estuarine ecosystems and life. Previous studies here include oyster culture techniques and water pollution. Special programs, lectures and exhibits at Interpretive Center. Trails and waterways (daily); guided trail walks and canoe tours (June-Aug; fee). Interpretive Center (June-Aug, daily; rest of yr, Mon-Fri). 4 mi S on Seven Devils Rd, in Charleston. Phone 541/888-5558.

State parks.

Sunset Bay. A 395-acre park with swimming beach on sheltered bay; fishing. Hiking. Picnicking. Tent & trailer sites. Observation point. Standard fees. 12 mi SW off US 101 on Cape Arago Hwy. Phone 541/888-4902.

Shore Acres. Former grand estate of Coos Bay lumberman, noted for its unusual botanical and Japanese gardens and spectacular ocean views (743 acres). Ocean beach. Hiking (on the Oregon Coast Trail). Picnicking. Standard fees. 13 mi SW off US 101 on Cape Arago Hwy. Phone 541/888-3732 or 541/888-8867.

Cape Arago. This 134-acre promontory juts $1/2$ mi into ocean. Two beaches; fishing. Hiking (on Oregon Coast Trail). Picnicking. Observation point (whale and seal watching). 14 mi SW off US 101 on Cape Arago Hwy. Phone 541/888-8867.

The Oregon Connection/House of Myrtlewood. Manufacturing of myrtlewood gift items. Tours. (Daily; closed Jan 1, Thanksgiving, Dec 25) 1125 S 1st St, just off US 101 in S Coos Bay. Phone 541/267-7804. **Free.**

Annual Event

Oregon Coast Music Festival. Variety of musical presentations ranging from jazz and dance to chamber and symphonic music. Also free outdoor picnic concerts. Phone 541/267-0938. Last 2 full wks July.

Motels

★ ★ **BEST WESTERN HOLIDAY.** *411 N Bayshore Dr, on US 101. 541/269-5111; res: 800/228-8655.* 77 rms, 2 story. July-Aug: S, D

$71-$91; each addl $5; suites $125-$140; kits. units $81-$91; lower rates rest of yr. Crib avail. TV; cable (premium). Indoor pool; whirlpool. Complimentary coffee in lobby. Restaurant adj open 24 hrs. Coin lndry. Ck-out noon. Exercise equipt; weights, bicycles. Microwaves avail. Whirlpools in suites. Cr cds: A, C, D, DS, MC, V.

D ☆ ✕ ☆ ☆ SC

★ ★ ★ **RED LION INN.** *1313 N Bayshore Dr, on US 101.* 541/267-4141; *FAX* 541/267-2884. 143 rms, 1-2 story. S $69-$85; D $79-$100; each addl $15; under 18 free. Crib free. Pet accepted, some restrictions. TV; cable (premium). Pool. Coffee in rms. Restaurant 6 am-10 pm. Rm serv. Bar 11-2 am; entertainment Fri, Sat. Ck-out noon. Meeting rms. Business servs avail. In-rm modem link. Free airport transportation. Microwaves avail. On Coos Bay. Cr cds: A, C, D, DS, ER, JCB, MC, V.

D ☞ ☆ ☆ ☆ SC

Restaurant

★ ★ **PORTSIDE.** *(8001 Kingfisher Rd, Charleston) 9 mi SW on US 101, at the Charleston Boat Basin.* 503/888-5545. Hrs: 11:30 am-11 pm. Res accepted. Bar. Semi-a la carte: lunch $4.95-$22.95, dinner $10.95-$24.95. Child's meals. Specializes in bouillabaisse, live lobster, fresh salmon. Own desserts. Entertainment Wed-Sun. Outdoor dining. Cr cds: A, D, MC, V.

Corvallis (C-4)

(See also Albany, Eugene, Salem)

Settled 1845 **Pop** 44,757 **Elev** 225 ft **Area code** 541 **E-mail** ccvb@visitcorvallis.com **Web** www.visitcorvallis.com

Information Convention & Visitors Bureau, 420 NW 2nd, 97330; 541/757-1544 or 800/334-8118.

Located in the heart of Oregon's fertile Willamette Valley and built on the banks of the Willamette River, Corvallis is a center for education, culture and commerce. It is the home of Oregon State University, the state's oldest institution of higher education. A prosperous business environment is supported by several international firms located here. Siuslaw National Forest headquarters is here.

What to See and Do

Avery Park. A 75-acre park on the Marys River. Bicycle, cross-country and jogging trails. Picnicking, playground, ballfield. Rose and rhododendron gardens, community gardens; 1922 Mikado locomotive. Playground (accessible to the disabled). (Daily) S 15th St and US 20. Phone 541/757-6918. **Free.**

Benton County Historical Museum. Located in the former Philomath College building. Features displays on history of the county; art gallery. Reference library (by appt). (Tues-Sat) 6 mi W at 1101 Main St in Philomath. Phone 541/929-6230. **Free.**

Oregon State University (1868). (14,500 students) On its 400-acre campus are Memorial Union Concourse Gallery (daily; phone 541/737-2416); Fairbanks Gallery (daily; phone 541/737-5009); Giustina Gallery at La Sells Stewart Center (Mon-Fri; phone 541/737-2402). Campus tours. Bounded by 11th and 53rd Sts, Monroe Ave & US 20. Phone 541/737-0123 or 541/737-1000. **Free.**

Siuslaw National Forest. Includes 50 mi of ocean frontage with more than 30 campgrounds; public beaches, sand dunes and overlooks; visitor center and nature trails in the Cape Perpetua Scenic Area. Marys Peak, highest peak in the Coast Range, has a road to picnic grounds and campground near the summit. Swimming; ocean, lake and stream fishing; hunting for deer, bear, elk and migratory birds; clam digging; boating. Hiking. Picnicking. Camping (fee in most areas); dune buggies (in designated areas). Forest contains 630,000 acres including the Oregon Dunes

National Recreation Area. W via OR 34. For further information contact Forest Supervisor, 97333; 541/750-7000.

Tyee Wine Cellars. Located on 460-acre Century farm. Offers tastings, tours, interpretive hikes, picnicking. (July-Sept, Fri-Mon; May-June & Oct-Dec, wkends; also by appt) 7 mi S via US 99W, 3 mi W on Greenberry Rd. Phone 541/753-8754. **Free.**

Annual Events

Da Vinci Days. Festival celebrating the relationship between art, science and technology. Phone 541/757-6363. 3rd wkend July.

Benton County Fair and Rodeo. Phone 541/757-1521. Late July-early Aug.

Fall Festival. Phone 541/752-9655. Sept.

Motels

★ ★ **BEST WESTERN GRAND MANOR INN.** *925 NW Garfield* (97330). 541/758-8571; *FAX* 541/758-0834. 55 rms, 3 story. S $71-$160; D $78-$160; each addl $6; suites $98-$160; under 12 free. Crib $6. TV; cable (premium). Heated pool. Complimentary continental bkfst. Restaurant nearby. Ck-out 11 am. Business servs avail. In-rm modem link. Exercise equipt; weight machine, bicycles. Refrigerators; some microwaves. Cr cds: A, C, D, DS, MC, V.

D ☆ ✕ ☆ ☆ SC

✔ ★ **ORLEANS.** *935 NW Garfield* (97330). 541/758-9125; res: 800/626-1900; *FAX* 541/758-0544. 61 rms, 3 story. No elvtr. S $45-$50; D $51-$54; each addl $4; suites $56-$64; under 12 free. Crib $5. Pet accepted, some restrictions. TV; cable. Pool privileges. Complimentary coffee in lobby. Restaurant nearby. Ck-out 11 am. Coin lndry. Whirlpool. Microwaves avail. Cr cds: A, D, DS, MC, V.

D ☞ ☆ ☆ ☆ SC

✔ ★ ★ **SHANICO INN.** *1113 NW 9th* (97330). 541/754-7474; *FAX* 541/754-2437; res: 800/432-1233. Web www.sdl.com/shanicoinn.html. 76 rms, 3 story. S $48; D $55-$65; each addl $5; suites $64; under 12 free. Crib free. Pet accepted, some restrictions. TV. Heated pool. Continental bkfst. Restaurant adj open 24 hrs. Ck-out noon. Meeting rm. Cr cds: A, C, D, DS, MC, V.

D ☞ ☆ ☆ ☆ SC

Inns

★ ★ ★ **ABED & BREAKFAST.** *2515 SW 45th St* (97330). 541/757-7321; res: 888/757-7321; *FAX* 541/753-4332. E-mail abed@proaxis.com; web www.proaxis.com/~abed. 4 rms, 2 share bath, 1 with A/C, 2 story. No rm phones. S $58-$72; D $68-$82; wkly rates. Children over 8 yrs only. TV in common rm; VCR avail (movies). Complimentary full bkfst. Ck-out 11 am, ck-in 4 pm. Business servs avail. Luggage handling. Concierge serv. Free guest lndry. Whirlpool. Built in 1950s; country atmosphere. Totally nonsmoking. Cr cds: A, C, D, DS, MC, V.

☆ ☆

★ ★ ★ **HARRISON HOUSE BED & BREAKFAST.** *2310 NW Harrison Blvd* (97330). 541/752-6248; res: 800/233-6248; *FAX* 541/754-1353. E-mail harrisonhouse@proaxis.com; web www.proaxis.com/harrison house/. 4 rms, all share bath, 2 with A/C, 2 story. S, D $50-$80; each addl $15; under 8 free; wkly, monthly rates. TV in some rms; cable (premium), VCR avail (movies). Complimentary full bkfst; afternoon refreshments. Rm serv 10 am-10 pm. Ck-out 11 am, ck-in 4 pm. Business servs avail. In-rm modem link. Luggage handling. Concierge serv. X-country ski 10 mi. Built in 1939; antiques. Totally nonsmoking. Cr cds: A, DS, MC, V.

☆ ☆ ☆ SC

Restaurants

★ ★ **GABLES.** *1121 NW 9th St.* 541/752-3364. Hrs: 5-9 pm; early-bird dinner Mon-Fri 5-6 pm. Res accepted. Continental menu. Bar 4:30-11 pm. Semi-a la carte: dinner $10.95-$25.95. Child's meals. Specializes in fresh seafood, steak, prime rib. Own desserts. Wine cellar dining area. Family-owned. Cr cds: A, D, DS, MC, V.

D

★ ★ **MICHAEL'S LANDING.** *603 NW Second St.* 541/754-6141. Hrs: 11:30 am-9 pm; Fri, Sat to 9:30 pm. Closed Dec 25. Res accepted. Bar to 11 pm; wkends to midnight. Semi-a la carte: lunch $5.25-$10.25, dinner $10.95-$18.95. Child's meals. Specializes in prime rib, pasta, seafood. Old RR depot overlooking river, built 1909. Cr cds: A, C, D, DS, MC, V.

D

Cottage Grove (D-4)

(See also Eugene)

Pop 7,402 **Elev** 641 ft **Area code** 541 **Zip** 97424
Information Cottage Grove Area Chamber of Commerce, 710 Row River Rd, PO Box 587; 541/942-2411.

Cottage Grove is the lumber, retail and distribution center for south Lane County. A Ranger District office of the Umpqua National Forest (see ROSEBURG) is located here.

What to See and Do

Chateau Lorane Winery. 30-acre vineyard located on 200-acre wooded estate features lakeside tasting room in which to enjoy great variety of traditional, rare and hand-made wines. (June-Aug, daily exc Mon; Mar-May & Sept-Dec, wkends & hols; also by appt) 12 mi W on Cottage Grove-Lorane Rd to Siuslaw River Rd. Phone 541/942-8028.   **Free.**

Cottage Grove Lake. Three-mi-long lake. Lakeside (W shore) and Wilson Creek (E shore) parks have swimming, boat launch and picnicking. Shortridge Park (E shore) has swimming, waterskiing, fishing and picnicking. Primitive and improved camping (showers, dump station) at Pine Meadows on E shore (Mid-May-mid-Sept, 14-day limit; no res; fee). S via I-5, Cottage Grove Lake exit 170, turn left, then 5 mi S on London Rd. For information phone 541/942-8657 or 541/942-5631. Per vehicle ¢¢¢

Cottage Grove Museum. Displays of pioneer homelife and Native American artifacts housed in a former Roman Catholic Church (1897), octagonal, with stained-glass windows made in Italy. Adj annex houses model of ore stamp mill showing how gold was extracted from the ore; working model of a green chain; antique tools. (Mid-June-Labor Day, Wed-Sun afternoons; rest of yr, wkends) Birch Ave & H St. Phone 541/942-3963. **Free.**

Covered Bridges. Five old-time covered bridges within 10-mile radius of town. Inquire at Chamber of Commerce.

Dorena Lake. Five-mi-long lake. Schwarz Park (camping fee), on Row River below dam, has fishing, picnicking and camping (dump station). Lane County maintains Baker Bay Park, on S shore, and offers swimming, waterskiing, fishing, boating (launch, marina, rentals), picnicking, concession and camping (fee); and Harms Park, on N shore, offers boat launching and picnicking. For further information inquire at Cottage Grove project office. 5 mi E on Row River Rd. Phone 541/942-1418. Schwarz Park per vehicle ¢¢¢

Annual Event

Bohemia Mining Days Celebration. Commemorates area's gold-mining days; parades; flower, art shows; rodeo, entertainment. 3rd wk July.

Motel

★ ★ ★ **BEST WESTERN VILLAGE GREEN.** *725 Row River Rd, just off I-5 exit 174.* 541/942-2491; FAX 541/942-2386. 96 rms. June-Oct: S $69-$99; D $79-$110; each addl $5; suites $99-$165; under 12 free; lower rates rest of yr. Crib free. Pet accepted. TV; cable (premium). Heated pool; whirlpool. Playground. Restaurant 6:30 am-9 pm. Bar 4 pm-midnight. Ck-out 11 am. Coin lndry. Meeting rms. Business servs avail. Sundries. Covered parking. Tennis. Some refrigerators. Private patios. 18-hole golf course adj. Cr cds: A, C, D, DS, MC, V.

D ✧ ☆ ≋ ⚡ ⚲ ⚐ ⚑ SC

Restaurant

★ **COTTAGE.** *2915 Row River Rd.* 541/942-3091. Hrs: 11 am-9 pm. Closed Sun; wk of Thanksgiving. Bar. Semi-a la carte: lunch, dinner $2.75-$19. Child's meals. Specializes in fresh seafood, steak, chicken. Salad bar. Own desserts. Bldg solar heated. Cr cds: MC, V.

D

Crater Lake National Park (E-5)

(57 mi N of Klamath Falls on US 97, OR 62)

One of Crater Lake's former names, Lake Majesty, probably comes closest to describing the feeling visitors get from these deep blue waters in the caldera of dormant Mt Mazama. More than 7,700 years ago, following climactic eruptions, this volcano collapsed and formed a deep basin. Rain and snow accumulated in the empty caldera, forming the deepest lake in the US (1,932 ft). Surrounded by 25 miles of jagged rim rock, the 21-square-mile lake is broken only by Wizard and Phantom Ship Islands. Entrance by road from any direction brings you to the 33-mile Rim Drive (July-mid-Oct or first snow), leading to all observation points, park headquarters and a visitor center at Rim Village (June-Sept, daily). The Sinnott Memorial Overlook with broad terrace permits a beautiful view of the area. On summer evenings, rangers give campfire talks at Mazama Campground (late June-Sept, phone 541/594-2211). The Steel Center located at Park Headquarters (daily) has exhibits about the natural history of the park and a movie is shown daily.

The park can be explored on foot or by car, by following spurs and trails extending from Rim Drive. Going clockwise from Rim Village, to the west, The Watchman Peak is reached by a trail almost one mile long that takes the hiker 1,800 feet above the lake with a full view in all directions; Mt Shasta in California, 105 miles away, is visible on a clear day. The road to the north entrance passes through the Pumice Desert, once a flood of frothy debris from the erupting volcano.

On the northeast side, Cleetwood Trail descends one mile to the shore and a boat landing where two-hour launch trips depart hourly each day in summer (fee). From the boats, Wizard Island, a small volcano, and Phantom Ship, a craggy mass of lava, can be seen up close.

Six miles farther on Rim Drive, going clockwise, is the start of a 2½-mile hiking trail, 1,230 feet to Mt Scott, soaring 8,926 feet, the highest point in the park. Just to the west of the beginning of this trail is a one mile drive to the top of Cloudcap, 8,070 feet high and 1,600 feet above the lake. Four miles beyond this point, a road leads seven miles from Rim Drive to The Pinnacles, pumice spires rising like stone needles from the canyon of Wheeler Creek.

Back at Rim Village, two trails lead in opposite directions. Counterclockwise, a 1½-mile trek mounts the top of Garfield Peak. The other trail goes to Discovery Point, where in 1853 a young prospector, John Hillman, became the first settler to see the lake.

In winter, the south and west entrance roads are kept clear in spite of the annual 45-foot snowfall; the north entrance road and Rim Drive are closed from mid-Oct-June, depending on snow conditions. A cafeteria is open daily at Rim Village for refreshments and souvenirs.

Depending on snow, the campground (fee) is open from mid-June-mid-Oct. Mazama, at the junction of the S and W entrance drives, has a camper store, fireplaces, showers, laundry facilities, toilets, water and tables; no reservations. There are six picnic areas on Rim Drive. The wildlife includes black bears—keep your distance and never feed them. There are also deer, golden-mantled ground squirrels, marmots and coyotes. Do not feed any wildlife in park.

The park was established in 1902 and covers 286 square miles. For park information contact Superintendent, Crater Lake National Park, PO Box 7, Crater Lake 97604; 541/594-2211. Golden Eagle Passport (see MAKING THE MOST OF YOUR TRIP). Per vehicle ¢¢¢

Note: Conservation measures may dictate the closing of certain roads and recreational facilities. In winter, inquire locally before attempting to enter the park.

Lodge

★ ★ ★ **CRATER LAKE LODGE.** (565 Rim Village Dr, Crater Lake 97604) 541/594-2255; res: 541/830-8700; FAX 541/594-2622. 71 rms, 4 story. No A/C. No rm phones. S, D $99-$120; under 12 free. Closed mid-Oct-mid-May. Complimentary coffee in lobby. Restaurant 7-10:30 am, 11:30 am-2:30 pm, 5-10 pm. Ck-out 11 am. Bellhops. Picnic tables, grills. On lake. Totally nonsmoking. Cr cds: MC, V.

Dalles
(see The Dalles)

Depoe Bay (C-3)

(See also Lincoln City, Newport)

Pop 870 **Elev** 58 ft **Area code** 541 **Zip** 97341
Information Chamber of Commerce, PO Box 21; 541/765-2889.

The world's smallest natural, navigable harbor, with six acres, Depoe Bay is a base for the US Coast Guard and a good spot for deep-sea fishing. The shoreline is rugged at this point. Seals and sea lions inhabit the area, and whales are so often seen that Depoe Bay claims to be the "whale watching capital of the Oregon coast." In the center of town are the "spouting horns," natural rock formations throwing geyserlike sprays high in the air. There are nine state parks within a few miles of this resort community.

What to See and Do

Depoe Bay Park. Covers 3 acres. Ocean observation building with view of bay, spouting horn and fishing fleets. Small picnic area. N on US 101.

Fogarty Creek State Park. A 142-acre park with beach area and creek, swimming (dressing rms); fishing. Hiking; picnicking. Standard fees. 2 mi N on US 101. Phone 541/265-9278.

Thundering Seas (Oregon State University School for the Crafts). Professional school for goldsmiths and silversmiths lies 60 ft above the Pacific Ocean; unusual museum. Tours (daily, phone ahead). Point St. Phone 541/765-2604. **Free.**

Annual Events

Classic Wooden Boat Show & Crab Feed. Last wknd Apr.

Fleet of Flowers Ceremony. After services on shore, flowers are cast on the water to honor those who lost their lives at sea. Memorial Day.

Salmon Bake. Depoe Bay Park. Salmon prepared in the Native American manner. 3rd Sat Sept.

Motels

★ ★ **INN AT OTTER CREST.** (301 Otter Crest Loop, Otter Rock 97369) 5 mi S, just W of US 101 exit Otter Rock. 541/765-2111; FAX 541/765-2047; res: 800/452-2101. E-mail ottercrest@newportnet.com. 120 units. S, D $99-$299. Crib free. TV; cable (premium), VCR avail. Heated pool; whirlpool. Restaurant 8 am-10 pm; mid-Oct-mid-June to 8 pm. Bar. Ck-out noon. Coin lndry. Meeting rms. Business servs avail. Bellhops. Sundries. Gift shop. Outdoor tennis. Sauna. Lawn games. Sun deck. Refrigerators; some microwaves. Private balconies. 2 baths in some units. On 35 acres; duck pond. Ocean view; beach access. Cr cds: A, C, D, DS, MC, V.

★ ★ **SURFRIDER OCEANFRONT RESORT.** 2 mi N at Fogarty Creek State Park. 541/764-2311; FAX 541/764-2634; res: 800/662-2378. 52 rms, 2 story, 20 kits. No A/C. June-Sept, wknds, hols: S, D $70-$90; each addl $5; studio rms, suites, kit. units $105-$125; under 12 free; lower rates rest of yr. Crib $10. TV; cable (premium). Indoor pool; whirlpool. Restaurant 7 am-10 pm. Bar 7-2:30 am. Ck-out 11 am. Gift shop. Free airport transportation. Sauna. Many fireplaces; some in-rm whirlpools. Many private patios; some balconies. All rms with ocean view. Cr cds: A, C, D, DS, MC, V.

Inn

★ ★ **CHANNEL HOUSE.** 35 Ellingson St. 541/765-2140; FAX 541/765-2191; res: 800/447-2140. E-mail cfinseth@newportnet.com; web www.channelhouse.com. 14 rms, 3 story, 9 suites, 2 kit. units. No elvtr. Mar-Dec: S, D $80-$150; each addl $30; suites $175-$225; kit. units $225; lower rates rest of yr. Children over 12 yrs only. TV; cable (premium). Complimentary bkfst. Restaurants nearby. Ck-out 11 am, ck-in 4 pm. Business servs avail. Street parking. Some balconies. Modern oceanfront building overlooking Depoe Bay. Totally nonsmoking. Cr cds: A, DS, MC, V.

Enterprise
(see Joseph)

Eugene (D-4)

(See also Corvallis, Cottage Grove)

Settled 1846 **Pop** 112,669 **Elev** 419 ft **Area code** 541 **E-mail** cvalco@cvalco.org **Web** www.cvalco.org
Information Lane County Convention & Visitors Association, 115 W 8th, Ste 190, PO Box 10286, 97440; 541/484-5307 or 800/547-5445.

Eugene sits on the west bank of the Willamette (Wil-AM-et) River, facing its sister city Springfield on the east bank. The Cascade Range rises to the east, mountains of the Coast Range to the west. Bicycling, hiking and jogging are especially popular here, with a variety of trails to choose from. Forests of Douglas fir support a lumber industry that accounts for 40 percent of the city's manufacturing. Eugene-Springfield is at the head of a series of dams built for flood control of the Willamette River Basin. Willamette National Forest headquarters are located here.

What to See and Do

Armitage State Park. A 57-acre park on partially wooded area on the S bank of the McKenzie River. Fishing; boating (ramp). Hiking. Picnicking. Standard fees. 6 mi N off I-5 on Coburg Rd. Phone 541/686-7592.

Camp Putt Adventure Golf Park. 18-hole course with challenging holes like "Pond O'Peril," "Thunder Falls " and "Earthquake." Lakeside patio with ice cream bar. (Late Mar-mid-Nov, daily) 4006 Franklin Blvd. Phone 541/741-9828. ¢¢

Fall Creek Dam and Lake. Winberry Creek Park has swimming beach; fishing; boating (ramp). Picnicking. (May-Sept) Some fees. North Shore Ramp has fishing; boat launching facilities. Picnicking. (Daily with low-level ramp) Cascara Campground has swimming; fishing; boating (ramp). Camping (May-Sept). Some fees. 20 mi SE on OR 58 to Lowell, then follow signs to Big Fall Creek Rd. N county road. For further information phone 541/937-2131.

Hendricks Park Rhododendron Garden. A 20-acre, internationally known garden features more than 6,000 aromatic plants, including rare species and hybrid rhododendrons from the local area and around the world (peak bloom mid-Apr-mid-May). Walking paths, hiking trails; picnic area. (Daily) Summit & Skyline Drs. Phone 541/687-5220. **Free.**

Hult Center. Performing arts center offering more than 300 events each year ranging from Broadway shows and concerts to ballet. 7th Ave & Willamette St; One Eugene Ctr. Phone 541/682-5000 tickets or 541/682-5746 (24-hr event recording). For tour information phone 541/682-5087.

Lane County Historical Museum. Changing exhibits depict history of county from mid-19th century to 1930s; includes artifacts of pioneer and Victorian periods; textiles; local history research library. (Wed-Fri, also Sat afternoons) 740 W 13th Ave. Phone 541/687-4239. ¢

Lookout Point and Dexter Dams and Lakes. The 14-mi-long Lookout Point Lake has Black Canyon Campground (May-Oct; fee) with trailer parking. Fishing. Picnicking. Hampton Boat Ramp with launching facilities and four camp sites (all yr; fee) with trailer parking. Fishing. Picnicking; closed to launching during low water (usually Oct-Apr). **Lowell Park** on 3-mi-long Dexter Lake has swimming, waterskiing; boating (moorage, ramp), sailboating. Picnicking. **Dexter Park** has waterskiing; fishing; boating (ramp), sailboating. Picnicking. The Powerhouse at Lookout Point Dam is open to the public (by appt). 20 mi SE on OR 58. For further information inquire at Project Office, Lookout Point Dam; 541/937-2131.

Owen Municipal Rose Garden. A 5-acre park with more than 300 new and rare varities of roses, as well as wild species (best blooms late June-early July); a recognized test garden for experimental roses. Also here is a collection of antiques and miniatures. Picnic area. (Daily) N end of Jefferson St, along the Willamette River. Phone 541/687-5220. **Free.**

Spencer Butte Park. Park has 305 acres of wilderness, with Spencer Butte Summit, at 2,052 ft, dominating the scene. Hiking trails. Panoramic views of Eugene, Cascade Mts. (Daily) 2 mi S of city limits on Willamette St. Phone 541/687-5220. **Free.** Starting at edge of park is

South Hills Ridgeline Trail. A 5-mi trail extending from Blanton Rd E to Dillard Rd; a spur leads to top of Butte. Trail offers magnificent views of the Cascade Mts, Coburg Hills and Mt Baldy; wildflowers along the trail reach peak bloom late Apr. Begins at 52nd St & Willamette St.

University of Oregon (1876). (17,000 students) The 250-acre campus includes more than 2,000 varieties of trees. Points of interest include the Museum of Natural History, Robinson Theatre, Beall Concert Hall, Hayward Field and the Erb Memorial Union. Campus tours depart from Information and Tour Services, Oregon Hall (daily exc Sun). Bounded by Franklin Blvd & 18th Ave, Alder & Moss Sts. Phone 541/346-3014. Also on campus are

Museum of Art. Diverse collections including large selection of Asian art representing cultures of China, Japan, Korea, Cambodia and American and British works of Oriental influence; official court robes of the Ch'ing dynasty (China, 1644-1911); Russian icon paintings from the 17th-19th centuries; Persian miniatures and ceramics; photography; works by contemporary artists and craftsmen from the Pacific Northwest, including those of Morris Graves. Special exhibits. Gift shop. (Wed-Sun afternoons; closed major hols) Phone 541/346-3027. **Free.**

Knight Library. With more than two million volumes, this is the largest library in Oregon. Main lobby features changing exhibits of rare books, manuscripts; Oregon Collection on 2nd floor. Fine arts pieces, wrought iron gates and carved panels. (Daily) Phone 541/346-3054.

(All buildings closed Jan 1, Martin Luther King Day, Memorial Day, July 4, Labor Day, Thanksgiving, Dec 25; hrs vary in summer, wkends and during school vacations.)

Whitewater rafting. Numerous companies offer trips on the McKenzie, North Umpqua, Descutes and Willamette rivers. Trips range from 2 hrs to 5 days. Contact Chamber of Commerce for details.

Willamette National Forest. More than 1.5 million acres. Home to more than 300 species of wildlife; includes Cascade Mt Range summit; Pacific Crest National Scenic Trail with views of snowcapped Mt Jefferson, Mt Washington, Three Fingered Jack, Three Sisters, Diamond Peak; Koosah and Sahalie Falls on the Upper McKenzie River; Clear Lake; the lava beds at summit of McKenzie Pass; Waldo Lake near summit of Willamette Pass. Fishing, hunting. Hiking. Skiing, snowmobiling. Camping (fee at some sites). E via US 20, OR 126. For further information contact Supervisor, 211 E 7th Ave, 97401.

Willamette Pass Ski Area. Double, 4 triple chairlifts; patrol, school, rentals (ski & snowboard). Lodge, restaurant, lounge. Longest run 2.1 mi; vertical drop 1,563 ft. Also 20 km of groomed nordic trails. (Mid-Nov-mid-Apr) Night skiing (late Dec-late Apr, Fri-Sat). S via I-5, E on OR 58. Phone 541/484-5030. ¢¢¢¢

Willamette Science & Technology Center. Participatory science center encourages hands-on learning; features exhibits illustrating physical, biological & earth sciences and related technologies. Planetarium shows (phone for schedule). (Wed-Sun afternoons) 2300 Leo Harris Pkwy. Phone 541/687-3619 or 541/687-STAR (planetarium). ¢¢; Planetarium ¢¢

Annual Events

Northwest Microbrew Expo & Willamette Winter Wine Festival. Early Feb.

Bach Festival. Numerous concerts by regional and international artists; master classes; family activities. Last wk June-1st wk July.

Lane County Fair. Mid-Aug.

Motels

✔★ **BARRON'S TRAVELODGE.** *1859 Franklin Blvd (97403), near University of Oregon.* 541/342-6383. 60 rms, 2-3 story. S $52-$61; D $70-$80; each addl $5; suites $80-$85; under 12 free. Crib free. Pet accepted, some restrictions. TV; cable. Complimentary continental bkfst. Coffee in rms. Restaurant adj 7 am-11 pm. Ck-out 11 am. Business servs avail. Sauna. Whirlpool. Microwaves avail; refrigerators in suites. Cr cds: A, D, DS, MC, V.

D ✔ ≈ ⊠ ⊠ SC

★★ **BEST WESTERN GRAND MANOR INN.** *(971 Kruse Way, Springfield 97477)* N on I-5, exit 195. 541/726-4769; FAX 541/744-0745. 65 suites, 3 story. S $63-$73; D $68-$85; each addl $5; under 12 free. Crib $5. TV; cable. Indoor pool. Complimentary continental bkfst. Restaurant adj open 24 hrs. Ck-out 11 am. Coin lndry. Meeting rms. Business servs avail. In-rm modem link. Exercise equipt; weights, bicycles, sauna. Refrigerators; some wet bars; microwaves avail. Some balconies. Cr cds: A, C, D, DS, MC, V.

D ≈ ⊠ ⊠ SC

★★ **BEST WESTERN NEW OREGON.** *1655 Franklin Blvd (97403), opp University of Oregon.* 541/683-3669; FAX 541/484-5556. E-mail neworegon@aol.com. 129 rms, 1-2 story. S $54-$62; D $68-$78; each addl $2; suites $89-$125. Crib free. Pet accepted, some restrictions. $25 deposit. TV; cable (premium). Indoor pool; whirlpool. Complimentary coffee in lobby. Restaurant adj 6 am-11 pm. Ck-out noon. Coin lndry. Business servs avail. In-rm modem link. Exercise equipt; bicycle, stair machine, saunas. Health club privileges. Refrigerators. Cr cds: A, C, D, DS, ER, JCB, MC, V.

D ✔ ≈ 🕏 ⊠ ⊠ SC

✔★ **CAMPUS INN.** *390 E Broadway (97401). 541/343-3376; res: 800/888-6313.* 58 rms, 2 story. S $46; D $48-$70; each addl $8. Pet accepted; $20 refundable. TV; cable (premium). Complimentary continental bkfst. Restaurant nearby. Ck-out 11 am. In-rm modem link. Cr cds: A, C, D, DS, MC, V.

✦ ⊠ ▨ SC

★ **ORLEANS.** *(3315 Gateway St, Springfield 97477) 3¹/2 mi NE, just E of I-5 exit 195A. 541/746-1314; FAX 541/746-3884; res: 800/626-1900.* 72 rms, 3 story. No elvtr. S $42-$46; D $46-$54; each addl $5; suites $58-$66; under 12 free. Crib $5. TV; cable. Complimentary coffee in lobby. Restaurant nearby. Ck-out 11 am. Coin lndry. Business servs avail. In-rm modem link. Health club privileges. Whirlpool. Microwaves avail. Cr cds: A, C, D, DS, MC, V.

D ⊠ ▨ SC

★ **PACIFIC 9 MOTOR INN.** *(3550 Gateway St, Springfield 97477) 3¹/2 mi NE, just E of I-5 exit 195A. 541/726-9266; FAX 541/744-2643; res: 800/722-9462.* 119 rms, 3 story. S $29.95; D $39.95; each addl $6; under 17 free. TV; cable. Pool. Restaurant opp 24 hrs. Ck-out 11 am. Cr cds: A, D, DS, MC, V.

D ≈ ⊠ ▨ SC

★★ **PHOENIX INN.** *850 Franklin Blvd (97403). 541/344-0001; res: 800/344-0131; FAX 541/686-1288.* 97 rms, 4 story. S $64; D $79; each addl $5; suites $110; under 17 free; wkly rates. TV; cable. Complimentary continental bkfst. Complimentary coffee in rms. Restaurant nearby. Ck-out noon. Meeting rms. Business servs avail. Valet serv. Coin lndry. Free airport, RR station transportation. Exercise equipt; bicycle, treadmill. Indoor pool; whirlpool. Refrigerators, microwaves; some bathrm phones. Cr cds: A, C, D, DS, MC, V.

D ⊠ ▨ ▨ SC

★★ **RODEWAY INN.** *(3480 Hutton St, Springfield 97477) just off I-5 exit 195A. 541/746-8471; FAX 541/747-1541.* 58 rms, 3 story. S $60-$70; D $70-$82; each addl $6; under 18 free. Pet accepted; $10. TV; cable, VCR avail (movies). Indoor pool; whirlpool. Complimentary continental bkfst. Restaurant adj open 24 hrs. Ck-out noon. Coin lndry. Meeting rms. Business servs avail. In-rm modem link. Exercise equipt; bicycles, stair machine. Microwaves avail. Cr cds: A, C, D, DS, ER, JCB, MC, V.

D ✦ ≈ ▨ ▨ SC

★★ **SHILO INN.** *(3350 Gateway St, Springfield 97477) 3¹/2 mi NE, just E of I-5 exit 195A. 541/747-0332; FAX 541/726-0587.* 143 rms, 2 story, 43 kits. S, D $65-$75; each addl $10; kit. units $79-$89; under 12 free; wkly, monthly rates. Pet accepted, some restrictions; $7/day. TV; cable (premium), VCR avail (movies). Pool. Complimentary continental bkfst. Restaurant 6 am-11 pm. Rm serv. Bar 11-2 am. Ck-out noon. Coin lndry. Meeting rms. Business servs avail. Free airport transportation. Some microwaves. Cr cds: A, C, D, DS, ER, JCB, MC, V.

D ✦ ≈ ⊠ ▨ SC

Motor Hotels

★★ **RED LION INN.** *205 Coburg Rd (97401), I-5 exit 194B, then I-105 1 mi to exit 1. 541/342-5201; FAX 541/485-2314.* 137 rms, 2 story. S $80-$85; D $95-$100; each addl $15; studio rms $80-$100; under 18 free. Crib free. Pet accepted, some restrictions. TV; cable, VCR avail. Heated pool; whirlpool. Restaurant 6 am-10 pm; closed Sun. Rm serv. Bar 3 pm-2 am, Sun to midnight; entertainment. Ck-out noon. Meeting rms. Business servs avail. In-rm modem link. Bellhops. Sundries. Free airport, RR station, bus depot transportation. Exercise equipt; weight machine, bicycle. Some private patios, balconies. Cr cds: A, C, D, DS, ER, JCB, MC, V.

D ✦ ≈ ✕ ▨ ▨

★★★ **VALLEY RIVER INN.** *1000 Valley River Way (97440), off I-5 exit 194B, northbound and southbound, follow signs to Valley River Center. 541/687-0123; FAX 541/683-5121; res: 800/543-8266.* E-mail reserve@valleyriverinn.com; web www.valleyriverinn.com. 257 rms, 2-3 story. S, D $135-$180; suites $175-$300; under 18 free. Crib free. Pet

accepted, some restrictions. TV; cable (premium), VCR avail. Heated pool; whirlpool, wading pool, poolside serv. Restaurant (see SWEETWATERS). Rm serv. Bar 11:30 am-midnight, Sun 9 am-11 pm; entertainment. Ck-out 11 am. Meeting rms. Business servs avail. In-rm modem link. Bellhops. Valet serv. Concierge. Free airport, RR station, bus depot transportation. Exercise equipt; bicycles, stair machine, sauna. Health club privileges. Private patios, balconies. Logging memorabilia. Some rms have views of Willamette River. Cr cds: A, C, D, DS, MC, V.

D ✦ ✦ ≈ ✕ ▨ ▨ SC

Hotel

★★★ **HILTON.** *66 E Sixth Ave (97401). 541/342-2000; FAX 541/302-6660.* 272 rms, 12 story. S $130; D $145; each addl $15; suites $290-$360; under 18 free. Pet accepted, some restrictions; $25. TV; cable (premium). Indoor pool; whirlpool. Restaurant 6:30 am-10 pm. Rm serv to 1 am. Bar; entertainment. Ck-out noon. Convention facilities. Business center. Concierge. Gift shop. Free covered parking. Free airport, RR station, bus depot transportation. Exercise equipt; weights, treadmills. Health club privileges. Some refrigerators; microwaves avail. Balconies. Luxury level. Cr cds: A, C, D, DS, ER, JCB, MC, V.

D ✦ ≈ ✕ ▨ ▨ SC ✦

Inn

★★★ **CAMPBELL HOUSE.** *252 Pearl St (97401), in historic Skinner Butte district. 541/343-1119; FAX 541/343-2258; res: 800/264-2519.* 12 rms, 3 story. May-Oct: S, D $80-$400; each addl $15; lower rates rest of yr. TV; cable, VCR (movies avail). Complimentary full bkfst. Coffee in rms. Restaurant nearby. Ck-out noon, ck-in 4 pm. Concierge serv. Luggage handling. Business servs avail. In-rm modem link. Health club privileges. Lawn games. Refrigerators; some microwaves. Built in 1892; on hill with views of city. Totally nonsmoking. Cr cds: A, DS, MC, V.

D ⊠ ▨

Restaurants

★★ **AMBROSIA.** *174 E Broadway (97401). 541/342-4141.* Hrs: 11:30 am-10 pm; Fri, Sat to 11 pm; Sun 4:30-10 pm. Closed some major hols. Italian menu. Bar. Semi-a la carte: lunch $8-$10, dinner $10-$17. Specializes in regional Italian dishes. Outdoor dining. Many antiques. Cr cds: MC, V.

D

✔★ **CAFE NAVARRO.** *454 Willamette St (97402). 541/344-0943.* Hrs: 11 am-2 pm, 5-9:30 pm; Sat from 9 am; Sun 9 am-2 pm. Closed Mon; also July 4, Thanksgiving, Dec 25. No A/C. Caribbean, Latin menu. Wine, beer. Semi-a la carte: bkfst, lunch $3.95-$6.95, dinner $7.50-$13.95. Totally nonsmoking. Cr cds: DS, MC, V.

D

★★ **CAFE ZENON.** *898 Pearl St (97401). 541/343-3005.* Hrs: 8 am-11 pm; Fri, Sat to midnight; Sun from 9:30 am; Sun brunch to 2 pm. Closed Thanksgiving, Dec 25. Wine, beer. Semi-a la carte: bkfst $5.25-$8, lunch $5.75-$9.50, dinner $8.75-$17.50. Sun brunch $5.75-$9.75. Specializes in local pork, lamb. Own desserts. Outdoor dining. Totally nonsmoking. Cr cds: MC, V.

D

★★★ **CHANTERELLE.** *207 E Fifth Ave (97401), in Fifth Pearl Bldg. 541/484-4065.* Hrs: 5-10 pm. Closed Sun, Mon; major hols. Res accepted. Continental menu. Serv bar. Complete meals: dinner $13.95-$23.95. Specializes in wild game, rack of lamb, seafood. Casual, intimate dining. Totally nonsmoking. Cr cds: A, D, JCB, MC, V.

D

★ **EXCELSIOR INN.** *754 E 13th (97401). 541/342-6963.* E-mail excelinn@pacinfo.com. Hrs: 7 am-midnight; Sun brunch 10 am-2 pm. Res accepted. Continental, Italian menu. Bar until 1 am. Semi-a la carte:

bkfst $3-$8, lunch $6-$12.50, dinner $13.95-$21.95. Sun brunch $6.95-$13.95. Child's meals. Specializes in fresh seafood. Patio dining. Intimate, informal dining. Totally nonsmoking. Cr cds: A, D, DS, MC, V.

D

★ ★ **NORTH BANK.** *22 Club Rd (97401), W of Ferry St Bridge.* *541/343-5622.* Web www.teleport.com/~casado/northbank. Hrs: 11:30 am-9:30 pm; Fri to 10 pm; Sat 5-10 pm; Sun 4:30-9 pm. Closed Dec 25. Res accepted. Bar. A la carte entrees: lunch $3.25-$8.95; dinner $9.95-$19.95. Specializes in fresh seafood, steak, prime rib. Parking. Outdoor deck overlooks Willamette River and Ferry St Bridge. Cr cds: A, D, DS, MC, V.

D

★ ★ **OREGON ELECTRIC STATION.** *140 E Fifth St (97401).* *541/485-4444.* Hrs: 11:30 am-2:30 pm, 5-10 pm; Fri to 10:30 pm; Sat 4:30-10:30 pm; Sun 4:30-9:30 pm. Closed July 4, Dec 25. Res accepted. Bar 11:30-1 am; Fri to 2 am; Sat 4 pm-2 am; Sun 4 pm-midnight. Semi-a la carte: lunch $3.75-$10.95, dinner $10.95-$29.95. Child's meals. Specializes in prime rib, seafood, chicken. Parking. Outdoor dining. Former RR station (1912); memorabilia. Cr cds: A, D, DS, MC, V.

D

★ ★ ★ **SWEETWATERS.** *(See Valley River Inn Motor Hotel)* *541/687-0123.* E-mail reserve@valleyriverinn.com; web www.valleyriverinn.com. Hrs: 6:30 am-2 pm, 5:30-9:30 pm; Sun from 7:30 am; Sun brunch 9 am-2 pm. Bar 11:30 am-midnight. Wine list. Semi-a la carte: bkfst $4-$8, lunch $7-$9, dinner $15-$22. Sun brunch $15.75. Child's meals. Specializes in seafood, fowl, Pacific Northwest regional cuisine. Parking. Outdoor dining. Fireplace. Overlooks Willamette River; view from every table. Cr cds: A, C, D, DS, MC, V.

D

★ ★ **TREEHOUSE.** *1769 Franklin Blvd (97403). 541/485-3444.* Hrs: 11:30 am-2 pm, 5-9:30 pm; Sat 5-10 pm; Sun 5-9 pm. Closed Jan 1, July 4, Dec 25. Res accepted. Bar to midnight. Semi-a la carte: lunch $6-$15, dinner $12-$25. Child's meals. Specialties: poulet grille, Indian-baked salmon, châteaubriand. Parking. Contemporary, rattan decor. Cr cds: DS, MC, V.

D

Unrated Dining Spot

GOVINDA'S VEGETARIAN BUFFET. *270 W 8th St.* *541/686-3531.* Hrs: 11:30 am-2:30 pm, 5-8 pm. Closed Sat, Sun; Jan 1, July 4, Dec 25. Res accepted. International vegetarian menu. A la carte entrees: lunch $2-$4, dinner $2-$4.50. Buffet: lunch, dinner $5-$6. Child's meals. Specializes in vegetable, rice and pasta dishes. Salad bar. Parking. Far Eastern atmosphere. Totally nonsmoking. No cr cds accepted.

D **SC**

Florence *(D-3)*

(See also Reedsport, Yachats)

Settled 1876 **Pop** 5,162 **Elev** 23 ft **Area code** 541 **Zip** 97439 **Web** www.presys.com/wtc/discoverflorence

Information Florence Area Chamber of Commerce, PO Box 26000; 541/997-3128.

At the northern edge of the National Dunes Recreation Area, with some of the highest sand dunes in the world, Florence is within reach of 17 lakes for fishing, swimming and boating. River and ocean fishing, crabbing and clamming are also popular. Along the Siuslaw River is "Old Town," an historic area with galleries, restaurants and attractions.

What to See and Do

C & M Stables. Experience spectacular scenery of Oregon coast on horseback. Beach (1¹/₂-2 hrs), dune trail (1-1¹/₂ hrs), sunset (2 hr, with or without meal), and coast range (¹/₂-day or all day) rides. Must be 8 yrs or older. (Daily; closed Thanksgiving, Dec 25) 8 mi N on US 101. Phone 503/997-7540. ¢¢¢¢

Heceta Head Lighthouse (1894). Picturesque beacon set high on rugged cliff. 12 mi N on US 101.

Sand Dunes Frontier. Excursions aboard 20-passenger dune buggies or drive-yourself Odysseys; miniature golf; flower garden; arcade, gift shop, snack bar. (Daily) 3¹/₂ mi S on US 101. Phone 541/997-3544. Dune buggy rides ¢¢¢¢

✖ **Sea Lion Caves.** Descend 208 ft under basaltic headland into cavern (1,500 ft long); home of wild sea lions. These mammals (up to 12 ft long) are generally seen on rocky ledges outside the cave in spring and summer and inside the cave in fall and winter. Self-guided tours; light jacket and comfortable shoes suggested. (Daily; closed Dec 25) 12 mi N on US 101. Phone 541/547-3111. ¢¢¢

Siuslaw Pioneer Museum. Exhibits preserve the history of the area; impressive display of artifacts and items from early settlers and Native Americans. Library rm; extensive genealogy records; hundreds of old photographs. (Jan-Nov, daily exc Mon; closed major hols) 85294 US 101S, 1 mi S. Phone 541/997-7884. **Free.**

State parks.

Jessie M. Honeyman Memorial. Park has 522 coastal acres with wooded lakes and sand dunes, an abundance of rhododendrons and an excellent beach. Swimming, waterskiing; fishing; boat dock & ramps. Hiking. Picnicking. Improved camping; tent & trailer sites (dump station). (Daily) Standard fees. 3 mi S on US 101. Phone 541/997-3641.

Devil's Elbow. A 545-acre park. Ocean beach; fishing. Hiking. Picnicking. Observation point. 13 mi N on US 101, below Heceta Head Lighthouse. Phone 541/997-3641. ¢¢

Carl G. Washburne Memorial. This 1,089-acre park is a good area for study of botany. Two-mi-long beach; swimming; fishing, clamming. Hiking. Picnicking. Tent & trailer campsites with access to beach. Elk may be seen in campgrounds and nearby meadows. 14 mi N on US 101. Phone 541/547-3416.

Darlingtonia. An 18-acre park with short loop trail through bog area noted for Darlingtonia, a carnivorous, insect-eating plant also known as cobra lilly. Picnicking. Viewing deck. 5 mi N on US 101. Phone 541/997-3641.

Westward Ho! Sternwheeler. One-hr cruises include Classical Continental Breakfast & Birdwatch, Jazzy Lunch Adventure, Afternoon Blues Cruise. Also 2-hr Sunset Buffet Cruise (Fri-Sun evenings, res required) and 30-min Bay Rides (Sun & hols). (Apr-Oct, daily) Old Town Dock. Phone 541/997-9691. ¢¢¢-¢¢¢¢¢

Annual Event

Rhododendron Festival. 3rd wkend May.

Motels

★ ★ **BEST WESTERN PIER POINT INN.** *85625 US 101S.* *541/997-7191; FAX 541/997-3828.* 55 rms, 3 story. Mid-June-early Sept: S $75-$95; D $95-$119; each addl $10; lower rates rest of yr. TV; cable (premium). Complimentary continental bkfst. Ck-out 11 am. Meeting rms. Sauna. Whirlpool. Balconies. Overlooks Siuslaw River. Cr cds: A, C, D, DS, MC, V.

D ⊠ 🦺 **SC**

★ ★ **HOLIDAY INN EXPRESS.** *2475 US 101. 541/997-7797; FAX 541/997-7895.* 51 rms, 2 story. S, D $55-$95; each addl $10; under 19 free. Crib free. TV; cable (premium). Complimentary continental bkfst. Restaurant adj 6 am-9 pm. Ck-out 11 am. Meeting rms. Exercise equipt; weight machine, bicycle. Whirlpool. Cr cds: A, C, D, DS, MC, V.

D 🏃 ⊠ 🦺 **SC**

✔★ **MONEY SAVER.** *170 US 101, just N of bridge.* 541/997-7131. 40 rms, 2 story. No A/C. June-Sept: S $46-$48; D $52-$60; each addl $6; lower rates rest of yr. Crib $6. Pet accepted, some restrictions; $5. TV; cable. Complimentary coffee in lobby. Restaurant nearby. Ck-out 11 am. Cr cds: A, DS, MC, V.

★ **RIVERHOUSE.** *1202 Bay St.* 541/997-3933. 40 rms, 2 story. No A/C. June-Sept: S, D $64-$120; each addl $6; higher rates hols; lower rates rest of yr. Crib $6. TV; cable. Complimentary coffee in lobby. Restaurant nearby. Ck-out 11 am. Coin lndry. On river. Cr cds: A, DS, MC, V.

Restaurant

★ ★ **WINDWARD INN.** *3757 US 101N.* 541/997-8243. Hrs: 7 am-9 pm; Fri-Sun to 9:30 pm. Closed Dec 25. Res accepted. Bar. Semi-a la carte: bkfst $2.95-$8.95, lunch $3.95-$10.95, dinner $6.95-$18.95. Child's meals. Specializes in steak, fresh seafood. Own baking. Pianist wkends. Cr cds: A, DS, MC, V.

D SC

Forest Grove (B-4)

(See also Beaverton, Hillsboro, Portland)

Settled 1845 **Pop** 13,559 **Elev** 175 ft **Area code** 503 **Zip** 97116 **Web** www.grovenet.org/forestgrove/chamber/index.html

Information Chamber of Commerce, 2417 Pacific Ave; 503/357-3006.

Forest Grove traces its beginning to missionaries who brought religion to what they called the "benighted Indian." The town is believed to have been named for a forest of firs which met a grove of oaks.

What to See and Do

Oregon Electric Railway. Collection of old trolleys includes double decker, interurbans. Trolley rides. Camping, picnic area. (May-Oct, Sat, Sun & hols) 16 mi NW via OR 8 to OR 6, exit milepost 38. Phone 503/357-3574. ¢¢

Pacific University (1849). (1,600 students) Founded as Tualatin Academy, it is one of the Northwest's oldest schools. On campus is art gallery and Old College Hall (academic yr, Tues, Thurs; also by appt). Tours of campus. Main entrance on College Way. Phone 503/357-6151.

Scoggin Valley Park and Hagg Lake. Features 11 mi of shoreline. Swimming, windsurfing; fishing; boating (ramps). Picnic sites. (Apr-Oct) 7 mi SW via OR 47, Scoggin Valley Rd exit.

Annual Events

Barbershop Ballad Contest. Phone 503/292-5673. 1st wkend Mar.

Hawaiian Luau. Pacific University. Hawaiian traditions celebrated in food, fashions & dance. Phone 503/357-6151. Mid-Apr.

Concours d'Elegance. Pacific University. Classic and vintage auto display. Phone 503/357-2300. Sun late June.

Founders Day Corn Roast. Phone 503/357-3006. Sept 21.

Motels

✔★ **FOREST GROVE INN.** *4433 Pacific Ave.* 503/357-9700; FAX 503/357-3135; res: 800/240-6504. 20 rms, 2 story, 4 kit. units. S $41-$46; D $46-$49; each addl $7; kit. units $65. Crib free. TV; cable (premium), VCR avail (free movies). Complimentary coffee in rms. Restau-

rant nearby. Ck-out 11 am. Business servs avail. Refrigerators. Cr cds: A, C, D, DS, ER, JCB, MC, V.

★ ★ **TRAVELODGE SUITES.** *3306 Pacific Ave.* 503/357-9000. 41 rms, 2 story. May-Sept: S $40-$55; D $59-$70; each addl $6; under 17 free; lower rates rest of yr. Crib free. TV; cable (premium), VCR avail. Indoor pool; whirlpool. Complimentary continental bkfst; coffee in rms. Restaurant adj 6-1 am. Bar 11 am-11 pm. Ck-out 11 am. Coin lndry. Meeting rms. Business servs avail. In-rm modem link. Exercise equipt; bicycles, stair machine. Refrigerators. Cr cds: A, C, D, DS, ER, JCB, MC, V.

D 🏊 🚴 🛏 🐾 SC

Fort Clatsop National Memorial (A-3)

(For accommodations see Astoria, Cannon Beach, Seaside)

(6 mi SW of Astoria off US 101A)

This site marks the western extremity of the territory explored by Meriwether Lewis and William Clark in their expedition of 1804-1806. The fort is a reconstruction of their 1805-1806 winter quarters. The original fort was built here because of its excellent elk hunting grounds, its easy access to ocean salt, its protection from the westerly coastal storms and the availability of fresh water.

The expedition set out on May 14, 1804, to seek "the most direct and practicable water communication across this continent" under orders from President Thomas Jefferson. The first winter was spent near Bismarck, North Dakota. In April, 1805, the party, then numbering 33, resumed the journey. On November 15, they had their first view of the ocean from a point near McGowan, Washington. The company left Fort Clatsop on March 23, 1806, on their return trip and was back at St Louis on September 23 of the same year. The Lewis and Clark Expedition was one of the greatest explorations in the history of the United States, and its journals depict one of the most fascinating chapters in the annals of the American frontier. The visitor center has museum exhibits and provides audiovisual programs. The canoe landing has replicas of dugout canoes of that period. Ranger talks and living history demonstrations are presented mid-June-Labor Day. (Daily; closed Dec 25) For further information contact Superintendent, Rte 3, Box 604 FC, Astoria 97103; 503/861-2471. Apr-Sept   ¢¢; Rest of year   **Free.**

Gleneden Beach

(see Lincoln City)

Gold Beach (F-2)

(See also Brookings, Port Orford)

Pop 1,546 **Elev** 51 ft **Area code** 541 **Zip** 97444 **E-mail** goldbeach@harborside **Web** www.harborside.com/gb

Information Chamber of Commerce & Visitors Center, 29279 Ellensburg Ave #3; 541/247-7526 or 800/525-2334.

Until floods in 1861 washed the deposits out to sea, placer mining in the beach sands was profitable here; hence the name. There is still some mining farther up the Rogue River. Gold Beach is at the mouth of the Rogue River, on the south shore; Wedderburn is on the north bank. Agate hunting is popular at the mouth of the Rogue River. The river is also well-known for steelhead and salmon fishing. Surf fishing and clamming are possible at many excellent beaches. The Siskiyou National Forest (see GRANTS PASS) is at the edge of town and a Ranger District office of the forest is located here.

What to See and Do

⭐ **Boat trips.**

Jerry's Rogue River Jet Boat Trips. A 6-hr (64-mi) round trip into wilderness area; 2-hr lunch or dinner stop at Agness. Also 8-hr (104-mi) and 6-hr (80-mi) round trip whitewater excursions. Rogue River Museum & Gift Shop (all yr). (May-Oct, daily). S end of Rogue River Bridge at port of Gold Beach Boat Basin. Phone 541/247-4571 or 800/451-3645. ¢¢¢¢¢

Official Rogue River Mail Boat Hydro-Jet Trips. A 64-mi round trip by jet boat up the wild and scenic Rogue River; 2-hr lunch stop at Agness. (May-Oct, daily) Res advised. Mail Boat Dock, 1/4 mi upstream from N end of Rogue River Bridge in Wedderburn, on N bank of the Rogue River. Phone 800/458-3511 or 541/247-7033.   ¢¢¢¢

Mail Boat Whitewater Trips. A 104-mi round trip by jet boat into wilderness and white water of the upper Rogue River. The narrated 7¹/₂-hr trip includes 2-hr lunch stop at a wilderness lodge. (May-Oct, daily) Also 80-mi round trip to the middle Rogue River. Narrated 6³/₄-hr trip departs twice daily; includes lunch or dinner stop. (Mid-June-Sept) Res advised for all trips. Mail Boat Dock. Phone 800/458-3511 or 541/247-7033.   ¢¢¢¢¢

Court's White Water Trips. A 104-mi round trip to Blossom Bar Rapids; stopover for lunch at Paradise Lodge with overnight option. Also 6-hr (64-mi) trip. Res advised. Departs from Jerry's Rogue River Jets, S end of Rogue River Bridge on US 101. Phone 541/247-6022, 541/247-6504. ¢¢¢¢¢

Cape Sebastian State Park. Approx 1,100 acres of open and forested land. Cape Sebastian is a precipitous headland, rising more than 700 ft above tide with a view of many mi of coastline. A short roadside through the forest area is marked by wild azaleas, rhododendrons and blue ceanothus in season. Trails; no rest rms or water. 7 mi S on US 101. Phone 541/469-2021.

Curry County Historical Museum. Collections and interpretive displays of early life in Curry County. (June-Sept, Tues-Sat afternoons; rest of yr, Sat afternoons) Fairgrounds. Phone 541/247-6113. **Donation.**

Prehistoric Gardens. Life-size sculptures of dinosaurs and other prehistoric animals that disappeared more than 70 million yrs ago are set among primitive plants, which have survived. (Daily) 14 mi N on US 101, located in Oregon's rain forest. Phone 541/332-4463.   ¢¢¢

Annual Events

Whale of a Wine Festival. Jan.

Clam Chowder Festival. 1st wkend May.

Curry County Fair. Last wkend July.

Motel

⭐ ⭐ **SHORE CLIFF INN.** 29346 Ellensburg Ave (US 101). 541/247-7091. 38 rms, 1-2 story. S, D $59-$75; each addl $5. TV; cable (premium). Complimentary coffee in lobby. Restaurant adj 6 am-10 pm. Ck-out 11 am. Balconies. On beach. Cr cds: MC, V.

Lodge

⭐ ⭐ ⭐ ⭐ **TU TU' TUN LODGE.** 96550 N Bank Rogue. 541/247-6664; res: 800/864-6357; FAX 541/247-0672. Web www.tututun.com. This richly appointed fishing lodge—the name is pronounced "Too Tootin'"—sits on the clear-blue Rogue River. Private decks of individually decorated rooms look out on the water and surrounding old-growth forest. 16 rms, 2 suites, 1 garden house. S, D $135-$310; each addl $10; suites $185-$195; garden house $200. 2 River Suites and Garden House avail all yr. Pool. Complimentary hors d'oeuvres. Dining rm open May-Oct (public by res):

bkfst 7:30-9:30 am, lunch sitting (registered guests only) 1 pm; dinner sitting 7 pm. Bar. Ck-out 11 am, ck-in 3 pm. Business center. In-rm modem link. Free airport transportation. Dock; guides, whitewater boat trips. 4-hole pitch & putt golf; horseshoes. Rec rm. Private patios, balconies. Library. Cr cds: DS, MC, V.

Inn

⭐ ⭐ **INN AT NESIKA BEACH.** 33026 Nesika Rd, 6 mi N on US 101. 541/247-6434. 4 rms, 2 story. No rm phones. S, D $100-$130. Complimentary full bkfst. Ck-out 11 am, ck-in 3 pm. Game rm. Lawn games. On bluff overlooking Pacific Ocean. Victorian-style house furnished with antiques. Totally nonsmoking. No cr cds accepted.

Restaurants

⭐ **THE CHOWDERHEAD.** 29430 Ellensburg (US 101). 541/247-0588. Hrs: 11 am-10 pm. Serv bar. Semi-a la carte: lunch $4.95-$9.95, dinner $10.75-$33. Child's meals. Specializes in seafood, steak. Salad bar. Rustic decor; dining rm with ocean view. Cr cds: DS, MC, V.

D

⭐ ⭐ **NOR'WESTER SEAFOOD.** Box 1157, at Port of Gold Beach. 541/247-2333. Hrs: 5-10 pm. Closed Dec, Jan. Continental menu. Bar. Semi-a la carte: dinner $12.95-$22.95. Child's meals. Specializes in seafood, steak. Overlooks bay and ocean. Cr cds: A, MC, V.

Grants Pass (F-3)

(See also Cave Junction, Jacksonville, Medford)

Pop 17,488 **Elev** 948 ft **Area code** 541

Information Visitor & Convention Bureau, PO Box 1787, 97526; 541/476-5510.

Grants Pass was named by the rail constructors who were here when news reached them of General Grant's victorious siege of Vicksburg in 1863. On the Rogue River, Grants Pass is the seat of Josephine County. Tourism is the chief source of income; agriculture and electronics are next in importance. Fishing in the Rogue River is a popular activity. A Ranger District office and headquarters of the Siskiyou National Forest is located here.

What to See and Do

Grants Pass Museum of Art. Permanent and changing exhibits of photography, paintings, art objects. (Tues-Sat afternoons; closed some major hols) In Riverside Park, on the Rogue River off of 7th & Park Sts. Phone 541/479-3290.   **Free.**

Oregon Caves National Monument (see). 28 mi SW on US 199 to Cave Junction, then 20 mi E on OR 46.

Rogue River Boat Trips. One-five-day whitewater scenic or fishing trips through the wilderness, past abandoned gold-mining sites; overnight lodges or camping en route. Some of these are seasonal; some all year. For details contact the Visitor & Convention Bureau. Also avail is

Hellgate Jetboat Excursions. Interpretive jet boat trips down the Rogue River: 2-hr scenic excursion (May-Sept, daily); 4-hr country dinner excursion (mid-May-Sept); 4-hr champagne brunch excursion (mid-May-Sept, wkends); 5-hr whitewater trip (May-Sept, daily). Depart from Riverside Inn. Phone 800/648-4874 or 541/479-7204.   ¢¢¢¢

Siskiyou National Forest. Over one million acres. Famous for salmon fishing in lower Rogue River gorge and early-day gold camps. Many species of trees and plants are relics of past ages; a botanist's paradise. An 84-mi stretch of Rogue River between Applegate River and Lobster

Creek Bridge is designated a National Wild and Scenic River; nearly half is in the forest. Boat, pack and saddle trips into rugged backcountry. Picnic sites. Camping. N, S and W off US 199 or W of I-5. For further information contact Visitor Information Office, PO Box 440, 200 NE Greenfield Rd; 541/471-6516.

Valley of the Rogue State Park. A 275-acre park with fishing; boat ramp to Rogue River. Picnicking. Improved tent & trailer sites (daily; dump station). Standard fees. 8 mi S on I-5. Phone 541/582-1118.

Annual Events

Boatnik Festival. Riverside Park. Parade, concessions, carnival rides, boat races; entertainment. A 25-mi whitewater hydroboat race from Riverside Park to Hellgate Canyon and back. Square dance festival at Josephine County Fairgrounds. Memorial Day wknd.

Parimutuel Horse Racing. Fairgrounds. Phone 541/476-3215. Late May-early July.

Josephine County Fair. Fairgrounds, Redwood Hwy and W Park St. Phone 541/476-3215. Mid-Aug.

Jedediah Smith Mountain Man Rendezvous & Buffalo Barbecue. Sportsman Park. Muzzleloader/black powder shoots, costume contests, exhibits. Phone 541/479-8929. Labor Day wknd.

Josephine County Air Fair. Airport, Brookside Dr. Antique aircraft, contests, airplane and helicopter rides. Phone 541/474-5285 or 541/474-0665. Early Sept.

Heritage Days. Phone 541/476-5510. Sept 15-Oct 15.

Motels

★ ★ **BEST WESTERN GRANTS PASS INN.** 111 NE Agness Ave (97526). 541/476-1117; FAX 541/479-4315. Web www.rogueweb .com/holiday. 84 rms, 2 story. June-Sept: S $72-$82; D $78-$88; each addl $5; suites $110-$129; under 19 free; lower rates rest of yr. Crib $5. TV; cable (premium), VCR avail. Heated pool; whirlpool. Coffee in rms. Restaurant 6 am-10 pm. Bar. Ck-out 11 am. Coin lndry. Business servs avail. In-rm modem link. Health club privileges. Some refrigerators. Whirlpool in suites. Rogue River 1 mi. Cr cds: A, C, D, DS, ER, JCB, MC, V.

⬜ 🏊 🍽 🐾 SC

★ ★ **BEST WESTERN INN AT THE ROGUE.** 8959 Rogue River Hwy (97527). 541/582-2200; FAX 541/582-1415. 54 rms, 2 story. June-Sept: S, D $69.50-$159; each addl $5; suites $129-$179; under 12 free; lower rates rest of yr. Crib $5. Pet accepted, some restrictions; $10. TV; cable (premium), VCR avail. Heated pool; whirlpool. Complimentary continental bkfst. Restaurant adj 6 am-10 pm. Bar 5-10 pm. Ck-out 11 am. Coin lndry. Meeting rms. Business servs avail. Exercise equipt; weights, bicycles. Some refrigerators, microwaves, minibars. Balconies. Cr cds: A, C, D, DS, MC, V.

⬜ 🐾 🏊 🍽 SC

✔★ **COMFORT INN.** 1889 NE Sixth St (97526). 541/479-8301; FAX 541/955-9721. 59 rms, 2 story. S $49.99; D $59.99-$64.99; each addl $5. Crib $5. TV; cable (premium). Heated pool. Complimentary continental bkfst. Restaurant adj open 24 hrs. Ck-out 11 am. Microwaves avail. Cr cds: A, D, DS, MC, V.

⬜ 🏊 🐾 SC

✔★ **DEL ROGUE.** 2600 Rogue River Hwy (OR 99) (97527). 541/479-2111. 14 rms, 1-2 story, 13 kits. (oven in 10). S $40; D $65; each addl $5-$10; suites, kit. units $45-$65; lower rates rest of yr. TV; cable. Restaurant nearby. Ck-out 11 am. Coin lndry. Many microwaves. Porches. Picnic tables, grills. Shaded grounds; on river. Cr cds: MC, V.

🐾 🏊

★ ★ **HOLIDAY INN EXPRESS.** 105 NE Agness Ave (97526), I-5 exit 55. 541/471-6144; FAX 541/471-9248. Web www.rogueweb.com /holiday. 80 rms, 4 story. Mid-May-mid-Sept: S $74; D $79-$84; each addl $5; suites $129; under 19 free; higher rates Boatnik Festival; lower rates rest of yr. Crib free. Pet accepted, some restrictions; $5/day. TV; cable

(premium). Heated pool; whirlpool. Complimentary continental bkfst. Restaurant adj 6 am-11 pm. Ck-out 11 am. Guest lndry. Meeting rms. Business center. In-rm modem link. Sundries. Health club privileges. Cr cds: A, C, D, DS, JCB, MC, V.

⬜ 🐾 🏊 🍽 SC 🏃

★ ★ **MORRISON'S ROGUE RIVER LODGE.** (8500 Galice Rd, Merlin 97532) NW on I-5 to Merlin, 12 mi W on Galice Rd. 541/476-3825; FAX 541/476-4953; res: 800/826-1963. E-mail mlrrrt@chatlink.com. 13 units, 2 with shower only, 4 rms in lodge, 9 cottages. July-Aug, MAP: S $120; D $190; each addl $90; AP rates avail mid-Sept-Nov; family rates; lower rates May-June. Closed rest of yr. TV. Heated pool. Restaurant (see MORRISON'S ROGUE RIVER LODGE). Ck-out 11 am. Meeting rms. Business center. Gift shop. Tennis. Lawn games. Guided raft trips. Some balconies. Picnic tables. On river. Cr cds: DS, MC, V.

🐾 🏊 🍽 🏃

★ ★ **REDWOOD.** 815 NE Sixth St (97526). 541/476-0878; FAX 541/476-1032. E-mail redwood@chatlink.com; web www.chatlink.com /~redwood. 26 rms, 9 kits. Mid-May-Sept: S $55-$80; D $60-$82; each addl $5; kit. units $68-$95; lower rates rest of yr. Crib $5. Pet accepted, some restrictions; $10. TV; cable (premium). Heated pool. Playground. Complimentary continental bkfst. Restaurant opp 6 am-10 pm. Guest lndry. Ck-out 11 am. Microwaves avail. Picnic tables. Cr cds: A, C, D, DS, MC, V.

⬜ 🐾 🏊 🍽 SC

★ **ROGUE VALLEY.** 7799 Rogue River Hwy (97527), I-5 exit 48. 541/582-3762. 8 rms, 6 with shower only, 1 story. June-Sept: S $45-49; D $72; each addl $5; lower rates rest of yr. Crib free. Pet accepted, some restrictions. TV; cable. Heated pool. Complimentary coffee in rms. Ck-out 11 am. Refrigerators; many microwaves. Picnic tables. On river. Cr cds: MC, V.

⬜ 🐾 🏊 🍽

✔★ **ROYAL VUE.** 110 NE Morgan Lane (97526). 541/479-5381; res: 800/547-7555 (exc OR), 800/452-1452 (OR). 60 rms, 2 story. S $40-$44; D $49-$66; suites $64. Crib $4. Pet accepted. TV; cable (premium), VCR avail. Heated pool; whirlpool, poolside serv. Coffee in rms. Restaurant 6 am-10 pm. Rm serv. Bar 11-2 am; entertainment Thur-Sun. Ck-out noon. Coin lndry. Sauna, steam rm. Refrigerator, minibar in suites. Balconies. Cr cds: A, C, D, DS, MC, V.

🐾 🏊 🍽 SC

★ ★ **SHILO INN.** 1880 NW Sixth St (97526). 541/479-8391; FAX 541/474-7344. 70 rms, 2 story. May-Sept: S, D $59-$79; each addl $10; under 12 free; lower rates rest of yr. Crib free. Pet accepted; $7. TV; cable (premium). Pool. Continental bkfst. Restaurant adj open 24 hrs. Ck-out noon. Meeting rm. Sauna, steam rm. Microwaves avail. Cr cds: A, C, D, DS, ER, JCB, MC, V.

⬜ 🐾 🏊 🍽 SC

Lodge

★ ★ **PARADISE RESORT.** 7000 Monument Dr (97526). 541/479-4333; FAX 541/479-0218. 16 rms. No rm phones. May-Oct: S $70-$90; D $90-$125; each addl $15; lower rates rest of yr. Crib free. Heated pool; whirlpool. Complimentary continental bkfst. Meeting rms. Free local airport transportation. Lighted tennis. Rec rm. Rustic decor; beamed ceilings. Situated in wooded area with pond, lake and views of Coastal Mts. Cr cds: MC, V.

🏃 🏊 🍽

Motor Hotel

★ ★ ★ **RIVERSIDE INN RESORT & CONFERENCE CENTER.** 971 SE Sixth St (97526). 541/476-6873; FAX 541/474-9848; res: 800/334-4567. Web www.riverside-inn.com. 174 rms, 3 story. S, D $65-$105; each addl $10; suites $140-$275; cottage $350; under 11 free. Crib $10. Pet accepted, some restrictions; $15. TV; cable, VCR avail (movies). 2 heated pools. Complimentary coffee in rms. Restaurant 6 am-10 pm. Bar 11-1 am. Ck-out 11 am. Meeting rms. Business servs avail. Sundries. Gift shop. Some in-rm whirlpools; microwaves avail. Balconies. Jet boat trips May-Sept. Cr cds: A, C, D, DS, MC, V.

Inns

★ ★ **FLERY MANOR.** *2000 Jumpoff Joe Creek Rd (97526). 541/476-3591.* E-mail flery@chatlink.com; web www.grantspass.com/b&b /flery. 4 rms, 3 story. No elvtr. S, D $75-$125; wkly rates. Children over 8 yrs only. TV in common rm; VCR avail (movies). Complimentary full bkfst; afternoon refreshments. Ck-out 11 am, ck-in 3-6 pm. Business servs avail. Luggage handling. Picnic tables, grills. Country decor; fireplace, antiques. Totally nonsmoking. Cr cds: MC, V.

★ ★ **HOME FARM BED & BREAKFAST.** *157 Savage Creek Rd (97527), I-5 exit 48, cross river, N on OR 99. 541/582-0980; res: 800/522-7967.* E-mail homefarm@chatlink.com. 4 rms. No rm phones. S $55-$70, D $60-$80; each addl $10; wkly rates. TV in parlor. Complimentary full bkfst. Ck-out 11 am, ck-in 3-6 pm. Luggage handling. Game rm. Lawn games. Picnic tables. Farm house built 1944; many antiques. On 4.5 acres. Totally nonsmoking. No cr cds accepted.

★ ★ **PINE MEADOW.** *(1000 Crow Rd, Merlin 97532) I-5 exit Merlin. 541/471-6277; res: 800/554-0806.* E-mail pmi@pinemeadow inn.com; web www.pinemeadowinn.com. 4 rms, 2 story. S, D $80-$110. Complimentary full bkfst. Ck-out 11 am, ck-in 4 pm. Luggage handling. Whirlpool. Midwest-style farm house furnished with turn-of-the-century antiques. 9 acres of private forest. Totally nonsmoking. Cr cds: DS, MC, V.

★ ★ **WEASKU.** *5560 Rogue River Hwy (97527), 8 mi N on Redwood Hwy 99, exit 48. 541/471-8000; res: 800/493-2758; FAX 541/471-7038.* Web www.riverside-inn.com. 7 rms, 2 with A/C, 2 story, 3 suites. S, D $85-$150; suites $250-$350. Children over 12 yrs only. TV; cable, VCR (movies). Complimentary continental bkfst. Ck-out noon, ck-in 3 pm. Business servs avail. Luggage handling. Gift shop. Health club privileges. Lawn games. Some fireplaces. Some balconies. Picnic tables. On river. Built in 1924; antiques. Totally nonsmoking. Cr cds: A, D, DS, MC, V.

Restaurants

★ ★ **MORRISON'S ROGUE RIVER LODGE.** *(See Morrison's Rogue River Lodge Motel) 541/476-3825.* E-mail mlrrrt@chatlink.com. Hrs: 7-9 am, dinner (1 sitting) 7:30 pm. Closed mid Nov-Apr. Res required. Bar. Complete meals: bkfst $8, dinner $20-$29. Specializes in Northwestern cuisine. Family-owned. Cr cds: DS, MC, V.

✔ ★ ★ **YANKEE POT ROAST.** *720 NW Sixth St (97526). 541/476-0551.* Hrs: 5-9 pm. Closed Tues; Dec 25. Serv bar. Semi-a-la carte: dinner $7.95-$15.95. Specializes in Yankee pot roast, fresh halibut. Restored historic home; built 1905. Cr cds: MC, V.

Hermiston (A-8)

(See also Pendleton, Umatilla)

Pop 10,040 **Elev** 457 ft **Area code** 541 **Zip** 97838

Information Greater Hermiston Chamber of Commerce, 415 S US Hwy 395, PO Box 185; 541/567-6151.

Centrally located between the major cities of the Northwest, Hermiston offers an abundant array of recreational opportunities. The Columbia River, second-largest river in the country, flows five miles to the north and the Umatilla River skirts the city limits; both are popular for fishing. The nearby Blue Mts offer a variety of summer and winter activities. Agriculture, processing and production form the economic base of this community, which has become a trading center for this area of the Columbia River Basin.

Seasonal Event

Stock Car Racing. Race City, USA, on US 395. Phone 541/567-8320. Apr-Oct.

Motel

★ **SANDS.** *835 N First St. 541/567-5516; FAX 541/567-5516.* 39 rms, 3 kit, 1-2 story. S $35; D $42; each addl $5; suites $58; wkly rates. Crib $3. Pet accepted; $5. TV; cable (premium). Pool. Restaurant adj 5 am-10 pm. Bar adj. Ck-out 11 am. Business servs avail. Cr cds: A, D, DS, MC, V.

Hillsboro (B-4)

(See also Beaverton, Forest Grove, Oregon City, Portland)

Pop 37,520 **Elev** 165 ft **Area code** 503 **E-mail** sueleblanc@hilchamber.org **Web** www.hilchamber.org

Information Greater Hillsboro Chamber of Commerce, 334 SE 5th Ave, 97123; 503/648-1102.

Motels

★ ★ **BEST WESTERN HALLMARK INN.** *3500 NE Cornell Rd (97124). 503/648-3500; FAX 503/640-2789.* 123 rms, 2 story. S, D $89-$109; each addl $5; under 12 free. Crib $5. TV; cable (premium), VCR avail (movies). Heated pool; whirlpool. Complimentary coffee in rm. Restaurant 6:30 am-9 pm. Bar. Ck-out 11 am. Coin lndry. Meeting rms. Business servs avail. Exercise equipt; weight machine, bicycles. Some in-rm whirlpools. Cr cds: A, C, D, DS, JCB, MC, V.

✔ ★ **PARK DUNES.** *622 SE 10th (97123). 503/640-4791; FAX 503/640-8127; res: 800/548-0163.* 58 rms, 2 story. S $55; D $60; each addl $7. Crib $7. TV; cable (premium), VCR avail (movies). Complimentary coffee in rms. Restaurant adj 6 am-10 pm. Ck-out 11 am. Coin lndry. Business servs avail. Refrigerators. Cr cds: A, C, DS, MC, V.

Hood River (A-5)

(See also The Dalles)

Settled 1854 **Pop** 4,632 **Elev** 155 ft **Area code** 541 **Zip** 97031
Information Chamber of Commerce Visitor Center, 405 Portway Ave; 541/386-2000 or 800/366-3530.

Hood River, located in the midst of a valley producing apples, pears and cherries, boasts a scenic view of Oregon's highest peak, Mt Hood; its slopes are accessible in all seasons by road. OR 35, called the Loop Highway, leads around the mountain and up to the snowline. The Columbia River Gorge provides perfect conditions for boardsailing in the Hood River Port Marina Park.

What to See and Do

Bonneville Lock & Dam. The dam consists of three parts, one spillway and two powerhouses. It has an overall length of 3,463 ft and extends across the Columbia River to Washington. A major hydroelectric project of the US Army Corps of Engineers. On the Oregon side is a five-story visitor center with underwater windows into the fish ladders and new navigation lock with viewing facilities. Audiovisual presentations and tours of fish ladders, and the original powerhouse (June-Sept, daily or by appt; Oct-May, self-guided; closed Jan 1, Thanksgiving, Dec 25). Stern wheeler boat tours (June-Sept; fee). State salmon hatchery adj. Fishing (salmon and sturgeon ponds). Picnicking. Powerhouse II and Visitor Orientation Bldg on Washington side, WA 14; underwater fish viewing, audiovisual presentations, fish ladder and powerhouse tours (June-Sept, daily or by appt; Oct-May, self-guided; closed Jan 1, Thanksgiving, Dec 25); accessible via Bridge of the Gods from I-84. 23 mi W on I-84. Phone 541/374-8820. **Free.**

Columbia Gorge. Stern wheeler makes daytime excursions, sunset dinner and brunch cruises, harbor tours and special holiday cruises. Res required exc for daily excursions (mid-June-Sept). Port of Cascade Locks. 10 mi W on I-84, exit 44. For schedule and prices phone 541/223-3928 or 541/374-8427. ¢¢¢¢

Hood River County Museum. Items from early settlers to modern residents. An outdoor display that includes stern wheeler paddle wheel, beacon light used by air pilots in the Columbia Gorge, steam engine from the *Mary.* (Mid-Apr-Oct, daily) Port Marina Park. Phone 541/386-6772. **Donation.**

Lost Lake. Swimming; fishing; boat rentals. Hiking. Picnicking, concession, day lodge. Camping. 28 mi SW off I-84 on Dee Secondary Hwy and paved Forest Service road in Mt Hood National Forest (see).

Mt Hood National Forest (see). S & W of city.

Mt Hood Scenic Railroad. Historic railroad (1906); 44-mi round-trip excursions. (Apr-Dec, schedule varies) 110 Railroad Ave. Phone 541/386-3556. ¢¢¢¢

Panorama Point. Observation point for Hood River Valley and Mt Hood. 1/2 mi S on OR 35 to Eastside Rd.

Winery tours.

Flerchinger Vineyards. Tours; tasting rm. (Daily). 4200 Post Canyon Dr. Phone 541/386-2882. **Free.**

Hood River Vineyards. Tours; tasting rm. (Mar-Nov, daily) 4693 Westwood Dr. Phone 541/386-3772. **Free.**

Annual Events

Blossom Festival. 3rd wkend Apr.

Return of the Sternwheeler Days. Celebration of the sternwheeler *Columbia Gorge*'s return to home port for the summer. Wine & cheese tasting, crafts, food. June.

Hood River County Fair. July.

Cross Channel Swim. Labor Day.

Hood River Valley Harvest Fest. Fresh local fruit, art & crafts, wine tasting, contests. 1st wkend Oct.

Motel

✔★ ★ **VAGABOND LODGE.** 4070 Westcliff Dr. 541/386-2992; FAX 541/386-3317. 40 rms, 23 A/C, 5 suites. S $41-$61; D $47-$77; each addl $6; suites $61-$82; lower rates winter. Crib $5. Pet accepted. TV; cable. Playground. Restaurant adj 7 am-9 pm. Ck-out 11 am. Picnic tables. On 5 wooded acres; overlooks Columbia River Gorge. Cr cds: A, C, D, MC, V.

Lodge

★ ★ ★ **SKAMANIA.** (PO Box 189, 1131 Skamania Lodge Way, Stevenson 97648) W on I-84, exit 44, cross Bridge of the Gods to WA 14, then E to Stevenson. 509/427-7700; FAX 509/427-2547; res: 800/221-7117. 195 rms, 4 story. May-Sept: S, D $95-$155; each addl $15; suites $185-$265; under 12 free. Crib free. TV; cable. Indoor pool; whirlpool. Playground. Complimentary coffee in rms. Restaurant 7 am-10 pm. Rm serv. Bar; entertainment wkends. Ck-out noon. Meeting rms. Business center. Bellhops. Sundries. Gift shop. Tennis. 18-hole golf, pro, greens fee $32, putting green, driving range. Exercise equipt; weights, rowers, sauna. Game rm. Lawn games. Refrigerators. Some balconies. Picnic tables. Cr cds: A, C, D, DS, MC, V.

Motor Hotel

★ ★ **BEST WESTERN HOOD RIVER INN.** 1108 E Marina Way, I-84N exit 64. 541/386-2200; FAX 541/386-8905. 149 rms, 2-3 story. May-Sept: S, D $79-$99; each addl $12; suites $81-$165; under 18 free; lower rates rest of yr. Crib free. TV; cable, VCR avail. Heated pool. Restaurant 6 am-9 pm. Rm serv. Bar; entertainment. Ck-out noon. Coin lndry. Business servs avail. In-rm modem link. Free airport transportation. Private patios. Beach access; windsurfing. In Columbia River Gorge. Cr cds: A, C, D, DS, MC, V.

 SC

Hotel

★ ★ ★ **COLUMBIA GORGE.** 4000 Westcliff Dr, I-84 exit 62. 541/386-5566; FAX 541/387-5414; res: 800/345-1921. 40 rms, 3 story. No A/C. S $125; D $150-$270; each addl $30. Pet accepted. TV; cable, VCR avail. Complimentary bkfst. Restaurant (see COLUMBIA RIVER COURT DINING ROOM). Bar 8 am-midnight. Ck-out noon. Business servs avail. Free RR station, bus depot transportation. Restored building (1920s) with formal gardens; "Jazz Age" atmosphere. Windsurfing nearby. Overlooks river, waterfall. Cr cds: A, C, D, DS, MC, V.

Inns

★ ★ **INN OF THE WHITE SALMON.** (172 W Jewett, White Salmon 98672) I-84 E to exit 64, E on WA 14 for 1 1/2 mi, left at flashing light, 1.6 mi to inn. 509/493-2335; res: 800/972-5226. 16 rms, 2 story, 5 suites. S $75; D $89-$115; suites $99-$115. Crib free. Pet accepted. TV. Complimentary full bkfst. Restaurant nearby. Ck-out noon, ck-in 3 pm. Luggage handling. Picnic tables. European-style inn built in 1937; antique decor, original art. Cr cds: A, C, D, DS, MC, V.

★ **STATE STREET.** 1005 State St. 541/386-1899. 4 rms, share bath, 2 story. No rm phones. Apr-Oct: S $50-$75; D $60-$80; each addl $10; under 10 free; lower rates rest of yr. Complimentary full bkfst. Restaurant nearby. Ck-out noon, ck-in 4 pm. Free RR station, bus depot transportation. Game rm. View of Columbia River and Mt Adams. Totally nonsmoking. Cr cds: MC, V.

Restaurant

★ ★ ★ **COLUMBIA RIVER COURT DINING ROOM.** *(See Columbia Gorge Hotel)* 541/386-5566. Hrs: 8 am-10 pm. Res accepted; required hols. Continental menu. Bar to midnight. Wine list. Complete meals: bkfst $22.95. Prix fixe: 3-course lunch $13.50. A la carte entrees: dinner $18-$30. Specialties: wilted spinach salad with apple smoked duck, fresh salmon, Hood River apple tarté. Own baking. Pianist evenings. Valet parking. View of river gorge. Totally nonsmoking. Cr cds: A, C, D, DS, MC, V.

Jacksonville (F-4)

(For accommodations see Ashland, Grants Pass, Medford)

Founded 1852 **Pop** 1,896 **Elev** 1,569 ft **Area code** 541 **Zip** 97530
E-mail jvillechamber@wave.net **Web** www.wave.net/upg/jvillechamber/
Information Historic Jacksonville Chamber of Commerce, PO Box 33; 541/899-8118.

Gold was discovered here in 1851 and brought prospectors by the thousands. An active town until the gold strike played out in the 1920s, Jacksonville lost its county seat to the neighboring town of Medford (see) in 1927. Now a national historic landmark, the town is one of the best preserved pioneer communities in the Pacific Northwest. Approximately 80 original buildings can be seen and some visited. A Ranger District office of the Rogue River National Forest (see MEDFORD) is located about 20 miles southwest of town, in Applegate Valley.

What to See and Do

⭐ **Jacksonville Museum.** In Old County Courthouse (1883), has exhibits of southern Oregon history, pioneer relics, early photographs, fashions, toys, Native American artifacts, quilts, natural history. (Memorial Day-Labor Day, daily; rest of yr, daily exc Mon; closed Jan 1, Thanksgiving, Dec 25) Children's Museum is in Old County Jail. (1883), 206 N 5th St. Phone 541/773-6536. ¢ Also maintained by the Southern Oregon Historical Society is

Beekman House (1875) Country Gothic house; former home of a prominent Jacksonville citizen. Living history exhibit. (Memorial Day-Labor Day, daily) 352 E California St. ¢

The Oregon Vortex Location of the House of Mystery. The Vortex is a spherical field of force half above the ground, half below. Natural, historical, educational and scientific phenomena are found in former assay office and surrounding grounds. Guided lecture tours (Mar-Oct, daily). Approx 10 mi NW on county road, at 4303 Sardine Creek Rd, in Gold Hill. Phone 541/855-1543. ¢¢

Seasonal Event

Britt Musical Festivals. Hillside estate of pioneer photographer Peter Britt forms a natural amphitheatre. Festivals in classical, jazz, folk, country, dance and musical theater. Phone 541/779-0847 or 800/882-7488. Mid-June-Sept 1.

Inns

★ ★ **JACKSONVILLE INN.** *175 E California St.* 541/899-1900; res: 800/321-9344; FAX 541/899-1373. 11 rms, 8 with shower only, 2 story, 3 suites, 3 cottages. S $80-$125; D $100-$145; each addl $10; suites, cottages $205-$245. Crib $10. TV in cottages; cable. Complimentary full bkfst. Restaurant (see JACKSONVILLE INN). Bar. Ck-out 11 am

(cottages 1:30 pm), ck-in 3 pm (cottages 4:30 pm). Meeting rms. Business servs avail. In-rm modem link. Sundries. Shopping arcade. Free airport transportation. Refrigerators; some bathrm phones, in-rm whirlpools, microwaves, fireplaces. Built in 1860s; gold-rush era atmosphere. Cr cds: A, D, DS, MC, V.

★ **THE STAGE LODGE.** *830 N Fifth St.* 541/899-3953; res: 800/253-8254. 27 rms, 2 suites, 2 story. Late May-Sept: S $69; D $72; each addl $5; suites $135; under 10 free; lower rates rest of yr. Crib $3. Pet accepted, some restrictions; $10. TV; cable. Complimentary continental bkfst. Ck-out 11 am, ck-in 2 pm. Some refrigerators, microwaves. Cr cds: A, D, DS, MC, V.

★ ★ **TOUVELLE HOUSE.** *455 N Oregon St.* 541/899-8938; res: 800/846-8422; FAX 541/899-3992. E-mail touvelle@wave.net; web www.wave.net/upg/touvelle. 6 rms, 3 story, 1 suite. May-Sept: S, D $105; each addl $30; hols (2-day min); lower rates rest of yr. Children over 12 yrs only. TV in common rm; cable (premium). Complimentary full bkfst. Restaurant nearby. Ck-out 11 am, ck-in 3 pm. Business servs avail. In-rm modem link. Luggage handling. Concierge serv. Gift shop. Free airport transportation. Heated pool; whirlpool. Picnic tables, grills. Built in 1916; antiques. Cr cds: A, D, DS, MC, V.

Restaurants

★ ★ ★ **JACKSONVILLE INN.** *(See Jacksonville Inn)* 541/899-1900. Hrs: 7:30-10:30 am, 11:30 am-2 pm, 5-10 pm; Mon 7:30-10:30 am, 5-10 pm; Sun 10 am-2 pm (brunch), 5-9 pm. Closed Thanksgiving, Dec 24, 25. Res accepted. Continental menu. Bar 11:30 am-midnight. Wine list. Semi-a la carte: bkfst $5.95-$9.95, lunch $6.95-$14.95, dinner $13.95-$41.95. Specializes in prime rib, fresh salmon in season, veal scaloppini. Patio dining. Building dates to gold-rush era. Totally nonsmoking. Cr cds: A, D, DS, MC, V.

★ ★ ★ **McCULLY HOUSE.** *240 E California.* 541/899-1942. Web www.wave.net/upg/mccully. Hrs: 5-10 pm. Res accepted. Bar. Semi-a la carte: dinner $8.50-$21.95. Specializes in fresh seafood, pasta, salads. Patio dining. One of first houses built in town (1861). 3 Guest rms avail. Totally nonsmoking. Cr cds: A, MC, V.

John Day (C-8)

Pop 1,836 **Elev** 3,085 ft **Area code** 541 **Zip** 97845
Information Grant County Chamber of Commerce, 281 W Main; 541/575-0547 or 800/769-5664.

John Day, named for a heroic scout in the first Astor expedition, was once a Pony Express stop on trail to The Dalles. Logging and cattle raising are the major industries in the area. Headquarters for the Malheur National Forest is located here; two Ranger District offices of the forest are also located here.

What to See and Do

Grant County Historical Museum. Mementos of gold-mining days, Joaquin Miller cabin, Greenhorn jail (1910). (June-Sept, Mon-Sat, also Sun afternoons) 2 mi S on US 395 at 101 S Canyon City Blvd in Canyon City. Phone 541/575-0362 or 541/575-1993. ¢

John Day Fossil Beds National Monument. The monument consists of three separate units in Wheeler and Grant counties of north central Oregon; no collecting within monument. Wayside exhibits at points of interest in each unit. 40 mi W on US 26, then 2 mi N on OR 19. Phone 541/987-2333. **Free.** These units include

Sheep Rock Unit. Here are outstanding examples of the buff and green layers of the fossil-bearing John Day Formation, Mascall Formation and Rattlesnake Formation. Visitor center offers picnicking and browsing among fossil displays. Self-guided Island in Time Trail and Story in Stone Trail include exhibits. 7 mi W of Dayville on OR 19.

Painted Hills Unit. Displays a colorful, scenic landscape of buff and red layers in the John Day Formation. Self-guided Painted Cove Trail and Leaf Hill Trail. Exhibits; picnicking. 9 mi NW of Mitchell, off US 26 on a county road.

Clarno Unit. Consists of hills, bluffs, towering rock palisades and pinnacles. Self-guided Trail of the Fossils features abundant plant fossils visible in the 35-50 million-yr-old rock. Picnicking. 20 mi W of Fossil on OR 218.

Kam Wah Chung & Co Museum. Originally constructed as a trading post on The Dalles Military Rd (1866-1867). Now houses Chinese medicine herb collection, shrine, kitchen, picture gallery, Doc Hay's bedroom. (May-Oct, daily exc Fri) 250 NW Canton, adj to city park. Phone 541/575-0028. ¢

Malheur National Forest. Nearly 1.5 million acres in southwestern part of Blue Mts include Strawberry Mt and Monument Rock wilderness areas. Trout fishing in Magone, Yellowjacket and Canyon Meadows Lakes, stream fishing, elk and deer hunting. Hiking. Winter sports. Picnicking. N & S on US 395; E & W on US 26. Camping, For further information contact Supervisor, PO Box 919; 541/575-3000. **Free.**

Annual Events

"62" Day Celebration. Canyon City, 1 mi S. Celebrates the discovery of gold in 1862. Medicine wagon and fiddling shows, parade, booths, barbecue, dancing, selection of queen. 2nd wkend June.

Grant County Fair and Rodeo. Grant County Fairgrounds. Oregon's oldest continuous county fair. 5 days late Aug.

Motels

✔★ **DREAMERS LODGE.** *144 N Canyon Blvd, just N of jct US 26, 395.* 541/575-0526; FAX 541/575-2733; res: 800/654-2849. 25 rms, 2 story. S $40-$42; D $46-$48; each addl $2; suites $45-$60. Crib $3. Pet accepted. TV; cable (premium). Complimentary coffee in rms. Restaurant nearby. Ck-out 11 am. Business servs avail. Free airport transportation. X-country ski 20 mi. Refrigerators. Cr cds: A, C, D, DS, MC, V.

★ **SUNSET INN.** *390 W Main St.* 541/575-1462; FAX 541/575-1471; res: 800/452-4899. 43 rms, 2 story. S $45-$48.50; D $65; each addl $5; suites $110. Crib $5. Pet accepted, some restrictions. TV, cable (premium). Indoor pool; whirlpool. Restaurant 5 am-11 pm. Bar. Ck-out 11 am. Meeting rms. Business servs avail. Free airport transportation. Cr cds: A, D, DS, MC, V.

D ✔ 🏊 ⛷ 🔥 SC

Joseph (B-10)

Pop 1,073 **Elev** 4,190 ft **Area code** 541 **Zip** 97846 **E-mail** wallowa@eoni.com **Web** www.eoni.com/~wallowa/

Information Wallowa County Chamber of Commerce, 107 SW First St, PO Box 427, Enterprise 97828; 541/426-4622 or 800/585-4121.

Joseph is located in the isolated wilderness of northeast Oregon. Remote from industry, the town attracts vacationers with its beautiful surroundings. There are fishing lakes here and hunting in the surrounding area. At the north end of Wallowa Lake is Old Joseph Monument, a memorial to the Nez Perce chief who resisted the US government. A Ranger District office of the Wallowa-Whitman National Forest (see BAKER) is located in nearby Enterprise.

What to See and Do

Hells Canyon National Recreation Area. Created by the Snake River, at the Idaho/Oregon border, Hells Canyon is the deepest gorge in North America—1½ mi from Idaho's He Devil Mt (elevation 9,393 ft) to the Snake River at Granite Creek (elevation 1,408 ft). Overlooks at Hat Point, southeast of Imnaha, and in Idaho (see GRANGEVILLE, ID); both are fire lookouts. The recreation area includes parts of the Wallowa-Whitman National Forest in Oregon, and the Nez Perce and Payette national forests in Idaho. Activities include float trips, jet boat tours, boat trips into canyon from Lewiston, ID (see) or the Hells Canyon Dam (see WEISER, ID); auto tours; backpacking and horseback riding. Developed campgrounds in Oregon and Idaho; much of the area is undeveloped, some is designated wilderness. Be sure to inquire about road conditions before planning a trip; some are rough and open for a limited season. 30 mi NE on County Road 350 in Wallowa-Whitman National Forest (see BAKER). For a commercial outfitters guide list and further information contact Hells Canyon National Recreation Area Office, 88401 OR 82, Enterprise 97828, phone 541/426-4978; for river information and float res contact PO Box 699, Clarkston, WA 99403, phone 509/758-1957.

Valley Bronze of Oregon. Company produces finished castings of bronze, fine and sterling silver and stainless steel. Showroom displays finished pieces. Tours of foundry depart from showroom (by res). (May-Nov, daily; rest of yr, by appt) 018 S Main. Phone 541/432-7445. Showroom **Free;** Foundry tours ¢¢

Wallowa Lake State Park. Park has 201 forested acres in an alpine setting formed by a glacier at the base of the rugged Wallowa Mts. Swimming, water sport equipment rentals; fishing; boating (dock, motor rentals). Picnicking, concession. Improved tent & trailer sites (dump station). Standard fees. Park at edge of Eagle Cap wilderness area; hiking and riding trails begin here. Horse stables nearby. 6 mi S on OR 82. Phone 541/432-4185.

Wallowa Lake Tramway. Gondola rises from valley to Mt Howard summit. Snack bar at summit. (June-Sept, daily; May, wkends, weather permitting) 6 mi S on OR 82. Phone 541/432-5331. ¢¢¢

Annual Event

Chief Joseph Days. PRCA rodeo, parades, Native American dances, cowboy breakfasts. Contact Chamber of Commerce. Last full wkend July.

Motels

★ **FLYING ARROW RESORT.** *59782 Wallowa Lake Hwy.* 541/432-2951. 20 cottages. June-Labor Day: cottages $60-$130; each addl $5; 5-day min stay; higher rates 1-day stay; lower rates rest of yr. TV; cable. Heated pool. Ck-out 11 am. Refrigerators; many fireplaces. Picnic tables, grills. On river. Cr cds: DS, MC, V.

✔★ **INDIAN LODGE.** *201 S Main St.* 541/432-2651; FAX 541/432-4949. 16 rms. May-Nov: S $35-$40; D $43-$46; each addl $5; lower rates rest of yr. TV; cable (premium). Complimentary coffee in rms. Restaurant nearby. Ck-out 11 am. Lake 1 mi. Cr cds: MC, V.

★ ★ **WALLOWA LAKE LODGE.** *60060 Wallawa Lake Hwy, 6 mi S on OR 82.* 541/432-9821; FAX 541/432-4885. 22 units, 3 story, 2 suites, 8 kit. cottages. No A/C. No elvtr. No rm phones. Late May-mid Oct: S, D $70-$130; family rates; lower rates rest of yr. Restaurant 7-10 am, 5:30-8:30 pm. Ck-out 11 am. Meeting rms. Gift shop. Downhill ski 16 mi. On Wallowa Lake; swimming. Totally nonsmoking. Cr cds: DS, MC, V.

Inn

★ ★ **CHANDLERS' BED, BREAD & TRAIL.** *700 S Main St.* 541/432-9765; res: 800/452-3781. 5 rms (2 share bath), 2 story. No A/C. No rm phones. S $50-70; D $60-80; each addl $10. Children over 11 yrs only. Complimentary full bkfst. Ck-out 11 am, ck-in 2 pm. Downhill/x-country ski 6 mi. Picnic tables. Cedar and log interiors with high vaulted ceilings. Totally nonsmoking. Cr cds: MC, V.

Klamath Falls (F-5)

Settled 1867 **Pop** 17,737 **Elev** 4,105 ft **Area code** 541

Information Klamath County Department of Tourism, 1451 Main St, 97601; 541/884-0666 or 800/445-6728.

The closest sizable town to Crater Lake National Park (see) with more than 100 good fishing lakes nearby, Klamath Falls is host to sports-minded people. Upper Klamath Lake, the largest body of fresh water in Oregon, runs north of town for 30 miles. White pelicans, protected by law, nest here each summer, and a large concentration of bald eagles winter in the Klamath Basin. Headquarters and a Ranger District office of the Winema National Forest are located here.

What to See and Do

Collier Memorial State Park and Logging Museum. A 655-acre park located at the confluence of Spring Creek and Williamson River. Open-air historic logging museum with display of tools, machines and engines; various types of furnished 1800s-era pioneer cabins; gift shop (daily; free). Fishing. Hiking. Picnicking. Tent & trailer campsites (hookups, dump station). Standard fees. 30 mi N, on both sides of US 97. Phone 541/783-2471.

Favell Museum of Western Art and Native American Artifacts. Contemporary Western art; working miniature gun collection; extensive display of Native American artifacts. Also art & print sales galleries. Gift shop. (Daily exc Sun; closed Jan 1, Thanksgiving, Dec 25) 125 W Main. Phone 541/882-9996. ¢¢

Ft Klamath Museum. Housed in a log replica of the original guardhouse built on the eight-acre Ft Klamath frontier post (established 1863 to promote peaceful relations between natives and early settlers). Contains displays of clothes, equipment, firearms, original artifacts from the fort and other relics of the period. Picnic area. (June-Labor Day, Thurs-Mon; closed hols) 36 mi NW via US 97, OR 62 to Ft Klamath. Phone 541/883-4208. **Donation.**

Jackson F. Kimball State Park. A 19-acre pine and fir timbered area at headwaters of Wood River, noted for its transparency and deep blue appearance. Fishing. Picnicking. Primitive campsites. Standard fees. 40 mi N on US 97, OR 62 to Ft Klamath, then 3 mi N on OR 232. Phone 541/783-2471.

Klamath County Baldwin Hotel Museum. Restored turn-of-the-century hotel contains many original furnishings. Guided tours (June-Sept, Tues-Sat; closed hols). 31 Main St. Phone 541/883-4207. ¢¢

Klamath County Museum. Local geology, history, wildlife and Native American displays; research library has books on history, natural history and anthropology of Pacific Northwest. (June-Sept, daily; rest of yr, daily exc Sun; closed hols) 1451 Main St. Phone 541/883-4208. ¢

Migratory Bird Refuge (in OR and CA). Major stopover on Pacific Flyway. There are six national wildlife refuges in the Klamath Basin. Upper Klamath and Klamath Marsh refuges lie to the N and Lower Klamath, Bear Valley, Tule Lake and Clear Lake lie to the S of the city. There is a visitor center with exhibits at refuge headquarters at Tule Lake (daily). Waterfowl (Mar-Apr, Oct-Nov); bald eagles (Dec-Mar); migratory birds (Mar-Apr); waterfowl and colonial bird nesting (summer). S on OR 39 and CA 139 to Tulelake, CA, then 5 mi W on East-West Rd. Phone 916/667-2231. **Free.**

Winema National Forest. This forest (more than 1 million acres) includes former reservation lands of the Klamath Tribe; high country of Sky Lakes; portions of Pacific Crest National Scenic Trail; recreation areas in Lake of the Woods, Recreation Creek, Mountain Lakes Wilderness and Mt Theilson Wilderness. Swimming; boating. Picnicking. Camping (some areas free). N, E and W, reached by US 97, OR 62 or OR 140. For information contact Supervisor, 2819 Dahlia St; 541/883-6714. Camping ¢¢¢

Annual Events

Bald Eagle Conference. Feb 13-15.

Klamath Memorial Rodeo & Powwow. May 24-25.

Klamath County Fair. Aug 6-9.

Jefferson State Stampede. Aug 8-9.

Motels

★ ★ **BEST WESTERN KLAMATH INN.** *4061 S Sixth St (97603), near Kingsley Field Airport.* 541/882-1200; FAX 541/882-2729. 52 rms, 2 story. S, D $59-$79; each addl $8. Crib $4. Pet accepted, some restrictions. TV; cable (premium), VCR avail. Indoor pool. Complimentary continental bkfst. Restaurant adj 6 am-10:30 pm. Ck-out noon. Meeting rms. Microwaves; some in-rm whirlpools, refrigerators. Cr cds: A, C, D, DS, MC, V.

★ ★ **BEST WESTERN OLYMPIC INN.** *2627 S Sixth St (97603).* 541/882-9665; FAX 541/884-3214. 71 rms, 3 story. June-Sept: S $69; D $79-$89; each addl $10; under 12 free; lower rates rest of yr. TV; cable (premium). Complimentary continental bkfst. Complimentary coffee in rms. Restaurant opp open 24 hrs. Ck-out 11 am. Meeting rms. Business servs avail. In-rm modem link. Exercise equipt; bicycle, stair machine. Heated pool; whirlpool. Refrigerators, microwaves. Cr cds: A, C, D, DS, ER, MC, V.

✔ ★ **CIMARRON MOTOR INN.** *3060 S Sixth St (97603).* 541/882-4601; FAX 541/882-6690; res: 800/742-2648. 163 rms, 2 story. S $45; D $50-$55; each addl $5. Pet accepted; $5. TV; cable (premium). Heated pool. Continental bkfst. Restaurant adj open 24 hrs. Ck-out noon. Meeting rm. Business servs avail. Cr cds: A, D, DS, MC, V.

★ ★ **COMFORT INN.** *2500 S Sixth St (97601).* 541/884-9999; FAX 541/882-4020. 57 rms, 2 story, 10 suites. S $50-$70; D $55-$75; each addl $8; suites $75-$125; under 17 free; family rates. Crib $4. TV; cable (premium), VCR avail. Indoor pool; whirlpool. Complimentary continental bkfst. Restaurant nearby. Ck-out noon. Coin lndry. Meeting rms. Business servs avail. Exercise equipt; weight machine, rower. Microwaves. Cr cds: A, C, D, DS, ER, JCB, MC, V.

★ ★ **QUALITY INN.** *100 Main St (97601).* 541/882-4666; FAX 541/883-8795; res: 800/732-2025. Web www.multi.com/molatore. 80 rms, 2 story, 4 suites. S $63; D $63-$95.50; each addl $5; suites $93.50; under 18 free. Crib free. Pet accepted, some restrictions. TV; cable (premium). Heated pool. Complimentary continental bkfst. Coffee in rms. Restaurant adj. Ck-out noon. Coin lndry. Meeting rms. Business servs avail. In-rm modem link. Some in-rm whirlpools, microwaves. Cr cds: A, C, D, DS, JCB, MC, V.

★ **SUPER 8.** *3805 US 97N (97601), near Oregon Tech.* 541/884-8880; FAX 541/884-0235. 61 rms, 3 story. No elvtr. June-mid-Sept: S $47.88-$51.88; D $51.88-$61.88; each addl $4; lower rates rest of yr. Crib free. TV; cable. Complimentary coffee in lobby. Restaurant nearby. Ck-out noon. Coin lndry. Whirlpool. Cr cds: A, C, D, DS, MC, V.

✔ ★ **TRAVELODGE.** *11 Main St (97601).* 541/882-4494; FAX 541/882-8940. 47 rms, 2 story. May-Oct: S $38-$42; D $48-$58; each addl $5; under 17 free. Pet accepted, some restrictions. TV; cable. Heated pool. Complimentary continental bkfst. Complimentary coffee in rms. Restaurant nearby. Ck-out 11 am. Some refrigerators, microwaves. Cr cds: A, C, D, DS, MC, V.

Motor Hotel

★ ★ ★ **SHILO INN SUITES.** *2500 Almond St (97601), 2 mi NW on US 97 N (Business), exit OIT.* 541/885-7980; FAX 541/885-7959. 143 suites, 4 story. June-Sept: S, D $99-$119; each addl $10; kit. units $149; under 12 free; golf plans; lower rates rest of yr. Crib free. Pet accepted, some restrictions; $7. TV; cable (premium), VCR (movies). Complimentary continental bkfst. Complimentary coffee in rms. Restaurant 6 am-11 pm. Rm serv. Bar 11-2 am. Ck-out noon. Meeting rms. Business center. In-rm modem link. Bellhops. Valet serv. Sundries. Coin lndry. Free airport, RR station transportation. Exercise equipt; bicycle, stair machine, sauna. Health club privileges. Indoor pool; whirlpool. Bathrm phones, refrigerators, microwaves, wet bars. Cr cds: A, D, DS, MC, V.

Restaurant

★ ★ **FIORELLA'S.** *6139 Simmer Ave (97603).* 541/882-1878. Hrs: 5-9 pm. Closed Sun, Mon; Dec 25. Res accepted. Northern Italian menu. Bar. Semi-a la carte: dinner $8.50-$19.95. Complete meals: dinner $11.50-$22.50. Child's meals. Specialties: pasticio, ravioli, gnocchi, filet mignon. Large wine selection. Cr cds: A, DS, MC, V.

La Grande (B-9)

(See also Baker City, Pendleton)

Settled 1861 **Pop** 11,766 **Elev** 2,771 ft **Area code** 541 **Zip** 97850

Information La Grande/Union County Visitors & Conventions Bureau, 1912 Fourth Ave, #200; 541/963-8588 or 800/848-9969.

Located in the heart of Northeast Oregon amid the Blue and Wallowa mountains, La Grande offers visitors breathtaking scenery and numerous exhilarating activities. Rafting and fishing enthusiasts enjoy the Grande Ronde River; hikers and mountain bikers navigate the Eagle Cap Wilderness and the tracks of the Oregon Trail. A Ranger District office of the Wallowa-Whitman National Forest (see BAKER) is located here.

What to See and Do

Catherine Creek State Park. A 160-acre park in pine forest along creek. Biking, hiking, fishing. Picnicking. Camping. Standard fees. 8 mi SE on OR 203. Phone 541/963-0430 or 541/963-6444.

Eastern Oregon State College (1929). (1,900 students) Campus overlooks the town. Liberal arts college. Rock and mineral collection displayed in science building (Mon-Fri; closed hols; free). Nightingale Gallery, concerts, theatrical productions, in Loso Hall; changing exhibits. 1410 L Avenue. Phone 541/962-3672.

Hilgard Junction State Park. A 233-acre park on the old Oregon Trail. Fishing. Picnicking. Camping (daily). Exhibits at Oregon Trail Interpretive Center (Memorial Day-Labor Day, daily). Standard fees. 8 mi W off I-84N. Phone 541/963-0430 or 541/963-6444.

Spout Springs Ski Area. At 5,100-ft. Area has 2 double chairlifts, T-bar, rope tow; patrol, school, rentals; restaurant. 13 mi of cross-country trails. (late Nov-Mar, Wed, Fri-Sun) Summer activities include mountain biking, camping. 45 mi N on OR 204, 3 mi SE of Tollgate in Umatilla National Forest. Phone 541/566-2164. ¢¢¢¢; Cross-country trail pass ¢¢¢

Turns of the Brick. Self-guided walking tour of 30 turn-of-the-century bldgs and ghost signs. Approx 1-hr tour includes McGlasson's Stationery (1890), Masonic Lodge & JC Penney Co (ca 1900), Fire Station Bldg (1898) and Helm Bldg (1891). Unique brickwork & architecture explained in brochure avail from La Grande Downtown Development Assn, 105 Fir, Ste 321; 503/963-0364. **Free.**

Annual Events

Union County Fair. Union County Fairgrounds. Early Aug.

Oregon Trail Days. Celebration of pioneer heritage includes historical events, arts & crafts; also a buffalo barbecue. Aug 14-16.

Motels

★ ★ **HOWARD JOHNSON.** *2612 Island Ave, 1 mi E on OR 82, just E of I-84N, exit 261.* 541/963-7195; FAX 541/963-4498. 146 rms, 2 story. S, D $70-$77; each addl $5; under 12 free; lower rates rest of yr. Crib $3.50. Pet accepted. TV; cable (premium). Heated pool; whirlpool. Complimentary continental bkfst. Restaurant adj open 24 hrs. Ck-out noon. Free lndry. Meeting rms. Business servs avail. Exercise equipt; weights, bicycles, sauna. Refrigerators. Private patios, balconies. Cr cds: A, C, D, DS, ER, MC, V.

✔ ★ **ROYAL MOTOR INN.** *1510 Adams Ave.* 541/963-4154; FAX 541/963-3588. 44 rms, 2 story. S, D $37-$42; each addl $5; under 17 free. Crib free. TV; cable (premium). Restaurant nearby. Ck-out 11 am. Cr cds: A, C, D, DS, MC, V.

★ **SUPER 8.** *2407 East R Ave.* 541/963-8080; FAX 541/963-2925. 64 rms, 2 story. 8 suites. Mid-May-Sept: S, D $50.88; each addl $5; suites $76.88-80.88; kit. unit $75.88; under 12 free; lower rates rest of yr. Crib $4. TV; cable (premium), VCR avail. Indoor pool; whirlpool. Complimentary continental bkfst in lobby. Restaurant nearby. Ck-out 11 am. Coin lndry. Meeting rms. Exercise equipt; weight machine, bicycles. Refrigerators. Cr cds: A, C, D, DS, MC, V.

Inn

★ ★ **STANG MANOR.** *1612 Walnut St.* 541/963-2400; 800 888/286-9463. 4 rms, 2 story. No A/C. S $70-$90; D $75-$90; each addl $15. Children over 10 yrs only. TV in living room, VCR avail. Complimentary full bkfst; afternoon tea. Restaurant nearby. Ck-out 11 am, ck-in 3:30 pm. Free RR station transportation. Picnic tables. Georgian Colonial design; grand staircase; antique furnishings. Totally nonsmoking. Cr cds: DS, MC, V.

Lakeview (F-6)

Founded 1876 **Pop** 2,526 **Elev** 4,798 ft **Area code** 541 **Zip** 97630
E-mail lakeview@triax.com **Web** www.triax.com/lakecounty/lakeco.htm

Information Lake County Chamber of Commerce, 126 North E St; 541/947-6040.

General John C. Frémont and Kit Carson passed through what is now Lake County in 1843. There are antelope and bighorn sheep in the area, many trout streams and seven lakes nearby. A supervisor's office of the Frémont National Forest is located here; also here is a district office of the Bureau of Land Management and an office of the US Department of Fish and Wildlife.

What to See and Do

Drews Reservoir. Fishing; boating (launch). Camping. 15 mi W on Dog Lake Rd.

Fremont National Forest. More than 2 million acres. Includes remnants of ice-age lava flows and the largest and most defined exposed geologic fault in North America, Abert Rim, on E side of Lake Abert. Abert Rim is most spectacular at the E side of Crooked Creek Valley. Many of the lakes are remnants of post-glacial Lake Lahontan. Gearhart Mt Wilderness is rough and forested with unusual rock formations, streams and Blue Lake. Fishing, hunting. Picnicking. Camping. E & W via OR 140, N & S via US 395 and OR 31. For information contact Supervisor, 524 North G St; 541/947-2151.

Geyser and Hot Springs. "Old perpetual," said to be largest continuous hot water geyser in the northwest. Spouts as high as 70 ft occur approximately every 90 seconds. Hot springs nearby. 1 mi N on US 395.

Paisley. Unspoiled old Western town. 45 mi N on OR 31.

Schminck Memorial Museum. Pressed-glass goblets, home furnishings, dolls, toys, books, clothing, quilts, guns, saddles, tools and Native American artifacts. (Feb-Nov, Tues-Sat; also by appt; closed hols) 128 S E St. Phone 541/947-3134. ¢

Annual Events

Junior Rodeo. Last wkend June.

World-Class Hang-Gliding Festival. July 4 wkend.

Lake County Fair and Roundup. Labor Day wkend.

Motels

★ ★ **BEST WESTERN SKYLINE MOTOR LODGE.** *414 North G St. 541/947-2194; FAX 541/947-3100.* 38 rms, 2 story. S $48-$56; D $54-$60; each addl $6; suites $70-$110; higher rates special events. Crib $10. TV; cable (premium). Indoor pool; whirlpool. Complimentary continental bkfst. Complimentary coffee in rms. Restaurant adj 6 am-8 pm. Ck-out 11 am. Business servs avail. In-rm modem link. Coin lndry. Downhill/x-country ski 10 mi. Refrigerators; microwaves avail. Cr cds: A, C, D, DS, MC, V.

✔★ **LAKEVIEW LODGE.** *301 North G St, just S of jct US 395, OR 140. 541/947-2181; FAX 541/947-2572.* Web bobkings@triax.com. 40 rms. S $38-$46; D $42-$50; each addl $4; family units $42-$60; kit. units $4-$6 addl; higher rates Labor Day wkend. Crib free. Pet accepted. TV; cable (premium). Complimentary coffee in rm. Restaurant nearby. Ck-out 11 am. Downhill/x-country ski 8 mi. Exercise equipt; bicycle, stair machine, sauna. Whirlpool. Microwaves avail. Cr cds: A, C, D, DS, MC, V.

Restaurant

★ ★ **PLUSH WEST.** *9 North F St. 541/947-2353.* Hrs: 5-10 pm. Closed Sun. Res accepted. Bar from 4 pm. Semi-a la carte: dinner $9.95-$16.95. Child's meals. Specializes in lemon chicken, Australian lobster, prime rib. Western decor; antique mirrors. Cr cds: MC, V.

Lincoln City (B-3)

(See also Depoe Bay, Newport, Tillamook)

Pop 5,892 **Elev** 11-115 ft **Area code** 541 **Zip** 97367 **E-mail** lcvcb@newportnet.com
Information Visitor & Convention Bureau, 801 SW US 101, Suite #1; 541/994-8378 or 800/452-2151.

Nicknamed the "kite capital of the world," Lincoln City is a popular recreation, art and shopping area offering many accommodations with ocean-view rooms.

What to See and Do

Alder House II. Set in a grove of alder trees, this is the oldest glass-blowing studio in Oregon. Watch molten glass drawn from a furnace and

shaped into pieces of traditional or modern design. (Mid-Mar-Nov; daily) 611 Immonen Rd, 1/2 mi E off US 101. **Free.**

Devil's Lake State Park. A 109-acre park with swimming; fishing; boating (ramp on E side of Devil's Lake). Tent & trailer sites (on NW side of lake). Standard fees. S of town, off US 101. Phone 541/994-2002.

Theatre West. Community theater featuring comedy and drama. (Thurs-Sat) 3536 SE US 101. For res phone 541/994-5663.

Motels

★ ★ **"D" SANDS.** *171 SW US 101. 541/994-5244; FAX 541/994-7484; res: 800/527-3925.* 63 kit. units, 3 story. No elvtr. May-Oct: S, D $115-$130; each addl $10; under 8 free; lower rates mid-wk off-season. Crib free. TV; cable (premium). Indoor pool; whirlpool. Complimentary coffee in lobby. Restaurant nearby. Ck-out 11 am. Business servs avail. Some fireplaces. Some private balconies. On ocean, beach. Cr cds: A, DS, MC, V.

★ ★ **BEST WESTERN LINCOLN SANDS INN.** *535 NW Inlet Ave. 541/994-4227; FAX 541/994-2232.* 33 kit. suites, 3 story. Suites $89-$349. Crib $10. Pet accepted, some restrictions. TV; cable (premium), VCR. Heated pool; whirlpool. Complimentary continental bkfst. Complimentary coffee in rms. Restaurant nearby. Ck-out 11 am. In-rm modem link. Sauna. Microwaves. Balconies. Picnic table. On beach. Cr cds: A, C, D, DS, MC, V.

★ **COHO INN.** *1635 NW Harbor Ave, just W of US 101. 541/994-3684; FAX 541/994-6244; res: 800/848-7006.* 50 rms, 3 story, 31 kits. No A/C. No elvtr. June-Oct: S, D $96; each addl $6; suites $104-$116; lower rates rest of yr. Pet accepted, some restrictions; $6. TV; cable (premium). Complimentary coffee in lobby. Ck-out 11 am. Business servs avail. Sauna. Whirlpool. Some fireplaces. Some private patios, balconies. Oceanfront; beach nearby. Cr cds: A, DS, MC, V.

★ **COZY COVE BEACH FRONT RESORT.** *515 NW Inlet Ave. 541/994-2950; FAX 541/996-4332; res: 800/553-2683.* 70 rms, 2-3 story, 33 kits. S, D $46-$130; suites $130-$220; kit. units $69-$90. TV; cable, VCR avail (free movies). Heated pool; whirlpool. Complimentary coffee in lobby. Restaurant nearby. Ck-out 11 am. Business servs avail. Sauna. Some in-rm whirlpools, fireplaces. Some private patios, balconies. Picnic tables. On beach. Cr cds: D, DS, MC, V.

★ ★ **DOCK OF THE BAY.** *1116 SW 51st St. 541/996-3549; res: 800/362-5229.* 24 kit. suites, 3 story. No elvtr. Mid-June-mid-Sept: 1-bedrm $109-$129; 2-bedrm $129-$189; lower rates rest of yr. TV, VCR avail. Restaurant nearby. Ck-out 11 am. Sauna. Whirlpool. Balconies. On bay; beach. Cr cds: MC, V.

✔★ **LINCOLN SHORES.** *136 NE US 101. 541/994-8155; FAX 541/994-5581; res: 800/423-6240.* 30 rms, 3 story, 4 kits. May-Oct: S $40-$80; D $50-$100; each addl $5; lower rates rest of yr. Crib avail. TV; cable. Coffee in rms. Restaurant nearby. Ck-out 11 am. Business servs avail. Many balconies. Just N of "D" River; near beach. Cr cds: A, C, D, DS, MC, V.

★ ★ **NORDIC.** *2133 NW Inlet Ave. 541/994-8145; FAX 541/994-2329; res: 800/452-3558 (western US), 800/243-3558 (CAN).* 52 rms, 3 story, 24 kits. No elvtr. June-Aug: S, D $79-$83; each addl $7; suites $97; kit. units $85-$97; lower rates rest of yr. Crib $7. TV; cable, VCR. Indoor pool; whirlpool. Complimentary continental bkfst. Restaurant nearby. Ck-out noon. Meeting rm. Business servs avail. Saunas. Game rm. Microwaves avail. Cr cds: C, D, DS, MC, V.

✔★ **PELICAN SHORES INN.** *2645 NW Inlet Ave, just W of US 101. 541/994-2134; FAX 541/994-4963; res: 800/705-5505.* 34 rms, 3 story, 19 kits. No elvtr. May-Sept: S, D $59-$89; each addl $5; suites, kit. units $99-$119; lower rates Sun-Thurs rest of yr. Crib free. TV; cable, VCR avail. Indoor pool. Coffee in lobby. Restaurant nearby. Ck-out 11 am. Business servs avail. Some fireplaces. On ocean; beach access. Cr cds: A, C, D, DS, MC, V.

★★ **SHILO INN-OCEANFRONT RESORT.** *1501 NW 40th Place. 541/994-3655; FAX 541/994-2199.* 247 rms, 3-4 story. Mid-June-mid-Sept: S $49-$102; D $84-$110; suites $169-$240; kit. unit $125-$160; under 12 free; lower rates rest of yr. Crib free. Pet accepted, some restrictions; $6/day. TV; cable (premium), VCR avail. Indoor pool; whirlpool. Restaurant adj 7-2 am. Rm serv. Bar 11-1 am. Ck-out noon. Coin lndry. Meeting rms. Business center. Free local airport, bus depot transportation. Exercise equipt; weight machine, stair machine, sauna. Health club privileges. Refrigerators, microwaves; some bathrm phones. Picnic tables. On beach. Cr cds: A, C, D, DS, ER, JCB, MC, V.

Lodge

★★★★ **SALISHAN.** *(US 101, Gleneden Beach 97388) 1 blk E of US 101. 541/764-2371; FAX 541/764-3681; res: 800/452-2300.* Web www.dolce.com. Nestled on a 700-acre hillside forest preserve on the Oregon coast, Salishan comprises multiple buildings connected by bridges and walkways. Views of the ocean, forest and golf course are available. Rooms feature wood-burning fireplaces, balconies and prints and lithographs by Oregon artists. 205 rms, 2-3 story. No elvtr. May-Oct: S, D $175-$265; each addl $15; under 6 free; lower rates rest of yr. Crib $10. Pet accepted, some restrictions; $15. TV; cable (premium), VCR avail. Indoor pool; whirlpool, hydrotherapy pool. Dining rm 7 am-10 pm (also see THE DINING ROOM AT SALISHAN). Rm serv. Bar noon-1:30 am; entertainment. Ck-out noon. Meeting rms. Business servs avail. Bellhops. Valet serv. Concierge. Shopping mall. Indoor/outdoor lighted tennis, pro. 18-hole golf, greens fee $50-$55, pro, putting green, covered driving range. Self-guided nature trail. Exercise rm; instructor, weights, bicycles, sauna. Massage. Game rm. Refrigerators. Art gallery. Library. Cr cds: A, C, D, DS, MC, V.

Motor Hotel

★★★ **INN AT SPANISH HEAD.** *4009 SW US 101. 541/996-2161; FAX 541/996-4089; res: 800/452-8127.* E-mail spanishhead@new portnet.com; web www.per2per.com/inn@spanishhead.htm. 120 kit. units, 10 story. S, D $125-$159; each addl $15; suites $195-$269; under 16 free. Crib free. TV; cable, VCR avail (movies). Heated pool; whirlpool. Restaurant 8 am-2 pm, 5-9 pm; Sun-Thurs in winter to 8 pm. Rm serv. Bar 2 pm to close; winter from 5 pm. Ck-out noon. Meeting rms. Business servs avail. Bellhops. Valet parking. Exercise equipt; treadmill, stair machine, sauna. Game rm. Many private balconies. Built on side of cliff; ocean view. Cr cds: A, C, D, DS, MC, V.

Restaurants

★★★ **BAY HOUSE.** *5911 SW US 101. 541/996-3222.* E-mail bayhouse@newportnet.com. Hrs: 5:30-9 pm; Sat from 5 pm. Closed Dec 25; also Mon, Tues Nov-April. Res accepted. Serv bar. Semi-a la carte: dinner $14.50-$25.95. Specializes in fresh seafood, game, pasta. Overlooking Siletz Bay. Cr cds: A, DS, MC, V.

★★ **CHEZ JEANNETTE.** *(7150 Old Hwy 101, Gleneden Beach 97388) S via US 101. 541/764-3434.* Hrs: 5:30-10 pm. Res accepted. French, Northwestern menu. Bar. Semi-a la carte: dinner $18-$25. Child's

meals. Specializes in seafood, rack of lamb, game. French cottage decor; built 1920. Cr cds: A, DS, MC, V.

★★★★ **THE DINING ROOM AT SALISHAN.** *(See Salishan Lodge) 541/764-2371.* Carved teak panels and natural Oregon woods complement the sparkling crystal and silver at this three-tiered, candlelit dining room, which has a panoramic view of Siletz Bay. Regional Amer menu. Specializes in Oregon lamb, fresh seafood, regional cuisine. Own baking. Hrs: 7 am-10 pm; Fri, Sat to 10:30 pm; Sun brunch 10 am-2 pm. Res accepted. Serv bar. Wine cellar. A la carte entrees: bkfst $6-$9, lunch $8-$12, dinner $10-$28. Sun brunch $21.50. Child's meals. Valet parking. Cr cds: A, C, D, DS, MC, V.

✔★ **DORY COVE.** *5819 Logan Rd, N on Logan Rd, adj to Roads End State Park. 541/994-5180.* Hrs: 11:30 am-8 pm; Sun from noon; summer to 9 pm. Wine, beer. Semi-a la carte: lunch $4-$10, dinner $9-$20. Child's meals. Specializes in seafood. Some tables have ocean view. Cr cds: A, DS, MC, V.

Madras (C-6)

(See also Prineville, Redmond)

Pop 3,443 **Elev** 2,242 ft **Area code** 541 **Zip** 97741
Information Chamber of Commerce, 197 SE 5th St, PO Box 770; 541/475-2350.

Although the area was explored as early as 1825, settlement here was difficult because of Native American hostility. Settlement east of the Cascades, considered a wall of separation between the Native Americans and the settlers, was officially forbidden in 1856. In 1858 the order was revoked, and in 1862 the first road was built across the Cascades to provide a passage for traders. Shortly thereafter, settlement began in earnest.

What to See and Do

Jefferson County Museum. Located in the old courthouse; old-time doctor's equipment; military memorabilia; homestead & farm equipment. (June-Sept, Tues-Fri afternoons) 34 SE D St, 1 blk off Main St. Phone 541/475-3808. **Donation.**

Rockhounding. Richardson's Recreational Ranch. All diggings accessible by road; highlight of ranch are famous agate beds, featuring Thunder Eggs and ledge agate material. Rockhound campground area (no hook-ups). Digging fee. 11 mi N on US 97, then right 3 mi to ranch office. Phone 541/475-2680.

The Cove Palisades State Park. A 4,130-acre park on Lake Chinook behind Round Butte Dam; scenic canyon of geological interest; spectacular views of the confluence of the Crooked, Deschutes and Metolius rivers forming Lake Billy Chinook in a steep basaltic canyon. Swimming; fishing; boating (ramp, dock, rentals, marina with restaurant, groceries). Houseboat rentals. Hiking. Picnicking. Tent & trailer sites (dump station). Standard fees. 15 mi SW off US 97. Phone 541/546-3412.

Annual Event

All Rockhounds Powwow Gem & Mineral Show. Jefferson County Fairgrounds. Field trips, entertainment, swapping. Late June or early July.

Motel

✔★★ **SONNY'S.** *1539 SW US 97. 541/475-7217; FAX 541/475-6547; res: 800/624-6137.* 44 rms, 2 story, 2 suites, 2 kits. S $47; D $55; each addl $7; suites $80-$105; kit. units $95; under 6 free. Crib $4. Pet accepted; $7. TV; cable (premium). Heated pool; whirlpool. Complimentary continental bkfst. Restaurant 11 am-10 pm. Bar 11 am-midnight. Ck-out 11 am. Coin Indry. Business servs avail. Lawn games. Some microwaves; refrigerators avail. Cr cds: A, C, D, DS, MC, V.

Resort

★ ★ ★ **KAH-NEE-TA.** (Box K, Warm Springs 97761) 14 mi NW on US 26 to Warm Springs, then 11 mi N. 541/553-1112; FAX 541/553-1071; res: 800/554-4786. 139 rms in 3-4 story lodge, 32 condos, 20 unfurnished teepees in village. Lodge: S, D $115-$140; suites $170-$275; condos: $109.95; village teepees for 5, $55; under 6 free in lodge; mid-wk packages (off season). Pet accepted. TV; cable (premium). 2 heated pools; whirlpools, poolside serv, private hot mineral baths at village. Dining rm 7 am-10 pm. Snacks. Salmon Bake Sat (Memorial Day-Labor Day). Bars 11 am-2 pm. Ck-out 11:30 am, ck-in 4:30 pm. Lodge meeting rms. Gift shop. Tennis. 18-hole golf, greens fee $32, pro, putting green, driving range. Exercise rm; instructor, weights, bicycles, sauna. Massage. Kayak float trips. Trails. Bicycles. Rec dir; entertainment. Game rm. Authentic Native American dances Sun May-Sept. Varied accommodations. Owned by Confederated Tribes of Warm Springs Reservation. RV and trailer spaces avail. Cr cds: A, C, D, DS, MC, V.

McKenzie Bridge (C-5)

Pop 200 (est) **Elev** 1,337 ft **Area code** 541 **Zip** 97413 **Web** www.el.com/to/Mckenzierivervalley/

Information McKenzie River Chamber of Commerce and Information Center, MP 24 McKenzie Hwy East (OR 126), PO Box 1117, Leaburg 97489; 541/896-3330 or -9011.

McKenzie Bridge and the neighboring town of Blue River are located on the beautiful McKenzie River, with covered bridges, lakes, waterfalls and wilderness trails of the Cascades nearby. Fishing, float trips, skiing and backpacking are some of the many activities available. Ranger District offices of the Willamette National Forest (see EUGENE) are located here and in Blue River.

What to See and Do

Blue River Dam & Lake. Saddle Dam Boating Site offers boat ramp. Mona Campground offers swimming; fishing. Picnicking (fee). Dam is a US Army Corps of Engineers project. Recreation areas administered by the US Forest Service. Camping (mid-May-mid-Sept; fee). 7 mi W on OR 126, then N on Forest Road 15 in Willamette National Forest. Phone 541/822-3317 (Blue River Ranger Station).

Carmen-Smith Hydroelectric Development. Salmon spawning facility near Trail Bridge Dam; three stocked reservoirs—Trail Bridge, Smith and Carmen (daily). Boat launching (free). Picnicking. Camping at Lake's End, N end of Smith Reservoir, at Ice Cap Creek on Carmen Reservoir and at Trail Bridge (10-day limit). 14 mi NE on OR 126, on Upper McKenzie River. Phone 541/484-2411 or the Ranger District stations. Camping ¢¢¢

Cougar Dam and Lake. Six-mi-long reservoir. Echo Park is a day-use area with boat ramp (free). Slide Creek campground offers swimming, waterskiing; fishing; boat ramp. Picnicking (free). Camping (fee). Delta and French Pete campgrounds offer fishing, picnicking. Campgrounds maintained and operated by US Forest Service. Dam is a US Army Corps of Engineers project. (May-Sept; most areas closed rest of yr, inquire) For further information inquire at Blue River Ranger Station. 5 mi W on OR 126, then S on Forest Rd 19 (Aufderheide Forest Dr) in Willamette National Forest (see EUGENE). Phone 541/822-3317 or 541/896-3614.

Motels

★ ★ ★ **EAGLE ROCK LODGE.** (49198 McKenzie Hwy, Vida 97488) I-5 exit 194A, E on OR 126. 541/822-3962; FAX 541/822-3237. E-mail erlodge@erlodge.com; web www.erlodge.com. 10 rms, 7 with shower only, 2 story. No A/C. S, D $65-$129; each addl $10; golf, rafting plans. TV avail. Complimentary full bkfst. Ck-out 11 am. X-country ski 5 mi. Refrigerators; some in-rm whirlpools, fireplaces; microwaves avail. Balconies. Picnic tables. Built 1930s. Totally nonsmoking. Cr cds: A, DS, MC, V.

✔★ **SLEEPY HOLLOW.** (54791 McKenzie Hwy, Blue River) 3 mi W on OR 126. 541/822-3805. 19 rms, 2 story. Apr-Oct: S $43.20; D $47.52-$56.16; each addl $10.80. Closed rest of yr. TV in some rms. Restaurant adj. Ck-out 11 am. Refrigerators. Cr cds: MC, V.

Restaurant

★ ★ **LOG CABIN INN.** 56483 McKenzie Hwy. 541/822-3432. Hrs (May-Nov): noon-9 pm; Sun brunch 10 am-2 pm. Phone for winter hrs. Res accepted. Bar 5 pm-midnight. Semi-a la carte: lunch $5.95-$8.95, dinner $10.95-$17.95. Sun brunch $8.95. Child's meals. Specializes in fish, game. Outdoor dining. Built as stagecoach stop in 1906. Cr cds: DS, MC, V.

McMinnville (B-4)

(See also Newberg, Oregon City, Salem)

Pop 17,894 **Elev** 160 ft **Area code** 503 **Zip** 97128

Information Chamber of Commerce, 417 N Adams; 503/472-6196.

McMinnville is in the center of a wine-producing area. Many of the wineries offer tours.

What to See and Do

Linfield College (1849). (2,100 students) Liberal arts. On the 100-acre campus are Renshaw Art Gallery, Linfield Anthropology Museum and the Linfield Theater. The music department offers concerts. Lectures and events throughout the yr. Phone 503/434-2000.

Annual Events

Turkey Rama/Oregon Hazelnut Festival. Mid-July.

Yamhill County Fair. Late July-early Aug.

Seasonal Event

Summer Theater & Drama Camp. Musical, comedy and drama productions by the Gallery Players of Oregon. Fri-Sun. Phone 503/472-2227. June-Aug.

Motels

✔★ **PARAGON.** 2065 S OR 99W. 503/472-9493; FAX 503/472-8470; res: 800/525-5469. 55 rms, 2 story. S $36; D $43; each addl $3; suites $86. Crib $2. Pet accepted; $5. TV; cable (premium), VCR avail. Heated pool. Complimentary continental bkfst. Restaurant nearby. Ck-out noon. Coin Indry. Meeting rm. Business servs avail. Refrigerators. Cr cds: A, D, DS, MC, V.

★ ★ **SAFARI MOTOR INN.** *345 N OR 99W. 503/472-5187; FAX 503/434-6380; res: 800/321-5543.* 90 rms, 2 story. S $38-$42; D $40-$50; each addl $3. Crib $3. TV. Restaurant 6 am-9 pm; Sun 7 am-3 pm. Bar from 4 pm. Ck-out noon. Meeting rms. Business servs avail. Whirlpool. Cr cds: A, C, D, DS, MC, V.

Inn

★ ★ **STEIGER HAUS.** *360 Wilson St. 503/472-0238.* 5 rms, 3 story. No A/C. No rm phones. S $65-$95; D $70-$100; each addl $20. Children over 10 yrs only. Complimentary full bkfst. Coffee in rms. Ck-out 11 am, ck-in 3-6 pm. Luggage handling. Lawn games. Picnic tables. Northern European country-style house; stained-glass windows. Totally nonsmoking. Cr cds: MC, V.

Guest Ranch

★ ★ **FLYING M RANCH.** *(23029 NW Flying M Rd, Yamhill 97148)* N on OR 47 to Yamhill, left on Oak Ridge Rd, left on Fairdale Rd, left on NW Flying M Rd. *503/662-3222; FAX 503/662-3202.* 28 rms in main building, 8 kit. cottages. S, D $50-$70; kit. cottages $75-$200. Pet accepted. TV in lounge. Dining rm 8 am-8 pm; Fri, Sat & hols to 10 pm. Box lunches. Picnics. Bar; entertainment Sun, dancing Fri, Sat. Ck-out 11 am, ck-in 4 pm. Grocery, coin lndry, package store 10 mi. Meeting rms. Business servs avail. Gift shop. Tennis. Swimming pond. X-country ski adj. Snowmobiling, sleighing. Hiking. Overnight trail rides. Lawn games. Fishing/hunting. Balconies. Picnic tables, grills. Cr cds: A, D, DS, MC, V.

Medford (F-4)

(See also Ashland, Grants Pass, Jacksonville)

Founded 1885 **Pop** 46,951 **Elev** 1,380 ft **Area code** 541
Information Visitors and Convention Bureau, 101 E 8th St, 97501; 541/779-4847 or 800/469-6307.

Medford is a name known throughout the US for pears: Comice, Bartlett, Winter Nellis, Bosc and d'Anjou. The city, on Bear Creek 10 miles from its confluence with the Rogue River, is surrounded by orchards. Trees make the city parklike; lumbering provides a large share of the industry. Mild winters and warm summers favor outdoor living and also encourage outdoor sports: boating and fishing on the Rogue River, fishing in 153 stocked streams and 17 lakes; camping and hunting in 56 forest camps within an 80-mile radius. The Rogue River National Forest headquarters is here.

What to See and Do

Butte Creek Mill. Water-powered gristmill (1872) grinds whole grain products with original mill stones. Museum (summer, Sat). Mill (daily exc Sun; closed hols). 10 mi N on OR 62 in Eagle Point. Phone 541/826-3531. **Free.**

Crater Rock Museum. Gem and mineral collection; Native American artifacts; fossils, geodes and crystals. Gift shop. (Tues, Thurs & Sat; closed major hols) N on I-5, exit 35 then S on OR 99 in Central Point at 2002 Scenic Ave. Phone 541/664-6081. **Donation.**

Joseph P. Stewart State Park. A 910-acre park located on lake formed by Lost Creek Dam. Swimming; fishing; boat dock & ramp to Rogue River. Hiking, bike trails. Picnicking. Tent & improved campsites (daily; dump station). Some fees. 35 mi NE on OR 62. Phone 541/560-3334.

Rogue River National Forest. Forest has 632,045 acres with extensive stands of Douglas fir, ponderosa and sugar pine. Rogue-Umpqua National Forest Scenic Byway offers a day-long drive through southern Oregon's dramatic panorama of mountains, rivers and forest; viewpoints. A part of the Pacific Crest National Scenic Trail and portions of three wilderness areas are included in the forest. For fishermen, the upper reaches of the Rogue River, other streams and lakes yield rainbow, cutthroat and brook trout. Union Creek Historic District, on OR 62 near Crater Lake National Park. Forest is in two separate sections, located in the Siskiyou Mts (W of I-5) and Cascade Range (E of I-5). Swimming. Hiking, backpacking. Downhill, cross-country skiing. Picnic areas. Camping. Some fees. S off I-5 and NE on OR 62, 140. For further information contact Information Receptionist, PO Box 520, 333 W 8th St; 541/776-3600.

Southern Oregon History Center. More than 2,000 items from Southern Oregon Historical Society's cultural history collection. Exhibits, public programs, research library. Gift shop. (Mon-Fri) 106 N Central Ave. Phone 541/773-6536. **Free.**

Tou Velle State Park. A 51-acre park. Fishing on Rogue River; boat ramp to Rogue River. Picnicking. 3 mi NE on I-5, then 6 mi N on Table Rock Rd. Phone 541/582-1118. ¢

Annual Events

Pear Blossom Festival. Parade; 10-mi run; band festival. 2nd wkend Apr.

Jackson County Fair. Jackson County Fairgrounds. Entertainment, dance, music, 4-H fair. 3rd wkend July.

Motels

★ ★ **BEST WESTERN.** *1015 S Riverside Ave (97501). 541/773-8266; FAX 541/734-5447.* 112 rms, 2 story, 14 suites. May-Oct: S $52-$60; D $58-$65; each addl $6; suites $89; under 12 free. Crib $6. TV; cable. Pool. Complimentary continental bkfst. Complimentary coffee in rms. Restaurant nearby. Bar 10-2 am. Ck-out 11 am. Meeting rms. Business servs avail. Downhill/x-country ski 20 mi. Some microwaves. Cr cds: A, C, D, DS, MC, V.

★ ★ ★ **BEST WESTERN PONY SOLDIER.** *2340 Crater Lake Hwy (97504), just E of I-5 exit 30. 541/779-2011; FAX 541/779-7304.* 72 rms, 2 story. May-Sept: S $75-$82; D $90-$96; each addl $5; under 12 free; lower rates rest of yr. Crib $3. Pet accepted, some restrictions. TV; cable (premium). Heated pool; whirlpool. Complimentary continental bkfst. Restaurant adj open 24 hrs. Ck-out noon. Free guest lndry. In-rm modem link. Downhill/x-country ski 20 mi. Health club privileges. Refrigerators, microwaves. Cr cds: A, C, D, DS, MC, V.

✔★ **CEDAR LODGE.** *518 N Riverside Ave (97501). 541/773-7361; FAX 541/776-1033; res: 800/282-3419.* www.prairieweb.j/arrons/hotel/usa/or/cedarlodge.htm. 79 rms, 1-2 story. May-Oct: S $32-$37; D $38-$45; each addl $5; suites $45-$62; kit. unit $52; under 12 free; wkly rates; lower rates rest of yr. Crib $5. Pet accepted, some restrictions. TV; cable. Heated pool. Restaurant adj 6 am-10 pm. Bar 10-2 am. Ck-out 11 am. Downhill/x-country ski 20 mi. Some microwaves. Cr cds: A, C, D, DS, MC, V.

★ ★ **HORIZON MOTOR INN.** *1154 E Barnett Rd (97504), E of I-5 exit 27. 541/779-5085; res: 800/452-2255.* Web www.horizoninns.com. 129 rms, 2 story. S $50-$58; D $55-$61; each addl $5; suites $100-$150; under 17 free. Crib $5. Pet accepted; $10. TV; cable (premium). Heated pool; whirlpool. Complimentary coffee in lobby. Restaurant 6 am-midnight. Bar. Ck-out noon. Airport transportation. Downhill/x-country ski 20 mi. Sauna. Some microwaves. Cr cds: A, C, D, MC, V.

✔★ **KNIGHTS INN.** *500 N Riverside Ave (97501). 541/773-3676; FAX 541/857-0493; res: 800/626-1900.* 83 rms, 2 story. S $35; D $39-$46; each addl $4. Crib $4. Pet accepted, some resrtictions. TV;

cable. Pool. Restaurant adj 6 am-9 pm. Ck-out 11 am. Downhill/x-country ski 20 mi. Microwaves avail. Cr cds: A, C, D, DS, MC, V.

[D] [≈] [≋] [⚐] [SC]

★ ★ **WINDMILL INN.** *1950 Biddle Rd (97504), I-5 exit 30, near Medford-Jackson County Airport.* 541/779-0050; res: 800/547-4747. 123 rms, 2 story. S $72; D $85; kit. units $95; under 18 free. Crib $3.50. Pet accepted. TV; cable; whirlpool. Complimentary continental bkfst. Restaurant adj 6 am-11 pm. Ck-out 11 am. Meeting rm. Business servs avail. Valet serv. Sundries. Free airport, bus depot transportation. Sauna. Health club privileges. Bicycles. Microwaves avail. Library. Cr cds: A, C, D, DS, MC, V.

[D] [⚐] [≈] [✈] [≋] [⚐] [SC]

Motor Hotels

★ ★ **DOUBLETREE.** *200 N Riverside Ave (97501).* 541/779-5811; FAX 541/779-7961. Web www.doubletreehotel.com. 186 rms, 2 story. S $76-$86; D $79-$89; each addl $10; suites $250; under 18 free. Crib free. Pet accepted; $50 deposit. TV; cable. 2 heated pools. Restaurant 6 am-10 pm; dining rm 11:30 am-2 pm, 5-10 pm; Sun 10 am-2 pm. Rm serv. Bar 3 pm-midnight; Fri, Sat to 2 am; entertainment. Ck-out noon. Coin lndry. Meeting rms. Business servs avail. In-rm modem link. Bellhops. Sundries. Free airport transportation. Downhill/x-country ski 20 mi. Health club privileges. Some private patios, balconies. Cr cds: A, C, D, DS, ER, MC, V.

[D] [⚐] [≈] [≋] [✈] [≋] [⚐] [SC]

✔ ★ ★ **RESTON.** *2300 Crater Lake Hwy (97504), E of I-5 exit 30, near Medford-Jackson County Airport.* 541/779-3141; FAX 541/779-2623; res: 800/779-7829. E-mail maryc@restonhotel.com; web www.restonhotel .com. 164 rms, 2 story. S, D $65; each addl $5; suites $120; under 18 free. Crib free. Pet accepted, some restrictions; $10. TV; cable. Indoor pool. Restaurant 6:30 am-1 pm, 5-10 pm. Rm serv. Bar 5 pm-midnight, Thurs-Sat to 2 am. Ck-out noon. Meeting rms. Business servs avail. Sundries. Airport transportation. Microwaves avail. Cr cds: A, C, D, DS, ER, MC, V.

[D] [⚐] [≈] [✈] [≋] [⚐] [SC]

★ ★ **ROGUE REGENCY INN.** *2345 Crater Lake Hwy (97504), at jct I-5, near Medford-Jackson County Airport.* 541/770-1234; FAX 541/770-2466; res: 800/535-5805. E-mail regency@rogueregency.com; web www.rogueregency.com. 125 rms, 4 story. S $77; D $87; each addl $10; suites $165-$250; under 18 free. Crib free. TV; cable (premium). Heated pool; whirlpool. Restaurant 6 am-10 pm. Rm serv. Bar 4 pm-midnight. Ck-out 11 am. Meeting rms. Free airport, bus depot transportation. Health club privileges. Refrigerators, microwaves, wet bars. Cr cds: A, C, D, DS, ER, JCB, MC, V.

[D] [≈] [✈] [≋] [⚐] [SC]

Restaurant

★ ★ **MON DESIR DINING INN.** *(4615 Hamrick Rd, Central Point 97502) I-5 exit 33 E 1/4 mi, then left on Hamrick Rd 1/4 mi.* 541/664-7558. Web www.so-menu.com. Hrs: 11 am-2 pm, 4-9 pm; Sat from 4 pm. Closed Sun, Mon. Res accepted. Continental menu. Bar. Semi-a la carte: lunch $4.75-$8.95, dinner $11.95-$24.95. Specializes in international cuisine. Outdoor dining. Converted mansion; fireplace, antiques; garden. Cr cds: DS, MC, V.

Mount Hood National Forest (B-5)

(See also Hood River, The Dalles)

(Crossed by US 26, approximately 50 mi E of Portland)

Mount Hood (11,235 ft) is the natural focal point of this 1,064,573-acre forest with headquarters in Gresham. Its white-crowned top, the highest point in Oregon, can be seen for miles on a clear day. It is also popular with skiers, who know it has some of the best slopes in the Northwest. There are five winter sports areas. Throughout the year, however, visitors can take advantage of the surrounding forest facilities for camping (93 camp and picnic sites), hunting, fishing, swimming, mountain climbing, golfing, horseback riding, hiking and tobogganing. The Columbia Gorge, which cuts through the Cascades here, has many spectacular waterfalls, including Multnomah (620 ft). There are nine routes to the summit, which has fumed and smoked several times since the once-volcanic peak was discovered. Only experienced climbers should try the ascent and then only with a guide. For further information contact the Mt Hood Visitor Center, 65000 E US 26, Welches 97067; 503/622-7674.

What to See and Do

River cruise. Two-hr narrated cruise of Columbia Gorge aboard the 599-passenger *Columbia Gorge,* an authentic sternwheeler. (Mid-June-Sept, 3 departures daily; res required for dinner cruise) Also here: museum; marina; travel information; picnicking; camping. 45 mi E of Portland via I-84 in Cascade Locks. Phone 503/223-3928. ¢¢¢¢

Skiing.

Timberline Lodge. Quad, triple, 4 double chairlifts; patrol, school, rentals; restaurant, cafeteria, concession, bar, lodge. Longest run more than 2 mi; vertical drop 3,700 ft. (Mid-Nov-Apr, daily) Chairlift also operates May-Aug (daily, weather permitting; fee). 6 mi N of US 26. Phone 503/272-3311 or 541/231-7979 (info), 541/222-2211 (snow conditions). ¢¢¢¢

Mt Hood Meadows. Quad, triple, 7 double chairlifts, free rope tow; patrol, school, rentals; restaurant, cafeteria, concession, bar, 2 day lodges. Longest run 3 mi; vertical drop 2,777 ft. Also 550 acres of expert canyon skiing. (Nov-May, daily) Groomed, ungroomed cross-country trails; night skiing (Wed-Sun). 11 mi NE of Government Camp on OR 35. Phone 503/337-2222 or 503/227-7669 (snow conditions). ¢¢¢¢

Motel

★ **MT HOOD INN.** *(Box 400, 87450 Government Camp Loop, Government Camp 97028) On US 26.* 503/272-3205; FAX 503/272-3307; res: 800/443-7777. 56 rms, 2 story, 4 suites. No A/C. S, D $95-$135; each addl $10; suites $115; under 12 free. Crib $5. Pet accepted; $5. TV; cable (premium), VCR avail. Complimentary continental bkfst. Restaurant nearby. Ck-out noon. Coin lndry. Meeting rms. Business servs avail. Downhill ski 1/4 mi; x-country ski adj. Whirlpool. Some refrigerators, wet bars. Picnic tables. Cr cds: A, D, DS, MC, V.

[D] [⚐] [≋] [≋] [⚐]

Resorts

★ ★ **RESORT AT THE MOUNTAIN.** *(68010 E Fairway, Welches 97067) Off US 26.* 503/622-3101; FAX 503/622-5677; res: 800/669-7666. 160 rms, 2 story, 60 kit. units. Mid-June-Oct: S, D $99-$155; each addl $20; kit. units from $155; under 18 free; ski, golf plans; lower rates rest of yr. Crib free. TV; VCR avail. Heated pool; whirlpool. Restaurant (see HIGHLANDS). Rm serv. Box lunches. Picnics. Bar 3 pm-1 am; entertainment Sat, Sun. Ck-out noon, ck-in 4 pm. Business servs avail. In-rm modem link. Gift shop. Grocery 1 mi. Coin lndry. Bellhops. Concierge. Valet serv. Sports dir. Social dir. Lighted tennis. 27-hole golf; greens fee $34, pro, putting green. Downhill/x-country ski 18 mi. Hiking trails. Bicycle rentals. Exercise equipt; weight machine, treadmill. Lawn games. Rec rm. Balconies. Picnic tables. 300-acres of forest at Salmon River. Scottish amenities reminiscent of Highlands. Cr cds: A, C, D, DS, JCB, MC, V.

★ ★ **TIMBERLINE LODGE.** *Timberline (97028), 6 mi NE of US 26.* 503/272-3311; FAX 503/272-3710; res: 800/547-1406. 70 rms, 4 story. No A/C. S, D $62-$162; with fireplace $162; each addl $15; under 11 free; ski package plans. Crib free. TV in 60 rms; cable, VCR avail (movies). Pool; whirlpool, sauna. Supervised child's activities (Dec-Mar); ages 4-12. Dining rm 8-10 am, noon-2 pm, 6-8:30 pm. Snack bar. Bars 11 am-11 pm. Ck-out noon, ck-in 4 pm. Business servs avail. Downhill ski on site. Some fireplaces. Rustic rms; hand-carved furniture. Cr cds: A, DS, MC, V.

Restaurants

★ ★ **B CRISTEN'S CHALET SWISS.** *(24371 E Welches Rd, Welches 97067) Off US 26.* 503/622-3600. Hrs: 5-10 pm; Sun to 9 pm. Closed Thanksgiving, Dec 24-25. Res accepted. Continental menu. Bar. Semi-a la carte: dinner $11.95-$18.95. Child's meals. Specializes in seafood, steak, pasta. Cr cds: A, DS, MC, V.

D

★ ★ ★ **HIGHLANDS.** *(See Resort At The Mountain)* 503/622-3101. Hrs: 7 am-9 pm; Sun brunch 10 am-2 pm. Res accepted. Bar to 1 am. Wine list. Semi-a la carte: bkfst $3.95-$7.95, lunch $5.50-$12, dinner $9.95-$19.95. Sun brunch $17.95. Child's meals. Specializes in prime rib, salmon, Northwest cuisine. Pianist Fri, Sat. Outdoor dining. Bright and cheerful atmosphere; view of pool and gardens. Totally nonsmoking. Cr cds: A, D, DS, MC, V.

D SC

★ ★ **SALAZAR'S OLD OREGON TRAIL.** *(71545 E US 26, Rhododendron)* W on US 26. 503/622-3775. Hrs: 4-10 pm; Sat & Sun from 6 am. Closed Tues. Res accepted; required hols. No A/C. Bar. Semi-a la carte: bkfst $1.99-$6.99, lunch $2.99-$6.99, dinner $6.95-$19.95. Child's meals. Specializes in pasta, seafood, steak. Many antiques. Cr cds: A, DS, MC, V.

Newberg (B-4)

(See also Beaverton, Hillsboro, McMinnville, Oregon City, Portland, Salem)

Founded 1889 **Pop** 13,086 **Elev** 176 ft **Area code** 503 **Zip** 97132
Information Chamber of Commerce, 115 N Washington; 503/538-2014.

Quakers made their first settlement west of the Rockies here and established Pacific Academy in 1885. Herbert Hoover was in its first graduating class (1888).

What to See and Do

Champoeg State Park. A 615-acre park on site of early Willamette River settlement, site of settlers' vote in 1843 for a provisional territorial government, swept away by flood of 1861. Fishing; boat dock on Willamette River. Hiking. Picnicking. Improved camping (dump station). Standard fees. Visitor information, interpretive center; monument. French Prairie Loop 40-mi auto or bike tour begins and ends here. (See SEASONAL EVENT) 5 mi W off I-5. Phone 503/678-1251. Per vehicle (Memorial Day wkend-Labor Day, wkends & hols) ¢¢ In the area are

Pioneer Mother's Memorial Log Cabin. A replica, much enlarged, of the type of log cabin built by early pioneers. Constructed of peeled hand-hewn logs, with a shake roof, it has a massive stone fireplace in the living room, a sleeping loft and two small bedrms; many pioneer items including an old Hudson's Bay heating stove, collection of guns & muskets dating from 1777-1853, a fife played at Lincoln's funeral, china

& glassware and original furnishings from pioneer homes. (Feb-Nov, Wed-Sun; closed Thanksgiving) Located in the park, on the banks of the Willamette River, at 8035 Champoeg Rd NE. Phone 503/633-2237. ¢

Newell House Museum. Reconstructed home of Robert Newell, onetime mountain man and friend of the Native Americans. Contains period furnishings, quilts, coverlets and examples of fine handiwork; collection of inaugural gowns worn by wives of Oregon governors; Native American artifacts. Old jail (1850) and typical pioneer one-rm schoolhouse. (Feb-Nov, Wed-Sun; closed Thanksgiving) Just W of park entrance at 8089 Champoeg Rd NE. Phone 503/678-5537. ¢

Visitor Center. Interpretive historical exhibits tell the story of "Champoeg: Birthplace of Oregon" films; tours. (Memorial Day-Labor Day, daily; winter Mon-Fri) 8239 Champoeg Rd NE. Phone 503/678-1251. **Donation.**

George Fox College (1891). (1,700 students) Founded as Pacific Academy; renamed in 1949 for English founder of the Society of Friends. Herbert Hoover was a student here; Hoover Bldg has displays. Brougher Museum has Quaker and pioneer exhibits. Campus tours. 414 N Meridian. Phone 503/538-8383, ext 222.

Hoover-Minthorn House Museum. Herbert Hoover lived here with his uncle, Dr. Henry Minthorn. Quaker house built in 1881 contains many original furnishings, photographs and souvenirs of Hoover's boyhood. (Mar-Nov, Wed-Sun; Dec & Feb, Sat & Sun; closed Jan) 115 S River St. Phone 503/538-6629. ¢

Seasonal Event

Vintage Celebration. Classic automobiles & airplanes, arts, wine tasting. Sat after Labor Day.

Motel

★ ★ **SHILO INN.** *501 Sitka Ave.* 503/537-0303; FAX 503/537-0442. 60 rms, 3 story. S, D $65-$79; each addl $10; suites $75; kit. units $79; under 12 free. Crib free. Pet accepted; $7/day. TV; cable (premium), VCR avail. Heated pool; whirlpool. Complimentary continental bkfst, coffee. Restaurant nearby. Ck-out noon. Coin lndry. Meeting rms. Business servs avail. Valet serv. Sundries. Exercise equipt; weights, bicycles, sauna. Bathrm phones, refrigerators, wet bars. Cr cds: A, C, D, DS, ER, JCB, MC, V.

Newport (C-3)

(See also Depoe Bay, Lincoln City, Yachats)

Settled 1882 **Pop** 8,437 **Elev** 160 ft **Area code** 541 **Zip** 97365 **E-mail** chamber@newportnet.com **Web** www.newport.net
Information Chamber of Commerce, 555 SW Coast Hwy; 541/265-8801 or 800/262-7844.

This fishing port at the mouth of the Yaquina River has been a resort for more than 100 years. Crabbing is a popular activity here; Dungeness crabs can be caught in the bay year-round.

What to See and Do

Hatfield Marine Science Center of Oregon State University. Conducts research on oceanography, fisheries, water quality, marine science education and marine biology; research vessel *Wecoma*; nature trail; aquarium-museum; films; special programs in summer. Winter & spring grey whale programs. Braille text and other aids for the hearing and visually impaired. (Daily; closed Dec 25) Marine Science Dr, S side of Yaquina Bay, just E of Newport Bridge, off US 101. Phone 541/867-0100. **Free.**

Lincoln County Historical Society Museums. Log Cabin Museum. Artifacts from Siletz Reservation; historical, pioneer and maritime exhibits.

(Daily exc Mon; closed Jan 1, Thanksgiving, Dec 25) 545 SW 9th St. Also **Burrows House Museum.** Victorian-era household furnishings, clothing; history of Lincoln County. (Same days as log cabin museum) 579 SW 9th St. Phone 541/265-7509.   **Free.**

Mineral collecting. Gemstones, marine fossils, other stones are found on beaches to N and S of Newport, particularly at creek mouths.

Oregon Coast Aquarium. Houses 190 species in unique habitats. Home of Keiko, the orca whale of *Free Willy* fame. (Daily; closed Dec 25) S side of Yaquina Bay. 2820 SE Ferry Slip Rd. Phone 541/867-3474.   ¢¢¢

Ripley's—Believe It or Not. Exhibits include replicas of a backwards fountain; King Tut's tomb; the Titanic; the Fiji mermaid. (Daily; closed Dec 25) 250 SW Bay Blvd. Phone 541/265-2206.   ¢¢¢

State parks.

Yaquina Bay. Over 30 acres. Ocean beach, fishing, picnicking. Agate beaches nearby. Old Yaquina Bay Lighthouse (1871) has been restored; exhibits. (Memorial Day-Labor Day, daily; rest of yr, wkends) N end of bridge on US 101. Phone 541/867-7451. **Donation.**

South Beach. Over 400 acres. Botanically interesting area, sandy beach, dunes. Fishing. Hiking. Picnicking. Improved campsites (dump station). Standard fees. 2 mi S on US 101. Phone 541/867-4715 or 541/867-7451.

Beverly Beach. A 130-acre park with beach access; fishing. Hiking. Picnicking. Tent & trailer sites (dump station, laundry tubs). Standard fees. 7 mi N on US 101. Phone 541/265-9278 or 800/452-5687.

Ona Beach. A 237-acre day-use park with ocean beach, swimming; fishing, boat ramp on creek. Picnicking. 8 mi S on US 101. Phone 541/867-7451.

Devil's Punch Bowl. An 8-acre park noted for its bowl-shaped rock formation that fills at high tide; ocean-carved caves, marine gardens. Beach. Trails. Picnicking. Observation point. 8 mi N off US 101. Phone 541/265-9278.

Undersea Gardens. Visitors descend beneath the sea for underwater show. Watch native sea life through viewing windows; guides narrate as scuba divers perform; features Armstrong, the giant octopus. (Daily; closed Dec 25) 250 SW Bay Blvd, on Yaquina Bay just off US 101 in the Bay Front district. Phone 541/265-2206.   ¢¢¢

Wax Works. Events of the past and future shown with animation and special effects. (Daily; closed Dec 25) 250 SW Bay Blvd. Phone 541/265-2206.   ¢¢¢

Yaquina Head. Lighthouse here is a popular spot for whale-watching and fully accessible tidal pool viewing. Also interpretive center. ½ mi N on US 101.

Annual Events

Seafood and Wine Festival. Last full wkend Feb.

Loyalty Days and Sea Fair Festival. Military ships, parade, sailboat races; entertainment. Phone 541/265-8801. 1st wkend May.

Motels

★ ★ **LITTLE CREEK COVE.** *3641 NW Ocean View Dr, just off US 101. 541/265-8587; FAX 541/265-4576; res: 800/294-8025.* E-mail lcc@newportnet.com; web www.newportnet.com/lcc. 29 kit. units, 2-3 story. No elvtr. S, D $99-$215; each addl $10. TV; cable (premium), VCR. Restaurant nearby. Ck-out noon. Business servs avail. Microwaves, fireplaces. Beach access. Cr cds: A, C, D, DS, MC, V.

★ ★ **SHILO INN OCEAN FRONT RESORT.** *536 SW Elizabeth St, just W of US 101. 541/265-7701; FAX 541/265-5687.* 179 rms, 4 story, 10 kits. Mid-June-mid-Sept: S, D $149-$205; each addl $15; kit. suites $199-$395; lower rates rest of yr. Pet accepted, some restrictions; $7/day. TV; cable (premium), VCR. Indoor pools. Restaurant 7 am-10 pm. Rm serv. Bar 11-2 am; entertainment Fri, Sat. Ck-out noon. Meeting rms. Coin

Indry. Business servs avail. Free airport transportation. Refrigerators, microwaves. On beach. Cr cds: A, C, D, DS, ER, JCB, MC, V.

★ **WHALER.** *155 SW Elizabeth St. 541/265-9261; FAX 541/265-9515; res: 800/433-9444.* 73 rms, 3 story. No elvtr. S, D $91-$135; package plans off-season. Crib $5. Pet accepted, some restrictions. TV; cable (premium). Continental bkfst. Restaurant nearby. Ck-out noon. Coin Indry. Free airport, bus depot transportation. Some refrigerators, microwaves. Ocean view. Cr cds: A, D, DS, MC, V.

Motor Hotel

★ ★ **EMBARCADERO.** *1000 SE Bay Blvd. 541/265-8521; FAX 541/265-7844; res: 800/547-4779.* 85 units, 3 story, 50 kits., 36 patio suites. No elvtr. June-Oct: S, D $109.95-$219.95; lower rates rest of yr. TV; cable, VCR avail. Indoor pool; whirlpools. Restaurant 7 am-9 pm. Bar 11 am-midnight. Ck-out noon. Coin Indry. Meeting rms. Business servs avail. Sundries. Airport transportation. Sauna. Marina; boat rentals. Private balconies. View of bay. Cr cds: A, C, D, DS, MC, V.

Restaurant

★ **WHALE'S TALE.** *452 SW Bay Blvd. 541/265-8660.* Hrs: 8 am-10 pm; Sat, Sun from 9 am. Closed Dec 24, 25; Jan 2-Feb 14; Wed in spring, fall, winter. Wine, beer. Semi-a la carte: bkfst $4-$8, lunch $4-$7, dinner $10.95-$18.95. Child's meals. Specializes in seafood, natural foods. Nautical decor. Local artwork. Cr cds: A, D, DS, MC, V.

North Bend (D-3)

(See also Bandon, Coos Bay, Reedsport)

Settled 1853 **Pop** 9,614 **Elev** 23 ft **Area code** 541 **Zip** 97459 **E-mail** bacc@ucinet.com **Web** www.ucinet.com/~bacc

Information Bay Area Chamber of Commerce, PO Box 210, Coos Bay 97420; 541/269-0215 or 800/824-8486. North Bend Information Center is located at 1380 Sherman Ave in town, phone 541/756-4613.

Commercial fisheries, lumbering and manufacturing thrive in this city on a peninsula in Coos Bay.

What to See and Do

Coos County Historical Society Museum. Local history; permanent and changing exhibits. (Tues-Sat) In Simpson Park, on US 101, N edge of town. Phone 541/756-6320 or 541/756-4847.   ¢

Oregon Dunes National Recreation Area. Area is 2 mi wide and 40 mi long. One of largest bodies of sand outside of the Sahara. (See REEDSPORT).

The Real Oregon Gift. Manufacturers of myrtlewood products. Tour of factory; gift shop. (Daily) 5 mi N on US 101. Phone 541/756-2220.   **Free.**

Motel

✔★ **BAY BRIDGE.** *33 US 101. 541/756-3151; res: 800/557-3156.* 16 rms, 3 kit. units. May-Oct: S $42-$52; D $52-$60; each addl $5; kit. units $59-$65; under 3 free; lower rates rest of yr. Crib $2. Pet accepted, some restrictions; $5/day. TV; cable. Complimentary coffee in lobby. Restaurant nearby. Ck-out 11 am. Some refrigerators. On Pacific Bay. Cr cds: A, C, D, DS, MC, V.

Restaurant

★ ★ **HILLTOP HOUSE.** *166 N Bay Dr. 541/756-4160.* Hrs: 11:30 am-2:30 pm, 4-10 pm. Res accepted. Semi-a la carte: lunch $4.25-$14.95, dinner $7.25-$29.95. Specializes in steak, seafood, pasta. View of bay harbor and sand dunes. Cr cds: A, MC, V.

Ontario (D-10)

(See also Caldwell, ID, Weiser, ID)

Founded 1883 **Pop** 9,392 **Elev** 2,154 ft **Area code** 541 **Zip** 97914
Information Visitors & Convention Bureau, 88 SW 3rd Ave; 541/889-8012 or 888/889-8012.

Ontario, the largest town in Malheur County, is a trading center at the eastern border of Oregon. Irrigation from the Snake River has made possible the cultivation of sugar beets, potatoes, onions, corn, hay and alfalfa seed, but there is still a vast wilderness of rangeland, lakes and reservoirs, mountains and canyons. Quartz crystals, jaspers, thundereggs, marine fossils, petrified wood and obsidian are abundant in the area.

What to See and Do

Fishing and hunting. Rainbow trout, crappie and bass are plentiful. Mallard and Canada geese are found on the Snake River; sage grouse, chukars, antelope, mule deer in the sagebrush areas; pheasant on irrigated land.

Owyhee Canyon. Fossils and utensils of Native Americans; petroglyphs. Boating. Fishing and hunting.

State parks.

Lake Owyhee. A 730-acre park with 52-mi-long lake created by Owyhee Dam. Fishing; boating (ramp). Picnicking. Improved camping (dump station). Standard fees. 33 mi SW off OR 201. Phone 541/339-2444.

Farewell Bend. A 72-acre park named by pioneers who left the Snake River at this point in their trek west. Swimming beach (bathhouse); fishing; boat ramp. Picnicking. Primitive & improved camping (dump station). Standard fees. 25 mi NW on I-84. Phone 541/869-2365.

Ontario. A 35-acre day-use area. Fishing; boat ramp. Picnicking. On I-84 at N end of town. Phone 541/869-2365.

Annual Events

American Musical Jubilee. Early June.

Obon Festival. Japanese dancing, food; art show. Mid-July.

Malheur County Fair. 1st wk Aug.

Motels

★ ★ **BEST WESTERN INN.** *251 Goodfellow St, I-84 exit 376. 541/889-2600; FAX 541/889-2259.* 61 rms, 2 story, 12 suites. S $51-$56; D $53-$72; each addl $4; suites $85-$95; under 14 free. Pet accepted, some restrictions; $30. TV; cable. Indoor pool. Complimentary continental bkfst. Restaurant nearby. Ck-out noon. Coin lndry. Exercise equipt; weight machine, bicycles. Some minibars. Refrigerator in suites. Cr cds: A, C, D, DS, ER, JCB, MC, V.

✔ ★ **COLONIAL MOTOR INN.** *1395 Tapadera Ave. 541/889-9615; res: 800/727-5014.* 84 rms, 2 story. S $27-$36; D $42-$45. Crib $2. TV; cable. Indoor pool; whirlpool. Restaurant adj 6 am-10 pm. Ck-out 11:30 am. Business servs avail. In-rm modem link. Sundries. Cr cds: A, DS, MC, V.

★ **HOLIDAY.** *615 E Idaho Ave, I-84, exit 376. 541/889-9188; FAX 541/889-4303.* 72 rms, 2 story. S $28.95; D $38.95; each addl $5. Crib $5. Pet accepted. TV; cable (premium). Heated pool. Restaurant open 24 hrs. Ck-out 11 am. Meeting rm. Business servs avail. Cr cds: A, D, DS, MC, V.

★ ★ **HOLIDAY INN.** *1249 Tapadera Ave. 541/889-8621; res: 800/525-5333 (exc OR), 800/345-5333 (OR).* 100 rms, 2 story. S $50-$58; D $54-$62; each addl $4; suites $58-$62; under 18 free. Crib free. TV; cable. Heated pool. Restaurant 6 am-midnight. Rm serv. Ck-out noon. Meeting rms. Local airport, RR station, bus depot transportation. Some private patios, balconies. Cr cds: A, C, D, DS, MC, V.

✔ ★ **MOTEL 6.** *275 NE 12th St, off I-84 exit 376 & US 30 Payette exit. 541/889-6617; FAX 541/889-8232.* 126 rms, 2 story. S $26.95; D $32.95; each addl $3; under 18 free. Crib free. TV; cable (premium). Heated pool (seasonal). Restaurants nearby. Ck-out noon. Cr cds: A, C, D, DS, MC, V.

★ **SUPER 8.** *266 Goodfellow St, I-84 exit 376. 541/889-8282; FAX 541/881-1400.* 63 rms, 2 story. S $44-$47; D $46-$52; each addl $4; under 13 free. TV; cable (premium). Indoor pool. Complimentary continental bkfst. Restaurant nearby. Ck-out 11 am. Coin lndry. Cr cds: A, C, D, DS, ER, MC, V.

Restaurant

★ ★ **NICHOLS STEAK HOUSE.** *(411 SW 3rd St, Fruitland 83619) Just off I-84 Fruitland exit. 208/452-3030.* Hrs: 11 am-9 pm; Fri to 10 pm; Sat 4-10 pm; Sun noon-8 pm. Closed Mon; hols. Wine, beer. Semi-a la carte: bkfst $1.50-$4, lunch $3-$10, dinner $9-$25. Child's meals. Specializes in prime rib, 22-oz T-bone. Salad bar. Western decor; antiques. Paintings by local artists. Cr cds: DS, MC, V.

Oregon Caves National Monument (F-3)

(For accommodations see Grants Pass; also see Cave Junction)

(20 mi E of Cave Junction on OR 46)

This area was discovered in 1874, when hunter Elijah Davidson followed a bear into the cave. After a visit in 1907, frontier poet Joaquin Miller called this "The Marble Halls of Oregon." In 1909 the cave and 480 acres of the Siskiyou Mts were made a national monument.

The cave has many chambers—Paradise Lost, Joaquin Miller's Chapel, Ghost Room and others. Guide service is required. The average temperature is 42°F. Evening talks are given by National Park Service naturalists in summer.

On the surface, the area is covered with a beautiful transition mountainside forest with abundant wildlife, birds, wildflowers and an interesting variety of trees and shrubs. A maintained and marked system of trails provides access to these areas; stay on the trail.

Forest Service campgrounds (fee) are located 4 mi and 8 mi NW on OR 46 in Siskiyou National Forest (see GRANTS PASS). (2nd Sat June-Labor Day) Phone 541/592-2166.

Cave tours (daily; closed Thanksgiving, Dec 25). Children under age 6 must be at least 3'-6" (42 inches) in height and complete a step test to be permitted into the cave. Cave tours are strenuous; recommended only for those in good physical condition. A jacket and walking shoes with nonslip soles should be worn. Lodge, dining rm (May-mid-Oct). For further information contact Oregon Caves Co, 19000 Caves Hwy, Cave Junction 97523; 541/592-3400. Cave tours ¢¢¢

Oregon City (B-4)

(See also Beaverton, Forest Grove, Newburg, Portland, Salem)

Settled 1829 **Pop** 14,698 **Elev** 55 ft **Area code** 503 **Zip** 97045
Information Oregon City Chamber of Commerce and Visitors Center, PO Box 226; 503/656-1619.

Below Willamette Falls, where the river spills over a 42-foot drop, is historic Oregon City. Steamers were built here in the 1850s and locks around the falls opened the upriver to navigation in 1873. Salmon fishing in the Willamette and Clackamas rivers is from early March-mid-May. The city is built on terraces and there is an enclosed elevator to an observation platform.

What to See and Do

Holmes Family Home (Rose Farm). Oldest standing American home in Oregon City, built in 1847. First Territorial governor gave his first address here in 1849; the upstairs ballroom was the scene of many social events. (Sun; closed hols & Jan-Feb) Holmes Lane & Rilance St. Phone 503/656-5146. ¢

John Inskeep Environmental Learning Center. Eight acres developed on former industrial site to demonstrate wildlife habitat in an urban setting. Includes extensive birds of prey exhibits, various plant and wildlife displays and plant nursery. Haggart Astronomical Observatory (Wed, Fri, Sat; fee). 19600 S Molalla on N side of Clackamas Community College's campus. Phone 503/657-6958, ext 2351. ¢

McLoughlin House National Historic Site. Georgian frame building built in 1845-1846 by Dr. John McLoughlin, chief factor of the Hudson's Bay Company, who ruled the Columbia River region from 1824-1846. Period furnishings; many are original pieces, most having come around Cape Horn on sailing ships. (Daily exc Mon; closed hols, also Jan) 713 Center St between 7th & 8th Sts. Phone 503/656-5146. ¢¢

Milo McIver State Park. On the Clackamas River, this 937-acre park offers a panoramic view of Mt Hood. Fishing; boating (ramp to river). Hiking, horseback trails. Picnicking. Improved campsites (dump station). Standard fees. 4 mi N on OR 213, then 12 mi SE via OR 212, 211. Phone 503/630-7150.

Oregon Trail Interpretive Center. Exhibits on journey made by early settlers over the Oregon Trail. (Daily; closed major hols) 1726 Washington St. Phone 503/657-9336. ¢

Stevens Crawford Museum (Mertie Stevens Residence, 1907). 15 furnished period rms. Working kitchen, bedrms, living rm, dining rm; doll collection. (Feb-Dec, daily exc Mon) 603 6th St. Phone 503/655-2866. ¢¢

The Old Aurora Colony Museum. Complex of buildings forming historical museum of the Aurora Colony, a German religious communal society, founded by Dr. William Keil (1856-1883). Includes Kraus House (1863), a colony house with original artifacts; Steinbach Cabin (1876); wash house used by colony women for washing, soap-making and canning; herb garden divided into various uses—teas, cooking, medicinal, fragrances. Exhibits of furniture, musical instruments, quilts, tools. Tours. (June-Aug, daily exc Mon; rest of yr, Wed-Sun; closed hols; also Jan) 15 mi SW via OR 99E at 15018 2nd St NE in Aurora. Phone 503/678-5754. ¢¢

Willamette Falls Locks. National Historical site; oldest multi-lift navagation lock, built 1873. Four locks, canal basin and guard lock operated by US Army Corps of Engineers. Picnic areas. Information Center. (Daily) On Willamette River, in West Linn. Phone 503/656-3381. **Free.**

Motor Hotel

★ **VAL-U INN.** *1900 Clackamette Dr at McLoughlin Blvd, just off I-205.* 503/655-7141; FAX 503/655-1927; res: 800/443-7777. 120 rms, 4 story. S $61; D $71-$76; each addl $5; suites $120; under 12 free. Crib $5. Pet accepted, some restrictions; $5. TV; cable (premium). Heated pool; whirlpool. Restaurant 6 am-10 pm; Sun 7 am-9 pm. Rm serv. Bar noon-1 am. Ck-out noon. Most balconies overlook river. Cr cds: A, C, D, DS, MC, V.

Pendleton (A-8)

(See also Hermiston, La Grande, Umatilla)

Founded 1868 **Pop** 15,126 **Elev** 1,068 ft **Area code** 541 **Zip** 97801
Information Chamber of Commerce, 501 S Main; 541/276-7411 or 800/547-8911.

Located on the old Oregon Trail, Pendleton is a trading center for the extensive cattle, wheat and green pea production in the area. Seat of Umatilla County, it is famous for its annual Round-up.

What to See and Do

Emigrant Springs State Park. A 23-acre park near summit of Blue Mts (nearly 4,000 ft); ponderosa pine forest. Winter sports. Picnicking, lodge. Tent & trailer sites. Oregon Trail display. Standard fees. 26 mi SE off I-84. Phone 541/983-2277.

Hamley's Western Store. Makers of fine Western saddles, custom leathercraft since 1883. Saddle making demonstrated. Tours (daily). 30 SE Court. Phone 541/276-2321. **Free.**

Pendleton Woolen Mills. Woolen manufacturing; carding, spinning, rewinding and weaving processes. Guided tours (30 min; Mon-Fri). 1307 SE Court Place. Phone 541/276-6911. **Free.**

Ukiah-Dale Forest State Park. A 3,000-acre scenic forest canyon extending along Camas Creek and N Fork of John Day River. Fishing. Camping. Standard fees. 50 mi S on US 395. Phone 541/983-2277.

⭐ **Umatilla Indian Reservation.** Created by the Walla Walla Valley Treaty of 1855. Firsthand view and understanding of a Native American community in transition. Historic significance as well as a lifestyle different from modern-day, American-style development. One of the first Catholic missions in the US is here. Reservation always open for unguided touring. Indian Lake has good fishing, camping and beautiful scenery. The foothills and lowlands of the Blue Mts provide excellent upland game and waterfowl hunting. In addition, the Umatilla Tribes have reestablished runs of chinook salmon and steelhead within the Umatilla River. Some fees. 5 mi E via Mission Hwy (US 30). Phone 541/276-3873.

Umatilla National Forest. More than one million acres, partly in Washington. Lewis and Clark passed through this region on the Columbia River in 1805. Includes spectacular views of the Tucannon, Umatilla, Grande Ronde, N Fork John Day and Wenaha River canyons. Remnants of historic gold mining can be found in the Granite, OR, area in sight of the Greenhorn Mt Range. N Fork John Day, N Fork Umatilla and the Wenaha-Tucannon wilderness areas may be reached on horseback or on foot. Stream fishing (steelhead, rainbow trout), big-game hunting (elk, deer); boating, river rafting. Hiking. Skiing, snowmobiling. Picnicking. Camping (fee at some campgrounds). NE & S of Pendleton. Reached by I-84, US 395, OR 11, 204, 82, 244, 207 & WA 12. For further information phone 541/276-3811. In forest are

Ski areas. Spout Springs. 21 mi NE on OR 11 to Weston, then 20 mi E on OR 204 to Tollgate (see LA GRANDE). **Ski Bluewood.** 45 mi NE to Walla Walla, WA, 29 mi NE on WA 12 to Dayton, then 23 mi SE on country road.

Annual Event

Pendleton Round-up. Stadium. Rodeo and pageantry of Old West, annually since 1910. Gathering of Native Americans, PRCA working cowboys and thousands of visitors. Phone 800/457-6336. Mid-Sept.

Motels

(Rates are higher during Pendleton Roundup)

★ **CHAPARRAL.** *SW 620 Tutuilla Rd, just S of I-84 exit 209.* 541/276-8654; FAX 541/276-5808. 51 rms, 1-3 story, 2 kits. S $39-$46; D $45-$48; each addl $5; kit. units $57-$60. Crib $4. Pet accepted; $5. TV; cable (premium). Complimentary coffee in rms, lobby. Restaurant adj open 24 hrs. Ck-out 11 am. Cr cds: A, D, DS, MC, V.

★ **TAPADERA INN.** *105 SE Court Ave.* 541/276-3231; FAX 541/276-0754; res: 800/722-8277. 47 rms, 2 story. Mid-May-mid-Sept: S $32.50-$42; D $38-$47; each addl $5; under 13 free; lower rates rest of yr. Crib $5. Pet accepted; $5. TV; cable (premium). Restaurant 6:30 am-9 pm. Rm serv. Bar 11-2 am. Ck-out noon. Meeting rms. Business servs avail. Cr cds: A, C, D, DS, MC, V.

✔★ **VAGABOND INN.** *201 SW Court Ave.* 541/276-5252; FAX 541/278-1213. 51 rms, 2 story. June-Sept: S $32-$36; D $40-$46; each addl $5; under 16 free; lower rates rest of yr. Closed during Pendleton Roundup. Crib free. Pet accepted; $5. TV; cable, VCR avail. Pool. Complimentary continental bkfst. Restaurant nearby. Ck-out noon. Cr cds: A, C, D, DS, MC, V.

Motor Hotel

★ ★ ★ **DOUBLETREE AT INDIAN HILLS.** *304 SE Nye Ave, at I-84N exit 210.* 541/276-6111; FAX 541/278-2413. 168 rms, 3 story. S $71; D $71-$81; each addl $10; under 18 free; wknd rates. Crib free. Pet accepted. TV. Heated pool. Restaurant 6 am-10:30 pm. Rm serv. Bar; entertainment. Ck-out noon. Meeting rms. Business servs avail. Free airport, RR station, bus depot transportation. Private patios, balconies. Cr cds: A, C, D, DS, ER, MC, V.

Restaurant

★ ★ **CIMMIYOTTI'S.** *137 S Main St.* 541/276-4314. Hrs: 4 pm-10 pm; Fri, Sat to 11 pm. Closed Sun. Res accepted. Bar. Semi-a la carte: dinner $8-$17. Child's meals. Specializes in beef, chicken, fish. Western motif. Cr cds: A, DS, MC, V.

Portland (B-4)

Founded 1851 **Pop** 437,319 **Elev** 77 ft **Area code** 503 **Web** www @pova.com

Information Portland Oregon Visitors Association, 26 SW Salmon St, 97204; 503/222-2223 or 888/606-6363.

Suburbs Beaverton, Forest Grove, Hillsboro, Newburg, Oregon City; also Vancouver, WA. (See individual alphabetical listings.)

Oregon's largest city sprawls across both banks of the Willamette River, just south of its confluence with the Columbia. The lush and fertile Willamette Valley brings it beauty and riches. Portland's freshwater harbor is visited by more than 1,400 vessels annually from throughout the world.

The city enjoys plentiful electric power, captured from river waters, which drives scores of industries with minimal amounts of smoke or smog.

Portland is surrounded by spectacular scenery. The Columbia River Gorge, Mt Hood, waterfalls, forests, ski slopes, fishing streams, hunting and camping areas are within easy access. It attracts many conventions, for which it is well-equipped with four large auditoriums, the Memorial Coliseum Complex and the Oregon Convention Center. Portland's reputation as "The City of Roses" is justified by its leadership in rose culture, as seen in its International Rose Test Garden and celebrated during the annual Portland Rose Festival, which attracts visitors worldwide. Mount St Helens (see WASHINGTON), in Washington's Gifford Pinchot National Forest, 50 miles to the northeast, can be seen from numerous vantage points in Portland.

Portland is also an educational center with Portland State University, the University of Portland (1901), Lewis & Clark College (1867) and Reed College (1911).

Transportation

Car Rental Agencies: See IMPORTANT TOLL-FREE NUMBERS.

Public Transportation: Buses, MAX light rail trains (Tri-County Metropolitan Transportation District), phone 503/238-RIDE.

Rail Passenger Service: Amtrak 800/872-7245.

Airport Information

Portland Intl Airport: Information 503/460-4234; lost and found 503/460-4277; weather 503/275-9792; cash machines, Main Terminal, N & S ends of Oregon Market Place.

What to See and Do

American Advertising Museum. Museum devoted to the history and evolution of advertising and its impact on culture. Permanent and changing exhibits on print and broadcast advertising; reference library. (Wed-Sun; closed hols) 50 SW 2nd Ave. Phone 503/226-0000. ¢¢

Children's Museum. Hands-on play spaces include grocery store, baby rm and clay shop. (Daily; closed major hols) 3037 SW 2nd Ave. Phone 503/823-2227. ¢¢

Council Crest Park. Highest point in Portland (1,073 ft) for views of Tualatin Valley, Willamette River, Mt Hood, Mt St Helens. S on SW Greenway Ave (follow blue and white scenic tour signs). Phone 503/823-2223. **Free.**

Crystal Springs Rhododendron Garden. Approx 2,500 rhododendrons of 1,000 varieties and other woodland plants in woodland setting (more than 6 acres) and formal gardens with lake. (Daily) SE 28th Ave, N of SE Woodstock Blvd. Phone 503/823-2223. ¢

Forest Park. Park has 4,800 acres of wilderness with 50 mi of hiking trails. Wildwood Trail begins at the Vietnam Veterans Living Memorial in Hoyt Arboretum and extends 27 mi, ending deep in the park beyond Germantown Rd. Bird-watching; small wild animals. Picnicking. (Daily) Off US 30, NW of Fremont Bridge. Phone 503/228-8733. A map is avail from Hoyt Arboretum visitor center or phone 503/823-2223. **Free.**

Gray Line bus tours. Contact 4320 N Suttle Rd, PO Box 17306, 97217; 503/285-9845 or 800/422-7042.

Grotto—The National Sanctuary of Our Sorrowful Mother. Religious sanctuary and botanical garden on 62 acres and 2 levels, created in 1924. Grotto carved in 110-ft cliff is surrounded by gardens. Elevator to the Natural Gallery in the woods featuring more than 100 statues. Landscaped top level with meditation chapel overlooking the Columbia River & Mt St Helens (fee). (Daily; closed Thanksgiving, Dec 25) NE 85th Ave at Sandy Blvd, on OR 30. Phone 503/254-7371. ¢

Howell Territorial Park and The Bybee House (1858). Restored house of early settlers; period furnishings. Pioneer orchard, agricultural museum on grounds. (June-Labor Day, wkend afternoons) 12 mi N via US 30, cross bridge to Sauvie Island, 1 mi W to Howell Territorial Park Rd. Phone 503/621-3344 or 503/222-1741. **Donation.**

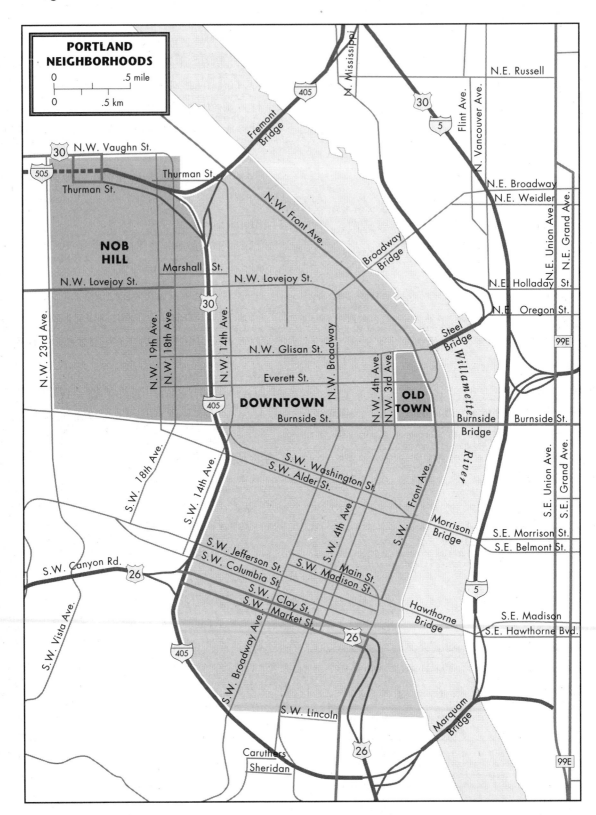

PORTLAND NEIGHBORHOODS

0   .5 mile

0   .5 km

Hoyt Arboretum. More than 214 acres, with displays of more than 700 kinds of woody plants and one of the nation's largest collections of needle-bearing trees; self-guided trails with Vietnam Veterans Living Memorial. Also guided nature walk (Apr-Oct, Sat & Sun afternoons). Park and visitor center (daily). Picnicking. 4000 SW Fairview Blvd. Phone 503/228-8733. **Free.**

Lewis & Clark College (1867). (3,400 students) Memorial Rose Garden with 1,500 plants; Tudor mansion (Mon-Fri), formal gardens. Tours of campus. SW Palatine Hill Rd, 3 mi E of I-5 Terwilliger exit. Phone 503/768-7000.

Metro Washington Park Zoo. Specializes in breeding rare and endangered species. Features Asian elephants, Humboldt penguins, chimpanzees, Oregon native plants and animals; bears; musk oxen; wolves; animals of the African plains & rain forests. Train travels through zoo to Washington Park, stopping near the International Rose Test Garden and Japanese gardens (fee). (Daily; closed Dec 25) 4001 SW Canyon Ct. Phone 503/226-1561. ¢¢¢

Mt Hood-Columbia Gorge Loop Scenic Drive. This 163-mi scenic drive along the Columbia River and through Mount Hood National Forest (see) offers splendid views of the river basin, visits to waterfalls, many state parks and spectacular mountain scenery. Drive E 17 mi on US 30, I-84 to Troutdale. At this point, for approx 24 mi, there are two routes: you may turn right and take the mountainous upper-level scenic route or continue on the main river-level freeway. The two roads rejoin about 10 mi W of Bonneville Dam (see HOOD RIVER). Continue E on US 30, I-84 for 23 mi to Hood River, turning S on OR 35 for 47 mi through Mount Hood National Forest to US 26. Drive NW on US 26, 56 mi back to Portland. A description of this tour may be found in a free visitors guide from the Portland Visitors Assn, phone 888/606-6363, or in "The Oregon Travel Guide" free from the Tourism Division, Oregon Economic Development Dept, 775 Summer St NE, Salem 97310.

Mt Tabor Park. Extinct volcano; view of city and mountains. Picnicking. Summer concerts. (Daily) SE 60th Ave & Salmon St. Phone 503/823-2223. **Free.**

Multnomah Falls. Chief among the 11 waterfalls along 11 mi of this highway; 620-ft drop in 2 falls, 4th-highest in US. Hiking. Restaurant. Visitor center. 32 mi E on I-84. (See MOUNT HOOD NATIONAL FOREST)

Oaks Amusement Park (1905). Thrill rides, children's area, roller rink (daily exc Mon; rentals), miniature golf; waterfront picnicking. Separate fees for activities. Park (two wks end of Mar, Apr-May, wkends; Mid-June-Sept, daily exc Mon). SE Oaks Park Way, E end of Sellwood Bridge. Phone 503/233-5777.

Oregon History Center. Regional repository of Northwest history; permanent and special exhibits; museum store; publishing house; regional research library (Wed-Sat). (Daily exc Mon; closed some hols) 1200 SW Park Ave. Phone 503/222-1741. ¢¢

Oregon Museum of Science and Industry. Six exhibit halls include interactive exhibits on space, biological, life, Earth, physical and computer science. Omnimax Theather (daily; fee); planetarium shows; laser light shows (fee). (Labor Day-Memorial Day, daily exc Mon; rest of yr, daily; closed Dec 25) 1945 SE Water Ave. Phone 503/797-4000. ¢¢¢

Peninsula Park and Community Center. Sunken rose gardens with 15,000 rose bushes; reflecting pond. Swimming (fee); wading pools. Tennis. Picnic grove, playground. Community Center (Mon-Fri). (Daily) N Portland Blvd & Albina Ave. Phone 503/823-2223. **Free.**

Pittock Mansion (1914). Restored and furnished French Chateau-esque mansion surrounded by 46 forested and landscaped acres. Spectacular views of rivers, the city and snowcapped mountains, including Mt St Helens and Mt Hood. (Daily; closed most hols, also 1st 3 wks Jan) 3229 NW Pittock Dr. Phone 503/823-3624. ¢¢

Police Historical Museum. Collection of early police uniforms, badges, photos and other police memorabilia. (Mon-Thurs; closed some hols) 1111 SW 2nd Ave, 16th floor. Phone 503/823-0019. **Free.**

✪ **Portland Art Museum.** Features 35 centuries of world art: European painting and sculpture from the Renaissance to the present; 19th- and 20th-century American art; noted collections of Northwest Coast Native American art, Asian, pre-Columbian, West African and classical Greek and Roman art; British silver; major print and drawings collection. Changing

exhibits. Lectures, films, concerts, special events. Gift shop; rental sales gallery. (Daily exc Mon; closed major hols) 1219 SW Park Ave at Jefferson St. Phone 503/226-2811. ¢¢

Portland State University (1946). (14,700 students) Art & photography exhibits in Smith Memorial Center and Neuberger Hall. Campus tours. Visitor information center at SW Broadway & College Sts. Phone 503/725-3000.

Professional sports.

NBA (Portland Trail Blazers). Rose Garden, 1 Center Court. Phone 503/234-9291.

State parks.

Willamette Stone. This two-acre historic site marks the initial point of all government land surveys of Oregon and Washington; trail to stone monument. No water, rest rms. 4 mi W at Skyline Blvd & W Burnside. **Free.**

Lewis and Clark. A 56-acre park with fishing; boating (ramp). Hiking. Picnicking. 16 mi E on I-84, exit 18. Phone 503/695-2261. **Free.**

Dabney. A 135-acre park with fishing in Sandy River. Hiking. Picnicking. 19 mi E off I-84 exit 18, at Stark St Bridge on US 30 Scenic Rte. Phone 503/695-2261. Per vehicle ¢¢

Rooster Rock. A 1¹/₂-mi beach on Columbia River in 927-acre park. Swimming; fishing; boating (ramp, docks). Hiking. Picnicking. Clothing optional beach area. E on I-84, milepost 25. Phone 503/695-2261. Per vehicle ¢

Crown Point. A 307-acre park with 725-ft-high point affords view of Columbia River Gorge with its 2,000-ft-high rock walls. Historic Vista House (1918), pioneer memorial of stone and marble. Visitor information service (summer). E on I-84, exit 22; on US 30 Scenic Rte. Phone 503/695-2261. **Free.**

Guy W. Talbot. A 371-acre park. Latourell Falls, 2nd-highest falls in the Columbia Gorge, drops 250 ft. Hiking. Picnicking. Observation point. E on I-84, exit 27; on US 30 Scenic Rte. Phone 503/695-2261. **Free.**

Benson. A 272-acre park with lake. Swimming; fishing; boating (no motors). Picnicking. E on I-84, exit 30. Phone 503/695-2261. Per vehicle ¢¢

✪ **Washington Park.** A 129-acre park on hill above city. Includes the International Rose Test Garden, with 8,000 bushes of more than 400 varieties (free); the Shakespeare Garden; Lewis and Clark monument; Sacajawea Memorial Statue. Two reservoirs. Archery, tennis. Picnic area. Sunken rose garden amphitheater has music productions, usually Aug-Sept (fee). Accessible via W Burnside St, SW Park Place, or Canyon Rd. Phone 503/823-2223 (wkdays). Also here is

Japanese Garden. 5¹/₂ acres; acclaimed one of the most authentic Japanese gardens outside of Japan. Traditional gardens include the Flat Garden (Hiraniwa), Strolling Pond Garden (Chisen-Kaiyu-Shiki), Tea Garden (Rojiniwa), Natural Garden (Shukeiyen) and the Sand and Stone Garden (Seki-tei); also an authentic Japanese pavilion. Special events include ikebana and bonsai exhibits. Gift shop. (Daily; closed Jan 1, Thanksgiving, Dec 25) Phone 503/223-1321. ¢¢

Water Tower in Johns Landing. Former three-story furniture factory (1903) with cobblestone courtyard; houses specialty shops and restaurants. (Daily; closed major hols) 5331 SW Macadam Ave. Phone 503/274-2786.

World Forestry Center. Educational exhibits on regional and international forests; 70-ft talking tree. Special exhibits, shows. (Daily; closed Dec 25) 4033 SW Canyon Rd. Phone 503/228-1367. ¢¢

Annual Events

Portland Rose Festival. Held for more than 80 yrs, this festival includes the Grand Floral Parade (res required for indoor parade seats) and two other parades; band competition; rose show; championship auto racing; hot-air balloons; air show; carnival; Navy ships. Phone 503/227-2681. Late May-June.

Portland Scottish Highland Games. 15 mi E at Mt Hood Community College in Gresham. Phone 503/293-8501. Mid-July.

Multnomah County Fair. Agricultural & horticultural exhibits; entertainment. Phone 503/289-6623. Late July.

Mt Hood Festival of Jazz. 15 mi E on I-84, in Gresham. International, national and local jazz acts presented in outdoor festival. Phone 503/666-3810. 1st wkend Aug.

Portland Marathon. World-class running event featuring international competition. Phone 503/226-1111. Early Oct.

Holiday Parade of Christmas Ships. Along Willamette & Columbia rivers. More than 50 boats cruise the two rivers in a holiday display. Phone 503/225-5555, code 2065. Early-mid-Dec.

Seasonal Events

Greyhound Racing. Multnomah Greyhound Park, NE 223rd Ave between NE Halsey and Glisan Sts, 12 mi E off I-84, exit 13 or 16A. Parimutuel betting. Matinee and evening races. Under 12 yrs not permitted at evening races. For schedule phone 503/667-7700. May-Oct.

Chamber Music Northwest. Nationally acclaimed summer chamber music festival offers 25 concerts featuring 40-50 artists. Mon, Tues, Thurs-Sat at Catlin Gabel School and Reed College. Catered picnic preceeding each concert. Children under 7 only permitted at Family Concert. Phone 503/223-3202. Mid-June-late July.

Horse racing. Portland Meadows, 1001 N Schmeer Rd, 6 mi N on I-5. Parimutuel betting. Thoroughbred & quarter horse racing. (Fri evenings, Sat & Sun matinee) Under 12 yrs not permitted at evening races. Phone 503/285-9144. Late Oct-Apr.

Portland Center Stage. Portland Center for the Performing Arts. Series of five contemporary and classical plays. Daily exc Mon. For fees, performance and title schedules phone 503/274-6588. Sept-Apr.

Additional Visitor Information

For further information contact the Portland Oregon Visitors Assn, 26 SW Salmon, 97204, phone 503/222-2223 or 888/606-6363. For a recorded message describing major theater, sports and music events in Portland for the current month, phone 503/225-5555, code 3608.

City Neighborhoods

Many of the restaurants, unrated dining establishments and some lodgings listed under Portland include neighborhoods as well as exact street addresses. Geographic descriptions of these areas are given, followed by a table of restaurants arranged by neighborhood.

Downtown: South of I-405, west of the Willamette River, north of SW Lincoln and east of I-30. **East of Downtown:** East of Willamette River. **West of Downtown:** West of I-30.

Nob Hill: West of Downtown; south of Vaughn St, west of I-405, north of Burnside St and east of NW 23rd St.

Old Town: Area of Downtown south of Glisan St, west of Front St and the river, north of Burnside St and east of NW 3rd St.

PORTLAND RESTAURANTS BY NEIGHBORHOOD
AREAS
(For full description, see alphabetical listings under Restaurants)

DOWNTOWN
Al-Amir. 223 SW Stark
Alessandro's. 301 SW Morrison
Atwater's. 111 SW 5th Ave
Bush Garden. 900 SW Morrison
Esplanade At Riverplace (Riverplace Hotel). 1510 SW Harbor Way
Heathman (Heathman Hotel). 1009 SW Broadway
Higgins. 1239 SW Broadway
Huber's. 411 SW 3rd Ave
Jake's Famous Crawfish. 401 SW 12th Ave
Jake's Grill (The Governor Hotel). 611 SW 10th St
London Grill (The Benson Hotel). 309 SW Broadway
Mandarin Cove. 111 SW Columbia
Pazzo Ristorante (Vintage Plaza Hotel). 422 SW Broadway

Red Star. 503 SW Alder
Widmer Gasthaus. 929 N Russell St

EAST OF DOWNTOWN
28 East. 40 NE 28th Ave
Caprial's. 7015 SE Milwaukie Ave
Esparza's Tex Mex Cafe. 2725 SE Ankeny St
Genoa. 2832 SE Belmont St
Ivy House. 1605 SE Bybee
Papa Haydn. 5829 SE Milwaukie
Perry's On Fremont. 2401 NE Fremont
Poor Richard's. 3907 NE Broadway
Rheinlander. 5035 NE Sandy Blvd
Ringside East. 14021 NE Glisan
Salty's On The Columbia. 3839 NE Marine Dr
Sayler's Old Country Kitchen. 10519 SE Stark
Sylvia's. 5115 NE Sandy Blvd
Winterborne. 3520 NE 42nd

WEST OF DOWNTOWN
Avalon Grill & Cafe. 4630 SW Macadam Ave
The Brewhouse. 2730 NW 31st Ave
Cafe Des Amis. 1987 NW Kearney
Chart House. 5700 SW Terwilliger Blvd
Couvron. 1126 SW 18th Ave
Delfina's. 2112 NW Kearney St
L'Auberge. 2601 NW Vaughn
Mazzi's Italian-Sicilian Food. 5833 SW Macadam Ave
Old Spaghetti Factory. 0715 SW Bancroft
Original Pancake House. 8601 SW 24th Ave
Paley's Place. 1204 NW 21st Ave
Plainfield's Mayur. 852 SW 21st Ave
Ringside. 2165 W Burnside St
Typhoon! 2310 NW Everett St

NOB HILL
Il Fornaio. 115 NW 22nd Ave
Tribeca. 704 NW 21st St
Wildwood. 1221 NW 21st Ave
Zefiro. 500 NW 21st Ave

OLD TOWN
Alexis. 215 W Burnside
Couch Street Fish House. 105 NW 3rd Ave
Dan & Louis Oyster Bar. 208 SW Ankeny St

Note: When a listing is located in a town that does not have its own city heading, it will appear under the city nearest to its location. In these cases, the address and town appear in parenthesis immediately following the name of the establishment.

Motels

★ ★ ★ **BEST WESTERN PONY SOLDIER.** *9901 NE Sandy Blvd (97220), near Intl Airport, east of downtown.* 503/256-1504; FAX 503/256-5928. 104 rms, 2 story, 15 suites. S $78.50-$84.50; D $78.50-$99.50; each addl $5; suites, kit. units $114.50-$123.50; under 13 free. Crib $3. TV; cable (premium). Heated pool; whirlpool. Complimentary continental bkfst. Restaurant adj 6 am-10 pm. Ck-out noon. Free lndry facilities. Meeting rms. Business servs avail. Valet serv. Sundries. Free airport transportation. Exercise equipt; weight machine, bicycle, sauna. Refrigerators. Balconies. Cr cds: A, C, D, DS, ER, MC, V.

⊡ ≋ ⅄ ⤫ ⤪ ⩔ SC

✔★ **CARAVAN.** *2401 SW 4th Ave (97201), south of downtown.* 503/226-1121; FAX 503/274-2681; res: 800/248-0506. 40 rms in 2 buildings, 2 story. S, D $55-$125; each addl $7. Crib $7. TV; cable (premium). Heated pool. Complimentary coffee in lobby. Restaurant 7 am-10 pm. Bar 11-2 am. Ck-out noon. Business servs avail. Some refrigerators. Balconies. Cr cds: A, C, D, DS, JCB, MC, V.

≋ ⤪ ⩔ SC

✔★ **CHESTNUT TREE INN.** 9699 SE Stark St (97216), east of downtown. 503/255-4444. 58 rms, 2 story. S $39; D $43; each addl $2. Crib free. TV; cable (premium). Complimentary coffee. Restaurant adj 6 am-11 pm. Ck-out noon. Business servs avail. Refrigerators. Cr cds: A, C, D, MC, V.

[D] [≈] [▧] [🔥]

★ **DAYS INN.** (9717 SE Sunnyside Rd, Clackamas 97015) I-205 Sunnyside exit. 503/654-1699; FAX 503/659-2702. 110 rms, 3 story. S $55-$95; D $62-$102; each addl $7; studio rms $65-$130; under 12 free. Crib free. TV; cable (premium). Heated pool; whirlpool. Sauna. Complimentary continental bkfst. Ck-out noon. Business servs avail. Some refrigerators. Cr cds: A, C, D, DS, JCB, MC, V.

[D] [≈] [▧] [🔥] [SC]

✔★★ **FAIRFIELD INN BY MARRIOTT.** 11929 NE Airport Way (97220), east of downtown. 503/253-1400; FAX 503/253-3889. 106 rms, 4 story. Apr-Sept: S, D $65; each addl $10; under 12 free; lower rates rest of yr. Crib free. TV; cable (premium). Heated pool; whirlpool. Complimentary continental bkfst. Restaurant nearby. Ck-out noon. Business servs avail. Sundries. Free airport transportation. Exercise equipt; bicycle, weight machine. Cr cds: A, D, DS, MC, V.

[D] [≈] [🏋] [▧] [🔥] [SC]

★★ **HOLIDAY INN EXPRESS.** (2323 NE 181st Ave, Gresham 97230) I-84 exit 13. 503/492-4000; FAX 503/492-3271. 71 rms, 3 story, 23 suites. May-Sept: S $70; D $77; each addl $7; suites $80-$120; under 18 free; lower rates rest of yr. Crib free. Pet accepted, some restrictions. TV; cable (premium), VCR avail (movies). Indoor pool; whirlpool. Complimentary continental bkfst. Coffee in rms. Restaurant adj 7 am-10 pm. Ck-out 1 pm. Coin lndry. Meeting rms. Business servs avail. Sundries. Valet serv. Exercise equipt; rower, stair machine, sauna. Some refrigerators. Cr cds: A, D, DS, JCB, MC, V.

[D] [🐾] [≈] [🏋] [▧] [🔥] [SC]

★★ **McMENAMINS EDGEFIELD.** (2126 SW Halsey St, Troutdale 97060) E on I-84, Wood Village exit 16A. 503/669-8610; FAX 503/492-7750; res: 800/669-8610. E-mail edge@mcmenamins.com; web www.mcmenamins.com. 103 rms, 100 share bath, 3 story. No rm phones. S, D $45-$180; each addl $15; under 6 free. Crib free. Complimentary full bkfst. Restaurant (see BLACK RABBIT). Bar 11-1 am. Ck-out 11 am. Business servs avail. Massage. Built 1911 as county poor farm; was converted to nursing home in 1960s. Renovated in style of European village complete with theater, winery and brewery. Herb gardens. Totally nonsmoking. Cr cds: A, DS, MC, V.

[D] [🦶] [▧] [🔥] [SC]

★★ **PHOENIX INN.** (14905 SW Bangy Rd, Lake Oswego 97034) S on I-5, exit 292, at OR 217. 503/624-7400; FAX 503/624-7405; res: 800/824-9992. 62 rms, 4 story. June-Sept: S, D $89; each addl $5; suites $119-$129; under 18 free; lower rates rest of yr. Crib free. TV; cable (premium). Indoor pool; whirlpool. Complimentary continental bkfst. Coffee in rms. Restaurant adj 11 am-10 pm. Bar 11 am-10 pm. Ck-out noon. Coin lndry. Meeting rms. Business servs avail. In-rm modem link. Bellhops. Valet serv. Sundries. Airport transportation avail. Exercise equipt; bicycle, treadmill. Refrigerators, minibars. Cr cds: A, C, D, DS, MC, V.

[D] [≈] [🏋] [🦶] [▧] [🔥] [SC]

★★ **PHOENIX INN.** (477 NW Phoenix Dr, Troutdale 97060) 503/669-6500; FAX 503/669-3500; res: 800/824-6824. 73 rms, 3 story. Mid-May-Sept: S $65-$75; D $79-$85; each addl $7; suites $115; under 17 free; lower rates rest of yr. Crib free. Pet accepted; $10. TV; cable (premium). Indoor pool; whirlpool. Complimentary continental bkfst. Restaurant adj open 24 hrs. Bar 11-2 am. Ck-out noon. Meeting rms. Business servs avail. Free airport transportation. Exercise equipt; bicycle, stair machine. Cr cds: A, D, DS, MC, V.

[D] [🐾] [≈] [🏋] [✕] [▧] [🔥] [SC]

★★ **RAMADA INN-AIRPORT.** 6221 NE 82nd Ave (97220), east of downtown. 503/255-6511; FAX 503/255-8417. 202 rms, 2 story. S, D $85-$120; each addl $10; suites $95-$250; under 18 free; wkend rates. Crib free. TV; cable (premium), VCR avail. Heated pool; whirlpool. Coffee

in rms. Restaurant 6:30 am-11 pm. Rm serv. Bar. Ck-out noon. Coin lndry. Meeting rms. Business center. Bellhops. Valet serv. Free airport transportation. Exercise equipt; weights, stair machine, sauna. Some private patios, balconies. Cr cds: A, C, D, DS, ER, JCB, MC, V.

[D] [≈] [🏋] [✕] [▧] [SC] [🦶]

★★ **RESIDENCE INN BY MARRIOTT-SOUTH.** (15200 SW Bangy Rd, Lake Oswego 97035) S on I-5, exit 292. 503/684-2603; FAX 503/620-6712. 112 kit. units, 2 story. 1 & 2-bedrm suites $120-$175. Crib $5. Pet accepted; $10/day. TV; cable (premium), VCR avail (movies free). Heated pool; whirlpool. Complimentary continental bkfst. Restaurant adj. Ck-out noon. Coin lndry. Business servs avail. Valet serv. Health club privileges. Fireplace in suites. Private patios, balconies. Picnic tables, grills. Cr cds: A, C, D, DS, JCB, MC, V.

[D] [🐾] [≈] [✕] [▧] [SC]

★★ **SHILO INN-WASHINGTON SQUARE.** (10830 SW Greenburg Rd, Tigard 97223) S on OR 217, Greenburg Rd exit. 503/620-4320; FAX 503/620-8277. 77 rms, 4 story, 6 kits. S, D $59-$89; each addl $10; kit. units $85; under 12 free; wkly, monthly rates. Crib free. Pet accepted; $7/day. TV; cable (premium), VCR avail (movies). Complimentary continental bkfst. Restaurant nearby. Ck-out noon. Coin lndry. Meeting rm. Business servs avail. Valet serv. Free airport transportation. Exercise equipt; weight machines, bicycles, sauna, steam rm. Cr cds: A, C, D, DS, ER, JCB, MC, V.

[D] [🐾] [🏋] [✕] [▧] [SC]

✔★ **SUPER 8.** (25438 SW Parkway Ave, Wilsonville 97070) I-5 exit 286. 503/682-2088; FAX 503/682-0453. 72 rms, 4 story. S $48.88; D $57.88-$65.88; each addl $4. Crib free. Pet accepted; $25 refundable. TV; cable (premium). Complimentary coffee in lobby. Restaurant opp open 24 hrs. Ck-out noon. Coin lndry. Meeting rm. Business servs avail. Cr cds: A, C, D, DS, MC, V.

[D] [🐾] [✕] [🔥]

✔★★ **WAYSIDE MOTOR INN.** (11460 SW Pacific Hwy, Tigard 97223) S on I-5, exit 294. 503/245-6421; FAX 503/245-6425; res: 800/547-8828. 117 rms, 4 story. S $51-$60; D $57-$70; each addl $6. Crib $5. TV; cable, VCR avail (movies free). Heated pool. Sauna. Complimentary continental bkfst. Restaurant adj open 24 hrs. Ck-out 11 am. Meeting rms. Business servs avail. Valet serv. Cr cds: A, C, D, DS, MC, V.

[D] [≈] [✕] [🔥] [SC]

Motor Hotels

★ **BEST WESTERN-ROSE GARDEN HOTEL.** 10 N Weidler (97227), east of downtown. 503/287-9900; FAX 503/287-3500. 181 rms, 5 story. S $70-$75; D $75-$85; each addl $5; suites $140; under 12 free. TV; cable (premium). Indoor pool. Restaurant 6:30 am-9:30 pm. Rm serv. Bar 11-2 am. Ck-out noon. Meeting rms. Business servs avail. Covered parking. Free RR station, bus depot transportation. Cr cds: A, C, D, DS, MC, V.

[D] [≈] [✕] [🔥] [SC]

★ **DAYS INN.** 1414 SW 6th Ave (97201), at Columbia, downtown. 503/221-1611; FAX 503/226-0447; res: 800/899-0248. 173 rms, 5 story. S $99-$109; D $104-$114; each addl $5; under 12 free. Crib free. TV; cable (premium). Heated pool. Restaurant 6:30 am-10 pm; Sat, Sun from 7 am. Rm serv. Bar 11 am-midnight. Ck-out noon. Meeting rms. Business servs avail. In-rm modem link. Valet serv. Cr cds: A, C, D, DS, MC, V.

[D] [≈] [✕] [🔥] [SC]

✔★ **DELTA INN.** 9930 N Whitaker Rd (97217), I-5 exit 306B, north of downtown. 503/289-1800; FAX 503/289-3778; res: 800/833-1800. 212 rms, 4 story. S, D $55-$65; each addl $5; under 12 free; wkly rates. Crib free. Pet accepted; $10/day. TV; cable (premium). Complimentary coffee. Restaurant adj 6 am-11 pm. Ck-out noon. Coin lndry. Meeting rm. Business servs avail. In-rm modem link. Sundries. Free airport, RR station, bus depot transportation. Park adj. Cr cds: A, C, D, DS, MC, V.

[D] [🐾] [✕] [▧]

★ ★ ★ **DOUBLETREE-COLUMBIA RIVER.** *1401 N Hayden Island Dr (97217), just W of I-5, Jantzen Beach exit, north of downtown.* 503/283-2111; FAX 503/283-4718. 351 rms, 3 story. S, D $150; each addl $15; suites $225-$350; under 18 free. Crib free. Pet accepted; $15. TV; cable, VCR avail. Heated pool. Restaurants 6 am-10 pm. Rm serv. Bars 11-2 am; entertainment. Ck-out noon. Convention facilities. Business servs avail. In-rm modem link. Bellhops. Valet serv. Gift shop. Barber, beauty shop. Free airport, RR station, bus depot transportation. Tennis adj. Putting green. Some refrigerators, bathrm phones. Whirlpool in some suites. Private patios, balconies. On Columbia River. Cr cds: A, C, D, DS, ER, JCB, MC, V.

D ⊮ ⩰ ⩛ 🐾

★ ★ ★ **DOUBLETREE-JANTZEN BEACH.** *909 N Hayden Island Dr (97217), just E of I-5 exit Jantzen Beach, north of downtown.* 503/283-4466; FAX 503/283-4743. 320 rms, 4 story. S, D $99-$109; each addl $15; suites $195-$350; under 18 free; package plans; wkend rates. Crib free. Pet accepted; $20. TV; cable, VCR avail. Heated pool. Coffee in rms. Restaurant 6 am-10 pm. Rm serv. Bar 10-2:30 am; entertainment. Ck-out noon. Convention facilities. Business servs avail. Bellhops. Valet serv. Sundries. Free airport transportation. Lighted tennis. Exercise equipt; weights, stair machine. Some bathrm phones, in-rm whirlpools. Private patios, balconies. On river; boat dock. Cr cds: A, C, D, DS, ER, JCB, MC, V.

D ⊮ 🛇 ⩰ 🏋 🐾 🔥 SC

★ ★ **HOLIDAY INN-AIRPORT.** *8439 NE Columbia Blvd (97220), 2½ mi N of I-84, on I-205, exit 23B/Columbia Blvd, near Intl Airport, east of downtown.* 503/256-5000; FAX 503/257-4742. 286 rms, 8 story. S, D $108; each addl $8; suites $175-$275. Crib free. TV; cable (premium), VCR avail. Indoor pool; whirlpool. Restaurant 6 am-10 pm. Rm serv. Bar. Ck-out noon. Coin lndry. Convention facilities. Business servs avail. Bellhops. Valet serv Mon-Fri. Gift shop. Free airport transportation. Exercise equipt; weight machine, stair machine, sauna. Game rm. Cr cds: A, C, D, DS, ER, JCB, MC, V.

D ⩰ 🏋 🛫 ⩛ 🔥 SC

★ ★ **RIVERSIDE INN.** *50 SW Morrison St (97204), downtown.* 503/221-0711; FAX 503/274-0312; res: 800/899-0247. 140 rms, 5 story. S $130-$145; D $140-$155; each addl $10; under 17 free. Crib free. Pet accepted, some restrictions; $10/day. TV. Coffee in rms. Restaurant 6:30-10 am, 4-11 pm; Sat, Sun 7 am-noon, 4-11 pm. Rm serv 5 pm-1 am. Bar 4 pm-2 am. Ck-out noon. Meeting rm. Business servs avail. Health club privileges. Balconies. Cr cds: A, C, D, DS, ER, MC, V.

D ⊮ ⩛ 🔥 🐾

★ ★ **SHILO INN.** *9900 SW Canyon Rd (97225), west of downtown.* 503/297-2551; FAX 503/297-7708; res: 800/222-2244. 142 rms, 2-3 story. S, D $79-$99; each addl $10; suites $99-$189; under 12 free. Crib free. TV; cable (premium), VCR avail (movies). Heated pool. Complimentary bkfst buffet. Restaurant 6 am-10 pm. Rm serv. Bar 11-2 am; entertainment exc Sun. Ck-out noon. Meeting rms. Business servs avail. Valet serv. Sundries. Free airport transportation. Exercise equipt; weight machine, bicycles. Refrigerators. Private patios, balconies. Cr cds: A, C, D, DS, ER, JCB, MC, V.

D ⩰ 🏋 ⩛ 🐾 SC

★ ★ **SWEETBRIER INN.** *(7125 SW Nyberg, Tualatin 97062) approx 10 mi S on I-5, exit 289.* 503/692-5800; FAX 503/691-2894; res: 800/551-9167. 100 rms, 32 suites. S $63-$83; D $73-$93; suites $90-$165; under 18 free; wkend rates. Crib free. Pet accepted; $100 refundable. TV; cable (premium). Playground. Complimentary coffee in rms. Restaurant 6:30 am-10 pm. Rm serv. Bar; entertainment Wed-Sat. Ck-out noon. Meeting rms. Business servs avail. In-rm modem link. Sundries. Valet serv. Refrigerator in suites. Some balconies, patios. Picnic tables. Cr cds: A, C, D, DS, JCB, MC, V.

D ⊮ 🛇 ⩛ 🔥 SC

Hotels

★ ★ ★ ★ **5TH AVENUE SUITES.** *506 SW Washington (97205), downtown.* 503/222-0001; FAX 503/222-0004; res: 800/711-2971. Built in 1912, this former department store has been completely renovated and redecorated in turn-of-the-century, American country-home style. Rooms are comfortable, light and airy. There are on-site business and fitness centers and the Red Star Tavern is open daily for breakfast, lunch and dinner. 221 rms, 10 story, 139 suites. S $150-$165; D $165-$180; each addl $15; suites $160-$225; under 18 free; wkend, hol rates. Pet accepted, some restrictions. Garage/valet parking $13. TV; cable (premium), VCR avail (movies). Pool privileges. Complimentary continental bkfst. Restaurant 6:30 am-10 pm. Rm serv 24 hrs. Bar 11-1 am. Ck-out noon. Meeting rms. Business center. In-rm modem link. Concierge. Exercise equipt; weights, treadmill. Refrigerators. Cr cds: A, C, D, DS, JCB, MC, V.

D ⊮ 🏋 ⩛ 🐾 🚶

★ ★ ★ **THE BENSON.** *309 SW Broadway (97205), at Oak St, downtown.* 503/228-2000; FAX 503/226-4603; res: 800/426-0670. 286 units, 13 story, 44 suites. S $145-$190; D $185-$210; each addl $25; suites $180-$600; under 18 free; wkend rates. Crib $25. Pet accepted; $50. Garage, valet $12/day. TV; cable, VCR avail. Restaurant (see LONDON GRILL). Rm serv 24 hrs. Bar 11-1 am; entertainment. Ck-out noon. Convention facilities. Business center. In-rm modem link. Concierge. Gift shop. Airport transportation. Exercise equipt; weights, treadmills. Minibars. Bathrm phone in suites. Cr cds: A, C, D, DS, ER, JCB, MC, V.

D ⊮ 🏋 ⩛ 🐾 🚶

★ ★ **COURTYARD BY MARRIOTT-AIRPORT.** *11550 NE Airport Way (97220), near Intl Airport, east of downtown.* 503/252-3200; FAX 503/252-8921. 150 rms, 6 story. June-Aug: S, D $79-$89; suites $110-$120; under 18 free; wkly rates; lower rates rest of yr. Crib free. TV; cable (premium), some VCRs. Heated pool; whirlpool, poolside serv. Coffee in rms. Restaurant 6 am-11 pm. Rm serv 5-10 pm. Bar 4-11 pm. Ck-out 1 pm. Coin lndry. Business servs avail. Exercise equipt; bicycles, stair machine. Free airport transportation. Refrigerator, wet bar in suites. Cr cds: A, C, D, DS, MC, V.

D ⩰ 🏋 🛫 ⩛ 🐾 SC

★ ★ ★ **CROWNE PLAZA.** *(14811 SW Kruse Oaks Blvd, Lake Oswego 97035)* 503/624-8400; FAX 503/684-8324. 161 rms, 6 story. June-Aug: S $134; D $149; suites $150-$265; under 18 free; lower rates rest of yr. Crib free. Pet accepted. Valet parking $5. TV; cable (premium). Indoor/outdoor pool; whirlpool. Complimentary coffee in rms. Restaurant 6 am-2 pm, 5-10 pm. Rm serv to midnight. Bar 2 pm-midnight. Ck-out noon. Meeting rms. Business servs avail. Sundries. Gift shop. Valet serv. Free RR transportation. Tennis privileges. Exercise equipt; bicycle, treadmill. Cr cds: A, D, DS, ER, JCB, MC, V.

D ⊮ 🛇 ⩰ 🏋 ⩛ 🐾 SC

★ ★ ★ **DOUBLETREE-LLOYD CENTER.** *1000 NE Multnomah St (97232), I-84 exit 1 (Lloyd Blvd), east of downtown.* 503/281-6111; FAX 503/284-8553. 476 rms, 15 story. S, D $99-$149; each addl $15; suites $269-$575; under 18 free. Crib free. Pet accepted. TV; cable, VCR avail. Pool; poolside serv. Coffee in rms. Restaurant 6 am-midnight. Bar; entertainment. Ck-out noon. Convention facilities. Business center. Valet parking. Free airport transportation. Exercise equipt; weights, bicycles. Some bathrm phones, in-rm whirlpools, refrigerators. Many private patios, balconies. Cr cds: A, C, D, DS, ER, JCB, MC, V.

D ⊮ ⩰ 🏋 ⩛ 🐾 🚶

★ ★ ★ **THE GOVERNOR.** *611 SW 10th (97205), at SW Alder Ave, downtown.* 503/224-3400; FAX 503/241-2122; res: 800/554-3456. 100 rms, 6 story, 32 suites. S $160-$185; D $185-$200; each addl $20; suites $195-$500; under 12 free; wkend rates. Crib free. Garage parking $13-$15. TV; cable, VCR avail. Indoor pool; whirlpool. Restaurant 6:30 am-11 pm (also see JAKE'S GRILL). Rm serv 24 hrs. Bar 11 am-midnight. Ck-out noon. Meeting rms. Business center. Concierge. Barber, beauty shop. Exercise rm; instructor, weights, treadmill, sauna. Refrigerators, minibars.

Some in-rm whirlpools, fireplaces. Some balconies. Cr cds: A, C, D, DS, JCB, MC, V.

⊡ ⇌ ✗ 🏃 🔥 🚶

★ ★ ★ **HEATHMAN.** *1001 SW Broadway (97205), downtown. 503/241-4100; FAX 503/790-7110; res: 800/551-0011.* 150 rms, 10 story. S $155-$180; D $175-$200; each addl $20; suites $250-$575; under 6 free; wkend rates. Crib $7. Garage in/out $12. TV; cable (premium), VCR avail (movies). Restaurant (see HEATHMAN). Rm serv 24 hrs. Afternoon tea. Bars 11-2 am; entertainment. Ck-out 1 pm. Meeting rms. Business servs avail. In-rm modem link. Concierge. Gift shop. Exercise equipt; bicycles, rowers. Health club privileges. Minibars. Cr cds: A, C, D, DS, ER, JCB, MC, V.

⊡ ✗ 🔥 🚶

★ ★ ★ **HILTON.** *921 SW 6th Ave (97204), downtown. 503/226-1611; FAX 503/220-2565.* 455 rms, 23 story. S $155; D $175; each addl $30; suites $400-$950; family, wkend rates. Garage in/out $14; valet $3 addl. Crib free. TV; cable (premium). Indoor pool; poolside serv. Restaurant 6:30 am-11:30 pm. Bar 11-1 am; entertainment Tues-Sat. Ck-out noon. Convention facilities. Business center. In-rm modem link. Gift shop. Barber, beauty shop. Exercise equipt; weights, treadmills, steam rm, sauna. Cr cds: A, C, D, DS, ER, JCB, MC, V.

⊡ ⇌ 🏃 🔥 🚶 🚶

★ ★ **IMPERIAL.** *400 SW Broadway (97205), at Stark St, downtown. 503/228-7221; FAX 503/223-4551; res: 800/452-2323.* 136 rms, 9 story. S $75-$90; D $80-$100; each addl $5; under 12 free. Crib free. TV; cable (premium). Pet accepted; $10. Restaurants 6:30 am-9 pm. Bar 11-1 am, Sat & Sun 1-9 pm. Ck-out 2 pm. Meeting rms. Business servs avail. In-rm modem link. Valet parking. Cr cds: A, C, D, DS, MC, V.

⊡ ⇦ 🔥 🚶

✔★ **MALLORY.** *729 SW 15th Ave (97205), just W of I-405, downtown. 503/223-6311; FAX 503/223-0522; res: 800/228-8657.* 143 rms, 8 story. S $65-$100; D $70-$110; each addl $5; suites $110-$120. Crib free. Pet accepted; $10. TV; cable (premium), VCR avail. Restaurant 6:30 am-9 pm; Sun from 7 am. Bar 11:30-1 am, Sun 1-9 pm. Ck-out 2 pm. Business servs avail. Some refrigerators. Cr cds: A, C, D, DS, MC, V.

⊡ ⇦ 🔥 🚶

★ **MARK SPENCER.** *409 SW 11th Ave (97205), downtown. 503/224-3293; FAX 503/223-7848; res: 800/548-3934.* 101 kit. units, 6 story. S, D $69-$105; each addl $10; suites $95-$110; studio rms $69; under 12 free; monthly rates. Crib free. Pet accepted; $200 refundable. Parking lot 1 blk $7. TV; cable, VCR avail. Complimentary coffee in lobby. Complimentary continental bkfst. Restaurant nearby. Ck-out noon. Coin Indry. Business servs avail. Health club privileges. Refrigerators. Rooftop garden. Cr cds: A, C, D, DS, MC, V.

⇦ ⇌ 🔥 SC

★ ★ ★ **MARRIOTT.** *1401 SW Front Ave (97201), downtown. 503/226-7600; FAX 503/221-1789.* 503 rms, 15 story. S $170-$190; D $180-$200; suites $350-$500; under 18 free. Crib free. Pet accepted. Valet parking in/out $14/day. TV; cable (premium), VCR avail. Indoor pool; whirlpool, poolside serv. Restaurant 6 am-11 pm; Fri, Sat to midnight. Bar 11:30-2 am; entertainment. Ck-out noon. Coin Indry. Convention facilities. Business center. Concierge. Gift shop. Barber, beauty shop. Exercise equipt; bicycles, rower, sauna. Massage. Game rm. Some bathrm phones, refrigerators; wet bar in suites. Some private patios, balconies. Japanese garden at entrance. Luxury level. Cr cds: A, C, D, DS, ER, JCB, MC, V.

⊡ ⇦ ⇌ 🏃 🔥 SC 🚶

★ ★ **RAMADA PLAZA.** *1441 NE Second Ave (97232), east of downtown. 503/233-2401; FAX 503/238-7016.* 240 rms, 10 story. S $96; D $106; under 18 free. Crib free. TV; cable (premium). Pool. Complimentary coffee in rms. Restaurant 6:30 am-2 pm, 5:30-10 pm. Bar. Ck-out noon. Meeting rms. Business servs avail. Free airport transportation. Exercise equipt; weights, stair machine. Cr cds: A, C, D, DS, ER, MC, V.

⊡ ⇌ 🏃 🔥 🚶

★ ★ ★ **RIVERPLACE.** *1510 SW Harbor Way (97201), downtown. 503/228-3233; FAX 503/295-6161; res: 800/227-1333.* 84 rms, 4 story. S, D $185-$245; condos $375-$475; suites $205-$700; under 18 free. Valet, garage parking in/out $15. Crib free. Pet accepted, some restrictions; $100. TV; cable (premium), VCR avail. Complimentary continental bkfst. Restaurant (see ESPLANADE AT RIVERPLACE). Rm serv 24 hrs. Bar 11-1 am; entertainment Wed-Sun evenings. Ck-out 1 pm. Meeting rms. Business servs avail. In-rm modem link. Concierge. Shopping arcade. Whirlpool, sauna. Health club privileges. Minibars; some bathrm phones. Some refrigerators, fireplaces in suites. Balconies. On river. Skyline, marina views. Cr cds: A, C, D, DS, ER, JCB, MC, V.

⊡ ⇦ 🔥 🚶

★ ★ ★ **SHERATON-PORTLAND AIRPORT.** *8235 NE Airport Way (97220), near Intl Airport, east of downtown. 503/281-2500; FAX 503/249-7602.* 215 rms, 5 story. S $115; D $127; each addl $10; suites $150-$395; under 18 free; wkend rates. Crib $5. TV; cable (premium). Indoor pool; whirlpool. Coffee in rms. Restaurant 5 am-10:30 pm; Sat, Sun 6 am-10 pm. Rm serv 24 hrs. Bars. Ck-out noon. Meeting rms. Business center. Concierge. Free airport transportation. Exercise equipt; weights, treadmill, sauna. Minibars. Cr cds: A, C, D, DS, JCB, MC, V.

⊡ ⇌ 🏃 ✗ 🔥 🚶

★ ★ ★ **SHILO INN SUITES-AIRPORT.** *11707 NE Airport Way (97220), near Intl Airport, east of downtown. 503/252-7500; FAX 503/254-0794.* 200 suites, 4 story. S, D $121-$157; each addl $15; under 13 free; higher rates Rose Festival. Crib free. TV; cable (premium), VCR (movies $3.50). Indoor pool; whirlpool. Complimentary bkfst; afternoon refreshments. Restaurant 6 am-11 pm. Rm serv to 10 pm. Bar 8-2 am; entertainment. Ck-out noon. Coin Indry. Meeting rms. Business center. In-rm modem link. Concierge. Free airport, RR station, bus depot transportation. Exercise equipt; weight machine, bicycles, sauna. Bathrm phones, refrigerators, wet bars. Cr cds: A, C, D, DS, ER, JCB, MC, V.

⊡ ⇌ 🏃 ✗ 🔥 🚶 SC 🚶

★ ★ **SILVER CLOUD INN.** *2426 NW Vaughn St (97210). 503/242-2400; FAX 503/242-1770; res: 800/551-7207.* 81 rms, 4 story. S $79; D $82; each addl $8; suites $91; under 14 free. Crib free. TV; cable (premium). Complimentary continental bkfst. Restaurant nearby. Ck-out noon. Meeting rms. Business servs avail. In-rm modem link. Free Indry. Exercise equipt; treadmill, weight machine. Whirlpool. Some refrigerators. Cr cds: A, D, DS, MC, V.

⊡ ✗ 🔥 🚶

★ ★ ★ ★ **VINTAGE PLAZA.** *422 SW Broadway (97205), downtown. 503/228-1212; FAX 503/228-3598; res: 800/243-0555.* This historic building's dramatic decor was inspired by Oregon vineyards; there's a winery theme throughout. 107 rms, 10 story, 23 suites. S $160-$175; D $175-$190; each addl $15; suites $195-$250; under 18 free; wkend rates. Crib free. Valet parking $13. TV; cable, VCR avail. Restaurant (see PAZZO RISTORANTE). Rm serv 24 hrs. Bar 11-1 am. Ck-out noon. Meeting rms. Business center. In-rm modem link. Concierge. Gift shop. Exercise equipt; bicycles, rowers. Minibars. Cr cds: A, C, D, DS, JCB, MC, V.

⊡ ✗ 🔥 🔥 🚶

Inns

★ ★ **GENERAL HOOKER'S.** *125 SW Hooker St (97201). 503/222-4435; FAX 503/295-6410; res: 800/745-4135.* 4 rms, 2 share baths, 1 shower only, 3 story. No elvtr. S $55-$115; D $70-$125; 2-day min. Children over 10 only. TV; cable (premium), VCR (movies). Complimentary continental bkfst; afternoon refreshments. Restaurant nearby. Ck-out 11 am, ck-in 3-5 pm. Health club privileges. Victorian house built in 1888. Totally nonsmoking. Cr cds: A, MC, V.

🚶 🔥

★ ★ **HERON HAUS.** *2545 NW Westover Rd (97210), in Nob Hill. 503/274-1846; FAX 503/243-1075.* 6 rms, 3 story. S $85; D $125-$250; each addl $65. TV; cable (premium), VCR avail (movies). Pool. Complimentary continental bkfst. Restaurant nearby. Ck-out noon, ck-in 4-6 pm. Business servs avail. In-rm modem link. Restored house (1904) in

NW hills overlooking city; library, morning rm. Totally nonsmoking. Cr cds: MC, V.

★ ★ **JOHN PALMER HOUSE.** *4314 N Mississippi Ave (97217), north of downtown.* 503/284-5893; FAX 503/284-1239; res: 800/518-5893. 7 rms, 2 story, 2 suites. May-Oct: S $65-$90; D, suites $70-$100; each addl $15; wkly rates; lower rates rest of yr. Children by appt. Crib free. Complimentary full bkfst. Ck-out 11 am, ck-in 3 pm. Business servs avail. RR station, bus depot transportation. Whirlpool. Picnic tables. Built in 1890; completely furnished with antiques. Totally nonsmoking. Cr cds: A, DS, MC, V.

★ ★ ★ **PORTLAND'S WHITE HOUSE.** *1914 NE 22nd Ave (97212), east of downtown.* 503/287-7131. 6 rms, 2 story. S $93-$111; D $102-$120; each addl $20; under 6 free. Crib free. TV avail. Complimentary full bkfst; afternoon refreshments. Complimentary coffee in rms. Restaurant nearby. Rm serv (bkfst). Ck-out 11 am, ck-in 2 pm. Business servs avail. Luggage handling. Street parking. Free airport, RR station, bus depot transportation. Game rm. Some balconies. White southern colonial mansion with Greek columns and fountain at entrance. Ballroom; antique stained-glass windows. Totally nonsmoking. Cr cds: MC, V.

Restaurants

★ **28 EAST.** *40 NE 28th Ave (97232), east of downtown.* 503/235-9060. Hrs: 11:30 am-3:30 pm, 5-10:30 pm; Fri to 11 pm; Sat 5-11 pm; Sun brunch 10 am-3 pm, also 5-9 pm. Closed Mon; most major hols. Res accepted. Northwestern cuisine. Bar. Semi-a la carte: lunch $5-$9; dinner $7-$18. Sun brunch $4-$8. Specialties: Asian marinated pork chops, pan-roasted rainbow trout. Outdoor dining. Open kitchen. Totally nonsmoking. Cr cds: A, MC, V.

D

★ ★ **AL-AMIR.** *223 SW Stark (97204), downtown.* 503/274-0010. Hrs: 11 am-10 pm; Fri to 1 am; Sat 4 pm-1 am; Sun 4-9 pm. Closed Jan 1, Thanksgiving, Dec 25. Res required Fri, Sat. Lebanese menu. Bar. Semi-a la carte: lunch $3.75-$7.50, dinner $7.50-$15.50. Child's meals. Specialties: maza al-amir, kebab. Entertainment Fri, Sat. Lebanese decor. Totally nonsmoking. Cr cds: A, D, DS, MC, V.

D

★ ★ **ALESSANDRO'S.** *301 SW Morrison (97204), downtown.* 503/222-3900. Hrs: 11:30 am-10 pm; Sat to 11 pm; Sun 2-10 pm. Closed major hols. Res required. Italian menu. Bar. Semi-a la carte: lunch $5.75-$11, dinner $10.50-$19.95. Complete meals: dinner $27.50. Specializes in Roman-style Italian seafood, poultry, veal. Parking. Totally nonsmoking. Cr cds: A, D, MC, V.

D

✔★ ★ **ALEXIS.** *215 W Burnside (97209), in Old Town.* 503/224-8577. Hrs: 11:30 am-2 pm, 5-10 pm; Fri to 11 pm; Sat 5-11 pm; Sun 4:30-9 pm. Closed major hols. Greek menu. Bar. Semi-a la carte: lunch $5.95-$8.95, dinner $8.95-$13.95. Specialties: deep fried squid, eggplant casserole, grape leaves stuffed with ground lamb. Belly dancer Fri, Sat. Greek decor. Cr cds: A, D, DS, MC, V.

D

★ ★ ★ **ATWATER'S.** *111 SW 5th Ave (97204), downtown.* 503/275-3622. Hrs: 5:30-9:30 pm; Fri, Sat to 10 pm; Sun 5-9 pm. Closed most major hols. Res accepted. Contemporary Amer menu. Bar to 1:30 am. Wine list. Semi-a la carte: dinner $15-$24. Child's meals. Specializes in salmon, lamb, duck. Entertainment Wed-Sat. Contemporary decor. Totally nonsmoking. Cr cds: A, C, D, DS, JCB, MC, V.

D

★ ★ ★ **AVALON GRILL & CAFE.** *4630 SW Macadam Ave (97201), west of downtown.* 503/227-4630. Hrs: 11:30 am-2 pm, 5:30-9:30 pm; Fri to 10 pm; Sat 11:30 am-10 pm; Sun brunch 10 am-2 pm, also

5:30-9:30 pm. Closed July 4, Dec 25. Res accepted. Bar. Wine list. Semi-a la carte: lunch $8-$12, dinner $17-$25. Sun brunch $15.95. Child's meals. Specializes in seafood, lamb. Entertainment. Outdoor dining. Views of the river. Totally nonsmoking. Cr cds: A, MC, V.

D

★ ★ **BLACK RABBIT.** *(See McMenamins Edgefield Motel)* 503/492-3086. E-mail edge@mcmenamins.com; web www.mcmenamins.com. Hrs: 7 am-10 pm. Res accepted. Bar 11-1 am. Semi-a la carte: bkfst $5.25-$9.25, lunch $6.25-$12.50, dinner $13.50-$21. Child's meals. Specializes in fresh Northwestern cuisine. Parking. Outdoor dining. Totally nonsmoking. Cr cds: A, DS, MC, V.

D

✔★ **THE BREWHOUSE.** *2730 NW 31st Ave (97210), west of downtown.* 503/226-7623. Hrs: 11 am-11 pm; Mon to 9:30 pm; Fri to 11:30 pm; Sat noon-11:30 pm; Sun noon-9:30 pm. Closed most major hols. Northwestern cuisine. Bar. Semi-a la carte: lunch $4.75-$9.95, dinner $5.50-$12.95. Child's meals. Specialties: MacTarnahan's fish & chips, haystack back ribs. Outdoor dining. Copper beer-making equipment at entrance. Totally nonsmoking. Cr cds: A, MC, V.

D

★ ★ **BUSH GARDEN.** *900 SW Morrison (97205), downtown.* 503/226-7181. Hrs: 11:30 am-1:45 pm, 5-9:45 pm; Sat 5-9:45 pm; Sun 5-8:45 pm. Closed most major hols. Res accepted. Japanese menu. Bar to 12:45 am; Fri, Sat to l:45 am. Semi-a la carte: lunch $5.75-$11.95, dinner $10.50-$24.95. Specializes in sashimi, sukiyaki. Sushi bar. Karaoke singing. Parking. Dining in tatami rms. Cr cds: A, D, DS, JCB, MC, V.

D

★ ★ ★ **CAFE DES AMIS.** *1987 NW Kearney (97209), west of downtown.* 503/295-6487. Hrs: 5:30-10 pm. Closed Sun; major hols. Res accepted. Country French menu. Serv bar. Semi-a la carte: dinner $12.50-$22. Specializes in filet of beef with garlic & port sauce, fresh fish. Own baking. Parking. Country French decor. Totally nonsmoking. Cr cds: A, MC, V.

D

✔★ **CAPRIAL'S.** *7015 SE Milwaukie Ave (97202), east of downtown.* 503/236-6457. Hrs: 11:30 am-3:30 pm, 5-8:30 pm; Fri to 9 pm; Sat noon-3:30 pm, 5-9 pm. Closed Sun, Mon; major hols. Res required. Eclectic menu. Wine, beer. Semi-a la carte: lunch $1.95-$8.25, dinner $14-$19. Specializes in pasta, seafood. Casual decor. Totally nonsmoking. Cr cds: MC, V.

D

★ ★ **CHART HOUSE.** *5700 SW Terwilliger Blvd (97206), west of downtown.* 503/246-6963. Hrs: 11:30 am-2 pm, 5-10 pm; Sat from 5 pm; Sun 5-9 pm. Res accepted. Bar to midnight. Semi-a la carte: lunch $6-$13, dinner $15-$25. Child's meals. Specializes in prime rib, steak, fresh seafood. Valet parking. Fireplace. 1,000 ft above Willamette River; panoramic view of Portland, Mt Hood and Mt St Helens. Totally nonsmoking. Cr cds: A, C, D, DS, MC, V.

D

★ ★ ★ **COUCH STREET FISH HOUSE.** *105 NW 3rd Ave, just N of OR 30, in Old Town.* 503/223-6173. Hrs: 5-10 pm; Fri, Sat to 11 pm; early-bird dinner 5-6:30 pm. Closed Sun; some major hols. Res accepted. Bar. Wine list. Semi-a la carte: dinner $16.95-$28.95. Specializes in Chinook salmon, live Maine lobster, Dungeness crab. Valet parking. Old San Francisco decor. Totally nonsmoking. Cr cds: A, C, D, DS, MC, V.

D

★ ★ **COUVRON.** *1126 SW 18th Ave (97205), west of downtown.* 503/225-1844. Hrs: 5:30-9 pm; Fri, Sat to 10 pm. Closed Sun, Mon; major hols. Res accepted. Continental, French menu. Wine list. Semi-a la carte: dinner $22-$32. 6-course menu $55. Specialties: foie gras, rack of lamb, salmon. Country French decor. Totally nonsmoking. Cr cds: A, DS, MC, V.

D

✔★ **DAN & LOUIS OYSTER BAR.** *208 SW Ankeny St (97204), in Old Town.* 503/227-5906. Hrs: 11 am-10 pm; Fri & Sat to 11 pm. Closed some major hols. Semi-a la carte: lunch $2.75-$6.50, dinner $5.95-$16.95. Child's meals. Specializes in stewed, broiled, fried, pan-fried & raw oysters. Antique seafaring decor. Ship models. 19th-century bldg (1907). Family-owned. Cr cds: A, D, DS, JCB, MC, V.

D SC ⌐

★ **DELFINA'S.** *2112 NW Kearney St (97210), west of downtown.* 503/221-1195. Hrs: 11:30 am-2:30 pm, 5-11 pm; Sat, Sun from 5 pm. Closed July 4, Thanksgiving, Dec 25. Res accepted. Italian menu. Bar 11:30-1 am; Sat, Sun from 5 pm. Semi-a la carte: lunch $6-$12, dinner $12-$20. Specializes in seafood, pasta. Valet parking. Outdoor dining. Original artwork. Cr cds: A, D, DS, MC, V.

D

✔★ **ESPARZA'S TEX MEX CAFE.** *2725 SE Ankeny St (97214), east of downtown.* 503/234-7909. Hrs: 11:30 am-10 pm. Closed Sun, Mon; most major hols. Tex-Mex menu. Bar. Semi-a la carte: lunch $4.75-$9.95; dinner $5.75-$11.50. Child's meals. Specialties: stuffed porkloin with buffalo spicy cactus, carne asada rib-eye steak. Western decor. Totally nonsmoking. Cr cds: A, MC, V.

★ ★ **ESPLANADE AT RIVERPLACE.** *(See Riverplace Hotel)* 503/228-3233. Hrs: 6:30 am-2 pm; 5-10 pm; Sat 6:30-11 am, 5-9 pm; Sun 6:30 am-2 pm, 5-9 pm; Sun brunch 11 am-2 pm. Res accepted. Continental menu. Bar 11-1 am. Wine cellar. Semi-a la carte: bkfst $3.50-$10.50, lunch $6.95-$15, dinner $13.50-$28. Sun brunch $9-$13. Child's meals. Specializes in Northwestern regional cuisine. Own desserts. Outdoor dining. Split-level dining; view of Willamette River & marina. Totally nonsmoking. Cr cds: A, C, D, DS, JCB, MC, V.

D ♥

★ ★ ★ **GENOA.** *2832 SE Belmont St, east of downtown.* 503/238-1464. Don't let the nondescript exterior of this storefront restaurant fool you—inside awaits an exquisite meal delivered with flawless service. The interior features antique sideboards and a 200-year-old Persian tapestry. Northern Italian menu. Specializes in authentic regional Italian dishes. Own baking. Hrs: 5:30-9:30 pm. Closed Sun; major hols. Res accepted. Prix fixe: 7-course dinner $50, 4-course dinner (Mon-Thurs) $40. Menu changes every two wks. Totally nonsmoking. Cr cds: A, C, D, DS, MC, V.

★ ★ ★ **HEATHMAN.** *(See Heathman Hotel)* 503/790-7752. Hrs: 6:30 am-11 pm. Res accepted. French, Amer menu. Bar 11-2 am. Wine cellar. Semi-a la carte: bkfst $4-$14, lunch $8-$18, dinner $13-$35. Specializes in Chinook salmon, halibut confit, Oregon lamb. Own baking. Entertainment. Valet parking. Outdoor dining. Built 1927. Formal decor. Cr cds: A, C, D, DS, ER, JCB, MC, V.

D

★ ★ **HIGGINS.** *1239 SW Broadway (97205), downtown.* 503/222-9070. Hrs: 11:30 am-2, 5-10:30 pm. Closed most major hols. Res accepted. Northwestern regional menu. Bar to 2 am. Semi-a la carte: lunch $6.75-$11.75; dinner $13.75-$19.75. Child's meals. Specializes in seafood, hamburger. Contemporary decor. Totally nonsmoking. Cr cds: A, C, D, DS, MC, V.

D

★ ★ **HUBER'S.** *411 SW 3rd Ave (97204), downtown.* 503/228-5686. Hrs: 11 am-midnight; Fri to 1 am; Sat noon-1 am. Closed Sun; major hols. Res accepted exc Fri evenings. Bar. Semi-a la carte: lunch $4.95-$9, dinner $6.50-$15. Specialties: roast turkey, flaming Spanish coffees. Originally a saloon established in 1879 that became a restaurant during Prohibition. Arched stained-glass skylight, mahogany paneling and terrazzo floor. Cr cds: A, D, DS, MC, V.

D ⌐

★ ★ **IL FORNAIO.** *115 NW 22nd Ave (97210), in Nob Hill.* 503/248-9400. Hrs: 11 am-11 pm; Fri to midnight; Sat 10 am-midnight; Sun 10 am-10 pm. Closed Thanksgiving, Dec 25. Res accepted. Italian menu. Bar. Semi-a la carte: lunch $4-$15, dinner $4-$19. Child's meals. Specialties: pizza con la luganega, pollo toscano, grigliata di vitello. Parking. Show

kitchen; wood-burning pizza oven & rotisserie. Totally nonsmoking dining rm. Cr cds: A, DS, MC, V.

D

★ ★ ★ **JAKE'S FAMOUS CRAWFISH.** *401 SW 12th Ave (97205), downtown.* 503/226-1419. Hrs: 11:30 am-11 pm; Fri to midnight; Sat 5 pm-midnight; Sun 5-10 pm. Closed July 4, Thanksgiving, Dec 25. Res accepted. Bar. Wine list. A la carte entrees: lunch $4.95-$10, dinner $8.95-$28.95. Specializes in fresh regional seafood. Own baking. Turn-of-the-century decor. Cr cds: A, C, D, DS, MC, V.

D ⌐

★ ★ ★ **JAKE'S GRILL.** *(See The Governor Hotel)* 503/220-1850. Hrs: 6:30 am-midnight; Fri to 1 am; Sat 7:30-1 am; Sun 7:30 am-11 pm. Res accepted. Bar. Semi-a la carte: bkfst $2.50-$11.95, lunch $4.95-$18.50, dinner $4.95-$9.95. Child's meals. Specializes in steak, salmon. Outdoor dining. Casual decor. Cr cds: A, D, DS, MC, V.

D

★ ★ ★ **L'AUBERGE.** *2601 NW Vaughn (97210), west of downtown.* 503/223-3302. Hrs: 5 pm-midnight; Fri, Sat to 1 am. Closed most major hols. Res accepted. French menu. Bar. Wine list. Complete meals: dinner $9.75-$36. Prix fixe: dinner $42, $60. Specializes in seafood, steak, lamb. Own baking. Parking. Outdoor dining. Tri-level dining; wall hangings, 2 fireplaces. Family-owned. Cr cds: A, C, D, DS, MC, V.

★ ★ ★ **LONDON GRILL.** *(See The Benson Hotel)* 503/295-4110. Hrs: 6:30 am-2 pm, 5-10 pm; Fri, Sat to 11 pm; Sun brunch from 9:30 am. Res accepted. Continental menu. Bar 11-2 am. Wine cellar. Semi-a la carte: bkfst $4.95-$9.95, lunch $9-$13, dinner $19.95-$25. Sun brunch $17.50. Child's meals. Specializes in Northwest salmon, Caesar salad, ostrich. Harpist Wed-Sat. Valet parking. Elegant dining in historic hotel. Jacket (dinner). Cr cds: A, C, D, DS, ER, JCB, MC, V.

D ⌐

★ ★ **MANDARIN COVE.** *111 SW Columbia, downtown.* 503/222-0006. Hrs: 11 am-2 pm, 4:30-10 pm; Sat noon-11 pm; Sun 4-10 pm. Res accepted. Mandarin, Chinese menu. Bar. Semi-a la carte: lunch $4.95-$6.50, dinner $6.50-$25.50. Specializes in Hunan and Szechwan meats and seafood. Valet parking. Cr cds: A, D, MC, V.

D

✔★ **MAZZI'S ITALIAN-SICILIAN FOOD.** *5833 SW Macadam Ave (97201), west of downtown.* 503/227-3382. Hrs: 11:30 am-11 pm; Fri to midnight; Sat 5 pm-midnight; Sun 5-11 pm. Closed Thanksgiving, Dec 24, 25. Italian menu. Bar. Semi-a la carte: lunch $3.25-$7.95, dinner $5.50-$14.50. Specializes in fresh seafood, calzone, homemade pasta. Salad bar (lunch). Parking. Mediterranean decor; fireplaces. Totally nonsmoking. Cr cds: A, MC, V.

D

✔★ **OLD SPAGHETTI FACTORY.** *0715 SW Bancroft (97201), west of downtown.* 503/222-5375. Hrs: 11:30 am-2 pm, 5-10 pm; Fri to 11 pm; Sat 1-11 pm; Sun noon-10 pm. Closed Thanksgiving, Dec 24-25. Italian menu. Bar. Semi-a la carte: lunch $3.25-$5.45, dinner $4.50-$8.25. Child's meals. Specializes in pasta. Own sauces. Parking. 1890s decor; dining in trolley car. Family-owned. Cr cds: D, DS, MC, V.

D

✔★ ★ **PALEY'S PLACE.** *1204 NW 21st Ave (97209), west of downtown.* 503/243-2403. Hrs: 5:30-10 pm; Fri, Sat to 11 pm. Closed Sun, Mon; major hols. Res accepted. Southern French menu. Serv bar. Wine list. Semi-a la carte: dinner $13-$19. Child's meals. Specializes in sweetbreads, seafood. Outdoor dining. Contemporary decor. Totally nonsmoking. Cr cds: A, MC, V.

★ ★ ★ **PAZZO RISTORANTE.** *(See Vintage Plaza Hotel)* 503/228-1515. Hrs: 7 am-10 pm; Fri to 11 pm; Sat 8 am-11 pm; Sun from 8 am. Closed some major hols. Res accepted. Italian menu. Bar 11:30 am-midnight; Fri & Sat to 1 am. A la carte entrees: bkfst $3.50-$6.25, lunch $8-$15, dinner $8-$18. Specializes in hardwood-grilled seafood, meat, fowl. Own bread, pasta. Outdoor dining. Italian marble floors, mahogany bar; also dining in wine cellar. Cr cds: A, C, D, DS, MC, V.

[D] [⤴]

★ ★ ★ **PLAINFIELD'S MAYUR.** *852 SW 21st Ave (97205), west of downtown.* 503/223-2995. Hrs: 5:30-10 pm. Closed Thanksgiving, Dec 25. Res accepted. East Indian menu. Serv bar. A la carte entrees: dinner $7.95-$15.95. Specialties: spiced lamb, lobster & spices, Tandoori chicken. Own baking. Parking. Patio dining. In 1901, shingle-style mansion; centerpiece of dining room is functioning Indian clay oven (tandoor). Cr cds: A, C, D, DS, MC, V.

[D] [⤴]

★ **POOR RICHARD'S.** *3907 NE Broadway (97232), at Sandy Blvd, east of downtown.* 503/288-5285. Hrs: 11:30 am-11 pm; Sat 4-11 pm; Sun noon-9 pm. Closed most major hols. Res accepted. Bar. Semi-a la carte: lunch $4.75-$7.50, dinner $6-$14.95. Child's meals. Specializes in steak, seafood. Parking. Colonial decor; fireplace. Family-owned. Cr cds: A, DS, MC, V.

[D] [⤴]

✔★ ★ ★ **RED STAR.** *503 SW Alder (97205), downtown.* 503/222-0005. Hrs: 7 am-2:30 pm, 5-10 pm; Fri to 11 pm; Sat 8 am-2:30 pm, 5-11 pm; Sun 8 am-10 pm. Closed most major hols. Res accepted. Bar. Semi-a la carte: bkfst $5.50-$8.25, lunch $4.25-$12.95, dinner $5.75-$16.95. Child's meals. Specialties: sage-roasted chicken with buttermilk mashed potatoes, rotisserie pork loin with sweet potato hash and roasted pear-onion jam. Wood-burning oven. Contemporary decor. Totally nonsmoking. Cr cds: A, C, D, DS, JCB, MC, V.

[D]

★ ★ **RHEINLANDER.** *5035 NE Sandy Blvd (97213), east of downtown.* 503/288-5503. Hrs: 11 am-10 pm; Sat to midnight; early-bird dinner 4:30-6 pm; Sat from 4 pm; Sun from 3:30 pm. Closed Labor Day, Dec 24, 25. Res accepted. German menu. Bar. Semi-a la carte: dinner $3.95-$16.95. Child's meals. Specialties: hasenpfeffer, homemade sausage, rotisserie chicken. Strolling accordionist; group singing. Parking. Family-owned. Cr cds: A, MC, V.

[D] [⤴]

★ ★ **RINGSIDE.** *2165 W Burnside St (97210), west of downtown.* 503/223-1513. Hrs: 5 pm-midnight; Sun 4-11 pm. Closed some major hols. Res accepted. Bar. Semi-a la carte: dinner $12.50-$38. Specializes in steak, prime rib, seafood. Valet parking. Fireplace. Prizefight pictures; sports decor. Family-owned. Cr cds: A, D, DS, MC, V.

[D] [⤴]

★ ★ **RINGSIDE EAST.** *14021 NE Glisan (97230), east of downtown.* 503/255-0750. Hrs: 11:30 am-2:30 pm, 5 pm-midnight; Sat from 5 pm, Sun from 4 pm. Closed most major hols. Res accepted. Bar. Semi-a la carte: lunch $4.50-$10.95, dinner $10.50-$36.75. Specializes in prime rib, steak, seafood. Parking. Cr cds: A, C, D, DS, MC, V.

[D] [⤴]

★ ★ **SALTY'S ON THE COLUMBIA.** *3839 NE Marine Dr (97211), east of downtown.* 503/288-4444. Web www.saltys.com. Hrs: 11:30 am-11 pm; Sun 2-10 pm; June-Sept to midnight; Sun brunch 9:30 am-2 pm. Closed Dec 25. Res accepted. Bar. Semi-a la carte: lunch $7.25-$18.95, dinner $14-$51. Sun brunch buffet $7.95-$15.95. Child's meals. Specializes in seafood, halibut supreme, blackened salmon. Free valet parking. Outdoor dining. Overlooks Columbia River. Cr cds: A, C, D, DS, MC, V.

[D] [⤴]

★ **SAYLER'S OLD COUNTRY KITCHEN.** *10519 SE Stark (97216), just E of I-205 Washington exit, east of downtown.* 503/252-4171. Hrs: 4-11 pm; Fri to midnight; Sat 3 pm-midnight; Sun noon-11 pm. Closed some major hols. Bar. Complete meals: dinner $8.95-$35. Child's meals. Specializes in steak, seafood, chicken. Parking. Family-owned. Cr cds: A, DS, MC, V.

[D] [SC] [⤴] [♥]

✔★ **SYLVIA'S.** *5115 NE Sandy Blvd (97213), east of downtown.* 503/288-6828. Hrs: 4-10 pm; Fri, Sat to 11 pm; early-bird dinner 4-6 pm. Closed Thanksgiving, Dec 24, 25. Res accepted; required for theater. Italian menu. Bar. Semi-a la carte: dinner $7.75-$15.50. Specializes in lasagne, fettucine Alfredo. Parking. Dinner theater adj. Family-owned. Cr cds: A, DS, MC, V.

[D] [⤴] [♥]

★ ★ **TRIBECA.** *704 NW 21st St (97209), on Nob Hill.* 503/226-6126. Hrs: 4:30-10 pm; Thur-Sat to 11 pm. Closed Jan 1, July 4, Dec 25. Res accepted. Northwestern cuisine. Bar. Semi-a la carte: dinner $9-$20. Specializes in crab cakes, mushroom strudel, salmon. Outdoor dining. Casual decor. Totally nonsmoking. Cr cds: A, MC, V.

[D]

✔★ ★ **TYPHOON!** *2310 NW Everett St (97201), west of downtown.* 503/243-7557. Hrs: 11:30 am-2:30 pm, 5-10 pm. Closed Sun; most major hols. Res accepted. Thai menu. Wine, beer. Semi-a la carte: lunch $5.95-$7.95, dinner $6.95-$17.95. Specialties: miang kum, drunken noodles. Outdoor dining. Thai decor. Cr cds: A, C, D, DS, MC, V.

[D]

★ **WIDMER GASTHAUS.** *929 N Russell St (97227), downtown.* 503/281-3333. Hrs: 11 am-11 pm; Fri, Sat to 1 am; Sun to 10 pm. Closed Jan 1, Thanksgiving, Dec 25. Res accepted. German menu. Bar. Semi-a la carte: lunch $5.95-$7.95, dinner $5.95-$13.95. Specializes in schnitzel, sauerbraten. Outdoor dining. Contemporary decor. Totally nonsmoking. Cr cds: A, DS, MC, V.

[D]

★ ★ ★ **WILDWOOD.** *1221 NW 21st Ave (97209), in Nob Hill.* 503/248-9663. Pacific Northwest menu. Specializes in mussels, breast of duck, salmon. Hrs: 11:30 am-2:30 pm, 5:30-10 pm; Fri, Sat to 10:30 pm; Sun 10 am-2 pm (brunch), 5-8:30 pm. Closed Jan 1, Thanksgiving, Dec 25. Res accepted. Bar. Wine cellar. Semi-a la carte: lunch $8-$13, dinner $16-$24. Sun brunch $5.50-$12. Outdoor dining. Art Deco decor, with blond wood, lofty ceilings, and an open-counter kitchen. Cr cds: A, MC, V.

[D]

★ ★ **WINTERBORNE.** *3520 NE 42nd (97213), east of downtown.* 503/249-8486. Hrs: 5:30-9:30 pm. Closed Sun-Tue; most major hols. Res accepted. French menu. Serv bar. Semi-a la carte: dinner $13.50-$19. Child's meals. Specializes in seafood. Contemporary decor. Totally nonsmoking. Cr cds: A, DS, MC, V.

[D]

★ ★ ★ **ZEFIRO.** *500 NW 21st Ave (97209), on Nob Hill.* 503/226-3394. Hrs: 11:30 am-2:30 pm, 6-10:30 pm; Fri, Sat to 11 pm. Closed Sun; major hols. Res accepted. Mediterranean menu. Bar to midnight. Wine list. Semi-a la carte: lunch $4.50-$11, dinner $14-$20. Specializes in caesar salad, oysters. Outdoor dining. Contemporary decor. Totally nonsmoking. Cr cds: A, C, D, MC, V.

[D]

Unrated Dining Spots

IVY HOUSE. *1605 SE Bybee, east of downtown.* 503/231-9528. Hrs: 11 am-11 pm; Sat 9 am-11 pm; Sun 9 am-10 pm; Sat, Sun brunch 9 am-4 pm. Closed Tues, Wed; Thanksgiving, Dec 24, 25. Res accepted. Continental menu. Wine, beer. A la carte entrees: lunch $3.65-$6.50. Semi-a la carte: dinner $7.95-$18.95. Sat, Sun brunch $3.25-$9.95. Specializes in European pastries, creamed soups, sandwiches. Parking. Outdoor dining. Cr cds: A, MC, V.

[⤴]

ORIGINAL PANCAKE HOUSE. *8601 SW 24th Ave, west of downtown.* 503/246-9007. Hrs: 7 am-3 pm. Closed Mon, Tues. Semi-a la carte: bkfst, lunch $5-$10. Specializes in omelettes, apple pancakes, cherry crêpes. Parking. Colonial decor. No cr cds accepted.

PAPA HAYDN. *5829 SE Milwaukie, east of downtown.* *503/232-9440.* Hrs: 11:30 am-11 pm; Fri, Sat to midnight. Closed Sun, Mon; major hols. Continental menu. Wine, beer. Semi-a la carte: lunch $4.95-$6.95, dinner $6.95-$13.95. Specializes in European pastries, desserts. Outdoor dining. Cr cds: A, MC, V.

PERRY'S ON FREMONT. *2401 NE Fremont, east of downtown.* *503/287-3655.* Hrs: 11 am-9 pm; Fri, Sat to 10 pm; Sun from noon. Closed most major hols. Beer. Semi-a la carte: lunch $4.50-$7.50. Child's meals. Specializes in desserts, fish & chips, soups. Outdoor dining. Murals. Totally nonsmoking. Cr cds: A, MC, V.

Port Orford (E-2)

(For accommodations see Bandon, Gold Beach)

Founded 1851 **Pop** 1,025 **Elev** 56 ft **Area code** 541 **Zip** 97465
Information Chamber of Commerce, 502 Battle Rock City Pk, PO Box 637; 541/332-8055.

Westernmost incorporated city in the contiguous United States, Port Orford overlooks the Pacific Ocean with spectacular views. This was the first settlement in Coos and Curry counties. Captain George Vancouver sighted this area in 1792 and named it for the Earl of Orford. The cedar trees that grow in the area (sometimes called Lawson cypress and later named for the Earl) are highly favored for boat construction.

What to See and Do

Battle Rock Wayside. Site of one of the fiercest Native American battles on the Oregon Coast (1851); explanation of battle is inscribed on a marker in the park. Battle Rock offers one of the best seascapes in the state and has an ocean beach, surfing. Hiking trail. S edge of town on US 101.

Cape Blanco State Park. A 1,880-acre park with unusual black sand ocean beach, observation point; historic lighthouse (1870). Fishing; boat ramp. Hiking. Picnicking. Improved campsites. Standard fees. 9 mi N off US 101. Phone 541/332-6774. In the park is the

Historic Hughes House (1898). Restored Victorian Gothic-style house. (May-Sept, Thurs-Mon & hols) **Donation.**

Fishing. Ocean fishing provides salmon, ling cod, perch, snapper and crabs. Fall fishing in the Elk and Sixes rivers provides catches of chinook salmon and trout. **Garrison Lake,** at the NW edge of town, is open all yr for trout and bass fishing. Also swimming, waterskiing; boat ramp.

Humbug Mt State Park. A 1,842-acre park with winding trail leading to summit (1,750 ft); peak looks out on virgin forest, trout streams, sand beach. Fishing. Hiking. Picnicking. Tent & trailer sites (dump station). Standard fees. 6 mi S on US 101. Phone 541/332-6774.

Prineville (C-6)

(For accommodations see Bend, Madras, Redmond)

Founded 1868 **Pop** 5,355 **Elev** 2,864 ft **Area code** 541 **Zip** 97754
E-mail pchamber@coinet.com
Information Prineville-Crook County Chamber of Commerce, 390 N Fairview; 541/447-6304.

Two-thirds of the population of Crook County lives in or near Prineville. Livestock, alfalfa, wheat, mint, sugar beets and lumbering are important in this county. Hunting, fishing and rockhounding are popular. The City of Prineville Railroad, 19 miles of main line connecting the Union Pacific and Oregon Trunk Railway, is one of the few municipally-owned railroads in the US. Two Ranger District offices and headquarters of the Ochoco National Forest are located here.

What to See and Do

Mineral collecting. Agates of various types, obsidian, petrified wood, geodes and other stones. More than 1,000 acres of digging space in Eagle Rock, Maury Mt, White Rock Springs and other areas. Obtain map from Chamber of Commerce.

Ochoco Lake State Park. A 10-acre juniper-covered promontory on the N shore of Ochoco Reservoir. Fishing; boating (ramp). Hiking. Picnicking. Improved tent & trailer sites. Standard fees. 7 mi E on US 26. Phone 541/447-4363.

Ochoco National Forest. An approx 848,000-acre forest plus 111,000-acre Crooked River National Grassland; central Oregon high desert; thunderegg deposits; stands of ponderosa pine. Fishing in streams, Walton and Delintment lakes, Haystack and Antelope reservoirs; hunting. Hiking trails. Winter sports. Picnicking. Camping (fee). E on US 26. Phone 541/447-6247.

Redmond (C-6)

(See also Bend, Madras, Prineville)

Pop 7,163 **Elev** 2,997 ft **Area code** 541 **Zip** 97756 **E-mail** rcc@empnet.com **Web** www.empnet.com/redmond
Information Chamber of Commerce, 446 SW 7th St; 541/923-5191 or 800/574-1325.

Popular with sports enthusiasts and tourists, this is also the agricultural, lumbering and industrial center of central Oregon. A Ranger District office of the Deschutes National Forest (see BEND) is located here. The US Forest Service Redmond Regional Air Center is located at Roberts Field.

What to See and Do

Firemen's Pond. Children's fishing pond. Three-acre lake stocked with bass, bluegill. Children under 14 & disabled persons only. (Mid-Apr-mid-Oct, daily) Lake Rd & Sisters Ave. Phone 541/548-6068. **Free.**

Petersen Rock Gardens. Model castles and bridges built with rock specimens; lagoons and flower beds; picnicking, fireplaces; museum. (Daily) 7930 SW 77th St, 7 mi S on US 97, then 2 1/2 mi W. Phone 541/382-5574. ¢

State parks.

Cline Falls. A 9-acre park on the banks of the Deschutes River. Fishing. Picnicking. 4 mi W on OR 126. Phone 541/388-6055.

Smith Rock. A 623-acre park with view of unusual multicolored volcanic & sedimentary rock formations and the Crooked River Canyon. Crooked River Gorge (403 ft deep) is 3 mi N. Fishing. Hiking, rock climbing. Picnicking. 9 mi NE off US 97. Phone 541/548-7501.

Peter Skene Ogden Wayside. A 98-acre park with canyon 400 ft wide, 304 ft deep. Picnicking. Observation point. 9 mi N on US 97. Phone 541/548-7501.

Annual Event

Deschutes County Fair and Rodeo. 1st wk Aug.

Motels

★ **BEST WESTERN RAMA INN.** *2630 SW 17th Place, off US 97 S.* *541/548-8080.* 49 rms, 2 story. S $57-$110; D $62-$130; under 12 free. Crib $4. TV; cable (premium), VCR avail. Indoor pool; whirlpool. Complimentary continental bkfst. Restaurant nearby. Ck-out 11 am. Coin lndry. Business servs avail. In-rm modem link. Free airport transportation.

Exercise equipt; weight machine, bicycles. Refrigerators. Cr cds: A, C, D, DS, ER, JCB, MC, V.

⊡ ≋ ⊀ ⋈ ⋈ SC

🖊★ **REDMOND INN.** *1545 US 97S.* 541/548-1091; res: 800/833-3259. 46 rms, 3 story, 6 kits. No elvtr. Mid-May-Sept: S $55; D $64; each addl $5; kit. units $63; under 12 free; lower rates rest of yr. Crib free. Pet accepted, some restrictions; $5. TV; cable. Heated pool. Complimentary continental bkfst. Restaurant opp 7 am-11 pm. Ck-out 11 am. Refrigerators, microwaves. Cr cds: A, D, DS, MC, V.

⊡ ⇌ ≋ ⋈ ⋈ SC

★ **VILLAGE SQUIRE.** *629 S 5th St.* 541/548-2105; res: 800/548-2102. 24 rms, 2 story. S $55; D $55-$60; each addl $5. Crib $5. Pet accepted. TV; cable (premium), VCR avail. Complimentary coffee in lobby. Restaurant nearby. Ck-out 11 am. Some refrigerators, microwaves. Cr cds: A, D, DS, MC, V.

⊡ ⇌ ≋ ⋈ SC

Hotel

★★ **QUALITY NEW REDMOND.** *521 S Sixth St.* 541/923-7378; FAX 541/923-3949. 48 rms, 3 story. S, D $48-$70; each addl $5; suites $65-$80; under 12 free. TV; cable. Complimentary continental bkfst. Restaurant 11 am-10 pm. Bar to midnight. Ck-out 11 am. Meeting rms. Shopping arcade. Free local airport transportation. Exercise equipt; bicycles, rower. Built 1927. Grand lobby; fireplace, wood beam ceiling, grandfather clock. Cr cds: A, D, DS, JCB, MC, V.

⊡ ⊀ ≋ ⋈ SC

Inn

★★★ **CASCADE COUNTRY INN.** *(15870 Barclay Dr, Sisters 97759)* 20 mi W on OR 126. 541/549-4666; res: 800/316-0089. 7 rms, 2 story, guest house. No rm phones. S, D $100-$125; guest house $125; winter rates vary; special events (2-day min). TV in some rms; cable, VCR avail (movies). Complimentary full bkfst. Ck-out 11:30 am, ck-in 3 pm. X-country ski 10 mi. Some fireplaces. Picnic tables, grills. Country setting; antiques. Totally nonsmoking. Cr cds: DS, MC, V.

⊡ ≋ ⋈

Resort

★★ **INN AT EAGLE CREST.** *5 mi W on OR 126.* 541/923-2453; FAX 541/923-1720; res: 800/682-4786. Web www.eagle-crest.com. 100 rms, 2 story, 38 kit. suites. Mid-Mar-Oct: S $67-$92; D $73-$97; kit. suites $89-$123; ski, golf plans; higher rates national hols; lower rates rest of yr. Crib free. TV; cable (premium), VCR avail. Heated pool; whirlpool. Playground. Supervised child's activities (mid-June-early Sept); ages 6-12. Dining rm 7 am-3 pm. Bar 4-9 pm. Ck-out noon, ck-in 4 pm. Coin lndry. Business servs avail. Grocery. Meeting rms. Gift shop. Beauty shop. Free airport transportation. Lighted tennis, pro. Two 18-hole golf, greens fee $40, pro, putting green, driving range. Hiking, bicycle trails. Exercise rm; instructor, weights, treadmills. Lawn games. Microwaves in suites. Balconies. Picnic tables, grills. On Deschutes River. Cr cds: A, DS, MC, V.

⊡ ⇌ ⥮ ⊀ ≋ ⊀ ⟰ ⋈ ⋈ SC

Restaurant

★★ **MRS BEASLEY'S.** *1555 S US 97.* 541/548-4023. Hrs: 6:30 am-10 pm; Sun brunch 9:30 am-2 pm. Closed Dec 25. Bar from 11:30 am. Semi-a la carte: bkfst $3-$6, lunch $4-$7, dinner $5-$24. Child's meals. Specializes in seafood, prime rib. Salad bar. Own baking. Cr cds: A, C, D, DS, MC, V.

⊡ SC

Reedsport (D-3)

(See also Coos Bay, Florence, North Bend)

Pop 4,796 **Elev** 10 ft **Area code** 541 **Zip** 97467 **E-mail** reewbycc@mail.coos.or.us **Web** www.coos.or.us/~reewbycc
Information Chamber of Commerce, PO Box 11; 541/271-3495 or 800/247-2155.

Surrounded by rivers, lakes and the ocean, the area has an abundance and variety of fish, particularly striped bass, steelhead and salmon. Two of the best bass fishing lakes in Oregon are nearby. Reedsport was originally marshland subject to flooding at high tides, so the earliest buildings and sidewalks were built 3-8 feet above ground. A dike was built after the destructive Christmastime flood of 1964 to shield the lower part of town.

What to See and Do

Dean Creek Elk Viewing Area. Area has 440 acres of pasture and bottomland where Roosevelt elk (Oregon's largest land mammal) and other wildlife can be viewed. Interpretive center. No hunting. (Daily) 3 mi E on OR 38. Contact Bureau of Land Management, 1300 Airport Lane, North Bend 97459; phone 541/756-0100. **Free.**

Oregon Dunes National Recreation Area. Large coastal sand dunes, forests and wetlands comprise this 32,000-acre area in Siuslaw National Forest (see CORVALLIS). Beachcombing; fishing; boating. Hiking, horseback riding, off-road vehicle areas. Picnicking. Camping (fee; some campgrounds closed Oct-May). Visitors center and headquarters in Reedsport at US 101 and OR 38 (Daily; closed hols). W off US 101. Phone 541/271-3611.

Salmon Harbor. Excellent boat basin for charter boats, pleasure and fishing craft. Fishing for silver and chinook salmon in ocean, a short run from mouth of the Umpqua River (May-Sept, daily; rest of yr, Mon-Fri). Phone 541/271-3407.

Umpqua Discovery Center. Interpretive displays centering on cultural and natural history of area; also Antarctic exploration featuring research vessel "HERO." (Daily; closed Jan 1, Thanksgiving, Dec 25) 409 Riverfront Way. Phone 541/271-4816. ¢¢

Umpqua Lighthouse State Park. This 450-acre park touches the mouth of the Umpqua River, borders the Umpqua Lighthouse Reservation and skirts the ocean shore for more than 2 mi, with sand dunes rising 500 ft (highest in US). Noted for its marvelous, seasonal display of rhododendrons. Swimming. Fishing. Hiking; trail to beach and around Lake Marie. Picnicking. Tent & trailer sites. Whale watching area. Standard fees. 6 mi S off US 101. Phone 541/271-4118.

William M. Tugman State Park. A 560-acre park in scenic coastal lake region. Swimming, bathhouse; fishing; boating (ramp to Eel Lake). Picnicking. Improved tent & trailer sites (dump station). Standard fees. 8 mi S on US 101. Phone 541/759-3604.

Motels

🖊★ **ANCHOR BAY INN.** *1821 Hwy 101.* 541/271-2149; FAX 541/271-1802; res: 800/767-1821. E-mail anchorbay@presys.com; web www.presys.com/chwy/r/reedspor.htm. 21 rms, 2 story, 4 kits. S $43-$48; D $51-$59; kit. units $60-$65. Pet accepted, some restrictions; $5/day. TV; cable (premium), VCR avail. Pool. Complimentary continental bkfst. Restaurant nearby. Ck-out 10 am. Coin lndry. Business servs avail. Some refrigerators, microwaves. Cr cds: A, DS, MC, V.

⇌ ≋ ⋈ ⋈ SC

★★ **BEST WESTERN SALBASGEON INN.** *1400 Highway Ave (US 101).* 541/271-4831; FAX 541/271-4832. 56 rms, 2 story, 9 suites, 2 kit. units. Late May-mid-Sept: S $64-$79; D $78-$98; each addl $5; suites $95-$130; kit. units $95-$120; lower rates rest of yr. Crib free. Pet accepted; $5. TV; cable (premium), VCR avail. Indoor pool; whirlpool. Complimentary continental bkfst. Restaurant nearby. Ck-out 11 am. Coin

Indry. Meeting rms. Business servs avail. Exercise equipt; stair machine, bicycle. Minibars; refrigerators. Near Scholfield River. Cr cds: A, C, D, DS, MC, V.

★ **SALBASGEON INN OF THE UMPQUA.** *45209 OR 38. 541/271-2025.* 12 rms, 2 story, 1 suite, 4 kit. units. Late May-mid-Sept: S $52-$68; D $65-$78; each addl $5; suite $71-$94; kit. units $73-$99; lower rates rest of yr. Pet accepted, some restrictions; $5/day. TV; cable (premium). Ck-out 11 am. Picnic tables. On Umpqua River. All rooms have river views. Cr cds: A, C, D, DS, MC, V.

Rockaway (A-3)

(See also Cannon Beach, Seaside, Tillamook)

Pop 970 **Elev** 16 ft **Area code** 503 **Zip** 97136
Information Rockaway Beach Chamber of Commerce 103 S First St, PO Box 198; 503/355-8108 or 800/331-5928.

Rockaway is an attractive resort area with a fine, wide beach.

Motels

★★ **SILVER SANDS.** *215 S Pacific, 1 blk W of US 101. 503/355-2206; FAX 503/355-9690; res: 800/457-8972.* 64 rms, 2 story, 40 kits. (no ovens). No A/C. May-Sept: S, D $79-$111; kit. units $89-$111; lower rates rest of yr. Crib free. TV; cable (premium). Indoor pool; whirlpool, sauna. Coffee in rms. Restaurant nearby. Ck-out 11:30 am. Refrigerators; some fireplaces. On ocean. Cr cds: A, C, D, DS, MC, V.

★ **SURFSIDE.** *101 NW 11th Ave. 503/355-2312; res: 800/243-7786.* 79 units, 1-2 story. No A/C. Mid-May-mid-Sept: S $44.50-$98.50; D $98.50-$149.50; kit. units $79.50-$149.50; lower rates rest of yr. Crib $5. Pet accepted; $10. TV; cable. Indoor pool. Complimentary coffee. Restaurant nearby. Ck-out 11 am. Some fireplaces. On ocean; beach access. Cr cds: A, DS, MC, V.

Roseburg (E-3)

Settled 1853 **Pop** 17,032 **Elev** 459 ft **Area code** 541 **Zip** 97470
Information Visitors and Convention Bureau, 410 Spruce St, PO Box 1262, 541/672-9731 or 800/444-9584.

Roseburg is in one of Oregon's big stands of virgin timber that supports lumbermills and plywood plants. Although roses were the local pride, the town's name came not from the flower but from Aaron Rose, an early settler. This is the seat of Douglas County and headquarters for Umpqua National Forest.

What to See and Do

Douglas County Museum of History & Natural History. Exhibits include early history and natural history displays of the region; photographic collection; research library. Also Regional Tourist Information. (Daily) 1 mi S via I-5, exit 123 at fairgrounds. Phone 541/440-4507. **Free.**

Umpqua National Forest. Paved scenic byway takes one through magnificent scenery to Diamond Lake, which offers fishing (rainbow, steelhead trout) and forest camps. Mt Thielsen (9,182 ft) and Mt Bailey (8,363 ft) tower above the lake. The Colliding Rivers Visitor Information Center

(daily) is located along OR 138 in Glide; Diamond Lake Visitor Center (summer) is located opp entrance to Diamond Lake Campground. The forest (nearly 1 million acres), named for Native Americans who once fished in the rivers, includes three wilderness areas: Boulder Creek, 19,100 acres, Mt Thielsen, 22,700 acres and Roque-Umpqua Divide, 29,000 acres. Also the Oregon Cascades Recreation Area, 35,500 acres. Picnicking, lodging. Hiking. Camping (fee). Direct access from OR 138, along North Umpqua River. For further information contact Forest Supervisor, 2900 NW Stewart Pkwy, PO Box 1008; 541/672-6601.

Wildlife Safari. A 600-acre drive-through animal park; 600 exotic specimens of African, Asian and North American wildlife in natural habitats; petting zoo; elephant and train rides (seasonal); guided and walk-through tours by res; restaurant. (Daily) 6 mi S on I-5, exit 119 to OR 42 for 4 mi, in Winston. Phone 541/679-6761. ¢¢¢

Wineries.

Hillcrest Vineyard. Wine tastings; tours. (Daily; closed hols) Approx 10 mi W; I-5 exit 125, W on Garden Valley Rd, Melrose Rd, Doerner Rd then N on Elgarose and follow signs. Phone 541/673-3709 or 800/736-3709. **Free.**

Callahan Ridge Winery. Tasting rm. (Daily) W of I-5; Garden Valley exit 125, 2 mi W to Melrose then 1 mi S to Busenbark Lane, then right. Phone 541/673-7901. **Free.**

Henry Estate Winery. Tours, tasting rm; picnic area. (Daily; closed major hols) 13 mi NW via I-5, 1 mi W of Umpqua on County 6. Phone 541/459-5120 or -3614. **Free.**

Annual Events

Greatest of the Grape. Mid-Feb.

Umpqua Valley Roundup. Wkend mid-June.

Roseburg Graffiti Week. 1st wk July.

Douglas County Fair. Early Aug.

Umpqua Valley Wine, Art and Jazz Festival. 15 mi N on I-5, in Oakland. Early Sept.

Motels

★ **BEST WESTERN DOUGLAS INN.** *511 SE Stephens St. 541/673-6625.* 52 rms, 2 story. June-Sept: S $49-$68; D $60-$76; each addl $5; lower rates rest of yr. Crib $5. TV; cable (premium). Complimentary coffee. Restaurant opp 6 am-10 pm. Ck-out noon. Business servs avail. In-rm modem link. Exercise equipt; weight machine, stair machine, sauna. Whirlpool. Cr cds: A, C, D, DS, ER, JCB, MC, V.

★★ **BEST WESTERN GARDEN VILLA.** *760 NW Garden Valley Blvd. 541/672-1601; FAX 541/672-1316.* 122 rms, 2 story. June-Sept: S $64-$70; D $68-$88; each addl $7; under 12 free; lower rates rest of yr. Crib $5. Pet accepted, some restrictions. TV; cable (premium). Heated pool. Complimentary continental bkfst. Restaurant adj 5 am-midnight. Ck-out noon. Coin lndry. Meeting rms. Sundries. Exercise equipt; weight machine, treadmill. Microwaves avail. Cr cds: A, C, D, DS, ER, JCB, MC, V.

✔★ **ORLEANS.** *427 NW Garden Valley Blvd, just E of I-5 Veterans Hospital exit 125. 541/673-5561; FAX 541/957-0318; res: 800/626-1900.* 72 rms, 1-2 story. S $39-$55; D $49-$65; each addl $5; under 12 free. Crib $5. TV; cable. Pool. Complimentary continental bkfst. Ck-out 11 am. Meeting rm. Business servs avail. Some microwaves. Cr cds: A, C, D, DS, MC, V.

★ **TRAVELODGE.** *315 W Harvard Blvd. 541/672-4836.* 40 rms, 1-2 story. S $55; D $75; each addl $5; under 17 free. Crib free. TV; cable (premium). Heated pool. Complimentary coffee in rms. Restaurant adj 5 am-midnight. Ck-out 11 am. Valet serv. Balconies. Picnic tables. On river. Cr cds: A, C, D, DS, ER, JCB, MC, V.

★ ★ **WINDMILL INN.** *1450 Mulholland Dr. 541/673-0901; res: 800/547-4747.* Web www.mind.net/windmills. 128 rms, 2 story. June-Sept: S $65-$71; D $71-$88; each addl $6; under 18 free; lower rates rest of yr. Crib $3.50. Pet accepted, some restrictions. TV; cable (premium). Pool; whirlpool. Complimentary continental bkfst. Restaurants 6 am-midnight. Bar. Ck-out 11 am. Guest lndry. Meeting rms. Business servs avail. In-rm modem link. Valet serv. Sundries. Free airport, bus depot transportation. Exercise equipt; bicycles, treadmill, sauna. Microwaves avail. Some balconies. Cr cds: A, C, D, DS, MC, V.

Salem (B-4)

(See also Albany, McMinnville, Newberg, Oregon City, Portland, Silverton)

Settled 1840 **Pop** 107,786 **Elev** 154 ft **Area code** 503 **E-mail** information@scva.org **Web** www.oregonlink.com/scva/

Information Convention & Visitors Association, 1313 Mill St SE, 97301; 503/581-4325 or 800/874-7012.

Capital and third-largest city in Oregon, Salem's economy is based on the state government, food processing, light manufacturing and wood products. Salem shares Oregon's sports attractions with other cities of the Willamette Valley.

What to See and Do

Bush House. Victorian mansion (1878) with authentic furnishings. (Daily exc Mon; closed hols) Bush's Pasture Park. 600 Mission St SE, 6 blks S of capitol. Phone 503/363-4714. ¢¢ Also here is

Bush Barn Art Center. Remodeled barn houses two exhibit galleries with monthly shows and a sales gallery featuring Northwest artists. (Daily exc Mon; closed hols) Phone 503/581-2228. **Free.**

Enchanted Forest. Features storybook theme. Other exhibits include reproduction of early mining town, haunted house (fee), log flume ride (fee), ice mountain bobsled ride (fee), old world village, theater featuring live comedy and children's shows, water & light show. Picnic area; refreshments; gift stores. (Mid-Mar-Sept, daily) 7 mi S, off I-5 Sunnyside-Turner exit 248, at 8462 Enchanted Way SE. Phone 503/363-3060. ¢¢¢

Gilbert House Children's Museum. Hands-on exhibits related to art, drama, music, science and nature. (Tues-Sat, also Sun afternoons) 116 Marion St. Phone 503/371-3631. ¢¢

Historic Deepwood Estate (1894). Queen Anne-style house and carriage house designed by W.C. Knighton. Povey Brothers stained-glass windows, golden oak woodwork; solarium; Lord & Schryver gardens with wrought-iron gazebo from 1905, boxwood gardens, perennial garden with English teahouse; nature trail. House (May-Sept, daily exc Sat; rest of yr, Mon, Wed, Fri, Sun; closed major hols). 1116 Mission St SE. Phone 503/363-1825. ¢¢

Honeywood Winery. Oregon's oldest producing winery. Tours, tasting rm, gift shop. (Daily; closed Thanksgiving, Dec 25) 1350 Hines St SE. Phone 503/362-4111. **Free.**

Mission Mill Village. Thomas Kay Woolen Mill Museum (1889) shows process of processing fleece into fabric. Jason Lee House (1841), John D. Boon House (1847), Methodist Parsonage (1841) and Pleasant Grove-Presbyterian Church (1858) help interpret missionary family life. Shops, park, picnicking. Tours of woolen mill, historic houses (daily; closed Jan 1, Thanksgiving, Dec 25). 1313 Mill St SE. Phone 503/585-7012. Tours ¢¢

State Capitol (1938). Marble, of modern Greek design. Atop the capitol is a fluted tower topped by a bronze, gold-leafed statue symbolic of the pioneers who carved Oregon out of the wilderness. Tours of capitol (June-Aug, daily; rest of yr by appt). Capitol building (daily; closed major

hols). Video; gift shop. Court & Summer Sts. Phone 503/986-1388. **Free.** N of here is the

Capitol Mall. Flanked by four state buildings in modern Greek style, including the Public Service, Transportation, Labor and Industries and State Library buildings. The grounds are an arboretum with historical statuary and monuments.

Willamette University (1842). (2,500 students) Oldest institution of higher learning west of Missouri River, with several historic buildings on campus including Waller Hall (1867) and the Art Bldg (1905) with the Hallie Brown Ford Art Gallery. The Mark O. Hatfield Library has special area for research and viewing of Senator Hatfield's public papers. Campus tours; picnic area. 900 State St, between 12th & Winter Sts. Phone 503/370-6300.

Annual Events

Salem Art Fair & Festival. Bush's Pasture Park. Arts & crafts booths & demonstrations, children's art activities & parade, ethnic folk arts, performing arts, street painting, 5K run, food; tours of historic Bush House. Phone Salem Art Assn 503/581-2228. 3rd wkend July.

West Salem Waterfront Parade. Mid-Aug.

Oregon State Fair. Fairgrounds, 2330 17th St NE. Horse racing, wine competition and tasting, agricultural exhibits, horse show, livestock, food, carnival, entertainment. Phone 503/378-3247. Aug 27-Sept 7.

Motels

(Rates may be higher during state fair)

★ ★ **BEST WESTERN NEW KINGS INN.** *3658 Market St NE (97301), off I-5 exit 256.* 503/581-1559; FAX 503/364-4272. 101 rms, 2 story. Mid-May-Oct: S $57-$67; D $60-$70; each addl $6; some lower rates rest of yr. Crib $4. TV; cable (premium). Indoor pool; whirlpool. Playground. Restaurant adj open 24 hrs. Ck-out noon. Coin lndry. Meeting rm. Business servs avail. Free airport, RR station, bus depot transportation. Tennis. Exercise equipt; weights, bicycles, sauna. Refrigerators. Cr cds: A, C, D, DS, MC, V.

✔ ★ **PHOENIX INN.** *4370 Commercial St SE (97302), I-5 exits 249 & 252.* 503/588-9220; FAX 503/585-3616; res: 800/445-4498. 89 rms, 4 story. S $56-$70; D $56-$77; each addl $5; suites $92-$110; under 17 free. Crib free. Pet accepted, some restrictions; $10. TV; cable (premium). Indoor pool; whirlpool. Complimentary continental bkfst. Restaurant adj 11 am-11 pm. Ck-out noon. Coin lndry. Meeting rms. Business servs avail. Exercise equipt; weight machine, treadmill. Refrigerators. Some suites with whirlpool. Cr cds: A, C, D, DS, MC, V.

★ ★ **SHILO INN.** *3304 Market St (97301), I-5 exit 256.* 503/581-4001; FAX 503/399-9385. 89 rms, 4 story. S, D $85-$95; each addl $10; under 12 free. Crib free. TV; cable (premium), VCR. Heated pool; whirlpool. Complimentary continental bkfst in lobby. Ck-out noon. Business servs avail. In-rm modem link. Free airport transportation. Exercise equipt; weight machine, bicycles, sauna. Refrigerators, wet bars. Cr cds: A, C, D, DS, ER, JCB, MC, V.

★ **TIKI LODGE.** *3705 Market St (97301), I-5 Market St exit.* 503/581-4441; FAX 503/581-4442. 50 rms, 20 with shower only, 2 story. Mid-May-Sept: S $49-$52; D $52-$58; each addl $4; under 12 free; wkly rates; lower rates rest of yr. Crib $2. Pet accepted. TV; cable (premium). Heated pool; sauna. Playground. Complimentary coffee in lobby. Restaurant adj open 24 hrs. Ck-out noon. Meeting rms. Business servs avail. Cr cds: A, D, DS, MC, V.

Motor Hotel

★ ★ **QUALITY INN.** *3301 Market St (97301), I-5 exit 256.* 503/370-7888; FAX 503/370-6305. 150 rms, 4 story. S $73-$78; D $78-

$83; each addl $5; suites $107-$112; under 18 free. Crib free. Pet accepted; $10. TV; cable (premium), VCR avail. Indoor pool; whirlpool, sauna. Complimentary coffee in rms. Restaurant 6:30 am-10 pm. Rm serv. Bar 11-1 am; entertainment Sat. Ck-out 11 am. Coin lndry. Meeting rms. Business servs avail. Bellhops. Sundries. Valet serv. Balconies. Cr cds: A, C, D, DS, ER, JCB, MC, V.

Inn

✓★ **STATE HOUSE.** 2146 State St (97301). 503/588-1340; res: 800/800-6712. 4 rms, 2 with shower only, 2 share bath, 3 story. S, D $50-$70; suites $55-$70; wkly rates; higher rates special events (2-night min). Crib free. TV; cable. Complimentary full bkfst. Complimentary coffee in rms. Ck-out 11:30 am, ck-in 2 pm. Refrigerators. Picnic tables. In 1920s residence. Totally nonsmoking. Cr cds: DS, MC, V.

Restaurants

★ ★ ★ **ALESSANDRO'S PARK PLAZA.** 325 High St SE (97301). 503/370-9951. Hrs: 11:30 am-2 pm, 5:30-9 pm; Sat from 5:30 pm. Closed Sun; major hols. Res accepted. Italian menu. Bar. Wine cellar. Semi-a la carte: lunch $5.75-$9.50, dinner $7.75-$16.75. Prix fixe: dinner $25-$35. Child's meals. Specializes in seafood, poultry, veal. Overlooks park, waterfall. Cr cds: A, DS, MC, V.

(D)

✓★ **CHELSEA'S.** 4053 Commercial St SE (97302). 503/585-1175. Hrs: 6:30 am-10 pm; Fri, Sat to 11 pm. Closed Thanksgiving, Dec 25. Wine, beer. Semi-a la carte: bkfst $2-$5.50, lunch, dinner $3.75-$10.95. Child's meals. Specializes in soups, desserts. Family-style dining. Cr cds: A, DS, MC, V.

(D SC)

Seaside (A-3)

(See also Astoria, Cannon Beach)

Pop 5,359 **Elev** 13 ft **Area code** 503 **Zip** 97138

Information Chamber of Commerce, 7 N Roosevelt, PO Box 7; 503/738-6391 or 800/444-6740.

Seaside is the largest and oldest seashore town in Oregon. It has a concrete promenade two miles long, and shallow ocean beaches provide good swimming and clam digging.

What to See and Do

Saddle Mt State Park. A 2,922-acre park with trail to 3,283-ft summit, one of the highest in the Coastal Range. Hiking. Picnicking. Primitive campsites. Standard fees. 13 mi SE on US 26, then 9 mi N. For information phone 503/861-1671 or 503/436-2844.

Seaside Aquarium. Deep-sea life and trained seals; seal feeding (fee); (Mar-Nov, daily; rest of yr, Wed-Sun; closed Thanksgiving, Dec 24, 25) 200 N Prom, on beach. Phone 503/738-6211. ¢¢

Motels

★ **ALOHA INN.** 441 2nd Ave, just W of US 101. 503/738-9581; res: 800/448-5544. 48 rms, 3 story, 10 kit. units. May-Oct: S $64; D $68; each addl $8; suites $106-$135; kit. units $77-$135; lower rates rest of yr. Crib free. Pet accepted; $10. TV; cable (premium). Indoor pool; whirlpool, sauna. Complimentary continental bkfst. Restaurant nearby.

Ck-out 11 am. Coin lndry. Meeting rm. Business servs avail. Some refrigerators. Cr cds: A, C, D, DS, MC, V.

✓★ **COAST RIVER INN.** 800 S Holladay Dr. 503/738-8474. 26 rms, 2 story, 5 kit. suites. No A/C. Many rm phones. May-Sept: S $45; D $59-$68; each addl $5; kit. suites $68-$200; under 5 free; winter wkly rates; lower rates rest of yr. Crib free. TV; cable (premium). Restaurant nearby. Ck-out 11 am. Meeting rms. Refrigerators. Cr cds: A, DS, MC, V.

★ ★ **EBB TIDE.** 300 N Promenade, at 3rd Ave. 503/738-8371; FAX 503/738-0938; res: 800/468-6232. 83 rms, 3 story, 45 kits. No A/C. No elvtr. May-Sept: S, D $80-$120; lower rates rest of yr. Crib $5. Pet accepted; $10/day. TV; cable (premium), VRC avail. Indoor pool; whirlpool. Restaurant nearby. Business servs avail. In-rm modem link. Refrigerators. On beach. Cr cds: A, C, D, DS, MC, V.

★ ★ **GEARHART BY THE SEA.** (1157 N Marion Ave, Gearhart) N on US 101, at jct N Marion Ave & 10th St. 503/738-8331; FAX 503/738-0881; res: 800/547-0115. 80 condominiums, 1-5 story. No A/C. Condominiums $119-$184; each addl $10. Crib $5. TV; cable, VCR avail (movies). Indoor pool. Restaurant 7 am-11 pm. Bar to 2:30 am. Ck-out 11 am. Coin lndry. Meeting rm. 18-hole golf, greens fee $25, pro, putting green. Balconies. Ocean view. Cr cds: DS, MC, V.

★ ★ **HI-TIDE.** 30 Avenue G. 503/738-8414; FAX 503/738-0875; res: 800/621-9876. 64 rms, 3 story, 64 kits. (no ovens). No A/C. No elvtr. May-Sept: S, D, kit. units $80-$115; lower rates rest of yr. TV; cable (premium), VCR avail. Indoor pool; whirlpool. Restaurant nearby. Ck-out noon. Business servs avail. On ocean. Cr cds: A, C, D, DS, MC, V.

✓★ **RIVERVIEW INN.** 555 Avenue G. 503/738-0670; FAX 503/738-0142. 21 rms, 2 story. No A/C. Late May-mid-Sept: S $50-$75; D $55-$65; family rates; lower rates rest of yr. Crib free. TV; cable (premium), VCR avail. Restaurant nearby. Ck-out 11 am. Meeting rms. Refrigerators. Balconies. Cr cds: DS, MC, V.

✓★ **ROYALE.** 531 Ave A. 503/738-9541. 26 rms, 1-2 story. No A/C. Mid-May-Sept: S $47; D $47-$57; each addl $4; family, wkly rates off-season; lower rates rest of yr. Crib free. TV; VCR avail. Complimentary coffee in rms. Restaurant nearby. Ck-out 11 am. Cr cds: A, C, D, DS, MC, V.

★ ★ **SHILO INN-SEASIDE SUITES EAST.** 900 S Holladay. 503/738-0549; FAX 503/738-0532. 58 rms, 3 story. Mid-Apr-early Sept: S, D $59-$124; higher rates hols; lower rates rest of yr. Crib free. TV; cable (premium), VCR avail. Indoor pool; whirlpool, steam rm, sauna. Complimentary continental bkfst. Restaurant nearby. Ck-out noon. Coin lndry. Business servs avail. Airport transportation. Bathrm phones. Cr cds: A, C, D, DS, ER, JCB, MC, V.

Motor Hotels

★ ★ **BEST WESTERN OCEANVIEW RESORT.** 414 N Promenade. 503/738-3334; FAX 503/738-3264. 104 rms, 5 story, 20 suites, 45 kit. units. No A/C. June-Aug: S, D, kit. units $69-$172; suites $195-$265; under 18 free; lower rates rest of yr. Crib free. Pet accepted, some restrictions; $15. TV. Indoor pool; whirlpool. Restaurant 7 am-10 pm. Rm serv. Bar 4 pm-midnight. Ck-out 11 am. Coin lndry. Meeting rms. Business servs avail. In-rm modem link. Many refrigerators. Balconies. On beach. Cr cds: A, C, D, DS, MC, V.

★★★ **SHILO INN.** *30 N Promenade. 503/738-9571; FAX 503/738-0674.* 112 rms, 5 story, 60 kit. units. No A/C. July-Labor Day: S $105-$215; D, kit. units $175-$215; each addl $15; under 12 free; lower rates rest of yr. Crib free. Free garage parking. TV; cable (premium), VCR avail (movies). Indoor pool; whirlpool. Restaurant 7 am-10 pm. Rm serv. Bar 11 am-2 pm. Ck-out noon. Coin lndry. Meeting rms. Business servs avail. Valet serv. Sundries. Gift shop. Free airport transportation. Exercise equipt; weight machine, bicycle, sauna. Game rm. Some balconies. On ocean. Cr cds: A, C, D, DS, ER, JCB, MC, V.

D ⊠ ✗ ⊼ ⊠ SC

Inns

★★ **ANDERSON'S BOARDING HOUSE.** *208 N Holladay Dr. 503/738-9055; res: 800/995-4013.* 7 rms, 2 story. No A/C. No rm phones. S $70-$110; D $75-$115; each addl $10. Crib free. TV; cable. Complimentary full bkfst. Restaurant nearby. Ck-out 11 am, ck-in 4 pm. Balconies. On river. Country Victorian house (1898); antiques. Totally nonsmoking. Cr cds: MC, V.

⊠ ⊠

★★★ **GILBERT.** *341 Beach Dr. 503/738-9770; FAX 503/717-1070; res: 800/410-9770.* 10 rms, 3 story, 2 suites. No A/C. S $74-$90; D $79-$95; each addl $10; suites $95. Closed Jan. Crib free. TV; cable. Complimentary full bkfst. Restaurant nearby. Ck-out 11 am, ck-in 3 pm. Bellhops. Free local airport, bus depot transportation. Queen Anne/Victorian house (1892); antiques. Totally nonsmoking. Cr cds: A, DS, MC, V.

⊠ ⊠

Restaurants

★ **CAMP 18.** *US 26, 25 mi E on US 26, at mile post 18. 503/755-1818.* Hrs: 7 am-9 pm; Sun brunch 10 am-2 pm. Closed Dec 25. Bar. Semi-a la carte: bkfst $2.95-$7.95, lunch $3.95-$7.95, dinner $10.95-$16.95. Sun brunch $10.95. Child's meals. Specializes in omelettes, family-style dinners. In log bldg. Cr cds: A, DS, MC, V.

★★ **DOOGER'S SEAFOOD & GRILL.** *505 Broadway. 503/738-3773.* Hrs: 11 am-10 pm. Closed first 2 wks Dec. Wine, beer. Semi-a la carte: lunch $4-$10.95, dinner $7.95-$22.95. Child's meals. Specializes in seafood, steak, homemade clam chowder. Totally nonsmoking. Cr cds: MC, V.

D

Silverton (B-4)

(For accommodations see Newberg, Oregon City, Salem)

Pop 5,635 **Elev** 249 ft **Area code** 503 **Zip** 97381
Information Chamber of Commerce, City Hall, 421 S Water St, PO Box 257; 503/873-5615.

What to See and Do

Cooley's Gardens. Largest producer of bearded iris in the world. Display gardens feature many varieties; over one million blossom in fields (mid-May-early June). 11553 Silverton Rd NE. Phone 503/873-5463. **Free.**

Country Museum/Restored Train Station. Ames-Warnock House (1908) contains local historical items dating from 1846. Southern Pacific Station (1906) contains larger items. (Mar-Dec, Thurs & Sun) Contact Chamber of Commerce. 428 S Water St. **Donation.**

Silver Falls State Park. Oregon's largest state park, 8,706 acres, has 10 waterfalls, of which 5 are more than 100 ft high; 4 may be viewed from road, the others from forested canyon hiking trail. Swimming. Bridle, bicycle trails. Picnicking. Tent & improved sites (dump station). Conference center. Standard fees. 15 mi SE on OR 214. Phone 503/873-8681.

Sweet Home (C-4)

(For accommodations see Albany)

Pop 6,850 **Elev** 525 ft **Area code** 541 **Zip** 97386 **E-mail** shchamber@jun.com **Web** www.peak.org/~wcarjs/sweethomeor/
Information Chamber of Commerce, 1575 Main St; 541/367-6186.

Gateway to Santiam Pass and the rugged Oregon Cascades, the area around Sweet Home is popular for fishing, boating, skiing, hiking and rock hounding. A Ranger District office of Willamette National Forest (see EUGENE) is located here.

What to See and Do

East Linn Museum. Nearly 5,000 artifacts of pioneer life in the area (1847). Period rms; rock collection and mining equipment; logging tools; maps, photos, portraits; guns, dolls, bottles; saddlery and blacksmith shop. (May-Sept, Tues-Sun; rest of yr, Thurs-Sun; also by appt; closed most major hols) 746 Long St, at jct OR 228, US 20. Phone 541/367-4580. **Donation.**

Foster Lake. Swimming, water sports; fishing; boating. 2 mi E on US 20 at Foster.

The Dalles (B-6)

(See also Biggs, Hood River)

Founded 1851 **Pop** 10,200 (est) **Elev** 98 ft **Area code** 541 **Zip** 97058 **E-mail** tdaccc@gorge.net
Information Chamber of Commerce, 404 W 2nd St; 541/296-2231 or 800/255-3385.

Once The Dalles was the end of the wagon haul on the Oregon Trail. Here the pioneers loaded their goods on boats and made the rest of their journey westward on the Columbia River. The falls and rapids that once made the river above The Dalles unnavigable are now submerged under water backed up by the Columbia River dams. The Dalles Dam is part of a system of dams extending barge traffic inland as far as Lewiston, Idaho, and Pasco, Washington. The port has berthing space for all types of shallow draft vessels. The chief source of income in the area is agriculture. The Dalles is noted for its cherry orchards and wheat fields located in the many canyons along the river.

What to See and Do

Celilo Converter Station. North terminal for transmission of direct current between Pacific Northwest and Pacific Southwest (south terminal at Sylmar, CA). Interpretive display with educational and historical exhibits; visitors may also view control rm, equipment. (Daily) 1 mi SE on US 197. Phone 541/296-4694 or 541/296-3615. **Free.**

⊠ **Columbia Gorge Discovery Center.** Over 26,000-sq-ft bldg is official interpretive center for the Columbia River Gorge National Scenic Area. Hands-on and electronic exhibits detail the volcanic upheavals and raging floods that created the Gorge, describe the history and importance of the river, and look to the Gorge's future. Also Early Explorers, Steamboats and Trains, Industry and Stewardship exhibits. Guided tours, seminars, classes and workshops (some fees). Library & collections (by appt). Cafe. (Daily; closed Jan 1, Thanksgiving, Dec 25) 3 mi NW at Crate's Point, 5000 Discovery Dr. Phone 541/296-8600. ¢¢¢ Admission includes

Wasco County Historical Museum. Reveals colorful history of over 10,000 yrs of county's occupation and importance of Columbia River on area history. Artifacts and exhibits feature Native Americans, missionaries, early pioneers and explorers; history of area railroad industry, farming and shipping. Interactive displays include a late 19th-century town, railroad depot and barn. (Schedule and phone same as Center) Also explore the

Oregon Trail Living History Park. Includes 80,000 sq ft of outdoor exhibits and gardens. Costumed interpreters demonstrate life of Oregon Trail emigrants, members of Lewis and Clark expedition and Native Americans. Footpaths wind through park; offers stunning views of river from high bluff. (Schedule and phone same as Center)

Ft Dalles Museum. Only remaining building of the 1856 outpost is the Surgeon's Quarters. Rare collection of pioneer equipment; stagecoaches, covered wagons. (Mar-Oct, daily; rest of yr, Wed-Sun; closed hols, also 1st 2 wks Jan) 15th & Garrison Sts. Phone 541/296-4547. ¢¢

Mayer State Park. A 613-acre park comprised of an undeveloped area with overlook on Rowena Heights; and a developed area, on the shores of the Columbia River, with swimming beach, windsurfing, dressing rms; fishing; boat ramp. Picnicking. 10 mi W, off I-84 exit 77. Phone 541/695-2261.

Mt Hood National Forest (see). W of city.

Sorosis Park. This 15-acre park overlooks the city from the highest point on Scenic Dr, with view of the Columbia River, Mt Adams and Mt Hood. Located on part of the bottom of ancient Lake Condon. The bones of three types of camels, the ancient horse and mastodons were found near here. Jogging trail; tennis courts. Picnic area. Rose Garden.

Riverfront Park. Swimming beach, windsurfing; fishing; boating (launch), jet boat excursions. Picnicking. Off I-84, exit 85.

The Dalles Dam and Reservoir. Two-mi train tour with views of historic navigation canal, visitor center, petroglyphs and fish ladder facilities (Memorial Day-Labor Day, daily; Apr-May & Oct-Mar, Wed-Sun). 3 mi E of town off I-84 and 1 mi E of The Dalles Hwy Bridge, which crosses the Columbia just below the dam (use I-84 exit 87 in summer, exit 88 off-season). Phone 541/296-1181. **Free.** On S shore, 8 1/2 mi E of dam is

Celilo Park. Swimming, sailboarding; fishing; boating (ramp). Picnicking, playground. Comfort station. Recreational areas with similar facilities also are on N and S shores. Adj to ancient fishing grounds, now submerged under waters backed up by The Dalles Dam.

Annual Events

Cherry Festival. 4th wkend Apr.

Ft Dalles Rodeo & Chili Cook-off. CASI sanctioned. Thurs-Sun, 3rd wk July.

Motels

✔★ **INN AT THE DALLES.** 3550 SE Frontage Rd, just S of I-84 exit 87. 541/296-1167; FAX 541/296-3920; res: 800/982-3496. 45 rms, 4 kits. S, D $34-$57; each addl $5; suites, kit. units $45-$75. Crib $5. TV; cable. Indoor pool. Coffee in lobby. Restaurant nearby. Ck-out 11 am. Business servs avail. Free airport transportation. View of Columbia River, Mt Hood, The Dalles Dam. Cr cds: A, C, D, DS, MC, V.

★★ **LONE PINE VILLAGE.** 351 Lone Pine Dr, I-84, exit 87, at US 197. 541/298-2800; FAX 541/298-8282; res: 800/955-9626. 56 rms, 2 story. June-Sept: S $52.20-$58; D $60.30-$67; each addl $6; suites $72-$81; under 12 free; lower rates rest of yr. Crib free. Pet accepted, some restrictions; $6. TV; cable (premium). Indoor pool; whirlpool. Complimentary full bkfst; coffee in lobby. Restaurant adj 6 am-10 pm. Bar. 3-11 pm. Ck-out noon. Coin lndry. Meeting rms. Business servs avail. Sundries. Gift shop. Free airport transportation. Golf privileges (par 3), pro, driving range. Exercise equipt; bicycle, stair machine. Lawn games. Refrigerators. Cr cds: A, D, DS, MC, V.

★★ **QUALITY INN.** 2114 W 6th St. 541/298-5161; FAX 541/298-6411. 85 rms, 2 story, 16 kits. S $59; D $65; kit. units $72-$79; each addl $5. Crib $2. Pet accepted; $2. TV; cable. Heated pool; whirlpool. Restaurant 6 am-10 pm; Fri, Sat to 11 pm. Ck-out 11 am. Coin lndry.

Meeting rms. Business servs avail. In-rm modem link. Health club privileges. Some fireplaces. Cr cds: A, D, DS, MC, V.

Motor Hotel

✔★ ★ **BEST WESTERN TAPADERA.** 112 W 2nd St, at Liberty St. 541/296-9107; FAX 541/296-3002. 65 rms, 2-4 story. S $51-$56; D $59-$63; each addl $7; under 12 free. Crib $8. Pet accepted. TV; cable (premium). Heated pool. Restaurant 6:30 am-9 pm. Rm serv. Bar 11 am-11 pm. Ck-out noon. Meeting rms. Business servs avail. In-rm modem link. Some refrigerators. Cr cds: A, C, D, DS, ER, JCB, MC, V.

Restaurant

✔★ **COUSINS'.** 2114 W 6th St. 541/298-2771. Hrs: 6 am-10 pm; Fri, Sat to 11 pm. Closed Dec 25. Bar. Semi-a la carte: bkfst $1.95-$7.95, lunch $4.25-$6.25, dinner $6.50-$11.50. Child's meals. Specialties: pot roast, turkey & dressing. Frontier motif. Cr cds: A, D, DS, MC, V.

D

Tillamook (B-3)

(See also Lincoln City, Rockaway)

Founded 1851 **Pop** 4,001 **Elev** 16 ft **Area code** 503 **Zip** 97141

Information Tillamook Chamber of Commerce, 3705 US 101N; 503/842-7525.

Located at the southern end of Tillamook Bay, this is the county seat. Dairying, cheese and butter making, timber and fishing are the main industries. There are many beaches for swimming, crabbing, clamming, beachcombing; boat landings, camping, picnicking and fishing sites are also in the area.

What to See and Do

Cape Lookout State Park. A 1,974-acre park with virgin spruce forest, observation point; one of most primitive ocean shore areas in state. Hiking trail to end of cape. Picnicking. Tent & trailer sites (dump station). Standard fees. 12 mi SW off US 101 on Whiskey Creek Rd. Phone 503/842-4981.

★ **Capes Scenic Loop Drive to Cape Meares and Oceanside.** (Approx 10 mi) W on 3rd St, NW on Bay Ocean Rd to Cape Meares; go S on Loop Rd to Cape Meares State Park. See Tillamook Bay County Boat Landing, Cape Meares Lake, beach with beachcombing; also Cape Meares Lighthouse; Native American burial Sitka spruce tree known as "Octopus Tree." Continue S to Oceanside, site of Three Arch Rocks Federal Sea Lion and Migratory Bird Refuge, and beach area with beachcombing and agates. Continue S to Netarts; see Netarts Bay Boat Landing and Whiskey Creek Fish Hatchery. Go S on Cape Lookout Rd to Pacific City and Cape Kiwanda, then back to US 101S. (Or take Whiskey Creek Rd from Netarts boat launching site, continue over Cape Lookout Mt through Sandlake, Tierra Del Mar to Pacific City. Exceptionally scenic, it also avoids traffic on US 101.)

Tillamook County Pioneer Museum. Possessions of early settlers, replica of pioneer home and barn; blacksmith shop; logging displays, war relics; relics from Tillamook Naval Air Station and Blimp Base; minerals, guns, books, vehicles, natural history and wildlife exhibits including nine dioramas; "great grandma's kitchen." (Mar-Sept, daily; rest of yr, daily exc Mon; closed Thanksgiving, Dec 25) 2106 2nd St at Pacific Ave. Phone 503/842-4553. ¢

Annual Events

Tilamook Dairy Parade & Rodeo. Fairgrounds. 4th wkend June.

Tillamook County Fair. Fairgrounds, 4603 3rd St. 1st full wk Aug.

Motels

★ **EL REY SANDS.** *815 Main Ave. 503/842-7511; res: 800/257-1185.* 22 rms, 2 story. S $47-$50; D $45-$65; suites $50. TV; cable (premium). Complimentary coffee in rms. Restaurant 5:30 am-8 pm. Ck-out 11:30 am. Cr cds: A, C, D, DS, MC, V.

★ ★ **MAR-CLAIR INN.** *11 Main Ave. 503/842-7571; res: 800/331-6857.* 47 rms, 1-2 story, 6 kits. No A/C. Mid-May-mid-Oct: S $56-$68; D $64-$74; suites, kit. units $79-$99; lower rates rest of yr. Crib $6. TV. Heated pool; whirlpool, sauna. Restaurant 7 am-9 pm. Ck-out 11 am. Sun deck. Cr cds: A, DS, MC, V.

Motor Hotel

★ ★ ★ **SHILO INN.** *2515 N Main. 503/842-7971; FAX 503/842-7960.* 100 rms, 2 story. July-Oct: S, D $69-$110; each addl $10; kit. units $110; under 12 free; higher rates during County Fair; lower rates rest of yr. Crib free. Pet accepted, some restrictions; $7. TV; cable (premium), VCR avail (movies). Indoor pool; whirlpool. Restaurant 6 am-11 pm. Bar 11-2 am. Ck-out noon. Coin lndry. Meeting rms. Business servs avail. Exercise equipt; weights, bicycle. Refrigerators. Cr cds: A, D, DS, MC, V.

Inn

★ ★ **SANDLAKE COUNTRY INN.** *(8505 Galloway Rd, Sandlake 97112) 11 mi S on US 101, right at Sandlake exit, 5 1/2 mi to Sandlake Grocery, right on Galloway Rd. 503/965-6745; FAX 503/965-7425.* 4 rms, 2 story, 1 suite, 1 kit. unit. No A/C. Some rm phones. S $75-$120; D $80-$125; each addl $10. TV; cable, VCR. Complimentary full bkfst. Ck-out 11 am, ck-in 3 pm. Concierge. Whirlpool. Balconies. Farmhouse built of timbers washed ashore from a ship wreck in 1890. Antiques. Totally nonsmoking. Cr cds: A, DS, MC, V.

Restaurant

★ **CEDAR BAY.** *2015 1st St, at Pacific St, on US 101. 503/842-8288.* Hrs: 11 am-9 pm; Sun noon-8 pm. Res accepted. No A/C. Bar to 11 pm. Semi-a la carte: lunch $4-$8, dinner $8-$20. Child's meals. Specializes in steak, prime rib, seafood. Cr cds: MC, V.

Umatilla (A-7)

(For accommodations see Hermiston, Pendleton)

Founded 1863 **Pop** 3,046 **Elev** 296 ft **Area code** 541 **Zip** 97882

Information Chamber of Commerce, PO Box 67; 541/922-4825 or 800/542-4944.

What to See and Do

Columbia Crest Winery. Located amidst 2,000 acres of European-style vinifera grapes. Tours, including wine production, cellar and tastings. Picnicking; gardens. (Self-guided tours, Mon-Fri; guided tours, Sat-Sun; closed major hols) 18 mi NW via WA 14, in Paterson, WA. Phone 509/875-2061. **Free.**

Hat Rock State Park. A 735-acre park on lake formed by McNary Dam. Swimming beach; fishing; boat ramp to the Columbia River. Hiking. Picnicking. Hat Rock is a large monolith that looks like a man's top hat; a landmark often referred to in diaries of early-day explorers and travelers. 9 mi E off US 730 near jct OR 207. Phone 541/567-5032.

McNary Lock and Dam. Single lift navigation lock. Dam is 7,365 ft long, 92 ft high. The Columbia River forms Lake Wallula, a 61-mi waterway partly in Washington. Swimming, waterskiing; fishing, hunting; boating (marinas). Picnicking. Primitive camping (2 areas; free). Tours of power, navigation and fish passage facilities (June-Sept, daily). (Daily) 2 mi E on US 730. Phone 541/922-4388. **Free.**

Umatilla Marina Park. Swimming beach; boating (launch, storage, gas, oil). Picnicking. RV trailer camping (fee). (Daily) NE edge of town on Columbia River. Phone 541/922-3939.

Annual Events

Sage Riders Rodeo. NRA sanctioned, 2nd wkend June.

Landing Days & Govenor's Cup Walleye Tournament. Labor Day wkend.

Yachats (C-3)

(See also Florence, Newport)

Pop 533 **Elev** 15 ft **Area code** 541 **Zip** 97498

Information Yachats Area Chamber of Commerce, US 101; PO Box 728; 541/547-3530.

Yachats (YA-hots) is a resort area on the central Oregon coast, west of Siuslaw National Forest. Derived from a Native American phrase meaning "waters at the foot of the mountain," Yachats is along a rocky shore with a fine sandy beach.

What to See and Do

Cape Perpetua Campground. Beachcombing; fishing. Hiking. Camping. Summer campfire programs (Sat, Sun). 3 mi S on US 101. Camping ¢¢¢ Nearby is

Cape Perpetua Visitor Center. Interpretive displays of oceanography, natural history of coastal area, movies. Nature trails, auto tour. (May, Thurs-Sun; June-Labor Day, daily; rest of yr, Sat-Sun; closed Dec 25) In Siuslaw National Forest. Phone 541/547-3289. **Free.**

Neptune State Park. This 302-acre park features Cook's Chasm (near N end), a long, narrow, deep fissure where the sea falls in with a spectacular fury; wind-depressed forest trees (near N end); slopes covered with huckleberry shrubs. A community of harbor seals makes its home on the rocks below Strawberry Hill. Surf fishing. Hiking. Picnicking. Observation point. 3 mi S on US 101. Phone 541/997-3641.

Tillicum Beach Campground. Ocean view, beachcombing. Camping. Summer evening campfire programs Sat & Sun. Camping 3 1/2 mi N on US 101. ¢¢¢

Yachats State Park. A 93-acre day-use park bordering the Yachats River, in the shadow of Cape Perpetua. Small picnic area. Observation point. On US 101. Phone 541/867-7451.

Motels

★ ★ **ADOBE.** *1555 US 101. 541/547-3141; FAX 541/547-4234; res: 800/522-3623 (western US).* 93 rms, 2-3 story, 5 kits. S, D $58-$100; each addl $8; suites $150; kit. units $110-$135. Crib $8. Pet accepted, some restrictions. TV; cable (premium), VCR. Complimentary coffee in rms. Restaurant 8 am-2:30 pm, 5-9 pm. Bar. Ck-out 11 am. Meeting rm. Business servs avail. Gift shop. Exercise equipt; weight machine, bicycle, sauna. Whirlpool. Refrigerators; some fireplaces. Whirlpool in suites. Some balconies. On ocean. Cr cds: A, C, D, DS, MC, V.

✔★ **FIRESIDE.** *1881 US 101N. 541/547-3636; FAX 541/547-3152; res: 800/336-3573.* 43 rms, 2 story. Mid-May-Sept: S, D $60-$130; each addl $7; kit. cottages $99-$135; some lower rates rest of yr. Crib $5. Pet accepted, some restrictions; $7/day. TV; cable, VCR avail. Complimentary coffee in rms. Restaurant nearby. Ck-out 11 am. Refrigerators; some fireplaces, microwaves. View of ocean. Cr cds: DS, MC, V.

★★ **SHAMROCK LODGETTES.** *¼ mi S on US 101. 541/547-3312; FAX 541/547-3843; res: 800/845-5028.* Web www.o-t-b.com. 19 rms, 11 kit. cottages. Mid-May-Sept: S, D, kit. units $70-$100; each addl $7; kit. cottages $91-$112; wkly rates; lower rates rest of yr. Crib $7. Pet accepted, some restrictions; $3/day. TV; cable (premium). Complimentary coffee in rms. Restaurant nearby. Ck-out 11 am. Massage. Refrigerators; some in-rm whirlpools; microwaves avail. Some private patios, balconies. Beach adj. Cr cds: A, D, DS, MC, V.

Inn

★★ **SEA QUEST.** *95354 US 101. 541/547-3782; res: 800/341-4878; FAX 541/547-3719.* Web www.seaq.com. 5 rms, 1 with shower only, 2 story. No rm phones. Apr-Nov: S, D $150-$160; each addl $15; wkends, hols (2-3-day min); lower rates rest of yr. Children over 14 yrs only. Complimentary full bkfst. Ck-out 11 am, ck-in 3 pm. Gift shop. Many in-rm whirlpools. On beach. Ocean view. Totally nonsmoking. Cr cds: MC, V.

South Dakota

Population: 696,004
Land area: 75,956 square miles
Elevation: 962-7,242 feet
Highest point: Harney Peak (Pennington County, in Black Hills)
Entered Union: November 2, 1889 (40th state, same day as North Dakota)
Capital: Pierre
Motto: Under God, The People Rule
Nickname: Mount Rushmore State
State flower: Pasque
State bird: Chinese ring-necked pheasant
State tree: Black Hills spruce
State fair: September 1-7, 1998, in Huron
Time zone: Central and Mountain
Web: www.state.sd.us

This land was once dominated by the proud and mighty Sioux. They, along with mountain men, who trapped for the American Fur Company, the Missouri Fur Company and the Hudson's Bay Company, slowly gave way to the settlers. Today most Sioux descendants live on nine reservations in South Dakota. Many South Dakota museums and shops display and sell Native American art and artifacts.

Many settlers, who came for the free land offered under the Homestead Act of 1862, built sod houses on the prairies; others, who came for gold discovered in 1874, set up gold rush camps in the Black Hills. Three groups of immigrants—Germans, Scandinavians, Czechs—retain their traditional customs and cookery in their home life. Several colonies of Hutterites prosper in the southeastern area.

In South Dakota, man's achievements are strikingly contrasted with nature's design. Here, near the town of Wall, are the Badlands, a colorful and spectacular result of eons of erosion. In the Black Hills the largest sculpture in the world, the Crazy Horse Memorial, is being created. The combination of natural wonders with Native American and frontier legend is a made-to-order attraction for tourists.

The wide-open spaces of eastern and central South Dakota are famous for pheasant and offer some of the finest hunting in the nation. The Missouri River, with its four great lakes, is a paradise for those who love water recreation. Walleye fishing in the area is superlative. Fishing for northern pike is also superb, especially in Lake Oahe, where they often reach trophy size.

Throughout the state, hundreds of markers inform visitors of history or natural phenomena. Many sites of natural, historical and cultural significance are also preserved in a number of the state parks and recreation areas.

When to Go/Climate

Unpredictable, sometimes erratic, weather conditions are common in South Dakota. Summers are hot and humid, although less so than in other midwestern states. September brings cold temperatures, while winter can get downright frigid, and it has been known to snow as late as May.

AVERAGE HIGH/LOW TEMPERATURES (°F)
RAPID CITY

Jan 34/11	**May** 68/42	**Sept** 74/46
Feb 38/15	**June** 78/52	**Oct** 63/35
Mar 46/22	**July** 86/58	**Nov** 47/23
Apr 58/32	**Aug** 85/56	**Dec** 36/13

SIOUX FALLS

Jan 24/3	**May** 71/46	**Sept** 73/49
Feb 30/10	**June** 81/56	**Oct** 61/36
Mar 42/23	**July** 86/62	**Nov** 43/23
Apr 59/35	**Aug** 83/59	**Dec** 28/9

Parks and Recreation Finder

Directions to and information about the parks and recreation areas below are given under their respective town/city sections. Please refer to those sections for details.

Key to abbreviations: I.P. = Interstate Park; N.B.C. = National Battlefield & Cemetery; N.B.P. = National Battlefield Park; N.F. = National Forest; N.G. = National Grassland; N.H. = National Historical Park; N.H.S. = National Historic Site; N.M. = National Monument; N.Mem. = National Memorial; N.M.P. = National Military Park; N.P. = National Park; N.Pres. = National Preserve; N.R. = National Recreational Area; N.R.R. = National Recreational River; N.Res. = National Reserve; N.S. = National Seashore; N.S.R. = National Scenic River; N.S.T. = National Scenic Trail; N.V.M. = National Volcanic Monument; S.B. = State Beach; S.C.P. = State Conservation Park; S.G. = State Garden; S.H.A. = State Historic Area; S.H.P. = State Historic Park; S.N.A. = State Natural Area; S.P. = State Park; S.R. = State Reserve; S.R.A. = State Recreation Area; S.Res.P. = State Resort Park; S.R.P. = State Rustic Park.

CALENDAR HIGHLIGHTS

JUNE

10K Volksmarch (Crazy Horse Memorial). Only time that top of the mountain is open to the public. Phone 605/673-4681.

JULY

Summer Festival (Brookings). Pioneer Park. Largest arts and crafts festival in the state. Entertainment, food. Phone 605/692-6125.

Corvette Classic (Spearfish). Main St. Sports car enthusiasts gather each summer for their convention. Highlight is Main St Show and shine, when hundreds of Corvettes line Main St. Phone 605/361-1243.

AUGUST

Central States Fair (Rapid City). Central States Fairground. Rodeo, carnival, horse and tractor pulls, auto races, demo derby. Phone 605/342-8325.

L. Frank Baum Oz Festival (Aberdeen). At Wylie Park. Oz characters, storytelling, book memorabilia, educational lectures. Art and food vendors, band concerts. Phone 800/645-3851.

SEPTEMBER

South Dakota State Fair (Huron). Largest farm machinery exhibit in midwest. Carnival, entertainment, horse shows, car races, rodeos, livestock. Phone 605/353-7340.

Corn Palace Festival (Mitchell). Music and entertainment. Phone Chamber of Commerce, 605/996-5667 or -6223 or 800/257-CORN.

NATIONAL PARK AND RECREATION AREAS

Place Name	Listed Under
Badlands N.P.	same
Black Hills	same
Black Hills N.F.	BLACK HILLS
Jewel Cave N.M.	same
Mount Rushmore N.Mem.	same
Wind Cave N.P.	same

STATE RECREATION AREAS

Place Name	Listed Under
Angostura Reservoir S.R.A.	HOT SPRINGS
Bear Butte S.P.	STURGIS
Custer S.P.	same
Farm Island S.R.A.	PIERRE
Fisher Grove S.P.	REDFIELD
Ft Sisseton S.P.	SISSETON
Hartford Beach S.P.	MILBANK
Lake Herman S.P.	MADISON
Mina S.R.A.	ABERDEEN
Oakwood Lakes S.P.	BROOKINGS
Platte Creek S.R.A.	PLATTE
Richmond Lake S.R.A.	ABERDEEN
Roy Lake S.P.	SISSETON
Snake Creek S.R.A.	PLATTE
Union County S.P.	BERESFORD

Water-related activities, hiking, riding, various other sports, picnicking and visitor centers, as well as camping, are available in many of these areas. Entrance fee (daily). Annual $20/carload permit is good at all state parks and recreation areas or $2/person daily (Custer, $3 May-Oct); under age 12 free. There is a camping fee at most areas ($6-$12/site/night; electricity $3). Cabins (where avail) $30/night. All areas open daily. Pets on leash

only. For further information write Division of Parks and Recreation, Department of Game, Fish and Parks, 523 E Capitol Ave, Pierre 57501-3182.

SKI AREAS

Place Name	Listed Under
Deer Mt Ski Area	LEAD
Terry Peak Ski Area	LEAD

FISHING & HUNTING

Nonresident: annual fishing license $49; family $59 (allows one limit); visitor's 5-day $29; 1-day $9; no license required for nonresidents under 16, but fish taken will be counted as part of string limit of a licensed accompanying adult. Nonresident: big game $150-$200; small game $95 (good for two 5-day periods). Nonresident waterfowl license $100 (good for 10 consecutive days except in southeast counties); nonresident turkey license $75; nonresident predator license $30.

All nonresident firearm licenses for deer and antelope are issued through a computer lottery.

Regulations, seasons and limits for both fish and game vary in different waters and areas of South Dakota. For detailed information write to Department of Game, Fish and Parks, 523 E Capitol Ave, Pierre 57501.

Driving Information

Children under 5 years must be in an approved child passenger restraint system anywhere in vehicle: ages 2-5 may use a regulation safety belt; age 1 and under must use an approved safety seat. For further information phone 605/773-4493.

INTERSTATE HIGHWAY SYSTEM

The following alphabetical listing of South Dakota towns in *Mobil Travel Guide* shows that these cities are within 10 miles of the indicated Interstate highways. A highway map, however, should be checked for the nearest exit.

Highway Number	Cities/Towns within 10 miles
Interstate 29	Beresford, Brookings, Sioux Falls, Sisseton, Vermillion, Watertown.
Interstate 90	Badlands National Park, Belle Fourche, Chamberlain, Deadwood, Mitchell, Murdo, Rapid City, Sioux Falls, Spearfish, Sturgis, Wall.
Interstate 229	Sioux Falls.

Additional Visitor Information

A state highway map and the annual *South Dakota Vacation Guide* are free from the South Dakota Department of Tourism, 711 E Wells Ave, Pierre 57501-3369. A periodical also worth looking at is *South Dakota Conservation Digest*, bimonthly, from South Dakota Department of Game, Fish and Parks, 445 E Capitol Ave, Pierre 57501.

There are thirteen information centers (mid-May-September, daily) at rest areas along I-90 near Chamberlain, Tilford, Salem, Spearfish, Valley Springs, Vivian and Wasta; and along I-29 near New Effington, Vermillion & Wilmot.

Aberdeen (A-5)

(See also Redfield, Webster)

Settled 1880 **Pop** 24,927 **Elev** 1,304 ft **Area code** 605 **Zip** 57401

Information Convention & Visitors Bureau, 516 S Main St, PO Box 1179, 57402-1179; 605/225-2414 or 800/645-3851.

The roots of Aberdeen's commerce are the three railroads that converge here and make it a wholesale and distribution center, giving it the fitting nickname "Hub City." Alexander Mitchell, a railroader of the 19th century, named the town for his Scottish birthplace. German-Russian immigrants arrived in 1884. Hamlin Garland, author of *Son of the Middle Border,* and L. Frank Baum, author of *The Wizard of Oz,* lived here.

What to See and Do

Dacotah Prairie Museum. Pioneer and Native American artifacts; area history & art. **Hatterscheidt Wildlife Gallery** features specimens from around the world. (Daily exc Mon; closed hols) 21 S Main St. Phone 605/626-7117. **Free.**

Mina State Recreation Area. On 300 acres. Swimming, bathhouses; fishing; boating (ramps, dock). Hiking. Picnicking (shelters), playground. Camping (electrical hookups). Interpretive programs. Standard fees. 11 mi W off US 12. Phone 800/710-2267.

Richmond Lake State Recreation Area. On 346 acres. Swimming, bathhouses; fishing; boating (ramps, dock). Hiking. Picnicking (shelters), playground. Camping (electrical hookups). Interpretive program. Standard fees. 10 mi NW via US 12, County 6 and County 13. Phone 800/710-2267.

Wylie Park. Man-made lake, swimming beach, waterslide, picnic areas, concession; zoo with buffalo, deer, elk. **Storybook Land,** a theme park inspired by children's stories and **Land of Oz** theme park. Camping (standard fees). (Late Apr-mid-Oct, daily) 1 mi N on US 281. Phone 605/626-3512. **Free.**

Annual Events

Parimutual horse racing. Brown County Fairgrounds. Quarter Horse & Thoroughbred racing. 3 wkends May.

Snow Queen Festival. 2 wkends in Jan.

L. Frank Baum Oz Festival. Aug 14-16.

Motels

★ **BREEZE INN.** *1216 6th Ave SW.* 605/225-4222; res: 800/288-4248. 20 rms, 3 kits. S $24; D $34.95-$36.95; each addl $2. Crib $2. Pet accepted. TV; cable. Restaurant adj. Ck-out 11 am. X-country ski 1 mi. Cr cds: C, D, DS, MC, V.

★ **SUPER 8.** *2405 6th Ave SE.* 605/229-5005; FAX 605/229-5005. 108 rms, 2-3 story. No elvtr. S $37.98; D $44.98; each addl $5. Crib free. TV; cable. Indoor pool; sauna. Restaurant nearby. Ck-out 11 am. Coin lndry. Business servs avail. In-rm modem link. Airport transportation. X-country ski 1 mi. Cr cds: A, C, D, DS, MC, V.

✔ ★ **WHITE HOUSE INN.** *500 6th Ave SW.* 605/225-5000; FAX 605/225-6730; res: 800/225-6000. 96 rms, 3 story. S $32; D $36-$38; each addl $3; suites $40-$55; under 12 free. Crib free. Pet accepted. TV; cable. Complimentary continental bkfst. Restaurant nearby. Ck-out 11 am. Business servs avail. Airport, RR station, bus depot transportation. X-country ski 1½ mi. Cr cds: A, C, D, DS, MC, V.

Motor Hotels

★ ★ **BEST WESTERN RAMKOTA INN.** *1400 8th Ave NW.* 605/229-4040; FAX 605/229-0480. 154 rms, 2 story. S, D $55.75-$63.75; each addl $6; suites $75-$150; under 18 free. Crib free. Pet accepted. TV; cable. Indoor pool; wading pool, whirlpool, sauna. Restaurant 6:30 am-10 pm. Bar 11-2 am. Ck-out noon. Meeting rms. Business servs avail. Free airport, RR station, bus depot transportation. X-country ski 2 mi. Cr cds: A, C, D, DS, ER, JCB, MC, V.

✔ ★ **HOLIDAY INN.** *Box 1007, 2727 6th Ave SE, near Municipal Airport.* 605/225-3600; FAX 605/225-6704. 153 rms, 2 story. S $40-$60; D $50-$65; each addl $8; under 18 free. Crib free. Pet accepted, some restrictions. TV; cable. Indoor pool. Playground. Restaurant 6 am-10 pm.

Rm serv. Bar 4 pm-2 am. Ck-out 11 am. Meeting rms. Business servs avail. Valet serv. Sundries. Free airport, bus depot transportation. X-country ski 1 mi. Rec rm. Cr cds: A, C, D, DS, JCB, MC, V.

Restaurants

★ ★ **THE FLAME.** *2 S Main St.* 605/225-2082. Hrs: 11 am-11 pm; Fri, Sat to midnight. Closed Sun; some major hols. Res accepted. Bar. Semi-a la carte: lunch $4.75-$8.95, dinner $7.75-$15.95. Child's plates. Specializes in steak, ribs, seafood. Family-owned. Cr cds: A, C, D, DS, MC, V.

✔ ★ **HONG KONG.** *1721 SE 6th Ave.* 605/229-2639. Hrs: 11 am-9 pm; Fri, Sat to 10 pm; Sun to 9 pm. Closed major hols. Res accepted. Chinese menu. Wine, beer. Semi-a la carte: lunch $4-$6, dinner $6-$8. Oriental decor. Cr cds: MC, V.

Badlands National Park (C-2)

Area code 605

(62 mi E of Rapid City via I-90, SD 240)

This fantastic, painted landscape of steep canyons, spires and razor-edged ridges was made a national monument by President Franklin D. Roosevelt in 1939 and became a national park in 1978. Its stark and simple demonstration of geologic processes has an unusual beauty. Soft clays and sandstones deposited as sediments 26 to 37 million years ago by streams from the Black Hills created vast plains, which were inhabited by the saber-toothed cat, the rhinoceros-like brontothere and ancestors of the present-day camel and horse. Their fossilized bones make the area an enormous prehistoric graveyard. Herds of bison, gone for many years, roam the area again. Pronghorn antelope, mule deer, prairie dogs and Rocky Mountain bighorn sheep can also be seen.

More than 600 feet of volcanic ash and other sediments were laid down. About 500,000 years ago, streams began carving the present structures, leaving gullies and multi-colored canyons.

The Ben Reifel Visitor Center with exhibits and an audiovisual program is open all year at Cedar Pass (daily; closed Jan 1, Thanksgiving, Dec 25). The "Touch Room" is open to children of all ages. Evening programs and activities conducted by ranger-naturalists are offered during the summer. Camping at Cedar Pass (fee) and Sage Creek (free). The White River Visitor Center, 60 miles SW of the Cedar Pass Visitor Center, features colorful displays on the history and culture of the Oglala Sioux. Vehicle fee; Golden Eagle, Golden Age and Golden Access Passports accepted (see MAKING THE MOST OF YOUR TRIP). For further information contact PO Box 6, Interior 57750; 605/433-5361.

Belle Fourche (B-1)

(For accommodations see Deadwood, Lead, Spearfish, Sturgis)

Founded 1890 **Pop** 4,335 **Elev** 3,023 ft **Area code** 605 **Zip** 57717
E-mail belchmbr@iwayl.iw.net

Information Chamber of Commerce, 415 5th Ave; 605/892-2676.

Belle Fourche, rich in Western heritage, is a destination for those in search of the West. Cowboys and sheepherders once fought a range war here. Belle Fourche, seat of Butte County, still ships the largest volume of livestock of any town in western South Dakota, Wyoming or Montana and is the wool-shipping capital of the nation. Industry includes bentonite (industrial clay) mills and mines. However, around July 4 there is little work done, for the Black Hills Roundup, one of the West's outstanding rodeos, keeps the town at fever pitch. The geographical center of the United States, with Alaska included, is marked at a point 20 miles north of Belle Fourche on US 85.

What to See and Do

Belle Fourche Reservoir and Orman Dam. Recreation on 52-mi shoreline. Swimming, waterskiing, windsurfing. Walleye and northern pike fishing. NE of town off US 85 or US 212.

Johnny Spaulding Cabin. Two-story cabin, built in 1876 and restored. Tourist information. (June-Aug, daily exc Sun) 801 State St, on US 212, opp Post Office. **Free.**

Tri-State Museum. Regional and historical exhibits; fossils; dolls. (Mid-May-mid-Sept, daily; closed Labor Day) 831 State St. Phone 605/892-3705. **Free.**

Annual Events

All Car Rally. Mid-June.

Black Hills Roundup. Rodeo. Phone 605/892-2676 for ticket prices and res. Early July.

Butte County Fair. 17 mi E on US 212, in Nisland. Mid-Aug.

Beresford (D-6)

(See also Sioux Falls, Vermillion)

Pop 1,849 **Elev** 1,498 ft **Area code** 605 **Zip** 57004

What to See and Do

Union County State Park. Approx 500 acres. Hiking, bridle trails. Picnicking, playground. Arboretum. Camping. Standard fees. 11 mi S off I-29. Phone 605/987-2263. ¢

Motel

✔★ **CROSSROADS.** *On SD 46, ¼ mi E of I-29 exit 46. 605/763-2020.* 32 rms. S $20-$24; D $28-$34.50; each addl $3. Crib $5. Pet accepted. TV. Restaurant adj 6 am-10 pm. Ck-out 11 am. Cr cds: C, D, DS, MC, V.

✈ ⊠ ⊠

Black Hills (C-1)

(For accommodations see Custer, Custer State Park, Deadwood, Hill City, Hot Springs, Keystone, Lead, Rapid City, Spearfish, Sturgis; also see Crazy Horse Memorial, Jewel Cave National Monument, Mount Rushmore National Memorial, Wind Cave National Park)

Magnificent forests, mountain scenery, ghost towns, Mount Rushmore National Memorial (see), Harney Peak (highest mountain east of the Rockies), Crazy Horse Memorial (see), swimming, horseback riding, rodeos, hiking, skiing and the Black Hills Passion Play make up only a partial list of attractions. Memories of Calamity Jane, Wild Bill Hickok, Preacher Smith (all buried in Deadwood) haunt the old Western towns. There are parks, lakes and picturesque mountain streams. Bison, deer, elk, coyotes, mountain goats, bighorn sheep and smaller animals make this area home.

Black Hills National Forest includes 1,247,000 acres—nearly half of the Black Hills. The forest offers 28 campgrounds, 20 picnic grounds and one winter sports area (see LEAD). Daily fees are charged at most campgrounds. Headquarters are in Custer (see). For information and a map ($4)

of the National Forest write Forest Supervisor, RR 2, Box 200, Custer 57730. Two major snowmobile trail systems, one in the Bearlodge Mountains and the other in the northern Black Hills, offer 330 miles of some of the best snowmobiling in the nation. There are also 250 miles of hiking, bridle and mountain biking trails.

There is a story that whimsically explains the formation of the Black Hills. Paul Bunyan, the legendary logger, had a stove so large that boys with hams strapped to their feet skated on the top to grease it for the famous camp flapjacks. One day when the stove was red hot, "Babe," Paul's favorite blue ox, swallowed it whole and took off in all directions. He died of a combination of indigestion and exhaustion. Paul, weeping so copiously his tears eroded out the Badlands, built the Black Hills as a cairn over his old friend.

Geologists, however, state that the Black Hills were formed by a great geologic uplift that pushed a mighty dome of ancient granite up under the sandstone and limestone layers. Water washed away these softer rocks, exposing the granite. This uplift was slow. It may still be going on. The Black Hills offer rich rewards in gold and silver from the famous Homestake and other mines. Pactola Visitor Center, on US 385 at Pactola Reservoir, west of Rapid City, has information and interpretive exhibits on Black Hills history, geology and ecology (Memorial Day-Labor Day).

Brookings (B-6)

(See also Madison, Watertown)

Founded 1879 **Pop** 16,270 **Elev** 1,623 ft **Area code** 605 **Zip** 57006 **E-mail** chamber@brookings.com **Web** www.brookings.com/chamber/ **Information** Chamber of Commerce/Convention & Visitor Bureau, 2308 6th St, PO Box 431; 605/692-6125 or 800/600-6125.

Research done at South Dakota State University has helped make Brookings the agricultural capital of the state; it has developed diversified farming and the manufacturing of devices for seed cleaning, counting and planting.

What to See and Do

Oakwood Lakes State Park. 255 acres. Swimming; fishing; boating, canoeing. Hiking. Picnicking, playground. Camping (electrical hookups, dump station). Visitor center (daily). Interpretive program. Standard fees. 8 mi N on I-29, then 9 mi W on county road. Phone 605/627-5441.

South Dakota Art Museum. Features Harvey Dunn paintings of pioneers, Oscar Howe paintings; Native American arts; South Dakota collection; changing exhibits. (Daily; closed Jan 1, Thanksgiving, Dec 25) Medary Ave at Harvey Dunn St. Phone 605/688-5423. **Donation.**

South Dakota State Univ (1881). (8,090 students) NE part of town. McCrory Gardens and South Dakota Arboretum, 65 acres of horticultural gardens including 15 acres of theme gardens. Walking tours. Guided tours on request. Phone 605/688-4541. Also here is

Agricultural Heritage Museum. Displays on historical development of South Dakota agriculture. Changing exhibits. (Daily; closed hols) Medary Ave & 11th St. Phone 605/688-6226. **Free.**

Annual Event

Summer Festival. Pioneer Park. Largest arts & crafts festival in the state. Entertainment, food. 2nd full wkend July.

Motels

✔★ ★ **BEST WESTERN STAUROLITE INN.** *2515 E 6th St, 1¼ mi E at jct US 14, I-29 exit 132. 605/692-9421; FAX 605/692-9429.* 102 rms, 2 story. S $43-$49; D $48-$56; each addl $2; suites $90; under 18 free. Crib free. Pet accepted. TV; cable. Indoor pool; wading pool; whirlpool. Restaurant 6 am-9 pm. Rm serv. Bar 4 pm-2 am; entertainment exc Sun. Ck-out 11 am. Meeting rms. Business servs avail. In-rm modem link. Bellhops. Valet serv. Sundries. Free airport, bus depot transportation.

X-country ski 1 mi. Private patios, balconies. Picnic tables. Cr cds: A, C, D, DS, ER, MC, V.

⚓ 🏌 🏊 🖈 🏇 SC

★ ★ ★ **HOLIDAY INN.** *2500 E 6th St, near Municipal Airport. 605/692-9471; FAX 605/692-5807.* 125 rms, 2 story. S $49-$61; D $54-$61; each addl $4; under 18 free. Crib free. Pet accepted. TV; cable. Indoor pool; whirlpool, sauna. Restaurant 6:30 am-10 pm. Rm serv. Bar 4 pm-2 am, closed Sun; entertainment. Ck-out noon. Coin lndry. Meeting rms. Business center. In-rm modem link. Bellhops. Valet serv. Sundries. Free airport transportation. X-country ski 1½ mi. Rec rm. Exercise equipt; stair machine, bicycles. Some balconies. Cr cds: A, C, D, DS, JCB, MC, V.

D ⚓ 🏌 🏊 🏂 ✈ 🖈 🏇 SC 🏃 ⛷

Restaurant

✔ ★ ★ **THE RAM.** *327 Main St. 605/692-2485.* Hrs: 11:30 am-10:30 pm. Closed Sun; most major hols. Res accepted. Bar 4:30 pm-2 am. Semi-a la carte: lunch $4.95-$9.25, dinner $5.25-$12.95. Specializes in prime rib, pasta, hamburgers. Three dining levels in restored 1920 bank. Cr cds: A, C, D, DS, MC, V.

Chamberlain (C-4)

(See also Platte, Winner)

Pop 2,347 **Elev** 1,465 ft **Area code** 605 **Zip** 57325

This town on the Missouri River is situated in the middle of the state, between corn-growing farms and western cattle ranches.

What to See and Do

American Creek Recreational Area. On Lake Francis Case; swimming (May-Oct, fee), sand beaches, waterskiing; fishing; boat docks. Picnicking; camping (May-Oct; fee). Park (daily; ranger, May-Oct). N end of Main St, SD 50. Phone 605/734-6772.

Big Bend Dam-Lake Sharpe. One of a series of six dams on the Missouri River built by the US Army Corps of Engineers as units in the "Pick-Sloan Plan" for power production, flood control and recreation. Guided tours of powerhouse (June-Aug, daily; rest of yr, by appt). Visitor center at dam site (mid-May-mid-Sept, daily). Many recreation areas along reservoir have swimming, fishing; boating (docks, ramps, fee); winter sports; picnicking; camping (May-mid-Sept, fee). 21 mi NW via SD 50. Phone 605/245-2255. **Free.**

Old West Museum. Antique cars, guns, tractors, glassware; old-time Main St; pioneer, Western and Native American displays of equipment, tools, artifacts. Buffalo, longhorn cattle on grounds. (Mid-Apr-Nov 1, daily) 3 mi W via I-90, exit 260. Phone 605/734-6157. ¢¢

Motels

★ ★ **BEST WESTERN LEE'S MOTOR INN.** *220 W King St. 605/734-5575.* 60 rms, 2 story. June-Aug: S $50; D $55-$68; family units $70-$80; family plan; lower rates rest of yr. Crib $5. TV; cable. Indoor pool. Ck-out 11 am. Cr cds: A, C, D, DS, MC, V.

🏊 🏇 🏇 SC

✔ ★ ★ **OASIS INN.** *(SD 16, Oacoma 57365) 2 mi W of Missouri River Bridge at I-90 exit 260. 605/734-6061; FAX 605/734-4161; res: 800/341-8000 (exc SD), 800/635-3559 (SD).* 69 rms, 2 story. June-mid-Oct: S $39-$50; D $60-$70; each addl $5; under 12 free; lower rates rest of yr. Crib free. Pet accepted. TV; cable. Restaurant adj 6 am-10:30 pm. Bar 5 pm-midnight. Ck-out 11 am. Coin lndry. Meeting rms. Sundries. Airport, bus depot transportation. Miniature golf. Whirlpool. Sauna. Picnic tables, grills. Pond. On river. Cr cds: A, C, D, DS, MC, V.

D ⚓ 🏇 🏇 SC

✔ ★ **RIVER VIEW INN.** *128 N Front, I-90 exit 263. 605/734-6057.* 29 rms, 2 story. May-Oct: S, D $50-$75; each addl $5. Closed rest of yr. Crib $5. TV; cable. Indoor pool; whirlpool. Sauna. Complimentary coffee in lobby. Restaurant nearby. Ck-out 10:30 am. Coin lndry. Meeting rms. Cr cds: DS, MC, V.

D 🏊 🏇 🏇 SC

★ **SUPER 8.** *Box 295, at I-90 Lakeview Heights exit 263. 605/734-6548.* 56 rms, 2 story. Mid-May-mid-Sept: S $45.88; D $49.88-$57.88; each addl $2; lower rates rest of yr. Crib $2. TV; cable. Restaurant nearby. Ck-out 11 am. Cr cds: A, C, D, DS, MC, V.

🏇 🏇 SC

Restaurant

✔ ★ **AL'S OASIS.** *2 mi W of Missouri River Bridge at I-90 exit 260. 605/734-6054.* Hrs: 6 am-10:30 pm; winter 7 am-9 pm. Closed Jan 1, Thanksgiving, Dec 25. Bar from 4 pm. Semi-a la carte: bkfst $2.75-$5.75, lunch $2.95-$7.25, dinner $6.95-$13.50. Child's meals. Specializes in buffalo burgers, steak, prime rib. Salad bar. Western artifacts display. Family-owned. Cr cds: A, DS, MC, V.

Crazy Horse Memorial (C-1)

(For accommodations see Custer)

(5 mi N of Custer off US 16, 385)

This large sculpture, still being carved from the granite of Thunderhead Mountain, was the lifework of Korczak Ziolkowski (1908-1982), who briefly assisted Gutzon Borglum on Mt Rushmore. With funds gained solely from admission fees and contributions, Ziolkowski worked alone on the memorial, refusing federal and state funding. The work is being continued by the sculptor's wife, Ruth, and several of their children.

The sculpture will depict Crazy Horse—the stalwart Sioux chief who helped defeat Custer and the US 7th Cavalry—astride a magnificent horse. It is meant to honor not only Crazy Horse and the unconquerable spirit of man, but all Native American tribes. It is merely a part of what is planned by Ziolkowski's family and the Crazy Horse Memorial Foundation. Near the mountain Ziolkowski visualized a great Native American center with a museum, medical training center and university.

Crazy Horse's emerging head and face are nearly nine-stories tall, the face is scheduled for completion by June 3, 1998. When completed in-the-round, the mountain carving will be 563 feet high and 641 feet long—the largest sculpture in the world. To date 8.4 million tons of granite have been blasted off the mountain. Audio-visual programs and displays show how the mountain is being carved.

The Indian Museum of North America is on the grounds and houses some 20,000 artifacts in three wings. A Native American educational and cultural center opened in 1997. The visitor complex also includes the sculptor's log studio-home and workshop filled with sculpture, fine arts and antiques. A restaurant is open daily (in season), daylight-dark; closed Dec 25. Phone 605/673-4681; or 605/673-2828 (museum). Inclusive fee per vehicle ¢¢¢¢; or per person ¢¢¢

Annual Events

10K Volksmarch. Only time that top of mountain is open to public. 1st full wkend June.

Night blasting. June 26 & Sept 6.

Custer (C-1)

(See also Hill City, Hot Springs, Keystone, Rapid City)

Settled 1876 **Pop** 1,741 **Elev** 5,318 ft **Area code** 605 **Zip** 57730
Information Custer County Chamber of Commerce, 615 Washington St; 605/673-2244 or 800/992-9818.

This is where a prospector with Lieutenant Colonel Custer's expedition of 1874 discovered gold, prompting the gold rush of 1875-1876. Main St was laid out in the 1880s, wide enough for wagons pulled by teams of oxen to make U-turns. Custer is the seat of Custer County, headquarters of the Black Hills National Forest (see BLACK HILLS) and center of an area of great mineral wealth. Gold, quartz, beryl, mica and gypsum are some of the minerals that are mined in commercial quantities. Lumbering, tourism and ranching are also important to the economy. Custer is a popular area for winter sports activities.

What to See and Do

 Crazy Horse Memorial (see). 5 mi N off US 16, 385.

Custer County Courthouse Museum (1881). Features historical and cultural memorabilia of Custer County. (June-Aug, daily) 411 Mt Rushmore Rd. Phone 605/673-2443. Also here is

    1875 Log Cabin. Way Park. Oldest cabin in the Black Hills. Preserved as a pioneer museum. (Days same as Courthouse Museum) **Free.**

Custer State Park (see). 5 mi E on US 16A.

Flintstones Bedrock City. Adventures with the modern stone-age family: Fred, Wilma, Barney, Betty, Pebbles, Bamm Bamm and Dino. Village tour; train ride; concessions. Campground. (mid-May-mid-Sept, daily) US 16, 385. Phone 605/673-4079. ¢¢¢

Golden Circle Tours. Mini-bus tours of the area. (May-Sept, daily) Write 40 N 5th St or phone 605/673-4349 for schedule. ¢¢¢¢

Jewel Cave Natl Monument (see). 14 mi W on US 16.

Mountain Man Show. Country music show with comedy; family entertainment. (Late May-Labor Day, daily) 2 mi N on US 16, 385, in Flinstone Theater. For res phone 605/673-2405.

Natl Museum of Woodcarving. Features woodcarvings by an original Disneyland animator and other professional woodcarvers; Wooden Nickel Theater, museum gallery, carving area and snack bar. (May-Oct, daily) 2 mi W on US 16. Phone 605/673-4404. ¢¢¢

Annual Event

Gold Discovery Days. Pageant of Paha Sapa, festival, carnival, parade. Late July.

Motels

    ★ **BAVARIAN INN.** *Box 152, 1 mi N on US 16, 385. 605/673-2802; FAX 605/673-4777; res: 800/657-4312.* 64 rms, 2 story. June-late Aug: S $65; D $68-$78; each addl $5; suites $90-$115; lower rates rest of yr. Crib free. Pet accepted. TV; cable (premium). 2 pools, 1 indoor; whirlpool, sauna. Playground. Coffee in rms. Restaurant 6:30-10:30 am, 4-10 pm. Bar 4:30 pm-2 am. Ck-out noon. Meeting rms. Gift shop. Lighted tennis. Game rm. Lawn games. Patios, balconies. Cr cds: A, C, D, DS, MC, V.

    ★ **SUPER 8.** *415 W Mt Rushmore Rd (US 16). 605/673-2200.* 40 rms. Mid-June-Labor Day: S $65.88; D $65.88-$76.88; suites $86.88; lower rates rest of yr. Crib free. TV; cable. Complimentary coffee in lobby. Restaurant nearby. Ck-out 11 am. Coin lndry. Cr cds: A, C, D, DS, MC, V.

Inn

    ✔★ ★ **CUSTER MANSION.** *35 Centennial Dr. 605/673-3333.* 5 rms, 2 story. No A/C. No rm phones. Mid-May-mid-Sept: S $50-$75; D $55-$95; each addl $10; wkly, family rates; lower rates rest of yr. TV in sitting rm. Complimentary full bkfst. Restaurant nearby. Ck-out 10:30 am, ck-in 3 pm. Balconies. Picnic tables. Built 1891; antiques. Totally nonsmoking. No cr cds accepted.

Restaurant

    ✔★ **SKYWAY.** *511 Mt Rushmore Rd (US 16). 605/673-4477.* Hrs: 6:30 am-10 pm. Closed Jan 1, Thanksgiving, Dec 25. Res accepted. Mexican, Amer menu. Bar. Semi-a la carte: bkfst $2.69-$5.99, lunch $3.75-$8, dinner $7-$12. Child's meals. Specializes in teriyaki chicken, chicken fried steak, Tex-Mex dishes. Salad bar. Contemporary dining. Cr cds: A, C, D, DS, MC, V.

SC ⬦

Custer State Park (C-1)

(See also Custer, Hill City, Hot Springs, Keystone)

Area code 605 **E-mail** craigp@gfp.state.sd.us **Web** www.state.sd.us/state/executive/gfp/gfp.html
Information Information Director, HC 83, PO Box 70, Custer 57730; 605/255-4515.

(5 mi E of Custer on US 16A)

This is one of the largest state parks in the US—73,000 acres. A mountain recreation area and game refuge, the park has one of the largest publicly owned herds of bison in the country (more than 1,400), as well as Rocky Mountain bighorn sheep, mountain goats, burros, deer, elk and other wildlife. Four man-made lakes and three streams provide excellent fishing and swimming. Near the park is the site of the original gold strike of 1874 and a replica of the Gordon stockade, built by the first gold rush party in 1874.

    Peter Norbeck Visitor Center (May-Oct, daily) has information about the park and naturalist programs, which are offered daily (May-Sept). Horseback riding, hiking, bicycle rentals. Jeep rides, paddle-boats. Camping. Hayrides, chuck-wagon cookouts. Standard fees. A park entrance license is required. Per vehicle ¢¢¢ or per person ¢¢

    The Black Hills Playhouse, in the heart of the park, is the scene of productions for 11 weeks (mid-June-late Aug, schedule varies); phone 605/255-4141.

Lodges

    ★ ★ **STATE GAME LODGE.** *(HC 83, Box 74, Custer 57730) 15 mi E of Custer on US 16A in park. 605/255-4541; FAX 605/255-4706; res: 800/658-3530.* 68 rms, 3 story, 21 cabins, 8 kits. No A/C in cabins, lodge, motel units. Some rm phones. Mid-May-mid-Oct: S, D $65-$230; 2 bedrm house $175-$250; 4 bedrm house $315; kit. cabins for 2-8, $85-$115. Closed rest of yr. Pet accepted. TV; cable. Dining rm 7 am-9 pm. Snack bar, box lunches. Bar noon-10 pm. Ck-out 10 am. Meeting rms. Gift shop. Grocery 1/4 mi, package store. Jeep rides into buffalo area. Hiking trails. Fireplace in lobby. Picnic tables. Served as "summer White House" for Presidents Coolidge and Eisenhower. Cr cds: A, DS, MC, V.

    ★ ★ **SYLVAN LAKE.** *(HCR 83, Box 74, Custer 57730) 8 mi N of Custer on SD 87, 89 in park. 605/574-2561; FAX 605/574-4943; res: 800/658-3530.* 35 rms in 3-story lodge, 31 cabins, 19 kits. No A/C. Mid-May-Oct: S, D $90-$125; kit. cabins $75-$200; cabins $85-$125; lower rates rest of yr. Crib $5. Restaurant 7 am-9 pm; dining rm 7 am-9 pm. Bar

11:30 am-midnight. Ck-out 10 am. Meeting rms. Gift shop. Grocery. Paddleboats. Hiking. Some fireplaces. Some private balconies. Picnic tables. Lake swimming. Cr cds: A, C, DS, MC, V.

Cottage Colonies

★ ★ **BLUE BELL LODGE & RESORT.** *(HCR 83, Box 63, Custer 57730) 12 mi SE of Custer.* 605/255-4531; res: 800/658-3530. 29 cabins, 13 kits. No A/C. Mid-May-early Oct: S, D $120; each addl $5; kit. units $80-$160; lower rates rest of yr. Crib $5. TV; cable. Restaurant 7 am-9 pm. Bar. Ck-out 10 am, ck-in after 2 pm. Coin lndry. Meeting rms. Grocery, package store opp. Campground; hiking trails. Hayrides. Chuckwagon cookouts. Overnight pack trips. Lawn games. Some refrigerators, fireplaces. Picnic tables, grills. Cr cds: A, DS, MC, V.

★ **LEGION LAKE RESORT.** *(HCR 83, Box 67, Custer 57730) 7 mi E of Custer.* 605/255-4521; FAX 605/255-4753; res: 800/658-3530. 25 cabins, 12 kits. May-Sept: S, D $67; kits. $90-$110; each addl $5. Closed rest of yr. Crib $5. Pet accepted; $5. Playground. Restaurant 7 am-9 pm. Ck-out 10 am. Grocery. Swimming beach; boating. Hiking. Bicycle rentals. On lake. Cr cds: A, DS, MC, V.

Deadwood (B-1)

(See also Belle Fourche, Lead, Rapid City, Spearfish, Sturgis)

Pop 1,830 **Elev** 4,537 ft **Area code** 605 **Zip** 57732
Information Deadwood-Lead Area Chamber of Commerce, 735 Main St; 605/578-1876.

This town is best known for gold and such Wild West characters as Calamity Jane, Preacher Smith and Wild Bill Hickok. The main street runs through Deadwood Gulch; the rest of the town crawls up the steep canyon sides. A bust of Hickok by Korczak Ziolkowski—creator of the Crazy Horse Memorial—stands on Sherman Street. At the height of the 1876 gold rush, 25,000 people swarmed over the hillsides to dig gold. When gold was first struck at Deadwood, nearly the entire population of Custer rushed to Deadwood; predictably, at the height of a newer strike, nearly the entire population of Deadwood rushed to the town of Lead. Recently legalized gambling has given Deadwood another boom.

The Nemo Ranger District office of the Black Hills National Forest (see BLACK HILLS) is located in Deadwood.

What to See and Do

Adams Museum. Exhibits of local interest. (May-Sept, daily; rest of yr, Mon-Sat) Sherman & Deadwood Sts. Phone 605/578-1714. **Free.**

Broken Boot Gold Mine. See how gold was mined in the historic gold camp days; underground guided tour. (Mid-May-Sept, daily) S edge of town on US 14A. Phone 605/578-9997. ¢¢

Casino gambling on historic Main St. Most facilities have dining and lodging avail. **First Gold Hotel,** 270 Main St, 605-578-9777 or 800/274-1876; **Four Aces,** 531 Main St, phone 800/825-ACES; **Gold Dust,** 688 Main St, phone 605/578-2100 or 800/456-0533; **Historic Franklin Hotel,** 700 Main St, phone 605/578-2241 or 800/688-1876; **Midnight Star,** 677 Main St, phone 800/999-6482; **Miss Kitty's,** 649 Main St, phone 605/578-1811; **Silverado,** 709 Main St, phone 605/584-7005; **Wild West Winners Club,** 622 Main St, phone 605/578-1100 or 800/500-7711.

Mt Moriah Cemetery. "Boot Hill" of Deadwood. Graves of Wild Bill Hickok, Calamity Jane, Preacher Smith, Seth Bullock and others. ¢

Old Style Saloon #10. Collection of Western artifacts, pictures, guns; this is the saloon in which Wild Bill Hickok was shot. Entertainment, gambling,

refreshments. (Daily; closed Dec 25) 657 Main St. Phone 605/578-3346. **Free.**

Sightseeing tours.

Boot Hill Tours. One-hr narrated open-air bus tours through historic Deadwood and Mt Moriah Cemetery ("Boot Hill"). Visit graves of Wild Bill Hickok & Calamity Jane. Res required for groups. (June-early Oct, daily) Departs from cafe at center of Main St. Phone 605/578-3758 for departure times. ¢¢¢

Original Deadwood Tour. One-hr narrated open-air bus tours through historic Deadwood and "Boot Hill." Res recommended. (May-late Sept, daily) Departs from Midnight Star, 677 Main St. Phone 605/578-2091 for departure times. ¢¢¢

Annual Event

Days of '76. Rodeo at Amusement Park, 1 mi N. Historic parade down Main St; re-enactment of early days. Last wkend July.

Seasonal Events

Ghosts of Deadwood Gulch Wax Museum. Old Town Hall, Lee & Sherman Sts. Audiovisual tour of more than 70 life-size wax figures depicting 19 historic episodes in the settling of the Dakota Territory. Daily. Phone 605/578-3583. Mid-May-Sept.

Trial of Jack McCall. Old Town Hall, Lee & Sherman Sts. Re-enactment of McCall's capture and trial for killing Wild Bill Hickok. Daily exc Sun. Phone 605/578-3583. June-Aug.

Motels

★ **DEADWOOD GULCH RESORT.** *PO Box 643, US 85S.* 605/578-1294; FAX 605/578-2505; res: 800/695-1876. 97 rms, 2 story. Late May-mid-Sept: S, D $90-$95; under 12 free; lower rates rest of yr. Crib free. TV; cable. Pool; whirlpool. Restaurant 6 am-10 pm. Bar 7-2 am. Ck-out 11 am. Meeting rms. Sundries. Gift shop. Game rm. Cr cds: A, DS, MC, V.

★ **GOLDDIGGERS.** *629 Historic Main St.* 605/578-3213; FAX 605/578-3762; res: 800/456-2023. 6 rms, 2 story, 3 suites. Late May-mid-Sept: S, D $89; each addl $7.50; suites $129; under 12 free; lower rates rest of yr. Crib free. TV; cable. Complimentary full bkfst. Complimentary coffee in rms. Restaurant 7 am-10 pm; Fri, Sat open 24 hrs; open 24 hrs May-Sept. Rm serv. Bar 7-2 am. Ck-out noon. Casino. Victorian theme in restored welding shop. Cr cds: A, DS, MC, V.

★ **MINERAL PALACE.** *601 Main St.* 605/578-2036; FAX 605/578-2037; res: 800/847-2522. 63 rms, 3 story. June-Aug: S, D $99-$109; each addl $5; suites $125-$195; under 18 free; ski plan; higher rates Christmas wk; lower rates rest of yr. Crib free. TV; cable. VCR avail (movies $3.50). Coffee in rms. Restaurant 6 am-10 pm. Rm serv. Bar 7-2 am. Ck-out 11 am. Meeting rms. Business servs avail. Bellhops. Concierge. Gift shop. Game rm. Refrigerator in suites. Cr cds: A, C, D, DS, MC, V.

Motor Hotel

★ ★ **BULLOCK HOTEL.** *633 Main St.* 605/578-1745; FAX 605/578-1382; res: 800/336-1876. 28 rms, 3 story. Late May-mid-Sept: S, D $65-$85; each addl $5; suites $155; under 12 free; lower rates rest of yr. Crib $10. TV; cable. Complimentary coffee. Restaurant 7 am-2 pm, 5-11 pm. Rm serv. Bar to 2 am; entertainment. Ck-out 11 am. Meeting rms. Bellhops. Minibar in suites. Restored Victorian hotel (1895). Cr cds: A, DS, MC, V.

Restaurant

★ ★ ★ **MIDNIGHT STAR.** *677 Main St, on top floor of Midnight Star Casino. 605/578-1555.* Hrs: 5-10 pm; Fri, Sat to midnight. Closed Dec 24, 25. Res accepted. Bar. Semi-a la carte: dinner $14.95-$27.95. Specialties: buffalo roulade, cajun seafood tortellini, filet mignon. Pianist. Elegant dining in atrium setting; skylight. Cr cds: A, C, D, DS, MC, V.

Hill City (C-1)

(See also Custer, Deadwood, Keystone, Rapid City)

Settled 1876 **Pop** 650 **Elev** 4,979 ft **Area code** 605 **Zip** 57745 **E-mail** HillsHeart@aol.com

Information Chamber of Commerce, PO Box 253; 605/574-2368 or 800/888-1798.

Hill City is a beautiful mountain town in the heart of the Black Hills. The Black Hills Institute of Geological Research and a Ranger District office of the Black Hills National Forest (see BLACK HILLS) are located here.

What to See and Do

1880 Train. Steam train runs on gold rush-era track; vintage railroad equipment. Two-hr round trip between Hill City and Keystone through natl forest, mountain meadowlands. Vintage car restaurant, gift shop. (Mid-May-mid-Oct, daily) Hill City Depot. Phone 605/574-2222. ¢¢¢¢

Recreation areas in Black Hills Natl Forest. **Sheridan Lake.** 4 mi NE on US 16, then 2 mi NE on US 385. Swimming beaches. **Pactola Lake.** 4 mi NE on US 16, then 12¹/₂ mi NE off US 385. Both areas offer fishing; boating (ramps, rental). Picnicking; camping supplies, grocery. Tent and trailer sites (fee). Visitor center (Memorial Day-Sept, daily). **Deerfield Lake.** 16 mi NW on Forest Highway. Fishing; waveless boating only (ramps). Picnicking. Camping (fee). Contact Forest Supervisor, RR 2, Box 200, Custer 57730.

Wade's Gold Mill. Authentic mill showing four methods of recovering gold. Panning for gold (fee). (May-Sept, daily) Deerfield Rd, ³/₄ mi NW. For tour schedule phone 605/574-2680. Tours ¢¢-¢¢¢

Annual Event

Heart of the Hills Celebration. Parade, barbecue, timber and logging show. 2nd wkend July.

Seasonal Events

Fife & Drum Corp Concerts. Main St. Free performances every Mon eve. Memorial Day-Labor Day.

Bank Robbery and Shoot Out. Main St. Tues-Thurs eves. Memorial Day-Labor Day.

Motel

★ ★ **BEST WESTERN GOLDEN SPIKE INN.** *106 Main St, ¹/₄ mi E on US 385. 605/574-2577; FAX 605/574-4719.* 61 rms, 2 story. Mid-June-Aug: S $74-$85; D $89-$102; each addl $5; lower rates Apr-mid-June & Sept-Nov. Closed rest of yr. Crib $5. TV; cable. Heated pool; whirlpool. Coffee in rms. Restaurant 6:30 am-9 pm. Ck-out 11 am. Coin lndry. Meeting rms. Gift shop. Bicycle rentals. Cr cds: A, C, D, DS, MC, V.

Restaurant

✔★ **THE ALPINE INN.** *225 Main St. 605/574-2749.* Hrs: 11 am-2:30 pm, 5-9:30 pm. Closed Sun; Thanksgiving; also Dec 24-mid-Jan.

No A/C. German, Amer menu. Wine, beer. Semi-a la carte: lunch $3.25-$5.25, dinner $5.95-$7.95. Filet mignon only entree on dinner menu. Outdoor dining (lunch). Old World German decor. No cr cds accepted.

Hot Springs (C-1)

(For accommodations see Custer, Keystone)

Settled 1879 **Pop** 4,325 **Elev** 3,464 ft **Area code** 605 **Zip** 57747

Information Chamber of Commerce, 801 S 6th St; 605/745-4140 or 800/325-6991 outside SD.

Hot Springs, seat of Fall River County, is on the southeast edge of Black Hills National Forest. Many local buildings are of pink, red and buff sandstone. A Ranger District office of the Nebraska National Forest (see CHADRON, NE) is located here.

What to See and Do

Angostura Reservoir State Recreation Area. On 1,480 acres. Swimming; fishing; boating, canoeing. Hiking. Picnicking, concession, lodging. Camping nearby. Interpretive program. Standard fees. 10 mi SE off US 18. Phone 605/745-6996.

Black Hills Wild Horse Sanctuary. Guided 2-hr tours. Camping & chuckwagon dinners avail. (Memorial Day-Labor Day) For res phone 605/745-5955 or 800/252-6652. ¢¢¢¢

Evans Plunge. Large indoor, natural warm water pool. Also health club with sauna, steam bath, spas and exercise equipment; indoor water slides. Outdoor pool with water slide open during summer months. (Daily exc Dec 25) 1145 N River St, N edge of town on US 385. Phone 605/745-5165. ¢¢¢

Fall River County Museum. Artifacts and memorabilia documenting history of Black Hills. In former school (1893). (June-early Sept, daily exc Sun) 300 N Chicago St. Phone 605/745-5147 or 605/745-4725. **Free.**

Historic District. Thirty-nine Richardsonian-Romanesque buildings, constructed of locally quarried sandstone. Architectural guide, narrated tours avail at the Chamber of Commerce. Near town center. **Free.**

Mammoth Site of Hot Springs. Excavation of a remarkable concentration of mammoth skeletons; to date the remains of 50 mammoths, a camel and giant short-faced bear have been unearthed. (Daily) Southern city limits on US 18 truck bypass. Phone 605/745-6017. ¢¢

Wind Cave Natl Park (see). 11 mi N on US 385.

Huron (C-5)

(See also Brookings, Mitchell)

Founded 1879 **Pop** 12,448 **Elev** 1,275 ft **Area code** 605 **Zip** 57350 **E-mail** peggyw@basec.net

Information Huron Convention & Visitors Bureau, 15 4th St SW; 605/352-0000 or 800/HURONSD.

Huron, seat of Beadle County, is also administrative center for a number of federal and state agencies. It is a trade and farm products processing center for a 10,500-square-mile area. Twelve city parks feature swimming, picnicking, golf, tennis and ballfields. The area offers excellent northern and walleye fishing, and good pheasant hunting brings enthusiasts here when the season opens in mid-October.

What to See and Do

Centennial Center. Gothic-style stone structure (1887) houses state centennial memorabilia, Native American artifacts, railroad items and memoirs of Hubert and Muriel Humpherey. (Mon-Fri, afternoons; also by appt) 48 Fourth St SE. Phone 605/352-1442. **Donation.**

Dakotaland Museum. Pioneer exhibits, log cabin. (Memorial Day-Labor Day, Mon-Fri) 8 blks W on US 14 at State Fairgrounds. Phone 605/352-4626. ¢

Gladys Pyle Historic Home (1894). This Queen Anne-style house was the residence of the first elected female US senator. Stained glass, carved woodwork, original furnishings. (Jan-Mar and wkends, by appt; rest of yr, Mon-Fri afternoons) 376 Idaho Ave SE. Phone 605/352-2528. ¢

Hubert H. Humphrey Drugstore. Mid-1930s atmosphere; owned by the former senator and vice-president until his death; still owned by Humphrey family. (Daily exc Sun) 233 Dakota S. Phone 605/352-4064. **Free.**

Laura Ingalls Wilder Memorial. Laura Ingalls Wilder wrote a series of children's books based on her childhood experiences in De Smet. Here are restored surveyors' house, the family home from 1879-1880; original family home (1887); replica of period schoolhouse; memorabilia; many other sites and buildings mentioned in her books. Guided tours (late May-mid-Sept, daily). 33 mi E at jct US 14 & SD 25 in De Smet. Phone 605/854-3383 or 605/854-3181. ¢¢

Annual Events

Laura Ingalls Wilder Pageant. 32 mi E on US 14, near De Smet. Fri-Sun, last wkend June & 1st 2 wkends July.

Meadowood Fair. Memorial Park. Art, craft exhibits, demonstrations; children's activities, entertainment, concessions. 1st wkend Aug.

South Dakota State Fair. State Fairgrounds, W on US 14, at 3rd St SW & Nevada Ave SW. Phone 605/353-7340. Sept 1-7.

Parade of Lights. Day after Thanksgiving.

Seasonal Event

State Fair Speedway. US 14 W. South Dakota's largest racing program. Phone 605/352-1896 or 605/352-1431. Late Apr-early Sept.

Motels

★ ★ ★ **CROSSROADS.** *100 4th St, at Wisconsin. 605/352-3204; FAX 605/352-3204, ext. 177.* 100 rms, 3 story. S $51-$61; D $56-$69; each addl $5; suites $130; family rates. Crib free. Pet accepted. TV; cable. Indoor pool; whirlpool, poolside serv. Sauna. Restaurants 6:30 am-10 pm. Rm serv. Bar 4 pm-2 am. Ck-out 11 am. Meeting rms. Business servs avail. In-rm modem link. Valet serv. Airport, RR station, bus depot transportation. Some refrigerator. Cr cds: A, C, D, DS, MC, V.

[D] [⟋] [≈] [⋈] [🔥] [SC]

✔ ★ ★ **DAKOTA PLAINS INN.** *Box 1433, US 14E. 605/352-1400; res: 800/648-3735.* 77 rms, 2 story. S $39; D $44; each addl $5; under 12 free. Crib free. Pet accepted. TV; cable. Pool. Restaurant adj 6-10 pm. Bar 11:30-2 am. Ck-out 11 am. Meeting rm. Business servs avail. In-rm modem link. X-country ski 1½ mi. Cr cds: A, DS, MC, V.

[⟋] [≈] [⋈] [🔥] [SC]

★ **SUPER 8.** *SD 37S. 605/352-0740.* 68 rms, 2 story. S $38.88-$65.88; D $40.88-$65.88; each addl $4. Crib $3. TV; cable. Indoor pool. Restaurant adj open 24 hrs. Ck-out 11 am. Business servs avail. X-country ski ½ mi. Cr cds: A, C, D, DS, MC, V.

[D] [≈] [🔥] [SC]

Restaurant

✔ ★ **HAROLD'S CAFE.** *225 Lincoln, 1 mi NW on SD 14 Business. 605/352-2301.* Hrs: 11 am-7 pm. Closed Thanksgiving, Dec 24-25.

Semi-a la carte: lunch $2-$4, dinner $4.25-$7. Child's meals. Specializes in broasted chicken. Own soups. Family-owned. No cr cds accepted.

Jewel Cave National Monument (C-1)

(For accommodations see Custer, Hill City; also see Newcastle, WY)

(13 mi W of Custer on US 16)

On a high rolling plateau in the Black Hills is Jewel Cave, with an entrance on the east side of Hell Canyon. More than 100 miles of passageways make this cave system the second longest in the US. Formations of jewel-like calcite crystals produce unusual effects. The surrounding terrain is covered by ponderosa pine. Many varieties of wildflowers bloom from early spring through summer on the 1,274-acre monument.

There is a guided 1¼-hr scenic tour of the monument (May-Sept) and a 1½-hr historic tour (Memorial Day-Labor Day; age six years or older only). There is also a 4-5-hr spelunking tour (June-Aug); advance reservations required; minimum age 16. Note: all tours recommended only for those in good physical condition. For spelunking wear hiking clothes and sturdy, lace-up boots. Visitor center. (Daily) Contact RR 1, PO Box 60 AA, Custer 57730; 605/673-2288. Tours: scenic or historic ¢; spelunking ¢¢¢¢

Keystone (C-1)

(See also Custer, Hill City, Rapid City)

Pop 232 **Elev** 4,323 ft **Area code** 605 **Zip** 57751
Information Chamber of Commerce, PO Box 653; 605/666-4896.

Keystone is the gateway to Mt Rushmore and Custer State Park. A former mining town supplying miners for the Peerless, Hugo and the Holy Terror Gold Mine, it was also home to Carrie Ingalls and the men who carved Mt Rushmore.

What to See and Do

Big Thunder Gold Mine. Authentic 1880s gold mine. Visitors may dig gold ore or pan it by the stream. Guided tours; historic film. (May-Oct, daily) 5 blks E of stop light. Phone 605/666-4847. ¢¢¢

☒ **Borglum Historical Center.** Exhibits on Gutzon Borglum and the carving of Mt Rushmore. Newsreels of carving in progress. Original models and tools, collection of his paintings, unpublished photos of the memorial, sculptures, historical documents. Full-size replica of Lincoln's eye. (Apr-Oct, daily) US 16A, in town. Phone 605/666-4449. ¢¢

Cosmos of the Black Hills. Curious gravitational and optical effects. Guided tours every 12 min. (Apr-Oct, daily) 4 mi NE, ½ mi off US 16. Phone 605/343-9802. ¢¢

☒ **Mt Rushmore Natl Memorial** (see). 3 mi SW off US 16A.

Parade of Presidents Wax Museum. Nearly 100 life-size wax figures depict historic scenes from nation's past. (May-Sept, daily) S on US 16A, at E entrance to Mt Rushmore. Phone 605/666-4455. ¢¢¢

Rushmore Aerial Tramway. This 15-min ride allows a view of the Black Hills and Mt Rushmore across the valley. (May-mid-Sept, daily) S on US 16A. Phone 605/666-4478. ¢¢¢

Rushmore Cave. Guided tours (May-Oct, daily). 5 mi E via SD 40, turn at Keystone traffic light. Phone 605/255-4467 or 605/255-4384. ¢¢¢

Rushmore Helicopter Sightseeing Tours. Helicopter rides over Mt Rushmore and nearby points of interest. (Late May-late Sept, daily) S on US 16A. Phone 605/666-4461. ¢¢¢¢

Motels

★ **BEST WESTERN FOUR PRESIDENTS.** *Box 690, on US 16A. 605/666-4472; FAX 605/666-4574.* 30 rms, 3 story. No elvtr. Mid-June-Sept: S $82; D $92; each addl $5; lower rates Apr-mid-June & Oct-Nov. Closed rest of yr. Crib $5. Pet accepted, some restrictions. TV. Complimentary coffee in rms. Restaurant adj 7 am-10 pm. Ck-out 10 am. Cr cds: A, C, D, DS, MC, V.

★ **FIRST LADY INN.** *702 US 16A. 605/666-4990; FAX 605/666-4676; res: 800/252-2119.* 39 rms, 3 story. No elvtr. Late May-early Sept: S $75; D $81; each addl $5; suites $125; lower rates rest of yr. Crib $5. Pet accepted. TV; cable. Complimentary coffee in rms. Ck-out 10 am. Whirlpool. Cr cds: A, DS, MC, V.

✔★ **KELLY INN.** *Box 654, S on US 16A at Cemetary Rd. 605/666-4483; FAX 605/666-4883; res: 800/635-3559.* 44 rms, 2 story. Mid-May-mid-Sept: S $62; D $67; each addl $5; under 4 free; lower rates rest of yr. Crib free. TV; cable. Restaurant nearby. Ck-out 11 am. Meeting rm. Whirlpool, sauna. Cr cds: A, D, DS, ER, MC, V.

Restaurant

★ **RAILHEAD.** *Swanzey St. 605/666-4561.* Hrs: 6 am-9 pm. Closed Nov-Apr. Semi-a la carte: bkfst $2.99-$7.50, lunch $3.95-$6.50, dinner $7.95-$16.95. Buffet: bkfst $7.99, lunch $8.95, dinner $9.95. Specializes in Black Hills trout, buffalo buffet. Country decor; antiques. Cr cds: DS, MC, V.

Lead (B-1)

(See also Belle Fourche, Deadwood, Rapid City, Spearfish, Sturgis)

Founded 1876 **Pop** 3,632 **Elev** 5,400 ft **Area code** 605 **Zip** 57754
Information Deadwood-Lead Area Chamber of Commerce, 735 Historic Main St, Deadwood 57732; 605/578-1876.

The chain of gold mines that began in Custer and spread through the Black Hills to Deadwood ended in Lead. The discovery of gold here in 1876 eventually led to the development of the Homestake Mine, one of the largest gold producers in this hemisphere. Lead is located on mountaintops with the Homestake Mine burrowing under the town.

What to See and Do

Black Hills Mining Museum. Exhibits trace development of mining in the Black Hills since 1876; includes guided tour of underground mine; gold panning; historic displays. (May-mid-Oct, daily) 323 W Main St. Phone 605/584-1605. ¢¢

Homestake Gold Mine Surface Tours (since 1876). A 1-hr tour of surface workings in an 8,000 ft mine; explanation of gold production. (May-Sept, daily; closed hols) 160 W Main St. Phone 605/584-3110. ¢¢

Skiing.

Terry Peak. 5 chairlifts, Mitey-Mite; patrol, school, rentals; snowmaking; 2 chalets; snack bar, cafeteria, bar. Longest run 1¼ mi; vertical drop 1,052 ft. (Thanksgiving-Easter, daily) 3 mi SW on US 85, then N, in Black Hills Natl Forest. Contact PO Box 774; 605/584-2165 or 800/456-0524. ¢¢¢¢

Deer Mt. Triple chairlift, 2 Pomalifts; patrol, school, rentals; cafeteria, bar. Cross-country trails. Night skiing. Halfpipe for snowboards. (Nov-Mar, daily exc Mon; closed Dec 25) 3 mi S on US 85. Contact PO Box 622, Deadwood 57732; 605/584-3230. ¢¢¢¢

Motel

★ **WHITE HOUSE INN.** *395 Glendale Dr. 605/584-2000; res: 800/654-5323.* 71 rms, 4 story. June-Sept: S $60; D $70-$75; each addl $10; suites $85-$110; under 16 free; lower rates rest of yr. Crib free. TV; cable (premium). Complimentary continental bkfst. Restaurant nearby. Ck-out 11 am. Meeting rms. Whirlpool. Cr cds: A, D, DS, MC, V.

Hotel

★ ★ **BEST WESTERN GOLDEN HILLS.** *900 Miners Ave. 605/584-1800; FAX 605/584-3933.* 100 rms, 5 story. S $89; D $99-$104; each addl $10; suites $185; under 18 free. Crib free. TV; cable (premium), VCR avail. Indoor pool; wading pool, whirlpool, lifeguard. Restaurant 6 am-1:30 pm, 5-10 pm. Bar 3 pm-2 am. Ck-out 11 am. Meeting rms. Business servs avail. Downhill/x-country ski 3 mi. Exercise rm; instructor, weight machines, bicycles, sauna. Refrigerator, wet bar; whirlpool in some suites. Cr cds: A, C, D, DS, ER, MC, V.

Madison (C-6)

(See also Brookings, Sioux Falls)

Founded 1875 **Pop** 6,257 **Elev** 1,670 ft **Area code** 605 **Zip** 57042
Information Greater Madison Chamber of Commerce, 315 S Egan St, PO Box 467; 605/256-2454.

Madison, seat of Lake County, is the marketing, processing and trade center for meat, grain and dairy products and has some diversified industry. Madison is well-known for its pheasant hunting, as well as fishing for walleye at many area lakes.

What to See and Do

Dakota State Univ (1881). (1,400 students) Karl E. Mundt Library contains archives of the South Dakota senator. The Dakota Prairie Playhouse offers varied entertainment; located off campus at 1205 N Washington Ave. Corner of Egan Ave & 8th St NE. Phone 605/256-5111. On campus is

Smith-Zimmermann State Museum. Local history. (Tues-Fri, afternoons; closed hols) Phone 605/256-5308. ¢

Lake Herman State Park. 226 acres. Swimming; fishing; boating, canoeing. Hiking. Picnicking, playground. Interpretive program, children's activities. Camping (electrical hookups, dump station). Standard fees. 2 mi W off SD 34. Phone 605/256-5003.

Prairie Village. Replica of pioneer town; 40 restored buildings, antique tractors, autos; steam merry-go-round (1893) and three steam trains. (May-Sept, daily) Limited camping. 2 mi W on SD 34. Phone 605/256-3644. ¢¢

Annual Events

Art in the Park. DSU campus. 2nd Sat June.

Steam Threshing Jamboree. Prairie Village. Antique farm machinery; plowing; parades, arts & crafts display; steam merry-go-round, train rides. Last wknd Aug.

Motels

★ **LAKE PARK.** *1515 NW 2nd, 1 mi W on US 81, SD 34. 605/256-3524.* 40 rms. M S $30; D $35. Crib $7. Pet accepted. TV; cable (premium). Heated pool. Restaurant adj. Ck-out 11 am. X-country ski 1 mi. Some refrigerators. Cr cds: A, C, D, DS, MC, V.

✔★ **SUPER 8.** *Box 5, at jct US 81, SD 34. 605/256-6931.* 34 rms, 2 story. S $31.88; D $35.88-$38.88; each addl $3-$4; under 12 free. Crib free. Pet accepted. TV; cable. Restaurant adj 6 am-10 pm. Ck-out 11 am. Cr cds: A, C, D, DS, MC, V.

D ✐ ⊠ 🐾 SC

Milbank (A-6)

(See also Watertown)

Pop 3,879 **Elev** 1,150 ft **Area code** 605 **Zip** 57252 **E-mail** chamber@cssd.com **Web** www.visitmilbank
Information Milbank Area Chamber of Commerce, 401 S Main; 605/432-6656 or 800/675-6656.

Milbank, the county seat of Grant County, is set in the Whetstone Valley, where granite production and the dairy industry figure prominently. Milbank is the birthplace of American Legion baseball, proposed here on July 17, 1925.

What to See and Do

Hartford Beach State Park. On 331 acres. Swimming, bathhouse; fishing; boating, canoeing. Hiking. Picnicking, playground. Camping (fee; hookups, dump station). Standard fees. 15 mi N on SD 15. Phone 605/432-6374.

Old Windmill (1882). Picturesque English-style gristmill (not operating), open to public. Operates as tourist information center May-Aug. E on US 12 near Milbank Insurance Co.

Motels

✔★ **LANTERN.** *1010 S Dakota St, 6 blks S of US 12 on US 77 & SD 15. 605/432-4591; res: 800/627-6075.* 30 rms. S $29-$32; D $33-$38; each addl $5; under 12 free. Crib $5. TV; cable (premium). Complimentary continental bkfst. Restaurant 5:30-10 pm. Ck-out 11 am. X-country ski 1 mi. Sauna. Cr cds: A, C, D, DS, MC, V.

🏊 ⊠ 🐾 SC

★ ★ **MANOR.** *Box 26, on US 12, 3/4 mi E of jct SD 15. 605/432-4527; res: 800/341-8000.* 30 rms, 1-2 story. S $30-$32; D $36-$42; each addl $4; under 16 free; higher rates Oct hunting season. Crib free. Pet accepted. TV. Indoor pool; whirlpool. Sauna. Restaurant 6 am-11 pm. Ck-out 11 am. X-country ski 1 mi. Cr cds: A, C, D, DS, MC, V.

✐ ✱ ≋ ⊠ 🐾 SC

★ **SUPER 8.** *Box 86, on US 12, 1 mi E of jct SD 15. 605/432-9288.* 39 rms, 2 story. S $33.88; D $44.88; each addl $3; under 12 free. Crib free. TV; cable (premium). Restaurant nearby. Ck-out 11 am. Meeting rm. Business servs avail. In-rm modem link. Cr cds: A, C, D, DS, MC, V.

D ⊠ 🐾 SC

Restaurant

✔★ **MILLSTONE.** *SD 12E. 605/432-6866.* Hrs: 6 am-11 pm; Sun from 7 am. Closed Thanksgiving, Dec 25. Res accepted. Semi-a la carte: bkfst $2.50-$5, lunch $3.75-$5, dinner $4-$8. Sun brunch $5.95. Child's meals. Specializes in hamburgers. Salad bar. Cr cds: MC, V.

SC

Mission (D-3)

(For accommodations see Murdo, Winner)

Pop 730 **Elev** 2,581 ft **Area code** 605 **Zip** 57555
Information Rosebud Sioux Tribal Office, PO Box 430, Rosebud 57570; 605/747-2381.

This is a trading center for the Rosebud Sioux Reservation.

What to See and Do

Buechel Memorial Lakota Museum. Lakota Sioux artifacts. (Late May-Sept, daily) 5 mi W on US 18, then 16 mi SW on Bureau of Indian Affairs Rd, in St Francis. Phone 605/747-2745. **Free.**

Ghost Hawk Park. Swimming; fishing. Picnicking, playground. Camping (fee). (Mid-May-Sept, daily) 3 mi NW of Rosebud on Bureau of Indian Affairs Rd; on Little White River.

Rosebud. Powwows can be seen Sat & Sun nights during summer. Inquire for swimming, fishing, golf in area. HQ for Rosebud Reservation. 5 mi W on US 18, then 8 mi SW on Bureau of Indian Affairs Rd. Phone 605/747-2381.

Annual Event

Rosebud Sioux Tribal Fair & Powwow. In Rosebud. Dances, traditional buffalo dinner; arts & crafts exhibits. Late Aug.

Mitchell (C-5)

Founded 1879 **Pop** 13,798 **Elev** 1,293 ft **Area code** 605 **Zip** 57301
E-mail mitcvb@mitchell.net **Web** www.dwu.edu/mitchell/index.htm
Information Dept of Tourism, 604 N Main St, PO Box 1026; 800/257-2676.

This is a tree-shaded town in the James River Valley, where agriculture is celebrated in a colorful, nine-day festival each September. The economy is based on agriculture, light industry and tourism. Pheasant shooting attracts hunters from the entire country.

What to See and Do

Balloon & Airship Museum. Exhibits detailing history of ballooning from 1700s to present; *Hindenburg* china, antiques. Video presentations. (Memorial Day-mid-Sept, daily; rest of yr, daily exc Wed, afternoons) 700 N Main St. Phone 605/996-2311. ¢¢

Enchanted World Doll Museum. More than 4,000 antique and modern dolls displayed in scenes from fairy tales and story books; dollhouses; accessories. (Apr-Nov, daily) 615 N Main. Phone 605/996-9896. ¢¢

Friends of the Middle Border Museum. Seven-building complex features Case Art Gallery; 1886 restored house, 1885 territorial school, 1900 railroad depot; pioneer life exhibits, horse-drawn vehicles, antique autos; American Indian Gallery; 1909 country church. (May-Sept, daily; rest of yr, by appt) 1311 S Duff St. Phone 605/996-2122. ¢¢

Lake Mitchell. Swimming, fishing, boating (rentals). Playground, grocery. Camping (electrical & sewer hookups, fee). (Mid-Apr-late Oct) Main St & Lakeshore Dr, 1 1/2 mi N on SD 37. Phone 605/995-4057 (in season) or 605/996-7180 (off-season).

⭐ **Oscar Howe Art Center.** Former Carnegie Library Bldg (1902) housing permanent gallery with original paintings by Sioux artist Oscar Howe. Changing exhibits; summer exhibits focus on Native American art and culture. (Memorial Day-Labor Day, daily exc Sun; rest of yr, Tues-Sat, also by appt; closed hols) 119 W Third. Phone 605/996-4111.

Prehistoric Indian Village Natl Historic Landmark Archaeological Site. 2 mi N via SD 37, exit 23rd Ave to Indian Village Rd, then N. On-going study of 1,000-yr-old Native American village. Boehnen Memorial Museum; excavation and exhibits; guided tours; visitor center. (May-Oct, daily; rest of yr, by appt) Phone 605/996-5473. ¢¢

✪ **The Corn Palace.** A huge building (seats 3,500), turreted, towered, dome-capped, flamboyantly Byzantine. Annually decorated, including scenic murals, entirely in colored corn and grasses. Erected in 1892, the structure has been rebuilt twice. (May-Sept, daily; rest of yr, Mon-Fri; closed hols) 604 N Main St. Phone 605/996-7311. **Free.**

Annual Events

Corn Palace Stampede. Rodeo. 3rd wkend July.

Corn Palace Festival. 2nd or 3rd wk Sept.

Motels

★ **ANTHONY.** *1518 W Havens St, near Municipal Airport.* *605/996-7518; FAX 605/996-7251; res: 800/477-2235.* 34 rms. June-Sept: S $30-$40; D $42-$48; each addl $4; lower rates rest of yr. Crib free. TV; cable. Heated pool. Restaurant adj 6 am-midnight. Ck-out 11 am. Coin lndry. Meeting rm. Business servs avail. Free airport, bus depot transportation. Cr cds: A, DS, MC, V.

≈ ✈ 🏒 🔥

✔★ **COACH LIGHT.** *1000 W Havens St, 1¹/₂ mi SW on I-90 Business.* *605/996-5686.* 20 rms. June-Oct: S $30; D $36-$38; each addl $3; lower rates rest of yr. Crib free. Pet accepted. TV; cable. Restaurant nearby. Ck-out 11 am. Airport, bus depot transportation. X-country ski 1¹/₂ mi. Cr cds: A, DS, MC, V.

🐾 ⛷ 🏒 🔥

★★ **COMFORT INN.** *I-90 & SD 37.* *605/996-1333; FAX 605/996-6022.* 60 rms, 2 story. May-Oct: S $53-$58; D $68-$78; each addl $5; under 19 free; lower rates rest of yr. Crib $3. TV; cable. Indoor pool; whirlpool, sauna. Complimentary continental bkfst. Restaurant adj 6 am-11 pm. Ck-out 11 am. Coin lndry. Meeting rm. Cr cds: A, C, D, DS, ER, JCB, MC, V.

D ≈ 🏒 🔥 SC

★★ **DAYS INN.** *I-90 & SD 37.* *605/996-6208; FAX 605/996-5220.* 65 rms, 2 story. S $38-$50; D $50-$70; each addl $5; under 12 free. Crib free. TV; cable. Indoor pool; whirlpool. Complimentary continental bkfst. Restaurant opp 6 am-11 pm. Ck-out 11 am. Coin lndry. X-country ski 1 mi. Cr cds: A, C, D, DS, MC, V.

D ⛷ ≈ 🏒 🔥 SC

★★ **ECONO LODGE.** *1313 S Ohlman, I-90 exit 330W.* *605/996-6647; FAX 605/996-7339.* 44 rms, 2 story. S $38.95; D $46.95; each addl $6; under 12 free. TV; cable (premium). Restaurant nearby. Ck-out 11 am. Cr cds: A, C, D, DS, MC, V.

🏒 🔥 SC

✔★ **MOTEL 6.** *1309 S Ohlman St, N of I-90 exit 330.* *605/996-0530; FAX 605/995-2019.* 122 rms. Mid-June-mid-Sept: S $29.95; D $35.95; under 17 free; lower rates rest of yr. Crib free. Pet accepted. TV. Heated pool. Restaurant nearby. Ck-out noon. X-country ski 2 mi. Cr cds: A, C, D, DS, MC, V.

D 🐾 ⛷ ≈ 🏒 🔥 SC

★ **SIESTA.** *1210 W Havens St.* *605/996-5544; FAX 605/996-4946; res: 800/424-0537.* 23 rms. Memorial Day-Labor Day: S $38; D $38-$48; each addl $4; lower rates rest of yr. Crib free. Pet accepted. TV; cable. Pool. Restaurant nearby. Ck-out 10 am. Cr cds: A, DS, MC, V.

🐾 ≈ 🏒 🔥 SC

★ **SUPER 8.** *Box 867, ¹/₂ blk N of I-90 on SD 37.* *605/996-9678; FAX 605/996-5339.* 107 rms, 3 story. S $38.88; D $43.88-$48.88; each addl $2. Crib $3. TV; cable. Indoor/outdoor pool; whirlpool. Restau-

rant adj open 24 hrs. Ck-out 11 am. Business servs avail. In-rm modem link. X-country ski 1 mi. Some in-rm whirlpools. Cr cds: A, C, D, DS, MC, V.

D ⛷ ≈ 🏒 🔥 SC

★★ **THUNDERBIRD LODGE.** *Box 984, 1 mi S on SD 37 at I-90 exit 332.* *605/996-6645; FAX 605/995-5883; res: 800/341-8000.* 48 rms, 2 story. June-Nov: S $38; D $52; each addl $5; suites $68; lower rates rest of yr. Crib $5. TV; cable (premium). Restaurant adj open 24 hrs. Ck-out 11 am. Coin lndry. Meeting rm. Airport transportation. X-country ski 1 mi. Whirlpool, sauna. Cr cds: A, C, D, DS, MC, V.

D ⛷ 🏒 🔥 SC

Motor Hotel

★★★ **HOLIDAY INN.** *1525 W Havens St, I-90 Business exit 330.* *605/996-6501; FAX 605/996-3228.* 153 rms, 2 story. June-Oct: S $74-$79; D $79-$84; each addl $5; under 19 free; lower rates rest of yr. Crib free. Pet accepted. TV; cable. Indoor pool; wading pool, whirlpool, sauna, poolside serv. Restaurant 6 am-10 pm. Rm serv. Bar 11-2 am. Ck-out noon. Coin lndry. Meeting rms. Business servs avail. In-rm modem link. Bellhops. Free airport, bus depot transportation. Putting green. Rec rm. Lawn games. Private patios, balconies. Cr cds: A, C, D, DS, JCB, MC, V.

D 🐾 ⛷ ≈ 🏒 🔥 SC

Restaurant

✔★★ **CHEF LOUIE'S.** *601 E Havens, N of I-90 exit 332.* *605/996-7565.* Hrs: 11 am-11 pm. Sun Jun-Aug to 8 pm; major hols. Res for pheasant dinners. Bar to 2 am. Semi-a la carte: lunch $4.25-$5.95, dinner $6.95-$19.95. Specializes in steak, seafood, pheasant. Cr cds: A, C, D, DS, MC, V.

Mobridge (A-3)

Founded 1906 **Pop** 3,768 **Elev** 1,676 ft **Area code** 605 **Zip** 57601
Information Chamber of Commerce, 212 Main; 605/845-2387.

The Milwaukee Railroad built a bridge across the Missouri River in 1906, at what was once the site of an Arikara and Sioux village. A telegraph operator used the contraction "Mobridge" to indicate his location. The name has remained the same. Today Mobridge is centered in farm and ranch country and is still home for a large Native American population. Located on the Oahe Reservoir, Mobridge is noted for its ample fishing and recreational activities.

What to See and Do

Klein Museum. Changing art exhibits; local pioneer artifacts and antiques; Sioux and Arikara artifacts; farm machinery collection; restored schoolhouse. (June-Aug, daily; Apr, May, Sept, Oct, daily exc Tues; closed Easter, Labor Day) 2 mi W on US 12. Phone 605/845-7243. ¢

Recreation Areas. Indian Creek. 2 mi E on US 12, then 1 mi S. **Indian Memorial.** 2 mi W off US 12. Both on Oahe Reservoir (see PIERRE). Swimming, bathhouse; boating (ramps, marinas); fishing. Picnicking, playgrounds. Tent & trailer sites (Memorial Day-Labor Day; hookups, dump station; fee). Phone 605/845-2252.

Scherr Howe Arena. Colorful murals by Oscar Howe, a Dakota Sioux and art professor at Univ of South Dakota, depict history and ceremonies of Native Americans. (Daily exc Sun; closed hols) Main St. Phone 605/845-3700. **Free.**

Sitting Bull Monument. Korczak Ziolkowski sculpted the bust for this monument. The burial ground on the hill affords beautiful view of Missouri River and surrounding country. 3 mi W on US 12, then 4 mi S on County 1806.

Motels

★ **SUPER 8.** *Box 156, 1/2 mi W on US 12, opp lake. 605/845-7215.* 31 rms, 2 story. S $34.52; D $39.83. Crib free. TV; cable. Restaurant nearby. Ck-out 11 am. Cr cds: A, C, D, DS, MC, V.

🖼 🖼 🖼

✔★ ★ **WRANGLER MOTOR INN.** *820 W Grand Crossing, 1/2 mi W on US 12. 605/845-3641; res: 800/341-8000.* 61 rms, 1-2 story. S $46-$56; D $56-$66; each addl $5; under 12 free. Crib $5. TV; cable. Indoor pool; whirlpool. Restaurant 6 am-10 pm. Rm serv. Bar 4 pm-2 am. Ck-out 11 am. Meeting rms. Business servs avail. Exercise equipt; weight machine, bicycles, sauna. Game rm. Rec rm. Overlooks Lake Oahe. Cr cds: A, D, DS, MC, V.

D 🖼 🖼 🖼 🖼 SC

Mount Rushmore National Memorial (C-1)

(For accommodations see Custer, Hill City, Keystone, Rapid City)

(25 mi SW of Rapid City off US 16A and SD 244)

The faces of four great American presidents—Washington, Jefferson, Lincoln and Theodore Roosevelt—stand out on a 5,675-foot mountain in the Black Hills of South Dakota, as grand and enduring as the contributions of the men they represent. Senator Peter Norbeck was instrumental in the realization of the monument. The original plan called for the presidents to be sculpted to the waist. It was a controversial project when sculptor Gutzon Borglum began his work on the carving in 1927. With crews often numbering 30 workers, he continued through 14 years of crisis and heartbreak and had almost finished by March, 1941, when he died. Lincoln Borglum, his son, brought the project to a close in October of that year. Today the memorial is host to almost three million visitors a year. To reach it, follow the signs south from I-90 on US 16. Then take US 16A through Keystone to SD 244 and the Memorial entrance. The orientation center, administrative and information headquarters, gift shop and a snack bar (daily) are on the grounds; also Buffalo Room Cafeteria (see KEYSTONE). Evening program followed by sculpture lighting and other interpretive programs (mid-May-mid-Sept, daily). Sculptor's studio museum (summer). Phone 605/574-2523. Per vehicle ¢¢

Murdo (C-3)

Founded 1906 **Pop** 679 **Elev** 2,326 ft **Area code** 605 **Zip** 57559

The old Ft Pierre-Custer stage route, and one of the main routes of the old Texas Cattle Trail, passed through the site where Murdo is now located. The town is named for pioneer cattleman Murdo McKenzie. Seat of Jones County, Murdo is still dominated by the cattle business. It is on the dividing line between Mountain and Central time.

Motels

★ **BEST WESTERN GRAHAM'S.** *301 W 5th St. 605/669-2441; FAX 605/669-3139.* 45 rms. June-mid-Sept: S $46-$50; D $52-$76; lower rates rest of yr. Crib $2. TV; cable (premium). Heated pool. Playground. Restaurant nearby. Ck-out 11 am. Business servs avail. Cr cds: A, C, D, DS, JCB, MC, V.

D 🖼 🖼 🖼 SC

✔★ **HOSPITALITY INN.** *302 W 5th St. 605/669-2425; res: 800/328-0529.* 29 rms, 1-2 story. June-Aug: S $35-$55; D $45-$75; each addl $4; wkly rates; lower rates rest of yr. Crib $1. Pet accepted. TV; cable.

Complimentary coffee. Restaurant nearby. Ck-out 11 am. Cr cds: A, C, D, DS, MC, V.

🖼 🖼 🖼

Restaurants

★ **STAR.** *2 blks SE on I-90 Business, 4 blks W of US 83. 605/669-2411.* Hrs: 7 am-10 pm. Closed Oct-early May. Semi-a la carte: bkfst $1.95-$5.50, lunch $3-$5.50, dinner $4.95-$16.75. Child's meals. Salad bar. Own pies. Family-owned. Cr cds: D, MC, V.

D

✔★ **TEEPEE.** *303 5th St. 605/669-2432.* Hrs: 7 am-10 pm. Closed Dec-Mar. Semi-a la carte: bkfst $1.50-$4.50, lunch $2-$6, dinner $5.95-$11.75. Child's meals. Specializes in chicken-fried steak, buffalo burgers. Salad bar. No cr cds accepted.

Pierre (B-3)

Settled 1880 **Pop** 12,906 **Elev** 1,484 ft **Area code** 605 **Zip** 57501 **E-mail** chamber@sd.cybernex.net **Web** www.pierre.org

Information Chamber of Commerce, 800 W Dakota, PO Box 548; 605/224-7361 or 888/962-2034

Pierre (PEER) is the capital of South Dakota, an honor for which it campaigned hard and won, in part, because of its central location—the geographic center of the state. The town's prosperity was built by cattlemen from the west, farmers from the east, local businessmen and government officials.

What to See and Do

Cultural Heritage Center. Pioneer life, Native American, mining and historic exhibits; the Verendrye Plate, a lead plate buried in 1743 at Ft Pierre by French explorers, the first known Europeans in South Dakota. (Daily; closed Jan 1, Thanksgiving, Dec 25) 900 Governors Dr. Phone 605/773-3458. ¢¢

Farm Island State Recreation Area. 1,184 acres. Swimming, bathhouse; fishing; boating, canoeing. Hiking. Picnicking, playground. Interpretive program. Camping (electrical hookups, dump station). Visitor center (May-Sept, daily). Standard fees. 4 mi E off SD 34. Phone 605/224-5605.

Fighting Stallions Memorial. Replica of a carving by Korczak Ziolkowski honors Governor George S. Mickelson and seven others who died in an airplane crash in 1993.

Oahe Dam and Reservoir. This large earthfill dam (9,300 ft long, 245 ft high) is part of the Missouri River Basin project. Lobby with exhibits (late May-early Sept, daily; rest of yr Mon-Fri; free). Recreation areas along reservoir offer waterskiing; fishing; boating. Nature trails. Picnicking. Primitive and improved camping (mid-May-mid-Sept; fee). 6 mi N on SD 1804, 1806. Phone 605/224-5862.

South Dakota Discovery Center & Aquarium. Hands-on science and technology exhibits; aquarium features native fish. (Daily, afternoons) 805 W Sioux Ave. For schedule phone 605/224-8295. ¢¢

State Capitol. Built of Bedford limestone, local boulder granite and marble. Guided tours (Mon-Fri). Capitol Ave E. Phone 605/773-3765. **Free.** Adj is

Flaming Fountain. On the northwest shore of Capitol Lake. The artesian well that feeds this fountain has a natural sulphur content so high that the waters can be lit. The fountain serves as a memorial to war veterans.

State Natl Guard Museum. Historical guard memorabilia. (Mon, Wed, Fri afternoons) 303 E Dakota. Phone 605/224-9991. **Free.**

Motels

★ **BEST WESTERN KINGS INN.** *220 S Pierre St. 605/224-5951; FAX 605/224-5301.* 104 rms, 2 story. S $44; D $49-$52; each addl $5; under 12 free. Crib free. Pet accepted. TV; cable. Restaurant 6 am-11 pm. Rm serv. Bar 11-2 am. Ck-out noon. Business servs avail. Sundries. X-country ski 1 mi. Whirlpool, sauna. Some refrigerators. Cr cds: A, C, D, DS, ER, MC, V.

★ ★ ★ **BEST WESTERN RAMKOTA INN.** *920 W Sioux, adj to River Centre convention facility. 605/224-6877; FAX 605/224-1042.* 151 rms, 2 story. S $57; D $64; each addl $6; suites $150; under 17 free. Crib avail. Pet accepted. TV; cable. Indoor pool; wading pool, whirlpool. Restaurant 6 am-10 pm. Rm serv. Bar. Ck-out noon. Coin lndry. Meeting rms. Business servs avail. Bellhops. Valet serv. Free airport, RR station, bus depot transportation. Exercise equipt; bicycles, stair machine, sauna. Game rm. Some refrigerators. Balconies. At Missouri River. Cr cds: A, C, D, DS, ER, MC, V.

★ **CAPITOL INN.** *815 Wells Ave. 605/224-6387; FAX 605/224-8083; res: 800/658-3055.* 81 rms, 2 story. S $19.95; D $21.95-$23.95; each addl $2; suites $58-$76. Crib free. Pet accepted. TV; cable. Pool. Restaurant nearby. Ck-out 11 am. Business servs avail. Some refrigerators. Balconies. Cr cds: A, C, D, DS, MC, V.

✔★ **DAYS INN.** *520 W Sioux Ave. 605/224-0411; FAX 605/204-0411.* 79 rms, 2 story. S $34-$45; D $38-$55; each addl $5. Crib free. TV; cable. Complimentary continental bkfst. Restaurant nearby. Ck-out 11 am. Business servs avail. X-country ski 1 mi. Cr cds: A, C, D, DS, MC, V.

★ **SUPER 8.** *320 W Sioux Ave. 605/224-1617; FAX 605/324-1617.* 78 rms, 3 story. S $36.98; D $41.98. Crib free. TV; cable (premium), VCR avail. Restaurant adj open 24 hrs. Ck-out 11 am. Cr cds: A, C, D, DS, MC, V.

Restaurant

★ **KOZY KORNER.** *217 E Dakota. 605/224-9547.* Hrs: 5 am-10 pm; winter from 6 am. Closed Dec 25. Res accepted. Semi-a la carte: bkfst $2.50-$5.75, lunch $3.35-$5.25, dinner $3.95-$8.95. Specializes in steak, seafood, soup. Salad bar. Own pies. Artwork displayed. No cr cds accepted.

Pine Ridge (D-2)

(For accommodations see Badlands National Park, Hot Springs; also see Chadron, NE)

Pop 2,596 **Elev** 3,232 ft **Area code** 605 **Zip** 57770

This is the administrative center for the Oglala Sioux nation at the Pine Ridge Indian Reservation.

What to See and Do

Red Cloud Indian School Heritage Art Museum. Features works by various Native American tribes. (June-Aug, daily; rest of yr, Mon-Fri) Holy Rosary Mission, 4 mi W on US 18. Phone 605/867-5491. **Free.**

✪ **Wounded Knee Historical Site.** Grounds where on Dec 29, 1890, almost 150 Minniconjou Sioux, including women and children, were shot by the US Army. A monument marks their mass grave. 8 mi E on US 18, then 7 mi N on unnumbered paved road to Wounded Knee.

Annual Event

Oglala Nation Fair & Rodeo. Powwow and dance contest with participants from 30 tribes; displays; activities. Phone 605/867-5821. Early Aug.

Platte (D-5)

Settled 1882 **Pop** 1,311 **Elev** 1,612 ft **Area code** 605 **Zip** 57369

Settled by immigrants from the Netherlands, Platte has a strategic location at the end of a railroad line.

What to See and Do

Ft Randall Dam-Lake Francis Case. Part of the Missouri River Basin project, Ft Randall Dam is 10,700 ft long and 165 ft high. Powerhouse guided tours (Memorial Day-Labor Day, daily). Many recreation areas along reservoir have swimming, fishing, boating, picnicking; camping (May-Oct; fee, electricity addl). The project also includes the former site of Ft Randall just below the dam. 7 mi E on SD 44, then 24 mi S on SD 50, then 6 mi S on US 18, 281, in Pickstown. Contact Lake Manager, PO Box 109, Pickstown 57367; 605/487-7847.

Platte Creek State Recreation Area. On 190 acres. Fishing; boating (ramp), canoeing. Picnicking, concession. Camping (electrical hookups, dump station). Standard fees. 8 mi W on SD 44, then 6 mi S on SD 1804. Phone 605/337-2587.

Snake Creek State Recreation Area. On 735 acres. Swimming, bathhouse; fishing; boating (ramp), canoeing. Picnicking, concession. Camping (electrical hookups, dump station). Interpretive program. Standard fees. 14 mi W off SD 44. Phone 605/337-2587.

Motels

★ **DAKOTA COUNTRY INN.** *RR 1, Box 240, 1/2 mi E on SD 44. 605/337-2607; res: 800/336-2607.* 30 rms. S $27; D $36-$42; each addl $3; higher rates pheasant season. Crib $2. TV; cable (premium). Complimentary coffee in lobby. Complimentary continental bkfst. Restaurant nearby. Ck-out 11 am. Business servs avail. In-rm modem link. Cr cds: A, DS, MC, V.

✔★ **KING'S INN.** *Box 54, 1/4 mi E on SD 44, 45, 50. 605/337-3385.* 34 rms. S $24-$28; D $31.95-$35.95. Crib $3. Pet accepted. TV; cable. Playground. Complimentary continental bkfst. Restaurant nearby. Ck-out 10 am. Cr cds: A, DS, MC, V.

Rapid City (C-1)

(See also Hill City, Keystone, Sturgis)

Founded 1876 **Pop** 54,523 **Elev** 3,247 ft **Area code** 605 **Web** rapidcitycvb.com

Information Convention & Visitors Bureau, 444 Mt Rushmore Rd N, PO Box 747, 57709; 605/343-1744 or 800/487-3223.

In the last few decades tourism has replaced gold mining as one of the chief industries of Rapid City. Founded only two years after gold was discovered in the Black Hills, Rapid City is a boom town that came to stay. It is the seat of Pennington County, second-largest city in South Dakota and home of Ellsworth Air Force Base. There is a substantial industrial life based on mining, lumbering and agriculture. The Pactola Ranger District office of the Black Hills National Forest (see BLACK HILLS) is located in Rapid City.

What to See and Do

Bear Country USA. Drive-through wildlife park with bears, mountain lions, wolves, elk, deer, buffalo, antelope, bighorn sheep, Rocky Mountain goats and moose. (Late May-mid-Oct, daily) 8 mi S via US 16. Phone 605/343-2290. Per adult ¢¢¢ or per vehicle ¢¢¢¢¢

Black Hills Caverns. Series of chambers connected by a fissure 160 ft high at some points; many types of formations, including amethyst and boxwork. Three different tours. (May 1-Oct 15, daily) 4 mi W on SD 44. Phone 605/343-0542. ¢¢

Black Hills Petrified Forest. Includes interpretive film on the Black Hills geology and petrifaction process; 5-blk walk through area of logs ranging from 5 ft-100 ft in length and up to 3 ft in diameter and stumps 3 ft-5 ft in height. Guided tours. Rock, fossil and mineral museum; gift and rock/lapidary shops. (Memorial Day-Labor Day, daily; weather permitting) Campground nearby. 11 mi NW on I-90, exit 46, then 1 mi E on Elk Creek Rd. Phone 605/787-4560. ¢¢¢

Black Hills Reptile Gardens. Includes reptile exhibit, alligator show, birds-of-prey show, snake lecture, jungle orchid trail. Children may ride giant tortoises and miniature horses. (Apr-Oct, daily) 6 mi S on US 16. Phone 605/342-5873. ¢¢¢

Chapel in the Hills. Replica of 12th-century Borgund Stavkirke. Vespers during summer months. SW off Jackson Blvd. Phone 605/342-8281.

Chuckwagon Suppers and Western Shows.

Circle B. Also covered wagon ride, shoot-outs. Supper (early June-Labor Day, daily; res required). 15 mi W via SD 44, then 1 mi N on US 385. Phone 605/348-7358. ¢¢¢¢

Flying T Chuckwagon. Supper and show (late May-mid-Sept, daily). Res suggested. 6 mi S via US 16; adj to Reptile Gardens. Phone 605/342-1905. ¢¢¢

Crystal Cave Park. Park with nature trail leading to replica of Native American village, petrified garden, rock and mineral display and cave; picnic grounds. (Mid-May-Sept, daily) 3 mi W via SD 44. Phone 605/342-8008. Cave tours ¢¢¢

Dahl Fine Arts Center. Visual arts center with three galleries. Mural Gallery with 200-ft cyclorama depicting 200 yrs of US history; narration. Two regional artists' galleries. (Daily; closed major hols) 713 7th St. Phone 605/394-4101. **Free.**

Dinosaur Park. Life-size steel and cement models of dinosaurs once numerous in the area. (Daily) W on Quincy St to Skyline Dr. Phone 605/343-8687. **Free.**

Gray Line Sightseeing Tours. Trips to Black Hills & Badlands. Phone 605/342-4461.

Marine Life Aquarium. Native and tropical fish; continuous shows of performing dolphins, sea lions and seals. (Mid-Apr-mid-Oct, daily) 3 mi S via US 16. Phone 605/343-7400. ¢¢¢

☆ **Mt Rushmore Natl Memorial** (see). 25 mi SW off US 16A.

Sitting Bull Crystal Cave. Believed to be only dogtooth spar cave in North America; fossils of sea life embedded in walls. (Mid-May-mid-Oct, daily) 9 mi S on US 16. Phone 605/342-2777. ¢¢¢

South Dakota School of Mines and Technology (1885). (2,358 students) Computer and scanning electron microscope laboratories. St Joseph St. On campus is

Museum of Geology. Exceptional display of minerals, fossils, gold samples and other geological material; first tyrannosaurus rex skull found in SD. (Mon-Sat, Sun afternoons; closed hols) O'Harra Memorial Bldg. Phone 605/394-2467. **Free.**

Stagecoach West. Lecture tours to Mt Rushmore, Custer State Park, Crazy Horse Memorial, Black Hills. (June-Sept, daily) Contact PO Box 264, 57709; 605/343-3113. ¢¢¢¢¢

Storybook Island. Fairyland park illustrating children's stories and rhymes; outdoor settings with music and animation. (Memorial Day-Labor Day, daily; weather permitting) Sheridan Lake Rd, 2 mi SW. Phone 605/342-6357. **Free.**

☆ **The Journey.** This important historical center utilizes state-of-the-art technology to reveal the geography, people and historical events that shaped the history of the Black Hills. Fully interactive exhibits take visitors back in time to discover the land as it was 2½ billion yrs ago, and trace its development to today. Home to five substantial collections of artifacts, memorabilia and specimens from the area. Gallery features traveling exhibits and is workplace for artists and craftspeople. Museum store. (Daily) Third & New York Sts. Phone 605/394-6923. ¢¢

Thunderhead Underground Falls. One of the oldest (1878) gold mining tunnels in Black Hills area; stalactites and gold-bearing granite formations. Falls are 600 ft inside mine. (May-Oct, daily) 10 mi W via SD 44. Phone 605/343-0081. ¢¢

Annual Events

Black Hills Powwow and Art Expo. Early July.

Central States Fair. Rodeo, carnival, horse and tractor pulls, auto races, demo derby. Early Aug.

Motels

★ **BEST WESTERN TOWN 'N COUNTRY INN.** *2505 Mt Rushmore Rd (57701).* 605/343-5383; FAX 605/343-9670. 100 rms, 1-2 story. June-late Aug: S $81; D $81-$91; each addl $5; under 12 free; lower rates rest of yr. Crib $5. TV; cable (premium). 2 pools, 1 indoor. Playground. Coffee in rms. Restaurant 7 am-9 pm. Ck-out 11 am. Gift shop. Free airport transportation. Some refrigerators. Cr cds: A, C, D, DS, MC, V.

⊠ ⊠ ⊠

★ **COMFORT INN.** *1550 N LaCrosse St (57701), just S of I-90 exit 59.* 605/348-2221; FAX 605/348-3110. 72 rms, 2 story. June-Aug: S, D $59-$139; each addl $5; higher rates Rally Week (mid-Aug); lower rates rest of yr. Crib $8. TV; cable. Indoor pool; whirlpool. Restaurant adj 7 am-10 pm. Ck-out 11 am. Game rm. Cr cds: A, C, D, DS, ER, JCB, MC, V.

D ⊠ ⊠ ⊠ SC

★★ **DAYS INN.** *1570 Rapp St (57701).* 605/348-8410; FAX 605/348-3392. 77 rms, 2 story, 16 suites. Mid-June-Aug: S $89; D $109; each addl $10; suites $109-$169; under 18 free; higher rates Sturgis Bike Rally (early Aug); lower rates rest of yr. Crib free. TV; cable (premium). VCR avail (movies). Indoor pool; whirlpool. Complimentary continental bkfst. Restaurant adj 6 am-10 pm. Ck-out 11 am. Coin lndry. Meeting rms. Business servs avail. In-room modem link. Bellhops. Valet serv. Sundries. Game rm. Refrigerator in suites. Cr cds: A, DS, MC, V.

D ⊠ ⊠ ⊠ SC

★ **FAIR VALUE INN.** *1607 La Crosse St (57701), S of I-90 exit 59.* 605/342-8118. 25 rms, 2 story. June-Aug: S, D $55-$75; each addl $3; higher rates motorcycle rally; lower rates rest of yr. Crib $3. TV; cable. Restaurant adj open 24 hrs. Ck-out 11 am. Cr cds: A, D, DS, MC, V.

D ⊠ ⊠

★★ **HOLIDAY INN EXPRESS.** *750 Cathedral Dr (57701).* 605/341-9300; FAX 605/341-9333. 63 rms, 3 story. June-mid-Sept: S $80; D $85; under 19 free; lower rates rest of yr. Crib free. TV; cable (premium). Indoor pool; whirlpool. Complimentary continental bkfst. Restaurant nearby. Ck-out 11 am. Coin lndry. Business servs avail. In-room modem link. Valet serv. Refrigerator in suites. Cr cds: A, C, D, DS, JCB, MC, V.

D ⊠ ⊠ ⊠ SC

★ **RAMADA INN.** *1721 LaCrosse St (57701).* 605/342-1300; FAX 605/342-0663. 139 rms, 4 story. June-Aug: S $79-$119; D $89-$139; each addl $10; suites $119-$159; under 18 free; higher rates special events; lower rates rest of yr. Crib free. Pet accepted. TV; cable (premium), VCR (movies). Indoor pool; whirlpool. Restaurant adj. Bar 7-12:30 am.

Ck-out noon. Meeting rms. Business servs avail. Bellhops. Game rm. Some bathrm phones, refrigerators. Cr cds: A, C, D, DS, MC, V.

★ **SUNBURST INN.** *620 Howard St (57701), I-90 exit 58.* 605/343-5434; FAX 605/343-7085; res: 800/456-0061. 98 rms, 2 story. July-mid-Aug: S $59; D $59-$69; each addl $5; under 17 free; lower rates rest of yr. Crib $3. TV; cable, VCR avail (movies $6). Pool. Complimentary coffee in lobby. Restaurant adj 11 am-10 pm. Ck-out 11 am. Cr cds: A, D, DS, MC, V.

★ **SUPER 8.** *2124 LaCrosse St (57701), at I-90 exit 59.* 605/348-8070; FAX 605/348-0833. 119 rms, 3 story. No elvtr. June-Aug: S $75; D $85; lower rates rest of yr. Crib free. Pet accepted. TV; cable (premium), VCR avail (movies). Complimentary coffee in lobby. Restaurant adj open 24 hrs. Ck-out 11 am. Sundries. Game rm. Cr cds: A, C, D, DS, JCB, MC, V.

Motor Hotel

★ ★ **HOWARD JOHNSON.** *Box 1795 (57709), 2211 LaCrosse St, I-90 exit 59.* 605/343-8550; FAX 605/343-9107. 272 rms, 2 story. June-Aug: S $84; D $94; each addl $10; suites $150; under 18 free; lower rates rest of yr. Crib free. TV; cable. Indoor/outdoor pool; whirlpool, pool-side serv. Playground. Restaurant 6 am-11 pm. Rm serv. Bar 11-2 am, Sun 1 pm-midnight; entertainment exc Sun. Ck-out noon. Coin lndry. Meeting rms. Business servs avail. Sundries. Airport, bus depot transportation. Exercise equipt; weights, bicycles, sauna, steam rm. Some refrigerators. Private patios, balconies. Cr cds: A, C, D, DS, ER, JCB, MC, V.

Hotels

★ ★ **ALEX JOHNSON.** *523 6th St (57701).* 605/342-1210; res: 800/888-2539. 143 rms, 6 story, 25 suites. June-Sept: S $98; D $102-$110; each addl $10; suites $115-$250; under 18 free; wkly, wkend & hol rates; lower rates rest of yr. Crib free. TV; cable. Restaurant 6 am-10 pm. Bar noon-2 am; entertainment Fri, Sat. Ck-out 11 am. Meeting rms. Concierge. Gift shop. Airport transportation. Refrigerators in suites. Renovated historic hotel (1928) pairing European and Native American decor. Cr cds: A, D, DS, MC, V.

★ ★ ★ **HOLIDAY INN-RUSHMORE PLAZA.** *505 N Fifth St (57701), I-90 exit 58.* 605/348-4000; FAX 605/348-9777. 205 rms, 8 story, 48 suites. S $90-$115; D $105-$125; each addl $15; suites $117-$250; under 18 free; wkend rates in winter. Crib free. TV; cable (premium). Indoor pool; whirlpool, poolside serv. Restaurant 6 am-10 pm. Bar 11-midnight. Ck-out noon. Convention facilities. Gift shop. Free airport, RR station, bus depot transportation. Exercise equipt; stair machine, treadmill, sauna. Refrigerator, wet bar in some suites. Next to Rushmore Plaza Civic Center. Cr cds: A, C, D, DS, JCB, MC, V.

Restaurants

✔★ **FIREHOUSE BREWING CO.** *610 Main St.* 605/348-1915. Hrs: 11-2 am; Sun to 10 pm. Closed Easter, Thanksgiving, Dec 25. Res accepted. Bar. Semi-a la carte: lunch $3.95-$7.50, dinner $6.95-$13.95. Child's meals. Specialties: cajun gumbo, beef brisket, buffalo steaks. Outdoor dining. In 1915 firehouse; microbrewery. Cr cds: A, DS, MC, V.

✔★ ★ **GREAT WALL.** *315 E North St (57701).* 605/348-1060. Hrs: 11 am-10 pm; Fri, Sat to 10:30 pm. Closed Thanksgiving, Dec 24, 25. Res accepted. Chinese menu. Wine, beer. Semi-a la carte: lunch $4.50-$6.95, dinner $5.75-$9.95. Child's meals. Specialties: Hunan-style orange chicken, mandarin-style sesame beef. Chinese decor. Cr cds: A, D, DS, MC, V.

Unrated Dining Spot

FLYING T CHUCKWAGON SUPPER & SHOW. *PO Box 9251 (57709), 6 mi S on US 16.* 605/342-1905. Hrs: one sitting at 7:30 pm. Closed mid-Sept-late May. Res accepted. Beer. Complete meals: dinner & show $12; age 4-10, $5. Western dinner of barbecued beef, baked potato, beans. Cr cds: MC, V.

D

Redfield (B-5)

(See also Aberdeen)

Pop 2,770 **Elev** 1,303 ft **Area code** 605 **Zip** 57469
Information Chamber of Commerce, 626 N Main St; 605/472-0965.

What to See and Do

Fisher Grove State Park. On 277 acres. Fishing; boating, canoeing. Hiking, golf. Picnicking, playground. Interpretive program. Camping (electrical hookups, dump station). Standard fees. 7 mi E on US 212. Phone 605/472-1212.

Spink County Historical Memorial Museum. Early-day furniture, household items, tools, machinery; collections of mounted birds, butterflies, other insects. (June-Aug, daily) SE corner of Courthouse Square. Phone 605/472-0758. ¢

Motels

✔★ **SUPER 8.** *826 W 4th St, jct US 212, 281.* 605/472-0720; FAX 605/472-0855. 27 rms, 2 story. S $31.88; D $36.88; each addl $3; under 12 free. Crib avail. TV; cable. Restaurant nearby. Ck-out 11 am. Cr cds: A, C, D, DS, MC, V.

★ **WILSON MOTOR INN.** *1 mi E on US 212.* 605/472-0550; res: 800/690-0551. 24 rms. S $24-$30; D $30-$40; each addl $4; higher rates special events. Crib $2.50. TV; cable. Ck-out 11 am. Cr cds: DS, MC, V.

Sioux Falls (C-6)

Founded 1856 **Pop** 100,814 **Elev** 1,442 ft **Area code** 605 **Web** siouxfalls.org
Information Chamber of Commerce & Convention and Visitors Bureau, 200 N Phillips Ave, Ste 102; 57101; 605/336-1620 or 800/333-2072.

At the falls of the Sioux River, this city has been developing at a constant pace since it was reestablished in 1865, having been abandoned in 1862 after threats of a Lakota attack. Its prosperity is based on diversified industry and farming. Cattle are shipped from a three-state area, slaughtered and packed here, then shipped east. Manufactured goods from the east are distributed throughout much of South Dakota from Sioux Falls.

Jean Nicolet saw the falls here in 1839 and described them impressively. The Dakota Land Company of Minnesota (1856) and the Western Town Company (1857) of Dubuque set out to develop the area and apparently worked together successfully. In September, 1858, the thirty-odd residents elected members to a Territorial Legislature, casting (it is said) votes for all their relatives as well as for themselves. On July 2, 1859, the first Sioux Falls newspaper, the *Democrat*, appeared.

Sioux Falls is the center for EROS (Earth Resources Observation Systems), an international center for space and aircraft photography of the Earth.

What to See and Do

Augustana College (1860). (2,100 students) Gilbert Science Center with Foucault pendulum, miniature dioramas of state wildlife. Center for Western Studies has museum and archival center on Western heritage. Art exhibits. Replica of Michelangelo's statue of Moses is on campus. Tours. 29th St & Summit Ave. Phone 605/336-5516.

EROS (Earth Resources Observation Systems). Data Center of Dept of the Interior aids in research and development of land and natural resource management. Houses millions of frames of satellite and aircraft photography of Earth. Visitors center containing audiovisual displays (Mon-Fri; closed federal hols); other buildings not open to public. NE off I-90 on County Rd 121. Phone 605/594-6511. **Free.**

Sherman Park. Formal flower garden, ballfields, picnicking. Kiwanis Ave from 12th to 22nd Sts. Also here are

Great Plains Zoo. More than 300 reptiles, birds and mammals from around the world; penguin exhibit; children's zoo. (Apr-Oct, daily; rest of yr, wkends) 805 S Kiwanis Ave. Phone 605/367-7003. Including museum ¢¢

Delbridge Museum of Natural History. Displays of five climatic ecozones; more than 150 mounted animals; hands-on exhibits. (Apr-Oct, daily; rest of yr, wkends) Phone 605/367-7003. Included in zoo admission.

⭐ **Siouxland Heritage Museums.** Unified museum system comprised of two sites:

Pettigrew Home & Museum. Restored Queen Anne historic house (1889) furnished to show life of state's first senator; galleries of Native American items and natural history of the Siouxland. (Daily exc Mon; closed hols) 8th St & Duluth Ave. Phone 605/367-7097. **Free.**

Old Courthouse Museum. Restored Richardsonian-Romanesque quartzite stone courthouse (1890) contains exhibits of Siouxland history, special exhibits on local culture. (Daily exc Mon; closed hols) 200 W 6th St. Phone 605/367-4210. **Free.**

Univ of Sioux Falls (1883). (900 students) Has Lorene B. Burns Indian Collection and Lucy Borneman Chinese Collection (academic yr, daily; summer, Mon-Fri; closed school vacations). The historic Yankton Trail crossed this area; marker indicates the site. 22nd St & Prairie Ave. Phone 605/331-5000. **Free.**

USS *South Dakota* Battleship Memorial. Memorial has the same dimensions as the battleship and is bordered by the ship's lifeline stanchions. Museum houses World War II mementos. (Memorial Day-Labor Day, daily) W 12th St & Kiwanis Ave. Phone 605/367-7060. **Free.**

Motels

⭐ **AMERICINN.** *3508 S Gateway Blvd (57106).* 605/361-3538; FAX 605/361-3538. 65 rms, 2 story. June-Aug: S $50.90-$54.90; D $56.90-$60.90; suites $70.90-$82.90; under 12 free; lower rates rest of yr. Crib free. TV; cable (premium). Indoor pool; whirlpool. Complimentary continental bkfst. Restaurant adj open 24 hrs. Ck-out 11 am. Meeting rms. X-country ski 1 mi. Cr cds: A, C, D, DS, MC, V.

⭐ **BUDGET HOST PLAZA INN.** *2620 E 10th St (57103).* 605/336-1550; FAX 605/339-0616; res: 800/283-4678. 38 rms. June-Sept: S $38.95; D $46.95-$55.95; each addl $4; under 10 free; lower rates rest of yr. Crib $3. Pet accepted. TV; cable. Heated pool. Restaurant adj open 24 hrs. Ck-out 11 am. Meeting rm. Cr cds: A, C, D, DS, ER, MC, V.

✔⭐⭐ **BUDGETEL.** *3200 Meadow Ave (57106), Empire Mall.* 605/362-0835; FAX 605/362-0835. 82 rms, 3 story. Late-May-Sept: S $46.99-$59.99; D $56.99-$69.99; suites $70.99-$84.99; under 18 free; lower rates rest of yr. Crib free. Pet accepted. TV; cable (premium). Indoor pool; whirlpool. Complimentary coffee in rms. Restaurant adj open 24 hrs. Ck-out 11 am. Meeting rms. X-country ski 2 mi. Some refrigerators. Cr cds: A, C, D, DS, MC, V.

✔⭐⭐ **COMFORT INN.** *3216 S Carolyn Ave (57106), Empire Mall.* 605/361-2822; FAX 605/361-2822. 67 rms, 2 story. Mid-May-mid-Sept: S $45.95-$65.95; D $50.95-$75.95; each addl $5; under 18 free; lower rates rest of yr. Crib free. Pet accepted. TV; cable (premium). Indoor pool; whirlpool. Complimentary continental bkfst. Restaurant adj open 24 hrs. Ck-out 11 am. Meeting rms. Game rm. Some refrigerators. Cr cds: A, C, D, DS, ER, JCB, MC, V.

⭐⭐ **COMFORT SUITES.** *3208 S Carolyn Ave (57106).* 605/362-9711; FAX 605/362-9711. 61 rms, 3 story. Mid-May-mid-Sept: S $59.95-$79.95; D $63.95-$89.95; each addl $5; under 18 free; lower rates rest of yr. Crib free. Pet accepted. TV; cable (premium). Indoor pool; whirlpool. Complimentary continental bkfst. Restaurant adj open 24 hrs. Ck-out 11 am. Business servs avail. X-country ski 1 mi. Cr cds: A, C, D, DS, ER, JCB, MC, V.

⭐ **DAYS INN-AIRPORT.** *5001 N Cliff Ave (57104), S of I-90 exit 399, near Joe Foss Field Airport.* 605/331-5959. 87 rms, 2 story. S $39-$48; D $48-$50; each addl $5. TV; cable. Complimentary continental bkfst. Ck-out noon. Business servs avail. Airport transportation. X-country ski 3 mi. Cr cds: A, C, D, DS, JCB, MC, V.

✔⭐ **DAYS INN EMPIRE.** *3401 Gateway Blvd (57106), W of I-29 exit 77.* 605/361-9240; FAX 605/361-5419. 76 rms, 2 story. S $38-$45; D $48-$55; each addl $5. Crib free. TV; cable. Complimentary continental bkfst. Restaurant adj open 24 hrs. Ck-out noon. Business servs avail. X-country ski 1 mi. Cr cds: A, C, D, DS, JCB, MC, V.

✔⭐ **EXEL INN.** *1300 W Russell St (57104).* 605/331-5800; FAX 605/331-4074. 105 rms, 2 story. S $31.99-$34.99; D $39.99-$41.99; each addl $4; under 18 free. Crib free. Pet accepted. TV; cable. Complimentary continental bkfst. Restaurant nearby. Ck-out noon. Coin lndry. X-country ski 1½ mi. Cr cds: A, C, D, DS, MC, V.

⭐⭐ **KELLY INN.** *Box 84711 (57118), 3101 W Russell St.* 605/338-6242; res: 800/635-3559. 42 rms, 2 story. June-Aug: S $44-$65; D $49-$70; each addl $5; under 12 free; lower rates rest of yr. Crib free. Pet accepted. TV; cable. Restaurant adj 6 am-11 pm. Ck-out 11 am. Coin lndry. Meeting rm. Airport transportation. Whirlpool, sauna. Cr cds: A, C, D, DS, ER, MC, V.

⭐ **MOTEL 6.** *3009 W Russell St (57104).* 605/336-7800; FAX 605/330-9273. 87 rms, 2 story. May-Sept: S $29.99; D $35.99; each addl $6; under 17 free; lower rates rest of yr. Crib free. Pet accepted, some restrictions. TV; cable. Heated pool. Restaurant adj 6 am-11 pm. Ck-out noon. Business servs avail. Cr cds: A, C, D, DS, MC, V.

✔⭐ **SELECT INN.** *3500 Gateway Blvd (57106).* 605/361-1864; FAX 605/361-9287. 100 rms, 2 story. S $29.90-$39.90; D $35.90-$39.90; each addl $3; under 12 free. Crib $3. Pet accepted. TV; cable, VCR avail (movies). Complimentary continental bkfst. Ck-out 11 am. Cr cds: A, C, D, DS, MC, V.

SUPER 8. *1508 W Russell St (57104), SE of I-29 exit 81.* *605/339-9330.* 95 rms, 3 story. No elvtr. S $27.29-$38.88; D $29.59-$47.88; each addl $5; under 12 free. Crib free. Pet accepted. TV; cable (premium). Restaurant adj open 24 hrs. Ck-out 11 am. Business servs avail. In-rm modem link. X-country ski 1 mi. Cr cds: A, C, D, DS, MC, V.

Motor Hotels

★ ★ ★ **BEST WESTERN RAMKOTA INN.** *2400 N Louise (57107), 2 mi NW on SD 38, at jct I-29 exit 81.* *605/336-0650; FAX 605/336-1687.* 227 rms, 2 story. S $67-$77; D $75-$85; each addl $8; suites $130-$180; under 18 free. Crib free. Pet accepted. TV; cable (premium), VCR avail. 2 pools, 1 indoor; wading pool, whirlpool, sauna, poolside serv. Playground. Restaurant 6 am-10 pm. Rm serv. Bar 11-2 am. Ck-out 11 am. Coin lndry. Convention facilities. Business servs avail. Bellhops. Valet serv. Sundries. Free airport, bus depot transportation. X-country ski 2 mi. Game rm. Rec rm. Cr cds: A, C, D, DS, ER, MC, V.

★ ★ **ENCORE INN.** *4300 Empire Place (57116).* *605/361-6684.* 106 rms, 3 story. S, D $79-$99; each addl $7; suites $130-$375; under 16 free. Crib free. TV; cable. Indoor pool; whirlpool. Coffee in rms. Restaurant 6:30 am-9 pm. Rm serv 6:30 am-11 pm. Ck-out noon. Meeting rms. Business servs avail. In-rm modem link. Bellhops. Valet serv. Sundries. Free airport, RR station, bus depot transportation. Refrigerator in suites. Cr cds: A, C, D, DS, ER, MC, V.

★ ★ ★ **HOLIDAY INN-CITY CENTRE.** *100 W 8th St (57102).* *605/339-2000; FAX 605/339-3724.* 302 rms, 10 story. S $79-$99; D $89-$109; each addl $10; suites $183; under 18 free. Crib free. TV; cable (premium), VCR avail. Indoor pool; whirlpool, poolside serv. Restaurants 6 am-10 pm. Rm serv. Bar noon-2 am. Ck-out noon. Meeting rms. Business center. In-rm modem link. Bellhops. Valet serv. Sundries. Gift shop. Free airport, bus depot transportation. Exercise equipt; weights, bicycles, sauna. Rec rm. Balconies. Cr cds: A, C, D, DS, JCB, MC, V.

 ★ ★ **HOWARD JOHNSON.** *3300 W Russell St (57101), at I-29 exit 81.* *605/336-9000.* 200 rms, 2 story. S $59-$68; D $59-$74; each addl $6; suites $85; under 18 free. Crib free. TV; cable. Indoor/outdoor pool; whirlpool, sauna. Playground. Restaurant 6 am-10 pm. Rm serv. Bar 1 pm-2 am, Sun to midnight; entertainment. Ck-out noon. Coin lndry. Meeting rms. Business servs avail. Bellhops. Valet serv. Sundries. Free airport, bus depot transportation. X-country ski 1 mi. Game rm. Private patios, balconies. Cr cds: A, C, D, DS, ER, JCB, MC, V.

★ ★ ★ **RAMADA INN CONVENTION CENTER.** *1301 Russell St (57104), E of I-29 exit 81, near Joe Foss Field Airport.* *605/336-1020; FAX 605/336-3030.* 200 rms, 2 story. S $57-$74; D $69-$84; each addl $8; under 18 free. Crib free. Pet accepted. TV; cable. Indoor pool; whirlpool, sauna. Restaurant 6 am-10 pm. Rm serv. Bar 4 pm-2 am, Sun to 10 pm; entertainment. Ck-out noon. Coin lndry. Meeting rms. Business servs avail. In-rm modem link. Bellhops. Valet serv. Sundries. Free airport, bus depot transportation. Putting green. X-country ski 2 mi. Cr cds: A, C, D, DS, ER, JCB, MC, V.

Restaurant

★ ★ **MINERVA'S.** *301 S Phillips (57102).* *605/334-0386.* Hrs: 11 am-2:30 pm, 5:30-10 pm; Sat 5-11 pm. Closed Sun; major hols. Res accepted. Continental menu. Bar 11 am-midnight. Semi-a la carte: lunch $4.95-$8.95, dinner $8.95-$28.95. Child's meals. Specializes in pasta, fresh seafood, aged steak. Salad bar. Cr cds: A, C, D, DS, MC, V.

Sisseton (A-6)

(See also Webster)

Pop 2,181 **Elev** 1,204 ft **Area code** 605 **Zip** 57262

What to See and Do

Ft Sisseton State Park. Established in 1864 to protect settlers, the fort housed 400 soldiers and contained more than 45 wooden, stone and brick buildings. The post was abandoned in 1889; during the 1930s it was used as a federal transient camp by the Works Progress Administration, which restored 14 of the fort's brick and stone buildings. Hiking trail, picnicking. Camping. Visitor center with historical exhibits (Memorial Day-Labor Day, daily). Standard fees. 20 mi W on SD 10, then S on SD 25. Phone 605/448-5701. ¢

Roy Lake State Park. On 509 acres. Swimming beach, bathhouse; fishing; boating, canoeing. Hiking. Picnicking, playground, concession. Camping (electrical hookups, dump station), cabins. Res accepted after Jan 1 annually. Standard fees. 18 mi W on SD 10, then 3 mi SW near Lake City. Phone 605/448-5701. ¢

Tekakwitha Fine Arts Center. Eight galleries featuring more than 200 works by Sisseton/Wahpeton Dakota Sioux. Gift shop. (Memorial Day-Labor Day, daily; rest of yr, Tues-Fri, also wkend afternoons; closed some major hols) 401 S 8th Ave. Phone 605/698-7058. **Donation.**

Annual Event

Ft Sisseton Historical Festival. Ft Sisseton State Park. Includes muzzle-loading rendezvous, cavalry and infantry drills, square dancing, melodrama, frontier crafts and Dutch oven cook-off. 1st wkend June.

Motel

 ★ **HOLIDAY.** *1 1/2 mi E at jct US 127, SD 10.* *605/698-7644.* 19 rms. S $22-$28; D $30-$34; each addl $3. Crib free. Pet accepted. TV; cable. Complimentary coffee. Restaurant nearby. Ck-out 11 am. Cr cds: A, C, D, DS, MC, V.

Restaurant

 ★ **AMERICAN HEARTH.** *SD 10.* *605/698-3077.* Hrs: 6 am-11 pm. Closed Dec 25. Res accepted. Semi-a la carte: bkfst $4-$6, lunch $4-$7, dinner $5-$9. Child's meals. Specializes in steak, breakfast. No cr cds accepted.

Spearfish (B-1)

(See also Belle Fourche, Deadwood, Lead, Rapid City, Sturgis)

Pop 6,966 **Elev** 3,643 ft **Area code** 605 **Zip** 57783
Information Chamber of Commerce, 106 W Kansas, PO Box 550; 605/642-2626 or 800/626-8013.

The fertile valley in which Spearfish lies is at the mouth of Spearfish Canyon, famous for its scenery and fishing. A Ranger District office of the Black Hills National Forest (see BLACK HILLS) is located in Spearfish.

What to See and Do

Black Hills State Univ (1883). (2,800 students) Located in the northern Black Hills overlooking the community. Library has Lyndle Dunn wildlife art, Babylonian tablets and Rachetts porcelain miniature dolls of First Ladies.

Donald E. Young Sports and Fitness Center open to public (fees). Walking tours. 1200 University Ave. Phone 605/642-6343.

City Campgrounds. Includes 150 campsites, 57 with hookups (addl fee). Fishing. (Mid-May-Oct, daily) I-90 exit 12, left at 2nd light, on S canyon St. Phone 605/642-1340. **¢¢¢**

DC Booth Historic Fish Hatchery (1899). One of the first in the West; facilities include ponds, visitor center, historic displays, restored Booth home. Visitor fish feeding. Historic buildings tour. 423 Hatchery Circle. Phone 605/642-7730. **Free.** Tour **¢**

High Plains Heritage Center and Museum. Western art, sculpture. Special events. (Daily; closed most major hols) 825 Heritage Dr. Phone 605/642-9378. **¢¢**

Star Aviation Air Tours. Airplane tours of the Gold Country, Devils Tower, Mt Rushmore and the Badlands. Min two persons per ride. Phone 605/642-4112, 800/742-8914 (SD), or 800/843-8010 (exc SD). **¢¢¢¢**

Annual Event

Corvette Classic. Main St. Sports car enthusiasts gather each summer for their convention. Highlight is Main St show & shine, when hundreds of corvettes line Main St. Phone 605/361-1243. July 17-20.

Seasonal Events

Black Hills Passion Play. Amphitheater, 400 St Joe St. Dramatization of last days of Jesus Christ, presented on 350-ft outdoor stage. Tues, Thurs & Sun. Phone 605/642-2646. June-Aug.

Matthews Opera House. 614 Main. For program schedule phone 605/642-7973. June-Aug.

Motels

(Advance reservations advised during Passion Play season)

★ **ALL AMERICAN INN.** *2275 E Colorado Blvd. 605/642-2350; FAX 605/642-9312; res: 800/606-2350 (SD).* 40 rms, 2 story. June-Aug: S $79; D $87; each addl $6; under 18 free; higher rates special events; lower rates rest of yr. Crib free. TV; cable (premium). Indoor pool; whirlpool. Complimentary continental bkfst. Ck-out 11 am. Cr cds: A, D, DS, MC, V.

D 🏊 ⛄ 🔥 SC

★ **COMFORT INN.** *2725 1st Ave, I-90 exit 14. 605/642-2337; FAX 605/642-0866.* 40 rms, 2 story. June-Aug: S $72; D $80; each addl $5; under 18 free; ski plan; higher rates special events; lower rates rest of yr. Pet accepted, some restrictions. TV; cable (premium). Indoor pool; whirlpool. Complimentary continental bkfst. Restaurant nearby. Ck-out 11 am. Coin lndry. Meeting rm. Cr cds: A, C, D, DS, JCB, MC, V.

D 🐾 🏊 ⛄ 🔥 SC

✔ ★ **DAYS INN.** *240 Ryan Rd, 1 mi S of I-90 exit 10. 605/642-7101; FAX 605/642-7120.* 50 rms, 2 story. June-Sept: S $49-$75; D $59-$80; each addl $5; suites $75; under 12 free; higher rates motorcycle rally; lower rates rest of yr. Crib free. TV; cable (premium). Complimentary continental bkfst. Restaurant nearby. Ck-out 11 am. Coin lndry. Cr cds: A, C, D, DS, MC, V.

D ⛄ 🔥 SC

★ ★ **FAIRFIELD INN BY MARRIOTT.** *2720 1st Ave E, I-90 exit 14. 605/642-3500; FAX 605/642-3500.* 57 rms, 3 story. May-Sept: S $65.95-$73.95; D $78.95; each addl $5; suites $85.95-$150; under 18 free; ski plan; lower rates rest of yr. Crib free. Pet accepted, some restrictions; $25 deposit. TV; cable (premium). Indoor pool; whirlpool. Complimentary continental bkfst. Ck-out 11 am. Meeting rm. Downhill/x-country ski 16 mi. Refrigerator in suites. Cr cds: A, D, DS, MC, V.

D 🐾 ⛵ 🏊 ⛄ 🔥 SC

★ ★ **KELLY INN.** *540 E Jackson. 605/642-7795; res: 800/635-3559.* 50 rms, 2 story. June-Aug: S $60; D $65; each addl $5; under 12 free; lower rates rest of yr. Crib free. Pet accepted. TV; cable (premium).

Complimentary coffee. Restaurant adj open 24 hrs. Ck-out 11 am. Coin lndry. Whirlpool, sauna. Some in-rm whirlpools. Cr cds: A, D, DS, MC, V.

D 🐾 🏊 🔥 🔥

Lodge

★ ★ **SPEARFISH CANYON.** *US 14A. 605/584-3435; FAX 605/584-3990; res: 800/439-8544.* 54 rms, 2 story. Mid-May-mid-Oct: S, D $79; each addl $6; suites $129-$195; under 12 free; wkend rates; higher rates Sturgis Black Hills Bike Rally (early Aug); lower rates rest of yr. Crib $10. TV; cable (premium). Whirlpool. Complimentary coffee in lobby. Restaurant opp 7 am-9 pm. Bar 8-2 am. Ck-out 11 am. Coin lndry. Meeting rms. Business servs avail. Bellhops. Gift shop. Downhill ski 6 mi; x-country ski on site. Refrigerator in suites. Minibars. Some balconies. Cr cds: A, DS, MC, V.

D ⛷ 🔥 🔥 SC

Restaurants

★ ★ **BELL STEAK HOUSE.** *539 W Jackson Blvd, W off I-90 exit 12. 605/642-2848.* Hrs: 11 am-1:30 pm, 5-9 pm; Fri to 10 pm; Sat 5-10 pm; Sun from 5 pm. Closed Dec 25. Res accepted. Bar 11 am-10 pm. Semi-a la carte: lunch $3.50-$7.25, dinner $4.75-$15.95. Child's meals. Specializes in prime rib, seafood. Salad bar. Cr cds: A, C, D, DS, MC, V.

SC ↗

✔ ★ **A LITTLE BIT OF ITALY.** *447 Main St. 605/642-5701.* Hrs: 11 am-midnight; Sun from noon. Closed Easter, Thanksgiving, Dec 25. Italian, Amer menu. Wine, beer. Semi-a la carte: lunch $4-$7, dinner $5.50-$10.95. Lunch buffet $4.25. Child's meals. Specializes in lasagne, fettucine Alfredo. Salad bar. Outdoor dining. Cr cds: A, D, DS, MC, V.

D SC ↗

Sturgis (B-1)

(See also Belle Fourche, Deadwood, Lead, Rapid City, Spearfish)

Founded 1878 **Pop** 5,330 **Elev** 3,440 ft **Area code** 605 **Zip** 57785

Information Chamber of Commerce, 606 Anna St, PO Box 504; 605/347-2556.

Originally a "bullwhackers" (wagon drivers) stop on the way to Ft Meade, this was once known as "Scooptown" because soldiers who came in were "scooped" (cleaned out) by such characters as Poker Alice, a famed cigar-smoking scoop-expert. Now Sturgis is a bustling Black Hills trade center.

What to See and Do

Bear Butte State Park. On 1,941 acres. Hiking trail to Bear Butte summit; ending point for 111-mi Centennial Trail through the Black Hills (see WIND CAVE NATIONAL PARK). Picnicking, playground. Camping. Visitor center has displays on Native American culture and history (May-Sept, daily). Park (daily). Standard fees. 6 mi NE off SD 79. Phone 605/347-5240.

Ft Meade Museum. On site of original Ft Meade (1878-1944), to which surviving members of the 7th Cavalry came after the Custer Massacre. Old cavalry quarters, post cemetery; museum has displays of artifacts, documents. Video presentation. (May-Sept, daily) 1 mi E on SD 34, 79. Phone 605/347-9822. **¢¢**

Motorcycle Museum & Hall of Fame. Vintage motorcycles; gift shop. (Daily) 2438 Junction Ave. Phone 605/347-4875. **¢¢**

Wonderland Cave. Scenic tours of underground caverns 60 million yrs old; two-level living cave with largest variety of crystal formations in the Northwest. Picnicking, snack bar; gift shop; hiking trails. (May-Oct, daily) S via I-90, exit 32, then 15 mi S on Vanocker Canyon Rd or S of Deadwood on SD 385. Phone 605/578-1728; 605/343-5043 (off-season). **¢¢¢**

Motels

★ **DAYS INN.** *HC 55, Box 348. 605/347-3027; FAX 605/347-0291.* 53 rms, 2 story. June-Aug: S $76; D $81; each addl $5; suites $86; under 13 free; higher rates motorcycle rally; lower rates rest of yr. Crib free. TV; cable (premium). Complimentary continental bkfst. Restaurant opp 6 am-11 pm. Ck-out 11 am. Coin lndry. Meeting rms. Business servs avail. Whirlpool, sauna. Cr cds: A, D, DS, MC, V.

★ **SUPER 8.** *Box 703, 1/2 blk SW of I-90 exit 30. 605/347-4447; FAX 605/347-2334.* 59 rms, 3 story. June-Sept: S $59.88; D $63.88-$68.88; each addl $3; lower rates rest of yr. Crib $5. Pet accepted. TV; cable (premium). Complimentary coffee in lobby. Restaurant adj open 24 hrs. Ck-out 11 am. Coin lndry. Exercise equipt; weights, bicycles, sauna. Whirlpool. Some balconies. Cr cds: A, C, D, DS, MC, V.

Vermillion (D-6)

(See also Beresford, Yankton; also see Sioux City, IA)

Settled 1859 **Pop** 10,034 **Elev** 1,221 ft **Area code** 605 **Zip** 57069 **E-mail** VDC@in.net **Web** mainstreetweb.com

Information Chamber of Commerce, 906 E Cherry St; 605/624-5571 or 800/809-2071.

Vermillion, the seat of Clay County, was settled originally below the bluffs of the Missouri River until the flood of 1881 changed the river's course, forcing residents to higher ground. Located in a portion of the state that was claimed twice by France and once by Spain before being sold to the United States, Vermillion has prospered and now prides itself as being a combination of rich farmland, good industrial climate and home to the University of South Dakota.

What to See and Do

Clay County Recreation Area. On 121 acres. Fishing; boating, canoeing (landing). Picnicking. 4 mi W, 1 1/2 mi S off SD 50, on banks of Missouri River. Phone 605/987-2263.

Univ of South Dakota (1862). (7,300 students) On campus is the DakotaDome, a physical education, recreation and athletic facility with an air-supported roof. Art galleries and theaters are located in the Warren M. Lee Center for the Fine Arts and Coyote Student Center. Tours. Dakota St, on SD 50 Bypass. Phone 605/677-5326. Also on campus is

Shrine to Music Museum. More than 6,000 antique musical instruments from all over the world and from all eras. (Daily; closed Jan 1, Thanksgiving, Dec 25) Clark & Yale Sts. Phone 605/677-5306. **Free.**

W.H. Over State Museum. State museum of natural and state history. Exhibits include life-size diorama of a Teton Dakota village; the Stanley J. Morrow collection of historical photographs; pioneer artifacts. Changing gallery. Gift shop. (Daily; closed hols) 1110 Ratingen St. Phone 605/677-5228. **Free.**

Motels

✔★ **BUDGET HOST TOMAHAWK.** *1313 W Cherry, jct SD 19, Business 50. 605/624-2601; res: 605/624-2449.* 20 rms. S $27; D $35; each addl $3; under 10 free; higher rates special events. Crib $2. TV; cable. Pool. Complimentary continental bkfst. Complimentary coffee in rms. Restaurant nearby. Ck-out 11 am. Business servs avail. Aiport, bus depot transportation. X-country ski 1 mi. Cr cds: A, C, D, DS, MC, V.

★ **COMFORT INN.** *701 W Cherry St (SD 50). 605/624-8333.* 46 rms, 2 story. S $38.95-$43.95; D $43.95-$59.95; each addl $5; under

18 free; higher rates some special events. Crib free. Pet accepted. TV; cable (premium). Indoor pool; whirlpool. Complimentary continental bkfst. Ck-out 11 am. Meeting rms. Business servs avail. Exercise equipt; bicycle, weights, sauna. Outdoor patio. Cr cds: A, C, D, DS, ER, JCB, MC, V.

Restaurant

✔★ **SILVER DOLLAR.** *1216 E Cherry (SD 50). 605/624-4830.* Hrs: 11 am-midnight. Closed Thanksgiving, Dec 25. Res accepted. Bar. Semi-a la carte: lunch $2.95-$5.95, dinner $3.95-$13.95. Specializes in chicken breast, prime rib. Cr cds: A, C, D, DS, MC, V.

Wall (C-2)

(See also Rapid City)

Founded 1907 **Pop** 834 **Elev** 2,818 ft **Area code** 605 **Zip** 57790

Established as a station on the Chicago & North Western Railroad in 1907, Wall is a gateway to Badlands National Park (see). The town is a trading center for a large area of farmers and ranchers, and it is noted for its pure water, which is brought up from wells 3,200 feet deep. A Ranger District office of the Nebraska National Forest (see CHADRON, NE) is located here.

What to See and Do

⊠ **Wall Drug Store.** World famous for roadside advertising, store features animated cowboy orchestra and chuck-wagon quartet; 80-ft dinosaur; art gallery; 23 Western shops; travelers' chapel; cafe. (Daily; closed major hols) On US 14, I-90, SD 240. Phone 605/279-2175. **Free.**

Motels

★ **BEST WESTERN PLAINS.** *Box 393, 712 Glenn St, I-90 Business exit 110. 605/279-2145; FAX 605/279-2977.* 74 rms, 1-2 story, 8 (2-rm) units. August: S, D $85; each addl $5; lower rates rest of yr. Crib $5. Pet accepted. TV; cable. Heated pool. Complimentary coffee in rms. Restaurant nearby. Ck-out 10:30 am. Gift shop. Rec rm. Cr cds: A, C, D, DS, MC, V.

★ **DAYS INN.** *10th St & Norris Ave, I-90 exit 110. 605/279-2000; FAX 605/279-2004.* 32 rms, 2 story. June-Aug: S $75; D $80-$85; each addl $5; under 12 free; higher rates motorcycle rally; lower rates rest of yr. Crib free. TV; cable. Complimentary coffee in lobby. Restaurant adj 5 am-10 pm. Ck-out 11 am. Whirlpool. Sauna. Pool privileges. Cr cds: A, DS, MC, V.

★ **SUPER 8.** *711 Glenn St, I-90 exit 110. 605/279-2688; FAX 605/279-2396.* 29 rms. June-Aug: S $64.88; D $70.88; each addl $2; lower rates rest of yr. Crib free. TV; cable (premium). Complimentary coffee in lobby. Restaurant nearby. Ck-out 11 am. Cr cds: A, C, D, DS, MC, V.

Restaurant

★ **WALL DRUG.** *510 Main St. 605/279-2175.* Hrs: 6 am-10 pm; winter to 6 pm. Closed some major hols. Res accepted. Wine, beer. Semi-a la carte: bkfst $2.20-$7.19, lunch, dinner $3.15-$10.69. Specializes in buffalo burgers, hot beef sandwiches. Salad bar. Original Western artwork; memorabilia. Cr cds: A, DS, MC, V.

Watertown (B-6)

(See also Brookings)

Founded 1879 **Pop** 17,592 **Elev** 1,739 ft **Area code** 605 **Zip** 57201 **Web** www.watertownsd.com

Information Convention & Visitors Bureau, 1200 33 St SE, Ste 209, PO Box 1113; 605/886-5814 or 800/658-4505.

Originally called Waterville, the settlement owed its boom to the railroads. Two large lakes, Kampeska and Pelican, are on the edges of town.

What to See and Do

Bramble Park Zoo. Municipal zoo (21 acres) features more than 400 birds and mammals of 100 different species. Live animal demonstrations; picnic area, playground; band concerts in summer. (Apr-Nov, daily) 901 Sixth Ave NW (SD 20). Phone 605/882-6269. ¢¢

Kampeska Heritage Museum. Exhibits depict pioneer history, local history through WWII and Native American artifacts. (Tues-Sat, afternoons) 27 1st Ave SE. Phone 605/886-7335. **Free.**

Lake Kampeska. Parks along shore offer swimming, bathhouses, water-skiing; fishing; boating (launch). Picnicking. Camping, trailer sites. Standard fees. There is also a 25-mi scenic drive around the lake. NW on SD 20. Phone 605/882-6260.

Mellette House (1883). Built by Arthur C. Mellette, last territorial and first state governor of South Dakota. Original Victorian furnishings, heirlooms, family portraits. (May-Sept, daily exc Mon; afternoons) 421 5th Ave NW. Phone 605/886-4730. **Free.**

Redlin Art Center. Houses over 100 of Terry Redlin's original oil paintings. Center also includes the only planetarium in the state, an amphitheater, gift shop and Glacial Lakes & Prairie Tourism Assoc. (Daily; closed hols) Jct US 212 & I-29. Phone 605/882-3877. Gallery **Free;** Planetarium ¢

Motels

★ ★ **BEST WESTERN RAMKOTA INN.** *1901 9th Ave SW, 4¹/₂ mi W of I-29 on US 212.* 605/886-8011; FAX 605/886-3667. 101 rms, 2 story. S $48-$51; D $56-$59; each addl $8; suites $125; under 18 free. Crib free. TV; cable. Indoor pool; whirlpool. Sauna. Restaurant 7 am-10 pm. Rm serv. Bar 4 pm-1 am; closed Sun. Ck-out noon. Meeting rms. Business servs avail. In-rm modem link. Valet serv. Sundries. Free airport, bus depot transportation. Cr cds: A, C, D, DS, ER, JCB, MC, V.

D ⛲ ⇌ ⋈ 🐾 SC

★ **SUPER 8.** *503 14th Ave SE, on US 81, 2 blks S of US 212.* 605/882-1900; FAX 605/882-1900, ext. 420. 58 rms, 3 story. No elvtr. S $38.88; D $47.88; each addl $6. Crib $1. TV; cable. Indoor pool; whirlpool. Sauna. Restaurant nearby. Ck-out 11 am. X-country ski 1 mi. Cr cds: A, C, D, DS, MC, V.

D ⛲ ⇌ ⋈ 🐾 SC

✔★ **TRAVEL HOST.** *1714 9th Ave SW, 1 mi W on US 212.* 605/886-6120; FAX 605/886-5352; res: 800/658-5512. 29 units, 2 story. S $28.90-$32.90; D $36.90-$41.90; each addl $5; under 12 free. Crib free. Pet accepted. TV; cable (premium). Complimentary continental bkfst. Restaurant adj 7 am-10 pm. Ck-out 11 am. Cr cds: A, C, D, DS, MC, V.

D ✔ ⋈ 🐾 SC

★ **TRAVELER'S INN.** *920 14th St SE (US 212), I-29 exit 177.* 605/882-2243; FAX 605/882-0968; res: 800/568-7074. 50 rms, 2 story. S $30-$37; D $41-$49; each addl $5; under 12 free. Crib free. TV; cable. Complimentary continental bkfst. Restaurant nearby. Ck-out 11 am. X-country ski 1¹/₂ mi. Cr cds: A, C, D, DS, MC, V.

D ⇌ ⋈ 🐾 SC

Webster (A-5)

(See also Aberdeen, Sisseton)

Founded 1881 **Pop** 2,017 **Elev** 1,847 ft **Area code** 605 **Zip** 57274
Information Chamber of Commerce, 513 Main, PO Box 123; 605/345-4668.

What to See and Do

Waubay Natl Wildlife Refuge. This 4,694-acre wildlife refuge has nature and bird-watching trails; 6-mi cross-country ski trails; 100-ft tall observation tower; outdoor classroom activities and wildlife exhibits. (Mon-Fri) 19 mi NE via US 12, then 7 mi N on County Rd 1, in Waubay. Phone 605/947-4521. **Free.**

Motels

★ **HOLIDAY.** *Box 478, ³/₄ mi NW on US 12.* 605/345-3323. 20 rms. S $24-$26; D $32; suites $44-$50. Crib free. TV. Restaurant adj 5-11 pm. Ck-out 10 am. Cr cds: DS, MC, V.

⇌ 🐾

✔★ **SUPER 8.** *PO Box 592, US 12W.* 605/345-4701. 27 rms, 2 story. S $36.88; D $41.88; each addl $5; under 12 free. Crib free. TV; cable. Complimentary coffee in lobby. Restaurant nearby. Ck-out 11 am. Cr cds: A, C, D, DS, MC, V.

⇌ 🐾 SC

Wind Cave National Park (C-1)

(For accommodations see Custer, Hill City, Hot Springs, Keystone)

(11 mi N of Hot Springs on US 385)

Wind Cave, one of many caves in the ring of limestone surrounding the Black Hills, is a maze of subterranean passages known to extend more than 79 miles. It is named for the strong currents of wind that blow in or out of its entrance according to atmospheric pressure. When the pressure is decreasing, the wind blows outward; when it increases, the wind blows in. It was the rushing sound of air coming out of the entrance that led to its discovery in 1881. The cave and surrounding area became a national park in 1903; today it comprises 44 square miles.

Wind Cave is a constant 53°F. Various 1-2-hr guided tours (daily; no tours Thanksgiving, Dec 25). Tours are moderately strenuous. A sweater or jacket is advised; shoes must have low heels and nonslip soles.

On the surface are prairie grasslands, forests and a wildlife preserve, the home of bison, pronghorn, elk, deer, prairie dogs and other animals. The Centennial Trail, a 111-mile, multi-use trail, takes visitors from one end of the Black Hills to the other. The trail begins here and ends at Bear Butte State Park (see STURGIS). In addition, there is hiking, bicycling, picnicking and camping at Elk Mountain near headquarters. Visitor center (daily; closed Thanksgiving, Dec 25). Hrs may vary in summer. Park (daily). Phone 605/745-4600. Tours ¢¢-¢¢¢¢

Winner (D-4)

Settled 1909 **Pop** 3,354 **Elev** 1,972 ft **Area code** 605 **Zip** 57580 **Web** www.state.sd.us/state/executive/tourism/adds/winner.htm

Information Chamber of Commerce, Tripp County Courthouse, PO Box 268; 605/842-1533.

Winner is a sports-oriented town; a pheasant-hunting autumn follows a baseball summer. It is the seat of Tripp County and one of the largest producers of cattle and wheat in the state.

Annual Events

Regional High School Rodeo. Early June.

Mid Dakota Fair. Mid-Aug.

Motels

★ **BUFFALO TRAIL.** *950 W First St, located at jct W US 18/183 & SD 44.* 605/842-2212; FAX 605/842-3199; res: 800/341-8000. 31 rms. S $30-$38; D $38-$42; each addl $5; higher rates hunting season. Crib $5. Pet accepted. TV; cable. Pool. Complimentary continental bkfst. Restaurant nearby. Ck-out 11 am. Free airport transportation. 9-hole golf privileges, putting green, driving range. Rec rm. Picnic tables, grills. Cr cds: A, C, D, DS, MC, V.

★ **WARRIOR INN.** *1/2 mi E on SD 44 at jct US 18, 183.* 605/842-3121; res: 800/658-4705. 39 rms. S $36; D $46; each addl $4; family rates. Crib $5. TV; cable. Indoor pool. Restaurant nearby. Bar 5 pm-1 am. Ck-out 11 am. Sundries. Free airport transportation. Cr cds: A, C, D, DS, MC, V.

Yankton (D-6)

(See also Beresford, Vermillion)

Settled 1859 **Pop** 12,703 **Elev** 1,205 ft **Area code** 605 **Zip** 57078 **E-mail** visitorinfo@yanktonsd.com **Web** www.yanktonsd.com

Information Chamber of Commerce, 218 W 4th St, PO Box 588-D; 605/665-3636.

First capital of Dakota Territory (1861-1883), Yankton has restored homes and mansions dating to territorial days.

What to See and Do

Dakota Territorial Capitol. Replica of first capitol of Dakota Territory. Original building (1862) was auctioned for scrap after the territorial capital was moved to Bismarck in 1883. Riverside Park. **Free.**

Dakota Territorial Museum. Museum in complex includes restored Dakota Territorial Legislative Council Bldg; railroad depot, caboose; rural schoolhouse; blacksmith shop; 1870 parlor, 1900 bedrm, grandma's kitchen; saloon; military display. (Memorial Day-Labor Day, daily exc Tues; rest of yr, by appt) 610 Summit Ave, in Westside Park. Phone 605/665-3898. **Free.**

Lewis & Clark Lake/Gavins Point Dam. This reservoir of Missouri River has 15 developed recreation areas for camping (fee), swimming beaches, boat and fishing access. Primitive areas for hunting, scenic drives, hiking. Other attractions include tour of powerhouse, visitor center, fish hatchery and aquarium, campground programs. 5 mi W on SD 52. Phone 402/667-7873. **Free.**

Annual Events

Riverboat Days. Entertainment, crafts, food, rodeo. 3rd wkend Aug.

Great Plains Oldtime Fiddlers Contest. Mid-Sept.

Dacotah Territorial Reunion. Late Sept.

Motels

★ **BEST WESTERN YANKTON INN.** *1607 E SD 50.* 605/665-2906; FAX 605/665-4318. 124 rms, 2 story. S $45-$66; D $49-$66; each addl $4; under 14 free. Crib free. Pet accepted. TV; cable, VCR avail (movies). Indoor pool; wading pool, whirlpool. Complimentary continental bkfst. Restaurant adj 6 am-10 pm. Ck-out 11 am. Meeting rms. Business servs avail. Bellhops. X-country ski 1 mi. Exercise equipt; bicycle, treadmill, sauna. Game rm. Some refrigerators. Opp lake. Cr cds: A, C, D, DS, ER, MC, V.

★ **BROADWAY.** *1210 Broadway, on US 81 at jct 15th St.* 605/665-7805. 37 rms. S $30.95-$39.95; D $35.95-$49.95; each addl $3. Crib $4. Pet accepted. TV; cable, VCR avail. Pool. Restaurant nearby. Bar 11-2 am. Ck-out 11 am. X-country ski 1 mi. Cr cds: A, DS, MC, V.

★ **COMFORT INN.** *2118 Broadway, US 81 N.* 605/665-8053; FAX 605/665-8165. 45 rms, 2 story. S $39.95; D $47.95-$65.95; each addl $4; under 19 free. Crib $5. Pet accepted, some restrictions. TV; cable. Whirlpool. Complimentary continental bkfst. Restaurant nearby. Ck-out 11 am. Business servs avail. In-rm modem link. Cr cds: A, C, D, DS, JCB, MC, V.

★ **DAYS INN.** *2410 Broadway, US 81 N.* 605/665-8717; FAX 605/665-8841. 45 rms, 2 story. S $38-$45; D $45-$50; each addl $4; under 13 free. Crib free. TV; cable. Whirlpool. Complimentary continental bkfst. Restaurant adj. Ck-out 11 am. Business servs avail. In-rm modem link. Cr cds: A, C, D, DS, MC, V.

★ **SUPER 8.** *2 mi E on SD 50.* 605/665-6510; FAX 605/665-6510. 58 rms, 3 story. No elvtr. S $31.88; D $36.88-$42.88; each addl $2. Crib $3. TV; cable. Restaurant adj open 24 hrs. Bar 3 pm-2 am. Ck-out 11 am. X-country ski 1 mi. Cr cds: A, C, D, DS, MC, V.

Washington

Population: 4,866,692
Land area: 68,192 square miles
Elevation: 0-14,410 feet
Highest point: Mount Rainier (Pierce County)
Entered Union: November 11, 1889 (42nd state)
Capital: Olympia
Motto: *Al-ki* (By and by)
Nickname: Evergreen State
State flower: Rhododendron
State bird: Willow goldfinch
State tree: Western hemlock
Time zone: Pacific
Web: www.tourism.wa.gov

The Stillaguamish, Steilacoom and Hoh, Puyallup, Tulalip and La Push, the Duckabush, the Dosewallips and the Queets, the Skookumchuck, the Sol Duc and the Pysht—all these are Washington towns and rivers. There are many more like them, named by Native Americans.

Ruggedly handsome Washington is like a bank in which nature has deposited some of her greatest resources. In addition to dramatic mountain ranges, expansive forests and inviting harbors, it is also a cornerstone of American hydroelectric technology. Here are the majestic spectacles of mighty Mt Rainier—revered as a god by the Native Americans—and the Olympic Peninsula, where one of the wettest and one of the driest parts of the country are only a mountain away from each other; also here is Puget Sound, a giant inland sea where 2,000 miles of shoreline bend into jewel-like bays.

Although British and Spanish navigators were the first Europeans to explore Washington's serrated shoreline, the first major discoveries were made in 1792, when an American, Captain Robert Gray, gave his name to Grays Harbor and the name of his ship, *Columbia,* to the great river. An Englishman, Captain George Vancouver, explored and named Puget Sound and christened Mt Baker and Mt Rainier, which he could see far inland. Fort Vancouver was the keystone of the British fur industry, dominating a Northwest empire. After conflicting US and British claims were resolved, Americans surged into this area by ship and wagon train.

Part of the Oregon Territory until separated in 1853, the state's eastern boundary was established in 1863, when Idaho became a territory. Entering the last decade of the 19th century as a state of the Union, Washington found itself no longer America's last territorial frontier.

Civilization has not dissipated Washington's natural wealth. On the contrary, after more than a century of logging operations, Washington retains 24 million acres of superb forests, and miracles of modern engineering have almost completely erased the wastelands through which the wagon trains of the pioneers passed on their way to the sea.

The mighty but capricious Columbia River meanders through the heart of northeast and central Washington, then runs for 300 miles along the Oregon-Washington border. Through a series of dams and the Grand Coulee Reclamation Project, the energies of the Columbia have been harnessed and converted into what is presently one of the world's great sources of water power. Irrigation and a vast supply of inexpensive power gave a tremendous push to Washington's economy, sparking new industries and making possible the state's production of huge crops of grains, vegetables and fruit.

Central Washington is the apple barrel of the country; dairying is a big industry in the western valleys. Forestry and wood products as well as the production of paper and allied products are of major importance in the western and northern sections of the state; one-third of the state is covered by commercial forests. In recent years Washington wines have enjoyed great popularity around the nation.

Since 1965, more than 25 percent of Washington's total manufacturing effort has been devoted to the production of transportation equipment, of which a large portion is involved in commercial jet aircraft. Along Puget Sound, industry means canning plants, lumber mills and pulp and paper plants; but even here there is a new economic dimension: petroleum refineries of four major companies have a daily capacity of 366,500 barrels of crude oil and gasoline; biotechnology and software development are growing industries. Tourism is the state's fourth largest industry, amounting to more than $8.8 billion a year.

When to Go/Climate

Moist air off the Pacific Ocean and Puget Sound creates the rainy conditions in western Washington and heavy snowfall in the Cascades. While the western slopes of the Cascades and Olympic Mountains are soaked with moisture, the eastern slopes and, indeed, the entire eastern part of the state is almost desert dry. Temperatures are seasonally mild, except for high in the mountains.

AVERAGE HIGH/LOW TEMPERATURES (°F)

SEATTLE

Jan 46/36	**May** 64/48	**Sept** 69/53
Feb 51/38	**June** 70/53	**Oct** 60/47
Mar 54/40	**July** 74/56	**Nov** 52/41
Apr 58/43	**Aug** 74/57	**Dec** 46/37

SPOKANE

Jan 33/21	May 66/42	Sept 72/46
Feb 41/26	June 75/49	Oct 59/36
Mar 48/30	July 83/54	Nov 41/29
Apr 57/35	Aug 83/54	Dec 34/22

Parks and Recreation Finder

Directions to and information about the parks and recreation areas below are given under their respective town/city sections. Please refer to those sections for details.

Key to abbreviations: I.P. = Interstate Park; N.B.C. = National Battlefield & Cemetery; N.B.P. = National Battlefield Park; N.F. = National Forest; N.G. = National Grassland; N.H. = National Historical Park; N.H.S. = National Historic Site; N.M. = National Monument; N.Mem. = National Memorial; N.M.P. = National Military Park; N.P. = National Park; N.Pres. = National Preserve; N.R. = National Recreational Area; N.R.R. = National Recreational River; N.Res. = National Reserve; N.S. = National Seashore; N.S.R. = National Scenic River; N.S.T. = National Scenic Trail; N.V.M. = National Volcanic Monument; S.B. = State Beach; S.C.P. = State Conservation Park; S.G. = State Garden; S.H.A. = State Historic Area; S.H.P. = State Historic Park; S.N.A. = State Natural Area; S.P. = State Park; S.R. = State Reserve; S.R.A. = State Recreation Area; S.Res.P. = State Resort Park; S.R.P. = State Rustic Park.

NATIONAL PARK AND RECREATION AREAS

Place Name	Listed Under
Colville N.F.	COLVILLE
Coulee Dam	same
Ft Vancouver N.H.S.	VANCOUVER
Gifford Pinchot N.F.	VANCOUVER
Klondike Gold Rush N.H.	SEATTLE
Mt Baker-Snoqualmie N.F.	BELLINGHAM, SEATTLE
Mount Rainier N.P.	same
Mount St Helens N.V.M.	same
North Cascades N.P.	SEDRO WOOLLEY
Okanogan N.F.	OMAK
Olympic N.P.	same
Olympic N.F.	OLYMPIA
San Juan Island N.H.	SAN JUAN ISLANDS
Umatilla N.F.	CLARKSTON
Wenatchee N.F.	WENATCHEE
Whitman Mission N.H.S.	WALLA WALLA

STATE RECREATION AREAS

Place Name	Listed Under
Alta Lake S.P.	CHELAN
Bay View S.P.	MOUNT VERNON
Belfair S.P.	BREMERTON
Birch Bay S.P.	BLAINE
Bogachiel S.P.	FORKS
Blake Island S.P.	BREMERTON
Brooks Memorial S.P.	GOLDENDALE
Conconully S.P.	OMAK
Deception Pass S.P.	ANACORTES
Federation Forest S.P.	ENUMCLAW
Fields Spring S.P.	CLARKSTON
Flaming Geyser S.P.	ENUMCLAW
Ft Canby S.P.	LONG BEACH
Ft Casey S.P.	COUPEVILLE
Ft Flagler S.P.	PORT TOWNSEND
Ft Worden S.P.	PORT TOWNSEND
Ginkgo/Wanapum S.P.	ELLENSBURG
Illahee S.P.	BREMERTON
Kitsap Memorial S.P.	PORT GAMBLE
Lake Chelan S.P.	CHELAN
Lake Cushman S.P.	UNION
Lake Sammamish S.P.	ISSAQUAH
Lake Sylvia S.P.	ABERDEEN
Larrabee S.P.	BELLINGHAM
Lewis & Clark Trail S.P.	DAYTON
Millersylvania S.P.	OLYMPIA
Moran S.P.	SAN JUAN ISLANDS
Moses Lake S.P.	MOSES LAKE
Mt Spokane S.P.	SPOKANE
Old Ft Townsend S.P.	PORT TOWNSEND
Potholes S.P.	MOSES LAKE
Rainbow Falls S.P.	CHEHALIS

CALENDAR HIGHLIGHTS

MARCH

Chocolate Fantasy (Yakima). Chocolate manufacturers from across the nation showcase candy, cookies and pies; sampling, "chocolate bingo." Phone 509/966-6309.

APRIL

Daffodil Festival (Tacoma). In Tacoma and Puyallup Valley. Flower show, coronation, four-city floral parade of floats, marine regatta, bowling tournament. Phone 253/627-6176.

MAY

Wooden Boat Festival (Olympia). Percival Landing in Harbor. Wooden boats on display, some open for public viewing. Wooden crafts fair. Phone 360/943-5404.

Ski to Sea Festival (Bellingham). Parades, carnival, art show, special events. Ski to Sea race; starts on Mt Baker, ends in Bellingham Bay and involves skiers, runners, canoeists, bicyclists and kayakers. Phone 360/734-1330.

JULY

Dixieland Jazz Festival (San Juan Islands). Friday Harbor and Roche Harbor. Phone 360/378-5509.

AUGUST

Seattle Seafair (Seattle). Citywide marine festival. Regattas, speedboat races, shows at Aqua Theater, parades, sports events, exhibits. Phone 206/728-0123.

Stampede and Suicide Race (Omak). Rodeo events; horses and riders race down a cliff and across the Okanogan River. Western art show. Native American dance contests. Encampment with more than 100 teepees. Phone 509/826-1002.

Southwest Washington Fair (Centralia). First held in 1909, this is the state's second oldest fair and one of the largest. Phone 360/736-6072.

SEPTEMBER

Northeast Washington Fair (Colville). Stevens County Fairgrounds. Parade, livestock and horse shows; arts and crafts exhibits; carnival. Phone 509/684-2585.

Western Washington Fair (Puyallup). Pacific Northwest's largest fair; includes three statewide youth fairs, livestock shows, agricultural and commercial exhibits, free entertainment, midway, rodeo, top-name grandstand acts. Phone 206/841-5045.

Central Washington State Fair & Rodeo (Yakima). Fairgrounds. Thoroughbred racing. Parimutuel wagering. Phone 509/248-3920.

Riverside S.P.	SPOKANE
Sacajawea S.P.	PASCO
Scenic Beach S.P.	BREMERTON
Schafer S.P.	ABERDEEN
Seaquest S.P.	KELSO
Sequim Bay S.P.	SEQUIM
Steamboat Rock S.P.	COULEE DAM
Squilchuck S.P.	WENATCHEE
Twanoh S.P.	UNION
Twenty-Five Mile Creek S.P.	CHELAN
Twin Harbors S.P.	WESTPORT
Wenberg S.P.	MARYSVILLE
Yakima Sportsman S.P.	YAKIMA

Water-related activities, hiking, riding, various other sports, picnicking and visitor centers, as well as camping, are available in many of these areas. The 248,882 acres owned or managed by the Washington State Parks & Recreation Commission provide unusually good camping and trailer facilities at most locations, with a camping fee of $5-$11/site; hookups $15-$16; 10-day limit in summer; 15 days rest of yr. Most parks are open daily: Apr-mid-Oct, 6:30 am-dusk; some are closed rest of yr. Pets on leash only. Further information may be obtained from the Washington State Parks & Recreation Commission, 7150 Cleanwater Lane, PO Box 42650, Olympia 98504-2650. For information, phone 800/233-0321.

SKI AREAS

Place Name	Listed Under
Alpental Ski Area	NORTH BEND
Crystal Mt Resort	MT RAINIER NATIONAL PARK
Hurricane Ridge Winter Use Ski Area	OLYMPIC NATIONAL PARK
Hyak Ski Area	NORTH BEND
Mission Ridge Ski Area	WENATCHEE
Mt Baker Ski Area	BELLINGHAM
Mt Spokane Ski Area	SPOKANE
Ski Acres Ski Area	NORTH BEND
Ski Bluewood Ski Area	DAYTON
Snoqualmie Ski Area	NORTH BEND
White Pass Village Ski Area	MT RAINIER NATIONAL PARK

FISHING & HUNTING

With 10,000 miles of bay and Pacific shoreline, 8,000 lakes and rivers that stretch from Oregon to Canada, Washington provides something for every fisherman's whim. Fish hatcheries dot the state, stocking nature's waterways and those artificially created by irrigation and navigation dams. If you like salmon and steelhead, Washington is the state to try your luck.

Nonresident freshwater fishing license $48; 3-day license $17. Steelhead tags $18. A food fish license is required for salmon and saltwater bottomfish; nonresident food fish license, $20. A shellfish/seaweed license is required for shellfish; nonresident license, $20. Razor clam season varies; contact the Dept of Fish & Wildlife for season dates, phone 360/902-2200. Nonresident hunting license $150; trapping $180; elk $120; bear tag $180; deer tag $60. Get hunting and freshwater fishing regulations and a complete list of license fees from Dept of Fish & Wildlife, 600 Capitol Way N, Olympia 98501-1091. Fishing and hunting regulation pamphlets are available in local sporting goods stores.

Driving Information

Safety belts are mandatory for all persons anywhere in vehicle. Children under 40 pounds in weight must be in an approved safety seat anywhere in vehicle. For further information phone 360/753-6197.

INTERSTATE HIGHWAY SYSTEM

The following alphabetical listing of Washington towns in *Mobil Travel Guide* shows that these cities are within 10 miles of the indicated Interstate highways. A highway map, however, should be checked for the nearest exit.

Highway Number	Cities/Towns within 10 miles
Interstate 5	Bellingham, Blaine, Centralia, Chehalis, Everett, Kelso, Longview, Marysville, Mount Vernon, Olympia, Puyallup, Seattle, Sedro Woolley, Snohomish, Tacoma, Vancouver.
Interstate 82	Ellensburg, Kennewick, Pasco, Richland, Sunnyside, Toppenish, Yakima.
Interstate 90	Bellevue, Ellensburg, Issaquah, Moses Lake, North Bend, Ritzville, Seattle, Spokane.
Interstate 182	Pasco, Richland.

Additional Visitor Information

Washington travel information and brochures on the state are available from the State Tourism Department of Community, Trade and Economic Development, 101 General Administration Bldg, PO Box 42500, Olympia 98504-2500; phone 800/544-1800 for a copy of *Washington State Lodging and Travel Guide*; phone 800/638-8474 or 360/586-2088 for tourism information. *This is Washington* (Superior Publishing Co, Seattle) and *Sunset Travel Guide to Washington* (Sunset Publishing, Menlo Park, CA) are also helpful.

There are 180 visitor information centers in Washington; most are open May-Sept. Visitors who stop by will find information and brochures most helpful in planning stops to points of interest. The locations for the official state visitor centers at points of entry are as follows: 7 mi S of Blaine, near the Canadian border, I-5 exit 270 northbound or southbound; at the Seattle/Tacoma (Sea-Tac) International Airport, airport terminal, baggage claim level (yr-round); east of Spokane at the Idaho/Washington border, I-90 exit 299 westbound; 404 E 15th St, Vancouver; in Oroville on US 97, near the Canadian border; at the Oregon border on US 97, near Maryhill State Park and Sam Hill Bridge; and on WA 401 near the Astoria Bridge.

Aberdeen (D-2)

(See also Hoquiam, Ocean Shores, Westport)

Settled 1878 **Pop** 16,565 **Elev** 19 ft **Area code** 360 **Zip** 98520 **E-mail** gchamber@techline.com **Web** www.chamber.grays-harbor.wa.us

Information Grays Harbor Chamber of Commerce, 506 Duffy St; 360/532-1924 or 800/321-1924.

Aberdeen and Hoquiam are twin cities on the eastern tip of Grays Harbor. Born as a cannery named for the city in Scotland, Aberdeen later blossomed as a lumber town, with one of the greatest stands of Douglas fir ever found in the Pacific Northwest at its back. Many Harbor residents are descendants of Midwestern Scandinavians who came here to fell the forests. Today, the town's commerce consists of wood-processing, fishing and ship building. The Port of Grays Harbor is located in town at the foot of Myrtle St.

What to See and Do

Aberdeen Museum of History. Special exhibits with 1880s-1940s furnishings and implements include kitchen and bedroom, general mercantile store, one-room school; farm and logging equipment and displays; blacksmith shop; pioneer church; fire trucks. Slide show, photographs. (June-Labor Day, Wed-Sun; rest of yr, wkends) 111 E 3rd St. Phone 360/533-1976. **Free.**

Grays Harbor Historical Seaport. Historical interpretive center; classes in long boat building. Includes a museum with informational and active exhibits on the history of sailing in the Pacific Northwest. Also replica of

Robert Gray's ship *Lady Washington* (seasonal; fee). (Daily; closed major hols) 813 E Heron St. Phone 360/532-8611. **Free.**

Lake Sylvia State Park. Approx 235 acres of protected timber. Swimming; fishing. Hiking. Picnicking, concession. Camping. Standard fees. 10 mi E on US 12, then 1 mi N on unnumbered road. Phone 360/249-3621.

Samuel Benn Park. Named for pioneer settler. Rose and rhododendron gardens; picnic facilities, playground, tennis. (Daily) East 9th & North I Sts. Phone 360/533-4100, ext 230. **Free.**

Schafer State Park. Approx 120 acres on Satsop River. Swimming; fishing. Hiking. Picnicking. Camping (hookups; dump station). (Apr-mid-Dec, daily; rest of yr, wkends & hols) Standard fees. 13 mi E on US 12, then 10 mi N on unnumbered road. Phone 360/482-3852.

Motels

★ **OLYMPIC INN.** *616 W Heron St. 360/533-4200; FAX 360/533-6223; res: 800/562-8618 (WA).* 55 rms, 2 story, 3 kits. No A/C. S $43-$70; D $53-$73; each addl $7; suites, kit. units $65-$97. Crib $7. TV; cable (premium). Restaurant nearby. Ck-out noon. Coin lndry. Meeting rm. Business servs avail. Many rms with refrigerators. Cr cds: A, C, D, DS, MC, V.

★ ★ **RED LION INN.** *52 W Wishkah. 360/532-5210; FAX 360/533-8483.* 67 rms, 2 story. June-Sept: S $68-$78; D $78-$98; each addl $10; under 18 free; lower rates rest of yr. Crib free. Pet accepted. TV; cable. Complimentary continental bkfst. Restaurant nearby. Ck-out noon. Sundries. Cr cds: A, C, D, DS, ER, MC, V.

Inn

★ ★ **ABERDEEN MANSION.** *807 N M St. 360/533-7079.* 4 rms, 2 story. No A/C. No rm phones. May-Oct: S, D $95-$125; lower rates rest of yr. Children over 12 yrs only. TV; cable. Complimentary full bkfst. Restaurant nearby. Ck-out 11 am, ck-in 4-6 pm. Luggage handling. Victorian house built in 1905; antiques. Totally nonsmoking. Cr cds: MC, V.

 ⊠ 🐾 SC

Restaurants

✔★ ★ **BILLY'S.** *322 E Heron. 360/533-7144.* Hrs: 11 am-11 pm; Fri, Sat to midnight; Sun noon-9 pm. Closed Easter, Thanksgiving, Dec 25. Bar. Semi-a la carte: lunch, dinner $4.50-$12.95. Child's meals. Specializes in burgers, salad. In 1904 building with antique furnishings. Cr cds: A, V.

D

★ ★ **BRIDGES.** *112 North G St. 360/532-6563.* Hrs: 11 am-9 pm; Fri & Sat to 10 pm; Sun 4-9 pm. Bar. Semi-a la carte: lunch $4.50-$10.95, dinner $6.50-$25.95. Child's meals. Specializes in prime rib, seafood, steak. Solarium. Family-owned. Smoking at bar only. Cr cds: A, D, DS, MC, V.

D 🔜 ♥

Anacortes (B-3)

(See also Coupeville, La Conner, Mount Vernon, Oak Harbor, San Juan Islands, Sedro Woolley)

Settled 1860 **Pop** 11,451 **Elev** 24 ft **Area code** 360 **Zip** 98221 **E-mail** anacortes@sos.net **Web** www.anacortes-chamber.com

Information Visitor Information Center at the Chamber of Commerce, 819 Commercial Ave, Ste G; 360/293-3832.

Anacortes, at the northwest tip of Fidalgo Island, houses the San Juan Islands ferries. The town's name honors Anna Curtis, wife of one of the founders.

What to See and Do

Deception Pass State Park. More than 3,000 acres of sheltered bays and deep forests with fjord-like shoreline. Swimming (lifeguards in summer), scuba diving; fishing, clamming; boating (ramp, dock). Hiking trails. Picnicking. Camping. Standard fees. 9 mi S on WA 20. Phone 360/675-2417.

San Juan Islands Trip. Ferryboats leave several times daily for major islands of the group. Either leave car at dock in Anacortes or disembark at any point and explore from paved roads. For schedules, fares contact Washington State Ferries, Colman Dock, Seattle 98104; 360/293-8166.

Washington Park. Approx 220 acres. Sunset Beach; saltwater fishing; boating (ramps; fee). Picnicking. Camping (14-day limit; electricity and water). Coin showers. Park (daily). 4 mi W on 12th St (Oakes Ave). Phone 360/293-1927. Camping ¢¢¢¢

Annual Events

Skagit Valley Tulip Festival. First 3 wkends Apr.

Barbershop Concert & Salmon Barbecue. Last wkend July.

Motels

★ ★ **ANACORTES INN.** *3006 Commercial Ave. 360/293-3153; FAX 360/293-0209; res: 800/327-7976.* 44 rms, 2 story, 5 kits. May-mid-Oct: S $65; D $70-$85; each addl $10; under 12 free; kit. units $10 addl. Pet accepted. TV; cable (premium). Heated pool. Coffee in rms. Restaurant nearby. Ck-out 11 am. Business servs avail. Refrigerators, microwaves. Cr cds: A, D, DS, MC, V.

🐾 ≋ ⊠ 🐾 SC

✔ **SHIP HARBOR INN.** *5316 Ferry Terminal Rd. 360/293-5177; FAX 360/299-2412; res: 800/852-8568 (US), 800/235-8568 (Canada).* E-mail shi@shipharborinn.com; web www.shipharborinn.com. 16 rms, 10 cottages, 1-2 story. No A/C. May-Sept: S, D $65-$95; each addl $5; under 12 free; lower rates rest of yr. Crib free. TV; cable. Playground. Complimentary continental bkfst. Restaurant adj 11 am-10 pm. Bar. Ck-out 11 am. Coin lndry. Meeting rm. Some refrigerators; microwaves avail. Private patios, porches. Picnic tables, grills. Cr cds: A, C, D, DS, MC, V.

D ⊠ 🐾 SC

Inn

★ ★ **CHANNEL HOUSE.** *2902 Oakes Ave. 360/293-9382; FAX 360/299-9208; res: 800/238-4353.* E-mail bed@sos.net; web www.anacortesb-b.com. 6 air-cooled rms, 2 story. No rm phones. S $59-$95; D $69-$105; each addl $20. Children over 12 yrs only. Complimentary full bkfst; afternoon refreshments. Restaurant nearby. Ck-out 11 am, ck-in 3 pm. Free local airport, bus depot, ferry terminal transportation. Whirlpool. Victorian-style residence (1902) built for an Italian count; many antiques, stained glass windows. Views of Puget Sound. Totally nonsmoking. Cr cds: A, DS, MC, V.

Restaurants

★ **BOOMER'S LANDING.** *209 T Ave, on waterfront at Guemes Channel.* 360/293-5108. Hrs: 11 am-9 pm; Fri, Sat to 10 pm. Closed Jan 1, Thanksgiving, Dec 25. Res accepted. Bar. Semi-a la carte: lunch $4.95-$8.95, dinner $10.95-$30.95. Child's meals. Specializes in steak, lobster, fresh seafood. Outdoor dining. Nautical decor. Cr cds: A, DS, MC, V.

[D]

★ ★ **SLOCUM'S.** *2201 Skyline Way.* 360/293-1261. Hrs: 7:30 am-10 pm; Sun brunch 10 am-2 pm. Closed Dec 25. Res accepted; required some hols. Bar. Semi-a la carte: lunch $4.95-$10.95, dinner $10.50-$20. Sun brunch $11.95. Child's meals. Specialties: prime rib, salmon Wellington, fresh seafood. Entertainment Fri, Sat. Outdoor dining. Nautical decor; models of famous sailboats; view of Skyline Marina. Cr cds: MC, V.

[D] [SC] [⌐]

Bellevue (C-3)

(See also Issaquah, Seattle)

Pop 86,874 **Elev** 125 ft **Area code** 425 **E-mail** 74117, 612@compuserve.com **Web** oasis.bellevue.k12.wa.us/cityofbellevue/

Information East King County Convention and Visitors Bureau, 520 112th Ave NE, Ste 101, 98004; 425/455-1926.

Incorporated in 1953, Bellevue has rapidly become the state's fourth largest city. It is linked across Lake Washington to Seattle by the Evergreen Floating Bridge.

What to See and Do

Bellevue Botanical Garden. 36-acres feature woodlands, meadows and display gardens including Waterwise Garden, Japanese Gardens and Fuchsia Display. Garden shop. Visitor Center. (Daily) 12001 Main St. Phone 425/462-2749. **Free.**

Chateau Ste Michelle. Located on an 87-acre estate; tours; wine tasting; summer concert series. Picnic area, gardens, gift shop with wine & picnic supplies. (Daily; closed major hols) N on I-405 to exit 23B, at 14111 NE 145th St in Woodinville. Phone 425/488-1133. **Free.**

Rosalie Whyel Museum of Doll Art. Features curated collection of dolls, teddy bears, toys and miniatures. Museum shop. (Daily; closed major hols) 1116 108th Ave NE. Phone 425/455-1116. ¢¢¢

Motels

★ ★ **BEST WESTERN BELLEVUE INN.** *11211 Main St (98004), just W of I-405 exit 12.* 425/455-5240; FAX 425/455-0654. 180 rms, 2 story. S $120; D $130; under 18 free; wkend rates. Crib free. Pet accepted; $30. TV; cable (premium), VCR avail. Heated pool; poolside serv. Coffee in rms. Restaurant 6:30 am-2 pm, 5-10 pm. Rm serv. Bar; entertainment Thurs-Sat. Ck-out noon. Meeting rms. Business servs avail. In-rm modem link. Bellhops. Valet serv. Sundries. Exercise equipt; treadmil, bicycle. Refrigerators; microwaves avail. Balconies. Cr cds: A, C, D, DS, ER, JCB, MC, V.

[D] [♥] [≈] [✕] [⋈] [⚒] [SC]

★ ★ **RESIDENCE INN BY MARRIOTT.** *14455 NE 29th Place (98007), off WA 520 148th Ave N exit.* 425/882-1222; FAX 425/885-9260. 120 suites, 2 story. S, D $160-$240. Crib $5. Pet accepted; $10/day. TV; cable (premium), VCR avail (free movies). Heated pool. Complimentary continental bkfst. Complimentary coffee in rms. Ck-out noon. Coin lndry. Meeting rms. Business servs avail. In-rm modem link. Valet serv. Lawn

games. Refrigerators, microwaves. Private patios, balconies. Picnic tables, grills. Cr cds: A, C, D, DS, JCB, MC, V.

[D] [♥] [≈] [⋈] [⚒]

★ ★ **SILVER CLOUD INN.** *(12202 NE 124th St, Kirkland 98034) N on I-405, exit 20-B, E on NE 124 St.* 425/821-8300; res: 800/205-6933; FAX 425/823-1218. 99 rms, 3 story. June-Sept: S $69-$97; D $77-$105; suites $98-$145; under 12 free; lower rates rest of yr. Crib free. TV; cable (premium). Complimentary continental bkfst. Restaurant adj open 24 hrs. Rm serv. Ck-out noon. Meeting rms. Business servs avail. In-rm modem link. Concierge. Sundries. Guest lndry. Exercise equipt; weight machine, bicycle. Heated pool; whirlpool. Refrigerators. Microwaves avail. Cr cds: A, C, D, DS, ER, MC, V.

[D] [≈] [✕] [⋈] [⚒] [SC]

Motor Hotels

★ ★ **WESTCOAST BELLEVUE HOTEL.** *625 116th Ave NE (98004), E of I-405, NE 8th St exit.* 425/455-9444; FAX 425/455-2154; res: 800/426-0670. 176 rms, 6 story. S $75-$85; D $85-$95; each addl $10; suites $100-$110; under 18 free. Crib free. TV; cable (premium). Heated pool; poolside serv. Complimentary coffee in rms. Restaurant 6 am-10 pm; Sat, Sun from 7 am. Rm serv. Bar 4-11 pm; closed Sun. Ck-out noon. Meeting rms. Business servs avail. In-rm modem link. Sundries. Exercise equipt; stair machine, bicycles. Cr cds: A, D, DS, MC, V.

[D] [≈] [✕] [⋈] [⚒] [SC]

Hotels

★ ★ ★ **BELLEVUE CLUB.** *11200 SE 6th (98004).* 425/454-4424; FAX 425/688-3101; res: 800/579-1110. Web www.bellevueclub.com. This four-story, neo-classical structure with Beaux Arts and Palladian influences is matched with interior spaces enveloped in beechwood paneling with French limestone floors and suspended, curved ceilings. The overall effect is clean, contemporary and inviting. The health-club facilities are outstanding, with everything from indoor tennis courts and two fully equipped weight-lifting and aerobic centers, to an Olympic-size swimming pool and running track. 67 rms, 2 with shower only, 4 story. S, D $190-$230; suites $370-$945; under 18 free. Crib free. Wkend rates. Valet parking $5. TV; cable (premium), VCR avail. Indoor pool; whirlpool, poolside serv, lifeguard. Supervised child's activities; ages 1-12. Complimentary coffee in lobby. Restaurant (see POLARIS). Rm serv 24 hrs. Bar 11 am-midnight; entertainment Thurs-Sat. Ck-out 1 pm. Guest lndry. Meeting rms. Business center. In-rm modem link. Concierge. Gift shop. Indoor tennis, pro. Extensive exercise rm; instructor, weights, bicycles, sauna, steam rm. Massage. Minibars; microwaves avail. Balconies. Cr cds: A, C, D, MC, V.

[D] [⚒] [≈] [✕] [⚒] [⚒]

★ ★ ★ **DOUBLETREE.** *300 112th Ave SE (98004), just W of I-405 exit 12.* 425/455-1300; FAX 425/455-0466. 353 rms, 10 story. S, D $180-$225; each addl $15; suites $250-$495; under 18 free; wkend rates. Crib free. TV; cable (premium), VCR avail. Heated pool; whirlpool, poolside serv. Complimentary coffee in rms. Restaurant 6 am-11 pm. Bar 11-2 am; closed Sun, Mon. Ck-out noon. Convention facilities. Business servs avail. In-rm modem link. Concierge. Gift shop. Barber, beauty shop. Exercise equipt; weight machine, bicycles. Some bathrm phones. Balconies. Glass-enclosed elvtrs in lobby; multi-story glass canopy at entrance. Luxury level. Cr cds: A, C, D, DS, ER, JCB, MC, V.

[D] [≈] [✕] [⋈] [⚒] [SC]

★ ★ **HILTON.** *100 112th Ave NE (98004), just off I-405 NE 4th St exit.* 425/455-3330; FAX 425/451-2473. 180 rms, 7 story. May-Oct: S $131-$181; D $141-$191; suites $209-$289; each addl $10; family, wkend rates; lower rates rest of yr. Crib free. TV; cable (premium), VCR avail. Indoor pool; whirlpool. Complimentary coffee in rms. Restaurants 5:30 am-10 pm. Bar 10-2 am. Ck-out noon. Meeting rms. Business center. In-rm modem link. Concierge. Exercise equipt; weight machine, bicycle, sauna. Cr cds: A, C, D, DS, ER, MC, V.

[D] [≈] [✕] [⋈] [⚒] [SC] [⚒]

★ ★ ★ **HYATT REGENCY BELLEVUE.** *900 Bellevue Way NE (98004), at Bellevue Place.* 425/462-1234; FAX 425/646-7567; res: 800/233-1234. 382 rms, 24 story, 29 suites. S $190-$215; D $215-$240; suites $250-$1,000; under 18 free. Crib free. Garage $7; valet parking $11. TV; cable (premium), VCR avail. Coffee in rms. Restaurant 6 am-10:30 pm. Bar 11-2 am. Ck-out noon. Convention facilities. Business center. In-rm modem link. Concierge. Shopping arcade. Barber, beauty shop. Some bathrm phones, refrigerators. Hotel connected to office/retail complex. Luxury level. Cr cds: A, C, D, DS, JCB, MC, V.

D 🏊 🐾 SC 🏃

★ ★ **SILVER CLOUD INN.** *10621 NE 12th (98004).* 425/637-7000; FAX 425/455-0531; res: 800/205-6937. 97 rms, 12 with shower only, 4 story. Mar-Sept: S $85; D $95-$135; each addl $8; suites $135; under 12 free; lower rates rest of yr. Crib free. TV; cable (premium). Heated pool; whirlpool. Complimentary continental bkfst. Restaurant nearby. Ck-out noon. Meeting rms. Business servs avail. In-rm modem link. No bellhops. Guest lndry. Exercise equipt; bicycles, weight machine. Refrigerators; microwaves avail. Cr cds: A, C, D, DS, ER, MC, V.

D 🏊 🏋 ⚓ 🐾 SC

★ ★ ★ **WOODMARK HOTEL ON LAKE WASHINGTON.** *(1200 Carillon Point, Kirkland 98033) N on Bellevue Way, continue onto Lake Washington Blvd NE.* 425/822-3700; FAX 425/822-3699; res: 800/822-3700. E-mail woodmarkhotel@compuserve.com; web thewoodmark.com. Stroll along a shoreline promenade or lie on the beach and soak in the panoramic views at this contemporary-style resort hotel, the only lodging on the shores of Lake Washington. 100 units, 4 story, 21 suites. S $165-$215; D $180-$230; suites $260-$1,200; under 18 free. Crib free. Overnight parking $9; valet. TV; cable. Complimentary evening refreshments. Complimentary coffee in rms. Restaurant 6:30 am-10 pm; Sat, Sun from 7 am. Bar 11 am-midnight. Ck-out noon. Meeting rms. Business servs avail. In-rm modem link. Concierge. Health club privileges. Refrigerators, minibars. Balconies. Marina; 3 lakeside parks. Cr cds: A, D, MC, V.

D 🏋 🐾 🐾 SC

Inn

✔ ★ ★ ★ **SHUMWAY MANSION.** *(11410 99th Place NE, Kirkland 98033) I-405N, exit 20A, then 1 1/2 mi W.* 425/823-2303; FAX 425/822-0421. 8 rms, 2 story. No A/C. Rm phone avail. S, D $70-$95; each addl $12; suite $105. Children over 12 yrs only. TV avail. Complimentary full bkfst; evening refreshments. Restaurant nearby. Ck-out 11 am, ck-in 3 pm. Business servs avail. In-rm modem link. Health club privileges. A 24-rm historic mansion (1909), restored and moved to present site in 1985. Overlooks Juanita Bay. Totally nonsmoking. Cr cds: A, MC, V.

🐾 🐾

Restaurants

★ ★ ★ **BISTRO PROVENÇAL.** *(212 Central Way, Kirkland 98033) I-405 Kirkland exit 18.* 425/827-3300. Hrs: 5:30-10:30 pm; Sun 5-9:30 pm. Closed major hols. Res accepted. French menu. Serv bar. Semi-a la carte: dinner $13-$21. Complete meals: dinner $23-$45. Specializes in seafood, rack of lamb. Own baking. French country inn decor. Casual elegance. Fireplace. Cr cds: A, C, D, MC, V.

★ ★ ★ **CAFE JUANITA.** *(9702 120th Pl NE, Kirkland 98034-4206) N on I-405, exit 20A, then approx 1 1/2 mi W.* 425/823-6533. Hrs: 5:30-9:45 pm. Closed some major hols. Res accepted. Italian menu. Serv bar. Wine cellar. A la carte entrees: dinner $14-$22.50. Child's meals. Specialties: pollo pistacchi, venison shank, coniglio con funghi. Own baking, pasta, ice cream. Outdoor dining. Casual dining in converted private home; open kitchen; wine-bottle accents. Family-owned. Totally nonsmoking. Cr cds: MC, V.

D

★ ★ **JAKE O'SHAUGHNESSEY'S.** *401 Bellevue Sq (98004), in Bellevue Sq Mall.* 425/455-5559. Hrs: 11:30 am-3 pm, 5-9 pm; Fri to 10 pm; Sun noon-3 pm, 4:30-9 pm. Closed Easter, Thanksgiving, Dec 25. Res

accepted. Bar 11 am-midnight. Semi-a la carte: lunch $3.95-$9.95, dinner $9.95-$19.95. Child's meals. Specializes in fresh salmon, prime rib, Caesar salad. Outdoor dining. Club atmosphere with aquatic decor; several dining areas; open kitchen. Totally nonsmoking. Cr cds: A, D, DS, MC, V.

D

✔ ★ ★ ★ **POLARIS.** *(See Bellevue Club Hotel)* 425/455-1616. Web www.bellevue.com. Hrs: 7-10 am, 11:30 am-1:30 pm, 6-9 pm; Fri, Sat to 10 pm. Res accepted. Continental menu. Bar to midnight. Semi-a la carte: bkfst $3-$9.25, lunch $5.50-$11.95, dinner $11.50-$20.95. Child's meals. Specializes in pasta, seafood, lamb. Outdoor dining. Contemporary decor. Totally nonsmoking. Cr cds: A, MC, V.

D

✔ ★ ★ **SPAZZO MEDITERRANEAN GRILL.** *10655 NE Fourth St (98004), on 9th floor of Key Bank Bldg.* 425/454-8255. Hrs: 11:30 am-10 pm; Fri to 11 pm; Sat 4-11 pm; Sun 4-10 pm. Closed Dec 25. Res accepted. Mediterranean menu. Bar. Semi-a la carte: lunch $6.95-$15.95, dinner $8.95-$23.95. Child's meals. Specializes in Italian, Greek and Spanish dishes. View of Lake Washington and downtown. Cr cds: A, D, DS, JCB, MC, V.

D

★ ★ ★ **THIRD FLOOR FISH CAFE.** *(205 Lake St S, Kirkland 98033) I-405 N to Kirkland.* 425/822-3553. Hrs: 5-9:30 pm; Fri, Sat to 10 pm; Sun 4:30-9 pm. Closed Jan 1, Thanksgiving, Dec 25. Res accepted. Bar 4 pm-midnight; Sun to 10 pm. Wine list. A la carte entrees: dinner $17-$35. Specialties: spice-crusted Pacific halibut, pan-seared sturgeon, lamb shank. Own pastries. Jazz Wed, Sat. Three window-walls overlook Lake Washington and marina; dark woods create intimate atmosphere. Totally nonsmoking. Cr cds: A, MC, V.

D

Bellingham (A-3)

(See also Blaine, Sedro Woolley; also see Vancouver, BC Canada)

Founded 1853 **Pop** 52,179 **Elev** 68 ft **Area code** 360 **E-mail** tourism@bellingham.org **Web** www.bellingham.org

Information Bellingham/Whatcom County Convention & Visitors Bureau, 904 Potter St, 98226; 360/671-3990 or 800/487-2032 (order information). The Bureau operates a Visitor Information Center off I-5 exit 253; daily; closed major hols.

This city, located on Bellingham Bay, has the impressive Mount Baker as its backdrop and is the last major city before the Washington coastline meets the Canadian border. The broad curve of the bay was charted in 1792 by Captain George Vancouver, who named it in honor of Sir William Bellingham. When the first settlers arrived here, forests stretched to the edge of the high bluffs along the shoreline. Timber and coal played major roles in the town's early economy.

Today, Bellingham has an active waterfront port, which supports fishing, cold storage, boat building, shipping, paper processing and marina operations. Squalicum Harbor's commercial and pleasure boat marina accommodates more than 1,800 vessels, making it the second largest marina on Puget Sound. The marina is a pleasant area to dine, picnic and watch the fishermen at work. The downtown area contains a mix of restaurants, art galleries, specialty shops and other stores. Bellingham is also home to Western Washington University, located on Sehome Hill, which affords a scenic view of the city and bay.

What to See and Do

Chuckanut Drive. A 10-mi drive, mostly along highway cut into mountain sides; beautiful vistas of Puget Sound and San Juan Islands. S from Fairhaven Park on WA 11 along Chuckanut Bay to Larrabee State Park.

City recreation areas. More than 2,000 acres of parkland offer a wide variety of activities. (Daily) Fee for some activities. For further information phone Parks and Recreation Dept, 360/676-6985. Areas include

Arroyo Park. Approx 40 acres of dense, second-growth forest in a canyon setting. Creek fishing. Hiking, nature and bridle trails. Off Chuckanut Dr on Old Samish Rd.

Bloedel Donovan Park. Swimming beach; fishing; boat launch (fee). Picnicking, playground; concession (summer). Community center with gym. Parking fee (summer). 2214 Electric Ave, NW area of Lake Whatcom.

Boulevard Park. Fishing; boat dock. Bicycle paths. Picnicking, playground. Craft studio. S State St & Bayview Dr.

Civic Field Athletic Complex. Contains multiple athletic fields and indoor community pool. Lakeway Dr & Orleans St.

Cornwall Park. Approx 65 acres. Wading pool; steelhead fishing in Squalicum Creek. Fitness trail; tennis, other game courts & fields. Picnicking, playground. Extensive rose garden in park. 2800 Cornwall Ave.

Fairhaven Park. Wading pool. Hiking trails; tennis. Picnicking, playground. Rose garden is test site for the American Rose Society. 107 Chuckanut Dr.

Lake Padden Park. Approx 1,000 acres with 152-acre lake. Swimming beach; fishing; boat launch (no motors). Hiking, bridle trails; 18-hole golf course (fee); tennis; athletic fields. Picnicking, playground. 4882 Samish Way.

Sehome Hill Arboretum. The 165-acre native plant preserve contains hiking and interpretive trails; scenic views of city, Puget Sound, San Juan Islands and mountains from observation tower atop hill. 25th St & McDonald Pkwy.

Whatcom Falls Park. Approx 240 acres. Children's fishing pond; state fish hatchery. Hiking trails; tennis; athletic fields. Picnicking, playground. 1401 Electric Ave, near Lake Whatcom.

✪ **Fairhaven District.** In the late 1800s, this area was a separate city that had hopes of becoming the next Chicago. The 1890s buildings are now restaurants and shops. Brass plaques detail history of the area. Walking tour brochures at the information gazebo, 12th & Harris. Centered at jct 12th St & Harris Ave.

Ferndale. Community founded in mid-1800s, with several preserved areas. **Hovander Homestead**, on Neilson Rd, is a county park with working farm and museum; interpretive center with nature trails and observation tower. Approx 9 mi NW off I-5, exit 262. Phone 360/384-3444. ¢¢

Larrabee State Park. Approx 2,000 acres. Scuba diving; fishing, clamming, crabbing, tide pools; boating (ramp). Hiking. Picnicking. Camping (hookups). Mountain viewpoints. Standard fees. 7 mi S on WA 11. Phone 360/676-2093.

Lynden Pioneer Museum. Exhibits on history of this Dutch community; antique car and buggy, farm equipment. (Daily exc Sun) Approx 12 mi N via WA 539, at 217 Front St, Lynden. Phone 360/354-3675. ¢

Maritime Heritage Center. Salmon life-cycle facility and learning center. Outdoor rearing tanks; indoor displays detail development from egg to adult. Park (daily). Learning Center (Mon-Fri; closed hols). 1600 C St. Phone 360/676-6806. **Free.**

Mt Baker-Snoqualmie Natl Forest. Mt Baker and Snoqualmie national forests were combined under a single forest supervisor in July, 1974. Divided into five ranger districts, the combined forest encompasses nearly 2 million acres. The Snoqualmie section lies E & SE of Seattle (see); the Mt Baker section lies E on WA 542 and includes the Mt Baker Ski Area. The forest extends from the Canadian border S to Mt Rainier Natl Park and includes rugged mountains and woodlands on the western slopes of the Cascades, the western portions of the Glacier Peak and Alpine Lakes, Henry M. Jackson, Noisy-Diobsud, Boulder River, Jackson, Clearwater, and Norse Peak wildernesses; 7 commercial ski areas; 1,440 mi of hiking trails; picnic areas & campsites. Mt Baker rises 10,778 ft in the north, forming a center for recreation all yr, famous for deep-powder snow skiing & snowboarding. Snoqualmie Pass (via I-90) & Stevens Pass (via US 2) provide all-yr access to popular, scenic destinations; Baker Lake provides

excellent boating & fishing. Contact Forest Service/National Park Service Information, phone 360/599-2714. E of forest is

North Cascades Natl Park. (See SEDRO WOOLLEY)

Mt Baker Ski Area. 2 quad, 6 double chairlifts, rope tow; patrol, school, rentals; restaurant, cafeteria, bar; lodge. Longest run 1.5 mi; vertical drop 1,500 ft. (Nov-Mar, daily; Apr, Fri-Sun; closed Dec 25) Also cross-country trails. Half-day rates (wkends, hols). 55 mi E on WA 542. Phone 360/734-6771 or 360/671-0211 (snow conditions). ¢¢¢¢¢

Western Washington Univ (1893). (11,000 students) A 189-acre campus; internationally acclaimed outdoor sculpture collection; contemporary art at Western Gallery, phone 360/650-3963. Theater (360/650-2829), music (360/650-3130), summer stock (360/650-3876). High St. Phone 360/650-3424.

Whatcom Museum of History & Art. Regional and historic displays; also changing art exhibits; in former city hall (1892) and three adj buildings. Fee for special exhibitions. (Daily exc Mon; closed most hols) 121 Prospect St. Phone 360/676-6981. **Free.**

Annual Events

Ski to Sea Festival. Parades, carnival, art show, special events. Ski to Sea race; starts on Mt Baker, ends in Bellingham Bay and involves skiers, runners, canoeists, bicyclists and kayakers. Memorial Day wkend.

Deming Logging Show. Log show grounds, in Deming. Log chopping, tree climbing, logger rodeo, salmon barbecue. 2nd wkend June.

Lummi Stommish. Lummi Reservation, 15 mi NW via I-5, exit 260 to WA 540. Water carnival with war canoe races, arts & crafts; salmon bake, Native American dancing. Wkend June.

Motels

★ ★ ★ **BEST WESTERN HERITAGE INN.** *151 E McLeod Rd (98226).* 360/647-1912; FAX 360/671-3878. 90 rms, 3 story. No elvtr. S $67-$80; D $77-$86; each addl $5; suites $135-$155; studio rms $67-$89; under 12 free. Crib free. TV; cable (premium), VCR avail. Heated pool; whirlpool. Continental bkfst. Restaurant 6 am-11 pm. Rm serv. Ck-out noon. Meeting rms. Business servs avail. Valet serv. Free airport transportation. Health club privileges. Some refrigerators, wet bars; microwaves avail. Cr cds: A, C, D, DS, MC, V.

D ≋ ⇆ ⋈ ⋈ SC

✔★ **DAYS INN.** *125 E Kellogg Rd (98226), I-5 exit 256, near Intl Airport.* 360/671-6200; FAX 360/671-9491. 70 rms, 3 story. July-Sept: S $49.95; D $54.95; each addl $5; suites $79-$99; under 12 free; lower rates rest of yr. Crib free. Pet accepted; $5. TV; cable (premium). Heated pool; whirlpool. Complimentary continental bkfst. Restaurant nearby. Ck-out 11 am. Coin lndry. Meeting rms. Health club privileges. Some refrigerators; microwaves avail. Cr cds: A, D, DS, MC, V.

D ✔ ≋ ⋈ ⋈ SC

★ ★ **HAMPTON INN.** *3985 Bennett Dr (98225), I-5 exit 258, near Intl Airport.* 360/676-7700; FAX 360/671-7557. Web www.hampton inn.com. 132 rms, 4 story. June-Sept: S $64-$69; D $74-$77 (up to 4); under 18 free; lower rates rest of yr. Crib free. TV; cable (premium). Pool. Complimentary continental bkfst. Complimentary coffee in rms. Rm serv 11 am-2 pm, 5-9 pm. Ck-out noon. Meeting rms. Business center. In-rm modem link. Free airport, RR station, ferry transportation. Exercise equipt; bicycles, treadmill. Cr cds: A, C, D, DS, ER, JCB, MC, V.

D ≋ ⋇ ✈ ⋈ ⋈ SC ⋀

★ ★ **QUALITY INN BARON SUITES.** *100 E Kellogg Rd (98226), I-5 exit 256, near Intl Airport.* 360/647-8000; FAX 360/647-8094. 86 suites, 3 story. June-mid-Sept: S $59.95-$79.95; D $69.95-$89.95; each addl $10; under 19 free; same rates Ski to Sea Festival; lower rates rest of yr. Crib free. TV; cable (premium), VCR avail. Heated pool; whirlpool. Complimentary continental bkfst. Coffee in rms. Ck-out noon. Coin lndry. Meeting rms. Business center. In-rm modem link. Free airport, bus depot transportation. Exercise equipt; weight machine, bicycles. Some refrigerators; microwaves avail. Balconies. Cr cds: A, C, D, ER, JCB, MC, V.

D ⚊ 🏃 ✈ ⬞ 🎣 SC ⚒

★ **RAMADA INN.** *215 Samish Way (98225). 360/734-8830; FAX 360/647-8956.* 66 rms, 3 story. June-Sept: S, D $90-$120; each addl $6; under 18 free; higher rates sporting events; lower rates rest of yr. Crib free. TV; cable (premium), VCR avail. Heated pool. Complimentary continental bkfst. Complimentary coffee in rms. Restaurant nearby. Ck-out noon. Business servs avail. Valet serv. Refrigerators. Balconies. Cr cds: A, D, DS, MC, V.

D 🐾 ⚊ ⬞ 🎣 SC

✔★ **TRAVELERS INN.** *3750 Meridian St (98225). 360/671-4600; FAX 360/671-6487.* 124 rms, 3 story. June-Sept: S $51.95; D $58.95; each addl $7; suites $64.95-$79.95; under 19 free; lower rates rest of yr. Crib free. Pet accepted, some restrictions. TV; cable (premium). Heated pool; whirlpool. Complimentary coffee in lobby. Restaurant nearby. Ck-out 11 am. Coin lndry. Meeting rms. Business servs avail. Some refrigerators. Cr cds: A, C, D, DS, MC, V.

D ⚊ ⬞ 🎣 SC

★ **VAL-U INN.** *805 Lakeway Dr (98226), I-5 exit 253. 360/671-9600; FAX 360/671-8323.* 82 rms, 3 story. June-Sept: S, D $51.50-$61.50; each addl $5; suites $75-$90; under 12 free; lower rates rest of yr. Crib $5. Pet accepted; $5. TV; cable (premium), VCR avail. Whirlpool. Complimentary continental bkfst. Restaurant nearby. Ck-out noon. Coin lndry. Meeting rms. Business servs avail. Valet serv. Free airport, RR station, ferry terminal transportation. Some refrigerators; microwaves avail. Cr cds: A, C, D, DS, MC, V.

D 🐾 ⬞ 🎣 SC

Motor Hotel

★ ★ ★ **BEST WESTERN LAKEWAY INN.** *714 Lakeway Dr (98226), just off I-5 Lakeway Dr exit 253. 360/671-1011; FAX 360/676-8519.* 132 rms, 4 story. S $64-$74; D $74-$84; each addl $10; suites $99-$119; under 13 free. Crib $5. Pet accepted, some restrictions. TV; cable (premium). Indoor pool; whirlpool. Complimentary full bkfst buffet. Coffee in rms. Restaurant 6 am-10 pm. Rm serv. Bar; entertainment Tues-Sat. Ck-out noon. Coin lndry. Meeting rms. Business center. Valet serv. Beauty shop. Free airport, bus depot transportation. Exercise equipt; weights, bicycles, sauna. Microwaves avail. Cr cds: A, C, D, DS, ER, JCB, MC, V.

D 🐾 ⚊ 🏃 ⬞ 🎣 SC ⚒

Restaurants

★ ★ **CHUCKANUT MANOR.** *(302 Chuckanut Dr, Bow 98232) 18 mi S on I-5 to exit 250, then 2 mi W. 360/766-6191.* Hrs: 11:30 am-10 pm; Sun from 10 am; Sun brunch to 2:30 pm. Closed Mon; major hols. Res accepted. Bar. Semi-a la carte: lunch $6-$12, dinner $14-$23. Sun brunch $12.95. Child's meals. Specializes in seafood, steak, Fri evening buffet. Overlooks Samish bay, San Juan Islands. Guest rms avail. Cr cds: A, C, D, MC, V.

D SC

★ ★ **MARINA.** *985 Thomas Glenn Dr (98225), on waterfront. 360/733-8292.* Hrs: 11:30 am-10:30 pm. Closed Dec 25. Res accepted Fri, Sat. Bar. A la carte entrees: lunch $5.95-$12.95, dinner $10.95-$29.95. Child's meals. Specializes in seafood, steak. Outdoor dining, views of bay. Cr cds: A, MC, V.

D

Blaine (A-3)

(See also Bellingham; also see Vancouver, BC Canada)

Pop 2,489 **Elev** 41 ft **Area code** 360 **Zip** 98231
Information Visitor Information Center, 215 Marine Dr; 360/332-4544 or 800/487-2032.

What to See and Do

Birch Bay State Park. Approx 190 acres. Swimming, scuba diving; fishing, crabbing, clamming. Picnicking. Camping (daily, res advised Memorial Day-Labor Day; hookups; dump station). Standard fees. 10 mi SW via I-5, exit 266, then 7 mi W via Grandview Rd, N via Jackson Rd to Helwig Rd. Phone 360/371-2800.

International Peace Arch (1921). The 67-ft-high arch is on the boundary line between the US and Canada and marks more than a century of peace and friendship between the two countries. The surrounding park is maintained by the state of Washington and Province of British Columbia; gardens, picnicking, playground. N at point where I-5 reaches Canadian border.

Semiahmoo Park. A cannery once located on this 1.5-mi-long spit was the last port of call for Alaskan fishing boats on Puget Sound. Restored buildings now house museum, gallery and gift shop (June-mid-Sept, Sat & Sun afternoons). Park (daily) offers clam digging. Picnicking; birdwatching. Off I-5, exit 274, on Semiahmoo Sandspit, Drayton Harbor. Phone Inn at Semi-Ah-Moo 360/371-2000. ¢¢

Annual Event

Peace Arch Celebration. Intl Peace Arch. Ceremony celebrates the relationship between the US and Canada; scouts and veterans from both nations. 2nd Sun June.

Resort

★ ★ ★ **INN AT SEMI-AH-MOO, A WYNDHAM RESORT.** *9565 Semiahmoo Pkwy (98230), 3 mi S of downtown, across Drayton Harbor; follow signs. 360/371-2000; FAX 360/371-5490.* Web www.semi.ah.moo .com. 198 units, 4 story, 14 suites. May-Oct: S, D $189-$419; each addl $20; suites $269-$499; under 19 free; golf plans; lower rates rest of yr. Crib free. Pet accepted; $50. TV; cable. Indoor/outdoor pool; whirlpool, poolside serv. Complimentary coffee in rms. Dining rms 6:30 am-2:30 pm, 5:30-11 pm. Box lunches, snack bar. Rm serv 6:30 am-11 pm. Bar 11-1 am; entertainment. Ck-out noon, ck-in 4 pm. Grocery 2 blks. Coin lndry, package store 7 mi. Meeting rms. Business servs avail. In-rm modem link. Concierge. Beauty shop. Sports dir. Indoor & outdoor tennis courts, pro. 18-hole golf, greens fee $75, pro, putting green, driving range. Beachcombing. 300-slip marina; boat & water sports. San Juan Island cruise yacht. Charter fishing, clam digging, oyster picking (seasonal). Bicycle rentals. Lawn games. Game rm. Exercise rm; instructor, weights, bicycles, sauna, steam rm. Spa. Some fireplaces. Some private patios, balconies. On 1,100-acre wildlife preserve. Cr cds: A, C, D, DS, ER, JCB, MC, V.

D 🐾 🐾 🏃 ⛷ ⚊ 🏃 🏂 ⬞ 🎣 SC

Bremerton (C-3)

(See also Seattle)

Founded 1891 **Pop** 38,142 **Elev** 60 ft **Area code** 360 **E-mail** kitspucb@pacific.telebyte.com **Web** www.kitsapeck.org
Information Kitsap Peninsula Visitor & Convention Bureau, 2 Rainier Ave, PO Box 270, 98364; 360/297-8200 or 800/416-5615.

The tempo of the Puget Sound Naval Shipyard is the heartbeat of Bremerton, a community surrounded on three sides by water. The six dry docks of the Naval Shipyard make Bremerton a home port for the Pacific fleet.

What to See and Do

Bremerton Naval Museum. Ship models, pictures, display of navy and shipyard history. Naval artifacts. (Tues-Sun; closed some major hols) 130 Washington Ave. Phone 360/479-SHIP. **Free.**

Kitsap County Historical Society Museum. Re-creation of 1800s pioneer settlements. Photos and documents of history to WWII era. (Tues-Sat; closed hols) 280 4th St. Phone 360/692-1949. ¢

State parks.

Belfair. Approx 80 acres. Swimming. Picnicking. Camping (hookups; res Memorial Day-Labor Day, by mail only). Standard fees. 15 mi SW via WA 3 in Belfair. Phone 360/275-0668.

Illahee. Approx 75 acres. Swimming, scuba diving; fishing, clamming; boating (ramp, dock). Hiking. Picnicking. Primitive camping. Standard fees. 3 mi NE off WA 306. Phone 360/478-6460.

Scenic Beach. Approx 90 acres. Swimming, scuba diving; limited fishing, oysters in season. Nature trail. Picnicking. Primitive camping. Standard fees. 12 mi NW on WA 3. Phone 360/830-5079.

Blake Island. More than 475 acres. Saltwater swimming beach, scuba diving; fishing; boating (dock). Hiking. Picnicking. Primitive camping. Standard fees. 6 mi SE, accessible only by boat. Phone 360/731-8330.

USS *Turner Joy*. Tours of Vietnam War era US Navy destroyer. (May-Sept, daily; rest of yr, Thurs-Mon; closed Dec 25) 300 Washington Beach Ave. Phone 360/792-2457. ¢¢

Annual Events

Armed Forces Day Parade. Mid-May.

Little Britches Rodeo. Mid-June.

Blackberry Festival. Late Aug.

Kitsap County Fair and Rodeo. Fairgrounds in Tracyton. Late Aug.

Seasonal Event

Mountaineers' Forest Theater. 8 mi W via WA 3, Kitsap Way, Seabeck Hwy, watch for signs. Oldest outdoor theater in the Pacific Northwest. Natural amphitheater surrounded by hundreds of rhododendrons beneath old-growth Douglas fir and hemlock. Log terraced seats. Family-oriented play. The 1/3-mile walk to theater is difficult for the physically disabled or elderly (assistance avail). Picnicking; concession. Contact 300 Third Ave W, Seattle 98119; 206/284-6310. Late May-early June.

Motels

★ ★ **FLAGSHIP INN.** 4320 Kitsap Way (98312). 360/479-6566; FAX 360/479-6745; res: 800/447-9396. 29 rms, 3 story. No elvtr. S $59.75; D $65.75-$71.75; each addl $6. Crib $6. TV; cable (premium), VCR (movies $2). Heated pool. Complimentary continental bkfst. Restaurant nearby. Ck-out noon. Business servs avail. In-rm modem link. Refrigerators. Balconies. On Oyster Bay. Cr cds: A, D, DS, MC, V.

🏊 ⛵ 🐾

✔★ ★ **MID WAY INN.** 2909 Wheaton Way (98310). 360/479-2909; FAX 360/479-1576; res: 800/231-0575. 60 rms, 3 story, 12 kit. units. S $59; D $63; each addl $7; kit. units $65; under 10 free; wkly rates. Crib $5. Pet accepted, some restrictions; $10. TV; cable (premium), VCR (free movies). Complimentary continental bkfst. Complimentary coffee in rms. Restaurant adj 4 pm-midnight. Ck-out 11 am. Coin lndry. Meeting rm. Business servs avail. Refrigerators. Cr cds: A, C, D, DS, MC, V.

D ⛵ ⛵ 🐾 SC

★ ★ **QUALITY INN.** 4303 Kitsap Way (98312). 360/405-1111; FAX 360/377-0597. 103 rms, 2-3 story, 77 kits. No elvtr. S $65-$80; D $80-$95; each addl $5; suites $75-$150. Crib free. Pet accepted; $50 refundable. TV; cable (premium), VCR avail (movies $5). Heated pool; whirlpool. Playground. Complimentary continental bkfst. Ck-out 11 am. Coin lndry. Meeting rm. Business servs avail. In-rm modem link. Exercise equipt; bicycle, weight machine. Picnic tables, grills. Cr cds: A, C, D, DS, ER, MC, V.

D ⛵ 🏊 🏃 ⛵ 🐾 SC

Motor Hotel

★ ★ ★ **SILVERDALE ON THE BAY-WEST COAST.** (3073 NW Bucklin Hill Rd, Silverdale 98383) approx 10 mi N on WA 3, Newberry Hill Rd exit to Bucklin Hill Rd. 360/698-1000; FAX 360/692-0932; res: 800/544-9799. 150 units, 2-3 story. S $70-$100; D $80-$110; each addl $10; suites $135-$325; under 18 free. Crib free. TV; cable. Indoor pool; whirlpool, poolside serv. Coffee in rms. Restaurant 6 am-11 pm. Rm serv. Bar 11-2 am; entertainment Fri-Sat. Ck-out noon. Meeting rms. Business servs avail. Bellhops. Valet serv. Lighted tennis. Exercise equipt; weight machine, treadmill, sauna. Game rm. Rec rm. Lawn games. Microwaves avail; refrigerator in suites. Private patios, balconies. Cr cds: A, C, D, DS, ER, JCB, MC, V.

D 🏃 🏊 🏃 ⛵ 🐾

Restaurants

★ ★ **BOAT SHED.** 101 Shore Dr (98310). 360/377-2600. Hrs: 11 am-midnight; Fri, Sat to 1 am; Sun 10 am-11 pm. Closed Jan 1, Thanksgiving, Dec 25. Bar to midnight; Fri, Sat to 1 am. Semi-a la carte: lunch $5.95-$9.95, dinner $5.95-$26.95. Specializes in seafood, steak, pasta. Outdoor dining. On waterfront. Cr cds: MC, V.

D ♥

★ ★ **YACHT CLUB BROILER.** (9226 Bayshore Dr, Silverdale 98383) 10 mi N on WA 3, exit Newberry Hill, to Bucklin Hill Rd, turn right. 360/698-1601. Hrs: 11 am-11 pm; Fri, Sat to midnight; Sun from 10 am; Sun brunch to 3 pm. Closed some major hols. Res accepted. Bar. Semi-a la carte: lunch $6-$12, dinner $10-$26. Sun brunch $4.95-$12. Child's meals. Specializes in Nebraska corn-fed prime steak, fresh salmon and halibut. Outdoor dining. Overlooks Silverdale Bay. Cr cds: A, C, D, MC, V.

D 🍽

Cashmere (C-5)

(See also Leavenworth, Wenatchee)

Founded 1881 **Pop** 2,544 **Elev** 853 ft **Area code** 509 **Zip** 98815
Information Chamber of Commerce, PO Box 834; 509/782-7404.

Cashmere, located in the Wenatchee Valley, has strong timber and fruit industries.

What to See and Do

Chelan County Historical Museum. Pioneer relics, Native Americans artifacts; Columbia River archaeology exhibit; water wheel (1891); mineral exhibit; "pioneer village" with 21 cabins, mining displays. Great Northern RR depot, passenger car and caboose. (See ANNUAL EVENTS) (Apr-Oct, daily; rest of yr, by appt) 600 Cottage Ave, E edge of town. Phone 509/782-3230. ¢¢

Liberty Orchards Co, Inc. Makes fruit-nut confections known as "aplets," "cotlets," "grapelets" & "fruit festives." Tour, samples. (May-Dec, daily; rest of yr, Mon-Fri; closed some hols) Children with adult only. 117 Mission St, off US 2. Phone 509/782-2191. **Free.**

Annual Events

Founders' Day. Chelan County Historical Museum. Last wkend June.

Chelan County Fair. 1st wkend after Labor Day.

Apple Days. Chelan County Historical Museum. Apple pie contest, old-time crafts, Pioneer Village in operation, cider making. 1st wkend Oct.

Motels

✔★ **VILLAGE INN.** *229 Cottage Ave. 509/782-3522; FAX 509/782-2619.* 21 rms, 2 story. S $45; D $50; higher rates festivals. TV; cable. Complimentary coffee in lobby. Restaurant nearby. Ck-out 11 am. Business servs avail. X-country ski 11 mi. Cr cds: A, DS, MC, V.

★ ★ **WEDGE MOUNTAIN INN.** *7335 US 2. 509/548-6694; res: 800/666-9664.* 28 rms, 2 story. May-Labor Day: S $63; D $68; each addl $5; lower rates rest of yr. TV; cable. Complimentary coffee in lobby. Restaurant adj 6 am-9 pm. Ck-out 11 am. Coin lndry. Balconies. Cr cds: A, DS, MC, V.

D ⇲ 🏊 ☒ SC

Centralia (D-3)

(See also Chehalis)

Founded 1875 **Pop** 12,101 **Elev** 189 ft **Area code** 360 **Zip** 98531
Information Twin Cities Chamber of Commerce, 500 NW Chamber of Commerce Way, Chehalis 98532; 360/748-8885.

Centralia was founded by a former slave named George Washington. George Washington Park is named for the founder, not for the country's first president.

What to See and Do

Borst Blockhouse (1852) and **Joseph Borst Family Farmstead** (1860). Fort built at confluence of Skookumchuck and Chehalis rivers as a strong point against Native American attacks; later moved to park entrance. Hewn log walls support upper fortification with loopholes for rifles, holes in second floor to shoot through. Early steam locomotive; rhododendron gardens, arboretum. Homestead is refurbished and restored to its original state of the 1860s. (May-Sept, Sat & Sun; rest of yr, by appt) W of town in Ft Borst Park, off I-5, S of Harrison Ave. Phone 360/736-7687. **Free.**

Schaefer County Park. Swimming in the Skookumchuck River; fishing. Hiking trails. Picnicking (shelter), playground. Horseshoe pits, volleyball. ½ mi N on WA 507. Phone 360/748-9121, ext 135. **Free.**

Annual Event

Southwest Washington Fair. 1 mi S on I-5. First held in 1909, this is the state's second oldest fair and one of the largest. 3rd wk Aug.

Motel

✔★ ★ **DAYS INN.** *702 Harrison Ave, I-5 exit 82. 360/736-2875; FAX 360/736-2651; res: 800/448-5544.* 89 rms, 2 story. June-Sept: S $55-$65; D $65-$75; each addl $4; suites $80; under 12 free; lower rates rest of yr. Crib $4. TV; cable. Heated pool. Complimentary continental bkfst. Restaurant opp open 24 hrs. Ck-out 11 am. Business servs avail. Cr cds: A, C, D, DS, MC, V.

Chehalis (D-3)

(For accommodations see Centralia)

Settled 1873 **Pop** 6,527 **Elev** 226 ft **Area code** 360 **Zip** 98532
Information Twin Cities Chamber of Commerce, 500 NW Chamber of Commerce Way; 360/748-8885 or 800/525-3323.

First called Saundersville, this city takes its present name, Native American for "shifting sands," from its position at the point where the Newaukum and Chehalis rivers meet. Farms and an industrial park give economic sustenance to Chehalis and neighboring Centralia.

What to See and Do

Historic Claquato Church (1858). Oldest church in state, original building on original site; handmade pews, pulpit. (Schedule varies) For information phone 360/748-4551 or -7755. 3 mi W on WA 6, on Claquato Hill.

Lewis County Historical Museum. Restored railroad depot (1912). Pioneer displays; Native American exhibits. Cemetery, genealogical history; artifacts, newspapers, books, photographs, written family histories, oral histories of pioneers. (Daily exc Mon; closed hols) 599 NW Front Way. Phone 360/748-0831. ¢

Rainbow Falls State Park. Approx 125 acres of woodland. Fishing. Hiking trails. Picnicking. Camping (dump station). Standard fees. 18 mi W on WA 6. Phone 360/291-3767.

Restaurant

★ **MARY McCRANK'S DINNER HOUSE.** *2923 Jackson Hwy. 360/748-3662.* Hrs: 11:30 am-8:30 pm; Sun noon-8 pm. Closed Mon; Dec 25. Res accepted. Beer, wine. Semi-a la carte: lunch $5.50-$8.95, dinner $10.95-$18.50. Child's meals. Old-fashioned home cooking. Own jams, jellies, breads, pies. Farmhouse atmosphere; fireplace; antiques. Established 1935. Totally nonsmoking. Cr cds: DS, MC, V.

D SC

Chelan (C-6)

(See also Wenatchee)

Settled 1885 **Pop** 2,969 **Elev** 1,208 ft **Area code** 509 **Zip** 98816 **E-mail** travel@kozi.com **Web** www.lakechelan.com
Information Lake Chelan Chamber of Commerce, Box 216; (509)682-3503 or 800/4-CHELAN.

Located in an apple-growing region, Chelan is a gateway to Lake Chelan and the spectacular northern Cascade mountains. A Ranger District office of the Wenatchee National Forest (see WENATCHEE) is located here.

What to See and Do

Lake Chelan. This fiord-like lake, the largest and deepest lake in the state, stretches NW for approx 55 mi through the Cascade mountains to the community of Stehekin in the North Cascades Natl Park (see SEDRO WOOLLEY); lake is nearly 1,500 ft deep in some areas. There are two state parks and several recreation areas along the lake.

Lake cruises. The passenger boats *Lady of the Lake II* and *Lady Express* make daily cruises on Lake Chelan to Stehekin. For details contact Lake Chelan Boat Co, 1418 W Woodin Ave, Box 186; 509/682-4584 (recording). ¢¢¢¢¢

State parks.

Alta Lake. More than 180 acres. Swimming; fishing; boating (ramps). Hiking. Snowmobiling, ice-skating. Camping (hookups). Standard fees. 20 mi N on US 97, then 2 mi W on WA 153. Phone 509/923-2473.

Lake Chelan. Approx 130 lakefront acres. Swimming; fishing; boating (ramps, dock). Picnicking. Camping (hookups; res required late May-Aug). (Apr-Oct, daily; rest of yr, wkends & hols) Standard fees. 9 ½ mi W via US 97 & South Shore Dr or Navarre Coulee Rd. Phone (800)452-5687.

Twenty-Five Mile Creek. Approx 65 acres. Fishing; boating (launch, mooring, gas). Hiking. Concession. Camping (hookups). Standard fees. 18 mi NW on South Shore Dr. Phone (800)452-5687.

Annual Events

Apple Blossom Festival. 8 mi W via WA 150 in Manson. Mother's Day wkend.

WPRA Rodeo. Last wkend July.

Motels

★ ★ ★ **CAMPBELL'S RESORT.** *104 W Woodin Ave, on US 97, on Lake Chelan.* 509/682-2561; FAX 509/682-2177; res: 800/553-8225 (WA). 148 rms, 1-4 story, 5 cottages, 20 kits. Mid-June-Labor Day: S, D $138; each addl $10; suites $180-$270; cottages $140-$198; family rates; higher rates Memorial Day wkend, Labor Day wkend; lower rates rest of yr. Crib $5. TV; cable. 2 heated pools; whirlpools, poolside serv. Restaurant 6:45 am-9:30 pm. Bar 11-1 am. Ck-out 11 am. Meeting rms. Business servs avail. In-rm modem link. Sundries. X-country ski 6 mi. Refrigerators; some minibars. Private patios, balconies, lanais. Sand beach; boat, seaplane moorage. Cr cds: A, C, DS, MC, V.

★ ★ **CARAVEL.** *322 W Woodin Ave (US 97).* 509/682-2582; res: 800/962-5736. 92 rms, 1-4 story, 40 kits. Mid-June-mid-Sept: S, D $92-$120; suites $180-$275; wkly rate for kit. units; lower rates rest of yr. Crib $5. TV; cable. Heated pool. Restaurant nearby. Ck-out 11 am. Some refrigerators, fireplaces. Boat moorage. Cr cds: A, C, D, DS, MC, V.

Cheney (C-9)

(See also Spokane)

Pop 7,723 **Elev** 2,350 ft **Area code** 509 **Zip** 99004
Information Chamber of Commerce, 201 First St, PO Box 65; 509/235-8480.

Cheney, on a rise of land that gives it one of the highest elevations of any municipality in the state, has been a university town since 1882. It is also a farm distribution and servicing center.

What to See and Do

Cheney Historical Museum. Features pioneer artifacts. (Mar-Nov, Tue & Sat afternoons) 614 3rd St. Phone 509/235-4343 or -2422. **Free.**

Eastern Washington Univ (1882). (8,000 students) Tours of campus. Phone 509/359-2397.On campus are a theater, recital hall and

Gallery of Art. Changing exhibits. (Academic yr, Mon-Fri; closed hols) Phone 509/359-2493. **Free.**

Museum of Anthropology. Teaching-research facility concerning Native Americans of North America. For tour information phone 509/359-2433. **Free.**

Turnbull Natl Wildlife Refuge. Located on the Pacific Flyway; more than 200 species of birds have been observed in the area; also a habitat for deer, elk, coyotes, beaver, mink, chipmunks, red squirrels and Columbia ground squirrels. Refuge named after Cyrus Turnbull, an early settler. A 2,200-acre public use area (daily). 4 mi S on Cheney-Plaza Rd, then 2 mi E. Phone 509/235-4723. Per vehicle (Mar-Oct) ¢

Annual Event

Rodeo Days. Rodeo, parade. 2nd wkend July.

Motel

✔ ★ **WILLOW SPRING.** *5 B Street, I-90 exit 270.* 509/235-5138; FAX 509/235-4528. 44 rms, 3 story, 12 kits. No elvtr. S $37; D $41-$52; each addl $4; kit. units $5 addl. Pet accepted; $5/day. TV; cable. Restaurant opp 7 am-10 pm. Ck-out 11 am. Coin lndry. Cr cds: A, D, DS, MC, V.

Clarkston (E-9)

(See also Pullman; also see Lewiston, ID)

Founded 1896 **Pop** 6,753 **Elev** 819 ft **Area code** 509 **Zip** 99403
Information Chamber of Commerce, 502 Bridge St; 509/758-7712.

Clarkston is located on the Washington-Idaho boundary at the confluence of the Clearwater and Snake rivers. The town became a shipping center when the construction of four dams on the lower Snake River brought barge transportation here. Many recreation areas are located near Clarkston, especially along the Snake River and in the Umatilla National Forest. River trips are available into Hells Canyon.

What to See and Do

Asotin County Museum. Main museum contains sculptures, pioneer equipment, pictures and clothing. On grounds are furnished pioneer house, shepherd's cabin, one-rm schoolhouse, 1882 log cabin, blacksmith shop, a windmill and Salmon River barge. (Tues-Sat; closed major hols) Approx 6 mi S on WA 129, at 215 Filmore St, Asotin. Phone 509/243-4659. **Free.**

Fields Spring State Park. Approx 800 forested acres in the Blue Mts. A one-mi uphill hike from parking lot to Puffer Butte gives view of three states. Wide variety of wildflowers and birdlife. Picnicking. Primitive camping. Standard fees. 30 mi S on WA 129. Phone 509/256-3332.

Petroglyphs. Ancient writings inscribed in cliffs of Snake River near Buffalo Eddy. Near town of Asotin.

Umatilla Natl Forest. Approx 319,000 acres of heavily forested mountain area extending into Oregon. Many recreation areas offer fishing, hunting, hiking and camping. Downhill skiing (see DAYTON). S of US 12, access near Pomeroy. For further information contact Supervisor, 2517 SW Hailey Ave, Pendleton, OR 97801; 503/276-3811.

Valley Art Center. Various types of art and crafts; changing monthly exhibits with featured artists and special showings. (Mon-Fri, closed major hols) Northwest Heritage Show is held for two months in summer. 842 6th St. Phone 509/758-8331. **Free.**

Annual Event

Asotin County Fair. Includes cowboy breakfast, barbecue, parade. Last Thurs-Sun Apr.

Motels

 BEST WESTERN RIVERTREE INN. *1257 Bridge St. 509-758-9551.* 61 units, 2 story, 20 kits. (no equipt). S $55; D $60; each addl $5; suites $80-$130; kit. units $85 addl; higher rates university football games. Crib $5. TV; cable. Heated pool; whirlpool. Restaurant opp 6-3 am. Ck-out noon. Business servs avail. Exercise equipt; bicycles, weight machine, sauna. Refrigerators. Balconies. Picnic tables, grills. Many rms with spiral staircase to loft. Cr cds: A, C, D, DS, MC, V.

★ ★ **QUALITY INN.** *700 Port Dr. 509/758-9500; FAX 509/758-5580.* 75 rms, 3 story. No elvtr. S $60-$89; D $65-$89; each addl $5; under 18 free. Crib $5. TV; cable. Pool. Restaurant 6 am-2 pm, 5-10 pm. Rm serv. Bar from 4 pm. Ck-out noon. Coin lndry. Meeting rms. Business servs avail. Valet serv. Balconies. On river; swimming. Convention center adj. Cr cds: A, C, D, DS, ER, JCB, MC, V.

Colville (B-8)

(See also Spokane)

Pop 4,360 **Elev** 1,635 ft **Area code** 509 **Zip** 99114 **E-mail** colvillecoc @plix.com
Information Chamber of Commerce, 121 E Astor, PO Box 267; 509/684-5973.

Once a brawling frontier town, Colville, the seat of Stevens County, has quieted down and now reflects the peacefulness of the surrounding hills and mountains. Many towns flourished and died in this area—orchards, mills and mines all had their day. The portage at Kettle Falls, a fort, and the crossing of several trails made Colville a thriving center.

What to See and Do

Colville Natl Forest. This million-acre forest is located in the NE corner of Washington bordering Canada. The forest extends along its western boundary from the Canadian border S to the Colville Reservation and E across the Columbia River to Idaho. Comprising conifer forest types, small lakes and winding valleys bounded by slopes leading to higher mountainous areas, the forest offers good hunting and fishing and full-service camping. Also here is Sullivan Lake, offering recreation opportunities including boating, fishing, swimming, developed and dispersed campground settings, hiking trails, and sightseeing. The bighorn sheep that inhabit adj Hall Mt can be viewed at a feeding station near the lake, which is cooperatively managed by the forest and the Washington Dept of Wildlife. For more information, contact the Forest Supervisor, Federal Bldg, 765 S Main St; 509/684-7000. Also located here are a Ranger District office and

Lake Gillette Recreation Area. Boating, swimming, fishing, picnicking; amphitheater with programs; camping (fee). (Mid-May-Sept) E via Tiger Hwy, WA 20. Phone 509/684-5657. **Free.**

Keller Heritage Center. Site of 3-story Keller home (1910), carriage house; blacksmith shop; farmstead cabin; gardens; museum; schoolhouse; machinery building; lookout tower. Local records, Native American artifacts. (May-Sept; daily) 700 N Wynne St. Phone 509/684-5968. **Donation.**

St Paul's Mission. A chapel was built by Native Americans near here in 1845, followed by the hand-hewn log church in 1847. It fell into disuse in the 1870s and in 1939 was restored to its original state. Self-guided tour. Located at Kettle Falls in Coulee Dam Natl Recreation Area (see COULEE DAM). (All yr) 12 mi NW, near intersection of Columbia River & US 395. Phone 509/738-6266. **Free.**

Annual Events

Colville Professional Rodeo. Father's Day wkend.

Rendezvous. Arts & crafts, entertainment. 1st wkend Aug.

Northeast Washington Fair. Stevens County Fairgrounds. Parade, livestock & horse shows; arts & crafts exhibits; carnival. Wkend after Labor Day.

Inn

★ ★ ★ **MY PARENTS' ESTATE.** *(Box 724, Kettle Falls 99141) 7 mi N on US 395. 509/738-6220.* 4 rms, 2 story. No rm phones. S $65; D $75-$100. Adults only. TV in sitting rm. Complimentary full bkfst. Ck-out 11 am, ck-in 4-6 pm. Built in 1873 as a convent for a mission. On 47 acres with gazebo, barn and gymnasium. Totally nonsmoking. Cr cds: MC, V.

Coulee Dam (B-7)

Founded 1934 **Pop** 1,087 **Elev** 1,145 ft **Area code** 509 **Zip** 99116
E-mail coulee@televar.com **Web** www.televar.com/~chamber/coulee
Information Grand Coulee Dam Area Chamber of Commerce, 306 Midway Ave, PO Box 760, Grand Coulee, 99133; 509/633-3074 or 800/COULEE2.

Established as a construction community for workers on the Grand Coulee Dam project, this town now is the home of service and maintenance employees of the dam and headquarters for the Coulee Dam National Recreation Area.

What to See and Do

Colville Tribal Museum. More than 8,000 years of history on 11 tribes. (Late May-Sept; daily; rest of yr, schedule varies) Mead Way. Phone 509/633-0751. **Free.**

✪ **Grand Coulee Dam.** Major structure of multipurpose Columbia Basin Project, built by Bureau of Reclamation. Water is diverted from the Columbia River to what in prehistoric days was its temporary course down the Grand Coulee (a deep water-carved ravine). The project will reclaim more than a million acres through irrigation and already provides a vast reservoir of electric power. One of the largest concrete structures in the world, the dam towers 550 ft high, has a 500-ft-wide base and a 5,223-ft-long crest. Power plants contain some of world's largest hydro-generators. Self-guided tours begin at Visitor Arrival Center (daily exc Jan 1, Thanksgiving, Dec 25). Major exhibits along tour route. Laser show (Memorial Day-Sept, nightly). Glass-enclosed elevator rides down face of third power plant forebay dam; water recreation; camping. Near jct WA 155, 174. Phone 509/633-3074 or 509/633-3838. **Free.**

Lake Roosevelt Natl Recreation Area. Totals 100,059 acres including Franklin D. Roosevelt Lake. Lake formed by Grand Coulee Dam serves as storage reservoir with 630-mi shoreline, extends 151 mi NE, reaching the Canadian border. Southern part is semi-arid; northern part mountainous, forested with ponderosa pine, fir, tamarack. Excellent for all sizes of motorboats with 151-mi waterway along reservoir and 200 mi of cruising water in Canada provided by Arrow Lakes, reached from Lake Roosevelt by the Columbia River. Thirty-two areas have been specially developed; most provide camping (fee), picnicking, swimming, boating and launching sites. Fishing all yr in Roosevelt Lake. Nine camping areas (mid-Apr-Oct; fee). Contact Superintendent, 1008 Crest, 99116; 509/633-9441. Within is

Ft Spokane. One of the last frontier military outposts of the 1800s. Four of 45 buildings remain; brick guardhouse is now visitor center and small museum. Built to maintain peace between the settlers and Native Americans, no shot was ever fired. Self-guided trail around old parade grounds; interpretive displays. (Mid-June-Labor Day; daily) Living history programs performed on wkends in summer. Nearby are beach and camping (fee). Phone 509/725-2715. **Free.**

Steamboat Rock State Park. Approx 900 acres. Swimming; fishing; boating (launch). Hiking. Picnicking. Camping (hookups; res recommended Memorial Day-Labor Day wkends) Standard fees. 11 mi S of Electric City on WA 155. Phone 509/633-1304 or 800/452-5687 (res).

Annual Events

Colorama Festival & PWRA Rodeo. 2nd wkend May.

Laser Light Festival. Memorial Day wkend.

Motels

 ✔★ **COULEE HOUSE.** *110 Roosevelt Way.* 509/633-1101; FAX 509/633-1416; res: 800/715-7767. 61 units, 2 story, 15 kits. S, D $50-$70; each addl $4; suites $98-$115; kit. units $62-$98. Crib $4. Pet accepted. TV; cable (premium). Heated pool; whirlpool. Restaurant adj 6 am-10 pm. Ck-out 11 am. Coin lndry. Business servs avail. Sundries. Some refrigerators, balconies. View of dam. Cr cds: A, D, DS, MC, V.

★ **PONDEROSA.** *10 Lincoln St.* 509/633-2100; FAX 509/633-2633; res: 800/633-6421. 35 rms, 2 story. S $49-$75; D $67; under 12 free. TV; cable (premium). Pool. Complimentary coffee in rms. Restaurant nearby. Ck-out 11 am. Business servs avail. Gift shop. Airport transportation. Some refrigerators. Private patios, balconies. View of dam. Cr cds: A, DS, MC, V.

Restaurant

✔★★ **SAGE INN.** *(Box 66, 413 Midway Ave, Grand Coulee 99133)* Just S on WA 155. 509/633-0550. Hrs: 7 am-10 pm. Res accepted; required some hols. Bar 11-2 am. Semi-a la carte: bkfst, lunch $2.50-$8, dinner $5-$15. Child's meals. Cr cds: MC, V.

D

Coupeville (B-3)

(See also Oak Harbor, Port Townsend)

Pop 1,377 **Elev** 80 ft **Area code** 360 **Zip** 98239
Information Central Whidbey Chamber of Commerce, PO Box 152; 360/678-5434.

One of the oldest towns in the state, Coupeville was named for Thomas Coupe, a sea captain and early settler, the only man to ever sail a full-rigged ship through Deception Pass. Fortified to protect the settlers and for the defense of Puget Sound, Coupeville was once the home of the only seat of higher education north of Seattle, the Puget Sound Academy. Today it is near Whidbey Island Naval Air Station, home of Naval Aviation for the Pacific Northwest.

What to See and Do

Alexander Blockhouse (1855). One of four such buildings built on Whidbey Island to protect settlers' homes from Native Americans during the White River Massacre. Near Front St, on waterfront.

Ft Casey State Park. Approx 140 acres. Scuba diving; saltwater fishing; boating (launch). Picnicking. Camping. Museum (early May-mid-Sept). Standard fees. 3 mi S. Phone 360/678-4519.

Motel

★ **HARBOUR INN.** *(1606 E Main, Freeland 98249) 20 mi S of Coupeville; 1 blk N off WA 525.* 360/331-6900. E-mail harborinn@whidbey.com. 20 rms, 2 story. No A/C. S $49-$72; D $54-$77; each addl $6.

Crib $6. Pet accepted, some restrictions; $6. TV; cable. Complimentary continental bkfst. Restaurant nearby. Ck-out 11 am. Refrigerators; microwaves avail. Cr cds: A, MC, V.

Inns

★★ **CAPTAIN WHIDBEY.** *2072 Captain Whidbey Inn Rd.* 360/678-4097; FAX 360/678-4110; res: 800/366-4097. E-mail captain@whidbey.net; web www.whidbey.net/~captain/. 32 units, 20 with bath, 3 kits. No A/C. S, D $85-$195; each addl $15; suites $135-$195; kit. cottages $150-$195. Complimentary full bkfst. Bar noon-midnight. Ck-out noon, ck-in 4 pm. Meeting rms. Business servs avail. Private beach; dock; boats, sailboats; clamming. Lawn games. Library. Fireplace in cottages. Turn-of-the-century log inn (1907) on sheltered cove. Cr cds: A, C, D, DS, MC, V.

★★★ **GUEST HOUSE.** *(3366 S WA 525, Greenbank 98253)* 10 mi S via WA 525, on Whidbey Island. 360/678-3115. Web www.whidbey.net. 5 kit. cottages, 1 luxury log house, 1 suite, 1 & 2 story. A/C in 1 unit. No rm phones. Mar-mid-Oct: cottages: S, D $150-$195; log house $285; suite $110; wkly rates; lower rates rest of yr. Adults only. TV; cable, VCR (free movies). Heated pool. Complimentary full bkfst. Restaurant nearby. Ck-out 11 am, ck-in 4 pm. Exercise equipt; bicycles, treadmill. Lawn games. In-rm whirlpools, microwaves. Fireplace in cottages. Private patios, balconies. Picnic tables, grills. Located on 25 acres with forest and meadows; marine and mountain views. Totally nonsmoking. Cr cds: A, DS, MC, V.

★★★ **INN AT LANGLEY.** *(400 First St, Langley 98260) S on WA 525 to Langley Rd then E.* 360/221-3033. 24 rms, 4 story. No A/C. No elvtr. S, D $189-$199; each addl $35; suites $269; wkends, hols (2-day min). Children over 12 yrs old. TV; cable (premium), VCR (movies). Complimentary continental bkfst. Complimentary coffee in rms. Dining rm, 1 sitting: 7 pm Fri, Sat. Restaurant nearby. Ck-out noon, ck-in 3 pm. Business servs avail. In-rm modem link. Concierge serv. In-rm whirlpools, refrigerators, fireplaces. Balconies. On ocean. Elegant atmosphere. Totally nonsmoking. Cr cds: A, MC, V.

D

Restaurant

✔★★ **CAFE LANGLEY.** *(113 First St, Langley 98260) S on WA 525 to Max Welton Rd, then E to Langley Rd to First St.* 360/221-3090. Hrs: 11:30 am-2:30 pm, 5-10 pm. Closed some major hols; also Tues Jan-Mar. Res accepted. No A/C. Mediterranean, Greek menu. Wine, beer. Semi-a la carte: lunch $5-$9, dinner $13.50-$17. Specialties: mixed grill, Mediterranean seafood stew, Washington lamb. Tile floors, hanging plants, some antiques. Totally nonsmoking. Cr cds: A, MC, V.

Crystal Mountain

(see Mount Rainier National Park)

Dayton (Columbia Co) (E-8)

(For accommodations see Walla Walla)

Settled 1859 **Pop** 2,468 **Elev** 1,613 ft **Area code** 509 **Zip** 99328 **E-mail** Daytoncc@televar.com **Web** HistoricDayton.com

Information Chamber of Commerce, 166 E Main St; 509/382-4825 or 800/882-6299.

Once an important stagecoach depot and stopping-off place for miners, Dayton is now the center of a farm area in which sheep, cattle, wheat, apples, peas, asparagus and hay are raised. Little Goose Lock & Dam, a multipurpose federal project and one of four such developments on the Snake River, is about 35 miles north of town. Vegetable canning and lumbering are local industries.

Dayton has many historic homes and buildings, including the Columbia County Courthouse (1886), oldest courthouse in the state still used for county government, and the Dayton Historic Depot (oldest in state).

What to See and Do

Kendall Skyline Drive. Scenic route through Blue Mts and Umatilla Natl Forest (see CLARKSTON). Usually open by July. Contact Chamber of Commerce for details. S of town.

Lewis and Clark Trail State Park. Approx 40 acres. Swimming; fishing. Hiking. Picnicking. Camping. Standard fees. *Closed due to flooding. Day-use area only is open.* 5 mi SW on US 12. Phone 509/337-6457.

Palouse River Canyon. Deeply eroded gorge pierces wheatlands of region; cliffs rise hundreds of feet above river. At Palouse Falls, river roars over 198-ft cliff into deep ravine of basaltic rock, continues south to join Snake River. Nearby are Lyons Ferry and Palouse Falls state parks. 18 mi N on US 12, then 22 mi NW on unnumbered roads.

Ski Bluewood. 2 triple chairlifts, platter pull, half pipe; patrol, school, rentals; cafeteria, bar. Longest run 2.5 mi; vertical drop 1,125 ft. (Jan-Feb, daily; mid-Nov-Dec & Feb-Mar, daily exc Mon) Snowboarding. Half-day rates. 22 mi S via 4th St (North Touchet Rd), in Umatilla Natl Forest. Phone 509/382-4725. ¢¢¢¢

Annual Events

Dayton Depot Festival. July 18 & 19.

Columbia County Fair. Dayton Fairgrounds. Sept 5-7.

Ellensburg (D-5)

(See also Yakima)

Settled 1867 **Pop** 12,361 **Elev** 1,508 ft **Area code** 509 **Zip** 98926 **E-mail** chamber@adsnet.net

Information Chamber of Commerce, 436 N Sprague; 509/925-3137.

Although this community has long abandoned its first romantic name, Robber's Roost, it cherishes the tradition and style of the West, both as a center for dude ranches and as the scene of one of the country's best annual rodeos. At the geographic center of the state, Ellensburg processes beef and dairy products. The county ranges from lakes and crags in the west through irrigated farmlands to sagebrush prairie along the Columbia River to the east.

A Ranger District office of the Wenatchee National Forest (see WENATCHEE) is located here.

What to See and Do

Central Washington Univ (1890). (7,000 students) Liberal arts and sciences, business, technology, education. 8th Ave & Walnut St. Phone 509/963-1111.

> **CWU Library.** Regional depository for federal documents; collection of microforms, maps, general materials. (Daily) 14th Ave & D St. Phone 509/963-1777. **Free.**

> **Sarah Spurgeon Art Gallery.** Features national, regional and advanced students' art exhibits in all media. (Sept-June, Mon-Fri; closed univ hols) In Randall Hall. Phone 509/963-2665. **Free.**

Gallery I. Seven exhibit and sales rooms surround a central atrium. (Daily exc Sun, afternoons) 408 1/2 N Pearl St, on 2nd floor of the Stewart Bldg (1889). Phone 509/925-2670. **Free.**

Ginkgo/Wanapum State Park. One of world's largest petrified forests (7,600 acres), with more than 200 species of petrified wood, including prehistoric ginkgo tree. Waterskiing, fishing, boating. Hiking. Picnicking. Camping (hookups). Standard fees. 28 mi E on I-90 exit 136, in Vantage. Phone 509/856-2700. **Free.**

✪ **Olmstead Place State Park-Heritage Site.** Turn-of-the-century Kittitas Valley farm, being converted to a living historical farm. Originally homesteaded in 1875. Eight buildings; wildlife, flowers & trees; 1/2-mi interpretive trail. Farm machinery. Tours. (June-Sept, wkends; rest of yr, by appt) (See ANNUAL EVENTS) 4 mi E via Kittitas Hwy on Squaw Creek Trail Rd. Phone 509/925-1943 or 509/856-2700. **Free.**

Wanapum Dam Heritage Center. Self-guided tour of center; fish-viewing room; powerhouse; petroglyph rubbings; exhibits detail life of the Wanapum, fur traders, ranchers, miners. (Daily) 29 mi E on I-90, then 3 mi S on WA 243. Phone 509/754-3541, ext 2571. **Free.**

Annual Events

Natl Western Art Show & Auction. Phone 509/962-2934. 3rd wkend May.

Ellensburg Rodeo. Kittitas County Fairgrounds. Calf roping, steer wrestling, bull riding, wild cow milking, Native American dances. 4 days Labor Day wkend.

Kittitas County Fair. Carnival, exhibits, livestock, crafts, contests, entertainment. 4 days Labor Day wkend.

Threshing Bee and Antique Equipment Show. Olmstead Place State Park. Steam & gas threshing, blacksmithing demonstrations, horse-drawn equipment, old-time plowing. 3rd wkend Sept.

Seasonal Event

Laughing Horse Summer Theatre. Tower Theatre, Central Washington Univ, 8th Ave & Anderson St. Company presents 4 plays in repertory. Phone 509/963-3400. Tues-Sat, early July-mid-Aug.

Motel

★ ★ **BEST WESTERN ELLENSBURG INN.** *1700 Canyon Rd.* 509/925-9801; FAX 509/925-2093. 105 rms, 2 story. S $59; D $64; each addl $5; suites $75; under 12 free; higher rates rodeo. Crib free. Pet accepted. TV; cable (premium). Indoor pool; wading pool, whirlpool. Restaurant 7 am-10 pm. Rm serv. Bar 11-2 am; entertainment. Ck-out noon. Meeting rms. Business servs avail. Valet serv. Exercise equipt; weights, treadmill. Cr cds: A, C, D, DS, JCB, MC, V.

Restaurants

✔ ★ ★ **CASA DE BLANCA.** *1318 S Canyon Rd.* 509/925-1693. Hrs: 10:30 am-10:30 pm. Closed Thanksgiving, Dec 25. Res accepted. Mexican, Amer menu. Bar. Semi-a la carte: lunch $3.50-$9, dinner

$6.50-$15. Child's meals. Specializes in prime rib, steak. Cr cds: A, DS, MC, V.

D **SC**

★ ★ **PUB MINGLEWOOD.** *402 N Pearl St. 509/962-2260.* Hrs: 11 am-10 pm. Closed Sun, Mon; Jan 1, July 4, Dec 25. Res accepted. Italian menu. Bar. Semi-a la carte: lunch $3.50-$7.95, dinner $8.95-$18.50. Child's meals. Specializes in pasta, burgers. Outdoor dining. Historic building; artwork, antique furniture. Cr cds: A, C, D, DS, MC, V.

D

Enumclaw (D-4)

(For accommodations see Tacoma, also see Puyallup)

Pop 7,227 **Elev** 750 ft **Area code** 360 **Zip** 98022 **E-mail** enumclaw@tx3.com **Web** www.enumclaw.com

Information Chamber of Commerce/Visitor Information; 1421 Cole St; 360/825-7666.

A Ranger District office of the Mount Baker-Snoqualmie National Forest (see BELLINGHAM, SEATTLE) is located here.

What to See and Do

Federation Forest State Park. Approx 620 acres of old growth timber. Catherine Montgomery Interpretive Center has displays on the state's seven life zones. Three interpretive trails, hiking trails and part of the Naches Trail, one of the first pioneer trails between eastern Washington and Puget Sound. Fishing, hiking, picnicking. 18 mi SE on WA 410. Phone 360/663-2207. **Free.**

Green River Gorge Conservation Area. Protects a unique 12-mi corridor of the Green River, which cuts through unusual rock areas, many with fossils. Views of present-day forces of stream erosion through caves, smooth canyon walls. 12 mi N on WA 169. **Free.** One of the many areas in the gorge is

Flaming Geyser State Park. Two geysers (actually old test holes for coal), one burning about six inches high and the other bubbling methane gas through a spring. Fishing, boating, rafting. Hiking. Picnicking, playground. Abundant wildlife, wildflowers. No camping. Standard fees. (Daily) Phone 206/931-3930.

Mud Mt Dam. One of the world's highest earth core and rock-fill dams. Vista-point structures; picnicking (shelters), playground; wading pool; nature trail. Day use only. (May-mid-Oct, daily; rest of yr, Mon-Fri) 7 mi SE via WA 410. Phone 360/825-3211. **Free.**

Annual Event

King County Fair. Fairgrounds. Phone 360/825-7777. 3rd wk July.

Motel

★ ★ **BEST WESTERN PARK CENTER HOTEL.** *1000 Griffin Ave. 360/825-4490; FAX 360/825-3686.* 40 rms, 2 story. June-Oct: S, D $63; each addl $5; under 12 free; lower rates rest of yr. Crib $10. Pet accepted; $10. TV; cable. Complimentary coffee in lobby. Restaurant 7 am-9 pm. Rm serv. Bar from 4 pm. Ck-out 11 am. Meeting rms. Business servs avail. In-rm modem link. Whirlpool. Some refrigerators, microwaves. Picnic tables. Cr cds: A, D, DS, MC, V.

D **⊷** **⊠** **▧** **SC**

Ephrata (C-6)

(See also Moses Lake, Quincy, Soap Lake)

Settled 1882 **Pop** 5,349 **Elev** 1,275 ft **Area code** 509 **Zip** 98823

Information Chamber of Commerce, 90 Alder NW, PO Box 275; 509/754-4656 or 800/345-4656.

Growth of this area is the result of the development of surrounding farmland, originally irrigated by wells, now supplied by the Columbia Basin irrigation project. Ephrata is the center of an area containing a series of lakes that offer fishing and water sports. There is excellent upland game bird hunting.

What to See and Do

Grant County Pioneer Village & Museum. Displays trace natural history, early pioneer development of area. Native American artifacts. Pioneer homestead and country village with 20 buildings (some original, restored), including church, schoolhouse, saloon, barbershop, Krupp-Marlin Jail, photography studio, bank, firehouse, livery stable, blacksmith shop; farm machinery exhibit. Guided tour. (Early May-Oct, daily exc Wed; rest of yr, guided tour by appt) 742 Basin St N. Phone 509/754-3334.   ¢

Oasis Park. Picnicking; 9-hole, par 3 golf (fee); children's fishing pond; playground; miniature golf (fee). Camping (fee); swimming pool (free to campers). (Daily) 1½ mi SW on WA 28. Phone 509/754-5102.

Annual Event

Sage & Sun Festival. Parade, sports events, arts & crafts shows. 2nd wkend June.

Motel

✔ ★ **SHARLYN.** *848 Basin St SW. 509/754-3575; res: 800/292-2965.* 19 rms, 2 story. S $40; D $50; each addl $8. TV; cable. Coffee in rms. Restaurant nearby. Ck-out 11 am. Business servs avail. Airport transportation. Cr cds: A, C, D, MC, V.

⊠ **▧**

Everett (B-3)

(See also Marysville, Seattle)

Founded 1890 **Pop** 69,961 **Elev** 157 ft **Area code** 425

Information Everett/Snohomish County Convention and Visitor Bureau, PO Box 1086, 98206; 425/252-5181.

This lumber, aircraft, electronics and shipping city is on a sheltered harbor where the Snohomish River empties into Port Gardner Bay. To the east is the snowcapped Cascade Mountain Range; to the west are the Olympic Mountains. Developed by Eastern industrial and railroad money, Everett serves as a major commercial fishing port and receives and dispatches a steady stream of cargo vessels. The Boeing 747 and 767 are assembled here.

Along the waterfront is an 1890s-style seaside marketplace, the Everett Marina Village.

What to See and Do

Boat tours. For information on companies offering sightseeing, dinner and whale watching cruises, contact the Convention & Visitors Bureau, 425/252-5181.

★ Boeing Everett Facility. Audiovisual presentation; bus tour of assembly facility. Gift shop. (Mon-Fri; closed hols) No children under 10 yrs. I-5

exit 189, approx 3 mi W on WA 526. For tour schedule phone 425/342-4801. **Free.**

Mukilteo. This town, just W of Everett, is the major ferry point from the mainland to the S tip of Whidbey Island. Its name means "good camping ground." A lighthouse built in 1905 is open for tours (Sat).

Recreation areas. There are many recreation areas in and near the city that offer swimming (fee), fishing, boat launch, hiking, picnicking, camping, nature centers, tennis and golf (fee). Phone 425/259-0300. **Free.**

Totem Pole. 80 ft high, carved by Tulalip Chief William Shelton. Rucker Ave & 44th St.

Annual Event

Salty Sea Days. Festival, parade, displays, food & carnival. Early June.

Seasonal Event

Auto racing. Evergreen Speedway, 15 mi SE via US 2, exit 194 off I-5. NASCAR super & mini stocks, SVRA modifieds, hobby stocks, figure eights; demolition events. Phone 360/794-7711. Apr-Sept.

Motels

★ ★ **BEST WESTERN CASCADIA INN.** *2800 Pacific Ave (98201). 425/258-4141; FAX 425/258-4755.* 134 rms, 3 story. S $65; D $93; each addl $4; suites $83-$149; under 18 free. Crib free. TV; cable (premium). Heated pool; whirlpool. Complimentary continental bkfst. Coffee in rms. Restaurant nearby open 24 hrs. Bar 11-1 am. Ck-out noon. Coin lndry. Meeting rms. Business servs avail. Health club privileges. Some refrigerators; microwaves avail. Cr cds: A, D, DS, MC, V.

✔★ **WELCOME MOTOR INN.** *1205 Broadway (98201). 425/252-8828; FAX 425/252-8880; res: 800/252-5512.* 42 rms, 2 story. July-Aug: S $38-$43; D $48-$52; each addl $5-$10; lower rates rest of yr. Crib $7. TV; cable (premium). Restaurant adj 5:30-10:30 pm. Ck-out 11 am. Microwaves avail. Cr cds: A, D, DS, MC, V.

Motor Hotel

★ ★ ★ **HOWARD JOHNSON PLAZA.** *3105 Pine St (98201), I-5 exit 193N, 194S. 425/339-3333; FAX 425/259-1547.* 247 rms, 7 story. S, D $99-$129; each addl $10; suites $195-$350; under 18 free. Crib free. TV; VCR avail. Indoor pool; whirlpool, poolside serv. Coffee in rms. Restaurant 6:30 am-10 pm. Rm serv. Bar 11-1:30 am; entertainment. Ck-out noon. Convention facilities. Business servs avail. Free covered parking. Exercise equipt; weight machines, bicycles, sauna. Some refrigerators; microwaves avail. Cr cds: A, C, D, DS, ER, JCB, MC, V.

Hotel

★ ★ ★ **MARINA VILLAGE INN.** *1728 W Marine View Dr (98201). 425/259-4040; FAX 425/252-8419; res: 800/281-7037.* 26 rms, 2 story, 16 suites. S, D $82-$160; each addl $20; suites $140-$229; under 18 free. Crib free. TV; VCR avail. Complimentary continental bkfst. Complimentary coffee in rms. Restaurant adj 7 am-10 pm. Ck-out noon. Business servs avail. Valet serv. Bathrm phones; many in-rm whirlpools. On Port Gardner Bay; view from many rms through large bay windows. Cr cds: A, C, D, DS, JCB, MC, V.

Forks (B-1)

Pop 2,862 **Elev** 375 ft **Area code** 360 **Zip** 98331
Information Chamber of Commerce, PO Box 1249; 360/374-2531 or 800/44-FORKS.

The major town in the northwest section of the Olympic Peninsula, Forks takes its name from the nearby junction of the Soleduck, Bogachiel and Dickey rivers. Timber processing is a major industry. A Ranger District office of the Olympic National Forest (see OLYMPIA) is located here.

What to See and Do

Bogachiel State Park. Approx 120 acres, on the shores of the Bogachiel River with swimming, fishing. Hiking. Camping (hookups, dump station). Standard fees. (Daily) 6 mi S on US 101. Phone 360/374-6356.

Olympic Natl Park (see). 3 mi E on unnumbered road.

Motels

★ ★ **FORKS.** *3 blks S on US 101. 360/374-6243; FAX 360/374-6760; res: 800/544-3416.* 73 rms, 1-2 story, 9 kits. Some A/C. June-Sept: S, D $45-$75; each addl $5; kit. units $5 addl; lower rates rest of yr. Crib $5. TV; cable. Heated pool; wading pool. Restaurant nearby. Ck-out 11 am. Coin lndry. Business servs avail. Cr cds: A, C, D, DS, MC, V.

✔★ **PACIFIC INN.** *352 Forks Ave (US 101). 360/374-9400; FAX 360/374-9402; res: 800/235-7344.* 34 rms, 2 story. Mid-May-Sept: S $48; D $53-$57; each addl $5; under 13 free; lower rates rest of yr. Crib $5. TV; cable. Complimentary coffee in lobby. Restaurant nearby. Ck-out 11 am. Coin lndry. Business servs avail. Cr cds: A, C, D, DS, MC, V.

Inn

★ **MANITOU LODGE.** *Kilmer Rd, 8 mi W on La Push Rd to Mora Rd, follow signs. 360/374-6295.* 7 rms, 2 story. No rm phones. June-Oct: S,D $60-$75; each addl $15; lower rates rest of yr. Children over 12 yrs only. Complimentary full bkfst. Ck-out 10:30 am, ck-in 4 pm. Exercise equipt; rower, bicycle. Balconies. Picnic tables, grills. Amidst 10 acres of rain forest. Totally nonsmoking. Cr cds: MC, V.

Resort

★ ★ **KALALOCH LODGE.** *157151 WA 101, 35 mi S on US 101. 360/962-2271; FAX 360/962-3391.* 8 rms in lodge, 10 motel rms, 2 story, 40 cabins, 34 kits. No A/C. No rm phones. June 7-Oct 5: lodge rms $76-$100; cabins $126-$176; suites $106; varied lower rates off season. Crib free. Pet accepted. Dining rm (public by res) 5-9 pm. Coffee shop 7 am-9 pm. Box lunches. Bar 4-10:45 pm; Sat, Sun from noon. Ck-out 11 am, ck-in 4 pm. Grocery. Gift shop. Fish/hunt guides. Some refrigerators, fireplaces. Some balconies. Cr cds: A, MC, V.

Goldendale (F-5)

Settled 1863 **Pop** 3,319 **Elev** 1,633 ft **Area code** 509 **Zip** 98620

Information Greater Goldendale Area Chamber of Commerce, Box 524; 509/773-3411.

Agriculture, aluminum smelting and an assortment of small industries comprise the major business of Goldendale, named for John J. Golden, a pioneer settler.

What to See and Do

Brooks Memorial State Park. More than 700 acres. Fishing. Hiking. Picnicking. Camping (hookups). Standard fees. 12 mi N on US 97. Phone 509/773-4611.

Goldendale Observatory. Nation's largest amateur-built Cassegrain telescope for public use; tours, demonstrations, displays, audiovisual programs. (Apr-Sept, Wed-Sun; rest of yr, schedule varies) 1602 Observatory Dr. Phone 509/773-3141.   **Free.**

Klickitat County Historical Museum. Furniture and exhibits from early days of Klickitat County, in 20-rm restored mansion. Gift shop. (Apr-Oct, daily; rest of yr, by appt) 127 W Broadway. Phone 509/773-4303. ¢¢

Maryhill Museum of Art. Constructed by Samuel Hill. Permanent exhibits include Rodin sculpture, European and American paintings, Russian icons, chess collection, French fashion mannequins, Native American baskets and artifacts. (Mid-Mar-mid-Nov, daily) 11 mi S on US 97, then 2 mi W on WA 14; 35 Maryhill Museum Dr. Phone 509/773-3733. ¢¢

Mt Adams Recreation Area. Lakes, streams, forests; excellent fishing, bird hunting. NW of town.

Annual Event

Klickitat County Fair and Rodeo. 4th wkend Aug.

Motels

✔★★ **FAR VUE.** 808 E Simcoe Dr. 509/773-5881; res: 800/358-5881. 48 rms, 2 story. S $42.50-$93; D $48.50-$93; each addl $6. Crib free. TV; cable. Heated pool. Restaurant 6 am-11 pm. Bar from 5 pm. Ck-out 11 am. Business servs avail. Free airport transportation. Refrigerators. View of Mt Adams & Mt Hood. Cr cds: A, C, D, MC, V.

D ≈ ⊠ 🐾 SC

★ **PONDEROSA.** 775 E Broadway St. 509/773-5842; FAX 509/773-4049. 28 rms, 2 story, 4 kits. S $34; D $40-$43; each addl $5; kit. units $5 addl. Pet accepted. TV; cable. Ck-out 11 am. Business servs avail. Cr cds: A, C, D, DS, MC, V.

✔ ⊠ 🐾 SC

Hoquiam (D-2)

(See also Aberdeen, Ocean Shores; also see Westport)

Settled 1859 **Pop** 8,972 **Elev** 10 ft **Area code** 206 **Zip** 98550

Information Grays Harbor Chamber of Commerce, 506 Duffy St, Aberdeen 98520; 360/532-1924 or 800/321-1924.

Twin city to Aberdeen, Hoquiam is the senior community of the two and the pioneer town of the Grays Harbor region. A deepwater port 12 miles from the Pacific, it docks cargo and fishing vessels, manufactures wood products and machine tools and cans the harvest of the sea.

What to See and Do

Hoquiam's "Castle." A 20-rm mansion built in 1897 by lumber tycoon Robert Lytle; antique furnishings; oak-columned entry hall; authentic Victorian atmosphere. (Summer, daily; rest of yr, wkends; closed Dec) 515 Chenault Ave. Phone 360/533-2005. ¢¢

Polson Park & Museum (1924). Restored 26-rm mansion; antiques; rose garden. (June-Aug, Wed-Sun; rest of yr, wkends) 1611 Riverside Ave. Phone 360/533-5862. ¢¢

Inn

★★ **LYTLE HOUSE.** 509 Chenault Ave. 360/533-2320; FAX 360/533-4025; res: 800/677-2320. 8 rms (2 with shared baths, 2 with shower only), 3 story. No A/C. No rm phones. Mid-May-Oct: S $65-$140; D $75-$150; each addl $15; lower rates rest of yr. Crib free. TV; cable, VCR avail. Complimentary full bkfst; afternoon refreshments. Restaurant nearby. Ck-out 11 am, ck-in 4-8 pm. Luggage handling. Business servs avail. Whirlpool. Built in 1897; antiques. Cr cds: A, D, MC, V.

D ⊠ 🐾 SC

Restaurants

✔★ **DUFFY'S.** 825 Simpson Ave. 360/532-1519. Hrs: 6 am-10 pm. Bar 11 am-11 pm. Semi-a la carte: bkfst $2.95-$8.50, lunch $3.25-$8.95, dinner $7.95-$13.95. Child's meals. Specializes in seafood, veal, wild blackberry pie. Family-style dining. Cr cds: A, D, DS, MC, V.

D

★★ **LEVEE STREET.** 709 Levee St. 360/532-1959. Hrs: 4:30-9:30 pm. Closed Sun, Mon; most major hols. Res accepted. No A/C. Complete meals: dinner $10.95-$19.95. Specialties: rack of lamb, chicken Oscar, crab-stuffed prawns. Overlooks Hoquiam River. Totally nonsmoking. Cr cds: A, DS, MC, V.

D ⊠

Issaquah (C-4)

(See also Bellevue, North Bend, Seattle)

Pop 7,786 **Elev** 100 ft **Area code** 425 **Zip** 98027

Information Chamber of Commerce, 155 NW Gilman Blvd; 425/392-7024.

Historic buildings and homes of Issaquah have been renovated and moved to a seven-acre farm site, called Gilman Village, where they now serve as specialty shops.

What to See and Do

Boehm's Chocolate Factory. The home of Boehm's Candies was built here in 1956 by Julius Boehm. The candy-making process and the Edelweiss Chalet, filled with artifacts, paintings and statues, can be toured. The Luis Trenker Kirch'l, a replica of a 12th-century Swiss chapel, was also built by Boehm. Tours by appt (May-Sept). 255 NE Gilman Blvd. Phone 425/392-6652.   **Free.**

Lake Sammamish State Park. Approx 430 acres. Swimming, fishing, boating (launch). Hiking. Picnicking. Standard fees. 2 mi W off I-90. Phone 425/455-7010.

Annual Event

Salmon Days Festival. Welcomes return of Northwest salmon to original home. Phone 425/392-0661. 1st full wkend Oct.

Motel

★ ★ **HOLIDAY INN.** *1801 12th Ave NW, at I-90 exit 15.* 425/392-6421; FAX 425/391-4650. 100 rms, 2 story. S $82; D $89; each addl $7; under 19 free. Crib free. TV; cable (premium). Heated pool; wading pool, poolside serv. Complimentary coffee in rms. Restaurant 6 am-2 pm, 5-10 pm. Rm serv. Bar. Ck-out noon. Coin lndry. Meeting rms. Business servs avail. In-rm modem link. Cr cds: A, C, D, DS, ER, JCB, MC, V.

Kelso (E-3)

(See also Longview)

Founded 1847 **Pop** 11,820 **Elev** 40 ft **Area code** 360 **Zip** 98626
Information Chamber of Commerce, 105 Minor Rd; 360/577-8058.

Kelso straddles the Cowlitz River and is an artery for the lumber industry. The river also yields a variety of fish from giant salmon to tiny smelt.

What to See and Do

Cowlitz County Historical Museum. Exhibits depict history of the area. (Daily exc Mon; closed hols) 405 Allen St. Phone 360/577-3119. **Free.**

Seaquest State Park. Approx 300 acres. Hiking. Picnicking. Camping (hookups). Nearby is Silver Lake with fishing (about 10,000 fish are caught here every summer). Standard fees. 10 mi N on I-5 exit 49, then 5 mi E on WA 504. Phone 360/274-8633.

Volcano Information Center. Pictorial and scientific exhibits on the eruption of Mt St Helens; Three-dimensional narrated topographical display of the devastation. Also visitor information on surrounding area. (May-Oct, daily; rest of yr, Wed-Sun; closed major hols) 105 Minor Rd, off I-5 exit 39. Phone 360/577-8058. **Free.**

Annual Event

Highlander Festival. Highland games, arts & crafts fair, entertainment, parade. Sept.

Motels

★ **COMFORT INN.** *440 Three Rivers Dr, I-5 exit 39.* 360/425-4600; FAX 360/423-0762. 57 rms, 2 story. S $60-$85; D $65-$85; each addl $5; under 18 free. Crib free. TV; cable (premium), VCR. Indoor pool; whirlpool. Complimentary continental bkfst. Restaurant nearby. Ck-out noon. Business servs avail. In-rm modem link. Valet serv. Game rm. Cr cds: A, C, D, DS, ER, JCB, MC, V.

★ ★ **DOUBLETREE.** *510 Kelso Dr, I-5 exit 39.* 360/636-4400; FAX 360/425-3296. 162 rms, 2 story. S, D $79; each addl $20; suites $175; under 18 free; wkend rates. Crib free. Pet accepted. TV; cable (premium), VCR avail. Heated pool; wading pool, poolside serv. Restaurant 6 am-10 pm; Fri, Sat to 11 pm. Rm serv. Bar 11-1:30 am; entertainment Fri, Sat. Ck-out noon. Meeting rms. Business servs avail. Cr cds: A, C, D, DS, ER, JCB, MC, V.

✓★ **MOUNT ST HELENS.** *(1340 Mt St Helens, Castle Rock 98611) 10 mi N on I-5, exit 49.* 360/274-7721. 32 rms, 2 story. AC upper level only. S $35; D $38-$48; each addl $6; under 6 free. Crib free. Pet accepted; $6. TV; cable. Complimentary coffee in lobby. Restaurant adj 6:30 am-11 pm. Ck-out 11 am. Coin lndry. Meeting rms. Some refrigerators. Cr cds: A, C, D, DS, MC, V.

Kennewick (E-7)

(See also Pasco, Richland)

Founded 1892 **Pop** 42,155 **Elev** 380 ft **Area code** 509
Information Chamber of Commerce, 1600 N 20th St, PO Box 550, Pasco 99301; 509/547-9755.

Huge hydroelectric dams harnessing the lower stem of the Columbia River have brought economic vitality to the "Tri-Cities" of Kennewick, Pasco and Richland. On the south bank of Lake Wallula and near the confluence of the Columbia, Snake and Yakima rivers, Kennewick has chemical and agricultural processing plants. Irrigation of the 20,500-acre Kennewick Highland project has converted sagebrush into thousands of farms, producing three cuttings of alfalfa annually, corn and beans. Appropriately enough, this city with the Native American name "winter paradise" enjoys a brief winter and is the center of the state's grape industry.

What to See and Do

Columbia Park. Approx 300 acres. Waterskiing; fishing; boating (ramps). 18-hole golf, driving range (fee); tennis. Picnicking. Camping (hookups; fee). Park open all yr (daily). 2 1/2 mi W on US 12 on Lake Wallula, formed by McNary Dam. Phone 509/783-3711. **Free.**

Two Rivers Park. Picnicking; boating (ramp), swimming, fishing. Park open all yr (daily). 5 mi E, off Finley Rd. Phone 509/783-3118. **Free.**

Motels

★ ★ ★ **CAVANAUGH'S AT COLUMBIA CENTER.** *1101 N Columbia Center Blvd (99336).* 509/783-0611; FAX 509/735-3087; res: 800/843-4667. 162 rms, 2 story. S $77, D $87; each addl $5; suites $90-$280; studio rms $75-$85; golf plans. Crib free. Pet accepted. TV; cable (premium), VCR avail. Pool; whirlpool. Restaurant 6:30 am-9 pm. Rm serv. Bar 11-2 am; entertainment Tues-Sat. Ck-out noon. Meeting rms. Business servs avail. Sundries. Airport, RR station, bus depot transportation. Private patios, balconies. Cr cds: A, C, D, DS, MC, V.

★ **NENDELS INN.** *2811 W 2nd (99336).* 509/735-9511; FAX 509/735-1944; res: 800/547-0106. 104 rms, 3 story, 19 kits. S $45; D $50-$53; each addl $5; kit. units $50; under 12 free; higher rates boat race wkends. Crib free. Pet accepted; $5. TV; cable. Heated pool. Restaurant nearby. Ck-out noon. Business servs avail. Some refrigerators. Cr cds: A, C, D, DS, MC, V.

✓★ ★ **SILVER CLOUD INN.** *7901 W Quinault Ave (99336).* 509/735-6100; FAX 509/735-3084. 125 rms, 4 story, 30 suites. S $45-$56; D $56-$60; each addl $6; suites $50-$100; under 18 free; higher rates boat races. Crib free. TV; cable (premium). 2 pools, 1 indoor; whirlpool. Complimentary continental bkfst, coffee. Restaurant opp open 24 hrs. Ck-out noon. Guest lndry. Meeting rms. Business servs avail. Concierge. Airport, RR station transportation. Exercise equipt; weights, bicycles. Refrigerators. Cr cds: A, C, D, DS, MC, V.

★ **TAPADARA INN.** *300 N Ely (99336), on WA 395.* 509/783-6191; FAX 509/735-3854. 61 rms, 2 story. May-Sept: S $40; D $47-$50; each addl $7; under 13 free; higher rates hydro races; lower rates rest of yr. Crib free. Pet accepted; $5. TV; cable (premium), VCR avail. Heated pool. Complimentary coffee in lobby. Restaurant adj 6 am-11 pm. Bar 11-2 am. Ck-out noon. Some refrigerators. Cr cds: A, C, D, DS, MC, V.

Restaurant

✓★ ★ BLACKBERRY'S. 329 N Kellogg (99336). 509/735-7253. Hrs: 7 am-9 pm; Sun, Mon to 2 pm. Closed some major hols. Wine. Semi-a la carte: bkfst $3.95-$6.95, lunch $3.95-$6.95, dinner $5.95-$12. Child's meals. Specializes in prime rib, chicken, salads. Antique oak furnishings. Totally nonsmoking. Cr cds: A, D, DS, MC, V.

La Conner (B-3)

(See also Anacortes, Mount Vernon)

Pop 656 **Area code** 360 **Zip** 98257
Information Chamber of Commerce, PO Box 1610; 360/466-4778.

A picturesque town along the Swinomish Channel, La Conner is a popular destination for weekend travelers. Many of the town's homes and businesses are housed in the clapboarded structures built by its founders around the turn of the century. Numerous boutiques, galleries and antique shops, some containing the works of local artists and craftspeople, line its streets.

What to See and Do

Museum of Northwest Art. Exhibits artist of the "Northwest School." (Tues-Sun; closed Jan 1, Thanksgiving, Dec 25) 121 S 1st St. Phone 360/466-4446. ¢¢

Skagit County Historical Museum. Exhibits depicting history of Skagit County. (Tues-Sun afternoons; closed Jan 1, Thanksgiving, Dec 25) 501 Fourth St. Phone 360/466-3365. ¢

Inns

★ ★ ★ COUNTRY INN. 107 Second St. 360/466-3101; FAX 360/466-5902. Web useattle.uspan.com/laconner/. 28 rms, 2 story. No A/C. S, D $89-$144; each addl $20; under 13 free. Crib free. TV; cable (premium). Complimentary continental bkfst. Dining rm 11:30 am-3 pm, 5-10 pm; Sun from 5 pm. Rm serv. Ck-out noon, ck-in 3 pm. Business servs avail. Free airport transportation. Cedar lodge building; many antiques, large fireplace in common area. Cr cds: A, C, D, DS, MC, V.

★ ★ THE HERON. 117 Maple Ave. 360/466-4626; FAX 360/466-3254. 12 rms, 3 story, 3 suites. No A/C. S, D $75-$95; suites $120-$160. Pet accepted, some restrictions. TV. Complimentary continental bkfst. Restaurant nearby. Ck-out 11 am, ck-in 3 pm. Whirlpool. Victorian-style inn. Stone fireplace in parlor. Cr cds: A, MC, V.

★ ★ ★ KATY'S. 503 S Third. 360/466-3366; res: 800/914-7767. 5 rms, 2 story, 2 share bath. No A/C. No rm phones. Mid-Mar-mid-Oct: S $60-$105; D $70-$115; each addl $20; lower rates rest of yr. Crib free. TV in 1 rm; cable, VCR avail (movies). Complimentary full bkfst; afternoon refreshments. Restaurant nearby. Ck-out 11 am, ck-in 4-6 pm. Luggage handling. Whirlpool. Many balconies. Picnic tables. Built in 1876; Victorian style. Cr cds: DS, MC, V.

★ ★ RAINBOW. 1075 Chilberg Rd. 360/466-4578. 8 rms, 3 share bath, 3 story. No rm phones. S $65-$85; D $75-$95; each addl $15. Complimentary full bkfst. Ck-out 11 am, ck-in 3-6 pm. Bus depot, RR station transportation. Whirlpool. Lawn games. Balconies. Picnic tables. Farmhouse (1907); view of mountains. Totally nonsmoking. Cr cds: DS, MC, V.

Leavenworth (C-5)

(See also Cashmere, Wenatchee)

Founded 1892 **Pop** 1,692 **Elev** 1,165 ft **Area code** 509 **Zip** 98826
E-mail info@leavenworth.org **Web** www.leavenworth.org
Information Chamber of Commerce, PO Box 327; 509/548-5807.

Surrounded by the Cascade Mountains, Leavenworth has an old world charm enhanced by authentic Bavarian architecture. Less than three hours from Seattle, the village is a favorite stop for people who enjoy river rafting, hiking, bicycling, fishing, golf or skiing. Two Ranger District offices of the Wenatchee National Forest (see WENATCHEE) are located here.

What to See and Do

Icicle Junction. Family fun park offers 18-hole Bavarian-theme miniature golf, excursion train, bumper boats, ice-skating, interactive arcade. Party facilities. Fee for each activity. (Summer, daily; winter hrs may vary) Jct US 2 & Icicle Rd. Phone 509/548-2400.

Natl Fish Hatchery. Raises chinook salmon and steelhead. Educational exhibits. Hiking, interpretive trails. Picniking. Fishing; boat ramp. Cross-country skiing. (Daily; closed Dec 25) 3½ mi S on Icicle Creek Rd. Phone 509/548-7641. **Free.**

Nutcracker Museum. Displays more than 3,000 nutcrackers. (May-Oct, daily; rest of yr, wkends; also by appt) 735 Front St. Phone 509/548-4708. ¢¢

Stevens Pass Ski Area. Quad, 4 triple, 6 double chairlifts; patrol, school, rentals; restaurant, cafeteria, bar; nursery. (Late Nov-mid-Apr, daily) 36 mi NW on US 2. Phone 206/973-2441. ¢¢¢¢

Annual Events

Bavarian Ice Fest. Snowshoe races, dogsled rides. Fireworks. Jan 17 & 18.

Maifest. Bandstand music, grand march, Maypole dance, art, chuck wagon breakfast. May 8-10.

Autumn Leaf Festival. Sept 25-27 and Oct 2-4.

Christmas Lighting. Sleigh rides, sledding. Dec 5 & 12.

Motels

★ ★ BEST WESTERN ICICLE INN. 505 US 2W. 509/548-7000; FAX 509/548-7050; res: 800/558-2438. 65 rms, 3 story. Mid-June-mid-Sept: S $75; D $85; each addl $10; under 12 free; higher rates special events; lower rates rest of yr. Crib free. TV; cable, VCR avail. Pool; whirlpool. Complimentary bkfst buffet. Ck-out 11 am. Meeting rms. Business servs avail. Exercise equipt; bicycles, treadmill. Some refrigerators. Balconies. Bavarian-style architecture. Cr cds: A, D, DS, JCB, MC, V.

★ ★ DER RITTERHOF. 190 US 2. 509/548-5845; res: 800/255-5845. 51 rms, 2 story, 5 kits. S, D $68-$74; each addl $8; kit. units $74. Crib free. Pet accepted. TV; cable, VCR avail. Heated pool; whirlpool. Restaurant opp 7 am-11 pm. Ck-out 11 am. Business servs avail. Putting green. X-country ski 1 mi. Lawn games. Private patios, balconies. Picnic table, grill. Cr cds: A, MC, V.

★ ★ ENZIAN MOTOR INN. 590 US 2. 509/548-5269; FAX 508/442-5269; res: 800/223-8511. 104 rms, 2-4 story. S $78-$88; D $92-$114; each addl $10; suites $152-$167; under 6 free. Crib free. TV; cable. 2 pools, 1 indoor; whirlpool. Complimentary full bkfst. Restaurant nearby.

Ck-out 11 am. Meeting rms. Exercise equipt; bicycles, stair machine. Some balconies. Cr cds: A, C, D, DS, MC, V.

Inns

✔★ **HAUS ROHRBACH PENSION.** *12882 Ranger Rd.* 509/548-7024; FAX 509/548-5038; res: 800/548-4477. 12 units, some share bath, 1-3 story, 3 suites. No elvtr. No rm phones. S $65-$95; D $75-$105; each addl $20; suites $160-$170; wkly rates. Crib free. Pool; whirlpool. Complimentary bkfst. Restaurant nearby. Ck-out 11 am, ck-in 2 pm. Free bus depot transportation. X-country ski 1 mi. Balconies. Picnic tables. Austrian chalet-style inn. At base of mountain. Totally nonsmoking. Cr cds: A, D, DS, MC, V.

★ ★ **RUN OF THE RIVER.** *9308 E Leavenworth.* 509/548-7171; FAX 509/548-7547; res: 800/288-6491. 6 air-cooled rms. No rm phones. S $80-$130; D $95-$150. Adults only. TV; cable. Complimentary full bkfst, coffee & tea. Ck-out 11 am, ck-in 3 pm. Business servs avail. X-country ski 2 mi. Whirlpool. Balconies. Picnic tables. Hand-hewn log furnishings and construction. Decks with views of forest and mountains; on bank of Icicle River. Totally nonsmoking. Cr cds: A, D, DS, MC, V.

Restaurant

✔★ **CAFE CHRISTA.** *801 Front St.* 509/548-5074. Hrs: 11 am-10 pm. Closed Thanksgiving, Dec 25. Res accepted; required hols. German, Amer menu. Wine, beer. Semi-a la carte: lunch $5-$8, dinner $9.95-$17. Specializes in Wienerschnitzel, Kassler Ripperspeer. Alpine atmosphere. View of downtown. Cr cds: MC, V.

Long Beach (E-1)

Pop 1,236 **Elev** 10 ft **Area code** 360 **Zip** 98631

Information Peninsula Visitors Bureau, PO Box 562; 360/642-2400 or 800/451-2542.

This seashore resort is on one of the longest hard sand beaches in the world, stretching 28 miles along a narrow peninsula, just north of where the Columbia River empties into the Pacific Ocean.

What to See and Do

Oysterville. Community founded in 1854; original settlers were lured by oysters found on tidal flats of Willapa Bay. Many original homes remain, as well as church & schoolhouse. 15 mi N via Sandridge Rd. For information on walking tours, phone 360/642-2400 or 800/451-2542.

Seascape scenic drive. 14 mi N from Seaview on WA 103, through Long Beach to Ocean Park.

State historic parks.

Ft Canby (1864). More than 1,880 acres overlooking mouth of Columbia River. Strategic base from pioneer days through World War II. The Lewis & Clark Interpretive Center, built near an artillery bunker on a hillside, has exhibits depicting the historic expedition and the contributions made by Native American tribes; also multimedia presentations (daily). Fishing. Hiking. Picnicking. Camping (hookups). Standard fees. (Daily) 2 mi S on WA 100, in Ilwaco. Phone 360/642-3078 or 800/452-5687 (res).

Ft Columbia. More than 580 acres. Site of former coastal artillery corps post with Endicott-period fortifications that protected mouth of Columbia River. Interpretive center in former barracks (Apr-Sept, daily) Also here is Columbia House, a former commander's residence. Hiking. Picnick-

ing. Grounds (Apr-Sept, Wed-Sun). 11 mi SE on US 101. Phone 360/777-8755. **Free.**

Motels

★ **ANCHORAGE MOTOR COURT.** *22nd NW & Boulevard N.* 360/642-2351; FAX 360/642-8730; res: 800/646-2351. 9 kit. units (1-2 bedrm). No A/C. July-Sept: S $58.50-$68.50; D $88.50; each addl $10; lower rates rest of yr. Crib free. Pet accepted, some restrictions; $5-$10. TV; cable. Playground. Restaurant nearby. Ck-out 11 am. Lawn games. Fireplaces (free firewood). Most units overlook ocean. Cr cds: A, DS, MC, V.

★ ★ **BREAKERS.** *Box 428, 1 mi N on WA 103.* 360/642-4414; FAX 360/642-8890. 114 rms, 3 story, 53 kits. No A/C. June-Labor Day: S, D $65-$77; suites $115-$175; kit. units $65-$77; lower rates rest of yr. Crib free. Pet accepted; $7. TV; cable. VCR avail. Heated pool; whirlpool. Restaurant nearby. Ck-out 11 am. Meeting rm. Business servs avail. Some refrigerators. Private patios, balconies. Public golf adj. Cr cds: A, D, DS, MC, V.

✔★ **CHAUTAUQUA LODGE.** *304 14th St NW.* 360/642-4401; FAX 360/642-2340; res: 800/869-8401. 180 units, 3 story, 60 kits. No A/C. June-Sept: S, D $55-$100; each addl $5; suites $115-$160; kit. units $85-$115; lower rates rest of yr. Crib $2. Pet accepted, some restrictions; $8. TV; VCR avail. Indoor pool; whirlpool, sauna. Restaurant adj 8 am-10 pm; winter from 11 am. Bar 4 pm-1 am. Ck-out 11 am. Coin lndry. Meeting rms. Business servs avail. Sundries. Rec rm. Refrigerators. Private patios, balconies. On beach. Cr cds: A, D, DS, MC, V.

★ **NENDELS EDGEWATER INN.** *409 10th St SW.* 360/642-2311; FAX 360/642-8018; res: 800/547-0106. 84 rms, 3 story. Mid-May-Sept: S, D $70-$108; lower rates rest of yr. Crib $3. Pet accepted, some restrictions. TV; cable (premium), VCR avail. Coffee in rms. Ck-out 11 am. Ocean view. Cr cds: A, D, DS, MC, V.

✔★ **OUR PLACE AT THE BEACH.** *1309 South Blvd.* 360/642-3793; FAX 360/642-3896; res: 800/538-5107. 25 rms, 1-2 story, 4 kits. May-Oct: S, D $45-$59; each addl $5; kit. units $64-$75; some lower rates rest of yr. Crib $1. Pet accepted; $5. TV. Coffee in rms. Restaurant nearby. Ck-out 11 am. Meeting rms. Business servs avail. Exercise equipt; bicycles, rowers, sauna. Whirlpool. Refrigerators. Picnic tables. Pathway to beach. Cr cds: A, C, D, DS, MC, V.

★ ★ **SHAMAN.** *115 3rd St SW, 1 blk W off WA 103.* 360/642-3714; FAX 360/642-8599; res: 800/753-3750. 42 rms, 2 story, 20 kits. No A/C. Mid-May-Sept: S $59-$84; D, kit. units $59-$79; lower rates rest of yr. Crib free. Pet accepted, some restrictions; $5. TV; cable, VCR avail (movies). Heated pool. Restaurant adj 7 am-11 pm. Ck-out 11 am. Business servs avail. Some refrigerators, fireplaces (log supplied). Cr cds: A, C, D, DS, MC, V.

★ **SUPER 8.** *500 Ocean Beach Blvd.* 360/642-8988; FAX 360/642-8986. 50 rms, 3 story. No A/C. May-Sept: S $64-$114; D $74-$124; each addl $5; under 12 free; lower rates rest of yr. Crib free. TV; VCR avail (movies avail $2.50). Complimentary continental bkfst. Restaurant adj 7 am-10 pm. Ck-out noon. Coin lndry. Meeting rms. Business servs avail. Sundries. Free airport transportation. Cr cds: A, C, D, DS, MC, V.

Inns

★ ★ **BOREAS BED & BREAKFAST.** *607 Boulevard Ave.* 360/642-8069. 4 rms, 2 with shower only, 2 share bath, 2 story. No A/C. No rm phones. May-Sept: S $75-$85; D $85-$95; each addl $10; family, wkly rates; 2-day min wkends, 3-day min hols; lower rates rest of yr. Complimentary full bkfst, afternoon tea/sherry. Restaurant nearby. Ck-out noon, ck-in 3 pm. Luggage handling. 1920s beachhouse with antiques; library. Totally nonsmoking. Cr cds: MC, V.

★ ★ **CHICK-A-DEE.** *(Box 922, 120 Williams St NE, Ilwaco 98624)* S on WA 103. 360/642-8686; FAX 360/642-8642. 10 rms, 2 story. No A/C. No rm phones. June-Nov: S, D $60-$150; each addl $15; lower rates rest of yr. Complimentary full bkfst; afternoon refreshments. Restaurant nearby. Ck-out noon, ck-in 2 pm. Business servs avail. Free airport transportation. Located in renovated church building. Totally nonsmoking. Cr cds: MC, V.

★ ★ **SCANDINAVIAN GARDENS INN.** *1610 California St.* 360/642-8877; FAX 360/642-8763; res: 800/988-9277. 5 rms (1 with shower only), 2 story, 1 suite. No A/C. No rm phones. S $65-$115; D $75-$125; each addl $15. Children over 2 yrs only. Full bkfst. Complimentary coffee in library. Restaurant nearby. Ck-out 11 am, ck-in 3-6 pm. Business servs avail. Free airport transportation. Whirlpool. Sauna. Game rm. Some refrigerators. Each rm decorated to theme of different Scandinavian country. Totally nonsmoking. Cr cds: DS, MC, V.

Restaurants

★ ★ **SANCTUARY RESTAURANT.** *(US 101 & Hazel St, Chinook)* 7 mi SE on US 101. 360/777-8380. Hrs: 5-9 pm. Closed Mon, Tues. Res accepted. Serv bar. Semi-a la carte: dinner $10.50-$17.95. Child's meals. Specializes in fresh local seafood, pasta, chicken. Outdoor dining. High ceiling, stained glass, soft lighting. Former church, built 1906. Cr cds: A, C, D, MC, V.

★ ★ ★ **SHOALWATER.** *(WA 103, Seaview 98644)* 1 mi S on WA 103, at 45th St. 360/642-4142. In this historic building (1896) filled with stained glass, natural wood and antiques, nationally acclaimed Northwest cuisine is served. Ingredients range from the freshest local fish to mushrooms and salad greens gathered from the peninsula's woods and gardens. Specializes in oysters, pasta, salmon. Own breads. Hrs: 11:30 am-3 pm, 5:30-9 pm; Sun brunch 10 am-2:30 pm. Closed Dec 25. Res accepted. No A/C. Bar from noon. Semi-a la carte: lunch $3.95-$8.50, dinner $13.50-$24. Child's meals. Cr cds: A, C, D, DS, MC, V.

Longview (E-3)

(For accommodations see Chehalis, Kelso)

Settled 1923 **Pop** 31,499 **Elev** 21 ft **Area code** 360 **Zip** 98632 **E-mail** longview-chamber@tdn.com
Information Longview Area Chamber of Commerce, 1563 Olympia Way; 360/423-8400.

Longview is the home of one of the largest forest products mill in the world. Factories produce pulp, fine and kraft papers, paper boxes, plywood, glassine, pig aluminum, concrete paint, caustic soda and chlorine. The first planned city in the West, Longview is a deepwater port fed by six railroad systems and several highways. Fishing for steelhead, smelt and salmon is excellent.

What to See and Do

Lake Sacajawea Park. A 120-acre park with 60-acre lake; picnic areas, playgrounds; gardens. Jogging, bike and fitness trail. Fishing, wildlife refuge. (Daily) Between Kessler & Nichols Blvds, US 30 & WA 432. **Free.**

Monticello Convention Site. Here residents of Washington met to petition the federal government to separate Washington Territory from Oregon. Olympia Way & Maple St.

Mt St Helens Visitor Center. (See MOUNT ST HELENS NATIONAL VOLCANIC MONUMENT) 10 mi N on I-5 to Castle Rock, then 5 mi E on WA 504.

Annual Events

Intl Festival. Lower Columbia College. Early May.

Cowlitz County Fair. Fairgrounds. Exhibits, entertainment, carnival, pro rodeo. Early Aug.

Marysville (B-4)

(See also Everett)

Settled 1872 **Pop** 10,328 **Elev** 15 ft **Area code** 360 **E-mail** chamber@marysville-tulalip.com **Web** www.marysville-tulalip.com
Information The Greater Marysville Tulalip Chamber of Commerce, 4411 76th St NE, 98270; 360/659-7700.

Natural surroundings, including lakes, rivers, and wooded countryside, make Marysville a popular spot for outdoor recreation.

What to See and Do

Tulalip Reservation. Within the community are St Anne's Church (1904) with old mission bell, the Native American Shaker Church and tribal community center. 6 mi NW via WA 506. Phone 360/651-4000.

Wenberg State Park. A 46-acre park. Swimming, fishing, boating (launch). Picnicking, concession (summer). Camping (some hookups). Standard fees. N via I-5 exit 206, 2 mi W to Lakewood Rd, then 3 mi N to E Lake Goodwin Rd, then S. Phone 360/652-7417.

Annual Events

Strawberry Festival. Parade, art show, races. Phone 360/659-7664. 3rd wk June.

Home-Grown Festival. 3rd & State Sts. Open-air market, arts & crafts booths, street fair. Early Aug.

Merrysville for the Holidays. Water-tower lighting, lighted holiday parade. Phone 360/659-3005. Early Dec.

Motel

✓ ★ **VILLAGE MOTOR INN.** *235 Beach Ave (98270).* 360/659-0005; FAX 360/658-0866. 45 rms, 3 story, 6 suites. S $50-$57; D $55-$62; each addl $5; suites $75-$130; under 12 free; monthly rates. Pet accepted, some restrictions. TV; cable (premium). Complimentary continental bkfst. Complimentary coffee in rms. Restaurant adj. Ck-out 11 am. Meeting rms. Business servs avail. In-rm modem link. Valet serv. Refrigerators avail. Cr cds: A, C, D, DS, MC, V.

Restaurant

★ **THE VILLAGE.** *220 Ash Ave (98270), SE of I-5 exit 199.* 360/659-2305. Hrs: 5 am-10 pm; Mon, Tues to 9 pm; Fri, Sat to midnight. Closed Dec 25. Bar. Semi-a la carte: bkfst $3.25-$7.50, lunch $4-$7, dinner $5-$12.95. Child's meals. Specializes in steak, seafood. Own pies. Totally nonsmoking. Cr cds: A, D, DS, MC, V.

D **SC**

Moclips (C-1)

Pop 700 (est) **Elev** 10 ft **Area code** 360 **Zip** 98562 **E-mail** wacoast @techline.com

Information Washington Coast Chamber, 2602 WA 109, Ocean City 98569; 360/289-4552 or 800/286-4452.

Motels

★ **HI-TIDE OCEAN BEACH RESORT.** *3 mi N of Pacific Beach just off WA 109, on Pacific Ocean. 360/276-4142; res: 800/662-5477 (WA).* 25 kit. suites, 2 story. No A/C. Mid-June-mid-Oct: kit. suites $84-$159; each addl $10; under 5 free; wkly rates; lower rates rest of yr. Crib free. Pet accepted; $10/day. TV; cable, VCR avail. Restaurant nearby. Ck-out 11 am. Business servs avail. Lawn games. Fireplaces. Health club privileges. Private patios, balconies. Cr cds: A, DS, MC, V.

D **≈** **⚑** **≈** **🔥** **SC**

★ ★ **OCEAN CREST RESORT.** *1 mi S; 1 mi N of Pacific Beach on WA 109. 360/276-4465; FAX 360/276-4149; res: 800/684-8439.* 45 rms, 1-3 story, 19 kits. (no oven in 5). No A/C. June-mid-Sept: S, D $56-$130; each addl $5.50-$11; kit. units $92-$130; lower rates rest of yr. Crib $3. TV; cable, VCR avail (movies $2). Indoor pool; whirlpool. Restaurant 8 am-9 pm. Bar. Ck-out 11 am. Coin lndry. Business servs avail. Sundries. Exercise equipt; weights, treadmill, sauna. Fireplaces. Some balconies. On cliff overlooking ocean. Cr cds: A, DS, MC, V.

D **≈** **🏃** **≈** **🔥** **SC**

Moses Lake (D-7)

(See also Ephrata)

Settled 1910 **Pop** 11,235 **Elev** 1,060 ft **Area code** 509 **Zip** 98837
Information Chamber of Commerce, 324 S Pioneer Way; 509/765-7888.

Because of the water impounded by Grand Coulee Dam, the recreational and agricultural resources of this area have blossomed. Swimming, fishing and hunting abound within a 25-mile radius. The city is also an important shipping and processing point for agricultural products.

What to See and Do

Adam East Museum. Native American artifacts; regional artwork; local history. (Tues-Sat afternoons; closed major hols) 3rd & Ash Sts. Phone 509/766-9395. **Free.**

Moses Lake Recreation Area. S & W of city. **Free.** Includes

Moses Lake. 18 mi long. NW off I-90, WA 17.

Potholes Reservoir. Formed by O'Sullivan Dam (10 mi S). Swimming, boating, waterskiing, fishing. 25 mi SW off WA 17, I-90 on WA 170.

Potholes State Park. Approx 2,500 acres. Water sports; fishing; boat launch. Hiking. Picnicking. Camping (hookups). Standard fees. 14 mi SW on WA 17 to WA 170.

Moses Lake State Park. A 78-acre park with swimming, fishing, boating (launch). Picnicking. (Wkends and hols; day use only) 2 mi W on I-90. Phone 509/765-5852.

Cascade Park. Swimming, boating (launch), fishing, waterskiing. Camping (fee). Park (mid-Apr-mid-Oct, daily). Valley Rd & Cascade Valley. Phone 509/766-9240.

Annual Events

Spring Festival. Memorial Day wkend.

Grant County Fair. Fairgrounds. Rodeo. 5 days mid-Aug.

Motels

★ **EL RANCHO.** *1214 S Pioneer Way, I-90 exit 179, then 1½ mi N. 509/765-9173; FAX 509/765-1137; res: 800/341-8000.* 21 rms, 9 kits. S $30-$40; D $40-$46; each addl $3; kit. units $4 addl; higher rates: Spring Festival, Grant County Fair. Crib $3.50. Pet accepted, some restrictions. TV; cable (premium). Heated pool. Restaurant nearby. Ck-out 11 am. Refrigerators. Cr cds: A, D, DS, MC, V.

⚑ **≈** **≈** **🔥** **SC**

✔ ★ **INTERSTATE INN.** *2801 W Broadway, at I-90 Business exit 176. 509/765-1777; FAX 509/766-9452; res: 800/777-5889.* 30 rms, 2 story. S $39-$42; D $49-$54; each addl $3; family, wkly rates. Crib $3.50. Pet accepted. TV; cable (premium), VCR avail. Indoor pool; whirlpool, sauna. Restaurant adj open 24 hrs. Ck-out 11 am. Business servs avail. Some refrigerators. Cr cds: A, C, D, DS, MC, V.

⚑ **≈** **≈** **🔥** **SC**

★ **MOTEL 6.** *2822 Wapato Dr. 509/766-0250; FAX 509/766-7762.* 111 rms, 2 story. S $28.99; D $34.99; each addl $6; under 18 free. Crib free. Pool. TV; cable (premium). Restaurant opp open 24 hrs. Ck-out noon. Cr cds: A, C, D, DS, MC, V.

≈ **≈** **🔥**

★ ★ **SHILO INN.** *1819 E Kittleson Rd. 509/765-9317; FAX 509/765-5058.* 100 rms, 2 story. 6 kits. Late May-mid-Sept: S, D $69-$85; each addl $6; kits. $89-$105; under 12 free; wkly rates; lower rates rest of yr. Crib free. TV; cable (premium). Indoor pool; whirlpool. Restaurant open 24 hrs. Serv bar (beer) 11-2 am. Ck-out noon. Coin lndry. Meeting rms. Business servs avail. Valet serv. Sundries. Gift shop. Free airport, bus depot transportation. Exercise equipt; weight machine, bicycles, sauna. Game rm. Bathrm phones, refrigerators, wet bars. Cr cds: A, C, D, DS, ER, JCB, MC, V.

D **≈** **🏃** **≈** **🔥** **SC**

Motor Hotel

★ ★ ★ **BEST WESTERN HALLMARK INN.** *3000 Marina Dr, I-90 exit 176. 509/765-9211; FAX 509/766-0493.* 160 rms, 2-3 story. S, D $75-$95; each addl $5; suites $100-$150; under 12 free. Crib free. Pet accepted, some restrictions. TV; cable (premium), VCR avail. Pool; wading pool, whirlpool, sauna. Restaurant 7 am-10 pm. Rm serv. Bar 11:30-2 am; entertainment exc Sun. Ck-out noon. Coin lndry. Meeting rms. Business servs avail. Valet serv. Free airport transportation. Tennis. Refrigerators. Many private patios, balconies. On lake; dock. Cr cds: A, C, D, DS, JCB, MC, V.

⚑ **🏃** **≈** **≈** **🔥** **SC**

Mount Rainier National Park (D-4)

(See also Packwood)

Majestic Mount Rainier, towering 14,411 feet above sea level and 8,000 feet above the Cascade Range of western Washington, is one of America's outstanding tourist attractions. More than two million people visit this 378-square-mile park each year to picnic, hike, camp, climb mountains or simply admire the spectacular scenery along the many miles of roadways.

The park's various "life zones," which change at different elevations, support a wide array of plant and animal life. Douglas fir, red cedar and western hemlock, some rising 200 feet into the air, thrive in the old-growth forests. In the summer, the subalpine meadows come alive with brilliant, multi-colored wildflowers. These areas are home to more than 130 species of birds and 50 species of mammals. Mountain goats, chipmunks and marmots are favorites among visitors, but deer, elk, bears, mountain lions and other animals can also be seen here.

Mount Rainier is the largest volcano in the Cascade Range, which extends from Mount Garibaldi in southwestern British Columbia to Lassen Peak in northern California. The eruption of Mount St Helens in 1980 gives a clue to the violent history of these volcanoes. Eruptions occurred at Mount Rainier as recently as the mid-1800s. Even today, steam emissions often form caves in the summit ice cap and usually melt the snow along the rims of the twin craters.

A young volcano by geologic standards, Mount Rainier was once a fairly symmetrical mountain rising about 16,000 feet above sea level. But glaciers and further volcanic activity shaped the mountain into an irregular mass of rock. The sculpting action of the ice gave each face of the mountain its own distinctive profile. The glaciation continues today, as Mount Rainier supports the largest glacier system in the contiguous United States, with 35 square miles of ice and 26 named glaciers.

Much of the park's beauty can be attributed to the glaciers, which at one time extended far beyond the park boundaries. The moving masses of ice carved deep valleys separated by high, sharp ridges or broad plateaus. From certain vantages, the valleys accentuate the mountain's height. The glaciers are the source of the many streams in the park, as well as several rivers in the Pacific Northwest. The meltwaters also nourish the various plants and animals throughout the region.

Winters at Mount Rainier are legendary. Moist air masses moving eastward across the Pacific Ocean are intercepted by the mountain. As a result, some areas on the mountain commonly receive 50 or more feet of snow each winter. Paradise, at 5,400 feet in elevation, made history in 1971-1972, when it received 93 feet of snow, the heaviest snowfall ever recorded in this country; the three-story Paradise Inn is often buried up to its roof by snow. Because the mountain's summit is usually above the storm clouds, the snowfall there is not as great.

The park's transformation from winter wonderland to summer playground is almost magical. Beginning in June or July, the weather becomes warm and clear, although the mountain is occasionally shrouded in clouds. The snow at the lower elevations then disappears; meltwaters fill stream valleys and cascade over cliffs; wildflowers blanket the meadows, and visitors descend on the park for its many recreational activities.

There are several entrances to the park. The roads from the Nisqually entrance to Paradise and from the southeast boundary to Ohanapecosh are usually open year-round but may be closed temporarily during the winter. Following the first heavy snow, around November 1, all other roads are closed until May or June. The entrance fee is $10 per vehicle. For further information contact Mount Rainier National Park, Tahoma Woods, Star Rte, Ashford 98304; 360/569-2211.

What to See and Do

Camping. Major campgrounds are located at Cougar Rock, Ohanapecosh and White River, and have fireplaces, tables, water and sanitary facilities. Smaller campgrounds are at Sunshine Point and Ipsut Creek. No hookups; dump stations at Cougar Rock and Ohanapecosh only. All areas closed during winter exc Sunshine Point. All sites open on first-come, first-served basis; 14-day limit. For group campsite res at Cougar Rock and Ipsut Creek phone 360/569-2211, ext 3301. Per site ¢¢¢

Fishing. No license required. Fishing season is open in lakes and ponds late Apr-Oct, in rivers and streams late May-Nov. Heavy snowfall restricts access to all water Nov-May. Most lakes are usually not ice-free until early July; ice-fishing not permitted. Specific regulations and details on special closure areas are available at ranger stations.

Hiking. More than 250 mi of trails wind throughout the park, offering unspoiled views of Mt Rainier, glaciers, meadows, lakes, waterfalls and deep valleys; many trails converge at Paradise and Sunrise; trails vary in degree of difficulty. The **Wonderland Trail**, a 93-mi trail that circles the mountain, is linked with several other trails in the park. A *Pictorial Map* (1986) of the park's topography and *50 Hikes in Mount Rainier National Park*, an illustrated book with maps and hiking details, are available for purchase. Hiking information centers (summer, daily) are located at Longmire and White River. Permit is required yr-round for overnight backpacking; available at ranger stations and visitor centers.

Interpretive programs and walks. Programs, including nature walks and evening slide shows, are offered at several locations. Schedules are posted in visitor centers and at other locations. (Late June-Labor Day)

Longmire. Longmire is often the first stop for visitors in this area of the park. Visitor center; lodging; cafe, limited groceries. Facilities usually open yr-round. Near the Nisqually entrance, in SW corner of park.

Mountain climbing. The park has many opportunities for climbers; one of the most popular climbs is the two-day trek to the summit of Mt Rainier. The guide service at Paradise conducts various programs for new and experienced climbers. Climbs should be attempted only by persons who are in good physical condition and have the proper equipment; deep crevasses and unstable ridges of lava are dangerous. All climbers must register with a park ranger. For guide service information phone Rainier Mountaineering, Inc, 360/569-2227 (summer) or 206/627-6242 (winter).

Paradise. This is the most visited area of the park, featuring subalpine meadows covered with wildflowers, and hiking trails that provide views of Nisqually, Paradise and Stevens glaciers. Visitor center with slide programs and films (May-mid-Oct, daily; rest of yr, wkends only); lodging (see MOTELS); cafe (summer, daily); snack bar (summer, daily; winter, wkends & hols only). The nearby Narada Falls drop 168 ft to Paradise River Canyon; viewpoints along stairway. Accessible from Nisqually entrance at SW corner of park, and from Stevens Canyon entrance at SE corner of park (summer only).

Skiing.

Paradise area. Cross-country skiing is popular here; equipment rentals and lessons are available at Longmire. For further information contact park HQ.

Crystal Mt Resort. 3 triple, 2 quad, 5 double chairlifts; patrol, school, rentals; restaurants, bars; day-care center, accommodations. Longest run 3¹/₂ mi; vertical drop 3,102 ft. (Nov-Apr, daily) Midweek, half-day and twilight rates. Also summer season (late June-Labor Day): swimming, fishing, hiking, mountain biking, tennis, volleyball; chairlift rides to summit (fee); poolside cafe; accommodations. E via WA 410, then 6 mi E on Crystal Mt Rd, on NE boundary of Mt Rainier Natl Park, in Mt Baker-Snoqualmie Natl Forest. Phone 360/663-2265. Winter ¢¢¢¢

White Pass Village. 4 double chairlifts, Pomalift, rope tow; patrol, school, rentals; accommodations, restaurant, bar, general store, service station. Longest run 2¹/₂ mi; vertical drop 1,500 ft. (Mid-Nov-mid-Apr, daily) Cross-country trails. On US 12, 12 mi E of Stevens Canyon (SE) entrance to the park. For schedule, fees phone 509/672-3100 or 509/453-8731. ¢¢¢¢

Sunrise. On NE side of mountain; accessible only July-mid-Sept. This is the highest point reached by paved road within Washington (6,400 ft). The drive to Sunrise is worth the time; the crowds are smaller, and this area offers spectacular views of the mountain and Emmons Glacier, the largest in the US outside Alaska. Visitor center, snack bar, picnic area.

✪ **Visitor centers.** Located at Longmire; at Paradise; at Sunrise (summer only); and at Ohanapecosh (summer only), near the Stevens Canyon entrance, in SE corner of park. All offer exhibits and publications.

Motels

★ ★ **NISQUALITY LODGE.** *(31609 State Rd (WA 706E), Ashford 98304)* 360/569-8804; FAX 360/569-2435. 24 rms, 2 story. May-Sept: S $67-$77; D $77; each addl $10; lower rates rest of yr. Crib $5. TV; VCR avail. Playground. Complimentary continental bkfst. Restaurant adj 7 am-9 pm. Ck-out 11 am. Whirlpool. Totally nonsmoking. Cr cds: A, C, D, MC, V.

D 🛇 🐾

★ ★ **PARADISE INN.** *(Ashford 98304)* In park, 20 mi E of Nisqually SW entrance. 360/569-2275; FAX 360/569-2770. 126 rms, 95 baths, 2-4 story. No A/C. No elvtr. No rm phones. Late-May-early Oct: S, D $66-$94; each addl $10; suites $124. Closed rest of yr. Crib $10. Restaurant 7-9 am, noon-2 pm, 5:30-8:30 pm. Bar noon-11 pm. Ck-out 11 am. Business servs avail. Bellhops. Sundries. Gift shop. Airport transportation. Naturalist programs nightly. Shake-shingle mountain lodge built with on-site timber in 1916. Totally nonsmoking. Cr cds: A, C, D, DS, MC, V.

Inn

★ ★ **ALEXANDER'S COUNTRY INN.** *(37515 State Rd (WA 706E), Ashford 98304) 360/569-2300; FAX 360/569-2323; res: 800/654-7615.* 12 rms (7 with shower only), 3 story, 2 guest houses. No A/C. No rm phones. May-Oct: S, D $89-$125; each addl $15; guest house $195-$250; under 5 free; lower rates rest of yr. Crib free. TV in parlor. Complimentary full bkfst; afternoon refreshments. Restaurant (see ALEXANDER'S COUNTRY INN). Ck-out 11 am, ck-in 3 pm. Concierge. Luggage handling. Built in 1912. Totally nonsmoking. Cr cds: MC, V.

Restaurant

✔ ★ ★ **ALEXANDER'S COUNTRY INN.** *(See Alexander's Country Inn)* 360/569-2300. Hrs: 7:30 am-9 pm. Closed mid-Oct-mid-May. Res accepted. Northwest regional menu. Semi-a la carte: bkfst $5.50-$8.50; lunch $5.95-$9.95, dinner $14.95-$18.95. Child's meals. Specializes in seafood, steak, pie. Country decor. Cr cds: MC, V.

D

Mount St Helens National Volcanic Monument (E-3)

(From I-5 exit 68: 48 mi E on US 12 to Randle, then S on Forest Service Rd 25; from I-5 exit 21: approx 35 mi NE on WA 503, Forest Service Rds 90, 25)

In 1978, two geologists who had been studying Mount St Helens warned that this youngest volcano in the Cascade Range could erupt again by the end of the century. On March 27, 1980, the volcano did just that, ending 123 years of inactivity. Less than two months later, on May 18, a massive eruption transformed this beautiful, snow-capped mountain and the surrounding forest into an eerie, desolate landscape with few signs of life.

The eruption sent a lateral blast of hot ash and gases out across the land at speeds up to 670 miles per hour, flattening 150 square miles of forest north of the volcano. An ash plume rising 13 miles into the atmosphere was spread eastward by the wind, coating many cities in Washington, Idaho and Montana with a fine grit. Rivers were choked with logs and mud; huge logging trucks were toppled like small toys; and the mountain, having lost 1,300 feet of its summit, was left with a gaping crater 2,000 feet deep, 1/2 mile wide and a mile long.

Among the 57 people missing or killed by the eruption was 83-year-old Harry Truman, who for many years owned a lodge on Spirit Lake, just north of the mountain. Truman refused to heed evacuation warnings, believing his "beloved mountain" would not harm him; he and his lodge are now beneath hundreds of feet of mud and water.

The monument, established in 1982, covers 110,000 acres within the Gifford Pinchot National Forestand provides a rare, natural laboratory in which scientists and visitors can view the effects of a volcanic eruption. Despite the destruction, the return of vegetation and wildlife to the blast zone has been relatively rapid. Within just weeks of the eruption, small plants and insects had begun to make their way through the ash. Today, herds of elk and other animals, as well as fir trees and wildflowers, have taken a strong foothold here.

Forest Service Road 25, which runs north-south near the eastern boundary, provides access to views of the volcano. The roads are usually closed from approximately November-May because of snow; some roads are narrow and winding.

Visitors are advised to phone ahead for current road conditions. Although volcanic activity at Mount St Helens has decreased greatly in the last few years, some roads into the monument could be closed if weather conditions dictate.

For further information, including a map with the locations of various facilities and attractions, contact the Monument Headquarters, 42218 NE Yale Bridge Rd, Amboy 98601; 360/247-3900.

What to See and Do

Ape Cave. At 12,810 ft in length, cave is said to be one of the longest intact lava tubes in continental US. Downslope portion of cave, extending approx 4,000 ft, is the most easily traveled. Upslope portion, extending nearly 7,000 ft, is recommended only for visitors carrying the proper equipment. All visitors are advised to carry three sources of light and wear sturdy shoes or boots and warm clothing; cave is a constant 42°F. An information station is also here; lantern rentals avail seasonally. On Forest Service Rd 8303, in southern part of monument.

Camping. There are no campgrounds within the monument, but many public and private campgrounds are located nearby. Primitive camping is usually allowed throughout the Gifford Pinchot Natl Forest (see VANCOUVER).

Hiking. An extensive system of trails offers hikers impressive views of the volcano and surrounding devastated areas. Trails vary in degree of difficulty. Some trails are accessible to wheelchairs. Temperatures can be very warm along the trails due to a lack of shade; hikers are advised to carry water.

Interpretive walks and programs. Presented at several locations. Details are available at the information stations, monument HQ or visitor centers.

✪ **Mount St Helens Visitor Center.** (Center cannot be reached directly from the NE side monument.) The center houses exhibits including a walk-through model of the volcano, displays on the history of the mountain and the 1980 eruption, and volcano monitoring equipment. A 10-min slide program and a 22-min movie are shown several times daily, and special programs are held throughout the yr. Also here are volcano viewpoints and a nature trail along Silver Lake. (Daily; closed some major hols) Outside the monument, off I-5 exit 49, 5 mi east of Castle Rock on WA 504. Contact 3029 Spirit Lake Hwy, Castle Rock 98611; 360/274-2100 or 360/274-2131.

Summit climb. Climbers are allowed to hike to the summit; free climbing permits are issued on a limited basis. Climb should be attempted only by persons in good physical condition. For climbing information contact the HQ or phone 360/247-3961 or 360/247-3900.

Visitor information stations. Located at Pine Creek, on Forest Service Rd 90 near the SE side of the monument; at Woods Creek, at the junction of Forest Service roads 25 and 76 near the NE side of the monument; and at Ape Cave. (Summer, daily; may remain open until Labor Day)

Volcano viewpoints. There are several viewpoints throughout the eastern side of the monument, particularly along Forest Service Rd 99; this road leads to Windy Ridge, with a spectacular view of the volcano and Spirit Lake. Lahar Viewpoint, on Forest Service Rd 83, provides an excellent view of mud flow activity on the south side of the mountain.

Mount Vernon (B-3)

(See also Anacortes, La Conner, Sedro Woolley)

Settled 1870 **Pop** 17,647 **Elev** 31 ft **Area code** 360 **Zip** 98273 **E-mail** chamber@sos.net **Web** www.mvcofc.org

Information Chamber of Commerce, 1700 E College Way, PO Box 1007; 360/428-8547.

Developed by disappointed gold miners who turned to farming and logging, Mount Vernon is a major commercial center. Centrally located between Puget Sound and the North Cascades, the Skagit Delta's deep alluvial soil produces flowers and flower bulbs, grass and vegetable seeds, small fruits and peas. Spring brings fields of daffodils, tulips and irises to the country; a map of the fields is available at the Chamber of Commerce. The city is named for George Washington's plantation.

What to See and Do

Bay View State Park. Approx 25 acres. Sand beach (no swimming). Picnicking; camping (hookups). Standard fees. Interpretive center nearby. 7 mi W via WA 20, then right on Bay View-Edison Rd. Phone 360/757-0227.

Hillcrest Park. Approx 30 acres with playgrounds, tennis & basketball courts; hiking trails; covered and open picnic facilities, barbecue pits. 13th St & Blackburn Rd, 1/2 mi E of I-5 to Cedardale Rd, 1/2 mi N to Blackburn Rd, then E 1/4 mi. Phone 360/336-6213. **Free.**

Little Mt. Observation area atop 934-ft mountain, providing view of Skagit Valley, Olympic Mts, Mt Rainier and San Juan Islands; surrounded by 480-acre forested park. Hiking. Picnicking. (Daily) SE of city on Blackburn Rd W. Phone 360/336-6213.

Annual Events

Tulip Festival. Festival planned around tulip fields as they bloom. Tulip field tours, arts & crafts, exhibits. Apr.

Skagit County Fair. 2nd wk Aug.

Motels

✔★ **BEST WESTERN COLLEGE WAY INN.** *300 W College Way, I-5 exit 227, then 1 blk W.* 360/424-4287; FAX 360/424-6036. 66 rms, 56 A/C, 2 story, 10 kits. Mid-June-Sept: S $55; D $60-$65; each addl $5; kit. units $10 addl; under 12 free; lower rates rest of yr. Crib free. Pet accepted. TV; cable (premium). Heated pool; whirlpool. Complimentary continental bkfst. Coffee in rms. Restaurant adj 7 am-11 pm. Ck-out noon. Meeting rm. Business servs avail. In-rm modem link. Health club privileges. Some refrigerators; microwaves avail. Private patios, balconies. Cr cds: A, C, D, DS, ER, MC, V.

[D] [✔] [≈] [✕] [🐾] [SC]

★ ★ **BEST WESTERN COTTON TREE INN.** *2300 Market St, I-5 exit 229.* 360/428-5678; FAX 360/428-1844. 120 rms, 3 story. S $69; D $74; each addl $5; under 18 free; wkly rates, golf plan. Crib free. Pet accepted. TV; cable (premium). Pool. Complimentary continental bkfst. Complimentary coffee in rms. Restaurant opp 4 am-9 pm. Bar noon-2 am. Ck-out noon. Coin lndry. Meeting rms. Business servs avail. In-rm modem link. Sundries. Valet serv. Health club privileges. Some refrigerators; microwaves avail. Cr cds: A, C, D, DS, ER, JCB, MC, V.

[D] [✔] [≈] [✕] [🐾] [SC]

Inns

★ ★ ★ **RIDGEWAY BED & BREAKFAST.** *1292 McLean Rd.* 360/428-8068; res: 800/428-8068; FAX 360/428-8880. E-mail ridgeway@halcyon.com. 8 rms, 3 share bath, 3 story, 1 suite, 1 cottage. No A/C. No rm phones. S $74-$124; D $79-$129; suite $159; cottage $129. Children over 11 yrs only (cottage only). TV in common rm; cable (premium), VCR avail (movies). Complimentary full bkfst; afternoon refreshments. Complimentary coffee in rms. Ck-out 11 am, ck-in 3-7 pm. Business servs avail. Gift shop. Free RR station, bus depot transportation. Lawn games. Some refrigerators, microwaves. Some balconies. Picnic tables. Built in 1928; Dutch colonial farmhouse. Totally nonsmoking. Cr cds: DS, MC, V.

[✕] [🐾]

★ ★ **WHITE SWAN.** *1388 Moore Rd, I-5 exit 221, 5 1/4 mi W on Fir Island Rd.* 360/445-6805. Web www.cnw.com/~wswan/. 3 rms in house, 2 baths, 1 kit. cottage. No A/C. No rm phones. S $75; D $80; cottage (2-4 persons) $125-$165. Complimentary continental bkfst. Ck-out 11 am, ck-in 3 pm. Queen Anne-style farmhouse (ca 1890). Wood stove in

parlor, wicker chairs on porch; sun deck on cottage. Totally nonsmoking. Cr cds: MC, V.

[✕] [🐾]

Neah Bay (B-1)

(For accommodations see Port Angeles, Sekiu)

Pop 916 **Elev** 0 ft **Area code** 360 **Zip** 98357

What to See and Do

Makah Cultural & Research Center. Exhibits on Makah and Northwest Coast Native Americans; 500-yr-old artifacts uncovered at the Ozette archaeological site, a Makah village dating back 2,000 yrs. Craft shop; dioramas; canoes; complete longhouse. (Memorial Day-mid-Sept, daily; rest of yr, Wed-Sun; closed Jan 1, Thanksgiving, Dec 25) WA 112, 1 mi E. Phone 360/645-2711. ¢¢

Newport (B-9)

(For accommodations see Spokane; also see Priest Lake Area, ID)

Settled 1890 **Pop** 1,691 **Elev** 2,131 ft **Area code** 509 **Zip** 99156 **E-mail** chamber@povn.com **Web** www.povn.com/~chamber

Information Chamber of Commerce, 324 W 4th St; 509/447-5812.

A shopping, distribution and lumbering center, Newport was born in Idaho. For a while there was a Newport on both sides of the state line, but the US Post Office interceded on behalf of the Washington community, which was the county seat of Pend Oreille County. Newport is known as "the city of flags"; flags from around the world are displayed on the main streets. A Ranger District office of the Colville National Forest (see COLVILLE) is located here.

What to See and Do

Historical Society Museum. In old railroad depot; houses historical artifacts of Pend Oreille County; two reconstructed log cabins. (Mid-May-Sept, daily) Washington & 4th Sts, in Centennial Plaza. Phone 509/447-5388. **Donation.** Also here is

Big Wheel. Giant Corliss steam engine that for years powered the town's foremost sawmill. Flag display. A visitor information center is located here. Centennial Plaza.

North Bend (C-4)

(See also Seattle)

Founded 1889 **Pop** 2,578 **Elev** 442 ft **Area code** 425 **Zip** 98045

Information City of North Bend, 211 Main Ave N, PO Box 896; 425/888-1211 or 425/340-0928.

A gateway to Mount Baker-Snoqualmie National Forest—Snoqualmie section (see SEATTLE)—and a popular winter sports area, North Bend also serves as a shipping town for a logging, farming and dairy region. A Ranger District office of the Mount Baker-Snoqualmie National Forest (see BELLINGHAM) is located here.

What to See and Do

Skiing.

Snoqualmie Ski Area. 6 double, 2 triple, quad chairlifts; 2 rope tows; 15 slopes & trails. Patrol, school, rentals; bar, restaurant, cafeteria; day care center. Vertical drop 900 ft. (Mid-Nov-Apr, daily exc Mon) Intermediate chairs; half-day & eve rates. 17 mi SE on I-90. Phone 425/434-6161 or 425/236-1600 (snow conditions). Shuttle bus to Ski Acres, Hyak & Alpental (Fri nights, wkends & hols); tickets interchangeable. ¢¢¢¢¢

Ski Acres. 2 triple, 6 double chairlifts, 5 rope tows; patrol, school, rentals; cross-country center; cafeteria, bar; day care center. Vertical drop 1,040 ft. (Hrs and fees same as Snoqualmie, exc closed Tues) Shuttle bus to Snoqualmie, Hyak & Alpental (Fri nights, wkends & hols); tickets interchangeable. 18 mi SE on I-90 at Snoqualmie Pass. Phone 425/434-6671 or 425/236-1600 (snow conditions). ¢¢¢¢

Alpental. 4 double chairlifts, 3 rope tows, platter pull; patrol, school, rentals; cafeteria, bar. Longest run 1 1/2 mi; vertical drop 2,200 ft. (Hrs, fees same as for Snoqualmie) Shuttle bus to Snoqualmie, Hyak & Ski Acres (Fri nights, wkends & hols); tickets interchangeable. 17 mi SE on I-90, then 1 mi N on Alpental Rd. Phone 425/434-6112 or 425/236-1600 (snow conditions). ¢¢¢¢

Hyak. 2 double chairlifts; patrol, school, rentals; cafeteria, bar. Vertical drop 960 ft. Shuttle bus to Ski Acres, Snoqualmie & Alpental. (Late Dec-mid-Mar; Fri, Sat & Sun) Tickets interchangeable. 19 mi SE on I-90, at Snoqualmie Pass. Phone 425/434-7600 or 425/236-1600 (snow conditions). ¢¢¢¢

Snoqualmie Falls. Perpetual snow in the Cascade Mts feeds the 268-ft falls. Power plant; park area; trail to bottom of falls. Salish Lodge (see LODGE) overlooks falls. 4 mi NW via WA 202.

Snoqualmie Valley Historical Museum. Displays, rm settings of early pioneer life from 1890s; photos, Native American artifacts; logging exhibits; farm shed; reference material. Slide shows; changing exhibits. (Apr-mid-Dec, Thurs-Sun; tours by appt) 320 S North Bend Blvd. Phone 425/888-3200. **Donation.**

Lodge

★ ★ ★ **SALISH LODGE AND SPA.** *(6501 Railroad Ave, Snoqualmie 98065) NW via WA 202.* 425/888-2556; FAX 425/888-2533; res: 800/826-6124. Web www.salish.com. Located at the crest of spectacular 268-foot Snoqualmie Falls, the lodge was used in filming the TV series *Twin Peaks.* Salish is dotted with antiques, and most rooms have a view of river, valley or falls. 91 units, 4 story. S, D $129-$269; each addl $25; suites $500-$575; higher rates Fri, Sat & hols June-Sept. Crib free. Pet accepted, some restrictions. TV; cable (premium), VCR. Complimentary coffee in rms. Restaurant (see SALISH LODGE AND SPA DINING ROOM). Rm serv. Bar 11-2 am. Ck-out noon. Meeting rms. Business servs avail. In-rm modem link. Concierge. Gift shop. Golf privileges. Downhill/x-country ski 20 mi. Exercise equipt; weight machines, bicycles, saunas. Spa. Refrigerators, whirlpools, minibars, bathrm phones, fireplaces. Private patios, balconies. Library. Cr cds: A, C, D, DS, JCB, MC, V.

Restaurant

★ ★ ★ **SALISH LODGE AND SPA DINING ROOM.** *(See Salish Lodge and Spa)* 425/831-6517. Web www.salish.com. Hrs: 7 am-10 pm. Res accepted. Bar 11-2 am; entertainment Fri, Sat. Wine cellar. Semi-a la carte: bkfst $12.95-$24.95, lunch $10.95-$15.95, dinner $17.50-$31.95. Sun brunch $21.95-$24.95. Child's meals. Specializes in multi-course country bkfst, potlatch-style salmon, Northwest game. Valet parking. Outdoor dining. Overlooks Snoqualmie Falls. Cr cds: A, C, D, DS, JCB, MC, V.

Oak Harbor (B-3)

(See also Anacortes, Coupeville, Everett, Port Townsend)

Settled 1849 **Pop** 17,176 **Elev** 115 ft **Area code** 360 **Zip** 98277 **E-mail** gohcc@whidbey.net **Web** www.whidbey.net/islandco

Information Chamber of Commerce Visitor Information Center, PO Box 883; 360/675-3535.

This trading center on Whidbey Island was first settled by sea captains and adventurers and then in the 1890s by immigrants from the Netherlands who developed the rich countryside. The town's name was inspired by the oak trees that cloaked the area when the first settlers arrived and which have been preserved. Side roads lead to secluded beaches and some excellent boating and fishing with marinas nearby.

What to See and Do

Holland Gardens. Gardens of flowers and shrubs surround blue and white windmill; Dutch provincial flags, tulips and daffodils decorate gardens during Holland Happening (see ANNUAL EVENTS). (Daily) SE 6th Ave W & Ireland St. **Free.**

Oak Harbor Beach Park. Authentic Dutch windmill; picnicking, barbecue pit; 1,800-ft sand beach, lagoon swimming, bathhouse, wading pools; tennis, baseball diamonds, playground; illuminated trails. Camping (hookups, dump station; fee). (Daily) Phone 360/679-5551. **Free.**

Whidbey Island Naval Air Station. Only active naval air station in the Northwest. Guided group tours (min 10 persons); res required several months in advance. Approx 5 mi N on WA 20. Phone 360/257-2286. **Free.**

Annual Events

Holland Happening. Tulip show, arts & crafts, Dutch buffet, carnival, culture foodfest, square dance exhibition, parade. Late Apr.

Whidbey Island Jazz Festival. Mid-Aug.

Motels

✓ ★ ★ ★ **AULD HOLLAND INN.** *33575 WA 20.* 360/675-2288; FAX 360/675-2817; res: 800/228-0148. 34 rms, 6 kits. May-Sept: S, D $55-$85; each addl $5; suites $115-$135; kit. units $5 addl; lower rates rest of yr. Crib $5. TV; cable, VCR avail (movies). Heated pool; whirlpool. Playground. Complimentary continental bkfst. Restaurant 5-9 pm. Bar from 4 pm. Ck-out 11 am. Coin lndry. Business servs avail. Valet serv. Tennis. Exercise equipt; weight machine, stair machine. Lawn games. Refrigerators, microwaves; some fireplaces. Also 24 mobile homes. Cr cds: A, D, DS, MC, V.

★ ★ ★ **BEST WESTERN HARBOR PLAZA.** *33175 WA 20.* 360/679-4567; FAX 360/675-2543. 80 rms, 3 story. July-Sept: S $89; D $99; each addl $10; under 18 free; lower rates rest of yr. Crib free. Pet accepted, some restrictions. TV; cable (premium). Heated pool; whirlpool. Complimentary continental bkfst. Coffee in rms. Restaurant adj 6 am-11 pm. Bar. Ck-out noon. Meeting rms. Business servs avail. In-rm modem link. Bellhops. Valet serv. Concierge. Exercise equipt; weight machine, bicycle. Refrigerators, microwaves. Balconies. Cr cds: A, C, D, DS, MC, V.

★ ★ **COACHMAN INN.** *32959 WA 20, at Goldie Rd.* 360/675-0727; FAX 360/675-1419; res: 800/635-0043. 102 rms, 2-3 story, 47 kits. S $60; D $70; each addl (after 4th person) $5; suites $125-$175; kit. units $80-$95; under 12 free. Crib $5. TV; VCR avail. Heated pool; whirlpool. Playground. Complimentary continental bkfst. Complimentary coffee in rms. Restaurant opp open 24 hrs. Ck-out noon. Coin lndry. Business servs avail. Exercise equipt; treadmills, bicycles. Refrigerators; microwaves avail. Picnic table, grill. Cr cds: A, C, D, DS, MC, V.

D ⌤ ⚲ ⛶ ⚒ SC

Ocean Shores (D-1)

(See also Aberdeen, Hoquiam, Westport)

Pop 2,301 **Elev** 21 ft **Area code** 360 **Zip** 98569 **E-mail** oschamber@techline.com **Web** www.oceanshores.com
Information Chamber of Commerce, Box 382; 360/289-2451 or 800/762-3224.

This 6,000-acre area at the southern end of the Olympic Peninsula is a seaside resort community with 6 miles of ocean beaches, 23 miles of lakes and canals and 12 miles of bay front. Clamming, crabbing and trout and bass fishing are popular.

Motels

★ ★ **CANTERBURY INN.** *Ocean Shores Blvd.* 360/289-3317; *FAX* 360/289-3420; *res:* 800/562-6678. 43 kit. units, 3 story. No A/C. Apr-Sept: S $80-$94; D $104-$118; each addl $10; suites $140-$160; under 14 free; lower rates rest of yr. Crib free. TV; cable. Indoor pool; whirlpool. Restaurant adj 4-9 pm. Ck-out noon. Meeting rm. Business servs avail. In-rm modem link. Sundries. Some fireplaces. Some patios, balconies. Cr cds: A, DS, MC, V.

D ⌤ ⚲ ⚒ SC

★ ★ **GREY GULL.** *Ocean Shores Blvd.* 360/289-3381; *res:* 800/562-9712 (WA). 36 kit. apts, 3 story. No A/C. Apr-Sept, hols & wkends in winter: kit. apts $98-$115; each addl $5; suites $110-$315; under 16 free; some lower rates rest of yr. Crib free. Pet accepted, some restrictions. TV; cable. Heated pool; whirlpool, sauna. Complimentary coffee. Restaurant nearby. Ck-out noon. Ck-in 4 pm. Coin lndry. Business servs avail. Refrigerators, fireplaces. Lanais, balconies. Cr cds: A, D, DS, MC, V.

D ⚑ ⌤ ⚲ ⚒ SC

★ ★ ★ **SHILO INN.** *707 Ocean Shores Blvd NW.* 360/289-4600; *FAX* 360/289-0355. 113 rms, 4 story. Apr-Oct: S, D $119-$199; each addl $15; under 13 free; lower rates rest of yr. Crib free. TV; cable (premium), VCR avail (movies). Indoor pool; whirlpool, sauna. Complimentary continental bkfst. Restaurant 7 am-9 pm. Rm serv. Bar to midnight. Ck-out noon. Meeting rms. Business servs avail. Sundries. Coin lndry. Free airport transportation. Exercise equipt; bicycles, weight machine. Some balconies. Cr cds: A, C, D, DS, ER, JCB, MC, V.

D ⚑ ⌤ ⚲ ⛶ ⚒ SC

Olympia (D-3)

(See also Centralia, Tacoma)

Founded 1850 **Pop** 33,840 **Elev** 100 ft **Area code** 360
Information Olympia/Thurston County Chamber of Commerce, PO Box 1427, 98507; 360/357-3362.

As though inspired by the natural beauties that surround it—Mt Rainier and the Olympic Mountains on the skyline and Puget Sound at its doorstep—Washington's capital city is a carefully groomed, parklike community. Although concentrating on the business of government, Olympia also serves tourists and the needs of nearby military installations. It is a deep-sea port and a manufacturer of wood products, plastics and mobile homes. The tiny village of Smithfield was chosen in 1851 as the site for a customhouse. The US Collector of Customs prevailed on the citizens to

rename the community for the Olympic Mts. Shortly afterwards, agitation to separate the land north of the Columbia from Oregon began. In 1853 the new territory was proclaimed, with Olympia as territorial capital. The first legislature convened here in 1854, despite Native American unrest that forced construction of a stockade ringing the town. (The 15-foot wall was later dismantled and used to plank the capital's streets.) The Olympia metropolitan area also includes the communities of Lacey and Tumwater, the oldest settlement in the state (1845) north of the Columbia River. The city today has a compact 20-square-block business section and a variety of stores, which attract shoppers from a wide area.

What to See and Do

✪ **Capitol Group.** On Capitol Way between 11th & 14th Aves. For information phone 360/586-8687 or 360/586-3460 (tours). In 35-acre park overlooking Capitol Lake and Budd Inlet of Puget Sound are

Legislative Bldg. A 287-ft dome with 47-ft lantern; neoclassical architecture; lavishly detailed interior. Guide service (daily). Phone 360/586-8687. **Free.**

Temple of Justice. Houses State Supreme Court. (Mon-Fri; closed hols) **Free.**

Library Bldg. Houses rare books; murals, mosaics. (Mon-Fri; closed hols) **Free.**

Capitol grounds. Grounds lined with Japanese cherry trees attract hundreds of visitors in the spring; plantings are changed seasonally. Also here is a replica of Tivoli Gardens Fountain in Copenhagen, Denmark; sunken gardens, state conservatory (Memorial Day-Labor Day, daily); World War I and Vietnam memorials. Grounds (daily).

Capitol Lake. Formed by dam at point where fresh water of Deschutes River empties into salt water of Budd Inlet. From top of dam thousands of salmon may be seen making their way upstream during spawning season starting in mid-Aug. Deschutes Pkwy skirts shore of Capitol Lake, providing scenic drive with dome of state capitol rising to the east. Boating, bicycle and running trails, playground, picnic tables, concession. (Daily) **Free.**

Millersylvania State Park. More than 800 acres along Deep Lake. Swimming, fishing; boating. Hiking. Picnicking. Camping (hookups). Standard fees. 10 mi S off I-5. Phone 360/753-1519.

Olympia Brewery. Guided tour (daily; closed Jan 1, Thanksgiving, Dec 25). Schmidt Place & Custer Way, just off I-5 exit 103, in Tumwater. Phone 360/754-5212. **Free.**

Olympic Natl Forest. More than 630,000 acres. Picturesque streams and rivers, winding ridges, rugged peaks, deep canyons, tree-covered slopes; rain forest, world's largest stand of Douglas fir, public-owned oyster beds; populous herd of Roosevelt elk. Swimming, fishing; hiking, hunting. Picnicking. Camping (May-Sept). NW of city, reached via US 101, exit 104. Contact Supervisor, Federal Bldg, 1835 Black Lake Blvd SW, 98502-5623; 360/956-2400.

Oyster beds. Big Skookum, Little Skookum, Mud, Oyster bays. Beds of rare Olympia oyster, found only in South Puget Sound.

Priest Point Park. Playgrounds, hiking trails, picnic facilities in heavily wooded area with view of Olympic Mts. (Daily) E Bay Dr, overlooks Budd Inlet. **Free.**

State Capital Museum. A 1920 Spanish-style stucco mansion houses art gallery; Native American art and culture exhibits; pioneer exhibits. (Daily exc Mon; closed hols) 211 W 21st Ave. Phone 360/753-2580. **Donation.**

Tumwater Falls Park. Gentle walk (1 mi) follows spectacular falls of the Deschutes River. Landscaped grounds, picnicking, playground. Good view of fall salmon run on man-made fish ladder. (Daily) S of city off I-5, 15 acres. Phone 360/943-2550. **Free.** Adj is

Tumwater Valley Athletic Club. 18-hole golf course. (All yr) Phone 360/943-9500. Indoor swimming pools. Tennis and racquetball courts. Fee for activities. Phone 360/352-3400.

Annual Events

Wooden Boat Festival. Percival Landing in Harbor. Wooden boats on display, some open for public viewing. Wooden crafts fair. 2nd wkend May.

Capital City Marathon and Relay. 8-km run, children's run, 5-10-km walk, wheelchair division. Phone 360/786-1786. Wkend before Memorial Day wkend.

Super Saturday. Evergreen State College. Arts, crafts, food fair. Early June.

Lakefair. Capitol Lake. Parade, carnival midway, boating and swimming competition, naval vessel tours, flower shows. Mid-July.

Thurston County Fair. Fairgrounds in Lacey. Late July-early Aug.

Harbor Day Festival & Tug Boat Races. Labor Day wkend.

Motel

★ ★ **BEST WESTERN TUMWATER.** *(5188 Capitol Blvd SE, Tumwater 98501)* S on I-5, exit 102. 360/956-1235. 89 rms, 2 story. June-Sept: S $54-$62; D $58-$73; each addl $2; under 18 free; lower rates rest of yr. Crib $5. Pet accepted, some restrictions; $5. TV; cable. Complimentary continental bkfst. Restaurant opp open 24 hrs. Ck-out 11 am. Guest lndry. Meeting rms. Business servs avail. In-rm modem link. Exercise equipt; weight machine, bicycles, sauna. Refrigerators. Cr cds: A, C, D, DS, JCB, MC, V.

Motor Hotels

★ ★ ★ **HOLIDAY INN SELECT.** *2300 Evergreen Park Dr (98502),* I-5 exit 104. 360/943-4000; FAX 360/357-6604. 191 rms, 3 story. S $79; D $89; each addl $10; suites $129-$149; under 18 free; some wkend rates. Crib free. TV; Cable (premium). Heated pool; whirlpool. Complimentary full bkfst. Complimentary coffee in rms. Restaurant 6 am-11 pm; Sun 7 am-2 pm. Rm serv. Bar 11:30-1 am. Ck-out noon. Coin lndry. Meeting rms. Business center. In-rm modem link. Valet serv. Exercise equipt; bicycles, weight machine. Lawn games. Wet bar in some suites. Some private patios, balconies. Cr cds: A, C, D, DS, ER, JCB, MC, V.

★ ★ **WEST COAST TYEE HOTEL.** *500 Tyee Dr (98512),* I-5 exit 102. 360/352-0511; FAX 360/943-6448; res: 800/386-8933. 146 rms, 2 story. S $76-$84 D $84; each addl $8; cabana suites $90-$150; studio rms $90; under 17 free; monthly rates. Crib free. TV; cable (premium). Heated pool. Restaurant 6:30 am-9 pm. Rm serv. Bar 11-1:30 am; entertainment Fri, Sat. Ck-out noon. Meeting rms. Business servs avail. In-rm modem link. Valet serv. Sundries. Beauty salon. Tennis. Some in-rm whirlpools. Health club privileges. Picnic tables. Cr cds: A, C, D, DS, MC, V.

Hotel

★ ★ **RAMADA INN-GOVERNOR HOUSE.** *621 S Capital Way (98501).* 360/352-7700; FAX 360/943-9349. 123 rms, 8 story. S $112-$130; D $122-$140; each addl $10; suites $125-$175; kit. units $79-$89; under 18 free; higher rates Lakefair. Crib free. TV; cable, VCR avail. Heated pool; whirlpool. Restaurant 6:30 am-9 pm. Bar 11:30-midnight. Ck-out noon. Coin lndry. Meeting rms. Business servs avail. In-rm modem link. Exercise equipt; weight machine, bicycles, sauna. Refrigerators. Balconies. Cr cds: A, C, D, DS, ER, JCB, MC, V.

Restaurants

★ ★ **BUDD BAY CAFE.** *525 N Columbia St (98501).* 360/357-6963. Hrs: 11 am-10 pm; Sun brunch 9 am-1 pm. Closed Dec 25. Res accepted. Bar to 2 am. Semi-a la carte: lunch $4.25-$12.95, dinner $5.95-$24.95. Sun brunch $15.95. Child's meals. Specializes in fresh seafood, pasta, prime rib. Outdoor dining. View of Budd Inlet and marina. Cr cds: A, D, DS, MC, V.

★ ★ ★ **FALLS TERRACE.** *106 S Deschutes Way (98501), I-5 exit 103.* 360/943-7830. Hrs: 11 am-9 pm; Sat 11:30 am-9 pm; Sun 11:30 am-8 pm; early-bird dinner Mon-Sat 4-5:45 pm. Closed some major hols. Bar to midnight. Semi-a la carte: lunch $5.99-$7.99, dinner $9.95-$26.95. Child's meals. Specializes in seafood, steak, prime rib. Multi-level dining; large windows offer unobstructed view of falls, river. Patio dining. Family-owned. Cr cds: A, D, DS, MC, V.

Olympic National Park (B-2 - C-2)

(See also Forks, Port Angeles, Sequim)

Web www.nps.gov/olym/
Information Park Headquarters, 600 E Park Ave, Port Angeles 98362; 360/452-0330.

(119 mi NW of Olympia on US 101)

In these 1,442 square miles of rugged wilderness are such contrasts as the wettest climate in the contiguous US (averaging 140-167 inches of precipitation a year) and one of the driest; seascapes and snow-cloaked peaks; glaciers and rain forests; elk and seals. With Olympic National Forest, State Sustained Yield Forest No 1, much private land and several Native American reservations, the national park occupies the Olympic Peninsula, due west of Seattle and Puget Sound.

The Spanish explorer Juan Perez spotted the Olympic Mountains in 1774, but the first major western land exploration did not take place until more than a century later. Since then, generations of adventurous tourists have rediscovered Mt Olympus, the highest peak (7,965 feet), several other 7,000-foot peaks and hundreds of ridges and crests between 5,000 and 6,000 feet high. The architects of these ruggedly contoured mountains are glaciers, which have etched these heights for thousands of years. About 60 glaciers are still actively eroding these mountains—the largest three are on Mt Olympus.

From approximately November through March, the west side of the park is soaked with water, while the northeast side is the driest area on the West Coast except southern California. The yearly deluge creates a rain forest in the western valleys of the park. Here Sitka spruce, western hemlock, Douglas fir and western red cedar grow to heights of 250 feet with 8-foot diameters. Mosses carpet the forest floor and climb tree trunks. Club moss drips from the branches.

Some 50 species of mammals inhabit this wilderness, including several thousand elk, Olympic marmot, black-tailed deer and black bear. On the park's 57-mile strip of Pacific coastline wilderness, deer, bear, raccoon and skunk can be seen; seals sun on the offshore rocks or plow through the water beyond the breakers. Mountain and lowland lakes sparkle everywhere. Lake Crescent is among the largest. Some roads are closed in winter.

What to See and Do

Camping. Limited to 14 days. Small camp trailers accommodated at most campgrounds. Campfire programs at some areas (July-Labor Day). ¢¢¢

Fishing. Streams and lakes have game fish including salmon, rainbow, Dolly Varden, eastern brook trout, steelhead and cutthroat. No license required in the park; permit or punch card is necessary for steelhead and salmon. Contact Park HQ for restrictions, phone 360/452-0330.

Hiking. Nearly 600 mi of trails. Obtain maps and trail guides in the park. Guided walks conducted July & Aug.

Mountain climbing. Something for everyone, from the novice to the experienced climber. Climbing parties must register at a ranger station.

Rain forests. Along Hoh, Queets and Quinault river roads. Hall of Mosses & Spruce Nature Trails and trail to Mt Olympus start at end of Hoh River Rd.

■ **Visitor Center & Park HQ.** Has information, natural history exhibits, displays of Native American culture, orientation slideshow. (Daily) 3002 Mt Angeles Rd. **Park HQ.** From here, one can enter the park on Heart O' the Hills Pkwy to Hurricane Ridge (there is limited access Nov-Apr). 600 E Park Ave in Port Angeles. Per vehicle ¢¢¢; Per person ¢¢ Here is

Skiing. Hurricane Ridge Winter Use Area. Pomalift, intermediate and beginner's runs; school, rentals; snack bar. (Late Dec-late Mar, Sat & Sun) Also snowshoeing and cross-country ski trails.

There is also a Visitor Center at Hoh Rain Forest (daily).

Resort

★ **SOL DUC HOT SPRINGS.** (Port Angeles 98362) 30 mi W of Port Angeles on US 101, then South 12 mi on Sol Duc Rd. 360/327-3583; FAX 360/327-3593. 32 cottages (1-bedrm), 6 kits. No A/C. Mid-May-Sept 23 & Apr, Oct wkends: S, D $83; each addl $12.50; kit. cabins $93; under 4 free. Closed rest of yr. Crib free. Pet accepted. Pool; wading pool, mineral pools. Dining rm 7:30-10:30 am, 5-9 pm. Ck-out 11 am, ck-in 4 pm. Grocery. Gift shop. Massage therapy. Picnic tables. Originally conceived as a European-style health spa (ca 1912). Mineral pools range in temperature from 98-106. Cr cds: A, DS, MC, V.

Omak (B-6)

(See also Winthrop)

Settled 1900 **Pop** 4,117 **Elev** 837 ft **Area code** 509 **Zip** 98841

Information Tourist Information Center, 401 Omak Ave, Rte 2, PO Box 5200; 509/826-4218 or 800/225-6625.

This lumber town is the largest in the north central part of Washington and is also known for its production of apples and its many orchards. The name of the town and nearby lake and mountain is derived from a Native American word meaning "good medicine." Omak is the "baby's breath capital of the world," a flower much used commercially by florists.

What to See and Do

Conconully State Park. Approx 80 acres along Conconully Reservoir; swimming, fishing, boating. Picnicking. Snowmobiling. Camping. Standard fees. (Daily) 5 mi N on US 97, then 10 mi NW on Conconully Hwy (unnumbered road). Phone 509/826-7408.

Okanogan Natl Forest. Nearly 1.75 million acres. In the northern part of the forest is 530,031-acre Pasayten Wilderness. In the southwestern part of the forest is 95,976-acre Lake Chelan-Sawtooth Wilderness. Hunting and fishing are plentiful; picnicking and camping at 41 sites, most of which have trailer spaces; eight boating sites. Thirty-eight mi W of town at Methow Valley Airport, between Winthrop and Twisp, is the North Cascades Smokejumper Base; visitors welcome. One-mi paved wheelchair trail to Rainy Lake at Rainy Pass. NE & NW of town, reached via US 97, WA 20. Contact Supervisor, 1240 S Second Ave, Okanogan 98840; 509/826-3275. **Free.**

Annual Event

Stampede and Suicide Race. Rodeo events; horses and riders race down a cliff and across the Okanogan River. Western art show. Native American dance contests. Encampment with more than 100 teepees. Phone 509/826-1002. 2nd wkend Aug.

Motels

✔★ **CEDARS INN.** (1 Apple Way, Okanogan 98840) S on WA 215 to jct WA 20 & US 97. 509/422-6431; FAX 509/422-4214. 78 rms, 3 story, 6 kits. No elvtr. S $46-$52; D, kit. units $52-$57; each addl $5; under 13 free; higher rates Stampede. Crib free. Pet accepted. TV; cable, VCR

avail (movies $2). Pool. Restaurant 6:30 am-10 pm. Bar 11 am-11:30 pm. Ck-out noon. Coin lndry. Meeting rms. Business servs avail. Cr cds: A, C, D, DS, MC, V.

✔★ **NICHOLAS.** 527 E Grape Ave, ½ mi N on WA 215. 509/826-4611. 21 rms. S $35; D $43-$47; each addl $4; higher rates Stampede wk. TV; cable. Complimentary coffee in rms. Restaurant nearby. Ck-out 11 am. Refrigerators. City park opp. Cr cds: A, C, D, DS, MC, V.

Orcas Island

(see San Juan Islands)

Othello (D-7)

(See also Moses Lake)

Pop 4,638 **Elev** 1,038 ft **Area code** 509 **Zip** 99344 **E-mail** othello@televar.com **Web** www.ncw.net:80/chambers/othello

Information Chamber of Commerce, 33 E Larch; 509/488-2683 or 800/684-2556.

Another beneficiary of the Grand Coulee project, Othello had a population of only 526 in 1950. The Potholes Canal runs by the town, linking the Potholes Reservoir and the smaller Scooteney Reservoir.

Annual Event

Adams County Fair. Carnival, entertainment, tractor pull, exhibits. Mid-Sept.

Motels

★ **ALADDIN MOTOR INN.** 1020 E Cedar. 509/488-5671. 52 rms, 2 story. S $40; D $45; each addl $5; kit units $43; higher rates hunting season. Crib $5. TV; cable. Pool. Restaurant opp 7 am-10 pm. Ck-out 11 am. Cr cds: A, D, MC, V.

✔★ **CABANA.** 665 Windsor St. 509/488-2605; res: 800/442-4581. 53 rms., 3 kit. units. S $26-$37; D $42-$48; each addl $5; kit. units $37-$65. Crib free. TV; cable. Heated pool. Restaurant nearby. Ck-out 11 am. Guest lndry. Some refrigerators. Cr cds: A, C, D, DS, MC, V.

Packwood (D-4)

Pop 950 (est) **Elev** 1,051 ft **Area code** 360 **Zip** 98361

Named for William Packwood, a colorful explorer who helped open this region, the town is a provisioning point for modern-day explorers of Mt Rainier National Park (see) and Snoqualmie and Gifford Pinchot National Forests. A Ranger District office of the Gifford Pinchot National Forest (see VANCOUVER) is located here. The area abounds in edible wild berries and mushrooms; no permit is needed for picking. Winter and spring are popular with game-watchers; elk, deer, bear and goats can be spotted in the local cemetery as well as in the nearby parks.

What to See and Do

Goat Rocks Wilderness. 105,600 acres of alpine beauty with elevations from 3,000-8,200 ft. Jagged pinnacles rising above snowfields, cascading streams, mountain meadows with wildflowers; this is the home of the pika and mountain goat. E & S of town, in Gifford Pinchot Natl Forest.

Motels

★ ★ **COWLITZ RIVER LODGE.** *13069 US 12. 360/494-4444; FAX 360/494-2075.* 32 rms, 2 story. June-Sept: S $50; D $60; each addl $5; under 6 free; lower rates rest of yr. Crib free. TV; cable. Complimentary continental bkfst. Restaurant opp 5 am-10 pm. Ck-out 11 am. Downhill ski 19 mi. Whirlpool. Cr cds: A, D, MC, V.

✔★ ★ **TIMBERLINE VILLAGE RESORT.** *13807 US 12. 360/494-9224.* 21 rms, 3 story. Some A/C. July-mid-Sept: S, D $50-$55; each addl $5; suites $70; under 10 free; lower rates rest of yr. Crib free. Pet accepted. TV; cable. Complimentary coffee in rms. Restaurant adj 8 am-10 pm. Ck-out 11 am. Downhill ski 18 mi. Cr cds: A, MC, V.

Pasco (E-7)

(See also Kennewick, Richland)

Founded 1880 **Pop** 20,337 **Elev** 381 ft **Area code** 509 **Zip** 99301 **Web** www.cbvcp.com/pascochamber/

Information Chamber of Commerce, 1600 N 20th, Ste A1, PO Box 550; 509/547-9755.

One of the "tri-cities" (see KENNEWICK and RICHLAND), Pasco has been nurtured by transportation throughout its history. Still a rail, air, highway and waterway crossroads, Pasco is enjoying increased farm and industrial commerce thanks to the Columbia Basin project.

What to See and Do

Ice Harbor Lock & Dam. The first of four dams on Lower Snake River between Pasco & Lewiston, ID. One of the world's highest (103 ft) single-lift navigation locks. There is a powerhouse on the S shore and a fish ladder on each side of the river. (Daily) Visitor Center (Apr-Oct, daily), fish viewing room, self-guided tours. Lake Sacajawea, with four developed parks, has swimming, waterskiing, picnicking, fishing, boat ramps; camping (May-Sept; hookups; fee). 9 mi E, off WA 124. For information contact Resource Mgr, Rte 6, Box 693, 99301; 509/547-7781. **Free.**

Kahlotus. Town redone in Old West atmosphere. Many of the businesses and buildings are museums in themselves. Near Palouse Falls (see DAYTON) and Lower Monumental Dam. 42 mi NE via US 395 & WA 260.

McNary Lock & Dam. Single-lift navigation lock. Dam is 7,365 ft long, 92 ft high and is the easternmost of four multipurpose dams on the lower Columbia River between Portland, OR & Pasco. The Columbia River forms Lake Wallula here. The 61-mi long lake reaches beyond the Tri-Cities up to Ice Harbor Dam on Snake River. Developed parks with boating, marinas, water skiing, swimming, fishing, picnicking and camping nearby. Self-guided tours of hydropower, navigation and salmon passage facilities. (Daily; guided tours in summer) 3 mi S of WA 14 in Umatilla, OR. For information contact Park Ranger, PO Box 1441, Umatilla, OR 97882; 541/922-4388. **Free.**

Preston Estate Vineyards. Self-guided tour of tasting room, oak aging casks, storage tanks and bottling line; park with picnic & play area, amphitheater, gazebo, pond. (Daily; closed major hols) 5 mi N via US 395, watch for road sign. Phone 509/545-1990. **Free.**

Sacajawea State Park. Site where Lewis and Clark camped in 1805. Approx 280 acres. Swimming, fishing, boating (launch, dock). Picnicking. (Daily) 2 mi SE off US 12. Phone 509/545-2361.

Annual Events

Jazz Unlimited. Columbia Basin Community College. Phone 509/547-0511. Usually 2nd & 3rd wkend Apr.

Tri-Cities Water Follies. Events scheduled throughout month of July leading to hydroplane races on Columbia River on last wkend of month. Phone 509/547-5531. July.

Motel

✔★ **VINEYARD INN.** *1800 W Lewis St, near Tri-Cities Airport. 509/547-0791; FAX 509/547-8632; res: 800/824-5457.* 165 rms, 2 story. 45 kits. S $40.50-$48; D $50-$60; each addl $5; kit. units, studio rms $50-$60; under 12 free; some wkend rates; higher rates hydro races. Crib $6. Pet accepted; $5/day. TV; cable (premium), VCR avail. Indoor pool; whirlpool. Complimentary continental bkfst. Restaurant 11 am-9 pm. Bar 11-2 am. Ck-out noon. Coin lndry. Business servs avail. Valet serv. Airport, RR station, bus depot transportation. Cr cds: A, C, D, DS, MC, V.

Motor Hotel

★ ★ ★ **DOUBLETREE MOTOR INN.** *2525 N 20th St, north of downtown. 509/547-0701; FAX 509/547-4278.* 279 rms, 2-3 story. S, D $89; each addl $10; under 18 free; some wkend rates. Crib free. Pet accepted. TV; cable. 2 heated pools; whirlpool, poolside serv. Restaurants 6 am-11 pm. Rm serv 7 am-10 pm. Bar 11-2 am; entertainment. Ck-out noon. Convention facilities. Business center. In-rm modem link. Bellhops. Valet serv. Sundries. Gift shop. Free airport, RR station, bus depot transportation. Exercise equipt; weight machine, bicycle. Refrigerator, wet bar in some suites. Private patios, balconies. Cr cds: A, C, D, DS, ER, JCB, MC, V.

Port Angeles (B-2)

(See also Neah Bay, Sequim)

Pop 17,710 **Elev** 32 ft **Area code** 360 **Zip** 98362

Information Chamber of Commerce, 121 E Railroad; 360/452-2363.

Sitting atop the Olympic Peninsula, Port Angeles has the Olympic Mountains at its back and Juan de Fuca Strait at its shoreline; just 17 miles across the Strait is Victoria, BC (see). Ediz Hook, a sandspit, protects the harbor and helps make it the first American port of entry for ships coming to Puget Sound from all parts of the Pacific; there is a US Coast Guard Air Rescue Station here. A Spanish captain who entered the harbor in 1791 named the village he found here Port of Our Lady of the Angels, a name that has survived in abbreviated form. The fishing fleet, pulp, paper and lumber mills as well as tourism are its economic mainstays today.

Port Angeles is the headquarters for Olympic National Park (see). It is an excellent starting point for expeditions to explore the many faces of the peninsula.

What to See and Do

Ferry service to Victoria, BC, Canada (see). A 90-min trip; departs from Coho ferry terminal to Victoria's Inner Harbour. (Daily; summer, 4 trips; spring & fall, 2 trips; rest of yr, 1 trip) Contact Black Ball Transport Inc, 10777 Main St, Suite 106, Bellevue 98004, phone 206/622-2222; or 604/386-2202 (Victoria). In Port Angeles phone 360/457-4491. (For Border Crossing Regulations see MAKING THE MOST OF YOUR TRIP.) Individuals ¢¢¢; Car & driver ¢¢¢¢

Olympic Natl Park (see). HQ, 600 Park Ave.

Olympic Raft & Guide Service. River rafting in Olympic Natl Park. Phone 360/452-1443.

Olympic Van Tours, Inc. Depart from Coho ferry terminal. Unique, interpretive sightseeing tours into Olympic Natl Park (3 & 8 hrs). Tours coincide with ferry schedule. Res advised. Also shuttle service to and from Seattle. For schedule and fees contact PO Box 2201; 360/452-3858.

Annual Event

Clallam County Fair. Mid-Aug.

Motels

★ ★ ★ **DOUBLETREE.** *221 N Lincoln. 360/452-9215; FAX 360/452-4734.* 187 rms, 2 story. No A/C. May-Sept: S $100-$130; D $115-$145; suites $145-$160; each addl $10; under 18 free; some lower rates rest of yr. Crib free. Pet accepted. TV; cable. Heated pool; whirlpool. Complimentary coffee in rms. Restaurant 5:30 am-midnight. Ck-out noon. Business center. Sundries. Health club privileges. Private balconies. Overlooks harbor. Cr cds: A, D, DS, ER, MC, V.

✔ ★ **HILL HAUS.** *111 E Second St. 360/452-9285; FAX 360/452-7935; res: 800/421-0706.* 23 rms, 3 story. No A/C. June-Sept: S, D $48-$96; each addl $12; lower rates rest of yr. TV; cable (premium). Complimentary coffee in rms. Restaurant nearby. Ck-out 11 am. Business servs avail. Some balconies. Cr cds: DS, MC, V.

★ ★ **UPTOWN.** *101 E Second St. 360/457-9434; res: 800/858-3812.* 35 rms, 1-3 story, 4 kits. No A/C. June-Oct: S, D $89-$130; each addl $5; kit. units $125; under 12 free; wkly, monthly rates; lower rates rest of yr. Crib free. Pet accepted, some restrictions. TV; cable (premium). Complimentary continental bkfst. Complimentary coffee in rms. Restaurant nearby. Ck-out 11 am. Refrigerators, microwaves. Scenic view. Cr cds: A, C, D, DS, MC, V.

Inns

★ ★ ★ **DOMAINE MADELEINE.** *146 Wildflower Ln, on Finn Hall Rd. 360/457-4174; FAX 360/457-3037.* E-mail domm@olypen.com; web www.northolympic.com/dm. This house sits on a bluff providing views of the Strait of Juan de Fuca and mountains. Many amenities are offered here including a gourmet bkfst. 5 rms, 1 with shower only, 2 story. Mid-Apr-mid-Oct: S $125-$150; D $145-$165; each addl $25; wkly rates; 2-day min wkends; lower rates rest of yr. Children over 12 yrs only. TV; cable (premium), VCR (movies). Complimentary full bkfst; afternoon refreshments. Ck-out 11 am, ck-in 4-6 pm. Luggage handling. Business servs avail. In-rm modem link. Airport, ferry transportation. Lawn games. Some refrigerators, microwaves. Picnic tables. Totally nonsmoking. Cr cds: A, DS, MC, V.

★ ★ **MAPLE ROSE.** *112 Reservoir Rd (98363), near Intl Airport. 360/457-7673; res: 800/570-2007.* E-mail maplerose@tenforward.com; web www.northolympic.com/maplerose. 5 rms, 4 story, 3 suites. No A/C. No elvtr. May-Sept: S, D $79-$89; each addl $15; suites $127-$147; under 9 free; wkends, hols (2-day min); lower rates rest of yr. Pet accepted; $15. TV; cable (premium), VCR (movies). Complimentary full bkfst. Complimentary coffee in rms. Restaurant nearby. Ck-out 11 am, ck-in 3-6 pm. Business center. In-rm modem link. Luggage handling. Free airport transportation. Putting green. Exercise equipt; weight machine, bicycle. Massage. Whirlpool. Some in-rm whirlpools, refrigerators, microwaves. Some balconies. Picnic tables, grills. Contemporary country inn. Totally nonsmoking. Cr cds: A, MC, V.

★ ★ **THE SEASUNS.** *1006 S Lincoln, near Intl Airport. 360/452-8248.* Web www.northolympic.com/seasons. 4 rms, 2 share bath, 2 story. No A/C. No rm phones. Mid-May-mid-Oct: S $85-$95; each addl $15; ski plans; lower rates rest of yr. Children over 12 yrs only. TV in common rm; cable, VCR avail (movies). Complimentary full bkfst; afternoon refreshments. Complimentary coffee in rms. Restaurant nearby. Ck-out 11 am, ck-in 4-6 pm. Luggage handling. Free airport transportation. Lawn games. Some balconies. Picnic tables, grills. Restored Dutch Colonial inn built in 1920s; pond, waterfall. Totally nonsmoking. Cr cds: MC, V.

★ ★ ★ **TUDOR INN.** *1108 S Oak. 360/452-3138.* E-mail tudor;info@aol.com. 5 rms, 2 story. No A/C. No rm phones. Mid-May-mid-Oct: S $80-$115; D $85-$120; lower rates rest of yr. Children over 12 yrs only. TV in sitting rm; VCR avail (free movies). Complimentary full bkfst; afternoon refreshments. Ck-out 11 am, ck-in 4-7 pm. Downhill/x-country ski 16 mi. View of Olympic Mts. Antiques, grand piano. English gardens. Totally nonsmoking. Cr cds: A, DS, MC, V.

Restaurants

★ ★ **BELLA ITALIA.** *117-B E First St. 360/457-6112.* Hrs: 11 am-11 pm; Sun brunch to 4 pm; winter hrs may vary. Closed Thanksgiving, Dec 25. Res accepted. Italian menu. Bar. A la carte entrees: lunch $5-$10, dinner $6-$18. Child's meals. Specializes in crab cakes, fresh seafood, organic pasta. Own pastries. Two dining rms divided by espresso & wine bar; windows overlook courtyard. Totally nonsmoking. Cr cds: A, D, DS, MC, V.

★ ★ **BUSHWHACKER.** *1527 E First St. 360/457-4113.* Hrs: 5-10 pm; Fri, Sat to 11 pm; Sun 4:30-9 pm. Closed July 4, Thanksgiving, Dec 24, 25. Northwest menu. Bar 4:30 pm-1 am Mon-Sat. Semi-a la carte: dinner $6.95-$19.95. Child's meals. Specializes in prime rib, salmon, halibut. Salad bar. Parking. Northwest decor. Cr cds: A, DS, MC, V.

★ ★ **C'EST SI BON.** *23 Cedar Park Dr. 360/452-8888.* Hrs: 5-11 pm. Closed Mon. Res accepted. Bar. Wine list. A la carte entrees: dinner $19.25-$22.50. Child's meals. Specializes in French cuisine. Parking. Outdoor dining on terrace with gazebo and rose garden. Romantic atmosphere. Cr cds: A, DS, MC, V.

✔★ **LANDINGS.** *115 E Railroad Ave, Ste. 101, adj Victoria ferry dock. 360/457-6768.* Hrs: 7 am-9 pm; 6 am-10 pm in summer. Closed Jan 1, Dec 25. No A/C. Bar. Semi-a la carte: bkfst $3-$8, lunch, dinner $3-$12. Specializes in seafood, hamburgers. Parking. Outdoor dining. Cr cds: A, C, D, DS, MC, V.

★ ★ ★ **TOGA'S.** *122 W Lauridsen Blvd. 360/452-1952.* Hrs: 5-10 pm. Closed Mon; some major hols; also Sept. Res required. No A/C. Continental menu. Semi-a la carte: dinner $13.95-$24.95. Child's meals. Specializes in beef fillets, prawns, lamb chops. Own baking. Outdoor dining. Intimate dining in private residence; windows offer mountain view. Totally nonsmoking. Cr cds: MC, V.

Port Gamble (C-3)

(For accommodations see Port Ludlow, Seattle)

Settled 1853 **Pop** 300 (est) **Area code** 360 **Zip** 98364
Information Pope & Talbot, Public Relations Dept, PO Box 217; 360/297-3341.

Captain William Talbot, a native of Maine, discovered the vast Puget Sound timberlands and located what has become the oldest continuously operating sawmill in North America here. Spars for the ships of the world were a specialty. The community, built by the company and still owned by it, gradually developed a distinctive appearance because of its unusual (to this part of the country) New England architectural style.

The company, realizing an opportunity to preserve a bit of the past, has rebuilt and restored more than 30 homes, commercial buildings and St Paul's Episcopal Church. Replicas of gas lamps and underground wiring have replaced street lighting. The entire town has been declared a historic district.

What to See and Do

Hood Canal Nursery. Self-guided tour covers storage & maintenance building, soil mixing, pump house and chemical storage, water reservoir, greenhouses with a capacity of 3$\frac{1}{2}$ million seedlings. (Mon-Fri) W edge of town. Phone 360/297-7555. **Free.**

Kitsap Memorial State Park. Over 50 acres. Saltwater swimming, scuba diving; fishing, boating (mooring). Hiking. Picnicking; shelters. Camping (dump station). Standard fees. 4 mi S on WA 3. Phone 360/779-3205.

Of Sea and Shore Museum. One of the largest shell collections in the country. Gift, book shop. (Mid-May-mid-Sept, daily exc Mon; rest of yr, wknds; closed Jan 1, Dec 25) Country Store Bldg, Rainier St. Phone 360/297-2426. **Free.**

Port Gamble Historic Museum. Exhibits trace the history of the area and the timber company. Displays arranged in order of time: replica of old saw filing rm; San Francisco office, captain's cabin from ship; individual rms from hotels and houses; Forest of the Future exhibit. (Memorial Day-Labor Day, daily) Downhill side of the General Store. Phone 360/297-8074. ¢

Port Ludlow (B-3)

(See also Port Gamble, Sequim)

Settled 1878 **Pop** 500 (est) **Elev** 0-30 ft **Area code** 360 **Zip** 98365

Inn

★ ★ ★ **INN AT LUDLOW BAY.** *1 Heron Rd. 360/437-0411; FAX 360/437-0310.* 37 rms, 3 story, 3 suites. No A/C. May-Sept: S, D $165-$200; each addl $35; suites $300-$450; lower rates rest of yr; under 18 free; golf plan; hol rates; 2-day min summer wknds. Crib avail. Pet accepted, some restrictions; $50 deposit. TV; VCR (free movies). Complimentary continental bkfst. Complimentary coffee in rms. Restaurant (see DINING ROOM AT INN AT LUDLOW BAY). Ck-out noon, ck-in after 3 pm. Luggage handling. Meeting rms. Business servs avail. In-rm modem link. 27-hole golf privileges; greens fee $50-$55, putting green, driving range. Lawn games. Refrigerators, some minibars. Balconies. Built in 1994 to resemble estate in Maine. Views of Olympics & Cascades Mts. On shore, beach. Totally nonsmoking. Cr cds: A, D, DS, MC, V.

Resort

★ ★ **PORT LUDLOW.** *200 Olympic Place. 360/437-2222; FAX 360/437-2482; res: 800/732-1239 (WA).* 190 multi-units, 1-2 story, 44 kits. No A/C. May-Oct: S, D $90-$115; suites $135-$420; each addl $10; lower rates rest of yr; under 12 free; golf plan. TV; cable, VCR avail (movies $5.95). Heated pool; whirlpool, lifeguard. Playground. Supervised child's activities (June-Sept); ages 4-12. Dining rm 7 am-10 pm. Box lunches, picnics. Bar 11-2 am; entertainment Tues-Sat (wknds winter). Ck-out noon, ck-in .4 pm. Grocery. Coin lndry. Convention facilities. Business center. Gift shop. Free airport transportation. Tennis. 27-hole golf, greens fee $55, driving range, putting green. Marina; boats, motors, sailboats. Bicycles. Lawn games. Exercise equipt; bicycles, treadmill, sauna. Picnic tables. Cr cds: A, MC, V.

Restaurant

★ ★ ★ **DINING ROOM AT INN AT LUDLOW BAY.** *(See Inn At Ludlow Bay) 360/437-0411.* Hrs: 5:30-9:30 pm. Closed Mon-Tues (winter). Res accepted. Northwestern menu. Bar. Wine cellar. Semi-a la carte: dinner $12-$24. Child's meals. Specializes in fresh game and seafood. Own herbs. Views of Bay, marina and Olympic Mts. Totally nonsmoking. Cr cds: A, D, DS, MC, V.

D

Port Townsend (B-3)

(See also Coupeville, Everett, Oak Harbor)

Settled 1851 **Pop** 7,001 **Elev** 100 ft **Area code** 360 **Zip** 98368 **E-mail** ptchambr@olympus.net **Web** www.olympus.net

Information Tourist Information Center, 2437 E Sims Way; 360/385-2722 or 888/ENJOY-PT.

Located on the Quimper Peninsula, at the northeast corner of the Olympic Peninsula, this was once a busy port city served by sailing vessels and sternwheelers. Captain George Vancouver came ashore in 1792 and named this spot Port Townshend, after an English nobleman. Port Townsend is a papermill town with boat building and farming.

What to See and Do

Rothschild House (1868). Furnished in original style; flower and herb gardens. (May-Oct, daily; rest of yr, Sat, Sun & hols only) Franklin & Taylor Sts. Phone 360/385-2722. ¢

State parks.

Old Ft Townsend (Historical). Approx 380 acres. Posted site of fort established in 1856, abandoned in 1895. Swimming, scuba diving; bank fishing. Hiking. Picnicking. Camping. (Mid-Apr-mid-Sept) Standard fees. 3 mi S on WA 20. Phone 360/385-4730

Ft Worden. Approx 340 acres. Home of Centrum Foundation, with poetry and visual arts symposiums; fiction writer's workshop; fiddletune, jazz and folk dance festivals; phone 360/385-3102. Park has many historic buildings, including several Victorian houses (overnight stays avail by res). Swimming, underwater park with scuba diving; fishing; boating (launch, moorage). Hiking, nature trails; tennis. Picnicking. Camping. Marine Science Center (Apr-Oct, Sat & Sun; summer hrs vary; fee). Coast Artillery Museum (summer months, Sat & Sun; fee). Youth hostel, phone 360/385-0655. Standard fees. 1 mi N. Phone 360/385-4730 or 800/233-0321.

Ft Flagler. More than 780 acres. Saltwater swimming, scuba diving; fishing; boating (launch, mooring). Hiking. Picnicking. Camping (res required Memorial Day-Labor Day). Nature study; forested areas, some military areas. Standard fees. 20 mi SE on Marrowstone Island. Phone 360/385-1259.

Annual Events

Heat Wave. Arts festival with numerous bands, theater productions, dancing, crafting. Also parade and masquerade ball. Phone 800/733-3608. Feb.

Jefferson County Fair. Agricultural and 4-H displays, livestock shows. Wkend mid-Aug.

Wooden Boat Festival. Displays, classes and lectures. 1st wkend after Labor Day.

House Tours. Phone 360/385-2722. 3rd wkend Sept.

Lodge

✓★ ★ **THE OLD ALCOHOL PLANT.** *(310 Alcohol Loop Rd, Port Hadlock 98339) 9 mi S. 360/385-7030; FAX 360/385-6955; res: 800/735-*

7030. 28 rms, 3 story. Mid-May-mid-Oct: S $49-$99; D $79-$99; each addl $10; suites $90-$250; under 14 free; wkly, monthly rates; lower rates rest of yr. Crib free. Pet accepted; $10. TV; cable (premium), VCR (movies $6). Restaurant 7 am-10 pm; Fri, Sat to 11 pm. Bar. Ck-out 11 am. Meeting rms. Exercise equipt; weights, bicycles. Game rm. Picnic tables. Former alcohol plant built 1910. Marina. Cr cds: A, D, DS, MC, V.

⊡ ⬙ ⬙ ✕ ⬙ ⬙ SC

Hotel

★ ★ **PALACE.** *1004 Water St. 360/385-0773; FAX 360/385-0780; res: 800/962-0741 (WA).* E-mail palace@olympus.net; web www.olympus.net/palace. 15 rms, 2 story. No A/C. No rm phones. May-mid-Sept: S, D $69-$139; each addl $10; suites $109-$129; under 13 free; lower rates rest of yr. Crib free. Pet accepted. TV; cable. Complimentary continental bkfst. Restaurant 6:30 am-10 pm. Ck-out noon. Meeting rms. Coin lndry. Some refrigerators. Cr cds: A, DS, MC, V.

⬙ ⬙ ⬙ SC

Inns

★ ★ **ANN STARRETT MANSION.** *744 Clay St. 360/385-3205; FAX 360/385-2976; res: 800/321-0644.* Web www.olympus.net/starrett/. 11 rms, 4 story. No A/C. Apr-Oct: S, D $75-$145; each addl $25; suites $155-$225; kit. unit $185; lower rates rest of yr. Children over 11 yrs only. Some TV; cable, VCR avail. Complimentary full bkfst. Restaurants nearby. Ck-out 11 am, ck-in 3-6 pm. Business servs avail. Free airport, bus depot, ferry terminal transportation. Antiques. Winding staircase; frescoed ceilings. View of Puget Sound, Mt Rainer, Cascades & Olympics. Totally nonsmoking. Cr cds: A, DS, MC, V.

⬙ ⬙

★ ★ **BISHOP VICTORIAN GUEST SUITES.** *714 Washington St. 360/385-6122; res: 800/824-4738.* E-mail bishop@waypt.com; web www.waypt.com/bishop. 14 kit. suites, 7 with shower only, 3 story. No A/C. No elvtr. May-Sept: kit. suites $71-$139; under 12 free; wkly rates; hols (2-day min); higher rates special events; lower rates rest of yr. Crib free. Pet accepted, some restrictions; $15. TV; cable, VCR avail (movies). Complimentary continental bkfst. Restaurant nearby. Ck-out 11 am, ck-in 3 pm. Business center. In-rm modem link. Luggage handling. Health club privileges. Refrigerators, microwaves; many fireplaces. Built in 1890 as an office/warehouse; converted to English inn. Totally nonsmoking. Cr cds: A, DS, MC, V.

⬙ ⬙ ⬙ SC ✦

★ ★ ★ **CHANTICLEER INN.** *1208 Franklin. 360/385-6239; res: 800/858-9421.* Web www.olympus.net/biz/chanticleer/chanticleer.html. 5 rms (3 with shower only), 2 story. S $70-$123; D $80-$133; each addl $10. Children over 12 yrs only. Complimentary full bkfst; afternoon refreshments. Restaurant nearby. Ck-out 10:30 am, ck-in 3-6 pm. Luggage handling. Victorian house built in 1876 furnished with antiques. Totally nonsmoking. Cr cds: MC, V.

⬙ ⬙

★ ★ **ENGLISH INN.** *718 F St. 360/385-5302; res: 800/254-5302.* E-mail nancy@englishinn.com; web www.english-inn.com. 5 rms, 1 with shower only, 2 story. No A/C. S $65-$85; D $75-$95; each addl $15. Children over 14 only. TV in sitting rm; cable, VCR avail (free movies). Whirlpool. Complimentary full bkfst; afternoon refreshments. Ck-out 11 am, ck-in 3-6 pm. Free bus depot, ferry terminal transportation. Built 1885; antiques. Rms named for British poets. Some rms with mountain view. Totally nonsmoking. Cr cds: A, D, DS, MC, V.

⬙ ⬙ SC

★ ★ **HOLLY HILL HOUSE.** *611 Polk St. 360/385-5619; res: 800/435-1454.* E-mail hollyhill@olympus.net; web www.acies.com.holly hill. 5 rms, 2 story, 1 suite. No A/C. No rm phones. S, D $78-$95; each addl $20; suite $165. Children over 12 yrs only. Complimentary full bkfst; afternoon refreshments. Ck-out 10:30 am, ck-in 3-6 pm. Built 1872; an-

tiques, stippled woodwork. Rare upside down Camperdown elm on grounds. Totally nonsmoking. Cr cds: MC, V.

⬙ ⬙

✔ ★ ★ **JAMES HOUSE.** *1238 Washington St. 360/385-1238; FAX 360/379-5551; res: 800/385-1238.* E-mail jameshouse@olympus.net; web www.jameshouse.com. 12 rms, 4 story. No A/C. May-Oct: S $60-$85; D $75-$125; suites $125-$165; lower rates rest of yr. Deposit required; 7-day notice for refund. Complimentary full bkfst. Restaurant nearby. Ck-out 11 am, ck-in 3 pm. Health club privileges. Fireplaces; microwaves avail. Some balconies. Restored Victorian guest house (1889); period furniture. Parlors, library. Most rms with view of mountains, bay. Totally nonsmoking. Cr cds: A, MC, V.

⬙ ⬙

★ ★ ★ **LIZZIE'S.** *731 Pierce St. 360/385-4168; FAX 360/385-9467; res: 800/700-4168.* E-mail wickline@olympus.net; web www.koike .com/lizzies. 7 rms, 2 story. No A/C. No rm phones. S, D $70-$135. Children over 10 yrs only. Complimentary full bkfst. Restaurants nearby. Ck-out 11 am, ck-in 4 pm. Italianate Victorian house (1887); sitting rms. Totally nonsmoking. Cr cds: DS, MC, V.

⬙ ⬙

★ ★ **MANRESA CASTLE.** *Seventh & Sheridan Sts. 360/385-5750; FAX 360/385-5883; res: 800/732-1281 (WA & OR).* Web www.olym pus.net/manresa. 40 rms, 3 story. No A/C. May-mid-Oct: S $65-$165; D $75-$175; each addl $10; lower rates rest of yr. TV; cable (premium). Complimentary continental bkfst. Dining rm 5-9 pm. Bar 4-11 pm. Ck-out 11 am. Business servs avail. Castle built 1892; period furniture. View of bay from many rms. Cr cds: DS, MC, V.

⬙

★ ★ ★ **OLD CONSULATE INN.** *313 Walker St. 360/385-6753; FAX 360/385-2097; res: 800/300-6753.* Web www.oldconsulateinn.com. 8 rms, 5 with shower only, 3 story, 3 suites. No rm phones. June-Sept: S, D $96-$130; each addl $45; suites $130-$195; 2-day min wkends; lower rates rest of yr. Children over 12 yrs only. 2 TVs; cable, VCR avail.Whirlpool. Complimentary full bkfst; afternoon refreshments. Ck-out 11 am, ck-in 3-6 pm. Luggage handling. Business servs avail. Free airport, ferry transportation. Queen Anne Victorian house built in 1889; many antiques. Totally nonsmoking. Cr cds: A, MC, V.

⬙ ⬙ SC

★ ★ ★ **RAVENSCROFT.** *533 Quincy St. 360/385-2784; FAX 360/385-6724; res: 800/782-2691.* E-mail ravenscroft@olympus.net; web https://www.olympus.net/ravenscroft/. 8 rms, 3 with shower only, 3 story, 2 suites. No A/C. Mid-May-mid-Oct: S, D $67-$170; suites $155-$170; 2-day min hols & special events; lower rates rest of yr. Children over 12 yrs only. TV in library; cable, VCR avail (free movies). Complimentary full bkfst; afternoon refreshments. Restaurants nearby. Ck-out 11 am, ck-in 3-6 pm. Business servs avail. Free airport transportation. Luggage handling. Croquet. Colonial decor; many antiques. Totally nonsmoking. Cr cds: A, DS, MC, V.

⬙ ⬙

★ ★ **THE SWAN HOTEL.** *222 Monroe St. 360/385-1718; res: 800/776-1718; FAX 360/379-1010.* E-mail swan@waypt.com; web www.waypt.com/bishop. 9 rms, 3 story, 5 kit. suites, 4 kit. cottages. May-Sept: kit. suites $105-$400; kit. cottages $85-$95; under 12 free; wkly rates; higher rates special events; lower rates rest of yr. Crib free. Pet accepted, some restrictions; $15 and daily fees. TV; cable, VCR avail (movies). Complimentary coffee in rms. Restaurant nearby. Ck-out 11 am, ck-in 3 pm. Meeting rms. Business servs avail. In-rm modem link. Free airport transportation. Refrigerators; microwaves avail. Some balconies. Cr cds: A, D, MC, V.

⊡ ⬙ ⬙ ⬙ SC

Restaurants

★ ★ **KHU LARB THAI.** *225 Adams St. 360/385-5023.* Hrs: 11 am-9 pm; Fri, Sat to 10 pm. Closed Wed (winter). Res accepted. Thai menu. A la carte entrees: lunch, dinner $6.95-$10.95. Attractive decor using Thai objets d'art. Cr cds: MC, V.

★ ★ **LONNY'S.** 2330 Washington St. 360/385-0700. Hrs: from 5 pm. Closed Tues; some major hols. Res accepted. Contemporary Italian, Amer menu. Bar. Wine cellar. Semi-a la carte: dinner $10.95-$18.95. Child's meals. Specializes in fresh seafood, local produce. Own baking, pasta. Elegant dining in rustic Italian atmosphere. Totally nonsmoking. Cr cds: MC, V.

★ ★ **MANRESA CASTLE.** (See Manresa Castle Inn) 360/385-5750. Web www.olympus.net/manresa. Hrs: 6-9 pm; Fri, Sat to 9:30 pm; Sun brunch 9 am-1 pm; winter Wed-Sat from 4 pm. Closed Jan 1, Dec 25. Res accepted. No A/C. Bar from 4 pm. Semi-a la carte: dinner $16-$24. Sun brunch $3.25-$8.50. Child's meals. Specialties: curry chicken, fresh Northwest salmon. Own breads, desserts. In 1892 castle; antique oak furnishings, ornate fireplace. Totally nonsmoking. Cr cds: DS, MC, V.

★ ★ **ORIGINAL OYSTER HOUSE.** 280417 US 101, 10 mi S. 360/385-1785. Hrs: 4-9 pm; Sun brunch from noon. Res accepted. Bar. Semi-a la carte: early bird dinner $9.95 Mon-Fri 4-6 pm, dinner $11.95-$18 Child's meals. Specializes in Northwest cuisine. Parking. Outdoor dining. Overlooking Discovery Bay, beach. Cr cds: D, DS, MC, V.

★ ★ **THE SILVERWATER CAFE.** 237 Taylor St. 360/385-6448. Hrs: 11:30 am-3 pm, 5-10 pm; Sun from 5 pm. Closed Easter, Thanksgiving, Dec 25. Northwestern menu. Bar. Wine, beer. Semi-a la carte: lunch $3.95-$7.50, dinner $7.95-$13.95. Child's meals. Specializes in fresh local seafood. Own desserts. Totally nonsmoking. Cr cds: MC, V.

Pullman (D-9)

(See also Clarkston)

Settled 1881 **Pop** 23,478 **Elev** 2,351 ft **Area code** 509 **Zip** 99163
Information Chamber of Commerce, 415 N Grand Ave; 509/334-3565 or 800/365-6948.

A university town and an agricultural storage and shipping center in the fertile Palouse Hills, this community is named for George M. Pullman, the inventor-tycoon who gave his name to the railroad sleeping car.

What to See and Do

Parks. Kamiak Butte County Park. 13 mi N on WA 27. Timbered area with rocky butte, trails leading to summit. Approx 300 acres. Picnicking, hiking, interpretive programs (summer). Camping (Apr-Oct; fee). Park (all yr). **Wawawai County Park.** 17 mi SW. Boating, picnicking, fishing, hiking. Earth-sheltered home (afternoon tours, call for dates). Camping (Apr-Oct; fee). Park (all yr). Phone 509/397-6238. **Free.**

Washington State Univ (1890). (16,000 students) E of town center. Guided tours at Office of Univ Affairs, French Administration Bldg, Rm 442 (Mon-Fri; closed school hols; phone 509/335-4527). On campus are

Museum of Art. Exhibitions, lectures, films. (Sept-May, daily, hrs vary) Fine Arts Center. Phone 509/335-1910 or 509/335-6607. **Free.**

Pullman Summer Palace Theater. Daggy Hall. (Late June, July & early Aug) Phone 509/335-7236.

Annual Event

Natl Lentil Festival. Food booths, arts & crafts, entertainment, parade, quilt show. Late Aug.

Motels

 ★ **AMERICAN TRAVEL INN.** S 515 Grand Ave. 509/334-3500; FAX 509/334-0549. 35 rms, 2 story. Mid-May-Sept: S, D $38-$47; each addl $4-$8; suites $52-$78; under 12 free; higher rates: graduation, football wknds, Mother's & Father's Day wknds. Crib free. TV; cable. Pool. Restaurant 6 am-3 pm. Ck-out 11 am. Sun deck. Cr cds: A, C, D, DS, MC, V.

★ ★ **QUALITY INN.** SE 1050 Bishop Blvd. 509/332-0500; FAX 509/334-4271. 66 rms, 2 story, 15 suites. S $60-$65; D $69.50-$72.50; each addl $7; suites $83-$138; under 18 free; higher rates college wknds. Crib free. TV; cable (premium), VCR avail. Heated pool; whirlpool, sauna. Restaurant 6:30 am-10 pm. Ck-out noon. Meeting rms. Business servs avail. In-rm modem link. Valet serv. Sundries. Airport transportation. Health club privileges. Refrigerator in suites. Cr cds: A, C, D, DS, ER, JCB, MC, V.

Puyallup (D-3)

(For accommodations see Tacoma; also see Enumclaw)

Founded 1877 **Pop** 23,875 **Elev** 40 ft **Area code** 206
Information Puyallup Area Chamber of Commerce, 322 2nd St SW, PO Box 1298, 98371; 206/845-6755.

Puyallup freezes the farm produce from the fertile soil and mild climate of the valley between Mt Rainier and Tacoma. A $2 million bulb industry (iris, daffodils, tulips) was born in 1923 when it was discovered the valley was ideal for growing. Ezra Meeker crossed the plains by covered wagon and named this city Puyallup (meaning "generous people") after a tribe that lived in the valley; Puyallups still live in the area.

What to See and Do

Ezra Meeker Mansion (1890). The 17-rm Victorian house of Ezra Meeker, pioneer, farmer, first town mayor, author and preserver of the Oregon Trail. Six fireplaces, period furnishings, stained-glass windows and hand-carved woodwork. (Mar-mid-Dec, Wed-Sun; closed Easter, Thanksgiving) 312 Spring St. Phone 206/848-1770. ¢

Pioneer Park. Life-size statue of Ezra Meeker. Playground; wading pool (summer). S Meridian St & Elm Pl. Phone 206/841-5457. **Free.**

Annual Events

Ezra Meeker Community Festival. Fine arts show, arts & crafts, entertainment; ice-cream social at Meeker Mansion. Late June.

Sumner Summer Festival. Early Aug.

Pierce County Fair. 6 mi S in Graham. Early Aug.

Western Washington Fair. Pacific Northwest's largest fair; includes three statewide youth fairs, livestock shows, agricultural and commercial exhibits, free entertainment, midway, rodeo, top-name grandstand acts. Phone 206/841-5045. 17 days Sept.

Quinault (C-2)

Pop 350 (est) **Elev** 221 ft **Area code** 360 **Zip** 98575

Information Grays Harbor Chamber of Commerce, 506 Duffy St, Aberdeen 98520; 360/532-1924 or 800/321-1924.

Quinault, on the shore of Lake Quinault, is the south entrance to Olympic National Park (see). In the heart of Olympic National Forest, it is the gateway to any of three valleys, the Hoh, Queets and Quinault, which make up the rain forest, a lush green ecological phenomenon. It also provides an entrance to the Enchanted Valley area of the park. The Quinault Reservation is two miles west.

A Ranger District office of the Olympic National Forest (see OLYMPIA) is located here.

Lodge

★ ★ **LAKE QUINAULT.** South Shore Rd, 2 mi NE of US 101. 360/288-2900; FAX 360/288-2901; res: 800/562-6672 (WA). 91 rms, 1-3 story. No A/C. No rm phones. June-Sept: S, D $105-$143; each addl $10; under 5 free; lower rates rest of yr. Indoor pool; sauna. Playground. Restaurant 7 am-9:30 pm. Bar noon-11:30 pm. Ck-out 11 am. Meeting rms. Business servs avail. Gift shop. Boat rental. Lawn games. Game rm. Some fireplaces. Some balconies. On lake, beach. Cr cds: A, MC, V.

Quincy (D-6)

(See also Ellensburg, Ephrata, Wenatchee)

Settled 1892 **Pop** 3,738 **Elev** 1,301 ft **Area code** 509 **Zip** 98848

Information Quincy Valley Chamber of Commerce, 119 F St SE, PO Box 668; 509/787-2140.

Although there are only about eight inches of rain a year in this area, irrigation has turned the surrounding countryside green. Quincy processes and markets farm produce; more than 80 crops are grown in the area. Deposits of diatomaceous earth (soft chalky material used for fertilizers, mineral aids and filters) are mined in the area and refined in Quincy. Fishing and game-bird hunting are good in the surrounding area.

What to See and Do

Crescent Bar Park. On Wanapum Reservoir in the Columbia River. Swimming, bathhouse, beaches; waterskiing, boating, fishing, marina; playground, picnicking. Camping (Apr-Oct; hookups; fee); restaurants, putting green, shops, pro shop, grocery. 9-hole golf (fee). Four tennis courts (fee). Park (all yr). 8 mi W off WA 28.

Annual Event

Farmer Consumer Awareness Day. Quincy High School, 16 Sixth Ave SE. Free tours to dairies, processing plants, packing houses, farms, harvesting operations. Exhibits, food booths, arts & Crafts, petting zoo, antique autos, farm equipment, games, parade, 2K & 5K run, entertainment. 2nd Sat Sept.

Motel

✔ ★ **TRADITIONAL INNS.** 500 SW F Street (WA 28). 509/787-3525; FAX 509/787-3528. 24 rms, 2 story. S, D $43-$67; under 13 free; wkly rates; higher rates Concerts in the Gorge. Pet accepted. TV; cable.

Complimentary coffee in lobby. Ck-out 11 am. Coin lndry. Refrigerators. Cr cds: A, C, D, DS, MC, V.

Richland (E-7)

(See also Kennewick, Pasco)

Pop 32,315 **Elev** 360 ft **Area code** 509 **Zip** 99352

Information Chamber of Commerce, 515 Lee Blvd, PO Box 637; 509/946-1651.

Although one of the "tri-cities" (see KENNEWICK and PASCO), Richland has an entirely different personality, due to the 560-square-mile Hanford Works of the Department of Energy (DOE)—formerly the US Atomic Energy Commission. In 1943, Richland was a village of 250, dedicated to fruit cultivation. A year later Hanford was established by the government as one of four main development points for the atomic bomb—the others, Oak Ridge, TN, Los Alamos, NM and the Argonne Laboratory, near Chicago. Hanford no longer is involved in the production of plutonium, the more than 16,000 employees are now dedicated to environmental cleanup and safe disposal of nuclear and hazardous wastes. Important companies in Richland include Siemens's Nuclear Fuels Inc., Battelle Northwest, Boeing Computer Services, Washington Public Power Supply Service (WPPSS), Kaiser Engineers and Fluor Daniel Hanford.

Once largely desert area, Richland today is surrounded by vineyards and orchards, thanks to irrigation from Grand Coulee Dam and the Yakima River Irrigation Projects. The city is at the hub of an area of spectacular scenery and outdoor activities within a short drive in any direction.

What to See and Do

CRESHT Museum. Displays, models, computer exhibits relating to US energy, science and environmental topics. (Daily exc Sun; closed major hols) 95 Lee Blvd. Phone 509/943-9000. **Free.**

Annual Events

Columbia Cup. Hydroplane races. July.

Benton-Franklin Fair & Rodeo. Franklin County Fairgrounds. Fair, parade, carnival. Aug.

Seasonal Event

NASCAR Auto Racing. June-Sept.

Motels

✔ ★ **BALI HI.** 1201 George Washington Way. 509/943-3101; FAX 509/943-6363. 44 rms, 2 story. S $37-$40; D $37-$50; each addl $5; studio rms $37-$45; higher rates hydroplane races. Crib free. TV; cable (premium). Heated pool. Complimentary coffee in rms. Restaurant adj 7 am-11 pm. Ck-out noon. Business servs avail. Refrigerators. Cr cds: A, C, D, DS, MC, V.

★ ★ ★ **DOUBLETREE.** 802 George Washington Way. 509/946-7611; FAX 509/943-8564. 150 rms, 2 story. S, D $72; each addl $10; under 18 free. Crib free. Pet accepted. TV. Heated pool; poolside serv. Coffee in rms. Restaurant 6 am-2 pm, 5-10 pm. Rm serv. Bar. Ck-out noon. Meeting rms. Bellhops. Valet serv. Sundries. Free airport, RR station, bus depot transportation. Boat dock; waterskiing. Private patios, balconies. Most rms with private lanais. Cr cds: A, C, D, DS, ER, JCB, MC, V.

✔ ★ **NENDELS INN.** 615 Jadwin Ave, 1 blk S of George Washington Way. 509/943-4611; res: 800/547-0106. 98 rms, 2 story, 16 kits. S

$39-$42, D $47; each addl $5; kit. units $50-$63; under 12 free; higher rates summer boat race wkends. Crib free. TV; cable (premium). Heated pool. Complimentary continental bkfst. Restaurant nearby. Ck-out noon. Business servs avail. Refrigerators. Cr cds: A, C, D, DS, MC, V.

★★ SHILO INN RIVERSHORE. *50 Comstock St, at George Washington Way. 509/946-4661; FAX 509/943-6741.* 150 rms, 2 story, 12 kits. Mid-May-mid-Sept: S, D $79-$99; each addl $9; kit. units $139-$155; under 13 free; higher rates hydroplane races; lower rates rest of yr. Crib free. Pet accepted; $7/day. TV; cable (premium), VCR (movies $3). Heated pool; wading pool, whirlpool. Restaurant 6 am-10 pm. Bar. Ck-out noon. Coin lndry. Meeting rms. Business servs avail. Valet serv. Airport, RR station, bus depot transportation. Tennis privileges, Golf privileges. Boats, waterskiing. Exercise equipt; treadmill, bicycle. Refrigerator in suites. On 12 acres. Cr cds: A, C, D, DS, ER, JCB, MC, V.

★ VAGABOND INN. *515 George Washington Way. 509/946-6117; FAX 509/943-2463.* 40 rms, 2 story. S $35-$55; D $38-$85; each addl $6; under 18 free. Crib free. Pet accepted; $10. TV; cable (premium), VCR avail. Heated pool. Restaurant nearby. Ck-out 11 am. Some refrigerators. Cr cds: A, C, D, DS, MC, V.

Motor Hotel

★★ BEST WESTERN TOWER INN. *1515 George Washington Way. 509/946-4121; FAX 509/946-2222; res: 800/635-3980.* 195 rms, 6 story. S, studio rms $54-$70; D $70-$80; each addl $10; suites $85-$125; under 17 free; higher rates boat races. Crib free. TV; cable (premium). Heated pool; wading pool, whirlpool. Sauna. Restaurant 6 am-9 pm. Rm serv. Bar; entertainment Thurs-Sat. Ck-out noon. Coin lndry. Meeting rms. Business servs avail. Bellhops. Free airport, RR station, bus depot transportation. Cr cds: A, D, DS, MC, V.

Restaurants

✔★ GIACCI'S. *94 Lee Blvd. 509/946-4855.* Hrs: 11 am-8 pm; Fri & Sat 11 am-4 pm, 5-9 pm. Closed Sun; major hols. Italian menu. Beer. Semi-a la carte: lunch $3-$7.95, dinner $8.95-$17. Child's meals. Specializes in linguine, parmigiana, ravioli. Own pasta. Outdoor dining. Cr cds: MC, V.

D

✔★ R.F. McDOUGALL'S. *1705 Columbia Dr SE. 509/735-6418.* Hrs: 11 am-11 pm. Closed Thanksgiving, Dec 25. Bar to 1 am. Semi-a la carte: lunch, dinner $3.50-$9.50. Specializes in hamburgers, pasta. Outdoor dining. Antique advertising signs in Western-style restaurant. Cr cds: A, DS, MC, V.

SC

Ritzville (D-8)

(See also Moses Lake)

Settled 1878 **Pop** 1,725 **Elev** 1,815 ft **Area code** 509 **Zip** 99169
Information Chamber of Commerce, PO Box 122; 509/659-1936.

Annual Events

BluesFest. 2nd Sat July.

Wheat Land Communities Fair. Parade, rodeo. Labor Day wkend.

Motel

★★ BEST WESTERN HERITAGE INN. *1405 Smitty's Blvd. 509/659-1007.* 42 rms, 2 story. May-mid-Nov: S $55; D $64-$70; each addl $8; suites $95-$145; under 18 free; lower rates rest of yr. Crib free. Pet accepted. TV; cable (premium), VCR avail. Heated pool; whirlpool. Complimentary continental bkfst. Restaurant adj open 24 hrs. Ck-out noon. Coin lndry. Meeting rms. Business servs avail. Gift shop. Cr cds: A, C, D, DS, ER, JCB, MC, V.

Restaurant

✔★ CIRCLE T INN. *214 W Main St. 509/659-0922.* Hrs: 6:30 am-10 pm. Closed Jan 1, Thanksgiving, Dec 25. Bar to 2 am. Semi-a la carte: bkfst $3.75-$6.50, lunch, dinner $4-$15.95. Specializes in steak, seafood. Own pies. Cr cds: MC, V.

San Juan Islands (A-3)

(See also Anacortes; also see Victoria, BC Canada)

Area code 360 **E-mail** chamber@sanjuanisland.org **Web** sanjuanisland.org
Information Chamber of Commerce, PO Box 98, Friday Harbor 98250; 360/378-5240.

These 172 islands nestled between the northwest corner of Washington and Vancouver Island, British Columbia, Canada, comprise a beautiful and historic area. Secluded coves, giant trees, freshwater lakes, fishing camps, modest motels, numerous bed & breakfasts and plush resorts characterize the four major islands. Over 500 miles of paved or gravel roads swing through virgin woodlands and along lovely shorelines. The islands are accessible by ferry from Anacortes (see).

San Juan Island gave birth in 1845 to the expansionist slogan "fifty-four forty or fight" and was the setting for the "pig war" of 1859, in which a British pig uprooted an American potato patch. The subsequent hostilities between the islands' 7 British and 14 American inhabitants reached such proportions that eventually Kaiser Wilhelm I of Germany was called in to act as arbiter and settle the boundaries. During the 13 years of controversy, the pig was the only casualty. This island was the last place the British flag flew within the territorial United States. Friday Harbor, most westerly stop in US on San Juan Islands ferry tour, is county seat of San Juan.

What to See and Do

Orcas Island. Largest in the chain; includes **Moran State Park** 15 mi NE. Has a 5,100-acre forest with swimming, fishing, boating (launch). Hiking. Picnicking. Primitive camping (res suggested in summer). Mt Constitution (2,409 ft) with view site and tower. Standard fees. Phone 360/376-2326.

⛴ **San Juan Island.** Friday Harbor on E shore serves as base for salmon fleet; major commercial center of islands. Fishing lakes, camping facilities, golf, International Seaplane Base and two airstrips are here. Also on San Juan is

San Juan Island Natl Historical Park. Commemorates settlement of boundary issue between the US and Great Britain. British Camp, 10 mi NW of Friday Harbor on Garrison Bay, has restored blockhouse, commissary, hospital, formal garden and barracks built during the British occupation. American Camp, 6 mi SE of Friday Harbor, has remains of redoubt, the American defensive earthwork; laundresses' and officers' quarters. Picnicking; information specialist at both camps (June-Sept, daily; rest of yr, Thurs-Sun). Office and information center in Friday Harbor, 1st & Spring Sts (June-Aug, daily; May & Sept, Mon-Fri; closed rest of yr; also closed major hols) For further information contact Superintendent, Box 429, Friday Harbor 98250; 360/378-2240. **Free.**

The Whale Museum. Art and science exhibits document the lives of whales and porpoises in this area. (Daily; closed major hols) 62 1st St N in Friday Harbor. Phone 360/378-4710. ¢¢

Annual Event

Dixieland Jazz Festival. Friday Harbor and Roche Harbor. Phone 360/378-5509. Last wkend July.

Inns

★ ★ **ARGYLE HOUSE.** (685 Argyle Ave, Friday Harbor 98250) 360/378-4084; res: 800/624-3459. Web www.pacificws.com/sj/argyle .html. 4 rms, shower only, 2 story, 1 guest house. No A/C. No rm phones. Mid-May-Sept: S, D $85-$100; guest house $125; wkly rates; lower rates rest of yr. Children over 10 yrs only. TV in common rm; cable, VCR avail (movies). Complimentary full bkfst; afternoon refreshments. Restaurant nearby. Ck-out 11 am, ck-in 3 pm. Luggage handling. Free airport transportation. Whirlpool. Lawn games. Picnic tables, grills. Built in 1910; country setting, gardens. Totally nonsmoking. Cr cds: MC, V.

⊠ 🖲 SC

★ ★ ★ **FRIDAY'S.** 35 First St (98250), San Juan Island, near ferry terminal. 360/378-5848; FAX 360/378-2881; res: 800/352-2632. E-mail information@friday-harbor.com; web friday-harbor.com. 10 rms, 6 share bath, 3 story. No A/C. No rm phones. June-Oct: S, D $90-$175; each addl $20; lower rates rest of yr. TV in some rms; cable (premium). Complimentary continental bkfst; afternoon refreshments. Restaurant nearby. Ck-out 11 am, ck-in 2 pm. Free airport transportation. Refrigerators; microwaves avail. Balconies. Built 1891. Antiques. Totally nonsmoking. Cr cds: MC, V.

⊠ 🖲

★ ★ **HARRISON HOUSE SUITES.** (235 C St, Friday Harbor 98250) 360/378-3587; res: 800/407-7933; FAX 360/378-2270. E-mail hhsuites@rockisland.com; web www.rockisland.com/~hhsuites. 5 rms. No A/C. May-Sept: S, D $85-$195; under 2 free; wkly rates; wkends (2-day min); lower rates rest of yr. Crib free. TV; cable (premium), VCR (movies). Complimentary continental bkfst. Complimentary coffee in rms. Restaurant nearby. Rm serv 24 hrs. Ck-out 3 pm, ck-in 11 am. Business servs avail. In-rm modem link. Luggage handling. Free guest lndry. Free airport, ferry transportation. Massage. Heated pool; whirlpool. Refrigerators, microwaves; many in-rm whirlpools; some fireplaces. Many balconies. Built in 1904; eclectic furnishings. Totally nonsmoking. Cr cds: A, DS, MC, V.

≋ ⊠ 🖲

★ ★ **HILLSIDE HOUSE.** (365 Carter Ave, Friday Harbor 98250) near Port of Friday Harbor Airport. 360/378-4730; FAX 360/378-4715; res: 800/232-4730. E-mail hillside@sanjuaninfo.com; web www.sanjuan info.com/house_1.html. 7 rms, 2 with shower only, 3 story. No A/C. Some rm phones. May-Sept: S, D $85-$165; each addl $25; lower rates rest of yr. Complimentary full bkfst. Restaurant nearby. Ck-out 11 am, ck-in 3 pm. Business servs avail. Luggage handling. Refrigerators. Near ocean. Gardens with aviary, fountain. Cr cds: A, DS, MC, V.

⊠ 🖲

★ ★ ★ **INN AT SWIFTS BAY.** (Rte 2, Box 3402, Lopez Island 98261) on Port Stanley Rd, 1 mi past park entrance. 360/468-3636; FAX 360/460-3637. Web www.swiftsbay.com. 5 air-cooled rms, 2 with shower only, 2 story. No rm phones. S, D $85-$175. Adults only. TV in den; VCR. Complimentary full bkfst; afternoon refreshments. Ck-out 11 am, ck-in 3-7 pm. Business servs avail. Exercise equipt; weight machine, bicycle, sauna. Whirlpool. Some fireplaces, refrigerators. Tudor-style inn in cedar grove; quiet atmosphere. Totally nonsmoking. Cr cds: A, DS, MC, V.

🏋 ⊠ 🖲

★ ★ **ORCAS HOTEL.** (Orcas 98280) at ferry landing, Orcas Island. 360/376-4300; FAX 360/376-4399. 12 air-cooled rms, 4 with bath, 3 story. No rm phones. May-Oct: S $59-$170; D $69-$170; each addl $15; lower rates rest of yr. Children over 12 yrs only. Complimentary continental

bkfst. Restaurant 8-11:30 am, 5-8:30 pm. Bar 11 am-10 pm. Ck-out 11 am, ck-in 1:30 pm. Business servs avail. Balconies. Victorian hotel built in 1904. View of island's ferry landing. Totally nonsmoking. Cr cds: A, DS, MC, V.

⊠ 🖲

★ ★ **PANACEA.** (595 Park St, Friday Harbor 98250) 360/378-3757; res: 800/639-2762. 4 rms, 2 with shower only. No A/C. No rm phones. May-Oct: S, D $135-$160; each addl $20; lower rates rest of yr. Children over 17 yrs only. TV; cable. Complimentary full bkfst. Ck-out 10 am, ck-in 2 pm. Some in-rm whirlpools. Picnic tables, grills. Craftsman-style home built in 1907. Totally nonsmoking. Cr cds: MC, V.

⊠ 🖲

★ ★ **SAN JUAN INN.** (50 Spring St, Friday Harbor 98250), ¹/₂ blk from ferry dock. 360/378-2070; FAX 360/378-6437; res: 800/742-8210. Web www.rockisland.com/~tucker/sjuan.html. 10 rms, 2 story. No A/C. Mid-May-mid-Oct: S, D $75-$175; wkly rates off season; lower rates rest of yr. Children over 5 yrs only. Complimentary continental bkfst. Ck-out 11 am, ck-in 2 pm. Restored inn; built 1873. Totally nonsmoking. Cr cds: A, DS, MC, V.

⊠ 🖲

★ ★ **TUCKER HOUSE.** (260 B St, Friday Harbor 98250) 360/378-2783; res: 800/965-0123; FAX 360/378-6437. Web www.rockis land/~tucker/sjinn.com/. 5 rms, 2 share bath, 2 story, 2 kit. units. No A/C. No rm phones. May-mid-Oct: S $85-$135; D $95-$135; each addl $25; wkly rates; lower rates rest of yr. Children over 18 yrs only. Crib free. Pet accepted, some restrictions; $15. TV; cable, VCR avail (movies). Complimentary full bkfst. Complimentary coffee in rms. Restaurant opp 11 am-10 pm. Ck-out 11 am, ck-in 2 pm. Luggage handling. Free airport transportation. Whirlpool. Some refrigerators, microwaves. Picnic tables. Victorian home built in 1898. Totally nonsmoking. Cr cds: A, DS, MC, V.

⊠ 🖲

✔ ★ ★ **TURTLEBACK FARM INN.** (Rte 1, Eastsound 98245) Crow Valley Rd, on Orcas Island. 360/376-4914; res: 800/375-4914; FAX 360/376-5329. 11 air-cooled rms, 2 story. Rm phones avail. S $70-$175; D $80-$185; each addl $25. Complimentary full bkfst; afternoon refreshments. Ck-out 11 am. Some refrigerators, fireplaces. Overlooks eighty acres of farmland. Totally nonsmoking. Cr cds: DS, MC, V.

D ⊠ 🖲

★ ★ ★ **WINDSONG BED & BREAKFAST.** (Deer Harbor Rd, Orcas 98280) 360/376-2500; res: 800/669-3948; FAX 360/376-4453. E-mail windsong@pacificrim.net; web www.pacificws.com/orcas/wingsong.html. 4 air-cooled rms, 3 with shower only. No rm phones. May-Oct: S $105-$130; D $115-$140; each addl $25; wkends, hols (2-day min); lower rates rest of yr. Children over 14 yrs only. TV in common rm; cable (premium), VCR avail (movies). Complimentary full bkfst. Complimentary coffee in rms. Ck-out 11 am, ck-in 2-5 pm. Luggage handling. Airport transportation. Whirlpool. Many fireplaces. Picnic tables, grills. Built in 1917 as a grammar school; first inn on Orcas Island. Totally nonsmoking. Cr cds: MC, V.

⊠ 🖲

Resorts

★ ★ **ROCHE HARBOR.** (Roche Harbor 98250) 10 mi NW on Roche Harbor Rd, on San Juan Island. 360/378-2155; FAX 360/378-6809; res: 800/451-8910. Web www.roche.harbor.com. 20 hotel rms, 4 with bath, 3 story, 9 kit. cottages (2-bedrm), 25 condos (1-3-bedrm). No A/C. No elvtr. May-Oct: S, D $79-$130; cottages $130-$195; condos $145-$245; under 6 free; lower rates rest of yr. Crib free. TV. Pool. Supervised child's activities (June-mid-Sept); ages 5-18. Restaurant opp 5-10 pm. Snack bar. Bar 11-1 am; entertainment (June-Aug). Ck-out 11 am, ck-in 3 pm. Business servs avail. Grocery. Coin lndry. Meeting rms. Business center. Gift shop. Airport transportation. Tennis. Swimming beach; boats. Hiking. Microwaves avail. Some balconies. Picnic area; grills. On harbor. Totally nonsmoking. Cr cds: A, MC, V.

🛥 🚵 ⊠ 🎿 🎣 ⊠ 🖲 🚶

★ ★ ★ **ROSARIO.** *(1 Rosario Way, Eastsound 98245)* on Orcas Island, 5 mi SE of Eastsound, on Puget Sound. 360/376-2222; FAX 360/376-3680; res: 800/562-8820. E-mail info@rosarioresort.com; web www.rosario-resort.com/. 86 rms, 33 suites, 2 with kit., 1-2 story. No A/C. June-mid-Oct: S, D $180-$200; each addl $20; suites $200-$400; kit. units $140-$280; under 12 free; lower rates rest of yr. Crib $5. TV; VCR avail (movies $3). 3 pools, 1 indoor; whirlpool, poolside serv. Restaurant (by res) 7 am-2 pm, 6-10 pm. Box lunches, snacks. Bar 11-1 am. Ck-out 11 am, ck-in 4 pm. Grocery. Coin lndry. Package store 5 mi. Meeting rms. Airport transportation. Tennis. Golf privileges. Boating (marina). Lawn games. Music rm; piano, organ concerts. Entertainment. Exercise rm; instructor, weights, bicycles, sauna. Some wet bars, fireplaces. Private patios, balconies. On 30-acre estate. Totally nonsmoking. Cr cds: A, D, DS, MC, V.

Cottage Colony

★ ★ ★ **LOPEZ FARM COTTAGES.** *(Fisherman Bay Rd, Lopez Island 98261)* 360/468-3555; res: 800/440-3556; FAX 360/468-3966. 4 kit. units, all with shower only. May-Oct: S, D $125; each addl $25; lower rates rest of yr. Complimentary continental bkfst. Ck-out 11 am, ck-in 3-7 pm. Grocery, coin lndry, package store 1¹/₂ mi. Free airport transportation. Hiking. Spa. Whirlpool. Refrigerators, microwaves, wet bars, fireplaces. On historic family farm. Totally nonsmoking. Cr cds: MC, V.

Restaurants

★ ★ ★ **CHRISTINA'S.** *(Horseshoe Hwy, Eastsound 98245)* on Orcas Island. 360/376-4904. Hrs: 5:30-10 pm. Closed Dec 25; also 1st 3 wks in Nov & Jan. Res accepted. Bar from 4 pm. Wine list. A la carte entrees: dinner $14.50-$26.50. Child's meals. Specializes in fresh Northwest seafood. Street parking. Outdoor dining. Extensive woodwork in several dining areas; large deck overlooks water. Totally nonsmoking. Cr cds: A, C, D, DS, MC, V.

★ ★ **DOWNRIGGER.** *10 Front St (98250), San Juan Island (98250), adj ferry dock.* 360/378-2700. Hrs: 11 am-10 pm. Res accepted. Bar. Semi-a la carte: lunch $4.95-$12.95, dinner $8.95-$22.95. Specializes in fresh local seafood, steak, pasta. Outdoor dining. Several dining levels with views of harbor. Totally nonsmoking. Cr cds: A, MC, V.

★ ★ **LA FAMIGLIA RISTORANTE.** *(Prune Alley at A Street, Eastsound 98245)* on Orcas Island, center of town. 360/376-2335. Hrs: 11 am-2 pm, 4:30 pm-closing. Res accepted. Italian, Amer menu. Serv bar. Semi-a la carte: lunch $3.25-$10.95, dinner $10.95-$17.95. Child's meals. Specialties: scallopine alla limone, seafood primavera. Outdoor dining. Rustic decor; oak furnishings. Totally nonsmoking. Cr cds: A, DS, MC, V.

Seattle (C-3)

Founded 1852 **Pop** 516,259 **Elev** 125 ft **Area code** 206 **Web** www.See Seattle.org

Information Seattle-King County Convention & Visitors Bureau, 520 Pike St, Ste 1325, 98101; 206/461-5840.

Suburbs Bellevue, Bremerton, Everett, Issaquah, Marysville, Port Gamble, Tacoma. (See individual alphabetical listings.)

Seattle has prospered from the products of its surrounding forests, farms and waterways, serving as provisioner to Alaska and the Orient. Since the 1950s it has acquired a new dimension from the manufacture of jet airplanes, missiles and space vehicles—which, along with tourism, comprise the city's most important industries.

The Space Needle, which dominated Seattle's boldly futuristic 1962 World's Fair, still stands, symbolic of the city's present-day, forward-looking character. The site of the fair is now the Seattle Center. Many features of the fair have been made permanent.

Seattle is on Elliott Bay, nestled between Puget Sound, an inland-probing arm of the Pacific Ocean, and Lake Washington, a 24-mile stretch of fresh water. The city sprawls across hills and ridges, some of them 500 feet high, but all are dwarfed by the Olympic Mountains to the west and the Cascades to the east. Elliott Bay, Seattle's natural harbor, welcomes about 2,000 commercial deep-sea cargo vessels a year. From Seattle's piers, ships wind their way 125 nautical miles through Puget Sound and the Strait of Juan de Fuca, two-thirds of them Orient-bound, the others destined for European, Alaskan and Eastern ports.

On the same latitude as Newfoundland, Seattle is warmed by the Japan Current, shielded by the Olympics from excessive winter rains, and protected by the Cascades from midcontinent winter blasts. Only twice has the temperature been recorded at 100°F; there isn't a zero on record.

Five families pioneered here and named the town for a friendly Native American chief. The great harbor, and the timber surrounding it, made an inviting combination; shortly thereafter a sawmill and a salmon-canning plant were in operation. Soon wagon trains were rolling to Seattle through Snoqualmie Pass, a tempting 3,022 feet, lower than any other in the Northwest.

Isolated at the fringe of the continent by the vast expanse of America, Seattle enjoyed great expectations but few women, an obvious threat to the growth and serenity of the community. Asa Mercer, a civic leader and first president of the Territorial University, went East and persuaded 11 proper young women from New England to sail with him around the Horn to Seattle to take husbands among the pioneers. This venture in long distance matchmaking proved so successful that Mercer returned East and recruited 100 Civil War widows. Today many of Seattle's families proudly trace their lineage to these women.

When a ship arrived from Alaska with a "ton of gold" in 1897, the great Klondike Gold Rush was on, converting Seattle into a boomtown—the beginning of the trail to fortune. Since then Seattle has been the natural gateway to Alaska because of the protected Inside Passage; the commercial interests of the two remain tightly knit. Another major event for Seattle was the opening of the Panama Canal in 1914, a tremendous stimulant for the city's commerce.

Transportation

Airport: See SEATTLE-TACOMA INTL AIRPORT AREA.

Car Rental Agencies: See IMPORTANT TOLL-FREE NUMBERS.

Public Transportation: Metro Transit System, phone 206/553-3000.

Rail Passenger Service: Amtrak 800/872-7245.

What to See and Do

Alki Beach. Site where Seattle's first settlers built cabins; monument; scenic views; lighthouse at Alki Point (adj); boat ramp on Harbor Ave SW; concessions. Alki Ave SW & 59th Ave SW, Southwest Side. **Free.**

⭐ **Boeing Field—King County Intl Airport.** Observation Park has viewing, picnicking facilities. Southeast Side. Phone 206/296-7380. **Free.** Also here is

Museum of Flight. Exhibits on aviation pioneers, industry. Spectacular Great Gallery focuses on modern flight, including space age; more than 40 aircraft on display, including A-12 Blackbird. Adj is Red Barn (1909), original Boeing Aircraft Mfg Bldg, featuring exhibits emphasizing aviation from its beginnings through the 1930s. (Daily; closed Thanksgiving, Dec 25) Phone 206/764-5720. ¢¢¢

Carkeek Park. Approx 190 acres on Puget Sound. Beach, picnic area; model airplane meadow, hiking trail (1 mi). (Daily) NW 110th St, Northwest Side. **Free.**

Charles and Emma Frye Art Museum. Collection of American and European paintings from late 19th century; art competitions; traveling and changing exhibits. (Daily; closed Thanksgiving, Dec 25) 704 Terry Ave, at Cherry St, downtown. Phone 206/622-9250. **Free.**

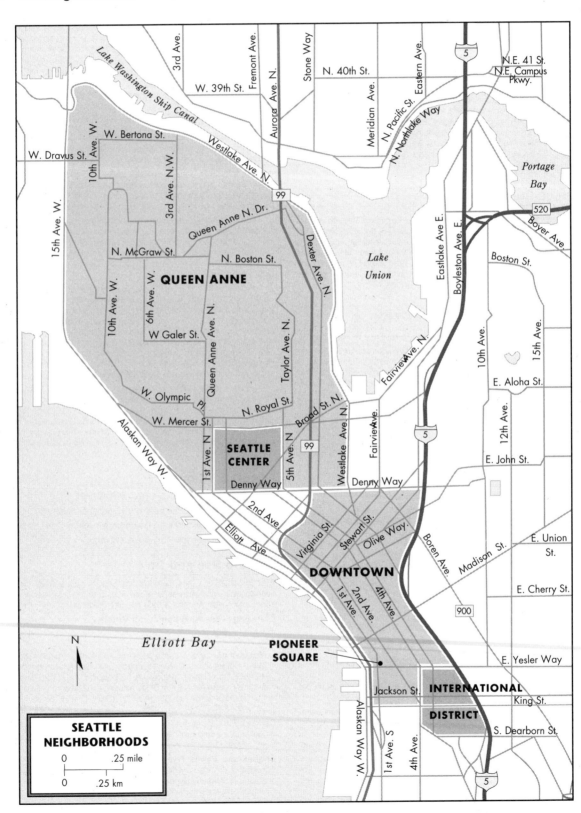

SEATTLE
NEIGHBORHOODS

0 _____ .25 mile

0 _____ .25 km

Discovery Park. More than 500 acres of urban wilderness on the Magnolia bluff. Former US Army post. Nature trails, meadows, forests, cliffs and beaches (no swimming). Picnicking, playground, tennis. Visitor center (daily; closed hols). Indian Cultural Center (Mon-Fri). Park (daily). Guided nature walks (Sat). 3801 W Government Way, Northwest Side. Phone 206/386-4236. **Free.**

Evergreen Floating Bridge. Almost 1¹/₂ mi long; connects downtown Seattle with Bellevue (see). On WA 520, near Montlake Pl, Southeast Side.

Ferry trips and cruises.

Ferry trips. Access to Olympic Peninsula, a number of interesting ferry trips. Seattle Ferry Terminal, Colman Dock, foot of Madison St. Contact Washington State Ferries, Colman Dock, 98104; 206/464-6400 or 800/843-3779 (WA). Per vehicle ¢¢-¢¢¢

Argosy Harbor Cruise. One-hr narrated harbor tour. (Daily) From Pier 55, foot of Seneca St. Phone 206/623-1445. ¢¢¢-¢¢¢¢

Tillicum Village. Narrated harbor cruise; baked-salmon dinner; stage show. (May-mid-Oct, daily; rest of yr, Sat; hrs vary) Res advised. Blake Island State Park. Excursion from Pier 56, ft of Seneca St. Phone 206/443-1244 or 800/426-1205. ¢¢¢¢¢

Gallant Lady Cruises. Six-day inclusive summer cruises to San Juan Islands; also extended cruises along British Columbia. Depart from Lake Union. For prices, schedule, contact PO Box 1250, Vashon 98070; 206/463-2073.

Freeway Park. Five-acre park features dramatic water displays. Free concerts (summer, Mon). (Daily). 6th & Seneca, downtown.

Gas Works Park. Views of downtown and Lake Union in 20-acre park. Towers of an old gas plant & imaginative reuse of industrial machinery. More than 26,000 boats/yr pass here to the ship canal. Your shadow marks the time on 28-ft sundial at top of Kite Hill. Kite-flying mound, picnic shelter, play barn, promenade. (Daily) N Northlake Way at Meridian N, Northwest Side. **Free.**

Golden Gardens. Saltwater swimming beach (no lifeguards; water temperature 54°F in summer); boat ramp (adj to Shilshole Bay Marina); picnic areas with views of Sound, mountains; volleyball courts. Teen activity center. (Daily) N end of Seaview Ave NW, Northwest Side. **Free.**

Green Lake Park. Two swimming beaches (mid-June-early Sept, daily); indoor pool (daily exc Sun; fee; phone 206/684-4961); wading pool (May-Sept, daily); Bathhouse Theater (phone 206/524-9110); tennis; 3-mi pedestrian and bicycle path around lake; fishing pier; boat rentals (phone 206/684-4074); picnic and playfield areas, playground; pitch 'n' putt golf; concessions. On Aurora Ave (WA 99), between N 65th & 72nd Sts, Northwest Side. **Free.**

Industrial tour.

Rainier Brewing Co. Guided tour of brewery; sample beer and root beer in Mountain Room. (Daily exc Sun & hols) Children must be able to walk and be accompanied by adult. (Mon-Fri) 3100 Airport Way S. Phone 206/622-2600. **Free.**

Intl District. Asian community with shops, restaurants and the Nippon Kan Theatre, a national historic site at Kobe Park, where a giant lantern overlooks the terraced community gardens. SE of downtown, 4th Ave to I-5 and Yesler to S Dearborn Sts, downtown.

Klondike Gold Rush Natl Historical Park-Seattle Unit. Visitor center in historic Pioneer Square District. Details gold rush stampede of 1897-1898; displays, photomurals, artifacts, slide & film programs; gold-panning demonstrations. (Daily; closed Jan 1, Thanksgiving, Dec 25) 117 S Main St, Southwest Side. Phone 206/553-7220. **Free.**

Lake Union. Boatyards, seaplane moorages, houseboat colonies on lake. Seen from George Washington Memorial Bridge, Northwest Side.

Lake Washington Canal. Chittenden Locks raise and lower boats to link salt and fresh water anchorages. More than 400,000 passengers and 6 million tons of freight pass through annually. Commodore Park and a salmon ladder with viewing windows are on the S side. Can be seen from Seaview Ave NW and NW 54th St, Northwest Side.

Lake Washington Floating Bridge. Can be seen from Lake Washington Blvd & Lakeside Ave. Connects downtown Seattle with Mercer Island via I-90.

Lincoln Park. Trails, picnic areas, tennis; beach, bathhouse; saltwater pool (mid-June-early Sept, daily; fee); wading pool (June-Sept, daily); fitness trail. (Daily) Fauntleroy Ave SW & SW Rose St, Southwest Side. **Free.**

Mt Baker-Snoqualmie Natl Forest. Snoqualmie Section. Includes several ski areas (see MT RAINIER NATIONAL PARK and NORTH BEND); eight wilderness areas; picnic and campsites, fishing, hunting. More than 1 million acres. E & S of city, reached via I-90. Contact Outdoor Recreation Information Center, 915 2nd Ave, Suite 442, 98174; 206/775-9702or 206/220-7450. (See BELLINGHAM) **Free.**

Museum of History and Industry. History of Seattle and Pacific Northwest, exhibits change frequently. (Daily; closed Jan 1, Thanksgiving, Dec 25) Tues free. 2700 24th Ave E, on N side of WA 520, just S of Husky Stadium, Southeast Side. Phone 206/324-1125. ¢¢¢

Myrtle Edwards/Elliott Bay. One mi of shoreline; paved bike trail; views of Puget Sound, the Olympic Peninsula and oceangoing vessels; Seamen's Memorial and a granite and concrete sculpture. N of Pier 70, Northwest Side. **Free.**

Nordic Heritage Museum. Center for Scandinavian community in Pacific Northwest. Represents all five Scandinavian countries. Historical exhibits; art gallery; performing arts. (Tues-Sat, also Sun afternoon) 3014 NW 67th St, Northwest Side. Phone 206/789-5707. ¢¢

⭐ **Pike Place Market.** Oldest continuously operating farmer's market in the country. Buy anything from artichokes to antiques. More than 225 permanent shops, restaurants; handcrafts. (Daily; closed major hols) First Ave & Pike St, in 9-acre historical district, downtown. Phone 206/682-7453. **Free.**

Pioneer Square. Restored buildings of early Seattle now house galleries, shops and restaurants. Bounded by 1st Ave, James St & Yesler Way, downtown.

Professional sports.

American League baseball (Seattle Mariners). Kingdome, 201 S King St. Phone 206/628-3555.

NBA (Seattle SuperSonics). Key Arena, at Seattle Center, 1st & Republic. Phone 206/281-5000.

NFL (Seattle Seahawks). Kingdome, 201 S King St. Phone 206/827-9777.

Schmitz Park. Section of forest as it was when first settlers arrived. Admiral Way SW & SW Stevens St, E of Alki Ave, Southwest Side. **Free.**

Seattle Art Museum. Collection of Asian and Chinese jades; modern art; ethnic art, including the Katherine White Collection of African art; changing exhibits. (Daily exc Mon; closed Jan 1, Thanksgiving, Dec 25). 100 University St, downtown. Phone 206/654-3100. ¢¢¢

⭐ **Seattle Center.** Site of 1962 World's Fair. 305 Harrison St, downtown. Phone 206/684-7200 or 206/684-8582 (recording). Its 74 acres include

Monorail. Provides a scenic 90-second ride between Center House and Westlake Center in downtown. Legacy of 1962 World's Fair, the Swedish-built train makes frequent runs throughout the day. (Daily, closed Jan 1, Thanksgiving, Dec 25) ¢

Space Needle. A 605-ft tower. At 520-ft level, visitors can take in spectacular view from observation deck. Shops, lounge and displays on observation deck; glass elevators. Two revolving restaurants at 500 ft; no elvtr charge when dining. (Daily) Phone 800/937-9582. ¢¢¢

Fun Forest Amusement Park. Rides (fees), games in parklike setting. (June-Labor Day, daily; Mar-June & early Sept-Nov, Fri-Sun) Phone 206/728-1585. **Free.**

Center House. Three floors of specialty shops, restaurants, conference facilities, administrative offices. (Daily) Phone 206/684-7200 or 206/684-8582 (recording).

Seattle Center Opera House, Playhouse, Arena, Key Arena. The Opera House is home of the Seattle Opera Assoc, Pacific Northwest Ballet and Seattle Symphony. Bagley Wright Theatre is home of Seattle Repertory Theatre (phone 206/443-2222). The Arena seats up to 6,000 for hockey, boxing, concerts. The Coliseum is home to the NBA Super-Sonics and seats up to 15,000 for sports, concerts, conventions and trade shows. Phone 206/684-7200.

Intl Fountain. Music and light show. (Daily)

Pacific Science Center. More than 200 hands-on exhibits plus IMAX Theater, live science demonstrations, planetarium shows, laser light shows and special events. Science playground. (Daily; closed Thanksgiving, Dec 25) 200 2nd Ave N. Phone 206/443-2001. ¢¢¢

Northwest Craft Center and Gallery. (Memorial Day-Labor Day, daily; rest of yr, daily exc Mon; closed Jan 1, Thanksgiving, Dec 25). Phone 206/728-1555. **Free.**

Seattle Univ (1891). (4,800 students) Landscaped urban campus with more than 1,000 varieties of exotic flowers, trees and shrubs; water fountain sculpture by George Tsutakawa. Tours of campus. Broadway & Madison St, downtown. Phone 206/296-6000.

Seward Park. Swimming beach (mid-June-early Sept, daily), bathhouse; picnic and play areas, tennis; amphitheater; Japanese lantern and *torii* (Japanese arch); fish hatchery. (Daily) Occupies peninsula off Lake Washington Blvd S & S Orcas St, Southeast Side. **Free.**

Shilshole Bay Marina. Moorage for 1,500 boats, fuel, repairs, launching ramp, marine supplies; restaurants. 7001 Seaview Ave NW, Northwest Side. Phone 206/728-3385.

Sightseeing tours.

Underground Tour. Informative, humorous lecture and guided walking tour of 5-block area where street level was raised 8-35 ft after the Seattle fire of 1889, leaving many storefronts and some interiors intact underground; 90-min tour goes both above and below ground. (Daily; closed major hols; advance res recommended) 610 1st Ave. Phone 206/682-1511 for information, 206/682-4646 for res (24 hrs). ¢¢¢

Gray Line bus tours. 720 S Forest St, 98134; 206/624-5077 or 800/426-7532.

Smith Cove. Navy ships at anchor; Seattle Annex, Naval Supply Center along N side of W Garfield St. Can be seen from Elliott Ave & W Garfield St, Northwest Side.

The Kingdome. Tours of King County's multipurpose covered stadium include visitors' locker room, VIP lounge, press box, field area (mid-Apr-mid-Sept, daily exc Sun). Concludes with visit to Royal Brougham Sports Museum. No tours when daytime events are scheduled. 201 S King St, downtown. Phone 206/296-3128. ¢¢

The Seattle Aquarium. Features 400,000-gallon underwater viewing dome; re-created Puget Sound habitats with tide that ebbs and flows; tropical Pacific exhibit; marine mammal exhibits of seals and sea otters. (Day after Labor Day-Memorial Day, daily) Pier 59, Waterfront Park, downtown. Phone 206/386-4320 (recording). ¢¢¢

Univ of Washington (1861). (34,400 students) Visitor Information Center, 4014 University Way NE. A 694-acre campus with 128 major buildings, stadium. Special exhibits in Henry Art Gallery (daily exc Mon; closed hols; fee). Thomas Burke Memorial-Washington State Museum (daily exc Mon; closed hols; free); Henry Suzzallo Library. Meany Hall for the Performing Arts, three theaters; health sciences research center & teaching hospital; Waterfront Activities Center; Washington Park Arboretum. Parking fee. Main entrance, 17th Ave NE & NE 45th St, Northeast Side. Phone 206/543-9198.

Volunteer Park. Tennis, play area, wading pool (June-Sept, daily), picnic area; conservatory (daily), formal gardens; observation deck in water tower (520 ft) with view of mountains, city, Puget Sound (daily). 15th Ave E & E Prospect St, Northeast Side. **Free.**

Warren G. Magnuson Park. Approx 200 acres; 1-mi shoreline. Swimming beach (mid-July-early Sept, daily); picnicking, playfield; small boat launch ramp, concessions. Fee for some activities. (Daily) NE 65th & Sand Point Way NE, Northeast Side.

Washington Park Arboretum. Arboretum Dr E winds over 200 acres containing more than 5,000 species of trees and shrubs from all parts of world. Rhododendrons, cherries, azaleas (Apr-June). Arboretum open daily all yr. Tours (Jan-Nov, Sun). On both sides of Lake Washington Blvd, between E Madison & Montlake, Southeast Side. Phone 206/543-8800. **Free.** Within is

Japanese Garden. Ornamental plants, glassy pools, 12-tier pagoda & teahouse. Tea ceremony (phone for dates). (Mar-Nov, daily) S end of arboretum. Phone 206/684-4725. ¢¢

✪ **Waterfront Drive.** Or take higher level Alaskan Way Viaduct along a parallel route to view harbor, sound, mountains. A trolley runs the length of the waterfront and continues into Pioneer Square and the International District. Follow Alaskan Way along Elliott Bay to see ships of many nations docked at piers.

Woodland Park Zoological Gardens. Displays more than 1,000 specimens, many in natural habitats, including nocturnal house, African savanna and Asian primates exhibits. Children's Zoo. (Daily) Phinney Ave N between N 50th & N 59th Sts, on WA 99, I-5 N 50th St exit, SW of Green Lake, Northwest Side. For hrs phone 206/684-4800 (recording). International Test Rose Gardens (free). ¢¢¢

Annual Events

Pacific Northwest Arts and Crafts Fair. 4 mi E in Bellevue. Art exhibits, handicrafts. Late July.

Seattle Seafair. Citywide marine festival. Regattas, speedboat races, shows at Aqua Theater, parades, sports events, exhibits. Phone 206/728-0123. Late July-early Aug.

Seasonal Event

A Contemporary Theater (ACT). One of the major resident theaters in the country, ACT is a professional (Equity) theater. Daily exc Mon. "A Christmas Carol," in Dec. 700 Union St. For res, information Phone 206/285-3220. May-Nov.

Seattle-Tacoma Intl Airport Area

For additional accommodations, see SEATTLE-TACOMA INTL AIRPORT AREA, which follows SEATTLE.

City Neighborhoods

Many of the restaurants, unrated dining establishments and some lodgings listed under Seattle include neighborhoods as well as exact street addresses. Geographic descriptions of these areas are given, followed by a table of restaurants arranged by neighborhood.

Downtown: South of Denny Way, west of I-5, north of S King St and east of Alaskan Way and Elliot Bay. **North of Downtown:** North of E Denny Way. **South of Downtown:** South of Dearborn St. **East of Downtown:** East of I-5.

International District: Southeast of Downtown; south of Yesler St, west of I-5, north of S Dearborn St and east of 4th Ave S.

Pioneer Square: Downtown area on and around Pioneer Square; bounded by 1st and James Sts, Yesler Way and 1st Ave S.

Queen Anne: South of W Nickerson St and Washington Ship Canal, west of Westlake Ave, north of Denny Way and east of Elliot Ave W and 15th St W.

Seattle Center: South of Mercer St, west of 5th Ave N, north of Denny Way and east of 1st Ave N.

SEATTLE RESTAURANTS BY NEIGHBORHOOD AREAS
(For full description, see alphabetical listings under Restaurants)

INTERNATIONAL DISTRICT
Four Seas. 714 S King St
Linyen. 424 Seventh Ave S

DOWNTOWN
Andaluca. 407 Olive Way
Assaggio Ristorante. 2010 Fourth Ave
Bombore. 89 University St
Brooklyn House. 1212 Second Ave
Buca Di Beppo. 701 Ninth Ave N
Cafe Campagne. 1600 Post Alley
Cafe Sophie. 1921 First Ave
Campagne. 86 Pine St
Chez Shea. 94 Pike St

Dahlia Lounge. 1904 Fourth Ave
El Gaucho. 2505 First Ave
Elliott's Oyster House. 1203 Alaskan Way
Etta's Seafood. 2020 Western Ave
Flying Fish. 2234 First Ave
Fullers (Sheraton Hotel). 1400 6th Ave
Georgian Room (Four Seasons Olympic Hotel). 411 University St
Hunt Club (Sorrento Hotel). 900 Madison St
Il Bistro. 93A Pike St
Ivar's Acres Of Clams. Pier 54
Labuznik. 1924 First Ave
Lampreia. 2400 First Ave
Las Margaritas. 1122 Post Ave
Marco's. 2510 First Ave
Maximilien-In-The-Market. 81A Pike Place
McCormick & Schmick's. 1103 First Ave
McCormick's Fish House. 722 Fourth Ave
Metropolitan Grill. 820 Second Ave
Obachine. 1518 Sixth Ave
Painted Table (Alexis Hotel). 1007 First Ave
Palace Kitchen. 2030 Fifth Ave
Palomino. 1420 Fifth Ave
Pink Door. 1919 Post Alley
Place Pigalle. 81 Pike St
Prego (Renaissance Madison Hotel). 515 Madison St
Queen City Grill. 2201 1st Ave
Reiner's. 1106 Eighth Ave
Roy's (The Westin Hotel). 1900 5th Ave
Ruth's Chris Steak House. 800 Fifth Ave
Sazerac (Hotel Monaco). 1101 4th Ave
Shiro's. 2401 Second Ave
Theoz. 1523 Sixth Ave
Tulio (Hotel Vintage Park). 1100 Fifth Ave
Union Square Grill. 621 Union St
Vina. 2207 First Ave
Virazon. 1329 First Ave
Wild Ginger. 1400 Western Ave

NORTH OF DOWNTOWN
Arnie's Northshore. 1900 N Northlake Way
Asia Grille. 2820 NE University Village
Bandoleone. 2241 Eastlake Ave E
Burrito Loco. 9211 Holman Rd NW
Cafe Lago. 2305 24th Ave E
Carmelita. 7314 Greenwood Ave N
Chinook's. 1900 W Nickerson
Cucina! Cucina!. 901 Fairview Ave N
Doong Kong Lau. 9710 Aurora Ave N
Franco's Hidden Harbor. 1500 Westlake Ave N
Ivar's Indian Salmon House. 401 NE Northlake Way
Jitterbug. 2114 N 45th St
Latitude 47°. 1232 Westlake N
Le Gourmand. 425 NW Market St
Pescatore. 5300 34th St NW
Piatti. 2800 NE University Village
Portage Bay Cafe (University Inn Motor Hotel). 4140 Roosevelt Way NE
Ray's Boathouse. 6049 Seaview Ave NW
Saleh Al Lago. 6804 E Greenlake Way
Serafina. 2043 Eastlake Ave E
Simpatico. 4430 Wallingford Ave
Stella's Trattoria. 4500 Ninth Ave
Surrogate Hostess. 746 19th Ave E
Szmania's. 3321 W McGraw
Union Bay Cafe. 3515 NE 45th St

EAST OF DOWNTOWN
Cactus. 4220 E Madison
Cafe Flora. 2901 E Madison
Dulces Latin Bistro. 1430 34th Ave
Kitto Japanese Noodle House. 614 Broadway E
Madison Park Cafe. 1807 42nd Ave E
Nishino. 3130 E Madison
Rover's. 2808 E Madison St

Z Ritz. 720 E Pike

PIONEER SQUARE
Al Boccalino. 1 Yesler Way
F.X. McRory's Steak, Chop & Oyster House. 419 Occidental Ave S
Il Terrazzo Carmine. 411 First Ave S
La Buca. 102 Cherry St
Trattoria Mitchelli. 84 Yesler Way

QUEEN ANNE
Adriatica. 1107 Dexter N
Canlis. 2576 Aurora Ave N
Chutney's. 519 First Ave N
Kaspar's. 19 W Harrison St
Paragon. 2125 Queen Anne Ave N
Pirosmani. 2220 Queen Anne Ave N
Ponti. 3014 Third Ave N

SEATTLE CENTER
Space Needle. 219 Fourth Ave N

Note: When a listing is located in a town that does not have its own city heading, it will appear under the city nearest to its location. In these cases, the address and town appear in parenthesis immediately following the name of the establishment.

Motels

★ ★ **BEST WESTERN LOYAL INN.** *2301 Eighth Ave (98121), at Denny Way, downtown.* 206/682-0200; FAX 206/467-8984. 91 rms, 4 story. July-Sept: S $88; D $106; each addl $6; suites $200; under 12 free; lower rates rest of yr. Crib $3. TV; cable. Complimentary continental bkfst. Restaurant opp open 24 hrs. Ck-out noon. Coin lndry. Business servs avail. In-rm modem link. Sauna. Whirlpool. Some refrigerators, wet bars; microwaves avail. Cr cds: A, C, D, DS, MC, V.

★ **QUALITY INN CITY CENTER.** *2224 8th Ave (98121), downtown.* 206/624-6820; FAX 206/467-6926. 72 rms, 7 story. May-Oct: S $105-$115; D $115-$125; each addl $10; suites $145-$185; under 18 free; lower rates rest of yr. Crib free. Pet accepted. TV; cable (premium), VCR avail (movies). Continental bkfst. Coffee in rms. Ck-out 1 pm. Meeting rms. Business servs avail. In-rm modem link. Valet serv. Sundries. Exercise equipt; weight machine, treadmill, sauna. Whirlpool. Some refrigerators; microwaves avail for suites. Balconies. Cr cds: A, C, D, DS, ER, JCB, MC, V.

D 🐾 🏋 🖾 🖎 SC

✔★ **TRAVELERS INN.** *(4710 Lake Washington Blvd NE, Renton 98056)* S on I-405 exit 7. 253/228-2858; FAX 253/228-3055; res: 800/633-8300. 116 rms, 2-3 story. No elvtr. S $42.99; D $49.99; each addl $4; suites $63.99-$79.99; under 18 free. Crib free. TV; cable (premium). Heated pool. Complimentary coffee in lobby. Restaurant adj open 24 hrs. Bar 11-2 am. Ck-out 11 am. Coin lndry. Business servs avail. Cr cds: A, D, DS, MC, V.

D 〰 🖾 🖎 SC

Motor Hotels

★ ★ **BEST WESTERN EXECUTIVE INN.** *200 Taylor Ave N (98109), at Seattle Center.* 206/448-9444; FAX 206/441-7929. E-mail executive.inn@juno.com. 123 rms, 5 story. July-Sept: S, D $100-$143; each addl $15; under 18 free; lower rates rest of yr. Crib free. TV; cable (premium), VCR avail. Complimentary coffee in rms Mon-Fri. Restaurant 6:30 am-10 pm; wkends from 7 am. Rm serv. Bar 11-2 am. Ck-out noon. Guest lndry. Meeting rms. Business servs avail. In-rm modem link. Bellhops. Valet serv. Sundries. Exercise equipt; weight machine, stair machine. Whirlpool. Some refrigerators. Cr cds: A, C, D, DS, JCB, MC, V.

★ ★ **BEST WESTERN-PIONEER SQUARE HOTEL.** *77 Yesler Way (98104), in Pioneer Square.* 206/340-1234; *FAX 206/467-0707.* Web www.pioneersquare.com. 75 rms, 4 story. S, D $109-$139; each addl $10; under 12 free. Crib free. Valet parking $13. TV; cable, VCR avail. Complimentary continental bkfst. Restaurant opp 7-4 am. Ck-out 11 am. Meeting rms. Business servs avail. In-rm modem link. Bellhops. Valet serv. Health club privileges. In restored building (1914). Cr cds: A, D, DS, JCB, MC, V.

⊡ ⋈ ⋒ SC

★ ★ ★ **EDGEWATER INN.** *2411 Alaskan Way (98121), Pier 67, west of downtown.* 206/728-7000; *FAX 206/441-4119; res: 800/624-0670.* 237 rms, 4 story. S $129-$170; D $129-$240; each addl $15; suites $350-$1,000; under 18 free. Crib free. Valet parking (fee). TV; cable (premium). Coffee in rms. Restaurant 6 am-11 pm. Rm serv. Bar 11-1:30 am; entertainment Tues-Sat. Ck-out noon. Meeting rms. Business center. In-rm modem link. Bellhops. Valet serv. Gift shop. Exercise equipt; bicycles, rower. Guest bicycles. Minibars. Some balconies. Built entirely over water; adj to ferry terminal. Cr cds: A, C, D, DS, ER, JCB, MC, V.

⊡ 🏃 ⋈ 🔥 SC 🏄

✔ ★ ★ **SIXTH AVENUE INN.** *2000 Sixth Ave (98121), downtown.* 206/441-8300; *FAX 206/441-9903; res: 800/648-6440.* 166 rms, 5 story, no ground floor rms. Mid-May-mid-Oct: S $81-$109; D $93-$121; each addl $12; suites $150; under 17 free. Crib free. TV; cable (premium). Restaurant 6:30 am-10 pm. Rm serv 7 am-9 pm. Bar 11 am-midnight. Ck-out noon. Meeting rms. Business servs avail. In-rm modem link. Bellhops. Valet serv. Sundries. Cr cds: A, C, D, MC, V.

⋈ ⋒ SC

★ ★ **UNIVERSITY INN.** *4140 Roosevelt Way NE (98105), north of downtown.* 206/632-5055; *FAX 206/547-4937; res: 800/733-3855.* E-mail Univinn@aol.com; web www.travelweb.com. 102 rms, 4 story. May-Oct: S, D $92-$112; suites $122-$132; each addl $10; under 18 free; wkly rates. Crib free. TV; cable (premium). Heated pool. Complimentary continental bkfst. Restaurant 6:30 am-3 pm. Ck-out noon. Coin lndry. Meeting rms. Business center. In-rm modem link. Valet serv. Exercise equipt; weight machine, bicycles. Cr cds: A, D, DS, MC, V.

⊡ ≈ 🏃 ⋈ 🔥 SC 🏄

Hotels

★ ★ ★ ★ **ALEXIS HOTEL.** *1007 1st Ave (98104), downtown.* 206/624-4844; *FAX 206/621-9009; res: 800/426-7033.* Web www.alexishotel.com. A charming small hotel, the Alexis is in an artfully restored 1901 building near the waterfront, the Public Market and the Seattle Art Museum. Each room is individually decorated. 109 rms, 6 story. S, D $210-$235; suites $245-$550; under 12 free; some wkend rates. Crib free. Pet accepted. Covered valet parking $18/day. TV; cable (premium), VCR avail. Restaurant 6:30 am-3 pm (also see PAINTED TABLE). Rm serv 24 hrs. Bar 11 am-midnight. Ck-out 1 pm. Meeting rms. Business servs avail. In-rm modem link. Concierge. Shopping arcade. Exercise equipt; treadmill, stair machine, steam rm. Massage. Refrigerators; some bathrm phones; microwaves avail. Wet bar, minibar, beverages, whirlpool in suites. Eight wood-burning fireplaces. Some balconies. Cr cds: A, C, D, DS, MC, V.

⊡ ☞ 🏃 🔥

★ **CAMLIN.** *1619 Ninth Ave (98101), at Pine St, downtown.* 206/682-0100; *FAX 206/682-7415; res: 800/426-0670.* 136 rms, 36 A/C, 4-10 story. S, D $83-$114; each addl $10; suites $175; under 18 free. Crib free. TV; cable (premium). Pool. Restaurant 6-10:30 am, 11:30 am-2 pm, 6-10 pm; Sat 6:30-11 am, 5:30-10:30 pm; Sun 6:30-11 am, 5-9 pm. Bar; entertainment Tues-Sat. Ck-out noon. Business servs avail. Some balconies. Motor entrance on 8th Ave. Cr cds: A, C, D, DS, JCB, MC, V.

≈ ⋈ ⋒ SC

★ ★ **CROWNE PLAZA.** *1113 Sixth Ave (98101), at Seneca St, downtown.* 206/464-1980; *FAX 206/340-1617.* E-mail cplaza@wolfenet.com; web www.crownwplaza.com. 415 rms, 34 story. June-Oct S, D $240; each addl $20; suites $260-$525; under 18 free; wkend rates; lower rates rest of yr. Crib free. Covered valet parking $18. TV; cable (premium), VCR avail. Coffee in rms. Restaurant 6 am-10 pm. Bar 11-2 am. Ck-out

noon. Meeting rms. Business servs avail. In-rm modem link. Concierge. Exercise equipt; weight machine, stair machine, sauna. Whirlpool. Refrigerators avail. Luxury level. Cr cds: A, C, D, DS, JCB, MC, V.

⊡ 🏃 ⋈ ⋒ SC

★ ★ ★ **DOUBLETREE GUEST SUITES.** *16500 Southcenter Pkwy (98188), I-5 Southcenter exit, south of downtown.* 206/575-8220; *FAX 206/575-4743.* Web www.doubletreehotels.com. 221 suites, 8 story. S, D $119-$238; each addl $15; under 18 free; wkend, seasonal rates. Crib free. TV; cable (premium), VCR avail. Indoor pool; outdoor pool privileges in summer; whirlpool. Coffee in rms. Restaurant 6 am-10 pm; wkends 7 am-11 pm. Bar 11-2 am; entertainment. Ck-out noon. Meeting rms. Business servs avail. Gift shop. Free airport transportation. Exercise equipt; weight machine, bicycles, sauna. Racquetball. Refrigerators; microwaves avail. Atrium lobby. Cr cds: A, C, D, DS, ER, JCB, MC, V.

⊡ ≈ 🏃 ⋈ 🔥 SC

★ ★ ★ ★ **FOUR SEASONS OLYMPIC HOTEL.** *411 University St (98101), downtown.* 206/621-1700; *FAX 206/682-9633.* This elegant Italian Renaissance-style landmark hotel occupies a central position in Seattle's social scene. Known for its opulent decor—oak paneling, antiques and Italian marble—its attentive service and the elegant Georgian Room and Garden Court restaurants, the hotel is a convenient tour base, since it's a short stroll from Pike Place Market and the Seattle Art Museum. 450 rms, 13 story. S $225-$255; D $265-$295; each addl $20; suites $330-$1,250; under 18 free; wkend rates. Crib free. Valet parking $21. TV; cable (premium), VCR avail (movies). Indoor pool; whirlpool, poolside serv. Restaurant (see GEORGIAN ROOM). Rm serv 24 hrs. Bar 11-1 am. Ck-out 1 pm. Convention facilities. Business center. In-rm modem link. Concierge. Shopping arcade. Barber, beauty shop. Airport transportation. Exercise equipt; weight machine, bicycles, sauna. Massage. Bathrm phones, minibars; some refrigerators. Cr cds: A, C, D, ER, JCB, MC, V.

⊡ ≈ 🏃 ⋈ 🔥 🏄

★ ★ ★ **HILTON.** *1301 Sixth Ave (98101), W of I-5 Seneca-Union exit, downtown.* 206/624-0500; *FAX 206/682-9029.* 237 rms, 28 story. S $165-$210; D $185-$230; each addl $15; suites $310-$475; under 18 free; some wkend rates. Crib free. Garage $13. TV; cable (premium). Complimentary coffee in rms. Restaurants 6 am-10 pm. Rm serv 24 hrs. Bar 11-2 am; pianist. Ck-out 1 pm. Meeting rms. Business servs avail. Concierge. Gift shop. Exercise equipt; weight machines, bicycles. Refrigerators, minibars. View of Puget Sound. Cr cds: A, C, D, DS, ER, JCB, MC, V.

⊡ 🏃 ⋈ ⋒

HOTEL MONACO. *(Too new to be rated) 1101 Fourth Ave (98101), downtown.* 206/621-1770; *res: 800/945-2240; FAX 206/621-7779.* Web www.monaco-seattle.com. 189 rms, 11 story, 45 suites. May-Sept: S $195; D $210; suites $240-$900; under 18 free; wkly, hol plans; lower rates rest of yr. Crib free. Pet accepted. Valet parking $18. TV; cable (premium), VCR. Complimentary coffee in rms. Restaurant (see SAZERAC). Rm serv 24 hrs. Bar 11:30 am-midnight. Ck-out noon. Meeting rms. Business center. In-rm modem link. Valet serv. Concierge. Gift shop. Exercise equipt; weights, treadmill. Massage. Health club privileges. Bathrm phones, refrigerators, minibars; some in-rm whirlpools; microwaves avail. Luxury level. Whimsical yet elegant decor with vibrant color scheme throughout. Cr cds: A, D, DS, MC, V.

⊡ ☞ 🏃 ⋈ ⋒ SC 🏄

★ ★ ★ **HOTEL VINTAGE PARK.** *1100 Fifth Ave (98101), at Spring St, downtown.* 206/624-8000; *FAX 206/623-0568; res: 800/624-4433.* Web www.hotelvintagepark.com. Built in 1922, this European-style lodging combines the luxury of an upscale hotel with the personality of a bed-and-breakfast. Guest rooms are named for Washington wineries and decorated in rich vineyard shades of dark green, plum and gold. 126 rms, 11 story. S $185-$205; D $200-$220; suites $215-$375; under 12 free; wkend rates; package plans. Crib free. Valet parking $16. TV; cable, VCR avail. Complimentary coffee in rms. Restaurant (see TULIO). Rm serv 24 hrs. Ck-out noon. Meeting rms. Business servs avail. In-rm modem link. Concierge. Exercise equipt delivered to rms. Health club privileges.

Bathrm phones, minibars. Wine tasting (Washington wines) in lobby Mon-Sat. Cr cds: A, C, D, DS, ER, JCB, MC, V.

[D] [🚲] [🛎️]

★ ★ ★ ★ **INN AT THE MARKET.** *86 Pine St (98101), downtown. 206/443-3600; FAX 206/448-0631; res: 800/446-4484.* Web usa.nia.com /innmarket. Adjacent to the Pike Place Market, this small, deluxe hotel emphasizes the informality of the Pacific Northwest rather than the amenities of a big hotel. Rooms are spacious, have contemporary furnishings and ceramic sculptures, and look out on the city, the market, the hotel courtyard or Elliott Bay. 69 rms, 4-8 story, 10 suites. May-mid-Oct: S, D $145-$210; each addl $15; suites $250-$350; under 16 free; some wkend rates; lower rates rest of yr. Crib free. Parking $15; valet. TV; cable (premium), VCR avail. Complimentary coffee in rms. Ck-out noon. Meeting rm. Business servs avail. Shopping arcade. Beauty shop. Health club privileges. Bathrm phones, refrigerators; microwaves avail. Cr cds: A, C, D, DS, JCB, MC, V.

[D] [🚲] [🛎️] [SC]

★ ★ **INN AT VIRGINIA MASON.** *1006 Spring St (98104), east of downtown. 206/583-6453; FAX 206/223-7545; res: 800/283-6453.* 79 air-cooled rms, 9 story. S, D $98-$155; suites $155-$215. TV; cable (premium), VCR (movies). Restaurant 7-10 am, 11:30 am-3 pm, 5-9 pm. Ck-out noon. Business servs avail. In-rm modem link. Concierge. Microwaves avail. English country-style apartment house (1928); Queen Anne-style furnishings. Totally nonsmoking. Cr cds: A, D, DS, JCB, MC, V.

[D] [🚲] [🛎️] [SC]

★ ★ ★ **MAYFLOWER PARK.** *405 Olive Way (98101), downtown. 206/623-8700; FAX 206/382-6997; res: 800/426-5100.* 172 rms, 12 story. S $135-$155; D $150-$170; each addl $15; suites $175-$350; mini-suites $175-$190; under 18 free. Crib free. Covered valet parking $9. TV; cable (premium). Restaurant 6:30 am-10 pm. Rm serv 24 hrs. Bar 11:30-2 am. Ck-out noon. Meeting rms. Business servs avail. In-rm modem link. Exercise equipt; weights, stair machine. Health club privileges. Cr cds: A, C, D, DS, MC, V.

[D] [🏃] [🛎️] [SC]

↩★ ★ ★ **MEANY TOWER.** *4507 Brooklyn Ave NE (98105), E of I-5 exit 45th St, north of downtown. 206/634-2000; FAX 206/547-6029; res: 800/899-0251.* E-mail meanytwr@aol.com. 155 rms, 15 story. June-Sept: S $145-$165; D $160-$180; each addl $15; under 14 free; lower rates rest of yr. Crib free. TV; cable. Restaurant 6 am-9:30 pm; Sat to 9 pm; Sun to 8:30 pm. Bar 11 am-11 pm; Fri, Sat to midnight. Ck-out noon. Meeting rms. Business servs avail. In-rm modem link. Exercise equipt; rower, weight machine. Game rm. View of mountains, lakes, city. 2 blks from Univ of WA campus. Cr cds: A, C, D, MC, V.

[D] [🏃] [🛎️] [SC]

★ **PACIFIC PLAZA.** *400 Spring St (98104), downtown. 206/623-3900; FAX 206/623-2059; res: 800/426-1165.* E-mail pph400 @aol.com. 160 rms, 8 story. S, D $95-$125; under 18 free; wkend rates. Crib free. Garage parking $12 in/out. TV; cable. Complimentary continental bkfst. Ck-out 11 am. Business servs avail. Cr cds: A, D, DS, JCB, MC, V.

[🛎️] [SC]

★ ★ **PLAZA PARK SUITES.** *1011 Pike St (98101), downtown. 206/682-8282; FAX 206/682-5315; res: 800/426-0670 (exc WA).* 193 suites, 9 story. Studios $125-$190; 1 bedrm $190-$220; 2 bedrm $290-$330; under 18 free. Crib free. Valet parking $13. TV; cable (premium), VCR avail. Heated pool; whirlpool. Complimentary continental bkfst. Complimentary coffee in rms. Restaurant. Ck-out noon. Coin lndry. Meeting rms. Business servs avail. In-rm modem link. Gift shop. Exercise equipt; weight machine, stair machine. Refrigerators, microwaves; many in-rm whirlpools, fireplaces. Balconies. Picnic tables. Cr cds: A, C, D, DS, ER, JCB, MC, V.

[D] [🏊] [🏃] [🛎️] [SC]

★ ★ **RENAISSANCE MADISON.** *515 Madison St (98104), I-5 S Madison St exit, downtown. 206/583-0300; FAX 206/622-8635.* 553 rms, 28 story. S, D $159-$179; suites $199-$800; wkend rates. Crib free. Covered parking $14. TV; cable, VCR avail. Indoor pool; whirlpool. Com-

plimentary coffee in rms. Restaurant 6:30 am-10 pm; Fri, Sat to 11 pm (also see PREGO). Rm serv 24 hrs. Bars 11-2 am. Ck-out 1 pm. Convention facilities. Business center. In-rm modem link. Concierge. Barber, beauty shop. Gift shop. Exercise equipt; stair machine, weight machine. Health club privileges. Free local transportation. Refrigerators, minibars. Luxury level. Cr cds: A, C, D, DS, ER, JCB, MC, V.

[D] [🏊] [🏃] [🛎️] [SC] [🏃]

★ ★ ★ **SHERATON.** *1400 6th Ave (98101), downtown. 206/621-9000; FAX 206/621-8441.* Web www.ITTsheraton.com. 840 units, 35 story. S $200, D $220; suites $275-$600; under 17 free; wkend rates. Crib free. Pet accepted, some restrictions. Valet parking $18. TV; cable (premium), VCR avail. Indoor pool; whirlpool. Complimentary coffee in rms. Restaurant 6 am-midnight (also see FULLER'S). Rm serv 24 hrs. Bar 11-2 am; entertainment. Ck-out noon. Convention facilities. Business center. In-rm modem link. Concierge. Drugstore. Barber. Exercise rm: instructor, weight machine, stair machine, sauna. Minibars; some bathrm phones. Rms with original Northwest art. Luxury level. Cr cds: A, C, D, DS, ER, JCB, MC, V.

[D] [🏊] [🏃] [🛎️] [SC] [🏃]

★ ★ **SILVER CLOUD INN.** *5036 25th Ave NE (98105), north of downtown. 206/526-5200; FAX 206/522-1450; res: 800/205-6940.* E-mail heather@scinns.com; web scinns.com. 144 rms, 4 story. July-Oct: S $91-$103; D $103-$115; each addl $10; suites $117-$142; under 12 free; lower rates rest of yr. Crib free. TV; cable (premium). Indoor pool; whirlpool. Complimentary continental bkfst. Restaurant nearby. Ck-out noon. Meeting rms. Business servs avail. In-rm modem link. Guest lndry avail. Exercise equipt; bicycle, stair machine. Refrigerators, microwaves avail. Cr cds: A, C, D, DS, ER, MC, V.

[D] [🏃] [🛎️] [SC]

★ ★ ★ ★ **SORRENTO.** *900 Madison St (98104), I-5 N James, S Madison exits, downtown. 206/622-6400; FAX 206/343-6155; res: 800/426-1265 (exc WA).* Web usa.nia.com/sorrento. Designed in 1909 to resemble an Italian villa, this deluxe hotel offers wonderful views of downtown and the waterfront. Standard rooms are quiet and comfortable; spacious corner suites have antiques and oversize baths. 76 rms, 6 story, 42 suites. S, D $180-$240; each addl $15; suites $220-$1,200; under 16 free. Crib free. Pet accepted. Covered parking; valet $17. TV; cable (premium), VCR avail. Restaurant (see HUNT CLUB). Bar 11:30-2 am. Ck-out noon. Meeting rms. Business servs avail. In-rm modem link. Concierge. Airport transportation. Exercise equipt; weight machines, treadmill. Massage. Refrigerators; many bathrm phones; microwaves avail. Cr cds: A, C, D, DS, JCB, MC, V.

[D] [🏃] [🛎️] [🔥]

★ ★ ★ **WARWICK.** *401 Lenora St (98121), at 4th Ave, downtown. 206/443-4300; FAX 206/448-1662; res: 800/426-9280.* 229 units, 19 story. May-Oct: S $190; D $210; each addl $10; suites $275-$500; under 18 free; lower rates rest of yr. Crib free. Covered valet parking $12. TV; cable, VCR avail. Indoor pool; whirlpool. Restaurant 6:30 am-2 pm, 5:30-10 pm. Rm serv 24 hrs. Bar 11-2 am; pianist Wed-Sat. Ck-out noon. Meeting rms. Business servs avail. In-rm modem link. Exercise equipt: weight machine, treadmill, sauna. Bathrm phones; many refrigerators, wet bars. In-rm whirlpool in suites. Balconies. Fireplace in lobby. Cr cds: A, C, D, DS, ER, JCB, MC, V.

[D] [🏊] [🏃] [🛎️] [SC]

★ ★ ★ **THE WESTIN.** *1900 5th Ave (98101), at Westlake, downtown. 206/728-1000; FAX 206/728-2259.* 865 rms, 40-47 story. S $135-$240; D $155-$260; each addl $25; suites $295-$1,200; under 18 free; wkend rates. Crib free. Garage $18. TV; cable (premium), VCR avail. Heated pool; whirlpool. Restaurants 6 am-10 pm; Thurs-Sun to 10:30 pm. Rm serv 24 hrs. Bar; entertainment exc Sun. Ck-out noon. Convention facilities. Business center. In-rm modem link. Concierge. Gift shop. Barber, beauty shop. Exercise equipt; weight machines, bicycles, sauna. Refrigerators, minibars. Sun deck. Tower rms with panoramic view. Cr cds: A, C, D, DS, ER, JCB, MC, V.

[D] [🏊] [🏃] [🛎️] [🔥]

Inns

★★ **BEECH TREE MANOR.** *1405 Queen Anne Ave N (98109), in Queen Anne.* 206/281-7037; FAX 206/284-2350. 7 rms, 2 share bath, 2 story. No A/C. No rm phones. Mid-May-mid-Oct: S $64-$94; D $74-$94; suite $110; each addl $10; wkly rates; lower rates rest of yr. Pet accepted. TV in sitting rm; cable (premium), VCR. Complimentary full bkfst. Restaurant nearby. Ck-out 11 am, ck-in 4-7 pm. Business servs avail. Street parking. Turn-of-the-century mansion (1903) furnished with many antiques. Totally nonsmoking. Cr cds: MC, V.

★★ **CHAMBERED NAUTILUS.** *5005 22nd Ave NE (98105), north of downtown.* 206/522-2536. E-mail chamberednautilus@msn.com. 6 rms, 3 story. No A/C. Rm phones avail. S $74-$105; D $79-$109; each addl $15. Complimentary refreshments. Restaurant nearby. Ck-out 11 am, ck-in 4-6 pm. Business servs avail. Street parking. Sundeck. Georgian colonial house (1915); library/sitting rm with fireplace. Cr cds: A, MC, V.

★★ **CHELSEA STATION ON THE PARK.** *4915 Linden Ave N (98103), north of downtown.* 206/547-6077; FAX 206/632-5107; res: 800/400-6077. 8 rms, 2 story, 6 suites. No A/C. June-Sept: S $84; D $89; each addl $10; suites $119; lower rates rest of yr. Children over 12 yrs only. Complimentary full bkfst; afternoon refreshments. Restaurants nearby. Ck-out 11 am, ck-in 3 pm. Business servs avail. In-rm modem link. Street parking. Microwaves avail. Colonial-style brick house (1929); antiques. Near Woodland Park Zoo. Totally nonsmoking. Cr cds: A, D, DS, MC, V.

★★★ **GASLIGHT.** *1727-1733 15th Ave (98122), east of downtown.* 206/325-3654; FAX 206/328-4803. Web www.gaslight-inn.com. 16 rms, 4 with shower only, 3 share bath, 3 story, 7 suites. No A/C. Some rm phones. S, D $68-$108; suites $128-$148; some wkly rates. TV; cable. Heated pool; poolside serv. Complimentary continental bkfst; afternoon refreshments. Restaurant nearby. Ck-out 11 am, ck-in 3-6 pm. Business servs avail. In-rm modem link. Luggage handling. Refrigerators. Picnic tables. Two buildings; one built 1906. Antiques. Cr cds: A, MC, V.

★★ **HILL HOUSE BED & BREAKFAST.** *1113 E John St (98102), east of downtown.* 206/720-7161; res: 800/720-7161; FAX 206/323-0772. E-mail hillhouse@uspan.com; web uspan.com/hillhouse. 5 rms, 2 share bath, 2 suites. No A/C. Some rm phones. Mid-May-mid-Nov: S, D $70-$90; suites $115; wkly rates; wkends, hols (2-4 day min); lower rates rest of yr. Children over 12 yrs only. TV in suites; cable (premium). Complimentary full bkfst. Restaurant nearby. Ck-out 11 am, ck-in (by appt). In-rm modem link. Restored 1903 Victorian inn. Cr cds: A, DS, MC, V.

★★★ **INN AT HARBOR STEPS.** *1221 First Ave (98101), downtown.* 206/748-0973; res: 888/728-8910; FAX 206/682-6045. Web www.harborsteps.com. 20 rms, 2 story. S, D $150-$200; each addl $15; hol rates. Crib $15. TV; cable, VCR avail. Complimentary full bkfst; afternoon refreshments. Complimentary coffee in rms. Restaurant 8 am-10 pm. Ck-out noon, ck-in 2 pm. Business servs avail. In-rm modem link. Luggage handling. Exercise equipt; weight machine, bicycle. Indoor pool; whirlpool. In-rm whirlpools, refrigerators, fireplaces. Balconies. Ocean and garden views. Cr cds: A, C, D, JCB, MC, V.

★ **PRINCE OF WALES.** *133 13th Ave E (98102), east of downtown.* 206/325-9692; FAX 206/322-6402; res: 800/327-9692. E-mail cnorton949@aol.com; web uspan.com/sbba. 4 rms, 2 with shower only, 3 story. Apr-Oct: S, D $99-$125; lower rates rest of yr. Children over 3 yrs only. Complimentary full bkfst; afternoon refreshments. Restaurant nearby. Ck-out 11 am, ck-in 4-6 pm. Business servs avail. Microwaves

avail. Built in 1903; furnished with antiques. Totally nonsmoking. Cr cds: DS, MC, V.

★★ **ROBERTA'S BED & BREAKFAST.** *1147 16th Ave E (98112), east of downtown.* 206/329-3326; FAX 206/324-2149. E-mail robertsbb@aol.com; web www.robertasbb.com. 5 rms, 3 story. S $82-$105; D $90-$125; each addl $20. Complimentary full bkfst. Complimentary coffee in rms. Ck-out 11 am. Business servs avail. Built 1903; many antiques. Extensive library. Totally nonsmoking. Cr cds: MC, V.

★★★ **SALISBURY HOUSE.** *750 16th Ave E (98112), east of downtown.* 206/328-8682; FAX 206/720-1019. E-mail cathy@salisbury house.com; web www.salisburyhouse.com. 4 rms, 3 with shower only, 2 story. No A/C. No rm phones. May-Oct: S $75-$115; D $85-$125; each addl $15; lower rates rest of yr. Children over 12 yrs only. Complimentary full bkfst. Restaurants nearby. Ck-out 11 am, ck-in 4-6 pm. Business servs avail. In-rm modem link. Built 1904; wraparound porch. Many antiques. Totally nonsmoking. Cr cds: A, D, MC, V.

Restaurants

★★★ **ADRIATICA.** *1107 Dexter N (98109), in Queen Anne.* 206/285-5000. Hrs: 5-11 pm; Fri, Sat to midnight. Closed some hols. Res accepted. Southern Mediterranean menu. Bar. Wine list. Semi-a la carte: dinner $10.50-$26. Specializes in lamb, pasta, seafood. Own pastries. Parking. Outdoor dining. Built 1922. European villa decor. Overlooks garden, Lake Union. Cr cds: A, D, MC, V.

★★★ **AL BOCCALINO.** *1 Yesler Way (98104), in Pioneer Square.* 206/622-7688. Hrs: 11:30 am-2 pm, 5-10 pm; Mon from 5 pm; Fri to 10:30 pm; Sat 5-10:30 pm; Sun 5-9:30 pm. Closed major hols. Res accepted. No A/C. Italian menu. Semi-a la carte: lunch $8-$12.50, dinner $11-$21. Specializes in fresh seafood, rissotto, veal chop. Bistro atmosphere. Cr cds: A, D, JCB, MC, V.

★★★ **ANDALUCA.** *407 Olive Way (98101), downtown.* 206/382-6999. Hrs: 6:30 am-2:30 pm, 5-10 pm; Fri, Sat to 11 pm; Sun 7 am-noon. Res required. Bar 11:30 am-closing. Semi-a la carte: bkfst $4.50-$8.25, lunch $7.50-$12.50, dinner $14.50-$23. Specializes in Northwestern cuisine with Mediterranean influence. Cr cds: A, C, D, DS, MC, V.

★★ **ARNIE'S NORTHSHORE.** *1900 N Northlake Way (98103), opp Gas Works Park, north of downtown.* 206/547-3242. Hrs: 11:30 am-9 pm; Sat 5-10 pm; Sun 10 am-9 pm; early-bird dinner Sun-Thurs 5-6 pm; Sun brunch to 2 pm. Closed Dec 25; also lunch Memorial Day, July 4, Labor Day. Res accepted. Bar to 2 am. Semi-a la carte: lunch $5.95-$10.95, dinner $10.95-$23.95. Sun brunch $5.95-$10.95. Specializes in Northwest seafood. Own sauces. Parking. Contemporary decor. Panoramic view of Lake Union, Seattle skyline. Cr cds: A, MC, V.

★★ **ASIA GRILLE.** *2820 NE University Village (98105), 3 mi N on I-5, exit NE 45th, north of downtown.* 206/517-5985. Hrs: 11:30 am-10 pm; Sun to 9 pm. Closed Thanksgiving, Dec 25. Res accepted (dinner). Asian menu. Bar. A la carte entrees: lunch $7.95-$10.95, dinner $7.95-$15.95. Child's meals. Specialties: spit-roasted garlic chicken, szechuan tuna. Outdoor dining. Bright, colorful Chinese decor. Cr cds: A, C, D, DS, MC, V.

★★ **ASSAGGIO RISTORANTE.** *2010 Fourth Ave (98121), downtown.* 206/441-1399. E-mail assaggiori@aol.com. Hrs: 11:30 am-2:30 pm, 5-10:30 pm; Fri to 11 pm; Sat 5-11 pm. Closed Sun; most major hols. Res accepted. Italian menu. Serv bar. Semi-a la carte: lunch $8.95-

$14.95, dinner $9.95-$20.95. Specializes in seafood, risotto. Outdoor dining. Italian decor. Totally nonsmoking. Cr cds: A, D, DS, MC, V.

[D]

✔★★ **BANDOLEONE.** *2241 Eastlake Ave E (98102), north of downtown.* 206/329-7559. Hrs: 5-11 pm; Fri, Sat to 11:30 pm; Sat, Sun brunch 9 am-2:30 pm. Closed Thanksgiving, Dec 24, 25. Res accepted. Latin Amer menu. Bar to 2 am. Semi-a la carte: dinner $8.50-$15.95. Sat, Sun brunch $4.50-$6.95. Child's meals. Specialties: ancho chile-marinated chicken, Jamaican jerk rack of lamb, pistachio-crusted Chilean sea bass. Own pastries. Latino music Sun. Validated parking. Outdoor dining. Casual, eclectic decor with original artwork. Cr cds: MC, V.

[D]

✔★★ **BOMBORE.** *89 University St (98101), downtown.* 206/624-8233. Web www.diningnw.com/bombore/. Hrs: 11:30 am-2:30 pm, 5-10 pm. Closed Sun; most major hols. Res accepted. Continental menu. Semi-a la carte: lunch $6.50-$13.95, dinner $8.50-$17.75. Specializes in pasta, seafood. Outdoor dining. Eclectic decor. Totally nonsmoking. Cr cds: A, DS, MC, V.

[D]

★★ **BROOKLYN HOUSE.** *1212 Second Ave (98101), downtown.* 206/224-7000. Hrs: 11 am-10 pm; Sat 4:30-10:30 pm; Sun 4:30-10 pm. Closed Dec 25. Res accepted. Bar. A la carte entrees: lunch $7-$14, dinner $12-$33. Child's meals. Specializes in seafood, steak. Oyster bar. Valet parking (dinner). Patio/courtyard dining. In 1890s building; artwork. Cr cds: A, D, DS, MC, V.

[D]

★ **BUCA DI BEPPO.** *701 Ninth Ave N (98109), downtown.* 206/244-2288. Hrs: 5-10 pm; Fri to 11 pm; Sat 4:30-11 pm; Sun from 4 pm. Closed Thanksgiving, Dec 24, 25. Res accepted Sun-Thurs. Italian menu. Bar. A la carte entrees: dinner $7.95-$19.95. Specialties: chicken cacciatore, tiramisu. Outdoor dining. Eclectic decor; mural on dome ceiling; some seating in kitchen. Totally nonsmoking. Cr cds: A, D, MC, V.

[D]

✔★ **BURRITO LOCO.** *9211 Holman Rd NW (98117), north of downtown.* 206/783-0719. Hrs: 11 am-10 pm. Closed some major hols. Mexican menu. Wine, beer. Semi-a la carte: lunch $3.25-$4.75, dinner $7.50-$8.95. Child's meals. Specialties: chile relleno, chicken en mole, tacos de carnitas. Outdoor dining. Colorful Mexican decor. Totally nonsmoking. Cr cds: MC, V.

[D]

✔★★ **CACTUS.** *4220 E Madison (98112), east of downtown.* 206/324-4140. Hrs: 11:30 am-2:30 pm, 5-10 pm; Sun 5-9:30 pm. Closed some major hols. Hispanic menu. Serv bar. Semi-a la carte: lunch $5.95-$9.95, dinner $7.95-$13.95. Child's meals. Specializes in flan, tapas, fresh fish. Outdoor dining. Southwestern atmosphere. Cr cds: DS, MC, V.

[D]

✔★★★ **CAFE CAMPAGNE.** *1600 Post Alley (98101), downtown.* 206/728-2233. Hrs: 8 am-10 pm; Fri, Sat to 11 pm; Sun brunch 8 am-3 pm. Closed some major hols. Res accepted. French menu. Bar. Semi-a la carte: bkfst $6.95-$11.95, lunch $5.95-$14.95, dinner $8.95-$14.95. Sun brunch $6.95-$12.95. Specialties: traditional cassoulet, house-made sausages, rotisserie meats. Outdoor dining. French bistro decor. Cr cds: A, C, D, MC, V.

[D]

✔★★ **CAFE FLORA.** *2901 E Madison (98112), east of downtown.* 206/325-9100. Hrs: 11:30 am-2:30 pm, 5:30-10 pm; Sat from 5 pm; Sun 5-9 pm; Sat, Sun brunch 9 am-2 pm. Closed Mon; some hols. Vegetarian menu. Wine, beer. Semi-a la carte: lunch $6.95-$9.95, dinner $9.95-$14.95. Sat, Sun brunch $5.95-$9.95. Child's meals. Specialties: Oaxca tacos, portabello Wellington, wheatberry burgers. Two large rms, one with stone fountain, decorated with original works of art. Totally nonsmoking. Cr cds: MC, V.

[D]

★★★ **CAFE LAGO.** *2305 24th Ave E (98112), north of downtown.* 206/329-8005. Hrs: 5-9:30 pm; Fri, Sat to 10 pm. Closed major hols; also 4th wk in Aug. Italian menu. Wine. A la carte entrees: dinner $10-$20. Specializes in pasta, wood-fired pizza, grilled fish. Trattoria atmosphere. Totally nonsmoking. Cr cds: DS, MC, V.

[D]

★★ **CAFE SOPHIE.** *1921 First Ave (98101-1010), downtown.* 206/441-6139. Hrs: 5-9 pm; Fri, Sat to 10 pm. Closed Sun; major hols. Res accepted. No A/C. Continental menu. Bar. A la carte entrees: dinner $14-$21. Child's meals. Specializes in European cuisine. Jazz Fri, Sat. Outdoor dining. Two dining areas: one with a romantic, intimate setting, the other with a library motif. Cr cds: A, C, D, DS, MC, V.

[D]

★★★ **CAMPAGNE.** *86 Pine St (98101), downtown.* 206/728-2800. Hrs: 5:30-10 pm. Closed some major hols. Res accepted. French menu. Bar to 2 am. A la carte entrees: dinner $20-$29. Complete meals: $25-$55. Specializes in fresh seafood, rack of lamb. Valet parking. Outdoor dining. View of Elliott Bay. Cr cds: A, C, D, MC, V.

[D]

★★★ **CANLIS.** *2576 Aurora Ave N (98109), in Queen Anne.* 206/283-3313. E-mail 74132.2463@compuserve.com; web www.canlis.com. Hrs: 5:30-10:30 pm. Closed Sun; major hols. Res accepted. Bar 5 pm-midnight. Extensive wine list. Semi-a la carte: dinner $20-$34. Specializes in seafood, steak. Own sauces. Piano bar from 7 pm. Valet parking. Fireplace. Open-hearth grill. Panoramic view of Lake Union, Cascade Mountains. Formal dining. Family-owned. Jacket. Cr cds: A, C, D, DS, JCB, MC, V.

[D]

★★ **CARMELITA.** *7314 Greenwood Ave N (98103), in Phinney Ridge area, north of downtown.* 206/706-7703. Hrs: 5-10 pm; Fri, Sat to 10:45 pm; Sat, Sun brunch 9 am-1:30 pm. Closed Mon; Jan 1, Dec 24, 25. No A/C. Vegetarian menu. Bar. Semi-a la carte: dinner $8.50-$13.95. Sat, Sun brunch $8.95. Child's meals. Specializes in vegetarian and vegan fare with Mediterranean influences. Own baking, pasta. Outdoor dining. Eclectic furnishings decorate this large dining area with high ceilings. Totally nonsmoking. Cr cds: MC, V.

[D]

✔★★★ **CHEZ SHEA.** *94 Pike St (98101), in Pike Place Market, downtown.* 206/467-9990. E-mail shea101@aol.com; web www.wct.net/chezshea. Hrs: 4:30 pm-midnight. Closed Mon; most major hols. Res accepted. Contemporary Amer menu. Bar. A la carte entrees: dinner $6-$12. Complete meals: 4-course dinner $39. Child's meals. Specializes in seafood. Contemporary decor. Totally nonsmoking. Cr cds: A, MC, V.

[D]

✔★★ **CHINOOK'S.** *1900 W Nickerson (98119), in Fisherman's Terminal, north of downtown.* 206/283-4665. Hrs: 11 am-10 pm; Fri to 11 pm; Sat 7:30 am-11 pm; Sun 7:30 am-10 pm. Closed Thanksgiving, Dec 25. Bar to midnight. Complete meals: bkfst $4.95-$9.95. Semi-a la carte: lunch $4.95-$11.95, dinner $5.95-$16.95. Child's meals. Specializes in Northwest seafood, salmon, halibut. Parking. Outdoor dining. On Fisherman's Wharf. Nautical decor. Cr cds: A, C, D, DS, MC, V.

[D]

★★ **CHUTNEY'S.** *519 First Ave N (98109), in Queen Anne.* 206/284-6799. Hrs: 11:30 am-2:30 pm, 5-10 pm; Fri, Sat to 10:30 pm; Sun from 5 pm. Closed Dec 25. Res accepted. Indian menu. Bar. Semi-a la carte: lunch, dinner $8.95-$13.95. Specialties: tandoori items, tikka masala, curried mussels. Own baking. Indian prints and carved deities decorate walls. Totally nonsmoking. Cr cds: A, C, D, DS, JCB, MC, V.

[D]

✔★★ **CUCINA! CUCINA!.** *901 Fairview Ave N (98109), north of downtown.* 206/447-2782. Hrs: 11:30-2 am. Closed Thanksgiving, Dec 25. Res accepted (lunch). Italian menu. Bar. A la carte entrees: lunch $4.95-$10.95, dinner $4.95-$14.95. Child's meals. Specializes in pizza, pasta, salads. Valet parking. Outdoor dining. Bicycles hang from ceiling in lounge. Cr cds: A, D, DS, JCB, MC, V.

D

★ ★ **DAHLIA LOUNGE.** *1904 Fourth Ave (98101), downtown.* *206/682-4142.* E-mail maureen@tomdouglas.com; web www.tom douglas.com. Hrs: 11:30 am-2:30 pm, 5:30-10 pm; Fri to 11 pm; Sat 5:30-11 pm; Sun 5-9 pm. Closed major hols. Res accepted. Semi-a la carte: lunch $6.50-$12, dinner $9.95-$22. Child's meals. Specializes in crab cakes, salmon, duck. Eclectic decor. Cr cds: A, C, D, DS, JCB, MC, V.

D

★ **DOONG KONG LAU.** *9710 Aurora Ave N (98103), north of downtown.* *206/526-8828.* Hrs: 11 am-10 pm. Res accepted. Chinese menu. Semi-a la carte: lunch $3.95-$5.95, dinner $5.95-$10.95. Specializes in northern Hakka cuisine. Parking. Chinese prints, fish tanks. Cr cds: A, D, DS, MC, V.

D 🍽

★ ★ **DULCES LATIN BISTRO.** *1430 34th Ave (98122), east of downtown.* *206/322-5453.* Hrs: 5-10 pm; Sun to 9 pm. Closed Mon; some major hols. Res accepted. Continental menu. Bar. Semi-a la carte: dinner $14.25-$18.50. Complete meal: dinner $25. Specialties: chiles rellenos, roasted red pepper ravioli, paella Valenciana. Own pasta, pastries. Classical guitarist Wed, Thurs, Sun. Bistro decor with deep gold and bronze accents; completely separate cigar rm. Cr cds: MC, V.

D

★ ★ ★ **EL GAUCHO.** *2505 First Ave (98121), downtown.* *206/728-1337.* Hrs: 5 pm-1 am; Sun to 11 pm. Closed most major hols. Res accepted. Continental menu. Bar to 2 am. Wine cellar. A la carte entrees: dinner $13-$30. Specialties: flaming shish kabob, chateaubriand, Angus steak. Own pastries. Pianist. Valet parking. Former union hall for merchent seamen; formal, elegant dining. Cr cds: A, C, D, JCB, MC, V.

D

★ ★ ★ **ELLIOTT'S OYSTER HOUSE.** *1203 Alaskan Way (98101), Pier 56, downtown.* *206/623-4340.* Hrs: 11 am-11 pm; Fri, Sat to midnight; winter hrs: 11 am-10 pm; Fri, Sat to 11 pm. Res accepted. Bar. Semi-a la carte: lunch $5.95-$15.95, dinner $10.95-$29.95. Child's meals. Specializes in Pacific salmon, fresh Dungeness crab, fresh oysters. Outdoor dining. View of bay. Cr cds: A, D, DS, JCB, MC, V.

D 🍽

★ ★ **ETTA'S SEAFOOD.** *2020 Western Ave (98121), downtown.* *206/443-6000.* E-mail maureen@tomdouglas.com; web www.tom douglas.com. Hrs: 11:30 am-10 pm; Fri to 11 pm; Sat 9 am-11 pm; Sun 9 am-10 pm. Closed major hols. Res accepted. Bar to 1 am. Semi-a la carte: lunch $5-$28, dinner $8-$30. Child's meals. Specializes in Northwestern seafood. Two dining rms. Totally nonsmoking. Cr cds: A, D, DS, JCB, MC, V.

D

★ ★ **F.X. McRORY'S STEAK, CHOP & OYSTER HOUSE.** *419 Occidental Ave S (98104), opp Kingdome, in Pioneer Square.* *206/623-4800.* Hrs: 11:30 am-2 pm, 5-10 pm; Sat noon-11 pm; Sun from 3 pm. Closed some major hols. Res accepted. Bar. Semi-a la carte: lunch $6-$12, dinner $10-$25. Child's meals. Specializes in steak, oysters, prime rib. Oyster bar. Outdoor dining. 1920s atmosphere. Cr cds: A, C, D, DS, MC, V.

D 🍽

✔★ ★ ★ **FLYING FISH.** *2234 First Ave (98121), downtown.* *206/728-8595.* Hrs: 5 pm-1 am. Closed most major hols. Res accepted. Bar to 2 am. Semi-a la carte: dinner $9-$16.95. Specialties: Thai crab cakes, whole fried snapper in lemon grass marinade. Outdoor dining. Eclectic decor. Totally nonsmoking. Cr cds: A, C, D, MC, V.

D **SC**

✔★ **FOUR SEAS.** *714 S King St (98104), in International District.* *206/682-4900.* Hrs: 10 am-midnight; Fri, Sat to 2 am. Res accepted. Cantonese, Mandarin menu. Bar. Semi-a la carte: lunch $5.75-$8.35, dinner $5.25-$15.95. Specialties: Hong Kong-style dim sum, garlic spareribs, moo goo gai pan. Parking. Hand-carved Oriental screens. Cr cds: A, D, DS, MC, V.

D 🍽

★ ★ **FRANCO'S HIDDEN HARBOR.** *1500 Westlake Ave N (98109), north of downtown.* *206/282-0501.* Hrs: 11 am-9 pm; Fri, Sat to 10 pm; Sun 4-10 pm. Closed Dec 25. Res accepted. Northwestern menu. Bar to 1 am; Sun 1-10 pm. Semi-a la carte: lunch $6-$11, dinner $9.95-$29.95. Child's meals. Specializes in prime rib, fresh seafood. Valet parking. Outdoor dining. Waterfront dining overlooking yacht harbor. Cr cds: A, D, DS, MC, V.

D

★ ★ ★ **FULLERS.** *(See Sheraton Hotel)* *206/447-5544.* Original works by Northwest artists are found on permanent display throughout the restaurant. A marble pool and fountain decorate the center of the dining area. Specializes in Northwest seafood, fowl, Ellensberg lamb. Own baking, pastas. Hrs: 11:30 am-2 pm, 5:30-10 pm; Sat from 5:30 pm. Closed Sun; some major hols. Res accepted. Bar. Wine list. A la carte entrees: lunch $10-$17, dinner $18-$30. Child's meals. Totally nonsmoking. Cr cds: A, C, D, DS, ER, JCB, MC, V.

D

★ ★ **GEORGIAN ROOM.** *(See Four Seasons Olympic Hotel)* *206/621-7889.* Hrs: 6:30 am-2 pm, 5:30-10 pm; Fri, Sat to 11 pm; Sat 6:30 am-noon; Sun 6:30 am-1:30 pm; Sun brunch in Garden Court 11:30 am-2 pm. Res accepted. Bar. Wine cellar. A la carte entrees: bkfst $4.50-$19.50, lunch $7.75-$19, dinner $14.50-$33. Sun brunch $14.50-$29. Specializes in Pacific Northwest seafood, rack of lamb. Own baking. Pastry chef. Jacket (dinner). Elegant dining in room of Italian Renaissance decor. Cr cds: A, C, D, JCB, MC, V.

D 🍽

★ ★ ★ **HUNT CLUB.** *(See Sorrento Hotel)* *206/343-6156.* Web www.usa.nia.com.sorrento. Hrs: 7 am-2:30 pm, 5:30-10 pm; Fri, Sat to 11 pm. Res accepted. Bar from 11:30 am. A la carte entrees: bkfst $6-$10, lunch $9-$18, dinner $18-$30. Specializes in seafood of the Northwest, game. Free valet parking. English hunt motif. Cr cds: A, C, D, DS, JCB, MC, V.

D

★ ★ ★ **IL BISTRO.** *93A Pike St (98101), downtown.* *206/682-3049.* Hrs: 5:30-10 pm; Fri, Sat to 11 pm. Closed some major hols. Res accepted. Italian menu. Bar to 2 am. A la carte entrees: dinner $11.95-$29.95. Specializes in fresh seafood, pasta, rack of lamb. Valet parking Thurs-Sat. Outdoor dining. Original art. Cr cds: A, C, D, MC, V.

D 🍽

★ ★ ★ **IL TERRAZZO CARMINE.** *411 First Ave S (98104), in Pioneer Square.* *206/467-7797.* Hrs: 11:30 am-2:30 pm, 5:30-10 pm; Fri, Sat to 10:30 pm. Closed Sun; most major hols. Res accepted. Italian menu. Bar. Semi-a la carte: lunch $8-$13, dinner $9.50-$28. Specializes in osso buco, venison ravioli. Outdoor dining. Elegant decor. Totally nonsmoking. Cr cds: A, C, D, DS, MC, V.

D

★ ★ **IVAR'S ACRES OF CLAMS.** *Pier 54 (98104), downtown.* *206/624-6852.* Hrs: 11 am-10 pm; Fri, Sat to 11 pm. Closed Thanksgiving, Dec 25. Res accepted. Bar. Semi-a la carte: lunch $6.95-$13.95, dinner $10.95-$19.95. Child's meals. Specializes in Northwestern king salmon, oven-roasted seafood brochettes, dungeness crab-topped prawns. On pier with windows overlooking waterfront; collection of old photos of the area. Cr cds: A, MC, V.

D 🍽

★ ★ **IVAR'S INDIAN SALMON HOUSE.** *401 NE Northlake Way (98105), on N shore of Lake Union, north of downtown.* *206/632-*

0767. Hrs: 11:30 am-2:30 pm, 4:30-10 pm; Fri to 11 pm; Sat noon-3:30 pm, 4-11 pm; Sun 3:30-10 pm; Sun brunch 10 am-2 pm. Closed Thanksgiving, Dec 25. Res accepted. Bar. Semi-a la carte: lunch $7-$15, dinner $13-$25. Sun brunch $14.95. Child's meals. Specializes in smoked salmon. Parking. Outdoor dining. Indian long house decor. View of lake. Family-owned. Cr cds: A, JCB, MC, V.

D SC

✔ ★ **JITTERBUG.** *2114 N 45th St (98103), north of downtown.* 206/547-6313. Hrs: 8 am-10 pm; Fri, Sat to 11 pm; June-Aug to 11 pm. Closed some major hols. Bar. Semi-a la carte: bkfst $2-$8.25, lunch $4-$8.25, dinner $8.25-$15.75. Child's meals. Specialties: Italian farmhouse egg rumble, charmoula chicken sandwich, transcontinental tango. Own pasta, pastries. Lively atmosphere; counter service. Cr cds: MC, V.

D ⌐

★ ★ ★ **KASPAR'S.** *19 W Harrison St (98119), in Queen Anne.* 206/298-0123. E-mail kaspars@aol.com; web www.uspan.com. Hrs: 5-10 pm; Fri, Sat to 11 pm. Closed Sun, Mon; Jan 1, July 4. Res accepted. Bar. A la carte entrees: dinner $13-$21. Child's meals. Specializes in Northwestern cuisine, vegetarian dishes, smoked salmon. Own ice cream & sorbets. Valet parking. 2 levels. Totally nonsmoking. Cr cds: A, MC, V.

D

✔ ★ **KITTO JAPANESE NOODLE HOUSE.** *614 Broadway E (98102), east of downtown.* 206/325-8486. Hrs: 11:30 am-10 pm; Fri, Sat to 11 pm. Closed Thanksgiving, Dec 25. Res accepted. Japanese menu. Wine, beer. Semi-a la carte: lunch $4.95-$12.95, dinner $5.75-$12.95. Specializes in tempura, noodles. Oriental decor. Totally nonsmoking. Cr cds: MC, V.

D

★ ★ **LA BUCA.** *102 Cherry St (98104), in Pioneer Square.* 206/343-9517. Hrs: 11:30 am-2:30 pm, 5-10 pm. Closed Jan 1, Thanksgiving, Dec 25. Res accepted. Italian menu. Serv bar. A la carte entrees: lunch $6.95-$10, dinner $8.95-$16. Child's meals. Specializes in classic Italian dishes. Own pastries. Rustic Italian trattoria with separate dining areas underground; one dates to 1890. Cr cds: A, C, D, DS, JCB, MC, V.

⌐

★ ★ ★ **LABUZNIK.** *1924 First Ave (98101), downtown.* 206/441-8899. Hrs: 4:30 pm-midnight. Closed Sun, Mon; major hols; also spring break, 3 wks July. Res accepted. Continental menu. Bar. Semi-a la carte: dinner $12.50-$29. Child's meals. Specializes in veal, pork, roast duck. Dining on 2 levels; sliding doors open to street. Original art. Cr cds: A, D, DS, MC, V.

D

★ ★ ★ **LAMPREIA.** *2400 First Ave (98121), downtown.* 206/443-3301. Hrs: 5-11 pm. Closed Sun, Mon; Thanksgiving. Res accepted. Italian, Mediterranean menu. Bar. Wine cellar. Semi-a la carte: dinner $9-$25. Tasting menu: dinner $40. Specializes in seasonal dishes. Own baking, pasta. Wine display at entrance changes frequently. Totally nonsmoking. Cr cds: A, MC, V.

D

✔★ **LAS MARGARITAS.** *1122 Post Ave (98101), downtown.* 206/623-7203. Hrs: 11 am-11 pm; Sun to 9 pm. Closed Dec 25. Res accepted. Mexican menu. Bar. Semi-a la carte: lunch $5.75-$7.95, dinner $2.75-$10.95. Child's meals. Specializes in regional cuisine, carnitas, fajitas. Cr cds: A, D, DS, MC, V.

D

★ ★ ★ **LATITUDE 47°.** *1232 Westlake N (98109), north of downtown.* 206/284-1047. Hrs: 11:30 am-2:30 pm, 5-9:30 pm; Fri, Sat from 5 pm; Sun 3-9 pm; Sun brunch 10 am-2 pm. Closed Dec 25. Res accepted. Bar to 2 am. Wine list. Semi-a la carte: lunch $5.95-$14.50, dinner $10-$18.50. Sun brunch $14.95. Child's meals. Specializes in seafood, steak, pasta. Valet parking. Entertainment. Outdoor dining. Enclosed patio overlooks Lake Union; moorage. Cr cds: A, D, DS, MC, V.

D ⌐

★ ★ ★ **LE GOURMAND.** *425 NW Market St (98107), at 6th Ave, north of downtown.* 206/784-3463. Hrs: 5:30-11 pm. Closed Sun-Tues; Easter, Thanksgiving, Dec 24, 25. Res accepted. French, Amer menu. Wine, beer. Complete meals: dinner $18-$30. Specialties: poached salmon with gooseberry & dill sauce, roast duckling with black currant sauce. Original artwork. Totally nonsmoking. Cr cds: A, MC, V.

D

✔★ **LINYEN.** *424 Seventh Ave S (98104), in International District.* 206/622-8181. Hrs: 11-2 am. Res accepted. Chinese menu. Bar. Semi-a la carte: lunch $2.80-$6, dinner $5.95-$15.25. Specializes in fresh Northwest fish and vegetables, lemon chicken, Hong Kong-style dim sum. Valet parking. Cr cds: A, D, DS, MC, V.

D ⌐

✔ ★ ★ **MADISON PARK CAFE.** *1807 42nd Ave E (98112), east of downtown.* 206/324-2626. Hrs: 8 am-2:30 pm; Sun to 2 pm; Fri, Sat also 5:30-10 pm. Closed Mon; some major hols. No A/C. Continental menu. Wine, beer. Semi-a la carte: bkfst $2.50-$7.25, lunch $2.50-$8.50, dinner $12.95-$16.95. Child's meals. Specializes in fresh seasonal pastas and seafoods, homemade bkfst pastries. Own pasta, pastries. Outdoor dining. French bistro atmosphere in converted house; brick courtyard. Totally nonsmoking. Cr cds: A, MC, V.

✔★ ★ **MARCO'S.** *2510 First Ave (98121), downtown.* 206/441-7801. Hrs: 11:30 am-2 pm, 5:30-11 pm; Fri, Sat to midnight; Sun from 5:30 pm. Closed most major hols. Res accepted. Continental menu. Bar. Semi-a la carte: lunch $6.95-$10.95, dinner $10.95-$15.95. Child's meals. Specializes in jerk chicken, fried sage leaves. Outdoor dining. Eclectic decor. Cr cds: A, MC, V.

D

★ ★ **MAXIMILIEN-IN-THE-MARKET.** *81A Pike Place (98101), Pike Place Market, downtown.* 206/682-7270. Hrs: 7:30 am-10 pm; Sun brunch 9:30 am-4 pm. Closed Jan 1, Thanksgiving, Dec 25. Res accepted. French menu. Bar. Semi-a la carte: bkfst $3-$7.25, lunch $5.50-$13, dinner $8.25-$24. French family supper Mon-Fri: $13.25-$24. Sun brunch $1.75-$8.50. Specializes in French-style Northwest seafood. French marketplace decor; antiques. View of bay, mountains. Cr cds: A, D, MC, V.

D

★ ★ **McCORMICK & SCHMICK'S.** *1103 First Ave (98101), downtown.* 206/623-5500. Hrs: 11:30 am-11 pm; Sat 4:30-11 pm; Sun 5-10 pm; summer hrs vary. Closed Thanksgiving, Dec 25. Res accepted. Bar to 12:30 am; Fri, Sat to 1:30 am; Sun to 11:30 pm. Semi-a la carte: lunch $4.95-$12.75, dinner $6.75-$20. Specializes in fresh seafood. Beamed ceilings, Irish bar. Original art. Cr cds: A, C, D, DS, JCB, MC, V.

D ⌐

★ ★ **McCORMICK'S FISH HOUSE.** *722 Fourth Ave (98104), downtown.* 206/682-3900. Hrs: 11:30 am-11 pm; Fri to midnight; Sat 4:30 pm-midnight; Sun from 4:30 pm. Closed Memorial Day, Thanksgiving, Dec 25. Res accepted. Bar. Semi-a la carte: lunch $5.95-$11.95, dinner $5.95-$19.95. Specializes in fresh seafood. Oyster bar. Outdoor dining. Vintage 1920s and 30s atmosphere; tin ceilings. Cr cds: A, C, D, DS, MC, V.

D ⌐

★ ★ ★ **METROPOLITAN GRILL.** *820 Second Ave (98104), at Marion St, downtown.* 206/624-3287. Hrs: 11 am-3:30 pm, 5-11 pm; Sat from 4:30 pm; Sun 4:30-10 pm. Closed Thanksgiving. Res accepted. Bar. Wine list. Semi-a la carte: lunch $6.95-$15.95, dinner $10.95-$27.95. Child's meals. Specialties: 28-day aged prime steak, Northwest seafood dishes. Cr cds: A, C, D, DS, JCB, MC, V.

D

★ ★ **NISHINO.** *3130 E Madison (98112), east of downtown.* 206/322-5800. Hrs: 5:30-10:30 pm; Sun to 9:30 pm. Closed some major hols. Res accepted. Japanese menu. Serv bar. Semi-a la carte: dinner $4-$16. Complete meal: dinner $45-$60. Specializes in omakase, sushi.

Outdoor dining. Subdued Japanese decor; rooftop dining. Totally non-smoking. Cr cds: A, MC, V.

[D]

★ ★ ★ **OBACHINE.** *1518 Sixth Ave (98101), downtown.* 206/749-9653. Hrs: 11:30 am-4:30 pm, 5:30-10 pm. Closed July 4, Thanksgiving, Dec 25. Res accepted. Pan-Asian menu. Bar 11:30 am-midnight. Wine list. A la carte entrees: lunch $5.95-$13.95, dinner $8.95-$18.95. Child's meals. Own pastries. Two-level dining areas feature dramatic colors, Asian artwork. Totally nonsmoking. Cr cds: A, D, MC, V.

[D]

★ ★ ★ **PAINTED TABLE.** *(See Alexis Hotel)* 206/624-3646. Hrs: 6:30-10 am, 11:30 am-2 pm, 5:30-10 pm; Sat, Sun 7:30 am-noon, 11:30 pm. Res accepted. Bar. Wine list. A la carte entrees: bkfst $3.50-$9.50, lunch $6.95-$14.95, dinner $7.95-$24.95. Specializes in Northwest regional produce and seafood. Own baking, sauces. Valet parking. In historic building (1901). Totally nonsmoking. Cr cds: A, C, D, DS, MC, V.

[D]

★ ★ ★ **PALACE KITCHEN.** *2030 Fifth Ave (98121), downtown.* 206/448-2001. E-mail maureen@www.tomdouglas.com; web www.tomdouglas.com. Hrs: 5 pm-1 am. Closed most major hols. Res accepted. Bar. Wine list. Semi-a la carte: dinner $14-$19. Child's meals. Specializes in applewood-grilled rotisserie dishes. Own baking, pasta. Central kitchen and bar dominate dining rm. Cr cds: A, D, DS, MC, V.

[D] [⤴]

★ ★ **PALOMINO.** *1420 Fifth Ave (98101), on 3rd floor of Pacific First Center, downtown.* 206/623-1300. Hrs: 11:15 am-10:30 pm; Tues, Thurs to 11:30 pm; Fri to 12:30 am; Sat 11-12:30 am; Sun 4-10 pm. Closed some major hols. Res accepted. Mediterranean menu. Semi-a la carte: lunch $6.95-$15.95, dinner $7.95-$19.95. Specializes in grilled salmon, spit-roasted chicken, wood oven-roasted prawns. Parking. Original art, exotic African wood. Overlooking atrium. Cr cds: A, D, DS, MC, V.

[D]

★ ★ **PARAGON.** *2125 Queen Anne Ave N (98109), in Queen Anne.* 206/283-4548. Hrs: 5-11 pm. Closed Dec 25. Res accepted. Contemporary Amer menu. Bar 4 pm-2 am. Semi-a la carte: dinner $9-$18. Specializes in risotto, seafood. Bistro decor. Totally nonsmoking. Cr cds: A, MC, V.

[D]

★ ★ **PESCATORE.** *5300 34th St NW (98107), north of downtown.* 206/784-1733. Hrs: 11 am-closing; Sat from 4 pm; Sun from 5 pm; Sun brunch 9 am-2:30 pm. Res accepted. Bar to 11:30 pm; Fri-Sun to 12:30 am. Semi-a la carte: lunch $5.95-$11.95, dinner $9.95-$19.95. Sun brunch $10.95-$19.95. Child's meals. Specializes in Italian seafood, pizza, and lasagne. Parking. Outdoor dining. Overlooks Chittendon Locks. Family-owned. Cr cds: A, C, D, DS, JCB, MC, V.

[D] [SC]

✔ ★ **PIATTI.** *2800 NE University Village (98105), north of downtown.* 206/524-9088. Hrs: 11:30 am-10 pm; Fri, Sat to 11 pm. Closed Dec 25. Res accepted. Italian menu. Bar. Semi-a la carte: lunch, dinner $6.95-$19.95. Child's meals. Specializes in regional Italian cuisine. Outdoor dining. Casual decor. Totally nonsmoking. Cr cds: A, D, MC, V.

[D]

★ ★ **PINK DOOR.** *1919 Post Alley (98101), Pike Place Market, downtown.* 206/443-3241. Hrs: 11:30 am-2:30 pm, 5:30-10 pm. Closed Sun, Mon; some major hols. Res accepted. No A/C. Italian menu. Bar to 11:30 pm; Fri, Sat to 1 am. Semi-a la carte: lunch $6.95-$11.50, dinner $6.95-$17.95. Child's meals. Specializes in rustic Italian dishes. Own baking, pasta. Entertainment. Outdoor dining. Eclectic decor with cherubs, mirrors and a swing; patio offers water view. Totally nonsmoking. Cr cds: A, MC, V.

★ ★ ★ **PIROSMANI.** *2220 Queen Anne Ave N (98109), in Queen Anne.* 206/285-3360. Hrs: 5:30-10 pm. Closed Sun, Mon; Easter, Thanksgiving, Dec 25. Res accepted. No A/C. Mediterranean, Georgian menu.

Wine, beer. Semi-a la carte: dinner $16-$22. Seasonal menu. Outdoor dining. Original art and Georgian artifacts are displayed in the dining rms of this 1906 house. Totally nonsmoking. Cr cds: A, D, DS, MC, V.

★ ★ ★ **PLACE PIGALLE.** *81 Pike St (98101), in Pike Place Market, downtown.* 206/624-1756. Hrs: 11:30 am-3 pm, 5:30-10 pm; Fri to 11 pm; Sat 11:30 am-3:30 pm, 6-10:30 pm. Closed Sun; most major hols. Res accepted. Northwest regional menu. Semi-a la carte: lunch $8-$14, dinner $15-$23. Specialties: rabbit reminiscence, seafood in tamarind broth, duck bijoux. Overlooks Elliott Bay. Casual decor. Cr cds: A, MC, V.

★ ★ ★ **PONTI.** *3014 Third Ave N (98109), in Queen Anne.* 206/284-3000. Hrs: 11:30 am-2:30 pm, 5-10 pm; Fri, Sat to 11 pm; Sun from 10 am; early bird dinner 5-6 pm. Closed Jan 1, July 4, Dec 25. Res accepted. Eclectic menu. A la carte entrees: lunch $8.95-$12.95, dinner $11.95-$19.95. Child's meals. Specializes in Pacific rim seafood. Valet parking. Patio dining. Formal dining in attractive surroundings. View of Lake Washington Canal. Cr cds: A, D, MC, V.

[D]

✔ ★ **PORTAGE BAY CAFE.** *(See University Inn Motor Hotel)* 206/632-5055. Hrs: 6 am-3 pm; Sat, Sun from 7 am. Closed Jan 1, Dec 25. Res accepted. Semi-a la carte: bkfst $2-$7.95, lunch $4-$8.25. Child's meals. Specialties: cafe linguine, blackened salmon. Outdoor dining. Bright, contemporary decor with floor-to-ceiling windows. Totally nonsmoking. Cr cds: A, D, DS, MC, V.

[D]

★ ★ ★ **PREGO.** *(See Renaissance Madison Hotel)* 206/583-0300. Hrs: 11:30 am-1:30 pm, 5:30-10 pm. Closed Dec 25. Res accepted. Italian menu. Bar. Semi-a la carte: lunch $6-$13, dinner $11-$25. Specializes in seafood, pasta. Original Matisse art. Views of skyline, Puget Sound. Cr cds: A, C, D, DS, ER, JCB, MC, V.

[D] [⤴]

★ ★ ★ **QUEEN CITY GRILL.** *2201 1st Ave (98121), downtown.* 206/443-0975. Web www.queencitygrill.com. Hrs: 11:30 am-11 pm; Fri, Sat to midnight. Closed some major hols. Res accepted. Bar. Wine cellar. A la carte entrees: lunch $7.95-$13.95, dinner $8.95-$19.50. Child's meals. Specialties: grilled Chilean sea bass with chili-lime butter, grilled ahi tuna, aged Colorado Angus steak. Own pastries, pasta. Exposed brick walls, original artwork and mahogany woodwork accent this dining rm. Cr cds: A, C, D, DS, MC, V.

[D] [⤴]

★ ★ ★ **RAY'S BOATHOUSE.** *6049 Seaview Ave NW (98107), north of downtown.* 206/789-3770. E-mail rays@rays.com; web www.rays.com. Hrs: 11:30 am-2 pm, 5-10 pm. Closed Jan 1, Dec 25. Res accepted. Bar to midnight. Wine cellar. Semi-a la carte: lunch $5.95-$9.95, dinner $10.95-$25. Child's meals. Specializes in Northwest seafood. Valet parking. Outdoor dining. View of Olympic Mts. Cr cds: A, D, DS, MC, V.

[D]

★ ★ ★ **REINER'S.** *1106 Eighth Ave (98101), downtown.* 206/624-2222. Hrs: 5-10 pm. Closed Sun, Mon; some major hols. Res accepted. Continental menu. Serv bar. Wine list. A la carte entrees: dinner $14.50-$24. Specializes in rack of lamb, crab cakes, calf's liver. Outdoor dining. Intimate dining in European atmosphere. Totally nonsmoking. Cr cds: A, MC, V.

[D]

★ ★ ★ **RELAIS.** *(17121 Bothell Way NE, Bothell 98011) I-5 N exit 177 E to WA 522 N.* 206/485-7600. Hrs: 5-9 pm; Sun brunch 11 am-3 pm. Closed Mon. Res accepted. No A/C. French menu. Bar. Wine list. Semi-a la carte: dinner $21-$30. Complete meals: dinner $55. Sun brunch $19.95. Specializes in lamb, seafood. Own desserts. Parking. Outdoor dining. Turn-of-the-century French decor. Original artwork, antiques. Cr cds: A, MC, V.

[D] [⤴]

★ ★ ★ ★ **ROVER'S.** *2808 E Madison St (98112), east of downtown.* 206/325-7442. Chef Thierry Rautureau's cozy white cottage with country-

French decor is an intimate theater for his contemporary regional cuisine with French influences. Only the freshest ingredients—including white asparagus from France, rabbit from Oregon and herbs and flowers from the restaurant's garden—make their way into the award-winning dishes here. Northwest contemporary menu with French accent. Specializes in seafood, Northwest game, vegetarian dishes. Hrs: from 5:30 pm. Closed Sun, Mon; most major hols. Res accepted. Extensive wine list. A la carte entrees: dinner $23-$39.50. Complete meals: dinner $49.50, $59.50 & $89.50. Outdoor dining. Totally nonsmoking. Cr cds: A, D, DS, MC, V.

D

★ ★ ★ ROY'S. (See The Westin Hotel) 206/256-7697. Hrs: 6 am-10 pm. Res accepted. Continental menu. Bar from 5 pm. Wine cellar. Complete meal: bkfst $8.75-$15.75. Semi-a la carte: bkfst $3.75-$9.75, lunch $4.25-$14, dinner $14.95-$23.95. Child's meals. Specializes in fresh seafood with Pacific Rim influence. Own desserts. Multi-leveled, semi-circular dining rm with nautical theme. Totally nonsmoking. Cr cds: A, C, D, DS, MC, V.

D

★ ★ ★ RUTH'S CHRIS STEAK HOUSE. 800 Fifth Ave (98104), downtown. 206/624-8524. Hrs: 5-10 pm. Closed some major hols. Res accepted. Bar. A la carte entrees: dinner $16-$29.95. Specializes in steak, seafood. Valet parking. Cr cds: A, D, MC, V.

D ↵

★ ★ ★ SALEH AL LAGO. 6804 E Greenlake Way (98115), north of downtown. 206/524-4044. E-mail salehj@msn.com. Dining is offered on two levels in this elegant atmosphere with faux-marble pillars and pale pink trim, mauve and lilac fabrics and carpet, and recessed lighting. The fine china and crystal is replaced annually. Italian menu. Specializes in central Italian cooking. Own pasta. Hrs: 11:30 am-1:30 pm, 5:30-9:30 pm. Closed Sun; major hols. Res accepted. Bar. A la carte entrees: lunch $9-$13, dinner $13-$18. Child's meals. Parking. Patio dining. Cr cds: A, D, MC, V.

D

★ ★ ★ SAZERAC. (See Hotel Monaco) 206/621-1770. Web www.monaco-seattle.com. Hrs: 6:30 am-10 pm. Res accepted. Bar. Wine list. Semi-a la carte: bkfst $5.95-$12.95, lunch $8.95-$15.95, dinner $14.95-$28.95. Child's meals. Specialties: spit-roasted whole fish with lemon-chili broth, molasses sweet-potato pasta cigars with sausage and sage-butter. Own baking, pasta. Valet parking. Outdoor dining. Contemporary decor with high ceiling, multi-level dining and open, elevated kitchen. Totally nonsmoking. Cr cds: A, D, DS, MC, V.

D

↵★ ★ SERAFINA. 2043 Eastlake Ave E (98102), north of downtown. 206/323-0807. Hrs: 11:30 am-2 pm, 5:30-10 pm; Fri to 11 pm; Sat 5:30-11 pm; Sun 5:30-10 pm. Closed some major hols. Res accepted. Italian menu. Bar. A la carte entrees: lunch $2.95-$8.95, dinner $7.95-$17.95. Specializes in rustic Italian dishes. Entertainment. Outdoor dining in European courtyard. Murals. Cr cds: MC, V.

D

★ ★ SHIRO'S. 2401 Second Ave (98121), downtown. 206/443-9844. Hrs: 11:30 am-1:45 pm, 5:30-10 pm; Sat from 5:30 pm. Closed Sun; major hols. Res accepted. Japanese menu. Wine, beer. Semi-a la carte: lunch $6.95-$14.50, dinner $16-$19.50. Specializes in sushi, full Japanese dinners. Casual decor with large windows, sushi bar. Totally nonsmoking. Cr cds: A, JCB, MC, V.

D

★ ★ SIMPATICO. 4430 Wallingford Ave (98103), north of downtown. 206/632-1000. Hrs: 5-10 pm; Fri, Sat to 11 pm. Closed major hols. Italian menu. Bar. Semi-a la carte: dinner $10.95-$17.95. Child's meals. Specializes in traditional Italian cuisine with Northwestern flair. Parking. Live jazz wkends. Outdoor dining. Intimate dining in converted school building that also houses shops. Cr cds: A, MC, V.

D

★ ★ SPACE NEEDLE. 219 Fourth Ave N (98109), in Seattle Center. 206/443-2100. Web www.spaceneedle.com. Hrs: 8 am-11 pm; Sun brunch to 3 pm. Res accepted. Bar 11 am-midnight. Semi-a la carte: bkfst $9.95-$14.95, lunch $14.95-$19.95, dinner $20.95-$31.95. Sun brunch $17.95-$21.95. Child's meals. Specializes in regional dishes. Valet parking. Revolving dining rm. Family-owned. Totally nonsmoking. Cr cds: A, D, DS, ER, JCB, MC, V.

D ♥

↵★ STELLA'S TRATTORIA. 4500 Ninth Ave (98105), northeast of downtown. 206/633-1100. Open 24 hrs. Sun brunch 4 am-3 pm. Closed Thanksgiving, Dec 25. Italian, Amer menu. Semi-a la carte: bkfst $2.95-$6, lunch $6-$8.50, dinner $7-$13. Sun brunch $2.95-$8. Child's meals. Outdoor dining. Lively atmosphere. Totally nonsmoking. Cr cds: A, DS, MC, V.

D

★ ★ ★ SZMANIA'S. 3321 W McGraw (98199), north of downtown. 206/284-7305. Hrs: 5-9:30 pm; Fri, Sat to 10 pm; Sun 4:30-9 pm. Closed Mon; most major hols. Res accepted. Continental menu. Bar. Wine list. Semi-a la carte: dinner $9-$20. Child's meals. Specialties: German dishes, seasonal Pacific Northwest regional dishes. Parking. Fireplace; open kitchen. Totally nonsmoking. Cr cds: A, D, MC, V.

D

★ ★ ★ THEOZ. 1523 Sixth Ave (98101), downtown. 206/749-9660. Hrs: 11:30 am-2:30 pm, 5-10:30 pm; Fri to 11 pm; Sun from 5 pm; early-bird dinner to 6 pm; Sat, Sun brunch 11 am-3 pm. Closed most major hols. Res accepted. Bar to 1 am; Fri to 2 am; Sat 4 pm-2 am. Wine list. Semi-a la carte: lunch $7.50-$9, dinner $12.50-$30. Sat, Sun brunch $9.50-$11. Specializes in northwestern American dishes with Latin American and Indonesian influences. Own baking. Sophisticated decor with Tandoori oven, partially open kitchen. Totally nonsmoking. Cr cds: A, MC, V.

D

↵★ TRATTORIA MITCHELLI. 84 Yesler Way (98104), in Pioneer Square. 206/623-3883. Hrs: 7-4 am; Mon to 11 pm; Sat from 8 am; Sun 8 am-11 pm. Closed Dec 25. Res accepted Sun-Thurs. Italian menu. Bar 11-2 am. Semi-a la carte: bkfst $2.75-$8.75, lunch $4.95-$9.95, dinner $6.75-$14.50. Complete meals: lunch (Mon-Fri) $4.95. Child's meals. Specializes in pizza, pasta, chicken. Outdoor dining. Antique furnishings. Cr cds: A, DS, MC, V.

D

★ ★ TULIO. (See Hotel Vintage Park) 206/624-5500. Hrs: 7-10 am, 11:30 am-2:30 pm, 5-10 pm; wkend hrs vary. Closed some major hols. Res accepted. Italian menu. Bar. Wine cellar. A la carte entrees: bkfst $5-$9, lunch $9-$15, dinner $9-$21. Child's meals. Specializes in regional Italian cuisine. Valet parking. Outdoor dining. Open view of wood-burning pizza oven. Cr cds: A, C, D, DS, ER, JCB, MC, V.

D

★ ★ ★ UNION BAY CAFE. 3515 NE 45th St (98105), north of downtown. 206/527-8364. Hrs: 5-10 pm; Sun 4:30-9 pm. Closed Mon; some major hols. Res accepted. Wine list. A la carte entrees: dinner $11.50-$18.75. Child's meals. Specializes in fresh seafood, organic produce, free-range chicken. Own pastries. Outdoor dining. Intimate dining in two dining rms with orginal artwork, wine and flower displays. Totally nonsmoking. Cr cds: A, C, D, DS, MC, V.

D

★ ★ ★ UNION SQUARE GRILL. 621 Union St (98101), downtown. 206/224-4321. Hrs: 11 am-3 pm, 5-10 pm; Fri, Sat to midnight. Closed some major hols. Res accepted. Bar. Wine list. Semi-a la carte: lunch $6.95-$15.95, dinner $15.95-$29.95. Specializes in steaks, chops, Northwestern seafood. Valet parking. Several dining areas; mahogany furnishings, dividers. Cr cds: A, C, D, DS, JCB, MC, V.

D

✔★ ★ ★ **VINA.** 2207 First Ave (98121), downtown. 206/443-1465. Hrs: 5-10 pm; Fri, Sat to 11 pm. Closed most major hols. Res accepted. Mediterranean menu. Bar to midnight. Semi-a la carte: dinner $10.95-$14.95. Specialties: smoked roasted chicken, Spanish paella. Elegent decor. Totally nonsmoking. Cr cds: MC, V.

[D]

★ ★ ★ **VIRAZON.** 1329 First Ave (98101), at Union St, downtown. 206/233-0123. Hrs: 11:30 am-2:30 pm, 5:30-9:30 pm; Mon to 2 pm; Fri, Sat 11:30 am-2:30 pm, 6-10 pm. Closed Sun; major hols. Res accepted. French menu. Beer. Wine list. A la carte entrees: lunch $5-$12, dinner $16-$29. Tasting menu: dinner $49. Child's meals. Specializes in seafood, 5-course tasting menu. Validated parking. Outdoor dining. The menu changes daily in this bright, European-style restaurant. Totally nonsmoking. Cr cds: A, D, JCB, MC, V.

[D]

★ ★ ★ **WILD GINGER.** 1400 Western Ave (98101), downtown. 206/623-4450. Hrs: 11:30 am-3 pm, 5-11 pm; Fri 5 pm-midnight; Sat to midnight; Sun 4:30-11 pm. Closed Thanksgiving, Dec 25. Res accepted. Southeast Asian, Chinese menu. Bar. Semi-a la carte: lunch $6.95-$12.95, dinner $9.95-$19.95. Specializes in fresh seafood, curry. Satay bar. Near Pike Place Market. Cr cds: A, C, D, DS, MC, V.

[D] [⇥]

★ ★ **Z RITZ.** 720 E Pike (98122), east of downtown. 206/329-6448. Hrs: 11:30 am-3 pm, 5:30-9:30 pm; Sat to 10:30 pm; Sun 5-9 pm; Sat, Sun brunch 9:30 am-2:30 pm. Closed some major hols. Res accepted. Mediterranean menu. Wine, beer. A la carte entrees: lunch $3.95-$8.95, dinner $8.95-$15.95. Sat, Sun brunch $5.95-$8.95. Child's meals. Specialties: couscous maison, lamb, veal. Own pastries. Outdoor dining. Cozy, intimate bistro atmosphere with private booths. Cr cds: MC, V.

[D] [⇥]

Unrated Dining Spot

SURROGATE HOSTESS. 746 19th Ave E, north of downtown. 206/324-1944. Hrs: 6 am-9 pm. Closed Jan 1, Dec 25. No A/C. Northwest country cooking. Wine, beer. Avg ck: bkfst $3-$7, lunch $4-$7, dinner $4-$11. Specializes in seafood, salads, desserts. Parking. Outdoor dining. Totally nonsmoking. No cr cds accepted.

[D]

Seattle-Tacoma Intl Airport Area (C-3)

(See also Seattle, Tacoma)

Services and Information

Information: 206/433-4645.

Lost and Found: 206/433-5312.

Airlines: Aeroflot, Air Canada, Alaska Arlns, America West, American, Asiana, British Airways, Canadian Arlns Intl, China Eastern, Continental, Delta, Eva Airways, Frontier Arlns, Hawaiian Arlns, Martinair Holland, Northwest, Reno Air, SAS, Southwest, Swissair, TWA, United, USAir, Western Pacific Arlns.

Motels

★ ★ **BEST WESTERN AIRPORT EXECUTEL.** (20717 Pacific Hwy S, Seattle 98198) 1 mi S on WA 99, at S 207th St. 206/878-3300; FAX 206/824-9000. 138 rms, 3 story. June-Sept: S $101-$121; D $107-$135; each addl $6; suites $213-$325; under 18 free; lower rates rest of yr. Crib

free. TV; cable (premium). Indoor pool; whirlpool. Complimentary continental bkfst. Complimentary coffee in rms. Restaurant 6 am-10 pm. Bar 3 pm-2 am. Ck-out noon. Meeting rms. Business servs avail. In-rm modem link. Bellhops. Valet serv. Free airport transportation. Exercise equipt; stair machine, bicycle, sauna. Cr cds: A, C, D, DS, JCB, MC, V.

[D] [≋] [🏃] [✈] [⇤] [🔥] [SC]

★ ★ **COMFORT INN.** (19333 International Blvd, Seattle 98188) 1 mi S on WA 99, at S 193rd St. 206/878-1100; FAX 206/878-8678. 119 rms, 4 story. S, D $75-$150; each addl $10; suites $135-$175; under 18 free. Crib free. TV; cable (premium); VCR avail. Complimentary continental bkfst. Restaurant adj open 24 hrs. Ck-out noon. Meeting rms. In-rm modem link. Bellhops. Sundries. Free covered parking. Free airport transportation. Exercise equipt; weight machine, bicycles. Whirlpool. Refrigerator in suites. Cr cds: A, C, D, DS, ER, JCB, MC, V.

[D] [🏃] [✈] [⇤] [🔥] [SC]

✔★ ★ **LA QUINTA.** (2824 S 188th St, Seattle 98188) 1 mi S on WA 99. 206/241-5211; FAX 206/246-5596. 142 rms, 6 story. Late May-Sept: S $74; D $82; each addl $8; lower rates rest of yr; under 18 free. Crib free. Pet accepted, some restrictions. TV; cable (premium). Pool; whirlpool. Complimentary continental bkfst. Restaurant opp. Ck-out noon. Coin lndry. Meeting rm. Business servs avail. In-rm modem link. Sundries. Free airport transportation. Exercise equipt; weights, stair machine. Luxury level. Cr cds: A, D, DS, MC, V.

[D] [🐾] [≋] [🏃] [✈] [⇤] [🔥] [SC]

★ ★ **RAMADA INN-SEATAC EAST.** (16838 International Blvd, Seattle 98188) 1/4 mi S on WA 99, at S 168th St. 206/248-0901; FAX 206/242-3170; res: 800/845-2968. 150 rms, 3 story. June-Sept: S, D $78-$87; each addl $10; suites $80; under 12 free; lower rates rest of yr. Crib free. Pet accepted. TV; cable (premium). Restaurant 7 am-10 pm. Ck-out noon. Meeting rm. Business servs avail. In-rm modem link. Sundries. Free airport transportation. Exercise equipt; weight machine, rower. Balconies. Cr cds: A, C, D, DS, ER, JCB, MC, V.

[D] [🐾] [🏃] [✈] [⇤] [🔥] [SC]

✔★ **TRAVELODGE.** (2900 S 192nd St, Seattle 98188) 206/241-9292; FAX 206/242-0681. 106 rms, 3 story. July-Sept: S, D $65-$90; each addl $6; under 18 free; lower rates rest of yr. Crib free. TV; cable (premium). Complimentary coffee in rms. Restaurant adj open 24 hrs. Ck-out noon. Coin lndry. Business servs avail. In-rm modem link. Free airport transportation. Sauna. Cr cds: A, C, D, DS, ER, JCB, MC, V.

[D] [✈] [⇤] [🔥] [SC]

Motor Hotels

★ ★ **BEST WESTERN EXECUTEL.** (31611 20th Ave S, Federal Way 98003) I-5 exit 143 S. 253/941-6000; FAX 253/941-9500. E-mail execute1@ricochet.net. 112 rms, 3 story. Mid-June-mid-Sept: S, D $99-$129; each addl $10; under 18 free. Crib free. Pet accepted; $20. TV; cable (premium). Heated pool; whirlpool. Restaurant 6 am-11 pm. Rm serv. Bar. Ck-out noon. Meeting rms. Business center. In-rm modem link. Bellhops. Valet serv. Free airport transportation. Health club privileges. Cr cds: A, C, D, DS, JCB, MC, V.

[D] [🐾] [≋] [⇤] [🔥] [SC] [🏂]

★ ★ **CLARION.** (3000 S 176th, Seattle 98188) 206/242-0200; FAX 206/242-1998. 211 rms, 3 story. June-Oct: S $60-$89; D $70-$99; each addl $10; under 19 free; higher rates Sea Fair; lower rates rest of yr. Crib free. TV; cable (premium); VCR avail. Complimentary coffee in rms. Restaurant 6 am-2 pm, 5-10 pm. Rm serv. Bar from 4 pm. Ck-out noon. Meeting rms. Business center. In-rm modem link. Coin lndry. Free airport transportation. Exercise equipt; treadmill, rowers, sauna. Massage. Indoor pool; whirlpool. Game rm. Some refrigerators, microwaves. Cr cds: A, C, D, DS, JCB, MC, V.

[D] [≋] [🏃] [✈] [⇤] [🔥] [SC] [🏃]

★ ★ **DOUBLETREE INN.** (205 Strander Blvd, Seattle 98188) I-5, I-405 Southcenter exit, south of downtown. 206/246-8220; FAX 206/575-4749. Web www.doubletreehotels.com. 198 rms, 2 story. S, D

$99-$178; each addl $10; suites $136-$142; under 18 free; wkend, seasonal rates. Crib free. TV; cable (premium), VCR avail. Heated pool; poolside serv. Playground. Restaurant 6 am-10 pm. Rm serv. Bar 11-2 am. Ck-out noon. Meeting rms. Business servs avail. Bellhops. Valet serv. Health club privileges. Microwaves avail. Some private patios. Cr cds: A, C, D, DS, ER, JCB, MC, V.

[D] [≈] [✕] [M] [SC]

★ ★ ★ **DOUBLETREE-SEATTLE AIRPORT.** (18740 Pacific Hwy S, Seattle 98188) 206/246-8600; FAX 206/431-8687. 850 rms, 14 story. S, D, suites $295-$550; under 18 free; wkend rates; lower rates rest of yr. Crib free. TV; cable, VCR avail. Heated pool; poolside serv. Coffee in rms. Restaurant (see MAXI'S). Rm serv 24 hrs. Bars 11:30-2 am; entertainment. Ck-out noon. Convention facilities. Business center. In-rm modem link. Bellhops. Valet serv. Concierge. Sundries. Gift shop. Barber, beauty shop. Free airport transportation 24 hrs. Exercise equipt; weight machines, stair machine. Many bathrm phones. Private patios, balconies. Many rms with view of lake, mountains. Outdoor glass-enclosed elvtrs. On 28 acres. Cr cds: A, C, D, DS, ER, JCB, MC, V.

[D] [≈] [✕] [✕] [M] [SC]

★ ★ ★ **HILTON SEATTLE AIRPORT.** (17620 International Blvd, Seattle 98188) at S 176th St. 206/244-4800; FAX 206/248-4495. E-mail debra_noonan@hilton.com; web www.hilton.com. 178 rms, 2-3 story. S, D $109-$159; suites $275-$350; under 18 free; wkend rates. Crib free. Pet accepted. TV; cable (premium), VCR avail. Heated pool; whirlpool, poolside serv. Complimentary coffee in rms. Restaurant 6 am-11 pm. Rm serv 24 hrs. Bar 11 am-midnight. Ck-out 1 pm. Meeting rms. Business center. In-rm modem link. Bellhops. Valet serv. Sundries. Free airport transportation. Exercise equipt; weight machine, bicycles. Private patios. Garden setting. Cr cds: A, C, D, DS, ER, JCB, MC, V.

[D] [⊶] [≈] [✕] [✕] [M] [SC] [✦]

★ ★ **HOLIDAY INN.** (17338 International Blvd, Seattle 98188) at S 173rd St. 206/248-1000; FAX 206/242-7089. 260 rms, 12 story. S, D $134-$144; suites $200-$250; each addl $10; family, wkend rates. Crib free. TV; cable (premium). Indoor pool; whirlpool. Restaurant 6 am-10 pm; Fri to 10:30 pm; Sat 7 am-10:30 pm; Sun from 7 am. Rm serv. Bars 11 am-11 pm. Ck-out noon. Coin lndry. Meeting rms. Business servs avail. In-rm modem link. Bellhops. Sundries. Gift shop. Free airport transportation. Exercise equipt; weight machine, bicycle. Microwaves avail. Revolving rooftop dining rm. Cr cds: A, C, D, DS, JCB, MC, V.

[D] [≈] [✕] [✕] [M] [SC]

★ ★ ★ **MARRIOTT SEA-TAC.** (3201 S 176th St, Seattle 98188) International Blvd (WA 99) to S 176th St. 206/241-2000; FAX 206/248-0789. 459 rms. S, D $111-$132; suites $200-$450; under 18 free; wkly, wkend rates. Crib free. Pet accepted. TV; cable (premium), VCR avail. Indoor pool; whirlpool, poolside serv. Restaurant 6 am-11 pm. Rm serv. Bar 11-2 am. Ck-out 1 pm. Convention facilities. Business center. In-rm modem link. Bellhops. Valet serv. Shopping arcade. Free airport transportation. Exercise equipt; weight machines, bicycles, sauna. Game rm. Microwaves avail. 21,000-sq ft atrium with trees, plants, totem poles, waterfall. Luxury level. Cr cds: A, C, D, DS, ER, JCB, MC, V.

[D] [⊶] [≈] [✕] [✕] [M] [SC] [✦]

★ ★ **QUALITY INN.** 17101 Pacific Hwy S (98188). 206/246-7000; FAX 206/246-1715. 138 rms, 3 story. June-Aug: S $79-$115; D $89-$125; each addl $10; suites $145; under 18 free; lower rates rest of yr. Crib free. TV; cable (premium). Heated pool. Complimentary continental bkfst. Coffee in rms. Restaurnt adj 6 am-11 pm. Ck-out noon. Meeting rms. Business servs avail. In-rm modem link. Bellhops. Beauty shop. Free airport transportation. Exercise equipt; treadmills, stair machine. Cr cds: A, C, D, DS, ER, JCB, MC, V.

[D] [≈] [✕] [✕] [M] [SC]

★ ★ ★ **RADISSON SEATTLE AIRPORT.** (17001 International Blvd (Pacific Hwy), Seattle 98188) N on International Blvd (WA 99) at 170th St. 206/244-6000; FAX 206/246-6835. 170 rms, 2 story. S $119-$159; D $129-$169; each addl $10; under 18 free; wkend rates. Crib free. TV; cable. Heated pool; poolside serv. Coffee in rms. Restaurant 6 am-10 pm. Rm serv. Bar 4 pm-1 am. Ck-out noon. Convention facilities. Business

servs avail. In-rm modem link. Bellhops. Sundries. Gift shop. Free airport transportation. Exercise equipt; stair machines, bicycles, sauna. Luxury level. Cr cds: A, C, D, DS, ER, JCB, MC, V.

[D] [≈] [✕] [✕] [✕] [M] [SC]

★ ★ **WESTCOAST SEA-TAC HOTEL.** (18220 International Blvd, Seattle 98188) at 182nd St. 206/246-5535; FAX 206/246-9733; res: 800/426-0670. 146 rms, 5 story. S $95-$105; D $105-$115; each addl $10; suites $150; under 18 free; some wkend rates. Crib free. TV; cable (premium), VCR avail. Heated pool; whirlpool, poolside serv. Restaurant 6 am-10 pm. Rm serv. Bar 11:30-2 am. Ck-out noon. Meeting rms. Business servs avail. Bellhops. Valet serv. Free valet parking. Free airport transportation. Exercise equipt; treadmill, stair machine, sauna. Cr cds: A, C, D, DS, ER, JCB, MC, V.

[D] [≈] [✕] [✕] [✕] [M] [SC]

Restaurant

★ ★ ★ **MAXI'S.** (See Doubletree Motor Hotel) 206/246-8600. Hrs: 5-10 pm; Sun 9 am-2 pm (brunch). Closed Dec 25. Res accepted. Continental menu. Bar to 2 am. Semi-a la carte: dinner $17.95-$39.95. Sun brunch $17.95. Child's meals. Specialties: tableside Caesar salad, tableside steak Diane. Valet parking. Elegant, multi-level dining areas offer views of mountains or airport. Family-owned. Cr cds: A, C, D, DS, MC, V.

[D] [SC] [➶]

Sedro Woolley (B-3)

(For accommodations see Anacortes, Bellingham, Mount Vernon)

Founded 1884 **Pop** 6,031 **Elev** 509 ft **Area code** 360 **Zip** 98284
Information Chamber of Commerce, 714-B Metcalf St; 360/855-1841 or 888/225-8365.

A thick growth of cedar once cloaked the Skagit River Valley, but it has been replaced with fertile farms, for which Sedro Woolley is the commercial center. Lumbering is still one of the main industries. The town represents the merger of the town of Sedro (Spanish for "cedar") and its onetime rival, Woolley, named for its founder.

A Ranger District station of the Mount Baker-Snoqualmie National Forest (see BELLINGHAM, SEATTLE) is located here.

What to See and Do

Lake Whatcom Railway. A seven-mi, round-trip steam train ride in antique Northern Pacific passenger cars through countryside. (July-Aug, Sat & Tues; Dec, Sat only; rest of yr, charter trips) 11 mi N on WA 9, in Wickersham. Phone 360/595-2218. ¢¢¢

North Cascades Natl Park. Authorized in 1968, this 504,781-acre area has beautiful alpine scenery, deep glaciated canyons, more than 300 active glaciers, hundreds of jagged peaks and mountain lakes. It is adjacent to the 576,865-acre Glacier Peak Wilderness dominated by 10,541-ft-high Glacier Peak and to Ross Lake and Lake Chelan Natl Recreation Areas. Camping along WA 20 in Ross Lake area (June-Sept, fee); fishing, climbing, hiking, backpacking (by permit). 50 mi E on WA 20 (portions of this road are closed in winter). Contact 2105 Hwy 20; 360/856-5700. **Free.**

Seattle City Light Skagit Hydroelectric Project. Four and one half-hr tours include 560-ft ride up mountain on incline lift, 4½-mi boat ride to Ross Dam & Powerhouse (tour) and return by boat to Diablo; family-style dinner. (Late June-Labor Day, Thurs-Mon) Res and advance payment required. Single 90-min tour also avail. (July-Labor Day, Thurs-Mon) 62 mi E of I-5/Mt Vernon on WA 20 (North Cascades Hwy) in Diablo, in Ross Lake Natl Recreation Area. Contact Skagit Tours, Seattle City Light, 1015 3rd Ave, Seattle 98104; 206/684-3030. Museum in tour center. ¢¢¢¢ Self-guided mini-tours at Ross Lake Natl Recreation Area include

Newhalem Visitor Information Center. Information on Skagit Project and Natl Park/Recreation Area. (Mid-June-Labor day, daily) **Free.**

Trail of the Cedars. (45 min) Informative nature walk on S bank of Skagit River. Begins at end of Main St, Newhalem. **Free.**

Gorge Powerhouse/Ladder Creek Falls & Rock Gardens. Begins at Gorge Powerhouse, Newhalem; self-guided tour of powerhouse, walk through Gorge Rock Gardens to Ladder Creek Falls. Gardens lighted at night. (Late June-Labor Day, daily) **Free.**

Swimming, hiking, camping, boating, fishing, windsurfing. Also fishing in Skagit River. Clear Lake. 3 mi S on WA 9. RV sites in town.

Annual Events

Loggerodeo. Logging contests, rodeos, parades. 1 wk late June-early July.

Christmas Lighting Festival. Parade, tree lighting. First wkend Dec.

Sequim (B-3)

(See also Neah Bay, Port Angeles, Port Townsend)

Pop 3,616 **Elev** 183 ft **Area code** 360 **Zip** 98382 **E-mail** sequim@tenforward.com **Web** www.cityofsequim.com

Information Sequim-Dungeness Valley Chamber of Commerce, 1192 E Washington St, PO Box 907; 360/683-6197 or 800/737-8462.

Sequim (pronounced SKWIM) is a Native American name meaning "quiet water."

What to See and Do

Dungeness Recreation Area. Approx 200 acres. Camping (Feb-Oct; fee). Access to Dungeness Natl Wildlife Refuge. (Daily) Clallam County Park, 6 mi NW. Phone 360/683-5847.

Olympic Game Farm. Wild animals; guided walking tour (summer; drive-through rest of yr). Endangered species breeding program. (Daily) 6 mi NW. Phone 360/683-4295. ¢¢-¢¢¢

Sequim Bay State Park. More than acres along Sequim Bay. Swimming, scuba diving; fishing, clamming, boating (dock). Hiking, tennis, ballpark. Picnicking. Camping (hookups). Standard fees. 4 mi SE on US 101. Phone 360/683-4235.

Annual Event

Irrigation Festival. Oldest community festival in the state; celebrates the bringing of water to the Sequim Prairie. Picnics, parades, flower shows, contests. 1st full wk May.

Motels

✓★ **BEST WESTERN BAY LODGE.** 268522 US 101. 360/683-0691; FAX 360/683-3748. E-mail sbl@olympus.net. 54 rms, 1 with shower only, 36 with A/C, 3 story, 14 suites. No elvtr. May-Sept: S $75-$100; D $85-$110; each addl $8; suites $95-$145; under 12 free; lower rates rest of yr. Crib free. Pet accepted; $25 refundable. TV; cable (premium). Heated pool. Complimentary coffee in lobby. Complimentary continental bkfst Mid-Oct-mid Mar. Restaurant adj 7 am-9 pm. Ck-out noon. Meeting rms. Business servs avail. 9-hole putting course. Lawn games. Refrigerators in suites. Balconies. Picnic tables. Cr cds: A, C, D, DS, ER, JCB, MC, V.

D 🐕 🏊 🖺 🖎 SC

✓★ **ECONO LODGE.** 801 E Washington St. 360/683-7113; FAX 360/683-7343. 43 rms, 2 story. May-Sept: S $69; D $79; each addl $6; under 18 free; lower rates rest of yr. Crib free. TV; cable, VCR avail (movies $8). Complimentary continental bkfst. Restaurant opp 6:30 am-10

pm. Ck-out 11 am. Guest lndry. Business servs avail. Lawn games. Refrigerators, microwaves. Cr cds: A, D, DS, MC, V.

🖺 🖎 SC

Inns

★★ **DIAMOND POINT INN.** (241 Sunshine Dr, Gardiner 98334) E on US 101, left on Diamond Point Rd, right On Eagle Creek Rd, right on Sunshine Rd. 360/797-7720; res: 888/797-0393; FAX 360/797-7723. 6 rms, 2 share bath, 2 story. No A/C. No rm phones. Apr-Sept: S, D $75-$105; each addl $20; lower rates Oct-Nov, Feb-Mar. Closed rest of yr. Children over 5 yrs only. Complimentary full bkfst. Ck-out 11 am, ck-in 3 pm. Business servs avail. Luggage handling. Whirlpool. Lawn games. Some refrigerators. Picnic tables, grills. Surrounded by 10 acres of evergreens. Totally nonsmoking. Cr cds: MC, V.

🖺 🖎 SC

✓★ **GRANNY SANDY'S ORCHARD.** 405 W Spruce. 360/683-4365. E-mail moorross@olypen.com. 4 rms, 3 shared baths, 2 story. No A/C. No rm phones. June-Sept: S $47-$72; D $57-$82; under 5 free; lower rates rest of yr. Crib free. Complimentary full bkfst. Restaurant nearby. Ck-out 11 am, ck-in 2 pm. Luggage handling. Business servs avail. Totally nonsmoking. Cr cds: MC, V.

🖺 🖎

★★★ **GREYWOLF.** 395 Keeler Rd. 360/683-5889; FAX 360/683-1487; res: 800/360-9653. E-mail grywolf@olypen.com. 5 rms, 2 story. No A/C. 1 rm phone. June-Oct: S, D $65-$130; each addl $20; lower rates rest of yr. Children over 12 yrs only. TV in sitting rm; VCR avail (free movies). Complimentary full bkfst; afternoon refreshments. Ck-out 11:30 am, ck-in 4 pm. Business servs avail. Bus depot, marina transportation. Gift shop. Exercise equipt; rower, bicycle. Whirlpool. Microwaves avail. Picnic tables, grills. Theme oriented rms with many antiques. Totally nonsmoking. Cr cds: A, DS, MC, V.

🏃 🖺 🖎

★★ **GROVELAND COTTAGE.** (4861 Sequim-Dungeness Way, Dungeness) 5 mi N. 360/683-3565; FAX 360/683-5181; res: 800/879-8859. 4 rms, 2 story. No A/C. June-Oct: S $70-$100; D $80-$110; each addl $15; wkly rates; lower rates rest of yr. Children over 12 yrs only. TV; cable, VCR (free movies). Complimentary full bkfst. Complimentary coffee in rms. Restaurant nearby. Ck-out noon, ck-in 3 pm. Meeting rm. Business servs avail. Picnic tables. Former merchant's residence (1886); many antiques, Oriental rugs. Library/sitting rm. Totally nonsmoking. Cr cds: A, D, DS, MC, V.

🖺 🖎

★★ **MARGIE'S INN ON THE BAY.** 120 Forrest St. 360/683-7011; res: 800/730-4011. Web www.northolympic.com/margie. 4 rms, 2 story. No rm phones. May-mid-Oct: S, D $69-$132; each addl $20; lower rates rest of yr. Children over 12 yrs only. TV; VCR avail (movies). Whirlpool. Complimentary full bkfst. Restaurant nearby. Ck-out 11 am, ck-in 4 pm. Located on ocean. Totally nonsmoking. Cr cds: A, DS, MC, V.

D 🖺 🖎

Restaurants

✓★★ **ANYTHING GOES.** 235 E Washington. 360/683-1061. Hrs: 11 am-2 pm, 4:30-8 pm; Fri to 9 pm; Sat 4:30-9 pm. Closed Sun; some major hols. Res accepted. No A/C. Continental menu. Semi-a la carte: lunch $3.50-$8, dinner $7-$15. Child's meals. Specializes in Italian dishes, seafood. Own pasta, pastries. Two dining rms feature many plants, murals and original artwork. Totally nonsmoking. Cr cds: MC, V.

D

✓★★ **BUCKHORN GRILL.** 268522 US 101. 360/683-9010. E-mail teruok@prodigy.net. Hrs: 7 am-2 pm, 4-9 pm; Sun from 8 am; Sat, Sun brunch 8 am-2 pm. Closed Wed; Jan 1, Dec 25. Res accepted. Bar 5-9 pm. Semi-a la carte: bkfst $3.95-$8.50, lunch $3.95-$7.95, dinner $3.95-$14.95. Sat, Sun brunch $3.95-$8.50. Child's meals. Specializes in crab cakes, lamb chops, pasta. Own pasta. Bright, two-level dining area with skylights; windows overlook scenic evergreens. Cr cds: DS, MC, V.

★ ★ **DUNGENESS INN.** *1965 Woodcock.* 360/683-3331. Hrs: 7 am-9 pm; early-bird dinner Mon-Fri 3-6 pm; Sat, Sun brunch to 11 am. Closed Dec 25. Res accepted. Bar. Semi-a la carte: bkfst $3.50-$7.95, lunch $3.75-$12.95, dinner $6.95-$17.95. Sat, Sun brunch $5.95. Child's meals. Specializes in seafood, steak. Two-level dining with windows offering panoramic view of golf course. Family-owned. Totally nonsmoking. Cr cds: MC, V.

✔★ **MOON PALACE.** *323 E Washington.* 360/683-6898. Hrs: 11:30 am-8:30 pm; Fri to 9 pm; Sat 3-9 pm; Sun noon-8 pm. Closed Mon; most major hols. Res accepted. Chinese menu. Bar from 2 pm. Semi-a la carte: lunch $3.95-$5.50, dinner $5.25-$9.95. Sun lunch buffet $5.95. Specializes in Cantonese, mandarin dishes. Parking. Oriental decor. Cr cds: A, DS, MC, V.

D **SC**

★ ★ **PARADISE.** *703 N Sequim Ave.* 360/683-1977. Hrs: 11 am-9 pm. Closed Mon; July 4, Thanksgiving, Dec 25. Res accepted. Bar. Semi-a la carte: lunch $3.95-$12.95, dinner $6.95-$24.75. Specializes in steak, seafood, pasta. Parking. Many plants. Etched-glass booth dividers. Cr cds: A, DS, MC, V.

D

Snohomish (B-4)

(For accommodations see Everett, Marysville)

Settled 1853 **Pop** 6,499 **Elev** 64 ft **Area code** 360 **Zip** 98290

Information Chamber of Commerce, 116 Ave B, Waltz Bldg, PO Box 135, 98291; 360/568-2526.

Snohomish is sustained by dairy farms, tourism and retail trade. The Boeing plant that manufactures 747s and 767s (see EVERETT) is nearby. Snohomish claims to be the antique capital of the Pacific Northwest, boasting 400 dealers and many individual shops.

What to See and Do

Blackman Museum. Restored 1878 Victorian house; vintage furnishings. (June-Sept, daily; Mar-May & Oct-Dec, Wed-Sun afternoons; closed rest of yr) 118 Ave B. Phone 360/568-5235. ¢ Nearby is

Mt Baker-Snoqualmie Natl Forest. E via US 2. (See BELLINGHAM, SEATTLE)

Pioneer Village. Six authentic pioneer buildings moved here include general store (ca 1910) and weaver's shop, which displays antique looms. (June-Sept, daily; rest of yr, by appt) 2nd St & Pine St. Phone 360/568-5235. ¢

Star Center Antique Mall. More than 165 antique shops housed in a former armory. Restaurant, children's play area. (Daily) 829 2nd St. Phone 360/568-2131.

Stevens Pass Ski Area. Road goes past Eagle Falls. (See LEAVENWORTH) 53 mi E on US 2.

Walking tour of historical houses. Contact Chamber of Commerce, 116 Ave B, Waltz Bldg, for brochure. Phone 360/568-2526. **Free.**

Soap Lake (C-6)

(See also Coulee Dam, Ephrata)

Pop 1,149 **Elev** 1,075 ft **Area code** 509 **Zip** 98851

The minerals and salts in Soap Lake (Native American name *Smokiam,* or "healing waters") give the community status as a health resort. They also whip into a soaplike foam that lines the shoreline on windy days. This is the south entrance to the Grand Coulee, the 50-mile channel of the prehistoric Columbia River.

Motel

✔★ ★ **NOTARAS LODGE.** *231 Main St.* 509/246-0462; FAX 509/246-1054. 20 kit. units, 2 story. S $48; D $55; each addl $7; suites $90-$110. Pet accepted; $50 refundable and $10/day. TV; cable. Restaurant 11 am-10 pm. Ck-out 11 am. Refrigerators. Some in-rm whirlpools. Balconies. Picnic tables. Some rms with skylights. Cr cds: MC, V.

Restaurant

★ ★ **DON'S.** *14 Canna.* 509/246-1217. Hrs: 11 am-10 pm; Fri to 11 pm; Sat 4-11 pm. Closed Dec 25. Bar. Semi-a la carte: lunch $4-$10.50, dinner $7.95-$26.95. Specializes in steak, seafood. Own baking. Collection of Louie Leininger photos. Cr cds: MC, V.

Spokane (C-9)

(See also Cheney; also see Coeur d'Alene & Sandpoint, ID)

Settled 1871 **Pop** 177,196 **Elev** 1,898 ft **Area code** 509 **E-mail** visitors@spokane.net **Web** www.spokane-areacvb.org

Information Spokane Area Visitor Information Center, 201 W Main, 99204; 509/747-3230 or 800/248-3230.

Spokane (Spo-KAN) is the booming center of the vast, rich "inland Northwest," an area including eastern Washington, northern Idaho, northeastern Oregon, western Montana and southern British Columbia. A large rail center, the Spokane area also produces wheat, apples, hops, silver, gold, zinc and lead. Spokane boasts more than 6,500 commercial and industrial firms. Thanks to the surrounding mountain ranges, Spokane enjoys what it likes to term New Mexico's climate in the winter and Maine's in the summer. The city itself is in a saucerlike setting amid pine-green hills with the Spokane River running through its 52 square miles.

Long a favorite Native American hunting and fishing ground, Spokane began as a sawmill, powered by Spokane Falls. This village, the name meaning "children of the sun," was the only point in a 400-mile-long north-south range of mountains where railroads could cross the Rockies and reach the Columbia Basin. Railroading sparked the city's early growth. The Coeur d'Alene gold fields in Idaho helped finance Spokane's continuing development and helped it to survive an 1889 fire that nearly leveled the city. Farming, lumbering, mining and railroading aided Spokane's growth during the first decade of the century.

In 1974, the Havermale and Cannon islands in the Spokane River were the site of EXPO 74. The area has since been developed as Riverfront Park.

What to See and Do

✖ **Auto tour.**

Loop drive. A 33-mi city drive to major points of interest; route, marked with "city drive" signs, begins at Sprague Ave & Stevens St. Among points included are

Cathedral of St John the Evangelist (Episcopal). Magnificent sandstone Gothic structure; stained-glass windows by Boston's Connick Studios; wood and stone carvings. Tours (Sat-Tues, Thurs; Sun after services). Recitals on 49-bell carillon (Thurs, Sun); also recitals on Aeolian-Skinner organ (schedule varies). 1125 S Grand Blvd, at Sumner Ave. Phone 509/838-4277.   **Free.**

Comstock Park. Picnicking, tennis courts. Pool (mid-June-Aug, daily; fee for adults). Park (Daily). 29th Ave & Howard St.   **Free.**

Manito Park. Duncan Formal Gardens (May-Sept, daily); conservatory (daily; closed Jan 1, Dec 25). Davenport Memorial Fountain with changing formations in 10-min cycle (May-Sept, daily); Japanese, lilac and rose gardens (Apr-Oct, daily). Duck pond; picnicking. Grand Blvd at 18th Ave. Phone 509/625-6622.   **Free.**

Cliff Park. Built around old volcanic island; Review Rock, half acre at base, offers highest point in city for viewing. (Daily) 13th Ave & Grove St.   **Free.**

Cheney Cowles Museum. Houses collections of regional history and Native American culture. Fine Arts Gallery has changing art exhibits. Adj is **Campbell House** (1898), a restored mansion of Spokane's "age of elegance." (Daily exc Mon; closed hols) W 2316 1st Ave. Phone 509/456-3931.   ¢¢

Spokane Falls. Viewed from Bridge Ave at Monroe St or ft of Lincoln St. Spokane River roars over rocks in series of cascades; illuminated at night. Adj is

Riverfront Park. A 100-acre recreational park features outdoor amphitheater, IMAX theater, opera house, game room. Spokane River runs through park; suspension bridges over Spokane River; ft bridges; skyride over falls. Miniature golf; roller coaster, Ferris wheel, carousel. Children's petting zoo. Ponds; ice rink. Restaurant, vending carts, picnicking. Some fees. Spokane Falls Blvd from Division St to Post St. Phone 509/625-6600or 800/336-7275 (WA).   **Free.**

Flour Mill (1890). When it was built it was the most modern mill west of the Mississippi River. Today it is the home of boutiques, designer shops, galleries, restaurants. Overlooks Spokane River. (Daily) W 621 Mallon, adj to Riverfront Park entrance. Phone 509/327-4668.   **Free.**

Finch Arboretum. Approx 70 acres; includes Corey Glen Rhododendron Gardens, creek, 2,000 specimen plantings of ornamental trees & shrubs. (Daily) 3404 W Woodland Blvd, off Sunset Blvd. Phone 509/625-6655.   **Free.**

Gonzaga Univ (1887). (4,700 students) Rodin sculptures on display. In center of campus is Bing Crosby's gift to his *alma mater,* Crosby Student Center; Academy Award Oscar, gold records, certificates, trophies on display in Crosbyana Room (daily). Tours of campus (includes Crosby Center & St Aloyisius Church; by appt). Boone Ave & Addison St. Phone 509/328-4220, ext 2234.

Mt Spokane State Park. More than 13,000 acres; includes Mt Spokane (5,881 ft), with excellent view from summit, and Mt Kit Carson (5,306 ft). Hiking, bridle trails. Downhill skiing, cross-country skiing, snowmobiling (special parking permit required). Picnicking. Camping. Standard fees. 25 mi NE on WA 206. Phone 509/456-4169.

Riverside State Park. Approx 7,300 acres along Spokane River. Fishing; boating (launch). Hiking; equestrian area. Snowmobiling. Picnicking. Camping. Also 600-acre off-road vehicle area; outdoor stoves; interpretive center. Standard fees. 6 mi NW via Downriver Dr. Phone 509/456-3964.

Skiing. Mt Spokane. Five double chairlifts; patrol, school, rentals; cafeteria, bar; lodge. Longest run 1½ mi; vertical drop 2,000 ft. (Dec-mid-Apr, Wed-Sun) 30 mi NE on WA 206, in Mt Spokane State Park. Phone 509/238-6281.   ¢¢¢¢¢

Worden's Winery. Tour and tasting of Gold Medal wines. Picnicking. (Daily; closed Jan 1, Dec 25) 7217 W 45th. Phone 509/455-7835.   **Free.**

Annual Events

Ag Expo. Convention Center. Agricultural fair. Mid-Jan.

Spokane Interstate Fair. Interstate Fairgrounds. Broadway & Havana Sts. Phone 509/535-1766. 9 days mid-Sept.

Seasonal Events

Horse racing. Playfair Race Course. N Altamont & E Main Sts. Wed, Fri-Sun, hols. Phone 509/534-0505. July-mid-Nov.

Spokane Civic Theatre. 1020 N Howard. Live productions. Phone 509/325-2507. Thurs-Sun, Oct-mid-June.

Motels

★ ★ **BEST WESTERN TRADE WINDS DOWNTOWN.** *W 907 3rd Ave (99204).* 509/838-2091; FAX 509/838-2094; res: 800/586-5397. 59 rms, 4 story. Apr-mid-Oct: S $63-$74; D $68-$79; each addl $5; under 12 free; lower rates rest of yr. Crib $3. TV; cable (premium). Pool. Complimentary continental bkfst. Restaurant opp 6 am-10 pm. Ck-out 1 pm. Coin lndry. Business servs avail. Private patios, balconies. Cr cds: A, C, D, DS, ER, MC, V.

⊠ ⊠ ⊠ SC

★ **BEST WESTERN TRADE WINDS NORTH.** *N 3033 Division St (99207).* 509/326-5500; FAX 509/328-1357. 63 rms, 3 story. No elvtrs. May-Sept: S $58; D $58-$60; each addl $4; under 13 free; lower rates rest of yr. Crib $3. TV; cable (premium). Indoor pool. Complimentary coffee in rms. Complimentary continental bkfst. Ck-out noon. Business servs avail. Balconies. Cr cds: A, C, D, DS, ER, MC, V.

⊠ ⊠ ⊠ SC

★ **COMFORT INN SPOKANE VALLEY.** *N 905 Sullivan Rd (99037), 15 mi E on I-90, exit 291.* 509/924-3838; FAX 509/921-6976. 76 rms, 2 story, 13 suites. May-Sept: S, D $63-$68; each addl $5; suites $80-$125; under 19 free; higher rates special events; lower rates rest of yr. Crib free. Pet accepted, some restrictions; $15. TV; cable, VCR avail. Pool; whirlpool. Complimentary continental bkfst. Restaurant nearby. Ck-out 11 am. Coin lndry. Meeting rms. Business servs avail. Valet serv. Refrigerator in suites. Cr cds: A, C, D, DS, JCB, MC, V.

D ⊠ ⊠ ⊠ ⊠ SC

★ ★ **COURTYARD BY MARRIOTT.** *N 401 Riverpoint Blvd (99202).* 509/456-7600; FAX 509/456-0969. 149 rms, 3 story. S, D $72-$79; suites $109-$119; under 12 free; wkly rates. Crib free. TV; cable, VCR avail. Indoor pool; whirlpool. Complimentary coffee in rms. Restaurant 6:30 am-10 pm. Bar 4-11 pm. Ck-out 1 pm. Coin lndry. Meeting rms. Business servs avail. Valet serv. Exercise equipt; weight machine, bicycles. Refrigerator in suites. Balconies. Cr cds: A, C, D, DS, MC, V.

D ⊠ ⊠ ⊠ ⊠ SC

✔ ★ **DAYS INN.** *1919 Hutchinson Rd (99212).* 509/926-5399; FAX 509/928-5974. 92 rms, 2 story. S, D $55-$70; each addl $5; suites $75-$80; family rates. Crib free. Pet accepted; $10. TV; cable. Complimentary continental bkfst, coffee. Restaurant adj. Ck-out noon. Meeting rms. Business servs avail. Cr cds: A, C, D, DS, MC, V.

D ⊠ ⊠ ⊠ SC

★ ★ **RAMADA INN.** *Box 19228 (99219), opp Intl Airport.* 509/838-5211; FAX 509/838-1074. 168 rms, 2 story. S $65-$85; D $75-$95; each addl $8; suites $95-$150; kit units $150; studio rms $85; under 18 free; some wknd rates. Crib free. Pet accepted. TV; cable. 2 pools, 1 indoor; whirlpool, sauna. Restaurant 6 am-11 pm. Rm serv. Bar; entertainment exc Sun. Ck-out noon. Business servs avail. Bellhops. Valet serv. Sundries. Free airport transportation. Cr cds: A, C, D, DS, ER, JCB, MC, V.

D ⊠ ⊠ ⊠ ⊠ ⊠ SC

✔ ★ **RODEWAY INN.** *W 827 1st Ave (99204).* 509/838-8271; FAX 509/838-0525. 81 rms, 4 story. Mid-May-Sept: S $40-$55; D $46-$65; each addl $10; suites $95; under 18 free; higher rates Bloomsday; lower rates rest of yr. Crib free. Pet accepted, some restrictions. TV. Heated pool. Complimentary continental bkfst. Restaurant 6 am-10 pm. Bar to 2 am. Ck-out 1 pm. Meeting rms. Business servs avail. Airport, RR station, bus depot transportation. Cr cds: A, D, DS, JCB, MC, V.

⊠ ⊠ ⊠ ⊠ SC

✔★ **SHANGRI-LA.** *W 2922 Government Way (99204), I-90 Business, Garden Springs Rd exit.* 509/747-2066; FAX 509/456-8696; res: 800/234-4941. 19 (1-3 rm) units, 2 story, 6 kits. S $42-$45; D $47-$50; each addl $5; suites $50-$63; kit units $47-$79. Crib free. TV; cable, VCR avail. Heated pool. Playground. Restaurant nearby. Ck-out 11 am. Lawn games. Free airport transportation. Some refrigerators. Picnic tables. Cr cds: A, C, D, DS, MC, V.

≋ ⊠ ⍦ SC

★ **SIERRA HOTEL.** *W 4212 Sunset Blvd (99204), I-90 Business, exit 277 Garden Springs.* 509/747-2021; FAX 509/747-5950. 137 rms, 2 story. S $50-$67; D $56-$75; each addl $8; under 19 free; some wkend rates. Crib free. TV; cable (premium), VCR avail. Heated pool; poolside serv. Restaurant 6 am-10 pm. Rm serv. Bar. Ck-out noon. Coin lndry. Meeting rms. Business center. In-rm modem link. Bellhops. Valet serv. Airport transportation. Lawn games. Cr cds: A, C, D, DS, ER, JCB, MC, V.

≋ ⊠ ⍦ SC ✈

Motor Hotels

★ **CAVANAUGH'S FOURTH AVENUE.** *E 110 4th Ave (99202), I-90 exit 281.* 509/838-6101; FAX 509/624-0733. 151 rms, 6 story. S $54-$78; D $58-$78; each addl $8; suites $78; under 18 free. Crib free. Pet accepted. TV; cable. Pool. Restaurant 6 am-10 pm. Rm serv. Bar. Ck-out noon. Coin lndry. Meeting rms. Business servs avail. Free airport, RR station, bus depot transportation. Minibar in suites. Cr cds: A, C, D, DS, ER, MC, V.

D ✔ ≋ ⊠ ⍦ SC

★★★ **CAVANAUGH'S RIVER INN.** *N 700 Division St (99202).* 509/326-5577; FAX 509/326-1120; res: 800/843-4667. 241 rms, 2 story. S $77-$94; D $82-$99; each addl $10; suites $160; under 17 free. Crib free. Pet accepted, some restrictions. TV; cable, VCR avail. 2 heated pools; wading pool, whirlpool, sauna, poolside serv. Restaurant 7 am-10 pm. Rm serv. Bar 11-2 am; entertainment exc Sun. Ck-out noon. Meeting rms. Business servs avail. Bellhops. Valet serv. Sundries. Gift shop. Airport, RR station, bus depot transportation. Tennis. On river. Cr cds: A, C, D, DS, ER, MC, V.

D ✔ ⍅ ≋ ⊠ ⍦ SC

★★ **DOUBLETREE.** *N 1100 Sullivan Rd (99220), I-90 exit 291.* 509/924-9000; FAX 509/922-4965. 237 rms, 2-3 story. S, D $79-$99; each addl $15; under 18 free. Crib free. Pet accepted, some restrictions. TV; cable. Heated pool; whirlpool. Coffee in rms. Restaurant 6 am-11 pm. Rm serv. Bar 11-2 am; entertainment Tues-Sat. Ck-out noon. Meeting rms. Bellhops. Valet serv. Sundries. Barber, beauty shop. Free airport transportation. Some bathrm phones, refrigerators. Private patios, balconies. Cr cds: A, C, D, DS, ER, JCB, MC, V.

✔ ≋ ⊠ ⍦

★★★ **QUALITY INN VALLEY SUITES.** *E 8923 Mission Ave (99212).* 509/928-5218; res: 800/777-7355. 127 rms, 3-4 story, 52 suites. June-Oct: S $79-$89; D $89-$100; each addl $5; suites $180-$300; under 18 free; wkly rates; golf, package plans; lower rates rest of yr. Crib $5. TV; cable (premium), VCR avail (movies). Indoor pool; whirlpool, poolside serv. Complimentary continental bkfst. Restaurant 6:30-9 am, 5-10 pm. Rm serv. Bar from 5 pm. Ck-out 11 am. Coin lndry. Meeting rms. Business center. Bellhops. Valet serv. Sundries. Gift shop. Barber, beauty shop. Free airport, RR station, bus depot transportation. Exercise equipt; weights, bicycles, sauna. Refrigerators. Balconies. Picnic tables. Cr cds: A, C, D, DS, ER, JCB, MC, V.

D ≋ ⍓ ⊠ ⍦ SC ✈

★ **SHILO INN.** *E 923 3rd Ave (99202).* 509/535-9000; FAX 509/535-5740; res: 800/222-2244. 105 rms, 5 story. S $65; D $65-$69; each addl $8; under 12 free; some wkend rates. Crib free. Pet accepted; $7/day. TV; cable (premium), VCR (movies). Indoor pool. Coffee in rms. Complimentary full bkfst. Restaurant 6:30 am-10 pm. Rm serv. Bar 11:30 am-11 pm. Ck-out noon. Meeting rms. Business servs avail. In-rm modem

link. Free airport transportation. Exercise equipt; weight machine, bicycle, sauna. Refrigerators. Cr cds: A, C, D, DS, ER, JCB, MC, V.

✔ ≋ ⍓ ⊠ ⍦ SC

Hotels

★★★ **DOUBLETREE.** *N 322 Spokane Falls Court (99201), 3 blks W of US 2/395.* 509/455-9600; FAX 509/455-6285. 369 rms, 15 story. S, D $99-$109; each addl $10; suites $125-$450; under 17 free; some wkend rates; higher rates: Bloomsday, AAUW dragster finals. Crib free. Valet parking. TV; cable (premium). Heated pool. Restaurant 6:30 am-10 pm. Bar 11-2 am; entertainment. Ck-out 1 pm. Convention facilities. Business servs avail. Concierge. Beauty shop. Free airport, RR station, bus depot transportation. Wet bar in some suites. On river in park. Cr cds: A, C, D, DS, ER, JCB, MC, V.

D ≋ ⊠ ⍦ SC

★★★ **WESTCOAST RIDPATH.** *W 515 Sprague Ave (99204), at Stevens St.* 509/838-2711; FAX 509/747-6970; res: 800/426-0670. 350 rms, 3-12 story. S $85-$105; D $90-$110; each addl $10; suites $115-$150; under 17 free; wkend rates. Crib free. TV; cable (premium), VCR avail. Heated pool; poolside serv. Restaurant 6 am-11 pm. Bar 11-2 am; entertainment exc Sun. Ck-out 1 pm. Meeting rms. Business center. In-rm modem link. Drugstore. Barber, beauty shop. Garage; free parking. Free airport, RR station, bus depot transportation. Some bathrm phones. Whirlpool in some suites. Private patios, balconies, sun deck. Cr cds: A, C, D, DS, JCB, MC, V.

D ≋ ⊠ ⍦ SC ✈

Inn

★★★ **FOTHERINGHAM HOUSE.** *2128 W 2nd Ave (99204).* 509/838-1891; FAX 509/838-1807. 4 rms, 1 with shower only, 3 share baths. No A/C. No rm phones. S, D $75-$90. Children over 12 yrs only. Complimentary full bkfst. Restaurant adj 11:30 am-9 pm. Ck-out 11 am, ck-in 2-4 pm. Queen Anne-style house built 1891 for mayor of Spokane. Many antiques. Totally nonsmoking. Cr cds: MC, V.

⊠ ⍦

Restaurants

★ **CHAPTER XI.** *105 E Mission Ave.* 509/326-0466. Hrs: 11:30 am-10 pm; Fri, Sat to 11 pm; Sun from 4 pm. Closed Thanksgiving, Dec 25. Bar. Semi-a la carte: lunch $6-$10, dinner $10-$28. Specializes in prime rib, stuffed shrimp, mud pie. Salad bar. Cr cds: A, D, DS, MC, V.

SC

★★ **CLINKERDAGGER.** *621 W Mallon (99201), I-90 Newport exit.* 509/328-5965. Hrs: 11:30 am-2:30 pm, 5-9 pm; Fri, Sat 5-10 pm; Sun 4-9 pm. Closed July 4, Dec 25. Res accepted. Bar to midnight. Semi-a la carte: lunch $4.95-$9.95, dinner $9.95-$18.95. Child's meals. Specializes in prime rib, fish. Parking. Outdoor dining. Converted flour mill; shops inside. Overlooks Spokane Falls. Cr cds: A, D, DS, MC, V.

★ **HILLARY'S AT THE STOCKYARDS INN.** *3827 E Trent Ave, I-90 Freya St exit.* 509/534-1212. Hrs: 11 am-2 pm, 5-10 pm; Sat from 4:30 pm. Closed Sun; major hols. Res accepted. Bar. Semi-a la carte: lunch $5.50-$9.95, dinner $8.95-$32.95. Buffet (Mon-Fri): lunch $6.50. Child's meals. Specializes in steak, prime rib. Entertainment. Parking. Rustic decor. Family-owned. Cr cds: A, MC, V.

✔★ **OLD SPAGHETTI FACTORY.** *S 152 Monroe St, I-90 Lincoln St exit.* 509/624-8916. Hrs: 4:30-9:30 pm; Fri, Sat to 11 pm; Sun 4-9 pm. Closed Thanksgiving, Dec 24, 25. Italian menu. Bar. Complete meal: dinner $4.50-$9.25. Specializes in fettucine, tortellini, spaghetti dishes. Converted warehouse. Cr cds: DS, MC, V.

★★★ **PATSY CLARK'S.** *W 2208 2nd Ave (99204).* 509/838-8300. Hrs: 5-9 pm; Fri, Sat to 10 pm; Sun 5-9 pm; Sun brunch 10 am-1:30 pm. Res accepted. Continental menu. Bar. Semi-a la carte: dinner $13.95-

$19.95. Sun brunch $15. Specializes in lamb tenderloin, seafood, roasted duck with Idaho lentils. Own baking. Pianist. Valet parking. Mansion designed and built in 1898 by Kirkland K. Cutter for prominent mining tycoon, Patrick "Patsy" Clark. Furnished with antiques, handmade furniture, Tiffany stained glass. Cr cds: A, D, DS, MC, V.

Sunnyside (E-6)

(For accommodations see Richland; also see Toppenish)

Founded 1893 **Pop** 11,238 **Elev** 743 ft **Area code** 509 **Zip** 98944
Information Chamber of Commerce, 520 S 7th St, PO Box 329; 509/837-5939 or 800/457-8089.

This is the home of one of the first irrigation projects of more than 100,000 acres in the state. Its selection as a site for a large settlement of the Christian Cooperative movement brought growth and prosperity to this community. Today the pioneer Sunnyside Canal Co has been absorbed by the US Reclamation Service. Irrigation continues to bring rich crops to the fields that circle the city.

The town is aptly named. Sunnyside averages over 300 days of sunshine every year with mild winters and dry summers.

What to See and Do

Darigold Dairy Fair. Tours of cheese-making plant. (Daily; closed major hols). 400 Alexander Rd. Phone 509/837-4321. **Free.**

Tucker Cellars Winery. Wine tasting. (Daily) Yakima Valley Hwy & Ray Rd. Phone 509/837-8701.

Washington Hills Cellar. Wine tasting. (Daily) 111 E Lincoln. Phone 509/839-WINE.

Tacoma (C-3)

Settled 1868 **Pop** 176,664 **Elev** 250 ft **Area code** 253
Information Tacoma-Pierce County Visitor & Convention Bureau, 1001 Pacific Ave, #400, PO Box 1754, 98402; 253/627-2836 or 800/272-2662.

In its gemlike setting on Puget Sound, midway between Seattle and Olympia, Tacoma maintains its wood and paper products and its shipping traditions. Its harbor is a port of call for merchant vessels plying the oceans of the world. Backed by timber, shipping facilities and low-cost water and power, more than 500 industries produce lumber, plywood, paper, millwork, furniture, foodstuffs, beverages, chemicals and clothing. Major railroad and shipbuilding yards are also located here. Health care is a major employer, and high-tech industry continues to grow rapidly. The nearest metropolitan center to Mt Rainier National Park (see), Tacoma is a base for trips to Olympic National Park (see) and Puget Sound. Mild weather keeps parks and gardens green throughout the year.

In 1833 the Hudson's Bay Co built its second post (Ft Nisqually) on the North Pacific Coast in the forest, 18 miles south of the present site of Tacoma. In 1841 Charles Wilkes, commander of a United States expedition, began a survey of Puget Sound from this point and named the bay around which Tacoma is built Commencement Bay. When the rails of the Northern Pacific reached tidewater here late in 1873, they sparked the industrial growth of the city.

What to See and Do

Emerald Downs. Thoroughbred horse racing. (Late June-early Nov, Thurs-Mon) 15 mi NE on I-5 to Auburn. Phone 253/931-8400 or 888/931-8400. ¢¢

Enchanted Village. Family entertainment park with rides for all ages; wax museum, antique toy & doll museum. Live entertainment. Concessions.

(Mid-May-Labor Day, daily; early Apr-mid-May & Sept after Labor Day, wkends) 36201 Enchanted Pkwy S in Federal Way. Phone 253/661-8000 or 253/925-8000. ¢¢¢-¢¢¢¢¢ Also here is

Wild Waves Water Park. A 24,000-sq-foot wave pool with body & mat surfing in ocean-size waves; raging river ride; adult activity pool; four giant water slides with flashing lights & music, 2 speed slides; spas; childrens' pool. Game room; raft rentals. (Memorial Day wknd-Labor Day wknd, daily) Admission includes entry to Enchanted Village. Phone 253/661-8000 or 253/925-8000. ¢¢¢¢

Ferry. Point Defiance to Vashon Island. Contact Washington State Ferries, Seattle Ferry Terminal, Colman Dock, Seattle 98104; 206/464-6400 or 800/84-FERRY. Per vehicle ¢¢

Ft Lewis. Army center of the Northwest, home of I Corps, the 7th Infantry Division and associated support units. Approx 86,000 acres with military buildings and living quarters. Museum with exhibits on Northwest military history (Wed-Sun; phone 253/967-7206). 11 mi SW on I-5. Phone 253/967-2662.

McChord AFB. The 62nd Airlift Wing and 446th AW (Reserves) are based here. Tours (Tues & Thurs; res required one month in advance). Museum (Tues-Sat, afternoons). 8 mi SW on I-5. Phone 253/984-5637.

Mt Rainier Natl Park (see). Nisqually entrance, approx 56 mi SE on WA 7.

Narrows Bridge. Fifth-longest span for a suspension bridge in US (2,800 ft). Total length: 5,450 ft between anchorages. Successor to "Galloping Gertie," which collapsed in 1940, four months and seven days after it had officially opened. W on Olympic Blvd; WA 16.

Nature Center at Snake Lake. Approx 50 acres of marshland, forest, thickets and ponds providing a wildlife haven in heart of urbanized Tacoma. Nature trails, observation shelters; natural science library. Interpretive center; lectures and workshops. Park (daily). 1919 S Tyler St. Phone 253/591-6439. **Free.**

Northwest Trek. One-hr naturalist-guided and narrated tram tour takes visitors on 5.5-mi ride through 600-acre wilderness and wildlife preserve, where native Northwest animals may be seen roaming free in their natural habitat; self-guided nature walks through wetlands and forest animal exhibits; nature trails including barrier-free trail; children's discovery center. Theater with 14-min film on history of facility. (Mar-Oct, daily; rest of yr, Fri-Sun & selected hols) 32 mi SE via I-5, WA 512, 161. Phone 360/832-6117. ¢¢¢

Pacific Lutheran Univ (1890). (3,500 students) Swimming pool. 9-hole golf course open to public; phone 253/535-7393. Self-guided tours. Off I-5, exit 127. Phone 253/535-7430. On campus are

Univ Gallery. Changing art exhibits (Mon-Fri). Rune stones sculpture on campus mall. Ingram Hall. Phone 253/535-7143 or 253/535-7430.

Robert Mortvedt Library. African tribal art. (Daily exc Sun) Phone 253/535-7500. **Free.**

Pioneer Farm. Replica of an 1887 homestead with animals; log cabin, barn, trading post & other outbuildings; furnished with turn-of-the-century antiques. "Hands on" program; guided tours. (Mid-June-Labor Day, daily; Mar-mid-June & after Labor Day-Thanksgiving, Sat & Sun only) 35 mi SE via WA 7, in the Ohop Valley. Phone 360/832-6300. ¢¢-¢¢¢

✪ **Point Defiance Park.** Approx 700 acres of dense forest, clay cliffs, driftwood-covered gravel beaches and formal gardens. On bold promontory, nearly surrounded by water. Boating, fishing, swimming, hiking, picnicking. Park (daily). 6 mi N, entrance at N 54th & Pearl Sts. **Free.** Features of the park are

Boathouse Marina. Bait & tackle shop. Boat & motor rentals. Moorage. Restaurant. Gift shop. (Daily; closed Thanksgiving, Dec 25) Phone 253/591-5325.

Point Defiance Zoo & Aquarium. Zoo has polar bear complex, musk ox habitat, tundra waterfowl, elephants, beluga whales, walrus, seals and otters; World of Adaptions, Southeast Asia Complex and "The Farm." Aquarium and 38 perimeter displays with hundreds of Pacific Northwest marine specimens. Reef Aquarium features sharks and other South Pacific sea life. (Daily; closed Thanksgiving, Dec 25) N 54th & Pearl Sts. Phone 253/591-5337. ¢¢¢

Never Never Land. Sculptured storybook characters in 10-acre forest setting. Each wknd storybook characters visit and special events take place. (May-Aug, daily; Apr & Sept, wkends only) Phone 253/591-5845. ¢

Ft Nisqually (1833). Restored fur-trading outpost of Hudson's Bay Co reflects period of English control when fur pelts were used as currency. Purchased by US in 1869, moved to this site in 1937. Two remaining buildings of original outpost are the Factor's House (1853) and the Granary (1843), oldest existing building in state; 8 other buildings reconstructed according to original specifications using handmade hardware, lumber. Living history presentations. Fee for some special events. (Memorial Day-Labor Day, daily; rest of yr, Wed-Sun) Phone 253/591-5339. Summer wknds ¢; Rest of yr **Free.**

Camp Six Logging Exhibit (Western Forest Industries Museum). Reconstructed steam logging camp set amid virgin timber. Dolbeer Donkey steam engine (one of two in existence), 110-ft spar pole, restored water wagon, bunkhouses. (Jan-Oct, Wed-Sun) Logging train ride (Apr-Sept, Sat, Sun & hols). A 90-ton shay steam locomotive operates in summer (wkends & hols). Santa train (3 wkends Dec). Phone 253/752-0047. Train rides ¢

Five-Mile Drive. Around Point Defiance Park. Contains old growth forest with some 200-ft-high Douglas firs, variety of other evergreens, deciduous trees, shrubs. Scenic views of Puget Sound, Olympic and Cascade mountains, Narrows Bridge. Drive closed to motor vehicles Sat mornings for cycling and walking.

Gardens. Formal gardens in park include an AARS rose garden, Japanese Garden, Northwest Native garden, Pacific Northwest dahlia trial garden, rhododendron garden and seasonal annual displays. **Free.**

St Peter's Church (Episcopal). Oldest church in city (1873); the organ came around Cape Horn in 1874; half-ton bell, also shipped around the Horn, is mounted on tower beside church. (Sun; also by appt) 2910 Starr St, at N 29th St. Phone 253/272-4406.

Tacoma Art Museum. Permanent collection; changing exhibits; children's gallery with hands-on art activities. (Daily exc Mon; closed Jan 1, Dec 25) 12th St & Pacific Ave. Phone 253/272-4258. ¢¢

Totem Pole. One of the tallest in US, carved from 105-foot cedar tree by Alaskan Native Americans; located in Firemen's Park with view of Commencement Bay and the Port of Tacoma. 9th & A Sts.

Univ of Puget Sound (1888). (2,800 students) 37 Tudor Gothic buildings on 72-acre campus. Many free cultural events, art gallery, theater, recital hall. Univ is older than state. 1500 N Warner St. Phone 253/756-3100 or 253/756-3148. Also here is

James R. Slater Museum of Natural History. Thompson Hall. Displays research specimens, particularly of Pacific Northwest flora and fauna; more than 11,000 birds, 4,600 egg sets; reptiles, amphibians, mammals and pressed plants. (Mon-Fri; closed hols) Phone 253/756-3356. **Free.**

Washington State History Museum. Exhibits include collections of pioneer, Native American & Alaskan artifacts and detail the history of the state and its people. Interactive, introductory & changing exhibits. Indoor & outdoor theaters. Museum Cafe & Shop. (Memorial Day-Labor Day, daily; rest of yr, daily exc Mon; closed major hols) 1911 Pacific Ave. Phone 888/238-4373. ¢¢ Adj is

Union Station. Built in 1911 by Northern Pacific Railroad, the station, with its 98-ft-high dome, has been restored. Now home to the federal courthouse. The rotunda houses the largest single exhibit of sculptured glass by Tacoma-native Dale Chihuly. (Mon-Fri; closed hols) Phone 253/572-9310. **Free.**

Wright Park. More than 800 trees of 100 varieties in one of finest arboretums in Pacific Northwest. W.W. Seymour Botanical Conservatory, located in park at S 4th & G Sts, contains tropical plants, seasonal displays and a botanical gift shop (phone 206/591-5330). Lawn bowling and horseshoe courts; playground, wading pool. (Daily) 6th Ave & I St. Phone 253/591-5331 or 253/591-3690. **Free.**

Annual Events

Daffodil Festival. In Tacoma and Puyallup Valley. Flower show, coronation, four-city floral parade of floats, marine regatta, bowling tournament. Phone 253/627-6176. 2 wks Apr.

Taste of Tacoma. Point Defiance Park. Entertainment, arts & crafts. Phone 253/305-1036. Early July.

Seasonal Events

Tacoma Little Theater. 210 N I St. Six shows, including comedies, dramas and musicals. Phone 253/272-2481. Sept-June.

Tacoma Symphony Orchestra. For details phone 253/272-7264. Late Sept-early Apr.

Motels

★ ★ **BEST WESTERN TACOMA INN.** *8726 S Hosmer St (98444), I-5 at 84th St exit.* 253/535-2880; FAX 253/537-8379. 149 rms, 2 story, 8 kits. S $64-$72; D $70-$80; each addl $6; kit. units $78-$84; under 18 free. Crib free. Pet accepted, some restrictions; $20. TV; cable (premium); poolside serv. Playground. Complimentary coffee in rms. Restaurant 6:30 am-10:30 pm. Rm serv. Bar 11-2 am; entertainment. Ck-out noon. Coin lndry. Meeting rms. Business servs avail. In-rm modem link. Valet serv. Putting green. Exercise equipt; weight machine, bicycles. Some refrigerators; microwaves avail. Private patios, balconies. Cr cds: A, C, D, DS, ER, JCB, MC, V.

D ✔ ≈ ⊼ ⊠ 🖋 SC

★ ★ **DAYS INN.** *6802 Tacoma Mall Blvd (98409), I-5 exit 129.* 253/475-5900; FAX 253/475-3540. 123 rms, 2 story. S, D $70-$89; each addl $10; suites $165; under 12 free. Crib free. Pet accepted. TV; cable (premium). Heated pool. Complimentary coffee in lobby. Restaurant 6:30 am-10 pm; Sat from 8 am; Sun 8 am-9 pm. Ck-out 11 am. Ck-in 3 pm. Meeting rms. Business center. In-rm modem link. Valet serv. Health club privileges. Refrigerator; microwaves avail. Cr cds: A, C, D, DS, ER, JCB, MC, V.

D ✔ ≈ ⊠ 🖋 SC ⏚

★ ★ **ROYAL COACHMAN MOTOR INN.** *5805 Pacific Hwy E (98424).* 253/922-2500; FAX 253/922-6443; res: 800/422-3051. 94 rms, 2 story. S $56-$65; D $68-$75; each addl $7; suites $140; kit. units $95-$120; under 12 free. Crib free. Pet accepted; $25 refundable. TV; cable (premium), VCR avail. Coffee in rms. Restaurant 6:30 am-9 pm. Ck-out noon. Coin lndry. Meeting rms. Business servs avail. Valet serv. Some refrigerators, microwaves, in-rm whirlpools. Cr cds: A, C, D, DS, ER, JCB, MC, V.

D ✔ ⊠ 🖋 SC

✔ ★ **TRAVELERS INN.** *3100 Pacific Hwy E (98424).* 253/922-9520; FAX 253/922-2002; res: 800/633-8300. 115 rms, 2 story. S $35.99; D $42.99; each addl $7.70; suites $56.99-$64.99; under 17 free. Crib free. TV; cable (premium). Heated pool. Complimentary coffee in lobby. Restaurant opp 6 am-10 pm. Ck-out 11 am. Guest lndry. Business servs avail. In-rm modem link. Refrigerator in suites. Cr cds: A, D, DS, MC, V.

D ≈ ⊠ 🖋 SC

Motor Hotels

★ ★ **BEST WESTERN EXECUTIVE INN.** *(5700 Pacific Hwy E, Fife 98424) I-5 exit 137.* 253/922-0080; FAX 253/922-6439. 140 rms, 4 story. May-Sept: S $79-$99; D $109-$129; each addl $8; suites $150-$175; under 19 free; hol rates; lower rates rest of yr. Crib free. Pet accepted, some restrictions; $25 deposit. TV; cable (premium), VCR avail. Indoor pool; whirlpool. Complimentary coffee in rms. Restaurant 6 am-10 pm. Rm serv from 7 am. Bar 11-2 am. Ck-out noon. Meeting rms. Business center. In-rm modem link. Bellhops. Sundries. Valet serv. Free airport, RR station, bus depot transportation. Health club privileges. Some refrigerators; microwaves avail. Cr cds: A, D, DS, JCB, MC, V.

[D] [icons] [SC]

★ ★ ★ **LA QUINTA.** *1425 E 27th St (98421), exit I-5 exits 134S, 135N.* 253/383-0146; FAX 253/627-3280. 158 rms, 7 story. S $68-$78; D $76-$88; each addl $8; under 18 free. Crib free. Pet accepted. TV; cable (premium). Heated pool; whirlpool. Complimentary continental bkfst. Restaurant 6:30 am-10 pm. Rm serv. Bar. Ck-out noon. Coin lndry. Meeting rms. Business center. In-rm modem link. Valet serv. Sundries. Exercise equipt; bicycles, treadmill. Microwaves avail. View of both Mt Rainier and Commencement Bay. Cr cds: A, C, D, DS, MC, V.

[D] [icons] [SC] [icon]

★ ★ ★ **SHILO INN.** *7414 S Hosmer (98408), S on I-5, exit 72nd St.* 253/475-4020; FAX 253/475-1236. 132 rms, 4 story, 11 kits. S $79; D $85-$89; each addl $10; kit. units $99; under 12 free. Crib avail. Pet accepted; $7. TV; cable (premium), VCR avail. Indoor pool; whirlpool. Complimentary continental bkfst. Restaurant opp 6 am-11 pm. Ck-out noon. Coin lndry. Meeting rms. Business servs avail. In-rm modem link. Valet serv. Exercise equipt; weight machine, treadmill, sauna, steam rm. Bathrm phones, refrigerators, microwaves. Cr cds: A, D, DS, ER, JCB, MC, V.

[D] [icons] [SC]

Hotel

★ ★ ★ **SHERATON.** *1320 Broadway Plaza (98402), downtown.* 253/572-3200; FAX 253/591-4105; res: 800/845-9466. 319 rms, 26 story. S $140-$155; D $150-$165; each addl $10; under 12 free; wknd rates. Crib free. TV; cable (premium), VCR avail. Pool privileges; whirlpool. Complimentary coffee in rms. Restaurant 6 am-11 pm (also see ALTEZZO). Bar to 2 am; entertainment Wed-Sat. Ck-out noon. Convention facilities. Business center. Concierge. Shopping arcade. Barber, beauty shop. Sauna. Health club privileges. Some bathrm phones, refrigerators. Minibars. Dramatic 4-level skylit winter garden lobby. Luxury level. Cr cds: A, C, D, DS, ER, JCB, MC, V.

[D] [icons] [SC] [icon]

Inns

★ ★ ★ **CHINABERRY HILL.** *302 Tacoma Ave N (98403).* 253/272-1282; FAX 253/272-1335. E-mail chinaberry@wa.net; web www.wa.net/chinaberry. 5 rms, 3 story, 1 guest house. No A/C. No rm phones. S, D $95-$145; each addl $25; guest house $200; wkly rates. Children over 12 yrs only (any age allowed in guest house). TV in some rms; cable (premium), VCR avail (movies). Complimentary full bkfst; afternoon refreshments. Restaurant nearby. Ck-out 11 am, ck-in 4-6 pm. Business servs avail. In-rm modem link. Luggage handling. Health club privileges. Whirlpool. Refrigerators; many in-rm whirlpools. Victorian inn built in 1889; antiques. Totally nonsmoking. Cr cds: A, DS, MC, V.

[icons]

★ ★ ★ **COMMENCEMENT BAY.** *3312 N Union Ave (98407).* 253/752-8175; FAX 253/759-4025. E-mail greatviews@aol.com; web www.bestinns.net/usa/wa/cb.html. 3 rms, 3 story. Apr-Oct: S, D $85-$115; lower rates rest of yr. Children over 12 yrs only. TV; cable (premium), VCR (free movies). Complimentary full bkfst. Restaurant nearby. Ck-out 11 am, ck-in 4-6 pm. Luggage handling. Business servs avail. Exercise equipt; weight machine, bicycles. Massage. Whirlpool. Game rm. Microwaves avail. Colonial house built in 1937. Cr cds: A, DS, MC, V.

[icons]

✔★ **KEENAN HOUSE.** *2610 N Warner St (98407).* 253/752-0702; FAX 253/756-0822. E-mail idvkeenan@aol.com. 6 rms, 2 with bath, 2 story. No A/C. No rm phones. S $60-$65; D $65-$75; wkly rates. Crib free. TV in sitting rm. Complimentary full bkfst. Restaurant nearby. Ck-out

11 am, ck-in 2 pm. Street parking. Picnic tables. Two Victorian houses (ca 1890); antiques. Totally nonsmoking. Cr cds: MC, V.

[icons]

★ ★ ★ **THE VILLA.** *705 N Fifth St (98403).* 253/572-1157; FAX 253/572-1805; 800 888/571-1157. E-mail villabb@aol.com; web www.tribnet.com/bb/villa.htp. 4 rms, 1 with shower only, 2 story. No A/C. Guest phone avail. S, D $90-$145; each addl $15; wkly rates. Children over 12 yrs only. TV; cable (premium). Complimentary full bkfst. Ck-out noon, ck-in 3-9 pm. Business servs avail. In-rm modem link. Italianate villa built 1925; landscaped grounds; antiques. Totally nonsmoking. Cr cds: A, MC, V.

[icons] [SC]

Restaurants

★ ★ ★ **ALTEZZO.** *(See Sheraton Hotel)* 253/591-4155. Hrs: 5:30-10 pm; Fri, Sat to 11 pm. Closed Mon. Res accepted. Italian menu. Bar. Wine list. A la carte entrees: dinner $8.95-$16.50. Own baking. Valet parking. Penthouse dining; view of bay and mountains. Cr cds: A, C, D, DS, MC, V.

[D] [SC]

✔★ ★ **BAVARIAN.** *204 North K St (98403), at Division St.* 253/627-5010. Hrs: 11 am-9 pm; Fri to 10 pm; Sat 3-10 pm; Sun 11:30 am-8 pm. Closed major hols. Res accepted. No A/C. German, Amer menu. Bar. Semi-a la carte: lunch $4.50-$8.50, dinner $10-$17. Specializes in schnitzel, steak, seafood. Parking. Cr cds: A, D, MC, V.

[SC]

★ ★ ★ **CLIFF HOUSE.** *6300 Marine View Dr (98422).* 253/927-0400. Hrs: 11:30-1 am. Closed Dec 25. Res accepted. Bar. Semi-a la carte: lunch $6.95-$14, dinner $12.95-$25.95. Specializes in European, Northwestern cuisine. Tableside cooking. Built on cliff; view of Commencement Bay and Mt Rainier. Cr cds: A, C, D, DS, MC, V.

[D]

✔★ ★ **COPPERFIELD'S.** *8726 S Hosmer St (98444).* 253/531-1500. Hrs: 6:30 am-10:30 pm; Sun brunch 9 am-2 pm. Res accepted. Bar. Semi-a la carte: bkfst $2.50-$13.95, lunch $4.25-$7.25, dinner $6.50-$14.95. Sun brunch $13.95. Specializes in salmon, prime rib, pasta. Parking. Garden-like setting; wicker furniture. Cr cds: A, C, D, DS, ER, JCB, MC, V.

[D]

★ ★ **HARBOR LIGHTS.** *2761 Ruston Way (98402).* 253/752-8600. Hrs: 11 am-11 pm; Fri to 2 am; Sat noon-2 am; Sun 2-9 pm. Closed most major hols. Res accepted. Bar. Semi-a la carte: lunch $5-$9.50, dinner $9.50-$32. Child's meals. Specializes in steak, seafood, veal. Parking. Outdoor dining. Marine view. Family-owned. Cr cds: A, C, D, DS, MC, V.

[D] [SC]

★ ★ **JOHNNY'S DOCK.** *1900 East D St (98421).* 253/627-3186. Hrs: 10 am-9 pm; Fri, Sat to 10 pm. Res accepted. Bar. Semi-a la carte: bkfst $5.50-$7.95, lunch $5.95-$12.95, dinner $10.95-$24.95. Child's meals. Specializes in steak, seafood. Parking. Outdoor dining. Waterfront view; moorage. Family-owned. Totally nonsmoking. Cr cds: A, D, DS, MC, V.

[D]

★ ★ **LOBSTER SHOP SOUTH.** *4013 Ruston Way (98402).* 253/759-2165. Hrs: 4:30-9 pm; Fri, Sat to 10:30 pm; Sun to 9 pm; early-bird dinner exc Sat 4:30-5:30 pm; Sun brunch 9:30 am-1:30 pm, dinner 3:30-9 pm. Closed Dec 25. Res accepted. Bar. Wine list. A la carte entrees: dinner $9.95-$25.95. Sun brunch $15.95. Child's meals. Specializes in steak, seafood, Australian lobster. Own pastries. Parking. Outdoor dining. Cr cds: A, C, D, DS, MC, V.

[D]

Toppenish (E-5)

(For accommodations see Sunnyside, Yakima)

Pop 7,419 **Elev** 755 ft **Area code** 509 **Zip** 98948 **E-mail** cowboyup@wolfenet.com **Web** www.wolfenet.com/~cowboyup
Information Chamber of Commerce, PO Box 28, 509/865-3262.

Toppenish is a Native American word meaning "people from the foot of the hills." The Yakama Indian Agency is here, and the nearby million-acre Yakama Reservation is an important tourist attraction. The cultural differences offer good opportunities for sightseeing and dining. The Toppenish area produces hops, fruits, vegetables and dairy products. Average rainfall is only about eight inches a year, but irrigation makes the countryside bloom.

What to See and Do

Ft Simcoe Historical State Park. 200 acres. Restoration of fort established 1856 to protect treaty lands from land-hungry settlers and to guard military roads. Five original buildings restored; interpretive center with army and Native American relics. Picnicking, hiking. Park (Apr-Sept, daily; rest of yr, wkends & hols) 28 mi W on WA 220, Fort Rd. Phone 509/874-2372. **Free.**

Historical Murals. Painted on downtown buildings. For map or guided tour contact Mural Society, 5A Toppenish Ave, or phone 509/865-6516.

Yakama Nation Cultural Center. Located on ancestral grounds of the Yakimas. Includes museum depicting history of the Yakima Nation, library, theater and restaurant. (Daily; closed Dec 25) S on US 97. Phone 509/865-2800. ¢¢

Annual Events

Native American Celebrations. Most at Yakama Reservation in White Swan, 23 mi W on WA 220. For details and locations phone 509/865-5121, ext 436. **Yakama Nation Treaty Day, Powwow and Rodeo.** June 5-7 at Culture Heritage Center. **Bull-O-Rama.** July 2-5.

Union (C-2)

(For accommodations see Bremerton)

Settled 1858 **Pop** 600 (est) **Elev** 10 ft **Area code** 360 **Zip** 98592

This resort town at the curve of the Hood Canal almost became the saltwater terminus of the Union Pacific Railroad, but the failure of a British bank was a blow to Union's commercial future. There are public beaches, a marina, free launching sites and a golf course in town.

What to See and Do

Lake Cushman State Park. Approx 600 acres. Swimming, fishing, boating (launch, fee). Hiking trails. Picnicking. Camping (Apr-Nov; hookups). Standard fees. 5 mi SW via WA 106, 5 mi N via US 101 to Hoodsport, then 7 mi NW via Lake Cushman Rd. Phone 360/877-5491.

Tollie Shay Engine & Caboose #7. Refurbished 3-cylinder locomotive and Simpson logging caboose with coal-burning stove and unique side-door design. Caboose used by Shelton-Mason County Chamber of Commerce as office and tourist information center. (May-Sept, daily exc Sun; rest of yr, Mon-Fri; closed legal hols) 5 mi W on WA 106, 10 mi S on US 101 in Shelton. Phone 360/426-2021. **Free.**

Twanoh State Park. 182 acres along Hood Canal. Swimming, scuba diving; boating (launch, dock); fishing, clamming. Hiking. Picnicking. Camping (hookups). Standard fees. 12 mi E on WA 106, off US 101. Phone 360/275-2222.

Vancouver (F-3)

(See also Portland, OR)

Founded 1824 **Pop** 46,380 **Elev** 89 ft **Area code** 360 **E-mail** chamber@pacifier.com **Web** www.vancouverusa.com
Information Greater Vancouver Chamber of Commerce, 404 E 15th St, Suite 11, 98663; 360/694-2588 or 800/377-7084.

Vancouver treasures a national historic site, Fort Vancouver, now completely encircled by the city. The fort served as a commercial bastion for the Hudson's Bay Company, whose vast enterprises stretched far to the north and across the sea to Hawaii, bringing furs from Utah and California and dominating coastal trade well up the shoreline to Alaska. Around the stockaded fort, the company's cultivated fields and pastures extended for miles; drying sheds, mills, forges and shops made it a pioneer metropolis. This community was a major stake in Britain's claim for all the territory north of the Columbia River, but by the treaty of 1846, Fort Vancouver became American. Settlers began to take over the Hudson's Bay Company lands, and an Army post was established here in 1849, continuing to the present day. In 1860, all of Fort Vancouver was turned over to the US Army.

The city is on the Columbia River, just north of Portland, Oregon. Vancouver has a diversified industrial climate, which includes electronics, paper products, fruit packing, malt production and the manufacture of textiles, furniture and machinery. The Port of Vancouver, one of the largest on the West Coast, is a deepwater seaport handling a wide range of commodities.

What to See and Do

Clark County Historical Museum. Exhibits include 1890s store, doctor's office, printing press, doll collection, dioramas of area history, Native American artifacts; railroad exhibit; genealogical and historical research libraries. (Tues-Sat; closed some major hols) 1511 Main St. Phone 360/695-4681. **Free.**

★ **Ft Vancouver Natl Historic Site.** Over 150 acres. After extensive research and excavation, the fort has been partially reconstructed by the Natl Park Service. Now at the fort site: Chief Factor's house, kitchen, wash house, stockade wall, gates, the bastion, bake house, blacksmith shop and trade shop-dispensary. Visitor center has museum exhibiting artifacts, information desk, video presentations. Tours, interpretive talks and living history programs are offered. (Daily; closed some major hols) 1501 E Evergreen Blvd. Phone 360/696-7655. ¢¢

Gifford Pinchot Natl Forest. Forest's 1,379,000 acres include 12,326-ft Mt Adams; 8,400-ft Mt St Helens (see MOUNT ST HELENS NATIONAL VOLCANIC MONUMENT); and 180,600 acres distributed among seven wilderness areas. Picnicking, hiking, swimming, boating; camping; fishing, hunting. Some fees. NE of city, reached via WA 14, 25, 503. Contact Public Affairs Assistant, PO Box 8944, 98668; 360/750-5001.

Officers' Row. Self-guided walking tour of 21 turn-of-the-century houses; two open to public.

Pearson Air Museum. At M.J. Murdock Aviation Center, one of the oldest operating airfields in the nation. Vintage aircraft and flying memorabilia. (Tues-Sun; closed some hols) 1115 E Fifth St. Phone 360/694-7026. ¢

Motels

★ **BEST WESTERN FERRYMAN'S INN.** *7901 NE 6th Ave (98665), I-5 exit 4. 360/574-2151; FAX 360/574-9644.* 134 rms, 2 story, 9 kit. S $54-$65; D $63-$78; each addl $5; suites $65-$90.50; kit. units $65-$70; under 12 free. Crib free. Pet accepted; $3. TV; cable (premium). Heated pool. Complimentary continental bkfst. Restaurant adj open 24 hrs. Ck-out noon. Coin lndry. Meeting rms. Business servs avail. Cr cds: A, C, D, DS, MC, V.

D ✦ ≈ ⊠ ⊼ SC

✔★★ **COMFORT INN.** *13207 NE 20th Ave (98686), I-5 exit 7.* 360/574-6000; FAX 360/573-3746. 58 rms, 2 story. S $50-$55; D $60-$70; each addl $6; suites $100; under 18 free. Crib $2. TV; cable (premium), VCR avail. Indoor pool; whirlpool. Complimentary continental bkfst, coffee. Restaurant opp 6:30 am-9 pm. Ck-out 11 am. Coin lndry. Meeting rms. Business servs avail. Exercise equipt; weights, bicycles. Refrigerators. Cr cds: A, C, D, DS, ER, JCB, MC, V.

⊡ ⊠ ✕ ⊠ ⊠ SC

★★ **COMFORT SUITES.** *4714 NE 94th Ave (98662), I-205 exit 30, near Vancouver Mall.* 360/253-3100; FAX 360/253-7998. 68 suites, 2 story. S $71-$81; D $76-$86; each addl $5; under 18 free. Crib free. TV; cable (premium), VCR avail (movies). Indoor pool; whirlpool. Complimentary continental bkfst. Restaurant nearby. Ck-out noon. Meeting rms. Business servs avail. Valet serv Mon-Fri. Airport transportation. Exercise equipt; bicycles, stair machine. Refrigerators, microwaves. Cr cds: A, C, D, DS, ER, JCB, MC, V.

⊡ ⊠ ✕ ⊠ ⊠ SC

★ **HOLIDAY INN EXPRESS.** *9107 NE Vancouver Mall Dr (98662), near Vancouver Mall.* 360/253-5000; FAX 360/253-3137. 56 rms, 2 story. S $66-$76; D $71-$81; each addl $5; under 18 free; special events (2-3 day min). Crib avail. TV; cable (premium), VCR avail. Complimentary continental bkfst. Sundries. Indoor pool; whirlpool. Cr cds: A, C, D, DS, ER, JCB, MC, V.

⊡ ⊠ ⊠ SC

✔★ **QUALITY INN.** *7001 NE WA 99 (98665), I-5 exit 4.* 360/696-0516; FAX 360/693-8343. 72 kit. suites, 2 story. S $62.50-$67.50; D $69.50-$74.50; each addl $5; under 18 free. Crib $5. Pet accepted, some restrictions; $5. TV; cable (premium). Heated pool; whirlpool. Complimentary continental bkfst. Restaurant nearby. Ck-out noon. Coin lndry. Business servs avail. Some balconies. Cr cds: A, C, D, DS, MC, V.

⊠ ⊠ ⊠ ⊠ SC

✔★ **RODEWAY INN.** *221 NE Chkalov Dr (98684), I 205 exit 28.* 360/256-7044; FAX 360/256-1231; res: 800/426-5110. 118 rms, 2 story. S $52; D $58; each addl $6; suites $85-$100; under 18 free. Crib free. Pet accepted; $15. TV; cable (premium). Indoor pool; whirlpool. Complimentary continental bkfst. Restaurant 6 am-10 pm. Ck-out noon. Meeting rms. Business servs avail. Valet serv. Free airport transportation. Health club privileges. Cr cds: A, C, D, DS, MC, V.

⊡ ⊠ ⊠ ⊠ ⊠ SC

★ **SHILO INN-HAZEL DELL.** *13206 WA 99 (98686), I-5 exit 7.* 360/573-0511; FAX 360/573-0396. 66 rms, 2 story, 6 kits. S, D $75; each addl $10; kit. units $55-$79; under 13 free. Crib free. Pet accepted; $7. TV; cable (premium). Indoor pool; whirlpool. Complimentary continental bkfst 6:30 am-10:30 pm. Bar. Ck-out noon. Coin lndry. Meeting rms. Business servs avail. Valet serv. Free airport transportation. Sauna, steam rm. Refrigerators. Cr cds: A, C, D, DS, ER, JCB, MC, V.

⊠ ⊠ ⊠ ⊠ SC

Motor Hotel

★★★ **DOUBLETREE.** *100 Columbia St (98660).* 360/694-8341; FAX 360/694-2023. 160 rms, 2-3 story. S, D $99-$120; suites $185-$339; under 18 free; wknd rates. Crib free. TV; cable, VCR avail. Heated pool. Coffee in rms. Restaurant 6 am-10 pm. Rm serv. Bar 11-2 am; entertainment, dancing Tues-Sun. Ck-out noon. Meeting rms. Business servs avail. In-rm modem link. Bellhops. Valet serv. Free airport transportation. Some private patios, balconies. Overlooks river. Cr cds: A, C, D, DS, ER, JCB, MC, V.

⊡ ⊠ ⊠ ⊠ SC

Walla Walla (E-8)

(See also Dayton)

Founded 1859 **Pop** 26,478 **Elev** 949 ft **Area code** 509 **Zip** 99362 **E-mail** w2chamb@bmi.net **Web** www.bmi.net/wwchamb/

Information Chamber of Commerce, 29 E Sumach, PO Box 644; 509/525-0850.

Walla Walla Valley was first the site of a Native American trail and then an avenue for exploration and settlement of the West. Lewis and Clark passed through the area in 1805. Fur traders followed and Fort Walla Walla was established in 1818 as a trading post at the point where the Walla Walla and Columbia rivers meet. One of the key figures in the area's history was Dr. Marcus Whitman, a medical missionary, who in 1836 founded the first settler's home in the Northwest—a mission seven miles west of present-day Walla Walla. The Whitmans were killed by Native Americans in 1847. No successful settlement was made until after the Indian Wars of 1855-1858.

In 1859 the city became the seat of Walla Walla County, which then included half of present-day Washington, all of Idaho and one-quarter of Montana. It also had the first railroad in the Northwest, first bank in the state, first meat market and packing plant and first institution of higher learning.

Walla Walla means "many waters," but local enthusiasts will tell you this is "the city they liked so much they named it twice." Agriculture is the major industry, with wheat the most important crop and green peas the second. Industries concentrate chiefly on food processing. And the Walla Walla Onion is known nationwide for its sweetness; a festival is held each July to honor the important crop. A Ranger District office of the Umatilla National Forest (see CLARKSTON, also see PENDLETON, OR) is located here.

What to See and Do

Ft Walla Walla Park. Camping (dump station; fee). (Apr-Sept, daily; limited facilities rest of yr) Dalles Military Rd. 1 mi W of WA 125, W edge of town. Phone 509/527-3770. Also in park is Audubon Society Nature Walk, outdoor amphitheater and

Ft Walla Walla Museum Complex. Fourteen original and replica buildings from mid-1800s. Schoolhouse, homestead cabin, railroad depot, blockhouse, doctor's office, blacksmith shop; largest horse-era agricultural museum in the West. Tours (Apr-Oct, by appt). Complex (Apr-Oct, daily exc Mon). Phone 509/525-7703. ¢¢

Pioneer Park. A 58-acre park with horticultural displays, exotic game bird display, playground, tennis courts, picnicking. Division & Alder Sts. Phone 509/527-4527. **Free.**

Whitman Mission Natl Historic Site. The memorial shaft, erected in 1897, overlooks the site of the mission established by Dr. Marcus and Narcissa Whitman in 1836. A self-guided trail with audio stations leads to mission grounds, Old Oregon Trail, memorial shaft and grave. Visitor center, museum; cultural demonstrations (summer, wknds). (Daily; closed some hols) 7 mi W on US 12, then ³/₄ mi S. Phone 509/522-6360. ¢

Motels

★★ **COMFORT INN.** *520 N 2nd Ave.* 509/525-2522; FAX 509/522-2565. 61 rms, 3 story. May-Sept: S $57; D $62-$67; each addl $8; suites $100-$125; under 18 free; higher rates special events; lower rates rest of yr. Crib free. Pet accepted, some restrictions. TV; cable (premium). Indoor pool. Complimentary continental bkfst. Restaurant adj 11 am-10 pm. Ck-out 1 pm. Meeting rm. Business servs avail. Gift shop. Some refrigerators. Cr cds: A, C, D, DS, MC, V.

⊡ ⊠ ⊠ ⊠ ⊠ SC

★ ★ **HOWARD JOHNSON.** *325 E Main St. 509/529-4360; FAX 509/529-7463; res: 800/634-7669, ext. 25.* 85 rms, 2 story. S, D $62.50-$74.50; under 12 free. Crib $5. TV; cable (premium). Pool; whirlpool, sauna. Complimentary continental bkfst. Ck-out noon. Free lndry facilities. Meeting rms. In-rm modem link. Exercise equipt; weight machine, bicycle. Some refrigerators. Some private patios, balconies. Cr cds: A, C, D, DS, ER, MC, V.

✔★ **TAPADERA BUDGET INN.** *211 N 2nd Ave. 509/529-2580; FAX 509/522-1380; res: 800/722-8277.* 30 rms, 2 story. S $34-$39; D $39.50-$47; each addl $6; under 12 free. Crib $6. TV; cable (premium). Continental bkfst. Restaurant adj 6 am-10 pm. Ck-out noon. Business servs avail. In-rm modem link. Cr cds: A, C, D, DS, MC, V.

★ **TRAVELODGE.** *421 E Main St. 509/529-4940; FAX 509/529-4943.* 39 rms, 2 story. S $50; D $58-$64; each addl $5; under 17 free. Crib free. TV; cable (premium). Pool; whirlpool. Restaurant nearby. Ck-out noon. Business servs avail. Cr cds: A, C, D, DS, ER, MC, V.

Restaurant

✔★ **RED APPLE.** *57 E Main St. 509/525-5113.* Open 24 hrs. Bar. Semi-a la carte: bkfst $3-$7, lunch $3-$6, dinner $4.25-$13. Specializes in steak, seafood. Entertainment Thurs-Sun. Parking. Cr cds: MC, V.

Wenatchee (C-5)

(See also Cashmere, Leavenworth)

Founded 1888 **Pop** 21,756 **Elev** 727 ft **Area code** 509
Information Wenatchee Area Visitor & Convention Bureau, PO Box 850, 98807; 509/662-2116.

The apple blossoms in the spring and the sturdy red of the grown fruit in the fall are the symbols of this community. Nestled among the towering mountains are fertile irrigated valleys where residents care for the orchards. Cherries, pears, peaches and apricots are also grown here. With the establishment in 1952 of a huge aluminum smelter and casting plant, Wenatchee no longer has an economy based only on agriculture. The headquarters of the Wenatchee National Forest is located here.

What to See and Do

Mission Ridge Ski Area. 4 double chairlifts, 2 rope tows; patrol, school, rentals; snowmaking; cafeteria; child care. Vertical drop 2,140 ft. (Mid-Nov-mid-Apr) Half-day rates. Limited cross-country trails. 12 mi SW on Squilchuck Rd. Phone 509/663-7631 or 800/374-1693 (snow conditions). ¢¢¢¢

North Central Washington Museum. Cultural Center; restored, operational 1919 Wurlitzer pipe organ; Great Northern Railway model; fine art gallery; apple industry exhibit; first trans-Pacific flight (Japan to Wenatchee) exhibit; archaeological and Native American exhibits. (Feb-Dec, daily; rest of yr, Mon-Fri; closed most major hols) 127 S Mission St. Phone 509/664-3340. ¢¢

Rocky Reach Dam. Visitors Center with underwater fish viewing gallery; theater. Powerhouse has Gallery of the Columbia and Gallery of Electricity; changing grounds; picnic and play areas. (Daily; closed Dec 25; also Jan-mid-Feb) On Columbia River. 7 mi N on US 97A. Phone 509/663-7522 or 509/663-8121. **Free.**

Squilchuck State Park. This 287-acre park offers day use and group camping. (Mar-Nov) Standard fees. 9 mi SW on Squilchuck Rd. Phone 509/664-6373.

Wenatchee Natl Forest. Approx 2 million forested, mountainous acres lying west of Columbia River. Trail system leads to jagged peaks, mountain meadows, sparkling lakes. Hunting, fishing, picnicking; winter sports (also see LEAVENWORTH); many developed campsites (some fees). Forest map available (fee). N, S & W of town. Contact Supervisor, 301 Yakima St, PO Box 811, 98807; 509/662-4335.

Annual Event

Washington State Apple Blossom Festival. Parades, carnival, arts & crafts, musical productions; "Ridge to River Relay." Last wknd Apr-1st wknd May.

Motels

★ **CHIEFTAIN.** *1005 N Wenatchee Ave (98801). 509/663-8141; FAX 509/663-8176; res: 800/572-4456 (WA).* 105 rms, 1-2 story. S $45; D $65-$80; each addl $5. Crib free. Pet accepted. TV; cable (premium). Heated pool; whirlpool. Restaurant 6 am-midnight. Bar; entertainment Tues-Sat. Ck-out noon. Meeting rms. Business servs avail. Private patios, balconies. Cr cds: A, C, D, DS, MC, V.

✔★ **HOLIDAY LODGE.** *610 N Wenatchee Ave (98801). 509/663-8167; res: 800/722-0852.* 59 rms, 2 story. S $36-$48; D $46-$65; each addl $5; under 12 free; higher rates: Apple Blossom season, some hols. Crib $5. TV; cable (premium), VCR avail. Heated pool; whirlpool. Complimentary continental bkfst. Restaurant nearby. Ck-out noon. Coin lndry. Business servs avail. Exercise equipt; weights, bicycle, sauna. Cr cds: A, C, D, DS, MC, V.

✔★ **RIVERS INN.** *580 Valley Mall Pkwy (98802), E Wenatchee. 509/884-1474; FAX 509/884-9179; res: 800/922-3199.* 55 rms, 2 story. S $47-$57; D $62-$67; each addl $5; under 12 free. Crib free. TV; cable, VCR avail. Heated pool; whirlpool. Complimentary continental bkfst. Restaurant 11:30 am-10 pm. Bar 11:30-2 am. Ck-out 11 am. Business servs avail. Some refrigerators. View of mountains. Cr cds: A, C, D, DS, MC, V.

Motor Hotel

★ ★ ★ **DOUBLETREE.** *1225 N Wenatchee Ave (98801). 509/663-0711; FAX 509/662-8175.* 149 rms, 3 story. S, D $79-$89; each addl $10; under 18 free; wknd rates. Crib free. Pet accepted. TV; cable. Heated pool; poolside serv. Restaurant 6 am-10 pm. Rm serv. Bar 11-2 am, Sun 4 pm-midnight; entertainment exc Sun. Ck-out 1 pm. Meeting rms. Business servs avail. In-rm modem link. Valet serv. Sundries. Free airport, bus depot transportation. Balconies. Cr cds: A, C, D, DS, JCB, MC, V.

Hotel

★ ★ ★ **WESTCOAST WENATCHEE CENTER.** *201 N Wenatchee Ave (98801). 509/662-1234; FAX 509/662-0782.* 147 rms, 9 story. S $87-$92; D $97-$102; each addl $10; suites $125-$200; under 18 free; ski rates; higher rates Apple Blossom Festival. Crib free. Pet accepted; $50 deposit. TV. Indoor/outdoor pool; whirlpool, poolside serv. Restaurant 6:30 am-10:30 pm. Bar 11-2 am; entertainment Tues-Sat. Ck-out noon. Meeting rms. Business servs avail. Free airport, RR station, bus depot transportation. Downhill ski 12 mi. Exercise equipt; weights, bicycles. Some refrigerators. Cr cds: A, C, D, DS, ER, JCB, MC, V.

Westport (D-1)

(For accommodations see Aberdeen, Ocean Shores; also see Hoquiam)

Settled 1858 **Pop** 1,892 **Elev** 12 ft **Area code** 360 **Zip** 98595
Information Westport-Grayland Chamber of Commerce, 2985 S Montesano St, PO Box 306, 98595-0306; 360/268-9422 or 800/345-6223.

Near the tip of a sandy strip of land separating Grays Harbor from the Pacific, Westport is home to probably the largest sports fishing fleet in the Northwest. Pleasure and charter boats take novice and experienced anglers alike across Grays Harbor Bay into the Pacific for salmon fishing in the summer and deep-sea fishing nearly all year. In the winter, commercial fleets set their pots for crab and have their catch processed at one of Westport's large canneries. Whale-watching excursions operate from March-May.

What to See and Do

Grays Harbor Lighthouse (1900). Tallest lighthouse on W coast (107 ft). Ocean Ave.

Maritime Museum. Shipwreck and Coast Guard memorabilia; also on grounds are Coast Guard vessel *U/B 41332* and Whale Display House. (June-Sept, Wed-Sun afternoons, also hols) 2201 Westhaven Dr. Phone 360/268-0078. **Donation.**

Twin Harbors State Park. More than 150 acres. Surf fishing, clamming, whale-watching. Hiking. Picnicking. Camping (hookups; res advised Memorial Day-Labor Day). Ocean swimming permitted, but hazardous. Standard fees. 3 mi S on WA 105. Phone 360/268-9717.

Westport Aquarium. Large tank aquariums; performing seals. (Feb-Oct, daily; Nov, wkends; closed some hols) 321 Harbor St. Phone 360/268-0471. ¢¢

Winthrop (B-6)

(See also Omak)

Pop 302 **Elev** 1,760 ft **Area code** 509 **Zip** 98862
Information Chamber of Commerce, Information Office, PO Box 39; 509/996-2125 or 888/463-8469.

Redesigning the entire town on an old West theme has transformed it into the "old Western town of Winthrop," complete with annual events in the same vein.

Fifty-five miles west on the North Cascades Highway (WA 20) is North Cascades National Park (see SEDRO WOOLLEY). A Ranger District office of the Okanogan National Forest (see OMAK) is located here.

What to See and Do

Shafer Museum. Log house built by town founder, Guy Waring (1897). Includes early day farming and mining implements. (Memorial Day-Sept, daily) Castle Ave. Phone 509/996-2712. **Free.**

Motel

✔★ **WINTHROP INN.** Box 265, 1 mi SE on WA 20. 509/996-2217; res: 800/444-1972. 30 rms, 2 story. May-Oct: S, D $54-$65; each addl $8; under 12 free; higher rates hols; varied lower rates rest of yr. Crib free. TV. Pool; whirlpool. Playground. Complimentary coffee in lobby. Restaurant nearby. Ck-out 11 am. Downhill ski 8 mi; x-country ski on site. Picnic tables. Private patios, balconies. Cr cds: MC, V.

Resort

★★★★ **SUN MOUNTAIN LODGE.** *Patterson Lake Rd, 9 mi SW on Patterson Lake Rd.* 509/996-2211; FAX 509/996-3133; res: 800/572-0493. E-mail smtnsale@methow.com; web www.travel-in-wa.com/ADS/sun_mtn.html. This resort on 3,000 acres of wilderness features stone fireplaces, handcrafted furniture and a lake with a beach. 102 rms, 2-3 story, 13 kit. cottages. Mid-June-Sept: S, D $147-$242; each addl $18; suites $252-$315; kit. cottages $157-$184; under 13 free; higher rates: wkends (2-day min) & hols (3-day min); lower rates rest of yr. Crib free. 2 pools; whirlpool, poolside serv. Playground. Supervised child's activities (July-Labor Day); ages 4-10. Reastaurant 7 am-10 pm. Rm serv. Bar. Ck-out noon. Meeting rms. Business servs avail. Concierge. Gift shop. Tennis. X-country ski on site. Exercise equipt; weight machine, bicycles. Rec rm. Lawn games. Stables. Hiking, bicycle trails. Many refrigerators. Balconies. Picnic tables. Cr cds: A, D, MC, V.

Restaurant

★★ **THE DINING ROOM.** *(See Sun Mountain Lodge Resort)* 509/996-2211. Hrs: 7 am-9 pm; Fri, Sat to 10 pm; winter to 8:30 pm; Fri, Sat to 9 pm. Res accepted. Bar from noon. Semi-a la carte: bkfst $4-$10, lunch $6.50-$10, dinner $15-$25. Child's meals. Specialties: gnocchi, tenderloin mignon, Washington fryer chicken breast. Outdoor dining. Large windows offer grand views of mountains. Totally nonsmoking. Cr cds: A, D, MC, V.

Yakima (D-5)

(See also Ellensburg, Toppenish)

Settled 1861 **Pop** 54,827 **Elev** 1,068 ft **Area code** 509
Information Yakima Valley Visitors & Convention Bureau, 10 North 8th St, 98901; 509/575-1300.

Yakima (YAK-e-ma) County ranks first in the US in production of apples, hops, sweet cherries and winter pears. Irrigation was started as early as 1875, when early settlers dug crude canals. Orchards and farms replaced sagebrush and desert. The city takes its name from the Yakama Nation whose reservation lies to the south. There are about 300 days of sunshine annually, with an average yearly rainfall of 8 inches.

What to See and Do

Ahtanum Mission. Founded in 1852, destroyed in Yakama Native American Wars, rebuilt in 1867; site of oldest irrigated apple orchards in valley (1872). 9 mi SW on unnumbered roads.

Historic North Front Street. Called "birthplace of Yakima" this 2-block section of downtown has restaurants and shopping.

Painted Rocks. Historic Yakima Nation pictographs. 7 mi NW on US 12.

Skiing. White Pass Village. 55 mi NW on US 12, in Mt Baker-Snoqualmie Natl Forest. (See MOUNT RAINIER NATIONAL PARK)

Yakima Interurban Trolley Lines. Trolley cars make trips around city and surrounding countryside. Boarding at car barns at 3rd Ave & W Pine St. (May-mid-Oct wkends; also evening rides July, Aug) 307 W Pine St. Phone 509/575-1700. ¢¢

Yakima Sportsman State Park. Approx 250 acres. Picnicking. Camping (hookups). Standard fees. 3 mi E on WA 24, Keyes Rd. Phone 509/575-2774.

Yakima Valley Museum. Exhibits relating to history of Yakima valley; Yakima Nation; fruit industry. Collection of horse-drawn vehicles. (Daily exc Mon; closed major hols) 2105 Tieton Dr, in Franklin Park. Phone 509/248-0747. ¢¢

Annual Events

Chocolate Fantasy. Chocolate manufacturers from across the nation showcase candy, cookies and pies; sampling, "chocolate bingo." Phone 509/966-6309. Mid-Mar.

Spring Barrel Tasting. Area wineries participate. Last wkend Apr.

Yakima Air Fair. Phone 509/248-3425. First wkend June.

Central Washington State Fair & Rodeo. Fairgrounds. Phone 509/248-7160. Late Sept-early Oct.

Seasonal Event

Yakima Meadows Racetrack. Fairgrounds. Thoroughbred racing. Parimutuel wagering. For schedule phone 509/248-3920.

Motels

★ ★ ★ **BEST WESTERN RIO MIRADA.** *1603 Terrace Heights Dr (98901), 1 blk E of I-82 exit 33.* 509/457-4444; FAX 509/453-7593. 96 rms, 4 story, 6 kits. S $53-$58; D $58-$63; each addl $8; kit. units $60-$65. Crib $4. TV; cable, VCR avail. Heated pool; whirlpool. Restaurant adj 6 am-10 pm. Bar 11-2 am. Ck-out noon. Coin lndry. Meeting rms. In-rm modem link. Valet serv. Sundries. Free airport, bus depot transportation avail. Many refrigerators. Private patios, balconies. View of river. Cr cds: A, C, D, DS, MC, V.

★ ★ ★ **HOLIDAY INN.** *9th St & Yakima Ave (98901), I-82 City Center exit.* 509/452-6511; FAX 509/457-4931. 171 rms, 2-3 story, 8 kits. S, D, kit. units $69-$95; each addl $10; suites $110-$195; under 19 free. Crib free. Pet accepted. TV; cable (premium), VCR avail. Heated pool; poolside serv. Complimentary continental bkfst. Restaurant 6:30 am-10 pm. Rm serv. Bar. Ck-out noon. Coin lndry. Meeting rms. Business servs avail. In-rm modem link. Free airport transportation. Some refrigerators. Some private patios, balconies. Cr cds: A, C, D, DS, JCB, MC, V.

★ ★ **MENDELS.** *1405 N 1st St (98901), I-82 exit N 1st St.* 509/453-8981; FAX 509/452-3241. 53 rms, 2 story. S $43; D $49-$52; each addl $6. Crib free. TV; cable (premium). Heated pool; 2 whirlpools. Restaurant adj 6 am-11 pm. Ck-out 11 am. Business servs avail. Cr cds: A, C, D, DS, MC, V.

★ **QUALITY INN.** *12 Valley Mall Blvd (98903), I-82 Union Gap exit.* 509/248-6924; FAX 509/575-8470. 85 rms, 2 story. S $52-$57; D $66-$69; each addl $8; under 18 free. Pet accepted. TV; cable, VCR avail. Heated pool. Complimentary continental bkfst. Restaurant adj open 24 hrs. Ck-out 11 am. Business servs avail. Valet serv. Free airport transportation. Sun deck. Cr cds: A, C, D, DS, MC, V.

★ ★ **RED LION INN.** *818 N 1st St (98901), I-82 exit N 1st St.* 509/453-0391; FAX 509/453-8348. 58 rms, 2 story. S $64-$79; D $74-$89; each addl $10; suites $120-$150; under 18 free. Crib free. Pet accepted, some restrictions. TV; cable (premium). Heated pool. Coffee avail. Restaurant adj open 24 hrs. Ck-out noon. Business servs avail. Cr cds: A, C, D, DS, ER, MC, V.

Motor Hotels

★ ★ ★ **CAVANAUGH'S AT YAKIMA CENTER.** *607 E Yakima Ave (98901).* 509/248-5900; FAX 509/575-8975. 152 rms, 2 story. June-Oct: S $66-$86; D $76-$96; suites $185-$285; each addl $10; under 12 free; lower rates rest of yr. Crib free. TV; cable (premium). 2 pools; poolside serv. Restaurant 6:30 am-10 pm. Rm serv. Bar 11-2 am; entertainment. Ck-out noon. Meeting rms. Business servs avail. Valet serv. Sundries. Airport, bus depot transportation. Health club privileges. Some refrigerators. Private patios, balconies. Cr cds: A, C, D, DS, MC, V.

★ ★ **RED LION INN/YAKIMA VALLEY.** *1507 N 1st St (98901), I-82 exit N 1st St.* 509/248-7850; FAX 509/575-1694. 209 rms, 2 story. S $75-$82; D $75-$92; each addl $10; suites $135-$250; under 18 free. Crib free. TV; cable. 2 heated pools; whirlpool, poolside serv. Restaurant 6 am-11 pm. Rm serv. Bar; entertainment exc Sun. Ck-out noon. Meeting rms. Business servs avail. In-rm modem link. Bellhops. Valet serv. Sundries. Health club privileges. Some bathrm phones, refrigerators. Private patios, balconies. Cr cds: A, C, D, DS, ER, JCB, MC, V.

Restaurants

★ ★ ★ **BIRCHFIELD MANOR.** *2018 Birchfield Rd (98901).* 509/452-1960. Sittings: Thurs, Fri 7 pm; Sat 6 & 8:45 pm. Closed Sun-Wed; some major hols. Res accepted; required Thurs-Sat. Wine cellar. Semi-a la carte: dinner from $19.95. Specializes in seafood, veal, lamb. Own baking, chocolates. Elegant dining in Victorian mansion (1910). Guest rms avail. Totally nonsmoking. Cr cds: A, D, MC, V.

★ ★ **DELI DE PASTA.** *7 N Front St (98901).* 509/453-0571. Hrs: 11:30 am-9 pm; Fri & Sat to 10 pm. Closed Sun; most major hols. Res accepted. Italian menu. Wine, beer. Semi-a la carte: lunch $5.50-$10, dinner $8.95-$19. Specializes in seafood, steak, gourmet pasta dishes. Outdoor dining. Small, intimate dining area. Totally nonsmoking. Cr cds: A, MC, V.

Wyoming

Population: 453,588
Land area: 96,988 square miles
Elevation: 3,100-13,804 feet
Highest point: Gannett Peak (Between Fremont, Sublette Counties)
Entered Union: July 10, 1890 (44th state)
Capital: Cheyenne
Motto: Equal rights
Nickname: Equality State, Cowboy State
State flower: Indian paintbrush
State bird: Meadowlark
State tree: Cottonwood
State fair: August 17-22, 1998, in Douglas
Time zone: Mountain
Web: www.state.wy.us

From the high western plateaus of the Great Plains, the state of Wyoming stretches across the Continental Divide and on into the Rocky Mountains. This is a land of scenic beauty and geographic diversity; mountain ranges, grasslands and desert area can all be found within Wyoming's borders.

The first Europeans to explore this region were French; brothers Louis and Francés François Verendrye trapped here in 1743. The first American to enter what is now Yellowstone National Park was John Colter, a member of the Lewis and Clark expedition, who was here during the winter of 1807-1808. The 1820s saw a number of trappers and fur traders become established in the area. The territory became the site of important stops along the pioneer trails to the West Coast in the 1840s-1860s.

The pioneer trails across Wyoming allowed pioneers to cross the rugged spine of the Rocky Mountains on an easy grade, following grass and water over the Continental Divide. Of the approximately 350,000 individuals who made their way along the various westward trails, some 21,000 died en route, claimed by disease, accidents and mountain snow. After 1847 thousands of Mormons came along the Mormon Trail to join Brigham Young's settlement at Salt Lake. The situation improved dramatically for those bound for the West when the Union Pacific Railroad pushed across Wyoming during 1867-1869. The "iron horse" made the journey considerably safer and easier, not to mention faster. Permanent settlement of the West then began in earnest.

The hard existence wrought from a sometimes inhospitable land bred a tough, practical people who recognized merit when they saw it. While still a territory, Wyoming in 1869 became the first area in the US to grant women the right to vote. Subsequently, Wyomingites were the first in the nation to appoint a woman justice of the peace, the first to select women jurors and the first to elect a woman, Nellie Tayloe Ross in 1924, governor. This reputation has earned Wyoming the nickname "the equality state."

The civic-mindedness of its citizens spread beyond the political arena with equal vigor. Wyoming introduced the nation's first county library system and instituted a public education system that today ranks among the finest in the US.

Cattle and sheep outnumber people by more than five to one in Wyoming, which is the least populated state in the country. It is, therefore, easy to see how the cowboy has become such a prominent symbol here. The "bucking horse" insignia has appeared on Wyoming license plates since 1936. It also appears in various versions everywhere on road signs, storefronts and newspapers.

Mineral extraction is the principal industry in Wyoming, which has the largest coal resources in the country. Tourism and recreation ranks second, with approximately four million visitors per year entering the state. Generally, they come to visit the numerous national parks, forests and monuments. But Wyoming offers a wide range of attractions, from abundant camping to rustic guest ranching, all set among some of the finest natural beauty to be found in the nation.

The country's first national park (Yellowstone), first national monument (Devils Tower) and first national forest (Shoshone) are all located in Wyoming.

When to Go/Climate

Wyoming's climate is relatively cool and dry, although spring can be wet in the lower elevations and winter actually can be dangerous. Blizzards are frequent and have been known to arise from November through June. Temperatures can vary greatly on any given day in both spring and fall.

AVERAGE HIGH/LOW TEMPERATURES (°F)

CHEYENNE

Jan 38/15	**May** 65/39	**Sept** 71/44
Feb 41/18	**June** 74/48	**Oct** 60/34
Mar 45/22	**July** 82/55	**Nov** 47/24
Apr 55/30	**Aug** 80/53	**Dec** 39/17

LANDER

Jan 31/8	**May** 66/40	**Sept** 72/44
Feb 37/14	**June** 77/49	**Oct** 60/34
Mar 46/22	**July** 86/56	**Nov** 43/20
Apr 56/31	**Aug** 84/54	**Dec** 32/9

Parks and Recreation Finder

Directions to and information about the parks and recreation areas below are given under their respective town/city sections. Please refer to those sections for details.

Key to abbreviations: I.P. = Interstate Park; N.B.C. = National Battlefield & Cemetery; N.B.P. = National Battlefield Park; N.F. = National Forest; N.G. = National Grassland; N.H. = National Historical Park; N.H.S. = National Historic Site; N.M. = National Monument; N.Mem. = National Memorial; N.M.P. = National Military Park; N.P. = National Park; N.Pres. = National Preserve; N.R. = National Recreational Area; N.R.R. = National Recreational River; N.Res. = National Reserve; N.S. = National Seashore; N.S.R. = National Scenic River; N.S.T. = National Scenic Trail; N.V.M. = National Volcanic Monument; S.B. = State Beach; S.C.P. = State Conservation Park; S.G. = State Garden; S.H.A. = State Historic Area; S.H.P. = State Historic Park; S.N.A. = State Natural Area; S.P. = State Park; S.R. = State Reserve; S.R.A. = State Recreation Area; S.Res.P. = State Resort Park; S.R.P. = State Rustic Park.

NATIONAL PARK AND RECREATION AREAS

Place Name	Listed Under
Bighorn Canyon N.R.	LOVELL
Bighorn N.F.	SHERIDAN
Bridger-Teton N.F.	JACKSON, PINEDALE
Devils Tower N.M.	same
Flaming Gorge N.R.	GREEN RIVER
Fort Laramie N.H.S.	same
Fossil Butte N.M.	KEMMERER
Grand Teton N.P.	same
Medicine Bow N.F.	LARAMIE
Shoshone N.F.	CODY
Thunder Basin N.G.	DOUGLAS
Yellowstone N.P.	same

STATE RECREATION AREAS

Place Name	Listed Under
Boysen S.P.	THERMOPOLIS
Buffalo Bill S.P.	CODY
Curt Gowdy S.P.	CHEYENNE
Edness K. Wilkins S.P.	CASPER
Glendo S.P.	WHEATLAND
Guernsey S.P.	WHEATLAND
Hot Springs S.P.	THERMOPOLIS
Keyhole S.P.	GILLETTE
Seminoe S.P.	RAWLINS
Sinks Canyon S.P.	LANDER

Water-related activities, hiking, various other sports, picnicking and visitor centers, as well as camping, are available in many of these areas. State parks are open all year, but some facilities may be closed Nov-Mar. Entrance fee per vehicle $3 nonresident, $2 resident; annual entrance pass $25. Entrance fee for state historical sites, $1. Camping is limited to 14 days per site unless otherwise posted (no reservations); $4/vehicle/night. Pets under control. Further information may be obtained from Wyoming State Parks & Historic Sites, 6101 Yellowstone Rd, Cheyenne 82002; 307/777-6323.

SKI AREAS

Place Name	Listed Under
Hogadon Ski Area	CASPER
Jackson Hole Ski Resort	JACKSON
Sleeping Giant Ski Area	CODY
Snowy Range Ski Area	LARAMIE
Snow King Ski Resort	JACKSON

CALENDAR HIGHLIGHTS

JUNE

Plains Indian Powwow (Cody). People from tribes throughout the western plains states and Canada gather to compete. Dancing and singing; ceremonial and traditional tribal dress.

JULY

Legend of Rawhide (Lusk). Live show performed since 1946. Concert, dances, art show, parade, pancake breakfast.

1838 Mountain Man Rendezvous (Riverton). Council fire, primitive shoots, hawk and knife throw, games, food. Camping available. Phone 307/856-7306.

Central Wyoming Fair and Rodeo (Casper). Fairgrounds. Phone 307/235-5775.

Red Desert Round-Up (Rock Springs). One of the largest rodeos in the Rocky Mountains region.

Cheyenne Frontier Days (Cheyenne). Frontier Park arena. One of the countrys most famous rodeos; originated in 1897. Parades, carnivals; pancake breakfast; entertainment, square dancing nightly.

AUGUST

Gift of the Waters Pageant (Thermopolis). Hot Springs State Park. Commemorates the deeding of the worlds largest mineral hot springs from the Shoshone and Arapahoe to the people of Wyoming in 1896. Pageant features Native American dances, parade, buffalo barbecue.

SEPTEMBER

Jackson Hole Fall Arts Festival (Jackson). Three-week celebration of the arts featuring special exhibits in more than 30 galleries, demonstrations, special activities. Also dance, theater, mountain film festival, Native American arts & culinary arts. Phone 307/733-3316.

FISHING & HUNTING

For anglers there are 16,000 miles of fishing streams, 270,000 acres of fishing lakes and 90 fish varieties, among which are 22 game fish. Throughout Wyoming pronghorn antelope, moose, elk, black bear, whitetail and mule deer and bighorn sheep roam the mountain ranges and meadows, which are open to hunters.

Nonresident hunting and fishing license for one elk and one season of fishing: $350. Nonresident deer permit: $150; bighorn sheep permit (1 male): $1,000; moose permit (1 bull): $750; bird license: $40; turkey: $40; small game (cottontail) license: $35; fishing license: annual $50 (10-day, $30; 5-day, $20; 1-day, $5). Most hunting licenses must be applied for well in advance of the hunting season and are issued via computer drawing. Feb 1 is the deadline for elk applications, Mar 31 for deer, antelope, bighorn sheep, and moose. Persons missing out may apply for any leftover licenses. All license holders except for those purchasing a 1-day or 5-day fishing license must purchase a conservation stamp for $5 before hunting or fishing; one time fee/person/yr.

Visitors may take a self-guided tour of the visitor center in the headquarters office building, 5400 Bishop Blvd, Cheyenne.

Further information can be obtained from the State of Wyoming Game and Fish Department, 5400 Bishop Blvd, Cheyenne 82006; 307/777-4600.

Driving Information

Safety belts are mandatory for all persons in front seat of vehicle. Children under 3 years or under 40 pounds in weight must be in an approved safety seat. For further information phone 307/777-4301.

INTERSTATE HIGHWAY SYSTEM

The following alphabetical listing of Wyoming towns in *Mobil Travel Guide* shows that these cities are within 10 miles of the indicated Interstate highways. A highway map, however, should be checked for the nearest exit.

Highway Number	Cities/Towns within 10 miles
Interstate 25	Buffalo, Casper, Cheyenne, Douglas, Sheridan, Wheatland.
Interstate 80	Cheyenne, Evanston, Green River, Laramie, Rawlins, Rock Springs.
Interstate 90	Buffalo, Gillette, Sheridan.

Additional Visitor Information

Detailed visitor information is distributed by Wyoming Division of Tourism, I-25 at College Drive, Cheyenne 82002; 307/777-7777 or 800/225-5996. There are several welcome centers in Wyoming; visitors will find the information provided at these stops most helpful in planning their stay in the state. Their locations are as follows: in the northern central part of Wyoming, N on I-90 in Sheridan; at the lower eastern corner, on I-25, S of I-80 in Cheyenne; on the western side, near Grand Teton National Park, on US 89 in Jackson, and in central Wyoming in Casper on Center St, S of I-25 (Mon-Fri); I-80 E at exit 6 in Evanston; I-80, 10 miles east of Laramie (late May-mid-Oct); on I-90 in Sundance (late May-mid-Oct).

Afton (D-2)

(See also Alpine)

Pop 1,394 **Elev** 6,239 ft **Area code** 307 **Zip** 83110
Information Chamber of Commerce, PO Box 1097; 307/886-3196 or 800/426-8833.

An arch across Main St composed of 3,000 elk horns marks the entrance to the town of Afton. For anglers and big-game hunters there are outfitters and experienced guides here who rarely send their clients home empty-handed. Afton is located in Star Valley, which is noted for its cheese. A Ranger District office of the Bridger-Teton National Forest (see JACKSON) is located here.

What to See and Do

Bridger-Teton Natl Forest. (see JACKSON).

Fishing. Excellent brown trout and cutthroat trout fishing year-round on Salt River (within 2 1/2 mi).

Intermittent spring. Spring flows out of mountain for about 18 min, then stops completely for the same period. The theory behind this phenomenon is that a natural siphon exists from an underground lake. Canyon suitable for hiking or horseback riding. Horses, guides avail. 7 mi E up Swift Creek Canyon.

Outfitting and Big Game Hunting. Inquire at the Chamber of Commerce.

Motels

(Air conditioning is rarely needed at higher altitudes)

★ **BEST WESTERN HI COUNTRY INN.** *689 S Washington, 1/4 mi S on US 89. 307/886-3856; FAX 307/886-9318.* 30 rms. No A/C. S $45-$50; D $50-$55; each addl $5. Crib free. Pet accepted, some restrictions. TV; cable. Heated pool; whirlpool. Restaurant adj 6 am-10 pm. Ck-out 11 am. X-country ski 12 mi. Cr cds: A, C, D, DS, MC, V.

✔★ **CORRAL.** *161 Washington (US 89). 307/886-5424.* 15 rms, 2 kits. No A/C. Apr-Oct: S $35; D $40-$45; each addl $5; kits. $5 addl.

Closed rest of yr. Crib $2. Pet accepted, some restrictions. TV; cable (premium). Restaurant nearby. Ck-out 10 am. Some refrigerators. Picnic tables, grills. Cr cds: A, C, D, DS, MC, V.

★ **MOUNTAIN INN.** *1 mi S on US 89. 307/886-3156; res: 800/682-5356.* 20 rms. No A/C. Mid-May-mid-Oct: S $55; D $60; each addl $5; lower rates rest of yr. Crib $5. Pet accepted. TV. Heated pool; whirlpool. Sauna. Restaurant nearby. Ck-out 11 am. Cr cds: A, C, D, DS, MC, V.

Alpine (C-2)

(See also Afton, Jackson)

Pop 200 **Elev** 5,600 ft **Area code** 307 **Zip** 83128

The Palisades Reservoir, just south of town, offers fishing, boating and tent and trailer camping.

Motel

(Air conditioning is rarely needed at higher altitudes)

★ ★ ★ **BEST WESTERN FLYING SADDLE LODGE.** *1/2 mi E on US 26. 307/654-7561; FAX 307/654-7563.* 20 rms, 6 cottages. June-Oct: S, D $60-$150; each addl $5. Closed rest of yr. Crib free. TV; cable (premium), VCR avail (movies free). Heated pool; whirlpools. Restaurant 7-11 am, 5-10 pm. Bar. Ck-out 11 am. Business servs avail. Sundries. Tennis. Some refrigerators, in-rm whirlpools. Western decor. On Snake River. Cr cds: A, C, D, DS, MC, V.

Motor Hotel

★ **ALPEN HAUS.** *Box 258, jct of US 26, 89. 307/654-7545; FAX 307/654-7287, ext. 331; res: 800/343-6755 (exc WY).* 45 rms, 3 story. S $58-$64; D $65-$71; each addl $7; under 12 free. Crib $10. Pet accepted. TV; cable (premium); VCR avail (movies). Playground. Restaurant 7 am-10 pm. Bar 11-1 am. Ck-out 11 am. Coin lndry. Meeting rm. Gift shop. X-country ski on site. Whirlpool. Some refrigerators, minibars. Some balconies. Ice cream parlor. Cr cds: A, C, D, DS, MC, V.

Buffalo (B-6)

(See also Sheridan)

Founded 1884 **Pop** 3,302 **Elev** 4,640 ft **Area code** 307 **Zip** 82834
E-mail nadgross@wyoming.com **Web** www.buffalo.com/chamber
Information Chamber of Commerce, 55 N Main; 307/684-5544 or 800/227-5122.

Buffalo began as a trading center at the edge of Fort McKinney, one of the last of the old military posts. In 1892, trouble erupted here between big cattlemen and small ranchers with their allies, the nesters, in the Johnson County Cattle War. Several people were killed before Federal troops ended the conflict.

Located at the foot of the Big Horn Mountains, Buffalo attracts many tourists, hunters and fishermen; the economy is dependent on tourism, as well as lumber, minerals and cattle. A Ranger District office of the Bighorn National Forest (see SHERIDAN) is located in Buffalo.

What to See and Do

Ft Phil Kearny Site. Cavalry post was the scene of a clash between Sioux, Arapahoe, Cheyenne and US soldiers; site of Fetterman and Wagon Box battles; visitor center. (Daily) 13 mi N on US 87. Phone 307/684-7629.

Johnson County-Jim Gatchell Memorial Museum. Collection of Native American artifacts, local and regional history, pioneer equipment; natural history display. (Memorial Day-Labor Day, daily; May 2-Memorial Day & Labor Day-Nov 1, Mon-Fri; rest of yr, by appt; closed July 4) 100 Fort St, adj to courthouse. Phone 307/684-9331. ¢

Annual Event

Johnson County Fair and Rodeo. Features working cowhands; parade. Rodeo held last 3 days of fair. Phone 307/684-7357. 2nd wk Aug.

Motels

✔★ **CANYON.** 997 Fort St. 307/684-2957; res: 800/231-0742. 18 rms, 3 kits. S $38; D $40-$48; each addl $3; kit. units $50-$55. Crib free. Pet accepted. TV; cable. Complimentary coffee in rms. Restaurant nearby. Ck-out 11 am. Airport transportation. Picnic tables. Cr cds: A, DS, MC, V.

★ **COMFORT INN.** 65 Hwy 16 E. 307/684-9564. 41 rms, 2 story. Late June-mid-Aug: S, D $79.95-$94.95; each addl $5; under 18 free; lower rates rest of yr. Crib $5. Pet accepted, some restrictions. TV; cable (premium). Complimentary continental bkfst. Restaurant nearby. Ck-out 11 am. Whirlpool. Cr cds: A, D, DS, MC, V.

✔★ **WYOMING.** 610 E Hart St, 1/2 mi NE on US 16. 307/684-5505; FAX 307/684-5442; res: 800/666-5505. 27 rms, 5 kit. June-Oct: S $36-$62; D $46-$91; each addl $8; kit. unit $60-$145; lower rates rest of yr. Pet accepted. TV; cable (premium). Heated pool; whirlpool. Restaurant adj 6 am-10:30 pm. Ck-out 11 am. Picnic tables. Cr cds: A, C, D, DS, MC, V.

Lodge

★ ★ **THE RANCH AT UCROSS.** (2673 US 14E, Clearmont 82835) 307/737-2281; FAX 307/737-2211; res: 800/447-0194. 31 rms, 2 story. S $95; D $115; each addl $20; under 19 free. Pet accepted. Heated pool. Complimentary full bkfst. Restaurant 6:30-9 am, 11:30 am-1 pm, 7-9 pm. Bar 5-9 pm. Ck-out 1 pm. Meeting rm. Business servs avail. Bellhops. Sundries. Gift shop. Tennis. On creek. Cr cds: MC, V.

Inn

✔★ **CLOUD PEAK INN.** 590 N Burritt. 307/684-5794; FAX 307/684-7653; res: 800/715-5794. 5 rms, 1 with shower only, 2 share bath, 2 story. Mid-May-mid-Sept: S $50-$70; D $55-$75; each addl $5; under 10 free; lower rates rest of yr. Crib free. Whirlpool. Complimentary full bkfst. Complimentary coffee in library. Ck-out 11 am, ck-in 4 pm. Luggage handling. X-country ski 12 mi. 1 balcony. Turn-of-the-century decor; antiques. Totally nonsmoking. Cr cds: A, MC, V.

Guest Ranch

★ ★ ★ **PARADISE.** Box 790, 12 mi W on US 16, then 4 mi NW on Hunter Creek Rd. 307/684-7876. 18 kit. cabins. AP, late May-mid-Sept: S $1,210/wk; D $2,420/wk; each addl $1,210/wk; ages 6-12, $1,107/wk; under 6, $880/wk. Closed rest of yr. Crib free. Heated pool; whirlpool. Playground. Free supervised child's activities. Complimentary coffee, tea in cabins. Dining rm, sittings 7:30-8:30 am, 12:30 pm, 7 pm. Lunch rides.

Cookouts. Bar 5-10 pm. Ck-out 10 am, ck-in 3 pm. Lndry facilities in most cabins. Package store 16 mi. Meeting rms. Free airport transportation. Lawn games. Entertainment. Fishing guides. Fireplaces. Private patios. Picnic tables. No cr cds accepted.

Restaurant

✔★ **COLONEL BOZEMAN'S.** 655 E Hart St. 307/684-5555. Hrs: 6 am-10 pm. Closed Dec 25. Semi-a la carte: bkfst $2.95-$6.95, lunch $2.25-$8.95, dinner $6.95-$16.95. Child's meals. Specializes in pasta, steaks, Mexican dishes. Cr cds: A, DS, MC, V.

Casper (D-7)

(See also Douglas)

Founded 1888 **Pop** 46,742 **Elev** 5,140 ft **Area code** 307 **E-mail** visitors @trib.com **Web** www.trib.com/ads/casper/

Information Chamber of Commerce Visitor Center, 500 N Center St, PO Box 399, 82602; 307/234-5311 or 800/852-1889.

Before oil was discovered, Casper was a railroad terminus in the cattle-rich Wyoming hinterlands, where Native Americans and emigrants on the Oregon Trail had passed before. Casper was known as an oil town after the first strike in 1890 in the Salt Creek Field, site of the Teapot Dome naval oil reserve that caused a top-level government scandal in the 1920s. World War I brought a real boom and exciting prosperity. A half-million dollars in oil stocks was traded in hotel lobbies every day; land prices skyrocketed and rents inflated while oil flowed through some of the world's biggest refineries. The crash of 1929 ended the speculation, but oil continued to flow through feeder lines to Casper. Oil continues to contribute to the area's economy; also important are tourism, agriculture, light manufacturing, coal, bentonite and uranium mining.

What to See and Do

Casper Mt and Beartrap Meadow Parks. Nordic ski trails (fee). Snowmobile trails (registration required), mountain bike trails. Picnicking. Camping (fee), shelters (res required). (Daily) 10 mi S. Phone 307/235-9325. Located on the mountain is

Lee McCune Braille Trail. Flora, fauna and geology are the focus of this trail (1/3 mi) geared for both the sighted and the visually impaired. The self-guided loop trail has signs in both Braille and English at 36 interpretive stations. Safety ropes are provided for guidance. **Free.**

Casper Planetarium. Three 1-hr shows every evening. (Early June-early Sept & Thanksgiving-Dec 24, daily) 904 N Poplar St. Phone 307/577-0310. ¢; Per family ¢¢

Edness K. Wilkins State Park. Approx 300 acres on the Oregon Trail, bordered by the historic Platte River. Day-use park. Swimming pond; fishing. Hiking paths. Picnicking. 4 mi E via I-25, Hat Six exit on US 87. Phone 307/577-5150. Per Vehicle ¢¢

⊠ **Ft Caspar Museum.** On grounds of restored fort; exhibits of Platte Bridge Station/Ft Caspar, Oregon Trail, pony express, Mormon Trail, military artifacts, city of Casper, central Wyoming. (Mid-May-mid-Sept, daily; rest of yr, daily exc Sat) Fort buildings closed in winter. 4001 Ft Caspar Rd. Phone 307/235-8462. **Free.**

Hogadon Ski Area. 2 chairlifts, Pomalift; patrol, school, rentals; snowmaking; cafeteria. Longest run 3/4 mi; vertical drop 600 ft. (Late Nov-mid-Apr, Wed-Sun, hols; closed Dec 25) 11 mi S via WY 251. Phone 307/235-8499 or 307/235-8281 (summer); 307/235-8369 (snow conditions). ¢¢¢¢

Independence Rock. "Register of the Desert," 193 ft high. Inscribed with more than 50,000 pioneer names, some dating back more than 100 yrs. Many names are obscured by lichen or worn away. 45 mi SW on WY 220.

Nicolaysen Art Museum & Discovery Center. Changing and permanent exhibits. (Daily exc Mon; closed major hols) 400 E Collins Dr. Phone 307/235-5247. ¢

Annual Events

Central Wyoming Fair and Rodeo. Fairgrounds, W of city. Phone 307/235-5775. Mid-July.

Central Wyoming Fair Race Meet. Fairgrounds. Horse racing; parimutuel wagering. Phone 307/235-5775. Aug-early Sept.

Motels

★ ★ **HAMPTON INN.** *400 West F Street (82601), I-25 exit Poplar St.* 307/235-6668; FAX 307/235-2027. 122 rms, 2 story. S $59; D $67; under 18 free. Crib free. Pet accepted; $6. TV; cable (premium). Heated pool; sauna. Complimentary continental bkfst. Coffee in rms. Ck-out 11 am. Business servs avail. In-rm modem link. Valet serv. Free airport transportation. Downhill ski 7 mi. Cr cds: A, C, D, DS, MC, V.

D ❧ ⚲ ≋ ⇴ 🐾 SC

✔★ **KELLY INN.** *821 N Poplar (82601).* 307/266-2400; FAX 307/266-1146; res: 800/635-3559. 103 rms, 2 story. S $35-$43; D $41-$51; each addl $5; under 16 free. Crib free. Pet accepted. TV; cable (premium), VCR avail (movies). Complimentary coffee in lobby. Restaurant nearby. Ck-out 11 am. Coin lndry. Meeting rms. Whirlpool. Sauna. Cr cds: A, C, D, DS, MC, V.

D ❧ ⇴ 🐾 SC

Motor Hotels

★ ★ **HILTON INN.** *PO Box 224 (82602), 1 blk N of I-25, N Poplar exit.* 307/266-6000; FAX 307/473-1010. 228 rms, 6 story. S $65; D $65-$75; suites $85-$175; under 18 free. Crib free. Pet accepted. TV; cable (premium). Indoor pool; whirlpool. Restaurant 6 am-10 pm. Rm serv. Bar 11-1:30 am. Ck-out noon. Meeting rms. Business servs avail. Sundries. Beauty shop. Free airport transportation. Downhill/x-country ski 7 mi. Some in-rm whirlpools. Cr cds: A, C, D, DS, MC, V.

D ❧ ⚲ ≋ ⇴ 🐾 SC

★ ★ **HOLIDAY INN.** *300 West F Street (82602), (US 20/26).* 307/235-2531; FAX 307/266-0160. 200 rms, 2 story. S, D $69; each addl $5; suites $75-$150; under 18 free. Crib $6. Pet accepted, some restrictions. TV; cable (premium). Indoor pool; whirlpool. Restaurant 6 am-2 pm, 5-10 pm. Rm serv. Bar. Ck-out noon. Coin lndry. Meeting rms. Business servs avail. In-rm modem link. Sundries. Free airport, bus depot transportation. Downhill/x-country ski 7 mi. Exercise equipt; weights, bicycle, sauna. Game rm. Picnic tables. On river. Cr cds: A, C, D, DS, MC, V.

D ❧ ⚲ ≋ 🏃 🚴 ⇴ 🐾 SC

Inn

✔★ ★ **HOTEL HIGGINS.** *(416 W Birch, Glenrock 82637) 18 mi E on I-25, 1 mi N exit 165.* 307/436-9212; FAX 307/436-9213; res: 800/458-0144. 8 rms. Most A/C. S $46; D $60; each addl $7-$15; suites $70. Complimentary full bkfst. Restaurant (see PAISLEY SHAWL). Bar 11:30-2 am. Ck-out noon, ck-in after noon. Original terrazzo floors, fixtures. Antiques, some original to building (1916). Cr cds: C, D, DS, MC, V.

🔥

Restaurants

★ ★ **ARMOR'S.** *3422 S Energy Lane.* 307/235-3000. Hrs: 5-9:30 pm; Fri, Sat to 10 pm. Closed Dec 25. Res accepted. Continental menu. Bar. Semi a la carte: dinner $8.95-$19.95. Child's meals. Specializes in veal, fettucine, prime rib. Picture windows with mountain view. Cr cds: A, C, D, DS, MC, V.

⬚

★ ★ ★ **PAISLEY SHAWL.** *(See Hotel Higgins Inn)* 307/436-9212. Hrs: 11:30 am-1:30 pm, 6-9:30 pm. Closed major hols. Res accepted. Continental menu. Bar. A la carte entrees: lunch $5-$9, dinner $12-$25. Complete meals: dinner $28. Specialties: lamb chops with honey mustard, shrimp scampi. Own baking. Outdoor dining. In 1916 building; turn-of-the-century decor. Cr cds: C, D, MC, V.

⬚

Cheyenne (F-8)

(See also Laramie)

Founded 1867 **Pop** 50,008 **Elev** 6,098 ft **Area code** 307 **Zip** 82001

Information Cheyenne Convention & Visitors Bureau, 309 W Lincolnway, PO Box 765, 82003; 307/778-3133 or 800/426-5009.

Cheyenne was named for an Algonquian tribe that roamed this area. When the Union Pacific Railroad reached what is now the capital and largest city of Wyoming on November 13, 1867, there was already a town. Between July of that year and the day the tracks were actually laid, 4,000 people had set up living quarters and land values soared. Professional gunmen, soldiers, promoters, trainmen, gamblers and confidence men enjoying quick money and cheap liquor gave the town the reputation of being "hell on wheels." Two railways and three transcontinental highways made it a wholesale and commodity jobbing point, the retail and banking center of a vast region. Cheyenne is the seat of state and county government. Agriculture, light manufacturing, retail trade and tourism support the economy of the area.

What to See and Do

Cheyenne Botanic Gardens. Wildflower, rose gardens; lily pond; Community garden. (Mon-Fri; wkends, hols, afternoons) 710 S Lions Park Dr. Phone 307/637-6458. **Donation.**

Cheyenne Frontier Days™ Old West Museum. Includes collections of clothing, weapons, carriages, Western art. Gift shop. (Jan 1-May 1, Tues-Sun; rest of yr, daily; closed major hols) 4501 N Carey Ave, (see ANNUAL EVENTS). Phone 307/778-7290. ¢¢

 Cheyenne Street Trolley. Two-hr historic tour of major attractions. (Mid-May-late Sept, daily) 309 W Lincolnway, Convention & Visitors Bureau. Phone 307/778-3133. ¢¢¢

Curt Gowdy State Park. The foothills of a mountain range separating Cheyenne and Laramie create the park formation. Two reservoirs provide trout fishing (no swimming); boating (ramps). Hiking. Picnicking. Camping (standard fees). 26 mi W on Happy Jack Rd (WY 210). Phone 307/632-7946.

Historic Governors' Mansion (1904). Residence of Wyoming's governors from 1905-1976; first governors' mansion in the nation to be occupied by a woman, Nellie Tayloe Ross (1925-1927). (Tues-Sat; closed hols) 300 E 21st St. Phone 307/777-7878. **Free.**

Holliday Park. One of world's largest steam locomotives, 4000-type U.P.R.R., on grounds. Canoeing. Tennis. Picnicking. lighted horseshoe pit. (May-Oct) Morrie Ave & 19th St. Phone 307/637-6429. **Free.**

State Capitol (1887). Beaux-arts building with murals in Senate and House chambers by Allen T. True. Ceiling of each chamber is of stained glass. Guided tours (Mon-Fri; closed hols). Head of Capitol Ave. **Free.**

Warren AFB. Museum traces history of base from 1867-present (Sat, Sun, also by appt). (See ANNUAL EVENTS) Tours (Thurs morning or by appt). W on Randall Ave. Phone 307/775-3381. **Free.**

Annual Events

Cheyenne Frontier Days™. Frontier Park Arena, N on Carey Ave. One of country's most famous rodeos; originated in 1897. Parades, carnivals; pancake breakfast; entertainment, square dancing nightly. Phone 307/778-7200 or 800/227-6336. Last full wk July.

Heritage Day. Warren AFB. Open house, featuring USAF *Thunderbirds* flying team. Phone 307/775-3381. Late July.

Laramie County Fair. Frontier Park. Includes livestock and farm exhibits. Early Aug.

Cheyenne Western Film Festival. Phone 307/635-4646 or 800/250-1878. Mid-Sept.

Motels

(Rates may be higher during Frontier Days)

✔★ **COMFORT INN.** 2245 Etchepare Dr. 307/638-7202; FAX 307/635-8560. 77 rms, 2 story. June-Aug: S, D $60; under 18 free. Crib free. Pet accepted. TV; cable (premium). Heated pool. Complimentary continental bkfst. Restaurant opp open 24 hrs. Ck-out noon. Ck-in 3 pm. Coin lndry. Meeting rm. Business servs avail. Cr cds: A, C, D, DS, MC, V.

D ✦ ≋ ⟩ 🐾 SC

★ **DAYS INN.** 2360 W Lincolnway. 307/778-8877; FAX 307/778-8697. 72 rms, 2 story. May-Sept: S, D $60-$65; each addl $5; suites $72; lower rates rest of yr. Crib free. TV; cable (premium), VCR avail (movies). Complimentary continental bkfst, coffee. Restaurant adj open 24 hrs. Ck-out noon. Meeting rm. Business servs avail. Whirlpool. Sauna. Cr cds: A, C, D, DS, JCB, MC, V.

D ⟩ 🐾 SC

★★ **FAIRFIELD INN BY MARRIOTT.** 1415 Stillwater. 307/637-4070. 62 rms, 3 story, 8 suites. May-Sept: S $62.95; D $69.95; each addl $6; suites $79.95; under 18 free; lower rates rest of yr. Crib free. TV; cable (premium). Indoor pool; whirlpool. Complimentary continental bkfst. Restaurant nearby. Ck-out 11 am. Business servs avail. Game rm. Refrigerator in suites. Cr cds: A, C, D, DS, MC, V.

D ≋ ⟩ 🐾 SC

★ **LA QUINTA.** 2410 W Lincolnway (US 30 Business). 307/632-7117; FAX 307/638-7807. 105 rms, 3 story. June-Aug: S $55; D $63; each addl $6; under 18 free; lower rates rest of yr. Crib free. Pet accepted. TV; cable (premium). Pool. Complimentary continental bkfst. Restaurant adj open 24 hrs. Ck-out noon. Meeting rms. In-rm modem link. Sundries. Cr cds: A, C, D, DS, MC, V.

D ✦ ≋ ⟩ 🐾 SC

✔★ **SUPER 8.** 1900 W Lincolnway, (US 30, I-80 Business). 307/635-8741. 61 rms, 3 story. No elvtr. May-Sept: S $41.98; D $46.88-$48.88; each addl $5; under 12 free; lower rates rest of yr. Crib free. TV; cable (premium), VCR avail (movies). Continental bkfst avail. Restaurant adj open 24 hrs. Ck-out 11 am. Cr cds: A, C, D, DS, JCB, MC, V.

D ⟩ 🐾 SC

Motor Hotels

★★★ **BEST WESTERN HITCHING POST INN.** Box 1769, 1700 W Lincolnway (US 30, I-80 Business), 1/2 mi E at I-25 & I-80. 307/638-3301; FAX 307/778-7194. 175 rms, 1-2 story. June-Labor Day: S $70-$80; D $80-$100; each addl $6; suites $85-$150; under 12 free; lower rates rest of yr. Crib free. Pet accepted. TV; cable (premium). 2 pools, 1 indoor; whirlpool. Playground. Restaurants 5:30 am-11 pm. Rm serv. Bar noon-2 am; entertainment. Ck-out noon. Coin lndry. Meeting rms. Business center. In-rm modem link. Bellhops. Gift shop. Free airport, RR station, bus depot transportation. Exercise equipt; weights, bicycles, sauna. Game rm. Bathrm phones, refrigerators. Private patios, balconies. Cr cds: A, C, D, DS, ER, JCB, MC, V.

D ✦ ≋ 🏃 ⟩ 🐾 SC ⚒

★★★ **HOLDING'S LITTLE AMERICA.** Box 1529 (82003), 1 1/2 mi W at jct I-25, I-80. 307/775-8400; FAX 307/775-8425; res: 800/445-6945. 188 rms, 2 story. S $62; D $69-$76; each addl $10; suites $79-$135; under 12 free. Crib free. TV; cable (premium). Pool. Restaurants open 24 hrs. Rm serv. Bar 11-2 am; entertainment Fri, Sat. Ck-out noon. Coin lndry. Meeting rms. Bellhops. Shopping arcade. Free airport, RR station, bus depot transportation. 9-hole golf, putting green. Exercise equipt; weights, tread-

mill. Many bathrm phones, refrigerators. Private patios, balconies. Spacious landscaped grounds. Cr cds: A, C, D, DS, MC, V.

D 🏃 ≋ 🏃 ⟩ 🐾 SC

Inn

★ **RAINSFORD INN.** 219 E 18th St, near Airport. 307/638-2337; FAX 307/634-4506. 7 rms, 2 with shower only, 2 share bath, 3 story. S, D $65-$95. Children over 13 yrs only. 5 cable TVs. Complimentary full bkfst. Restaurant nearby. Ck-out 11 am, ck-in 4 pm. Free airport transportation. Turn-of-the-century house; many antiques. Totally nonsmoking. Cr cds: A, D, DS, MC, V.

D 🏃 ⟩ 🐾 SC

Restaurant

★★ **POOR RICHARD'S.** 2233 E Lincolnway, (US 30, I-80 Business). 307/635-5114. Hrs: 11 am-2:30 pm, 5-10 pm; Fri, Sat to 11 pm; Sat brunch 11 am-2:30 pm; Sun 5-10 pm. Closed Dec 25. Bar to 11 pm. Semi-a la carte: lunch $3.95-$6.95, dinner $6-$22.50. Sat brunch $4.75-$7.25. Child's meals. Specializes in steak, fresh seafood. Salad bar. Patio dining. Cr cds: A, C, D, DS, MC, V.

D 🍴 ♥

Cody (B-4)

Founded 1896 **Pop** 7,897 **Elev** 5,002 ft **Area code** 307 **Zip** 82414 **E-mail** chamberc@wave.park.wy.us **Web** wave.park.wy.us/~chamberc/chamber.html

Information Cody County Chamber of Commerce, 836 Sheridan Ave, PO Box 2777; 307/587-2777 or 307/587-2297 (tourism).

Buffalo Bill Cody founded this town, gave it his name and devoted time and money to its development. He built a hotel and named it after his daughter Irma, arranged for a railroad spur from Montana and, with the help of his friend Theodore Roosevelt, had what was then the world's tallest dam constructed just west of town.

Cody is located 52 miles east of Yellowstone National Park (see); everyone entering Yellowstone from the east must pass through here, making tourism an important industry. A Ranger District office of the Shoshone National Forest is located here.

What to See and Do

★ **Buffalo Bill Historical Center.** Four-museum complex; gift shops. (May-Oct, daily; Mar-Apr, Nov, daily exc Mon) (See ANNUAL EVENTS) 720 Sheridan Ave. Phone 307/587-4771. ¢¢¢ Admission includes

Buffalo Bill Museum. Personal and historical memorabilia of the great showman and scout including guns, saddles, clothing, trophies, gifts and posters.

Cody Firearms Museum. More than 5,000 projectile arms on display. Comprehensive collection begun in 1860 by Oliver Winchester.

Whitney Gallery of Western Art. Paintings, sculpture; major collection and comprehensive display of western art by artists from the early 1800s through today.

Plains Indian Museum. Extensive displays of memorabilia and artifacts representing the people of the Plains tribes and their artistic expressions; clothing, weapons, tools and ceremonial items.

Buffalo Bill State Park. Wildlife is abundant in this area. Fishing; boating (ramps, docks). Picnicking. Primitive camping. 6 mi W on US 14, 16, 20, on Buffalo Bill Reservoir. Phone 307/587-9227. Camping ¢¢; Along the adj reservoir is

Buffalo Bill Dam and Visitor Center (1910). A 350-ft dam, originally called the Shoshone Dam. The name was changed in 1946 to honor

Buffalo Bill, who helped raise money for its construction. The Visitor Center has a natural history museum, dam over-look, gift shop. (May-Sept, daily) E end of reservoir. Phone 307/527-6076. **Free.**

Shoshone Natl Forest. This 2,466,586-acre area is one of the largest in the natl forest system. Includes magnificent approach route (Buffalo Bill Cody's Scenic Byway) to the east gate of Yellowstone Natl Park (see) along north fork of the Shoshone River. The Fitzpatrick, Popo Agie, North Absaroka, Washakie and a portion of the Absaroka-Beartooth wilderness areas all lie within its boundaries. Includes outstanding lakes, streams, big-game herds, mountains and some of the largest glaciers in the continental US. Fishing; hunting. Camping. Standard fees. W on US 14, 16, 20. Contact Forest Supervisor, PO Box 2140; 307/527-6241.

Shoshone river trips.

Red Canyon River Trips. 4 different tours, from 2-4 hrs each. (June-mid Sept, daily) 1374 Sheridan Ave. Phone 307/587-6988 or 800/293-0148. ¢¢¢¢

River Runners. Whitewater trips; 1¹/₂-hr-half-day trips. (June-Labor Day, daily) 1491 Sheridan Ave. Phone 307/527-7238 or 800/535-RAFT. ¢¢¢¢

Wyoming River Trips. 1¹/₂-hr-half-day trips. (Mid-May-late Sept, daily) 1701 Sheridan Ave, located at Holiday Inn Complex. Phone 307/587-6661 or 800/586-6661. ¢¢¢¢

Sleeping Giant Ski Area. Chairlift, T-bar; patrol, school, rentals; snack bar. Longest run ³/₄ mi; vertical drop 500 ft. (Dec-mid-Apr, Fri-Sun, hols; closed Dec 25) Cross-country trails, snowmobiling. 46 mi W on US 14, 16, 20. Phone 307/587-4044; 307/527-7669 (snow report). ¢¢¢¢

Trail Town & the Museum of the Old West. Twenty-four reconstructed buildings dating from 1879-1899 and cemetery on site of Old Cody City along the original wagon trails. Buildings include cabin used as rendezvous for Butch Cassidy and the Sundance Kid and cabin of Crow scout Curley, the only one of General Custer's troops that escaped from the Battle of Little Bighorn. Cemetery includes remains of Jeremiah "liver eating" Johnson. (Mid-May-mid-Sept, daily) 2 mi W on Yellowstone Hwy. Phone 307/587-5302. ¢¢

Wyoming Vietnam Veteran's Memorial. Black granite memorial lists names of state residents who died or are missing in action in Vietnam. Off US 16/20 W of the airport.

🗹 **Yellowstone Natl Park** (see). 52 mi W on US 14, 16, 20.

Annual Events

Cowboy Songs and Range Ballads. Buffalo Bill Historical Center. Early Apr.

Frontier Festival. Buffalo Bill Historical Center. Demonstrations of pioneer skills, cooking crafts; musical entertainment. Early June.

Plains Indian Powwow. People from tribes throughout the western plains states and Canada gather to compete. Dancing and singing; ceremonial and traditional tribal dress. Late June.

Cody Stampede. Rodeo; parade. Phone 307/587-5155. Early July.

Yellowstone Jazz Festival. Elks Club lawn. Mid-July.

Seasonal Event

Cody Nite Rodeo. Stampede Park. Phone 307/587-5155. Nightly, June-last Sat in Aug.

Motels

★ ★ **COMFORT INN.** 1601 Sheridan Ave. 307/587-5556; FAX 307/527-7757. 75 rms, 2 story. June-mid-Sept: S, D $90-$125; each addl $6; under 19 free; lower rates rest of yr. Crib free. TV; cable. Complimentary continental bkfst. Restaurant adj 6 am-10 pm. Ck-out noon. Business servs avail. Free airport transportation. Cr cds: A, C, D, DS, ER, JCB, MC, V.

D ⊠ 🐾 SC

★ ★ **DAYS INN.** 524 Yellowstone Ave. 307/527-6604; FAX 307/527-7341. 52 rms, 2 story. Mid-May-Oct: S $115; D $125-$135; suites $150; each addl $10; under 12 free; lower rates rest of yr. Crib free. TV; cable (premium). Indoor pool; whirlpool. Complimentary continental bkfst. Restaurant nearby. Ck-out 11 am. Check-in 3 pm. Coin lndry. Cr cds: A, D, DS, MC, V.

D ⊠ ≍ 🐾 SC

★ ★ **HOLIDAY INN.** 1701 Sheridan Ave, (US 14, 16, 20, WY 120), in Buffalo Bill Village. 307/587-5555; FAX 307/527-7757. 190 rms, 2 story. Mid-June-Aug: S, D $90-$125; each addl $6; under 19 free; lower rates rest of yr. Crib free. TV; cable. Pool. Restaurant 6 am-10 pm. Rm serv. Bar 4-11 pm. Ck-out noon. Meeting rms. Business servs avail. Valet serv. Sundries. Free airport transportation. Bathrm phones. Cr cds: A, C, D, DS, JCB, MC, V.

D ⊠ ≍ 🐾 SC

★ ★ **KELLY INN.** US 16 & 26th St, near Regional Airport. 307/527-5505; res: 800/635-3559. 50 rms, 2 story. June-mid-Sept: S $69; D $82; each addl $5; lower rates rest of yr. Crib free. Pet accepted. TV; cable. Complimentary coffee in lobby. Restaurant nearby. Ck-out 11 am. Business servs avail. Coin lndry. Whirlpool, sauna. Cr cds: A, D, DS, MC, V.

D 🐾 ⊠ 🐾

★ ★ **UXU RANCH.** (1710 North Fork Hwy, Wapiti 82450) 35 mi W on US 14. 307/587-2143; FAX 307/587-8307; res: 800/373-9029. 10 cabins. No A/C. No rm phones. AP: wkly: S $1,200; D $2175; each addl $975; ages 3-5 $495; under 3 free. Closed Oct-May. Supervised children's activities. Restaurant 8-9 am, 12:30-1:30 pm, 7:30-8:30 pm. Bar noon-11 pm; entertainment. Ck-out 11 am. Gift shop. Downhill ski 15 mi; x-country ski on site. Rec rm. Lawn games. Rustic former logging camp in forest setting. Cr cds: MC, V.

🐾 ⅋ ≍ ⊠ 🐾

Lodges

✔ ★ **ABSAROKA MOUNTAIN.** (1231 E Yellowstone Hwy, Wapiti 82450) 40 mi W on US 14, 16, 20, on Gunbarrel Creek in Shoshone Natl Forest; 12 mi E of Yellowstone Natl Park. 307/587-3963. 16 cabins. No A/C. AP, June-Sept: S, D $60-$84; each addl $6; lower rates May. Closed rest of yr. Crib $10. Pet accepted, some restrictions. Playground. Dining rm 7:30-9:30 am, 6-8 pm. Bar 6-10 pm. Ck-out 11 am, ck-in 2 pm. Airport transportation. Lawn games. Picnic tables. Log cabins; western decor. Cr cds: DS, MC, V.

🐾 🐾 ⅋ 🐾

★ **CODY'S RANCH RESORT.** 2604-MG Yellowstone Hwy, 26 mi W on US 14, 16, 20. 307/587-2097. 14 cabins. No A/C. Mid-June-late Aug: S, D $115; each addl $15; wkly & package rates (3-day min); lower rates May-mid-June, late Aug-Sept. Closed rest of yr. Dining rm 7:30-9 am, 6-8 pm. Bar 4-10:30 pm. Ck-out 10 am. Airport transportation. Whirlpool. River rafting. Chuck wagon cookout. Private porches. Picnic tables. On stream. Cr cds: DS, MC, V.

D 🐾 ⅋ ⊠ 🐾

★ ★ **ELEPHANT HEAD.** (1170 Yellowstone Hwy, Wapiti 82450) 41 mi W on US 14, 16, 20; 11 mi E of Yellowstone Natl Park. 307/587-3980; FAX 307/527-7922. 11 cabins. No A/C. Mid-May-mid-Oct: S $54-$64; D $54-$84; AP avail. Closed rest of yr. Pet accepted. Playground. Western movies nightly. Dining rm 7:30-9:30 am, 11:30 am-1:30 pm, 6:30-8:30 pm. Bar 5:30-10 pm. Ck-out, ck-in noon. Picnic tables, grills. On river in Shoshone Natl Forest. Trail rides avail. Cr cds: A, DS, MC, V.

🐾 🐾 ⅋ ⊠

★ **GOFF CREEK.** Box 155, 42 mi W on US 14, 16, 20; 10 mi E of Yellowstone Natl Park. 307/587-3753; res: 800/859-3985. 14 cabins. No A/C. Mid-May-mid-Oct: S $85; D $90; each addl $5; duplex cabins $100-$180; lower rates rest of yr. Crib $5. Pet accepted. TV; VCR avail. Dining rm 7-9:30 am, 5-8 pm. Bar noon-11 pm. Ck-out 11 am. Sundries.

White water rafting. Lawn games. Private patios. Picnic tables. Trail rides avail. Cr cds: MC, V.

★ **SHOSHONE.** *349 Yellowstone Hwy, 46 mi W on US 14, 16, 20; 4 mi E of Yellowstone Natl Park.* 307/587-4044; FAX 307/587-2681. 16 cabins, 3 kits. (no equipt). No A/C. No rm phones. May-Oct: S $60-$70; D $66-$86; each addl $10; kit. units $20 addl. Closed rest of yr. Crib $2. Pet accepted. Dining rm 7-9 am, noon-1:30 pm, 6-8 pm. Ck-out 10 am. Coin lndry. Sundries. Lawn games. Downhill ski opp. X-country ski. Cookouts. Fireplace, trophies in lodge. Most cabins have porches. Scenic location on Grinnell Creek. Cr cds: A, DS, MC, V.

Guest Ranches

★ **BLACKWATER CREEK RANCH.** *1516 N Fork Hwy, 37 mi W on US 14, 16, 20; 15 mi E of Yellowstone Natl Park.* 307/587-5201. 15 cabins. No A/C. AP: S $1,050/wk; D $2,100/wk; under 10 $900/wk. Pool. Dining rm 7:30-8:30 am, 12:30-1:30 pm, 6:30-7:30 pm; closed mid-Sept-June. Cookouts. Bar. Ck-out 9:30 am, ck-in after 2 pm. Free airport transportation. Whitewater rafting. Horseback riding. Guided trips to Cody and Yellowstone. Hiking. Rodeos. Rec rm. Whirlpool. Lawn games. Square dancing. Picnic tables. On Shoshone River & Blackwater Creek. Cr cds: MC, V.

★ ★ **CASTLE ROCK.** *412 County Rd 6NS, 17 mi SW via Southfork & Lower Southfork Rds.* 307/587-2076; FAX 307/527-7196; res: 800/356-9965. 9 cabins. No A/C. No rm phones. AP, June-mid-Sept, wkly: D $1,160-$1,400/person; each addl $900-$1,100. Heated pool. Supervised child's activities (June-Sept); ages 3-10. Dining rm in lodge. Box lunches, cookouts. Ck-out 10 am, ck-in 3 pm. Meeting rms. Business servs avail. Free airport transportation. Whitewater rafting. Day & pack trips. Hiking. Mountain climbing. Mountain bikes. Lawn games. Soc dir. Rec rm. Game rm. Entertainment. Fishing/hunting guides. Clean and store. Some fireplaces. On the Shoshone River in the Southfork Valley. Cr cds: A, MC, V.

★ ★ **CROSSED SABRES.** *(Box MG, Wapiti 82450) Approx 43 mi W on US 14, 16, 20.* 307/587-3750. 17 cabins. No A/C. May-Sept (1-wk min), AP: S $1,156/wk; D $1,912/wk; 7-17 yrs $856/wk; under 7 $756/wk. Closed rest of yr. Crib free. Dining rm. Ck-out 11 am, ck-in 3 pm. Coin lndry. Overnight pack trips. Float, rodeo, Yellowstone and Cody trips. Entertainment; movies, square dancing. Game rm. Fish guides (fee). Some fireplaces. Picnic tables. No cr cds accepted.

★ ★ **DOUBLE DIAMOND X.** *3453 Southfork Rd, 35 mi SW.* 307/527-6276; FAX 307/587-2708; res: 800/833-7262. 12 units, 5 cabins, 7 rms in lodge. AP, June-Sept, wkly: S, D $1,210-$1,460; children 6-14 $880-$1,020; under 6, $550; lower rates May, Sept-Oct. Closed rest of yr. Indoor pool; whirlpool. Supervised child's activities (June-Sept). Cookouts. Ck-out 11 am. Guest lndry. Meeting rms. Gift shop. Free airport transportation. Hiking. Entertainment nightly in summer. Square dancing. Fishing/hunting trips. On south fork of Shoshone River. Cr cds: MC, V.

★ ★ **HIDDEN VALLEY RANCH RESORT.** *153 Hidden Valley Rd.* 307/587-5090; FAX 307/587-5265; res: 800/894-7262. 9 cabins, shower only. June-Sept, AP: S $95-$195; D $190-$290; each addl $75; under 3 free; wkly rates; lower rates rest of yr. Crib free. Pet accepted. Heated pool; whirlpool. Box lunches, picnics. Bar; entertainment. Ck-out noon, ck-in 3 pm. Coin lndry. Bellhops. Gift shop. Meeting rms. Business servs avail. Free airport transportation. X-country ski on site. Horse stables. Hiking. Fishing/hunting guides, clean & store. Lawn games. Picnic tables. On creek. Totally nonsmoking. Cr cds: A, DS, MC, V.

★ ★ **RIMROCK DUDE RANCH.** *2728 Northfork Hwy, 27 mi W on US 14, 16, 20.* 307/587-3970; FAX 307/527-4633; res: 800/208-7468. 9 cabins, 1-2 bedrms. No A/C. AP, June-Aug, wkly: S $1,100; D $2,000. Closed rest of yr. Crib free. Dining rm. Cookouts. Free airport transportation. Pack trips. Guided trip to Yellowstone Park. Float trip on Shoshone River. Trip to Cody Rodeo. Clean & store. Rec rm. Refrigerators; some fireplaces, porches. Cr cds: MC, V.

★ ★ **SEVEN D.** *774 Sunlight Rd, 17 mi N on WY 120, E on WY 296 to Sunlight Rd, 8 mi to ranch.* 307/587-9885. 11 cabins (1-4-bedrm). No A/C. No rm phones. AP, June-mid-Sept, wkly: D $1,250/person; each addl $1,175/person; under 12, $998/person; lower rates Sept. Closed rest of yr. Supervised child's activities (June-Aug). Dining rm in lodge. Box lunches, cookouts. Ck-out 9:30 am, ck-in 3 pm. Guest lndry. Airport transportation. Horse corrals. Pack trips. Hiking. Trap shooting. Square dancing. Lawn games. Rec rm. Fishing/hunting guides. On creek in Shoshone National Forest. No cr cds accepted.

Restaurants

★ ★ ★ **FRANCA'S.** *1421 Rumsey Ave.* 307/587-5354. Hrs: 6-10 pm. Closed Mon, Tues; mid-Mar-mid-May. Res accepted. Italian menu. Wine list. Semi-a la carte: dinner $12.50-$26. Specializes in seafood, pasta, dessert. Elegant decor. Totally nonsmoking. No cr cds accepted.

✔ ★ **LA COMIDA.** *1385 Sheridan Ave.* 307/587-9556. Hrs: 11 am-10 pm. Closed Jan 1, Thanksgiving, Dec 25. Res accepted. Mexican, Amer menu. Bar. Semi-a la carte: lunch $2.75-$9.95, dinner $3.50-$15.50. Child's meals. Specializes in fajitas, tacoritos, spinach enchiladas. Own desserts. Outdoor dining. Mexican decor; wall hangings. Cr cds: A, DS, MC, V.

★ **MAXWELL'S.** *937 E Sheridan St.* 307/527-7749. Hrs: 11 am-9 pm. Closed most major hols. Res accepted. Italian, Amer menu. Serv bar. Semi-a la carte: lunch $3.75-$5.25, dinner $3.75-$17.25. Child's meals. Specializes in pasta, steaks, chicken marsala. Outdoor dining. Cr cds: DS, MC, V.

Devils Tower National Monument (A-8)

(28 mi NW of Sundance on WY 24, 7 mi N of US 14)

The nation's first national monument, Devils Tower, was set aside for the American people by President Theodore Roosevelt in 1906. Located on 1,347 acres approximately 5 miles west of the Black Hills National Forest (see SOUTH DAKOTA), this gigantic landmark rises from the prairie like a giant tree stump 867 feet high. Sixty million years ago volcanic activity pushed molten rock toward the earth's surface. As it cooled Devil's Tower was formed. Towering 1,267 feet above the prairie floor and Ponderosa pine forest, the flat-topped formation appears to change hue with the hour of the day and glows during sunsets and in moonlight.

The visitor center at the base of the tower offers information about the area, a museum and bookstore. (Apr-Oct, daily). A self-guided trail winds around the tower for nature and scenery lovers. There are picnicking and camping facilities with tables, fireplaces, water and restrooms (Apr-Oct). Contact Superintendent, PO Box 10, Devils Tower 82714; 307/467-5283. ¢-¢¢

Douglas (D-7)

(See also Casper)

Founded 1886 **Pop** 5,076 **Elev** 4,842 ft **Area code** 307 **Zip** 82633
E-mail jackalope@chalkbuttes.com **Web** www.chalkbuttes.com/jackalope
Information Douglas Area Chamber of Commerce, 121 Brownfield Rd; 307/358-2950.

Cattlemen were attracted here by plentiful water and good grass. Homesteaders gradually took over, and agriculture became dominant. The town was named for Stephen Douglas, Lincoln's celebrated debating opponent. A Ranger District office for the Medicine Bow National Forest (see LARAMIE) is located in Douglas.

What to See and Do

Ft Fetterman State Museum. Located on a plateau above the valleys of LaPrele Creek and the North Platte River. Museum in restored officers' quarters; additional exhibits in ordnance warehouse. Picnic area. (Memorial Day-Labor Day, daily) 10 mi NW on WY 93 at Ft Fetterman State Historic Site. Phone 307/358-2864 or 307/777-7695.   **Free.**

Medicine Bow Natl Forest. S of town on WY 91 or WY 94 (see LARAMIE).

Thunder Basin Natl Grassland. Approximately 572,000 acres; accessible grasslands, sagebrush and some ponderosa pine areas. Bozeman and Texas trails cross parts of the grasslands. Large herds of antelope, mule deer; sage grouse. Hunting. N on WY 59. Phone 307/358-4690.   **Free.**

Wyoming Pioneer Memorial Museum. Large collection of pioneer and Native American artifacts; guns; antiques. (June-Sept, daily; rest of yr, Mon-Fri; closed winter hols) State Fairgrounds, W end of Center St. Phone 307/358-9288.   **Free.**

Annual Events

High Plains Old Time Country Music Show & Contest. Douglas High School Auditorium. 307/358-2950. Late Apr.

Jackalope Days. Carnival, entertainment, exhibitors. Usually 3rd wkend June.

Wyoming State Fair. Includes rodeo events, horse shows, exhibits. Phone 307/358-2398. Aug 17-22.

Motel

(Rates may be higher during state fair)

✓★ **BEST WESTERN DOUGLAS INN.** *1450 Riverbend Dr.* 307/358-9790; FAX 307/358-6251. 116 rms, 2 story. S $65-$75; D $73-$85; each addl $8; under 19 free. Crib free. Pet accepted, some restrictions. TV; cable (premium). Indoor pool; whirlpool. Complimentary coffee in lobby. Restaurant 6 am-2 pm, 5-10 pm. Rm serv. Bar 4:30 pm-2 am, Sun noon-10 pm. Ck-out 11 am. Coin lndry. Meeting rms. Business servs avail. Valet serv. Sundries. Exercise equipt; weights, star machine, sauna. Game rm. Cr cds: A, C, D, DS, MC, V.

D ✔ ≊ ✗ ⤢ ⋌ SC

Dubois (C-3)

(See also Grand Teton National Park)

Founded 1886 **Pop** 895 **Elev** 6,940 ft **Area code** 307 **Zip** 82513 **Web** www.wyo.com/~duboiscc/
Information Chamber of Commerce, 616 W Ramshorn St, PO Box 632-E; 307/455-2556.

On the Wind River, 56 miles from Grand Teton National Park (see), Dubois is surrounded on three sides by the Shoshone National Forest (see CODY). The Wind River Reservation (Shoshone and Arapahoe) is a few miles east of town. Dubois, in ranching and dude ranching country, is a good vacation headquarters. There are plentiful rockhounding resources, and a large herd of Bighorn sheep roam within five miles of town. A Ranger District office of the Shoshone National Forest (see CODY) is located here.

What to See and Do

Big game hunting for elk, deer, moose, bear and mountain sheep.

Fishing for six varieties of trout in nearby streams.

National Bighorn Sheep Interpretive Center. Major exhibit, "Sheep Mt," features full-size bighorns and the plants and animals that live around them. Other exhibits promote education, research and conservation of the sheep and their habitats. (Memorial Day-Labor Day, daily; winter hrs vary) 907 Ramshorn, off US 26, 287. Phone 307/455-3429.   ¢

Wind River Historical Center. Exhibits & displays depicting natural and social history of the Wind River Valley; includes Native American, wildlife and archaeological displays; also Scandinavian tie-hack industries. (Mid-May-mid-Sept, daily; rest of yr, by appt) W on US 26, 287 at 909 W Ramshorn. Phone 307/455-2284; or 307/455-2520 (off-season).   **Free.**

Annual Events

Pack Horse Races. Phone 307/455-2926 or 307/455-2853. Memorial Day wkend.

Wind River Rendezvous. Phone 307/455-2556. 2nd wkend Aug.

Motel

(Air conditioning is rarely needed at higher altitudes)

✓★ **SUPER 8.** *1414 Warm Springs Dr.* 307/455-3694; FAX 307/455-3640. 32 rms, 2 story. July-Aug: S $40.88; D $44.88-$49.88; suite $85; each addl $5; under 12 free; higher rates July 4 wkend; lower rates rest of yr. Crib free. Pet accepted. TV; cable (premium). Whirlpool. Complimentary coffee. Ck-out 11 am. Cr cds: A, D, DS, MC, V.

D ✔ ⤢ ⋌ SC

Guest Ranches

★★ **ABSAROKA RANCH.** *Box 929, Dunoir Valley.* 307/455-2275. 4 cabins. AP (1-wk min), mid-June-mid-Sept: $975/person; family rates; lower rates early June-mid-June. Closed rest of yr. 10% serv charge. Crib free. Supervised child's activities (June-Sept). Dining rm. Cookouts. Box lunches. Ck-out 11 am, ck-in 2 pm. Horse stables. Hiking. Sauna. Lawn games. Game rm. On creek. Totally nonsmoking. No cr cds accepted.

⤢ ⧖ ⤢ ⋌

★★★ **BROOKS LAKE LODGE.** *458 Brooks Lake Rd, off US 26/287.* 307/455-2121. 6 rms in main bldg, 6 cabins (1- and 2-bedrm). July-late Sept, 3-day min: S $210; D $350-$390; each addl $155-$175; family rates; wkly rates; lower rates late Sept, Jan-Mar. Closed rest of yr. Crib free. Whirlpool. Complimentary coffee in rms; full bkfst. Restaurant 7:30-9 am, 1 pm sitting, 7:30 pm sitting. Box lunches. Picnics, cookouts. Bar 6-10 pm; entertainment. Ck-out 11 am, ck-in 3 pm. Guest lndry. Gift shop. Meeting rms. Business servs avail. Boats. X-country ski on site, rental equipt avail. Horse stables. Snowmobiles, tobogganing, dog sled rides. Hiking. Lawn games. Some refrigerators, minibars. Picnic tables. Scenic location in mountains. Cr cds: A, MC, V.

★ ★ ★ **LAZY L & B RANCH.** *1072 E Fork Rd, 10 mi E on Fork Rd, follow ranch sign 12 mi to ranch. 307/455-2839; FAX 307/455-2634; res: 800/453-9488.* 12 cabins. AP (1-wk min), Memorial Day-Sept: S $970 person; D $895/person; under 13 yrs $795. Closed rest of yr. Pet accepted. Heated pool. Supervised child's activities (May-Aug). Dining rm. Cookouts. Ck-out Sat 10 am, ck-in Sun 1 pm. Gift shop. Airport transportation. River swimming. Hiking. Hayrides. Children's petting farm. Lawn games. Rec rm. 1,800 acres on mountain range bordering Shoshone National Forest. Totally nonsmoking. No cr cds accepted.

Evanston (F-2)

(See also Green River, Kemmerer)

Settled 1869 **Pop** 10,903 **Elev** 6,748 ft **Area code** 307 **Zip** 82930
Information Chamber of Commerce, 36 10th St, PO Box 365, 82931-0365; 307/789-2757 or 800/328-9708.

Coal from the mines at Almy, six miles north of Evanston, supplied trains of the Union Pacific Railroad, which operated a roundhouse and machine shop in Evanston beginning in 1871. By 1872, the mines employed 600 men.

While cattle and sheep ranching remain important industries, the discovery of gas and oil has triggered a new "frontier" era for the town. Evanston is also a trading center and tourist stopping point.

What to See and Do

Ft Bridger State Museum. Museum in barracks of partially restored fort named for Jim Bridger, scout and explorer. Pioneer history and craft demonstrations during summer; restored original buildings. (May-Sept, daily; rest of yr, wkends; closed mid-Dec-Feb) Picnicking. (See ANNUAL EVENTS) 30 mi E on I-80, at Ft Bridger State Historic Site. Phone 307/782-3842. ¢

Annual Events

Chili Cook-off. Uinta County fairgrounds. Usually 3rd Sat June.

Uinta County Fair. Fairgrounds, US 30 E. 4-H, FFA exhibits; carnival, food. 1st full wk Aug.

Mountain Man Rendezvous. Ft Bridger State Museum (see). Black powder gun shoot, Native American dancing, exhibits, food. Labor Day wkend.

Cowboy Days. PRCA rodeo with carnival, entertainment, parade, exhibits, booths, cookouts. Labor Day wkend.

Seasonal Event

Horse Racing. Wyoming Downs. 12 mi N on WY 89. Thoroughbred and quarter horse racing. Parimutuel wagering. Wkends & hols. Phone 307/789-0511. Memorial Day-Labor Day.

Motels

★ ★ ★ **BEST WESTERN DUNMAR.** *1601 Harrison Dr, W entrance I-80 exit #3, 1¼ mi W of I-80 exit 3. 307/789-3770; FAX 307/789-3758.* 166 rms. May-Sept: S $72; D $80-$84; each addl $6; suites $85-$195; under 18 free; lower rates rest of yr. Crib $6. TV; cable. Heated pool. Restaurant 5:30 am-10 pm. Bar 10-2 am; Sun noon-10 pm. Ck-out noon. Meeting rms. Gift shop. Exercise equipt; weights, bicycle. Many

bathrm phones, refrigerators, wet bars. Cr cds: A, C, D, DS, ER, JCB, MC, V.

✔ ★ **PRAIRIE INN.** *264 Bear River Dr. 307/789-2920.* 31 rms. S $40; D $44-$48; each addl $6. Crib $2. TV; cable (premium). Complimentary continental bkfst. Restaurant nearby. Ck-out 11 am. Cr cds: A, C, D, DS, MC, V.

Fort Laramie National Historic Site (E-8)

(For accommodations see Torrington)

(20 mi NW of Torrington on US 26, then W on WY 160; 3 mi SW of town of Fort Laramie)

Fort Laramie played an important role in much of the history of the old west. It was one of the principal fur-trading forts in the Rocky Mountain region from 1834-1849 and one of the the most important army posts on the Northern plains from 1849-1890. The first stockade built here, owned at one time by Jim Bridger and his fur-trapping partners, was Fort William, located on the strategic route to the mountains later to become the Oregon, California and Mormon trails. In 1841, the decaying Fort William was replaced with an adobe-walled structure called Fort John on the Laramie River.

Mormons, on the way to Utah in 1847, stopped here, as did tens of thousands of emigrants who paused in their trek for mail, supplies and repairs. As the gold rush to California brought more people west, the Federal government saw the need for a protective army garrison here and bought the fort for $4,000 from the American Fur Company. Fort Laramie was an important way station for the Pony Express, which was replaced one year later by the transcontinental telegraph. In 1851 and 1868, two major treaties were signed at or near the fort. The completion of the Trans-Continental Railroad in 1869 and cessation of Native American hostilities by 1880 finally reduced Fort Laramie's military importance; it was abandoned in 1890. The 67 buildings were auctioned off for little more than the value of the lumber. Only 22 structures remained by the time the historical site was established. Several are in ruins, but 11 are restored and refurnished. At present, the Sutler's store, "Old Bedlam" (at various times bachelor officer's quarters and the post commander's office), surgeon's quarters and six other buildings are open. There are ranger-conducted tours and living history demonstrations (early June-mid-Aug). Self-guided tours; 20-min audiovisual orientation program. (Daily; closed Jan 1, Thanksgiving, Dec 25) Visitor center and museum located in commissary storehouse (1884). Braille guidebooks avail. Contact the Superintendent, HC 72 Box 389, Ft Laramie 82212; 307/837-2221. ¢

Gillette (B-7)

(See also Buffalo, Devils Tower National Monument)

Pop 17,635 **Elev** 4,608 ft **Area code** 307 **E-mail** gillettecvb@vcn.com
Web www.vcn.com/gillette_f.html
Information Convention & Visitors Bureau, 1810 S Douglas Hwy #A, 82718; 307/686-0040 or 800/544-6136.

What to See and Do

Keyhole State Park. Within sight of Devils Tower (see). Surrounding mountains form the western boundary of the Black Hills. Antelope, deer and wild turkeys are common to this area. Reservoir is excellent for water sports. Swimming; fishing; boating (ramps, marina). Picnicking; lodging.

Camping; tent & trailer sites (standard fees). 45 mi E via I-90, then 8 mi N on Pine Ridge Rd. Phone 307/756-3596. Per vehicle ¢

Motel

✔★ BEST WESTERN TOWER WEST LODGE. *109 N US 14/16 (82716). 307/686-2210; FAX 307/682-5105.* 190 rms, 2 story. No elvtr. S $60; D $75; each addl $5; suites $125-$150; under 12 free. Crib free. TV; cable (premium), VCR avail (movies). Indoor pool; whirlpool. Complimentary coffee in rms. Restaurant 6 am-10 pm. Rm serv to 9 pm. Bar; entertainment. Ck-out noon. Coin lndry. Meeting rm. Business servs avail. In-rm modem link. Bellhops. Valet serv. Free airport transportation. Exercise equipt; weights, bicycles, sauna. Game rm. Refrigerators avail. Cr cds: A, C, D, DS, MC, V.

≈ ✗ ⊠ ⚓ SC

Motor Hotel

★ HOLIDAY INN. *2009 S Douglas Hwy (82718). 307/686-3000; FAX 307/686-4018.* 158 rms, 3 story. July-mid-Sept: S $85; D $93; each addl $8; suites $120-$150; under 18 free; lower rates rest of yr. Crib free. Pet accepted. TV; cable (premium). Indoor pool; whirlpool. Restaurant 6 am-10 pm. Rm serv. Bar 4:30 pm-2 am; entertainment Mon-Sat. Ck-out noon. Coin lndry. Meeting rms. Business servs avail. Valet serv. Gift shop. Free airport transportation. Exercise equipt; weights, bicycles, sauna. Game rm. Rec room. Cr cds: A, C, D, DS, MC, V.

D ✔ ≈ ✗ ⊠ ⚓ SC

Restaurant

✔★ HONG KONG. *1612 W 2nd St (82716). 307/682-5829.* Hrs: 11 am-9:30 pm. Closed Dec 25. Res accepted. Chinese menu. Serv bar. Semi-a la carte: lunch $4-$5.50, dinner $5-$12.95. Specializes in Hunan beef, lemon chicken. Cr cds: A, C, DS, MC, V.

Grand Teton National Park (B-2)

(See also Dubois, Jackson, Yellowstone National Park)

(7 1/2 mi S of south border of Yellowstone National Park on US 89/191/287; 4 mi N of Jackson on US 26/89/191)

These rugged, block-faulted mountains began to rise about nine million years ago, making them some of the youngest on the continent. Geologic and glacial forces combined to buckle and sculpt the landscape into a dramatic setting of plateaus, cirques and craggy peaks that cast their reflections across numerous clear alpine lakes. The Snake River winds gracefully through Jackson Hole ("hole" being the old fur trapper's term for a high-altitude plateau surrounded by mountains).

John Colter passed through the area during 1807-1808. French-Canadian trappers in the region thought the peaks resembled breasts and applied the French word *teton* to them.

Entering from the north, from Yellowstone National Park (see), US 89/191/287 skirts the eastern shore of Jackson Lake to Colter Bay, continuing to Jackson Lake Junction, where it turns eastward to the entrance at Moran Junction (at US 26). The Teton Park Road begins at Jackson Lake Junction and borders the mountains to Jenny Lake, then continues to park headquarters at Moose. US 89/191/26 parallels Teton Park Road on the east side of the Snake River to the south entrance from Moran Junction. All highways have a continuous view of the Teton Range, which runs from north to south. US 26/89/191 are open year-round from Jackson to Flagg Ranch, 2 miles south of Yellowstone National Park's South Gate,

as is US 26/287 to Dubois. Secondary roads and Teton Park Road are open May-October.

The park is open year-round (limited in winter), with food and lodging available in the park from mid-May through September and in Jackson (see). There are three visitor centers with interpretive displays: Moose Visitor Center (daily; closed Dec 25); Colter Bay Visitor Center & Indian Arts Museum (mid-May-late Sept, daily); and Jenny Lake Visitor Center (June-Labor Day). Ranger-led hikes are available (mid-June-mid-Sept, daily; inquire for schedule), and self-guided trails are marked. A 24-hour recorded message gives information on weather; phone 307/739-3611.

The park can be explored by various means. There is hiking on more than 200 miles of trails. Corrals at Jackson Lake Lodge and Colter Bay have strings of horses accustomed to mountain trails; pack trips can be arranged. Boaters and fishermen can enjoy placid lakes or wild streams; the Colter Bay, Signal Mountain and Leek's marinas have ramps, guides, facilities and rentals. Climbers can tackle summits via routes of varying difficulty; the more ambitious may take advantage of Exum School of Mountaineering and Jackson Hole Mountain Guides classes that range from a beginner's course to an attempt at conquering the 13,770-foot Grand Teton, considered a major North American climbing peak.

Horses, boats and other equipment can be rented. Bus tours, an airport, auto rentals, general stores and guide services are available. Five National Park Service campgrounds are maintained: Colter Bay, Signal Mountain, Jenny Lake, Lizard Creek and Gros Ventre (fee). Slide-illustrated talks on the park and its features are held each night (mid-June-Labor Day) at the amphitheaters at Colter Bay, Signal Mountain and Gros Ventre.

Many river and lake trips are offered. Five-, ten- and twenty-mile trips on rubber rafts float the Snake River. Visitors can choose an adventure to suit their individual tastes (see JACKSON). A self-guided trail tells the story of Menor's Ferry (1894) and the Maude Noble Cabin. Jenny Lake has boat trips and boat rentals. Jackson Lake cruises are available, some reaching island hideaways for breakfast cookouts. Boat rentals also are available at Jackson Lake. The Grand Teton Lodge Company offers a full-day, guided combination bus and boat trip covering major points of interest in the park (early June-mid-Sept); phone 307/543-2855.

A tram with a vertical lift of 4,600 feet operates at Teton Village, rising from the valley floor to the top of Rendezvous Peak, just outside the park's southern boundary (see JACKSON).

The Chapel of the Transfiguration, located in Moose, is a log chapel with a large picture window over the altar framing the mountains. (Daily; services held late May-Sept)

The park is home to abundant wildlife, including pronghorn antelope, bighorn sheep, mule deer, elk, moose, grizzly and black bear, coyote, beavers, marmots, bald eagles and trumpeter swans. Never approach or feed any wild animal. Do not pick wildflowers.

A park boat permit is required. A Wyoming fishing license is required for any fishing and may be obtained at several locations in the park. Camping permits are required for backcountry camping.

Grand Teton and Yellowstone National parks admission is $20/car. Contact Superintendent, PO Drawer 170, Moose 83012; 307/739-3399 or 307/739-3600 (recording).

CCInc Auto Tape Tours. This 90-min cassette offers a mile-by-mile self-guided tour of the park. Written by informed guides, it provides information on history, points of interest and flora & fauna of the park. Tapes may be purchased directly from CCInc, PO Box 227, 2 Elbrook Dr, Allendale, NJ 07401; 201/236-1666 or from the Grand Teton Lodge Co, 307/543-2855. ¢¢¢

Motels

(Reservations advised for accommodations within the national park; air conditioning is rarely needed at higher altitudes)

★ ★ DORNAN'S SPUR RANCH CABINS. *(10 Moose Lane, Moose 83012) 307/733-2522; FAX 307/739-9098.* E-mail spur@sisna .com; web www.sisna.com/jackson/dornan/spur1.htm. 12 kit. cottages. No A/C. June-Oct: 1-bdrm $125-$150 (up to 4); 2-bdrm $175 (up to 6); lower rates rest of yr. Restaurant adj 7 am-9 pm. Ck-out 11 am. Totally nonsmoking. Cr cds: DS, MC, V.

✔★ **HATCHET.** *(US 26/287, Moran 83013) 7¹/₂ mi E of Moran jct.* 307/543-2413; FAX 307/543-2413. 22 cabins. No A/C. Memorial Day-Labor Day: S, D $80; each addl $5. Closed rest of yr. Pet accepted; $20 deposit. Restaurant 6:30 am-9:30 pm. Ck-out 11 am. Gift shop. Sundries. Picnic tables. Totally nonsmoking. Cr cds: DS, MC, V.

Lodges

★★ **COWBOY VILLAGE RESORT AT TOGWOTEE.** *(US 26/287, Moran 83013) 17 mi E of Moran jct.* 307/543-2847; FAX 307/543-2391; res: 800/543-2847. Web www.cowboyvillage.com. 89 units, 3 story, 54 kit. cabins. No A/C. No elvtr. Mid-Nov-mid-Apr: S $241/person; D $211/person; suites $233/person; cabins $239/person; under 13, $40; lower rates June-mid-Oct. Closed rest of yr. TV; cable (premium). Dining rm 7 am-9:30 pm. Rm serv. Bar noon-midnight. Ck-out 11 am. Coin lndry. Sundries. Gift shop. Free airport transportation in winter. X-country ski on site. Snowmobiling. Whirlpools. Rec rm. Cabins have private porches, picnic tables, grills. Cr cds: A, D, DS, MC, V.

★★ **JACKSON LAKE.** *(Moran 83013) on US 89/287 in park.* 307/543-3100; res: 800/628-9988; FAX 307/543-3143. Web www.gtlc .com. 385 rms, 3 story. Mid-May-mid-Oct: S, D $99-$175; each addl $8.50; suites $315-$460; under 12 free. Closed rest of yr. Crib free. Heated pool; lifeguard. Dining rms 6 am-10:30 pm. Box lunches. Bar 11-1 am; entertainment exc Sun. Ck-out 11 am. Convention facilities. Business servs avail. Airport transportation. Bellhops. Concierge. Shopping arcade. Nightly programs July-Aug. Evening cookout rides. Float trips. Many private patios, balconies. Lounge has 2 fireplaces, 60-ft picture window. View of Mt Moran, Grand Tetons. Cr cds: A, D, MC, V.

★★ **SIGNAL MOUNTAIN.** *(Moran 83013) 4¹/₂ mi W on Interpark Rd, 3 mi SW of jct US 89/287 in park.* 307/543-2831; FAX 307/543-2569. E-mail 102547.1642@compuserv.com. 79 cabins, 1-2 story, 30 kits. No A/C. S, D $78-$160; each addl $8; kit. units $155. Pet accepted, some restrictions. Crib free. Restaurant 7 am-10 pm in season. Bar noon-midnight. Ck-out 11 am. Meeting rms. Gift shop. Some refrigerators, fireplaces; microwaves avail. Private patios, balconies. Marina; boat rentals; guided fishing trips. Scenic float trips on Snake River. On lake; campground adj. Cr cds: A, DS, MC, V.

Inn

★★★ **THE INN AT BUFFALO.** *(18200 E US 26/287, Moran 83013) 6 mi E of Moran entrance to Grand Teton Natl Park.* 307/543-2010; FAX 307/543-0935. E-mail innatbuff@blissnet.com. 5 rms, 2 with shower only. No A/C. No rm phones. June-mid-Oct: S $125-$165; D $135-$185; each addl $20; under 5 free; lower rates rest of yr. TV in common rm; VCR avail (free movies). Complimentary full bkfst. Ck-out 11 am, ck-in 4 pm. X-country ski 11 mi. Whirlpool. Country inn with scenic views. Totally nonsmoking. Cr cds: A, MC, V.

Guest Ranches

★★★ **GROS VENTRE RIVER.** *(Moose 83012) 8 mi S to Gros Ventre Jct then 7 mi E on Gros Ventre Rd.* 307/733-4138; FAX 307/733-4272. Web www.ranchweb.com/grosventre. 8 cabins, 4 kits. No A/C. No rm phones. AP, mid-June-mid-Sept, wkly: S $1,956-$2,220; D $1,122-$1,518; each addl $975; lower rates rest of yr. Crib free. TV, VCR in rec rm. Playground. Dining rm in lodge. Box lunches, cookouts. Ck-out 10 am, ck-in 3 pm. Meeting rms. Free airport transportation. Swimming in pond.

Canoes. Hiking. Mountain bikes. Lawn games. Rec rm. Some fireplaces. Scenic float trips on Snake River. Along the Gros Ventre River, ranch is completely surrounded by national park & forest lands. On 160 acres. No cr cds accepted.

★★★★ **JENNY LAKE LODGE.** *(Jenny Lake Rd, Moran 83013) 14 mi SW of Moran, in park.* 307/733-4647; FAX 307/543-0324. Restored 100-year-old homesteader cabins moved from all around the area to the base of the Grand Teton range accommodate guests at the property. Homemade quilts and down comforters are representative touches. 37 cabins. No A/C. No rm phones. MAP, late May-early Oct: S, D $278-$357; each addl $115; suite cabins $480-$490. Closed rest of yr. Crib free. Restaurant (see JENNY LAKE LODGE DINING ROOM). Serv bar. Ck-out 11 am, ck-in 4 pm. Bellhops. Gift shop. Airport transportation. Bicycles; trail rides. Golf, tennis & swimming privileges nearby. Some refrigerators. Wood stove in suites, lounge. Private patios. Cr cds: A, D, MC, V.

★★★★ **LOST CREEK RANCH.** *(Moose 83012) Approx 8 mi N of Moose on US 26, 89, 187, 189, then 2 mi E on gravel rd.* 307/733-3435; FAX 307/733-1954. E-mail ranch@lostcreek.com. Tiled and carpeted cabins, some with wood-burning fireplaces, nestle on 110 acres thick with pine and aspen. Animal heads and original artwork in the lodge vie with views of the Grand Teton Mountains for guests' attention. 10 cabins, 7 with kit. No A/C. AP, June-Sept, wkly rates: 1-4 persons $4,298-$9,620; each addl $860; under 6 free. Closed rest of yr. Crib free. Heated pool; whirlpool. Supervised child's activities (June-Aug). Coffee in cabins. Dining rm sittings: bkfst 7:30-8:30 am, lunch 12:30 pm, dinner 7 pm (children's dinner at 6 pm if desired). Ck-out 10 am, ck-in 3 pm. Free lndry serv. Meeting rms. Business servs avail. Airport transportation. Tennis. Hayrides. Extensive exercise rm; instructor, weight machines, rowers, sauna, steam rm. Massage. Lawn games. Entertainment (evenings). Game rm. Scenic float trips. Riding instruction avail. Wkly trips to rodeo. Yellowstone Natl Park tour. Hiking in Grand Teton Natl Park. Refrigerators, fireplaces. Private porches. Picnic tables, grills. No cr cds accepted.

★★★ **MOOSE HEAD RANCH.** *(Moose 83012) 13 mi N of Moose, on US 26, 89, 187.* 307/733-3141; res: 904/877-1431 (off season); FAX 307/739-9097. 14 cabins, 1-2 bedrm. No A/C. No rm phones. AP (includes riding), mid-June-Aug (5-day min): S $300; D $420; under 6, $100; 2-bedrm house (up to 6 people) $1,150-$1,600. Closed rest of yr. Crib free. Complimentary coffee in cabins. Dining rm 8-9 am, 12:30-1:30 pm, 7-8 pm. Grocery, package store 13 mi. Meeting rm. Free airport transportation. Horseback riding instruction, trips; hiking trails. Rec rm. Lawn games. Refrigerators. Some fireplaces in cabins. Private porches. Library. On 120 acres; series of man-made trout ponds. No cr cds accepted.

Cottage Colonies

★ **COLTER BAY CABINS.** *(83013). 10 mi N of Moran Jct.* 307/543-3100; res: 800/628-9988; FAX 307/543-3046. 208 cabins, 192 with shower only, 9 share bath. No A/C. No rm phones. S $32-$85; D $32-$110; each addl $8; under 12 free. Closed mid-Oct-mid-May. Crib free. Pet accepted, some restrictions. Restaurant 6:30 am-10 pm. Ck-out 11 am, ck-in 4 pm. Airport transportation. Boat rentals, lake cruises. On Jackson Lake. Cr cds: A, D, MC, V.

★★ **FLAGG RANCH.** *(US 89, Moran 83013) 5 mi N.* 307/543-2861; res: 800/443-2311; FAX 307/543-2484. E-mail info@flaggranch .com; web www.flaggranch.com. 92 2-4-rm cabins. No A/C. Late June-Aug: S, D $89-$125; each addl $4; under 18 free; lower rates rest of yr. Crib free. Complimentary coffee in rms. Restaurant 6:30 am-9 pm. Bar 4-11 pm. Ck-out 11 am, ck-in 4 pm. Meeting rms. Business servs avail.

Bellhops. Concierge. Gift shop. Grocery store. Airport transportation. On river. Cr cds: MC, V.

Restaurant

★ ★ ★ **JENNY LAKE LODGE DINING ROOM.** *(See Jenny Lake Lodge Guest Ranch)* 307/733-4647. Hrs: 7:30-9 am, noon-1:30 pm, 6-8:45 pm. Closed Oct-May. Res required dinner. No A/C. Serv bar. Wine list. Complete meals: bkfst $12.50, lunch $7-$9, dinner $38.50. Buffet: dinner (Sun) $38.50. Child's meals. Specialties: range-fed buffalo, fresh Pacific salmon, Rocky Mt trout. Classical guitarist Mon, Fri. Dining in restored cabin. Totally nonsmoking. Cr cds: A, D, MC, V.

D

Unrated Dining Spot

MOOSE CHUCK WAGON. *(PO Box 39, Moose 83012)* Opp (across bridge) Park Service headquarters visitors center. 307/733-2415. Hrs: 7-11 am, noon-3 pm, 5-8 pm. No A/C. Closed Sept-May. A la carte entrees: bkfst $2.50-$4.75, lunch $3.35-$6.75. Buffet: dinner $10. Specializes in beef & barbecue cooked over wood fires. Outdoor dining; inside giant teepees when raining. View of Tetons, Snake River. Family-owned. Cr cds: MC, V.

Green River (E-3)

(See also Evanston, Kemmerer, Rock Springs)

Settled 1862 **Pop** 12,711 **Elev** 6,109 ft **Area code** 307 **Zip** 82935
Information Chamber of Commerce, 1450 Uinta Dr; 307/875-5711 or 800/FLGORGE.

Green River, seat of Sweetwater County, is known as the trona (sodium sesquicarbonate) capital of the world. As early as 1852, Jim Bridger guided Captain Howard Stansbury on a Native American trail through the area. By 1862, a settlement here consisted mainly of the overland stage station, located on the east bank of the Green River. In 1868, Major John Wesley Powell, started from here on his expedition of the Green and Colorado rivers. This point of departure is now known as Expedition Island. The Green River, one of Wyoming's largest, is the northern gateway to the Flaming Gorge National Recreation Area.

What to See and Do

Flaming Gorge Natl Recreation Area. This area, administered by the US Forest Service, surrounds Flaming Gorge Reservoir in Wyoming (see ROCK SPRINGS) & Utah. Firehole campground and Upper Marsh Creek boat ramp are on the east shore of the reservoir; two other sites (Buckboard Crossing and Squaw Hollow) are on the west shore. Lucerne, Buckboard Crossing, Firehole and Antelope Flats have camping and boat-launching ramps. Upper Marsh Creek and Squaw Hollow are boat ramp sites only. (Check road conditions locally before traveling during winter or wet periods.) There is usually ice fishing Jan-Mar. The Flaming Gorge Dam, administered by the US Bureau of Reclamation, the HQ, three visitor centers and several other recreation sites are located along the south half of the loop in Utah. Campground fees; res required for group sites. S on WY 530 or US 191. For information contact District Ranger, Box 278, Manila, UT 84046; 801/784-3445. Camping ¢¢¢

Sweetwater County Historical Museum. Historical exhibits on southwestern Wyoming; Native Amertican, Chinese and pioneer artifacts; photographic collection. (July-Aug, daily exc Sun; rest of yr, Mon-Fri; closed hols) Courthouse, 80 W Flaming Gorge Way. Phone 307/872-6435. **Free.**

Motor Hotel

★ ★ **LITTLE AMERICA.** *I-80 at exit 68 (82929). 307/875-2400; FAX 307/872-2666; res: 800/634-2401.* 140 rms, 18 with shower only, 2 story. May-Sept: S $59; D $66-$72; each addl $6; suites $78; under 12 free; lower rates rest of yr. Crib free. TV; cable (premium). Heated pool. Playground. Restaurant open 24 hrs. Bar noon-1 am. Ck-out noon. Meeting rms. Business center. Sundries. Shopping arcade. Coin Indry. Exercise equipt; bicycle, treadmill. Some refrigerators. Some balconies. Cr cds: A, C, D, DS, MC, V.

Greybull (B-5)

(See Lovell)

Pop 1,789 **Elev** 3,788 ft **Area code** 307 **Zip** 82426
Information Chamber of Commerce, 333 Greybull Ave; 307/765-2100.

Just north of town are the rich geological sites Sheep Mountain and Devil's Kitchen. Sheep Mountain looks like a natural fortress surrounded by flatland when seen from the Big Horn Mountains. A Ranger District office of the Bighorn National Forest (see SHERIDAN) is located here.

What to See and Do

Greybull Museum. History and fossil displays; Native American artifacts. (June-Labor Day, daily exc Sun; Apr-May & Sept-Oct, Mon-Fri afternoons; rest of yr, Mon, Wed & Fri afternoons; closed Jan 1, Thanksgiving, Dec 25) 325 Greybull Ave. Phone 307/765-2444. **Free.**

Annual Event

Days of '49 Celebration. Parades, rodeo, running races, demolition derby. Concert, dances. 2nd wkend June.

Jackson (C-2)

(See also Alpine, Grand Teton National Park, Pinedale)

Pop 4,472 **Elev** 6,234 ft **Area code** 307 **Zip** 83001
Information Jackson Hole Area Chamber of Commerce, 555 E Broadway, PO Box E; 307/733-3316.

Jackson, uninhibitedly western, is the key town for the mountain-rimmed, 600-square-mile valley of Jackson Hole, which is surrounded by mountain scenery, dude ranches, national parks, big game and other vacation attractions. Jackson Hole is one of the most famous ski resort areas in the country, known for its spectacular views and its abundant ski slopes. It has three Alpine ski areas, five Nordic ski areas and miles of groomed snow-mobile trails. Annual snowfall usually exceeds 38 feet, and winter temperatures average around 21°F. The Jackson Hole area, which includes Grand Teton National Park, the town of Jackson and much of the Bridger-Teton National Forest, has all the facilities and luxuries necessary to accommodate both the winter and summer visitor. Jackson Hole offers winter sports, boating, chuck wagon dinner shows, live theater productions, symphony concerts, art galleries, rodeos, horseback riding, mountain climbing, fishing and several whitewater and scenic float trips. Two Ranger District offices of the Bridger-Teton National Forest are located in Jackson.

What to See and Do

Astoria Hot Springs. Swimming in a continuous flow of hot mineral water from two to nine ft deep (mid-May-mid-Sept, daily). Fishing. Hiking. Playground; basketball. Camping (res advised). Float trips (by appt). 17 mi S of

Jackson, 3 1/2 mi from Hoback Junction. Phone 307/733-2659. Swimming ¢¢; Camping ¢¢¢¢¢

Bridger-Teton Natl Forest. With more than 3.3 million acres, the forest literally surrounds the town of Jackson. Bridger-Teton was the site of one of the largest earth slides in US history, the Gros Ventre Slide (1925), which dammed the Gros Ventre River (to a height of 225 ft high and a width of nearly 1/2 mi), forming Slide Lake, which is approximately three mi long. There are scenic drives along the Hoback River Canyon, the Snake River Canyon and in Star Valley. Unspoiled backcountry includes parts of Gros Ventre, Teton and Wind River ranges along the Continental Divide and the Wyoming Range. Teton Wilderness (557,311 acres) and Gros Wilderness (247,000 acres) are accessible on foot or horseback. Swimming; fishing; rafting. Hiking, mountain biking. Winter sports areas. Camping (fee). Also in the forest is Bridger Wilderness (see PINEDALE). Fishing, big game hunting; boating. For further information contact Forest Supervisor, 340 N Cache, PO Box 1888; 307/739-5500.

★ **Grand Teton Natl Park** (see).

Gray Line bus tours. For information on tours in Jackson, Grand Teton and Yellowstone Natl Parks contact PO Box 411; 307/733-4325 or 800/443-6133.

Jackson Hole Museum. Regional museum of early West, local history and archeology. (Late May-Sept, daily) 105 N Glenwood. Phone 307/733-2414 or 307/733-9605. ¢¢

Natl Elk Refuge. This 25,000-acre refuge is the winter home of thousands of elk and many waterfowl. Visitor center with slide show, exhibits & horse-drawn sleigh rides (Mid-Dec-Mar, daily). 2 miles N of town. Phone 307/733-9212. Sleigh rides ¢¢¢

Natl Wildlife Art Museum. Art museum with large collection of North American wildlife paintings and sculpture; traveling exhibits, special programs. Overlooks Natl Elk Refuge. (Daily) Rungus Rd, N of town. Phone 307/733-5771. Call ahead for admission fees.

River excursions.

Barker-Ewing Float Trips. 10-mi scenic trips on the Snake River, within Grand Teton Natl Park; meals avail. Res necessary. Phone 307/733-1800 or 800/365-1800. ¢¢¢¢¢

Natl Park Float Trips. 10-mi scenic excursions in Grand Teton Natl Park. (May-Sept) Bus service from Jackson and Moose Village, 12 mi N. Phone 307/733-6445. ¢¢¢¢¢

Lewis and Clark Expeditions. Scenic 3 1/2- and 6-hr whitewater float trips through Grand Canyon of Snake River. (June-mid-Sept, daily) 145 W Gill St. Phone 307/733-4022 or 800/824-5375. Also raft & canoe rentals. ¢¢¢¢¢

Mad River Boat Trips, Inc. Three-hr whitewater Snake River Canyon trips (daily). Also combination scenic/whitewater trips, lunch/dinner trips. Res suggested. Phone 307/733-6203 or 800/458-RAFT. ¢¢¢¢¢

Triangle X Float Trips. Trips include 5- and 10-mi floats; sunrise and evening wildlife floats; also cookout supper floats. Most trips originate at Triangle X Ranch. Booking offices are also located on the southwest corner of Jackson Square. (Early June-late Sept) On the Snake River in Grand Teton Natl Park. Phone 307/733-5500. ¢¢¢¢¢

Solitude Float Trips. 5- and 10-mile scenic trips within Gand Teton Natl Park. Res suggested. Phone 307/733-2871.

Skiing.

Snow King Ski Resort. 3 double chairlifts, surface tow; school, rental/repair shop; snack bar, resort facilities. Vertical drop 1,571 ft. (Dec-Apr, daily) 6 blks S of Town Square. Phone 307/733-5200. ¢¢¢¢¢

Jackson Hole Ski Resort. 2 1/2-mi aerial tramway, 3 quad, triple, 3 double chairlifts, 2 surface tows; patrol, school, rentals; bar, restaurants, cafeterias; daycare; lodging. Longest run 4 1/2 mi; vertical drop 4,139 ft. (Dec-mid-Apr, daily) Cross-country trails. Also summer swimming, tennis, horseback riding, hiking. 12 mi NW at Teton Village. Phone 307/733-2292; 307/733-2291 (snow report). ¢¢¢¢¢ Also here is

Aerial Tramway. Makes 2 1/2-mi ride to top of Rendezvous Mt for spectacular views. Free guided nature hike. (Late May-early Oct) For schedule phone 307/733-2291. ¢¢¢¢

Teton Country Prairie Schooner Holiday. Four-day guided covered wagon trip between Yellowstone and Grand Teton national parks (see). Activities include hiking, horseback riding, swimming and canoeing. Meals, tents & sleeping bags included. (Mid-June-late Aug) Phone 307/733-5386 or 800/772-5386. ¢¢¢¢¢ Also avail is

Covered Wagon Cookout & Wild West Show. Ride covered wagons to outdoor dining area; eating area covered in case of rain. Western entertainment. Departs from Bar-T-Five Corral (late May-mid-Sept, daily). For res phone 307/733-5386. ¢¢¢¢¢

Teton County Historical Center. Fur trade exhibit. Research library. (Daily) 105 Mercill Ave. Phone 307/733-9605. **Free.**

Teton Mt Bike Tours. Guided mountain bike tours for all ability levels. Mountain bike, helmet, transportation and local guides. Day, multi-day and customized group tours avail. Phone 800/733-0788. ¢¢¢¢¢

Wagons West. Covered wagon treks through the foothills of the Tetons. Gentle riding horses, chuckwagon meals, campfire entertainment. Special guided horseback treks and hiking trips into surrounding mountains. Two-, four- and six-day furnished trips. (June-Labor Day, daily exc Sun) Res necessary. Depart from motels in Jackson. Phone 307/886-9693 or 800/447-4711. ¢¢¢¢¢

Seasonal Events

Jackson Hole Rodeo. Snow King Ave. Phone 307/733-2805. Sat, Memorial Day-Aug 31.

The Shootout. Town Square. Real-life Western melodrama. Nightly exc Sun, Memorial Day wknd-Labor Day.

Grand Teton Music Festival. 12 mi NW in Teton Village. Symphony and chamber music concerts. Virtuoso orchestra of top professional musicians from around the world. Many different programs of chamber music and orchestral concerts. Box office, phone 307/733-1128 or 800/959-4863. Early July-late Aug.

Jackson Hole Fall Arts Festival. Three-wk celebration of the arts featuring special exhibits in more than 30 galleries, demonstrations, special activities. Also dance, theater, mountain film festival, Native American arts & culinary arts. Phone 307/733-3316. Mid-Sept-early Oct.

Motels

(Reservations advised June-Aug)

✔★ **4 WINDS.** *150 N Millward St. 307/733-2474; res: 800/228-6461.* 21 rms, 1-2 story. June-Labor Day: S, D $72-$89; each addl $5; lower rates mid-late May, after Labor Day-mid-Oct. Closed rest of yr. Crib $2. TV; cable (premium). Complimentary coffee in lobby. Restaurant adj 7 am-10 pm. Ck-out 10 am. Picnic tables, grill. City park, playground adj. Cr cds: A, DS, MC, V.

★★ **BEST WESTERN LODGE AT JACKSON HOLE.** *80 Scott Lane. 307/739-9703; FAX 307/739-9168.* E-mail 103034.256@compuserve.com. 154 rms, 3 story. Mid-June-mid-Sept: S, D $189; each addl $10; under 12 free; ski plan; lower rates rest of yr. Crib free. TV; cable, VCR (movies). Indoor/outdoor pool; whirlpools. Complimentary continental bkfst. Complimentary coffee in rms. Restaurant nearby. Ck-out 11 am. Coin lndry. Meeting rms. Business servs avail. In-rm modem link. Bellhops. Gift shop. Valet serv. Downhill/x-country ski 12 mi. Sauna. Health club privileges. Refrigerators, microwaves, minibars. Cr cds: A, C, D, DS, JCB, MC, V.

★★ **BUCKRAIL LODGE.** *110 E Karns Ave. 307/733-2079; FAX 307/734-1663.* 12 rms. No A/C. No rm phones. Mid-June-mid-Sept: S, D $85-$95; each addl $5; lower rates Apr-mid-June & mid-Sept-mid-Oct. Closed rest of yr. Crib $5. TV; cable (premium). Restaurant nearby. Ck-out 11 am. Whirlpool. Picnic table, grill. Totally nonsmoking. Cr cds: A, DS, MC, V.

★ ★ **DAYS INN.** *350 S Hwy 89. 307/733-0033; FAX 307/733-0044.* 90 rms, 3 story. June-Labor Day: S, D $99-$149; each addl $10; suites $154-$209; under 12 free; lower rates rest of yr. Crib free. TV; cable (premium), VCR avail (movies). Complimentary continental bkfst. Coffee in rms. Restaurant adj. Ck-out 11 am. Sauna. Whirlpool. Some in-rm whirlpools, refrigerators, fireplaces; microwaves avail. Cr cds: A, C, D, DS, MC, V.

D ⚡ 🏊 SC

★ ★ **FLAT CREEK.** *1935 N US 89. 307/733-5276; FAX 307/733-0374; res: 800/438-9338.* 72 rms, 2 story, 12 kit. units. July-Aug: S $85; D $95; kit. units $115; lower rates rest of yr. Crib $5. TV; cable. Ck-out 11 am. Coin lndry. Exercise equipt; bicycle, rower. Sauna. Whirlpool. Refrigerators, microwaves. Cr cds: A, D, DS, MC, V.

D 🍴 🏊 ⚡

★ ★ **FRIENDSHIP INN-49ER.** *330 W Pearl St. 307/733-7550; FAX 307/733-2002; res: 800/451-2980.* 148 rms, 1-2 story. June-Sept: S $102; D $106; each addl $4; suites $130-$170; lower rates rest of yr. Crib free. Pet accepted, some restrictions. TV; cable (premium). Complimentary continental bkfst. Restaurant nearby 6 am-10 pm. Ck-out 11 am. Meeting rm. Downhill/x-country ski 12 mi. Exercise equipt; weight machines, treadmill. Health club privileges. Whirlpool. Some in-rm whirlpools, refrigerators, microwaves, fireplaces. Cr cds: A, C, D, DS, JCB, MC, V.

D 🐾 ⚡ 🍴 🏊 ⚡

★ **FRIENDSHIP INN-ANTLER.** *43 W Pearl St. 307/733-2535; FAX 307/733-4158; res: 800/522-2406.* 104 rms, 1-2 story, 2 suites. June-mid-Sept: S $76-$92; D $82-$96; each addl $5; suites $120; family rm (up to 6 persons) $112; lower rates rest of yr. Crib free. Pet accepted, some restrictions. TV; cable (premium). Restaurant opp 7 am-10 pm. Ck-out 11 am. Meeting rm. Downhill/x-country ski 12 mi. Exercise equipt; treadmill, stair machine. Whirlpool. Some fireplaces, in-rm whirlpools; microwaves avail. Cr cds: A, C, D, DS, MC, V.

D 🐾 ⚡ 🏊 ⚡

★ ★ **HITCHING POST LODGE.** *460 E Broadway, 4 blks E of town square. 307/733-2606; FAX 307/733-8221; res: 800/821-8351.* E-mail hitching-post@wyoming.com. 33 rms in cabins, 16 kit. units. No A/C. Mid-June-mid-Sept: S $78 D $88-$92; kit. units $149-$179; each addl $5; lower rates rest of yr. Crib free. TV; cable (premium). Pool. Complimentary continental bkfst. Restaurant nearby. Ck-out 11 am. Coin lndry. Whirlpool. Refrigerators, microwaves. Picnic tables. Cr cds: DS, MC, V.

🏊 ⚡

★ ★ **TRAPPER INN.** *235 N Cache. 307/733-2648; FAX 307/739-9351; res: 800/341-8000.* 54 rms, 2 story. June-mid-Sept: S, D $88-$115; each addl $6; under 12 free; higher rates special events; lower rates rest of yr. Crib free. TV; cable (premium). Complimentary coffee. Restaurant nearby. Ck-out 11 am. Coin lndry. Meeting rm. Whirlpools. Many refrigerators, microwaves. Cr cds: A, C, D, DS, JCB, MC, V.

D 🏊 ⚡

★ ★ **WYOMING INN.** *930 W Broadway. 307/734-0035; FAX 307/734-0037; res: 800/844-0035.* 73 rms, 3 story, 4 kit. units. July-Aug: S, D $179-$219; each addl $10; kit. units $199; under 13 free; lower rates rest of yr. Pet accepted. TV; cable. Complimentary continental bkfst. Coffee in rms. Restaurant nearby. Ck-out 11 am. Free guest lndry. Meeting rm. Business servs avail. Free airport transportation. Some refrigerators, fireplaces, whirlpools. Totally nonsmoking. Cr cds: A, DS, MC, V.

D 🐾 🏊 ⚡ SC

Lodges

★ ★ ★ **ALPENHOF.** *(3255 W McCollister Dr, Teton Village 83025) 12 mi NW on Teton Village Rd. 307/733-3242; FAX 307/739-1516; res: 800/732-3244 (exc WY).* E-mail alpenhof@sisna.com; web www.jacksonhole.com/alpenhof. 43 rms, 3 story. No A/C. Mid-June-Aug: D $99-$191; each addl $10; suites $235-$375; varied rates winter season. Closed mid-Oct-Nov & Apr-mid-May. Crib $10. TV; cable (premium). Heated pool; whirlpool. Restaurant (see ALPENHOF). Rm serv. Bar. Ck-out 11 am,

ck-in 3 pm. Coin lndry. Bellhops. Downhill/x-country ski on site. Sauna. Massage. Game rm. Some private balconies. Sun deck. Fireplace in lounge. Cr cds: A, C, D, DS, MC, V.

🐾 🏊 ⚡

★ ★ ★ **RUSTY PARROT.** *175 N Jackson. 307/733-2000; res: 800/458-2004; FAX 307/733-5566.* Three blocks northwest of the town square, this log-and-riverstone getaway offers easy access to shops and restaurants. Antiques and a roaring fireplace set a romantic tone. 32 rms, 3 story. No elvtr. S, D $200-$250; each addl $30; suite $450; ski plans. Crib free. TV; cable (premium), VCR avail. Complimentary full bkfst. Afternoon tea. Rm serv. Ck-out 11 am, ck-in 4 pm. Bellhops. Valet serv. Concierge. Downhill ski 12 mi; x-country ski 15 mi. Whirlpool. Spa. Balconies. Fireplace in 13 rms. Library/sitting rm. Totally nonsmoking. Cr cds: A, C, D, DS, MC, V.

D 🐾 🏊 ⚡

Motor Hotels

★ ★ ★ **BEST WESTERN INN AT JACKSON HOLE.** *(Box 328, Teton Village 83025) 12 mi NW on Teton Village Rd. 307/733-2311; FAX 307/733-0844.* E-mail 103034.256@compuserve.com. 83 rms, 4 A/C, 4 story, 11 suites, 30 kit. units. S, D $149; each addl $10; suites, kit. units $179-$230; under 15 free. Crib free. TV; cable. Heated pool; whirlpools, poolside serv. Restaurant 7 am-11 pm. Rm serv. Bar 11:30-1:30 am. Ck-out noon. Coin lndry. Meeting rms. Bellhops. Valet serv. Downhill ski ¼ mi; x-country ski on site. Sauna. Massage. Some fireplaces; microwaves avail. Balconies. Cr cds: A, C, D, DS, ER, JCB, MC, V.

D 🐾 🏊 🏊 ⚡ SC

★ ★ **SNOW KING RESORT.** *400 E Snow King Ave. 307/733-5200; FAX 307/733-4086; res: 800/522-5464.* 204 rms, 7 story. Late May-late Sept: S $170; D $180; each addl $10; suites $200-$420; under 14 free; ski plan; lower rates rest of yr. Crib free. Pet accepted, some restrictions. TV; cable. Heated pool; whirlpools, poolside serv. Restaurants 6:30 am-10 pm. Rm serv. Bar noon-2 am. Ck-out noon. Coin lndry. Meeting rms. Business servs avail. Bellhops. Valet serv. Concierge. Sundries. Gift shop. Barber, beauty shop. Free airport transportation; free shuttle to Jackson Hole ski area. Alpine Slide. Exercise equipt; treadmill, stair machine, sauna. Massage. Downhill ski adj; x-country ski 5 mi. Game rm. Located at foot of Snow King Mountain. Cr cds: A, C, D, DS, MC, V.

D 🐾 🏂 🏊 🍴 🏊 ⚡ SC

★ ★ ★ **SPRING CREEK RESORT HOTEL & CONFERENCE CENTER.** *1800 Spirit Dance Rd, 3 mi NW on WY 22, then 3½ mi on Spring Gulch Rd. 307/733-8833; FAX 307/733-1524; res: 800/443-6139 (exc WY).* E-mail info@springcreekresort.com; web www.springcreekresort.com. 117 rms, some kits. S, D $250; each addl $15; studio rms $275; condo units $450-$950; under 12 free; package plans. TV; cable (premium), VCR avail (movies). Heated pool; whirlpool. Complimentary coffee in rms. Restaurant 7:30 am-10 pm. Rm serv 7:30-10 am, noon-2 pm, 6-10 pm. Bar. Ck-out 11 am. Meeting rms. Business center. Bellhops. Valet serv. Concierge. Sundries. Gift shop. Airport transportation. Tennis. Downhill ski 12 mi; x-country ski. Lawn games. Refrigerators, fireplaces; some in-rm steam baths; microwaves avail. Private decks, balconies with view of Tetons. Picnic tables. Cr cds: A, D, DS, MC, V.

🏂 ⚡ 🏊 🏊 ⚡ SC ⚡

★ ★ ★ **WORT HOTEL.** *50 N Glenwood. 307/733-2190; FAX 307/733-2067; res: 800/322-2727.* 60 units, 2 story. Mid-June-mid-Sept: S, D $179; each addl $15; suites $225-$425; under 12 free; varied lower rates rest of yr. TV; cable (premium). Restaurant 6:30 am-10 pm. Rm serv. Bar 11-2 am. Ck-out 11 am. Meeting rms. Business servs avail. Bellhops. Valet serv. Downhill/x-country ski 15 mi. Exercise equipt; rower, bicycle. Whirlpools. Renovated 1940s hotel. Old West decor. Cr cds: A, C, D, DS, MC, V.

D 🏊 🍴 🏊 ⚡ SC

Inns

★ ★ ★ **DAVY JACKSON.** *85 Perry Ave. 307/739-2294; FAX 307/733-9704; res: 800/584-0532.* E-mail davyjackson@wyoming.com; web www.davyjackson.com. 12 rms, 3 story. June-Sept: S, D $185-$215; each addl $15; under 12 free; lower rates rest of yr. Crib free. TV; cable. Complimentary full bkfst; afternoon refreshments. Restaurant nearby. Ck-out noon, ck-in 3 pm. Airport transportation. Whirlpool. Some in-rm whirlpools, fireplaces. Victorian decor; many antiques. Cr cds: A, DS, MC, V.

★ ★ ★ **HUFF HOUSE INN.** *240 E Deloney, 2 blks E of town square. 307/733-4164; FAX 307/739-9091.* E-mail huffhousebnb@blissnet.com; web www.JacksonHoleNet.com/B&Bs/. 9 rms, 2 with shower only, some A/C, 2 story. Feb-Mar, June-Sept: S, D $125-$190 (2-day min); each addl $20; under 10 free; lower rates rest of yr. TV; cable, VCR avail (movies). Complimentary full bkfst. Restaurant nearby. Ck-out 11 am, ck-in 3 pm. Luggage handling. Downhill/x-country ski 1 mi. Game rm. Some in-rm whirlpools. Victorian house built in 1917. Totally nonsmoking. Cr cds: DS, MC, V.

★ ★ ★ **NOWLIN CREEK INN.** *660 E Broadway. 307/733-0882.* E-mail nowlin@sisna.com; web www.jacksonwy.com/bed&brk/bed&brk.html. 5 rms, 2 story. June-Sept: S $150/ D $160; each addl $20; under 12 free; lower rates rest of yr. Complimentary full bkfst. Restaurant nearby. Ck-out 11 am, ck-in 4 pm. Luggage handling. Whirlpool. Western ranch furnished with antiques. Totally nonsmoking. Cr cds: A, DS, MC, V.

★ ★ ★ **WILDFLOWER.** *3725 Teton Village Rd. 307/733-4710; FAX 307/739-0914.* 5 rms, 2 story. No A/C. No rm phones. S, D $140-$230; each addl $25; under 12 free. TV; cable (premium). Complimentary full bkfst. Restaurant nearby. Ck-out 11 am, ck-in 3-5 pm. Concierge serv. Downhill ski 4 mi. Whirlpool. Log house on 3 acres; pond; mountain views. Totally nonsmoking. Cr cds: MC, V.

Resorts

★ ★ **JACKSON HOLE RACQUET CLUB.** *3535 N. Moose-Wilson Rd, 9 mi W on Teton Village Rd. 307/733-3990; FAX 307/733-5551; res: 800/443-8616.* E-mail jhcondos@wyoming.com; web www.av@alpinevacation.com. 130 condo units. No A/C. June-Sept: 1-bedrm $97-$179; 2-bedrm $175-$359; 3-bedrm $169-$315; 4-bedrm $195-$349; house $175-$359; min stay required; higher rates Dec 25; lower rates rest of yr. Crib free. TV; cable. Heated pool; whirlpool. Dining rm 6-10 pm. Bar 4 pm-2 am. Ck-out 11 am. Guest lndry. Meeting rms. Mid-stay maid serv/5-day stay. Beauty shop. Downhill/x-country ski 4 mi. Exercise rm; instructor, weights, bicycles, sauna, steam rm. Massage. Refrigerators, microwaves, fireplaces. Private patios, balconies. Cr cds: A, DS, MC, V.

★ ★ ★ **TETON PINES.** *3450 N Clubhouse Dr, 7 mi W on Teton Village Rd. 307/733-1005; FAX 307/733-2860; res: 800/238-2223.* 16 suites. Mid-June-Sept: S, D $300-$385; 2-bedrm $650; golf plan; lower rates rest of yr. Crib free. TV; cable, VCR avail. Pool; whirlpool. Complimentary continental bkfst. Coffee in rms. Restaurant (see THE GRILLE AT THE PINES). Rm serv. Ck-out 11 am, ck-in 4 pm. Grocery ½ mi. Coin lndry 7 mi. Package store ½ mi. Meeting rms. Business servs avail. Bellhops. Free airport transportation. Tennis, pro. 18-hole golf, greens fee $60-$140, pro, putting green, driving range. Downhill ski 5 mi; x-country ski on site, rentals. Health club privileges. Refrigerators, wet bars, microwaves; some fireplaces. Cr cds: A, D, MC, V.

Restaurants

★ ★ ★ ★ **ALPENHOF.** *(See Alpenhof Motor Hotel) 307/733-3462.* E-mail alpenhof@sisna.com; web www.jacksonhole.com/alpenhof. Etched glass, wood beams and lots of greenery complete an elegant Bavarian motif at the base of the Jackson Hole ski area. Continental menu. Own baking. Hrs: 7:30-10:30 am, 5:30-9:30 pm. Closed early Apr-mid-May & mid-Oct-early Dec. Res accepted. No A/C. Bar 11:30-2 am. Wine list. Semi-a la carte: bkfst $3-$7.95, dinner $13.95-$24.95; special dinner for 2, $50-$60. Child's meals. Tableside preparation. Parking. Totally nonsmoking. Cr cds: A, C, D, DS, MC, V.

★ ★ **ANTHONY'S.** *62 S Glenwood. 307/733-3717.* Hrs: 5:30-9:30 pm. Closed Thanksgiving, Dec 25. Italian menu. Bar. Semi-a la carte: dinner $10-$16. Specializes in lemon chicken, cajun fettuccine, homemade bread. Art-deco Italian decor. Totally nonsmoking. Cr cds: A, MC, V.

★ ★ ★ **BLUE LION.** *160 N Millward St. 307/733-3912.* Hrs: 5:30-10 pm. No A/C. Res accepted. Continental menu. Bar. Semi-a la carte: dinner $15-$25. Specializes in fresh seafood, lamb, fresh elk. Own baking. Outdoor dining; bi-level deck. In renovated old house. Herb garden. Totally nonsmoking. Cr cds: A, DS, MC, V.

★ ★ ★ **CADILLAC GRILLE.** *55 N Cache. 307/733-3279.* Hrs: 11:30 am-3 pm, 5:30-10:30 pm. Res accepted. Bar to midnight. A la carte entrees: lunch $4.95-$8.95. Semi-a la carte: dinner $14-$23.50. Child's meals. Specializes in wild game, steak, fresh seafood. Own baking. Outdoor dining. Contemporary art decor. Cr cds: A, MC, V.

✔ ★ ★ **CALICO.** *2650 Teton Village Rd. 307/733-2460.* Hrs: 4-10 pm. Italian menu. Bar. Semi-a la carte: dinner $7.50-$15.95. Child's meals. Specializes in pasta, pizza, seafood. Outdoor dining. Old West decor. Cr cds: A, MC, V.

★ ★ **GOULOFF'S.** *(3600 Teton Village Rd, Teton Village) 10 mi NW. 307/733-1886.* Hrs: 5:30-10 pm. Closed Sun, Mon; Apr, Nov. Res accepted. No A/C. Bar. Semi-a la carte: dinner $14.25-$21.95. Child's meals. Specializes in wild game, pistachio chicken. Parking. Casual atmosphere. Cr cds: A, MC, V.

★ ★ ★ **THE GRILLE AT THE PINES.** *(See Teton Pines Resort) 307/733-1005.* Hrs: 11:30 am-2:30 pm, 6-9 pm. Closed Sun. Res accepted. Bar. Semi-a la carte: lunch $6.50-$9.95, dinner $13-$26.50. Specializes in wild game, fresh seafood. Parking. Outdoor dining. View of Tetons. Paintings of local scenes displayed. Cr cds: A, D, MC, V.

✔ ★ **JEDEDIAH'S.** *135 E Broadway. 307/733-5671.* Hrs: 7 am-2 pm, 5:30-9:30 pm. Closed Thanksgiving, Dec 25. Res accepted. Semi-a la carte: bkfst $2.95-$8.95, lunch $4.50-$8.50, dinner $6-$15. Child's meals. Specialties: sourdough pancakes, buffalo burgers. Outdoor dining. Rustic decor in old house (1910); Western antiques. Cr cds: A, DS, MC, V.

✔ ★ ★ **LAME DUCK.** *680 E Broadway. 307/733-4311.* Hrs: 5-10 pm. Closed Thanksgiving, Dec 25. Chinese menu. Serv bar. Semi-a la carte: dinner $3.95-$15.95. Child's meals. Specializes in seafood, sushi, sashimi. Parking. Outdoor dining. 2 tearooms. Totally nonsmoking. Cr cds: A, MC, V.

★ ★ **MILLION DOLLAR COWBOY STEAK HOUSE.** *25 N Cache St, opp Town Square. 307/733-4790.* Hrs: 5:30-10 pm. Closed Thanksgiving, Dec 25; Apr-mid-May, Nov. Bar. Semi-a la carte: dinner $14.95-$29.95. Specializes in steak, fresh seafood, wild game. Knotty pine furnishings, Western decor. Cr cds: A, DS, MC, V.

★ ★ **OFF BROADWAY.** *30 S King St. 307/733-9777.* Hrs: 5:30-10 pm. Closed Dec 25. Res accepted. Serv bar. Semi-a la carte: dinner

$11.50-$17. Child's meals. Specializes in fresh seafood, pasta, Thai dishes. Outdoor dining. Totally nonsmoking. Cr cds: A, MC, V.

★ ★ ★ **THE RANGE.** *225 N Cache St. 307/733-5481.* Hrs: 5:30-10 pm. Res accepted. Bar. Semi-a la carte: dinner $16-$29. Child's meals. Specialties: linguine roma tomatoes, breast of turkey, fresh artichoke pâté. Metropolitan high plains decor. Cr cds: A, MC, V.

★ ★ ★ **SNAKE RIVER GRILL.** *84 E Broadway. 307/733-0557.* Hrs: 5:30-10:30 pm. Closed Dec 25; Apr, Nov. Res accepted. Serv bar. Wine list. Semi-a la carte: dinner $12.95-$29.95. Child's meals. Specialties: free-range veal chop, grilled venison, grilled Idaho red-rainbow trout. Outdoor dining. Upscale Western ranch decor and atmosphere; stone fireplace. Totally nonsmoking. Cr cds: A, MC, V.

★ ★ ★ **STRUTTING GROUSE.** *Jackson Hole Golf & Tennis Club, 7 mi N on US 89. 307/733-7788.* Hrs: 11 am-9 pm. Closed Oct-mid-May. Res accepted. Bar. A la carte entrees: lunch $5-$9.25, dinner $16.95-$26.95. Specializes in fresh salmon, bison medallions, venison sausage. Parking. Outdoor dining (lunch). Western decor; gardens. View of golf course, mountains. Cr cds: A, D, MC, V.

★ ★ **SWEETWATER.** *King & Pearl Sts. 307/733-3553.* Hrs: 11:30 am-3 pm, 5:30-10 pm. Closed Thanksgiving, Dec 25. Res accepted. Greek, Amer menu. Bar. Semi-a la carte: lunch $4.95-$8.25, dinner $11.95-$24. Child's meals. Specializes in lamb, seafood, Greek phyllo pies. Outdoor dining. Western decor. In log house built by pioneers. Totally nonsmoking. Cr cds: A, D, DS, MC, V.

✔ ★ ★ **VISTA GRANDE.** *2550 Teton Village Rd, 6 mi NW on WY 22, then 1½ mi N on Teton Village Rd. 307/733-6964.* Hrs: 5:30-10 pm. Closed part of Nov. Mexican menu. Bar. Semi-a la carte: dinner $7.50-$14.95. Child's meals. Parking. Mexican decor. View of mountains. Cr cds: A, MC, V.

Unrated Dining Spots

BAR J. *6 mi NW on Teton Village Rd. 307/733-3370.* Sittings: 7:30 pm (dinner), 8:30 pm (show). Closed Oct-May. Res accepted. Complete meals: dinner $13; children 4-8 yrs, $5. Specializes in barbecue-chuck wagon dinner with beef or chicken & beans. Western show. On working cattle ranch. Cr cds: A, MC, V.

THE BUNNERY. *130 N Cache St, in Hole in the Wall Mall. 307/733-5474.* Hrs: 7 am-9:30 pm. Closed Thanksgiving, Dec 25. Wine, beer. Semi-a la carte: bkfst $2.95-$5.95, lunch $3.95-$6.95, dinner $6.95-$9.95. Child's meals. Specializes in whole grain waffles, broiled sandwiches. Own baking. Cr cds: MC, V.

SC

Kemmerer (E-2)

(For accommodations see Evanston, Green River)

Pop 3,020 **Elev** 6,959 ft **Area code** 307 **Zip** 83101

A Ranger District office of the Bridger-Teton National Forest (see JACKSON) is located here.

What to See and Do

Fossil Butte Natl Monument. On 8,198 acres is one of the most extensive concentrations of fossilized aquatic vertebrates, plants and insects (some 50 million yrs old) in the United States. (Daily) 11 mi W on US 30N. Phone 307/877-4455. **Free.**

Lander (D-4)

(See also Riverton)

Settled 1875 **Pop** 7,023 **Elev** 5,360 ft **Area code** 307 **Zip** 82520 **E-mail** landerchamber@rmisp.com **Web** www.landerchamber.org

Information Chamber of Commerce, 160 N 1st St; 307/332-3892 or 800/433-0662.

Lander was once called the place where the rails end and the trails begin. Wind River Range, surrounding the town, offers hunting and fishing, mountain climbing and rock hunting. The annual One-Shot Antelope Hunt opens the antelope season and draws celebrities and sports enthusiasts from all over the country. Sacajawea Cemetery (burial place of Lewis and Clark's Shoshone guide) is located in Fort Washakie, 15 mi NW on US 287. A Ranger District office of the Shoshone National Forest (see CODY) is located in Lander.

What to See and Do

Fremont County Pioneer Museum. Seven exhibit rms and outdoor exhibit area document the pioneer, ranching, Native American and business history of the area. (Mon-Fri, also Sat afternoons) 630 Lincoln St. Phone 307/332-4137. **¢-¢¢**

Sinks Canyon State Park. In a spectacular canyon, amid unspoiled Rocky Mt beauty, lies the middle fork of the Popo Agie River, which disappears into a cavern and rises again several hundred yards below in a crystal-clear, trout-filled spring pool. Abundant wildlife in certain seasons. Visitor center; observation points. Fishing (exc in the Rise of the Sinks). Hiking, nature trails. Groomed cross-country ski and snowmobile trails nearby. Limited tent & trailer sites (standard fees); other sites nearby. 7 mi SW on WY 131. Phone 307/332-6333.

South Pass City. An example of a once flourishing gold mining town. During the gold rush of 1868-1872, two thousand people lived here. Women were first given equal suffrage by a territorial act introduced from South Pass City and passed in Cheyenne on December 10, 1869. The town is currently being restored and has more than 20 historic buildings on display (mid-May-Sept, daily). 33 mi S on WY 28, then 3 mi W. Phone 307/332-3684. **¢**

Motels

★ ★ **BEST WESTERN THE INN AT LANDER.** *260 Grandview St. 307/332-2847; FAX 307/332-2760.* 48 rms, 2 story. May-Sept: S $62; D $70; each addl $5; suites $75-$90; under 12 free; wkly rates; lower rates rest of yr. Crib $5. TV; cable. Heated pool; whirlpool. Complimentary continental bkfst. Restaurant nearby. Ck-out 11 am. Meeting rms. Sundries. Free airport transportation. Exercise equipt; bicycle, treadmill. Some refrigerators. Cr cds: A, DS, MC, V.

D ≈ ✗ ⇲ 🛏 **SC**

✔ ★ **BUDGET HOST PRONGHORN.** *150 E Main St. 307/332-3940; FAX 307/332-2651.* 54 rms, 2 story. May-Sept: S $39-$43; D $42-$53; each addl $5; suites $61; under 12 free; lower rates rest of yr. Crib $5. Pet accepted, some restrictions. TV; cable (premium). Complimentary continental bkfst. Restaurant 6 am-11 pm. Ck-out 11 am. Coin lndry. Meeting rms. Whirlpool. Some refrigerators. On river. Cr cds: A, C, D, DS, MC, V.

Laramie (F-7)

(See also Cheyenne)

Founded 1868 **Pop** 26,687 **Elev** 7,165 ft **Area code** 307 **Zip** 82070
E-mail actb@lariat.org **Web** www.laramie.org
Information Albany County Tourism Board, 800 S Third St; 307/745-4195 or 800/445-5303.

Laramie had a rugged beginning as a lawless leftover of the westward-rushing Union Pacific. The early settlement was populated by hunters, saloonkeepers and brawlers. When the tracks pushed on, Laramie stabilized somewhat, but for six months vigilantes were the only law enforcement available against desperate characters who operated from town. Reasonable folk finally prevailed; schools and businesses sprang up, and improved cattle breeds brought prosperity. A Ranger District office of the Medicine Bow National Forest is located here.

What to See and Do

Laramie Plains Museum. Victorian mansion (1892); each rm finished in a different wood; collections include antique furniture, toys, china, ranching memorabilia, Western artifacts. Special seasonal displays. (Daily) 603 Ivinson Ave. Phone 307/742-4448. ¢¢

Lincoln Monument. World's largest bronze head (12½ ft high, 3½ tons), by Robert Russin of the Univ of Wyoming. 8 mi SE on I-80.

Medicine Bow Natl Forest. The more than one million acres include the Snowy Range Scenic Byway; one 30-mi stretch on WY 130, west from Centennial, is particularly scenic with elevations as high as 10,800 ft at Snowy Range Pass. Winter sports areas. Picnic grounds. Camping (fee); commercial lodges. W on WY 130, SW on WY 230, E on I-80 or N via US 30, WY 34, I-25, local roads. For further information contact the Forest Supervisor, 2468 Jackson St; 307/745-2300.

Snowy Range Ski Area. Triple, 2 double chairlifts, T-bar; 25 runs; school, rentals; snowmaking; guided snowmobile tours; cafeteria, bar. Vertical drop 1,000 ft; longest run 2 mi. Cross-country trails nearby. (Mid-Nov-mid-Apr, daily) 32 mi W on WY 130 (Snowy Range Rd). Phone 307/745-5750. ¢¢¢¢¢

Univ of Wyoming (1886). (10,650 students) The state's only 4-yr university. Its campus has the highest elevation of any in the US. The UW Visitor Information Center, 1408 Ivinson Ave has displays, community and campus literature. Between 9th & 30th Sts, 1 blk N of US 30 (Grand Ave). Phone 307/766-4075 or 307/766-1121. On campus are

American Heritage Center & Art Museum. Nine galleries feature display of paintings, graphics and sculpture from the 16th century to the present. Manuscripts, rare books, artifacts relating to Wyoming and the West. Research facilities. (Daily exc Mon; closed hols) 2111 Willet Dr. Phone 307/766-6622. ¢¢

Geological Museum. Houses rocks, minerals, vertebrate, invertebrate, mammal and plant fossils, including 1 of 5 brontosaurus skeletons in the world. (Mon-Fri) S.K. Knight Geology Bldg. Phone 307/766-4218. **Free.**

Wyoming Territorial Prison and Old West Park. Western heritage park with living history programs. Frontier town, Territorial Prison, US Marshals' Museum (fee), dinner theater (fee), playground, gift shop. (May-Sept, daily) 975 Snowy Range Rd, just off I-80. Phone 745-6161, ext 5 or 800/845-2287, ext 5. **Free.**

Motels

★ **BEST WESTERN FOSTER'S COUNTRY INN.** *1561 Jackson St, (WY 130, 230) at jct I-80 Snowy Range exit 311.* 307/742-8371; FAX 307/742-0884. 112 rms, 2 story. Mid-May-mid-Sept: S $54; D $60; each addl $6; under 12 free; higher rates special events; lower rates rest of yr. Crib $6. Pet accepted. TV; cable. Indoor pool; whirlpool. Restaurant open 24 hrs. Bar 8-2 am. Ck-out noon. Coin lndry. Meeting rms. Gift shop.

Free airport, RR station, bus depot transportation. Cr cds: A, C, D, DS, MC, V.

✔★ **CAMELOT.** *523 Adams, I-80, Snowy Range exit 311.* 307/721-8860; res: 800/659-7915. 33 rms, 2 story. S $45; D $65-$75; each addl $6. Crib $3. TV; cable. Restaurant opp open 24 hrs. Ck-out 11 am. Coin lndry. Cr cds: A, C, D, DS, MC, V.

★ **ECONO LODGE.** *1370 McCue St.* 307/745-8900; FAX 307/745-5806. 51 rms, 2 story. June-Aug: S, D $89-$189; each addl $10; under 13 free; lower rates rest of yr. Crib free. Pet accepted. TV; cable, VCR avail (movies). Indoor pool. Complimentary coffee in lobby. Restaurant nearby. Ck-out noon. Meeting rm. Some refrigerators. Cr cds: A, C, D, DS, MC, V.

★ **HOLIDAY INN.** *2313 Soldier Springs Rd, at jct US 30, 287; I-80 exit 313.* 307/742-6611; FAX 307/745-8371. 100 rms, 2 story. Mid-May-mid-Sept: S $60; D $68; each addl $8; under 12 free; lower rates rest of yr. Crib free. Pet accepted. TV; cable (premium). Indoor pool; whirlpool. Restaurant 6 am-10 pm. Rm serv. Bar. Ck-out noon. Coin lndry. Meeting rms. Gift shop. Free airport transportation. Game rm. Cr cds: A, C, D, DS, MC, V.

Inn

★ ★ ★ **A. DRUMMOND'S RANCH.** *399 Happy Jack Rd (82007).* 307/634-6042. 4 rms, 2 share bath, 2 story. No A/C. Mid-May-mid-Sept: S $60-$75; D $70-$150; each addl $15; under 8 free; wkly rates; MAP avail; lower rates rest of yr. Crib free. TV in sitting rm, VCR avail (free movies). Playground. Complimentary full bkfst. Ck-out 11 am, ck-in 4 pm. Business servs avail. X-country ski 8 mi. Whirlpool. Stable facilities $15. Secluded setting. Totally nonsmoking. Cr cds: MC, V.

Lovell (A-5)

(See also Greybull)

Pop 2,131 **Elev** 3,837 ft **Area code** 307 **Zip** 82431
Information Lovell Area Chamber of Commerce, 287 E Main, PO Box 295; 307/548-7552.

A Ranger District office of the Bighorn National Forest (see SHERIDAN) is located here.

What to See and Do

Bighorn Canyon Natl Recreation Area. The focus of the area is 71-mi-long Bighorn Lake, created by the Yellowtail Dam in Ft Smith, MT. Boats may travel through Bighorn Canyon, which cuts across the northern end of the Bighorn Mts in north-central Wyoming and south-central Montana. The solar-powered Bighorn Canyon Visitor Center is just east of town on US 14A (daily). The Ft Smith Visitor Contact Station is in Ft Smith, MT (daily). Both centers are closed Jan 1, Thanksgiving, Dec 25. Yellowtail Visitor Center at the dam has tours (summer). Recreational and interpretive activities are available at both ends of the area. Fishing; boating. Picnicking. Camping. S entrance 2 mi E on US 14A, then 8 mi N on WY 37. For further information contact Bighorn Canyon Visitor Center, Hwy 14A E; 307/548-2251. Adj and accessible from town is

Pryor Mt Wild Horse Range. This 32,000-acre refuge, est in 1968, provides a sanctuary for wild horses descended from Native American ponies and escaped farm and ranch horses. Administered jointly by the Natl Park Service and the Bureau of Land Management.

Annual Event

Mustang Days. Parade; rodeo; exhibits; entertainment, dancing; barbecue; 7-mi run. Late June.

Motel

★ **SUPER 8.** *595 E Main.* 307/548-2725. 35 rms, 2 story. S $36.88; D $40.88-$44.88; each addl $3; under 12 free. Crib free. TV; cable (premium). Restaurant adj 6 am-10 pm. Ck-out 11 am. Coin lndry. Cr cds: A, C, D, DS, MC, V.

D ⊣ 🖎 SC

Restaurant

★ **BIGHORN.** *605 E Main.* 307/548-6811. Hrs: 6 am-9 pm. Closed Jan 1, Dec 25. Bar. Semi-a la carte: bkfst $2.75-$6.99, lunch $2.50-$5.75, dinner $8-$16. Child's meals. Specializes in seafood. Salad bar. Cr cds: A, D, DS, MC, V.

D SC ⌐

Lusk (D-8)

(See also Douglas)

Founded 1886 **Pop** 1,504 **Elev** 5,015 ft **Area code** 307 **Zip** 82225 **E-mail** luniacc@coffey.com **Web** www.wyoming.com/~adventure/lusk **Information** Chamber of Commerce, PO Box 457; 307/334-2950 or 800/223-LUSK.

Raising livestock has always been important in Lusk; fine herds of Simmental Angus and sheep are the local pride. Hunting is excellent for deer and antelope.

What to See and Do

Stagecoach Museum. Relics of pioneer days, Native American artifacts; stagecoach. (May-June & Sept-Oct, Mon-Fri; July & Aug, daily exc Mon) 322 S Main. Phone 307/334-3444. ¢

Annual Events

Legend of Rawhide. Live show performed since 1946. Concert, dances, art show, parade, pancake breakfast. 2nd wkend July.

Senior Pro Rodeo. Labor Day wkend.

Motels

✔★ **BEST WESTERN PIONEER COURT.** *731 S Main (US 18, 20, 85).* 307/334-2640; FAX 307/3342642. 30 rms. S $42; D $55-$66; each addl $4. Crib $4. TV; cable. Pool. Complimentary coffee in lobby. Restaurant nearby. Ck-out 11 am. Cr cds: A, C, D, DS, JCB, MC, V.

≈ ⊣ 🖎

★ **COVERED WAGON.** *730 S Main, (US 18, 20, 85).* 307/334-2836; res: 800/341-8000. 51 rms. June-mid-Oct: S $55; D $64-$68; each addl $5; suite $155; some lower rates rest of yr. Crib $2. TV; cable (premium). Indoor pool; whirlpool. Sauna. Playground. Complimentary coffee in lobby. Restaurant nearby. Ck-out 11 am. Coin lndry. Meeting rm. Lawn games. Cr cds: A, C, D, DS, MC, V.

D ≈ ⊣ 🖎 SC

Newcastle (B-9)

Founded 1889 **Pop** 3,003 **Elev** 4,317 ft **Area code** 307 **Zip** 82701 **Web** www.trib.com/NEWCASTLE

Information Newcastle Area Chamber of Commerce, PO Box 68; 307/746-2739 or 800/835-0157.

Originally a coal mining town, Newcastle is now an oil field center with its own refinery. It is also a tourist center, with fishing, hunting and recreational facilities nearby. A Ranger District office of the Black Hills National Forest (see BLACK HILLS, SD) is located here.

What to See and Do

Anna Miller Museum. Museum of NE Wyoming, housed in stone cavalry barn. Log cabin from Jenney Stockade, oldest building in the Black Hills, and an early rural schoolhouse. More than 100 exhibits. (Mon-Fri, Sat by appt) Delaware & Washington Park. Phone 307/746-4188. **Free.**

Beaver Creek Loop Tour. Self-guided driving tour designed to provide the opportunity to explore a diverse and beautiful country. 45-mi tour covering 23 marked sites. Phone 307/746-2739. **Free.**

Pinedale (D-3)

(See also Jackson)

Settled 1878 **Pop** 1,181 **Elev** 7,175 ft **Area code** 307 **Zip** 82941 **Information** Chamber of Commerce, 32 E Pine, PO Box 176; 307/367-2242.

Pinedale is a place where genuine cowboys can still be found, and cattle drives still occur. Mountains, conifer and aspen forests and lakes and rivers combine to make this a beautiful vacation area. There are fossil beds in the area, and rockhounding is popular. Cattle and sheep are raised on nearby ranches. A Ranger District office of the Bridger-Teton National Forest (see JACKSON) is located in Pinedale.

What to See and Do

Bridger-Teton Natl Forest. Lies along the Wind River Range, E, N & W of town. Fishing, hunting. Hiking. Camping (fee). In forest is

Bridger Wilderness. Approx 400,000 acres of mountainous terrain entered only by foot or horseback. Trout fishing in snow-fed streams and more than 1,300 mountain lakes; hunting for big game. Backpacking. Permits required for some activities. Pack trips arranged by area outfitters.

Hunting. In-season hunting for elk, moose, deer, bear, antelope, mountain bighorn sheep, birds and small game in surrounding mountains and mesas.

Museum of the Mountain Man. Houses exhibits on fur trade, western exploration, early history. (May-Oct, daily) Fremont Lake Rd. Phone 307/367-4101. ¢¢

🔲 **Scenic Drives. Skyline.** Up into the mountains 14 mi the fauna changes from sagebrush to an alpine setting. Lakes, conifers, beautiful mountain scenery; wildlife often seen. **Green River Lakes.** N via WY 352 to the lakes with Square Top Mt in the background; popular with photographers. Wooded campground, trails, backpacking.

Water sports. Fishing for grayling, rainbow, mackinaw, brown trout, golden and other trout in most lakes and rivers; ice-fishing, mostly located N of town. Swimming, waterskiing; boating, sailing regattas, float trips on New Fork and Green rivers.

Winter recreation. Cross-country skiing, groomed snowmobile trails, ice-fishing, skating.

Annual Event

Green River Rendezvous. Rodeo grounds, Sublette County. Noted historical pageant commemorating the meeting of fur trappers, mountain men and Native Americans with the Trading Company's wagon trains at Ft Bonneville. Mid-July.

Motels

★ ★ **BEST WESTERN PINEDALE INN.** *850 W Pine. 307/367-6869; FAX 307/367-6897.* 58 rms, 2 story. June-Labor Day: S, D $85; suites $95; under 12 free; lower rates rest of yr. Crib $5. Pet accepted. TV; cable. Indoor pool; whirlpool. Sauna. Complimentary continental bkfst. Restaurant nearby. Ck-out 11 am. Meeting rms. Exercise equipt; bicycle, treadmill. Some refrigerators. Cr cds: A, D, DS, MC, V.

★ **WAGON WHEEL.** *407 S Pine. 307/367-2871.* 15 rms. No A/C. S $65; D $65-$70; each addl $5. Crib $8. TV; cable (premium). Restaurant nearby. Ck-out 10 am. Cr cds: A, C, D, DS, MC, V.

★ **THE ZZZZ INN.** *327 S Pine. 307/367-2121.* 34 rms. No A/C. May-Oct: S $50-$65; D $55-$75; each addl $5. Closed rest of yr. Pet accepted. TV; cable. Restaurant nearby. Ck-out 11 am. Cr cds: A, C, D, DS, MC, V.

Restaurant

★ ★ **McGREGORS PUB.** *21 N Franklin St. 307/367-4443.* Hrs: 11:30 am-2 pm, 5:30-10 pm; Sat, Sun from 5:30 pm. Closed some major hols. Res accepted. No A/C. Bar. Semi-a la carte: lunch $4.95-$6.95, dinner $10.95-$29.95. Child's meals. Specializes in prime rib, scallops, pasta. Own desserts, bread. Outdoor dining. Contemporary ranch decor. Cr cds: C, D, DS, MC, V.

Rawlins (E-6)

Founded 1867 **Pop** 9,380 **Elev** 6,755 ft **Area code** 307 **Zip** 82301
E-mail rcccoc@trib.com
Information Rawlins-Carbon County Chamber of Commerce, 519 W Cedar, PO Box 1331; 307/324-4111 or 800/228-3547.

Rawlins, a division point of the Union Pacific Railroad, is located 20 miles east of the Continental Divide. In 1867, General John A Rawlins, Chief of Staff of the US Army, wished for a drink of cool, clear water. Upon finding the spring near the base of the hills and tasting it, he said, "If anything is ever named after me, I hope it will be a spring of water." The little oasis was named Rawlins Springs, as was the community that grew up beside it. The city name was later shortened to Rawlins.

What to See and Do

Carbon County Museum. Houses artifacts of mining and ranching ventures. (Schedule varies) 9th & Walnut Sts. Phone 307/328-2740. **Donation.**

Seminoe State Park. Seminoe Dam impounds a 27-mi-long reservoir surrounded by giant white sand dunes and sagebrush. Pronghorn antelope & sage grouse inhabit area. Swimming; fishing (trout, walleye); boating (ramps). Hiking. Picnicking. Tent & trailer sites (standard fee). 6 mi E on I-80 to Sinclair, then 35 mi N on County Rd 351. Phone 307/328-0115 or 307/320-3013.

Wyoming Frontier Prison. Located on 49 acres, construction was begun in 1888. The prison operated from 1901-1981. Tours (fee). (May-Sept, daily; rest of yr, by appt) 5th & Walnut. Phone 307/324-4422. Museum **Free.** Tour **¢¢**

Annual Event

Carbon County Fair and Rodeo. Fairgrounds, Rodeo Park off Spruce St. Includes parades, exhibits, livestock, contests, demolition derby, old-timer rodeo. 2nd full wk Aug.

Motels

★ **DAYS INN.** *2222 E Cedar St. 307/324-6615.* 121 rms, 2 story. June-mid-Sept: S $50; D $50-$55; each addl $5; under 13 free; lower rates rest of yr. Crib free. Pet accepted. TV; cable. Indoor pool. Restaurant 6-9 am, 11 am-2 pm, 5-9 pm. Rm serv. Bar 5 pm-2 am. Ck-out noon. Coin lndry. Meeting rms. Business servs avail. Game rm. Cr cds: A, C, D, DS, MC, V.

✔★ **SLEEP INN.** *1400 Higley Blvd, I-80 exit 214. 307/328-1732; FAX 307/328-0412.* 81 rms, many with shower only, 2 story. June-Sept: S $48; D $53; each addl $5; under 19 free; lower rates rest of yr. Crib free. TV; cable (premium), VCR avail (movies $3.50). Complimentary coffee in lobby. Restaurant adj open 24 hrs. Ck-out 11 am. Meeting rms. Business servs avail. In-rm modem link. Sauna. Cr cds: A, D, DS, MC, V.

★ **SUPER 8.** *2338 Wagon Circle Rd, I-80 Spruce St exit. 307/328-0630; FAX 307/328-1814.* 47 rms, 2 story. June-mid-Sept: S, D $49-$54; each addl $5; under 5 free; lower rates rest of yr. TV; cable. Complimentary coffee in lobby. Restaurant adj 6 am-midnight. Ck-out 11 am. Coin lndry. Exercise equipt; weight machine, bicycles. Cr cds: A, DS, MC, V.

Inn

✔★ ★ ★ **FERRIS MANSION.** *607 W Maple. 307/324-3961.* 4 rms, 2 with shower only, 2 story. No A/C. No rm phones. Mar-mid-Nov: S, D $58-$65. Children over 10 yrs only. TV; cable (premium). Complimentary continental bkfst. Restaurant nearby. Ck-in 11 am, ck-out 4 pm. Built in 1903; furnished with antiques. Totally nonsmoking. Cr cds: DS, MC, V.

Riverton (C-5)

(See also Lander, Thermopolis)

Founded 1906 **Pop** 9,202 **Elev** 4,964 ft **Area code** 307 **Zip** 82501
E-mail riverton@wyoming.com
Information Chamber of Commerce, 1st & Main, Depot Bldg; 307/856-4801.

Riverton is the largest city in Fremont County. Resources extracted from the region include natural gas, oil, iron ore, timber and phosphate. Irrigation from the Wind River Range has placed 130,000 acres under cultivation, on which barley, alfalfa hay, beans, sunflowers and grain are grown. The town is surrounded by the Wind River Reservation, where Arapaho and Shoshone live.

What to See and Do

Riverton Museum. Shoshone and Arapaho displays; mountain man display. General store, drugstore, post office, saloon, homesteader's cabin, church, bank, dentist's office, parlor, school, beauty shop. Clothing, quilts, cutters, buggies. 700 E Park St. Phone 307/856-2665. **Free.**

Annual Events

Wild West Winter Carnival. Depot Bldg. Early Feb.

State Championship Old-time Fiddle Contest. 21 mi NE via US 26, 789 in Shoshoni. Divisional competition. Late May.

Powwows. Shoshone and Arapaho tribal powwows are held throughout the summer.

1838 Mountain Man Rendezvous. Council fire, primitive shoots, hawk & knife throw, games, food. Camping avail. Phone 307/856-7306. Early July.

Fremont County Fair & Rodeo. 1st full wk Aug.

Motel

★ ★ **SUNDOWNER STATION.** *1616 N Federal, (US 26, WY 789).* 307/856-6503; res: 800/874-1116. 60 rms, 2 story. S $42-$44; D $44-$48; each addl $4; under 12 free. Crib free. Pet accepted. TV; cable. Heated pool; sauna. Restaurant 5:30 am-10 pm. Bar 4 pm-11 pm. Ck-out 11 am. Meeting rms. Sundries. Free airport transportation. Balconies. Cr cds: A, C, D, DS, MC, V.

Motor Hotel

★ ★ **HOLIDAY INN.** *900 E Sunset.* 307/856-8100; FAX 307/856-0266. 121 rms, 2 story. S $59; D $65; each addl $6; under 19 free. Pet accepted. TV; cable. Indoor pool; whirlpool, poolside serv. Restaurant 6 am-10 pm. Rm serv. Bar 4 pm-2 am. Ck-out noon. Coin lndry. Meeting rms. Sundries. Beauty shop. Airport transportation. Game rm. Bathrm phones. Cr cds: A, C, D, DS, JCB, MC, V.

Rock Springs (E-4)

(See also Green River)

Pop 19,050 **Elev** 6,271 ft **Area code** 307 **Zip** 82901

Information Rock Springs Chamber of Commerce, 1897 Dewar Dr, PO Box 398, 82902-0398; 307/362-3771 or 800/46-DUNES.

Rock Springs traces its roots to a spring, which offered an ideal camping site along a Native American trail and, later, a welcome station on the Overland Stage route. Later still, Rock Springs became a supply station that provided millions of tons of coal to the Union Pacific Railroad. Noted for its multiethnic heritage, the town's first inhabitants were primarily Welsh and English immigrants brought in by the railroad and coal companies. West of town are large deposits of trona (sodium sesquicarbonate), used in the manufacture of glass, phosphates, silicates, soaps and baking soda.

What to See and Do

Flaming Gorge Reservoir. This manmade lake, fed by the Green River, is 90 mi long with approx 375 mi of shoreline, which ranges from low flats to cliffs more than 1,500 ft high. Surrounded by a natl recreation area (see GREEN RIVER), the reservoir offers excellent fishing. SW via I-80.

Annual Events

Desert Balloon Rally. Early July.

Red Desert Round-Up. One of the largest rodeos in the Rocky Mts region. Late July.

Motels

★ **COMFORT INN.** *1670 Sunset Dr (US 30), at I-80 Dewar exit.* 307/382-9490; FAX 307/382-7333. 103 rms. Mid-May-mid-Sept: S

$60.80; D $66.80; each addl $6; lower rates rest of yr. Crib $5. Pet accepted; $6. TV; cable (premium). Heated pool; whirlpool. Playground. Complimentary continental bkfst. Restaurant adj. Ck-out 11 am. Coin lndry. Business servs avail. In-rm modem link. Exercise equipt; weights, treadmill. Bathrm phones. Cr cds: A, C, D, DS, MC, V.

✔ ★ ★ **LA QUINTA.** *2717 Dewar Dr.* 307/362-1770; FAX 307/362-2830. 130 rms, 2 story. June-Aug: S $46; D $52; each addl $5; under 18 free; lower rates rest of yr. Crib free. Pet accepted. TV; cable (premium). Heated pool. Complimentary continental bkfst. Restaurant adj open 24 hrs. Ck-out noon. Meeting rms. Business servs avail. In-rm modem link. Valet serv. Cr cds: A, C, D, DS, MC, V.

Motor Hotels

★ ★ **HOLIDAY INN.** *1675 Sunset Dr (US 187).* 307/382-9200; FAX 307/362-1064. 114 rms, 4 story. May-Sept: S, D $56-$70; each addl $6; under 18 free; lower rates rest of yr. Crib free. Pet accepted. TV; cable (premium). Indoor pool; wading pool, whirlpool, poolside serv. Restaurant 6 am-2 pm, 5-10 pm. Rm serv. Bar 11-2 am, Sun noon-10 pm. Ck-out noon. Coin lndry. Meeting rms. Business servs avail. Bellhops. Airport transportation. Balconies. Cr cds: A, C, D, DS, MC, V.

★ **INN AT ROCK SPRINGS.** *2518 Foothill Blvd.* 307/362-9600; FAX 307/362-8846; res: 800/442-9692. 150 rms, 3 story. S, D $52-$78; under 17 free. Crib free. TV; cable (premium). Indoor pool; whirlpool. Coffee in rms. Restaurant 6:30 am-9 pm. Rm serv. Bar. Ck-out noon. Business servs avail. Bellhops. Airport, RR station, bus depot transportation. Game rm. Some minibars. Balconies. Cr cds: A, D, DS, MC, V.

Restaurant

★ **LOG INN.** *W Purple Sage Rd, I-80 Flaming Gorge exit 99.* 307/362-7166. Hrs: 5-10 pm. Closed some major hols. Res accepted. Bar. Semi-a la carte: dinner $10.50-$32. Specializes in deep-fried lobster, barbecued ribs, blackened prime rib steaks. Log building; rustic decor. Cr cds: A, D, DS, MC, V.

Sheridan (A-6)

(See also Buffalo)

Founded 1882 **Pop** 13,900 **Elev** 3,745 ft **Area code** 307 **Zip** 82801

Information Convention and Visitors Bureau, PO Box 7155; 800/453-3650.

Sheridan, named for General Philip Sheridan, was not settled until the Cheyenne, Sioux and Crow were subdued after a series of wars in the region. While the land, rich with grass, was ideal for grazing livestock, ranchers only moved in their herds after the tribes were driven onto reservations. For years the town had a reputation for trouble because of rustling and boundary disputes. Nevertheless, the first dude ranch in history was established near Sheridan in 1904.

Today, the town is a tourist center with dude ranches, hotels and motels and sportsmen's facilities. The nearby Big Horn Range, once a favored hunting ground of Native Americans, is rich in big game and fishermen's retreats. A Ranger District office of the Bighorn National Forest is located in Sheridan.

What to See and Do

⭐ **Bighorn Natl Forest.** The Big Horn Mts rise abruptly from the arid basins below to elevations of more than 13,000 ft. Fallen City, a jumble of huge rock blocks, is viewed from US 14, as are Sibley Lake and Shell Canyon and Falls. From Burgess Junction, US 14A passes by Medicine Mt, site of the "medicine wheel," an ancient circular structure. US 16 features Meadowlark Lake and panoramic views of Tensleep Canyon and the 189,000-acre Cloud Peak Wilderness. Forest has resorts, campgrounds (fee); backpacking & horseback trails; skiing at Antelope Butte Ski Area (60 mi W on US 14) and High Park Ski Area (40 mi E of Worland). Fishing, hunting. Cross-country skiing, snowmobiling. More than 1,100,000 acres W and S of town, traversed by 3 scenic byways; US 14 (Bighorn Scenic Byway), US 14A (Medicine Wheel Passage) & US 16 (Cloud Peak Skyway). Contact the Forest Supervisor, 1969 S Sheridan Ave; 307/672-0751.

Bradford Brinton Memorial. Historic ranch house built in 1892; purchased in 1923 by Bradford Brinton and enlarged to its present 20 rms. Contains collections and furnishings that make this a memorial to the art and history of the West. More than 600 oils, watercolors and sketches by American artists including Russell and Remington. Also bronzes, prints and rare books, ranch equipment, saddles and Native American artifacts. (Mid-May-Labor Day, daily; also early Dec-Dec 24) 7 mi S on US 87, then 5 mi SW on WY 335. Phone 307/672-3173. ¢

King's Saddlery Museum. Collection of saddles; also Western memorabilia, Native American artifacts, old photographs, carriages. (Daily exc Sun; closed some major hols) 184 N Main St, behind store. Phone 307/672-2702. **Free.**

Main St Historic District. Take a walking tour of Sheridan, which boasts the largest collection of original late-1800s and early-1900s buildings in the state. For brochure, phone 307/672-8881. **Free.**

Trail End Historic Center. Home of John B. Kendrick, Governor of Wyoming (1915-1917), later US Senator (1917-1933). Historical and family memorabilia. Mansion of Flemish-revival architecture; beautifully carved and burnished woodwork is outstanding. Botanical specimens on landscaped grounds. (Daily; closed major hols) 400 Clarendon Ave adj to Kendrick Park. Phone 307/674-4589.

Annual Events

Sheridan-Wyo PRCA Rodeo. Carnival & parade. Mid-July.

Sheridan County Rodeo. 2nd wkend Aug.

Motels

⭐ **BEST WESTERN SHERIDAN CENTER MOTOR INN.** *612 N Main St, (US 14, 87, I-90 Business).* 307/674-7421; FAX 307/672-3018. 138 rms, 2 story. June-Aug: S $61.95; D $66.95-$68.95; each addl $6; under 12 free; lower rates rest of yr. Crib free. TV; cable; VCR avail (movies). 2 pools, 1 indoor; whirlpool. Sauna. Complimentary coffee in rms. Restaurant 6:30 am-9:30 pm. Bar noon-midnight. Ck-out 11 am. Meeting rms. Valet serv. Sundries. Free airport, bus depot transportation. Game rm. Some balconies. Cr cds: A, C, D, DS, MC, V.

⊠ ⊠ 🐾 SC

⭐ ⭐ **DAYS INN.** *1104 Brundage Lane.* 307/672-2888. 46 rms, 2 story. June-Aug: S, D $60-$75; each addl $5; suites $85-$125; under 12 free; lower rates rest of yr. Crib $4. TV; cable (premium). Indoor pool; whirlpool. Sauna. Complimentary continental bkfst. Restaurant nearby. Ck-out 11 am. Coin lndry. Meeting rms. Near airport. Cr cds: A, D, DS, MC, V.

D ⊠ ⊠ 🐾 SC

Motor Hotel

⭐ ⭐ **HOLIDAY INN.** *1809 Sugarland Dr, I-90 exit 25.* 307/672-8931; FAX 307/672-6388. 212 rms, 5 story. S $76-$86; D $86-$108; each addl $10; suites $135-$200; under 19 free. Crib free. Pet accepted. TV; cable. Indoor pool; whirlpool, poolside serv. Restaurant 6 am-10 pm. Rm

serv. Bar 4 pm-1:45 am. Ck-out noon. Coin lndry. Meeting rms. Business servs avail. In-rm modem link. Bellhops. Sundries. Gift shop. Beauty shop. Airport, bus depot transportation. Exercise equipt; stair machine, treadmill, sauna. Game rm. Putting green. Some refrigerators. Picnic area. Cr cds: A, C, D, DS, JCB, MC, V.

D ⊠ ⊠ 🏃 🎣 🛪 ⊠ 🐾 SC

Inn

⭐ ⭐ ⭐ **SPAHN'S BIGHORN MOUNTAIN.** *(PO Box 579, Big Horn 82833)* I-90 exit 25 or 33 to Big Horn, continue on WY 335 to end of pavement, then 1/2 mi on gravel rd, follow sign. 307/674-8150. 2 rms, 3 story lodge, 2 cabins. No rm phones. June 20-Aug 19: S, D $80-$125; each addl $20; lower rates rest of yr. Complimentary full bkfst. Ck-out 11 am, ck-in 4-8 pm. Balconies. Antiques. Wildlife trips. Totally nonsmoking. Cr cds: MC, V.

⊠ 🐾

Restaurant

⭐ ⭐ **GOURMET GALLEY.** *856 Broadway.* 307/674-5049. Hrs: 11 am-3 pm, 5-9 pm. Closed Sun; Memorial Day, July 4, Thanksgiving. Res accepted. Bar. Semi-a la carte: lunch $5.25-$9.75, dinner $9.75-$20. Child's meals. Specializes in steak, chicken, seafood. Entertainment. Outdoor dining. Former home of Buffalo Bill. Cr cds: A, D, DS, MC, V.

Teton Village

(see Jackson)

Thermopolis (C-5)

(See also Riverton)

Founded 1897 **Pop** 3,247 **Elev** 4,326 ft **Area code** 307 **Zip** 82443
E-mail hotspot@wyoming.com **Web** www.wyoming.com/~hotspot/
Information Chamber of Commerce, PO Box 768; 307/864-3192 or 800/SUN-N-SPA.

The world's largest mineral hot springs are at Thermopolis, which lies in a beautiful section of Big Horn Basin where canyons, tunnels and buttes abound. The town is surrounded by rich irrigated farm and grazing land.

What to See and Do

Boysen State Park. Surrounded by the Wind River Reservation. Boysen Reservoir is 18 mi long and 3 mi wide. Beach on E shore, waterskiing; fishing for trout and walleye (all yr); boating (ramp, marina). Picnicking, restaurant, lodging. Tent & trailer sites (standard fees). 16 mi S on US 20. Phone 307/876-2772.

Hot Springs County Museum and Cultural Center. Home of "Hole-in-the-Wall" bar. Displays of arrowheads, minerals, gems; petroleum industry; country schoolhouse; agricultural building; railroad caboose; also period rms and costumes. (Daily exc Mon; closed some major hols) 7th & Broadway. Phone 307/864-5183. ¢¢

Hot Springs State Park. Beautiful terraces and mineral cones. Big Horn Spring, a hot mineral spring pours out millions of gallons every 24 hrs at 135°F. The warm waters pour into the Big Horn River. Mineral swimming pools, indoor & outdoor, public bathhouse (massage avail). Terrace walks. Picnicking, playgrounds. Campgrounds nearby. A state buffalo herd is also quartered here. Across the Big Horn River, 1 mi N on US 20. Phone 307/864-2176.

Wind River Canyon. Formations visible in canyon walls range from early to recent geologic ages. S on US 20.

Wyoming Dinosaur Center. Exhibits mounted dinosaurs and dioramas, fossils, guided tours of excavation sites. (Daily) Carter Ranch Rd. Phone 307/864-2997 or -3775. ¢¢¢-¢¢¢¢¢

Annual Events

Gift of the Waters Pageant. Hot Springs State Park. Commemorates the deeding of the world's largest mineral hot springs from the Shoshone and Arapahoe to the people of Wyoming in 1896. Pageant features Native American dances, parade, buffalo barbecue. 1st wkend Aug.

Currier & Ives Winter Festival. Downtown. Town is decorated in 19th-century holiday style. Christmas choir, sleigh rides. Beard contest; cookie contest. Nov-Dec.

Motel

★ **SUPER 8.** *175 Lane 5 (US 20S). 307/864-5515; FAX 307/864-5447.* 52 rms, 2 story. June-Sept: S $66.88; D $68.99-$70.88; each addl $5; suite $150; under 10 free; lower rates rest of yr. Crib $4. TV; cable (premium). Indoor pool; whirlpool. Complimentary coffee in lobby. Restaurant nearby. Ck-out 11 am. Meeting rms. Coin lndry. Cr cds: A, D, DS, JCB, MC, V.

⊡ ⇆ ⋈ 🐾 SC

Torrington (E-9)

Pop 5,651 **Elev** 4,098 ft **Area code** 307 **Zip** 82240 **E-mail** gcc @prairieweb.com **Web** www.prairieweb.com/goshen_cty_wy/

Information Goshen County Chamber of Commerce, 350 W 21st Ave; 307/532-3879.

The town was a way station for the Oregon Trail, the Texas Trail, the Mormon Trail and the pony express. It is now a livestock marketing center.

What to See and Do

Ft Laramie Natl Historic Site (see). 20 mi NW on US 26, then W on WY 160; 3 mi SW of town of Ft Laramie. ¢

Homesteader's Museum. Historical items from the area's homesteading, ranching and settlement period (1830-1940). Ranch collection, furnished homestead shack; artifacts, photographs, archaeological materials. Changing exhibits. (Summer, daily; winter, Mon-Fri; closed hols) 495 Main St. Phone 307/532-5612. **Donation.**

Western History Center. Exhibits on prehistory, archeology, paleontology. Tours to dig sites (fee). (Tues-Sun, also by appt) 265 Main. Phone 307/837-3052. **Donation.**

Annual Events

Goshen County Fair & Rodeo. Mid-Aug.

Septemberfest. Early Sept.

Motel

✔★ **SUPER 8.** *1548 S Main St (US 85). 307/532-7118.* 56 rms, 3 story. No elvtr. May-Sept: S $41; D $47-$45; each addl $7; lower rates rest of yr. Crib $5. TV; cable. Complimentary coffee in lobby. Restaurant opp 5:30 am-10 pm. Ck-out 11 am. Cr cds: A, C, D, DS, MC, V.

⋈ 🐾 SC

Wheatland (E-8)

(See also Cheyenne, Torrington)

Pop 3,271 **Elev** 4,748 ft **Area code** 307 **Zip** 82201 **Web** www/wyoming .com/~platte/

Information Platte County Chamber of Commerce, 65 16th St, PO Box 427; 307/322-2322.

The southern edge of Medicine Bow National Forest(see LARAMIE) is 20 miles west.

What To See and Do

Glendo State Park. Rising out of Glendo Resevoir's E side at Sandy Beach are a series of sand dunes, some reaching from the Great Divide Basin to the sand hills in Nebraska. Chips, scrapers and arrowheads dating back 8,000 yrs are sometimes found. Abundant wildlife. Near historic crossings. Swimming, waterskiing; fishing, hunting; boating (marina, ramp, rentals). Picnicking, restaurant, grocery, lodging. Tent & trailer sites (standard fees). N on I-25. Phone 307/735-4433.

Guernsey State Park. On the shores of Guernsey Reservoir; high bluffs surround the park with Laramie Peak on the west. Surrounding area is rich in historical interest including the Oregon Trail. Museum (mid-May-Labor Day, daily; free) has exhibits on early settlers, the Oregon Trail, geology. Park offers swimming, waterskiing. Camping (standard fees). Some facilities may be closed Nov-Apr. 12 mi N on I-25, then 12 mi E on US 26, then N on WY 317. Phone 307/836-2334. Per vehicle ¢¢

Annual Events

Chugwater Chili Cookoff. Diamond Guest Ranch. Music, dancing, food. Family activities. Phone 307/322-2322. 2nd Sat June.

Guernsey Old Timer's Assoc Rodeo. Parade, barbecue. July 3-4.

Summer Fun Fest & Antique Tractor Pull. Phone 307/322-2322. 2nd Sat July.

Platte County Fair and Rodeo. Includes parade, livestock sale, barbecue, pig wrestling. Phone 307/322-9504. Early Aug.

Motel

✔★ **BEST WESTERN TORCHLITE MOTOR INN.** *1809 N 16th. 307/322-4070; FAX 307/322-4072.* 50 rms, 2 story. S $40-$75; D $45-$75; each addl $5. Crib $8. Pet accepted. TV; cable (premium). Ck-out 11 am. Business servs avail. Airport transportation. Refrigerators. Cr cds: A, C, D, DS, MC, V.

⊡ ✔ ⋈ 🐾 SC

Yellowstone National Park (A-2 - B-3)

(See also Cody; also see West Yellowstone, MT)

Pop 350 (est) **Area code** 307 **Zip** 82190

In 1872, the Congress of the United States set aside more than 3,000 square miles of wilderness in the Wyoming Territory, establishing the world's first national park. More than a century later, Yellowstone boasts a marvelous list of sights, attractions and facilities: A large freshwater lake, the highest in the nation (7,733 feet); a waterfall almost twice as high as Niagara; a dramatic, 1,200-foot-deep river canyon; and the world's most famous geyser—Old Faithful.

Most of the park has been left in its natural state, preserving the area's beauty and delicate ecological balance. The widespread fires at Yellowstone in 1988 were the greatest ecological event in the more than hundred-year-old history of the park. Although large areas of forest land were affected, park facilities and attractions remained generally undamaged. Yellowstone is one of the world's most successful wildlife sanctuaries. Within its boundaries live a variety of species, including grizzly and black bears, elk, deer, pronghorn and bison. Although it is not unusual to encounter animals along park roads, they are more commonly seen along backcountry trails and in more remote areas. Never approach, feed or otherwise disturb any wild animal. Visitors should stay in their cars with the windows up if approached by wildlife. Animals may look friendly, but are unpredictable.

The Grand Loop Road, a main accessway within the park, winds approximately 140 miles past many major points of interest. Five miles south of the North Entrance is Mammoth Hot Springs, the park headquarters and museum (year-round). The visitor center provides a general overview of the history of the park. High terraces with water spilling from natural springs are nearby. Naturalist-guided walks are conducted on boardwalks over the terraces (summer).

The Norris Geyser Basin is 21 miles directly south of Mammoth Hot Springs. The largest thermal basin in the world provides a multitude of displays; springs, geysers, mud pots and steam vents hiss, bubble and erupt in a showcase of thermal forces at work. The visitor center has self-explanatory exhibits and dioramas (June-Labor Day, daily). A self-guided trail (2 1/2 miles) offers views of the Porcelain and Back basins from boardwalks (mid-June-Labor Day). The Museum of the National Park Ranger is also nearby.

At Madison, 14 miles southwest of Norris, the West Entrance Road (US 20/91 outside the park) joins the Grand Loop Road. Heading south of Madison, it is a 16-mile trip to Old Faithful. Along the route are four thermal spring areas; numerous geysers, mud pots and pools provide an appropriate prologue to the spectacle ahead. Old Faithful has not missed a performance in the more than 100 years since eruptions were first recorded. Eruptions occur on the average of every 75 minutes, although intervals have varied from 30 to 120 minutes. A nearby visitor center provides information, exhibits and a film and slide program (May-Oct, mid-Dec-mid-Mar, daily).

From Old Faithful it is 17 miles east to West Thumb. Yellowstone Lake, the highest natural freshwater lake in the US is here. Early explorers thought that the shape of the lake resembled a hand-with the westernmost bay forming its thumb. A variety of rare species of waterfowl make their home along its 110 miles of shoreline. The 22-mile road from the South Entrance on the John D. Rockefeller Jr. Memorial Parkway (US 29/287 outside the park) meets the Grand Loop Road here.

Northeast of West Thumb, about 19 miles up the western shore of Yellowstone Lake, the road leads to Lake Village and then to Fishing Bridge. Although fishing is not permitted at Fishing Bridge (extending one mile downstream, to the north and one-quarter mile upstream, to the south of Fishing Bridge), the numerous lakes and rivers in the park make Yellowstone a fisherman's paradise. At Lake Village the road splits—27 miles east is the East Entrance from US 14/16/20, 16 miles north is Canyon Village. Canyon Village is near Upper Falls (109-foot drop) and the spectacular Lower Falls (308-foot drop). The colorful and awesome Grand Canyon of the Yellowstone River can be viewed from several points; there are self-guided trails along the rim and naturalist-led walks (summer). Groomed cross-country ski trails are open in winter. Museum (mid-May-late Sept, daily).

Sixteen miles north of Canyon Village is Tower. Just south of Tower Junction is the 132-foot Tower Fall, which can best be observed from a platform at the end of the path leading from the parking lot. The Northeast Entrance on US 212 is 29 miles east of Tower; Mammoth Hot Springs is 18 miles west.

The rest of the park is wilderness, with more than 1,100 miles of marked foot trails. Some areas may be closed for resource management purposes; inquire at one of the visitor centers in the area before hiking in backcountry. Guided tours of the wilderness can be made on horseback; horse rentals are available at Mammoth Hot Springs, Roosevelt and Canyon Village.

Do not pick wildflowers or collect any natural objects. Read all regulations established by the National Park Service and comply with them—they are for the protection of all visitors as well as for the protection of park resources.

Recreational vehicle campsites are available by reservation at Fishing Bridge RV Park (contact TW Recreational Services, Inc, at 307/344-7901 for general information or 307/344-7311 for reservations). During July and August, demand often exceeds supply and many sites are occupied by mid-morning. Overnight vehicle camping or stopping outside designated campgrounds is not permitted. Reservations for Bridge Bay Campground are available through local Mistix outlets, by mail or by phoning 800/365-2267. There are ten additional National Park Service campgrounds at Yellowstone; these are operated on a first-come, first-served basis, so it is advisable to arrive early to secure the site of your choice. Campfires are prohibited except in designated areas or by special permit obtained at ranger stations. Backcountry camping is available by permit only, up to 48 hours in advance, in person, at ranger stations.

Fishing in Yellowstone National Park requires a permit (free at any visitor center or ranger station). Rowboats, powerboats and tackle may be rented at Bridge Bay Marina. Permits are also required for all vessels (motorized, $10; nonmotorized, $5) and must be obtained in person at any of the following locations: South Entrance, Bridge Bay Marina, Mammoth Visitor Center, Grant Village Visitor Center, Lake Ranger Station and Lewis Lake Campground. Information centers near Yellowstone Lake are located at Fishing Bridge and Grant Village (both Memorial Day-Labor Day, daily).

At several locations there are visitor centers, general stores for provisions, photo shops, service stations, tent & trailer sites, hotels and lodges. There are bus tours through the park from mid-June to Labor Day (contact TW Recreational Services, Inc, at 307/344-7901). Cars can be rented in some of the gateway communities.

CCInc Auto Tape Tours, two 90-min cassettes, offer a mile-by-mile self-guided tour of the park. Written in cooperation with the National Park Service, it provides information on geology, history, points of interest and flora and fauna. Tapes may be obtained at gift shops throughout the park. Tapes also may be purchased directly from CCInc, PO Box 227, 2 Elbrook Dr, Allendale, NJ 07401; 201/236-1666. ¢¢¢¢

TourGuide Self-Guided Car Audio Tours. Produced in cooperation with the National Park Service, this system uses the random-access capability of CD technology to instantly select narration on topics like wildlife, ecology, safety, history and folklore. Visitors rent a self-contained player (about the size of a paperback book) that plugs into a car's cigarette lighter and broadcasts an FM signal to its radio. A screen on the unit displays menus of chapters and topics, which may be played in any order for an individualized, narrated auto tour (total running time approx 5 hrs). Players may be rented at selected park hotels (contact TW Recreational Services, Inc, 307/344-7901). For further information contact TIS, Inc, 1018 Burlington Ave, Suite 101, Missoula, MT 59801; phone 406/549-3800 or 800/247-1213. Per day ¢¢¢¢

The official park season is May 1 through Oct 31. However, US 212 from Red Lodge, MT to Cooke City, MT (outside the Northeast Entrance) is not open to automobiles until about May 30 and closes about Oct 1. In winter, roads from Gardiner to Mammoth Hot Springs and to Cooke City, MT are kept open, but the road from Red Lodge is closed; travelers must return to Gardiner to leave the park. The west, east and south entrances are closed to automobiles from Nov 1 to about May 1, but are open to oversnow vehicles from mid-Dec-mid-Mar. Dates are subject to change. For current road conditions and other information, phone park headquarters at 307/344-7381. Entrance permit, $10/vehicle/visit, good for seven days; Grand Teton permit also honored. For further information phone 307/344-7381 (no campground reservations).

Note: Weather conditions or conservation measures may dictate the closing of certain roads and recreational facilities. In winter, inquire before attempting to enter the park.

Motel

(Reservations advised for accommodations within the national park)

★ **GRANT VILLAGE.** *18 mi E of Old Faithful, then 2 mi S of Loop Rd on Yellowstone Lake. 307/344-7311; FAX 307/344-7456.* Web www.amfac.com. 300 rms in 6 bldgs, 2 story. No A/C. Late May-Sept: S, D $80-$100; each addl $9; under 12 free. Closed rest of yr. Restaurant 6:30 am-10 pm. Bar 5 pm-midnight. Ck-out 11 am. Coin lndry. Meeting rms. Gift shop. On lake. Cr cds: A, C, D, DS, JCB, MC, V.

Hotels

★ ★ ★ **LAKE YELLOWSTONE.** *1/2 mi S of Lake jct on Loop Rd in park.* 307/344-7311; FAX 307/242-7652. Web www.amfac.com. 194 rms. No A/C. Late May-late Sept: S, D $90-$145; each addl $8; suite $385; under 12 free. Closed rest of yr. Crib free. Restaurant (see LAKE YEL-LOWSTONE DINING ROOM). No rm serv. Bar 11:30 am-midnight. Ck-out 11 am. Overlooks Yellowstone Lake. Cr cds: A, C, D, DS, JCB, MC, V.

✔★ **MAMMOTH HOT SPRINGS HOTEL & CABINS.** *5 mi S of North Entrance on Loop Rd in park.* 307/344-7311. Web www.amfac.com. 97 rms, 69 baths, 4 story, 126 cabins, 75 baths. No A/C. Late May-mid-Sept: S, D $45-$115; each addl $9; suites $255; cabins with whirlpool $120; under 12 free; lower rates rest of yr. Closed Oct-Nov & Mar-Apr. Crib free. Restaurant opp 7 am-10 pm. No rm serv. Bar 11:30 am-midnight.

Ck-out 11 am. Meeting rm. Gift shop. X-country ski on site. Cr cds: A, C, D, DS, JCB, MC, V.

★ ★ **OLD FAITHFUL INN.** *On Loop Rd, adj to Old Faithful Geyser in park.* 307/344-7311. Web www.amfac.com. 325 rms, 246 baths, 1-4 story. No A/C. Many rm phones. Early May-mid-Oct: S, D $55-$140; each addl $8; suites $330; under 12 free. Closed rest of yr. Crib free. Restaurant 6:30-10 am, 11:30 am-2:30 pm, 5-10 pm. No rm serv. Bar 11:30 am-midnight. Ck-out 11 am. Some refrigerators. Some rms have view of Old Faithful. Historic log structure (1904). Cr cds: A, C, D, DS, JCB, MC, V.

Restaurant

★ ★ **LAKE YELLOWSTONE DINING ROOM.** *(See Lake Yel-lowstone Hotel)* 307/344-7311. E-mail chef@imt.net; web www.amfac .com. Hrs: 6:30-10:30 am, 11:30 am-2:30 pm, 5-10 pm. Closed Oct-May. Res accepted. Bar 11:30 am-11:30 pm. Semi-a la carte: bkfst $2.75-$5.95, lunch $3.75-$8.95, dinner $10.95-$21.95. Buffet: bkfst $6.75. Child's meals. Specializes in grilled salmon, grilled duck, roasted tenderloin. String quartet or pianist. Overlooks lake. Totally nonsmoking. Cr cds: A, C, D, DS, JCB, MC, V.

Canada

Population: 24,343,181
Land area: 3,851,809 square miles (9,976,357 square kilometers)
Highest point: Mt Logan, Yukon Territory, 19,850 feet (6,050 meters)
Capital: Ottawa
Speed limit: 50 or 60 MPH (80 or 100 KPH), unless otherwise indicated

Just north of the United States, with which it shares the world's longest undefended border, lies Canada, the world's largest country in terms of land area. Extending from the North Pole to the northern border of the United States and including all the islands from Greenland to Alaska, Canada's area encompasses nearly 4 million square miles (10.4 million square kilometers). The northern reaches of the country consist mainly of the Yukon and Northwest territories, which make up the vast, sparsely-populated Canadian frontier.

Jacques Cartier erected a cross at Gaspé in 1534 and declared the establishment of New France. Samuel de Champlain founded Port Royal in Nova Scotia in 1604. Until 1759, Canada was under French rule. In that year, British General Wolfe defeated French General Montcalm at Québec and British possession followed. In 1867, the British North America Act established the Confederation of Canada, with four provinces: New Brunswick, Nova Scotia, Ontario and Québec. The other provinces joined later. Canada was proclaimed a self-governing Dominion within the British Empire in 1931. The passage in 1981 of the Constitution Act severed Canada's final legislative link with Great Britain, which had until that time reserved the right to amend the Canadian Constitution.

Today, Canada is a sovereign nation—neither a colony nor a possession of Great Britain. Since Canada is a member of the Commonwealth of Nations, Queen Elizabeth II, through her representative, the Governor-General, is the nominal head of state. However, the Queen's functions are mostly ceremonial with no political power or authority. Instead, the nation's chief executive is the prime minister; the legislative branch consists of the Senate and the House of Commons.

Visitor Information

Currency. The American dollar is accepted throughout Canada, but it is advisable to exchange your money into Canadian currency upon arrival. Banks and currency exchange firms typically give the best rate of exchange, but hotels and stores will also convert it for you with purchases. The Canadian monetary system is based on dollars and cents, and rates in *Mobil Travel Guide* are given in Canadian currency. Generally, the credit cards you use at home are also honored in Canada.

Goods and Services Tax (GST). Most goods and services in Canada are subject to a 7% tax. Visitors to Canada may claim a rebate of the GST paid on *short-term accommodations* (hotel, motel or similar lodging) and on *most consumer goods* purchased to take home. Rebates may be claimed for cash at participating Canadian Duty Free shops or by mail. For further information and a brochure detailing rebate procedures and restrictions contact Revenue Canada, Customs and Excise, Visitors' Rebate Program, Ottawa, ON K1A 1J5; phone 613/991-3346 or 800/66-VISIT (in Canada).

Driving in Canada. Your American driver's license is valid in Canada; no special permit is required. In Canada the liter is the unit of measure for gasoline. One US gallon equals 3.78 liters. Traffic signs are clearly understood and in many cities are bilingual. All road speed limits and mileage signs have been posted in kilometers. A flashing green traffic light gives vehicles turning left the right-of-way, like a green left-turn arrow. The use of safety belts is generally mandatory in all provinces; consult the various provincial tourism bureaus for specific information.

Holidays. All Canada observes the following holidays, and these are indicated in text: New Year's Day, Good Friday, Easter Monday, Victoria Day (usually 3rd Mon May), Canada Day (July 1), Labour Day, Thanksgiving (2nd Mon Oct), Remembrance Day (November 11), Christmas and Boxing Day (December 26). See individual provinces for information on provincial holidays.

Liquor. The sale of liquor, wine, beer and cider varies from province to province. Restaurants must be licensed to serve liquor, and in some cases liquor may not be sold unless it accompanies a meal. Generally there are no package sales on holidays. Minimum legal drinking age also varies by province. **Note:** It is illegal to take children into bars or cocktail lounges.

Daylight Saving Time. Canada observes Daylight Saving Time beginning the first Sunday in April through the last Sunday in October, except for most of the province of Saskatchewan, where Standard Time is observed year-round.

Tourist information is available from individual provincial and territorial tourism offices (see Border Crossing Regulations in MAKING THE MOST OF YOUR TRIP).

Province of Alberta

Pop 2,513,100 **Land area** 246,423 sq mi (661,185 sq km) **Capital** Edmonton

Information Travel Alberta, Box 2500, Edmonton T5J 2Z4; 403/427-4321 or 800/661-8888.

With a history of ancient indigenous civilizations, missionary settlements, fur trading, "gold fever" and frontier development, Alberta thrives today as a vital industrial, agricultural and recreational center. It possesses the widest variety of geographical features of any province in Canada, including a giant plateau "badlands" rich in dinosaur fossils, rolling prairie and vast parkland. All along its western border are the magnificent Canadian Rockies.

Easily accessible from Montana, you can enter Alberta from Waterton Lakes National Park and drive north to Calgary, where you intersect with the Trans-Canada Highway and can enjoy a variety of attractions. The view of the Rockies from the Calgary Tower and the excitement of the Calgary Stampede are not to be missed.

From Calgary drive northwest to Banff, Lake Louise and Jasper National Park for some of the finest mountain scenery, outdoor activities, resorts and restaurants on the continent.

Heading due north from Calgary, visit Red Deer, a town famous for agriculture, oil and its beautiful parkland setting. Farther north is the provincial capital, Edmonton. A confident, multicultural city, it is noted for its oil, its "gold rush" past and its parks, cultural activities, magnificent sports facilities and rodeos. Northwest of Edmonton, Alberta provides paved access to "Mile 0" of the Alaska Highway at Dawson Creek, BC. There is also paved access to the Northwest Territories—Canada's "frontier" land.

Drive southeast from Calgary and enter an entirely different scene— cowboy and Indian territory. Fort Macleod brings you back to the early pioneer days. Lethbridge is famous for its replica of the most notorious 19th-century whiskey fort—Fort Whoop-Up—and the Nikka Yuko Japanese Gardens. Farther east, visit Medicine Hat, known for its parks, pottery and rodeos. Alberta is truly a vacation destination for all seasons and tastes.

Alberta observes Mountain Standard Time and Daylight Saving Time in summer. Hunting is not permitted in national or provincial parks and a separate fishing license is required. For information on hunting and fishing in other areas of the province, contact the Fish and Wildlife Division, Dept of Forestry, Lands and Wildlife, 9920 108th St, Edmonton T5K 2C9.

In addition to national holidays, Alberta observes Heritage Day (1st Mon Aug) and Family Day (3rd Mon Feb).

Safety belts are mandatory for all persons anywhere in vehicle. Children under 6 years or under 40 pounds in weight must be in an approved child safety seat. For further information phone 403/427-8901.

Banff (D-3)

(See also Calgary, Lake Louise)

Pop 6,800 (est) **Elev** 4,538 ft (1,383 m) **Area code** 403
Information Banff-Lake Louise Tourism Bureau, 224 Banff Ave, PO Box 1298, T0L 0C0; 403/762-8421.

Banff came to be because of the popularity of the hot springs in the area. The Banff Hot Springs Reservation was created in 1885 and by 1887 became Rocky Mountains Park. Today we know this vast recreation area as Banff National Park, offering the visitor activity all year, plus the beauty of the Rocky Mountains.

Banff comes alive each summer with its music and drama festival, put on by the Banff Centre. In winter, the Rockies provide some of the best skiing on the North American continent, including helicopter, downhill and cross-country. The town of Banff itself has exciting nightlife, sleigh rides, Western barbecues and indoor recreational activities. The area offers sightseeing gondola rides, boat and raft tours, concerts, art galleries, museums, hot springs, ice field tours, hiking and trail rides.

What to See and Do

Cave & Basin Centennial Centre. The birthplace of Canada's national park system and a national historic site. Hot springs, cave, exhibits, trails, theater (daily; closed Jan 1, Dec 25). W on Cave Ave. Phone 403/762-1557. ¢¢

Jasper National Park (see). 179 mi (287 km) N on Hwy 93.

Natural History Museum. More than 60 displays, slide and film shows depicting the national parks; prehistoric life, precious stones, trees & flowers, origins of the earth and formations of mountains and caves. (Daily; closed Dec 25) 112 Banff Ave, upstairs at Clock Tower Mall. Phone 403/762-4747. **Free.**

Sightseeing tours.

Rocky Mountain Raft Tours. 1-hr round-trip excursions (4 trips daily); also 3-hr round-trips (2 trips daily). Trip durations approximate; includes transportation time to departure site. (June-mid-Sept) For schedule and fees contact Rocky Mt Raft Tours, PO Box 1771, T0L 0C0; 403/762-3632.

CCInc Auto Tape Tours. This 90-min cassette offers a mile-by-mile self-guided tour. Written by informed guides, it provides information on history, glaciers, points of interest and flora & fauna of the area. Tapes are available at The Thunderbird on Banff Ave, opposite the park Information Center. Rental includes player and tape: Banff tour or combination Banff/Jasper. Tapes also may be purchased directly from CCInc, PO Box 227, 2 Elbrook Dr, Allendale, NJ 07401; 201/236-1666. ¢¢¢¢

Seasonal Event

Banff Festival of the Arts. St Julien Rd. Mainstage productions and workshops in opera, ballet, music theater, drama, concerts, poetry reading, visual arts. Some events free. For information contact The Banff Centre Box Office, PO Box 1020, T0L 0C0; 403/762-6300. June-Aug.

Motels

★ **BEST WESTERN SIDING 29 LODGE.** *(453 Marten St, Banff AB T0L 0C0)* 451 Marten St. 403/762-5575; FAX 403/762-8866. 51 rms, 3 story, 10 suites. No A/C. June-Sept: S, D $140-$170; suites $175-$250; lower rates rest of yr. Crib $10. Pet accepted. TV; cable. Indoor pool; whirlpool. Complimentary coffee in lobby. Restaurant adj 7-11 am, 5-11 pm. Ck-out 11 am. Business servs avail. Downhill ski 5 mi; x-country ski 2 mi. Some refrigerators. Some balconies. Cr cds: A, C, D, DS, ER, JCB, MC, V.

★ ★ **CHARLTON'S CEDAR COURT.** *(513 Banff Ave, Banff AB T0L 0C0)* 403/762-4485; FAX 403/762-2744; res: 800/661-1225 (Canada). 63 rms, 3 story, 16 kits. No A/C. June-Sept: S, D $155-$175; each addl $15; kit. units $175; under 16 free; lower rates rest of yr. Crib free. TV; cable; VCR avail (movies). Indoor pool; whirlpool, steam rm. Complimentary coffee in lobby. Restaurant nearby. Ck-out 11 am. Business servs avail. In-rm modem link. Free covered parking. Downhill ski 2 mi; x-country ski 1 mi. Cr cds: A, D, ER, JCB, MC, V.

★ ★ **CHARLTON'S EVERGREEN COURT.** *(459 Banff Ave, Banff AB T0L 0C0)* 403/762-3307; FAX 403/762-2744; res: 800/661-1225 (Canada). 52 rms, 2 story, 18 kit. units. No A/C. June-Sept: S, D $155-$175; each addl $15; kit. units $175; under 16 free; ski plans; lower rates rest of yr. Crib free. TV; VCR avail (movies). Heated pool; whirlpool. Continental bkfst 7-10:30 am. Complimentary coffee in lobby. Restaurant adj 7 am-10:30 pm. Ck-out 11 am. Business servs avail. In-rm modem link. Dowhill/x-country ski 2 mi. Some in-rm whirlpools. Cr cds: A, D, ER, JCB, MC, V.

★ ★ ★ **DOUGLAS FIR RESORT.** *(Box 1228, Banff AB T0L 0C0)* 5 mi S of Trans-Canada Hwy 1 via Lynx St, Wolf St to Tunnel Mountain Rd. 403/762-5591; FAX 403/762-8774; res: 800/661-9267. 133 condo units, 3 story, 9 chalets. No A/C. S, D $188-$198; each addl $10; suites, chalets $238-$278; under 15 free. TV; cable, VCR avail. Indoor pool; whirlpool, water slides. Ck-out 11 am. Coin lndry. Business servs avail. Underground parking. Tennis. Downhill ski 5 mi; x-country ski adj. Exercise equipt; weights, bicycles, sauna, steam rm. Refrigerators, fireplaces. Private patios, balconies. Picnic tables, grills. Gazebo. Cr cds: A, D, ER, MC, V.

⊠ ⚐ 🏃 ≈ 🍴 🐾

★ **HIDDEN RIDGE CHALETS.** *(600 Tunnel Mountain Rd, Banff AB T0L 0C0)* 403/762-3544; FAX 403/762-2804; res: 800/661-1372. 83 kit. units, 1-2 story. No A/C. June-Sept: S, D $165-$190; each addl $15; under 14 free; higher rates Dec 25; lower rates rest of yr. Crib free. TV; cable. Complimentary coffee in rms. Restaurant nearby. Ck-out 11 am. Business servs avail. Whirlpool. Downhill/ x-country ski 5 mi. Balconies. Picnic tables. Cr cds: MC, V.

⊠ 🐾

✔★ **RED CARPET INN.** *(425 Banff Ave, Banff AB T0L 0C0)* 403/762-4184; FAX 403/762-4894; res: 800/563-4609 (CN only). 52 rms, 3 story. No A/C. June-mid-Oct: S $100-$125; D $140-$150; lower rates rest of yr. Crib avail. Pet accepted. TV; VCR avail. Restaurant adj 7 am-11 pm. Business servs avail. Free garage parking. Whirlpool (winter only). Balconies. Cr cds: A, MC, V.

⚐ ≈ 🐾

✔★ ★ **RUNDLE MOUNTAIN MOTEL & GASTHAUS.** *(PO Box 147, Canmore, Banff AB T0L 0M0)* 15 mi E on Hwy 1, Canmore exit, on Mountain Ave. 403/678-5322; FAX 403/678-5813; res: 800/661-1610 (W CAN). 51 rms, 2 story, 14 suites, 18 kit. units. No A/C. Mid-June-mid-Sept: S, D $93-$113; each addl $10; suites $195; kit. units $103-$195; family, wkly rates; ski plans; lower rates rest of yr. TV; cable. Indoor pool; whirlpool. Playground. Complimentary coffee in rms. Restaurant 7 am-10 pm. Ck-out 11 am. Meeting rms. Refrigerators. Picnic tables. Cr cds: A, D, ER, MC, V.

D ⊠ ≈ 🐾

★ ★ **RUNDLESTONE LODGE.** *(537 Banff Ave, Banff AB T0L 0C0)* 403/762-2201; FAX 403/762-4501; res: 800/661-8630. 80 rms, 3 story, 8 suites. June-Sept: S $130-$170; D $145-$175; each addl $10; suites $175-$225; under 5 free; lower rates rest of yr. TV; cable. Complimentary continental bkfst. Restaurant nearby. Ck-out 11 am. Coin lndry. Meeting rms. Business servs avail. In-rm modem link. Bellhops. Sauna. Whirlpool. Balconies. Cr cds: A, D, DS, MC, V.

D ⊠ 🐾

★ ★ **TUNNEL MOUNTAIN CHALETS.** *(Box 1137, Banff AB T0L 0C0)* 5 mi S of Trans-Canada Hwy 1 via Moose St, Otter St to Tunnel Mountain Rd. 403/762-4515; FAX 403/762-5183; res: 800/661-1859. 24 kit. condo units, 2 story, 51 kit. chalets. No A/C. Mid-June-mid-Sept: S, D $179-$210; each addl $15; under 15 free; lower rates rest of yr. Crib free. TV; cable (premium), VCR avail. Sauna. Indoor pool; whirlpools. Complimentary coffee in rms. Restaurant nearby. Ck-out 11 am. Meeting rms. Business servs avail. Free garage parking. Downhill ski 5 mi; x-country ski 1 mi. Picnic tables, grills. Cr cds: A, C, MC, V.

⊠ ≈ ⚐ 🐾 SC

Lodge

★ ★ **TIMBERLINE.** *(Box 69, Banff AB T0L 0C0)* off Trans-Canada Hwy 1 at base of Mt Norquay. 403/762-2281; FAX 403/762-8331. 52 rms, 2 story. No A/C. June-late Sept: S, D $115-$145; each addl $15; suites $158-$185; kit. chalet $275; under 12 free; MAP avail; lower rates rest of yr. TV; cable. Dining rm 7 am-11 pm. Rm serv. Bar 11 am-midnight. Ck-out 11 am. Meeting rms. Business servs avail. Valet serv. Downhill/x-country ski 1/2 mi. Outdoor whirlpool. Some refrigerators. Balconies. Picnic tables, grills. Cr cds: A, MC, V.

⊠ 🏃 ≈ 🐾

Motor Hotels

★ ★ **BANFF PARK LODGE.** *(222 Lynx St, Banff AB T0L 0C0)* 403/762-4433; FAX 403/762-3553; res: 800/661-9266. 211 rms, 3 story. June-Sept: S, D $199; each addl $15; suites $279; under 16 free; higher rates Christmas hols; lower rates rest of yr. TV; cable (premium), VCR

avail. Heated pool; whirlpool, steam rms. Restaurant 7 am-midnight. Rm serv. Bar; entertainment exc Sun. Ck-out 11 am. Business servs avail. In-rm modem link. Bellhops. Shopping arcade. Barber, beauty shop. Heated underground parking. Downhill/x-country ski 2 mi. Private patios, balconies. Cr cds: A, C, D, ER, JCB, MC, V.

D ⊠ ≈ 🐾 SC

★ ★ ★ **BANFF ROCKY MOUNTAIN RESORT.** *(Box 100, Banff AB T0L 0C0)* Banff Ave at Tunnel Mt Rd, just off Trans-Canada Hwy 1. 403/762-5531; FAX 403/762-5166; res: 800/661-9563. 171 condo units, 2 story. Mid-June-mid-Sept: condos $200-$275; each addl $15; under 16 free; higher rates Christmas hol; lower rates rest of yr. Crib free. Pet accepted. TV, cable. Indoor pool; whirlpool. Playground. Restaurant 7-11 am, 6-9:30 pm. Rm serv 3-10 pm. Bar 11-1 am. Ck-out 11 am. Meeting rms. Business servs avail. Tennis. Downhill/x-country ski 2 mi. Exercise equipt; weight machine, bicycle, sauna. Refrigerators, fireplaces. Balconies. Picnic tables, grill. Cr cds: A, C, D, ER, JCB, MC, V.

D ⚐ ⊠ 🏃 ≈ 🍴 🏃 🐾 SC

✔★ ★ **BANFF VOYAGER INN.** *(555 Banff Ave, Banff AB T0L 0C0)* 403/762-3301; FAX 403/762-4131; res: 800/879-1991. 88 rms, 2 story. No A/C. June-Sept: S, D $99-$119; each addl $15; under 17 free; ski plans; lower rates rest of yr. Crib free. TV; cable (premium). Heated pool; whirlpool, sauna. Restaurant 7-11 am, 5:30-9:30 pm. Bar 11-2 am. Ck-out 11 am. Meeting rms. Business servs avail. Downhill/country ski 2 mi. Balconies. Cr cds: A, MC, V.

⊠ ≈ 🐾

★ ★ **BEST WESTERN-GREEN GABLES INN.** *(Hwy 1A, Box 520, Canmore AB T0L 0M0)* 15 mi E on Hwy 1, at Canmore exit. 403/678-5488; FAX 403/678-2670; res: 800/661-2133. 61 rms, 2 story, 10 kit. units. June-mid-Sept: S, D $129-$149; each addl $10; suites $159-$199; kit. units $149; under 18 free; ski plans; lower rates rest of yr. Crib free. TV; cable (premium). Complimentary continental bkfst. Complimentary coffee in rms. Restaurant 7 am-2 pm, 5-10 pm (see also CHEZ FRANÇOIS). Bar 5-10 pm. Ck-out 11 am. Meeting rms. Business servs avail. Downhill ski 15 mi; x-country ski 2 mi. Exercise equipt; weights, bicycles. Whirlpool. Refrigerators. Balconies. Cr cds: A, D, DS, ER, MC, V.

D ⊠ 🍴 ≈ 🐾 SC

★ ★ **BUFFALO MOUNTAIN LODGE.** *(Box 1326, Banff AB T0L 0C0)* 5 mi S off Trans-Canada Hwy 1 via Moose St, Otter St to Tunnel Mountain Rd. 403/762-2400; FAX 403/762-4495; res: 800/661-1367. 85 rms, 20 kit. units. No A/C. Early June-late Sept: S, D, kit. units $210-$280; each addl $20; under 12 free; ski plan. Crib free. TV; cable, VCR avail. Complimentary coffee, tea in rms. Restaurant 7 am-10 pm. Rm serv. Bar 11 am-11 pm. Ck-out 11 am. Meeting rms. Business servs avail. In-rm modem link. Bellhops. Downhill/x-country ski 3 mi. Steam rm. Whirlpool. Some refrigerators, fireplaces. Balconies. Cr cds: A, D, ER, MC, V.

⊠ 🐾 SC

★ ★ **DYNASTY INN.** *(501 Banff Ave, Banff AB T0L 0C0)* 403/762-8844; FAX 403/667-1464. 98 rms, 3 story. Mid-June-late Sept: S, D $155-$205; each addl $12; under 12 free; ski plan, wkend rates; lower rates rest of yr. Crib free. Garage parking. TV; cable. Restaurant nearby. Ck-out 11 am. Business servs avail. In-rm modem link. Bellhops. Downhill/x-country ski 3 mi. Sauna. Whirlpool. Balconies. Cr cds: A, MC, V.

⊠ ≈ 🐾

★ ★ **GREENWOOD INN.** *(511 Box Valley Tr, Canmore AB T0L 0M0)* approx 10 mi E on Hwy 1. 403/678-3625; FAX 403/678-3765; res: 800/263-3625. 171 rms, 3 story. Late June-early Sept: S, D $119-$139; each addl $10; suites $185-$225; under 16 free; lower rates rest of yr. Crib free. TV; cable. Pool; whirlpool, steam rm. Restaurant 7 am-11 pm. Rm serv. Bar. Ck-out 11 am. Meeting rms. Business servs avail. In-rm modem link. Valet serv. Downhill ski 14 mi, x-country ski 2 mi. Balconies. Cr cds: A, C, D, ER, MC, V.

D ⊠ ≈ 🐾

✔★ ★ **HIGH COUNTRY INN.** *(419 Banff Ave, Banff AB T0L 0C0)* 403/762-2236; FAX 403/762-5084; res: 800/661-1244. 70 rms, 3 story.

June-early Oct: S, D $115-$120; each addl $10; under 12 free; lower rates rest of yr. Crib free. TV; cable. Indoor pool; whirlpools. Restaurant 7:30 am-10:30 pm (see also TICINO SWISS-ITALIAN). Ck-out 11 am. Meeting rms. Business servs avail. Free garage parking. Downhill/x-country ski 2 mi. Cr cds: A, MC, V.

★ ★ **INNS OF BANFF.** (600 Banff, Banff AB T0L 0C0) 403/762-4581; FAX 403/762-2434; res: 800/661-1272. 180 rms, 4 story. June-Sept: S, D $180-$200; each addl $20; under 16 free; ski plans; lower rates rest of yr. Crib free. TV; cable. Indoor pool; whirlpool. Sauna. Restaurant 7 am-2 pm, 6-10 pm. Rm serv. Bar 2-10 pm. Ck-out 11 am. Meeting rms. Business servs avail. Bellhops. Gift shop. Downhill/x-country ski 2 mi. Refrigerators. Balconies. Scenic mountain location. Cr cds: A, D, ER, JCB, MC, V.

★ ★ **IRWIN'S MOUNTAIN INN.** (429 Banff Ave, Banff AB T0L 0C0) 403/762-4566; FAX 403/762-8220; res: 800/661-1721. 65 rms, 3 story. No A/C. June-Sept: S $115-$195; D $140-$220; each addl $10; suites $150-$220; under 16 free; lower rates rest of yr. Crib free. TV; cable (premium). Indoor pool; whirlpool. Complimentary coffee in rms. Restaurant 7-11 am, 5-11 pm. Ck-out 11 am. Meeting rms. Business servs avail. In-rm modem link. Gift shop. Valet serv. Coin lndry. Downhill ski 5 mi; x-country ski 1 mi. Exercise equipt; bicycle, treadmill, sauna. Some refrigerators. Cr cds: A, MC, V.

★ ★ **QUALITY RESORT.** (1720 Bow Valley Trail, Canmore AB T0L 0M0) 403/678-6699; FAX 403/678-6954. 119 rms, 3 story. June-Oct: S, D $159-$189; kit. units $219-$249; under 18 free; lower rates rest of yr. Crib free. TV; VCR (movies). Indoor pool; whirlpool. Sauna. Playground. Supervised child's activties (July-Aug); ages 7-15. Complimentary coffee in rms. Restaurant 6 am-11 pm. Rm serv. Bar to 1 am. Ck-out 11 am. Meeting rms. Business servs avail. Lighted tennis. Downhill ski 18 mi; x-country ski 1 mi. Health club privileges. Bicycles rental. Some refrigerators. Some balconies. Cr cds: A, C, D, DS, ER, JCB, MC, V.

Hotels

★ ★ **BANFF CARIBOU LODGE.** (521 Banff Ave, Banff AB T0L 0C0) 403/762-5887; FAX 403/762-5918; res: 800/563-8764. 200 rms, 4 story. June-Oct: S $160-$175; D $175-$190; each addl $15; suites $225-$275; under 16 free; hol rates; ski plans; lower rates rest of yr. Crib avail. TV; cable (premium). Playground. Restaurant 6:30 am-11 pm. Bar. Ck-out 11 am. Meeting rm. Business servs avail. Downhill ski 2 mi; x-country ski 1 mi. Exercise equipt; bicycles, rowers, sauna. Whirlpool. Some balconies. Cr cds: A, D, ER, MC, V.

★ ★ **BANFF INTERNATIONAL.** (333 Banff Ave, Banff AB T0L 0C0) 403/762-5666; FAX 403/762-4895; res: 800/665-5666. 165 rms, 3 story. No A/C. June-Sept: S, D $189-$229; each addl $15; under 13 free; lower rates rest of yr. TV; cable. Restaurant 7-10:30 am. No rm serv. Business servs avail. In-rm modem link. Gift shop. Free covered parking. Downhill/x-country ski 1 mi. Whirlpool, sauna. Cr cds: A, D, ER, JCB, MC, V.

★ ★ ★ **BANFF SPRINGS.** (Box 960, Banff AB T0L 0C0) Spray Ave. 403/762-2211; FAX 403/762-5755; res: 800/441-1414. 815 rms, 9 story. No A/C. Mid-May-mid-Oct: S, D $190-$425; each addl $21; suites $425-$975; under 18 free; lower rates rest of yr. Crib free. Pet accepted; $20. Garage $6.50/day, valet $11. TV; cable. 2 pools, 1 indoor; whirlpool. Restaurant (see BANFF SPRINGS). Bar 11:30-1 am. Ck-out noon. Convention facilities. Business servs avail. In-rm modem link. Concierge. Shopping arcade. Beauty shop. Tennis, pro. 27-hole golf, greens fee $90, pro, putting green, driving range. Downhill ski 2 mi. Exercise equipt; weights, bicycles, sauna. Bowling. Rec rm. Minibars. Picnic tables. An-

tiques throughout. Located in wooded area overlooking Bow River Valley. Elaborate landscaping. Cr cds: A, C, D, DS, ER, JCB, MC, V.

★ ★ **MOUNT ROYAL.** (138 Banff Ave, Banff AB T0L 0C0) 138 Banff Ave. 403/762-3331; FAX 403/762-8938; res: 800/267-3035. 136 rms, 3-4 story. Late June-Sept: S, D $185; each addl $18; suites $245; under 16 free; ski plans; lower rates rest of yr. Crib free. Pet accepted, some restrictions. TV; cable. Restaurant 7 am-10 pm. Bar 11:30-1 am. Ck-out 11 am. Meeting rms. Beauty shop. Airport transportation. Downhill/x-country ski 5 mi. Exercise equipt; weight machine, bicycles, sauna. Whirlpool. Cr cds: A, D, ER, JCB, MC, V.

★ ★ **PTARMIGAN INN.** (337 Banff Ave, Banff AB T0L 0C0) 403/762-2207; FAX 403/762-3577; res: 800/661-8310. 167 rms, 3 story. No A/C. June-Sept: S $133; D $140; each addl $12; suites $210; under 16 free; ski plans; lower rates rest of yr. Pet accepted, some restrictions; $25. Free garage. TV; cable. Restaurant 7 am-11 pm. Bar 5 pm-midnight; entertainment wkends. Ck-out 11 am. Meeting rms. Business servs avail. Gift shop. Downhill/x-country ski 2 mi. Sauna. Whirlpool. Balconies. Cr cds: A, D, DS, ER, JCB, MC, V.

★ ★ ★ **RIMROCK RESORT HOTEL.** (Mountain Ave, Banff AB T0L 0C0) 403/762-3356; FAX 403/762-4132; res: 800/661-1587. 346 rms, 9 story, 45 suites. May-Sept: S, D $135-$325; each addl $20; suites $270-$650; under 18 free; wkly, wkend & hol rates; ski plan; lower rates rest of yr. Crib free. Garage parking $6; valet $10. TV; cable. Indoor pool; whirlpool, poolside serv. Restaurant (see THE PRIMROSE). Rm serv 24 hrs. Bar. Ck-out noon. Convention facilities. Business servs avail. In-rm modem link. Concierge. Shopping arcade. Barber, beauty shop. Downhill ski 3 mi; x-country ski on site. Exercise rm; instructor, weight machine, treadmill, sauna. Massage. Health club privileges. Game rm. Rec rm. Minibars. Balconies. Cr cds: A, C, D, DS, ER, JCB, MC, V.

Inn

✔★ ★ **LADY MACDONALD COUNTRY INN.** (1201 Bow Valley Trail, Canmore AB T0L 0M0) 15 mi E on Hwy 1A. 403/678-3665; FAX 403/678-9714; res: 800/567-3919. 11 rms, 2 story. No A/C. June-Sept & Dec hols: S $100-$160; each addl $10; under 6 free; lower rates rest of yr. Pet accepted, some restrictions; $10. TV; cable (premium). Complimentary full bkfst. Restaurant adj open 24 hrs. Ck-out 11 am. Business servs avail. In-rm modem link. Luggage handling. Downhill ski 10 mi; x-country ski 2 blks. Picnic tables. Victorian-style architecture; Shaker pine furniture. Cr cds: A, MC, V.

Restaurants

★ ★ **BALKAN.** (120 Banff Ave, Banff AB T0L 0C0) 403/762-3454. Hrs: 11 am-11 pm. Closed Dec 25. Res accepted. Greek, Amer menu. Semi-a la carte: lunch $6.50-$10, dinner $9.95-$20. Child's meals. Greek menu. Own desserts. Greek wall hangings, statues. Cr cds: JCB, MC, V.

★ ★ ★ **BANFF SPRINGS.** (See Banff Springs Hotel) 403/762-2211. Res accepted. No A/C. Bar 11:30 am-midnight. Child's meals. Own baking. Entertainment. Valet parking. Alberta Dining Room: 7-10 am, 6-9 pm; Sun brunch 11 am-2 pm. Continental menu. Complete meals: bkfst $12.50. Semi-a la carte: dinner $22-$45. Sun brunch $22.95. Rob Roy: 6-10 pm. A la carte entrees: dinner $20-$32. Specializes in steak, flambéed desserts. Waldhaus: noon-10 pm. German menu. Semi-a la carte: lunch $5-$12, dinner $16-$27. Specializes in fondues, schnitzel. Historical castle, built 1888. View of mountains. Cr cds: A, C, D, DS, ER, JCB, MC, V.

★ ★ **THE BISTRO.** *(229 Bear St, Banff AB T0L 0C0)* in Wolf & Bear Mall. 403/762-8900. Hrs: noon-midnight. Res accepted. Continental menu. Semi-a la carte: lunch $6.50-$15.50, dinner $10-$24. Child's meals. Specializes in seafood, bistro-style cuisine. Parking. Modern decor. Cr cds: A, MC, V.

D

★ ★ **CABOOSE STEAK & LOBSTER.** *(Lynx & Elk Sts, Banff AB T0L 0C0)* in railroad station. 403/762-3622. Hrs: 5-10 pm. Closed Dec 25. Res accepted. Bar 9 pm-2 am. A la carte entrees: dinner $10-$28. Specializes in prime rib, steak, seafood. Salad bar. Parking. Antiques and memorabilia from the railroad era. Porter's cart used as salad bar. Cr cds: A, D, ER, JCB, MC, V.

D

★ ★ **CHEZ FRANÇOIS.** *(See Best Western-Green Gables Inn Motor Hotel)* 403/678-6111. Hrs: 7 am-2:30 pm, 5-11 pm; Sun brunch 11 am-2:30 pm. Res accepted. French menu. Bar. Semi-a la carte: bkfst $3.95-$8.50, lunch $5.50-$12.95, dinner $10.95-$22.95. Sun brunch $6.50-$12.95. Child's meals. Parking. Outdoor dining. Cr cds: A, D, ER, MC, V.

★ ★ **GIORGIO'S TRATTORIA.** *(219 Banff Ave, Banff AB T0L 0C0)* 403/762-5114. Hrs: 4:30-11 pm. Northern Italian menu. Bar. A la carte entrees: dinner $9.50-$20. Specializes in veal, pasta, lamb. Cr cds: A, MC, V.

D

★ **GRIZZLY HOUSE.** *(207 Banff Ave, Banff AB)* 403/762-4055. Hrs: 11:30 am-midnight. Res accepted. Swiss menu. Bar. A la carte entrees: lunch $5-$15, dinner $12-$40. Specializes in fondue, steak. Outdoor dining. Carved totem poles, Indian crafts, antiques. Family-owned. Cr cds: A, MC, V.

★ ★ **LE BEAUJOLAIS.** *(212 Buffalo St, Banff AB)* 403/762-2712. Hrs: 6-11 pm. Res accepted. Air-cooled. French menu. Wine cellar. A la carte entrees: dinner $22-$27. Complete meals: dinner $36-$45. Child's meals. Specializes in seafood, beef, rack of lamb. Own baking. Scenic view of mountains. Frequented by movie, TV & political personalities. Cr cds: A, MC, V.

✔★ ★ **PEPPERMILL.** *(726 9th St, Canmore AB T0L 0M0)* 403/678-2292. Hrs: 5-10 pm. Closed Tues; Dec 25; also Nov. Res accepted. Swiss menu. Complete meal: dinner $9-$19.50. Child's meals. Specializes in peppersteak, seafood. Swiss atmosphere. Casual decor. Cr cds: A, MC, V.

D

★ ★ ★ **THE PRIMROSE.** *(See Rimrock Resort Hotel)* 403/762-3356. Hrs: 6:30 am-2 pm, 6-10 pm. Res accepted; required Fri, Sat. Continental menu. Bar. Wine list. Semi-a la carte: bkfst $7.75-$14.75, lunch $8-$23.75, dinner $15.50-$25. Buffet: bkfst $13. Child's meals. Specializes in pasta, veal, seafood. Valet parking. Large windows provide beautiful view. Cr cds: A, C, D, ER, JCB, MC, V.

D

★ ★ ★ **TICINO SWISS-ITALIAN.** *(See High Country Inn Motor Hotel)* 403/762-3848. Hrs: 5:30-10:30 pm. Res accepted. Swiss, Italian menu. Wine list. A la carte entrees: dinner $12-$26. Child's meals. Specializes in veal dishes, beef & cheese fondue, pasta. European atmosphere. Family-owned. Cr cds: A, JCB, MC, V.

D

Calgary (D-3)

(See also Banff)

Founded 1875 **Pop** 720,000 (est) **Elev** 3,439 ft (1,049 m) **Area code** 403 **E-mail** destination@visitor.calgary.ab.ca **Web** www.visitor.calgary.ab.ca **Information** Convention & Visitors Bureau, 237 8th Ave SE, Rm 200, T2G 0K8; 403/263-8510 or 800/661-1678.

Calgary, called "the gateway to the Canadian Rockies," was founded in 1875 by the North West Mounted Police at the confluence of the Bow and Elbow rivers. Surrounding the city are fertile farmlands and, to the west, the rolling foothills of the Rockies. It is partially due to this lush land that ranching and grain farming have played such a large part in the development of the city. In fact, Calgary is a principal centre for Canada's agri-businesses.

Calgary is also the major oil center in Canada. Since 1914, the petroleum industry has centered its activities here. Today more than eight percent of Canada's oil and gas producers are headquartered in Calgary. As a result, Calgary has experienced a phenomenal growth rate. But the city has retained some of its earlier "small town" atmosphere, and Calgarians are still noted for their warmth and hospitality.

Site of the 1988 Olympic Winter Games, Calagary offers a broad array of pursuits for outdoors enthusiasts, ranging from its numerous golf courses to hiking and whitewater rafting in its foothills and alpine environs. Cultural activities abound as well, and Calgary also provides its share of nightlife.

What to See and Do

Calaway Park. Amusement park with 19 rides, attractions, entertainment, games, shops, concessions. (July-Aug, daily; late May-June & Sept-Oct, wkends) 6 mi (10 km) W via Hwy 1, Springbank exit. Phone 403/240-3822. All-inclusive fee ¢¢¢¢

Calgary Centre for Performing Arts. Three theaters noted for their excellent acoustics house the Calgary Philharmonic, Theatre Calgary and other performing arts. Guided tours avail. 205-8 Ave SE. Phone 403/294-7455.

Calgary Science Centre. Star Theatre, Pleiades Mystery Theatre, astronomy displays, exhibitions, observatory and self-guided tours; science and technology demonstrations. Souvenir shop, snack bar. Admission varies with program. (Daily; closed Dec 25) 7th Ave & 11th St SW. Phone 403/221-3700. ¢¢

⊠ **Calgary Tower.** A 626-ft (191-m) tower with a spectacular view of Calgary and the Rocky Mountains; revolving restaurant (see PANORAMA), observation terrace, lounge, souvenir shop. (Daily) 101 9th Ave SW. Phone 403/266-7171. ¢¢

Canada Olympic Park. Premiere site of XV Olympic Winter Games. Olympic Hall of Fame & Museum. Winter sports include double, 2 triple chairlifts, T-bar; ski school, rentals; snowmaking. Winter facilities (Nov-Mar, daily). Tours, special events (all yr). Trans-Canada Hwy & Bowfort Rd NW. Phone 403/247-5452. Lift ¢¢¢¢

Devonian Gardens. Approx 2½ acres (1.25 hectares) of indoor vegetation in the heart of the city; waterfalls, fountains, ponds with rainbow trout, goldfish & koi; seating for concerts; art displays; playground; reflecting pool. Below the gardens are stores and restaurants. (Daily) 7th Ave between 2nd & 3rd Sts SW. Phone Calgary Parks & Recreation, 403/268-3830. **Free.**

Energeum. Public visitor center that involves guests in the story of Alberta's energy resources. Hands-on exhibits cover geology, exploration, conservation and more; 1958 limited-edition Buick; theater with films, demonstrations, special events. (June-Aug, daily exc Sat; rest of yr, Mon-Fri) 640 5th Ave SW. Phone 403/297-4293. **Free.**

Fort Calgary Historic Park (1875). Riverside park of 40 acres (16 hectares), site of original North West Mounted Police (NWMP) fort, at confluence of Bow and Elbow rivers. Abandoned in 1914, the site of the fort is now being rebuilt. Interpretive center focuses on NWMP, Calgary history.

Exhibit hall, audiovisual presentation, Discovery Room. Excellent views of rivers and St George's Island. Adjacent is **Deane House** (1906), restored & open to public as restaurant; guided tours (by appt; phone 403/269-7747). (Daily) 750 9th Ave SE. Phone 403/290-1875. ¢

Glenbow Museum. Museum, art gallery, library & archives. Regional, national and international fine arts; displays of native cultures of North America and the development of the West; mineralogy, warriors, African and personal adornment. (Daily exc Mon; closed some hols) 130 9th Ave SE. Phone 403/268-4100 or 403/237-8988 (recording). ¢¢

Heritage Park Historical Village. Re-creates life in western Canada before 1914. More than 100 exhibits; steam train, paddle-wheeler, horse-drawn & electric streetcars, wagon rides, antique midway. (Mid-May-early Sept, daily; mid-Sept-early Oct, wkends & hols) 1900 Heritage Dr SW. Phone 403/259-1910 (recording) or 403/259-1900. ¢¢¢

Museum of the Regiments. One of North America's largest military museums, honors 4 Calgary Regiments. Films. Traveling art exhibits. (Daily exc Wed) 4520 Crowchild Trail SW. Phone 403/974-2850. **Free.**

Professional sports.

NHL (Calgary Flames). Canadian Airlines Saddledome. 14th Ave & 5th St SE. Phone 403/777-2177.

★ **Royal Tyrrell Museum of Palaeontology.** World's largest display of dinosaurs in state of the art museum setting. More than 35 complete dinosaur skeletons; "Palaeoconservatory" with more than 100 species of tropical and subtropical plants that once thrived in this region; hands-on exhibits, including several computer information terminals and games throughout. Souvenir shop, cafeteria. Inquire locally about summer bus service from Calgary. (Late May-Labour Day, daily; rest of yr, daily exc Mon; also Mon hols; closed Dec 25) 80 mi (128 km) NE via Hwy 9 in Drumheller. Phone 403/823-7707 or 403/294-1992 (from Calgary). ¢¢

Spruce Meadows. One of North America's finest equestrian facilities. Devoted to hosting the best show jumping tournaments on the continent, training young riders & young horses and breeding a super sport horse by the crossing of the North American Thoroughbred and the German Hanoverian. (Daily; closed Jan 1, Dec 25) (See ANNUAL EVENTS) Fee during tournaments. 3 mi (5 km) SW via Hwy 22X. Phone 403/974-4200. ¢¢

The Calgary Zoo, Botanical Garden & Prehistoric Park. One of Canada's largest zoos, with more than 1,400 animals; botanical garden; Canadian Wilds (25 acres) features Canadian ecosystems populated by their native species. Prehistoric Park. (Daily) St George's Island, 1300 Zoo Rd NE. Phone 403/232-9300 or 403/232-9372. ¢¢¢

Annual Events

Calgary Winter Festival. Music, entertainment, sports competitions, children's activities, carnival, dance. Phone 403/268-2688. 11 days mid Feb.

Calgary Stampede. Stampede Park. "The World's Greatest Outdoor Show." Parade, rodeo, chuck wagon races, stage shows, exhibition, square dances, marching bands, vaudeville shows. Phone 403/261-0101 or 800/661-1260. 10 days early July.

The Masters. Spruce Meadows. Only internationally sanctioned outdoor horse jumping show held in North America; offers the world's richest show jumping purse. Phone 403/254-3200. Early Sept.

Motels

(Rates may be higher Stampede Week)

✔★ **COMFORT INN.** (2363 Banff Trail NW, Calgary AB T2M 4L2) 403/289-2581; FAX 403/284-3897. 70 rms, 2 story. Apr-Sept: S $59.99-$139.99; D $79.99-$169.99; each addl $5; under 16 free; wkend rates; lower rates rest of yr. Crib $5. TV; cable. Sauna. Indoor pool; whirlpool. Complimentary continental bkfst. Coffee in rms. Restaurant adj 6 am-midnight. Ck-out 11 am. Business servs avail. In-rm modem link. Refrigerators. Some balconies. Cr cds: A, C, D, DS, ER, JCB, MC, V.

▨ ⊠ ⅏ SC

★ ★ **GLENMORE INN.** (2720 Glenmore Trail SE, Calgary AB T2C 2E6) at Ogden Rd. 403/279-8611; FAX 403/236-8035; res: 800/661-

3163 (CAN). 73 rms, 2 story. June-Aug: S, D $92-$102; each addl $10; under 18 free; lower rates rest of yr. Crib free. TV; cable (premium), VCR avail. Sauna. Whirlpool. Coffee in rms. Restaurant 6:30 am-11 pm. Rm serv. Bar 11-1 am. Ck-out noon. Meeting rms. Business servs avail. Valet serv. Cr cds: A, C, D, ER, MC, V.

⅏ SC

★ ★ **HOLIDAY INN EXPRESS.** (2227 Banff Trail NW, Calgary AB T2M 4L2) 1 blk N of Trans-Canada Hwy 1. 403/289-6600; FAX 403/289-6767. 64 rms, 3 story. S, D $60-$150; each addl $10; suites $100-$175; under 18 free. Crib free. TV; cable. Sauna. Heated pool; whirlpool. Complimentary coffee in rms. Complimentary continental bkfst. Restaurant adj. Ck-out noon. Meeting rms. Business servs avail. In-rm modem link. Valet serv. Cr cds: A, D, DS, ER, JCB, MC, V.

D ▨ ⊠ ⅏ SC

★ **QUALITY INN.** (2359 Banff Trail NW (1A), Calgary AB T2M 4L2) 1 blk N of Trans-Canada Hwy 1. 403/289-1973; FAX 403/282-1241. 101 rms, 2 story. July-Sept: S, D $69-$129; suites $89-$249; under 18 free; lower rates rest of yr. Crib free. Pet accepted. TV; cable, VCR avail (movies). Sauna. Indoor pool. Restaurant 7 am-2 pm, 5-10 pm. Rm serv. Bar 11-2 am. Ck-out 11 am. Meeting rms. Business servs avail. In-rm modem link. Balconies. Cr cds: A, C, D, DS, ER, MC, V.

✎ ▨ ⊠ ⅏ SC

★ ★ **TRAVELODGE SOUTH.** (7012 Macleod Trail S, Calgary AB T2H 0L3) 403/253-1111; FAX 403/253-2879. 62 rms, 2 story. June-Oct: S $100; D $120; each addl $5; under 17 free; lower rates rest of yr. Crib free. TV; cable (premium), VCR avail (movies). Pool. Complimentary coffee in rms. Restaurant adj. Ck-out noon. Business center. In-rm modem link. Cr cds: A, D, ER, MC, V.

D ▨ ⊠ ⅏ SC ⚹

Motor Hotels

★ ★ ★ **BEST WESTERN HOSPITALITY INN.** (135 Southland Dr SE, Calgary AB T2J 5X5) at Macleod Trail (Hwy 2S). 403/278-5050; FAX 403/278-5050. 261 rms, 8 story. S, D $92-$107; each addl $5; suites $115-$275; under 16 free; wkend rates. Crib free. TV; cable. Indoor pool; whirlpool. Coffee in rms. Restaurant 6:30 am-11 pm. Rm serv. Bar 11-2 am. Ck-out noon. Convention facilities. Business servs avail. In-rm modem link. Bellhops. Gift shop. Barber, beauty shop. Some minibars. Some private patios, balconies. Cr cds: A, C, D, DS, ER, MC, V.

D ▨ ⊠ ⅏ SC

★ ★ ★ **BLACKFOOT INN.** (5940 Blackfoot Trail SE, Calgary AB T2H 2B5) 403/252-2253; FAX 403/252-3574; res: 800/661-1151. 200 rms, 7 story. S $135; D $145; each addl $10; suites $150; under 16 free; monthly rates. Crib free. Pet accepted. TV; cable, VCR avail. Heated pool; whirlpool, poolside serv. Restaurant 7 am-midnight. Rm serv. Bar 11:30-1:30 am; entertainment Mon-Fri. Ck-out 1 pm. Meeting rms. Business servs avail. In-rm modem link. Bellhops. Sundries. Gift shop. Exercise equipt; bicycles, rowers, sauna. Minibars. Cr cds: A, D, ER, MC, V.

D ✎ ✎ ⊠ ⚹ ⊠ ⅏

★ ★ **HIGHLANDER.** (1818 16th Ave NW (Trans-Canada Hwy 1), Calgary AB T2M 0L8) 403/289-1961; FAX 403/289-3901; res: 800/661-9564 (CAN). 130 rms, 4 story. Mid-June-Sept: S $79; D $99; suites $125; each addl $6; under 16 free; higher rates special events; lower rates rest of yr. Crib free. Pet accepted. TV; cable (premium), VCR avail. Heated pool; poolside serv. Restaurant 6:30 am-11:30 pm; pianist in dining rm Thurs-Sun. Rm serv. Bar 11-1:30 am. Ck-out noon. Meeting rms. Business servs avail. Bellhops. Gift shop. Airport transportation. Balconies. Cr cds: A, C, D, ER, JCB, MC, V.

D ✎ ✎ ⊠ ⊠ ⅏ SC

★ ★ **HOLIDAY INN.** (4206 Macleod Trail SE, Calgary AB T2G 2R7) 403/287-2700; FAX 403/243-4721. 154 rms, 4 story. May-Sept: S $104-$109; D $109-$114; each addl $5; under 19 free; wkend, wkly rates; lower rates rest of yr. Crib free. Pet accepted. TV; cable (premium), VCR avail. Heated pool. Restaurant 7 am-10 pm. Rm serv. Bar 11 am-midnight.

Ck-out noon. Coin lndry. Meeting rms. Business servs avail. Bellhops. Valet serv. Some refrigerators. Cr cds: A, C, D, DS, ER, JCB, MC, V.

[D] [icons] SC

★ ★ **HOLIDAY INN-CALGARY AIRPORT.** *(1250 McKinnon Dr NE, Calgary AB T2E 7T7)* Trans-Canada Hwy 1 & 19th St NE. 403/230-1999; FAX 403/277-2623. 170 rms, 5 story. S $94-$105; D $94-$125; each addl $10; under 18 free. Pet accepted. TV; cable. Sauna. Indoor pool. Restaurant 6:30 am-10 pm. Rm serv. Bar 11-1 am. Ck-out 11 am. Meeting rms. Business servs avail. Gift shop. Free airport transportation. Cr cds: A, C, D, DS, ER, JCB, MC, V.

[D] [icons] SC

✔★ **NITE INN.** *(4510 Macleod Trail S, Calgary AB T2G 0A4)* 403/243-1700; FAX 403/243-4719. 60 rms, 6 story. D $99; each addl $10; under 18 free. Pet accepted. TV; cable. Complimentary coffee in rms. Restaurant 7 am-9 pm. Rm serv. Bar 11-2 am. Meeting rms. Business servs avail. Cr cds: A, C, D, DS, ER, MC, V.

[D] [icons] SC

★ ★ **QUALITY AIRPORT INN.** *(4804 Edmonton Trail NE, Calgary AB T2E 3V8)* 403/276-3391; FAX 403/230-7267. 117 rms, 7 story. S, D $85-$90; each addl $5; suites $114; under 18 free. Crib $10. Pet accepted, some restrictions. TV; cable. Restaurant 6:30 am-10 pm. Rm serv. Bar 11-2 am; entertainment. Ck-out 11 am. Meeting rms. Business servs avail. In-rm modem link. Free airport transportation. Sauna. Cr cds: A, D, DS, ER, MC, V.

[icons] SC

✔★ **STAMPEDER INN.** *(3828 Macleod Trail S, Calgary AB T2G 2R2)* 403/243-5531; FAX 403/243-6962; res: 800/361-3422. 102 rms, 3 story. S, D $70-$140; suites $95-$150; each addl $10; under 16 free. Crib free. Pet accepted. TV; cable. Heated pool; whirlpool. Coffee in rms. Restaurants 7 am-10 pm. Rm serv. Bar 11-2 am, closed Sun. Ck-out 11 am. Meeting rms. Business servs avail. Bellhops in summer. Valet serv. Gift shop. Cr cds: A, C, D, DS, ER, MC, V.

[D] [icons] SC

Hotels

✔★ ★ **BEST WESTERN KANANASKIS INN.** *(Kananaskis Village AB T0L 2H0)* 60 mi SW on Trans-Canada Hwy 1 and Kananaskis Trail (Hwy 40). 403/591-7500; FAX 403/591-7633. 96 rms, 3 story, 32 kit. suites. S, D $125-$295; each addl $10; suites $250-$295; kit. units $155-$190; under 16 free; ski, golf plans. Crib free. TV; cable (premium), VCR avail. Indoor pool; whirlpool, steam rm. Complimentary coffee in rms. Restaurant 7 am-10 pm. Bar. Ck-out 11 am. Meeting rms. Business servs avail. In-rm modem link. Gift shop. Free covered parking. Tennis. 36-hole golf; greens fee, putting green, driving range. Downhill ski 4 mi. Private patios, balconies. Cr cds: A, C, D, DS, ER, JCB, MC, V.

[D] [icons]

★ ★ **BEST WESTERN PORT O'CALL INN.** *(1935 McKnight Blvd NE, Calgary AB T2E 6V4)* 403/291-4600; FAX 403/250-6827. 201 rms, 7 story. S, D $110-$140; suites $220; under 18 free. TV; cable. Indoor pool; whirlpool, steam rm. Restaurant 6:30 am-11 pm. Bar 11:30-1 am. Ck-out noon. Meeting rms. Business servs avail. In-rm modem link. Gift shop. Barber, beauty shop. Free garage parking. Free airport transportation. Exercise equipt; weight machine, bicycle. Some minibars. Balconies. Cr cds: A, D, DS, ER, JCB, MC, V.

[D] [icons] SC

★ ★ ★ **CALGARY AIRPORT.** *(2001 Airport Rd NE, Calgary AB T2E 6Z8)* at Intl Airport. 403/291-2600; FAX 403/291-3419; res: 800/441-1414. 296 rms, 8 story. S $155-$195; D $165-$205; each addl $15; suites $270-$370; under 18 free. Pet accepted, some restrictions. TV; cable; VCR avail. Indoor pool; whirlpool. Restaurant 6:30 am-10 pm. Rm serv 24 hrs. Bar 11:30-1 am. Ck-out noon. Convention facilities. Business servs

avail. Gift shop. Exercise equipt; weights, bicycles, sauna. Minibars. Atrium. Cr cds: A, C, D, DS, ER, JCB, MC, V.

[D] [icons] SC

★ ★ **CARRIAGE HOUSE INN.** *(9030 Macleod Trail S, Calgary AB T2H 0M4)* 403/253-1101; FAX 403/259-2414; res: 800/661-9566 (CAN). 175 rms, 10 story. S, D $100-$121; each addl $5; suites $170; under 16 free; wkly rates. Crib free. Pet accepted, some restrictions; $5. TV; cable (premium), VCR avail. Heated pool (in season); whirlpool, poolside serv. Restaurant 6:30 am-11 pm. Bar 11-2 am; entertainment. Ck-out noon. Meeting rms. Business servs avail. In-rm modem link. Gift shop. Sauna. Health club privileges. Game rm. Bathrm phones, minibars. Cr cds: A, C, D, DS, ER, JCB, MC, V.

[D] [icons] SC

★ ★ ★ **THE COAST PLAZA AT CALGARY.** *(1316 33rd St NE, Calgary AB T2A 6B6)* 403/248-8888; FAX 403/248-0749; res: 800/661-1464. 248 rms, 7 & 12 story. S, D $125-$140; each addl $10; suites $250; under 18 free. Crib free. Pet accepted; $10. TV; cable, VCR avail. Heated pool; whirlpool. Sauna. Complimentary coffee in rms. Restaurant 6:30 am-11 pm. Bar 11-2 am; entertainment. Ck-out noon. Convention facilities. Business servs avail. Gift shop. Free airport transportation. Luxury level. Cr cds: A, C, D, DS, ER, MC, V.

[D] [icons] SC

✔★ ★ ★ **CROSSROADS.** *(2120 16th Ave NE, Calgary AB T2E 1L4)* Trans-Canada Hwy 1. 403/291-4666; FAX 403/291-6498; res: 800/661-8157 (exc Alaska). 185 rms, 10 story. S, D $89-$99; each addl $5; suites $205; under 12 free. Crib free. TV; cable (premium). Pool; whirlpool. Restaurant 6 am-11:30 pm; Sat, Sun 7 am-11 pm. Sun brunch 10 am-2 pm. Bar 11-2 am; entertainment. Ck-out 11 am. Meeting rms. Business center. In-rm modem link. Gift shop. Free airport transportation. Exercise equipt; weight machine, bicycle, sauna. Some refrigerators. Balconies. Cr cds: A, C, D, ER, MC, V.

[icons] SC

★ ★ ★ **DELTA-BOW VALLEY.** *(209 4th Ave SE, Calgary AB T2G 0C6)* 403/266-1980; FAX 403/266-0007; res: 800/268-1133. 398 rms, 25 story. S, D $190-$210; each addl $15; suites $185-$450; under 18 free; wkend, family rates. Garage $6, valet $8. TV; cable (premium). Indoor pool; whirlpool, poolside serv. Supervised child's activities (wkends), ages 3-16. Restaurant 7 am-10 pm. Dining rm 11:30 am-2 pm, 5:30-10:30 pm; Sat from 5:30 pm. Rm serv 6-2 am. Bar 11:30-1 am; pianist Mon-Fri. Ck-out 1 pm. Convention facilities. Business servs avail. In-rm modem link. Gift shop. Exercise equipt; weights, bicycles, sauna. Sun deck. Canadian artwork on display. Overlooks river. Cr cds: A, C, D, DS, ER, JCB, MC, V.

[D] [icons] SC

★ ★ ★ **HOTEL KANANASKIS.** *(Kananaskis Village, Calgary AB T0L 2H0)* 60 mi SW on Trans-Canada Hwy 1 and Kananaskis Trail (Hwy 40). 403/591-7711; FAX 403/591-7770; res: 800/441-1414. 68 air-cooled rms, 3 story. S, D $200-$275; each addl $20; suites $340-$550; under 18 free; ski plans. Crib free. Garage $4. TV; cable, VCR avail (movies). Indoor/outdoor pool; whirlpool. Restaurant 7-1 am. Bar. Ck-out noon. Meeting rms. Business center. In-rm modem link. Concierge. Shopping arcade. Barber, beauty shop. Airport, bus depot transportation. Tennis. 36-hole golf; greens fee, pro, putting green, driving range. Downhill ski 1 mi; x-country ski on site. Exercise equipt; weights, bicycles, sauna. Bathrm phones, minibars. Private patios, balconies. Cr cds: A, C, D, DS, ER, JCB, MC, V.

[D] [icons] SC

★ ★ ★ **INTERNATIONAL.** *(220 4th Ave SW, Calgary AB T2P 0H5)* 403/265-9600; FAX 403/265-6949; res: 800/243-1166. 247 suites, 35 story. S $130-$144; D $144-$156; under 16 free; wkend rates. Crib free. Garage $4. TV; cable (premium), VCR avail. Indoor pool; whirlpool. Restaurant 6:30 am-11 pm. Bar 11-1 am. Ck-out 1 pm. Meeting rms. Business servs avail. In-rm modem link. Concierge. Gift shop. Barber. Exercise equipt; weights, bicycles, sauna. Refrigerators, minibars. Balconies. Cr cds: A, C, D, ER, MC, V.

[D] [icons] SC

★ ★ ★ **LODGE AT KANANASKIS.** *(Kananaskis Village, Calgary AB T0L 2H0)* 60 mi SW on Trans-Canada Hwy 1 and Kananaskis Trail *(Hwy 40).* 403/591-7711; FAX 403/591-7770; res: 800/441-1414. 250 air-cooled rms, 3 story. S, D $185-$260; each addl $20; suites $300-$550; under 18 free; ski plans. Crib free. Pet accepted; $20/day. Covered parking $4. TV; cable, VCR avail (movies). Indoor/outdoor pool; whirlpool. Restaurant 6-4 am. Bar; entertainment. Ck-out noon. Convention facilities. Business center. In-rm modem link. Concierge. Shopping arcade. Barber, beauty shop. Tennis. 36-hole golf course; greens fee, pro, putting green, driving range. Downhill ski 1 mi; x-country ski on site. Exercise equipt; weights, sauna, steam rm. Game rm. Rec rm. Minibars; some bathrm phones. Private patios, balconies. Cr cds: A, C, D, DS, ER, JCB, MC, V.

[D] [🏂] [🏃] [🏋] [⛷] [⛸] [🏊] [✈] [🚶] [▨] [SC] [🏃]

★ ★ ★ **MARRIOTT PLAZA.** *(110 9th Ave SE, Calgary AB T2G 5A6)* in Calgary Center. 403/266-7331; FAX 403/262-8442. 376 rms, 23 story. S, D $159; each addl $20; suites $179; under 18 free; wknd rates; higher rates, special events. Crib free. Garage $7-$11/day. TV; cable (premium). Heated pool; whirlpool, poolside serv. Restaurant 6:30 am-2 pm, 5-10:30 pm; Sat, Sun 7 am-10:30 pm, dining rm 11:45 am-2:30 pm, 6-11:30 pm. Rm serv 24 hrs. Bar 11 am-midnight. Ck-out noon. Meeting rms. Business center. In-rm modem link. Concierge. Exercise equipt; bicycles, sauna. Health club privileges. Minibars. Convention facilities, shopping arcade adj. Luxury level. Cr cds: A, C, D, DS, ER, JCB, MC, V.

[D] [▨] [🏋] [▨] [▨] [SC] [🏃]

★ ★ ★ **PALLISER.** *(133 9th Ave SW, Calgary AB T2P 2M3)* 403/262-1234; FAX 403/260-1260; res: 800/441-1414. 405 rms, 12 story. S, D $260; each addl $25; suites $300-$600; under 18 free. Crib free. Pet accepted, some restrictions. TV; cable (premium). Restaurant 6:30 am-10 pm. Rm serv 24 hrs. Bar 11-2 am. Ck-out noon. Convention facilities. Business center. In-rm modem link. Concierge. Shopping arcade. Barber, beauty shop. Airport transportation. Exercise equipt; weight machine, bicycles. Minibars. Luxury level. Cr cds: A, C, D, ER, JCB, MC, V.

[D] [🏂] [🏋] [▨] [🔥] [SC] [🏃] [🏃]

★ ★ **PRINCE ROYAL SUITES.** *(618 5th Ave SW, Calgary AB T2P 0M7)* 403/263-0520; FAX 403/298-4888; res: 800/661-1592. 301 air-cooled kit. suites, 28 story. S $110-$120; D $115-$145; each addl $15; under 16 free. TV; cable. Restaurant 6:30 am-11 pm. Bar from noon. Ck-out noon. Coin lndry. Meeting rms. Airport transportation. Business servs avail. In-rm modem link. Exercise equipt; weights, bicycles, sauna, steam rm. Refrigerators. Cr cds: A, C, D, DS, ER, JCB, MC, V.

[🏋] [▨] [🔥] [SC]

★ ★ ★ **SHERATON CAVALIER.** *(2620 32nd Ave NE, Calgary AB T1Y 6B8)* 403/291-0107; FAX 403/291-2834. 306 rms, 8 story. S $195; D $205; each addl $15; suites $250-$280; under 18 free. Crib free. Pet accepted, some restrictions. TV; cable (premium). Sauna. Indoor pool; wading pool, whirlpools, poolside serv, 2 water slides. Coffee in rms. Restaurant 6:30 am-10 pm. Bar 11-12:30 am. Ck-out noon. Convention facilities. Business servs avail. In-rm modem link. Gift shop. Free airport transportation. Game rm. Minibars. Cr cds: A, C, D, ER, MC, V.

[D] [🏂] [▨] [▨] [▨] [SC]

★ ★ ★ **THE WESTIN.** *(320 4th Ave SW, Calgary AB T2P 2S6)* 403/266-1611; FAX 403/233-7471; res: 800/228-3000. 525 rms, 17 & 19 story. S $119-$178; D $129-$188; each addl $10; suites $285-$660; under 18 free; wkend rates. Crib free. Pet accepted, some restrictions. TV; cable (premium), VCR avail. Indoor pool; whirlpool, poolside serv. Restaurant 6:30 am-11 pm (also see OWL'S NEST). Rm serv 24 hrs. Bar 11:30-1 am. Ck-out 1 pm. Lndry facilities. Convention facilities. Business servs avail. In-rm modem link. Concierge. Barber. Indoor valet parking. Exercise equipt; weights, bicycles, sauna. Minibars. Downtown; skywalk to adj shopping mall. Cr cds: A, C, D, DS, ER, JCB, MC, V.

[D] [🏂] [▨] [🏋] [▨] [🔥] [SC]

Guest Ranches

✔★ **KANANASKIS.** *(Calgary AB T0L 1X0)* 403/673-3737; FAX 403/673-2100. 33 cabins (1-2-bedrm). No A/C. May-mid-Oct: D $90-$110;

each addl $15; under 4 free. Closed rest of yr. Crib free. TV lounge. Dining rm 7:30 am-2 pm, 5-8:30 pm. Box lunches. Barbecues. Bar 4 pm-1 am. Ck-out 11 am, ck-in 4 pm. Grocery nearby. Meeting rms. Business servs avail. Gift shop. Hiking. Trail rides. Whitewater rafting. Lawn games. Whirlpool. Picnic tables. On Bow River. Cr cds: MC, V.

[D] [🏂] [🏋] [🏊] [▨]

★ ★ **RAFTER SIX.** *(Calgary AB T0L 1X0)* 403/673-3622; FAX 403/673-3961. 18 rms in 3 story lodge, 8 cabins, 4 chalets. No A/C. AP: S, D $415-$740; 3-day min. TV in sitting rm. Heated pool; whirlpool. Playground. Dining rm 7:30 am-9 pm. Bar 4 pm-midnight. Ck-out noon. Coin lndry. Meeting rms. Business servs avail. Gift shop. Hiking. Hayrides. Entertainment. Horseback riding, chuck wagon bkfst, barbecues. Wilderness camping facilities. Lawn games. Some fireplaces. Balconies. Rustic; authentic Western Canadian ranch decor, furnishings; original Indian design door murals. Cr cds: A, MC, V.

[🏋] [🏊] [🏃] [▨] [▨] [SC]

Restaurants

★ ★ **ATRIUM STEAKHOUSE.** *(2001 Airport Road NE, Calgary AB)* in Intl Airport. 403/291-2600. Hrs: 6:30 am-10 pm; Terrace from 5 pm. Sun brunch (Atrium) 11 am-2 pm. Res accepted. Bar 11-1 am. Atrium: Continental menu. Semi-a la carte: bkfst $6-$14, lunch $7.50-$19, dinner $18-$26. Sun brunch $18.95. Parking. Bright atmosphere; fresh flowers. Cr cds: A, C, D, DS, ER, JCB, MC, V.

[D] [♥]

★ ★ ★ **CAESAR'S STEAK HOUSE.** *(512 4th Ave SW, Calgary AB T2P 0J6)* 403/264-1222. Hrs: 11 am-midnight; Sat from 4:30 pm. Closed Sun; major hols. Res accepted. Continental menu. Bar. Wine list. Semi-a la carte: lunch $8-$18, dinner $17-$35. Child's meals. Specializes in steak, seafood, ribs. Valet parking. Greco-Roman motif; marble pillars, statues. Cr cds: A, C, D, ER, JCB, MC, V.

[D]

★ ★ ★ **HY'S CALGARY STEAK HOUSE.** *(316 4th Ave SW, Calgary AB T2P 0H8)* 403/263-2222. Hrs: 11:30 am-2:30 pm, 5:30-11 pm. Closed Sun; major hols. Res accepted. Continental menu. Bar to 11:30 pm. Semi-a la carte: lunch $9.50-$15, dinner $16.95-$25. Specializes in steak. Parking. Rustic decor; antiques. Family-owned. Cr cds: A, C, D, DS, ER, JCB, MC, V.

[D]

★ ★ ★ **INN ON LAKE BONAVISTA.** *(747 Lake Bonavista Dr SE, Calgary AB T2J 0N2)* 403/271-6711. Hrs: 11:30 am-2 pm, 5-11 pm; Sun 5-9 pm; Sun brunch 10:30 am-2 pm. Res accepted. French, continental menu. Bar. Wine list. A la carte entrees: lunch $6.75-$12.50, dinner $16.50-$30. Sun brunch $16.95. Child's meals. Specializes in beef, seafood. Entertainment. Outdoor dining. On lake. Cr cds: A, C, D, ER, MC, V.

[♥]

✔★ ★ **THE KEG STEAKHOUSE & BAR.** *(7104 Macleod Trail S, Calgary AB T2H 0L3)* 403/253-2534. Hrs: 11:30 am-11 pm; wkends to 2 am. Closed Dec 25. Res accepted. International menu. Bar. Semi-a la carte: lunch $6.99-$10.99, dinner $12.99-$19.99. Child's meals. Specializes in prime rib, steak. Patio dining. 4-tier dining area; 2 fireplaces. Cr cds: A, MC, V.

[D] [🗗]

★ ★ ★ **MAMMA'S RISTORANTE.** *(320 16th Ave NW, Calgary AB T2M 0H6)* 403/276-9744. Hrs: 11:30 am-2 pm, 5-11 pm. Closed Sun. Res required. Italian menu. Wine cellar. Semi-a la carte: lunch $7.95-$14.95, dinner $9.95-$24.95. Specializes in pasta, veal, game birds. Own baking. Parking. Formal dining rm with chandeliers. Italian paintings. Cr cds: A, D, DS, ER, MC, V.

[D] [🗗]

✔★ ★ **MESCALERO.** *(1315 1st St SW, Calgary AB T2R 0V5)* 403/266-3339. Hrs: 11:30 am-midnight; Sat, Sun brunch 11 am-3 pm. Closed Dec 25. Res accepted. Mexican, Southwestern menu. Bar. A la carte entrees: lunch $5-$13, dinner $5-$24. Sun brunch $5-$12. Specializes in applewood grilled items. Parking. Outdoor dining. Rustic decor; imported Southwestern furnishings. Cr cds: A, ER, MC, V.

D

★ ★ ★ **OWL'S NEST.** (See The Westin Hotel) 403/267-2823. Hrs: 11:30 am-2 pm, 5:30-11 pm. Closed Sun exc special occasions. Res accepted. Continental menu. Bar. Wine cellar. A la carte entrees: lunch $7.90-$13.75, dinner $20.75-$30.25. Child's meals. Specialties: rack of lamb, Alaska king crab Provençale. Own desserts. Pianist (dinner). Parking. Lavish decor. Cr cds: A, C, D, ER, JCB, MC, V.

D

★ ★ ★ **PANORAMA.** (101 9th Ave SW, Calgary AB T2P 1J9) Tower Center. 403/266-7171. Hrs: 8 am-3 pm, 5-10 pm. Res accepted. Continental menu. Bar 11:30 am-midnight. Complete meals: bkfst $10, lunch $10-$15, dinner $19-$29.50. Child's meals. Revolving restaurant atop Calgary Tower; panoramic view of city, mountains (fee). Cr cds: A, C, D, ER, MC, V.

D **SC**

★ ★ **QUINCY'S ON SEVENTH.** (609 7th Ave SW, Calgary AB T2P 0Y9) 403/264-1000. Hrs: 11 am-11 pm; Sat from 5 pm. Closed most major hols. Res accepted. Bar. A la carte entrees: lunch $7.95-$15.95, dinner $9.95-$22.95. Child's meals. Specializes in steak, prime rib. Antique furnishings. Cr cds: A, C, D, ER, JCB, MC, V.

SC

✔★ ★ **REGENCY PALACE.** (328 Centre St S, Calgary AB T2G 2B8) Dragon City Plaza. 403/777-2288. Hrs: 10 am-11 pm. Res accepted. Chinese menu. Bar. Semi-a la carte: lunch $1.95-$4.95, dinner $4.95-$12.95. Specializes in duck, chicken, seafood. Salad bar. Outdoor dining. Oriental decor. Cr cds: A, D, MC, V.

D

★ ★ **RIVER CAFE.** (Prince's Island Park, Calgary AB T2G 0K7) 403/261-7670. Hrs: 11 am-11 pm; Sat, Sun from 10 am. Sun brunch 10 am-3 pm. Closed Dec 25; also Jan-Feb. Res accepted. Bar. Semi-a la carte: lunch $8-$20, dinner $28-$35. Sun brunch $5-$12. Specialties: cedar-planked arctic char, rack of lamb. Outdoor dining. Country decor. Totally nonsmoking. Cr cds: A, D, ER, MC, V.

D

★ ★ **SILVER DRAGON.** (106 3rd Ave SE, Calgary AB T2G 0B6) in Chinatown. 403/264-5326. Hrs: 10:30-1 am; wkends 10-2 am. Res accepted; required Sat & Sun. Chinese menu. Wine. Semi-a la carte: lunch $6-$15, dinner $8-$30. Specializes in Cantonese, Peking-style cuisine. Oriental decor. Family-owned. Cr cds: A, C, D, ER, JCB, MC, V.

★ ★ **SMUGGLER'S INN.** (6920 Macleod Trail, Calgary AB T2H 0L3) 403/253-5355. Hrs: 11:30 am-midnight; Fri, Sat to 1 am; Sun 4:30-11 pm. Sun brunch 10:30 am-2:30 pm. Closed Jan 1, Dec 25. Res accepted. Continental menu. Bar to 2 am. Complete meals: lunch $6-$10. Semi-a la carte: dinner $7-$25. Specializes in Alberta beef, seafood, prime rib. Salad bar. Entertainment. Parking. Patio dining. Rustic atmosphere; antique furnishings. Family-owned. Cr cds: A, C, D, ER, MC, V.

D ⌐

★ ★ **TEATRO.** (200 8 Ave SE, Calgary AB T2G 0K7) downtown, on Olympic Square. 403/290-1012. Hrs: 11:30 am-11 pm; Sat 5 pm-midnight; Sun 5-10 pm. Closed Jan 1, Dec 24, 25. Res accepted. Italian menu. Bar. A la carte entrees: lunch $10-$16, dinner $16-$26. Specialties: lobster and scallop lasagna, grilled venison rack. Parking. Outdoor dining. In old Dominion Bank bldg (1911); specializes in Italian market cuisine. Cr cds: A, D, ER, MC, V.

D

Edmonton (B-4)

Settled 1795 **Pop** 854,200 (metro) **Elev** 2,192 ft (671 m) **Area code** 403 **E-mail** ede@wnet.gov.edmonton.ab.ca **Web** www.wnet.gov.edmonton .ab.ca/edmonton

Information Edmonton Tourism, 9797 Jasper Ave NW, T5J 1N9; 403/496-8400 or 800/463-4667.

As capital of a province whose economic mainstays are petroleum and agriculture, Edmonton has all the brash confidence of its position as a major supplier of one of the world's most sought after resources, yet traces of the practical reticence nurtured by its past still linger.

The first Fort Edmonton, established in 1795, was named for Edmonton, England, now a suburb of London. The fort was relocated several times before its fifth site location near the present Alberta Legislature Building. With the close of the fur trade era, a settlement grew up around the fort and became the nucleus of the city. The sixth fort, a reconstruction from the fur-trading days, is now a major attraction in the city's river valley.

In the 1890s, Edmonton became a major supply depot for the gold rush to the Yukon, since it was on the All-Canadian Route to the Klondike. Thousands of men stopped for days, weeks or months before making the final 1,500-mile (2,400-kilometer) trip to Yukon gold. Many decided to stay in the town, turning a quiet village into a prosperous city. Each July, the city returns to the colorful era of the gold rush for 10 days of fun and frolic called Edmonton's Klondike Days (see ANNUAL EVENTS).

Edmonton prides itself in having more park area per capita than any other city in Canada. The park area winds along the banks of the North Saskatchewan River, Edmonton's most prominent physical characteristic. Capital City Recreation Park encompasses 3,000 acres (1,214 hectares) with 18 miles (29 kilometers) of biking and hiking trails along the river valley.

What to See and Do

Alberta Legislature Building. Tours of historic structure; Interpretive Centre includes displays of Alberta's history and legislature. Cafeteria. (Daily; closed most hols) 108 St & 97 Ave. Phone 403/427-7362. **Free.**

Citadel Theatre. Five-theater complex, located in downtown Edmonton, is one of Canada's finest centers for the performing arts. Glass-enclosed atrium area; waterfall, plants. Three theater series (Sept-May). 9828 101 A Ave. For schedule, fees phone 403/426-4811 or 403/425-1820 (tickets).

Commonwealth Stadium. Built for the XI Commonwealth Games; seating capacity is 61,356. Home of the Canadian Football League Edmonton Eskimos. The Stadium Recreation Centre houses gym, weights, racquetball and squash courts. 11000 Stadium Rd. Phone 403/944-7400. ¢¢

Devonian Botanic Garden. Approx 200 acres (80 hectares) including alpine and herb gardens, peony collection and native plants; outstanding 5-acre Japanese garden; nature trails; aspen & jackpine forests; Lilac Garden. Concession. (May-Sept, daily) 6 mi W via Yellowhead Hwy 16, then 9 mi S on Hwy 60. Phone 403/987-3054. ¢¢

★ **Edmonton Space & Science Centre.** Multipurpose facility, including 220-seat planetarium theater; IMAX film theater (fee) with 4-story screen; extensive science exhibit hall, dealing with latest discoveries in science, astronomy and space exploration; artifacts (moon rock, telescopes). Challenger Learning Centre lets visitors cooperate in teams to complete a space flight simulation. Book, gift store. (Summer, daily; rest of yr, daily exc Mon) Varied fees for laser shows and IMAX films. 11211 142 St, in Coronation Park. For fees and showtimes, phone 403/451-3344. ¢¢¢-¢¢¢¢

Elk Island National Park. Forests, meadowlands, quiet lakes and beaver ponds form an island in the area developed by man. A 75-square-mile sanctuary for many species; moose, elk, deer, lynx, trumpeter swans, beaver and coyote; large herd of plains bison and a small herd of rare wood bison; more than 200 species of birds. Camping (summer), hiking, golf, cross-country skiing. Visitor center and interpretive center (summer, wkends). Park (all yr). 28 mi (45 km) E on Yellowhead Hwy 16. Phone

403/922-2950 or 403/922-5790 (recording). Entrance fee/day ¢¢ Camping/night ¢¢¢¢

Fort Edmonton Park. Canada's largest historical park is a re-creation of four sites of historic Edmonton, including Ft Edmonton, the Hudson's Bay Company Trading Post that gave the city its name, 1885 Street, 1905 Street & 1920 Street. Demonstrations of artifacts and skills of earlier times by costumed interpreters. Steam train & streetcar rides. (Victoria Day-Labour Day, daily; rest of yr, days vary) Whitemud Dr & Fox Dr. Phone 403/496-8787. ¢¢¢ Adj is

John Janzen Nature Centre. Natural history events and programs; hands-on exhibits; active beehive, gopher colony and nature trails; nature shop. (Daily; closed Dec 25) Phone 403/496-2939. **Free.**

Kinsmen Sports Centre. Built for the XI Commonwealth Games. Swimming, diving, weight training; all types of racquet sports. Children under 8 must be accompanied by an adult. 9100 Walterdale Hill. Phone 403/496-7300. ¢¢

Muttart Conservatory. Glass pyramids house controlled growing environments: tropical, arid and temperate. A fourth pyramid is a floral showcase, which is changed every few weeks. (Daily) 98 Ave & 96A St. Phone 403/496-8755. ¢¢

Old Strathcona Model and Toy Museum. Dedicated to models and toys made of paper and card; famous buildings, castles, trains, space ships, animals; 18th- and 19th-century children's card toys, paper dolls and soldiers; operational N scale model railroad. (Wed-Sun, limited hrs; summer also Mon & Tues afternoons; closed some hols) 8603 104 St. Phone 403/433-4512. **Donation.**

Parks. Capital City Recreation Park, winding through the city's river valley, is one of Canada's most extensive park systems. Bicycle, walking and cross-country ski trails link the major parks, where barbecue, picnic facilities, public rest rooms and food concessions may be found. Contact River Valley Parks; 403/496-7275.

Professional sports.

NHL (Edmonton Oilers). Edmonton Coliseum, 7424 118th Ave. Phone 403/474-8561.

Provincial Museum of Alberta. Contains excellent displays reflecting the many aspects of Alberta's heritage. Exhibits on natural & human history, including aboriginal peoples, wildlife, geology, live insects, dinosaurs and ice-age mammals. (Victoria Day-Labour Day, daily; rest of yr, daily exc Mon; closed Dec 25) 12845 102 Ave. Phone 403/427-1786 (recording) or 403/453-9100. ¢¢

⭐ **Reynolds-Alberta Museum.** Interprets the mechanization of ground and air transportation, agriculture and selected industries in Alberta from the turn of the century. More than 100 major artifacts in museum building, hangar and on 156-acre grounds. Displays include vintage steam-powered farm equipment, automobiles and aircraft; multimedia orientation show (17 min). (Daily; closed Jan 1, Good Friday, Dec 25) Approx 40 mi (64 km) S via Hwy 2A in Wetaskiwin. Phone 403/361-1351. ¢¢¢ Also here is

Canada's Aviation Hall of Fame. More than 100 aviators have been inducted into the hall of fame; many artifacts. Vintage planes, free-standing exhibits; videos, large aviation library.

University of Alberta. (30,000 students) One of Canada's largest major research universities; 18 faculties and many research institutes. Tours (by appt). 114 St & 89 Ave. Phone 403/492-2325. On campus is

Rutherford House (1911). Jacobethan-revival home was residence of Alberta's first premier. Restored and refurnished to reflect lifestyle of post-Edwardian era. Costumed interpreters reenact life in 1915 with activities such as baking on wood stove, historical dramas, craft demonstrations and musical performances. (Daily; closed Jan 1, Dec 25) Phone 403/427-3995. ¢

Valley Zoo. Features a wide variety of birds and mammals, fish and reptiles. Train, merry-go-round, pony and camel rides; gift shop. (Daily) 134 St & Buena Vista Rd. Phone 403/496-6911. ¢¢

⭐ **West Edmonton Mall and Canada Fantasyland.** Mile-long (1.6-km) shopping and recreation complex with more than 800 stores and services; 110 eating establishments, 19 movie theaters, aviary, aquaria, dolphin shows; 80-ft (24-m) replica of a Spanish Galleon, 4 submarines, water park with wave pool & water slides, bungee jumping, ice-skating rink, car

museum, amusement park with 14-story, looping rollercoaster, 18-hole miniature golf course. (Daily) 8770 170 St. Phone 403/444-5200.

Annual Events

Jazz City Festival. Jazz concerts, workshops, outdoor events. Late June-early July.

Edmonton's Klondike Days. Entertainment, exhibits, midway, parade; events include Sourdough Raft Race, Sunday promenade, band extravaganza, chuckwagon races. Mid-late July.

Heritage Festival. William Hawrelak Park. More than 40 ethnic groups show Alberta's multicultural heritage in pageantry of color and music. Early Aug.

Folk Music Festival. 3 days of music at Alberta's largest outdoor music festival. Mid-Aug.

Fringe Theatre Event. Old Strathcona district. Dance, music, plays, mime, mask, street entertainers; more than 700 performances. Mid-late Aug.

Canadian Finals Rodeo. Edmonton Coliseum. Professional indoor rodeo to decide national championships. Mid-Nov.

Motels

★ ★ **BEST WESTERN CITY CENTRE INN.** *(11310 109th St, Edmonton AB T5G 2T7)* 403/479-2042; FAX 403/474-2204. 110 rms, 2 story. S $63-$68; D $77-$84; suites $77-$84; under 14 free; wkend rates. Crib free. TV; cable (premium), VCR avail (movies). Heated pool; whirlpool, water slide. Restaurant open 24 hrs. Rm serv. Bar. Ck-out noon. Meeting rms. Business servs avail. In-rm modem link. Local airport transportation. Exercise equipt; bicycle, rower. Some balconies. Cr cds: A, C, D, ER, MC, V.

D ≈ 🏋 🖐 SC

✔★ **WEST HARVEST INN.** *(17803 Stony Plain Rd, Edmonton AB T5S 1B4)* 403/484-8000; FAX 403/486-6060; res: 800/661-6993 (W CAN). 161 rms, 3 story. S $59; D $69; each addl $10; under 16 free. Crib free. TV; cable. Restaurant 7 am-11 pm. Rm serv. Ck-out 11 am. Meeting rms. Business servs avail. Barber, beauty shop. Game rm. Some refrigerators, in-rm whirlpools. Cr cds: A, ER, MC, V.

🖐 SC

Motor Hotels

★ ★ **BEST WESTERN CEDAR PARK INN.** *(5116 Calgary Trail N (Hwy 2), Edmonton AB T6H 2H4)* 403/434-7411; FAX 403/437-4836. 190 rms, 5 story. S, D $72-$92; each addl $5; suites $135-$150; family rates. Crib free. Pet accepted, some restrictions. TV; cable. Sauna. Heated pool. Restaurant 7 am-11 pm; also 24-hr snack shop. Rm serv. Bar 11:30-1 am. Ck-out noon. Meeting rms. Business servs avail. In-rm modem link. Gift shop. Free airport transportation. Cr cds: A, D, DS, ER, JCB, MC, V.

✔ ≈ 🖐 SC

★ ★ **CHATEAU LOUIS.** *(11727 Kingsway Ave, Edmonton AB T5G 3A1)* 403/452-7770; FAX 403/454-3436; res: 800/661-9843. 147 rms, 3 story. S $65; D $70; each addl $6; suites $100-$125; wkend rates; under 12 free. Crib $3. Pet accepted, some restrictions. TV; cable, VCR (movies $5). Complimentary coffee in rms. Restaurant 6 am-midnight; Sat from 7 am; Sun, hols from 8 am. Rm serv 24 hrs. Bars 11-2 am; entertainment. Ck-out noon. Meeting rms. Business servs avail. In-rm modem link. Valet serv. Airport transportation. Some minibars. Outdoor patio dining. Some in-rm whirlpools in suites. Cr cds: A, C, D, ER, MC, V.

✔ 🖐 SC

★ ★ ★ **HOLIDAY INN-THE PALACE.** *(4235 Calgary Trail N, Edmonton AB T6J 5H2)* 403/438-1222; FAX 403/438-0906. 130 rms, 5 story, 40 suites. S, D $85-$140; each addl $10; suites $125-$300; under 19 free. Crib avail. TV; cable, VCR avail. Complimentary coffee in rms. Restaurant 6:30 am-11 pm. Rm serv. Bar. Ck-out 11 am. Meeting rms. Business servs avail. In-rm modem link. Valet serv. Gift shop. Beauty shop. Free airport transportation. Exercise equipt; weights, bicycle. Refrigerator avail. Balconies. Cr cds: A, C, D, DS, ER, MC, V.

⊠ 🕴 ⛵ 🧹 SC

★ ★ **NISKU INN.** *(Edmonton Intl Airport AB T5J 2T2) off Hwy 2, opp Intl Airport.* 403/955-7744; FAX 403/955-7743; res: 800/661-6966. 160 rms, 2 story. S $89; D $99; each addl $8; suites $129-$189; under 18 free; wkend rates. Crib free. Pet accepted, some restrictions. TV; cable, VCR avail (movies). Indoor pool; whirlpool. Restaurant 6 am-11 pm. Rm serv. Bar 11:30-2 am. Ck-out noon. Meeting rms. Business center. In-rm modem link. Sundries. Gift shop. Free airport transportation 24 hrs. Downhill ski 10 mi. Sauna. Some in-rm whirlpools. Courtyard atrium. Cr cds: A, D, ER, MC, V.

⊠ 🖊 ⛵ ⚐ ⛷ 🕴 🧹 SC 🎿

✔★ ★ **ROYAL INN.** *(10010 178th St, Edmonton AB T5S 1T3)* 403/484-6000; FAX 403/489-2900; res: 800/661-4879 (CAN). 194 rms, 4 story. S $59-$95; D $59-$103; each addl $8; wkend rates. Crib free. Pet accepted. TV; cable, VCR. Restaurants 6:30 am-10 pm. Rm serv. Bar noon-1 am. Ck-out 11 am. Meeting rms. Business servs avail. In-rm modem link. Bellhops. Valet serv. Sundries. Gift shop. Exercise equipt; bicycles, treadmill, steam rm. Whirlpool. Refrigerator in suites; some in-rm whirlpools. Cr cds: A, ER, MC, V.

⊠ 🖊 🕴 🧹 SC

Hotels

★ ★ ★ **COAST TERRACE INN.** *(4440 Calgary Trail North, Edmonton AB T6H 5C2)* 403/437-6010; FAX 403/431-5801; 800 888/837-7223. 223 rms, 4 story. S, D $90-$180; suites $99-$199; under 18 free; wkend rates; package plans. Pet accepted, some restrictions. TV; cable. Heated pool; whirlpool. Restaurant 6 am-11 pm. Rm serv 24 hrs. Bar 11:30-1 am; entertainment. Ck-out 1 pm. Meeting rms. Business servs avail. In-rm modem link. Bellhops. Gift shop. Barber, beauty shop. Underground parking. Exercise equipt; weights, bicycles, sauna, steam rm. Minibars. Balconies. Luxury level. Cr cds: A, D, DS, ER, JCB, MC, V.

⊠ 🖊 ⛵ ⚐ 🕴 🛉 🧹 SC

★ ★ ★ **CONVENTION INN.** *(4404 Calgary Trail, Edmonton AB T6H 5C2)* 403/434-6415; FAX 403/436-9247; res: 800/661-1122. 237 rms, 11 story. S, D $75-$150; each addl $10; suites $115-$325; under 16 free. Crib free. TV; cable. Heated pool; whirlpool. Complimentary continental bkfst. Restaurants open 24 hrs. Bar 11-2 am; entertainment. Ck-out noon. Meeting rms. Business center. Barber, beauty shop. Free indoor parking; valet. Exercise equipt; weight machine, bicycle. Minibars. Cr cds: A, D, ER, MC, V.

⊠ ⚐ 🕴 🧹 SC 🎿

★ ★ ★ **CROWNE PLAZA CHATEAU LACOMBE.** *(10111 Bellamy Hill, Edmonton AB T5J 1N7)* 403/428-6611; FAX 403/425-6564. 307 rms, 24 story. S $150; D $165; each addl $15; suites $180-$275; under 18 free; wkend rates. Crib free. Pet accepted, some restrictions. TV; cable, VCR avail. Restaurant 6:30 am-9 pm; Fri, Sat to 11 pm (also see LA RONDE). Bar 11-1 am. Ck-out 1 pm. Meeting rms. Business servs avail. In-rm modem link. Garage parking; valet. Exercise equipt; weights, bicycles. Minibars. Some balconies. Luxury level. Cr cds: A, C, D, DS, ER, MC, V.

⊠ 🖊 🕴 🧹 🧹 SC

★ ★ **DELTA EDMONTON CENTRE SUITE.** *(10222 102nd St, Edmonton AB T5J 4C5) at Eaton Centre Shopping Mall.* 403/429-3900; FAX 403/428-1566; res: 800/877-1133 (US), 800/268-1133 (CAN). 169 rms, 7 story, 126 suites. S $178-$198; D $188-$208; each addl $10; suites $178-$225; under 18 free; wkend rates. Crib free. Valet parking $7.50. TV; cable, VCR avail. Coffee in rms. Restaurant 6:30 am-10 pm. Bar 11 am-midnight. Ck-out noon. Free lndry facilities. Meeting rms. Business center. In-rm modem link. Concierge. Barber, beauty shop. Exercise

equipt; bicycle, rower, steam rm. Miniature golf. Minibars. Cr cds: A, C, D, ER, MC, V.

⊠ 🕴 ⚐ 🧹 🎿

★ ★ ★ **EDMONTON INN.** *(11830 Kingsway Ave, Edmonton AB T5G 0X5)* 403/454-9521; FAX 403/453-7360; res: 800/661-7264 (CAN). 431 rms, 6-9 & 15 story. S, D $110-$120; each addl $10; suites to $385; under 18 free; wkend rates. Crib free. Pet accepted, some restrictions. TV; cable. Restaurants 6:30 am-midnight; Sat, Sun from 7 am. Bar; entertainment. Ck-out 11 am. Convention facilities. Business servs avail. In-rm modem link. Gift shop. Beauty shop. Local airport transportation. Some refrigerators. Balconies. Cr cds: A, D, DS, ER, MC, V.

⊠ 🖊 ⚐ 🧹 SC

★ ★ ★ **FANTASYLAND.** *(17700 87th Ave, Edmonton AB T5T 4V4) in West Edmonton Mall.* 403/444-3000; FAX 403/444-3294; res: 800/661-6454 (CAN). 354 rms, 12 story. Mid-June-early Sept: S, D $138-$208; each addl $10; suites, theme rms $198-$240; under 17 free; lower rates rest of yr. Crib $7. Some covered parking; valet $3.50. TV; cable, VCR avail. Restaurant 7 am-11 pm. Rm serv 24 hrs. Bar noon-1 am. Ck-out noon. Convention facilities. Business center. Concierge. Shopping arcade. Barber, beauty shop. Exercise equipt; weights, bicycles, stair machines. Mall attractions include indoor amusement park, water park, movie theaters. Cr cds: A, D, ER, JCB, MC, V.

⊠ 🕴 ⚐ 🧹 🎿

★ ★ ★ ★ **HOTEL MACDONALD.** *(10065 100th St, Edmonton AB T5J 0N6)* 403/424-5181; FAX 403/424-8017; res: 800/441-1414. Restored to its 1915 glory, this chateau-like property on the North Saskatchewan River features ornamental plasterwork and original artwork in the lobby. Gardens and gazebos grace the spacious grounds. 198 rms, 8 story. S $139-$220; D $159-$240; each addl $20; suites $300-$2,500; under 18 free; wkend rates. Crib free. Pet accepted, some restrictions. Valet parking. TV; cable (premium). Indoor pool; wading pool, whirlpool, poolside serv. Restaurant (see HARVEST ROOM-LIBRARY). Rm serv 24 hrs. Bar 11-1 am. Ck-out 1 pm. Meeting rms. Business servs avail. In-rm modem link. Concierge. Gift shop. Exercise rm; instructor, weight machine, bicycles, sauna. Massage. Sun deck. Game rm. Minibars. Cr cds: A, C, D, DS, ER, JCB, MC, V.

⊠ 🖊 ⛵ ⚐ 🕴 🧹 🧹 SC

★ ★ ★ **HOWARD JOHNSON PLAZA.** *(10010 104th St, Edmonton AB T5J 0Z1)* 403/423-2450; FAX 403/426-6090. 138 rms, 9 story. S, D $109-$186; each addl $10; suite $135; under 17 free; wkend rates. Crib free. Parking (fee). TV; cable. Indoor pool; whirlpool. Restaurant 6:30 am-10 pm; Sat, Sun from 7:30 am. Bar 11:30-1 am. Ck-out noon. Meeting rms. Business center. In-rm modem link. Shopping arcade. Barber, beauty shop. Exercise equipt; weight machine, bicycles, sauna. Health club privileges. Balconies. Cr cds: A, C, D, ER, MC, V.

⊠ ⚐ 🕴 🧹 🧹 SC 🎿

★ ★ ★ **INN ON 7TH.** *(10001 107th St, Edmonton AB T5J 1J1)* 403/429-2861; FAX 403/426-7225; res: 800/661-7327 (AB). 172 rms, 14 story. S $118; D $128; suites $170; each addl $10; under 12 free. Crib free. Pet accepted. TV; cable (premium). Restaurant 6:30 am-9 pm. Bar 11 am-11 pm. Ck-out 11 am. Meeting rms. Business servs avail. Cr cds: A, D, DS, ER, MC, V.

⊠ 🖊 ⚐ 🧹 SC

★ ★ ★ **MAYFIELD INN.** *(16615 109th Ave, Edmonton AB T5P 4K8)* 403/484-0821; FAX 403/486-1634; res: 800/661-9804. 322 rms, 10 story, 115 suites, 10 kits. S, D $85; each addl $10; suites $128-$225; kit. units $125; under 16 free; wkend rates. Crib free. TV; cable. Heated pool; whirlpool. Complimentary bkfst buffet Mon-Fri (exc hols). Restaurant 6:30 am-midnight. Bar; entertainment. Ck-out 1 pm. Meeting rms. Business servs avail. In-rm modem link. Barber, beauty shop. Exercise equipt; weight machines, bicycles, sauna, steam rm. Airport transportation. Dinner theater. Cr cds: A, D, ER, JCB, MC, V.

⊠ ⚐ 🕴 🧹 🧹

✔★ ★ **RAMADA INN.** *(5359 Calgary Trail, Edmonton AB T6H 4J9)* 403/434-3431; FAX 403/437-3714. 122 rms, 7 story. S, D $59-$79;

each addl $5; suites $69-$109; under 18 free. Crib free. TV; cable. Indoor pool; wading pool, whirlpool. Restaurant 6:30 am-10 pm. Bar to 2 am. Ck-out 11 am. Meeting rms. Business servs avail. Valet serv. Coin lndry. Free airport transportation. Game rm. Some balconies. Cr cds: A, D, ER, MC, V.

D ≋ ⊠ 🔥 SC

★ ★ ★ **RENAISSANCE.** (10155 105th St, Edmonton AB T5J 1E2) 403/423-4811; FAX 403/423-3204; res: 800/468-3571. 300 rms, 21 story. S $149-$189; D $159-$199; each addl $10; suites $250-$400; under 18 free; wkend rates. Crib free. Garage $7.50. TV; cable, VCR avail. Indoor pool; whirlpool. Complimentary coffee in rms. Restaurants 6:30 am-11 pm. Rm serv 24 hrs. Bar 11-1 am. Ck-out 1 pm. Meeting rms. Business center. In-rm modem link. Gift shop. Exercise equipt; weight machines, bicycles, steam rm. Luxury level. Cr cds: A, C, D, DS, ER, JCB, MC, V.

D ≋ 🏋 ⊠ 🔥 SC 🏊

★ ★ ★ **SHERATON EDMONTON.** (10235 101st St, Edmonton AB T5J 3E9) downtown. 403/428-7111; FAX 403/441-3098; res: 800/268-9275 (US). 313 rms, 26 story. S, D $159-$179; each addl $20; suites $209. Crib free. TV; cable (premium), VCR avail. Heated pool. Coffee in rms. Restaurant 6:30 am-11 pm. Rm serv 24 hrs. Bar 11:30-2 am; entertainment. Ck-out noon. Meeting rms. Business center. Shopping arcade. Valet parking. X-country ski 2 mi. Minibars. Atrium lobby; garden lounge. Connected by walkway to Edmonton Centre. Cr cds: A, C, D, ER, JCB, MC, V.

D ≋ ≋ ⊠ 🔥 🏊

★ ★ **TOWER ON THE PARK.** (9715 110th St, Edmonton AB T5K 2M1) 403/488-1626; FAX 403/488-0659; res: 800/661-6454 (CAN). 98 kit. suites, 14 story. Crib $5. Pet accepted. TV; cable. Complimentary continental bkfst. Coffee, tea in rms. Ck-out noon. Meeting rms. Business servs avail. Covered parking. Lndry facilities. Balconies. Italian marble, mirrored lobby. Cr cds: A, D, ER, MC, V.

🏊 ⊠ 🔥

★ ★ ★ **THE WESTIN.** (10135 100th St, Edmonton AB T5J 0N7) downtown. 403/426-3636; FAX 403/428-1454. 413 rms, 12-20 story. S $129-$165, D $139-$175; each addl $20; suites $330-$350; under 18 free; wkend rates. Crib free. Valet parking $13, garage $10. TV; cable. Heated pool. Restaurant 6:30 am-11 pm. Rm serv 24 hrs. Bar 11-1 am. Ck-out 1 pm. Meeting rms. Business center. X-country ski 2 mi. Exercise equipt; bicycles, stair machines, sauna. Massage. Minibars; some bathrm phones. Luxury level. Cr cds: A, C, D, DS, ER, JCB, MC, V.

D ≋ ≋ 🏋 🔥 SC 🏊

Restaurants

✔★ ★ **BUON APPETITO.** (9707 110th St, Edmonton AB T5K 2L9) 403/482-5858. Hrs: 11:30 am-2:30 pm, 5-10 pm; Sat, Sun from 5 pm. Closed Mon; most major hols. Res accepted. Italian menu. Bar. Semi-a la carte: lunch $6.95-$9.95; dinner $7.50-$15. Child's meals. Specializes in lamb, sausage. Salad bar. Overlooking the River Valley. Cr cds: MC, V.

D

✔★ ★ **CHIANTI CAFE.** (10501 82nd Ave, Edmonton AB) at Strathcona Square Market. 403/439-9829. Hrs: 11 am-midnight; Sun from 4 pm. Closed Dec 25. Res accepted. Italian menu. Bar. Semi-a la carte: lunch, dinner $4.25-$13.95. Specializes in pasta, veal, seafood. Outdoor patio dining. Renovated historic post office building. Cr cds: A, D, DS, ER, MC, V.

D ⊡

★ ★ **CLAUDE'S ON THE RIVER.** (9797 Jasper Ave, Edmonton AB) 403/429-2900. Hrs: 6-10 pm. Closed Sun; Dec 25. Res accepted. French menu. Wine list. Complete meals: dinner $38. Specializes in rack of lamb, seafood. Menu changes weekly. Underground parking. Cr cds: A, C, D, ER, MC, V.

D ⊡

✔★ **FIORE.** (8715 109th St, Edmonton AB T6G 2L5) 403/439-8466. Hrs: 11 am-11 pm; Sat noon-midnight; Sun to 10 pm. Closed Dec 25. Res accepted. Italian menu. Bar. Semi-a la carte: lunch $5-$8.50; dinner $8-$15. Child's meals. Specializes in pasta, seafood. Outdoor dining. Casual decor. Cr cds: A, C, D, DS, ER, MC, V.

D

★ ★ ★ **HARVEST ROOM-LIBRARY.** (See Hotel Macdonald) 403/424-5181. Hrs: 6:30 am-10 pm; Sat, Sun from 7 am; Sun brunch 10:30 am-1:30 pm. Res accepted. Continental, Pacific Northwest menu. Bar 11:30-1 am; Sun to midnight. Wine cellar. Semi-a la carte: bkfst $7.75-$11.95, lunch $6.25-$12.50. A la carte: dinner $18-$34. Buffet: lunch $10.95. Sun brunch $23. Child's meals. Specialties: cream of wild mushroom & artichoke soup, young lamb loin with rosemary, slow-roasted Alberta prime rib. Valet parking. Terrace dining overlooking Saskatchewan River and city. Elegant dining in historic hotel. Cr cds: A, C, D, DS, ER, JCB, MC, V.

D SC ⊡

★ ★ ★ **HY'S STEAK LOFT.** (10013 101A Ave, Edmonton AB) 403/424-4444. Hrs: 11:30 am-2 pm, 5:30-11 pm; Sun 5-10 pm. Closed some major hols. Res accepted. Continental menu. Bar 11:30 am-11 pm. Wine cellar. A la carte entrees: lunch $8-$13, dinner $18.50-$25.50. Child's meals. Specializes in Alberta beef. Elegant dining. Cr cds: A, D, DS, ER, MC, V.

D ⊡

✔★ ★ **JAPANESE VILLAGE.** (10126 100th St, Edmonton AB) 403/422-6083. Hrs: 11:30 am-2 pm, 5-10:30 pm; Fri, Sat 5-11 pm; Sun 4:30-10 pm. Closed Victoria Day, Nov 11, Dec 24 & 25. Res accepted. Japanese menu. Serv bar. Semi-a la carte: lunch $5.95-$10.95, dinner from $14.95. Complete meals: dinner $15.60-$34. Child's meals. Specializes in sushi, tempura, Teppanyaki cooking. Cr cds: A, D, ER, JCB, MC, V.

★ ★ ★ **L'ANJOU.** (10643 123 St, Edmonton AB) 403/482-7178. Hrs: 6-8:30 pm. Closed Sun-Tues; some major hols. Res required. French country menu. Bar. Complete meals: dinner $27-$35. Child's meals. Parking. Five-course meal only Fri, Sat. French country decor. Cr cds: A, D, MC, V.

D

★ ★ ★ **LA BOHEME.** (6427 112th Ave, Edmonton AB) 403/474-5693. Hrs: 10 am-midnight; Sun 11 am-9 pm. Closed Dec 25. Res required. French, Moroccan menu. Bar. Wine cellar. A la carte entrees: lunch, dinner $7.95-$15.95. Complete meals: dinner $30. Sun brunch $11.75. Specializes in seafood, lamb. Own pastries. Parking. Outdoor dining. Romantic European atmosphere. Guest rms avail. Cr cds: A, MC, V.

★ ★ ★ **LA RONDE.** (See Crowne Plaza Chateau Lacombe Hotel) 403/428-6611. Hrs: 5:30-10:30 pm; Sun brunch 10:30 am-2 pm. Res accepted. Bar. A la carte entrees: dinner $18-$25. Sun brunch $19.95. Child's meals. Specializes in Alberta beef, fresh fish. Dancing Thurs-Sat. Parking. Revolving restaurant with panoramic view of city. Cr cds: A, D, ER, JCB, MC, V.

D ⊡

★ ★ ★ **LA SPIGA RISTORANTE.** (10133 125th St, Edmonton AB) 403/482-3100. Hrs: 5-11 pm; Sat to midnight. Closed Sun; most major hols. Res accepted; required Fri, Sat. Northern Italian menu. Serv bar. Wine list. A la carte entrees: dinner $13-$21. Specializes in rack of lamb. Own desserts. Parking. Outdoor dining. Mansion built 1915; beamed ceilings, fireplaces. Cr cds: A, D, ER, MC, V.

✔★ ★ **SELECT.** (10180 101st St, Edmonton AB) 403/429-2752. Hrs: 11:30 am-7 pm; Thurs to 10 pm; Fri, Sat to midnight. Closed Sun; Jan 1, Dec 25. Res accepted. Continental menu. Bar. A la carte entrees: lunch $3.75-$11.95, dinner $5.95-$19.95. Specializes in gourmet pizza (12 varieties). Jazz combo Thurs-Sat. Parking free after 5 pm. Natural slate floor; original artwork. Cr cds: A, D, ER, MC, V.

D ⊡

Unrated Dining Spot

CRÊPERIE. *(10220 103rd St, Edmonton AB)* 403/420-6656. Hrs: 11:30 am-11 pm; Fri to midnight; Sat noon-midnight; Sun 5-10 pm. Closed Dec 25. Res accepted; required Fri, Sat. French menu. Bar. A la carte entrees: lunch $6-$10, dinner $6-$14. Child's meals. Specializes in crêpes, country French dishes. Menu changes twice wkly. Cr cds: A, D, ER, MC, V.

Fort Macleod (E-4)

(See also Lethbridge)

Settled 1874 **Pop** 3,139 **Elev** 3,105 ft (1,046 m) **Area code** 403 **E-mail** edo@town.fortmacleod.ab.ca **Web** www.fortmacleod.com

Information Tourism Action Committee, PO Box 1959, T0L 0Z0; 403/553-2500 or 403/553-3204.

Fort Macleod was the first North West Mounted Police post in Alberta, named in honor of Colonel James F. Macleod, who led the force on its march westward. The fort was successful in stamping out the illegal whiskey trade that had flourished previously in the area. Today, the region has an abundance of mixed and grain farming.

What to See and Do

Fort Museum. Museum complex depicts history of North West Mounted Police, Plains tribes, and pioneer life in Fort Macleod, the first outpost in the Canadian west. A special feature is the Mounted Patrol Musical Ride (July-Aug, 4 times daily). (May-Oct, daily; rest of yr, Mon-Fri; closed some hols) 25th St & 3rd Ave. Phone 403/553-4703. ¢¢

Head-Smashed-In Buffalo Jump Interpretive Centre. Buffalo jump site dating back approx 6,000 yrs. Interpretive tours, theater, cafeteria. (Daily; closed Easter, Dec 25) (2 mi (3 km) N on Hwy 2, then 10 mi (16 km) W on Spring Point Rd (S-785). Phone 403/553-2731. ¢¢¢

Remington-Alberta Carriage Centre. Displays one of the largest collections of horse-drawn vehicles in North America; Over 200 carriages, wagons & sleighs. Gallery has interactive displays, audio-visual productions, carriage factory. (Daily) 35 mi S on Hwy 2 at 623 Main St in Cardston. Phone 403/653-5139. ¢¢¢

Waterton Lakes National Park (see). 30 mi SW on Hwy 3, then on Hwy 6.

Annual Event

Annual Powwow & Tipi Village. At Head-Smashed-In Buffalo Jump. Celebration features open tipi village, traditional native dances, games, food. 3rd wkend July.

Motel

✔★ **SUNSET.** *(104 Hwy 3W, Fort Macleod AB T0L 0Z0)* at W edge of town. 403/553-4448; res: 888/554-2784; FAX 403/553-2784. E-mail sunsetmo@telusplanet.net. 22 rms, 3 kits. June-Sept: S $46; D $52; each addl $4; kit. units $74-$85; varied lower rates rest of yr. Crib free. Pet accepted. TV; cable. Coffee in office. Restaurant nearby. Ck-out 11 am. Refrigerators. Cr cds: A, D, DS, ER, MC, V.

Restaurant

★ **SCARLET & GOLD INN.** *(2323 Seventh Ave (Hwy 3), Fort Macleod AB)* 403/553-3337. Hrs: dining rm 4:30-11:30 pm; Sun noon-10 pm; coffee shop 6 am-10 pm. Closed Jan 1, Dec 25, 26. Bar noon-midnight. Semi-a la carte: bkfst $2.85-$8.10, lunch $4.75-$11, dinner $7.75-

$16.95. Child's meals. Specializes in prime rib, steaks. Cedar building. Royal Canadian Mounted Police theme. Cr cds: A, MC, V.

Jasper National Park (C-1)

Area code 403

Information Jasper Tourism & Commerce, 632 Connaught Dr, PO Box 98, T0E 1E0; 403/852-3858.

(222 mi or 357 km W of Edmonton via Yellowhead Highway)

Established in 1907 and located in the Canadian Rockies, Jasper is one of Canada's largest and most scenic national parks. In its more than 4,200 square miles (10,878 square kilometers) are waterfalls, lakes, canyons, glaciers and wilderness areas filled with varied forms of wildlife, in the midst of which is the resort town of Jasper.

Park naturalists offer year-round interpretive programs, trips and campfire talks. There are also guided wilderness trips, a sky tram, skating, skiing, ice climbing, rafting and cycling trips. The park, the Rockies and the resort atmosphere of Jasper make this trip enjoyable any time of the year.

What to See and Do

Marmot Basin. Quad, triple, 3 double chairlifts, 2 T-bars; patrol, school, rentals; repair shop; nursery, 3 cafeterias, bar. Vertical drop 2,300 ft (700 m). (Early Dec-late Apr) 13 mi (19 km) S of Jasper via Icefield Pkwy (93A). Phone 403/852-3816 or 403/488-5909 (snow conditions). Tows/lifts ¢¢¢¢

Miette Hot Springs. Pool uses natural hot mineral springs. Lodge (phone 403/866-3750). (Mid-May-early Sept) 38 mi (61 km) E of Jasper via Hwy 16, Pocahontas Junction. Contact Canadian Parks Service, PO Box 10, Jasper, T0E 1E0; 403/852-6161. ¢¢

Sightseeing tours.

Jasper Tramway. Two 30-passenger cars take 1¼-mi (2-km) trip up Whistlers Mt. Vast area of alpine tundra at summit; hiking trails, picnicking; restaurant, gift shop. (Apr-mid-Oct, daily) 4 mi (6 km) S of Jasper, exit Jasper-Banff Hwy to Whistlers Mt Rd. Phone 403/852-3093. ¢¢¢

Boat cruise. Maligne Tours, Ltd. Narrated cruise (1½ hr) on Maligne Lake to world-famous Spirit Island. (June-Sept, daily) Fishing supplies & boat rentals. Whitewater raft trips on Maligne River. Hiking; horseback riding. 30 mi (48 km) S of Jasper via Hwy 16, Maligne Rd exit. Phone 403/852-3370. Cruise ¢¢¢¢¢

Other tours. Various tours are offered by bus, raft, gondola and "snocoach" to Lake Louise, Jasper, Calgary, Banff and the Athabasca Glacier. For further information contact Brewster Transportation & Tours, PO Box 1140, Banff, T0L 0C0; 403/762-6700.

Motels

(Because of the altitude, air conditioning is rarely necessary)

★★ **AMETHYST LODGE.** *(200 Connaught Dr, Jasper National Park AB T0E 1E0)* 200 Connaught Dr. 403/852-3394; FAX 403/852-5198; res: 800/661-9935 (W CAN). 97 rms, 3 story. June-Sept: S, D $151-$205; each addl $10; under 15 free; lower rates rest of yr. Pet accepted, some restrictions. TV; cable (premium). Complimentary coffee in rms. Restaurant 7-10 am, 5-10 pm; also noon-2 pm in season. Bar 4 pm-midnight. Ck-out 11 am. Meeting rms. Business center. Bellhops. Free RR station, bus depot transportation. Downhill/x-country ski 15 mi. 2 whirlpools. Balconies. Cr cds: A, D, ER, JCB, MC, V.

★ ★ **LOBSTICK LODGE.** (Box 1200, Jasper National Park AB T0E 1E0) Juniper at Geikie St. 403/852-4431; FAX 403/852-4142; res: 800/661-9317 (W CAN). 138 rms, 3 story, 43 kits. No A/C. June-Sept: S, D $151; each addl $10; suites, kit. units $166; under 15 free; MAP avail; ski plans; lower rates rest of yr. Crib free. Pet accepted, some restrictions. TV; cable (premium). Sauna, steam rm. Heated pool; 2 whirlpools. Restaurant 7-11 am, 5-10 pm; summer 6:30-11 am, 5-11 pm. Bar 5 pm-midnight. Ck-out 11 am. Coin lndry. Business servs avail. Downhill/x-country ski 15 mi. Cr cds: A, D, ER, JCB, MC, V.

★ ★ **MARMOT LODGE.** (86 Connaught Dr, Jasper National Park AB T0E 1E0) 86 Connaught Dr. 403/852-4471; FAX 403/852-3280; res: 800/661-6521 (W CAN). 107 rms, 47 A/C, 2 story, 32 kits. June-Sept: S, D $131-$178; each addl $10; suites $178-$325; under 16 free; ski plan; lower rates rest of yr. Pet accepted, some restrictions. TV; cable. Heated pool; whirlpool, sauna. Complimentary coffee. Restaurant 6:30-11 am, 5-10 pm. Bar 4:30 pm-1 am. Ck-out 11 am. Coin lndry. Meeting rm. Business servs avail. Valet serv. RR station, bus depot transportation. Downhill/x-country ski 15 mi. Fireplace in some kit. units. Private patios, balconies. Grills. Ski waxing rm & lockers in winter. Cr cds: A, D, JCB, MC, V.

Lodges

✔ ★ ★ ★ **ALPINE VILLAGE.** (Box 610, Jasper National Park AB T0E 1E0) 1½ mi S on Hwy 93, then ¼ mi E on Hwy 93A. 403/852-3285. 37 log cabins, 5 lodge suites, 29 kits. No A/C. S, D $85; each addl $10; suites, kit. units $85-$190. Closed mid-Oct-Apr. TV; cable. Playground. Ck-out 11 am. Many fireplaces. Grills. Whirlpool. Cr cds: MC, V.

★ ★ **OVERLANDER MOUNTAIN.** (Hinton AB T7V 1X5) 403/866-2330. 29 rms, 2 story. No A/C. No rm phone. May-Oct: S, D $100-$140; each addl $20; kit. units $125; lower rates rest of yr. Crib free. Pet accepted. Complimentary coffee in rms. Restaurant 7:30-10:30 am, 5:30-9:30 pm. Ck-out noon. Meeting rms. Business servs avail. X-country ski 15 mi. Some refrigerators. Some balconies. Cr cds: A, MC, V.

Motor Hotels

★ ★ ★ **CHATEAU JASPER.** (96 Geikie St, Jasper National Park AB T0E 1E0) 96 Geikie St. 403/852-5644; FAX 403/852-4860; res: 800/661-9323 (CAN). 119 rms, 3 story. Early June-late Sept: S, D $250-$350; each addl $25; under 16 free; lower rates rest of yr. Crib free. TV; cable; VCR avail. Indoor pool; whirlpool. Complimentary coffee in rms. Restaurants 7 am-10 pm (also see LE BEAUVALLON). Rm serv. Bar 11-midnight; entertainment. Ck-out 11 am. Meeting rms. Business servs avail. In-rm modem link. Bellhops. Sundries. Free underground parking. Free RR station, bus depot transportation. Downhill/x-country ski 15 mi. Some whirlpools. Cr cds: A, D, DS, ER, JCB, MC, V.

★ ★ **SAWRIDGE HOTEL JASPER.** (82 Connaught Dr, Jasper National Park AB T0E 1E0) 403/852-5111; FAX 403/852-5942; res: 800/661-6427 (CAN). 154 rms, 3 story. June-Sept: S, D $195; each addl $20; suites $220-$280; under 16 free; lower rates rest of yr; MAP avail. Crib free. TV; cable. Indoor pool; whirlpool. Restaurant 6:30 am-10:30 pm. Rm serv. Bar 4:30 pm-2 am. Ck-out 11 am. Meeting rms. Business servs avail. Valet serv. Free RR station, bus depot transportation. Downhill/x-country ski 5 mi. Some refrigerators; whirlpool in suites. Balconies. Ski lockers. Cr cds: A, D, DS, ER, JCB, MC, V.

Resort

★ ★ ★ **JASPER PARK LODGE.** (Box 40, Jasper National Park AB T0E 1E0) 2 mi E off Hwy 16. 403/852-3301; FAX 403/852-5107; res: 800/441-1414. 442 units, 5 cabins. No A/C. Late May-mid-Oct: S, D $364-$544; each addl $22; under 18 free; MAP avail; lower rates rest of yr. Crib free. Pet accepted, some restrictions. TV; cable. Heated pool; whirlpool, lifeguard. Supervised child's activities; ages 2 and up. Dining rm (see EDITH CAVELL). Box lunches. Rm serv. Bar 11-1 am. Ck-out noon, ck-in 4:30 pm. Business servs avail. In-rm modem link. Shopping arcade. Airport, RR station, bus depot transportation. Tennis, pro. 18-hole golf, greens fee $45-$75, putting green, driving range. Swimming. Rowboats, canoes, sailboats. Whitewater rafting. Downhill ski 15 mi; x-country ski on site. Bicycles. Lawn games. Soc dir; entertainment, dancing, movies. Rec rm. Game rm. Exercise rm; instructor, weights, bicycles, sauna, steam rm. Massage. Fishing guides. Minibars; some refrigerators, fireplaces. Some private patios, balconies. Cr cds: A, C, D, DS, ER, JCB, MC, V.

Restaurants

★ **CANTONESE.** (608 Connaught Dr, Jasper National Park AB) 403/852-3559. Hrs: 11 am-11 pm. Closed late Nov-mid-Dec. Res accepted. Chinese, Amer menu. Bar. Semi-a la carte: lunch, dinner $6-$17.50. Child's meals. Specializes in dim sum cuisine. Chinese decor. Family-owned. Cr cds: D, ER, MC, V.

★ ★ ★ **EDITH CAVELL.** (See Jasper Park Lodge Resort) 403/852-6073. Hrs: 6-9 pm; Fri, Sat to 10 pm. Res accepted. French menu. Bar. Semi-a la carte: dinner $35-$40. Child's meals. Specialties: wild mushroom chowder, beef tenderloin. Entertainment. Jacket. Cr cds: A, C, D, DS, ER, JCB, MC, V.

✔ ★ **L & W.** (Patricia & Hazel Sts, Jasper National Park AB) 403/852-4114. Hrs: 11-1 am. Closed Dec 25; also Nov. Greek, Amer menu. Bar. A la carte entrees: bkfst $2-$7, lunch $7-$15, dinner $8-$19. Child's meals. Specializes in pasta, pizza. Salad bar. Parking. Outdoor dining. Garden-like setting. Family-owned. Cr cds: A, D, MC, V.

★ ★ ★ **LE BEAUVALLON.** (See Chateau Jasper Motor Hotel) 403/852-5644. Hrs: 7 am-1 pm, 5:30-9:30 pm; summer 6:30 am-2 pm, 5:30-10 pm; Sun brunch 10:30 am-1:30 pm. Res accepted; required late May-Sept. Continental menu. Bar. Wine cellar. Semi-a la carte: bkfst $7-$13, lunch $8-$12, dinner $15-$40. Buffet: dinner (late May-Sept) $18. Sun brunch $15. Child's meals. Specializes in game, beef, seafood. Own baking. Harpist. Parking. Cr cds: A, D, ER, JCB, MC, V.

✔ ★ **SOMETHING ELSE.** (526 Patricia, Jasper National Park AB T0E 1E0) 403/852-3850. Hrs: 8 am-midnight. Greek, Italian, Amer menu. Serv bar. Semi-a la carte: bkfst $4-$7.50, lunch $6-$10, dinner $10-$16. Child's meals. Own pizza. Outdoor dining. Open kitchen. Cr cds: A, D, ER, MC, V.

★ ★ **TOKYO TOM'S PLACE.** (410 Connaught Dr, Jasper National Park AB) 403/852-3780. Hrs: 11:30 am-11 pm; Oct-mid-May 5-10 pm. Closed Dec 25. Res accepted; required Fri, Sat. Japanese, Chinese menu. Bar. A la carte entrees: lunch $6.50-$10, dinner $11-$19. Specializes in sushi, live lobster & crab. Cr cds: A, MC, V.

★ ★ **TONQUIN PRIME RIB.** (94 Geikie St, Jasper National Park AB) 403/852-4966. Hrs: 7-10:30 am, 5-11 pm. Res accepted; required in season. Continental menu. Bar 4 pm-2 am. Buffet: bkfst $6.50-$7.50. A la carte entrees: bkfst $3.25-$8.95, dinner $14-$39. Child's meals. Specializes in prime rib, seafood. Parking. Outdoor dining. Views of mountains. Cr cds: A, D, ER, MC, V.

Lake Louise (D-2)

(See also Banff)

Pop 1,600 (est) **Elev** 5,018 ft (1,520 m) **Area code** 403
Information Banff-Lake Louise Tourism Bureau, PO Box 1298, Banff, T0L 0C0, phone 403/762-8421 or Lake Louise Info Centre, phone 403/522-3833.

In the heart of the Canadian Rockies, Lake Louise is probably best known as one of the finest year-round resort towns in this area, along with Banff (see) and Jasper. The Rockies provide miles of summer hiking trails, natural beauty for the photographer and excellent skiing for a great part of the year. Lake Louise' also provides the resort atmosphere of nightlife and fun. During the summer, be sure to view the town from the gondola. The ride takes you to Mount Whitehorn where there is a lodge, and you can hike, picnic, explore and relax. Other popular activities include canoeing, fishing, climbing, biking, riding, tennis and sightseeing tours.

Motels

(Because of the altitude, air conditioning is rarely necessary)

★★ **CASTLE MOUNTAIN VILLAGE.** *(Lake Louise AB T0L 1E0)* 18 mi (29 km) E on Trans-Canada Hwy 1, just N of Castle Junction, in Banff National Park. 403/522-2783; FAX 403/762-8629. 21 kit. cottages, 8 with shower only, 7 suites. No A/C. No rm phones. S, D $150-$210. Crib $5. Pet accepted; $10. TV. Restaurant nearby. Ck-out 10:30 am. Coin lndry. Gift shop. Grocery store. Downhill ski 20 mi; x-country ski on site. Exercise equipt; weights, rowers. Some in-rm whirlpools, fireplaces. Cr cds: MC, V.

★★ **EMERALD LAKE LODGE.** *(Field BC V0A 1G0)* 20 mi W on Trans-Canada Hwy 1 in Yoho National Park. 250/343-6321; FAX 604/343-6724; res: 800/663-6336. 85 suites in 24 cabin-style bldgs, 2 story. No A/C. June-Sept: suites $260-$410; under 12 free; ski plans; lower rates rest of yr. Crib free. TV; VCR avail. Restaurant 6-11 pm. Bar. Ck-out 11 am. Meeting rms. Business servs avail. X-country ski on site; rentals. Sauna. Whirlpool. Boat rentals. Ice rink (winter). Game rm. Fireplaces. Private balconies. Picnic tables. On Emerald Lake in Canadian Rockies; canoeing. Cr cds: A, ER, MC, V.

★★ **MOUNTAINEER LODGE.** *(101 Village Rd, Lake Louise AB T0L 1E0)* 403/522-3844; FAX 403/522-3902. 78 rms in motel and lodge, 2 story. No A/C. No rm phones. Mid-June-Sept: S, D $150-$220; each addl $10; suites $180-$220; under 10 free; lower rates May-mid-June & late Sept-Oct. Closed rest of yr. Crib free. TV; cable (premium). Complimentary coffee in lobby. Restaurant opp 7 am-11 pm. Ck-out 11 am. Business servs avail. Sauna. Whirlpool. Cr cds: A, MC, V.

Lodge

★ **DEER LODGE.** *(Lake Louise AB T0L 1E0)* 2¼ mi SE off Trans-Canada Hwy 1. 403/522-3991; FAX 403/522-3883; res: 800/661-1595. 73 rms, 3 story. June-Sept: S, D $135-$195; each addl $20; under 12 free; lower rates rest of yr. Crib free. Dining rm 7-11 am, 6-9 pm. Bar 11 am-midnight. Ck-out 11 am. Business servs avail. Downhill ski 3 mi; x-country ski adj. Sauna. Outdoor whirlpool. Some balconies. Former trading camp (1921); rustic setting. Cr cds: A, D, MC, V.

Hotels

★★★ **CHATEAU LAKE LOUISE.** *(2½ mi SE off Trans-Canada Hwy 1, Lake Louise AB T0L 1E0)* 403/522-3511; FAX 403/522-3834; res: 800/441-1414. 511 rms, 8 story. Mid-May-mid-Oct: S $275; D $445; each addl $20; suites $560-$1,350; under 18 free; lower rates rest of yr. Pet accepted; $20. Covered parking $5/day. TV; cable, VCR avail. Steam rm. Indoor pool; whirlpool. 6 dining rms (also see WALLISER STUBE and VICTORIA DINING ROOM). Bars noon-2 am; entertainment. Ck-out noon. Convention facilities. Business servs avail. In-rm modem link. Shopping arcade. Airport transportation. Downhill ski 5 mi; x-country ski on site. Sleigh rides, ice-skating. Minibars. Some balconies. Resort-like hotel on Lake Louise, surrounded by rolling lawns and large flower gardens. Cr cds: A, C, D, DS, ER, JCB, MC, V.

★★★ **POST.** *(200 Pipestone, Lake Louise AB T0L 1E0)* 403/522-3989; FAX 403/522-3966; res: 800/661-1586 (US). 98 units, 3 story, 5 kit. units, 2 cottages. S, D $190-$330; suites $360-$450; kit. units $350-$380; cottages $310; ski plans. Closed Nov. Crib free. TV; cable (premium), VCR avail. Sauna, steam rm. Indoor pool; whirlpool. Restaurant (see POST HOTEL). No rm serv. Bar noon-midnight; entertainment (in season). Ck-out 11 am. Meeting rms. Business servs avail. Bus depot transportation. Downhill/x-country ski 1 mi. Some in-rm whirlpools, fireplaces. Private patios, balconies. Picnic tables. On river. Cr cds: A, MC, V.

Resorts

★★ **BAKER CREEK CHALETS.** *(Bow Valley Pkwy, Lake Louise AB T0L 1E0)* 403/522-3761; FAX 403/522-2270. 33 units (11 with shower only, 27 with kits.), 25 chalets (1- or 2-bdrm). S, D $150-$200; chalets $115-$225; family rates; lower rates winter. Crib $15. Complimentary coffee in rms. Restaurant 8 am-11 pm. Rm serv. Box lunches. Bar. Ck-out 11 am, ck-in 3 pm. Gift shop. Grocery, coin lndry 7 mi. Downhill ski 7 mi; x-country ski on site. Hiking. Refrigerators. Balconies. Picnic tables. Near river. Cr cds: MC, V.

★ **PARADISE LODGE & BUNGALOWS.** *(105 Lake Louise Dr, Lake Louise AB T0L 1E0)* 403/522-3595; FAX 403/522-3987. 24 rms in lodge, 21 cottages (shower only). No rm phones. June-Sept: suites $180-$215; cottages $125-$140; kit. cottages $150-$160; lower rates May & Oct. Closed rest of yr. Crib $6. TV; cable. Playground. Restaurant nearby. Ck-out 11 am, ck-in 4 pm. Business servs avail. Refrigerators. Balconies. Picnic tables. Cr cds: MC, V.

Restaurants

★★★ **POST HOTEL.** *(See Post Hotel)* 403/522-3989. Hrs: 7 am-2 pm, 5-10 pm. Closed Nov. Res accepted; required dinner. Continental menu. Bar. Wine cellar. A la carte entrees: bkfst $8-$15.50, lunch $8.50-$20, dinner $25-$37. Child's meals. Specializes in Alberta lamb, fresh seafood, Alberta beef. Pianist exc Sun. Rustic setting; mountain view. Cr cds: A, MC, V.

★★★ **VICTORIA DINING ROOM.** *(See Chateau Lake Louise Hotel)* 403/522-3511. Hrs: 7-9 am, 11:15 am-1 pm, 6-9 pm; Sun brunch 11:30 am-2 pm. Res accepted. No A/C. Continental menu. Wine list. Bar from noon. Buffet: bkfst $15, lunch $17.50. Complete meals: dinner $22-$43. Sun brunch $24.95 Child's meals. Specializes in prime rib, salmon. Salad bar (Sun lunch). Own baking. Entertainment. Valet parking. Cr cds: A, C, D, DS, ER, JCB, MC, V.

★★ **WALLISER STUBE.** *(See Chateau Lake Louise Hotel)* 403/522-3511. Hrs: 4-11:30 pm. Res accepted. No A/C. Swiss menu. Bar. Complete meals: dinner $12.50-$26. Child's meals. Specialties: fondue, cheese & beef. Swiss decor. Cr cds: A, C, D, DS, ER, JCB, MC, V.

Lethbridge (E-4)

(See also Fort Macleod)

Settled 1870 **Pop** 60,610 **Elev** 2,983 ft (909 m) **Area code** 403 **E-mail** west@albertasouth.com **Web** www.albertasouth.com

Information Chinook Country Tourist Association, 2805 Scenic Dr S, T1K 5B7; 403/320-1222 or 800/661-1222.

Lethbridge, in chinook country, sits amid ranchland and irrigated farms. The chinook, an Alberta winter phenomenon, is a warm wind that reportedly can raise temperatures as much as 40 degrees within 10 minutes.

Originally known to the Blackfoot as *Sik-okotoks* or "place of black rocks," Lethbridge was named after William Lethbridge, first president of the North-West Coal & Navigation Company. Among the many beautiful parks and gardens are the Brewery Gardens at the western edge of town; Indian Battle Park, site of the last battle between Native American nations in North America (1870), today a semi-wilderness; and Henderson Lake Park.

In 1869, traders from the United States came north and built so-called "whiskey forts." One of the most notorious was Fort Whoop-Up near Lethbridge. The arrival of the North West Mounted Police in 1874 soon stamped out this illegal whiskey trade. The city has rebuilt this fort, and the flag that signaled the arrival of the latest load of whiskey is now the official flag of Lethbridge.

What to See and Do

Alberta Birds of Prey Centre. Living museum featuring hawks, owls, falcons and other birds of prey from Alberta and around the world. Interpretive center has educational displays, wildlife art. Daily flying demonstrations; picnicking. (May-mid-Nov, daily, weather permitting) Approx 5 mi (8 km) E via Crowsnest Hwy (Hwy 3), on 16 Ave in Coaldale. Phone 403/345-4262 or 800/661-1222, operator 20. ¢¢

Fort Whoop-Up. This is a replica of the original fort, a major whiskey trading post in southern Alberta in the 1870s. Interpretive gallery, theater; tours, train tours. (Mid-May-Sept, daily; rest of yr, Tues-Fri, Sun afternoons) In Indian Battle Park. Phone 403/329-0444. ¢¢

Nikka Yuko Japanese Garden. Built to commemorate Canada's Centennial in 1967, the authentic garden is a symbol of Japanese-Canadian friendship. Buildings and bridges were built in Japan and reassembled in Lethbridge. The garden is an art form of peace & tranquility. (Mid-May-late Sept, daily) Henderson Lake Park. Phone 403/328-3511. ¢¢

Sir Alexander Galt Museum. Displays relate to early development of area. Featured exhibits include indigenous culture, pioneer life, civic history, coal mining, farming history, irrigation, ethnic displays. Video presentations. (Daily; closed some major hols) W end 5th Ave S. Phone 403/320-3898. **Free.**

Annual Events

"Ag-Expo" Agricultural Exposition. Early Mar.

Whoop-Up Days. Fair, exhibitions, horse racing, rodeo, grandstand show. Early Aug.

International Air Show. Aug.

Motor Hotel

★ ★ **BEST WESTERN HEIDELBERG INN.** *(1303 Mayor Magrath Dr, Lethbridge AB T1K 2R1)* 403/329-0555; FAX 403/328-8846. 67 rms, 9 story. S $65; D $70-$75; each addl $5; under 18 free. Crib free. TV; cable, VCR avail. Coffee in rms. Restaurant 6 am-11 pm. Bar 4 pm-1:30 am. Ck-out noon. Valet serv. Sundries. Sauna. Cr cds: A, C, D, DS, ER, JCB, MC, V.

Hotel

★ ★ ★ **LETHBRIDGE LODGE.** *(320 Scenic Dr, Lethbridge AB T1J 4B4)* 403/328-1123; FAX 403/328-0002; res: 800/661-1232. 191 rms, 4 story. S $81-$88; D $83-$90; each addl $7; suites $106-$130; under 18 free. Crib free. Pet accepted, some restrictions. TV; cable. Heated pool; whirlpool. Restaurant 6:30 am-11 pm. Bar 11 am-midnight; entertainment exc Sun. Ck-out noon. Meeting rms. Business servs avail. Health club privileges. Some refrigerators. Overlooks gorge & Univ of Lethbridge. Cr cds: A, D, ER, MC, V.

Restaurants

★ ★ **BEEFEATER STEAK HOUSE.** *(1917 Mayor Magrath Dr S, Lethbridge AB)* 403/320-6211. Hrs: 11 am-midnight; Sun to 9 pm; Sun brunch 10 am-2 pm. Res accepted. Continental menu. Bar. Semi-a la carte: lunch $5.95-$9.95, dinner $9.95-$24.95. Sun brunch $9.95. Child's meals. Specializes in Alberta prime rib, steak, seafood. Own desserts. Outdoor dining. Atrium, garden setting. Cr cds: A, D, ER, MC, V.

★ ★ ★ **COCO PAZZO ITALIAN CAFÉ.** *(1264 3rd Ave S, Lethbridge AB T1J 0J9)* downtown. 403/329-8979. Hrs: 11 am-11 pm; Thur-Sat to midnight; Sun 5-9 pm. Closed some major hols. Res accepted. Italian menu. Bar. Semi-a la carte: lunch $4.95-$7.95, dinner $7.25-$16.50. Child's meals. Specializes in wood fired Italian pizza, Alberta beef. Outdoor dining. Casual Italian cafe dining. Cr cds: A, MC, V.

✔ ★ ★ **NEW DYNASTY.** *(103 Seventh St S, Lethbridge AB)* 403/328-1212. Hrs: 11 am-midnight; Fri, Sat to 2 am; Sun to 9:30 pm. Closed Dec 25. Res accepted. Chinese menu. Bar. Semi-a la carte: lunch $5-$7, dinner $8-$12. Child's meals. Specialties: shredded ginger beef, moo shu pork, shrimp & scallops with bacon wrap. Modern Oriental decor. Cr cds: A, D, MC, V.

★ ★ **SVEN ERICKSEN'S.** *(1715 Mayor Magrath Dr, Lethbridge AB)* 403/328-7756. Hrs: 11 am-midnight; Sun 10 am-9 pm; Sun brunch to 1:30 pm. Closed Dec 25, 26. Res accepted. Bar. Semi-a la carte: lunch $4.75-$7.95. Complete meals: dinner $8.95-$24.95. Sun brunch $4.95-$6.75. Child's meals. Specializes in prime rib, seafood, roast beef. Own baking. Entertainment Sat. Provincial decor; display of old photos, Lethbridge memorabilia; antique clock. Family-owned. Cr cds: A, ER, MC, V.

Medicine Hat (E-5)

Settled 1883 **Pop** 42,929 **Elev** 2,365 ft (721 m) **Area code** 403 **E-mail** east@albertasouth.com **Web** www.absouth.com

Information Medicine Hat & District Convention and Visitor Bureau, 8 Gehring Rd SE, PO Box 605, T1A 7G5; 403/527-6422.

The city of Medicine Hat is famous for its industries. Rich in clays and natural gas, the area was a natural site for brick, tile and petrochemical plants. Its hot summer temperatures make it ideal for market gardens and greenhouses. There are many beautiful parks and excellent recreational facilities.

The name Medicine Hat is a translation of the Blackfoot name "Saamis" meaning "headdress of a medicine man." Supposedly a Cree medicine man lost his war bonnet in the river during a fight between the Cree and Blackfoot.

Natural gas was discovered here in 1883, and in 1909 the huge Bow Island gas field was founded. Because of these gas fields, the British poet Rudyard Kipling referred to the early settlement as "the town with all hell for a basement." Medicine Hat came into being with the arrival of the Canadian Pacific Railway.

What to See and Do

Cypress Hills Provincial Park. Oasis of mixed deciduous & coniferous forests in the middle of a predominantly grassland region. At a maximum elevation of 4,810 ft (1,466 m) above sea level, the hills are the highest point in Canada between the Rocky Mountains and Labrador. The area offers a swimming beach, boating, canoeing, fishing, camping (fee), golf course, hiking trails and nature interpretive programs. E on Trans-Canada Highway 1, then S on Hwy 41. For further information contact PO Box 12, Elkwater T0J 1C0; 403/893-3777 or 403/893-3782 (camping, May-Sept). Fort Walsh National Historic Park is nearby.   **Free.**

✪ **Dinosaur Provincial Park.** A UNESOUR World Heritage Site. Discoveries of extensive fossil concentrations in this area in the late 1800s led to the designation of this area as a provincial park. More than 300 complete skeletons have been recovered for display in museums world-wide. The 22,000-acre park consists mainly of badlands; large areas have restricted access and can be seen only on interpretive tours. Facilities include canoeing; fishing. Interpretive trails, dinosaur displays (at their actual site of discovery) along public loop drive. Picnicking. Primitive camping (firewood & water provided). Guided tours & hikes, amphitheater events and talks (summer; fee; inquire in advance). A field station of the Royal Tyrell Museum of Palaeontology in Drumheller is located here; also John Ware Cabin, with displays. Park (daily). Field station (mid-May-mid-Oct, daily; rest of yr, Mon-Fri). Some fees. Approx 25 mi (40 km) W on Hwy 1, then N on Hwy 884, W on Hwy 544. Phone 403/378-4342.

Medicine Hat Museum & Art Gallery. Displays depict the history of the Canadian West, featuring pioneer items, local fossils, relics and Native artifacts. The archives contain a large collection of photographs and manuscripts. (Daily; closed Jan 1, Good Friday, Dec 25) 1302 Bomford Crescent SW. Phone 403/527-6266 or 403/526-0486.   **Free.**

Annual Event

Exhibition and Stampede. Stampede Park. Cattle & horse shows, professional rodeo, midway rides.1st wkend Aug.

Motels

★ ★ **BEST WESTERN INN.** (722 Redcliff Dr, Medicine Hat AB T1A 5E3) 1½ mi W, 3 blks N of Hwy 3, near Municipal Airport. 403/527-3700; FAX 403/526-8689. 110 rms, 2 story, 24 suites, 11 kits. S $69; D $75-$79; suites $119; kit. units $73-$83. Crib $3. Pet accepted. TV; cable (premium). 2 indoor pools; 2 whirlpools. Complimentary continental bkfst. Restaurant adj 6 am-10:30 pm. Bar. Ck-out 11 am. Coin lndry. Meeting rms. Business servs avail. Sundries. Exercise equipt; weight machine, stair machine, sauna. Game rm. Refrigerators, microwaves. Cr cds: A, C, D, DS, ER, MC, V.

★ **SUPER 8.** (1280 Transcanada Way SE, Medicine Hat ON T1B 1J5) opp Southview Mall. 403/528-8888; FAX 403/526-4445. 70 rms, 3 story, 8 kit. units. Late June-early Sept: S $59.88; D $63.88-$68.88; each addl $4; suite $114.88; kit. units $78.88; under 12 free; wkly rates; higher rates Exhibition and Stampede; lower rates rest of yr. Crib free. Pet accepted. TV; cable. Indoor pool; whirlpool. Complimentary continental bkfst. Restaurant opp open 24 hrs. Ck-out 11 am. Business servs avail. Cr cds: A, D, DS, ER, MC, V.

Motor Hotels

★ ★ ★ **MEDICINE HAT LODGE.** (1051 Ross Glen Dr SE, Medicine Hat AB T1B 3T8) at jct Trans-Canada Hwy 1 & Dunmore Rd. 403/529-2222; FAX 403/529-1538; res: 800/661-8095. 190 rms, 4 story. S, D $79-$87; suites $109-$239; under 18 free. Crib free. Pet accepted. TV; cable, VCR avail. Indoor pool; wading pool, whirlpool. Coffee in rms. Restaurant 6:30 am-11 pm. Rm serv. Bar noon-1 am. Ck-out noon.

Meeting rms. Business servs avail. In-rm modem link. Bellhops. Sundries. Gift shop. Barber, beauty shop. Exercise equipt; bicycles, treadmill, sauna. Game rm. Balconies. Cr cds: A, C, D, DS, ER, MC, V.

 ✎ ≋ ✈ ⩔ ⋈ SC

↙★ **TRAVELODGE.** (1100 Redcliff Dr SW, Medicine Hat AB T1A 5E5) off Trans-Canada Hwy 1. 403/527-2275; FAX 403/526-7842; res: 800/442-8729. 130 rms, 2 story. S $69; D $69-79. Crib free. TV; cable (premium). Heated pool; wading pool, whirlpool. Coffee in rms. Restaurant 6 am-11 pm; Sun 7 am-9 pm. Rm serv. Bar 11-2 am. Ck-out noon. Meeting rms. Business servs avail. Valet serv. Exercise equipt; bicycle, treadmill, sauna. Some refrigerators. Cr cds: A, C, ER, MC, V.

≋ ✈ ⩔ ⋈ SC

Restaurant

★ ★ **BEEFEATER STEAK HOUSE.** (3286 13th Ave SE, Medicine Hat AB) 403/526-6925. Hrs: 11 am-midnight; Sat from 4:30 pm; Sun 4:30-10 pm. Closed Dec 25, 26. Res accepted. Bar. Semi-a la carte: lunch $5.25-$12.50, dinner $8.50-$44. Child's meals. Specializes in beef, seafood. Salad bar. English motif. Cr cds: A, D, ER, MC, V.

⊒

Red Deer (C-3)

Settled 1885 **Pop** 58,252 **Elev** 2,816 ft (860 m) **Area code** 403 **Web** www.visitor.red-deer.ab.ca

Information Visitor & Convention Bureau, Heritage Ranch Visitor Information Centre, PO Box 5008, T4N 3T4; 403/346-0180 or 800/215-8946.

The city of Red Deer sits in the valley of the Red Deer River, which winds through the lush green parkland of central Alberta. Sylvan and Pine lakes are among the popular recreation lakes surrounding the city. Agriculture and the petroleum industry are the mainstays of the economy. To the west is the David Thompson Highway, leading through the foothills into Alberta's Canadian Rockies and Banff National Park (see BANFF).

In the early 1870s the Calgary-Edmonton Trail crossed the river at a point known as Red Deer Crossing. With the coming of the railway, traffic increased and a trading post and stopping place were established. When the Northwest Rebellion broke out in 1885, a small regiment was stationed at Fort Normandeau. A reconstruction of this fort stands near Red Deer.

The river was originally called *Was-ka-sioo*, the Cree word for elk, because of the abundance of these animals. Early Scottish fur traders thought the elk were related to the red deer of their native land, hence the present name for the river and city.

What to See and Do

Canyon Ski Area. Triple, double chairlifts, 2 T-bars, handle tow; nordic jump; patrol, school, rentals; snowmaking; day lodge; bar, cafeteria. Longest run ½ mi (1 km); vertical drop 500 ft (164 m). (Nov-Mar, daily) Cross-country skiing. 6 mi (10 km) E on Ross St. Phone 403/346-5589, 403/346-5588 (snow conditions), 403/346-7003 (off-season). ¢¢¢¢¢

Cronquist House (1911). Victorian farmhouse in park setting at Bower Ponds. (Mon-Fri, also Sun afternoon; tours by appt) Kerry Wood Dr. Phone 403/346-0055.

Fort Normandeau. Rebuilt 1885 army fort and interpretive center with displays of cultural history. Slide program, living history interpreters. (May-Sept, daily) Picnic area, canoe launch. (see ANNUAL EVENTS) 2 mi (3 km) W off Hwy 2 on 32nd St. Phone 403/346-2010 or 403/347-7550.   **Free.**

Red Deer and District Museum. Displays cover pre-history and early settlement of Red Deer; changing exhibits. Also here are Heritage Square and Red Deer and District Archives. (Daily; extended hrs July-early Sept;

closed Jan 1, Dec 25) 4525 47 A Ave, adj to Recreation Centre. Phone 403/343-6844. **Donation.**

Waskasoo Park. Large River Valley park extending throughout city. Includes 47 mi (75 km) of bicycle & hiking trails, equestrian area, fishing, canoeing, water park, 18-hole golf. Picnicking (shelters). Campground (fee). Natural & cultural history interpretive centers; other attractions located within park. Fee for activities. (Daily) Phone 403/342-8159. **Free.**

Annual Events

Fort Normandeau Days. Fort Normandeau. Native American ceremonies & dances, parade, children's activities. Late May.

Highland Games. Westerner Park. Last Sat June.

International Folk Festival. Ethnic performers, displays, ethnic foods, fireworks. July 1.

Westerner Days. Fair & exhibition, midway, livestock shows, chuckwagon races. Mid-July.

Motels

★ ★ **NORTH HILL INN.** (7150 50th Ave (Hwy 2A), Red Deer AB T4N 6A5) 403/343-8800; FAX 403/342-2334; res: 800/662-7152 (AB). 98 rms, 3 story. S $62; D $66; under 12 free; wkend rates; golf plans. Crib free. Pet accepted, some restrictions. TV; cable (premium), VCR avail. Heated pool; whirlpool, sauna. Restaurant 6 am-10 pm. Rm serv. Bar; entertainment. Ck-out 11 am. Meeting rms. Business center. In-rm modem link. Downhill ski 10 mi; x-country ski 3 mi. Luxury level. Cr cds: A, D, ER, MC, V.

★ **RAINBOW MOTOR INN.** (2803 50th Ave (Hwy 2A), Red Deer AB T4R 1H1) 403/343-2112; FAX 403/340-8540; res: 800/223-1993 (AB, BC, SK). 88 rms, 2 story, 12 kits. S, D $47-$55; each addl $6; kit. units $53-$68; under 12 free. Crib free. Pet accepted, some restrictions. TV; cable (premium), VCR avail (movies). Restaurant 6:30 am-9 pm; wkends from 7 am. Ck-out noon. Meeting rm. Business servs avail. In-rm modem link. Downhill ski 10 mi; x-country ski 3 mi. Refrigerators. Picnic tables. Courtyard. Cr cds: A, C, D, ER, MC, V.

★ **TRAVELODGE.** (2807 50th Ave, Red Deer AB T4R 1H1) 403/346-2011; FAX 403/346-1075; res: 800/578-7878. 136 rms, 3 story, 10 kits. S $59; D $64; suites $90; under 12 free. Crib avail. Pet accepted, some restrictions. TV; cable. Indoor pool; whirlpool. Restaurant 6:30 am-1 pm, 5-10 pm. Rm serv. Ck-out 11 am. Business servs avail. Coin lndry. Downhill ski 10 mi; x-country ski 3 mi. Cr cds: A, D, ER, MC, V.

Hotels

★ ★ ★ **BLACK KNIGHT INN.** (2929 50th Ave (Hwy 2A), Red Deer AB T4R 1H1) 403/343-6666; FAX 403/340-8970; res: 800/661-8793 (AB). 98 rms, 8 story. S, D $70-$85; each addl $6; suites $88-$165; under 18 free; golf plans. Crib free. TV; cable (premium). Heated pool; whirlpool. Restaurant 6:30 am-10 pm. Bar 11-1 am. Ck-out noon. Meeting rms. Business servs avail. In-rm modem link. Gift shop. Downhill ski 10 mi; x-country ski 3 mi. Whirlpool in some suites. Cr cds: A, ER, MC, V.

★ ★ ★ **CAPRI CENTRE.** (3310 Gaetz Ave, Red Deer AB T4N 3X9) at the top of the South Hill. 403/346-2091; FAX 403/346-4790; res: 800/662-7197 (AB). 175 rms, 14 story, 22 kits. S $70-$85; D $70-$100; each addl $15; suites, kit. units $145-$300; under 16 free. Pet accepted, some restrictions. TV; cable, VCR avail. Heated pool; whirlpool. Restaurant 7 am-midnight. Bar 11-2 am; entertainment. Ck-out noon. Meeting rms. Business center. In-rm modem link. Shopping arcade. Barber, beauty shop. Airport transportation. Downhill ski 10 mi; x-country ski 3 mi. Exer-

cise equipt; weights, bicycles, sauna, steam rm. Some refrigerators. Some balconies. Cr cds: A, C, D, ER, MC, V.

★ ★ ★ **HOLIDAY INN.** (6500 67th St, Red Deer AB T4P 1A2) 403/342-6567; FAX 403/343-3600. 97 rms, 4 story. S, D $70-$89; suites from $140; under 10 free; golf packages. Crib free. Pet accepted. TV; cable (premium). Complimentary coffee in rms. Restaurant 6 am-11 pm; Bar 11-2 am. Ck-out 11 am. Business center. In-rm modem link. Barber, beauty shop. Downhill ski 10 mi; x-country ski 2 mi. Exercise equipt; weights, bicycles, sauna. Whirlpool. Cr cds: A, C, D, DS, ER, JCB, MC, V.

Restaurant

★ **HOULIHANS.** (#11 6791 Gaetz Ave, Red Deer AB T4N 4C9) in Pines Plaza. 403/342-0330. Hrs: 11 am-11 pm; Sat from 4:30 pm. Closed Sun; most major hols. Res accepted Mon-Thurs. Bar. Semi-a la carte: lunch $5-$7, dinner $8-$10. Child's meals. Specializes in prime rib, beef Wellington. Various dining levels with fountain in center. Cr cds: A, D, ER, MC, V.

Waterton Lakes National Park (F-3)

E-mail Angelege-mcintyre@pch.gc.ca **Web** www.worldweb.com/parks canada-waterton

Information Superintendent, Waterton Lakes National Park, Waterton Park, T0K 2M0; 403/859-2224 (winter) or 403/859-5133 (summer).

Waterton Lakes National Park was established in 1895, taking its name from the lakes in the main valley, which were named for the 19th-century English naturalist Squire Charles Waterton. In 1932 it was linked with Glacier National Park in Montana (see), the whole area now known as Waterton-Glacier International Peace Park. This park contains 203 square miles (526 square kilometers) on the eastern slope of the Rocky Mountains, just north of the US-Canadian border.

Travelers from the US can reach the park via the Chief Mountain Highway along the east edge of Glacier National Park (mid-May-mid-Sept). The trails are well-maintained and afford an introduction to much of the scenery that is inaccessible by car. Whether by foot, car or boat, exploring the park and its many wonders will make the trip most worthwhile.

The Red Rock Parkway goes from the town of Waterton Park to Red Rock Canyon after branching off Alberta Highway 5. A buffalo paddock is located on Highway 6, just inside the northeastern park boundary. Also from the town of Waterton Park, you can drive to Cameron Lake, via the Akamina Parkway. Separate fees are charged at most parks.

Motel

(Because of the altitude, air conditioning is rarely necessary)

★ ★ **ASPEN VILLAGE INN.** (111 Windflower Ave, Waterton Lakes National Park AB T0K 2M0) 403/859-2255; FAX 403/859-2033. E-mail travel@watertoninfo.ab.ca; web www.watertoninfo.ab.ca. 37 rms, 1-2 story, 2 suites, 12 kit. units. No A/C. No elvtr. Mid-May-Oct: S, D $122-$193; each addl $10; suites $159-$215; kit. units $126-$174; under 16 free; lower rates Easter-mid-June & Oct-Thanksgiving. Closed rest of yr. Crib $10. TV. Playground. Complimentary coffee in rms. Restaurant adj 7:30 am-9 pm. Ck-out 11 am. Gift shop. Sundries. Whirlpool. Grills. Cr cds: A, D, DS, ER, MC, V.

Lodges

★ ★ **CRANDELL MOUNTAIN.** *(102 Mount View Rd, Waterton Lakes National Park AB T0K 2M0)* 403/859-2288. 17 rms, 2 story, 8 kit. units. No A/C. No rm phones. June-Sept: S $99-$149; D $104-$149; each addl $10; kit. units $119-$169; 2-day min hols; lower rates rest of yr. Crib $7. Pet accepted, some restrictions. TV. Coffee in rms. Restaurant opp 7:30 am-10 pm. Ck-out 10 am. Meeting rms. Some fireplaces. Cr cds: A, DS, ER, MC, V.

✔ ★ ★ ★ **KILMOREY.** *(117 Evergreen Ave, Waterton Lakes National Park AB T0K 2M0)* 403/859-2334; FAX 403/859-2342. E-mail travel@watertoninfo.ab.ca; web www.watertoninfo.ab.ca. 23 rms, 3 story, 3 suites. No A/C. No elvtr. No rm phones. S, D $86-$133; each addl $10; suites $117-$171; under 16 free; special package rates. TV in lobby. Dining rm 7:30 am-10 pm. Rm serv. Ck-out 11 am, ck-in 3 pm. Country-style inn built in 1923. On Emerald Bay in Waterton Park. Cr cds: A, D, DS, ER, MC, V.

Inn

★ **PRINCE OF WALES.** *(In Waterton Lakes National Park, Waterton Lakes National Park AB T0K 2M0)* 602/207-6000; FAX 403/859-2630. 82 rms, 5 story. No A/C. S $169-$221; D $175-$227; each addl $15; under 12 free. Closed late Sept-mid May. Crib free. Dining rm 6:30-9:30 am, 11:30 am-2 pm, 5-9 pm. Tearoom 2-5 pm. Bar 11:30 am-midnight. Ck-out 11 am. Bellhops. Gift shop. Large, gabled inn (built 1927) overlooking lake & mountains. Cr cds: MC, V.

Restaurant

★ ★ ★ **COBBLESTONE MANOR.** *(173 Seventh Ave W, Cardston ON)* 26 mi E on Hwy 5. 403/653-1519. Hrs: 4:30-10 pm. Closed early Jan-Mar; Sun Oct-Dec, Apr-mid-May. Res accepted. British, Amer menu. Complete meals: dinner $7.95-$17.95. Child's meals. Specializes in steaks, soups, home-style cooking. Own baking. Historic house (1889) built of rock with inlaid panels of fine wood from all over the world; antique furniture & woodwork. Cr cds: A, MC, V.

Province of British Columbia

Pop 3,100,000 (est) **Land area** 344,817 sq mi (893,073 sq km) **Capital** Victoria **Web** travel.bc.ca

Information Tourism British Columbia, Box 9830, Stn Prov Govt, Victoria V8W 9W5; 800/663-6000.

This huge territory, with its mixture of climate, geography, products and people, began its modern history in 1843, while under British control. In 1871 British Columbia joined the Confederation and its steady progression can be traced through fur trading and gold rushes to urban development. Bordered on the south by Washington and on the north by the Yukon, the province has a wide range of weather conditions from the balmy warm breezes in Victoria to cold arctic winds in the far north. Thus many recreational possibilities, including skiing, sailing, swimming, spelunking and river rafting can be enjoyed.

Vacation choices range from shopping for indigenous art, to gold panning, to flying over the magnificent wilderness of the Queen Charlotte Islands. No trip to British Columbia would be complete without a visit to Vancouver and Victoria. International in character, Vancouver boasts all the attractions of a modern city while preserving its vital past. Museums,

galleries, parks, gardens and fine dining blend well with beaches and marinas in this lovely peninsular city.

Victoria, the capital, is located on Vancouver Island and is noted for its many gardens and parks. Victoria offers sights that include the Parliament buildings, the Royal British Columbia Museum, with its Natural History Gallery, and reconstructed areas that reflect the past.

Most of British Columbia is on Pacific Standard Time and observes Pacific Daylight Saving Time in summer. Tourists should note that there is strong anti-litter legislation in British Columbia which applies to boaters and hikers as well as drivers and pedestrians.

In addition to national holidays, British Columbia observes British Columbia Day (1st Mon Aug).

Safety belts are mandatory for all persons anywhere in vehicle. Children under 40 pounds in weight must be in an approved passenger restraint anywhere in vehicle: 20-39 pounds may use an approved safety seat facing forward if in parents' or guardians' vehicle, or a regulation safety belt if in someone else's vehicle; under 20 pounds must be in an approved safety seat facing rear. For further information phone 250/387-3140.

Kamloops (D-4)

Pop 64,048 **Elev** 1,181 ft (360 m) **Area code** 250 **E-mail** chamber@netshop.net **Web** www.city.kamloops.bc.ca

Information Chamber of Commerce and Visitor InfoCentres, 1290 W Trans-Canada Hwy, V2C 6R3; 250/374-3377 or 800/662-1994.

Kamloops is located at the junction of the North and South Thompson rivers and is a trade center for a farming, mining, ranching, lumbering and fruit-growing region. Kamloops trout are world famous; there are 200 lakes within 60 miles (96 kilometers) of the city.

What to See and Do

Kamloops Wildlife Park. More than 300 animals, both native and international. Nature trail. Miniature railroad (seasonal, fee). Park (daily). 11 mi (18 km) E, at 9055 E Trans-Canada Hwy 1. For further information contact PO Box 698, V2C 5L7; 250/573-3242. ¢¢¢

Secwepemc Native Heritage Park. Located on the Kamloops Reserve, park interprets culture and heritage of the Secwepemc people. Includes archaeological site, full-scale winter village model, indoor museum exhibits, native arts & crafts. Tours avail. (Summer, daily; rest of yr, Mon-Fri) N across Yellowhead Bridge, then 1st right. Phone 250/828-9801. ¢¢¢

St Joseph's Church. Historic church (1870) constructed by Oblate missionaries and Kamloops; originally a log building. Restored in 1985 by the local community. Period religious artifacts, elaborate gilded altar. Guided tours. (July-Labour Day, Wed-Sun, limited hrs; rest of yr, by appt) On Kootenay Way; N via Mt Paul Way to Chilcotin St. Phone 250/828-9700. **Free.**

Annual Event

International Air Show. Fulton Field. Concession, beer garden. 1st Wed Aug.

Motels

★ ★ **HOSPITALITY INN.** *(500 W Columbia St, Kamloops BC V2C 1K6)* 250/374-4164; FAX 604/374-6971; res: 800/663-5733 (BC). 77 rms, 2 story, 15 kits. June-Sept: S $92.50; D $96.50; each addl $6; kit. units $6 addl; under 12 free; lower rates rest of yr. Crib $6. TV; cable (premium). Sauna. Pool; whirlpool. Restaurant 7 am-10 pm. Ck-out 11 am. Meeting rms. Business servs avail. Refrigerators. Private patios. Cr cds: A, D, DS, ER, MC, V.

★ ★ **PANORAMA INN.** *(610 W Columbia St, Kamloops BC V2C 1L1)* 250/374-1515; FAX 250/374-4116; res: 800/663-3813. 94 rms, 2-3 story, 11 suites, 40 kits. May-Sept: S $79-$85; D $85-$89; each addl $8; suites $95-$125; kits. $8 addl; under 12 free; lower rates rest of yr. Crib free. TV; cable. Sauna. Heated pool; whirlpool. Coffee in rms. Restaurant 7 am-11 pm. Ck-out 11 am. Business servs avail. In-rm modem link. Private balconies. View of city. Cr cds: A, D, DS, ER, MC, V.

D ≈ ⊠ 🔥 SC

★ ★ **RAMADA INN.** *(555 W Columbia St, Kamloops BC V2C 1K7)* 250/374-0358; FAX 604/374-0691; res: 800/663-2832. 114 rms, 3 story, 12 kits. May-Sept: S $95; D $105; each addl $5; suites $100-$175; kit. units $10 addl; under 12 free; lower rates rest of yr. Crib free. TV; cable (premium), VCR avail. Sauna. Pool; whirlpool. Restaurant 6 am-11 pm. Rm serv. Bar; entertainment. Ck-out noon. Meeting rms. Business servs avail. Valet serv. Whirlpool, sauna. Refrigerators. Cr cds: A, C, D, ER, MC, V.

≈ ⊠ 🔥 SC

✔ ★ ★ **SAGE BRUSH.** *(660 W Columbia St, Kamloops BC V2C 1L1)* 250/372-3151; FAX 604/372-2983. 60 rms, 2 story, 30 kits. May-mid-Sept: S $60; D $68-$78; each addl $5; kit. units $5 addl; higher rates hols; lower rates rest of yr. TV; cable (premium). Sauna. Heated pool; whirlpool. Restaurant 6 am-11 pm. Ck-out 11 am. Business servs avail. Refrigerators. Cr cds: A, D, MC, V.

≈ ⊠ 🔥 SC

★ ★ **STAY 'N SAVE.** *(1325 Columbia St W, Kamloops BC V2C 2P4)* 250/374-8877; FAX 250/374-0507. 83 rms, 3 story, 25 kit. units. S $89; D $99; each addl $10; suites $120; kit. units $99-$130; under 17 free; ski plans. Crib free. Pet accepted. TV; cable. Heated pool; whirlpool. Complimentary coffee in lobby. Restaurant adj open 24 hrs. Ck-out 11 am. Coin lndry. Meeting rms. Business servs avail. In-rm modem link. Valet serv. X-country ski 15 mi. Exercise equipt; bicycle, stair machine, sauna. Picnic tables. Cr cds: A, D, ER, MC, V.

D ✔ ⊁ ≈ 🕈 ⊠ 🔥 SC

★ ★ **TRAVELODGE.** *(430 Columbia St, Kamloops BC V2C 2T5)* 250/372-8202; FAX 604/372-1459. 68 rms, 2 story. May-Oct: S, D $84-$94; each addl $5; under 18 free; lower rates rest of yr. Crib free. TV; cable, VCR avail. Sauna. Heated pool; whirlpool. Restaurant 7 am-9 pm. Ck-out 11 am. Meeting rm. Business servs avail. Cr cds: A, C, D, ER, MC, V.

D ≈ ⊠ 🔥 SC

Motor Hotels

★ ★ ★ **COAST CANADIAN INN.** *(339 St Paul St, Kamloops BC V2C 2J5)* 250/372-5201; FAX 250/372-9363; res: 800/663-1144. 94 rms, 5 story. May-Sept: S $110; D $120; each addl $10; under 18 free; ski plans; lower rates rest of yr. Crib free. TV; cable (premium), VCR avail (movies). Pool. Restaurant 6:30 am-10 pm. Rm serv 24 hrs. Bar 1 pm-1 am; entertainment exc Sun. Ck-out 1 pm. Meeting rms. Business center. In-rm modem link. Bellhops. Minibars. Cr cds: A, D, DS, ER, JCB, MC, V.

≈ ⊠ 🔥 SC ✗

★ ★ **DAYS INN.** *([B85 W Trans-Canada Hwy 1, Kamloops BC V2E 2J7)* 250/374-5911; FAX 250/374-6922; res: 800/561-5002 (AB, BC). 60 rms. June-Sept: S $99; D $109; each addl $10; suites $125-$250; kits. $150-$250; under 12 free; lower rates rest of yr. Crib free. Pet accepted, some restrictions. TV; cable (premium), VCR avail. Heated pool; whirlpool. Restaurant 7 am-9 pm. Ck-out noon. Meeting rms. Business servs avail. Refrigerators. Cr cds: A, D, ER, MC, V.

✔ ≈ ⊠ 🔥 SC

★ ★ **STOCKMEN'S HOTEL.** *(540 Victoria St, Kamloops BC V2C 2B2)* 250/372-2281; FAX 250/372-1125; res: 800/663-2837 (CAN). 150 rms, 5 story. May-Sept: S $105-$115; D $115-$125; each addl $10; suites $150-$175; under 14 free; lower rates rest of yr. Crib free. TV; cable (premium), VCR avail. Coffee in-rms. Restaurant 6 am-10 pm. Bar 11-1

am exc Sun. Ck-out noon. Meeting rms. Business servs avail. Cr cds: A, D, DS, ER, JCB, MC, V.

D ⊠ 🔥 SC

Kelowna (D-4)

(See also Penticton)

Pop 78,000 (est) **Elev** 1,129 ft (344 m) **Area code** 250 **E-mail** kelownachamber@awinc.com **Web** www.kelownachamber.org.
Information Visitors and Convention Bureau, 544 Harvey Ave, V1Y 6C9; 250/861-1515.

Kelowna is located on the shores of Okanagan Lake, between Penticton (see) and Vernon, 80 miles (128 kilometers) north of the US border. The name Kelowna is a corruption of an indigenous word for grizzly bear. The history of Europeans in the area dates back to the fur brigades in the 19th century. Father Pandosy established a mission here in 1858. The apple trees that were planted by him were the beginning of one of the largest fruit-growing districts in Canada.

The Civic Centre complex, located in downtown Kelowna, includes government buildings, community theater, a curling rink, regional library and centennial museum. The city also has 31 parks, seven on the lakeshore. Among the facilities in these parks are soccer fields, lawn bowling greens and tennis courts.

Kelowna is a playground at almost any time of year. Water sports, golf, cricket, curling, baseball and skiing are only a few of the sports played in the area. The winter highlight is the annual Snowfest.

Annual Events

Snowfest. "Smockey" game, Light Up Parade, polar bear dip, snowshoe relay, belly flop contest. Late Jan.

Black Mountain Rodeo. Mid-May.

Kelowna Regatta. Mid-July.

Okanagan Wine Festival. Races, ethnic events, baking contest, dance, wine tasting (also see PENTICTON). Phone 250/861-1515. May & Oct.

Motels

★ ★ **BEST WESTERN INN.** *(2402 Hwy 97N, Kelowna BC V1X 4J1)* 250/860-1212; FAX 604/860-0675. 99 rms, 2 story, 30 suites. May-Sept: S $89-$109; D $99-$119; each addl $10; suites $99-$142; under 12 free; ski, golf packages; lower rates rest of yr. Crib free. TV; cable (premium), VCR avail. Heated pool; whirlpools. Complimentary coffee in-rms. Restaurant 7 am-10 pm. Bar. Ck-out 11 am. Business servs avail. Tennis. Refrigerators. Private patios, balconies. Cr cds: A, C, D, DS, ER, JCB, MC, V.

D ⊁ ✗ ≈ ⊠ 🔥 SC

★ ★ **HOLIDAY INN EXPRESS.** *(2429 Hwy 97N, Kelowna BC V1X 4J2)* at Banks Rd. 250/763-0500; FAX 250/763-7555. 120 rms, 4 story. May-Oct: S, D $109-$139; each addl $10; suites $179; under 19 free; golf plans; lower rates rest of yr. Crib free. TV; cable (premium). Indoor pool; whirlpool. Complimentary continental bkfst. Restaurant adj 6 am-8:30 pm. Ck-out noon. Meeting rm. Business center. In-rm modem link. Bellhops. Valet serv. Exercise equipt; weight machine, bicycle. Some in-rm whirlpools. Cr cds: A, D, DS, ER, JCB, MC, V.

D ≈ ✗ ⊠ 🔥 SC ✗

★ **SANDMAN HOTEL.** *(2130 Harvey Ave (Hwy 97N), Kelowna BC V1Y 6G8)* 250/860-6409; FAX 250/860-7377; res: 800/726-3626. 120 rms, 3 story. S $77-$87; D $85-$89; each addl $5; kit. units $10 addl; under 12 free. Crib free. Pet accepted, some restrictions. TV; cable. Sauna. Pool; whirlpool. Restaurant open 24 hrs. Bar 11-1 am. Ck-out noon. Meeting rms. Business servs avail. Sundries. Refrigerators. Balconies. Cr cds: A, C, D, DS, ER, JCB, MC, V.

★ ★ **STAY 'N SAVE.** *(1140 Harvey Ave (Hwy 97), Kelowna BC V1Y 6E7) 250/862-8888; FAX 250/862-8884.* 101 rms, 3 story, 12 suites, 26 kits. Mid-May-Sept: S, D $89-$109; each addl $10; suites $120; kit. units $109; under 16 free; lower rates rest of yr. Crib free. TV; cable. Heated pool; whirlpool. Restaurant adj 6:30 am-10 pm. Ck-out 11 am. Coin lndry. Meeting rms. Business servs avail. Exercise equipt; bicycles, sauna. Cr cds: A, D, ER, MC, V.

Motor Hotels

★ ★ ★ **BEST WESTERN VERNON LODGE.** *(3914 32nd St, Vernon BC V1T 5P1) 30 mi N on Hwy 97. 604/545-3385; FAX 604/545-7156.* 131 rms, 3 story. S $91; D $101; each addl $10; suites $125-$160; under 15 free. TV; cable (premium). Heated pool; whirlpool. Restaurant 7 am-5 pm; dining rm 5-10 pm. Rm serv. Bar. Ck-out noon. Meeting rms. Business servs avail. Valet serv. Sundries. Downhill/x-country ski 14 mi. Private patios, balconies. Cr cds: A, D, DS, ER, MC, V.

★ ★ **RAMADA LODGE.** *(2170 Harvey (Hwy 97N), Kelowna BC V1Y 6G8) 250/860-9711; FAX 250/860-3173; res: 800/665-2518.* 135 rms, 3 story, 39 suites. Mid-May-mid-Sept: S, D $90-$99; each addl $10; suites $105-$199; under 19 free; ski, golf plans; lower rates rest of yr. Crib free. TV; cable (premium), VCR avail. Sauna. Indoor pool; whirlpool. Complimentary coffee in rms. Restaurant open 24 hrs. Rm serv. Bar 11-1 am; entertainment. Ck-out noon. Meeting rms. Business servs avail. Valet serv. Sundries. Some covered parking. Some in-rm whirlpools. Cr cds: A, C, D, DS, ER, MC, V.

★ ★ **VILLAGE GREEN HOTEL.** *(4801 27th St, Vernon BC V1T 4Z1) 27th St & 48th Ave. 604/542-3321; FAX 250/549-4252.* 138 rms, 2-6 story. S $80; D $90; each addl $10; suites $120-$210; under 13 free. Crib free. TV; cable (premium). Sauna. 2 heated pools; whirlpool, poolside serv. Restaurant 6 am-10 pm. Rm serv. Bar noon-1 am; entertainment. Ck-out noon. Meeting rms. Business servs avail. Bellhops. Valet serv. Sundries. Tennis. Golf privileges. Downhill/x-country ski 12 mi. Refrigerators. Private patios, balconies. Cr cds: A, C, D, DS, ER, JCB, MC, V.

Hotel

★ ★ ★ **COAST CAPRI.** *(1171 Harvey Ave (Hwy 97), Kelowna BC V1Y 6E8) 250/860-6060; FAX 250/762-3430; res: 800/663-1144.* 185 rms, 4-7 story. May-mid-Sept: S $115-$135; D $125-$145; each addl $10; suites $175; under 18 free; ski, golf plans; lower rates rest of yr. Crib free. TV; cable, VCR avail. Sauna. Heated pool; whirlpool, poolside serv. Coffee in rms. Restaurant 6:30 am-10 pm. Rm serv 24 hrs. Bar. Ck-out noon. Meeting rms. Business center. In-rm modem link. Drugstore. Barber, beauty shop. Balconies. Cr cds: A, C, D, ER, MC, V.

Nanaimo (E-3)

(See also Vancouver, Victoria)

Founded 1874 **Pop** 47,069 **Elev** 100 ft (30 m) **E-mail** information@tourism.nanaimo.bc.ca. **Web** tourism.nanaimo.bc.ca.

Information Tourism Nanaimo, Beban House, 2290 Bowen Rd, V9T 3K7; 250/756-0106 or 800/663-7337.

Nanaimo is located on Vancouver Island, off the west coast of British Columbia, a main entry port for ferries from Vancouver and Horseshoe Bay. Because of its location, it serves as a fine starting point to other attractions on the island, as well as being a vacation highlight in itself. The name comes from the indigenous term "Sne-ny-mos" that referred to the gathering of the tribes. In 1849 coal was discovered and was mined here for 100 years.

What to See and Do

Bastion. Built in 1853 as a Hudson's Bay Company fort. Now a museum; cannon firing ceremony (summer months at noon). Restored to original appearance. (July-Aug) Front & Bastion Sts. Along harbor basin below is

Queen Elizabeth Promenade. Named to commemorate the vessel and landing of the first settlers in the area (1854); boardwalk offers pleasant view of waterfront & tidal lagoon.

Bowen Park. Swimming pool (fee), tennis courts, fitness circuit, game fields, picnic shelters, recreation complex, lawn bowling; totem poles, rose garden, rhododendron grove, petting farm, duck ponds, fish ladder. 500 Bowen Rd. ¢¢

Cyber City. Adventure park with laser tag, bumper cars, miniature golf, virtual reality arcade, spaceball. Restaurant. (Daily) 1815 Bowen Rd. Phone 250/755-1828. **Free.**

Ferry trips. BC Ferries. Service between Nanaimo and Horseshoe Bay, north of Vancouver (1½ hrs); or Nanaimo and Tsawassen, south of Vancouver, near US border (2 hrs). For current schedule & fare information contact BC Ferry Corporation, 1112 Fort St, Victoria, V8V 4V2; 250/669-1211 (Vancouver) or 250/386-3431 (Victoria).

Nanaimo Art Gallery & Exhibition Centre. Gallery with changing exhibits of art, science and history. (Daily; closed statutory hols) On Malaspina College campus. Phone 250/755-8790. **Free.**

Nanaimo District Museum. Walk-in replica of coal mine; turn-of-the-century shops, restored miner's cottage; dioramas; Chinatown display; changing exhibits. Tours avail. (May-Aug, daily; rest of yr, Tues-Sat; closed some hols) 100 Cameron St. Phone 250/753-1821. ¢

Newcastle Island Provincial Marine Park. Boat docking (fee); camping (fee), hiking & bicycle trails, picnicking; pavilion with historical displays, concession (May-Sept). Dance and barbecue events in summer. No land vehicle access. Access by foot/passenger ferry from Maffeo Sutton Park (May-mid-Oct; fee); private boat rest of yr. **Free.**

Petroglyph Park. Established to preserve the many ancient indigenous rock carvings. 2 mi (3 km) S on Trans-Canada Hwy 1.

Annual Events

Polar Bear Swim. Prizes for all participants; free ice cream, bananas and suntan lotion. Jan 1.

Nanaimo Marine Festival. Bathtub race (3rd or 4th Sun July) across the Straits of Georgia to Vancouver; many other events. Begins 1 wk prior to race day.

Vancouver Island Exhibition. Beban Park. Early or mid-Aug.

Motels

★ **DAYS INN HARBOURVIEW.** *(809 Island Hwy S, Nanaimo BC V9R 5K1) 250/754-8171; FAX 250/754-8557.* 79 rms, 2 story, 16 kits. June-Sept: S $83; D $93; each addl $10; suites $120; kit. units $85-$115;

under 13 free; lower rates rest of yr. Crib $5. Pet accepted; $7/day. TV; cable (premium), VCR avail. Indoor pool; whirlpool. Restaurant 6 am-10 pm. Rm serv. Ck-out 11 am. Coin lndry. Meeting rms. Business servs avail. Sundries. Some refrigerators. Overlooking Nanaimo's inner harbour. Cr cds: A, D, DS, ER, JCB, MC, V.

✔★ **TALLY-HO.** (1 Terminal Ave (Trans-Canada Hwy 1), Nanaimo BC V9R 5R4) 250/753-2241; FAX 250/753-6522; res: 800/663-7322. 101 rms, 3 story. S, D $80-$110; each addl $10; suites $150; under 14 free; wkend rates. Crib free. TV; cable, VCR avail. Heated pool (seasonal). Restaurant 6:30 am-9 pm. Bar 11:30-1:30 am. Ck-out noon. Meeting rms. Business servs avail. Valet serv. Sundries. Cr cds: A, C, D, ER, MC, V.

Hotel

★★ **COAST BASTION INN.** (11 Bastion St, Nanaimo BC V9R 2Z9) 250/753-6601; FAX 250/753-4155; res: 800/663-1144. 179 rms, 14 story. Mid-May-mid-Sept: S, D $120-$130; each addl $10; suites $198-$208; under 18 free; package plans; lower rates rest of yr. Crib free. Pet accepted. TV; cable (premium). Restaurant 6:30 am-9 pm. Bar 11:30-1 am; entertainment exc Sun. Ck-out 1 pm. Meeting rms. Business servs avail. Gift shop. Barber, beauty shop. Exercise equipt; weight machine, bicycles, sauna. Whirlpool. Many minibars. Balconies. Ocean 1 blk; swimming. Cr cds: A, D, MC, V.

Resort

★★ **SCHOONER COVE.** (3521 Dolphin Dr, Nanoose Bay BC V0R 2R0) 15 mi (20 km) from BC Ferry terminal. 250/468-7691; FAX 250/468-5744; res: 800/663-7060 (CAN). 31 units. May-Sept: S, D $93-$109; each addl $10; under 12 free; lower rates rest of yr. TV; cable, VCR avail (movies). Pool; whirlpool. Dining rm 6 am-10 pm. Rm serv. Box lunches. Bar 11-1 am. Ck-out noon. Grocery. Coin lndry. Meeting rms. Business servs avail. Tennis. 18-hole golf privileges opp, greens fee $37, pro, driving range. Boats (rentals). 405-slip marina. Balconies. Picnic tables. Extensive landscaping; outstanding views. Cr cds: A, D, MC, V.

Cottage Colony

★★ **YELLOW POINT LODGE.** (RR 3, 3700 Yellow Point Rd, Ladysmith BC V0R 2E0) 15 mi S via Trans-Canada Hwy 1, follow signs. 250/245-7422. 9 rms in main bldg, 4 story, 44 cottages, 19 with bath. No A/C. No elvtr. No rm phones. AP, May-Sept: S, cottages (1 or 2-bedrm) $58-$109; D $105-$172; each addl $58; suites $109-$172; higher rates Christmas hols; lower rates rest of yr. Children over 16 yrs only. Saltwater pool; whirlpool. Dining rm, 3 sittings: 8:30-9:30 am, 12:30 pm, 6:30 pm. Serv bar 11 am-11 pm. Ck-out noon, ck-in 3 pm. Coin lndry 8 mi. Meeting rms. Grocery 4 mi. Package store. Airport, RR station, bus depot transportation. Tennis. Sauna. Beach; ocean swimming. Boats. Bicycles. Lawn games. Rec rm. Some refrigerators. Balconies. Picnic tables. Surrounded by 180 acres of preserved private forest; on Straits of Georgia. Cr cds: MC, V.

Penticton (E-4)

(See also Kelowna)

Pop 23,181 **Elev** 1,150 ft (351 m) **Area code** 250 **E-mail** jpearmai@vip.net **Web** www.penticton.org

Information Visitor Info Centre, 888 Westminster Ave W, V2A 8S2; 250/493-4055 or 800/663-5052.

Penticton is situated between the beautiful Okanagan and Skaha lakes on an alluvial plain. Beyond the lakes is fertile orchard land and rolling hills. Penticton is famous for its peaches and other fruits. Because of its prime location, Penticton is sometimes called the land of peaches and beaches. The growing of grapes and the manufacturing of wine has become very important in the Okanagan Valley, producing some very fine wines.

What to See and Do

Agriculture Canada Research Station. Beautiful display of ornamental gardens; canyon view; picnicking. Guided tours (July-Aug). 6 mi (10 km) N on Hwy 97. Phone 250/494-7711. ¢

Dominion Radio Astrophysical Observatory. Guided tours (July-Aug, Sun). Visitor Centre (daily). 9 mi (15 km) SW via Hwy 97, 5 1/2 mi (9 km) S on White Lake Rd. Phone 250/493-2277. **Free.**

Okanagan Game Farm. Excellent selection of wild animals in natural setting. More than 900 animals on 600 acres (243 hectares). Gift, coffee shop; picnicking. (Daily) 5 mi (8 km) S on Hwy 97. Phone 250/497-5405. ¢¢¢

Penticton Museum. Collection of Salish artifacts; taxidermy, ghost town and pioneer exhibits. Changing exhibits. At 1099 Lakeshore Dr W are two historic 1914 steamships: SS *Sicamous*, a 200-ft sternwheeler, and SS *Naramata*, a 90-ft steam tug (donation). (Daily exc Sun; closed statutory hols) 785 Main St. Phone 250/492-6025. **Free.**

Wonderful Water World. Waterpark has waterslides, miniature golf, slot car racing on 110-ft track. Concessions, picnic area. Campground on site. (Late May-Labour Day, daily) 225 Yorkton Ave. Phone 250/493-8121. ¢¢¢¢

Annual Events

Midwinter Breakout. Festival for the entire family. 2nd & 3rd wk Feb.

British Columbia Square Dance Jamboree. In King's Park. Street dancing; dancing under the stars on perhaps North America's largest outdoor board floor. Early Aug.

Peach Festival. Parade, entertainment, aquatic events. Mid-Aug.

Ironman Canada Championship Triathlon. Qualifier for Hawaiian Ironman. Late Aug.

Okanagan Wine Festival. Wine tasting, grape stomping, seminars & dinners (also see KELOWNA). Late Sept-mid-Oct.

Motels

✔★★ **BEL-AIR.** (2670 Skaha Lake Rd, Penticton BC V2A 6G1) 250/492-6111; FAX 250/492-8035; res: 800/766-5770. 42 rms, 2 story, 16 kits. Mid-June-mid-Sept: S $64; D $68; each addl $5; kit. units $84-$98; lower rates rest of yr. Crib $5. TV; cable (premium). Sauna. Heated pool; whirlpool. Restaurant nearby. Ck-out 11 am. Coin lndry. Picnic tables, grills. Cr cds: A, MC, V.

★★★ **BEST WESTERN INN.** (3180 Skaha Lake Rd (Hwy 97A), Penticton BC V2A 6G4) 250/493-0311; FAX 250/493-5556. 67 rms, 2 story, 24 kits. Mid-June-mid-Sept: S $108-$150; D $120-$150; each addl $10; kit. units $135-$145; suites $195-$275; lower rates rest of yr. Crib $10. TV; cable (premium). 2 pools, 1 indoor; whirlpool. Playground. Restaurant 7 am-10 pm. Ck-out 11 am. Coin lndry. Business servs avail. In-rm modem link. Valet serv. Refrigerators. Picnic tables, grills. Cr cds: A, C, D, DS, ER, JCB, MC, V.

★ ★ **RAMADA COURTYARD INN.** *(1050 Eckhardt Ave W, Penticton BC V2A 2C3) 250/492-8926; FAX 250/492-2778.* 50 rms. Mid-May-mid-Sept: S, D $95; each addl $10; under 12 free; lower rates rest of yr. Pet accepted, some restrictions. TV; cable (premium). Heated pool. Restaurant nearby open 24 hrs. Bar. Ck-out 11 am. Coin lndry. Meeting rms. Business servs avail. Valet serv. Lawn games. Some refrigerators, fireplaces. Private patios. Picnic tables, grill. Cr cds: A, D, DS, ER, MC, V.

★ ★ **SANDMAN HOTEL.** *(939 Burnaby Ave W, Penticton BC V2A 1G7) off Hwy 97. 250/493-7151; FAX 604/493-3767.* 141 rms, 3 story. Mid-May-Sept: S $71; D $81; each addl $5; under 16 free; lower rates rest of yr. Crib free. TV; cable (premium). Sauna. Indoor pool; whirlpool. Restaurant open 24 hrs. Bar noon-1 am. Ck-out noon. Meeting rms. Business servs avail. Valet serv. Sundries. Cr cds: A, C, D, DS, ER, JCB, MC, V.

✔ ★ ★ **SPANISH VILLA.** *(890 Lakeshore Dr, Penticton BC V2A 1C1) 250/492-2922; FAX 604/492-2922; res: 800/552-9199.* 60 rms, 1-2 story, 45 kits. Mid-June-Sept: S $58-$130; D $62-$130; each addl $20; suites, kit. units $80-$150; lower rates rest of yr. Crib $5. TV; cable. Indoor pool. Playground. Ck-out 11 am. Coin lndry. Meeting rms. Business servs avail. In-rm modem link. Valet serv. Free airport transportation. Refrigerators. Private patios. Opp beach. Cr cds: A, D, DS, ER, MC, V.

★ ★ **TRAVELODGE.** *(950 Westminster Ave (Hwy 97A), Penticton BC V2A 1L2) 250/492-0225; FAX 250/493-8340.* 34 rms, 3 story. Mid-May-mid-Sept: S, D $85-$105; each addl $8; kit. units $8 addl; under 17 free; lower rates rest of yr. TV; cable (premium). Sauna. 2 pools, heated; whirlpool. Restaurant 7 am-1:30 pm. Ck-out noon. Meeting rms. Refrigerators. Private patios, balconies. Picnic tables. Cr cds: A, C, D, ER, MC, V.

Hotel

★ ★ ★ **CLARION LAKESIDE RESORT.** *(21 Lakeshore Dr W, Penticton BC V2A 7M5) 250/493-8221; FAX 250/493-0607; res: 800/663-1144.* 204 rms, 6 story. July-Aug: S, D $175-$195; each addl $15; under 16 free; golf plans; lower rates rest of yr. Crib free. Pet accepted, some restrictions. TV; cable (premium), VCR avail. Indoor pool; whirlpool. Supervised child's activities (late May-Labor Day); ages 3-17. Restaurant 7 am-11 pm. Bar noon-2 am; seasonal entertainment. Meeting rms. Business servs avail. In-rm modem link. Gift shop. Beauty shop. Tennis. Golf privileges. Downhill/x-country ski 20 mi. Exercise rm; instructor, weights, bicycles, sauna. Game rm. Balconies. On Okanagan Lake; swimming, boat rides. Cr cds: A, D, ER, MC, V.

Restaurant

★ ★ **EDWARDS.** *(2007 Main St, Penticton BC) 250/492-0007.* Hrs: 6:30 am-10 pm; Sun brunch 11 am-2 pm. Wine, beer. Semi-a la carte: bkfst $4.95-$9.45, lunch, dinner $5-$14. Sun brunch $12.99. Child's meals. Specializes in smörgasbord. Salad bar. Early California decor; stained glass. Cr cds: MC, V.

Revelstoke (D-5)

Pop 5,544 **Elev** 1,499 ft (457 m) **Area code** 250 **E-mail** cocrev@mindlink.bc.ca **Web** www.revelstokecc.bc.ca/mountns

Information Chamber of Commerce, 204 Campbell Ave, PO Box 490, V0E 2S0, phone 250/837-5345; or visit the Travel Info Centre, Trans-Canada Hwy 1 & BC 23N, phone 250/837-3522.

Located in the towering Monashee and Selkirk ranges of the Columbia Mountains, between the scenic Rogers and Eagle passes, Revelstoke is the gateway to Mt Revelstoke National Park, with Glacier National Park just to the east. Visitors may enjoy many activities all year. Especially popular is the skiing; with an annual average of 40 feet (13 m) of snow, Revelstoke offers multiple opportunities for downhill, cross-country, cat helicopter, ski touring adventures and snowmobiling. Tennis, fishing, hiking, golfcaving, mountaineering and swimming are also available throughout this exciting alpine city.

What to See and Do

Beardale Castle Miniatureland. Indoor attraction constructed in a European-style village setting. Handcrafted authentic miniature exhibits include prairie town, Swiss mountain village and medieval German village, each with a model railway running through it. Also animated toyland exhibits. (May-Sept, daily) 26 mi (42 km) W via Trans-Canada Hwy 1 at Craigellachie. Phone 250/836-2268. ¢¢

Provincial Building & Court House (1912). Provincial building contains the original oak staircase connecting the three floors and basement; courtroom same as when built; marble walls in foyer; pillars; lighted dome. Tour (Mon-Fri, by appt; closed hols). 1123 W 2nd St. Phone 250/837-7636. **Free.**

Revelstoke Dam Visitor Centre. Displays, films and photographs describe construction and operation of the hydroelectric powerhouse and relate the history of Revelstoke Dam. Self-guided tours. (Apr-Oct, daily) 3 mi (5 km) N via Hwy 23. Phone 250/837-6515. **Free.**

Three Valley Gap. Historic ghost town (guided tours; fee); lake. Lodging, restaurant. Cowboy show (nightly; fee). (Mid-Apr-mid-Oct, daily) 12 mi (19 km) W on Trans Canada Hwy 1. Phone 250/837-2109. ¢¢¢

Annual Event

Revelstoke Sno Fest. Outhouse races, parade, casino, dances, entertainment, cross-country skiing, downhill races, sno pitch, ice sculpture, snow golf tournaments. Phone 250/837-9351. Jan.

Motels

★ ★ ★ **BEST WESTERN WAYSIDE INN.** *(1901 Laforme Blvd (Trans-Canada Hwy 1), Revelstoke BC V0E 2S0) 250/837-6161; FAX 250/837-5460.* 88 rms, 2 story, 25 kits. S $89-$129; D $99-$139; each addl $6-$8; suites $190; under 12 free. Crib free. TV; cable (premium). Saunas. Indoor pool; whirlpool. Coffee in rms. Restaurant 6:30 am-9 pm. Bar. Ck-out noon. Meeting rms. Business servs avail. Downhill/x-country ski 5 mi. Some refrigerators. Heli-skiing offered Jan-mid-Apr. Cr cds: A, C, D, DS, ER, JCB, MC, V.

✔ ★ **CANYON MOTOR INN.** *(Box 740, Revelstoke BC V0E 2S0) Trans-Canada Hwy 1 & Columbia River Bridge. 250/837-5221.* 40 rms, 1-2 story, 12 kits. May-Oct: S $44-$76; D $50-$100; each addl $7; kit. units $7 addl; lower rates rest of yr. Crib free. Pet accepted. TV; cable. Restaurant 6 am-10 pm. Rm serv. Ck-out noon. Coin lndry. Meeting rms. Sundries. Downhill/x-country ski 5 mi. Sauna. Whirlpool. Refrigerators. Private patios, balconies. Picnic tables. On riverbank. RV park on property. Cr cds: A, D, DS, ER, MC, V.

★ **SANDMAN INN.** (Box 2329, Revelstoke BC V0E 2S0) 1 mi NW on Trans-Canada Hwy 1, Fraser Dr. 250/837-5271; FAX 604/837-2032; res: 800/663-6900. 83 rms, 2 story, 10 kits. S $94; D $94-$104; each addl $5; kit. units $10 addl; under 18 free. Crib free. TV; cable (premium). Sauna. Heated pool; whirlpool. Restaurant open 24 hrs. Bar 4 pm-1 am. Ck-out 11 am. Meeting rms. Business servs avail. Valet serv. Downhill/x-country ski 5 mi. Refrigerators. Balconies. Cr cds: A, C, D, DS, ER, JCB, MC, V.

🐾 ≋ ⇲ ⚓ SC

★ ★ ★ **THREE VALLEY GAP MOTOR INN.** (Box 860, Revelstoke BC V0E 2S0) 12 mi W on Trans-Canada Hwy 1. 250/837-2109; FAX 250/837-5220. 165 rms, 2-6 story. No A/C. Mid-Apr-mid-Oct: S $69-$79; D $73-$85; each addl $4; suites $75-$150; family rates. Closed rest of yr. Crib free. TV. Heated pool; whirlpool. Restaurants 7 am-9 pm. Ck-out 11 am. Meeting rms. Sundries. Rec rm. Private patios, balconies. On lake. Cr cds: A, D, DS, ER, MC, V.

≋ ⇲ ⚓

Restaurant

★ **FRONTIER.** (1 mi W on Trans-Canada Hwy 1 & Hwy 23N, Revelstoke BC) 250/837-5119. Hrs: 5 am-9 pm. Continental, Canadian menu. Serv bar. Semi-a la carte: bkfst $1.75-$7.25, lunch $2.75-$7.25, dinner $4.25-$16.95. Child's meals. Specializes in steak, chicken. Salad bar (dinner). Rustic; view of mountains. Cr cds: DS, ER, MC, V.

Vancouver (E-3)

(See also Nanaimo, Victoria; also see Bellingham, WA)

Settled 1886 **Pop** 456,000 (est) **Elev** 38 ft (12 m) **Area code** 604 **Web** www.travel.bc.ca/vancouver

Information Tourism Vancouver InfoCentre, 200 Burrard St, V6C 3L6; 604/683-2000.

Surrounded by the blue waters of the Strait of Georgia and backed by the mile-high peaks of the Coast Range, Vancouver enjoys a natural setting surpassed by few other cities on this continent. The waters that wash the city's shores protect it from heat and cold, making it a pleasant place to visit all year.

Captain George Vancouver, searching these waters for the Northwest Passage, sailed into Burrard Inlet and landed here in 1792. Fur traders, gold prospectors and other settlers soon followed. In 1886 Vancouver was incorporated as a city, only to be destroyed by fire several months later. The city was rebuilt by the end of that same year. In the next four years rail transportation from the east, along with the traffic of sailing vessels of the Canadian Pacific fleet, assured the future of its growth. Today Vancouver is one of Canada's largest cities—a major seaport, cultural center, tourist spot and gateway to the Orient.

Vancouver's population is primarily English, but its large number of ethnic groups including Germans, French, Scandinavians, Dutch, Chinese and Japanese give the city an international flavor. Tourism, logging, mineral extraction equipment, marine supplies, chemical and petroleum products and machine tools are among the city's major industries.

Vancouver is on the Canadian mainland, not on Vancouver Island as some people think. The downtown area, which includes many of the points of interest we list, is a "peninsula on a peninsula." It juts out from the rest of Vancouver into Burrard Inlet, making it an especially attractive spot with beaches and marinas within easy walking distance of the city's busy heart. To the north, across Burrard Inlet is North Vancouver; to the south is the mouth of the Fraser River and the island municipality of Richmond; to the east is Burnaby and beyond that, the Canadian mainland.

For Border Crossing Regulations see MAKING THE MOST OF YOUR TRIP.

What to See and Do

Burnaby Art Gallery. Monthly exhibitions of local, national and international artists. Collection of contemporary Canadian works on paper. Housed in Ceperley Mansion, overlooking Deer Lake and the surrounding gardens. (Daily exc Mon) 6344 Deer Lake Ave in Burnaby. Phone 604/291-9441. ¢

Burnaby Village Museum. Living museum of the period before 1925, with costumed attendants; more than 30 full-scale buildings with displays & demonstrations. (Early Apr-late Dec, days vary) 6501 Deer Lake Ave in Burnaby, 9 mi (15 km) E. Phone 604/293-6501 (recording). ¢¢¢

Capilano Suspension Bridge & Park. Park flanks 1 mi (1.6 km) of the canyon through which the Capilano River flows. A 450-ft (137-m) gently swaying footbridge spans the canyon at a height of 230 ft (70 m). Park contains gardens, totem poles and large Trading Post. Guided tours; native wood carver on site; Story Centre; restaurants. (Daily; closed Dec 25) N on Capilano Rd in N Vancouver. Phone 604/985-7474. ¢¢¢

Chinatown. This downtown area is the nucleus of the third-largest Chinese community in North America (only San Francisco's and New York's are larger.) At the heart lies the Chinese Market where 100-yr-old duck eggs may be purchased; herbalists promise cures with roots and powdered bones. The Dr. Sun Yat-Sen Classical Chinese Garden provides a beautiful centerpiece. Chinese shops display a variety of items ranging from cricket cages to cloisonné vases. Offices of three Chinese newspapers, and one of the world's narrowest buildings, are located within the community's borders. Resplendent Oriental atmosphere offers fine examples of Chinese architecture, restaurants and nightclubs. East Pender St between Gore & Carrall Sts.

Exhibition Park. Approx 165 acres (70 hectares). Concert, convention, entertainment facilities. Thoroughbred racing (late spring-early fall) and Playland Amusement Park (Apr-June, wkends; July-Oct, daily; also evenings). Free tours of Challenger Relief Map. (See ANNUAL EVENTS) Hastings St between Renfrew & Cassiar Sts. Phone 604/253-2311.

Fort Langley National Historic Site. Restoration of Hudson's Bay Company post built in 1840 on the Fraser River; reconstructed palisade, bastion and four buildings plus one original building. Demonstrations of fur trade activities and period crafts of 1858. (Mar-Oct, daily; Nov-Feb, hrs vary; closed Jan 1, Dec 25, 26) 35 mi (48 km) E off Trans-Canada Hwy 1 or BC 7. Phone 604/888-4424 (recording). ¢¢

★ **Gastown.** The original heart of Vancouver, named for "Gassy Jack" Deighton, who opened a saloon here in 1867. Restored late 19th- and early 20th-century buildings now house antique shops, boutiques, art galleries, coffeehouses, restaurants and nightclubs. Historic landmarks, cobblestone streets and unique steam clock. Area bounded by Alexander, Columbia, Water and Cordova Sts. Adj is

Harbour Centre-The Lookout. Glass elevators to 360° viewing deck 553 ft (167 m) above street level; multimedia presentation, historical displays, tour guides. Revolving restaurant. (Daily; closed Dec 25) 555 W Hastings St. Phone 604/689-0421. Deck ¢¢¢

Gordon Southam Observatory. (Fri-Sun & hols, weather permitting) Phone 604/738-7827. **Free.**

Granville Island. Originally dredged for industrial purposes in 1913 from the False Creek Tidal Flats, now restored to retain flavor of boomtown industry. Public Market area houses many specialty shops. Electronic irrigation has helped Norway and red maples, which are cultivated here to adapt to the saline soil. Parks, supervised playground, craft studios, an art college, tennis, theaters. Harbor tours. (Daily; closed Mon in winter) 37-acre (15-hectare) area in heart of city, beneath S end of Granville Bridge. Phone 604/666-5784.

Industrial tours. The Tourism Vancouver Travel InfoCentre has information on available tours.

Irving House Historic Centre (1864). 302 Royal Ave, in New Westminster, 12 mi (19 km) S via Hwy 1A. Fourteen rms of period furniture 1864-1890. Adj is **New Westminster Museum**, on back of property, which has displays on local history, household goods, May Day memorabilia. (May-mid-Sept, daily exc Mon; rest of yr, Sat & Sun; closed Jan 1, Dec 25, 26) Phone 604/527-4640. **Donation.**

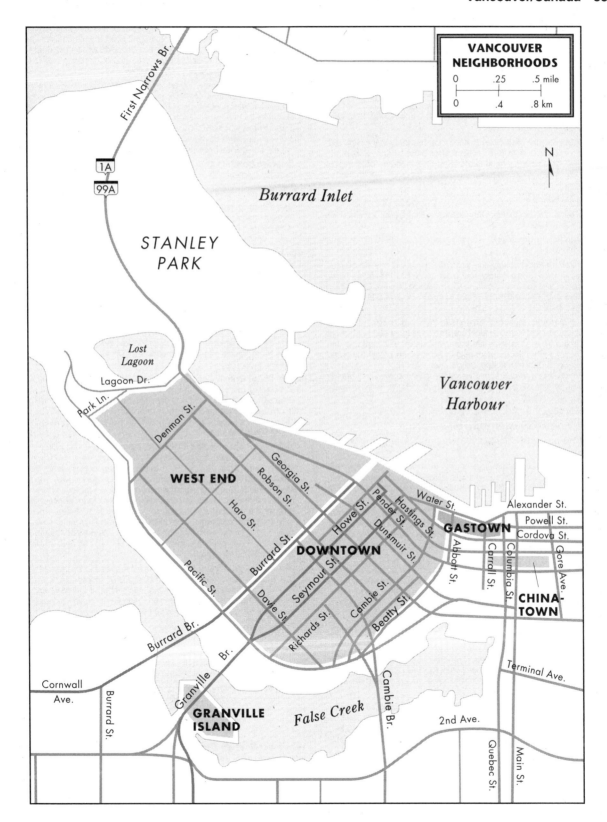

VANCOUVER
NEIGHBORHOODS

| 0 | .25 | .5 mile |
| 0 | .4 | .8 km |

First Narrows Br.

1A
99A

Burrard Inlet

STANLEY
PARK

*Lost
Lagoon*

Lagoon Dr.

Park Ln.

*Vancouver
Harbour*

Denman St.

Georgia St.

Robson St.

WEST END

Haro St.

Burrard St.

Water St.

Alexander St.

Howe St.

Pender St.

Hastings St.

Powell St.

GASTOWN

Cordova St.

Dunsmuir St.

DOWNTOWN

Abbott St.

Carrall St.

Columbia St.

Gore Ave.

Pacific St.

Davie St.

Seymour St.

Richards St.

Cambie St.

Beatty St.

CHINA-
TOWN

Burrard Br.

Granville Br.

Cornwall
Ave.

Burrard St.

Terminal Ave.

Cambie Br.

GRANVILLE
ISLAND

False Creek

2nd Ave.

Quebec St.

Main St.

N

Maritime Museum. Changing maritime exhibits highlighting exploration, marine industries, model ships and a harbor. Restored Arctic Schooner *St Roch,* first ship to navigate the Northwest Passage both ways; open to the public. (May-Sept, daily; rest of yr, daily exc Mon; closed Dec 25) Combined rate with Vancouver Museum. Foot of Cypress St. Phone 604/257-8300 (recording). ¢¢

Old Hastings Mill (ca 1865). One of few buildings remaining after fire of 1886; now houses indigenous artifacts, memorabilia of Vancouver's first settlers. (June-mid-Sept, daily; rest of yr, Sat & Sun afternoons) 1575 Alma Rd. Phone 604/734-1212. **Free.**

Pacific Space Centre. Visitors experience a journey through the night sky, backward or forward in time, or a search for other worlds. Shows are dramatic, informative, easy to understand. Shows (summer, daily; rest of yr, daily exc Mon). 1100 Chestnut St. Phone 738-7827 (recording) or 604/738-4431. ¢¢¢

Professional sports.

NBA (Vancouver Grizzlies). General Motors Place, 800 Griffiths Way. Phone 604/899-4601.

NHL (Vancouver Canucks). General Motors Place, 800 Griffiths Way. Phone 604/899-4600.

Queen Elizabeth Park. Observation point affords view of city, harbor and mountains; Bloedel Conservatory has more than 100 free-flying birds; tropical, desert and seasonal displays. (Daily; closed Dec 25) Off Cambie St & W 33rd Ave. Phone 604/257-8584 (conservatory) or 604/257-8570 (recording). ¢¢

***Samson V* Maritime Museum.** Last steam-powered paddlewheeler to operate on the Fraser River now functions as a floating museum. Displays focus on the various paddlewheelers and paddlewheeler captains that have worked the river, and on river-related activities such as fishing and lumbering. (Sat & Sun afternoons; July & Aug, Wed-Sun; closed Jan 1, Dec 25, 26) Moored on the Fraser River at the Westminster Quay Market in New Westminster, 12 mi (19 km) S via Hwy 1A. Phone 604/527-4640. **Donation.**

Sightseeing trips.

Grouse Mountain tramway. Phone 604/984-0661.

Gray Line bus tours. Contact 399 W 6th St, Suite 200, V54 1L1; 604/879-3363.

Harbour Cruises Ltd. Boat/train excursion (6¹/2 hrs); also sunset dinner cruises; harbor tours, private charters. (May-Sept) Departures from northern foot of Denman St. For schedule and fees, phone 604/688-7246.

SeaBus Harbour Ride. Makes 15-min crossing on twin-hulled catamaran design vessels every 15 min (30 min evenings and Sun). Part of regional public transit system. Operates between Waterfront Station & Lonsdale Quay, across Burrard Inlet. Transit information 604/521-0400. ¢-¢¢

Royal Hudson Excursion. 6-hr round-trip steam train ride 80 mi (129 km) to Squamish; 2-hr stopover with optional tours. (June-Sept, Wed-Sun) Also train/boat combinations. Res requested; payment required 48 hrs in advance with res. 1311 W 1st St, N Vancouver. Phone 604/631-3500. ¢¢¢¢

British Columbia Ferry Corp. Trips to Nanaimo (2 hrs) or to Swartz Bay, near Victoria (1¹/2 hrs); both destinations are on Vancouver Island. Terminals at Horseshoe Bay, N of Vancouver via Trans-Canada Hwy 1, and Tsawwassen, near US border, S of Vancouver via Hwy 99, 17. For current schedule & fare information contact BC Ferry Corporation, 1112 Fort St, Victoria V8V 4V2; 604/669-1211 (Vancouver) or 250/386-3431 (Victoria).

Simon Fraser University (1965). (20,000 students) Located on Burnaby Mt; architecturally outstanding buildings. Original campus was completed in only 18 months. Hrly guided tours (July-Aug, daily; free). 10 mi (16 km) E off BC 7A (Hastings St) in Burnaby. Phone 604/291-3210 or 604/291-3111.

Skiing.

Grouse Mountain. All-yr recreational facility. Aerial tramway, 4 double chairlifts, 2 T-bars, 3 rope tows; 13 runs; patrol, school, rentals; lounge, restaurants. (Dec-mid-Apr, daily) Night skiing. Skyride (all yr; fee). Playground, hiking trails. "Our Spirit Soars" multimedia presentation; logging shows; helicopter tours, chairlift rides, horse-drawn wagon rides. 8 mi (13 km) N at 6400 Nancy Greene Way (top of Capilano Rd) in North Vancouver. Phone 604/984-0661. ¢¢¢¢¢

Seymour Ski Country. Three double chairlifts, rope tow; night skiing; patrol, school, rentals; cafeteria. (Mid-Nov-Apr, daily) Cross-country and snowshoe trails (Dec-Mar, daily). Chairlift also operates July-Aug (daily). 9 mi (15 km) NE off Mt Seymour Pkwy, in Mount Seymour Provincial Park. Phone 604/986-2261. Provincial park is a large semi-wilderness with scenic roadside viewpoints overlooking Vancouver; picnic areas; hiking, self-guided interpretive trails. Park (all yr, daily). Ski area ¢¢¢¢

Cypress Bowl Ski Area. Four double chairlifts, rope tow; patrol, school, rentals; cafeteria. Cross-country trails; hiking trails. Snowshoe/winter hiking trail. (Dec-mid-Apr, daily) Phone 926-6007 (recording) or 604/926-5612. Provincial park offers spectacular views of Vancouver and the surrounding area and an accessible old-growth forest; scenic lookouts; picnic areas; hiking, self-guided interpretive trails. Park (all yr, daily). 7¹/2 mi (12 km) NW via BC 99, in Cypress Provincial Park. Ski area ¢¢¢¢

Stanley Park. Approx 1,000 acres (405 hectares) of beautifully landscaped gardens, lakes, totem poles, trails; swimming pool and sand beaches, golf, tennis. Children's farmyard (fee), miniature train (daily; fee). Horse-drawn tours avail from AAA Horse & Carriage Ltd (May-mid-Oct; phone 604/681-5115). NW of downtown. Phone 604/257-8400. Also here is

Vancouver Aquarium. One of the largest in North America; more than 8,000 marine and freshwater animals from around the world in five major viewing areas; killer whales, Beluga whales; Amazon Rain Forest gallery; North Pacific and Tropical galleries. (Daily) Phone 604/268-9900. ¢¢¢¢

University of British Columbia (1915). (28,000 students) The 990-acre (401-hectare) campus features museums, galleries (some fees), many spectacular gardens; almost 400 buildings complement the natural grandeur of the area. Free guided campus tours (May-Aug). Beautifully situated on scenic Point Grey, 8 mi (13 km) SW via Burrard St, 4th Ave. Phone 604/822-5355. Includes

Museum of Anthropology. World-renowned collection of artifacts from many cultures, with emphasis on art of first peoples of the Northwest Coast. **Great Hall** displays 30-ft totem poles and huge feast dishes; **Masterpiece Gallery** contains intricate works in gold, silver, wood and stone; unique European ceramics collection; outdoor exhibit area has replicas of traditional Haida buildings. "Visible storage" concept allows 90% of the museum's collection to be viewed at all times. Changing exhibits; public programs. Guided tours (free exc if by appt). (July-Aug, daily; rest of yr, daily exc Mon; closed Dec 25, 26) Free admission Tues in winter, Tues evenings in summer. 6393 NW Marine Dr. Phone 604/822-3825 (recording). ¢¢¢

UBC Botanical Garden. Seven separate areas include Asian, Physick, B.C. Native, Alpine and Food gardens. (Daily; closed Jan 1, Dec 25) 6804 SW Marine Dr. Phone 604/822-9666. **Nitobe Garden,** authentic Japanese tea garden located behind Asian Centre (mid-Mar-early Oct, daily; rest of yr, Mon-Fri). Phone 604/822-6038. ¢¢

Frederic Wood Theatre. Summer stock and winter main stage productions. For tickets and information, phone 604/822-2678.

VanDusen Botanical Garden. Approx 55 acres (22 hectares) of flowers and exotic plants. Seasonal displays, mountain views, restaurant. (Daily; closed Dec 25) 5251 Oak St. Phone 604/878-9274. ¢¢

Vancouver Art Gallery. Changing exhibits of contemporary and historical art, featuring masterworks of Emily Carr. Guided tours (by appt). Fine arts library. Restaurant, gift shop. (June-Sept, daily; rest of yr, daily exc Tues; closed Jan 1, Dec 25) 750 Hornby St. Phone 604/662-4719 (recording) or 604/682-4668. ¢¢

Vancouver Museum. One of Canada's largest civic museums. Decorative arts, Vancouver history, Northwest Coast indigenous culture and touring exhibits. (May-Sept, daily; rest of yr, daily exc Mon; closed Dec 25) Combined rate with Maritime Museum. 1100 Chestnut St, 1¹/2 mi (2¹/2 km) SW via Burrard, Cypress Sts. Phone 604/736-4431. ¢¢

Annual Events

Hyack Festival. 12 mi (19 km) S via Hwy 1A in New Westminster. Commemorates birthday of Queen Victoria, held yearly since 1871; 21-gun salute; band concerts, parade, carnival, sports events. Phone 604/522-6894. 10 days mid-May.

International Bathtub Race. 34-mi (55-km) race from Nanaimo to Vancouver. Phone 800/663-7337. 3rd or 4th Sun July.

Pacific National Exhibition Annual Fair. Exhibition Park. Second-largest fair in Canada. Hundreds of free exhibits, major theme event, concerts, thrill shows, world championship timber show; petting zoo, thoroughbred horse racing, commercial exhibits, roller coaster, agricultural shows, horse shows, livestock competitions, horticultural exhibits. Phone 604/253-2311. Usually mid-Aug-early Sept.

Christmas events. Christmas Carol Ship, and lighted ship parade; New Year's Day Polar Bear swim.

Seasonal Events

A symphony orchestra, opera company and many theater groups present productions around town, especially at the Queen Elizabeth Theatre & Playhouse and Orpheum Theatre. Consult local paper for details.

Special Event

Sumo Basho. Pacific Coliseum. Championship event of Japan's most popular sporting event, to be held in Canada for the first time. Approx 50 rikishi (Sumo athletes) will compete. Phone 604/682-2222. June 6-7.

Additional Visitor Information

There are many more interesting things to see and do in Vancouver and the suburbs of Burnaby and New Westminster to the east, Richmond to the south, North Vancouver and West Vancouver. The Tourism Vancouver InfoCentre has pamphlets, maps, ferry schedules and additional information at Plaza Level, Waterfront Centre, 200 Burrard St, V6C 3L6; 604/683-2000.

City Neighborhoods

Many of the restaurants, unrated dining establishments and some lodgings listed under Vancouver include neighborhoods as well as exact street addresses. Geographic descriptions of these areas are given, followed by a table of restaurants arranged by neighborhood.

Chinatown: North of Pender St, east of Carrall St, south of Hastings St and west of Gore St.

Downtown: North of Beatty St, east of Pacific Blvd, south of Burrard St and west of Port Roadway. **South of Downtown:** South of Beatty St. **East of Downtown:** East of Port Roadway. **West of Downtown:** West of Burrard St.

Gastown: North of Cordova St, east of Cambie St, south of Water St and west of Columbia St.

Granville Island: South of Downtown; bordered by Johnston St, Cartwright St and Duranleau St.

West End: North of Burrard St, east of Pacific St, south of Park Lane and west of Port Roadway.

VANCOUVER RESTAURANTS BY NEIGHBORHOOD AREAS
(For full description, see alphabetical listings under Restaurants)

CHINATOWN
Phnom Penh. 244 E Georgia St

DOWNTOWN
Bacchus (Wedgewood Hotel). 845 Hornby St
Chartwell (Four Seasons Hotel). 791 W Georgia St
Five Sails (Pan Pacific Vancouver Hotel). 300-999 Canada Place
Hy's Encore. 637 Hornby St

A Kettle Of Fish. 900 Pacific
Le Crocodile. Smythe & Burrard Sts
Top Of Vancouver. 555 W Hastings
Umberto's. 1380 Hornby St
William Tell (Georgian Court Hotel). 773 Beatty St

SOUTH OF DOWNTOWN
Bishop's. 2183 W 4th Ave
Greens And Gourmet. 2681 W Broadway

EAST OF DOWNTOWN
Cannery. 2205 Commissioner St
Pink Pearl. 1132 E Hastings St

WEST OF DOWNTOWN
Teahouse. 7501 Stanley Park Dr
Tojo's. 777 W Broadway #202

GASTOWN
Umberto Al Porto. 321 Water St

GRANVILLE ISLAND
Star Anise. 1485 W 12th St

WEST END
Cloud 9 (Landmark Hotel). 1400 Robson St
Delilah's. 1739 Comox St
Piccolo Mondo. 850 Thurlow St
True Confections. 866 Denman St

Note: When a listing is located in a town that does not have its own city heading, it will appear under the city nearest to its location. In these cases, the address and town appear in parenthesis immediately following the name of the establishment.

Motels

★ ★ **BEST WESTERN EXHIBITION PARK.** *(3475 E Hastings St, Vancouver BC V5K 2A5)* east of downtown. 604/294-4751; FAX 604/294-1269. 58 rms, 3 story, 22 suites. June-Sept: S $125-$150; D $140-$175; each addl $10; suites $180-$210; under 12 free; higher rates some special events; lower rates rest of yr. Crib free. TV, VCR avail (movies). Continental bkfst. Complimentary coffee. Restaurant adj 6:30 am-11 pm. Ck-out noon. Business servs avail. In-rm modem link. Coin lndry. Sundries. Free parking. Sauna. Whirlpool. Refrigerators. Cr cds: A, D, DS, ER, MC, V.

D ⤢ 🐾 SC

★ ★ **BEST WESTERN KINGS INN.** *(5411 Kingsway, Burnaby BC V5H 2G1)* 2 mi S on Kingsway (Hwy 1A/99A). 604/438-1383; FAX 604/438-2954. 141 rms, 2 story. May-Sept: S $110; D $120; each addl $10; suites, kit. units $130-$135; under 14 free; lower rates rest of yr. Crib free. TV; cable, VCR avail. Pool. Complimentary coffee in rms. Restaurant 7 am-10 pm. Bar 11 am-midnight. Ck-out noon. Coin lndry. Business servs avail. Sundries. Health club privileges. Cr cds: A, C, D, DS, ER, JCB, MC, V.

D ⤢ ⤢ 🐾 SC

★ ★ **DELTA TOWN & COUNTRY.** *(6005 CN 17 at CN 99, Delta BC V4K 4E2)* 604/946-4404; FAX 604/946-5916. 48 rms, 2 story. May-late Oct: S $85-$90; D $90-$95; each addl $10; suites $130-$150; under 16 free; lower rates rest of yr. Crib free. TV; VCR avail. Sauna. Pool; poolside serv. Complimentary coffee in rms. Restaurant 6 am-10 pm. Bar to midnight. Ck-out 11 am. Meeting rms. Business servs avail. In-rm modem link. Gift shop. Valet serv. Lighted tennis. Lawn games. Cr cds: A, D, ER, MC, V.

D ⤢ ⤢ ⤢ 🐾 SC

↙★ ★ **TRAVELODGE SURREY.** *(13245 King George Hwy (99A), Surrey BC V3T 2T3)* 15 mi SE on Hwy 99A. 604/588-0181; FAX 604/588-0180. 54 rms, 1-2 story, 41 kits. June-Aug: S $60; D $65-$70; each addl $6; kits. $70-$80; suites $80-$110; under 17 free; lower rates rest of yr.

Crib free. TV; cable (premium). Complimentary coffee in rms. Restaurant nearby. Ck-out 11 am. Coin lndry. Business servs avail. Sundries. Refrigerators. Cr cds: A, C, D, DS, ER, JCB, MC, V.

[D] [X] [N] [SC]

Motor Hotels

★ ★ **BEST WESTERN ABERCORN INN.** (9260 Bridgeport Rd, Richmond BC V6X 1S1) 9 mi S, near Intl Airport. 604/270-7576; FAX 604/270-0001. 98 rms, 3 story. June-Sept: S $120-$185; D $135-$185; each addl $15; under 17 free; higher rates special events; lower rates rest of yr. Crib free. TV; cable. Complimentary coffee in rms. Restaurant 6:30 am-10 pm. Rm serv. Bar 11-1 am. Ck-out noon. Meeting rms. Business servs avail. In-rm modem link. Bellhops. Concierge. Valet serv. Free airport transportation. Minibars. Cr cds: A, C, D, DS, ER, JCB, MC, V.

[D] [X] [N] [N] [SC]

★ ★ **BEST WESTERN SANDS.** (1755 Davie St, Vancouver BC V6G 1W5) 1 blk from English Bay, in the West End. 604/682-1831; FAX 604/682-3546. 121 rms, 5 story. May-Oct: S, D $159; each addl $15; suites $195-$265; under 12 free; lower rates rest of yr. Crib free. TV; cable. Restaurant 7-1 am. Rm serv 8 am-8 pm. Bars noon-2 am. Ck-out noon. Meeting rms. Business servs avail. In-rm modem link. Bellhops. Valet serv. Free covered parking. Exercise equipt; weights, bicycles, sauna. Balconies. Cr cds: A, C, D, DS, ER, JCB, MC, V.

[D] [X] [N] [N] [SC]

✔ ★ **BILTMORE.** (395 Kingsway (Hwy 1A/99A), Vancouver BC V5T 3J7) south of downtown. 604/872-5252; FAX 604/874-3003; res: 800/663-5713. 100 rms, 7 story. Apr-Oct: S, D $79-$110; each addl $8; under 12 free; lower rates rest of yr. Crib free. TV; cable. Pool. Restaurant 6:30 am-8 pm; Sat from 7 am; Sun 8 am-2 pm. Bar noon-2 am. Ck-out noon. Meeting rms. Business servs avail. Valet serv. Cr cds: A, D, DS, ER, MC, V.

[N] [N] [N]

★ ★ **EXECUTIVE INN.** (7211 Westminster Hwy, Richmond BC V6X 1A3) Approx 10 mi S on Hwy 99, then 2½ mi W on Westminster Hwy. 604/278-5555; res: 800/663-2878. 153 units, 3 story, 30 kit. units. May-Sept: S $119; D $139; each addl $10; suites $139-$209; under 13 free; lower rates rest of yr. Crib free. TV; cable (premium). VCR avail. Indoor pool. Coffee in rms. Restaurant 6:30 am-10 pm. Rm serv. Bar 5 pm-midnight. Ck-out noon. Meeting rms. Business center. In-rm modem link. Bellhops. Gift shop. Free airport transportation. Health club privileges. Many refrigerators; some in-rm whirlpools. Cr cds: A, D, ER, MC, V.

[D] [N] [N] [SC] [image]

★ ★ **QUALITY HOTEL-DOWNTOWN.** (1335 Howe St, Vancouver BC V6Z 1R7) downtown. 604/682-0229; FAX 604/662-7566. 157 units, 7 story, 25 suites. May-Sept: S $140; D $160; each addl $16; suites $170-$190; under 18 free; lower rates rest of yr. Crib free. Pet accepted. Garage $6. TV; cable. Pool. Restaurant 7 am-10 pm. Rm serv. Bar 11:30-1 am. Ck-out 11 am. Meeting rms. Business servs avail. Bellhops. Valet serv. Some refrigerators. Cr cds: A, C, D, DS, ER, JCB, MC, V.

[D] [X] [N] [N] [SC]

✔ ★ **STAY 'N SAVE-AIRPORT.** (10551 St Edward Dr, Richmond BC V6X 3L8) Hwy 99 exit 39, near Vancouver Airport. 604/273-3311; FAX 604/273-9522; res: 800/663-0298. 206 rms, 3 story. Mid-May-Sept: S $104; D $114; each addl $10; suites $120-$130; kits. $10 addl; under 16 free; lower rates rest of yr. Crib free. Pet accepted. TV; cable, VCR avail (movies free). Complimentary coffee in rms. Restaurant 6:30 am-11 pm. Ck-out 11 am. Coin lndry. Meeting rms. Business servs avail. Valet serv. Free airport transportation. Exercise equipt; stair machine, bicycles. Whirlpool. Cr cds: A, C, D, ER, MC, V.

[D] [X] [X] [N] [N] [SC]

Hotels

★ ★ **BEST WESTERN CHÂTEAU GRANVILLE.** (1100 Granville St, Vancouver BC V6Z 2B6) at Helmcken, downtown. 604/669-7070; FAX 604/669-4928. 148 rms, 15 story, 90 suites. May-Oct: S, D $133-$180; each addl $20; under 16 free; wkend rates; lower rates rest of yr. Crib free. Covered parking $5. TV; cable (premium). Restaurant 7-10 pm. Bar noon-1 am. Ck-out 11 am. Meeting rms. Business servs avail. Refrigerators, minibars. Private patios, balconies. Cr cds: A, C, D, DS, ER, JCB, MC, V.

[D] [N] [N] [SC]

★ ★ **BLUE HORIZON.** (1225 Robson St, Vancouver BC V6E 1C3) in the West End. 604/688-1411; FAX 604/688-4461; res: 800/663-1333. 214 rms, 31 story. May-mid-Oct: S, D $185-$210; each addl $15; suites $290; under 16 free; lower rates rest of yr. Crib free. Covered parking $8. TV; cable (premium). Indoor pool; whirlpool. Restaurant 6:30 am-10 pm. No rm serv. Bars noon-2 am. Ck-out noon. Meeting rms. Business servs avail. In-rm modem link. Exercise equipt; weight machine, bicycles, sauna. Refrigerators. Balconies. Cr cds: A, D, DS, ER, JCB, MC, V.

[D] [N] [X] [N] [N] [SC]

✔ ★ **CLARION VILLA.** (4331 Dominion St, Burnaby BC V5G 1C7) 8 mi E via Trans-Canada Hwy 1, Willingdon Ave S exit. 604/430-2828; FAX 604/430-9230. 275 rms, 21 story. S $131; D $141; each addl $10; suites $175-$1,000; under 18 free. Crib free. TV; cable. 2 pools, 1 indoor; poolside serv. Restaurant 6:30 am-10 pm. Rm serv. Bar 11-1 am. Ck-out noon. Meeting rms. Business center. In-rm modem link. Gift shop. Barber. Free covered parking. Refrigerators. Balconies. Cr cds: A, C, D, ER, MC, V.

[D] [N] [N] [N] [SC] [image]

★ ★ ★ **COAST PLAZA AT STANLEY PARK.** (1733 Comox St, Vancouver BC V6G 1P6) in the West End. 604/688-7711; FAX 604/688-5934; res: 800/663-1144. 267 rms, 35 story, 190 kits. No A/C. May-Oct: S $245-$295; D $285-$335; each addl $20; suites $295-$400; kit. units $10 addl; under 18 free; package plans. Crib free. TV; cable (premium). VCR avail. Indoor pool. Restaurants 6:30 am-10:30 pm. Rm serv 24 hrs. Bar noon-2 am. Ck-out 1 pm. Coin lndry. Meeting rms. Business servs avail. In-rm modem link. Concierge. Shopping arcade. Barber, beauty shop. Valet parking. Free downtown transportation. Exercise rm; instructor, weights, stair machine, steam rm, sauna. Refrigerators, minibars. Balconies. Luxury level. Cr cds: A, C, D, DS, ER, JCB, MC, V.

[D] [N] [X] [N] [N] [SC]

★ ★ ★ **DELTA PACIFIC.** (10251 St Edwards Dr, Richmond BC V6X 2M9) 8 mi S via Hwy 99. 604/278-9611; FAX 604/276-1121; res: 800/877-1133 (US), 800/268-1133 (CAN). 460 rms, 2, 11 & 17 story. Apr-Oct: S, D $155-$185; each addl $15; suites $250-$350; under 18 free; lower rates rest of yr. Crib free. Pet accepted. TV; cable. 3 pools, 1 indoor; whirlpool, poolside serv. Playground. Supervised child's activities; ages 5-12. 2 restaurants 6:30 am-11 pm. Rm serv 24 hrs. Bar 11-1 am. Ck-out noon. Convention facilities. Business center. In-rm modem link. Gift shop. Beauty shop. Golf privileges. Lighted & indoor tennis. Exercise rm; instructor, weight machine, treadmill, sauna. Massage. Squash courts. Private patios, balconies. Cr cds: A, C, D, DS, ER, JCB, MC, V.

[D] [N] [X] [X] [N] [X] [N] [N] [SC] [image]

★ ★ ★ **DELTA VANCOUVER AIRPORT.** (3500 Cessna Dr, Richmond BC V7B 1C7) 9 mi S, near Intl Airport. 604/278-1241; FAX 604/276-1975; res: 800/268-1133 (CAN). 415 rms, 11 story. May-Sept: S, D $260; each addl $20; suites $395-$495; under 18 free; lower rates rest of yr. Crib free. TV; cable, VCR avail. Heated pool; poolside serv in season. Restaurant 6 am-10:30 pm. Bars 11-1 am. Ck-out 1 pm. Business center. In-rm modem link. Concierge. Gift shop. Airport transportation. Exercise equipt; weights, treadmill. On Fraser River; marina. Cr cds: A, C, D, DS, ER, JCB, MC, V.

[D] [N] [X] [X] [N] [N] [SC] [image]

★ ★ **EXECUTIVE INN.** (4201 Lougheed Hwy, Burnaby BC V5C 3Y6) between Gilmore and Willingdon Sts. 604/298-2010; FAX 604/298-1123; res: 800/590-3932. 125 suites, 4 story. May-Sept: S, D $115-$160; each addl $10; under 12 free; wkend rates; lower rates rest of yr. Crib free. TV; cable (premium), VCR avail. Pool; whirlpool. Complimentary coffee in rms. Restaurant 6:30 am-10 pm. Bar 11 am-11 pm. Ck-out noon. Meeting rms. Business center. In-rm modem link. Health club privileges. Exercise equipt; weights, treadmill. Refrigerators. Balconies. Cr cds: A, D, ER, MC, V.

D ≈ 💃 ⛷ 🏋 SC 🏃

★ ★ ★ **FOUR SEASONS.** (791 W Georgia St, Vancouver BC V6C 2T4) downtown. 604/689-9333; FAX 604/684-4555. Web www.fshr.com. Tasteful pastel-hued decor, outstanding service and large, luxurious rooms create an atmosphere of calm in this bustling high-rise above the Pacific Centre shopping mall and adjacent to the Vancouver Stock Exchange. Notable are the glamorous atrium bar/restaurant and a partially covered pool on a sun terrace. 385 rms, 28 story. May-Oct: S, D $280-$495; each addl $25; suites $450-$2,200; under 18 free; wkend rates; lower rates rest of yr. Crib free. Pet accepted. Garage $20/day. TV; cable (premium), VCR (movies). Heated pool; whirlpool. Restaurant 6:30 am-11 pm (also see CHARTWELL). Rm serv 24 hrs. Bar 11:30-1 am. Ck-out noon. Meeting rms. Business center. In-rm modem link. Concierge. Shopping arcade. Tennis privileges. Downhill ski 10 mi. Exercise rm; instructor, weights, bicycles, sauna. Shuffleboard. Minibars. Cr cds: A, C, D, ER, JCB, MC, V.

D 💃 ➤ 🏂 ⛷ ≈ 💃 🏋 🏃

★ ★ ★ **GEORGIAN COURT.** (773 Beatty St, Vancouver BC V6B 2M4) downtown. 604/682-5555; FAX 604/682-8830; res: 800/663-1155. 180 rms, 12 story. May-Oct: S $170; D $190; each addl $20; suites $195-$450; under 18 free; lower rates rest of yr. Crib free. Pet accepted, some restrictions. Parking $7. TV; cable (premium). Restaurant (see WILLIAM TELL). Bar. Ck-out 1 pm. Meeting rms. Business servs avail. In-rm modem link. Concierge. Gift shop. Exercise equipt; weight machine, bicycles, sauna. Whirlpool. Bathrm phones, minibars. Balconies. Italian marble in bathrms. Cr cds: A, C, D, ER, JCB, MC, V.

D 💃 🏋 💃 🏃 SC

★ ★ **HOLIDAY INN DOWNTOWN.** (1110 Howe St, Vancouver BC V6Z 1R2) downtown. 604/684-2151; FAX 604/684-4736. 242 rms, 7 story. May-Oct: S $169; D $189; each addl $10; suites $199-$235; under 18 free; lower rates rest of yr. Crib free. Valet parking $8.95. TV; cable (premium), VCR avail. Sauna. Indoor pool. Complimentary coffee. Restaurant 6:30 am-10 pm. Rm serv 24 hrs. Bars 11-2 am; entertainment on wkends. Ck-out noon. Meeting rms. Business center. Concierge. Gift shop. Some refrigerators. Balconies. Cr cds: A, C, D, DS, ER, JCB, MC, V.

D ≈ 💃 🏃 SC 🏃

★ ★ **HOLIDAY INN VANCOUVER CENTER.** (711 W Broadway, Vancouver BC V5Z 3Y2) at Heather St, south of downtown. 604/879-0511; FAX 604/872-7520. 200 rms, 16 story. May-Oct: S $179; D $199; each addl $20; suites $275-$325; under 19 free; wkend rates; lower rates rest of yr. Crib free. Pet accepted, some restrictions. TV; cable. Indoor pool. Restaurant 7 am-10 pm. Bar 11-1 am. Ck-out noon. Meeting rms. Business servs avail. In-rm modem link. Gift shop. Exercise rm; instructor, weights, bicycles, sauna. Massage. Refrigerator in suites. Balconies. Cr cds: A, C, D, DS, ER, JCB, MC, V.

D 💃 ≈ 🏋 💃 🏃 SC

★ ★ **HOTEL GEORGIA.** (801 W Georgia St, Vancouver BC V6C 1P7) downtown. 604/682-5566; FAX 604/682-8192; res: 800/663-1111. 313 rms, 11 story. May-Oct: S $145-$175; D $160-$190; each addl $30; suites $250-$500; under 16 free; lower rates rest of yr. Crib free. Garage $12. TV; cable (premium), VCR avail. Restaurant 6:30 am-10 pm. Bars 11:30-1:30 am; entertainment. Ck-out noon. Meeting rms. Business center. Shopping arcade. Barber, beauty shop. Some refrigerators, minibars. Cr cds: A, C, D, ER, JCB, MC, V.

💃 🏃 SC 🏃

★ ★ ★ **HOTEL VANCOUVER.** (900 W Georgia St, Vancouver BC V6C 2W6) downtown. 604/684-3131; FAX 604/662-1929; res: 800/441-1414. 550 rms, 14 story. Late Apr-early Oct: S $180-$340; D $205-$365;

each addl $25; suites $305-$1,830; family, wkend rates; lower rates rest of yr. Pet accepted. TV; cable (premium), VCR avail. Indoor pool; wading pool, whirlpool. Restaurant 6 am-10 pm. Rm serv 24 hrs. Bars 11-1 am; entertainment. Ck-out noon. Meeting rms. Business center. In-rm modem link. Concierge. Shopping arcade. Beauty shop. Exercise rm; instructor, weights, bicycles, sauna. Refrigerator in suites. Luxury level. Cr cds: A, C, D, DS, ER, JCB, MC, V.

D 💃 ≈ 🏋 💃 🏃 SC 🏃

★ ★ ★ **HYATT REGENCY.** (655 Burrard St, Vancouver BC V6C 2R7) on Discovery Square, downtown. 604/683-1234; FAX 604/689-3707. 644 rms, 34 story. May-Oct: S, D $295-$320; each addl $25; suites $795-$1,295; under 18 free; wkend rates; lower rates rest of yr. Crib free. Garage $18.50. TV; cable, VCR. Heated pool. Restaurant 6:30 am-10 pm. Bars 11-1 am. Ck-out noon. Convention facilities. Business center. In-rm modem link. Concierge. Shopping arcade. Exercise equipt; weight machine, treadmill, sauna. Health club privileges. Some bathrm phones. Some balconies. Luxury level. Cr cds: A, C, D, DS, ER, JCB, MC, V.

D ≈ 🏋 💃 🏃 SC 🏃

★ ★ **LANDMARK.** (1400 Robson St, Vancouver BC V6G 1B9) in the West End. 604/687-0511; FAX 604/687-2801; res: 800/830-6144. 358 rms, 42 story. May-Oct: S $160-$180; D $180-$200; each addl $20; suites $350-$450; under 18 free. Crib free. Parking $7. TV; cable (premium). Restaurant (see CLOUD 9). Rm serv 6 am-11 pm. Bar. Ck-out noon. Meeting rms. Business center. In-rm modem link. Exercise equipt; bicycle, treadmill, sauna. Whirlpool. Some refrigerators. Balconies. Beach 4 blks. Cr cds: A, C, D, DS, ER, JCB, MC, V.

D 🏋 💃 🏃 SC 🏃

★ ★ ★ **THE METROPOLITAN.** (645 Howe St, Vancouver BC V6C 2Y9) downtown. 604/687-1122; FAX 604/689-7044; res: 800/667-2300. 197 rms, 18 story. May-Oct: S $325; D $345; each addl $20; suites $425-$1,500; under 18 free; wkend rates. Crib free. Pet accepted. Covered parking $16. TV; cable (premium), VCR avail. Indoor pool; whirlpool, poolside serv. Complimentary coffee, tea in rms. Restaurant 6:30 am-11 pm. Rm serv 24 hrs. Bar 11:30-1 am. Ck-out 1 pm. Convention facilities. Business center. In-rm modem link. Concierge. Exercise rm; instructor, weights, bicycles, sauna, steam rm. Bathrm phones, refrigerators. Private patios, balconies. Library. Artwork, antiques; elaborate floral arrangements. Elegant Oriental touches. Cr cds: A, C, D, DS, ER, JCB, MC, V.

D 💃 ≈ 🏋 💃 🏃 SC 🏃

★ ★ ★ **PACIFIC PALISADES.** (1277 Robson St, Vancouver BC V6E 1C4) in the West End. 604/688-0461; FAX 604/688-4374; res: 800/663-1815. 233 suites, 20-23 story. May-Oct: S $210-$275; D $235-$310; each addl $25; suites to $800; under 16 free; lower rates rest of yr. Crib free. Parking $12. TV; cable, VCR avail. Indoor pool; whirlpool. Restaurant 6:30 am-10 pm. Rm serv 24 hrs. Bar 11:30-1 am; entertainment Thurs-Sat. Ck-out noon. Meeting rms. Business center. In-rm modem link. Concierge. Garage parking. Exercise rm; instructor, weights, treadmill, sauna. Some balconies. Cr cds: A, D, ER, JCB, MC, V.

D ≈ 🏋 💃 🏃 SC 🏃

★ ★ ★ **PAN PACIFIC VANCOUVER.** (300-999 Canada Place, Vancouver BC V6C 3B5) adj trade & convention center, downtown. 604/662-8111; FAX 604/685-8690; res: 800/663-1515. Dramatically positioned at the cruise-ship complex, looking over the bay toward Stanley Park and the mountains, this ultra-modern luxury hotel has comfortable Asian-accented rooms with fine views. There's a well-equipped gym and sports center and several bars, cafes and restaurants. 506 rms, 23 story. Mid-Apr-late Oct: S, D, studios $400-$430; each addl $30; suites $525-$2,000; under 18 free; wkend rates; lower rates rest of yr. Crib free. Pet accepted. Garage $20; valet. TV; cable, VCR avail. Heated pool; whirlpool. Restaurant 6:30 am-11 pm (also see FIVE SAILS). Rm serv 24 hrs. Bar 11:30-1 am. Ck-out 1 pm. Convention facilities. Business center. In-rm modem link. Concierge. Shopping arcade. Barber, beauty shop. Exercise rm; instructor, weights, bicycles, sauna, steam rm. Massage. Bathrm phones, refrigerators; some in-rm steam baths. Cr cds: A, C, D, ER, JCB, MC, V.

D 💃 ≈ 🏋 🏂 💃 🏃 🏃

★ ★ ★ **RADISSON.** (8181 Cambie Rd, Richmond BC V6X 3X9) 604-276-8181; FAX 604/279-8381. 184 rms, 11 story. S, D $205; each addl $15; suites $225-$370; under 18 free. Crib free. TV; cable (premium), VCR avail. Indoor pool. Complimentary coffee in rms. Restaurant 6:30 am-2 pm, 5-10 pm. Rm serv 24 hrs. Bar to midnight. Ck-out 1 pm. Meeting rms. Business servs avail. In-rm modem link. Shopping arcade. Barber, beauty shop. Valet serv. Free airport transportation. Exercise equipt; bicycles, weight machine. Refrigerators. Cr cds: A, D, DS, ER, JCB, MC, V.

D ≈ ✕ ▲ ⊠ ⊞

★ ★ ★ **RENAISSANCE HARBOURSIDE-VANCOUVER.** (1133 W Hastings, Vancouver BC V6E 3T3) downtown. 604/689-9211; FAX 604/689-4358. 439 rms, 19 story. May-Oct: S $205-$305; D $230-$330; each addl $25; suites $350-$1,000; under 19 free; lower rates rest of yr. Crib free. Pet accepted. Covered parking $12. TV; cable (premium). Indoor pool. 2 restaurants 6:30 am-11 pm. 2 bars; entertainment exc Sun. Ck-out noon. Convention facilities. Business servs avail. In-rm modem link. Exercise equipt; weights, bicycles, sauna. Minibars; refrigerators. Balconies. Cr cds: A, C, D, DS, ER, JCB, MC, V.

D ✍ ≈ ✕ ▲ ⊠ ⊞ SC

★ ★ ★ ★ **SUTTON PLACE.** (845 Burrard St, Vancouver BC V6Z 2K6) downtown. 604/682-5511; FAX 604/682-5513; res: 800/961-7555. E-mail info@suttonplace.com; web www.travelweb.com/sutton.html. This European-style hotel has a lively late-night bar and a restaurant that serves afternoon tea. Compact rooms have Regency-style furnishings and skyline views. 397 rms, 21 story, 47 suites. Mid-Apr-Oct: S $195-$395; D $215-$415; each addl $20; suites $445-$1,500; under 18 free; lower rates rest of yr. Crib free. Garage, valet parking $15. TV; cable (premium), VCR avail (movies). Indoor pool; whirlpool, poolside serv. Restaurant 6:30 am-11 pm. Rm serv 24 hrs. Bar 11:30-1:30 am; entertainment. Ck-out noon. Convention facilities. Business center. In-rm modem link. Concierge. Gift shop. Exercise equipt; weights, bicycles, sauna, steam rm. Massage. Bathrm phones, refrigerators. Sun deck. Cr cds: A, C, D, DS, ER, JCB, MC, V.

D ≈ ✕ ▲ ⊠ ⊞ ⚓

★ ★ ★ **WATERFRONT CENTRE.** (900 Canada Place Way, Vancouver BC V6C 3L5) at Burrard Inlet, in the West End. 604/691-1991; FAX 604/691-1838. 489 units, 23 story. May-Oct: S, D $280-$395; each addl $25; suites $465-$1,700; under 18 free; lower rates rest of yr. Crib free. Pet accepted; $50. Garage parking $15.70. TV; cable, VCR avail. Heated pool; whirlpool, poolside serv. Restaurant 6:30 am-midnight. Rm serv 24 hrs. Bar from 11 am; entertainment exc Sun. Ck-out noon. Convention facilities. Business center. In-rm modem link. Concierge. Shopping arcade. Exercise equipt; weight machine, bicycles. Minibars. Waterfront hotel, flanked by terraced gardens, is linked by an enclosed walkway to Trade and Convention Centre & cruise ship terminal. Luxury level. Cr cds: A, C, D, DS, ER, JCB, MC, V.

D ✍ ≈ ✕ ▲ ⊠ ⊞ ⚓

★ ★ ★ **WEDGEWOOD.** (845 Hornby St, Vancouver BC V6Z 1V1) downtown. 604/689-7777; FAX 604/688-3074; res: 800/663-0666. 93 rms, 14 story. May-Nov: S $200-$300; D $220-$320; each addl $20; suites $400-$520; under 14 free; wkend rates; package plans; lower rates rest of yr. Crib free. Garage $15. TV; cable (premium), VCR avail. Complimentary coffee in rms. Restaurant (see BACCHUS). Rm serv 24 hrs. Bar noon-2 am; entertainment. Ck-out 1 pm. Meeting rms. Business center. Exercise equipt; weights, stair machine, sauna. Refrigerators. Private patios, balconies. Old World charm. Cr cds: A, C, D, ER, JCB, MC, V.

D ✕ ▲ ⊠ ⊞ ⚓

★ ★ ★ ★ **THE WESTIN BAYSHORE HOTEL, VANCOUVER.** (1601 W Georgia St (BC 99), Vancouver BC V6G 2V4) Stanley Park area, in the West End. 604/682-3377; FAX 604/687-3102. Web www.westin.com. The closest thing you'll find to a resort in the downtown area, the elaborately landscaped Bayshore is perched on the harbor, five minutes away from Stanley Park. Rooms in the tower section are largest and offer water views. 517 rms, 9 & 20 story. Apr-Oct: S $199-$265; D $224-$299; each addl $25; suites $335-$1,600; under 18 free; lower rates rest of yr. Crib free. Parking $11/day. TV; cable (premium), VCR avail. 2 pools, 1 indoor; whirlpool, poolside serv. Complimentary coffee in rms. Restaurant 6:30 am-10 pm. Rm serv 24 hrs. 2 bars 11:30-1 am. Ck-out 1 pm. Conven-

tion facilities. Business servs avail. In-rm modem link. Concierge. Shopping arcade. Barber, beauty shop. Valet parking. Exercise rm; instructor, weights, bicycles, sauna, steam rm. Massage. Bathrm phones, refrigerators. Balconies. Cr cds: A, C, D, DS, ER, JCB, MC, V.

D ≈ ✕ ✦ ⊠ ⚓ SC

Inns

★ ★ **BEAUTIFUL BED & BREAKFAST.** (428 W 40th Ave, Vancouver BC V5Y 2R4) downtown. 604/327-1102; FAX 604/327-2299. 5 rms, 3 share bath, 2 story. No A/C. No rm phones. Apr-Oct: S $95-$210; D $120-$210; each addl $15-$25; lower rates rest of yr. Children over 14 yrs only. 2 TVs; cable. Complimentary full bkfst. Restaurant nearby. Ck-out 11 am, ck-in 5-6 pm. Business servs avail. Downhill/x-country ski 10 mi. Balconies. Colonial-style house with sculptured gardens. Totally nonsmoking. No cr cds accepted.

☀ ⊠ ⚓

★ ★ ★ **RIVER RUN COTTAGES.** (4551 River Rd W, Ladner BC V4K 1R9) 604/946-7778; FAX 604/940-1970. 4 cottages, 1 story. Apr-Dec: S, D $80-$160; each addl $20; under 5 free; lower rates rest of yr. Pet accepted. Complimentary full bkfst; afternoon refreshments. Restaurant nearby. Ck-out noon, ck-in 3 pm. Luggage handling. Business servs avail. On river. Totally nonsmoking. Cr cds: MC, V.

✦ ⊠ ⚓

✔ ★ ★ ★ **WEST END GUEST HOUSE.** (1362 Haro St, Vancouver BC V6E 1G2) in the West End. 604/681-2889; FAX 604/688-8812. 8 air-cooled rms, 3 story. S $95-$195, D $110-$210. Children over 12 yrs only. TV; cable. Complimentary full bkfst; afternoon refreshments. Restaurant nearby. Ck-out 11 am, ck-in 3 pm. Business servs avail. Former residence (1906) of one of first photographers in Vancouver. Period furnishings. Totally nonsmoking. Cr cds: A, DS, MC, V.

⊠ ⚓

Restaurants

★ ★ ★ **BACCHUS.** (See Wedgewood Hotel) 604/689-7777. Hrs: 6:30 am-11 pm. Res accepted. Northern Italian menu. Bar from 11 am. Wine list. Semi-a la carte: bkfst $5.25-$13.95, lunch $11-$15, dinner $14-$27. Sun brunch $8-$14. Afternoon tea 2-4 pm $12.95. Child's meals. Specializes in lamb, seafood. Pianist exc Sun. Valet parking. European decor; many antiques and original artwork. Jacket (dinner). Cr cds: A, D, ER, JCB, MC, V.

D

★ ★ ★ **BEACH HOUSE AT DUNARAVE PIER.** (150 25th St, West Vancouver BC) on Dundarave Pier. 604/922-1414. Hrs: 11:30 am-11 pm; Sat, Sun from 10:30 am; summer hrs vary; Sun brunch 10:30 am-5 pm. Res accepted. Bar. A la carte entrees: lunch $8.95-$13.95, dinner $9.95-$21. Sun brunch $8.95-$13. Child's meals. Specializes in rack of lamb, pasta, fresh seafood. Valet parking. Heated outdoor patio. View of ocean & Vancouver bay. Cr cds: A, D, ER, MC, V.

D

★ ★ ★ **BISHOP'S.** (2183 W 4th Ave, Vancouver BC) south of downtown. 604/738-2025. Hrs: 5:30-11 pm; Sun to 10 pm. Closed Dec 24-26. Res required. Serv bar. Wine list. Semi-a la carte: dinner $18-$30. Child's meals. Specializes in fresh West Coast cuisine. Contemporary decor; large fresh flower arrangements. Cr cds: A, D, ER, MC, V.

★ ★ ★ **CANNERY.** (2205 Commissioner St, Vancouver BC) at foot of Victoria Dr, east of downtown. 604/254-9606. Hrs: 11:30 am-2:30 pm, 5:30-10 pm; Sat 5:30-10:30 pm. Closed Dec 24-26. Res accepted. Bar. Wine list. Semi-a la carte: lunch $8.95-$15.95, dinner $17.95-$31.95. Child's meals. Specializes in fresh seafood, mesquite-grilled dishes. Parking. Nautical motif; view of harbor. Cr cds: A, D, DS, ER, JCB, MC, V.

✔ ★ **CAPILANO HEIGHTS CHINESE.** (5020 Capilano Rd, North Vancouver BC) 6 mi N on Capilano Rd, opp Cleveland Dam.

604/987-9511. Hrs: noon-10 pm; Sat from 4:30 pm; Sun 4:30-9 pm. Closed Dec 25 & 26. Res accepted. Chinese menu. Bar. A la carte entrees: lunch $7-$17, dinner $10-$20. Specialties: prawns & broccoli with black bean sauce, Peking duck (24-hr notice). Parking. Cr cds: A, MC, V.

D

★ ★ **CHARTHOUSE.** *(3866 Bayview, Richmond BC V7E 4R7) 604/271-7000.* Hrs: 11:30 am-10 pm. Closed Dec 25. Res accepted. Semi-a la carte: lunch $5.95-$10.95, dinner $9.95-$21.95. Sun brunch $8.95. Child's meals. Specializes in seafood, beef. Outdoor dining. Casual decor. Cr cds: A, MC, V.

D

★ ★ ★ **CHARTWELL.** *(See Four Seasons Hotel) 604/689-9333.* Hrs: 6:30 am-10 pm. Res accepted. Bar. Wine cellar. A la carte entrees: bkfst $9-$19, lunch $17-$23, dinner $18-$41. Specializes in Salt Spring Island lamb. Own baking. Seasonal menu. Parking. Cr cds: A, C, D, ER, JCB, MC, V.

D

★ ★ **CHEZ MICHEL.** *(1373 Marine Dr, West Vancouver BC) 604/926-4913.* Hrs: 11:30 am-2 pm, 5:30-10:30 pm. Closed Sun; major hols. Res required. French menu. Wine, beer. Semi-a la carte: lunch $8.95-$11.95, dinner $12.95-$19.95. Specialties: prawns Niçoise, rack of lamb au jus, bouillabaisse. Parking. Local art on display. View of English Bay and Burrard Inlet. Cr cds: A, D, ER, MC, V.

D ⏏

★ ★ **CLOUD 9.** *(See Landmark Hotel) 604/687-0511.* Hrs: 6:30 am-10 pm; Sun from 7 am; Sun brunch 10 am-2 pm. Res accepted. Continental menu. Bar. Semi-a la carte: bkfst $7.50-$15. A la carte entrees: lunch $8-$15, dinner $17-$40. Sun brunch $14-$25. Child's meals. Specializes in fresh seafood, baked salmon. Parking. Revolving dining rm on 42nd floor of hotel. Cr cds: A, C, D, DS, ER, JCB, MC, V.

D

★ ★ ★ **DELILAH'S.** *(1739 Comox St, Vancouver BC V6G 1P5) in the West End. 604/687-3424.* Hrs: 5:30 pm-1 am. Closed Dec 24-26. Continental menu. Bar. Wine list. Complete meals: dinner 2-course $18.50, 5-course $29. Specializes in rack of lamb, grilled salmon. Eclectic decor with Art Nouveau touches. Ceilings painted in oils by local artist. Cr cds: A, D, ER, MC, V.

D

★ ★ ★ **FIVE SAILS.** *(See Pan Pacific Vancouver Hotel) 604/662-8111.* Hrs: 6-11 pm. Res accepted. Bar. Wine list. A la carte entrees: dinner $38-$45. Specializes in Pacific Rim cuisine. Own baking. Valet parking. Formal contemporary decor. View of harbor & mountains. Cr cds: A, C, D, ER, JCB, MC, V.

D

★ ★ **HY'S ENCORE.** *(637 Hornby St, Vancouver BC) downtown. 604/683-7671.* Hrs: 11:30 am-11 pm; Sat, Sun from 5:30 pm. Bar. A la carte entrees: lunch $10-$22. Complete meals: dinner $22-$40. Specializes in steak. Baronial decor. Cr cds: A, C, D, DS, ER, JCB, MC, V.

D

★ ★ ★ **A KETTLE OF FISH.** *(900 Pacific, Vancouver BC) downtown. 604/682-6853.* Hrs: 11:30 am-2 pm, 5:30-9:30 pm; Fri, Sat 5:30-10 pm. Closed Jan 1, Dec 24 eve, 25, 26. Res accepted. Serv bar. Complete meals: lunch $6.95-$12.95, dinner $13.95-$32. Specializes in fresh seafood. English country garden atmosphere. Cr cds: A, D, JCB, MC, V.

D

★ ★ ★ **LE CROCODILE.** *(Smythe & Burrard Sts, Vancouver BC) downtown. 604/669-4298.* Hrs: 11:30 am-2:30 pm, 5:30-10 pm; Sat from 5:30 pm. Closed Sun; major hols. Res accepted. French, continental menu. Serv bar. Wine list. A la carte entrees: lunch $9.50-$16.95, dinner $14.95-$22.95. Specializes in veal, salmon. Own baking. Own ice cream.

Valet parking. Outdoor dining. Modern French decor; antiques. Cr cds: A, D, ER, MC, V.

D

✔ ★ **PHNOM PENH.** *(244 E Georgia St, Vancouver BC) in Chinatown. 604/682-5777.* Hrs: 10 am-9 pm. Closed Tues. Res accepted. Cambodian, Vietnamese menu. Bar. Complete meals: lunch, dinner $5-$12. Specialties: hot & sour soup, barbecued chicken with lemon grass, marinated butter beef. Cr cds: A, MC.

★ ★ ★ **PICCOLO MONDO.** *(850 Thurlow St, Vancouver BC V6E 1W2) in the West End. 604/688-1633.* Hrs: 11:30 am-2:30 pm, 5:30-10 pm; Sat from 5:30 pm. Closed Sun. Res accepted. Italian menu. Bar. Semi-a la carte: lunch $9.75-$15, dinner $15-$27. Specialties: tortellini della nonna, scaloppini a la Marsala, Tuscan dishes. Extensive wine selection. Cr cds: A, D, ER, MC, V.

D ⏏

★ ★ **PINK PEARL.** *(1132 E Hastings St, Vancouver BC) east of downtown. 604/253-4316.* Hrs: 9 am-3 pm, 5-10 pm; Fri, Sat to 11 pm. Res accepted. Chinese menu. Bar 11-1 am. A la carte entrees: bkfst, lunch $6-$14, dinner $14-$28. Specialties: Peking duck, spiced crab. Parking. Very large dining area. Cr cds: A, D, ER, MC, V.

D

★ ★ ★ **STAR ANISE.** *(1485 W 12th St, Vancouver BC V6H 1M6) Granville Island. 604/737-1485.* Hrs: 11:30 am-2:30 pm, 5:30-11 pm; Summer hrs 5:30-11 pm. Closed Dec 24-26. Res accepted. Northwestern menu. Bar. Wine cellar. Semi-a la carte: lunch $12-$14, dinner $17-$21. Specializes in local seafood & game, tandoori salmon. Own desserts, pastries, ice cream. Parking. Relaxing, elegant dining. Art by local artists. Cr cds: A, C, D, ER, MC, V.

D

★ ★ ★ **TEAHOUSE.** *(7501 Stanley Park Dr, Vancouver BC V6G 3E2) at Ferguson Point in Stanley Park, west of downtown. 604/669-3281.* Hrs: 11:30 am-2:30 pm, 5:30-10 pm; Sun from 10:30 am. Closed Dec 25. Res accepted. Continental, West coast menu. Wine cellar. A la carte entrees: lunch $11.75-$17.95, dinner $9.95-$15.95. Sat, Sun brunch $9.95-$15.50. Specializes in seafood, poultry, pasta. Own baking. Outdoor dining. Glass conservatory; view of harbor. Cr cds: A, MC, V.

D

★ ★ **TOJO'S.** *(777 W Broadway #202, Vancouver BC V5Z 4I7) west of downtown. 604/872-8050.* Hrs: 5-11 pm. Closed Sun. Res accepted. Japanese menu. Bar. Semi-a la carte: dinner $15-$28. Complete meals: dinner $45-$100. Specializes in traditional Japanese dishes. Sushi bar. Parking. Patio dining with view of Japanese garden. Tatami rms available. Cr cds: A, ER, MC, V.

D ⏏

★ ★ **TOP OF VANCOUVER.** *(555 W Hastings, Vancouver BC V6B 4N6) downtown. 604/669-2220.* Hrs: 11:30 am-2:30 pm, 5-10 pm; summer to 11 pm; Sun brunch to 2:30 pm. Res accepted. Bar. A la carte entrees: lunch, dinner $13-$42. Sun brunch $26.95. Child's meals. Specializes in local seafood, pasta. Revolving restaurant 550 ft above street level. Cr cds: A, MC, V.

D

★ ★ **UMBERTO AL PORTO.** *(321 Water St, Vancouver BC) in Gastown. 604/683-8376.* Hrs: 11:30 am-11 pm. Closed Sun; major hols. Res accepted. Italian menu. Bar. Semi-a la carte: lunch $9-$15, dinner $10-$22. Child's meals. Specializes in pasta. Sun room dining. In original Hudson's Bay Co building; tiled floors. Tuscan-style Mediterranean decor. Cr cds: A, C, D, ER, JCB, MC, V.

D

★ ★ ★ **UMBERTO'S.** *(1380 Hornby St, Vancouver BC) downtown. 604/687-6316.* Hrs: 5:30-11 pm. Closed Mon; Jan 1, Dec 25. Res accepted. Northern Italian menu. No A/C. Serv bar. Wine list. A la carte entrees: dinner $14-$30. Specialties: rack of lamb, osso buco, filet of veal.

Valet parking. Outdoor dining. In converted Victorian house (1896); Italian, Tuscan decor. Cr cds: A, ER, JCB, MC, V.

★ ★ ★ **WILLIAM TELL.** *(See Georgian Court Hotel)* 604/688-3504. Hrs: 6:30 am-9:30 pm; Sun 6:30 am-noon, 5:30-8 pm. Res accepted. Swiss, continental menu. Bar. Semi-a la carte: bkfst $6.50-$9.50, lunch $6-$13.25, dinner $18.75-$28. Specializes in veal, fresh seafood. Own baking, ice cream. Valet parking. European decor. Cr cds: A, D, ER, JCB, MC, V.

D

Unrated Dining Spots

GREENS AND GOURMET. *(2681 W Broadway, Vancouver BC)* south of downtown. 604/737-7373. Hrs: 9 am-10 pm. Closed Dec 25. International health food menu. Juice bar. Wine, beer. Semi-a la carte: bkfst, lunch $3.25-$7.95, dinner $3.25-$8.95. Specialties: Greek moussaka, spinach pie. Organic salad bar. Guitarist Fri-Sun. Parking. California-style dining. Totally nonsmoking. Cr cds: MC, V.

D SC

TRUE CONFECTIONS. *(866 Denman St, Vancouver BC V6G 2L8)* in the West End. 604/682-1292. Hrs: 4 pm-midnight; Fri to 1 am; Sat & Sun 1 pm-1 am. Dessert menu. Wine, beer. A la carte entrees: lunch, dinner $2.50-$7. Specialties: devil's food cake with marshmallow icing, white chocolate raspberry cheesecake. 13-foot refrigerated display case is filled daily with fresh cakes, pies and other desserts. Outdoor dining (May-Oct). Totally nonsmoking. Cr cds: A, MC, V.

D

Vancouver Island

(See also Nanaimo, Vancouver, Victoria, BC; also see Anacortes, WA, Bellingham, WA, Seattle, WA)

The largest of the Canadian Pacific Coast Islands, Vancouver Island stretches almost 300 miles (480 kilometers) along the shores of western British Columbia. It is easily accessible by ferry from the city of Vancouver on the mainland as well as from other parts of British Columbia and the state of Washington. With most of its population located in the larger cities on the eastern coast, much of the island remains a wilderness and is very popular with outdoor enthusiasts.

The Vancouver Island Mountain Range cuts down the middle of the island, providing spectacular snowcapped scenery, fjords and rocky coastal cliffs. Several provincial parks are dedicated to the preservation of wildlife: Columbia black-tailed deer and eagles are common to the southern tip; Roosevelt elk, black bears and cougars inhabit the northern forests; and whales, sea lions and seals are found along the shores. The surrounding ocean, as well as the inland lakes and rivers offer fishermen some of the world's best salmon and trout. Among the variety of activities to enjoy are sailing, canoeing, boating, scuba diving, camping, climbing and caving.

The southern portion of the island contains more than half the island's total population and includes Victoria (see), British Columbia's capital city. Here, countryside resembles rural Britain with its rolling farmland, rows of hedges and colorful flower gardens. Spain claimed the Sooke Inlet in the 18th century, giving the familiar Spanish names to much of the area. Later, British farmers arrived as well as thousands of prospectors looking for gold. A spectacular and demanding coastal trail—the West Coast Trail, which runs from Port Renfrew to Bamfield—and countless paths through Pacific rain forests traverse East Sooke Park on the southwest coast. On the southeast coast, Malahat Dr on the Island Highway provides a dramatic panorama of the Gulf Islands and the Saanich Peninsula. Inland is the Cowichan Valley, with many lakes and rivers teeming with fish. Whippletree Junction in Duncan is a reminder of the role played by Oriental settlers in the island's mining and railway construction history. Just outside of Duncan are the British Columbia Forest Museum and Demonstration Forest and the Native Heritage Centre.

Island-hopping is pleasant in the Gulf Islands, located in the sheltered waters of the Strait of Georgia. These beautiful, isolated islands have become home to many artists. Salt Spring, the largest island, has a traditional market on Saturday in the town of Ganges, where handmade crafts are featured.

Nanaimo (see) is the dominant town in the central region, an area known for excellent sandy beaches and beautiful parks. The spectacular waterfalls found on Englishman River and the natural caves in Horne Lake Provincial Park on the Qualicum River are worth a special trip. MacMillan Provincial Park contains the famous Cathedral Grove and features Douglas fir trees 800 years old with circumferences of 30 feet (9 meters). In the center of the island is the Alberni Valley, named for the Spanish sea captain who landed at the port in 1791 searching for gold and native treasures along the coast. Located in the valley are several parks with excellent swimming and fishing, the tallest falls found in North America—Della Falls—and a bird sanctuary and fish hatchery. From Port Alberni the mountain highway winds its way to the peaceful fishing village of Tofino, the northern boundary of the Long Beach section of the Pacific Rim National Park. The park encompasses 80 miles (129 kilometers) of rugged shoreline: Long Beach, only seven miles (11 kilometers) is the best-known and most easily accessible; south of Long Beach lies the Broken Island Group of Barkley Sound, 98 islands clustered in a huge bay surrounded by the Mackenzie Mountains; and south of Barkley Sound is the famous West Coast Lifesaving Trail of 45 miles (77 kilometers), originally a route to civilization for shipwrecked sailors, now a test of strength and endurance for experienced hikers. Pacific Rim is especially popular among amateur naturalists who enjoy watching the whales and other sea life.

Settlements along the northern coast are primarily lumber towns or small villages. Cumberland, which once had the largest Chinese population in Canada, began as a coal mining town. A popular area among sports enthusiasts is Forbidden Plateau and Mt Washington, excellent for skiing and hiking. The Campbell River is where the famous Tyee and Coho salmon are found in abundance. The Quinsam River fish hatchery keeps the area well-stocked. Inland from Campbell River is the largest untouched wilderness area on the island—Strathcona Provincial Park. In the center of the park is the Golden Hinde, the island's highest peak (more than 7,000 feet/2,200 meters). Much of the rugged, mountainous wilderness is a wildlife sanctuary, but it also accommodates campers, hikers, climbers and canoe and kayak enthusiasts. Nootka Sound, on the west coast, discovered by Captain Cook, remains pristine, with few towns and no roads along the coast. On the east coast, a major highway runs north of Kelsey Bay. Although this section of the north island is more heavily populated, it is still able to preserve its wilderness character. Visiting the tiny villages in this section is like stepping back in time to the days of the first settlers. Cape Scott, at the northernmost tip of the island, can be reached by a hiking trail which winds through Cape Scott Provincial Park, a stormy coastal wilderness with magnificent forests and various wildlife.

Adding to the beauty of Vancouver Island is its moderate climate, especially in the south where the land is protected from the open sea by mainland British Columbia on the southeast and Washington state on the southwest. On the west coast, however, winter storms can be bitter, and there is much rainfall throughout the year. All in all, Vancouver Island is an exciting place to visit with its fascinating terrain, sparkling waters, abundant wildlife and delightful people.

Victoria (E-3)

(See also Nanaimo, Vancouver, BC; also see San Juan Islands, WA)

Founded 1843 **Pop** 64,379 **Elev** 211 ft (64 m) **Area code** 250 **E-mail** info@travel.victoria.bc.ca

Information Tourism Victoria, 812 Wharf St, V8W 1T3; 250/953-2033 or 800/663-3883.

Bordered by Juan de Fuca Strait on one side and majestic mountains on the other, Victoria is situated on the southeast tip of Vancouver Island. Established in 1843 as a trading post of the Hudson's Bay Company, the city was later called Fort Victoria. In the late 1850s, Victoria became the provisioning and outfitting base for miners on their way to British Columbia's goldfields. In 1866, Vancouver Island was administratively linked with the mainland and Victoria became the provincial capital in 1871.

A major port with two harbors—the outer for ocean shipping and cruising, and the inner for coastal shipping, pleasure boats, ferries to the US mainland, amphibian aircraft and fishing—Victoria has a distinctly English flavor with many Tudor-style buildings and a relaxed way of life. It is a center of Pacific Northwest indigenous culture.

Victoria is a city of parks and gardens; even the five-globed Victorian lampposts are decorated with baskets of flowers in summer. One may take a horse-drawn carriage or double-decker bus tours through many historic and scenic landmarks; inquire locally for details. In winter, temperatures rarely go below 40°F (4°C). Victoria's climate is Canada's most moderate, making it a delightful place to visit any time of year.

What to See and Do

Art Gallery of Greater Victoria. Said to be the finest collection of Japanese art in Canada. Major holdings of Asian ceramics and paintings. Canadian and European art, with focus on prints and drawings. Decorative arts. Lectures, films, concerts. Only Shinto shrine outside Japan is located here. Japanese garden, bonsai. Gift shop. (Daily; closed some major hols) 1040 Moss St. Phone 250/384-4101. ¢¢

BC Forest Museum. Logging museum; old logging machines and tools, hands-on exhibits, logging camp, 1.5-mi (2.4 km) steam railway ride, sawmill, films, nature walk, picnic park, snack bar, gift shop. (May-Sept, daily) 40 mi (64 km) N on Hwy 1, near Duncan. Phone 250/746-1251. ¢¢

Beacon Hill Park. Approx 180 acres (75 hectares) with lakes, wildfowl sanctuary, children's petting farm, walks and floral gardens, cricket pitch; world's second-tallest totem pole; beautiful view of the sea. For a list of additional recreational areas contact Tourism Victoria. From Douglas St to Cook St, between Superior St & waterfront. **Free.**

Carr House (1863). Italianate-style birthplace of famous Canadian painter/author Emily Carr. Ground floor restored to period. (Mid-May-Sept, daily; rest of yr, by appt) 207 Government St. Phone 250/383-5843. ¢¢

Centennial Square. Includes fountain plaza; Elizabethan knot garden of herbs and flowers. Occasional noontime concerts. Douglas & Pandora Sts.

Craigdarroch Castle (1890). Historic house museum with beautifully crafted wood, stained glass; furnished with period furniture and artifacts. (Daily; closed Jan 1, Dec 25, 26) 1050 Joan Crescent. Phone 250/592-5323. ¢¢¢

Craigflower Farmhouse & Schoolhouse Historic Site. Farmhouse built in 1856 in simple Georgian style. 1854 schoolhouse is oldest in western Canada. Some original furnishings. (May-Oct, Sun; rest of yr, by appt) Craigflower Rd at Admirals Rd, 4 mi (6 km) NW. Phone 250/387-4697. ¢¢

Dominion Astrophysical Observatory. Public viewing through 72-in (185-cm) telescope; display galleries (Mon-Fri). Tours (Apr-Oct, Sat evenings). 10 mi (16 km) NW at 5071 W Saanich Rd. Phone 250/363-0012 (recording). **Free.**

Empress Hotel. Historically famous building constructed by Canadian Pacific Railroad in 1908 and restored in 1989. Victorian in tradition, including afternoon tea and crumpets served in the lobby. (See HOTELS) 721 Government St. Also here are

> **Crystal Garden.** Glass building formerly housed the largest saltwater pool in the British Empire. Tropical gardens, waterfall, fountain, aviary, monkeys, free-flying butterflies, exotic fish pool; restaurant, shops. (Daily) 713 Douglas St, behind Empress Hotel. Phone 250/381-1277. ¢

> **Miniature World.** More than 80 miniature, three-dimensional scenes of fact, fiction and history. Two large doll houses; very large rail diorama; villages; world's smallest operational sawmill. (Daily; closed Dec 25) 649 Humboldt St, at Empress Hotel. Phone 250/385-9731. ¢¢¢

Ferry trips. Black Ball Transport, Inc: between Victoria, BC and Port Angeles, WA (see), car ferry, phone 250/386-2202; Washington State Ferries: between Sidney, BC and Anacortes, WA, phone 250/381-1551; British Columbia Ferry Corp: between Victoria and British Columbia mainland or smaller island destinations, car ferry, phone 250/386-3431 or 604/669-1211 (Vancouver).

Fort Rodd Hill National Historic Site. A coastal artillery fort from 1895-1956; casemated barracks, gun and searchlight positions, loopholed walls. Grounds (daily; closed Jan 1, Dec 25, 26). Historic lighthouse (1860) adj. 603 Fort Rodd Hill Rd, 8 mi (13 km) W, then 1/2 mi (1 km) S of BC 1A. For further information contact the Superintendent, 603 Fort Rodd Hill Rd, V9C 2W8; 250/363-4662. **Free.**

Hatley Castle (Royal Roads University, 1908). Once the private estate of James Dunsmuir, former Lieutenant-Governor of British Columbia. Buildings are noted for their beauty, as are the grounds, with their Japanese, Italian and rose gardens. Grounds (daily). 6 mi (10 km) W via Trans-Canada Hwy 1 and 1A, Colwood exit, on Hwy 14 (Sooke Rd) in Colwood. Phone 250/391-2511. **Free.**

Helmcken House (1852). Second-oldest house in British Columbia; most furnishings are original. Extensive 19th-century medical collection. (May-Oct, daily; rest of yr, by appt) E of museum. Phone 250/387-4697. ¢¢

Maritime Museum. Located in Old Provincial Courthouse. Depicts rich maritime heritage of the Pacific Northwest from early explorers through age of sail & steam; Canadian naval wartime history; large collection of models of ships used throughout the history of British Columbia. The *Tilikum*, a converted dugout that sailed from Victoria to England during the years 1901-1904, is here. Captain James Cook display. On view, *Trekka* (1954), one of the smallest boats to circumnavigate the globe. (Daily; closed Jan 1, Dec 25) 28 Bastion Sq. Phone 250/385-4222. ¢¢

Pacific Undersea Gardens. Underwater windows for viewing of more than 5,000 marine specimens; scuba diver shows. (Daily; closed Dec 25) 490 Belleville St. Phone 250/382-5717. ¢¢¢

Parliament Buildings. Built in 1893-1897 mostly of native materials, beautifully illuminated at night; houses British Columbia's Legislative Assembly. Guided tours (mid-June-Labour Day, daily; rest of yr, Mon-Fri; closed statutory hols exc summer). Foreign language tours. Advance notice suggested for group tours. 501 Belleville St, at Inner Harbour. Phone 250/387-3046. **Free.**

Point Ellice House Museum (1861). Original Victorian setting, furnishings. Afternoon tea served in restored garden. (Mid-June-Sept, Thurs-Mon; rest of yr, by appt) Pleasant St, off Bay St. Phone 250/387-4697. ¢¢

Royal British Columbia Museum. Exhibits include natural and human history, indigenous history and art; re-creation of a turn-of-the-century town. Natural history gallery, "Living Land-Living Sea" depicts natural history of British Columbia from ice age to present. (Daily; closed Dec 25) 675 Belleville St. Phone 250/387-3701. ¢¢¢ Nearby are

> **Carillon.** Bells made in Holland; presented to the province by citizens of Dutch descent. Concerts; inquire locally for private tour.

> **Thunderbird Park.** Collection of authentic totem poles and indigenous carvings, representing the work of the main Pacific Coastal tribes. Indigenous carvers may be seen at work in the Carving Shed.

Royal London Wax Museum. More than 250 figures in theatrical settings. (Daily; closed Dec 25) 470 Belleville St, downtown on Inner Harbour. Phone 250/388-4461. ¢¢¢

Sightseeing tours.

> **Scenic Drives. North.** Malahat Dr (Trans-Canada Hwy 1), a continuation of Victoria's Douglas St, through Goldstream Park over Malahat Dr to Mill Bay, Cowichan Bay, Duncan and the BC Forest Museum. **North.** On the continuation of Victoria's Blanshard St (Hwys 17 & 17A) through rural communities, pastoral valleys known as the Saanich Peninsula where, on 50 acres (20 hectares) of manicured lawns, ponds, fountains and formal gardens bloom the world-famous Butchart Gardens. **North.** Around the sea shore along Dallas Road through beautiful, traditionally English residential areas, to Beach Dr, Oak Bay and beyond to Cordova Bay. **West.** Leave the city behind on Trans-Canada Hwy 1 to Hwy 14, which winds through rural communities to the village of Sooke, where the population is still engaged in fishing, clamming and logging. Unspoiled beaches, hiking trails, rocky seashores are accessible from this West Coast road. Continuation on Hwy 14 will lead to Jordan River and to Port Renfrew, with its beautiful Botanical Beach.

> **Capital City Tally-Ho & Sightseeing Company.** English horse-drawn carriage sightseeing tours: of city highlights, departing from Inner Harbour beside Parliament Buildings; or past Victorian homes and through 200-acre (81-hectare) Beacon Hill Park and its extensive flower gardens

(departs from Menzies & Belleville Sts). Fully narrated. (Apr-Sept, daily) 2044 Milton St. Phone 250/595-8108. ¢¢¢-¢¢¢¢

Gray Line bus tours. Several bus tours of Victoria and vicinity are offered (all yr). Contact 700 Douglas St, V8W 2B3; 250/388-5248.

The Butchart Gardens. Approx 50 acres (20 hectares). The "sunken garden" was created in the early 1900s by the Butcharts, on the site of their depleted limestone quarry, with topsoil brought in by horse-drawn cart. Already a tourist attraction by the 1920s, the gardens now include the Rose, Japanese and Italian gardens; also Star Pond, Concert Lawn, Fireworks Basin, Ross Fountain and Show Greenhouse. Subtly illuminated at night (mid-June-mid-Sept). Fireworks (July-Aug, Sat evenings). Musical stage show (July-Aug, wkday evenings). Restaurants; Seed & Gift Store. 13 mi (21 km) N on Benvenuto Ave, near Brentwood Bay. For hrs and fees, phone 250/652-5256 (recording) or 250/652-4422. ¢¢

Vancouver Island (see). SW of mainland and accessible by ferry, aircraft and jet catamaran.

Annual Event

Victorian Days. Citizens dress in period costumes of 100 yrs ago; antique car display, parades, yacht race. Mid-May.

Motels

★ ★ **BEST WESTERN INNER HARBOR.** (412 Quebec St, Victoria BC V8V 1W5) 250/384-5122. 74 rms, 7 story. Mid-May-mid-Oct: S $94-$140; D $110-$160; each addl $15; suites $190-$355; under 12 free; lower rates rest of yr. Crib free. TV; cable, VCR avail. Heated pool; whirlpool. Complimentary continental bkfst. Restaurant nearby. Ck-out 11 am. Coin lndry. Sauna. Refrigerators, microwaves. Cr cds: A, D, DS, ER, MC, V.

D 🏊 ⊗ 🐾 SC

★ ★ **HOLIDAY INN-VICTORIA.** (3020 Blanshard St, Victoria BC V8T 5B5) 250/382-4400; FAX 250/382-4053. 126 rms, 3 story. June-Sept: S $140; D $170; each addl $20; suites $180-$200; under 18 free; lower rates rest of yr. Crib free. TV; cable (premium). Complimentary coffee in rms. Restaurant 6:30 am-9 pm. Rm serv. Bar 11-1 am. Ck-out noon. Coin lndry. Meeting rms. Business servs avail. In-rm modem link. Valet serv. Sundries. Gift shop. Barber, beauty shop. Exercise equipt; weight machine, bicycles, sauna. Whirlpool. Refrigerator, microwave, wet bar in suites. Balconies. Cr cds: A, C, D, DS, ER, JCB, MC, V.

D 🏋 ✈ 🐾 SC

★ **PAUL'S MOTOR INN.** (1900 Douglas St, Victoria BC V8T 4K8) 250/382-9231; FAX 250/384-1435. E-mail laurelpoint@ampsc.com; web www.islandnet.com/~cvcprod/laurel.html. 78 rms, 2 story. No A/C. May-Sept: S $83-$113; D $87-$117; each addl $5; under 11 free; lower rates rest of yr. Crib free. TV; cable. Restaurant open 24 hrs. Bar noon-2 am. Ck-out noon. Meeting rms. Business servs avail. Valet serv. Cr cds: A, ER, MC, V.

⊗ 🐾

★ ★ **QUALITY INN HARBOURVIEW.** (455 Belleville St, Victoria BC V8V 1X3) 250/386-2421; FAX 250/383-7603. E-mail grandpac@octonet.com; web www.victoriabc.com/accom/quality. 86 rms, 3 story, 11 kit. units. No A/C. June-Sept: S, D $145-$165; kit. units $160-$180; under 18 free; golf plans; lower rates rest of yr. Crib free. Pet accepted, some restrictions. TV; cable, VCR avail. Complimentary coffee in rms. Restaurant 7 am-10 pm. Bar 11-1 am. Ck-out 11 am. Meeting rms. Business servs avail. In-rm modem link. Bellhops. Valet serv. Sundries. Coin lndry. Free garage parking. Exercise equipt; weights, rowers, sauna. Massage. Indoor pool; wading pool; whirlpool. Opp ocean. Cr cds: A, D, DS, ER, JCB, MC, V.

D 🐾 🏊 🏋 ✈ 🐾 SC

✔★ **STAY 'N SAVE.** (3233 Maple St, Victoria BC V8X 4Y9) at Mayfair Shopping Center. 250/475-7500; FAX 250/475-7599; res: 800/663-0298. 117 rms, 3 story. July-Aug: S, D $99-$119; each addl $10; suites $120-$130; under 16 free; golf plans; lower rates rest of yr. Crib free.

Pet accepted, some restrictions. TV; cable. Complimentary coffee in rms. Restaurant 6:30 am-10 pm. Ck-out 11 am. Coin lndry. Meeting rms. Business servs avail. In-rm modem link. Health club privileges. Cr cds: A, D, ER, MC, V.

D 🐾 ✈ 🐾 SC

Motor Hotels

★ ★ **DAYS INN ON THE HARBOUR.** (427 Belleville St, Victoria BC V8V 1X3) 250/386-3451. E-mail welcome2@daysinn-vic.com. 71 rms, 4 story, 18 kit. units. No A/C. May-mid-Oct: S, D $163-$193; kit. units $173-$203; under 12 free; family, wkly rates; lower rates rest of yr. Crib free. TV; cable, VCR avail (movies). Complimentary coffee in rms. Restaurant 7 am-10 pm. Bar noon to 1:30 am. Ck-out noon. Meeting rms. Business servs avail. Valet serv. Heated pool; whirlpool. Refrigerator, microwave in kit. units. Cr cds: A, D, DS, ER, JCB, MC, V.

🏊 ✈ 🐾 SC

★ ★ **EMBASSY INN.** (520 Menzies St, Victoria BC V8V 2H4) 1 blk S of Inner Harbour. 250/382-8161; FAX 250/382-4224; res: 800/268-8161. 103 rms, 3-4 story, 70 A/C, 45 kits. July-Sept: S $99-$135; D $99-$140; each addl $15; suites $140-$174; kit. units $15 addl; under 14 free; lower rates rest of yr. Crib free. TV; cable (premium). Heated pool. Complimentary coffee in rms. Restaurant 7 am-9:30 pm. Bar 11 am-11 pm. Ck-out 11 am. Coin lndry. Business center. In-rm modem link. Valet serv. Sundries. Free parking. Microwaves avail. Cr cds: A, D, MC, V.

🏊 ✈ 🐾 SC 🏃

★ ★ **ROYAL SCOT INN.** (425 Quebec St, Victoria BC V8V 1W7) 1/2 blk W of Parliament Bldgs. 250/388-5463; FAX 250/388-5452; res: 800/663-7515. E-mail royalscot@commercial.net; web www.com.net /vault/royal/royal.html. 150 kit. suites, 4 story. No A/C. Mid-May-Sept: S, D $120-$305; each addl $15; under 16 free; wkly, monthly rates; lower rates rest of yr. TV; cable, VCR avail (movies $2.50). Indoor pool; whirlpool. Complimentary coffee in rms. Restaurant 7 am-9 pm. Ck-out 11 am. Coin lndry. Meeting rms. Business servs avail. Bellhops. Valet serv. Gift shop. Free covered parking. Exercise equipt; weight machines, bicycle, sauna. Rec rm. Some bathrm phones; microwaves avail. Balconies. Cr cds: A, D, ER, MC, V.

🏊 🏋 ✈ 🐾

Hotels

★ ★ ★ **THE BEDFORD REGENCY.** (1140 Government St, Victoria BC V8W 1Y2) 250/384-6835; FAX 250/386-8930; res: 800/665-6500. E-mail bedfordreg@aol.com. 40 rms, 12 with shower only, 6 story. No A/C. May-early Oct: S, D $165-$215; each addl $25; under 6 free; lower rates rest of yr. Crib free. TV; cable (premium). Continental bkfst. Restaurant 7-11 am. No rm serv. Bar 11:30 am-midnight. Ck-out 11 am. Meeting rms. Business servs avail. Some in-rm whirlpools, fireplaces. Cr cds: A, MC, V.

✈ 🐾 SC

★ ★ **BEST WESTERN CARLTON PLAZA.** (642 Johnson St, Victoria BC V8W 1M6) 250/388-5513; FAX 250/388-5343. 103 rms, 6 story, 47 kit. suites. May-mid-Oct: S, D $129-$149; each addl $20; kit. suites $169-$189; under 18 free; wkly rates; lower rates rest of yr. Crib free. Garage parking; valet $8. TV; cable (premium). Complimentary coffee in rms. Restaurant 7 am-9 pm. Ck-out 11 am. Coin lndry. Business center. In-rm modem link. Shopping arcade. Barber, beauty shop. Health club privileges. Cr cds: A, C, D, DS, ER, JCB, MC, V.

D ⊗ 🐾 SC 🏃

★ ★ **CHÂTEAU VICTORIA.** (740 Burdett Ave, Victoria BC V8W 1B2) 250/382-4221; FAX 250/380-1950; res: 800/663-5891. Web www.chateauvictoria.com. 60 rms, 118 suites, some A/C, 19 story, 49 kits. May-mid-Oct: S $117; D $147; each addl $15; suites $172-$270; under 18 free; package plans; lower rates rest of yr. Crib free. TV; cable (premium); VCR avail (movies). Indoor pool; whirlpool. Complimentary coffee in rms. Restaurants 6:30 am-10 pm. Bar 11:30 am-midnight. Ck-out 11 am. Meeting rms. Business servs avail. In-rm modem link. Free parking. Exercise equipt; weight machine, bicycle. Microwaves avail. Cr cds: A, D, DS, ER, JCB, MC, V.

[D] [≈] [✕] [≈] [⋏] [SC]

★ ★ ★ **CLARION GRAND PACIFIC.** (540 Quebec St, Victoria BC V8V 1W5) 250/386-0450; FAX 250/383-7603. E-mail grandpac@octonet.com; web www.victoriabc.com/accom/clarion. 145 rms, 8 story, 19 suites. June-Sept: S, D $289-$349; suites $369-$589; under 18 free; golf plans; lower rates rest of yr. Crib free. Pet accepted, some restrictions. TV; cable, VCR avail. Complimentary coffee in rms. Restaurant 7 am-10 pm. Rm serv 24 hrs. Bar 11-1 am. Ck-out 11 am. Meeting rms. Business center. In-rm modem link. Concierge. Coin lndry. Free garage parking. 18-hole golf privileges. Exercise rm; instructor, weights, weight machine, sauna. Massage. Indoor pool; wading pool, whirlpool. Refrigerators, minibars. Opp ocean. Cr cds: A, D, DS, ER, JCB, MC, V.

[D] [✔] [✕] [≈] [⋏] [≈] [⋏] [SC] [⚓]

★ ★ ★ **COAST VICTORIA HARBOURSIDE.** (146 Kingston, Victoria BC V8V 1V4) 250/360-1211; FAX 250/360-1418. 132 rms, 8 story. May-Oct: S $220; D $250; each addl $30; suites $270-$560; under 18 free; lower rates rest of yr. Crib free. Pet accepted. TV; cable, VCR avail. 2 pools, 1 indoor; whirlpool. Complimentary coffee in rms. Restaurant 6:30 am-10 pm. Rm serv 24 hrs. Bar. Ck-out noon. Meeting rms. Business servs avail. In-rm modem link. Concierge. Sundries. Valet serv. Exercise equipt; bicycles, weight machine, sauna. Refrigerators; microwaves avail. Balconies. Cr cds: A, C, D, DS, ER, JCB, MC, V.

[D] [≈] [✕] [⋏] [≈] [SC]

★ ★ ★ **EMPRESS.** (721 Government St, Victoria BC V8W 1W5) Inner Harbour area. 250/384-8111; FAX 250/381-4334; res: 800/441-1414. E-mail swilkins @emp.mhs.compuserve.com; web vvv.com/empress/. 475 rms, 7 story. No A/C. Mid-May-Sept: S, D $255-$315; each addl $25; suites $405-$1,700; under 18 free; lower rates rest of yr. Crib free. Garage $14.50. TV; cable (premium), VCR avail. Indoor pool; whirlpool, wading pool. Restaurants 6 am-10 pm. Bar 11:30-1 am; entertainment exc Sun. Ck-out noon. Convention facilities. Business servs avail. In-rm modem link. Shopping arcade. Exercise equipt; weight machine, bicycles, sauna. Minibars; some refrigerators; microwaves avail. Opened in 1908. Cr cds: A, C, D, DS, ER, JCB, MC, V.

[D] [≈] [✕] [⋏] [≈]

★ ★ **EXECUTIVE HOUSE.** (777 Douglas St, Victoria BC V8W 2B5) 250/388-5111; FAX 250/385-1323; res: 800/663-7001. E-mail executivehouse@executivehouse.com; web www.executivehouse.com. 179 rms, 17 story, 100 kits. No A/C. May-mid-Oct: S, D $99-$195; each addl $15; kit. units $15 addl; suites $195-$595; under 18 free; lower rates rest of yr. Pet accepted; $15/day. Garage $2. TV; cable. Complimentary coffee. Restaurant 7 am-10 pm. Bars 11-1 am; entertainment. Ck-out noon. Meeting rm. Business servs avail. Exercise equipt; weights, bicycles, sauna, steam rm. Massage. Whirlpool. Many refrigerators; some bathrm phones. Private patios, balconies. Cr cds: A, D, DS, ER, JCB, MC, V.

[✔] [✕] [≈] [⋏] [SC]

★ ★ ★ **HARBOUR TOWERS.** (345 Quebec St, Victoria BC V8V 1W4) 1 blk S of Inner Harbour. 250/385-2405; FAX 250/385-4453; res: 800/663-5896. E-mail harbour@pacificcoast.net; web www.islandnet.com/~cvcprod/harbour.html. 184 rms, 12 story, 49 kits. No A/C. June-mid-Oct: S $150-$200; D $170-$225; each addl $15; suites $215-$375; under 16 free; lower rates rest of yr. Crib free. Garage parking $2/day. TV; cable (premium). Indoor pool; whirlpool. Complimentary coffee in rms. Restaurant 6:30 am-10 pm. Rm serv to 1 am. Bar 11-1 am; Sat noon-2 am. Ck-out 11 am. Meeting rms. Business center. In-rm modem link. Gift shop. Airport transportation. Exercise equipt; weight machine, bicycles, sauna. Refrigerators, minibars, microwaves. Balconies. Luxury level. Cr cds: A, D, ER, JCB, MC, V.

[D] [≈] [✕] [⋏] [≈] [⋏] [SC] [⚓]

★ ★ ★ **LAUREL POINT INN.** (680 Montreal St, Victoria BC V8V 1Z8) 1 blks W of Ferry Dock. 250/386-8721; FAX 250/386-9547; res: 800/663-7667. E-mail laurelpoint@ampsc.com; web www.islandnet .com/~cvcprod/laurel.html. 202 rms, 4-6 story. Mid June-Oct: S, D $185-$250; each addl $15; suites $350-$650; under 12 free; lower rates rest of

yr. Crib free. TV; cable. Indoor pool; whirlpool, poolside serv. Restaurant 7 am-10:30 pm. Rm serv 24 hrs. Bar 11:30-1:30 am; entertainment. Ck-out noon. Meeting rms. Business servs avail. Gift shop. Free garage parking. Sauna. Private patios, balconies. On harbor. Cr cds: A, D, ER, JCB, MC, V.

[D] [≈] [≈] [⋏]

★ ★ ★ **OAK BAY BEACH.** (1175 Beach Dr, Victoria BC V8S 2N2) 250/598-4556; FAX 250/598-6180; res: 800/668-7758. 51 rms, 3 story. No A/C. June-Sept, mid-Dec-early Jan: S, D $169-$209; each addl $18; suites $239-$399; lower rates rest of yr. Crib free. TV; cable, VCR avail. Restaurant 7 am-9 pm. Bar from 11:30 am. Ck-out noon. Meeting rms. Business servs avail. In-rm modem link. Tennis, golf adj. Some microwaves, bathrm phones. Some balconies. Tudor-style hotel (1927); some four poster beds, many antiques. On beach. Cr cds: A, D, ER, MC, V.

[≈] [⋏]

★ ★ ★ **OCEAN POINTE RESORT, HOTEL & SPA.** (45 Songhees Rd, Victoria BC V9A 6T3) across Johnson St bridge. 250/360-2999; FAX 250/360-1041; res: 800/667-4677. E-mail ocean_pointe@pinc.com; web www.oprhotel.com. 250 rms, 143 with A/C, 8 story, 27 suites. Mid-May-mid-Oct: S, D $219-$279; each addl $15; suites $395-$650; kits. avail; under 13 free; wkly, wkend, hol rates; lower rates rest of yr. Crib free. Pet accepted; $75. TV; cable, VCR avail. Indoor pool; whirlpool, poolside serv. Restaurants 7 am-10 pm (also see THE VICTORIAN). Rm serv 24 hrs. Bar 11-1 am. Ck-out noon. Meeting rms. Business center. In-rm modem link. Concierge. Gift shop. Beauty shop. Lighted tennis. Exercise rm; instructor, weight machines, treadmill, sauna. Spa. Minibars; microwaves avail. Balconies. On harbor. Cr cds: A, C, D, ER, JCB, MC, V.

[D] [✔] [≈] [⋏] [≈] [✕] [⋏] [≈] [⋏] [SC] [⚓]

★ ★ **QUEEN VICTORIA INN.** (655 Douglas St, Victoria BC V8V 2P9) 250/386-1312; FAX 250/381-4312; res: 800/663-7007. E-mail queenvic@ampsc.com; web www.queenvictoriainn.com. 128 rms, 7 story, 20 suites, 84 kit. units. Mid-May-Sept: S, D $110-$150 each addl $20; suites $190-$215; kit. units $15 addl; under 15 free; lower rates rest of yr. Crib free. Garage parking $3/day. TV; cable (premium). Indoor pool. Restaurant 6:30 am-9 pm. Ck-out noon. Business servs avail. Exercise equipt; stair machine, bicycle. Some bathrm phones. Balconies. Cr cds: A, C, D, DS, ER, JCB, MC, V.

[D] [≈] [≈] [⋏] [SC]

★ ★ ★ **RAMADA HUNTINGDON MANOR.** (330 Quebec St, Victoria BC V8V 1W3) 1 blk S of Inner Harbour. 250/381-3456; FAX 250/382-7666; res: 800/663-7557. E-mail huntingdon@visual.net; web www.visual .net/storefront/huntingdon. 116 rms, 40 A/C, 3 story, 58 kits. Mid-June-mid-Sept: S, D $149-$179; each addl $15; suites $169-$229; kit. units $15 addl; under 18 free; wkly rates; lower rates rest of yr. Crib free. TV; cable. Coffee in rms. Restaurant 7 am-9 pm. Bar 3-10 pm. Ck-out 11 am. Coin lndry. Meeting rms. Business servs avail. Sauna. Massage. Whirlpool. Refrigerators, microwaves. Some private patios, balconies. Opp harbor. Cr cds: A, D, DS, ER, MC, V.

[D] [≈] [⋏] [SC]

★ ★ ★ **SWANS.** (506 Pandora Ave, Victoria BC V8W 1N6) 250/361-3310; FAX 250/361-3491; res: 800/668-7926. E-mail swans@islandnet.com; web www.island.net.com/~swans/hotel.htm. 29 rms, 4 story. No A/C. July-Sept: S, D $165-$175; each addl $20; under 12 free; lower rates rest of yr. Crib $15. Garage $8. TV; cable, VCR avail (movies $3.50). Complimentary coffee in rms. Restaurant 7-1 am. Bar 11:30-2:30 am; entertainment Sun-Thurs. Ck-out noon. Coin lndry. Meeting rms. Business servs avail. Refrigerators, microwaves. Some balconies. Brewery, beer & wine shop on premises. Cr cds: A, D, ER, JCB, MC, V.

[D] [≈] [⋏] [SC]

★ ★ ★ **VICTORIA REGENT.** (1234 Wharf St, Victoria BC V8W 3H9) on Inner Harbour. 250/386-2211; FAX 250/386-2622; res: 800/663-7472. E-mail regent@epinc.com. 45 rms, 8 story, 30 suites. July-Sept: S, D $169; each addl $20; suites $219-$695; under 16 free; wkly rates in winter; golf, package plans. Crib free. TV; cable (premium), VCR avail. Restaurant 7 am-11 pm. Ck-out noon. Meeting rms. Business servs avail. In-rm modem link. Free covered parking. Health club privileges. Refrigerators, microwaves; some fireplaces, in-rm whirlpools. Balconies. Marina. View of Inner Harbour & city. Cr cds: A, D, DS, ER, JCB, MC, V.

D ⊠ ☕ SC

Inns

★ ★ ★ **ABIGAIL'S HOTEL.** *(906 McClure St, Victoria BC V8V 3E7)* 250/388-5363; FAX 250/388-7787; res: 800/561-6565. E-mail inn keeper@abigailshotel.com; web www.abigailshotel.com. 16 rms, 4 story. No A/C. No elvtr. S, D $145-$289; each addl $30. Complimentary full bkfst; afternoon refreshments. Restaurant nearby. Ck-out 11 am, ck-in 3-9 pm. Business servs avail. In-rm modem link. Gift shop. Some refrigerators, fireplaces. Renovated Tudor-style building (1930). Antiques. Flower garden. Totally nonsmoking. Cr cds: A, MC, V.

⊠ 🔥

★ ★ **ANDERSEN HOUSE.** *(301 Kingston St, Victoria BC V8V 1V5)* 250/388-4565; FAX 250/388-4563. E-mail andersen@islandnet.com; web www.islandnet.com/~andersen/. 5 rms, 3 with shower only, 3 story, 2 suites, 1 kit. unit. No A/C. Mid-May-mid-Oct: S $145-$185; D $155-$195; each addl $35; suites $165-$205; lower rates rest of yr. Children over 12 yrs only. TV in some rms; cable. Complimentary full bkfst. Complimentary coffee in rms. Restaurant nearby. Ck-out 11 am, ck-in 1 pm. Luggage handling. Street parking. Some refrigerators. Some balconies. Picnic tables. Built in 1891; eclectic mix of antiques and modern art. A 1927 motor yacht is avail as guest rm. Totally nonsmoking. Cr cds: MC, V.

⊠ ⊠

★ ★ ★ **BEACONSFIELD.** *(998 Humboldt St, Victoria BC V8V 2Z8)* 250/384-4044; FAX 250/380-4052. E-mail beaconsfield@island net.com; web www.islandnet.com/beaconsfield. 9 rms, 4 story. No A/C. No elvtr. Rm phones avail. Mid-June-Sept: S, D $200-$350; each addl $65. Complimentary full bkfst; afternoon refreshments. Restaurant nearby. Ck-out 11 am, ck-in 3 pm. Business servs avail. Restored Edwardian mansion (1905); period antique furnishings, stained glass, mahogany floors. Library. Totally nonsmoking. Cr cds: MC, V.

⊠ 🔥

★ ★ **HATERLEIGH HERITAGE INN.** *(243 Kingston, Victoria BC V8V 1V5)* 250/384-9995; FAX 250/384-1935. E-mail paulk@tnet.net; web vvv.com/~paulk. 6 rms, 2 story. No rm phones. June-mid-Oct: S, D $165-$250; lower rates rest of yr. Complimentary full bkfst; afternoon refreshments. Restaurant nearby. Ck-out 11 am, ck-in 4 pm. Luggage handling. Built in 1901; antiques. Totally nonsmoking. Cr cds: MC, V.

⊠ 🔥

★ ★ **HOLLAND HOUSE.** *(595 Michigan St, Victoria BC V8V 1S7)* 250/384-6644; FAX 250/384-6117. Web www.islandnet.com /~holndhus/. 10 rms, 3 story. No A/C. May-Oct: S, D $120-$235; each addl $25; under 4 free; lower rates rest of yr. Crib free. TV; cable. Complimentary full bkfst; afternoon refreshments. Ck-out 11 am, ck-in 2 pm. Business servs avail. Some fireplaces. Balconies. Many antique furnishings; 4-poster beds. Totally nonsmoking. Cr cds: A, MC, V.

⊠ 🔥

✔★ ★ ★ **OLDE ENGLAND INN.** *(429 Lampson St, Victoria BC V9A 5Y9)* via Johnson St Bridge. 250/388-4353; FAX 250/382-8311. 60 rms, 3 story, 6 kits. No A/C. No elvtr. Apr-Oct: S, D $82-$210; each addl $10; lower rates rest of yr. Crib $10. TV; cable. Restaurant 8 am-10 pm. Ck-out 11 am. Business servs avail. Luggage handling. Gift shop. Microwaves avail. Tudor-style mansion (1909); many antiques, including canopied beds used by European monarchs. Replica of William Shakespeare's 16th-century birthplace on grounds. Cr cds: A, C, D, DS, ER, JCB, MC, V.

⊠ 🔥

★ ★ ★ **PRIOR HOUSE.** *(620 St Charles, Victoria BC V8S 3N7)* 250/592-8847; FAX 250/592-8223. E-mail innkeeper@priorhouse.com; web www.priorhouse.com. 6 air-cooled rms, 3 story. Some rm phones. May-Oct: S, D $115-$265; each addl $35; 2-day min wkends, Aug; lower rates rest of yr. Complimentary full bkfst; afternoon refreshments. Restaurant nearby. Ck-out noon, ck-in 4 pm. Business servs avail. Lawn games.

Fireplaces; microwave avail. Balconies. Edwardian mansion (1912) built by King's representative. Crystal chandeliers, oak woodwork. Totally nonsmoking. Cr cds: MC, V.

⊠ 🔥

★ ★ ★ ★ **SOOKE HARBOUR HOUSE.** *(1528 Whiffen Spit Rd, Sooke Harbour BC V0S 1N0)* 23 mi NW via Hwy 1A & Hwy 14, thru Sooke, left on Whiffen Spit Rd. 250/642-3421; res: 800/889-9688; FAX 250/642-6988. E-mail shh@islandnet.com; web sookenet.com/shh. This elegant country inn by the sea offers all the amenities of an exclusive resort with a homey, yet elegant, atmosphere. All 13 rooms have an ocean view, balcony or terrace and fireplace. Staff will arrange everything from scuba diving excursions to fishing charters. 13 rms, 1 with shower only, 2 story. No A/C. Apr-Oct, MAP: S, D $290-$360; each addl $35; under 12 free; lower rates rest of yr. Closed 3 wks Jan. Crib free. Pet accepted; $20. TV avail; cable (premium), VCR avail (movies). Whirlpool. Restaurant (see SOOKE HARBOUR HOUSE). Rm serv 24 hrs. Ck-out noon, ck-in 3 pm. Luggage handling. Business servs avail. Free airport transportation. Massage. Lawn games. Refrigerators; microwaves avail. Balconies. Picnic tables. On ocean. Totally nonsmoking. Cr cds: A, D, ER, JCB, MC, V.

D ✦ ⊠ 🔥

Resort

★ ★ ★ ★ **THE AERIE.** *(600 Ebedra Ln, Malahat BC V0R 2L0)* 30 km (20 mi) N on Rte 1, Spectacle Lake turn. 250/743-7115; FAX 250/743-4766. E-mail aerie@relaischateaux.fr; web www.aerie.bc.ca. This resort is perched high above Malahat with views of the San Juan Islands and the Olympic Mountains. Guest rooms feature sleigh beds with down duvets, soaking tubs and handmade wood furniture. 23 rms, 3 story, 13 suites. May-mid-Oct: S, D $120-$245; each addl $25; suites $275-$395; 2-day min wkends, hols; lower rates rest of yr. Children over 10 yrs only. TV; cable (premium). Indoor pool; whirlpool. Complimentary full bkfst. Complimentary coffee in rms. Restaurant (see AERIE DINING ROOM). Rm serv. Ck-out noon, ck-in 3 pm. Bellhops. Business servs avail. In-rm modem link. Tennis. 18-hole golf privileges, greens fee $45, putting green, driving range. Exercise equipt; weight machine, bicycle, sauna. Spa. Some refrigerators. Some balconies. Picnic tables. Totally nonsmoking. Cr cds: A, D, ER, MC, V.

🏂 👣 🏊 🏋 🐾 ⊠ 🔥

Restaurants

★ ★ ★ **AERIE DINING ROOM.** *(See The Aerie Resort)* 250/743-7115. E-mail aerie@relaischateaux.fr; web www.aerie.bc.ca. Hrs: 6-9:30 pm. Res accepted. French menu. Bar. A la carte entrees: dinner $27-$29.50. Complete meals: dinner $60. Child's meals. Specializes in fresh seafood, lamb, game. Parking. Outdoor dining. Elegant formal dining rm with view of Olympic Mts. Cr cds: A, D, ER, MC, V.

D

★ ★ ★ **ANTOINE'S.** *(2 Centennial Square, Victoria BC V8W 1P7)* adj City Hall. 250/384-7055. Hrs: 11:30 am-2 pm, 5:30-10 pm. Closed Jan 1. Res required. Continental menu. Bar. Wine list. A la carte entrees: lunch $10-$12, dinner $22-$30. Complete meals: dinner $22-$45. Specializes in local seafood. Parking. Overlooks large fountain in Centennial square. Cr cds: A, MC, V.

⊐ ♥

★ ★ ★ **BLUE CRAB BAR & GRILL.** *(See Coast Victoria Harbourside Hotel)* 250/480-1999. Hrs: 6:30-11 pm; Sun brunch 11 am-2:30 pm; early-bird dinner 5-6:30 pm. Res accepted. Seafood menu. Bar 11-1 am. Semi-a la carte: bkfst $5-$9.25, lunch $8.50-$14.25, dinner $16-$27. Sun brunch $10. Child's meals. Specializes in fresh local seafood. Contemporary decor; view of harbor and skyline. Totally nonsmoking. Cr cds: A, C, D, DS, ER, JCB, MC, V.

D SC

★ ★ ★ **CAMILLE'S.** *(45 Bastion Square, Victoria BC V8W 1J1)* 250/381-3433. Hrs: 5:30-10 pm. Closed Jan 1, Dec 24, 25. Res accepted.

Bar. Semi-a la carte: dinner $14.95-$21.95. Specializes in seafood. Entertainment. Romantic atmosphere. Cr cds: A, MC, V.

D

★ ★ ★ **DEEP COVE CHALET.** *(11190 Chalet Rd, Victoria BC V8L 4R4) 18 mi N on 17 to 17A (Warn Rd). 250/656-3541.* Web www.kcorp.com/~. Hrs: noon-2:30 pm, 5:30-10 pm. Closed Mon. Res accepted. French menu. Bar. Wine cellar. Semi-a la carte: lunch $15-$35, dinner $20.50-$70. Complete meals: lunch $15-$22, dinner $20-$40. Many daily specials. Pianist Fri, Sat. Parking. Outdoor dining. View of Deep Cove Bay. Built in 1914; originally teahouse for a railroad station. Cr cds: A, MC, V.

D

★ ★ **GATSBY MANSION.** *(309 Belleville St, Victoria BC V8V 1X2) just W of Parliament Bldg. 250/388-9191.* E-mail huntingdon@visual.net; web vvv.com/storefront/huntingdon. Hrs: 10 am-11 pm. Res accepted. Continental menu. Serv bar. Semi-a la carte: bkfst, lunch $4.95-$8.95, dinner $14.95-$23.95. Specializes in seafood, steak, poultry. Parking. Outdoor dining. Restored 3-story mansion (1897); antiques; garden. Cr cds: A, D, ER, MC, V.

★ ★ **HERALD STREET CAFFE.** *(546 Herald St, Victoria BC V8W 1S6) 250/381-1441.* Hrs: 11:30 am-3 pm, 5:30-10:30 pm; Mon, Tues from 5:30 pm; Fri, Sat to midnight; Sun brunch 11 am-3 pm. Res accepted. Eclectic menu. Bar. Semi-a la carte: lunch $7-$11, dinner $11.95-$32.95. Sun brunch $8.50-$10.95. Specializes in seafood. Eclectic decor. Cr cds: A, ER, MC, V.

D

★ ★ **IL TERRAZZO.** *(555 Johnson St, Victoria BC V8W 1M2) at Waddington Alley. 250/361-0028.* Hrs: 11:30 am-3:30 pm, 5-11 pm; Fri, Sat to midnight; Sun 5-10 pm. Closed Jan 1, Dec 25. Res accepted. No A/C. Italian menu. Bar. A la carte entrees: lunch $7.95-$11.95, dinner $13.95-$21.95. Child's meals. Specializes in wood oven-baked meats and game, Northern Italian dishes. Own baking, pasta. Outdoor dining. Two-level dining area features fireplaces, wood-fired pizza oven. Cr cds: A, MC, V.

D

✔ ★ **INDIA TANDOORI HUT.** *(1548 Fort St, Victoria BC V8S 5J2) 250/370-1880.* Hrs: 11 am-2 pm, 5-9:30 pm; Sat brunch to 2 pm. Closed Dec 25. Res accepted. No A/C. East Indian menu. Bar. A la carte entrees: lunch $5-$18, dinner $11-$19. Sat brunch $7.99. Specialties: tandoori chicken, lamb curry, chicken marsala. Own baking. Outdoor dining. Colorful Indian decor. Cr cds: MC, V.

D SC

✔ ★ ★ **J & J WONTON NOODLE HOUSE.** *(1012 Fort St, Victoria BC V8V 3K4) 250/383-0680.* Hrs: 11 am-2:30 pm, 3:30-8:30 pm. Closed Sun; some major hols. Chinese menu. Bar. Semi-a la carte: lunch $3.95-$11, dinner $5.95-$16.95. Child's meals. Specialties: spicy beef noodle soup, sizzling hot pan prawns, spicy tofu hot pot. Own baking, noodles. Casual Chinese decor. Totally nonsmoking. Cr cds: MC, V.

D

✔ ★ ★ **JACK LEE'S CHINESE VILLAGE.** *(755 Finlayson St, Victoria BC V8T 4W4) 250/384-8151.* Hrs: 11:30 am-9:30 pm; Fri, Sat to 10:30 pm; Sun 4-8:30 pm. Closed first 2 wks Jan, Thanksgiving, Dec 25. Res accepted. Chinese menu. Bar. Semi-a la carte: lunch $7.50. Complete meals: dinner $12.95-$15. Specializes in Szechuan & Cantonese dishes. Parking. Family-owned. Cr cds: A, MC, V.

D

★ ★ **JAPANESE VILLAGE STEAK & SEAFOOD HOUSE.** *(734 Broughton St, Victoria BC V8W 1E1) 250/382-5165.* Hrs: 11:30 am-2 pm, 5-10:30 pm; Sat 5-11:30 pm; Sun 5-10 pm. Closed major hols. Res accepted. Japanese menu. Serv bar. Complete meals: lunch $6.50-$11.50, dinner $16.50-$34.50. Child's meals. Specialties: teppan-style

steak, salmon, lobster. Entertainment Sun evenings. Tableside cooking, sushi bar. Japanese decor. Cr cds: A, D, ER, JCB, MC, V.

★ ★ **LA VILLE D'IS.** *(26 Bastion Sq, Victoria BC V8W 1H9) 250/388-9414.* Hrs: 11:30 am-2 pm, 5:30-10 pm; Sat from 5:30. Closed Sun; also Jan. Res accepted. No A/C. French menu. Serv bar. A la carte entrees: lunch $7-$18, dinner $18.75-$26. Complete meals: lunch $9.95-$19.95. Child's meals. Specializes in mussels, rack of lamb, fresh lobster soufflé. Outdoor dining. Brittany decor. Cr cds: A, D, ER, MC, V.

★ ★ ★ **THE MARINA.** *(1327 Beach Dr, Victoria BC V8S 2N4) 250/598-8555.* Hrs: 11:30 am-10 pm; Fri, Sat to 11 pm; Sun from 10 am; Sun brunch to 2:30 pm. Closed Dec 25. Res accepted. Continental menu. Bar. Wine list. Semi-a la carte: lunch $7.25-$13.95, dinner $9.95-$24.95. Sun brunch $21.95. Child's meals. Specialties: oyster Jim, seafood hot pot, chocolate fetish. Own baking. Outdoor dining. Two-level dining area with large windows overlooking marina. Cr cds: A, D, ER, JCB, MC, V.

D

★ ★ ★ **MICHELINE'S.** *(512 Yates St, Victoria BC V8W 1K8) 250/388-0188.* Hrs: 5:30-10:30 pm. Closed Jan 1, Dec 25; Sun, Mon Nov-Apr; also mid-Jan-mid-Feb. Res accepted. No A/C. Continental menu. Bar. Wine list. A la carte entrees: dinner $13.50-$25. Child's meals. Specializes in fresh seafood, rack of lamb. Own baking, ice cream, sorbet. Old bldg with exposed brick wall, orginal artwork. Cr cds: MC, V.

D

★ ★ **REBECCA'S.** *(1127 Wharf St, Victoria BC V8W 1T7) 250/380-6999.* Hrs: 11:30 am-11 pm; Sun from 11 am; Sun brunch to 3 pm. Closed Jan 1, Dec 24, 25. Res accepted. Bar. A la carte entrees: lunch $5.95-$11.95, dinner $9.95-$22.95. Sun brunch $5.95-$10.95. Specializes in local seafood, breads, desserts. Overlooks harbor; open kitchen. Family-owned. Cr cds: A, MC, V.

D

★ ★ ★ **SOOKE HARBOUR HOUSE.** *(See Sooke Harbour House Inn) 250/642-3421.* E-mail shh@islandnet.com; web sookenet.com/shh. Well worth a trip from Victoria, this restaurant in a 1931 clapboard farmhouse uses just-caught seafood and some 200 varieties of herbs grown on the property. Sitting on the terrace on a summer evening, you may catch a glimpse of the sea mammals that play nearby. Continental menu. Specializes in fresh seafood. Hrs: 5:30-9:30 pm. Res accepted. Bar. A la carte entrees (Apr-Oct): dinner $20-$30. Semi-a la carte (winter): dinner $40-$45. Cr cds: A, D, ER, JCB, MC, V.

D

✔ ★ ★ **SPINNAKER'S BREW PUB.** *(308 Catherine St, Victoria BC V9A 3S8) across Johnson St bridge. 250/386-2739.* E-mail spinnakers@spinnakers.com; web www.spinnakers.com. Hrs: 7 am-11 pm. Closed Dec 25. Res accepted. No A/C. Bar from 10 am. Semi-a la carte: bkfst $1.99-$8.95, lunch $4.50-$11.95, dinner $4.50-$14.95. Child's meals. Specializes in pasta, pot pies, fish & chips. Own baking, pasta. Jazz, blues Fri, Sat. Outdoor dining. Views of harbor and city skyline; brewing vats can be seen from bar. Cr cds: A, ER, MC, V.

D

★ ★ ★ **THE VICTORIAN.** *(See Ocean Pointe Resort & Spa Hotel) 250/360-5800.* E-mail ocean-pointe@pinc.com; web www.oprhotel.com. Hrs: 6-10:30 pm. Closed Sun; also 1st 3 wks Jan. Res accepted. Bar 11-1 am. A la carte entrees: dinner $21-$27. Complete meals: dinner $39-$49. Child's meals. Specializes in fresh seafood, rack of lamb. Valet parking. View of Inner and Outer Harbour. Totally nonsmoking. Cr cds: A, C, D, ER, JCB, MC, V.

D

Whistler (D-3)

(See also Vancouver)

Pop 4,500 (est) **Elev** 2,200 ft **Area code** 604 **Web** www.whistler-resort .com

Information Whistler Resort Assn, 4010 Whistler Way, V0N 1B4, phone 604/932-3928 or 800/944-7853; or the Activity & Information Centre, phone 604/932-2394.

The winning combination of Blackcomb and Whistler mountains makes this an internationally famous ski area. It is also a popular summer vacation area. Five lakes dot the valley in Whistler, offering ample opportunity to fish, swim, boardsail, canoe, kayak, sail, or waterski; all of the lakes are accessible by the Valley Trail network that winds its way through Whistler.

The alpine slopes for a time give way to extensive hiking and mountain biking trails, but even in summer there is skiing to be found; Whistler is where enthusiasts will find the only lift-serviced, summertime public glacier skiing in North America.

What to See and Do

Skiing. Patrol, school, sport shop; snowmaking; cafeterias, restaurants, bars; nursery, lodge. Cross-country skiing (17.5 mi), heliskiing, snowboarding, sleigh rides, snowshoeing. Multiday, dual-mountain rates. (Mid-Nov-Apr, daily) Gondola & some lifts also operate in summer.

Blackcomb. 6 high-speed quad chairlifts (1 covered), 3 triple chairlifts, 3 handletows, 2 T-bars, platter lift, magic carpet lift. More than 100 runs; longest run 8 mi, vertical drop 5,280 ft. Glacier skiing (mid-June-Aug, weather permitting). High-speed gondola.

Whistler. 3 high-speed quad, double, 3 triple chairlifts, 2 handletows, 2 T-bars, platter pull. More than 100 runs; longest run 7 mi, vertical drop 5,020 ft. 2 high-speed gondolas.

Motor Hotels

★ ★ **CRYSTAL LODGE.** (4154 Village Green, Whistler BC V0N 1B0) 604/932-2221; FAX 604/932-2635; res: 800/667-3363. 137 rms, 2-3 story, 40 kit. suites. Late Jan-Apr: S, D $195-$230; each addl $25; kit. suites $250-$270; suites from $450; ski, golf plans; higher rates Christmas hols; lower rates rest of yr. Crib free. Garage parking $7. TV; cable, VCR avail. Heated pool; whirlpools, steam rm, poolside serv. Restaurant 7 am-10 pm. Bar noon-1 am; entertainment. Ck-out 10 am. Coin lndry. Meeting rms. Business servs avail. Bellhops. Valet serv. Concierge. Shopping arcade. Airport, RR station transportation. Downhill/x-country ski adj. Cr cds: A, D, DS, ER, JCB, MC, V.

★ **LISTEL WHISTLER HOTEL.** (4121 Village Green, Whistler BC V0N 1B4) 4121 Village Green. 604/932-1133; FAX 604/932-8383; res: 800/663-5472. 98 rms, 3 story. Mid-Dec-mid-Apr: S, D $229; each addl $30; suites $395; family rates; ski, golf plans; higher rates New Year's hols; lower rates rest of yr. Crib free. Parking $8; valet. TV; cable. Sauna. Heated pool; whirlpool. Restaurant 7-10:30 am, 5:30-11 pm. Bar 11:30 am-midnight. Ck-out 10 am. Coin lndry. Meeting rms. Business servs avail. Bellhops. Valet serv. Sundries. Gift shop. Downhill/x-country ski adj. Refrigerators; bathrm phone in suites. Cr cds: A, C, D, DS, ER, JCB, MC, V.

Hotels

★ ★ ★ **CHATEAU WHISTLER RESORT.** (4599 Chateau Blvd., Whistler BC V0N 1B4) 604/938-8000; FAX 604/938-2020; res: 800/441-1414. 342 rms, 10-12 story. Mid-Dec-mid-May: S, D $350-$375; each addl $30; suites $475-$1,100; under 17 free; ski, golf plans; higher rates Christmas hols; lower rates rest of yr. Crib free. Pet accepted; $10. Valet parking $15. TV; cable. Indoor/outdoor pool; whirlpool, poolside serv. Supervised child's activities (June-Sept). Restaurants 7 am-11 pm. Rm serv 24 hrs. Bar 11 am-midnight; entertainment, dancing. Ck-out 11 am. Meeting rms. Concierge. Shopping arcade. Tennis, pro. 18-hole golf, greens fee $109 (incl cart), pro, putting green. Downhill/x-country ski adj. Exercise equipt; weights, rowers, sauna. Refrigerators avail. Minibars; some bathrm phones. Large, chateau-style hotel at foot of Blackcomb Mt. Cr cds: A, D, DS, ER, JCB, MC, V.

★ ★ ★ **DELTA WHISTLER RESORT.** (4050 Whistler Way, Whistler BC V0N 1B0) 604/932-1982; FAX 604/932-7332; res: 800/268-1133. 292 rms, 8 story, 99 kit. units. Early Dec-mid-Apr: S, D $335; each addl $30; suites $470-$595; kit. units $390; family rates; ski, golf plans; higher rates Christmas hols; lower rates rest of yr. Crib free. Pet accepted. Garage parking $12. TV; cable (premium). Pool; whirlpool, poolside serv. Complimentary tea, coffee. Restaurant 6 am-10 pm. Bar 11-1 am. Ck-out 11 am. Coin lndry. Convention facilities. Business servs avail. Concierge. Shopping arcade. Indoor tennis, pro. Downhill/x-country ski adj. Exercise equipt; weights, stair machine, steam rm. Minibars; some bathrm phones. Rms overlook valley, mountains. Cr cds: A, C, D, ER, JCB, MC, V.

Restaurants

★ ★ ★ **LA RUA.** (4557 Blackcomb Way, Whistler BC V0N 1B0) In Le Chamois Hotel. 604/932-5011. Hrs: 5:30-11 pm. Res required. Continental menu. Bar. Wine cellar. Semi-a la carte: dinner $13.95-$24.95. Specializes in Northwestern cuisine, seafood. Valet parking. Outdoor dining. Formal dining in Mediterranean-style decor; many antiques. Jacket. Totally nonsmoking. Cr cds: A, D, ER, JCB, MC, V.

★ ★ **RIMROCK CAFE.** (2101 Whistler Rd, Whistler BC V0N 1B0) 604/932-5565. Hrs: 6-10 pm. Res accepted. No A/C. Bar. Semi-a la carte: dinner $16-$25. Specializes in fresh Northwest seafood, oysters. Parking. Outdoor dining. Works of local artists. Built on and around a very large rock. Cr cds: A, MC, V.

★ ★ ★ **RISTORANTE ARAXI.** (4222 Village Square, Whistler BC V0N 1B4) Whistler Village Square. 604/932-4540. Hrs: 10:30 am-3 pm, 5:30-10:30 pm. Res accepted. Italian menu. Bar. Wine list. A la carte: lunch $8-$12.95, dinner $10.50-$19.95. Specializes in fresh salmon in pastry, fresh grilled double lamb chops, fresh game. Outdoor dining. Mediterranean decor. Cr cds: A, MC, V.

✔ ★ **SUSHI VILLAGE.** (4272 Mountain Square, Whistler BC V0N 1B4) Westbrook Hotel, 2nd floor. 604/932-3330. Hrs: noon-2:30 pm, 5-10 pm; summer hrs vary. Japanese menu. Bar. Complete meals: lunch $7.95-$13.25, dinner $7.95-$31.25. Specialties: sushi, chicken teriyaki. Sushi bar. Tatami rms or traditional dining facilities. Cr cds: A, D, ER, JCB, MC, V.

★ ★ **TRATTORIA DI UMBERTO.** (4417 Sundial Place, Whistler BC V0N 1B0) 604/932-5858. Hrs: noon-2:30 pm, 5:30-10 pm. Res accepted. Italian menu. Bar. Semi-a la carte: lunch $5-$15, dinner $5-$26. Child's meals. Specialties: rack of lamb, prawns sauteed in tomato & garlic sauce, Tuscan cuisine. Outdoor dining. Large tile mosaic imported from the Vatican. Cr cds: A, D, ER, JCB, MC, V.

★ ★ ★ **VAL D'ISÈRE.** (Whistler Village Centre, Whistler BC V0N 1B0) St Andrews House, 2nd floor. 604/932-4666. Hrs: 5:30-10:30 pm. Closed mid-Oct-mid-Nov. Res accepted. No A/C. French country menu. Wine list. Semi-a la carte: dinner $14.50-$22.50. Specialties: venison, Alsace-style onion pie. Overlooks large courtyard. Cr cds: A, D, ER, JCB, MC, V.

Province of Manitoba

Pop 1,026,241 **Land area** 211,470 sq mi (547,705 sq km) **Capital** Winnipeg **Web** www.gov.mb.ca/travel-manitoba

Information Travel Manitoba, Dept RK8, 155 Carlton St, 7th Floor, Winnipeg R3C 3H8; 204/945-3777 or 800/665-0040, ext RK8.

Manitoba is the most eastern of Canada's three prairie provinces. The capital city, Winnipeg, houses more than half of the province's population. Much of the remainder of the province is unspoiled recreational area. Entry into Manitoba can be made from Ontario on the east, Saskatchewan on the west or from Minnesota and North Dakota on the south.

Many summer festivals are held that reflect the varied ethnic settlements in the province. Most representative of all ethnic backgrounds is Folklorama, a festival of the nations, which takes place in Winnipeg in August.

Manitoba is also known for its 12 provincial parks and numerous recreation and heritage parks. Riding Mountain National Park is located near Dauphin. Fishing is good from May to September and water-related activities can be enjoyed in the many resorts and beaches on Lake Winnipeg, Lake Manitoba and lakes in the provincial parks.

Outstanding attractions in Winnipeg include the zoo in Assiniboine Park, the Forks National Historic Site, the Manitoba Museum of Man and Nature and the Winnipeg Art Gallery. The internationally acclaimed Royal Winnipeg Ballet, the Winnipeg Symphony Orchestra, the Manitoba Opera and the Manitoba Theatre Centre have made Winnipeg a mecca for all who enjoy fine music and theater.

Manitoba observes Central Standard Time and Daylight Saving Time in summer.

In addition to national holidays, Manitoba observes Civic Holiday (1st Mon Aug).

Seat belts are mandatory for all persons anywhere in vehicle. Children under 5 years or 50 pounds in weight must be in an approved safety seat anywhere in vehicle. For further information phone 204/945-4603.

Brandon

Pop 42,000 (est) **Elev** 1,342 ft (409 m) **Area code** 204 **E-mail** bedb@docker.com **Web** www.docker.com/~bedb/brandon.html

Information Brandon Economic Development Board, 1043 Rosser Ave, R7A 0L5; 204/728-3287 or 888/799-1111.

Brandon has been named the "Wheat City" in honour of its rich agricultural heritage and reputation as a prosperous farming community. It is also the setting for the province's largest agricultural fairs.

What to See and Do

Commonwealth Air Training Plan Museum. Display of World War II aircraft, vehicles; photos, uniforms, flags and other mementos of Air Force training conducted in Canada (1940-1945) under the British Commonwealth Air Training Plan. (Daily) McGill Field, Hangar #1. Phone 204/727-2444. ¢¢

Annual Events

Royal Manitoba Winter Fair. Keystone Centre. Manitoba's largest winter fair. Equestrian events, heavy horses, entertainment. Late Mar.

Manitoba Summer Fair. Keystone Centre. Competition, children's entertainment, midway, dancing. June.

Manitoba Fall Fair. Keystone Centre. Manitoba's largest livestock show and sale; tractor pull, rodeo. Oct.

Motels

✔★★ **COLONIAL INN.** *(1944 Queens Ave, Brandon MB R7B 0T1)* 204/728-8532; FAX 204/727-5969. 87 rms, 2 story. S $42.95; D $51.95-$53.95. Crib free. TV; cable, VCR avail (movies). Indoor pool; wading pool, whirlpool. Restaurant 6 am-9 pm; Sun 7 am-8 pm. Ck-out noon. Business servs avail. Valet serv. Cr cds: A, C, D, ER, MC, V.

★ **COMFORT INN.** *(925 Middleton Ave, Brandon MB R7C 1A8)* 204/727-6232; FAX 204/727-2246. 81 rms, 2 story. Apr-Oct: S $56.99-$78.99; D $64.99-$86.99; each addl $4; under 18 free; wkend rates; lower rates rest of yr. Crib free. Pet accepted. TV; cable. Complimentary coffee in lobby. Complimentary continental bkfst. Restaurant nearby. Ck-out 11 am. Business servs avail. In-rm modem link. Sundries. Valet serv. Cr cds: A, D, DS, ER, JCB, MC, V.

★ **REDWOOD MOTOR INN.** *(345 18th St N, Brandon MB R7A 6Z2)* 204/728-2200. 60 rms. S $44.95; D $49.95-$54.95. TV; cable, VCR avail (movies). Indoor pool; whirlpool. Complimentary coffee. Restaurant nearby. Ck-out noon. Business servs avail. In-rm modem link. Sundries. Cr cds: A, C, D, ER, MC, V.

Motor Hotels

★★ **ROYAL OAK INN.** *(3130 Victoria Ave W, Brandon MB R7B 0N2)* 204/728-5775; FAX 204/726-5828; res: 800/852-2709 (MB). 96 rms, 2 story. S $64-$82; D, suites $72-$82; each addl $10; under 17 free; package plans. Pet accepted. TV; cable, VCR avail (movies). Indoor pool; wading pool, whirlpool, poolside serv. Restaurant 7 am-10 pm; Sun 8 am-10 pm. Bar 11:30 am-midnight. Ck-out noon. Coin lndry. Meeting rms. Business servs avail. Valet serv. Sundries. RR station, bus depot transportation. Exercise equipt; bicycles, rower. Cr cds: A, C, D, ER, MC, V.

★★★ **VICTORIA INN.** *(3550 Victoria Ave W, Brandon MB R7B 2R4)* 204/725-1532; FAX 204/727-8282; res: 800/852-2710 (MB). 131 rms, 2 story. S $60.95-$75.95; D $68.95-$85.95; suites $75.95; studio rms $75-$125; package plans. Crib free. Pet accepted.TV; cable. Indoor pool; whirlpool, poolside serv. Restaurant 7 am-10 pm; Sun 8 am-9 pm. Rm serv. Bar 11:30-2 am. Ck-out noon. Meeting rms. Business servs avail. In-rm modem link. Sundries. Exercise equipt; weights, bicycles, sauna. Poolside balconies. Cr cds: A, D, ER, MC, V.

Inn

✔★ **THE CASTLE.** *(149 2nd Ave, Minnedosa MB R0J 1E0)* 204/867-2830. 4 rms (1 shared bath), 2 story. S $45; D $55-$60; each addl $10; suites $90; under 5 free. Pet accepted. TV in sitting rm. Complimentary full bkfst. Restaurant nearby. Ck-out noon, ck-in 1 pm. Downhill ski 5 mi; x-country 2 mi. Built in 1901; antiques, art collection. Totally nonsmoking. Cr cds: MC.

Restaurant

★★★ **KOKONAS.** *(1011 Rosser Ave, Brandon MB)* in Scotia Towers. 204/727-4395. Hrs: 11:30 am-11 pm; Sat from 11:30 am; Sun 5-9 pm. Res accepted. Continental menu. Bar to 1 am. Semi-a la carte: lunch $5.25-$10.95, dinner $8.95-$29.95. Lunch buffet $7.95. Specializes in steak, seafood. Nightly prime rib buffet. Salad bar. Own pastries. Cr cds: A, D, ER, MC, V.

D

Turtle Mountain Provincial Park

(For accommodations see Brandon, MB; also see Bottineau, ND)

(Adjacent to International Peace Garden on US-Canada border)

Turtle Mountain is one of Manitoba's smaller provincial parks, with 47,000 acres (19,020 hectares) of forested hills, ponds and lakes. Its lakes provide a good environment for western painted turtle, beaver, muskrat and mink. Arbor and Eagle islands have stands of elm, oak and ash that have not been touched by fire, thereby remaining excellent examples of mature deciduous forests. Swimming, hiking trails, interpretive programs, fishing and boating are available, as well as snowmobile and cross-country skiing trails and a winter day-use area at Lake Adam. Camping (primitive and improved) at Lake Adam, Lake William, and Lake Max campgrounds (hookups, dump stations).

Not far from the park is the town of Boissevain, where the annual Canadian Turtle Derby is held in mid-July. A large statue of Tommy Turtle welcomes the visitor at the south end of town. For further information phone 204/534-7204.

Winnipeg

Pop 650,000 (est) **Elev** 915 ft (279 m) **Area code** 204 **E-mail** wpginfo@tourism.winnipeg.mb.ca **Web** www.tourism.winnipeg.mb.ca
Information Tourism Winnipeg, 320-25 Forks Market Rd, R3C 4S8; 204/943-1970 or 800/665-2004.

Winnipeg, the provincial capital, is situated in the heart of the continent and combines the sophistication and friendliness of east and west. The city offers much for any visitor, including relaxing cruises on the Assiniboine and Red rivers, Rainbow Stage summer theater in Kildonan Park, the Manitoba Theatre Centre, the Winnipeg Symphony, the Manitoba Opera and the renowned Royal Winnipeg Ballet. Sports fans will enjoy the Blue Bombers in football and the Manitoba Moose hockey team. Shopping, nightlife, gourmet restaurants—Winnipeg has it all.

What to See and Do

"Dalnavert." Restored Victorian residence (1895) of Sir Hugh John Macdonald, premier of Manitoba, depicting lifestyle and furnishings of the period. Gift shop. Guided tours (Mar-Dec, Tues-Thurs, Sat & Sun; rest of yr, Sat & Sun only) 61 Carlton St. Phone 204/943-2835. ¢¢

Assiniboine Park. A 376-acre (152-hectare) park features colorful English and formal gardens; the Leo Mol Sculpture Garden; conservatory with floral displays; duck pond; playgrounds; picnic sites; cricket and field hockey area; refreshment pavilion; miniature train; bicycle paths; fitness trail. **Assiniboine Park Zoo** has collection of rare and endangered species, tropical mammals, birds and reptiles; children's discovery area featuring variety of young animals (daily; fee exc Tues). Park (daily). 2355 Corydon Ave. Phone 204/986-3989. Park **Free.**

Birds Hill Provincial Park. A 8,275-acre (3,350-hectare) park situated on a glacial formation called an *eskar.* Large population of white-tailed deer; many orchid species. Interpretive, hiking, bridle, bicycle trails; snowshoe, snowmobile, cross-country skiing trails (winter). Interpretive programs. Camping, swimming and picnicking at 81½-acre (33-hectare) lake (seasonal). Riding stables (phone 204/222-1137). (Daily) 8 mi N on Hwy 59. Phone 204/222-9151. Per vehicle (May-Sept) ¢¢

⭐ Centennial Centre. Complex includes concert hall, planetarium, Museum of Man and Nature, Manitoba Theatre Centre Building. 555 Main St. For free tours of concert hall phone 204/956-1360.

Manitoba Museum of Man & Nature. Seven galleries interpret Manitoba's human and natural history: Orientation; Earth History (geological background); Grasslands (prairie); Arctic-Subarctic; Boreal Forest; *Nonsuch* (full-size replica of a 17th-century ship); and Urban. (Victoria Day-Labour Day, daily; rest of yr, daily exc Mon) 190 Rupert Ave. Phone 204/956-2830 or 204/943-3139 (program information). ¢¢ Also here is

Manitoba Planetarium. Circular, multipurpose audiovisual theater. Wide variety of shows; subjects include UFOs, cosmic catastrophes and the edge of the universe. In the **Touch the Universe Gallery,** visitors can learn about science through hands-on exhibits (separate admission fee). (Same days as museum) Phone 204/943-3142 (recording). ¢¢

Legislative Building. Example of neoclassical architecture. Grounds contain statues of Queen Victoria, Lord Selkirk, George Cartier. Tours (June-Aug, Mon-Fri; Sept-June, by appt) Broadway & Osborne. Phone 204/945-5813. **Free.**

Lower Fort Garry National Historic Site. Hudson's Bay Company fur trade post restored to the 1850s. Original buildings: blacksmith shop, farmhouse, Ross cottage, furloft, Governor's house, sales shop; indigenous encampment. Visitor center with exhibits and artifacts of the fur trade society; costumed tour guides. Restaurant, gift shop. (Mid-May-Labour Day, daily) 20 mi (32 km) N on Hwy 9. Phone 204/785-6050. ¢¢

Oak Hammock Marsh Wildlife Management Area. More than 8,000 acres (3,238 hectares) of marshland and grassland wildlife habitat. Attracts up to 300,000 ducks and geese during spring (Apr-mid-May) and fall migration (Sept-Oct). nature trails; picnic sites; marsh boardwalk; viewing mounds, drinking water. Conservation center with displays, interpretive programs (daily; fee). 14 mi (23 km) N via Hwy 7 or 8, then 5 mi (8 km) to Hwy 67. Phone 204/945-6784. **Free.**

Paddlewheel/Gray Line/River Rouge boat & bus tours. Floating restaurant, moonlight dance and sightseeing cruises (May-Sept); also guided tours on double-decker buses. Bus/cruise combinations available. Contact PO Box 3930, Postal Station B, R2W 5H9; 204/942-4500. ¢¢¢-¢¢¢¢¢

Ross House (1854). Oldest building in the original city of Winnipeg; first post office in western Canada. Displays and period-furnished rms depict daily life in the Red River Settlement. (Mid-May-Labour Day, Wed-Sun) 140 Meade St N, between Euclid & Sutherland Aves. Phone 204/943-3958 or 204/947-0559. **Free.**

Royal Canadian Mint (1976). One of the world's most modern mints; striking glass tower, landscaped interior courtyard. Tour allows viewing of coining process; coin museum. (Early May-late Aug, Mon-Fri; closed statutory hols) 520 Lagimodière Blvd. Phone 204/257-3359. ¢

Saint-Boniface Museum (1846). Housed in oldest structure in the city, dating to the days of the Red River Colony; largest oak log construction in North America. 494 ave Taché. Phone 204/237-4500.

Seven Oaks House Museum. Oldest habitable house in Manitoba (1851). Log construction, original furnishings, housewares. Adjoining buildings include general store, post office. (Mid-June-Sept, daily; mid-May-mid-June, Sat & Sun) Rupertsland Ave, in West Kildonan area. Phone 204/339-7429 or 204/986-3031. ¢

The Forks National Historic Site. Situated on 56 acres at the confluence of the Red and Assiniboine rivers. Riverside promenade; walkways throughout. Historical exhibits, heritage theater, children's programs, playground; evening performances. Special events. (May-Sept, daily) Grounds (all yr). Adj area open in winter for skating, cross-country skiing. Pioneer Blvd, opp Water & Pioneer Aves at Provencher Bridge. Phone 204/983-2007 or 204/983-5988. **Free.**

Winnipeg Art Gallery. Canada's first civic gallery (1912). Eight galleries present changing exhibitions of contemporary, historical and decorative art, plus North America's largest collection of Inuit art. (Summer, daily; rest of yr, daily exc Mon; closed hols) Programming includes tours, lectures, films, concerts. Cafeteria. 300 Memorial Blvd. Phone 204/786-6641. ¢¢

Annual Events

Festival du Voyageur. In St-Boniface, Winnipeg's "French Quarter." Winter festival celebrating the French-Canadian voyageur and the fur-trade era. Phone 204/237-7692. 10 days mid-Feb.

Red River Exhibition. Large event encompassing grandstand shows, band competitions, displays, agricultural exhibits, parade, entertainment, midway, petting zoo, shows, food. Phone 204/772-9464. Late June-early July.

Winnipeg Folk Festival. Birds Hill Provincial Park, 8 mi N on Hwy 59. More than 100 regional, national and international artists perform; nine stages; children's village; evening concerts. Juried crafts exhibit and sale; international food village. Phone 204/231-0096. Early July.

Folklorama. Pavilions throughout city. Multicultural festival featuring up to 40 pavilions. Singing, dancing, food, cultural displays. Phone 204/982-6210 or 800/665-0234. Aug.

Seasonal Events

Winnipeg Symphony Orchestra. Centennial Concert Hall. Classical, pops and children's concerts. Phone 204/949-3999 (box office). Sept-May.

Canada's Royal Winnipeg Ballet. Centennial Concert Hall. Performs mix of classical and contemporary ballets. Phone 204/956-2792. Oct-May.

Manitoba Opera Association. Portage Place. Phone 204/942-7479. Nov-May.

Motels

★ **COMFORT INN.** *(1770 Sargent Ave, Winnipeg MB R3H 0C8) near Intl Airport.* 204/783-5627. 81 rms, 2 story. Mid-June-mid-Sept: S $57.99-$63.99; D $65.99-$71.99; each addl $4; under 18 free; wkend rates; lower rates rest of yr. Crib free. Pet accepted. TV; cable. Complimentary coffee in lobby. Continental bkfst avail. Restaurant nearby. Ck-out 11 am. Business servs avail. In-rm modem link. Valet serv. Cr cds: A, D, JCB, MC, V.

✔★ ★ **COUNTRY INN & SUITES BY CARLSON.** *(730 King Edward St, Winnipeg MB R3H 1B4) near Intl Airport.* 204/783-6900; FAX 204/775-7197. 77 units, 3 story, 36 suites. S $65-$95; D $75-$105; each addl $10; under 18 free; wkend rates. Crib free. Pet accepted, some restrictions. TV; cable (premium), VCR (free movies). Complimentary coffee in rms. Complimentary continental bkfst. Restaurant adj 7 am-11 pm. Ck-out noon. Coin lndry. Business servs avail. Sundries. Valet serv. Refrigerators. Cr cds: A, C, D, DS, ER, MC, V.

Motor Hotels

✔★ **AIRLINER INN.** *(1740 Ellice Ave, Winnipeg MB R3H 0B3) near Intl Airport.* 204/775-7131; FAX 204/788-4685; res: 800/665-8813 *(CAN).* 155 rms, 5 story. S, D $54-$72; each addl $5; under 16 free; wkend rates; package plans. Crib $5. TV; cable, VCR avail. Sauna. Indoor pool; whirlpool, poolside serv. Complimentary continental bkfst. Restaurant 7 am-11 pm. Rm serv. Bar 11-1 am; entertainment, dancing. Ck-out 1 pm. Coin lndry. Meeting rms. Business servs avail. Bellhops. Valet serv. Sundries. Gift shop. Free airport transportation. Cr cds: A, C, D, ER, MC, V.

★ ★ **BEST WESTERN INTERNATIONAL INN.** *(1808 Wellington Ave, Winnipeg MB R3H 0G3) near Intl Airport.* 204/786-4801; FAX 204/786-1329. 288 rms, 5 story. S $78; D $83; each addl $5; suites $175; under 16 free; wkend rates. Crib $5. Pet accepted. TV; cable, VCR avail (movies free). 2 pools, 1 indoor; whirlpool, sauna, poolside serv. Restaurant 7 am-midnight; dining rms 5:30-midnight. Rm serv. Bar 11:30-2 am. Ck-out 2 pm. Meeting rms. Business servs avail. In-rm modem link.

Bellhops. Gift shop. Free airport transportation. Game rm. Some refrigerators. Cr cds: A, D, DS, ER, JCB, MC, V.

★ ★ ★ **HOLIDAY INN-SOUTH.** *(1330 Pembina Hwy, Winnipeg MB R3T 2B4)* 204/452-4747; FAX 204/284-2751. 169 rms, 11 story. S $125; D $136; each addl $11; suites $200; under 19 free; wkend rates. Crib free. Pet accepted. TV; cable, VCR avail. Indoor pool; wading pool, whirlpool, poolside serv. Coffee in rms. Restaurant 6:30 am-11 pm; wkend hrs vary. Rm serv. Bar from 11:30 am. Ck-out noon. Coin lndry. Meeting rms. Business servs avail. In-rm modem link. Bellhops. Valet serv. Sundries. Free airport transportation. Cr cds: A, C, D, DS, ER, JCB, MC, V.

Hotels

✔★ **CHARTER HOUSE.** *(330 York Ave, Winnipeg MB R3C 0N9)* 204/942-0101; FAX 204/956-0665. 90 rms, 5 story. S, D $75-$125; under 18 free; wkly, wkend rates. Crib avail. Pet accepted. TV; cable, VCR avail (movies). Heated pool; poolside serv. Restaurant 7 am-11 pm. Dining rm 11:30 am-2:30 pm, 5-11 pm; Sat from 5 pm; Sun 5-9 pm. Bar 11-1 am. Ck-out noon. Meeting rms. Business servs avail. In-rm modem link. Health club privileges. Balconies. Cr cds: A, C, D, DS, ER, MC, V.

★ ★ ★ **CROWNE PLAZA-DOWNTOWN.** *(350 St Mary Ave, Winnipeg MB R3C 3J2)* 204/942-0551; FAX 204/943-8702. 389 rms, 18 story. S $155; D $165; each addl $15; suites $195-$495; under 20 free. Crib avail. TV; cable (premium). 2 pools, 1 indoor; whirlpool; wading pool, lifeguard. Complimentary coffee in rm. Restaurants 6:30-1 am. Rm serv 24 hrs. Ck-out 1 pm. Coin lndry. Meeting rms. Business center. In-rm modem link. Airport transportation. Exercise rm; instructor, weights, bicycles, sauna. Refrigerators. Balconies. Luxury level. Cr cds: A, C, D, DS, ER, JCB, MC, V.

★ ★ ★ **DELTA.** *(288 Portage Ave, Winnipeg MB R3C 0B8)* 204/956-0410; FAX 204/947-1129; res: 800/268-1133 *(CAN),* 800/877-1133 *(US).* 272 rms, 29 story. S, D $129-$199; each addl $15; suites $229; under 18 free; wkend rates. Crib free. Pet accepted. Garage parking $3.75-$7; valet $3. TV; cable (premium), VCR avail (movies). Indoor pool; whirlpool, poolside serv. Supervised child's activities. Coffee in rms. Restaurant 6:30 am-10 pm; Sat, Sun from 7 am. Rm serv 24 hrs. Bars 11:30-1 am. Ck-out 1 pm. Meeting rms. Business center. In-rm modem link. Concierge. Gift shop. Exercise equipt; weights, rowers, sauna. Minibars. Adj to skywalks major downtown businesses & shopping. Cr cds: A, D, ER, JCB, MC, V.

★ ★ ★ **HOLIDAY INN-AIRPORT WEST.** *(2520 Portage Ave, Winnipeg MB R3J 3T6)* 204/885-4478; FAX 204/831-5734. 227 rms, 15 story, 8 kits. S $105; D $115; each addl $10; suites $145-$175; under 19 free; wkend rates. Crib free. TV; cable. Indoor pool; wading pool, whirlpool, poolside serv, lifeguard. Supervised child's activities, ages 3-11. Coffee in rms. Restaurant 6:30 am-11 pm. Bar 11:30-2 am; entertainment, dancing. Ck-out 1 pm. Coin lndry. Meeting rms. Business center. In-rm modem link. Free airport transportation. Exercise equipt; bicycles, stair machine, rower, sauna. Some minibars; refrigerators. Some balconies. Cr cds: A, C, D, DS, ER, JCB, MC, V.

★ ★ ★ **RADISSON SUITE-AIRPORT.** *(1800 Wellington Ave, Winnipeg MB R3H 1B3) near Intl Airport.* 204/783-1700; FAX 204/786-6588. 149 suites, 6 story. S $125; D $155; each addl $15; under 17 free; wkend & hol rates. TV; cable; VCR (free movies). 2 pools, 1 indoor; whirlpool, poolside serv. Complimentary coffee in rms. Restaurant 7 am-10 pm. Rm serv 24 hrs. Bar 11:30-1 am. Ck-out noon. Meeting rms. Business servs avail. Gift shop. Free airport transportation. Exercise equipt; weights, bicycles, sauna. Refrigerators, wet bars. Cr cds: A, C, D, DS, ER, JCB, MC, V.

★ ★ ★ **SHERATON.** *(161 Donald St, Winnipeg MB R3C 1M3) 204/942-5300; FAX 204/943-7975.* 266 rms, 21 story. S $130-$145; D $140-$155; each addl $15; under 18 free; wkend rates. Crib free. Pet accepted. Underground parking, valet $7.50/day. TV; cable (premium). Indoor pool; whirlpool, poolside serv. Coffee in rms. Restaurant 6:30 am-11 pm. Rm serv 24 hrs. Bar 11-1 am. Ck-out noon. Convention facilities. Business servs avail. In-rm modem link. Concierge. Gift shop. Airport transportation avail. Sauna. Health club privileges. Many refrigerators. Many balconies. Cr cds: A, D, ER, MC, V.

D ✦ ≈ ⇥ 🖐 **SC**

Restaurants

★ ★ **AMICI.** *(326 Broadway, Winnipeg MB R3C 0S5) 204/943-4997.* Hrs: 11:30 am-2 pm, 5-10 pm; Sat from 5 pm. Closed Sun; most major hols. Res accepted. Italian menu. Bar to 11 pm. Semi-a la carte: lunch $6-$14.75, dinner $14.50-$36. Child's meals. Specializes in venison, veal, wild boar. Contemporary decor. Cr cds: A, C, D, ER, MC, V.

D

★ ★ ★ **HY'S STEAK LOFT.** *(216 Kennedy, Winnipeg MB) 204/942-1000.* Hrs: 5 pm-midnight; Sun to 9:30 pm. Closed major hols. Res accepted. Bar 4 pm-midnight; Sat from 5 pm. Wine list. Semi-a la carte: dinner $17-$31. Specializes in steak, seafood. Bi-level dining; old English decor. Cr cds: A, C, D, ER, MC, V.

★ ★ **ICHIBAN JAPANESE STEAKHOUSE.** *(189 Carlton St, Winnipeg MB) 204/925-7400.* Hrs: 4:30-10 pm. Fri, Sat to 10:30 pm. Closed major hols. Res accepted. Japanese menu. Bar 4:30-10 pm, Fri, Sat to 10:30. Semi-a la carte: dinner $12.95-$24.95. Specialties: imperial dinner, empress dinner, sushi. Tableside cooking. Japanese garden atmosphere. Cr cds: A, C, D, ER, MC, V.

D

Index

Establishment names are listed in alphabetical order followed by a symbol identifying their classification, and then city, state and page number.' Establishments affiliated with a chain appear alphabetically under their chain name, followed by the state, city and page number. The symbols for classification are: [H] for hotel; [I] for inns; [M] for motels; [L] for lodges; [MH] for motor hotels; [R] for restaurants; [RO] for resorts, guest ranches, and cottage colonies; [U] for unrated dining spots.

Notes

Notes

Notes

Notes

Notes

Notes

Mobil Travel Guide

Looking for the Mobil Guides . . . ?

**Call toll-free 800/533-6478 around the clock
or use the order form below.**

Please check the guides you would like to order:

☐ 0-679-03506-0
America's Best Hotels & Restaurants
$11.00 (Can $14.95)

☐ 0-679-03498-6
California and the West (Arizona, California, Nevada, Utah)
$15.95 (Can $21.95)

☐ 0-679-03500-1
Great Lakes (Illinois, Indiana, Michigan, Ohio, Wisconsin, Canada: Ontario)
$15.95 (Can $21.95)

☐ 0-679-03501-X
Mid-Atlantic (Delaware, District of Columbia, Maryland, New Jersey, North Carolina, Pennsylvania, South Carolina, Virginia, West Virginia)
$15.95 (Can $21.95)

☐ 0-679-03502-8
Northeast (Connecticut, Maine, Massachusetts, New Hampshire, New York, Rhode Island, Vermont, Canada: New Brunswick, Nova Scotia, Ontario, Prince Edward Island, Québec)
$15.95 (Can $21.95)

☐ 0-679-03503-6
Northwest and Great Plains (Idaho, Iowa, Minnesota, Montana, Nebraska, North Dakota, Oregon, South Dakota, Washington, Wyoming, Canada: Alberta, British Columbia, Manitoba)
$15.95 (Can $21.95)

☐ 0-679-03504-4
Southeast (Alabama, Florida, Georgia, Kentucky, Mississippi, Tennessee)
$15.95 (Can $21.95)

☐ 0-679-03505-2
Southwest & South Central (Arkansas, Colorado, Kansas, Louisiana, Missouri, New Mexico, Oklahoma, Texas)
$15.95 (Can $21.95)

☐ 0-679-03499-4
Major Cities (Detailed coverage of 45 major U.S. cities)
$17.95 (Can $25.00)

☐ 0-679-00047-X
Southern California (Includes California south of Lompoc, with Tijuana and Ensenada, Mexico)
$12.00 (Can $16.95)

☐ 0-679-00048-8
Florida
$12.00 (Can $16.95)

☐ 0-679-03548-6
On the Road with Your Pet (More than 3,000 Mobil-rated Lodgings that Welcome Travelers with Pets)
$12.00 (Can $16.95)

☐ My check is enclosed.

☐ Please charge my credit card

Total cost of book(s) ordered $ _____

Shipping & Handling (please add $2 for first book, $.50 for each additional book) $ _____

Add applicable sales tax (In Canada and in CA, CT, FL, IL, NJ, NY, TN and WA.) $ _____

TOTAL AMOUNT ENCLOSED $ _____

☐ VISA ☐ MasterCard ☐ American Express

Credit Card # _____

Expiration _____

Signature _____

Please ship the books checked above to:

Name _____

Address _____

City _____ State _____ Zip _____

Please mail this form to: Mobil Travel Guides, Random House, 400 Hahn Rd., Westminster, MD 21157

M⊙bil
Travel
Guide

Northwest & Great Plains
Idaho
Iowa
Minnesota
Montana
Nebraska
North Dakota
Oregon
South Dakota
Washington
Wyoming

Canada:
Alberta
British Columbia
Manitoba

California & the West
Arizona
California
Nevada
Utah

Southwest & South Central
Arkansas
Colorado
Kansas
Louisiana
Missouri
New Mexico
Oklahoma
Texas

Great Lakes
Illinois
Indiana
Michigan
Ohio
Wisconsin

Canada:
Ontario

Southeast
Alabama
Florida
Georgia
Kentucky
Mississippi
Tennessee

Mid-Atlantic
Delaware
District of Columbia
Maryland
New Jersey
North Carolina
Pennsylvania
South Carolina
Virginia
West Virginia

Northeast
Connecticut
Maine
Massachusetts
New Hampshire
New York
Rhode Island
Vermont

Canada:
New Brunswick
Nova Scotia
Ontario
Prince Edward Island
Quebec

MAKE THE MOST OF YOUR TRAVELING TIME . . .

with Random House AudioBooks.

WITH MORE THAN 500 TITLES TO CHOOSE FROM, LISTEN TO GREAT BOOKS WHILE STILL ADMIRING THE SCENERY . . . YOU'LL REACH YOUR DESTINATION IN NO TIME.

  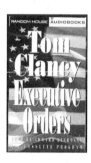 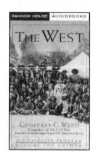

For a complete listing of Random House AudioBooks,
Fax: (212) 572-6074; call (212) 572-6004; write: Random House Audio, Dept. CC,
201 East 50th Street, New York, NY 10022

- -

Please send me the following Random House AudioBooks:

The Perfect Storm by Sebastian Junger (abridged, 3 hours)
Read by Stanley Tucci • ISBN: 0-679-46035-7   _____ @ $18.00 = _____

Unnatural Exposure by Patricia Cornwell (abridged, 4 hours)
Read by Blair Brown • ISBN: 0-679-45786-0   _____ @ $24.00 = _____

Executive Orders by Tom Clancy (abridged, 6 hours)
Read by Edward Herrmann • ISBN: 0-679-43696-0   _____ @ $25.95 = _____

The West by Geoffrey C. Ward (abridged, 4 hours)
Read by the Author • ISBN: 0-679-45615-5   _____ @ $24.00 = _____
(Quantity)

Shipping/Handling*	= _____
Subtotal	= _____
Sales Tax (where applicable)	= _____
Total Enclosed	= _____

*Please enclose $4.00 to cover shipping and handling (or $6.00 if total order is more than $30.00).
☐ If you wish to pay by check or money order, please make it payable to Random House Audio Publishing.
☐ To charge your order to a major credit card, please fill in the information below.

Charge to   ☐ American Express   ☐ Visa   ☐ MasterCard

Account No._____ Expiration Date_____

Signature_____

Name_____

Address_____

City_____ State_____ Zip_____

Send your payment with the order form above to:
Random House Audio Publishing, Dept. CC, 23-2, 201 East 50th Street, New York, NY 10022.
Prices subject to change without notice. Please allow 4-6 weeks for delivery.

Also available wherever books are sold.

HELP US GET TO KNOW YOU AND RECEIVE A FREE KEY CHAIN!

Please complete and return this postage paid card to Mobil Travel Guide. The information on you and your travel habits will help us improve the Guide to better serve you in the future. The first 500 respondents who successfully complete and return this questionnaire will receive a free Mobil key chain with our thanks and appreciation. The information supplied herein will be treated in confidence; names and addresses will not be released to mailing list houses or any other associations or organizations.

Please circle the appropriate letter or number, or fill in the blank, as necessary.

1. 1.__Mr.   2.__Mrs.   3.__Ms.   4.__Miss

_____
First Name   Initial   Last Name

_____
Street   Apt. No.

_____
City   State   Zip Code

2. Date of Purchase: Month___ Date___ Year___

3. How many round trips of 200 miles or more via any method of transportation have you taken in the last year? _____
a) How many of these were for leisure/pleasure? _____
b) How many of these were for business? _____

4. What is the duration of your average trip?
a) Leisure/pleasure travel? _____
b) Business travel? _____

5. How many of these trips were by car?
a) Leisure/pleasure travel? _____
b) Business travel? _____

6. Do you use the Mobil Travel Guide in your car?
a) Yes   b) No

7. What cities/towns/states or regions were your destinations for your last three (3) leisure/pleasure trips?

_____   _____   _____

8. What cities/towns/states or regions were your destinations for your last three (3) business trips?

_____   _____   _____

9. What kinds of activities do you prefer when you travel for leisure/pleasure? Circle all that apply.
a) Sightseeing-Historical
b) Sightseeing-Scenic
c) Camping/hiking
d) Sports and recreation
e) Shopping
f) Rest and relaxation
g) Visiting museums/galleries
h) Fine dining
i) Going to the beach

10. How much do you typically spend (on a per-night basis) for your accommodations when you travel for leisure/pleasure?
$_____ per night

11. How much do you typically spend (on a per-night basis) for your accommodations when you travel for business?
$_____ per night

12. What are your restaurant preferences when you travel for leisure/pleasure?
a) 4 or 5 Star   c) Family
b) Moderately priced   d) Fast food chain

13. What are your restaurant preferences when you travel for business?
a) 4 or 5 Star   c) Family
b) Moderately priced   d) Fast food chain

14. What kind of resources are used to plan your trips?
a) Leisure/pleasure travel?
i) Travel books/guides
ii) Magazines
iii) Internet
iv) Friends/family recommendations
v) Travel agent
vi) Other _____
b) Business travel?
i) Travel books/guides
ii) Magazines
iii) Internet
iv) Friends/family recommendations
v) Travel agent
vi) Other _____

15. If your vacation/business travel requires you to rent an automobile, how likely would you be to buy a travel guide of the area if offered (1: Not likely 5: Very likely)
1 2 3 4 5

16. Did you purchase the Mobil Travel Guide primarily for (choose one)?
a) Leisure/pleasure travel
b) Business travel
c) Maps
d) Coupons
e) Other _____

17. How did you hear about the Mobil Travel Guide?
a) Advertisement
b) Friends and family
c) Colleague
d) Point of sale (bookstore, service station)
e) Other _____

18. Where did you purchase the Mobil Travel Guide?
a) Furnished by employer
b) It was a gift
c) Chain bookstore Which? _____
d) Independent bookstore Which? _____
e) Travel store Which? _____
f) Department store
g) Drug store
h) Gift shop
i) Newsstand
j) Service station
k) Other _____

19. When was the last time you purchased a Mobil Travel Guide?
a) Never   d) Three to five years ago
b) Last year   e) More than five years ago
c) Two years ago

20. Why did you choose the Mobil Travel Guide in lieu of other options (choose three)?
a) Price
b) Quality ratings of accommodations
c) Quality ratings of restaurants
d) Factual information on accommodations
e) Factual information on restaurants
f) Information on things to see and do in the area
g) Maps
h) Discount coupons
i) Background information on states, cities and towns
j) Other _____

006

CUT ALONG DOTTED LINE

FOLD AND TAPE (OR SEAL) FOR MAILING—PLEASE DO NOT STAPLE

SKOKIE, IL 60076
SUITE 803
4709 W. GOLF RD.
Mobil Travel Guide

POSTAGE WILL BE PAID BY ADDRESSEE

FIRST CLASS   PERMIT NO. 253   SKOKIE, IL
BUSINESS REPLY MAIL

NO POSTAGE
NECESSARY
IF MAILED
IN THE
UNITED STATES

86

21. What three (3) features would you like to see more of?
a) Accommodation choices
b) Details/comments on accommodations
c) Restaurant choices
d) Details/comments on restaurants
e) Things to see and do in the area
f) State/city background information
g) Maps
h) Icons/Easy-to-use symbols
i) Discount Coupons
j) Other_____

22. In your opinion, does the Mobil Travel Guide improve Mobil Corporation's image?
a) Yes   c) Not sure
b) No

23. You are:
a) Female   b) Male

24. Your age is:
a) 18–24   d) 45–54
b) 25–34   e) 55–64
c) 35–44   f) 65+

25. You are:
a) Single/never married   c) Separated/divorced
b) Married   d) Widowed

26. The ethnic group that best describes you is:
a) African-American   d) Caucasian/White
b) Asian   e) Hispanic
c) Other_____

27. Highest level of education:
a) Some High School
b) High School Graduate
c) Some College
d) Technical Certification
e) College Degree (2- or 4-Year)
f) Some Post College Study
g) Advanced Degree

28. Your occupation is:
a) Professional
b) Executive, Managerial, Administrative
c) Military
d) Clerical, Sales, Technical
e) Precision, Crafts, Repair
f) Retired
g) Other_____

29. Your spouse/significant other's occupation is:
a) Professional
b) Executive, Managerial, Administrative
c) Military
d) Clerical, Sales, Technical
e) Precision, Crafts, Repair
f) Retired
g) Other

30. How many children do you have living at home in the following age groups?
a) None   f) 10–11 Years
b) < 1 Year   g) 12–14 Years
c) 1–2 Years   h) 15–18 Years
d) 3–5 Years   i) Over 18
e) 6–9 Years

31. Which choice best describes your household income level?
a) Under $10,000
b) $10,000–$19,999   g) $60,000–$69,999
c) $20,000–$29,999   h) $70,000–$79,999
d) $30,000–$39,999   i) $80,000–$89,999
e) $40,000–$49,999   j) $90,000–$99,999
f) $50,000–$59,999   k) >$100,000

32. Which types of credit cards do you use most for travel?
a) American Express, Diners Club, Discover, Carte Blanche
b) Bank Card (Mastercard, Visa)
c) Gas, Department Store
d) None of the Above

33. What type of vehicle do you drive on your trips?
a) Luxury   d) Mini Van
b) Mid Size   e) Sport Utility
c) Compact   f) RV

34. Do you belong to an automobile club?
a) Yes Which? _____
b) No

35. What other products/services do you purchase specifically for travel?
a) Tire/Auto Service
b) Luggage
c) Travel Store Items
d) Maps
e) Other_____

YOU CAN HELP MAKE THE *MOBIL TRAVEL GUIDE* MORE ACCURATE AND USEFUL

ALL INFORMATION WILL BE KEPT CONFIDENTIAL

Your Name_____
(Please Print)

Street_____

City, State, Zip_____

Were children with you on trip? ☐ Yes ☐ No

Number of people in your party _____

Your occupation_____

Establishment name_____

Hotel ☐ Resort ☐ Other ☐
Motel ☐ Inn ☐ Restaurant ☐

Street_____ City_____ State _____

Do you agree with our description? ☐ Yes ☐ No; if not, give reason _____

Please give us your opinion of the following:

DECOR	CLEANLINESS	SERVICE	FOOD
☐ Excellent	☐ Spotless	☐ Excellent	☐ Excellent
☐ Good	☐ Clean	☐ Good	☐ Good
☐ Fair	☐ Unclean	☐ Fair	☐ Fair
☐ Poor	☐ Dirty	☐ Poor	☐ Poor

1998 *GUIDE* RATING _____ ★
CHECK YOUR SUGGESTED RATING BELOW:
☐ ★ good, satisfactory ☐ ★★★★ outstanding
☐ ★★ very good ☐ ★★★★★ one of best
☐ ★★★ excellent in country
☐ ✓ unusually good value

Comments:_____

Date of visit_____

First ☐ Yes
visit? ☐ No

2.

Establishment name_____

Hotel ☐ Resort ☐ Other ☐
Motel ☐ Inn ☐ Restaurant ☐

Street_____ City_____ State _____

Do you agree with our description? ☐ Yes ☐ No; if not, give reason _____

Please give us your opinion of the following:

DECOR	CLEANLINESS	SERVICE	FOOD
☐ Excellent	☐ Spotless	☐ Excellent	☐ Excellent
☐ Good	☐ Clean	☐ Good	☐ Good
☐ Fair	☐ Unclean	☐ Fair	☐ Fair
☐ Poor	☐ Dirty	☐ Poor	☐ Poor

1998 *GUIDE* RATING _____ ★
CHECK YOUR SUGGESTED RATING BELOW:
☐ ★ good, satisfactory ☐ ★★★★ outstanding
☐ ★★ very good ☐ ★★★★★ one of best
☐ ★★★ excellent in country
☐ ✓ unusually good value

Comments:_____

Date of visit_____

First ☐ Yes
visit? ☐ No

3.

Establishment name_____

Hotel ☐ Resort ☐ Other ☐
Motel ☐ Inn ☐ Restaurant ☐

Street_____ City_____ State _____

Do you agree with our description? ☐ Yes ☐ No; if not, give reason _____

Please give us your opinion of the following:

DECOR	CLEANLINESS	SERVICE	FOOD
☐ Excellent	☐ Spotless	☐ Excellent	☐ Excellent
☐ Good	☐ Clean	☐ Good	☐ Good
☐ Fair	☐ Unclean	☐ Fair	☐ Fair
☐ Poor	☐ Dirty	☐ Poor	☐ Poor

1998 *GUIDE* RATING _____ ★
CHECK YOUR SUGGESTED RATING BELOW:
☐ ★ good, satisfactory ☐ ★★★★ outstanding
☐ ★★ very good ☐ ★★★★★ one of best
☐ ★★★ excellent in country
☐ ✓ unusually good value

Comments:_____

Date of visit_____

First ☐ Yes
visit? ☐ No

FOLD AND TAPE (OR SEAL) FOR MAILING—PLEASE DO NOT STAPLE

CUT ALONG DOTTED LINE

_____

_____

_____

_____
Please make any general comment here. Thanks!

Have you sent us one of these forms before? ☐ Yes ☐ No

HOW CAN WE IMPROVE THE MOBIL TRAVEL GUIDE?

Mobil Travel Guides are constantly being revised and improved. All attractions are updated and all listings are revised and evaluated annually. You can contribute to the accuracy and usefulness of the guides by sending us your reactions to the places you have visited. Your suggestions for improving the guides are also welcome. Just complete this prepaid mailing form or address letters to: *Mobil Travel Guide*, 4709 W. Golf Rd., Suite 803, Skokie, IL 60076. The editors appreciate your comments.

The Mobil Travel Guide is available at Mobil Service Stations, bookstores, or by mail from the Mobil Travel Guide, Random House, 400 Hahn Rd., Westminster, MD 21157, or call toll-free, 24 hours a day, 1-800/533-6478.

Major Cities: Detailed coverage of 45 Major Cities.

Southwest and South Central: Arkansas, Colorado, Kansas, Louisiana, Missouri, New Mexico, Oklahoma, Texas.

Northwest and Great Plains: Idaho, Iowa, Minnesota, Montana, Nebraska, North Dakota, Oregon, South Dakota, Washington, Wyoming; Western Canada.

Great Lakes: Illinois, Indiana, Michigan, Ohio, Wisconsin; Ontario, Canada.

Southeast: Alabama, Florida, Georgia, Kentucky, Mississippi, Tennessee.

Mid-Atlantic: Delaware, District of Columbia, Maryland, New Jersey, North Carolina, Pennsylvania, South Carolina, Virginia, West Virginia.

Northeast: Connecticut, Maine, Massachusetts, New Hampshire, New York, Rhode Island, Vermont; Eastern Canada.

California and the West: Arizona, California, Nevada, Utah.

Revised editions are now being prepared for publication next year:

98

NO POSTAGE
NECESSARY
IF MAILED
IN THE
UNITED STATES

BUSINESS REPLY MAIL
FIRST CLASS   PERMIT NO. 253   SKOKIE, IL

POSTAGE WILL BE PAID BY ADDRESSEE

Mobil Travel Guide
4709 W. GOLF RD.
SUITE 803
SKOKIE, IL 60076

Mobil Travel Guide®

The Guide That Saves You Money When You Travel!

Las Vegas TRAVEL

UP TO 20% OFF

ENJOY 20% OFF, PLUS FREE FUN BOOKS, MEAL AND SHOW DISCOUNTS.

Call Las Vegas Travel for a 20% discount for most major casino hotels in Las Vegas.

Mention this coupon to receive free fun books, free meals and discounts on Las Vegas shows. Call **800-449-4697** for more information. For golf reservations call **800-627-4465**.

OFFER EXPIRES JUNE 30, 1999

National Car Rental.

ONE CAR CLASS UPGRADE

PRESENT THIS CERTIFICATE AT A NATIONAL RENTAL COUNTER TO RECEIVE A ONE CAR-CLASS UPGRADE ON A COMPACT THROUGH FULL-SIZE 2-DOOR CAR. VALID AT PARTICIPATING NATIONAL LOCATIONS IN THE U.S.

Reservations recommended. Contact your Travel Agent or National at **800-CAR RENT**®. Subject to terms and conditions on reverse side.

Discount #5130876   PC #013354-5   Type 7

OFFER EXPIRES JUNE 30, 1999

ASTROLAND AMUSEMENT PARK
"Home of the World Famous CYCLONE"

1000 Surf Ave. • Brooklyn, NY
718-265-2100

FREE BAND

ENJOY ONE COMPLIMENTARY PAY-ONE-PRICE BAND.

Valid for one complimentary Pay-One-Price Band when a second Pay-One-Price Band of equal or greater value is purchased. Not valid on kiddie rides. Offer valid June 21 thru September 7, 1998.

VALID DURING THE 1998 OPERATING SEASON

ONE HOUR MOTO**PHOTO**®

50% OFF FILM DEVELOPING

ONE HOUR MOTOPHOTO INVITES YOU TO ENJOY 50% OFF THE REGULAR PRICE OF PROCESSING AND PRINTING 35MM COLOR PRINT FILM.

Limit one roll; standard size prints only. Not valid with other coupons or extra set promotions. Coupon may not be combined with any other discount or coupon. Club members take an additional 10% off coupon price. *Participating stores only.*

ZZ70101

OFFER EXPIRES JUNE 30, 1999

Alamo

ONE FREE UPGRADE

CERTIFICATE IS VALID FOR ONE FREE UPGRADE TO THE NEXT CAR CATEGORY (WITH SAME TRANSMISSION IN EUROPE).

Just reserve a compact through a premium 4-door car in the United States or Canada, or a Group B through F in Europe or Mexico. Valid on rentals of at least 3 days. For reservations, contact your travel agent or call Alamo at **1-800-354-2322**. Be sure to request ID Number 422325, Rate Code BY and coupon code **UM5B** at time of reservation. For interactive reservations, **UM5B** access us at **www.goalamo.com**. See terms, conditions and blackout dates on reverse side of this coupon.

OFFER EXPIRES JUNE 15, 1999

 SUPER 8 MOTELS

10% OFF

RECEIVE A 10% DISCOUNT AT ALL SUPER 8 MOTEL LOCATIONS, OVER 1,600 MOTELS.

Mention 8800/10185 when calling Super 8 Motels at 1-800-800-8000 to make reservations. E-Mail Address: **http://www.super8motels.com**

OFFER EXPIRES JUNE 30, 1999

10% OFF

RECEIVE A 10% DISCOUNT OFF ALL TIME AND MILEAGE CHARGES ON CRUISE AMERICA OR CRUISE CANADA VEHICLES ONLY.

For reservations call: **800-327-7799** US and Canada.

OFFER EXPIRES JUNE 30, 1999

Please note: All offers may not be available in Canada. Call
(410) 825-3463 if you are unable to use an 800 number
listed on the coupon.

TERMS AND CONDITIONS: ≋**National** Car Rental.

Valid for car classes indicated on front at participating National locations in the U.S. (Not valid in Manhattan, NY.) • Subject to availability and blackout dates. • Rate and time parameters, local rental and minimum rental day requirements apply. • Cannot be used in multiples or with any other certificate, special discount or promotion. • Standard rental qualifications apply. • Minimum rental age at most locations is 25.

In addition to rental charges, where applicable, renter is responsible for: Optional loss Damage Waiver, up to $15.99 per day; a per mile charge in excess of mileage allowance; taxes; surcharges; additional charges if car is not returned within a prescribed rental period; drop charge and additional driver fee; optional refueling charge; optional insurance benefits.

RENTAL AGENT INSTRUCTIONS: 1. Rental Screen 1: • Key Promo Coup # from the front side. **2.** Rental Screen 3: • Key Discount # from the front side in "RATE RECAP #" field. • Key applicable rate in "RATE RECAP #" field. • Change rate for one car class lower than class of car actually rented. **3.** Write RA# and rental date below. **4.** Retain certificate at rental. Send certificate to Headquarters, Attn: Travel Industry Billing. RA#_____ Rental Date ___/___/___

TASTE PUBLICATIONS INTERNATIONAL

Las Vegas TRAVEL

Advance reservations required. For show, wedding, or casino information call 900-RESORT CITY. Valid Sunday thru Thursday only, except holidays and during city-wide conventions. May not be used in conjunction with any other discount or promotion.

800-449-4697 – One Toll-Free Call Gives You All These:

Luxor • Monte Carlo • Tropicana • Circus Circus • Caesar's Palace
New York-New York • Bally's • The Orleans • Rio Suite Hotel • Plaza
Stardust • Stratosphere • Boomtown • Sahara • Westward Ho
Holiday Inn Board • Excalibur • Flamingo Hilton • Las Vegas Hilton
Lucky Lady • The Plaza • San Remo • And so many more.

TASTE PUBLICATIONS INTERNATIONAL

ONE HOUR MOTOPHOTO®

TASTE PUBLICATIONS INTERNATIONAL

 ASTROLAND AMUSEMENT PARK
CONEY ISLAND "Home of the World Famous CYCLONE"

Not valid with other discount offers or on holidays.
Valid Monday-Friday in season.

TASTE PUBLICATIONS INTERNATIONAL

SUPER 8 MOTELS

Not valid in conjunction with other discounts or promotions.
Each Super 8 Motel is independently owned and operated.

TASTE PUBLICATIONS INTERNATIONAL

Alamo

TERMS AND CONDITIONS:

• Upgrade is subject to availability at time of rental; as certain car categories may be sold out. Valid on self-drive rentals only.
• Only one certificate per rental; not to be used in conjunction with any other discounted or promotional rate. Cannot be used with any Alamo Express Plus(SM) or a Quicksilver(SM) rental.
• Please make your reservations at least 24 hours before arrival. Travel agents please include /SI-C-UM5B in the car sell. Valid only on Association Rate Codes.
• You must present this certificate at the Alamo counter on arrival. It is void once redeemed.
• Certificate has no cash value and does not include taxes (including in California, VLF taxes ranging up to $1.89 per day), registration fee/tax reimbursements, airport concession recoupment charges, fuel, other optional items, or airport access fees, if any.
• Any used portion is non-refundable.
• Reproductions will not be accepted and expired or lost certificates cannot be replaced.
• Offer valid through March 1, 1998 through June 15, 1999. The following blackout dates apply: In the United States and Canada: 4/09-4/11/98, 5/21-5/23/98, 7/02-7/04/98, 7/16-8/15/98, 9/03-9/05/98, 10/08-10/10/98, 11/25-11/27/98, 12/17-12/31/98, 2/11-2/13/99 and 4/1-4/3/99. In the United Kingdom, Germany, Belgium, The Netherlands and Switzerland: 6/15-7/31/98 and 12/20-12/31/98. In Ireland, Greece, Portugal, the Czech Republic, and Malta: 7/15-9/30/98 and 12/20-12/31/98. In Mexico: 7/15-8/31/98 and 12/15/98-1/31/99.
• Offer is valid at airport and airport serving locations and at participating European or Mexican locations operating under the name of Alamo.
• Coupon not valid on plan code A1.

TASTE PUBLICATIONS INTERNATIONAL

CRUISE AMERICA   CRUISE CANADA
MOTORHOME RENTAL & SALES   MOTORHOME RENTAL & SALES

Offer not available in conjunction with other discount offers or promotional rates. Excludes other rental charges, deposits, sales tax, and fuels. Normal rental conditions and customer qualification procedures apply. Members must reserve vehicle through Central Reservations only, at least one week in advance of pick up and mention membership affiliation at time of reservation.

TASTE PUBLICATIONS INTERNATIONAL

Mobil Travel Guide.

The Guide That Saves You Money When You Travel!

 Audio Diversions

$25.00 VALUE

FREE 1ST YEAR MEMBERSHIP IN THE "LITERATURE FOR LISTENING CLUB™."

Membership gives you 10% off on all purchases and rentals. When renting you get twice as long (30 days) to listen to your selections with over 2,600 titles to choose from. You will never run out of choices. Call 800-628-6145.

OFFER EXPIRES JUNE 30, 1999

Budget. All The Difference In The World.™

15% OFF

TAKE 15% OFF WEEKLY OR WEEKEND STANDARD RATES.

Valid on Economy through Full-Size Cars. For reservations call: **800-455-2848**. Be sure to mention **BCD#: T445311**.

OFFER EXPIRES JUNE 30, 1999

 *Empire State Building Observatories*

UP TO FOUR ADMISSIONS

ENJOY $1.00 OFF ADULT ADMISSIONS AND $1.00 OFF CHILDREN ADMISSIONS.

Offer good for up to four admissions upon presentation of coupon at ticket office. Open daily 9:30 am - midnight. Last elevator to the top at 11:30 pm.

OFFER EXPIRES JUNE 30, 1999

 DAYS INN Follow the Sun™

10% SPECIAL DISCOUNT

FOLLOW THE SUN TO DAYS INNS.

Now you can save even more at any of our more than 1,700 Days Inns throughout the United States and internationally. Just present this coupon upon check-in and we'll take 10% off our regular room rate for your entire length of stay! Advance reservations recommended so call now! For reservations and location information call **800-DAYS-INN**.

OFFER EXPIRES JUNE 30, 1999

 CRUISE AMERICA **CRUISE CANADA** **KOA**

FREE CAMPING STAY

CAMP FREE WHEN YOU RENT A KOA DEAL MOTOR HOME FROM CRUISE AMERICA.

Call **800-327-7778** and request a KOA DEAL Motor Home rental and learn how to camp free at participating KOA Kampgrounds.

OFFER EXPIRES JUNE 30, 1999

 **BUSCH GARDENS** AND **WATER COUNTRY USA** WILLIAMSBURG, VA.

UP TO $21.00 OFF

BUSCH GARDENS WILLIAMSBURG AND WATER COUNTRY USA INVITE YOU TO ENJOY $3.50 OFF THE ONE-DAY REGULAR OR CHILD'S ADMISSION PRICE.

For information on opening schedule call **800-343-SWIM**. See reverse for details.

OFFER EXPIRES JUNE 30, 1999

 AVIS We try harder.®

UP TO $20.00 OFF

SAVE FROM $10.00 TO $20.00 ON A WEEKEND RENTAL.

Rent an Intermediate through Full Size 4-Door car for a minimum of two consecutive weekend days and you can save $5.00 per day, up to a total of $20.00 off for four weekend rental days, when you present this coupon at a participating Avis location in the U.S. Subject to complete Terms and Conditions on back. For information and reservations, call the special Avis reservation number: **800-831-8000**. Be sure to mention the special Avis Worldwide Discount (AWD) number for this offer A291814. Avis features GM cars. Offer cannot be used in conjunction with any other coupon, promotion or offer.

Coupon #MUGD717 for a 2 day rental • Coupon #MUGD718 for a 3 day rental • Coupon #MUGD719 for a 4 day rental

OFFER EXPIRES JUNE 30, 1999

Taste Publications International, The Mobil Travel Guide, and Fodor's Travel Publications, Inc., will not be responsible if any establishment breaches its contract or refuses to accept coupons. However, Taste Publications International will attempt to secure compliance. If you encounter any difficulty, please contact Taste Publications International. We will do our best to rectify the situation to your satisfaction. ©1998 Taste Publications International

TASTE PUBLICATIONS INTERNATIONAL • 1031 CROMWELL BRIDGE ROAD • BALTIMORE, MD 21286

Budget

TERMS AND CONDITIONS

Be sure to mention BCD# T445311 when reserving an economy through full-size car and present this certificate at participating U.S. Budget locations (except in the New York metro area) to receive your member savings discount. This offer requires a one-day advance reservation, and is subject to vehicle availability. Vehicle must be returned to the original renting location except where intra-inter metro area drop-offs are permitted. Local age and rental requirements apply. Locations that rent to drivers under 25 may impose an age surcharge. Offer is not available with CorpRate, government or tour/wholesale rates, or with any other promotion. Refueling services, taxes, surcharges, and optional items are extra. Blackout dates may apply. Limit one certificate per rental.

TASTE PUBLICATIONS INTERNATIONAL

Audio Diversions

Good Books are for listening too!

More than 2,600 titles carefully drawn from among the best in travelbooks, adventure, biographies, business, children's, classics, education, how to's, foreign language, inspirational, literature, motivational, mystery, and self help books, Audio Diversions is sure to have what you need. Rentals are 10% off plus come with addressed and stamped packages for easy return.

10 % off everything.

TASTE PUBLICATIONS INTERNATIONAL

DAYS INN
Follow the Sun™

Available at participating properties. This coupon cannot be combined with any other special discount offer. Limit one coupon per room, per stay. Not valid during blackout periods or special events. Void where prohibited. No reproductions accepted.

TASTE PUBLICATIONS INTERNATIONAL

Empire State Building Observatories
Managed by:
Helmsely Spear, Inc.

Built in 1931, this 1,454 foot high skyscraper was climbed by King Kong in the movie classic. View Manhattan from the 86th floor observatory with outdoor promenade. Also enjoy the enclosed 102nd floor and exhibits of the eight wonders of the world.

TASTE PUBLICATIONS INTERNATIONAL

BUSCH GARDENS

Present this coupon when purchasing your ticket at any Busch Gardens Williamsburg or Water Country USA General admission price. Children two and under are admitted FREE. Admission price includes all regularly scheduled rides, shows and attractions. This coupon has no cash value and cannot be used in conjunction with any other discount. Prices and schedule subject to change without notice. Busch Gardens Williamsburg and Water Country USA have a "no solicitation" policy. Limit six tickets per coupon.

1   2   3   4   5   6

PLU #R364 C365   Please circle number of admissions.

TASTE PUBLICATIONS INTERNATIONAL

KOA

KOA has over 550 locations throughout the U.S. and Canada. Cruise America and Cruise Canada have over 100 rental centers.

TASTE PUBLICATIONS INTERNATIONAL

AVIS We try harder

TERMS AND CONDITIONS (*Save up to $20.00 on a Weekend Rental*)

Offer valid on an Intermediate (Group C) through a Full Size 4-door (Group E) car for a 2-day minimum rental. Coupon must be surrendered at time of rental; one per rental. Coupon valid at Avis corporate and participating licensee locations in the continental U.S. Weekend rental period begins Thursday noon, and car must be returned by Monday 11:59 p.m. or a higher rate will apply. Offer not available during holiday and other blackout periods. Offer may not be available on all rates at all times. An advance reservation is required. Cars subject to availability. Taxes, local government surcharges and optional items, such as LDW, additional driver fee and refueling, are extra. Renter must meet Avis age, driver and credit requirements. Minimum age is 25. Offer expires June 30, 1999.

RENTAL SALES AGENT INSTRUCTION AT CHECKOUT: **1.** In AWD, enter A291814. **2.** For a 2 day rental, enter MUGD717 in CPN. **3.** For a 3 day rental, enter MUGD718 in CPN. **4.** For a 4 day rental, enter MUGD719 in CPN. **5.** Complete this information:
RA#_____ Rental Date __/__/__ **6.** Attach to COUPON tape.

TASTE PUBLICATIONS INTERNATIONAL

Mobil Travel Guide®

The Guide That Saves You Money

When You Travel!

FREE FANNY PACK

YOURS FREE WHEN YOU JOIN NPCA NOW!

Join NPCA and save our national treasures! We are offering a special one-year introductory membership for only $15.00! Enjoy the many benefits of a NPCA membership and receive: a free National Parks and Conservation Association Fanny Pack, a free PARK-PAK, travel information kit, an annual subscription to the award-winning National Parks magazine, the NPCA discount photo service, car rental discounts and more.
See reverse for order form.   MTG98

OFFER EXPIRES JUNE 30, 1999

Ripley's Believe It or Not!®

BUY ONE GET ONE FREE!*
(Limit 6 people)

*Receive one complimentary admission with purchase of an equal value ticket.

Not valid with any other offers. Not for resale.
Valid only at locations listed. Coupon non-relinquishable.

Ripley's and Believe It or Not! are registered
trademarks of Ripley Entertainment Inc.
PLU-MOBIL

OFFER EXPIRES JUNE 30, 1999

ADVENTURE WORLD THE GREAT ESCAPE.

$7.00 OFF

SAVE $7.00 OFF EACH REGULAR ADMISSION (UP TO 6 PEOPLE) WHEN YOU PRESENT THIS COUPON AT ANY ADVENTURE WORLD TICKET WINDOW.

One (1) coupon good for up to six people and cannot be combined with any other discount, sold, or be redistributed, and not valid with Junior or Senior admission. Valid 1998/1999 season. Call for details **301-249-1500**, for dates and time.
Code: 1017

OFFER EXPIRES JUNE 30, 1999

CHOICE HOTELS INTERNATIONAL

10% OFF

ENJOY A 10% DISCOUNT AT PARTICIPATING COMFORT, QUALITY, CLARION, SLEEP, ECONO LODGE AND RODEWAY INN HOTELS AND SUITES.

The next time you're traveling call **800-4-CHOICE** and request Mobil discount #00052333. Advance reservations required. Kids 18 and under stay free and 1,400 hotels will provide free continental breakfast.

OFFER EXPIRES JUNE 30, 1999

Travel Discounters

UP TO $100.00 OFF

RECEIVE UP TO $100.00 OFF WHEN YOU BUY AN AIRLINE TICKET FROM TRAVEL DISCOUNTERS. CALL 800-355-1065 AND MENTION CODE MTG IN ORDER TO RECEIVE THE DISCOUNT.

Savings are subject to certain restrictions and availability. Valid for flights on most major airlines. See reverse for discount chart.

OFFER EXPIRES JUNE 30, 1999

General Cinema   LOEWS THEATRES SONY THEATRES   UNITED ARTISTS

THEATER DISCOUNT

Valid at all participating theatres.
Please send me:
_____ Sony/Loews at $4.50 each = _____
_____ United Artists at $4.50 each = _____
_____ General Cinema at $5.00 each = _____
Add $1.00 for handling. Allow 2-3 weeks for delivery. Orders over $75.00 will be sent via certified mail and may require additional processing time.
Limit 20 tickets per order.

OFFER EXPIRES JUNE 30, 1999

 American Tourister Samsonite

COMPANY STORE   SAVE 20% OFF

SHOPPING SPREE!

20% off selected merchandise when you visit any American Tourister or Samsonite Company Store. All stores carry first quality luggage, accessories and gifts to fit all your travel needs at 35%-50% off comparable prices.
Call 1-800-547-BAGS for a location nearest you.

OFFER EXPIRES JUNE 30, 1999

Read each coupon carefully before using. Discounts only apply to the items and terms specified in the offer at participating locations. Remove the coupon you wish to use.

Atlantic City, NJ	Myrtle Beach, SC
Branson, MO	Newport, OR
Buena Park, CA	Niagara Falls, Canada
Cavendish, P.E.I.	Orlando, FL
Grand Prairie, TX	San Antonio, TX
Hollywood, CA	San Francisco, CA
Jackson Hole, WY	St. Augustine, FL
Key West, FL	Wisconsin Dells, WI

TASTE PUBLICATIONS INTERNATIONAL

☐ YES! I want to preserve and protect our National Parks by becoming a National Parks and Conservation Association Member.
☐ I have enclosed a check in the amount of $15.00 for my one-year membership.
☐ Charge my annual dues to my ☐ Visa ☐ MasterCard ☐ Amex

Acct. #: _____ Exp. Date: _____

Signature: _____

Name: _____

Address: _____

City: _____ State: _____ Zip: _____

Phone: _____

Please allow 6-8 weeks for delivery of your fanny pack and first issue of National Parks Magazine.

Make checks payable and mail to: NPCA, 1776 Massachusetts Ave. NW, Washington, DC 20036-1904

TASTE PUBLICATIONS INTERNATIONAL

CHOICE HOTELS
INTERNATIONAL

Discount is limited to availability at participating hotels and cannot be used with any other discount. Kids stay free in same room as parents. Advance reservations through **1-800-4-CHOICE** required.

TASTE PUBLICATIONS INTERNATIONAL

ADVENTURE WORLD
THE GREAT ESCAPE.

13710 Central Ave. · Largo, MD

301-249-1500

From Washington, DC metro area,
take I-495/I-95 to exit 15A (Rt. 214 east, Central Ave.).
Adventure World located 5 miles on left.

From Baltimore metro area,
take I-695 to I-97 south to Exit 7, Rt. 3/301 south, to Rt. 214/Central Ave. west.
Adventure World located 3 miles on right.

TASTE PUBLICATIONS INTERNATIONAL

Prices are subject to change. A self-addressed stamped envelope must be enclosed to process your order. No refunds or exchanges. Mail order only, not redeemable at box office. Passes have expiration dates, generally one year from purchase. In some cases, tickets cannot be used during the first two weeks of a first-run movie.

Name: _____

Address: _____

City: _____ State: _____ Zip: _____

Make check payable to:
Taste Publications International, 1031 Cromwell Bridge Road, Baltimore, MD 21286.

TASTE PUBLICATIONS INTERNATIONAL

Travel Discounters

Minimum ticket price	Save
$200.00	$25.00
$250.00	$50.00
$350.00	$75.00
$450.00	$100.00

TASTE PUBLICATIONS INTERNATIONAL

COMPANY STORE

American Tourister   Samsonite

20% Off Selected Merchandise.
SHOPPING SPREE!
Call 1-800-547-BAGS

Not valid with any other promotional offer. Not valid on sale or previously purchased merchandise. Not valid on Kodak, Hasbro, Safety 1st or Ex Officio Products.

TASTE PUBLICATIONS INTERNATIONAL

Mobil
Travel Guide.

The Guide That Saves You Money

When You Travel!

 **Six Flags** Theme Parks — UP TO **$24.00 OFF**

Save up to $24.00 on admission to Six Flags Theme Parks.

$4.00 savings per ticket, up to six (6) admissions.

NLU 758000T 7580 1C

OFFER EXPIRES DECEMBER 31, 1998

 FLOWERS U·S·A

Because it's from you.™
1-800-225-3232

SAVE 20%

Receive a 20% discount on all floral and gift purchases from FLOWERS USA. Whether you are traveling or at home, celebrate birthdays, anniversaries, holidays and more with fresh cut flowers, floral arrangements, plants, gourmet food baskets, chocolates, fruits and balloons. To receive your savings, call **1-800-225-3232** and ask for referral code E59.

OFFER EXPIRES JUNE 30, 1999

National Audubon Society — # FREE BACKPACK

Sign me up for a 1-year membership at the special low rate of $20.00 and send me my Free Backpack upon receiving my payment. Member benefits include Six bi-monthly issues of AUDUBON magazine, savings on select Audubon nature products and discounts on exciting trips and tours, automatic membership in your local chapter (if there's one in your area), invitations to Audubon sanctuaries and Nature centers located around the country, and your official Audubon welcome pack, and more!

See reverse for order form.

OFFER EXPIRES JUNE 30, 1999

The One Accessory Every RV Needs
$5.00 OFF

With the world's largest selection of RV accessories and supplies, the Camping World catalog is a must for every RV. It's like having a store next door. Shop 24 hours a day, 7 days a week. Call today for a FREE catalog and receive $5 off your first order of $25 or more.

Call 1-800-845-7875   CAMPING WORLD.

Mention Code MT

OFFER EXPIRES JUNE 30, 1999

 Howard Johnson — # 10% OFF

Howard Johnson Makes You Feel at Home.

You're invited to stay at one of nearly 600 Howard Johnson Plazas, Hotels, Inns, and Express Inns throughout the United States, Canada and Mexico. And, if you present this certificate upon check-in, we'll take 10% off the regular room rate for your stay up to 7 nights. So make your reservation today! Call **1-800-I-GO-HOJO®** and ask for the TravelDeal discount.

1-800-I-GO-HOJO®

OFFER EXPIRES JUNE 30, 1999

 (NYI) — # SAVE $5.00

Great Photos With Any Camera

How to take great vacation pictures with your Point-and-Shoot camera. Learn to take better vacation pictures with this fun and easy video program! Whether you use a point-and-shoot, a "cardboard" camera, or an SLR, you'll be taking better pictures in just a few hours after watching this tape …or your money back. Guaranteed! From New York Institute of Photography - World's Largest Photography School. Founded 1910.
Regularly: $19.95 – Your Price: **ONLY $14.95**.
To order, call **1-800-453-3686**, Dept. TG.
Add $4.95 shipping and handling.

OFFER EXPIRES JUNE 30, 1999

 DOLLAR RENT A CAR — DOLLAR MAKES SENSE? — # FREE UPGRADE

Free One Car Class Upgrade Certificate

For worldwide reservations, call your professional travel agent or:

1-800-800-4000, Reference ID# PC3007
www.dollarcar.com.

OFFER EXPIRES JUNE 30, 1999

Coupons may not be used in conjunction with any other promotion or discount offers. **Example:** special promotional pricing. If in doubt, please check with the establishment.

Present this coupon at any Six Flags Theme Park main gate ticket booth on any regular operating day through December 31, 1998 and save $4.00 off a one-day full-price adult admission. Valid for up to six (6) tickets. Coupon must be presented at time of purchase and tickets must be used the same day. Not valid on Six Flags Wild Safari Animal Park, Six Flags Hurricane Harbor, Six Flags WaterWorld or Wet 'n Wild individual park tickets. Cannot be combined with any other discount admission offer including Child, Sr. Citizen, Two-day and After 4pm tickets. Coupon cannot be resold or redeemed for cash and is void if reproduced. Call parks for operating schedule.

Six Flags Over Texas Arlington, TX 817-640-8900	Six Flags AstroWorld Houston, TX 713-799-8404	Six Flags Fiesta Texas San Antonio, TX 210-697-5050	Six Flags Over Georgia Atlanta, GA 770-948-9290
Six Flags St. Louis St. Louis, MO 314-938-5300	Six Flags Great America Chicago, IL 847-249-2133	Six Flags Magic Mountain Los Angeles, CA 805-255-4100	Six Flags Great Adventure Jackson, NJ 908-928-2000

TASTE PUBLICATIONS INTERNATIONAL

FLOWERS U·S·A

Because it's from you.™
1-800-225-3232

Offer does not apply to service charge and applicable tax. Discount cannot be combined with any other offers. Void where prohibited.

TASTE PUBLICATIONS INTERNATIONAL

RV Accessories and Supplies
Call 1-800-845-7875
for a FREE Catalog
Code MT

TASTE PUBLICATIONS INTERNATIONAL

National 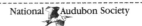 Audubon Society

Mail this coupon to:
National Audubon Society, Membership Data Center
P.O. Box 52529, Boulder, CO 80322-2529

Yes! Please enroll me as a 1-year member for $20.00 to the National Audubon Society.
Check one: ____ Payment enclosed. ____ Bill me later.

Name: _____
Address: _____
City: _____ State: _____ Zip: _____

5MB96

TASTE PUBLICATIONS INTERNATIONAL

SAVE $5.00 — Great Photos With Any Camera
How To Take Great Vacation Photos

GUARANTEED: You'll take better photos after just watching this video…or your money back. Regularly: $19.95 – Your Price: **ONLY $14.95**. To order, call **1-800-453-3686**, Dept. TG. Or write to: NYI, 211 East 43rd St., New York, N.Y. 10017 Dept T

Add $4.95 shipping and handling.

TASTE PUBLICATIONS INTERNATIONAL

Call 1-800-I-GO-HOJO® and ask for the 10% TravelDeal discount.

Children under 18 always stay free in their parent's room*. Advance reservations required. Original certificate must be presented at check-in.

* Children 17 and under stay free in their parent's room with existing bedding.

TASTE PUBLICATIONS INTERNATIONAL

DOLLAR MAKES SENSE®

This coupon entitles you to a one-class upgrade to the next higher car group at no extra charge. Simply make a reservation for a compact or intermediate class car, then present this certificate to any *Dollar*® rental agent when you arrive. You'll receive an upgrade to the next car class at no additional charge. Upgrade subject to vehicle availability. This certificate must be surrendered at time of rental, may not be used in conjunction with any other certificate or promotion, has no cash value, and expires 6/30/99. Upgrade certificate valid at participating locations only. Renter must meet age and credit requirements. FASTLANE℠ Instructions: Proceed to special documents window, use document code UPG.

TASTE PUBLICATIONS INTERNATIONAL